lonely planet

New Zealand

**Jeff Williams
Christine Niven
Peter Turner**

LONELY PLANET PUBLICATIONS
Melbourne • Oakland • London • Paris

NEW ZEALAND

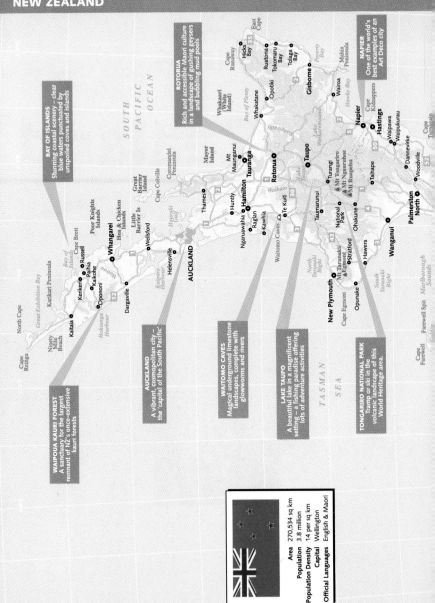

BAY OF ISLANDS
Stunning coastal scenery – clear blue waters dotted by unspoiled coves and islands

ROTORUA
Rich and accessible Maori culture in a landscape of gushing geysers and bubbling mud pools

NAPIER
One of the world's best examples of an Art Deco city

WAIPOUA KAURI FOREST
A sanctuary for the largest remnant of NZ's once-extensive kauri forests

AUCKLAND
A vibrant, cosmopolitan city – the capital of the South Pacific

WAITOMO CAVES
Magical underground limestone landscapes, complete with glowworms and rivers

LAKE TAUPO
A beautiful lake in a magnificent setting – a fishing paradise offering lots of adventure activities

TONGARIRO NATIONAL PARK
Tramp or ski in the volcanic landscape of this World Heritage area.

SOUTH PACIFIC OCEAN

TASMAN SEA

Area	270,534 sq km
Population	3.8 million
Population Density	14 per sq km
Capital	Wellington
Official Languages	English & Maori

North Cape
Cape Reinga
Ninety Mile Beach
Karikari Peninsula
Great Exhibition Bay
Kaitaia
Kaikohe
Opononi
Kerikeri
Paihia
Russell
Cape Brett
Bay of Islands
Whangarei
Hen & Chicken Islands
Poor Knights Islands
Little Barrier Is
Great Barrier Island
Wellsford
Dargaville
Helensville
Kaipara Harbour
Hokianga Harbour
Hauraki Gulf
AUCKLAND
Coromandel Peninsula
Cape Colville
Mayor Island
Mt Maunganui
Tauranga
Whakatane
Opotiki
Bay of Plenty
Whakaari (White Island)
Thames
Huntly
Hamilton
Raglan
Kawhia
Ngaruawahia
Te Kuiti
Waitomo Caves
Rotorua
Taupo
Turangi
Taumarunui
National Park
Mt Tongariro
Mt Ngauruhoe
Mt Ruapehu
Ohakune
Taihape
Raetihi
New Plymouth
Cape Egmont
Mt Taranaki/Egmont
Opunake
Stratford
Hawera
Wanganui
Palmerston North
Woodville
Dannevirke
Waipukurau
Waipawa
Hastings
Napier
Cape Kidnappers
Hawke Bay
Wairoa
Mahia Peninsula
Gisborne
Poverty Bay
Tolaga Bay
Tokomaru Bay
Ruatoria
Hicks Bay
East Cape
Cape Runaway
Lake Taupo
Lake Waikaremoana
Waikato
North Taranaki Bight
South Taranaki Bight
Farewell Spit
Cape Farewell
Marlborough Sounds

New Zealand
10th edition – October 2000
First published – December 1977

Published by
Lonely Planet Publications Pty Ltd ABN 36 005 607 983
90 Maribyrnong St, Footscray, Victoria 3011, Australia

Lonely Planet Offices
Australia Locked Bag 1, Footscray, Victoria 3011
USA 150 Linden St, Oakland, CA 94607
UK 10a Spring Place, London NW5 3BH
France 1 rue du Dahomey, 75011 Paris

Photographs
Many of the images in this guide are available for licensing from
Lonely Planet Images.
email: lpi@lonelyplanet.com.au

Front cover photograph
Sunset on Mt Ngauruhoe, Tongariro National Park, North Island
(Ross Barnett, LPI)

North Island title page photograph
Cape Reinga Lighthouse, Northland (David Wall, LPI)

South Island title page photograph
Stirling Point Signpost, Bluff, Southland (David Wall, LPI)

ISBN 1 86450 122 7

text & maps © Lonely Planet 2000
photos © photographers as indicated 2000

Printed by SNP Offset Sdn Bhd
Printed in Malaysia

Contents – Text

NEW ZEALAND

ELEVATION

3000 m
2000 m
1000 m
500 m
200 m
0

TE PAPA, WELLINGTON
'Our Place' is a fascinating museum which encapsulates the history and culture of this small, diverse nation.

KAIKOURA
Share the ocean with dusky dolphins or watch whales backflip.

THE TRANZALPINE
Take this great rail journey across plains and mountains from the South Pacific Ocean to the Tasman Sea.

MT COOK (AORAKI)
The highest mountain in NZ has fantastic scenery and walks and the mighty Tasman Glacier.

QUEENSTOWN
A stunning setting for adrenaline-pumping activities

OTAGO PENINSULA
An amazing variety of wildlife exists in this small area – albatross, penguins, Hooker's sea lions, seals and dolphins.

THE CATLINS
A living natural history museum, with unique flora and fauna, tracts of rainforest, waterfalls and kelp-strewn beaches.

ABEL TASMAN NATIONAL PARK
Walk or kayak past beautiful beaches, bays and turquoise waters.

THE WEST COAST
A rugged, remote wilderness with seascapes, pristine forests and lakes, and the mighty Franz Josef and Fox Glaciers extending almost to the sea

FIORDLAND
Calm water mirrors the sheer peaks surrounding the 22km-long Milford Sound

To Chatham Islands

To Bounty Islands &
Antipodes Islands

To Campbell Island

To The Snares & Auckland Islands

SOUTH
PACIFIC
OCEAN

TASMAN
SEA

COOK STRAIT

Kapiti
Island

Masterton
Upper Hutt
Lower Hutt
WELLINGTON
Cape Palliser
Picton
Blenheim
Nelson
Takaka
Tasman Bay
Richmond
St Arnaud
Murchison
Karamea
Karamea Bight
Westport
Reefton
Punakaiki
Greymouth
Hokitika
Ross
Lewis Pass
Hanmer Springs
Kaikoura
Pegasus Bay
CHRISTCHURCH
Lyttelton
Banks Peninsula
Akaroa
Arthur's Pass
Methven
Mt Hutt
Ashburton
Canterbury Bight
Temuka
Timaru
Waimate
Oamaru
Whataroa
Franz Josef
Fox Glacier
Mt Cook Village
Mt Cook (Aoraki)
Twizel
Palmerston
Otago Peninsula
DUNEDIN
Haast
Haast Pass
Mt Aspiring
Jackson Bay
Wanaka
Glenorchy
Queenstown
Cromwell
Alexandra
Milton
Balclutha
Chaslands Mistake
Milford Sound
Te Anau
Manapouri
Lumsden
Gore
Winton
Invercargill
Bluff
George Sound
Doubtful Sound
Dusky Sound
West Cape
Puysegur Point
Stewart Island (Rakiura)
Oban
Halfmoon Bay
Mason Bay
Foveaux Strait

200 km
100 miles

New Zealand
10th edition – October 2000
First published – December 1977

Published by
Lonely Planet Publications Pty Ltd ABN 36 005 607 983
90 Maribyrnong St, Footscray, Victoria 3011, Australia

Lonely Planet Offices
Australia Locked Bag 1, Footscray, Victoria 3011
USA 150 Linden St, Oakland, CA 94607
UK 10a Spring Place, London NW5 3BH
France 1 rue du Dahomey, 75011 Paris

Photographs
Many of the images in this guide are available for licensing from
Lonely Planet Images.
email: lpi@lonelyplanet.com.au

Front cover photograph
Sunset on Mt Ngauruhoe, Tongariro National Park, North Island
(Ross Barnett, LPI)

North Island title page photograph
Cape Reinga Lighthouse, Northland (David Wall, LPI)

South Island title page photograph
Stirling Point Signpost, Bluff, Southland (David Wall, LPI)

ISBN 1 86450 122 7

text & maps © Lonely Planet 2000
photos © photographers as indicated 2000

Printed by SNP Offset Sdn Bhd
Printed in Malaysia

Although the authors and Lonely Planet try to make the information as accurate as possible, we accept no responsibility for any loss, injury or inconvenience sustained by anyone using this book.

Contents – Text

BAY OF PLENTY 302

CENTRAL PLATEAU 340

WANGANUI & MANAWATU 370

THE EAST COAST 390

WELLINGTON REGION 421

MARLBOROUGH & NELSON 454

THE WEST COAST 498

Contents – Maps

MAP INDEX

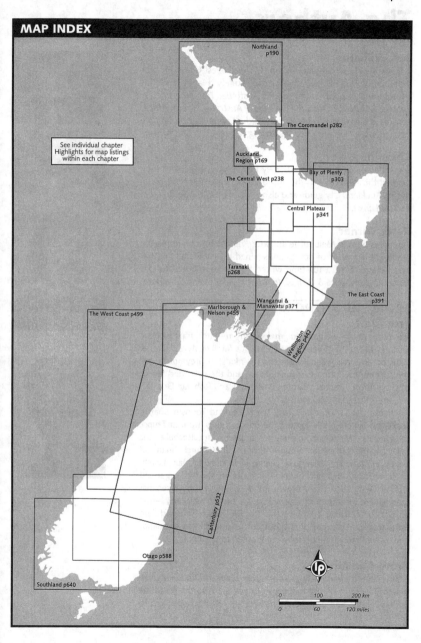

See individual chapter Highlights for map listings within each chapter

Northland p190

The Coromandel p282

Auckland Region p169

Bay of Plenty p303

The Central West p238

Central Plateau p341

Taranaki p268

Wanganui & Manawatu p371

The East Coast p391

The West Coast p499

Marlborough & Nelson p455

Wellington Region p442

Canterbury p532

Otago p588

Southland p640

| 0 | 100 | 200 km |
| 0 | 60 | 120 miles |

The Authors

Jeff Williams

Jeff is a Kiwi from Greymouth, on NZ's wild West Coast. He predominantly works as a writer for Lonely Planet and has co-authored or contributed to LP's *Australia*, *Tramping in New Zealand*, *Outback Australia*, *Western Australia*, *South Africa*, *Lesotho & Swaziland*, *USA*, *Virginia & the Capital Region*, *Middle East*, *Istanbul to Cairo on a Shoestring*, *West Africa* and *Africa*.

Christine Niven

Christine began working for Lonely Planet as an editor but soon jumped the fence to join the authors. She wrote the first edition of LP's *Auckland* city guide and also worked on *India*, *South India* and *Sri Lanka*.

Peter Turner

Peter was born in Melbourne and after various forays around the world and a variety of occupations joined Lonely Planet in 1986 as an editor. Now a full-time writer, he has contributed to LP's *Malaysia*, *Singapore & Brunei*, *Indonesia*, *Jakarta* and *Singapore*.

FROM THE AUTHORS
From Jeff

There are many to thank for making my research trips to New Zealand so fruitful. Thanks to Whitebait's family (Myra, Linda & Winston, Rosemary & Bernard, and their kids) in Greymouth; my son Callum; co-author Christine Niven; and the extended family of Greg Alford, Rebecca Turner, Errol Hunt and Rob van Driesum at Lonely Planet in Melbourne.

Thanks also to Graeme Ching (New Zealand Tourism Board), Mark and Simon in Wellington; the one and only Trout in Taupo; the Duchess, Mr Worm, Maurice, Margaret, Gary, Rochelle, Eric Foley and the staff of Canterbury Tourism in Christchurch; Brian and Lesley in Dunedin; Willy and Valerie in Invercargill; Iain Leitch, Graham, Rusty, Nick and Glyn in Queenstown; the well-organised staff at Destination Queenstown for organising a superb seminar (and saving me hours of foot slogging); the Animal Party – the answer to 'NZ Thirst' (Rabbit – Minister for Dodgy Transport, and Rat – Roving Ambassador without Portfolio & VIP) in Auckland; and to hundreds of others who contributed to this book.

From Christine

Many people generously gave of their time and knowledge to help my research. A big thank you to you all. Also thanks to the editors, cartos and designers who worked on this book, and to Jeff for his advice.

This Book

New Zealand is one of Lonely Planet's oldest books with a long list of contributors: Tony Wheeler did the first edition way back in 1977 and the next two were updated by Simon Hayman. The fourth edition was updated by Mary Covernton, and Tony updated the fifth edition with Robin Tinker. Nancy Keller updated the sixth edition, and also the seventh edition along with Jeff Williams. Peter Turner and Jeff updated the eighth and ninth editions.

For this historic 10th edition (only the third Lonely Planet book to reach two digits), Jeff wrote the new 'Maori Culture & Arts' section and revised all the introductory chapters, plus Wellington Region and all the South Island chapters. Christine Niven updated the rest of the North Island.

From the Publisher

The production of *New Zealand 10* was coordinated in-house by Barbara Benson (design and maps) and Errol Hunt (editing). Barbara was assisted with the maps by Corrine Waddell, Chris Love, Chris Thomas and Jenny Jones; Jane Hart did the final design check. Errol was assisted with editing by Hilary Ericksen, Anne Mulvaney, Bruce Evans and Kim Hutchins; Chris Wyness, Hilary, Martin Heng, Rebecca Turner and Tony Davidson did the final layout checks. Simon Bracken and Margie Jung designed the book's cover, Pablo Gastar created those excellent chapter ends and Kusnandar drew up the climate charts. Martine Lleonart briefed the authors before they started researching. Quentin Frayne edited the Language section – *tino pai* Quentin – while Leonie Mugavin did sterling work with health and travel information. Val Tellini at LPI coordinated images and photographers.

Ferne McKenzie at the Department of Conservation and Betty Moss at the Alexander Turnbull Library provided much assistance – Ferne with the magnificent shots in the 'Fauna & Flora' section and Betty with historical images. Thanks to Te Papa Museum for permission to use their images in the 'Maori Culture & Arts section'.

Thanks to Jeff and Christine for answering all our extra questions, and to various family and friends (you know who you are) who checked obscure facts for us. Thanks to Tim Uden for providing chocolate fishes for the workforce, Jenny Blake for the NZ flag, Barbara for entertaining us with her Maori pronunciation and the 1999 East Coast rugby team for inspiration.

THANKS
Many thanks to the travellers who used the last edition and wrote to us with helpful hints, advice and interesting anecdotes. Your names appear in the back of this book.

Foreword

ABOUT LONELY PLANET GUIDEBOOKS

The story begins with a classic travel adventure: Tony and Maureen Wheeler's 1972 journey across Europe and Asia to Australia. Useful information about the overland trail did not exist at that time, so Tony and Maureen published the first Lonely Planet guidebook to meet a growing need.

From a kitchen table, then from a tiny office in Melbourne (Australia), Lonely Planet has become the largest independent travel publisher in the world, an international company with offices in Melbourne, Oakland (USA), London (UK) and Paris (France).

Today Lonely Planet guidebooks cover the globe. There is an ever-growing list of books and there's information in a variety of forms and media. Some things haven't changed. The main aim is still to help make it possible for adventurous travellers to get out there – to explore and better understand the world.

At Lonely Planet we believe travellers can make a positive contribution to the countries they visit – if they respect their host communities and spend their money wisely. Since 1986 a percentage of the income from each book has been donated to aid projects and human rights campaigns.

Updates Lonely Planet thoroughly updates each guidebook as often as possible. This usually means there are around two years between editions, although for more unusual or more stable destinations the gap can be longer. Check the imprint page (following the colour map at the beginning of the book) for publication dates.

Between editions up-to-date information is available in two free newsletters – the paper *Planet Talk* and email *Comet* (to subscribe, contact any Lonely Planet office) – and on our Web site at www.lonelyplanet.com. The *Upgrades* section of the Web site covers a number of important and volatile destinations and is regularly updated by Lonely Planet authors. *Scoop* covers news and current affairs relevant to travellers. And, lastly, the *Thorn Tree* bulletin board and *Postcards* section of the site carry unverified, but fascinating, reports from travellers.

Correspondence The process of creating new editions begins with the letters, postcards and emails received from travellers. This correspondence often includes suggestions, criticisms and comments about the current editions. Interesting excerpts are immediately passed on via newsletters and the Web site, and everything goes to our authors to be verified when they're researching on the road. We're keen to get more feedback from organisations or individuals who represent communities visited by travellers.

> Lonely Planet gathers information for everyone who's curious about the planet – and especially for those who explore it first-hand. Through guidebooks, phrasebooks, activity guides, maps, literature, image library, TV series and Web site we act as an information exchange for a worldwide community of travellers.

Research Authors aim to gather sufficient practical information to enable travellers to make informed choices and to make the mechanics of a journey run smoothly. They also research historical and cultural background to help enrich the travel experience and allow travellers to understand and respond appropriately to cultural and environmental issues.

Authors don't stay in every hotel because that would mean spending a couple of months in each medium-sized city and, no, they don't eat at every restaurant because that would mean stretching belts beyond capacity. They do visit hotels and restaurants to check standards and prices, but feedback based on readers' direct experiences can be very helpful.

Many of our authors work undercover, others aren't so secretive. None of them accept freebies in exchange for positive write-ups. And none of our guidebooks contain any advertising.

Production Authors submit their raw manuscripts and maps to offices in Australia, USA, UK or France. Editors and cartographers – all experienced travellers themselves – then begin the process of assembling the pieces. When the book finally hits the shops, some things are already out of date, we start getting feedback from readers and the process begins again ...

WARNING & REQUEST

Things change – prices go up, schedules change, good places go bad and bad places go bankrupt – nothing stays the same. So, if you find things better or worse, recently opened or long since closed, please tell us and help make the next edition even more accurate and useful. We genuinely value all the feedback we receive. Julie Young coordinates a well travelled team that reads and acknowledges every letter, postcard and email and ensures that every morsel of information finds its way to the appropriate authors, editors and cartographers for verification.

Everyone who writes to us will find their name in the next edition of the appropriate guidebook. They will also receive the latest issue of *Planet Talk*, our quarterly printed newsletter, or *Comet*, our monthly email newsletter. Subscriptions to both newsletters are free. The very best contributions will be rewarded with a free guidebook.

Excerpts from your correspondence may appear in new editions of Lonely Planet guidebooks, the Lonely Planet Web site, *Planet Talk* or *Comet*, so please let us know if you *don't* want your letter published or your name acknowledged.

Send all correspondence to the Lonely Planet office closest to you:

Australia: Locked Bag 1, Footscray, Victoria 3011
USA: 150 Linden St, Oakland, CA 94607
UK: 10A Spring Place, London NW5 3BH
France: 1 rue du Dahomey, 75011 Paris

Or email us at: talk2us@lonelyplanet.com.au

For news, views and updates see our Web site: www.lonelyplanet.com

HOW TO USE A LONELY PLANET GUIDEBOOK

The best way to use a Lonely Planet guidebook is any way you choose. At Lonely Planet we believe the most memorable travel experiences are often those that are unexpected, and the finest discoveries are those you make yourself. Guidebooks are not intended to be used as if they provide a detailed set of infallible instructions!

Contents All Lonely Planet guidebooks follow roughly the same format. The Facts about the Destination chapters or sections give background information ranging from history to weather. Facts for the Visitor gives practical information on issues like visas and health. Getting There & Away gives a brief starting point for researching travel to and from the destination. Getting Around gives an overview of the transport options when you arrive.

The peculiar demands of each destination determine how subsequent chapters are broken up, but some things remain constant. We always start with background, then proceed to sights, places to stay, places to eat, entertainment, getting there and away, and getting around information – in that order.

Heading Hierarchy Lonely Planet headings are used in a strict hierarchical structure that can be visualised as a set of Russian dolls. Each heading (and its following text) is encompassed by any preceding heading that is higher on the hierarchical ladder.

Entry Points We do not assume guidebooks will be read from beginning to end, but that people will dip into them. The traditional entry points are the list of contents and the index. In addition, however, some books have a complete list of maps and an index map illustrating map coverage.

There may also be a colour map that shows highlights. These highlights are dealt with in greater detail in the Facts for the Visitor chapter, along with planning questions and suggested itineraries. Each chapter covering a geographical region usually begins with a locator map and another list of highlights. Once you find something of interest in a list of highlights, turn to the index.

Maps Maps play a crucial role in Lonely Planet guidebooks and include a huge amount of information. A legend is printed on the back page. We seek to have complete consistency between maps and text, and to have every important place in the text captured on a map. Map key numbers usually start in the top left corner.

Although inclusion in a guidebook usually implies a recommendation we cannot list every good place. Exclusion does not necessarily imply criticism. In fact there are a number of reasons why we might exclude a place – sometimes it is simply inappropriate to encourage an influx of travellers.

Introduction

Fresh air, magnificent scenery and outdoor activities are the feature attractions of New Zealand. It's not a big country but for sheer variety it's hard to beat. Visitors who come expecting a pristine, green, well-organised little country are not disappointed and the country's reputation for being 'clean and green' is well deserved.

New Zealand is like a microcosm of all the world's attractions. You can trek on the slopes of active volcanoes, or in remote, rugged patches of virgin rainforest, through thermal areas of geysers and boiling mud, or kauri forests with some of the largest and oldest trees on Earth. You can swim with dolphins, watch whales, see glaciers descending into rainforests, fish for trout in cold, pristine streams and see fur seals and penguins swimming around your boat as

you cruise on remote fiords. The adventurous can go white-water rafting, cave rafting, rock and mountain climbing, tandem sky-diving, bungy jumping, skiing down long glaciers, and much more. Plus there are many chances to experience the fascinating Maori culture and the warmth of New Zealand's friendly people.

The major cities each have their own unique character. There's also a growing cultural life with some great nightlife, live theatre, dancing and arty cafes. Arts and crafts are popular and many New Zealand cities have fine art galleries.

Getting around is easy with cycling, hitching and driving through the country all popular ways to travel. Finding affordable accommodation is also easy, although it's a good idea to book ahead in the high season.

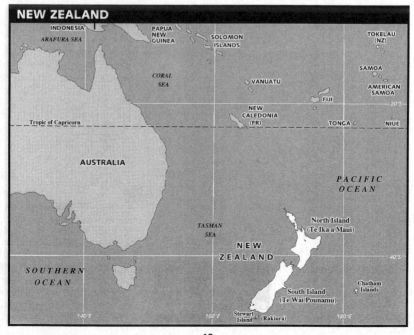

The food is fresh and there's plenty of it, and even the wine is excellent.

Travellers do have one consistent complaint about New Zealand, though: that they haven't allowed themselves enough time in the country. Look at the map of the world and it doesn't appear to be a big country. However, once you arrive in New Zealand, it soon becomes apparent how much there is to see and do.

If time is no object, we'd recommend allowing at least six weeks for a visit. Of course you can still enjoy New Zealand in less time and some travellers make a mad dash through the country, rushing from activity to activity, and have a great trip.

This book will help to show you all there is to see and do in New Zealand, and to plan your travels. Have a great time. It's a beautiful country.

Facts about New Zealand

HISTORY

It is known from archaeological evidence that there were established communities in New Zealand from around AD 1000 onwards – perhaps much earlier.

Although different tribes have differing legends of the initial settlement of NZ, many oral histories tell of the discovery of NZ by the navigator Kupe in about AD 800. Kupe sailed to Aotearoa from Hawaiki, the ancestral homeland. It was Kupe's wife Hine-te-aparangi who named the new land Aotearoa – 'The Land of the Long White Cloud'. Kupe visited the North and South Islands then returned to Hawaiki from Hokianga to report his find. Despite the similar names, Hawaiki was not Hawaii, it was probably Ra'iatea (in Maori, Rangiatea), near Tahiti.

Other legends tell of the so-called Great Migration in AD 1350, when a fleet of migratory canoes – including *Te Arawa, Aotea* and *Tainui* – left Hawaiki to settle Aotearoa. This 'history', although still widely believed, was a dubious adaptation of Maori legends by early Western historians. While the canoes named almost certainly existed, it is unlikely that they travelled in a fleet.

For the early creation mythology see the 'Maori Culture & Arts' special section.

Early Settlement

Recent evidence indicates that Polynesians, who were to become the Maori, arrived in NZ in a series of migrations over several generations from around AD 1000.

These migrations had been preceded by an eastward seaborne expansion of Austronesians (from the Melanesian/Indonesian chain) some three thousand years earlier. The Lapita people (named after a location in New Caledonia where their distinctive pottery was found) reached Fiji, Tonga and Samoa around 1500 BC. Almost 1000 years later they fanned out further east, reaching as far as Tahiti (Society Islands). Another 1000 years later they were on the move again – to Easter Island, Hawaii, and eventually NZ.

Driven from their homeland by land shortages, war or religious dissent, the settlers on these great canoe voyages found in NZ temperate islands far larger than any islands of the Pacific. Apart from bats, the land was devoid of mammals for hunting but the sea provided abundant food resources. Of the birdlife, the most spectacular was the huge flightless moa, over 3m tall.

This initially plentiful food supply became one of the staples of early Polynesians, especially on the east of the South Island, where the moa was hunted for its food and feathers. Agriculture was not well developed in this early 'Archaic' period of settlement, perhaps because the climate was so much colder than the Polynesian homeland. There is evidence to suggest that there were three areas of settlement based on different resources. The warmer north where kumara (sweet potato) cultivation was possible; a transitional area where such cultivation was marginal; and the far colder south where cultivation wasn't an issue.

Widespread agricultural societies based on the imported Polynesian crops of kumara, taro and yams came later; this second era of settlement, sometimes known as the 'Classic Maori' period was only possible with the development of a sophisticated system to protect root crops from frost.

Probably the most devastating effect of the arrival of humans in the untouched environment was the destruction of flora and fauna. Widespread forest fires led to extensive deforestation and there was a transition of large areas of fernland to tussock grassland.

The giant moa was extinct by about 400 years ago; seal populations were confined to smaller remnants in the south; and the introduced rats *(kiore)* and dogs *(kuri)* wreaked havoc on populations of ground-dwelling birds.

With natural resources so reduced it was necessary for the Maori to develop another food supply. Over two centuries (approximately 1300 to 1500) the northern tribes became cultivators of fern root and kumara. Over this time, under increasing pressure for land and again beginning in the north, the Maori became more warlike and many tribes were wiped out by a process of conquest and enslavement. Cannibalism became prevalent at this time, as did the development of *pa* (forts) for protection against warring tribes.

The Moriori, who inhabited the Chatham Islands, are believed to have settled there from the main NZ islands about 500 years ago. They retained an Archaic culture long after it had vanished from the mainland.

One version of history you may hear is that the Moriori were the first settlers of NZ. Based soley on a study by historian S Percy Smith (1840–1922), this theory said that the Moriori (or Maruiwi) were a Melanesian people and were forcibly displaced by the arrival later of the Polynesian Maori. Although discredited since the early 20th century the theory was taught to NZ schoolkids until relatively recently and still finds favour among many adults.

European Exploration

In 1642 Dutch explorer Abel Tasman, who had just sailed around Australia from Batavia (modern-day Jakarta, Indonesia), sailed up the west coast of NZ but didn't stay long after his only landing attempt resulted in three members of his crew being killed. He christened the land Niuew Zeeland, after the Netherlands province of Zeeland.

The Dutch, after this first uncomfortable look, were none too keen to return and NZ was left alone until British navigator and explorer James Cook sailed around it in the *Endeavour* in 1769.

Because Tasman had only sailed up the west coast, there had been speculation that this could be the west coast of the fabled great southern continent. In the logical European cosmology, it was thought that a large southern land must exist to balance the large landmasses in the northern hemisphere.

Cook sailed right around the coast of NZ on three voyages altogether, mapping as he went, and many places still bear the names he gave them. He made friendly contact with the Maori inhabitants on several occasions, with one exception – at Poverty Bay some Maori were killed. Luckily his Polynesian interpreter, Tupaia, was Ra'iatean and spoke a language very similar to NZ Maori. Cook was impressed with their bravery and spirit, and with the potential of this lightly populated land. After finishing his sail around the coasts of both the North and South Islands and determining that it was not the great southern continent, Cook claimed the entire land for the British Crown and continued on to Australia.

The French explorer Jean-François Marie de Surville, was sailing around NZ at the same time as Cook but the two never did bump into one another. They came close, off the coast of the North Island, but each was unaware of the other's presence.

New Zealand's first European settlers were temporary – sealers (who soon reduced the seal population to next to nothing) and then whalers (who did the same to the whales). They introduced diseases and prostitution, created such a demand for preserved heads that Maori chiefs began chopping off their slaves' heads to order (previously they'd only preserved the heads of warriors who had died in battle) and, worst of all, brought in European firearms. When they exchanged greenstone *mere* (clubs) for muskets, the Maori soon embarked on wholesale slaughter of one another. In what became known as the Musket Wars, Northland's Ngapuhi tribe, led by Hongi Hika, embraced the new technology and sent raiding parties throughout the central North Island as far south as Hawkes Bay on the East Coast and Taranaki in the west.

By 1830 the Maori population was falling dramatically.

European Settlement

The first missionary, Samuel Marsden, brought Christianity to NZ in 1814, and other missionaries soon followed. The Bible was translated into Maori – the first time the Maori language had been written. By the middle of the 19th century tribal warfare had abated, cannibalism was fairly well stamped out and the raging impact of European diseases also curbed. But the

Maori people now found themselves spiritually assaulted and much of their tradition and culture was irrevocably altered. Their numbers continued to decline.

During the early 19th century European settlers (called Pakeha in Maori) arrived in increasing numbers, some on settlement campaigns organised from Britain; in the 1830s entrepreneurs from Australia raced to carve out holdings in the new land. Growing lawlessness from less savoury settlers and a deterioration in Maori-Pakeha relations resulted in petitions for British intervention.

The British were not keen on further colonising – what with burning their fingers in America, fighting in Canada and stretching

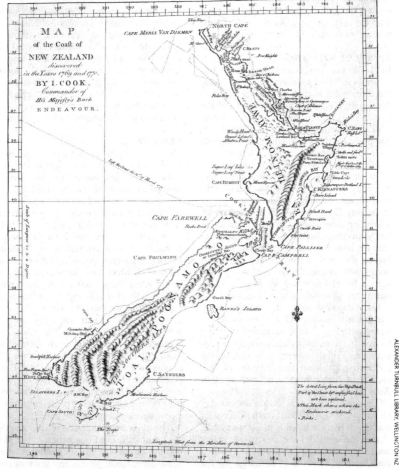

Map of the coast of New Zealand discovered in the years 1769 and 1770, by I Cook, commander of His Majesty's bark Endeavour (B Longmate, 1773)

their involvement in other places, not to mention having Australia to worry about. The need to establish law finally prompted them to dispatch James Busby as the British Resident in 1833. It was a low-key effort, illustrated by poor Busby having to pay his own fare from Australia. Once he'd set up shop in Kororareka (now called Russell) in Northland, his efforts to protect the settlers and keep law and order were made somewhat difficult without the support of forces, arms and authority. He was soon dubbed 'the man of war without guns'.

Treaty of Waitangi

In 1838 the lawlessness problem, unscrupulous 'purchases' of Maori land and the threat of a French colonising effort at Akaroa in the South Island all stirred the British to seek annexation of NZ. Captain William Hobson was sent to replace Busby and persuade the Maori chiefs to relinquish their sovereignty to the British Crown.

The Treaty of Waitangi was drawn up in 1840 within a few days of Hobson's arrival in NZ, and on 5 February over 400 Maori gathered in front of Busby's residence at Waitangi in the Bay of Islands to hear the treaty read. The Maori chiefs had some objections, so the treaty was amended and they withdrew to debate the issue throughout the night. The following day, with a truly British display of pomp and circumstance, the treaty was signed by Hobson and 45 Maori chiefs, mostly from the Bay of Islands region.

Over the next seven months the treaty was carried throughout NZ by missionaries, traders and officials, eventually being signed by over 500 chiefs. Hobson proclaimed British sovereignty, becoming NZ's first governor and establishing his capital at Kororareka – he moved it to Auckland a year later.

Though the treaty was short and seemed to be simple, it was a controversial document that is still hotly debated in modern-day NZ. Under the terms of the treaty, the chiefs ceded their sovereignty *(kawanatanga)* to the Queen of England in exchange for the Queen's protection and the granting to Maori people all citizenship rights, privileges and

duties enjoyed by citizens of England. The term kawanatanga, however, did not have the same connotation in Maori as 'sovereignty' does in English – the Maori chiefs thus had a different understanding to the British as to what they were signing.

The treaty guaranteed the Maori possession of their land, fisheries and resources (their *tino rangatiratanga*) and stipulated that they could only sell their land to the Crown. The Queen's agent would then sell the land to settlers in an orderly and fair fashion.

The treaty seemed to promise benefits for both sides, but when settlers arrived and needed land and the Maori didn't want to sell, conflict inevitably resulted. The admirable idea that the government should be a go-between in all Maori-Pakeha deals to ensure fairness fell apart when the government was too tight-fisted to pay the price.

Land Wars

The first visible revolt came when Hone Heke chopped down the flagpole at Kororareka which flew the British flag. Despite new poles and more guards, Hone Heke or his followers managed to chop the pole down four times; on the last occasion it was covered with iron to foil further attempts. In 1845, Hone Heke attacked and razed the town of Kororareka. In the skirmishes that followed, the British governor posted a £100 reward for his head, to which the chief responded by offering a matching £100 for the governor's head. See the Bay of Islands in the Northland chapter for more about the war.

The Northland war was only one in a series of conflicts between the Maori and Europeans. The original benign intent of the Treaty of Waitangi began to ebb under the pressure of ever-increasing numbers of European settlers. Many land sales were disputed, as chiefs sold land that belonged to the whole tribe or sold land of other tribes, resulting in a new development of tribal conflict.

The government pressed on with developing the colony. The Constitution Act of 1852 divided the country into six provinces which administered local government and took over the responsibility for land purchases and sales. Alarmed, Maori became increasingly reluctant to sell land. In the Waikato region, a number of tribal chiefs united to elect a Maori 'King' in 1858 and resisted land sales and European settlement in the Waikato and King Country region until the 20th century (see the Central West chapter).

Pressures between Maori and European escalated into several fully fledged wars with troops from England and Australia aiding the NZ militia. Known collectively as the Land Wars (or Maori Wars), fighting took place in many parts of the country: Northland (1844–46), Taranaki (1860–61 and 1865–69), Waikato/King Country (1863–67) and the East Coast (1868–72). See individual chapters for more historical information.

The most bitterly fought conflicts were in Taranaki. The force of arms enabled imperial troops to vanquish the Taranaki tribes, but later, related skirmishes erupted in the East Coast region with the rise of Hauhauism, a Maori religious movement which aimed to oust the Europeans. Also around that region, Te Kooti (see the boxed text in the East Coast chapter) led raiding parties against European settlers until he finally retreated to the King Country in 1872.

After the Land Wars the government confiscated huge parcels of Maori land, which, with new legislation allowing private land sales, resulted in the loss of the prime Maori land over the rest of the 19th century.

Late 19th Century

While development in the North Island languished because of the conflicts, the South Island prospered, helped first by farming and then by the discovery of gold. After 1870, the North Island economy began to recover but it remained the poorer cousin until the 20th century. In 1876 the colonial government abolished the provincial governments and centralised power in Wellington, which had become the capital in 1865.

European settlement and influence grew and NZ became a productive agricultural country. Sheep farming, the backbone of modern NZ, flourished as refrigerated ships made it possible to sell NZ meat in Europe. NZ became what has been called

Tukaroto Matutaera Potatau Te Wherowhero Tawhiao, second Maori king – d. 1894

'an efficient offshore farm' for England, exporting agricultural products, especially mutton, wool, sheepskin and dairy products, and importing manufactured goods.

Towards the end of the 19th century NZ went through a phase of sweeping and unprecedented social change. After years of lobbying spearheaded by the remarkable Kate Sheppard, women were given the vote in 1893, 25 years before Britain or the USA and 75 years before Switzerland. An eminent leader at the time, Richard 'King Dick' Seddon and his Liberal Party were responsible for many of the reforms. Their farsighted social reforms and pioneering legislation included old-age pensions, minimum wage structures and the introduction of arbitration courts and child health services.

Meanwhile the Maori people suffered. NZ grew through immigration (a selective policy), but by 1900 the Maori population had dropped to an estimated 42,000. The Maori were given the vote in 1867, but continued to lose the struggle to hold on to their culture and ancestral lands.

Richard Seddon wheeling a barrow of clay at the turning of the first sod of the Lawrence–Roxburgh railway works (circa 1900)

Early 20th Century

New Zealand had became a self-governing British colony in 1856 and a dominion in 1907. By the 1920s it controlled most of its affairs, but it was not a fully independent country until 1947.

Meanwhile NZ fought for the British in the Boer War of 1899–1902 and in WWI. The Kiwi soldiers earned a reputation for skill and bravery, but also suffered heavy losses, with one in every three men aged between 20 and 40 killed or wounded fighting for Britain in WWI. NZ troops also helped the British in WWII, fighting in the European and Middle East arenas. But after 1941, when war was declared in the Pacific and NZ was directly threatened, a division was also established in the south-west Pacific.

The post-war years were good to NZ, as the world rebuilt and prices for agricultural products were high. NZ had one of the highest per-capita incomes in the world and a social welfare system envied by many countries.

During the Korean War (1950–53), NZ again sent troops as part of a Commonwealth brigade. Australia, NZ and the USA signed the Anzus defence pact, pledging mutual aid in the event of any attack. In response to the perceived threat of communism, NZ also joined the anti-communist Seato (South-East Asia Treaty Organisation).

During the 1960s and '70s an increased amount of NZ aid was directed to Pacific countries and in 1971 NZ joined the South Pacific Forum, designed for Pacific governments to discuss common problems.

Race Relations

The most important event in the history of NZ race relations was the signing of the Treaty of Waitangi in 1840. Though it signalled the annexation of the country by Britain, its motives – to stop lawlessness and the rampant grab for Maori land – were at least partly humanitarian. In exchange for granting sovereignty over NZ to Britain, the Maori chiefs were promised full exclusive and undisturbed possession of their lands, forests, fisheries and other properties, and the same rights and privileges as British subjects.

As settlement progressed, the terms of the treaty were increasingly ignored. Disputes over land resulted in the Land Wars of the 1860s, which eventually broke the back of Maori resistance. Maori land was appropriated and the treaty, which was never ratified by a NZ parliament, was all but dead.

Despite romantic notions of the Maori people, partly inspired by the 'noble savage' sentiments fashionable in the 19th century, Europeans remained largely separate from Maori society. Though intermarriage was common, for the most part Maori retreated to the more isolated rural areas.

At the turn of the 20th century, when race relations looked their bleakest, the Maori began to organise and develop leaders skilled in Pakeha and Maori affairs. The setting aside of Maori seats in parliament gave the Maori a political voice. In the South Island the Ngai Tahu people petitioned parliament over land grievances. The Maori also elected members of parliament specifically to lobby over these issues. The Young Maori Party, composed of Pakeha-educated Maori, pressed for greater education and health services for Maori communities.

Apirana Ngata of the Ngati Porou tribe was an inspiring leader who became Minister of Native Affairs in 1928, establishing Maori land development schemes and stressing the importance of Maori culture. Ngata was a member of the Young Maori Party with Hone Heke (the nephew of the warrior chief of the same name, of the Ngapuhi tribe), James Carroll (Ngati Kahungunu tribe), Maui Pomare (Tainui) and Peter Buck (also known as Te Rangi Hiroa) of the Ngati Toa tribe. These politicians lobbied the Labour Party heavily and when Labour achieved power in 1935, the government introduced legislation guaranteeing equality in employment, and increased spending on health, housing and education. Though the Maori were conspicuous on the rugby field and keen to sign up to defend the realm in times of war, up until WWII interaction between Pakeha and Maori communities remained minimal.

Despite disparities in education, wealth and power-sharing between Maori and Pakeha, Maori people did enjoy greater acceptance and equality under the law than the indigenous peoples of other European colonised countries. New Zealanders are proud of their record of racial harmony. *Return to Paradise* by James Michener tells of the outraged local reaction when WWII GIs stationed in NZ tried to treat the Maori like American blacks.

The postwar economic boom saw the greatest change in Maori society, as Maori migrated to the cities with the promise of jobs. Urban Maori mixed with Europeans as never before, as the government pursued the policies of assimilation fashionable at the time. But assimilation meant the dominance of European culture and though Maori culture survived, particularly in rural areas, Maori lost contact more than ever with their language and traditions.

In the late 1960s a new Maori voice arose and called for a revival in Maoritanga (Maori culture). Young activists combined with traditional leaders to provide a new direction, calling for the government to address Maori grievances. The contentious Treaty of Waitangi, always on the Maori agenda,

came to the fore as never before, and the concept of 'tino rangatiratanga' became a catch cry for greater self-determination. Increasing radicalism saw Maori take to the streets and engage in land occupations. In the 1970s, historic land disputes involved Raglan golf course and Bastion Point, in Auckland. The rise of black power groups and gangs such as the Mongrel Mob, a prominent Maori 'biker' group, unsettled many in the European community.

The focus on Maori issues spurred the government to give the Maori language greater prominence in schools and the media, to institute the Race Relations Act, banning discrimination, and to introduce the Waitangi Tribunal in 1975 to investigate Maori land claims. Though some claims have resulted in the return of Maori land, the implications for private land ownership has seen claims delayed for many years.

In an attempt to extricate itself from the terms of the tribunal, the government in 1994 proposed a massive once-and-for-all 'fiscal envelope' of $1 billion to pay out all Maori land claims over the following 10 years. Settlements have already been made, including the notable $170 million reparation to the Tainui in 1995 for lands confiscated in 1884 and an agreement between the Crown and the Ngai Tahu in 1997.

Perhaps the greatest effect of the Maori revival has been the growing interest in Maoritanga. Maori language, literature, arts and culture are experiencing a renaissance. The establishment of Te Kohanga Reo (language nests) in schools, with sessional or all-day immersion in Maori language and culture, is a strong step towards the preservation of Maori identity. The Maori population is now overwhelmingly urban and largely integrated into European society, but the loss of traditional culture is being redressed as more and more Maori learn the language and return to *marae*.

Many Pakeha also have a growing awareness of Maori culture. Certainly government and intellectuals have embraced the new Maori revival and see an understanding of Maori culture and at least a basic knowledge of Maori as an advantage. However, there is an undercurrent of unease in the wider community, especially with radical Maori aspirations that call for Maori sovereignty – the establishment of a separate Maori government and judicial system.

The Maori occupation of the Moutoa Gardens in Wanganui in 1995, which created great acrimony in the town and other parts of NZ, points to the difficulties of adjustment for the dominant European culture. Though NZ is not the utopia of racial harmony it is sometimes portrayed to be, there is no denying the genuine attempts by the European community to accommodate Maori aspirations. The overall good relations between both communities continues, and NZ's record on race relations remains strong.

Recent History

New Zealand's economy, along with much of the rest of the world, took a nose dive in the 1970s and '80s. The loss of its traditional European market for agricultural products, combined with the oil-crisis price hikes of many of its mineral and manufactured imports, caused a dramatic deterioration in the country's economy. Robert Muldoon's National Party government of the day tried to buy NZ's way out of trouble by running up large foreign debts and investing in wayward industrial development programs.

In 1984 a Labour government was elected and, in a reversal of political roles, set about a radical restructuring of the economy; dubbed 'Rogernomics' after the finance minister, Roger Douglas. While the reforms produced economic gains, they also resulted in rising unemployment, which increasingly threatened Labour's chances of re-election. As Douglas pressed on with the privatisation of state industries and proposals of a flat income tax rate and deregulation of the labour market, Prime Minister David Lange decided enough was enough and sacked him. After the party reinstated Douglas, Lange shocked the nation by resigning in 1989. Labour was in disarray, and the National Party led by Jim Bolger swept to power in 1990.

The 1970s and '80s also saw a resurgence of Maori culture, as Maori leaders and activists pushed for social justice and highlighted Maori grievances. In 1975 the Treaty of Waitangi, which in 1877 was ruled 'a simple nullity', was reconsidered. The parliament passed the Treaty of Waitangi Act, establishing a Waitangi Tribunal to investigate Maori claims against the British Crown dating from 1975. In 1985 the act was amended to include claims dating back to the original signing of the treaty in 1840. Financial reparations were made to many Maori tribes whose lands were found to have been unjustly confiscated.

In 1983 Australia and NZ signed the Closer Economic Relations Trade Agreement, permitting free and unrestricted trade between the two countries. As NZ increasingly saw itself as a Pacific nation, rather than an 'efficient offshore farm' for the UK, its UK trade declined in proportion to its increased trade with Australia, the USA, Japan and the rest of Asia.

In 1984 NZ took a strong stand on nuclear issues by refusing entry to nuclear-equipped and powered warships. In response, the USA suspended its obligations to NZ within the Anzus defence pact. Although this brave policy has caused many problems for the Kiwis they have continued to stick by it.

NZ also became a leader in the Pacific in its opposition to nuclear testing by the French at Moruroa Atoll in French Polynesia. In 1985 French secret service agents sank the Greenpeace ship *Rainbow Warrior* in Auckland's harbour (see the boxed text 'The *Rainbow Warrior* Trail' in the Northland chapter). In 1995 the French restarted testing in French Polynesia despite world-wide condemnation. NZ was again at the forefront of international protests and dispatched the navy frigate HMNZS *Tui* with a protest flotilla to Moruroa; the NZ ambassador to France was recalled as a mark of NZ's outrage. After a number of controversial detonations the French finally stopped testing.

In the 1990s the National Party government pressed on with Labour's free-market economics with greater privatisation, substantial cuts in welfare and a deregulation of the labour market that emasculated unions. National's majority was slashed in the 1993 elections and it held government by just one seat. Through a referendum in 1993 NZ adopted a Mixed Member Proportional (MMP) system (see Government & Politics later in the chapter).

In the 1996 election the National Party, led by Jim Bolger, formed a government in coalition with the minority NZ First Party and its maverick leader, the charismatic Winston Peters. In a bloodless coup Bolger was ousted and replaced by Jenny Shipley, the country's first woman prime minister. The most notable event during this period was the visit of Bill Clinton, who attended the meeting of APEC and commented favourably on both NZ's beauty and its golf potential.

In late November 1999, Labour won a general election and Helen Clark became NZ's first *elected* woman prime minister (in fact, with Shipley as Leader of the Opposition, women lead three of NZ's five major parties at present). Labour formed a coalition with the left-wing Alliance party, but are dependent on the support of the Greens.

A significant event of the 1990s – probably the greatest cause for national celebration – was NZ's 1995 win in the America's Cup yachting race, followed by its successful defence in 2000 (see the boxed text in the Auckland chapter).

GEOGRAPHY

New Zealand stretches 1600km from north to south. It consists of two large islands and some smaller islands, plus a few far-flung islands hundreds of kilometres away. NZ's territorial jurisdiction extends to Tokelau and the mostly uninhabited islands of the Chathams, Kermadec, Auckland, Antipodes, Snares, Solander and Bounty, and to the Ross Dependency in Antarctica.

The North Island (115,000 sq km) and the South Island (151,000 sq km) are the two major landmasses. Stewart Island (1700 sq km) lies directly south of the South Island. The country is 10,400km south-west of the USA, 1700km south of Fiji and 2250km east of Australia, its nearest large neighbour. Its western coastline faces the Tasman Sea, which separates NZ and Australia.

NZ's land area (270,534 sq km) is greater than that of the UK (244,800 sq km), but almost 36 times smaller than that of the USA. With only 3,800,000 people, almost 70% of whom live in the five major cities, NZ has a lot of wide open spaces. Its coastline, with many bays, harbours and fiords, is long compared with its landmass.

A notable feature of NZ's geography is the great number of rivers. There's a lot of rainfall in NZ and all that rain has to go somewhere. The Waikato River in the North Island is NZ's longest river (425km). Also in the North Island, the Whanganui River is the country's longest navigable river, which has always made it an important waterway. NZ also has many beautiful lakes; Lake Taupo is the largest, Waikaremoana and Wanaka are two of the most beautiful and Lake Hauroko the deepest (462m).

GEOLOGY

Both the North Island and South Island have some high mountains, formed by two distinct geological processes associated with the westward movement of the Pacific tectonic plate.

When one tectonic plate slides underneath another one, it forms a subduction zone. The North Island is on the southern reaches of the subduction zone where the oceanic Pacific Plate is sliding underneath the continental Indo-Australian Plate. The resulting volcanic activity has created a number of large volcanoes and thermal areas, and some equally impressive volcanic depressions.

A rough 'line' of volcanoes, some of which are still active, extends south from the steaming Whakaari (White Island) in the Bay of Plenty past Putauaki (Mt Edgecumbe), Tarawera and the highly active thermal areas in and around Rotorua and Lake Taupo. The latter, NZ's largest lake, was formed by a gigantic volcanic explosion in AD 186 and still has thermal areas bubbling away nearby. South of Lake Taupo are the North Island's spectacularly large volcanoes Tongariro, Ruapehu, Ngauruhoe and the smaller Pihanga. Further south-west is the lone volcanic cone of Mt Taranaki/Egmont.

Other parts of the North Island also have evidence of volcanic activity; in Auckland, for example, there are over 50 volcanic cones, including most of its famous 'hills' (One Tree Hill, Mt Eden etc) that rise up from the plains.

The North Island has some ranges of hills and mountains produced by folding and uplift, notably the Tararua and Ruahine ranges in the southern part of the North Island. In general, though, most of the high places of the North Island were formed by volcanic activity – particularly the high central plateau.

In the South Island the geological process is different. Here the two tectonic plates are smashing into each other, resulting in a process called 'crystal shortening'. This has caused the Southern Alps to rise as a spine, virtually extending along the entire length of the South Island. Thrust faulting, folding and vertical slips all combine to create a rapid uplift of the Southern Alps. Though the Southern Alps receive a lot of rainfall, and hence a lot of erosion, their rate of uplift is enough to keep pace and they are continuing to rise, as much as 10mm a year. Most of the east side of the South Island is a large plain known as the Canterbury Plains. Banks Peninsula, on the east coast, was formed by volcanic activity and joined to the mainland by alluvial deposits washed down from the Southern Alps.

CLIMATE

Lying between 34°S and 47°S, NZ is in Roaring Forties latitude, meaning it has a prevailing wind blowing over it from west to east year-round, ranging from gentle, freshening breezes to occasional raging gales in winter. Coming across the Tasman Sea, this breeze is relatively warm and moisture-laden. When the wind comes up from the south, it's coming from Antarctica and is icy; a southerly wind always means cold weather.

Because of their different geological features, the North and South Islands have two distinct rainfall patterns. In the South Island, the Southern Alps act as a barrier for the moisture-laden winds coming across the Tasman Sea, creating a wet climate on the west side of the mountains and a dry climate on the east side: the annual rainfall on the west side is over 7500mm but is only about 330mm on the east.

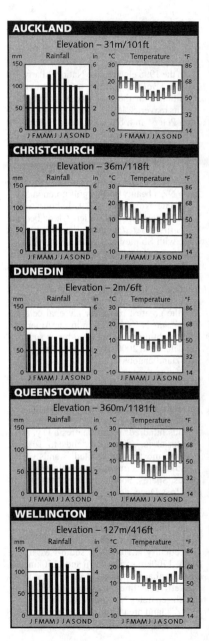

The South Island's geography also creates a wind pattern in which the prevailing wind, after losing its moisture, blows eastwards as a dry wind, gathering heat and speed as it blows downhill and across the Canterbury Plains towards the Pacific coast. In summer this katabatic or föhn wind can be hot, dry and fierce. In the Grey River valley on the South Island's West Coast there's another kind of downhill wind, locally called 'the Barber'.

In the North Island, the western sides of the high volcanoes get a lot more rain than the eastern sides but the rain shadow is not as pronounced, as there is not such a complete barrier as the Alps. Rainfall is more evenly distributed over the North Island, averaging around 1300mm per year.

It is a few degrees cooler in the South Island than the North Island. Winter is from June to August and summer from December to February. But there are regional variations: it's quite warm and pleasant up in the Northland region at any time of year. Higher altitudes are always considerably cooler, and it's usually windy in Wellington, which catches the winds whistling through the Cook Strait.

Snow is mostly seen in the mountains, though there can be snowfalls, even at sea level, in the South Island, particularly in the extreme south. Some of the plains and higher plateaus also receive snow in winter, notably the Canterbury Plains in the South Island and the high plateau around the Tongariro National Park in the North Island, especially on the 'desert' (east) side. Snow is seldom seen near sea level on the west coast of either island and not at all in the far north.

One of the most important things travellers need to know about the NZ climate is that it's a maritime climate, as opposed to the continental climate typical of larger landmasses. This means the weather can change with amazing rapidity. If you're tramping at high altitudes the extreme changeability of the weather can be a life-or-death matter.

ECOLOGY & ENVIRONMENT

The special colour 'Fauna & Flora' section following this chapter outlines the sad story of the decimation of many of NZ's bird species. It also focuses on the brave attempts to bring some species back from the brink of extinction.

NATIONAL PARKS

In addition to NZ's 13 national parks there are numerous forest areas. NZ has 19 forest, three maritime and two marine parks. The excellent pamphlet *Exploring New Zealand's Parks* outlines the national, maritime and forest parks. See the map 'New Zealand Parks' in the Activities chapter.

The Department of Conservation (Te Papa Atawhai), commonly referred to as DOC, looks after parks, tracks, walkways, huts and general tramping facilities. It also administers hundreds of scenic, historic, scientific and nature reserves, and wildlife refuges and sanctuaries. It also has responsibility for the three World Heritage areas – Tongariro National Park, Te Wahipounamu (south-west NZ, incorporating Fiordland, Mt Aspiring, Mt Cook and Westland national parks) and NZ's Subantarctic Islands.

The local DOC office (see the list in the Activities chapter) is usually the best place for information on nature and outdoor attractions in any area. DOC produces excellent pamphlets on almost any natural attraction. In some towns the visitor centres have the same information and a collection of DOC pamphlets. Also check out www.doc.govt.nz on the Web.

GOVERNMENT & POLITICS

The governmental structure of NZ is modelled on the British parliamentary system, with elections based on universal adult suffrage. The minimum voting age is 18 and candidates are elected by secret ballot. The maximum period between elections is three years but the government of the day can call an early election. Voting is not compulsory, but more than 80% of eligible voters usually turn up.

NZ is a constitutional monarchy. The traditional head of state, the reigning British monarch, is represented by a resident governor-general, who is appointed for a five-year term. An independent judiciary makes up another tier of government.

The difference between the British Westminster system and the NZ model is that NZ has abolished the upper house and governs solely through the lower house. Known as the House of Representatives, it has 120 seats. The government runs on a party system – the party that wins a majority of seats in an election automatically becomes the government and its leader the prime minister (PM). The main parties are the Labour Party (traditionally a workers' party) and National Party (conservative).

The two-party system has traditionally made it difficult for other parties to gain much power. But election results in 1993 were so close that the National Party was only voted in by a one-seat majority, ahead of the Labour Party and the smaller Alliance and NZ First Parties, both with two seats.

In a 1993 referendum on electoral reforms, New Zealanders voted overwhelmingly for proportional representation. The government introduced the MMP (Mixed Member Proportional) electoral system, a limited form of proportional voting based on the German electoral system. Under MMP, electors have two votes: one vote for a candidate in their electorate and the second for a political party. NZ has 60 general electorates and five Maori electorates (Maori voters can choose to vote in either a general or Maori electorate). The remaining 55 seats are allocated to the parties according to the percentage of party votes received.

After the country's first MMP elections, in 1996, the minority NZ First Party and the National Party formed the country's first coalition government, even though the Labour Party achieved the highest number of votes. National leader Jim Bolger was returned as PM and Winston Peters became the coalition treasurer and deputy PM.

While Bolger was overseas in November 1997 the party replaced him with Jenny Shipley, the transport minister. Shipley became the country's first woman PM and the government stumbled on in the uncertainties created by MMP.

The 1999 election saw Labour, headed by Helen Clark, win power after forming a coalition with the leftist Alliance Party. The

Greens achieved the balance of power after the allocation of MMP party votes. NZ First lost all but a handful of seats. The far-right ACT Party is also represented.

The composition of parliament as it entered the new millennium was made more significant with the election of the first trans-sexual (in the Labour Party) and first Rastafarian (Greens).

ECONOMY

New Zealand is a modern country that enjoys a standard of living equivalent to that of other developed countries.

The NZ economy has undergone a radical restructuring from 1984, first under Labour and then the National government, moving from a welfare-state, government-involved economy towards a private open-market economy.

By the 1980s NZ had lost its traditional UK market for agricultural produce, had incurred huge foreign debts and the economy was stagnant and restricted by government controls.

First the financial market was deregulated by floating the NZ dollar and abolishing exchange controls. Restrictions on overseas borrowing and foreign investment were also reduced. Tariffs were lowered, agricultural subsidies abolished and the taxation system was reformed by introducing a goods and services tax (GST), while lowering company and personal income taxes.

The initial changes resulted in a drop in the NZ dollar, an influx of foreign capital, even larger capital speculation, and an increase in private foreign debt. Inefficient, government-protected industries faced with foreign competition went to the wall.

The bubble burst in 1987 with the worldwide stock market collapse, which hit NZ's speculation boom the hardest. Inflation and unemployment topped 10%, growth was nonexistent and the country questioned the restructuring. The main engineer of the economic reforms, Labour's finance minister Roger Douglas, pressed on with a program of privatisation.

With the economy in the doldrums and the country enduring all the pain but no gain from the reforms, Labour was booted out of office in 1990. The incoming National government continued with the free-market reforms, tackling areas a Labour government never could. Welfare programs were cut (the state-funded health insurance system was abolished), privatisation was increased and, most significantly, the labour market was deregulated.

The economy continued to languish in the early 1990s but recently has shown dramatic improvement. The government is running a budget surplus, and public debt at around 24.7% of GDP in 1998, has dropped from 51.6% of GDP in 1990. The economy is enjoying unprecedented growth of around 5%, inflation is under 2% and unemployment is around 7%. NZ is receiving plaudits from around the world for its market reforms, and business confidence is bursting.

The reforms have had a major effect on the NZ economy and society. Though still overwhelmingly reliant on agriculture for export income, NZ has made progress in its efforts to diversify its economy. Business efficiency and profit has increased in the manufacturing, finance and service industries. NZ also has a broader world outlook, both in its trade and in general. Since 1960, when Britain bought over half of NZ's exports, NZ has shifted its focus elsewhere, especially to Asia. Australia is now NZ's single-largest trading partner, accounting for over 20% of all trade, but Asia takes 30% of exports, the USA 16.1% and the UK only 9.3%. NZ is also attracting greater investment from Asia, especially Japan and Singapore, and the Auckland property boom is spurred by Asian money.

The reforms have also had their pitfalls. As the corporate philosophy engulfs NZ, the once-sacrosanct ideals of equality in society have taken a back seat. Income disparity has grown substantially. In the new user-pays NZ, social services have been cut back, or rather sold off to private enterprise, resulting in higher charges and the axing of some nonprofitable services.

Tourism, service industries, manufacturing, small-scale industry and agriculture are important in the NZ economy. In a recent count the sector of trade, restaurants and hotels accounted for the largest proportion of GDP, followed by the sector of financing, insurance, real estate and business services, then by manufacturing and then agriculture.

With all the sheep, cattle and farms you see around NZ – the country is reckoned to have around 48 million sheep (12.5 per person) and nearly nine million cattle – it's not surprising that agriculture is an important part of the economy. In strictly dollar amounts it accounts for only about 10% of the entire GDP and employs about the same percentage of the country's workforce, but over 50% of all land in the country is devoted to pasture. Agricultural products from sheep, cattle, fish and forestry are NZ's chief exports (50%). Farming is a scientific proposition in NZ, with constant research carried out and the most modern scientific farming methods used.

Principal exports, in order of importance, are: meat (beef and veal bring in slightly more revenue than lamb and mutton), dairy products, fish, forest products (almost entirely pine and other non-native trees), fruits and vegetables (especially kiwi fruit, apples and pears) and wool. Main imports are machinery and mechanical appliances, electrical machinery and equipment, textiles, motor cars and other goods.

Tourism is also a major source of foreign revenue, although it is estimated as being 0.2% of the world total. Tourist arrivals numbered 1.46 million in 1998. The tourism industry aimed to increase this number to three million by 2000, but current arrivals, and the downturn in the Asian economies, indicate that this will not be achieved.

POPULATION & PEOPLE

Of NZ's population of around 3.8 million, 75.8% are NZ European (Pakeha), 13.8% are NZ Maori, 5.3% are Pacific Island Polynesians and about 4.5% are Asian.

Many Pacific islands are experiencing a rapid population shift from remote and undeveloped islands to the 'big city'. Auckland is very much the big city of the South Pacific, with the greatest concentration of Polynesians on earth. It sometimes causes a great deal of argument, discussion and tension, and much of it is not between the recent Pacific immigrants and the Pakeha population, but between the islanders and the Maori, or among the various islander groups themselves.

Asian migration is also increasing. NZ has a sizeable Indian community, mostly from Fiji, and has attracted east Asian migrants, many of them through NZ's recent immigration incentives. Central Auckland has a particularly east Asian character.

With only about 14 people per sq km, NZ is lightly populated by many countries' standards but is more densely populated than Australia with its stretches of empty country (2.3 people per sq km). Over the last 20 years or so the economic situation has led to a mass exodus of New Zealanders to Australia and further afield, though improving economic conditions have helped slow emigration.

The South Island once had a greater population than the North Island but is now the place to go for elbow room – its population is barely more than that of Auckland. The nation's capital is Wellington but Auckland is the largest city. Despite its rural base, NZ is very much an urban country. Altogether, the population of the 15 largest urban areas is nearly 70% of NZ's population – Auckland alone has 29% of the entire population.

EDUCATION

New Zealanders place a high value on education and virtually all of them are literate. Education is mandatory and free for all children between the ages of five and 16; in fact most children start school by the age of five and many have also attended preschool before then, all subsidised by the state. Correspondence education is available for children who live in remote places. Kohanga Reo kindergartens and Te Kura Kaupapa primary schools use the Maori language as the means of instruction.

NZ has eight universities and a number of teacher training institutions and polytechnics. NZ is gaining a reputation, especially in Asian countries, as a good place to learn English. But this trend may be affected by the recent downturn in many Asian economies. There are numerous language schools throughout NZ (although most are in Auckland) and some student visas permit foreign students to study for up to four years.

ARTS

New Zealand has a multifaceted arts scene, with both Maori and Pakeha engaged in all kinds of traditional and modern arts. Although there are distinct 'Maori arts' and 'European arts', there is rarely a ruling over who can practise particular arts. For example, there are Pakeha who enjoy carving in bone and painting in traditionally Maori styles; Maori songs, *poi* dances and a little bit of Maori language are taught in all schools. Likewise, there are many Maori who excel in the traditionally European arts such as theatre and music. Dame Kiri Te Kanawa is one of the world's best-known operatic divas (see the boxed text 'Dame Kiri Te Kanawa' in The East Coast chapter). Another opera singer of world standing is Dame Malvina Major.

Though the written word was not traditionally a part of Maori culture, NZ is experiencing a movement of dynamic Maori writing in fiction, nonfiction and poetry (see Maori & Pacific Literature later in this section).

Maori Arts

For information on Maori Arts see the special 'Maori Culture & Arts' section.

Theatre & Dance

New Zealanders take part in all the traditional European-based art forms. There's a lively literary scene (see Literature later in this section), poetry readings, many dance styles and live theatre. Wellington is particularly known for its theatre scene, with traditional as well as improvisational and avant-garde live theatre companies. Other major centres – Auckland, Palmerston North, Christchurch and Dunedin – also have active theatre and dance scenes. Smaller towns often actively support a community theatre group.

Music

As with theatre, so with music – the major centres have the liveliest music scenes but even smaller towns can have some interesting music. There's plenty of opportunity for going out in the evening and hearing live music in the larger centres, with a choice of everything from a symphony concert and the ballet to a rock, jazz or blues band. Irish music – both the acoustic ballad minstrel variety and the rousing Irish dance-band style – is very popular in NZ.

Rock New Zealand rock music doesn't begin and end in Dunedin, though over the last 10 years you could be forgiven for thinking so. In terms of innovative and alternative music, Dunedin is NZ's music capital.

In the 1970s and '80s, Split Enz was NZ's best-known and most successful band. Originally an unusual and eccentric group, their style became more mainstream in the '80s. Like many other NZ bands who achieved success, Split Enz based themselves in Australia and found themselves referred to as 'a great Australian band'. After its break-up in the mid-1980s, band member Neil Finn formed another successful 'Australian' band, Crowded House (at least Crowded House had some Australian members). For more details on the origins of Split Enz, see the boxed text 'A Blind Date with Destiny' in the Central West chapter.

Kiwi bands following the Split Enz tradition and achieving great things overseas include Garageland, Weta and Shihad.

NZ bands have long been renowned not only for their 'alternative' feel but also for their imaginative names. Examples (all of which are or were quite good bands) include Sneaky Feelings, Straitjacket Fits, Look Blue Go Purple, Headless Chickens and the Jean-Paul Sartre Experience. Possibly the prize example, however, is an outfit called the Great Unwashed, who later renamed themselves The Clean – signifying a major change in musical direction, perhaps?

Recently, there has been a development towards a distinctly Kiwi style, mixing accepted overseas styles with Polynesian influences. Lately this style has been exemplified by Bic Runga, a Chinese-Maori artist and the Tokelauan group Te Vaka.

The evergreen Dave Dobbyn's popular *Slice of Heaven* is an anthem for the tourist industry, and his many other compositions have distinctly NZ themes.

Visual Arts

The larger centres have a variety of museums and art galleries with contemporary and traditional art, and smaller towns often have a gallery, which may combine arts and crafts. All the visual arts are represented in NZ, including painting, sculpture, ceramics and a wide variety of handicrafts.

Frances Hodgkins (1869–1947) is NZ's most famous painter, but like author Katherine Mansfield, she achieved her fame overseas and never returned to NZ after 1913. Her European-influenced oils are hung in galleries worldwide.

New Zealand's most famous portrait painter was Charles Frederick Goldie (1870–1947) whose portraits of Maori with *moko* (tattoos) are so realistic as to be almost photo-like.

The best known of recent NZ painters is Modernist Colin McCahon (1919–87) who expressed bold often controversial themes, and incorporated cryptic messages on his canvases.

Literature

New Zealand has an active literary scene. Probably the most internationally famous NZ writer is Katherine Mansfield (1888–1923), who was born and raised in NZ and later moved to England, where she did most of her writing (see the boxed text 'Katherine Mansfield' in the Wellington chapter). See also Books in the Facts for the Visitor chapter.

Frank Sargeson (1903–82) is another classic NZ author. Within the country he is probably as well known as Mansfield, especially for his three-volume autobiography, novels and many short stories. But, since he lived all his life in NZ, his work did not become as widely known overseas.

For a wide-ranging collection of fiction by NZ women, try *In Deadly Earnest* compiled by Trudie McNaughton.

For short stories see the *Oxford Book of New Zealand Short Stories,* edited by Vincent O'Sullivan, and *Some Other Country: New Zealand's Best Short Stories* chosen by Marion McLeod & Bill Manhire. For students of NZ literature there's the *Oxford History of New Zealand Literature in English,* edited by Terry Sturm, or the *Penguin History of New Zealand Literature* by Patrick Evans.

Maurice Shadbolt is the author of several fine historical novels about NZ – so far he's published nine novels, four collections of short stories and several nonfiction books. His best-known novel is probably *The Season of the Jew,* which was chosen by the *New York Times* as one of the best books of 1987. This book follows a band of Maori in the East Coast Land War (see the boxed text about their leader, Te Kooti, in the Bay of Plenty chapter).

Janet Frame is another popular novelist, poet and short-story writer. Her three-volume autobiography *(To the Island, An Angel at my Table* and *Envoy from Mirror City)* became famous after the film *An Angel at My Table* by acclaimed Kiwi director Jane Campion. *Janet Frame: An Autobiography* is a fascinating insight into her life. Frame's many works are widely available (see the boxed text 'Shiver with a Sense of Yesterdays' in the Otago chapter).

Shonagh Koea is another popular author; her better-known works include *The Woman Who Never Went Home, The Grandiflora Tree, Staying Home and Being Rotten* and *Fifteen Rubies by Candlelight.*

Other favourite authors include Maurice Gee, whose novel *Going West* won the NZ Wattie Book of the Year Award in 1993; Fiona Kidman *(The Book of Secrets);* Owen Marshall *(Tomorrow We Save the Orphans);* Philip Temple *(Beak of the Moon);* and Dame Ngaio Marsh, who writes murder mysteries.

Maori & Pacific Literature Two books of the series *Te Ao Marama – Contemporary Maori Writing,* edited by Witi Ihimaera, have been published. *Volume One: Te Whakahuatanga o te Ao – Reflections of Reality* is an anthology of written and oral Maori literature; *Volume Two: He Whakaatanga o te Ao – The Reality* (1993) has prominent Maori authors examining crucial issues affecting Maori people. Witi Ihimaera, of the Rongowhakaata tribe, is a prolific author of novels and short stories. Some of his better-known novels include *The Matriarch, Tangi* and *Pounamu, Pounamu.* His *Bulibasha* is a zany look at the life of Maori sheep-shearing gangs in the East Coast region of the North Island.

Keri Hulme received international acclaim when *The Bone People* won the British Booker McConnell Prize for fiction in 1985. She has published several other novels and books of poetry.

Alan Duff is a controversial author who writes about Maori people in modern NZ society. His novels and nonfiction have all generated heated debate. His first novel, *Once Were Warriors,* was made into the eponymous film which received international acclaim; his second novel was *One Night Out Stealing.* In 1993 his nonfiction *Maori: The Crisis and the Challenge* sparked a rage of controversy.

Other significant Maori authors include novelists Apirana Taylor and Patricia Grace *(Potiki),* and poet Hone Tuwhare.

NZ also has some important Pacific islander authors. Albert Wendt, a Samoan author who is a professor of English at the University of Auckland, is one of the finest. His novels include *Leaves of the Banyan Tree, Pouliuli, Sons for the Return Home, Ola* and *Black Rainbow;* he has also published two poetry books and two collections of short stories. The excellent *The Shark that Ate the Sun: Ko e Ma go ne Kai e La* by Niuean John Puhiatau Pule is about the Pacific island experience in NZ.

Children's Literature This is a particularly fertile area of writing, with many NZ writers achieving international success.

David Hill deals with the sensitive subject of children with disabilities in *See Ya, Simon.* Rural life is the setting for Jack Lasenby's *Uncle Trev* and *Harry Wakatipu.* Sports, especially sailing and swimming, are the impetus for some of Tessa Duder's novels (the *Alex* series, *Jellybean* and *Night Race to Kawau*), while William Taylor's novels, aimed at 11- and 12-year-olds, focus on the plight of the underdog.

One of NZ's most successful writers of children's literature is Margaret Mahy; she is author of over 100 titles and winner of the international Carnegie Medal for *The Changeover* and *The Haunting*.

Poetry James K Baxter, who died in 1972, is possibly the best-known NZ poet. Others include RAK Mason, Allen Curnow, Denis Glover, Hone Tuwhare and the animated Sam Hunt. *Contemporary New Zealand Poetry Nga Kupu Titohu o Aotearoa* edited by Miriama Evans, Harvey McQueen & Ian Wedde is an excellent collection of NZ poetry written both in English and Maori. Wedde and McQueen also edited the comprehensive *Penguin Book of New Zealand Verse*.

Cinema

The history of NZ film doesn't really begin until the late 1970s. From some early stumbling attempts, notable feature films have survived the test of time and launched the careers of NZ directors and actors.

Sleeping Dogs (1977) is an accomplished psychological drama that was at the forefront of the new film industry; it also launched the careers of actor Sam Neill and director Roger Donaldson.

Bad Blood (1981) is a British-NZ production about the gun-toting psychosis of macho NZ, based on the true story of Stan Graham, a nutter oddly afforded hero status in NZ, who went berserk in a rural town during WWII. *Smash Palace* (1981), about a marriage break-up and custody case, was a local success. *Came a Hot Friday* (1984), directed by Ian Mune, is one of NZ's better comedies.

Other films of note are *Utu* (Revenge; 1983), an amateurish but breakthrough Maori film; *Meet the Feebles* (1989), a sick piece of splatter puppetry but not without innovation; and *The Quiet Earth* (1985), an end-of-the-world sci-fi movie with wit and imagination. *Goodbye Pork Pie* (1980), an exuberant NZ road movie directed by Geoff Murphy, was a box office hit in NZ, as was

the later *Footrot Flats* (1986), starring NZ's favourite cartoon character, The Dog.

NZ films moved into art-house cinemas with Vincent Ward's *Vigil* (1984), a brooding film about a girl's coming of age in the rain-drenched backblocks of NZ. It proved too ponderously artistic for many Kiwi filmgoers but wowed them at Cannes. Ward's follow-up *The Navigator* (1988) is a strange modern/medieval hunt for the Holy Grail.

NZ's best-known director is Jane Campion. Her greatest films explore NZ themes. *An Angel at My Table* (1990), based on Janet Frame's autobiography, shows the fine character development typical of her films. Campion's masterpiece, *The Piano* (1993), about the trials of a mute woman in NZ's pioneer days, received Cannes and Academy Award success.

Suddenly the world noticed NZ's already accomplished movie industry. *Once Were Warriors* (1994), a brutal tale of modern urban Maori life, stunned movie-goers around the world. The sequel *What Becomes of the Broken Hearted?* (1999) had nowhere as near as much impact.

Peter Jackson followed *Meet the Feebles* and other equally tasteless (but excellent) flicks with *Heavenly Creatures* (1994), achieving critical acclaim. It's based on a famous 1950s case of matricide by two schoolgirls. Jackson achieved another coup in 1999 – currently he is directing the Tolkein trilogy *Lord of the Rings,* the biggest film project ever to be undertaken in this country.

Skarfies (1999) relates the misadventures of a group of students, known as 'scarfies' (because they wear university scarfs). Almost a cult movie now, it was made on a shoestring budget. The dark comedy *Savage Honeymoon* (2000) laughs at life in Auckland's west.

SOCIETY & CONDUCT

Maori culture has always been an integral part of NZ and is a strong and growing influence, although NZ culture is essentially European, transplanted by the British to these far-off islands.

European New Zealanders used to hold so strongly to their British traditions that they earned the tag of 'South Seas Poms'. While British culture is still a strong focus for many, a growing diversity of migrants and a wider global outlook has seen a distinct change in NZ society in recent years. Resurgent Maori culture and the new corporate philosophy have also helped to shape a new world view. NZ has always been proud of its traditions, but more than ever the country is exploring its identity.

Though the majority of NZ's population comes from English stock, other notable early influences were the Scots and the Dalmatians, the latter coming to dig kauri gum in Northland. Scottish immigrants came in large numbers and their influence is most evident in the far south, where Scottish games are held, the bagpipes still blow and a distinct Scottish brogue can be heard.

More recently, Polynesians have brought their cultures with them from Pacific island nations. In Auckland you can go to a Samoan rugby match on Saturday afternoon, dance the *tamure* at a Cook Islands nightclub that night and go to a Tongan-language church service on Sunday. The Indians and the Chinese are NZ's other two major immigrant groups.

Through a common history and culture based on British traditions and a strong geographical link, NZ shares many cultural attributes with, and has long been influenced by, neighbouring Australia. Many Kiwis have migrated to Australia, or at least travelled to and worked there, but Kiwis are keen to distance themselves from their brasher and patronising cousins across the Tasman.

New Zealanders are intensely proud of their country. Aware of their country's small size and relative insignificance on the world stage, national achievements, particularly world-beating sporting achievements, are greeted with great fanfare. NZ also values its independence and is not afraid to take on the world, as it has done in its anti-nuclear stance, a policy so widely supported that not even conservative governments have been game to reverse it despite intense international pressure.

New Zealanders value hard work, resourcefulness, honesty, fairness, independence and ruggedness – legacies of their pioneering history. For the visitor, perhaps the most immediately obvious trait of all New Zealanders is their friendliness.

RELIGION

The most common religion in NZ is Christianity. Twenty-four per cent of the population is Anglican (Church of England), 18% is Presbyterian and 15% is Roman Catholic. Other denominations include the Methodist (5%) and Baptist churches, the Church of Latter-Day Saints (Mormon Church), Jehovah's Witnesses, the Pentecostal Church, Assembly of God and the Seventh-Day Adventist Church. Other faiths, including Hinduism, Judaism, Islam and the Baha'i faith, are also represented.

The Ratana and Ringatu faiths, with significant followings, are Maori forms of Christianity. Ringatu was founded by Te Kooti (see the boxed text in the Bay of Plenty chapter) after a divine revelation while he was imprisoned on the Chathams. Revitalised by the Tuhoe prophet Rua Kenana in the early 20th century, the Church still has a considerable following in the Bay of Plenty, and on the 11th of each month its devotees begin an intensive period of worship which culminates in a communion ritual known as a 'love-feast'.

The Ratana Church was founded by Tahupotiki Wiremu Ratana (1870–1939). He performed faith healing and soon attracted a loyal following of adherents – to them he was Te Mangai, 'The Mouthpiece of God'. The Ratana faith has since its founding been an influential force in Maori politics – at one time four Maori seats were held by Ratana members. Ratana Pa near Raetihi, with its twin-towered temple, is the spiritual centre for its 40,000 plus members.

About 20% of Kiwis have no religion.

FAUNA & FLORA

FAUNA
Birds

There is not an enormous variety of endemic birdlife in New Zealand but the avifauna here evolved in relative peace with very little threat, and no large competitors. In such a peaceful environment, flightless birds such as ground-dwelling parrots, kiwi and moa not only survived but thrived.

The balance was altered by the arrival of humans – first the Maori, then the Pakeha – as well as the predatory species which both groups introduced. Many species vanished in a blink of the eye relative to NZ's evolutionary history.

Thus, one NZ bird you *won't* see is the famous moa (see later in this section). Similarly, the huia, with its remarkably different male and female bills, is extinct. The subantarctic fairy tern is currently the bird closest to extinction; only 36 remain. Other species in peril are the Chatham Island oyster catcher (around 100), the kakapo (60) and even the famous kiwi itself!

Kiwi

There are six identified varieties of kiwi: the brown kiwi (Apteryx australis), of which there are several subspecies (Okarito, Southern Tokoeka and Haast Tokoeka); the little spotted kiwi (A. owenii); and the great spotted kiwi (A. haastii). The best known of all NZ's birds, the kiwi has become the country's most recognised symbol and a nickname for New Zealanders themselves. In theory the kiwi is named for its distinctive call ('kee-wee') but if you hear one in the wild you might wonder why the bird wasn't named a 'kyyheeekkkkk'.

It's a small, tubby, flightless bird and, because it's nocturnal, is not easy to observe. Kiwi have defunct vestigial wings, feathers that are more like hair than real feathers and lousy eyesight, but strong legs. Most active at night, they are fairly lazy, sleeping for up to 20 hours a day. They spend the rest of the time poking around for worms, sniffed out with the nostrils on the end of their bill.

The female kiwi is larger than the male and much fiercer. She lays an egg weighing up to half a kilogram, huge in relation to her size and about 20% of her body weight. After performing that mighty feat,

Dinornis ingens – restoration from skeleton and feathers (FW Frohawk, 1906)

ALEXANDER TURNBULL LIBRARY, WELLINGTON NZ

Kiwi

LEE FOSTER

Title Page: Silver fern (underside)
Photograph by David Wall

Great spotted kiwi

Royal albatross *(toroa)* with chick

Westland black petrel

she leaves the male to hatch it while she guards the burrow. So when the kiwi hatches it associates with its father, completely ignoring its mother.

Brown kiwi are found in the forests of Northland, the Central Plateau and eastern ranges of the North Island, Fiordland and Stewart Island. Little spotteds are confined to Kapiti and Little Barrier Islands. The great spotted is found in the South Island in north-west Nelson, the central West Coast and Arthur's Pass National Park.

Kiwi are threatened – rare enough that no species of kiwi, with the exception of the Stewart Island brown, can be easily seen in the wild. However, the nocturnal bird can be observed in many artificially dark 'kiwi houses' in NZ (in Kaitaia, Whangarei, Auckland Zoo, Otorohanga, Rotorua, Taupo, Napier, Mount Bruce in the Wairarapa, Waikanae, Wellington Zoo, Christchurch and Queenstown).

For another picture of the kiwi (as well as the tuatara, white heron, yellow-eyed penguin, blue duck, NZ falcon, kokako and mohua) see the boxed text 'Pictures in Your Wallet' under Money in the Facts for the Visitor chapter.

Royal Albatross

New Zealand waters host 14 of the world's 24 species of albatross. The huge Royal albatross *(Diomedea epomorphora;* Maori: *toroa),* with a wingspan of over 3m, ranges throughout the world and breeds on island groups to the south and east of NZ. These birds spend more than 80% of their lives at sea and can cover almost 200,000km over the course of a year. New Zealand's one mainland breeding colony is Taiaroa Head on the Otago Peninsula, where they can be observed by visitors (see the Otago chapter).

There is nothing quite like seeing these enormous birds swoop past at eye level. On land, however, they are clumsy, lumbering creatures. In winter you may see a wandering albatross *(Diomedea exulans)* over NZ waters.

Westland Black Petrel

Near Punakaiki, on the South Island's West Coast, are the world's only breeding grounds of the largest burrowing petrel. Westland black petrels *(Procellaria westlandica)* come to land only during the breeding season – from March to December. Eggs are laid in

May and chicks hatch in July/August. From August to November chicks are fed by one of the parents every three days. In December the fledglings leave the colony to breed, not to return for another seven years.

Their daily flights to and from feeding grounds are best observed near Punakaiki. They fly out individually each morning but congregate offshore for the flight in at dusk. During the breeding season thousands can be seen coming in at once. (See Punakaiki & Paparoa National Park in the West Coast chapter.)

Fiordland Crested Penguin

This penguin (*Eudyptes pachyrhynchus;* Maori: *pokotiwha*) lives around the south-west coast of the South Island and around Stewart Island. Believed to be the rarest species of penguin in the world, it is (sensibly perhaps?) very timid.

The bird is identifiable by its yellow crest, which distinguishes it from the yellow-eyed penguin.

You are most likely to see these birds when you're travelling down the West Coast in Te Wahipounamu World Heritage region, especially near the beach by Lake Moeraki (see the West Coast chapter), and in Milford Sound (see the Southland chapter).

Little Blue Penguin

The little blue penguin (*Eudyptula minor;* Maori: *korora*) is common in coastal waters from the top of the North Island to Stewart Island. There are five subspecies (North Island, Cook Strait, South Island, Chatham Island and White-flippered).

The smallest species of penguin, the little blue can be seen coming ashore at night, most notably on beaches along the Otago coast. Its upper parts are blue, underparts white and bill black. In Australia it is known as the fairy or little penguin.

Yellow-eyed Penguin

The yellow-eyed penguin (*Megadyptes antipodes;* Maori: *hoiho*) is the world's second-rarest species of penguin, its numbers having diminished because of the loss of its coastal habitat. It can still be seen along the south-eastern coast of the South Island (see Otago Peninsula in the Otago chapter). A streaked yellow head and eye are its most conspicuous characteristics.

Fiordland crested penguins *(pokotiwha)*

Little blue penguin *(korora)*

Yellow-eyed penguin *(hoiho)*

Australasian gannet *(takapu)*

Spotted shags

White heron *(kotuku)*

Australasian Gannet

This gannet *(Morus serrator;* Maori: *takapu)* has three mainland breeding colonies: Farewell Spit (see the Marlborough & Nelson chapter), Muriwai (see Around Auckland in the Auckland chapter) and Cape Kidnappers (at Hawkes Bay on the North Island's East Coast). Juveniles migrate to Australia and return in four years to breed. These birds dive from great heights, with wings folded back, to catch fish. The yellow head and white body is the most obvious feature of adult birds but immature gannets are speckled brown. On land they may seem ungainly but in the air they're poetry in motion.

Cormorants & Shags

Cormorants and shags are all referred to as 'shags' in NZ, and distinction is seldom made between the seven species. The black shag *(Phalacrocorax carbo novahollandiae;* Maori: *kawau),* NZ's largest shag, is common on inland lakes and along sheltered parts of the coastline. It is seen in flocks near shellbanks and sandspits or perched on rocks.

Three other species of *Phalacrocorax* are found in NZ: the pied shag, little black shag and the little shag. The little black is distinguished from the immature little shag by its long, narrow bill.

The NZ king shag *(Leucocarbo carunculatus)* is one of the rarest shags in the world and only found in coastal waters on the southern side of Cook Strait. Pink feet are its distinguishing feature.

The Stewart Island shag *(L. chalconotus)* is found in coastal waters from the Otago Peninsula to Stewart Island.

The spotted shag *(Stictcarbo punctatus punctatus),* recognised by the black spots on its back, is found in coastal waters around Auckland, the Marlborough Sounds and on the Otago and Banks Peninsulas.

White Heron

This heron *(Egretta alba modesta;* Maori: *kotuku)* is widely spread throughout the world but seen in relatively few numbers in NZ. It is believed that there are only 200 kotuku in the country. The sole breeding colony is at Whataroa (see Ross to Okarito in the West Coast chapter) and the best time to see them is from September to November. After that, they scatter to wetlands and tidal lagoons throughout NZ.

In ancient times some Maori believed that seeing a kotuku was a once-in-a-lifetime experience, and it is still considered a sign of good luck to spot one now.

Blue Duck

This endemic and threatened species of duck *(Hymenolaimus malacorhynchos;* Maori: *whio)* is found in fast-flowing rivers of the high country of the North and South Islands, but no farther north than East Cape on the East Coast.

Strong swimmers, they feed both on the surface and underwater. You can be almost certain that it is a whio if you see a bluish-grey duck surfing and feeding in fast-flowing, turbulent water.

Weka

Weka

The four subspecies of weka are found in a wide range of habitats, usually in scrub and on forest margins. The North Island weka *(Gallirallus australis greyi)* is found on Kapiti Island, in Northland and Poverty Bay. The western South Island weka *(G. australis australis)* is found in the north and western regions of the South Island, while the eastern South Island weka *(G. australis hectori)* is found in the drier east. The Stewart Island weka *(G. australis scotti)* has been introduced to Kapiti Island.

A flightless bird, the weka is most active at dusk, but it can be seen scrounging during the day in areas where humans leave rubbish.

NZ falcon *(karearea)* on eggs

New Zealand Falcon

The falcon *(Falco novaeseelandiae;* Maori: *karearea)* is distinguished from the larger Australasian harrier (also common in NZ) by its rapid flight and longer, straighter tail. It inhabits high country in the South Island, and it's rarely seen north of central North Island. It has a rapid 'kek-kek-kek' call and feeds mostly on smaller passerine birds.

Pukeko

This brightly coloured bird *(Porphyrio porphyrio melanotus)* is common throughout the wetter areas of NZ, especially near swamps and lake edges where there are clumps of rushes; often seen on the roadside as you drive past such areas.

The pukeko is a good swimmer and a good flier. It has very large feet, which can look a little strange

Pukeko

Black stilt (kaki)

DOC – CR VEITCH

Takahe

DOC – P MORRISON

New Zealand dotterel (tuturiwhatu)

DOC – MF SOPER

dangling below it as the bird takes off. Pukeko emit a high-pitched screech when disturbed.

Black Stilt

The Mackenzie Country of south Canterbury is the home of the black stilt (Himantopus novaezelandiae; Maori: kaki), one of the world's rarest wading birds. It is found in swamps and beside braided riverbeds in South Island river systems. A single remnant population of just 37 adults survives in the wild.

A captive breeding and release program for the endangered black stilt has been established by the Department of Conservation (DOC) near Twizel in the South Island. Juvenile birds are hand-reared (isolated from predators) and released into the wild at nine months of age. In 1998, 15 were released to the wild but most died of iodine deficiency. The release of 19 in September 1999 was more successful. (For more information see Twizel in the Canterbury chapter.)

Takahe

The takahe (Porphyrio [Notornis] mantelli hochstetteri) was first classified by botanists in 1849 but was believed extinct by the early 20th century. However, it was found again in the Murchison Mountains, Fiordland, in 1948. There are about 130 birds still in Fiordland, another 60 on predator-free islands, and some in captivity. You can see them at Te Anau (see the Southland chapter) and Mt Bruce (see Wairarapa in the Wellington Region chapter).

The takahe is a flightless bird with similar colouring to that of the pukeko. It feeds on tussock shoots, alpine grasses and fern roots, and its habitat is tussock and small patches of beech forest.

New Zealand Dotterel

The dotterel (Charadrius obscurus; Maori: tuturiwhatu), a threatened species (1500 remain), is found north of the Bay of Plenty and Raglan and occasionally on Stewart Island. There are several breeding colonies on the sandy beaches of the eastern side of the Coromandel. Its nest is a simple sand scrape, sometimes lined with dry grass; the birds nest from August to December. Listen for the 'pweep' when they are disturbed – then back off, as you are too close.

Wrybill

If you fail to recognise this bird, with its unique bill with the tip bent to the right, put the binoculars away and take up stamp collecting. Wrybills *(Anarhynchus frontalis;* Maori: *ngutuparore)* migrate within NZ, first nesting in the shingle riverbeds of Canterbury and Otago then moving north to spend autumn and winter in the warmer estuaries and mud flats of the North Island. The wrybill swings its bill sideways through mud to trap marine organisms from the sludge.

Kakapo

The kakapo *(Strigops habroptilus)* is severely endangered. The only remaining populations are on predator-free islands in the Marlborough Sounds and offshore of Stewart Island. There are only 60 or so birds left; few enough that they have been individually named by DOC staff – from Alice to Zephyr.

The largest parrot in the world (males sometimes weigh up to 4kg), the kakapo is flightless, although it can glide a shortway downhill and uses its wings for balance. The name means literally 'night parrot' in Maori – the kakapo is nocturnal.

You will only be able to observe this bird with the assistance of DOC, and they'll want a pretty good reason before they let you disturb the birds.

Kaka

There are two subspecies of kaka. The North Island kaka *(Nestor meridionalis septentrionalis)* inhabits lowland forest in the North Island and forested offshore islands. The South Island kaka *(N. meridionalis meridionalis)* inhabits forests in the Nelson, the West Coast, Fiordland and Stewart Island. The South Island kaka is slightly larger than its northern cousin and has a whitish (sometimes grey) crown; both birds are generally bronze in colour with crimson tones on their underparts.

Kea

The kea *(Nestor notabilis)* is a large parrot decked out in unparrot-like drab green except for bright red underwings. They inhabit South Island high-country forests and mountains and are amusing, fearless, cheeky and inquisitive birds. There are plenty of opportunities to observe them at the Fox and Franz Josef Glaciers and in Arthur's Pass National Park. At

'Alice' – one of DOC's precious kakapo

Kaka

Kea

Red-crowned parakeet *(kakariki)*

Morepork *(ruru)*

NZ wood pigeon *(kereru)*

the car parks at the terminal of the glaciers they hang around waiting for tourist hand-outs. Signs warn you of their destructive tendencies – they occasionally supplement their diet of bugs and berries with windscreen rubber.

Parakeets

New Zealand has two species of indigenous parakeet – the yellow-crowned *(Cyanoramphus auriceps auriceps)* and red-crowned *(C. novaezelandiae novaezelandiae)*; both are known to the Maori as *kakariki* (which is also the Maori word for 'bright green').

The yellow-crowned is seen high in the canopy of forests in the North, South and Stewart Islands, and on many outlying islands. The red-crowned is not likely to be seen on the mainland but rather in lowland forest on offshore islands. Both species lay their eggs from October to January and the males help feed the chicks.

Morepork

The endemic owl *(Ninox novaeseelandiae novaeseelandiae;* Maori: *ruru)* is found throughout NZ, with the exception of the east of the South Island. It is the only endemic owl and differs from the introduced little owl *(Athene noctua)* in that it has a rounded head and larger tail.

The morepork gets its name from its cry of 'quorquo', which, with a *lot* of imagination, sounds like 'more pork' (in other countries the bird is called a mopoke). It would probably eat pork if offered, but usually favours insects such as moths and the large bush weta (see Other Fauna).

New Zealand Pigeon

When you first encounter the NZ pigeon *(Hemiphaga novaeseelandiae novaeseelandiae)* in the forest it is likely that you will be startled by its heavy, thumping wingbeat as it flies from tree to tree. Also called the wood pigeon or *kereru*, it is easily identified by its bright green colouring and white 'apron'.

The bird is widespread in NZ forests and is occasionally seen eating in open fields. A large bird, it is NZ's only endemic species of pigeon. The West Coast, the Catlins, Fiordland and Stewart Island are good places to see them. Their numbers have dropped alarmingly in Northland forests – partly due to illegal hunting.

Rifleman

There are two subspecies of rifleman, NZ's smallest bird. The South Island rifleman (*Acanthisitta chloris chloris*; Maori: *titipounamu*) is found throughout that island, especially in mountainous beech forests. It has also been seen feeding in exotic forests, gorse and even in suburban hedges. The North Island rifleman (*A. chloris granti*) is found on the Barrier Islands and in forests south of Te Aroha in the Waikato. The rifleman has a short tail and short, spiralling flight, flitting from tree to tree when feeding.

Rock wren

Rock Wren

This bird (*Xenicus gilviventris*) inhabits subalpine and alpine fields in the South Island. Not much larger than the rifleman, it is recognised by its long legs and its curious habit of bobbing up and down. It literally jumps from rock to rock, looking for insects and spiders. During winter it lives in rock crevices under the snow.

Fantail

There are two subspecies of fantail, the North Island (*Rhipidura fuliginosa placabilis*; Maori: *piwakawaka*) and South Island (*R. fuliginosa fuliginosa*); both are common in forests, scrubland and can even be seen in suburban gardens. The South Island fantail has more white on its outer tail feathers. Although most fantails are pied (dark brown and white), there are black variants of both species.

Pied fantail (*piwakawaka*) on nest

The fantail has a reputation as a friendly bird because of its habit of following trampers through the bush. It is attracted to the insects you disturb as you brush past the undergrowth. In Maori tradition, the fantail is sometimes considered a harbinger of doom.

Whitehead & Mohua (Yellowhead)

The whitehead (*Mohoua albicilla*; Maori: *popokatea*) inhabits forest and scrubland in the North Island. Like the mohua, its most conspicuous feature is the single colour of the head. It doesn't occur north of Te Aroha, except on Tiritiri and Little Barrier Islands.

The mohua (*M. ochrocephala*), or yellowhead, is about the size of a house sparrow and unmistakable in forests because of its bright yellow head. The mohua is very rare and difficult to observe; there are about 200 in the forests around Arthur's Pass, several hundred in Fiordland and a few in the Catlins. If you

Mohua (yellowhead)

Chatham Island black robin

DOC – D MERTON

North Island kokako

DOC – R COLBOURNE

Tui (parson bird)

DOC – CR VEITCH

see a similar bird in open grassland, it's probably an introduced yellowhammer.

Chatham Island Black Robin

In 1976 there were only a handful of black robins *(Petroica traversi)* left, all on Little Mangere Island in NZ's Chatham Islands. Over the following few years attempts were made to transfer the birds to safer habitats on other islands. These relocations were largely unsuccessful and in 1980 there were only five black robins left. Such a small population would usually spell extinction of the species but, as a last resort, wildlife authorities began a cross-fostering program using endemic warblers and, later, tom tits.

The robins must have sensed that the time for their emergence was right. By the end of summer 1984 there were 19 robins, and at the end of the following summer there were 38. The tom tits were ideal foster parents. The future of the black robin is no longer bleak and one of the most courageous attempts to save an endangered species has succeeded. There are now around 250.

The North Island *(P. australis longipes)* and South Island robins *(P. a. australis)* are both greyish in colour.

Kokako

The depletion of its habitat and the introduction of predators have severely endangered populations of the North Island kokako *(Callaeas cinerea wilsoni)*. It is a member of the wattlebird family and distinguished by its blue wattle (the skin hanging from its throat).

The kokako is a weak flier and would most likely be seen bounding and gliding through the unmodified lowland North Island forests. DOC has had recent success breeding this bird in captivity.

The South Island kokako, orange-wattled, is thought to be extinct, although it *may* survive in remote parts of the South Island and Stewart Island.

Tui

The tui *(Prosthemadera novaeseelandiae novaeseelandiae)* is found throughout NZ's forests. Conspicuous by its white throat feathers (hence its alternative name, 'parson bird'), it is also identified by its voice. The tui is perhaps the most beautiful singing bird in NZ. Parts of its song are an almost liquid call similar to that of the bellbird, but it adds clicks, grunts, chuckles and other sounds from its extremely large repertoire of sounds. It may also mimic other birds.

Tui are widely distributed and you can see them around much of the country, even in built-up areas. However, forest areas are their prefered habitat. Pelorus Sound, Ulva Island and Oban (Stewart Island) are particularly fertile spotting grounds.

Saddleback

There are two subspecies of saddleback (you've guessed it by now!): the North Island *(Philesturnus carunculatus rufusater;* Maori: *tieke)* and South Island *(P. carunculatus carunculatus).* The first (of which there are about 5000) is found on islands off the East Coast region and on rat-free Kapiti Island near Wellington, and the second on small islands off the coast of Stewart Island. They differ in that the North Island saddleback has a narrow, buff-coloured band in front of the saddle. Both are weak fliers and tend to flit through the forest in short rapid movements. You will often be greeted by their distinctive chattering call when you enter their territory.

Bellbird

The bellbird *(Anthornis melanura melanura;* Maori: *makomako)* is common in both native and exotic forests and is easily identified by its beautiful bell-like call. It is found all over NZ, except Northland. A member of the honeyeater family, like the tui and the stichbird, it has a curved honeyeater beak and short tail feathers. Among trees from which it takes nectar are rata, pohutukawa and kowhai.

Moa

New Zealand's most famous extinct bird, the flightless, herbivorous *Dinornithiformes* resembled an oversized ostrich. There were numerous types and sizes, the largest of them – the giant moa – were as tall as 3.5m and weighed over 200kg. Their flesh was an integral part of the early Maori diet, their bones had many uses and the large eggs were used to carry water.

Most species of moa had been extinct for a few centuries by the time Europeans arrived. Moa skeletons and reconstructions are displayed in many NZ museums, and their bones can be seen in the Honeycomb Caves, near Karamea in the South Island (see the West Coast chapter).

North Island saddlebacks *(tieke)*

DOC – CR VEITCH

Bellbird *(makomako)*

DOC – CR VEITCH

Marine Mammals

Perhaps one of the greatest delights of a trip to NZ, especially the South Island, is a chance to observe the wealth of marine mammals. There are 76 species of whales and dolphins on this globe and NZ, as small as it is, is blessed with 35 of these species. Kaikoura, in Canterbury, is particularly blessed, as nearly half of that number of whales and dolphins have been seen in waters off its shores.

Of the 66 species of toothed whales and dolphins, the largest and the smallest are seen in NZ waters – the sperm whale and the Hector's dolphin. There are also baleen whales, seals and sea lions.

Many species of whales and seals were once hunted in NZ waters – but no longer. The whales, dolphins, seals and sea lions attract not the bludgeon and harpoon but the entranced eyes of foreign and local observers. The tourist dollars pouring into Kaikoura and elsewhere are worth many times the money made by the previous slaughter for oil and skins.

Sperm Whale

Physeter macrocephalus is the largest of the toothed whales – the male often reaches up to 20m in length, while the female is much smaller, with a maximum length of 12m. This is the whale 'watchers' come to Kaikoura to see. Adult males weigh from 35 to 50

DAVID WALL

Sperm whale

tonnes and females just over 20 tonnes; both live for up to 70 years. They dive for long periods (around 45 minutes).

They are hard to locate in the open ocean and the only real giveaway is a blow from their spout, or their sonar clicks, detected with hydrophones. Because they each require a huge feeding area, whales are normally seen singly. The sperm whales have a single blowhole, offset on the left side of their head.

Humpback Whale

Sadly, sightings of the humpback *(Megaptera novaengliae)* are rare. Once there were an estimated 100,000 in the world's oceans, but now the number is believed to be about 2000. These whales sieve their food through baleen (fine bones), hence their classification as Mysticeti (baleen whales). The males are a little smaller than the females, who usually reach 16m in length and about 50 tonnes in weight. Humpbacks have unique tail fluke patterns, long flippers (up to one third of their length) and throat grooves.

Orca (Killer Whale)

Orca *(Orcinus orca)* are the largest of the dolphins and among the largest predators on earth, feeding on other dolphins and whales, as well as seals, sea birds, penguins and sharks. They are classified as members of the Odontoceti (toothed whales and dolphins). They grow up to 9.5m in length (females 7m) and to 8000kg in weight (females 4000kg).

They are distinguished by their huge dorsal fins, which often reach nearly 2m high. Both sexes have up to 12 pairs of teeth in each jaw. The orca vocalises both for socialising and to keep contact when foraging for food. There is no record of an unprovoked attack by an orca, as powerful as it is, on humans.

Long-finned Pilot Whale

Of the two species of pilot whale, the long- and short-finned, it is the long-finned *(Globicephala melas)* which is seen the most in NZ waters. This is the species which has become notorious for large-scale strandings (NZ has one of the highest rates of whale strandings in the world). Long-finned pilot whales grow to over 6m in length (females 5.5m) and to 3000kg in weight (females 2500kg).

Humpback whale

Stranded pilot whales

DAVID WALL

Bottlenose dolphin

DAVID WALL

A dusky dolphin jumping for joy

Bottlenose Dolphin

This is the 'Flipper' dolphin. It is one of the larger species, often reaching 4m in length, although those seen in NZ waters are about 3.5m. The bottlenose *(Tursiops truncatus)* is gregarious, but occasionally goes 'solo'.

The bottlenose is the most recorded dolphin in history, probably because of its commensal fishing activities with people. They are also known to feed cooperatively among themselves after encircling a shoal of fish. See Opononi in the Northland chapter for the story of Opo, NZ's most famous dolphin.

Dusky Dolphin

Dusky dolphins *(Lagenorhynchus obscurus)* can reach lengths of over 2m, but usually average 1.6m to 1.8m. What they lack in size they make up for in spirit. These are the most playful dolphins and those which 'dolphin swimming' participants are most likely to encounter (see the boxed text 'Dolphin Swimming' in the Canterbury chapter). While in the water, you will see them executing noisy head-first re-entry leaps and somersaults.

They feed on small schooling fish and often round up hundreds of fish in a tight ball, from which members of the pod take turns at feeding. They congregate near the shore from late October to May; after that the pods break up, as winter comes on, and the dolphins move offshore.

Hector's Dolphin

This dolphin *(Cephalorhynchus hectori)* is confined to NZ waters. They have a rather dumpy shape, a distinctive rounded fin and reach a length of only 1.4m. Like the dusky dolphin they feed on small schooling fish, but they stay relatively close to shore year-round.

Even though they are the world's rarest dolphin there is a good chance you will see them when travelling in the South Island. Kaikoura, Banks Peninsula (Canterbury) and Porpoise Bay (Southland) are all good locations.

Some years back Greenpeace reported that 230 Hector's, about 30% of the population of the area, had been killed in gill nets around Banks Peninsula over four years; DOC has since declared the area a marine mammal sanctuary.

Common Dolphin

This dolphin *(Delphinus delphis)* is the most wide-spread of dolphins, found all around the world. They grow up to 2.5m long, although they are likely to average just over 2m. They dive to nearly 300m and can stay underwater for five or so minutes.

Near Kaikoura, they are often seen alongside pods of duskys, but are considered more an offshore (pelagic) species. Common dolphins are recognised by the golden coloration on their sides.

New Zealand Sea Lion

These sea lions *(Neophoca hookeri)*, sometimes referred to as Hooker's sea lions, are visitors to the South Island. They are much larger than the NZ fur seal.

When a pup was born on the Otago Peninsula in 1995 it was an incredible event – it is believed this hadn't occurred on the mainland for about 700 years. (There have been more mainland births since.)

See Otago Peninsula in the Otago chapter for information about seeing these creatures (on tours to a protected beach).

New Zealand Fur Seal

This seal *(Arctocephalus forsteri)* is most commonly seen in NZ waters. Mature male seals (bulls) are about 2m in length and females (cows) are about 1.6m; their average weight is about 140kg. Once slaughtered for their skins, fur seals are now thriving as a protected species. You can see them basking on rocks, but they will probably enter the safety of the water if you get too close. Fur seals differ from sea lions in that they have a broader bear-shaped head, prominent ears and larger front flippers.

You can swim with these seals near Kaikoura. They are a popular distraction for sea kayakers in the Abel Tasman National Park region, and you will see them from boats in Milford and Doubtful Sounds.

Elephant Seal

This seal *(Mirounga leonina)*, with a distinctive trunk-like nose, is not commonly seen in NZ. There is a small breeding colony at the Nuggets in the fauna-rich Catlins. The seals are found in their thousands on NZ's subantarctic islands. The male grows to over 4m long and can weigh more than 4000kg, making it the largest seal species.

New Zealand (Hooker's) sea lion

Subantarctic fur seal

Elephant seal (male)

New Zealand's dinosaur, the tuatara

Other Fauna

Reptiles

The **tuatara** *(Sphenodon punctatus)* is a lizard-like reptile dating back to the age of the dinosaurs (about 220 million years). It is the only surviving member of the order Rhynchocephalia. Active at night, it eats insects, small mammals and birds' eggs. It also has a rudimentary 'third eye' in the centre of its forehead, grows to up to 60cm in length and may live for 100 years. The tuatara is found on protected offshore islands (eg, The Brothers and Stephens Island in the Marlborough Sounds), for which you need special permission to visit. Some specimens are kept in captivity in places such as the Wellington Zoo, Otorohanga Kiwi House, and Southland Museum in Invercargill (where they have been successfully bred).

If you hear something croaking during the night, you can be sure it's not one of the three species of native NZ **frogs** – they lack a vocal sac, so can only produce a high-pitched squeak. They're also remarkable in not having a free-swimming tadpole stage, instead undergoing metamorphosis in a capsule. You'd be lucky to spot one of these creatures anyway: one species of frog is restricted to the high parts of the Coromandel Peninsula, another to the summit of Stephens Island, Marlborough Sounds, and the other is only found in remnant rainforest in the Marlborough Sounds.

There are no snakes in NZ.

Creepy Crawlies

There are four species of **weta**, large invertebrates with a fearsome appearance. The cave weta has long legs and a small body (only 35mm), perfectly adapted for movement on cave walls. In contrast, the bush weta has a large body (50mm) and looks fearsome with a large head and snapping mandibles. It can deliver a painful nip with those scary mandibles, but it's really pretty harmless. The wingless alpine weta, also known as the 'Mt Cook flea', lives in rock crevices above the snowline. The largest, the giant weta, grows to 100mm in length but is confined now to offshore islands in the north of the country.

There is only one (slightly) dangerous spider in NZ, the rare **katipo** (see Health in the Facts for the Visitor chapter).

Giant weta

DAVID WALL

DOC – M AVISS

Bats

There are two species of indigenous bat (in Maori, *pekapeka*), which were NZ's only land mammals before the arrival of humans. The two species are prosaically named long-tailed and short-tailed. Long-tailed bats *(Chalinolobus tuberculatus)* are similar to the fruit bats or flying foxes of Australia and the Pacific Islands, but the short-tailed bat *(Mystacina tuberculata)* is endemic to NZ. You may see both species of bat flitting around forest margins at sunset seeking insects.

Long-tailed bat

Introduced Animals

All of the deliberately introduced species of mammals have done their fair share of damage. Probably the most infamous is the **brush-tailed possum** *(Trichosurus vulpecula)*. There are now more than 70 million possums in NZ, eating an estimated 7 million tonnes of vegetation per year and doing terrible damage to particular trees including rata, totara, kowhai, pohutukawa and kohekohe.

Short-tailed bat

Other introduced pests are rabbits, chamois, thar, Virginia (white-tailed) deer, red deer, pigs (both large, wild Captain Cookers and smaller kune kune), goats and stoats. In a classic case of *There Was an Old Lady Who Swallowed a Fly*, stoats were introduced to NZ to eat the (introduced) rabbits, but preferred the taste of kiwi.

Fish

New Zealand is renowned as an angler's paradise, largely due to the introduction of rainbow and brown trout, perch, carp, Atlantic salmon and quinnat salmon to its rivers and estuaries.

Sitting at a major confluence of warm and cold ocean currents, NZ's offshore waters have a great variety of tropical and cold-water species of fish, and its thousands of kilometres of coastline are home to tasty crustaceans such as the crayfish (also known as lobster; in Maori they are called *koura*).

New Zealand boasts its own species of 'trout', which is actually the giant kokopu, one of five galaxiid species found in NZ waters. The others are the inanga (which is 'whitebait' in its imago stage), koaro, banded kokopu and short-jawed kokopu. The giant kokopu can be seen at the World Heritage Visitor Centre in Haast.

Mt Cook lily

FLORA

When the first Europeans arrived in the 1800s, about 70% of NZ was covered in native forest. Much of it was soon cleared for timber (like the large kauri forests) or to make way for farming.

Despite that, NZ still has some magnificent areas of native forest and bush. About 10% to 15% of its total land area is native flora, much of it in protected parks and reserves.

The variety of vegetation in NZ is enormous. Heading south from the giant kauri forests of Northland, there are the luxuriant lowland kohekohe forests of the Bay of Plenty; rainforests dominated by rimu, various beeches, tawa, matai and rata, and a great range of tree ferns; the podocarp and hardwood forests of the lower parts of the North Island, with its kahikatea, tawa, rimu, rata and kohekohe; the summer-flowering alpine and subalpine herb fields; and the windswept scrub of the smaller islands.

In the South Island the vegetation changes dramatically as you climb into the mountains. The lowland supplejacks give way to rimu, miro, and then tree ferns at about 800m. Above 1000m the totara, wineberry, fuchsias, rata and kaikomako are gradually left behind, to be replaced by subalpine scrub. At about 1200m the scrub gives way to tussock grasses and alpine herb fields, and at the extreme heights only some hardy lichens hang onto the exposed rock.

Like the Australian species, most of the 72 NZ orchids are not large or brilliantly coloured; one exception is the beautiful *Earina autumnalis*, which has perfumed cream flowers.

Various introduced species have been planted in large tracts for the timber industry. The most obvious imports are the massive plantations of radiata or Monterey pine and Douglas fir (Oregon).

The Maori language has bestowed marvellous names on some of the native plants of NZ, names that are almost unpronounceable to Pakeha – tawhairauriki, kowhai ngutukaka, whauwhaupaku, mingimingi, hangehange, kumarahou, and pua o te reinga, to name a handful. Some of the English names are nearly as colourful and it's interesting to speculate about their derivation – gum digger's soap, wild Irishman, seven-finger, bog pine, flower of Hades and Dieffenbach's Spaniard.

Dracophyllum species

Trees

The progenitors of NZ's two major forest groups, the podocarps and the southern beeches, were found in the ancient supercontinent of Gondwanaland. When the continents drifted apart and the land bridges were eventually lost, over 60 million years ago, NZ's flora evolved in isolation. Of the country's 2000 or so flowering plants, about 75% are only found in NZ.

The podocarps are part of an ancient family, *Podocarpaceae*, which evolved before flowering plants. Fossil pollen indicates that trees very similar to kahikatea and rimu have been here for more than 60 million years. The *Nothofagus* (beech) species found in NZ are very similar to those found in the south of South America, adding weight to the Gondwanaland theory.

For more information, see these books: *Which Native Tree?* and *Which Native Fern?* by Andrew Crowe and *New Zealand Trees and Ferns* by Murdoch Riley.

Kahikatea (white pine)

Kahikatea

The white pine *(Dacrycarpus dacrydioides)* is NZ's tallest tree, reaching 60m and taking hundreds of years to mature. An adult tree has green scaly leaves. The immature fruit is yellow, ripening into an orange-red berry that bears a seed at its tip – favoured by the NZ pigeon (kereru) and the Maori. It is not surprising that the Maori also snared many pigeons on this tree.

Kamahi in flower

Kamahi

Pronounced 'car-my', the hardy black birch *(Wein-mannia racemosa)* is found throughout NZ, from Auckland down to Stewart Island. It grows to a height of 25m and attains a diameter of over 1m. It has grey bark with white blotches, glossy, dark-green leaves, small lilac-coloured flowers and rusty red seeds.

Kauri

Kauri trees *(Agathis australis)* only grow in Northland and on the Coromandel Peninsula. These large native trees were once ruthlessly cut down for their excellent timber and Northland is covered with evidence of the kauri days (see Trounson Kauri Park and Waipoua Kauri Forest in the Northland chapter). A

The blotchy bark of the kauri

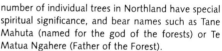

Flowers of the kowhai

number of individual trees in Northland have special spiritual significance, and bear names such as Tane Mahuta (named for the god of the forests) or Te Matua Ngahere (Father of the Forest).

Kauri gum was an important ingredient in varnish and at one time there were many 'gum diggers' who roamed the forests, poking in the ground for hard lumps of kauri gum.

Kauri grow to at least 30m and are believed to attain an age of about 2000 years. Their bark has a distinctive blotchy mosaic which feels as good as it looks.

Kowhai

This tree *(Sophora microphylla)* grows to about 11m and has small green leaves and groups of bright yellow flowers – in fact the Maori word for 'yellow' is *kowhai*. There are three species of this, NZ's national flower, and all are similar in appearance. The tree is found in open areas, near rivers and on the edge of forests. They're popular trees with birds, especially tui, which seek honey from the flowers.

Matai

The black pine *(Prumnopitys taxifolia)* is one of the most majestic of NZ's trees and is found throughout the North and South Islands. It grows to 30m and often achieves a very wide girth (one particular matai, massive and very accessible, is at Lake Ianthe on the South Island's West Coast; see that chapter). Its thick, grey bark falls off to reveal blotchy red patches underneath. It has small, flat leaves, male and female flowers on the same long, yellow spikes and produces edible purple berries.

Miro

The miro *(Prumnopitys ferrugineus)*, another member of the pine family, grows to 25m. It is found throughout lowland forests in NZ. Very slow-growing, it may take 500 years to reach maturity. It has pointed leaves which could be mistaken for matai.

Pohutukawa

This beautiful tree *(Metrosideros excelsa)* is predominantly found in the north of the North Island but it has been successfully planted throughout the South

Pohutukawa flowers

Island. Its magnificent crimson flowers appear in December, making it popularly known as the 'Christmas tree'; thin brown seeds appear in May. It can grow up to 20m in height and 2m across at its base, and is found close to the sea; good places to see it are along the beaches of the Coromandel Peninsula, Bay of Plenty and East Coast.

Pohutukawa of special significance include the 600-year-old Te Waha o Rerekohu at Te Araroa (see the East Coast chapter), and the 800-year-old tree, at Cape Reinga, whose roots form the gateway to the Underworld; see Ancestors (Tipuna) in the 'Maori Culture & Arts' special section.

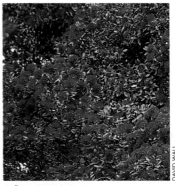

A flowering rata

Rata

The rata is another tree with beautiful crimson flowers like the pohutukawa, except that its leaves are shiny and pointed at both ends. The northern rata *(Metrosideros robusta)*, reaching a height of 25m, grows in the North Island and in Nelson in the South Island. Southern rata *(M. umbellata)* predominates in the South Island but is also found in Northland.

What is the nature of the rata? It starts as a climber (epiphyte) on a host tree which it eventually strangles. When this happens the aerial roots disappear and the tree takes on a gnarled appearance.

Rimu

The red pine *(Dacrydium cupressinum)* is the most easily recognised of the podocarps. The tree is found throughout NZ in areas of mixed forest and grows to a height of more than 50m, with a girth of about 1.5m. The distinctive, narrow, prickly leaves drape down and often have little red cones at the tips of the leafy clusters. The fruit appears as a black nut at the tip of the seed.

It was once the most common of the lowland podocarps but its popularity as a building timber has led to its drastic depletion.

Rimu (red pine)

Cabbage Tree

The beautiful broad-leafed mountain cabbage tree *(Cordyline indivisa;* Maori: *ti kouka)* is found in moist mountain areas where there is plenty of light. It grows to 20m and, when mature, its stems hang downwards. The name comes from an old misunderstanding: James Cook's crew ate the leaves of

Cabbage tree *(ti kouka)*

DOC – R MORRIS

Totara

DAVID WALL

Nikau palm

a similar tree, the nikau palm, but ti kouka ended up with the name.

Beeches

New Zealand has several species of beech *(Nothofagus spp)*. The silver beech *(Nothofagus menziesii;* Maori: *tawhai)* is found in stands in mixed forest on both islands and occurs in subalpine regions. It can grow up to 30m in height and has a silver-grey trunk of up to 2m in diameter. The small rounded leaves have serrated edges, the small flowers are green and brown, and the fruit is small and woody.

It is closely related to the other beeches, including the red beech *(N. fusca)* and black beech *(N. solandri var. solandri)*.

The beautiful mountain beech *(Nothofagus solandri var. cliffortioides;* Maori: *tawhairauriki)* occurs in mountain and subalpine areas from the North Island's Central Plateau to the far south of the South Island. It grows to 22m in favoured sites (but usually to about 15m) and its trunk is about 1m in diameter. Its leaves are dark and pointy, as opposed to the light leaves of the tawhai. It has small red flowers and woody fruit. It is seen in splendour in Arthur's Pass National Park and near the Lewis Pass.

Totara

This tree *(Podocarpus totara)* has special significance in NZ, as it was favoured for Maori war canoes because of its soft wood. It can grow to be extremely old, attaining an age of 1000 years or more. One particular totara, named Pouakani, in Pureora Forest Park in the North Island, is said to be more than 1700 years old. The totara has long, pointy leaves, and the male and female cones occur on separate trees. Its red-and-pink stalks attract birds.

Nikau

The nikau *(Rhapalostylis sapida)* is found throughout lowland areas of the North Island and the north of the South Island, as far south as Banks Peninsula. The best place to see nikau is on the north of the West Coast, from Punakaiki to Karamea; their appearance there could fool you into thinking you are in the tropics. They can grow to 10m in height and in ancient times their fronds were interwoven and used for roofing material by the Maori.

Ferns

One of the prominent features of the NZ bush is the proliferation of tree ferns which are intertwined with the undergrowth. There are over 80 species of fern and five species of soft fern. Perhaps the most unusual appearance-wise are the **mauku** (hen and chickens fern; *Asplenium bulbiferum*) and the **raurenga** (kidney fern; *Trichomanes reniforme*), and the rarest would be the **para** (horseshoe or king fern; *Marattia salicina*). A common sight on NZ hillsides is the bracken fern *(Pteridium aquilinum)*, growing to 3m or more.

The **mamaku** (black tree fern; *Cyathea medullaris*) is the largest of the NZ ferns and grows to a height of 20m, with the fronds extending to 7m. It grows throughout the country, and is common in damp forest gullies.

The **ponga** (silver tree fern; *Cyathea dealbata*) is one of NZ's national symbol; it adorns the jumpers of many of NZ's sports representatives and is shown in logos such as NZ wool and NZ tourism. It grows to up to 10m in height and the fronds, which extend up to 4m, are white on the underside and dull green on the upper side.

The **piupiu** (crown fern; *Blechnum discolor*) is found throughout the country and is noticeable because its bright green fronds, up to 1.5m in length, often form a significant part of the ground cover. When the frond is turned over it reveals a silvery-grey side. Interestingly, it is the colour of the two types of fronds of *Blechnum* species, one brown and one green, which denotes whether they are fertile or sterile. The brown fronds look as though they are dead or dying, but they produce the reproductive spores. Other ferns produce spores seen as brown spots on the underside of green fronds.

Piupiu (crown fern)

Tree ferns

Facts for the Visitor

SUGGESTED ITINERARIES

Those with special interests, particularly tramping and other outdoor activities, should also see the Activities chapter. These itineraries assume you are on a tour or have your own transport; reliance on public transport will add more time, as will time out for tramping.

One Week – North Island

Day 1 Auckland – wander around the central city, ascend the Skytower and explore the rejuvenated America's Cup Village; dine in Ponsonby or Parnell

Day 2 Auckland to the Bay of Islands – cruise out to the Hole in the Rock; swim with dolphins; visit historic Waitangi or Russell

Day 3 Return to Auckland via the Waipoua Kauri Forest on Northland's west coast; visit the Matakohe Kauri Museum

Day 4 Auckland to Rotorua – visit mud pools and geysers; attend a Maori *hangi* and concert evening; visit one of the city's many tourist complexes

Day 5 Tour more of the thermal wonders of the Rotorua and Taupo regions including Waiotapu and the Huka Falls

Day 6 Rotorua to Waitomo – go underground and see the magnificent display of glowworms

Day 7 Return to Auckland and visit the museum with its excellent Maori collection

Two Weeks – North Island

Days 1 & 2 Auckland – cruise out to Rangitoto or Waiheke Islands in the Hauraki Gulf

Days 3, 4 & 5 Auckland to Bay of Islands – add a trip to the Far North and Cape Reinga; return to Auckland via the west coast

Day 6 Auckland to Rotorua

Day 7 Rotorua to Waitomo – take a detour to the west coast village of Kawhia, rich in Maori history

Day 8 Waitomo to Tongariro National Park – visit volcanic landscape; ski the slopes in winter; take one of many interesting short walks

Day 9 Tongariro to Wellington – stop off along the Kapiti Coast; 'fly by wire'; feast on a seafood lunch

Day 10 Wellington – visit Te Papa National Museum; cafe crawl at night; rollerblade along the waterfront

HIGHLIGHTS

New Zealand has so many superb physical features that you tend to take the country's beauty for granted after a while. Here's our list of not-to-be-missed sights or things to do in NZ – first the North Island:

- **The Great Outdoors** – NZ has some of the finest tramping (bushwalking) in the world, plus challenging cycling and great skiing. The range of other adventurous pursuits below, on and above ground, is bewildering, and they all take advantage of the unforgettable scenery.

- **Northland** – The best of this region includes magnificent west coast kauri forests with giant 1500-year-old trees; the stunning Bay of Islands on the east; and the places of Maori mythology in the Far North.

- **Rotorua & Taupo** – There's thermal activity (boiling mud pools, hissing geysers and eerie volcanic landscapes) and abundant Maori culture such as concerts and hangi. NZ's largest lake, Taupo, is surrounded by things to do and see, and has the stunning volcanic plateau as a backdrop. Many activities are offered – from easy walks through volcanic areas to thrilling skydives above the lake.

- **Waitomo Caves** – The Waitomo region is riddled with limestone caves with stalactites and stalagmites, and these are decorated by stellar-like glowworms.

- **Wellington** – Visit museums and a Maori *marae* for an insight into NZ culture. Te Papa in Wellington shouldn't be missed – stay an extra day in the nation's capital to learn the intricacies of NZ's complex racial mix. A visit to a Maori marae or an invitation to a local hangi may be your warmest memory.

HIGHLIGHTS

If you thought the scenery of the North Island was magnificent, you aint seen nothing yet! The mountains and forests of the South Island are even *more* spectacular, and attractions here include:

• **Kaikoura** – Whale-watching trips and swimming with dolphins, seals and sharks have made this place famous, and there are myriad other adventure activities.

• **The South Island's West Coast** – Nowhere else do glaciers so close to the equator come this near to sea level. The glaciers (the Fox and the Franz Josef) are just one highlight on this rugged coast. There are also lush native forests, a scenic coastal road, the famous *TranzAlpine* rail link, sparkling lakes and friendly hamlets and towns.

• **Mt Cook** – Also known as Aoraki, the highest mountain in the country has fantastic scenery, good walks and skiing, and mighty glaciers cascading from its flanks.

• **Queenstown** – The home of the bungy jump, on the shores of Lake Wakatipu, is NZ's outdoor activity capital. Additionally, you get the fantastic natural setting thrown in for free. If an adrenaline activity exists in NZ, chances are you can do it here.

• **Fiordland** – As wild and remote as it gets. Doubtful Sound and Milford Sound are spectacular fiords (similar to those in Norway). The region attracts trampers of all nationalities, keen to tackle the world-famous tracks.

• **The Wildlife of the South-Eastern Coast** – This coastline, especially the Otago Peninsula and the Catlins, is a wildlife enthusiast's dream, with an amazing array of fauna – albatross, fairy and yellow-eyed penguins, Hector's dolphins, seals and sea lions. A must!

Day 11 Wellington to Napier – indulge yourself at the vineyards in Wairarapa and Hawkes Bay; stroll past the Art Deco architecture of Hastings and Napier

Day 12 Napier to Taupo – enjoy fishing or adventure activities, such as jet-boating and sky-diving; explore the lake by boat

Day 13 Taupo to Rotorua – relax in the hot pools of 'Roto-Vegas' and catch up on things you missed, such as the luge or zorbing

Day 14 Rotorua to Auckland

One Week – South Island

Day 1 Christchurch – catch the tram to the museum, cathedral and Arts Centre; sip coffee in Oxford Terrace; watch a play at the old Court Theatre

Day 2 Christchurch to Greymouth – travel the superb road crossing or on the *TranzAlpine* train; visit Arthur's Pass National Park; take in the rugged scenery

Day 3 Greymouth to Franz Josef and Fox Glaciers – visit the two glaciers which almost reach the sea (Fox is south); see pristine lakes reflect lofty mountains; tramp in native forest; ascend a glacier with a guide

Day 4 Franz Josef to Queenstown – visit the World Heritage region; take in the lakes and mountains; cross the scenic Haast Pass

Day 5 Queenstown – here a bungy jump is essential for many; ski in winter; enjoy the stunning mountain backdrop

Day 6 Queenstown to Mt Cook – take in the overpowering Aoraki (Mt Cook); go walking; traverse the scenic national parks by helicopter or ski-landing plane

Day 7 Mt Cook to Christchurch

Two Weeks – South Island

Days 1 & 2 Christchurch – sidetrip to the Port Hills and the French village of Akaroa

Day 3 Christchurch to Kaikoura – try whale-watching or swim with dolphins, seals and sharks; indulge in a crayfish (lobster) meal

Day 4 Kaikoura to Nelson – visit the wineries near Blenheim; take in the scenic Marlborough Sounds

Day 5 Nelson – detour to Golden Bay; sea kayak or walk in Abel Tasman National Park

Day 6 Nelson to Punakaiki – raft in the Buller Gorge; walk in Paparoa National Park; visit the Pancake Rocks and other dramatic coastal scenery

Days 7, 8 & 9 Punakaiki to Queenstown via the Glaciers

Day 10 Queenstown to Te Anau – see caves with water rushing through; take a boat or plane trip; enjoy the region's walks; spot the rare takahe

Day 11 Te Anau to Milford and Doubtful Sounds – revel in the sounds' overwhelming scenery

Day 12 Te Anau to Dunedin via the Catlins – travel the Southern Scenic Route; visit the tuatara at Southland Museum; explore the treasures of the Catlins

Day 13 Dunedin – see the albatross, seals, sea lions and penguins of Otago Peninsula; partake in the pub and student cafe scenes; enjoy the city's architecture

Day 14 Dunedin to Christchurch

One Month

Combine the two week options for both the South and North Islands, and vary as suits, eg, substitute a trip to Napier with an exploration of delightful Mt Taranaki/Egmont in the north, or Mt Cook for the Catlins and the *TranzAlpine* train journey for Golden Bay in the south. You might decide to sacrifice Northland for a tramp in the Central Plateau.

Two Months

If you really want to experience much of what NZ has to offer then two months is a good duration.

In the North Island, you could add the forests and beaches of Coromandel (two to three days), Great Barrier Island (two to three days), Lake Waikaremoana and Urewera National Park (two to three days), the Bay of Plenty (two days), East Cape and Gisborne (three days), Taranaki (three days) and canoeing on the Whanganui River (three to four days).

Tramping highlights include Lake Waikaremoana, Tongariro Crossing, Tongariro Northern Circuit, Totara Flats in the Tararua Ranges, and Mt Egmont/Taranaki (see the Activities chapter).

In the South Island, add the beautiful waterways of Marlborough Sounds (three days), Kahurangi National Park and Farewell Spit (three days), Nelson Lakes National Park (three days), Hanmer Springs hot pools (one day), Karamea and Westport (two days), the Haast World Heritage region (two days), Wanaka with Mt Aspiring National Park, skiing and fine walks (four days), Stewart Island (two to seven days), Central Otago cycle trails (two days), Lake Tekapo (two days) and Methven rafting, skiing and walks (two to three days).

The South Island is a paradise for trampers with the Routeburn, Milford and the Abel Tasman Coastal Tracks (walk or sea kayak). There's also the Kepler, Heaphy, Greenstone, Caples, Rakiura and Queen Charlotte walks (see the Activities chapter).

It's easy to spend extra days anywhere – particularly in the main destinations, eg the Bay of Islands, Rotorua, Auckland, Taupo, Wellington, Kaikoura, Nelson, Queenstown, Dunedin and Christchurch. Chances are the highlight of your trip will be time spent somewhere we haven't even mentioned.

PLANNING
When to Go

New Zealand's busiest tourist season is during the warmer months, from around November to April, with some exceptions – ski resort towns, obviously, will be packed out in winter.

The peak travel time in NZ is the summer school holidays, from 20 December to late January. During these holidays, when both New Zealanders and international visitors are out on the road, transport and every type of accommodation is likely to fill up, especially the more economical places, so book as far ahead as possible. It may be more pleasant to visit NZ either before or after this hectic period, when the weather is still warm. To a lesser extent Easter weekend (April/May), Labour Day weekend (late October) and the mid-year school holidays are also busy.

The main tourist season for overseas visitors is from December to March, when accommodation can still be hard to find in the tourist areas, transport services are in demand, tramping trails can be crowded etc. Accommodation should be booked at least a day or two in advance. January and February are the best beach-weather months, but December and March are usually warm and even hot in some areas.

November and April are slightly cooler – not beach weather – but these months are noticeably quieter and accommodation is easier to find. In many ways they are the best months to travel.

October and May are even quieter and cheaper months to travel. Though snow falls at higher altitudes, the weather is cool but mild in much of the country. The main tourist industry starts to wind down; while most services and activities still operate, a few close.

June to September is a paradise for winter sports enthusiasts but, away from the busy ski areas, some accommodation, transport services and activities close due to lack of patronage. Some of the tramping trails are closed because of snow and ice, as are some of the pass roads. However, NZ is not like some countries where the weather is so miserable that there's no point in going. Winter is cold – freezing in the far south and at higher altitudes – but parts of the North Island, particularly Northland, and the Nelson region of the South Island have mild winters where nights are cold but days can be sunny and pleasant. You'll need warm clothes but there are many things to see and do in NZ year-round.

Maps

Many excellent maps are widely available in NZ – everything from street maps and road atlases to detailed topographical maps.

Automobile Association (AA) members (or members of affiliate organisations) can present their cards at any AA office and get many free maps. The AA city, town, regional and highway maps are some of the best available. For car touring off the beaten track, pick up a set of its superb 1:350,000 district maps. You don't have to be a member to buy its road atlases and large maps of the North and South Islands. The Shell road atlas, Wises' maps and road atlases, and the Minimap series are also excellent and available at AA offices and bookshops.

Land Information New Zealand (formerly known as DOSLI) publishes several excellent map series – street, country and holiday maps, maps of national parks and forest parks, detailed topographical maps for trampers, and more. Its maps are available at Land Information NZ offices, some bookshops and Department of Conservation (DOC) offices.

What to Bring

New Zealand may be a small, compact country but it has widely varying and very changeable weather. A T-shirt-and-shorts day at the Bay of Islands can also bring snow and sleet to a high pass in the Southern Alps. In fact, on any of NZ's mountains you can often meet T-shirt and snow-gear weather on the same day. So be prepared – if you're tramping, proper gear can save your life. Good camping and sports equipment is available in NZ but is expensive, although it can be hired quite cheaply.

Bring waterproof gear and a warm down sleeping bag even if you're not camping or tramping. A sleeping bag will save a lot of money in budget accommodation where linen costs extra.

Come prepared for NZ's 'dress standards' too. An amazing number of restaurants, bars, clubs and pubs have draconian dress rules, so bring a set of 'smart casual' clothes.

NZ is a modern, well-organised country and you should be able to find most requirements. Clothing and luxury items are expensive by world standards though, so bring them with you.

RESPONSIBLE TOURISM

For hints on how to tramp with the least impact upon the delicate ecosystems of NZ's national parks, see Tramping in the Activities chapter. In particular, carry out cigarette butts – they're highly toxic and the filters take years to break down.

At all times practise the correct etiquette on Maori *marae*, and do not photograph carvings and artworks without permission of the appropriate tribal representatives.

Observe all signs which relate to appropriate distances when approaching wildlife. Don't risk crushing the nesting burrow of a yellow-eyed penguin or the sand scrape of the rare NZ dotterel just to get a better photograph.

TOURIST OFFICES
Local Tourist Offices

Almost every city or town has a tourist information centre – any town big enough to have a pub and a corner shop seems to have an information centre. Many are united by VIN, the Visitor Information Network, affiliated with the New Zealand Tourism Board (NZTB). These bigger information centres have trained staff, abundant information on local activities and attractions and free brochures and maps. Staff also act as travel agents, booking almost all activities, transport and accommodation. Use the centres: they are an excellent resource for travellers everywhere in NZ.

Their only problem is that they can be understaffed and some are too busy.

Smaller tourist offices funded by local councils or business communities don't have the resources of the VIN network and are usually staffed by helpful volunteers. They may not be able to take bookings.

Tourist Offices Abroad

The NZTB has representatives in various countries around the world. The board's head office is at PO Box 95, Wellington, New Zealand (☎ 04-472 8860), its Web site is www.purenz.com and overseas offices include:

Australia (☎ 02-9247 5222) Level 8, 35 Pitt St, Sydney, NSW 2000
Germany (☎ 69-971 2110) Friedrichstrasse 10-12, 60311 Frankfurt am Main
UK (☎ 020-7930 1662) New Zealand House, Haymarket, London SW1Y 4TQ
USA
  California: (☎ 310-395 7480) 501 Santa Monica Blvd, Suite 300, Santa Monica, CA 90401
  New York: (☎ 212-832 8482) 780 3rd Avenue, Suite 1904, New York, NY 10017-2024

VISAS & DOCUMENTS
Passport

Almost everyone needs a passport to enter NZ. If you enter on an Australian or NZ passport, or on a passport containing an Australian or NZ residence visa, your passport must be valid on arrival. All other passports must be valid for at least three months beyond the time you intend to stay in NZ, or one month beyond the intended stay if the issuing government has an embassy or consulate in NZ able to issue and renew passports.

All important documents should be photocopied – leave one copy at home and take another with you, separate from originals.

Visas

Australian citizens or holders of current Australian resident return visas do not need a visa or permit to enter NZ and can stay indefinitely if they do not have any criminal convictions. Australians do not require a work permit.

Citizens of the UK, and other British passport holders who can show they have permanent UK residency, do not need a visa; they are issued on arrival with a visitor permit to stay for up to six months.

Citizens of the following countries do not need a visa and are given a three-month, extendable visitor permit upon arrival:

Austria, Bahrain, Belgium, Brazil, Brunei, Canada, Chile, Czech Rep, Denmark, Finland, France, Germany, Greece, Ireland, Israel, Italy, Japan, Korea (South), Kiribati, Kuwait, Liechtenstein, Luxembourg, Malaysia, Malta, Monaco, Nauru, Norway, Oman, Portugal, Qatar, Saudi Arabia, Singapore, South Africa, Spain, Sweden, Switzerland, Thailand, Tuvalu, UAE, Uruguay, USA

Citizens of all other countries require a visa to enter NZ, available from any NZ embassy or consulate (see the list later in this chapter). Visas are normally valid for three months. Check at the immigration Web site (www.immigration.govt.nz).

To qualify for a visitor permit on arrival or for a visa, you must be able to show the following:

• Your passport, valid for three months beyond the time of your intended stay in NZ.
• Evidence of sufficient funds to support yourself for the time of your intended stay, without working. This is calculated to be NZ$1000 per month (NZ$400 per month if your accommodation has been prepaid) and can be in the form of cash, travellers cheques, bank drafts or the main credit cards.
• An onward ticket to a country where you have right of entry, with firm bookings if travelling on a special rate air fare.

Evidence of sufficient funds can be waived if a friend or relative in NZ sponsors you (ie will guarantee your accommodation and maintenance). Requirements can change, so always check the situation before departure.

Work & Student Visas It is illegal to work on a visitor permit. If you have an offer of employment, you should apply for a work permit, valid for up to three years, before arriving in NZ. Permission to work is granted only if no NZ job seekers can do the job you have been offered. A work permit can be applied for in NZ after arrival but, if granted, it will only be valid for the remaining time you are entitled to stay as a visitor.

Citizens of Canada, Japan and the UK aged 18 to 30 years can apply for a Working Holiday Work Visa, valid for a 12-month stay. It allows you to work while travelling around the country, but must be applied for in your home country before you enter NZ; it is only issued to those seeking a genuine working holiday, not for permanent work.

You can study on a visitor permit if it is one single course not more than three months long. For longer study, you must obtain a student permit.

Visa Extensions Visitor permits can be extended for stays of up to nine months, if you apply for further permits and meet normal requirements. 'Genuine tourists' and a few other categories of people can be granted stays of up to 12 months.

Apply for extensions at any New Zealand Immigration Service office:

Auckland (☎ 09-914 4100, fax 914 4119) 450 Queen Street
Manukau Leyton House, Great South Rd, Manukau City, Auckland
Hamilton (☎ 07-838 3566) 5th floor, Westpac Building, Victoria St
Palmerston North (☎ 06-359 1956) State Insurance Bldg, Rangitikei St; PO Box 948
Wellington (☎ 04-384 7929) Level 7, Regional Council Centre, 142–146 Wakefield St; PO Box 27149
Christchurch (☎ 03-365 2520) Carter House, 81 Lichfield St; PO Box 22-111
Dunedin (☎ 03-477 0820) 6th floor, Evan Parry House, 43 Princes St; PO Box 557

Be careful not to overstay or you'll be subject to removal from the country. Extensions are easy to get provided you meet the requirements.

Documents
No special documents other than your passport are required in NZ. Since no vaccinations are required to enter the country, an international health certificate is not necessary.

Bring your driving licence. A full, valid driving licence from your home country is all you need to rent and drive a car in NZ. Members of automobile associations should bring their membership cards – it can be useful if recognised by the AA.

An ISIC card (International Student Identity Card) entitles you to certain discounts, particularly on transport. The international Youth Hostel Association card (YHA card) is well worth having even if you don't intend staying in hostels. This card provides a 50% discount on domestic air travel and a 30% discount on major bus lines, plus dozens of discounts on activities. A VIP Backpackers Card (from hostels belonging to the VIP group) offers the same benefits and can be bought in NZ or Australia from VIP hostels.

Travel Insurance
A travel insurance policy to cover theft, loss and medical problems is a good idea. Some policies offer lower and higher medical-expense options; the higher ones are chiefly for countries such as the USA, which have extremely high medical costs. There is a wide variety of policies available, so check the small print.

Some policies specifically exclude 'dangerous activities', which can include scuba diving, motorcycling, even tramping. A locally acquired motorcycle licence is not valid under some policies.

You may prefer a policy which pays doctors or hospitals directly rather than you having to pay on the spot and claim later. If you have to claim later make sure you keep all documentation. Some policies ask you to call back (reverse charges) to a centre in your home country where an immediate assessment of your problem is made.

Check that the policy covers ambulances or an emergency flight home.

EMBASSIES & CONSULATES
NZ Embassies & Consulates
New Zealand embassies and consulates in other countries include:

Australia
High Commission: (☎ 02-6270 4211, fax 6273 3194) Commonwealth Ave, Canberra, ACT 2600
Consulate-General: (☎ 02-9247 1999, fax 9247 1754) 14th floor, Gold Fields Building, 1 Alfred St, Circular Quay, Sydney, NSW 2000; GPO Box 365
Canada
High Commission: (☎ 613-238 6097, fax 238 5707) Suite 727, Metropolitan House, 99 Bank St, Ottawa, Ont K1P 6G3
Consulate-General: (☎ 604-684 7388, fax 684 7333) Suite 1200-888 Dunsmuir St, Vancouver, BC V6C 3K4
France (☎ 01 45 00 24 11, fax 01 45 01 26 39) Embassy, 7ter, rue Léonard de Vinci, 75116 Paris
Germany
Embassy: (☎ 30-206 210, fax 206 21114) Atrium Friedrichstrasse, Friedrichstrasse 60, 10117, Berlin
Consulate-General: (☎ 40-442 5550, fax 4425 5549) Heimhuderstrasse 56, 20148 Hamburg
Ireland (☎ 01-676 2464, fax 676 2489) Consulate-General, 46 Upper Mount St, Dublin 2
Netherlands (☎ 70-346 9324, fax 363 2983) Embassy, Carnegielaan 10, 2517 KH The Hague
UK (☎ 09069 100 100, fax 020-7973 0370) High Commission, New Zealand House, Haymarket, London SW1Y 4TQ
USA
Embassy: (☎ 202-328 4848, fax 667 5227), 37 Observatory Circle NW, Washington, DC 20008
Consulate-General: (☎ 310-207 1605, fax 207 3605) Suite 1150, 12400 Wilshire Blvd, Los Angeles, CA 90025
Consulate: (☎ 206-525 9881, fax 525 0271) 6810 51st Ave NE, Seattle, WA 98115

Embassies & Consulates in NZ
The capital city, Wellington (area code ☎ 04), houses the consulates and embassies of many countries, including:

Australia (☎ 473 6411) 72–78 Hobson St
Canada (☎ 473 9577) 61 Molesworth St
France (☎ 384 2555) 34–42 Manners St
Germany (☎ 473 6063) 90–92 Hobson St
Netherlands (☎ 473 8652) 10th floor, Investment Centre, cnr Featherston and Ballance Sts
UK (☎ 472 6049) 44 Hill St, Thorndon
USA (☎ 472 2068) 29 Fitzherbert Terrace, Thorndon

Your Own Embassy
It's important to realise what your own embassy – the embassy of the country of which you are a citizen – can and can't do to help you if you get into trouble.

Generally speaking, it won't be much help in emergencies if the trouble you're in is remotely your own fault. Remember that you are bound by the laws of the country you are in. Your embassy will not be sympathetic if you end up in jail after committing a crime locally, even if such actions are legal in your own country.

In genuine emergencies you might get some assistance, but only if other channels have been exhausted. For example, if you need to get home urgently, a free ticket home is exceedingly unlikely – the embassy would expect you to have insurance. If you have all your money and documents stolen, it might assist with getting a new passport, but a loan for onward travel is out of the question.

CUSTOMS
Customs allowances are 200 cigarettes (or 50 cigars or 250g of tobacco), 4.5L of wine or beer and one 1125mL bottle of spirits or liqueur.

Goods up to a total combined value of NZ$700 are free of duty and GST. Personal effects are not normally counted. If you do not exceed your $700 passenger concession, and do not have any alcohol or tobacco in your possession, you can import two extra bottles of duty-free liquor.

As in most countries the customs people are fussy about drugs.

MONEY
Currency
New Zealand's currency is dollars and cents. There are $5, $10, $20, $50 and $100

notes and $0.05 (5 cents), $0.10, $0.20 and $0.50, $1 and $2 coins. Unless otherwise noted, all prices quoted in this book are in NZ dollars.

There are no limitations on the import or export of foreign currency. Unused NZ currency can be changed before you leave the country.

Exchange Rates

The currencies of Australia, the UK, USA, Germany and Japan are all easily changed, and at consistently good rates. Most banks will exchange these and several other currencies, but rates may be slightly worse for less frequently changed currencies.

country	unit		NZ$
Australia	A$1	=	$1.30
Canada	C$1	=	$1.40
euro	€1	=	$2.00
France	10FF	=	$3.05
Germany	DM1	=	$1.02
Ireland	IR£1	=	$2.50
Japan	¥100	=	$1.90
UK	£1	=	$3.20
USA	US$1	=	$2.03

Exchanging Money

Banks are open from 9 am to 4.30 pm from Monday to Friday. Exchange rates may vary a few cents between banks. At most banks there's no service charge for changing travellers cheques.

Moneychangers (bureaux de change) work in the major tourist areas and at airports. They have slightly longer weekday hours (9 am to 9 pm) and are usually open on Saturday and sometimes Sunday. Thomas Cook offices have competitive rates and change a wider variety of currencies than most banks.

ATMs & Credit Cards

Some banks allow ATM access to overseas savings accounts, via networks such as Cirrus and Plus, but check with your bank before departure to see if this is available in NZ. You can get cash advances over the counter at banks or via 24-hour ATMs that display Visa or MasterCard symbols.

Pictures in Your Wallet

New Zealand currency carries pictures of several native species and famous locals. If you want to see a photo of the 'Father of the Atom', Ernest Rutherford (and you're fairly wealthy), just check inside your wallet.

Coins show a tuatara ($0.05, 5 cents), a stylised tattooed face ($0.10), a kiwi ($0.20), James Cook's ship the Endeavour ($0.50), another kiwi ($1) and a white heron or kotuku ($2). All coins have NZ's head of state, Queen Elizabeth II, on the reverse.

Each banknote depicts a native bird and a famous New Zealander: the $5 note shows the yellow-eyed penguin (hoiho) and mountaineer Sir Edmund Hillary; $10 has a blue duck (whio) and suffragette Kate Sheppard; $20 has the NZ falcon (kareerea) and Queen Elizabeth II (who might be surprised if you called her a famous New Zealander); $50 has the kokako and Maori politician Sir Apirana Ngata; and $100 has the mohua (yellowhead) and Ernest Rutherford, the atom-splitting physicist.

Visa, MasterCard, Bankcard, JCB and Diners Club credit cards are the most widely recognised. Money can be sent by telegraphic transfer, bank to bank, or – more easily – through a credit card.

Many NZ businesses allow EFTPOS (electronic funds transfer at point of sale) purchases, using your ATM card to pay over the counter.

Costs

While it is possible to travel quite economically in NZ, it's just as easy to spend up big. If you stay in backpacker accommodation, it will cost around $17 to $20 per person. In motor camps, costs are about $25 for singles or $35 for two in simple cabins, and about half that for camping. Basic DOC camp sites are even cheaper.

Guesthouses, homestays and B&Bs charge around $80 a night for two, but it can be that much per person. Cheaper hotels

GARETH McCORMACK

Dense forest and thermal pools – Waiotapu in the North Island

DAVID WALL

Jagged mountains and glassy waters – Milford Sound in the South Island

Wata (Provision House) at Otumatua on the North Shore of Cooks Strait (Charles Heaphy, 1841)

A Reconstruction of the Signing of the Treaty of Waitangi, 1840 (LC Mitchell, 1949)

Death of Major Von Tempskey at Te-Ngutu-o-te-Manu, New Zealand, 7th September 1868 (Kennett Watkins, 1893)

charge about \$40/60 for singles/doubles, while motels start at \$60 to \$70 for two.

Backpackers, motor camps and motels have kitchens for guests' use, allowing you to cook your own food – a big money saver. Eating out can cost anywhere from around \$5 for simple takeaways to around \$60 for two for dinner at medium-priced places.

The average long-distance (three- to five-hour) bus ride might cost around \$30, or 30% less with approved VIP/YHA/BBH cards. Hiring or buying a car may be just as economical for a small group. Hitchhiking and cycling are popular and essentially free ways of getting around.

Some of the many activities that attract people to NZ cost nothing – such as tramping, swimming and bird-watching. But the activities industry is huge and activities can be major part of the budget.

Security

Travellers cheques are always the safest way to carry money and their exchange rate is slightly better than that for cash in NZ. American Express, Visa, MasterCard and Thomas Cook travellers cheques are widely recognised.

Credit cards are a convenient way to carry money if you avoid interest charges by always keeping your account in the black and your bank doesn't charge exorbitant fees. Get a card equipped for ATM withdrawals.

For long stays, it may be worth opening a bank account. Westpac and the Bank of New Zealand (BNZ) have many branches around the country and you can request a card for 24-hour ATM access.

Tipping

Tipping is becoming more widespread, although many Kiwis still regard it as a foreign custom. Nevertheless, it is on the increase, principally in the major tourist centres. You should tip in a restaurant if you feel you have received exceptional service. The tip should be about 5% to 10% of the bill.

Taxes

GST (Goods and Services Tax) adds 12.5% to the price of just about everything in NZ.

Prices quoted almost invariably include GST, but look out for any small print announcing that the price is GST exclusive.

POST & COMMUNICATIONS
Post

New Zealand post shops (they're not called post offices any more) are open from 9 am to 5 pm on weekdays. You can have mail addressed to you care of 'Poste Restante, Main Post Shop' in whichever town you require. Mail is usually held for 30 days. Post shops acting for post restante in the main centres are Wellesley St, Auckland; Bunny St, Wellington; Cathedral Square, Christchurch; and Metro, 283 Princess St, Dunedin.

Within NZ, standard post costs \$0.45 for medium letters and postcards, and \$0.80 for letters larger than 120mm by 235mm; delivery time is two days between major centres, and a bit longer for rural areas. Or there's Fast Post, promising next-day delivery between Auckland, Wellington and Christchurch, and two-day delivery for rural areas. Fast Post costs \$0.80/\$1.20 for medium/large letters. In both cases the maximum thickness is 10mm.

For international mail, use Fast Post; just affix a Fast Post sticker or use a Fast Post envelope. This way it costs \$1 to send postcards anywhere in the world.

The cost and average delivery times for international airmail letters with a maximum weight of 200g and thickness of 20mm (prices given are for medium/large/ extra large letters) to various destinations are:

Australia & South Pacific
\$1/1.50/3, three to eight days delivery
North America & East Asia
\$1.50/2.50/6, four to 10 days delivery
Europe, Africa, Middle East & South America
\$1.80/2.80/6.80, six to 12 days delivery

Telephone

The phone system has been deregulated and opened to competition. Telecom still operates the public phone and local call networks, and the benefits of competition only affect NZ subscribers. From private phones, local calls cost $0.20 for unlimited time or are free for those subscribers who pay higher rent, while rates for long-distance calls through the various suppliers are competitive but constantly changing.

The big losers are those forced to use pay phones. Local calls cost a flat rate of $0.50, out-of-area calls start at around $0.50 per minute, international calls have a minimum charge of $3 and the cost builds up at an alarming rate.

Almost all pay phones in NZ are now card-operated. Cardphones accept $5, $10, $20 or $50 cards, available from visitor centres, newsagencies, backpackers and hotels or shops displaying the lime-green 'phonecards available here' sign. The larger cities have some credit-card phones. Long-distance and international calls can be dialled directly from pay phones. For international calls dial ☎ 00, then the country code, area code and number.

To avoid the high charges of making long-distance calls from public phones, use the various callcards available. These pre-paid phonecards (to values of $10 to $50) offer discounted rates. Usually, you dial an ☎ 0800 (toll-free) number and then follow the instructions before making overseas calls. Companies offering the cards include Eziphone, NetTel and Smartel. The cards are available from many backpackers and some retail outlets.

Lonely Planet's eKno Communication Card is aimed specifically at travellers and provides cheap international calls as well as a range of messaging services including free email. However, for local calls alone you're usually better off with a local phonecard and you should compare eKno rates with local cards if you're going to be making a lot of calls. You can join online at www.ekno.lonelyplanet.com, or by phone from NZ by dialling ☎ 0800-11 44 84. Once you have joined, to use eKno from NZ, dial ☎ 912 8211 from Auckland or ☎ 0800-11 44 78 elsewhere.

Many places to stay have cardphones for guests, on which you can also receive calls. Make a short call to someone long distance or overseas and get them to ring you back. Alternatively, you could make a reverse-charge call (see Country Direct later in this section).

Emergency calls are not charged. Toll-free numbers in NZ are preceded by a ☎ 0800 or ☎ 0508 code, although cardphones may require you to insert a card, even though the call is not charged. The ☎ 0900 code attracts a charge higher than local calls. Mobile phone numbers are preceded by the ☎ 021 or ☎ 025 code and also attract a higher rate.

Useful numbers include:

Directory assistance in NZ	☎ 018
Emergency (police, ambulance, fire brigade)	☎ 111
International direct dial access code	☎ 00
International directory service	☎ 0172
International tolls operator	☎ 0170
Local and national tolls operator	☎ 010
New Zealand country code	☎ 64
Tolls help desk	☎ 123

NZ Area Codes Regional area codes in NZ are:

Auckland and Northland	☎ 09
Coromandel Peninsula, Bay of Plenty, Waikato and Central Plateau	☎ 07
East Coast, Hawkes Bay, Wanganui, Manawatu and Taranaki	☎ 06
Wellington Region	☎ 04
South Island	☎ 03

When dialling within a region you still have to use the area code between towns, often for a town just a few kilometres down the road.

Country Direct The toll-free Country Direct service enables you to phone directly to an operator in an overseas country for reverse-charge calls, bypassing the NZ operator. The connection fee and call is then charged to the number you dial. Details, including Country Direct numbers, are listed in the front of telephone directories or are available from the NZ international operator. The access number varies, depending on the number of phone companies in the country you call, but is usually ☎ 000 9 (followed by the country code).

Telecards and call-back services from your telephone company, allowing you to make calls throughout the world and have them charged to your account, usually work out cheaper than Country Direct dialling. Set this up before you leave home.

Fax

Many hotels, motels and even backpackers have fax machines. Most towns of any size have at least one business offering fax services, and post shops often do too. The charge to send a fax is about $5, plus the telephone toll charges. Receiving a fax costs around $1 per page.

Email & Internet Access

Many businesses are on the Internet, which means that you can send and receive email at most hotels, backpackers and even camping grounds. A small fee usually applies.

Various computer stores and Internet providers in even the smaller cities offer email services, which are usually more expensive. There are Internet cafes in all the major centres.

INTERNET RESOURCES

The World Wide Web is a rich resource for travellers. You can research your trip, hunt down bargain air fares, book hotels, check on weather conditions or chat with locals and other travellers about the best places to visit (or avoid!).

There's no better place to start your Web explorations than the Lonely Planet Web site (www.lonelyplanet.com). Here you'll find succinct summaries on travelling to most places on earth, postcards from other travellers and the Thorn Tree bulletin board, where you can ask questions before you go or dispense advice when you get back. You can also find travel news and updates to many of our most popular guidebooks, and the subWWWay section links you to the most useful travel resources elsewhere on the Web.

A Web search on NZ will turn up thousands of useful sites and as many useless ones. Many have been included in the relevant chapters. Good starting points are:

Air New Zealand
www.airnz.co.nz
Akiko News, general information and lots of links, and plenty of 'Pink pages'.
http://nz.com/guide
Ansett Airlines
www.ansett.co.nz
AraNui A great links site.
www.lincoln.ac.nz/libr/nz/
Bushwise NZ Information for women travellers about accommodation and activities.
www.bushwise.co.nz
Department of Conservation Information on national parks, walks (including the Great Walks and bookings) plus press reports on endangered species and new developments.
www.doc.govt.nz
KiwiNewZ An up-to-date site with lots of links, although its primary focus is Queenstown and the Southern Lakes region.
www.KiwiNewZ.com
NZ Government General information on the country, government services and regulations (immigration and census figures).
www.govt.nz
New Zealand Tourism Board Highlights, itineraries, events, links etc.
www.purenz.com
Notice Board A useful site for travellers as it allows them to keep an easily accessible diary that friends can access back in their home countries; useful tips and information.
www.notice-board.com
Queenstown This is the site for the world's outdoor adventure capital.
www.queenstown-nz.co.nz
Telecom The NZ Telephone directory online.
www.whitepages.co.nz
Tranz Rail
www.tranzrail.co.nz
VIP Backpackers Resorts
www.vip.co.nz
Youth Hostel Association
www.yha.org.nz

BOOKS

For details of NZ literature, including poetry, children's books and contemporary Maori and Pacific islander literature, see Literature under Arts in the Facts about New Zealand chapter.

Whitcoulls and London Bookshops are two large chains with a wide variety of books, including sections specialising in NZ books. The larger cities have a good selection of other general and specialist bookshops, including Smith's in Christchurch, a browser's heaven.

Lonely Planet

Tramping in New Zealand describes nearly 50 walks in all parts of NZ. The *Cycling New Zealand* guide is a comprehensive coverage of all the main routes, and it has heaps of tips. The *Auckland* city guide describes the 'City of Sails' and surrounds in detail.

Guidebooks

Innumerable specialist travel guides have been written about tramping, skiing, cycling, scuba diving, surfing, fishing, birdwatching and many other activities. See the Activities chapter for details.

The *Mobil New Zealand Travel Guide* by Diana & Jeremy Pope is an excellent resource for history, background information and interesting stories about the places you visit. It comes in two volumes – *North Island* and *South Island*.

The Reader's Digest *Guide to New Zealand* was written by Maurice Shadbolt, one of the country's pre-eminent authors, who provides wonderful insights into NZ's history, culture and attractions. The coffee-table format is packed with wonderful photographs by Brian Brake, as well as historical pictures. Another good Reader's Digest book is *Wild New Zealand* with comprehensive descriptions of 24 of the wilderness regions.

The *Bateman New Zealand Encyclopedia* covers all aspects of NZ, especially history, geography and biography.

History

Although a little outdated, *A History of New Zealand* by Keith Sinclair is a readable and entertaining general history, from the Maori account of the creation to the present.

The *People and the Land – Te Tangata me Te Whenua: An Illustrated History of New Zealand 1820–1920* by Judith Binney, Judith Bassett & Erik Olssen is also good.

The *New Zealand Historical Atlas: Visualising New Zealand – Ko Papatuanuku e*

Takoto Nei is the most exciting NZ publication (1997) for years. Numerous colour spreads cover the prehistory, history and demography of the islands in detail. The text is easy to read and the graphs, diagrams, maps and illustrations highlight interesting aspects of the country's development – Maori migration, the kauri harvest, the sheep-meat industry, sport and leisure, women in paid work, suburban streets etc. The atlas is well worth the $75 price tag.

Two Worlds: First Meetings between Maori and Europeans 1642–1772 by Anne Salmond is an account of the first contact between the Maori and the European explorers. It's a fascinating anthropological history telling the story as it was experienced by both sides.

The 19th-century Land Wars between Europeans and Maori are looked at in a new and interesting way in *The New Zealand Wars* by James Belich.

Christopher Pugsley's *Anzac* is a pictorial account of NZ troops' involvement in the ill-fated Gallipoli campaign in 1915 during WWI, an important element of the national psyche.

Maori: A Photographic and Social History by Michael King is an excellent illustrated history of the Maori people.

The Old-Time Maori by Makereti, first published in London in 1938, was the first ethnographic account of the Maori written by a Maori scholar. It's fascinating reading.

One of the most important and controversial elements of NZ history is the Treaty of Waitangi. Many books have been written about the treaty and the debates surrounding it. One of the best is *The Treaty of Waitangi* (as well as *An Illustrated History of the Treaty of Waitangi*) by Claudia Orange.

Several books have been written about the Greenpeace ship, the *Rainbow Warrior*, sunk by the French government in Auckland's harbour in 1985, including the illustrated *Making Waves: The Greenpeace New Zealand Story* by Michael Szabo.

Biography

Some fascinating history has been told through biography. *The Dictionary of New*

Zealand Biography is a multivolume collection of hundreds of short NZ biographies.

A People's History: Illustrated Biographies from The Dictionary of New Zealand Biography, *Volume One, 1769–1869,* edited by WH Oliver, contains over 100 biographies of early New Zealanders, illustrated with historic photos.

Three biographies about Maori elders are particularly interesting: *Eruera: The Teachings of a Maori Elder* by Eruera Stirling, as told to Anne Salmond, won the NZ Wattie Book of the Year Award, one of NZ's highest literary awards. *Te Puea* by Michael King tells the story of the Maori King Movement's Te Puea Herangi, one of the most influential women in modern Maori history. *Whina*, also by King, tells the story of the Ngapuhi elder Whina Cooper, another important Maori figure, who organised her first public protest at 18 and welcomed an international audience to the XIV Commonwealth Games in Auckland in 1990 at age 95.

The Book of New Zealand Women – Ko Kui Ma Te Kaupapa edited by Charlotte Macdonald, Merimeri Penfold & Bridget Williams is a large anthology of over 300 biographical essays of NZ women – a great resource.

Contemporary Autobiography One of NZ's favourite characters, the late Barry Crump was a writer and rugged adventurer, more the Bukowski than the bastard of the bush. He is the author of many popular books, including *A Good Keen Man* (1960), *Hang On a Minute Mate* (1961) and many others published after these, which still sell even after all these years.

Being Pakeha by Michael King is the autobiography of one of NZ's foremost Maori historians, who is a Pakeha.

An Autobiography by the poet Lauris Edmonds (1924–2000) is a frank account of an emergent writer's life. Her poetry, written in a relaxed style, is a delight to read; some of the best is in *Wellington Letter: A Sequence of Poems* (1980).

Mihi Edwards is a contemporary Maori elder who writes readable books telling the story of her life growing up Maori in Pakeha culture and how Maori were punished if they spoke their language in school. Her books include *Mihipeka: Early Years* and *Mihipeka: Time of Turmoil*.

Maori Culture

In recent years NZ has experienced a renaissance of interest in Maori culture, a subject covered by many excellent books. Maori language books are mentioned in the Language chapter at the end of the book.

Te Marae: A Guide to Customs & Protocol by Hiwi & Pat Tauroa is a useful little 'how-to' book for non-Maori visiting a marae for the first time.

Hui: A Study of Maori Ceremonial Gatherings by Anne Salmond is an excellent, more scholarly book about Maori gatherings on the marae with insights into Maori culture.

Te Ao Hurihuri: Aspects of Maoritanga edited by Michael King is a collection of writings on many aspects of Maori culture, written by a number of respected Maori authors.

Tikanga Whakaaro: Key Concepts in Maori Culture by Cleve Barlow is a book in English and Maori in which the author explains 70 terms central to Maori culture.

Maori Customs and Crafts compiled by Alan Armstrong is only a small book in the Pocket Guide series but describes and illustrates many different Maori customs and crafts.

A number of good books have been written about the rich legends, myths and stories of the Maori people. An excellent one is the illustrated *Maori Myths and Tribal Legends* retold by Antony Alpers. Another smaller volume is the illustrated *Maori Myth and Legend* by AW Reed.

Traditional Maori Stories, introduced and translated by Margaret Orbell, is a fine book of Maori stories in English and Maori.

A good, accessible overview of Maori culture is *The Maori: Heirs of Tane* by David Lewis, illustrated by Werner Forman.

Greenstone Trails: The Maori and Pounamu by Barry Brailsford is a fascinating archaeological and historical account of trails used by the Maori when they crossed the Southern Alps to trade the precious stone. His *Song of the Waitaha* and *The Tatooed Land* are also interesting reading, introducing the author's own prehistory theories.

Chatham Islands

Moriori: A People Rediscovered by Michael King tells about the Moriori people of the Chatham Islands and debunks some of the common notions about them. King also wrote *A Land Apart: The Chatham Islands of New Zealand*, with photographs by Robin Morrison, which is a good coverage of the history and stories of these remote islands.

Photography

There are innumerable coffee-table books of NZ photographs. You'll find at least a dozen in almost any large bookstore in NZ, with titles like *New Zealand – the Glorious Islands, New Zealand – A Special Place, Beautiful New Zealand* and so on. Two of NZ's best photographers, Craig Potton and Robin Morrison, have published a number of books.

Art & Architecture

There are plenty of high-quality art books on NZ's well-known artists and Maori arts and crafts. The magnificent *Taonga Maori: A Spiritual Journey Expressed through Maori Art* by the Australian Museum (Sydney) has colour photographs and insightful text on some of the best Maori art.

Architecture is not what people usually think of when contemplating NZ, but the book *The New Zealand House* by Michael Fowler (architect) & Robert van de Voort (photographer) is a fascinating presentation of an amazing variety of NZ home architecture, with colour photos of everything from grand Victorian palaces to homemade rolling caravan inventions.

Cartoons

No overview of Kiwi publishing could be complete without mention of NZ's favourite comic strip, *Footrot Flats* by Murray Ball. Many books have been published of the adventures of the focal character, The Dog, a mongrel black-and-white sheepdog, and his master Wal, the farmer. It's a delightful look

into rural NZ farming life as told from the sheepdog's point of view.

Publication Warning

Most books are published in different editions by different publishers in different countries. As a result, a book might be a hardcover rarity in one country while it's readily available in paperback in another. Fortunately, bookshops and libraries search by title or author, so your local bookshop or library is best placed to advise you on the availability of these recommendations.

FILMS

See Cinema under Arts in the Facts about New Zealand chapter for NZ films.

CD-ROMS

One of the more interesting CD-ROMs on NZ is the *TVNZ New Zealand Encyclopedia*, covering history, culture and many other topics, with over 2300 illustrations, 54 maps and 20 minutes of videos. Of interest to birdwatchers, *Birds of New Zealand* covers all NZ birds. Other CD-ROMs include *Coast to Coast*, an interactive tourist guide. Order it from New Zealand Video Tours (☎ 09-415 9343), Web site: www.nzvt.co.nz.

NEWSPAPERS & MAGAZINES

There is no national paper although the *New Zealand Herald* (Auckland), the *Dominion* (Wellington) and the *Press* (Christchurch) have wide circulations. Backing up the city newspapers are numerous local dailies, some OK, some not. The closest to a national weekly news magazine is the *Listener*, an excellent publication which provides a weekly TV and radio guide, plus articles on the arts, social issues and politics. International publications (eg *Time* and *Newsweek*) are available in most towns.

Local magazines of merit are *Cuisine*, which features innovative uses of local produce, and *North & South*, which has articles on all aspects of NZ culture.

RADIO & TV

There are four national commercial TV stations (in some areas only a couple can be received) plus Sky, a subscriber television service with news, sports, movie and documentary channels.

Many regional or local commercial radio stations broadcast on the AM and FM bands. Of particular interest are National Radio (837kHz), good for current affairs, Concert FM (96FM) for classical and jazz and Radio Pacific (95.6FM) for talkback. There are also university stations (good for less-safe music than the commercial stations) in the big cities, and tribal-based stations.

VIDEO SYSTEMS

Three video systems are used in the world, and each one is completely incompatible with the others. Video recorders in NZ operate on the PAL system, used in Australia and most of Europe.

PHOTOGRAPHY & VIDEO

Photographic and video supplies, equipment and maintenance are all readily available, but prices are generally higher than in other countries.

Fuji and Kodak are the most popular films, with Agfa also available. Film and processing prices can vary, so it pays to shop around. For prints, one-hour photo developing shops are all over NZ. Slide film is very expensive and processing usually takes about a week.

The native bush in NZ is dense and light levels can be very low – more-sensitive (eg, 400 ASA) film will help.

TIME

Being close to the international date line, NZ is one of the first places in the world to start the new day (Pitt Island in the Chatham Islands gets the first sunrise each new year). NZ is 12 hours ahead of GMT (Greenwich Mean Time, also known as UTC) and two hours ahead of Australian Eastern Standard Time.

In summer NZ observes daylight-saving time, where clocks are put forward by one hour on the last Sunday in October; clocks are wound back on the first Sunday of the following March. Ignoring daylight-saving time, when it is noon in NZ it is 10 am in Sydney, 8 am in Singapore, midnight in London, 8 pm the previous day in New York and 5 pm the previous day in San Francisco. The Chathams are 45 minutes ahead of the mainland.

ELECTRICITY

Electricity is 230V AC, 50Hz, as in Europe and Australia; Australian-type three-blade plugs are used. Appliances designed for DC supply or different voltages need a transformer. It's not usually possible to operate appliances such as clocks or computers under a different frequency.

WEIGHTS & MEASURES

New Zealand uses the metric system, but you'll still encounter vestiges of the old imperial system. If you go sky diving they'll take you up to 9000 feet rather than 2743m and if you ask someone how much they weigh, the answer may be in kilograms, pounds or stones (a stone is 14 pounds).

LAUNDRY

Laundries are rare in NZ, but virtually every accommodation place provides a coin-operated washing machine and a dryer You can wash a full load of clothes for about $2 and dry it for $2, using coins or tokens.

HEALTH

There are no vaccination requirements to enter NZ, which is largely a clean, healthy, disease-free country with few health concerns. Medical attention is of a high quality but the state-subsidised health system has long since disappeared. A visit to a general practitioner costs around $35 and hospital services are expensive – take out travel insurance with decent medical coverage.

The same health precautions apply as in other developed countries. Of extra note for trampers in NZ is the presence of giardia in some lakes, rivers and streams, but it is rare. There is also a risk of catching amoebic meningitis if you bathe in natural hot thermal pools (see Infectious Diseases under Environmental Hazards).

NZ has no dangerous animals, no snakes and only one poisonous spider (the rarely encountered katipo – see Cuts, Bites & Stings).

Medical Kit Check List

Following is a list of items you should consider including in your medical kit – consult your pharmacist for brands available in your country.

☐ **Aspirin or paracetamol (acetaminophen in the USA)** – for pain or fever
☐ **Antihistamine** – for allergies, eg, hay fever; to ease the itch from insect bites or stings; and to prevent motion sickness
☐ **Cold and flu tablets, throat lozenges and nasal decongestant**
☐ **Multivitamins** – consider these for long trips, when dietary vitamin intake may be inadequate
☐ **Antibiotics** – consider including these if you're travelling well off the beaten track; see your doctor, as they must be prescribed, and carry the prescription with you
☐ **Loperamide or diphenoxylate** –'blockers' for diarrhoea
☐ **Prochlorperazine or metaclopramide** – for nausea and vomiting
☐ **Rehydration mixture** – to prevent dehydration, which may occur, for example, during bouts of diarrhoea; particularly important when travelling with children
☐ **Insect repellent, sunscreen, lip balm and eye drops**
☐ **Calamine lotion, sting relief spray or aloe vera** – to ease irritation from sunburn and insect bites or stings
☐ **Antifungal cream or powder** – for fungal skin infections and thrush
☐ **Antiseptic (such as povidone-iodine)** – for cuts and grazes
☐ **Bandages, Band-Aids (plasters) and other wound dressings**
☐ **Water purification tablets or iodine**
☐ **Scissors, tweezers and a thermometer** – note that mercury thermometers are prohibited by airlines

Trampers face the usual health dangers, especially hypothermia. Many of NZ's most popular tramps are in alpine regions and walkers must be well-equipped against the rain and cold. Good equipment can save your life, as can good advice. Consult DOC before undertaking walks and heed its warnings.

Predeparture Planning

Health Insurance Make sure that you have adequate health insurance. See Travel Insurance under Visas & Documents earlier in this chapter for details.

Immunisations You don't need any vaccinations to visit NZ. It's always a good idea to keep your tetanus immunisation up to date no matter where you are – boosters are necessary every 10 years and protection is highly recommended.

Nutrition Good, well-prepared food is plentiful in NZ but you should take care to make sure your diet is well balanced. Cooked eggs, tofu, beans, lentils and nuts are all safe ways to get protein. Fruit is a good source of vitamins. Try to eat plenty of grains (including rice) and bread. If your diet isn't well balanced or if your food intake is insufficient, it's a good idea to take vitamin and iron pills.

Other Preparations Make sure you're healthy before you start travelling. If you are going on a long trip make sure your teeth are OK. If you wear glasses take a spare pair and your prescription.

If you require a particular medication take an adequate supply, as it may not be available locally. Take part of the packaging showing the generic name rather than the brand, which will make getting replacements easier. It's a good idea to have a legible prescription or letter from your doctor to show that you legally use the medication to avoid any problems.

Basic Rules

Water Tap water is clean, delicious and safe to drink in NZ. Water in lakes, rivers and streams is often OK, but giardia (see Infectious Diseases later) has been found in these sources. DOC can advise on the occurrence of giardia in national parks and forest areas it administers. Water from these sources should be purified before drinking.

Water Purification The simplest way of purifying water is to boil it. Vigorous boiling should be satisfactory. Note: at high altitude water boils at a lower temperature, so germs are less likely to be killed. Boil it for longer in these environments.

Consider purchasing a water filter for a long trip. There are two main kinds of filter. Total filters take out all parasites, bacteria and viruses and make water safe to drink. They are often expensive, but they can be more cost effective than buying bottled water. Simple filters (which can even be a nylon mesh bag) take out dirt and larger foreign bodies from the water so that chemical solutions work much more effectively; if water is dirty, chemical solutions may not work at all.

It's very important when buying a filter to read the specifications, so that you know exactly what it removes from the water and what it doesn't. Simple filtering will not remove all dangerous organisms, so if you cannot boil water it should be treated chemically. Chlorine tablets will kill many pathogens, but not some parasites like giardia and amoebic cysts. Iodine is more effective in purifying water and is available in tablet form. Follow the directions carefully and remember that too much iodine can be harmful.

Environmental Hazards

Hypothermia Too much cold can be dangerous, particularly if it leads to hypothermia. Hypothermia is a real and present danger in NZ, due to the country's extremely changeable weather. Visitors die from hypothermia every year, mostly because they have gone out walking without adequate preparation, not realising that within the space of a few minutes a bright, warm day can change to freezing winds, rain and hail. Always be prepared for cold, wet or windy conditions even if you're just out walking or hitching; it's especially important if you're tramping out in the bush, away from civilisation.

Hypothermia occurs when the body loses heat faster than it can produce it and the core temperature of the body falls. It is surprisingly easy to progress from very cold to dangerously cold due to a combination of wind, wet clothing, fatigue and hunger, even if the air temperature is above freezing. It is best to dress in layers; silk, wool and some of the new artificial fibres are all good insulating materials. A hat is important, as a lot of heat is lost through the head. A strong, waterproof outer layer (and a 'space' blanket for emergencies) is essential. Carry basic supplies, including food containing simple sugars to generate heat quickly and fluid to drink.

Symptoms of hypothermia are exhaustion, numb skin (particularly toes and fingers), shivering, slurred speech, irrational or violent behaviour, lethargy, stumbling, dizzy spells, muscle cramps and violent bursts of energy. Irrationality may take the form of sufferers claiming they are too warm and trying to take off their clothes.

To treat mild hypothermia, first get the person out of the wind and/or rain, remove their clothing if it's wet and replace it with dry, warm clothing. Give them hot liquids – not alcohol – and some high-energy, easily digestible food. Do not rub victims: instead, allow them to slowly warm themselves. This should be enough to treat the early stages of hypothermia. The early recognition and treatment of mild hypothermia is the only way to prevent severe hypothermia, which is a critical condition.

Motion Sickness Eating lightly before and during a trip will reduce the chances of motion sickness. If you are prone to motion sickness try to find a place that minimises movement – near the wing on aircraft, close to midships on boats, near the centre on buses. Fresh air usually helps; reading and cigarette smoke don't. Commercial motion-sickness preparations, which can cause drowsiness, have to be taken before the trip commences. Ginger (available in capsule form) and peppermint (including mint-flavoured sweets) are natural preventatives.

Sunburn You can get sunburnt surprisingly quickly, even through cloud. Use a sunscreen, a hat, and a barrier cream for your nose and lips. Calamine lotion, or a commercial after-sun preparation, is good for mild sunburn. Protect your eyes with good quality sunglasses, particularly if you will be near water, sand or snow.

Infectious Diseases

Diarrhoea Simple things like a change of water, food or climate can all cause a mild bout of diarrhoea, but a few rushed toilet trips with no other symptoms is not indicative of a major problem.

Dehydration is the main danger with any diarrhoea, particularly in children or the elderly as dehydration can occur quite quickly. Under all circumstances *fluid replacement* (at least equal to the volume being lost) is the most important thing to remember. Weak black tea with a little sugar, soda water, or soft drinks allowed to go flat and diluted 50% with clean water are all good replacements.

Giardiasis This is caused by a common parasite, *Giardia lamblia*. Symptoms include stomach cramps, nausea, a bloated stomach, watery, foul-smelling diarrhoea and frequent gas. Giardiasis can appear several weeks after you have been exposed to the parasite. The symptoms may disappear for a few days and then return; this can go on for several weeks.

You should seek medical advice if you think you have giardiasis but if this is not possible, tinidazole or metronidazole are the recommended drugs. Treatment is a 2g single dose of tinidazole or 250mg of metronidazole three times daily for five to 10 days.

Fungal Infections These occur more commonly in hot weather and are usually found on the scalp, between the toes (athlete's foot) or fingers, in the groin and on the body (ringworm). You get ringworm (which is a fungal infection, not a worm) from infected animals or other people. Moisture encourages these infections.

To prevent fungal infections wear loose, comfortable clothes, avoid artificial fibres, wash frequently and dry yourself carefully. If you do get an infection, wash the infected area at least daily with a disinfectant or medicated soap and water, and rinse and dry well. Apply an antifungal cream or powder such as tolnaftate. Try to expose the infected area to air or sunlight as much as possible and wash all towels and underwear in hot water, change them often and let them dry in the sun.

HIV & AIDS Infection with the human immunodeficiency virus (HIV) may lead to acquired immune deficiency syndrome (AIDS), which is a fatal disease. Any exposure to blood, blood products or body fluids may put the individual at risk. The disease is often transmitted through sexual contact or dirty needles – vaccinations, acupuncture, tattooing and body piercing can be potentially as dangerous as intravenous drug use.

Amoebic Meningitis This very serious disease can be a danger if you bathe in natural hot thermal pools. Fortunately, it's no danger if you know how to protect yourself from it.

The amoeba that causes the disease can enter your body through the orifices of your head, usually the nose but occasionally the ears as well. Once it gets inside the nose it bores through the tissues and lodges in the brain. It's easy not to catch the disease – just keep your head out of water!

Symptoms of amoebic meningitis may have a slow onset – it could be several days or even several weeks before the first symptoms are noticed. Symptoms may at first be similar to the flu, later progressing to severe headaches, stiffness of the neck, hypersensitivity to light and then even coma. It can be treated with intravenous anti-amoebic drugs.

Cuts, Bites & Stings

Bees & Wasps Bee and wasp stings are usually painful rather than dangerous. However, in people who are allergic to them severe breathing difficulties may occur and they require urgent medical care. Calamine lotion or a sting relief spray will give relief and ice packs will reduce the pain and swelling.

Mosquitoes & Sandflies Mosquitoes appear after dusk. In some parts of the country – notably the West Coast of the South Island and especially in summer – they can come in huge clouds. Avoid bites by covering bare skin and using an insect repellent.

Insect screens on windows and mosquito nets on beds offer good protection, as does burning a mosquito coil or using a pyrethrum-based insect spray.

Another six-legged New Zealander that can drive you wild is the tiny black sandfly. Sandfly bites can be even more irritating than mosquito bites; since the insects live on the ground, sandfly bites are mainly on the feet and ankles. Wearing shoes, thick socks and plenty of insect repellent is practically a necessity where sandflies are present.

The most effective insect repellent, DEET (N,N-diethyl-m-toluamide), is an ingredient in many commercially available repellents. Look for a repellent with at least a 28% concentration of DEET. Note that DEET breaks down plastic, rubber and synthetic fabrics, so be careful what you touch after using it. It poses no danger to natural fibres.

Other good insect repellents include Off! and Repel, which come in a stick or a spray form and will not eat through plastic the way DEET repellents do. Plenty of vitamin B1 in your system is thought to deter sandflies and mosquitoes. Two NZ dietary icons, kumara and marmite, are good sources.

Leeches & Ticks Leeches may be present in damp rainforest conditions; they attach themselves to your skin to suck your blood. Trampers often get them on their legs or in their boots. Salt or a lighted cigarette end will make them fall off. Do not pull them off, as the bite is then more likely to become infected. Clean and apply pressure if the point of attachment is bleeding. An insect repellent may keep them away.

You should always check all over your body if you have been walking through a potentially tick-infested area as ticks can cause skin infections and other more serious diseases. If a tick is found attached, press down around its head with tweezers, grab the head and gently pull upwards. Avoid pulling the rear of the body as this may squeeze the tick's gut contents through the attached mouth parts into the skin, increasing the risk of infection and disease. Smearing chemicals on the tick will not make it let go and is not recommended.

Spiders Of NZ's many spiders, the only poisonous one is the retiring little katipo *(Latrodectus katipo)*. The katipo's shiny black body, about 6mm long, has a bright red patch on the rear of the abdomen. Males and immature females have white markings alongside the famous red patch. Only mature females are venomous. Although mention of its name strikes fear into the hearts of brave souls, it's very rare to meet anyone who has ever seen a katipo, and its bite is not that dangerous. If you're lucky enough to be bitten by one you'll be a legend among New Zealanders; seek medical assistance when you've finished boasting.

WOMEN TRAVELLERS

New Zealand is quite an easy country for women travellers, with very few hassles. Women should, however, exercise the same degree of caution as they would in any other country. Observe all the commonsense habits of safety, such as not walking through isolated urban areas alone when it's dark, not hitchhiking alone etc.

GAY & LESBIAN TRAVELLERS

Legislation decriminalising sex between consenting males over 15 was finally passed in 1985 (sex between consenting women was never a criminal act). The Human Rights Act 1993 makes it unlawful to discriminate against a person on the grounds of their sexual orientation, in regards to employment, access to public places, provision of goods and services, accommodation and education facilities.

Numerous gay and lesbian organisations are found throughout the country, with the biggest concentration in Auckland. Auckland is also home to the HERO Festival held annually in February. Various cultural events are held and up to 200,000 people line the streets to witness the parade. The Devotion Festival in November is Wellington's biggest gay and lesbian pride celebration.

NZ has a Gay & Lesbian Tourism Association (☎ 04-384 1877, 0800-367 429, fax 384 5187, ✆ seretariat@nzglta.org.nz), PO Box 11-582, Wellington 6001, to promote gay and lesbian tourism to NZ. Travel Gay New

Zealand (fax 04-382 8246) is an information and reservation service covering gay destinations and accommodation. Their Web site (http://webnz.com/tpac/gaynz/) is a good source for information. Other good Web sites include www.gaynz.com and www.akiko.co.nz/glb/.

For further contacts, and for gay and lesbian venues, see the Information and Entertainment sections in the Auckland and Wellington Region chapters.

DISABLED TRAVELLERS

New Zealand generally caters well for disabled travellers. Most hostels, hotels, B&Bs etc have wheelchair access and disabled bathrooms, as required by law for new establishments. Many government facilities and tourist attractions are similarly equipped. Disabled travellers usually receive discounts on transport.

A good contact point is the Disability Information Service (☎ 03-366 6189, fax 379 5939) at 314 Worcester St, Christchurch.

SENIOR TRAVELLERS

Senior travellers over the age of 60 receive a discount on most transport; proof of age may be required. Discounts on entry to attractions, activities and other services may also be available but sometimes only for NZ citizens.

Life for many NZ seniors revolves around the bowling club and the garden (NZ has many wonderful private gardens open to the public, if you're interested), but many seniors are also active. It is not uncommon to meet septuagenarians on the tramping tracks, and many clubs and activities cater for seniors. NZ retirees are out in force touring their country, often pulling a caravan or driving a motor home, and many B&Bs are run by older couples delighted to meet like-minded travellers from overseas.

TRAVEL WITH CHILDREN

NZ is an ideal country to travel with children. Health problems are not a major issue, getting around is easy and many attractions and activities cater for children. However, all those theme attractions with hands-on activities and rides for the kids can be very expensive for families.

Family passes are usually available at attractions, though. Children's prices are quoted in this book, but usually apply to children from four to 14 years of age. For children younger than four, admission is often free or only a token amount applies.

Backpackers don't really cater for children, but also don't discourage them. The YHAs are better set up for families and often have specific family rooms set aside, but families can also get a four-bed share room to themselves in most backpackers.

B&Bs are mostly for couples and some even ban children. Motels, and particularly camping grounds, are well set up for children and often have playgrounds and game rooms. Children cost extra on top of double rates, but the charge is usually half the extra adult rate at motels and camping grounds, and the real 'littlies' may be free. Holiday homes and self-contained cottages are ideal for families. They are more spacious and often better value than tourist flats or motel units. The best way to find them is to inquire at information centres.

Major car hire companies, at least, have car seats for children but they are not always high quality. Good cradle restraints for babies are hard to get – you're better off bringing your own. If you can get a good deal on a motor home, it can be an economical and enjoyable way of seeing the country.

DANGERS & ANNOYANCES

Violent crime occurs but is not common in NZ. The newspapers report on murders and bashings in great detail, but this is more a reflection of the lack of crime (or perhaps lack of news). Auckland is the 'crime capital' of the country, but very safe by most standards. Of course, normal precautions should be taken in rough areas and around drunken yahoos on Saturday nights.

Theft, primarily from cars, can be a problem and is on the rise. Don't leave any valuables in a car, either outside accommodation or, particularly, at tourist parking areas, such as car parks at the start of walks. If you must leave your belongings in the car, make sure they are hidden from view.

The biggest dangers in NZ, though, may come not from your fellow humans but from nature. Remember to take all the recommended precautions when tramping, especially in the mountains; see Tramping in the Activities chapter for advice on tramping safety.

Sharks exist in NZ waters but are well fed by the abundant marine life and rarely pose a threat to humans. However, attacks do occasionally occur. Take notice of any local warnings when swimming, surfing or diving.

LEGAL MATTERS

Marijuana (aka 'New Zealand Green', 'electric puha' or 'dac') is widely indulged in but illegal – at least for now. Don't get caught carrying the stuff – fines can be stiff. Penalties for importing illegal drugs are severe.

Despite widespread campaigns, drink-driving still seems to be a national sport, but penalties are tough. The legal drinking age has recently been lowered to 18, and the legal blood alcohol limit is 0.08mg per 100mL of blood. Drivers under 20 face even more-stringent penalties than fully licensed drivers.

The legal dictum is pretty much 'buyer beware'. There's been so much deregulation that consumer rights are minimal and regulatory authorities, where they exist, often have little power. Fortunately most Kiwi businesses are honest.

The Commerce Commission, with offices in Auckland, Wellington and Christchurch, oversees the Fair Trading Act and can offer advice. The Citizens Advice Bureau, with offices in Wellington, Auckland (☎ 09-524 0298), Rotorua and Christchurch, is a referral service for legal, consumer and other advice. Like most British-based legal systems, lawsuits in NZ are prohibitively expensive and weighted against small complainants – this isn't the USA.

BUSINESS HOURS

Office hours are generally from 9 am to 5 pm Monday to Friday. Most government offices are open from around 8.30 am to 4.30 pm Monday to Friday. Shops are usually open from 9 am to 5.30 pm Monday to Friday plus Saturday morning (9 am to 12.30 pm), with late-night shopping to 9 pm one night of the week – usually Thursday or Friday.

Many small convenience stores (called 'dairies' in NZ) stay open for longer hours and the larger supermarkets are open until 8 pm or later daily.

PUBLIC HOLIDAYS & SPECIAL EVENTS

Christmas is in the middle of the summer school holidays, which means lots of crowds and higher prices. Public holidays include:

New Year	1–2 January
Waitangi Day	6 February
Easter	March/April
Anzac Day	25 April
Queen's Birthday	1 June
Labour Day	October
Christmas Day	25 December
Boxing Day	26 December

In addition, each province in NZ has its own anniversary day holiday (a hangover from the old days when each province was separatly administered). Provincial holidays (dates can vary) include:

Wellington	22 January
Auckland	29 January
Northland	29 January
Nelson	1 February
Otago	23 March
Southland	23 March
Taranaki	31 March
Hawkes Bay	1 November
Marlborough	1 November
Westland	1 December
Canterbury	16 December

When these holidays fall between Friday and Sunday, they are usually observed on the following Monday; if they fall between Tuesday and Thursday, they are held on the preceding Monday.

Some of the more noteworthy cultural events and festivals include:

January

Auckland Anniversary Day Regatta Auckland's biggest yacht race

Summer City Program Two months of festivals and entertainment around the city of Wellington (beginning of January to end of February)

February

Marlborough Food & Wine Festival Blenheim (2nd weekend)

Art Deco Festival Balls, dinners, fancy dress and Art Deco tours of Napier (3rd weekend)

International Festival of the Arts A month of national and international culture, Wellington (even-numbered years only)

Aotearoa Traditional Maori Performing Arts Festival Wellington (odd-numbered years)

March

Golden Shears Sheep Shearing Competition A major event in this rather sheepish country, Masterton

Ngaruawahia Regatta Maori canoe race, north of Hamilton

Wildfoods Festival Tasty and healthy wild food from the land, sea and air. Held in Hokitika.

Pasifika Polynesian Festival Traditional arts, entertainment, sports and food celebrating Auckland's Pacific communities

April

Highland Games Hastings

June

NZ Agricultural Field Days A major agricultural show at Mystery Creek near Hamilton

September

NZ Trout Festival Fishing contest, Rotorua

November

Canterbury Show Week Christchurch

December

Festival of Lights Light-up of New Plymouth and Pukekura Park over Christmas

There are smaller annual events held all over NZ. Each town seems to have its annual fair (or show), often involving simple sports like wheelbarrow and sugar bag races, wood chopping and sheep-shearing contests.

COURSES

People from around the world, especially Asia and the Pacific countries, come to NZ to study English. Typically each language school arranges for its students to live with NZ families, so that English is used outside as well as inside the classroom. Schools also arrange a variety of extracurricular evening and weekend activities for students.

Auckland has the highest concentration of language schools, but there are a few in other parts of the country as well. The Auckland Travel & Information Centre keeps a complete, up-to-date list.

Those wishing to learn Maori can do so at polytechnics in the major towns, many of which run evening courses.

Jade (known as greenstone) and hard-stone carving is also popular, and an excellent course is run at Tai Poutini Polytechnic in Greymouth, close to the source of greenstone.

WORK

New Zealand has a moderately high unemployment rate, so it's fussy about foreigners taking jobs from its citizens. An ordinary visitor permit or visa does not give you the right to work in NZ – so if you work you are breaking the law. Apply for a work permit before arriving in NZ or within the country at any NZ Immigration Service office. Generally, you need to be sponsored by an employer with an offer of definite employment in an occupation that is in demand. Special working holiday visas are available to citizens of Canada, Japan and the UK aged 18 to 30, and Australians can work; see Visas & Documents earlier in this chapter.

Fruit picking is readily available and popular work for visitors. Apples, kiwi fruit and other types of fruit and vegetables are picked in summer and early autumn; pay rates are so low that many New Zealanders won't touch this work. The main picking season is from around January to April, though there may be some agricultural work year-round. Picking is hard work and you are paid according to the amount you pick.

Places where you may find picking work include the Bay of Islands (Kerikeri and Paihia), rural Auckland, Tauranga, Gisborne and Hawkes Bay (Napier and Hastings) in the North Island; Nelson (Tapawera and Golden Bay), Marlborough and Central Otago (Alexandra and Roxburgh) in the South Island.

ACCOMMODATION

It's essential to book ahead in the main tourist areas at peak times: the summer holidays from Christmas to the end of January, and Easter. At these times prices rise, and finding a room can be difficult. International tourism also puts a strain on accommodation and is at its busiest from October to April, particularly during February and March.

Accommodation guides are available from the information centres, and include the *AA Accommodation New Zealand Guide, New Zealand Camping Guide, B&B Directory of New Zealand, YHA New Zealand Hostel Accommodation Guide, VIP Backpackers Accommodation Guide* and *BBH Backpacker Accommodation*.

Visitor centres have lists of all types of accommodation in their areas, often with illustrations to help in your choice. Prior to travelling you can contact visitor centres (their email addresses and fax numbers are given in this book) to find local fax numbers, email addresses or price updates.

Camping & Cabins

Kiwi camping grounds are some of the best in the world, and motor camps have excellent facilities for tent campers, caravans and campervans, plus on-site vans and cabins of different degrees of luxury.

Camping grounds and motor camps are found all over the country and often in prime locations. Most have well-equipped kitchens and dining areas. They're great places to meet people.

Camp or caravan sites are usually charged at a per-person rate, typically around $9 to $12 per adult, half-price for children, but rates may be for a minimum of two people.

At most sites the kitchen and showers are free but a few have coin-operated hotplates and hot showers. At most sites laundry facilities are coin operated ($2).

Why Isn't It Listed?

There are literally thousands of businesses offering accommodation in NZ, and thousands more offering food, tours or other services useful to travellers. To keep this book to a reasonable size we can only list a few such places in any given town. While we try to give a good selection, there's always a chance we've omitted the best place in town (or it has opened since we visited). What can you do about this?

• Contact the local visitors centre for more information before you leave home.
• Let your fingers do the surfing – check out some of the Web sites we've listed and search for others. Many hotels have their own site on the Internet these days.
• When you arrive in a new town, book into a hostel for one night, then the next day look around and see if you can find something even better.
• If you do find somewhere magnificent and we haven't listed it, write and tell us about it (or revel in having it all to yourself).

Camping becomes less practical in NZ in winter, especially in the south.

DOC Camping Grounds DOC operates over 120 camping grounds around NZ, often in beautiful locations. Its camping grounds are in reserves and national parks, maritime parks, forest parks and farm parks – DOC offices have lists.

Standard DOC camping grounds are basic, with minimal facilities that include cold running water, toilets, fireplaces and not much else, but they also have minimal charges (around $3 to $6 per adult). Informal camping grounds are free, but have almost no facilities, apart from a cold-water tap and places to pitch tents. Some DOC camping grounds are fully serviced like motor camps and have on-site managers.

Standard and informal camping grounds operate on a first-come, first-served basis, and fees are paid by a self-registration system. Since the low fees are used for the maintenance of the camping grounds, it's important to pay them (usually into an honesty box) even when there's no warden.

DOC also operates numerous backcountry huts, most of which can only be reached on foot. See Tramping in the Activities chapter for more information.

Cabins & Tourist Flats Many camping grounds and motor camps have cabins. Standard cabins are simply freestanding rooms with bare mattresses. You provide your own sleeping gear (a sleeping bag is fine) and towels, or linen can usually be hired. Rooms cost around $25 to $30 for two.

Many motor camps now offer hostel-style bunkrooms, often a cabin filled with dorm beds, but they are cheap at around $14 per person and often empty. Alternatively, backpacker beds are offered in two-, three- or four-bed cabins.

Better equipped cabins are called 'tourist flats'. Closer to motel standard, they have kitchens and/or bathrooms and may be serviced, with linen provided. On-site caravans ('trailer homes' in US parlance) are another camping-ground possibility.

Hostels

Hundreds of backpacker hostels offer cheap accommodation all over NZ. You rent a bed, usually for around $15 to $20 a night. Bunkrooms may be for 10 or more people, sometimes segregated, sometimes not. Some places have smaller bunkrooms or 'share rooms' with three or four beds, and almost all have at least a few twin ($35 to $40) or double (around $45) rooms. Sometimes single rooms (about $25 to $30) are offered, though they are rare and, unless the place is empty, you'll have to pay for a double.

YHA The YHA also goes under the banner of Hostelling International (HI), but the term YHA is still common in NZ. YHA hostels are only open to members. Join the YHA in your home country or in NZ at any YHA hostel for $30 for foreign travellers, more for Kiwis. Nonmembers can also stay at hostels by paying an extra instalment of $4 per night on a membership card. After six nights stay you

become a full member. If you have a YHA card make sure you bring it as it entitles you to discounts on buses (usually a 30% discount), airlines and for many activities.

NZ also has a number of Associate YHA Hostels – privately owned premises affiliated to the YHA – which are also open to nonmembers at the same rates.

Private Backpackers New Zealand has long led the world in this type of accommodation and nearly every town or tourist area has at least one or two private backpackers, and large cities have 20 plus.

These backpackers (private or independent hostels) have about the same facilities and prices as YHAs – a communal kitchen, laundry, dining area and lounge area. Some have bars, a spa or two, swimming pools, information racks, and almost all can advise on transport and onward accommodation bookings. Some have camping sites available; you share the common facilities.

The two biggest groups are VIP Backpackers Resorts (☎ 09-827 6016), Web site: www.vip.co.nz, and Budget Backpacker Hostels or BBH (☎ 0800-788 336), Web site: www.backpack.co.nz. Both have widely available books (see earlier in this section) which list their members' places. They also offer discounts on activities and transport (trains, planes, automobiles and buses), obtainable on presentation of your membership card. With the $30 VIP card you get $1 off the listed accommodation price.

The 80 VIP places tend to be the large city backpackers, but there are a few exceptions. The over 260 BBH places range from farmstays and homestays to bigger city hostels (all rated annually).

Recently a new group, Nomads (✉ info@ nomads-backpackers.com), set up in NZ with similar intentions. Some backpackers places choose not to belong to any group.

B&Bs & Guesthouses

B&B accommodation in private homes is by far the biggest category of accommodation, and B&Bs are everywhere.

Although breakfast is definitely on the agenda at the real B&B places, it may or may not feature at guesthouses. Breakfast may be 'continental' (ie not much) or a substantial meal of fruit, eggs, bacon, toast, tea and coffee. Many guesthouses pride themselves on the size, quality and 'traditional value' of their breakfasts. If you like to start the day heartily it's worth considering this when comparing prices. A big breakfast is worth about $10.

Guesthouses may be spartan, cheap, ultra-basic 'private' (unlicensed) hotels. Most are comfortable, relaxed but low-key places, patronised by people who don't enjoy the impersonal atmosphere of many motels. Others are very fancy indeed.

Guesthouses are often slightly cheaper than B&Bs. B&Bs usually start at around $40 a single, if available, or $60 a double – that will get you a standard room with a shared bathroom. Doubles with a bathroom start at around $80. Really luxurious B&Bs can cost well over $130.

Many B&Bs also offer an evening meal for an extra charge. A few B&Bs have a kitchen where guests can do their own cooking.

Farmstays (Farm Holidays)

New Zealand has been called the world's most efficient farm, so farmstays are one way of understanding the real NZ. Farmstays are popular and many offer guests the chance to 'have a go' at all the typical farm activities and be treated as one of the household. Choose from dairy, sheep, high country, cattle or mixed-farming farms.

Costs vary widely. Some have rooms in the homestead for $100 or more a double, including meals, but most offer B&B for more like $80 per day, with an extra $20 or so for dinner. Some farms have separate cottages where you fix your own food. Information centres have listings.

Farm Hosting in NZ (FHINZ; ☎ 06-376 4582), at Kumeroa Lodge Stud, RD1 Woodville, produces a booklet ($15) that lists farms throughout NZ providing lodging in exchange for four hours work per day.

WWOOF An economical way of staying on a farm and doing some work is joining Willing Workers on Organic Farms (WWOOF). Membership provides you with a list of over 300 organic farms throughout the country where, in exchange for your 'conscientious work', the farm owner will provide food, accommodation and some hands-on experience in organic farming. You must contact the farm owner or manager by telephone or letter; you cannot simply turn up at a farm without warning.

To join WWOOF and receive the booklet, phone ☎ 03-544 9890, or write to PO Box 1172, Nelson.

Motels

New Zealand motels have all the facilities of motels everywhere, and more. Many motel units have fully equipped kitchens, though some studio units only have a fridge, and tea- and coffee-making equipment. Most motels provide you with a small carton of fresh milk and often have a laundry for guests.

Many visitors find NZ motels a definite notch below international standards. Some motels date from the 1960s and look like it. Though comfortable enough, they are drab, prefabricated affairs. Newer motels are often cheap constructions but usually brighter with better decor, and some are definitely luxurious.

Motel rooms typically cost around $70 to $80 a double, and then $15 for every extra person. The more luxurious new motels charge around $95 and up. The difference in price between a single or double room, if there is one, is usually minimal. In tourist towns, motels can really hike prices in the main tourist season, but often discount in the off season.

A motor inn is part motel, part hotel, offering motel-style accommodation and usually a bar and restaurant.

Hotels

Many traditional, older-style pubs have rooms, but they are often just a sideline enterprise and the main emphasis is on the bar. At the other end of the scale are the five-star hotels in the big cities. At the cheapest pubs, singles/doubles might cost as low as $25/35, though $35/60 is more common, while at the most luxurious new establishments a room could cost $200 or more.

Holiday Homes & Cottages

Holiday homes (baches or cribs) or self-contained cottages can be rented in many country areas. They can be good for longer stays in one area, although many can be rented for only one or two nights. Prices are usually reasonable – typically $60 to $120, which, for a whole house or self-contained bungalow, is good value.

There is also the possibility of swapping homes temporarily with people from another country. The contact is Worldwide Home Exchange Club, 18–20 London Rd, Tunbridge Wells, Kent TN1 1YL, England.

FOOD

New Zealand is no longer in culinary no-person's land. The preparation of food was once ruled by strict adherence to the *Edmond's Cookery Book,* a slavish reflection of Anglo-Saxon stodge. Over the last ten years the NZ food scene has taken off like a rocket – the country is fast approaching the point where it can boast a distinctly 'Kiwi cuisine'. You may hear this referred to as 'Pacific Rim' at times.

There's no doubt that the styles of Asia, Europe and other parts of the Pacific have been plundered with abandon. The borrowings, however, have been gloriously applied to our fresh produce, especially the abundant and varied seafoods.

Almost every town in a tourist area will have an upmarket brasserie, cafe or restaurant that features Kiwi cuisine, especially towns close to the coastline.

You could expect, depending on season, such delights as a lamb burger with vegetables and prosciutto, yellow-fin tuna and wasabi caviar salad, pork fillets filled with kumara and apple stuffing accompanied by rice and spinach pilaf, paua risotto with crayfish stock, oysters in seaweed tempura batter, tuatua and pumpkin fritters, feijoa or kiwi-fruit ice cream.

It's not surprising that in the dishes above there is more than a smattering of seafood. Green-lipped mussels, available all over NZ, are easily the best in the world and cheap. Oyster fans shouldn't leave NZ without tasting the superb oysters (the best come from Bluff on the South Island). Scallops are also good eating. Crayfish (lobster) is a speciality in some areas, though most of it is exported and hard to find. Other exotics include the now-rare and expensive shellfish toheroa or slightly less pricey tuatua. In some places, such as Ninety Mile Beach in the North Island, and in the right season, a few minutes of digging in the sand at the beach can yield bucketfuls of shellfish, including tuatua, pipi and periwinkles.

Saltwater fish favourites include hoki, hapuka, groper, snapper, kingfish and orange roughie. NZ also has good freshwater fish, with incredibly large rainbow and brown trout, in rivers and lakes all over the country. You can't buy trout in the shops but there are many opportunities to catch one yourself (see Fishing in the Activities chapter).

Eels, plentiful in NZ's rivers and creeks, are another local delicacy, especially smoked eel. Smoked fish is also popular.

Old favourite meats such as lamb, pork and beef are still readily available, but treated with much more flair these days. You can have them with roast vegetables (as Kiwis did in the old days) or embellish them with exotic sauces and accompany them with innovative salads. Cervena (venison) is a regular feature on many menus.

There was also a time when you couldn't get anything but white bread, cheddar cheese and instant coffee. You don't have to shop around too much to find a French bread stick, brioche, ciabatta or bagel these days; a fantastic variety of cheeses from Kikurangi creamy blue to Legato goats' cheese; and cafes serving good coffee abound (see the boxed text 'Bean There Done That' in the Wellington chapter).

NZ took an obscure fruit, the Chinese gooseberry, and marketed it internationally as 'kiwi fruit'. It's now grown worldwide, but NZ produces the largest and juiciest variety, and it's still a perennial feature on Kiwi cuisine menus. Other exotic fruits, such as nashi, persimmons and the sweet, highly perfumed feijoa, are included in restaurant menus.

The magazine *Cuisine,* published every two months ($8.95), is testament to the variety of food now available in the country.

Fast Food

New Zealand has plenty of fast-food joints, including those symbols of US culinary imperialism: McDonald's, Pizza Hut and KFC. Burger Wisconsin is a popular newcomer to the chain choices, and is found in larger towns.

Fish and chips (also known as 'fush and chups') is an English institution that NZ excels at. Not only can you get some superb fresh fish, deep fried in batter, but fish and chip shops also offer mussels, scallops, oysters, paua fritters and other seafood delights, served with hot, crisp chips. (For Americans, 'chips' in NZ are thickly cut French fries.) Try kumara chips for a variation.

New Zealanders are just about as tied to the meat pie as Australians but they probably do a better job of them. The NZ meat pie must, by law, have no more than 25% offal content. In Australia up to 90% is permitted. The Kiwis win this one!

Other snacks popular in NZ include nachos, potato skins and hamburgers like the great 'Kiwi burger' with a fried egg, beetroot and salad.

The larger towns have pie carts, generally open from late at night to first thing in the morning. They serve all the fast food faves. The most famous are the White Lady in Shortland St, Auckland, and the one in Bunny St outside Wellington station. They no longer serve pies with pea & 'pud' (mashed spud or potato), the source of their name.

Cafes & Tearooms

New Zealand's traditional cafes or coffee shops, called tearooms, are nothing to get excited about. They're usually located in the smaller towns, open from around 9 am to 5 pm weekdays and perhaps on Saturday morning, serving fare such as tea, scones (as part of Devonshire teas with jam and cream) and sandwiches.

In the larger cities, more-fashionable cafes have proliferated. These cafes serve espresso (or cappuccino, cafe latte etc), croissants, sinfully rich desserts and baked focaccia with a variety of ingredients. Cafes are also often popular late-night hangouts for espresso or wine, light meals and music.

Pub Food

Pubs offer some of the best value for money. Counter meals (pie and chips, stews etc) have more or less died out, though some bars still sell pies from a pie warmer. A lot of pubs now have bistro meals – simple but good food such as schnitzel, steak, roasts or fish with chips and salad or coleslaw. Average main courses range from $8 to $12 and they are usually excellent value.

Restaurants

Just about every sizeable town has one or two decent restaurants which would not be out of place in a piazza in Europe. The main cities have a variety of international cuisines and top quality restaurants.

A lot of restaurants now offer main meals that are marinated, smoked, sauteed or provençal, doused in booze and accompanied by a variety of colourful things you're not really meant to eat. Menus in better NZ restaurants almost invariably feature venison, lamb, beef and fish dishes. With such excellent fresh produce, it is hard to go wrong, but the chefs are not always as innovative as their menus, especially in the smaller towns. Even in the countryside, you will find some real gems, but expect to pay $25 or more for a main course in better restaurants. With an entree (appetiser), dessert and drinks, a meal in a good restaurant will cost around $50 per person.

Fully licensed restaurants are now more common, but many restaurants are still BYO, where you 'bring your own' wine, beer etc. Food prices are generally lower than in licensed restaurants.

Vegetarian New Zealand has a number of great vegetarian restaurants, mainly in the big cities. Auckland has several cheap and excellent vegetarian restaurants, including Gopals, run by the Hare Krishnas. In small 'alternative' lifestyle regions like Golden Bay, west of Nelson, you'll find a good selection.

Self-Catering

As many places to stay provide cooking facilities for guests, buying and cooking your own food will save you a lot of money travelling around NZ.

NZ has several large supermarket chains – Pak N Save, New World and ShopRite for example – usually open until around 8 pm seven days a week. Large supermarkets are found in the cities and towns that serve a large rural community.

When the supermarkets are shut, the good old corner dairy is the place to go. A dairy is a small shop found on many street corners throughout NZ, selling milk, food, newspapers, chocolate, sweets – a bit of everything, but mostly food. They're open longer hours than other shops and are more widespread, but their selection is limited and prices higher.

DRINKS
Beer

New Zealanders are great drinkers, and both the beer and the pubs are pretty good. Almost all the beer is now brewed by only two companies, New Zealand Breweries and Dominion Breweries (DB). Steinlager, the various types of DB (Bitter, Export etc) and Lion Red are probably the most popular beers. Down in the deep south you'll come across some different labels such as Speights. Monteith's, from the South Island's wild West Coast, as dark as the bituminous coal dug by the miners who drank it, now comes in six delightful varieties.

Small boutique breweries are popular and found in the main cities and towns. Probably the best of the boutique beers are from Marlborough and Nelson – Pink Elephant and Mac's. 'Dark' drinkers will appreciate the Black Mac. If your constitution is up to it seek out Hooker's Ale, a beer with a kick like an enraged moa.

Cans aren't popular and most beer is sold in bottles anyway, which is cheaper. In a pub the cheapest beer is on tap. You can ask for a 'seven', originally seven fluid ounces but now a 200mL glass, the closest metric equivalent; a 'twelve' is a 12-fluid ounce glass (350mL); a 'handle' is a half-litre or litre mug with a handle and often called a pint or half-pint (old ways die hard); or a jug, which is just that (and costs $6).

Drinks at public bars are the cheapest, while lounge or fancier bars tend to mark their drinks up more, but prices vary widely.

In public bars you can pretty much wear anything, but lounge bars have a lot of 'neat dress required' signs. The bars with entertainment are normally lounge bars, which can sometimes make things awkward for the traveller with jeans, sandals and T-shirt.

The legal drinking age is 18.

Wine

New Zealand has a thriving wine-producing industry and many wineries have established international reputations, particularly for their whites (the climate is not as good for reds).

A few notable wine-producing areas are Henderson near Auckland, Martinborough in the Wairarapa, Hawkes Bay, Blenheim in the Marlborough region of the South Island, the Waipara Valley near Christchurch, and Central Otago. Winery visits and tours are popular in these places and, of course, there's free wine tasting. New wineries are constantly opening, as NZ wine continues to achieve a better reputation. The best-known regions are Marlborough, noted for its sauvignon blanc, and Hawkes Bay, noted for its chardonnay.

An unusual NZ speciality is kiwi fruit wine. There are lots of different varieties – still and bubbly, sweet and dry – and even a liqueur. You may not like it, but NZ is the best place to try it.

ENTERTAINMENT

As in many countries, there's plenty of nightlife in the major cities but not much in the small towns, where everything seems to shut with a bang after dark, except the pub and the takeaways, and even they might be closed by around 9 or 10 pm.

In the cities there's plenty of entertainment. Most sizeable towns have a cinema (eg Takaka's delightful Village Theatre), and the cities have big complexes such as Hoyts, and a couple of arthouse theatres (often featuring NZ productions such as *Scarfies* and *Once Were Warriors*).

Live theatre is also popular and Wellington has a very active group of professional theatres. Christchurch has a couple, with the Court Theatre in the Arts Centre being the most famous. In the larger cities there are regular performances by the New Zealand Symphony Orchestra, the National Ballet, and operatic and chamber music groups. Many visitors wish to see a Maori cultural performance in towns such as Rotorua and Queenstown.

Discos and live-music venues are found in most towns and cities – usually buzzing on weekends only in the towns, but all week in Auckland, Wellington and Christchurch. Dunedin, with its large student population, has a vibrant live-music scene and its probably NZ's live music and pubbing capital. Many of Wellington's plethora of cafes also feature live music. At The Casbah in Queenstown you can go on-line and relay images of you partying to those having a dull time back home.

Cafe strips, as exciting as those in Europe, can be found in Ponsonby and Parnell in Auckland, around Courtney Place and Cuba Mall in Wellington, Oxford Terrace in Christchurch, and along George St in Dunedin. Queenstown is alive all year round, and the regular gang of adrenaline junkies congregates at several venues.

SPECTATOR SPORTS

Rugby union (see the boxed text) is practically a national mania, with cricket taking a distant second place. NZ also excels at hockey and netball, although these sports attract fewer spectators.

As you travel you'll see rugby matches played everywhere by teams of all ages and both sexes. In rugby season, when they're not playing, they're inside watching it on television. A variant of the game, rugby league, is also very popular.

All cities have major stadiums, where you can see top national, and sometimes international, rugby and league teams. Just front up to a game (usually held on a Saturday or Sunday in winter) and buy your ticket at the gate. It could be just as much fun, and considerably cheaper, to watch a passionate third-grade semifinal at one of the smaller regional centres – such as West Coast versus North Otago at Greymouth's Rugby Park.

New Zealanders are also big punters and breed fine racehorses. Almost every town worth its salt has a racetrack with weekend meets at various times of year.

NZ FREELANCE COLLECTION; ALEXANDER TURNBULL LIBRARY, WELLINGTON NZ

George Nepia during a match at Athletic Park against Wellington (photographer unknown, 1935). Nepia was captain of the Maori All Blacks and this was his final game. (Wellington won 11 to 9).

Rugby – a National Obsession

No book about NZ would be complete without mention of the national obsession – rugby union football. Try to escape the euphoria when the All Blacks, the national team, steamroll their international opponents at Dunedin's Carisbrooke (the 'House of Pain'). Look at the fear on the faces of the opposition as the All Blacks perform their fearsome *haka* at the start of a match.

The Game Rugby union, almost always simply called 'rugby' in NZ, is played on a field 100m long and 69m wide, with H-shaped goals at each end. The object is to run the ball across the opponents' goal line and ground it (this is called a 'try' and worth five points), or kick it over the goal posts (a 'conversion' for two points, or a 'penalty' or 'drop goal' for three points).

There are 15 players in each side – eight forwards (two burly props, a hooker, two locks, two flankers and the No 8) and seven backs (fullback, two wingers, centre, inside centre, flyhalf and halfback).

National Most of NZ's 140,000 rugby players play club rugby. The next step up is provincial rugby, where 26 regional teams drawn from all the rugby clubs in that province compete for the national championship and for the Ranfurly Shield. As you might expect, the smaller provinces are never really competitive against large cities, so the competition is split into three divisions.

Five NZ teams (loosely based around first-division provincial teams Canterbury, Waikato, Wellington, Auckland and Otago) play in the annual Super 12 competition against three Australian and four South African teams. Kiwi teams had won all five titles up to 2000.

International The NZ Rugby Football Union was founded in 1892 and the country quickly became a stronghold of the game. Only the Pacific nations (and white South Africa) match NZ in their devotion to rugby. The national team is the All Blacks, and they are good! Whether up or down, it's almost unknown for NZ to fall out of the top three teams world wide. Historically, only South Africa nears NZ's international win rate, although Australia has been far more competitive in the last 10 years.

SHOPPING

You don't go to NZ intending to come back with a backpack full of souvenirs – a photograph of some flawless moment may be your best reminder – but there are some things worth checking out.

Woollen Goods

New Zealand produces beautiful woollen gear, particularly jumpers (sweaters) made from hand-spun, hand-dyed wool. Hand-knitted jumpers are something of an art form in NZ and although not cheap – around $150 to $300 – they are of the highest quality. Other knitted goods include hats, gloves, scarves and mufflers.

Woollen Swann-Dri jackets, shirts and pullovers are so practical and warm that they're just about the NZ national garment in the countryside, especially for farmers and hunters. Most common are the red-and-black or blue-and-black plaid ones, though they do also come in a few solid colours. You can buy Swann-Dris (affectionately called 'Swannies') in outdoor-gear shops and again, though not cheap – a good pullover could cost you around $200 – they're top quality and should keep you warm for at least the next decade.

Sheepskins are also a popular buy – the ones sold in the top tourist shops are beautiful and pure white, with long, thick, straight combed wool. Numerous other sheepskin goods include toasty warm slippers.

Greenstone (Pounamu)

Jade, called greenstone or *pounamu* in NZ, is made into ornaments, brooches, earrings, cuff links and *tiki*. The latter are tiny, stylised Maori figures, usually depicted with their tongue stuck out in a warlike challenge, worn on a thong or chain around the neck.

Rugby – a National Obsession

International rugby's highest level of competition is the World Cup, first held in 1987 (when NZ won). The All Blacks finished third in 1991 (Australia won the final against England), and second in 1995 (against South Africa and the infamous 'Susie the waitress'). In 1999 the whole country went into mourning when the All Blacks capitulated in the semifinals to a gallant French team. To make matters worse NZ's traditional rivals, Australia, won the final.

All Black's and ex-All Blacks are revered for life in NZ and many Kiwis will be able tell you exactly who played in what position many years back (not to mention who should be playing now!). Great All Blacks over the years include the famous King Country lock Colin 'Pine Tree' Meads, who played for NZ 55 times between 1957 and 1971; and shrewd Waikato fullback Don Clarke, who set a NZ scoring record only broken 24 years later by prolific Auckland flyhalf Grant Fox.

There have been a disproportionately large number of Maori All Blacks, the most famous of which was East Coast's George Nepia, who played in all 32 All Black games of 1924, yet was excluded from the 1928 tour to South Africa because of his race. More recently there was North Harbour's Wayne 'Buck' Shelford – NZ pubs still resound with theories about his sacking as All Black captain in 1990.

Many Polynesian New Zealanders have also played for the All Blacks, including Auckland winger Bryan 'BG' Williams, who was for a time Samoa's national coach. Auckland flanker Michael Jones is a hero in his parents' Samoa as well as in NZ, while the government of Tonga once considered naming a new volcanic island there after the Counties/Wellington winger Jonah Lomu.

Womens' Rugby The dominance of rugby in NZ is illustrated by the fact that Kiwi women also play rugby – over 5000 of them play at club, provincial and international levels. The national side, the Black Ferns, lost only one test (out of 19) in the 1990s. In 1998 they blitzed all opposition to win the first full international womens' rugby world cup – their closest game was a 32 point victory against the USA in the final.

Errol Hunt

They've got great *mana,* or power, but they also serve as fertility symbols, so beware!

See Arts in the 'Maori Culture & Arts' special section for more about greenstone.

Bone Carvings

Maori bone carvings are another fine art form undergoing something of a renaissance. Maori artisans have always made bone carvings, but nowadays they feed the tourist industry. Tiki, very interesting human and animal figures, such as dolphins and sea birds, are carved from bone. Bone fish-hook pendants, carved in traditional Maori and modernised styles, are most common and worn on a thong or a chain around the neck.

Paua (Abalone)

Abalone shell, called paua in NZ, is carved into some beautiful ornaments and jewellery, and some *really* tacky ones. Shells are used as ashtrays in places where paua is plentiful, but it's illegal to take natural paua shells out of NZ. Only processed ornaments can be taken with you.

Woodcarvings

Another distinctive Maori art form, woodcarvings are worth checking out, particularly in Rotorua. Carvers produce tremendous forms such as leaping dolphins, as well as the sometimes highly intricate traditional Maori carvings. Expect to pay a small fortune for high-quality work. Of course, many poor examples are turned out for the tourist trade and they tend to dominate the market.

Other Arts & Crafts

New Zealanders have a reputation as great do-it-yourselfers and there are a lot of excellent shops selling art and craft, with everything from hand-painted scarves and ceramics to homemade jams and preserves. The quality of the pottery and weaving is particularly fine; they make good presents to take back home and don't take up much room in your luggage. Nelson, in particular, is noted for its excellent pottery and the quality of its local clay.

Fashion

City Kiwis have an independent flair when it comes to fashion and consequently there are some great little clothes shops around.

In Auckland, check out Ponsonby Rd, the markets and in the centre around High and O'Connell Sts. The more mainstream designers congregate around the central city and Parnell districts in Auckland. Thornton Hall is a successful womens' label you'll find in all the major cities.

The outdoor clothing market has also become very competitive and the durable yet stylish Canterbury sports clothing label is known internationally. NZ is making quite a name for itself with high-quality outdoor fashion.

Activities

New Zealand is a haven for visitors who seek to combine adventure with the wide open spaces. The land, air and water are not sacrosanct, and the Kiwis and their visitors move over or through these media in just about every way imaginable. They jet-boat, white-water sledge, raft, boogy board, canoe, kayak, surf, surf raft, scuba dive and ski through the water; they bungy jump, parapente, skydive, abseil, fly, helicopter and barrel roll through the air; and they tramp, mountain bike, ski, horse ride, rock climb, 'zorb' and ice climb across terra firma. Beneath the surface caving, cave rafting, *tomo* (hole or entrance to a cave) exploring and hydro-sliding are all pursued.

For an indication of the lengths to which Kiwis will go to experience something different, read *Classic New Zealand Adventures* by Jonathan Kennett et al. It has every adventure including a sedate river paddle, pillocking (or 'surfing') across mud flats on a rubbish-bin lid, and bridge swinging.

The various adrenaline-pumping activities do have an element of risk. Perceived danger is part of the thrill and travellers should be aware that adventure sports, particularly those on fast-flowing rivers, such as rafting and kayaking, do entail risk. Chances of a mishap are perhaps minuscule, but make sure that the company you choose takes adequate safety precautions.

TRAMPING

Tramping (that's Kiwi talk for bushwalking, hiking or trekking) is the best way to experience NZ's natural beauty and is very well organised. The country has thousands of kilometres of tracks – many well marked, some only a line on the map. Tramping is made easy by NZ's excellent network of huts, enabling trampers to avoid lugging tents and cooking gear. Many tracks are graded, though others are only for experienced, fit walkers.

This section should open your eyes to the possibilities of tramping, however before attempting any track you should consult the appropriate authority for the latest information. There are literally hundreds of tracks to be enjoyed all over NZ. The famous ones – such as the Milford, Routeburn or Abel Tasman – attract many visitors (and crowds) while equally fine but unknown tracks are all but deserted.

The so-called Great Walks are the most popular tracks. Their beauty does indeed make them worth experiencing, but please don't go and then be upset that they are crowded. Of *course* these tracks are sometimes crowded, especially in summer, when people from all over the world come to tramp.

The most walked tracks in NZ are the Abel Tasman Coastal Track, the Routeburn, the Milford, the Tongariro Northern Circuit, the Kepler, and Lake Waikaremoana.

If you want to avoid the crowds, Department of Conservation (DOC) offices and park headquarters can advise and help you plan some enjoyable walks on lesser known tracks. DOC offices are in every city and in dozens of towns, and give free information about tramping in their areas. Every national park, forest park and maritime park has its own DOC headquarters. DOC information centres (see regional chapters for contact details) for national and maritime parks are found at:

Abel Tasman National Park Totaranui, Nelson, Motueka, Takaka
Arthur's Pass National Park Arthur's Pass township
Bay of Islands Maritime & Historic Park Russell
Egmont National Park Dawson Falls and North Egmont on Mt Taranaki/Egmont
Fiordland National Park Te Anau
Hauraki Gulf Maritime Park Auckland
Kahurangi National Park Karamea, Motueka, Takaka, Nelson
Marlborough Sounds Maritime Park Picton, Blenheim, Havelock
Mt Aspiring National Park Wanaka, Makarora

Mt Cook National Park Mt Cook Village
Nelson Lakes National Park St Arnaud, Lake Rotoroa
Otago Goldfields Park Dunedin, Alexandra
Paparoa National Park Punakaiki
Stewart Island Stewardship Area Oban (Halfmoon Bay)
Te Wahipounamu World Heritage Area Haast township
Tongariro National Park Whakapapa on Mt Ruapehu, Ohakune Mountain Road
Westland National Park Franz Josef and Fox Glaciers
Whanganui National Park Pipiriki, Taumarunui, Wanganui
Urewera National Park Aniwaniwa, Lake Waikaremoana

In addition to 13 national parks and 19 forest parks, NZ has council parks, farm parks, regional parks and more, all of which have walks. (In NZ a walk is defined as a fairly easy day walk or less, often suitable for families, while a tramp is a longer trek that requires you to be suitably equipped and where some experience may be necessary.)

When to Go

The most crowded season is during the school summer holidays, two weeks before Christmas until the end of January – a good period to avoid if you can. The best weather is from January to March, though most tracks can be walked enjoyably any time from about November to April. June and July, mid-winter, are not the time to be out on the tracks. Some are closed in winter because of avalanche danger. It's best to time your walks so that the most southerly are done in summer.

Surprisingly, most people on the tracks are from outside NZ. Kiwis do tramp, but they tend to avoid the popular tracks, making use of local knowledge rather than posted tracks or seeking the really wild and untouched regions.

What to Bring

For an enjoyable tramp the primary considerations are your feet and shoulders. Make sure your footwear is adequate and that your pack is not too heavy. Having adequate, waterproof rain gear is also very important, especially on the South Island's West Coast where you can get drenched to the skin in minutes if your rain gear is not up to the challenge.

Books

DOC produces very good books with detailed information on the flora and fauna, geology and history of NZ's national parks. DOC leaflets outline thousands of walking tracks throughout the country.

Jim DuFresne's *Tramping in New Zealand* is a Lonely Planet guide, describing nearly 50 walks of various lengths and degrees of difficulty in all parts of the country. Mark Pickering's *New Zealand's Top Ten Tracks* contains many of the obvious ones (Milford, Routeburn etc). *101 Great Tramps,* by Mark Pickering & Rodney Smith, has suggestions for two- to six-day tramps around the country. Also worth a scan is John Cobb's *Walking Tracks of NZ's National Parks.*

Tramping in North Island Forest Parks, by Euan & Jennie Nicol, and *Tramping in South Island Forest Parks,* by Joanna Wright, are good for shorter walking and tramping possibilities, from half-hour walks to tramps taking several days. The descriptions of flora, fauna and history in these books are outstanding.

Maps

Land Information New Zealand's (LINZ) topographical maps are the best, but bookshops don't usually have a good selection. LINZ has map sales offices in the main cities and major towns, and a local DOC office will often sell LINZ's maps of the tracks in its immediate area.

LINZ (formerly known as DOSLI) has various series of maps. Park maps cover national, state and forest parks, and Trackmaps cover some of the more popular walking tracks. There are also Holidaymaker maps, Touringmaps, Terrainmaps, Streetfinder maps and larger Aotearoa and Pacific maps covering all of NZ and some Pacific islands. The most detailed are the Topomaps series of topographical maps, but you may need two or three maps to cover one track. The maps cost about $13.50 each.

NEW ZEALAND PARKS

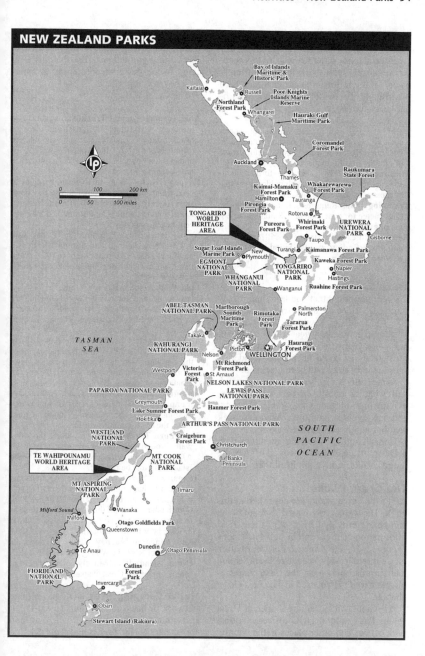

Bay of Islands Maritime & Historic Park
Kaitaia
Russell
Poor Knights Islands Marine Reserve
Northland Forest Park
Whangarei
Hauraki Gulf Maritime Park
Coromandel Forest Park
Raukumara State Forest
Auckland
Thames
Whakarewarewa Forest Park
Kaimai-Mamaku Forest Park
Hamilton
Tauranga
Pirongia Forest Park
Rotorua
TONGARIRO WORLD HERITAGE AREA
Pureora Forest Park
Whirinaki Forest Park
UREWERA NATIONAL PARK
Taupo
Gisborne
Sugar Loaf Islands Marine Park
New Plymouth
Turangi
Kaimanawa Forest Park
EGMONT NATIONAL PARK
TONGARIRO NATIONAL PARK
Kaweka Forest Park
Napier
WHANGANUI NATIONAL PARK
Hastings
Wanganui
Ruahine Forest Park
ABEL TASMAN NATIONAL PARK
Marlborough Sounds Maritime Park
Palmerston North
Rimutaka Forest Park
Tararua Forest Park
TASMAN SEA
KAHURANGI NATIONAL PARK
Takaka
Picton
Nelson
WELLINGTON
Haurangi Forest Park
Westport
Mt Richmond Forest Park
St Arnaud
Victoria Forest Park
NELSON LAKES NATIONAL PARK
PAPAROA NATIONAL PARK
LEWIS PASS NATIONAL PARK
Greymouth
Lake Sumner Forest Park
Hanmer Forest Park
Hokitika
ARTHUR'S PASS NATIONAL PARK
SOUTH PACIFIC OCEAN
WESTLAND NATIONAL PARK
Craigeburn Forest Park
Christchurch
Banks Peninsula
TE WAHIPOUNAMU WORLD HERITAGE AREA
MT COOK NATIONAL PARK
MT ASPIRING NATIONAL PARK
Timaru
Milford Sound
Milford
Wanaka
Otago Goldfields Park
Queenstown
Te Anau
Dunedin
Otago Peninsula
Catlins Forest Park
FIORDLAND NATIONAL PARK
Invercargill
Oban
Stewart Island (Rakiura)

0   100   200 km
0   50   100 miles

Track Classification

Tracks are classified according to their difficulty and many other features. In this chapter we loosely refer to the level of difficulty as one of the following: easy, medium, hard or difficult. The widely used track classification system is:

Path Easy and well formed; allows for wheelchair access or constructed to 'shoe' standard (ie walking boots not required). Suitable for people of all ages and fitness levels.

Walking Track Easy and well formed; constructed to 'shoe' standard. Suitable for people of most ages and fitness levels.

Tramping Track Requires skill and experience; constructed to 'boot' standard. Suitable for people of average physical fitness.

Route Requires a high degree of skill, experience and route-finding ability. Suitable for well-equipped trampers.

Track Safety

It's very important that you learn and follow some basic rules of safety when tramping in NZ. Thousands of Kiwis and overseas visitors tramp in NZ every year without incident, but every year a few die in the mountains. Most fatalities could have been avoided if simple safety rules had been observed.

Some trails are only for the experienced, and weather conditions are changeable, making high-altitude walks subject to snow and ice even in summer. Always check weather conditions before leaving.

Consult and register your intentions with a DOC office before heading off on the longer walks. Above all, heed their advice.

The Great Walks

All of the Great Walks are described in this book. The walks are covered in detail in the pamphlets provided by DOC offices (and information centres) and in Lonely Planet's *Tramping in New Zealand*. For information on a particular walk, see the relevant section later in this book – eg, the Lake Waikaremoana Circuit is covered in The East Coast chapter.

All Great Walks require a special Great Walks Pass, sold at DOC offices, national park offices and other places in the vicinity of each walk. Prices differ between the walks, but are generally not expensive. They allow you either to use the huts or to camp in the designated camping grounds, whichever you prefer.

The Great Walks are:

Abel Tasman Coastal Track An easy, two- to three-day walk along the coast and close to beaches and bays in Abel Tasman National Park (South Island). NZ's most popular walk is inundated with people, and a booking system has now been introduced.

Heaphy Track A four- to five-day, medium to hard tramp of 77km through forest and limestone (karst) landscape of Kahurangi National Park (South Island). The last day is a magnificent beach walk.

Kepler Track This 67km, four- to five-day walk in Fiordland National Park (South Island) is a medium to hard tramp. It climbs to the top of a mountain and includes alpine, lake and river-valley scenery.

Lake Waikaremoana Track A three- to four-day, easy to medium tramp in Urewera National Park (North Island), with great views of the lake and surrounding bush-clad slopes. Plans have been mooted to introduce a booking system.

Milford Track This 54km, four-day walk in Fiordland National Park (South Island) is one of the best known in the world. It includes views of river valleys, glaciers, waterfalls and an alpine pass crossing. Bookings are essential.

Rakiura (Stewart Island) Track A three-day tramp, mostly on duckboards, for which medium fitness is required. The track goes along the coast and through forest.

Routeburn Track A medium, 40km, three-day walk through the stunning alpine scenery of Mt Aspiring and Fiordland National Parks (South Island). It must be booked.

Tongariro Northern Circuit A four-day, medium to hard tramp through the active volcanic landscape of Tongariro National Park (North Island). Part of this tramp can be done as the one-day Tongariro Crossing (see Other Tracks, later in this section).

The Whanganui Journey A canoe trip down the Whanganui River in Whanganui National Park (North Island). It's obviously not a walk but it, too, is one of the Great Walks.

Hut & Camping Fees DOC has a huge network of back-country huts (over 950 at last count) in the national, maritime and forest parks. Hut fees range from $4 to a

New Zealand's Environmental Care Code

Toitu te whenua – Care for the land

• **Protect plants and animals** Treat NZ's unique forests and rare birds with care and respect.

• **Remove rubbish** Litter is unattractive, harmful to wildlife and can increase vermin and disease. Plan your visits so as to reduce rubbish, and carry out what you carry in.

• **Bury toilet waste** In areas without toilet facilities, bury your toilet waste in a shallow hole well away from waterways, tracks, camp sites and huts.

• **Keep streams and lakes pure** When cleaning and washing, wash well away from the water source. Because soaps and detergents are harmful to water life, drain used water into the soil to allow it to be filtered. If you suspect the water may be contaminated, boil it for at least three minutes, filter it or chemically treat it.

• **Take care with fires** Portable fuel stoves are less harmful to the environment and are more efficient than fires. If you do use a fire, keep it small, use only dead wood and make sure it is out by dousing it with water and checking the ashes before leaving.

• **Camp carefully** When camping, leave no trace of your visit.

• **Keep to the track** By keeping to the track, you lessen the chance of damaging fragile plants.

• **Consider others** People visit the back country and rural areas for many reasons. Be considerate of other visitors who also have a right to enjoy the natural environment.

• **Respect cultural heritage** Many places in NZ have a spiritual and historical significance. Treat these places with consideration and respect.

• **Look** Take a last look before leaving an area: will the next visitor know that you have been there?

Enjoy your visit. Enjoy your outdoor experience. Protect the environment for your own sake, for the sake of those who come after you and for the environment itself.

---

maximum of $35 per night for adults, paid with tickets purchased in advance at any DOC office or park visitor centre. You can buy $4 tickets in booklets and they are valid for 15 months. Children under 11 years of age can use all huts free of charge. Children 11 and older are charged half-price and use a special 'youth ticket'. If you plan to do a lot of tramping, DOC also sells an annual hut pass, available at all huts except the Great Walks huts.

Huts are classed into four categories and, depending on the category, a night's stay may use one or two tickets, except on Great Walks where special passes are needed. When you arrive at a hut, date the tickets and put them in the box provided. Accommodation is on a first come, first served basis. A list of all huts and their categories is available at any DOC office.

The Milford, Routeburn and Abel Tasman Tracks operate on a system of their own and are best booked through DOC via email (✉ greatwalksbooking@doc.govt.nz).

Other Tracks

In addition to the Great Walks there are numerous other tramping possibilities in all forest and national parks. These are merely some of the possibilities:

North Island

Coromandel Track An easy to medium, three-day walk in the Kauaeranga Valley in the Coromandel Forest Park, Coromandel Peninsula.

Great Barrier Forest Track A four-day, easy to medium loop walk on Great Barrier Island, with historic kauri dams, forests and hot springs.

Mt Holdsworth Circuit & Totara Flats Track Two three-day tramps in Holdsworth and Tararua Forest Park respectively. The first is a medium to hard walk over the top of alpine Mt Holdsworth. The second is a medium tramp mostly along the Totara River Valley.

Ninety Mile Beach–Cape Reinga Walkway A 50km, three-day, easy tramp in Northland. A beach walk with camping.

Round the Mountain, Mt Taranaki (Egmont) A 55km walk of four days or more in Egmont National Park. It is medium to hard tramping through mountainous country.

Tongariro Crossing A long one-day, medium tramp Tongariro National Park, introducing the fit tramper to an active volcanic landscape.

South Island

Arthur's Pass tramps there are many walks to choose from in Arthur's Pass National Park, most of which are difficult.

Banks Peninsula Walk A two-day (medium) or four-day (easy) walk over the hills and along the coast of Banks Peninsula, crossing private and public land near Akaroa.

Dusky & George Sound Tracks Part of the great wealth of tramping in Fiordland National Park, a World Heritage region. The Dusky is very challenging, as is the George Sound route.

Greenstone & Caples Tracks These two tracks are on stewardship land, just outside Fiordland National Park. They're close to the Routeburn and a good way to start or finish this popular track.

Hollyford Track There are several variants on this track in the Fiordland National Park. It will take eight days if you walk in and walk out, four days if you fly one way. It includes lake, alpine, rainforest and coastal scenery.

Inland Pack Track A medium tramp in Paparoa National Park, following river valleys through the karst landscape near Punakaiki on the West Coast.

Kaikoura Coast Track A three-day walk over private and public land along the spectacular coast, 50km south of Kaikoura.

Matukituki Valley walks There are good walks in the Matukituki Valley, Mt Aspiring National Park, near Wanaka.

Mt Somers Subalpine Walkway A medium, three-day walk in Canterbury foothills, through river valleys, subalpine forest and pastures.

North-West Circuit This eight- to 10-day route is just one of the many possibilities on Stewart Island (Rakiura). The whole island has wilderness possibilities.

Queen Charlotte Track A three- to four-day, medium walk in Marlborough Sounds from which you get great views of the sounds and pass many historic places.

Rees-Dart Track A 70km, four- to five-day, hard walk in Mt Aspiring National Park, through river valleys and traversing an alpine pass.

St James Walkway This 66km, five-day, medium walk in Lake Sumner Forest Park/Lewis Pass Reserve passes through excellent subalpine scenery.

Travers–Sabine Circuit & D'Urville Valley Tracks These five- to six-day circular tracks in Nelson Lakes National Park, are for experienced trampers only, 80km and 65km respectively. Both include alpine passes and river valleys.

Wangapeka & Leslie-Karamea Tracks The Wangapeka is a four- to five-day, medium tramp through river valleys and over passes. The Leslie-Karamea is a 90km to 100km, five- to seven-day tramp for the experienced only, which includes river valleys, gorges and passes. Both tracks are in Kahurangi National Park.

Getting There & Away

Getting to and from tracks can be a real problem, except for the most popular, which are serviced by trampers' transport. Having a vehicle only simplifies the problem of getting to one end of the track. Otherwise you have to take public transport or hitch in, and if the track starts or ends at the end of a dead-end road, hitching will be difficult.

SKIING & SNOWBOARDING

New Zealand is one of the most popular places for skiing and snowboarding in the southern hemisphere. In addition to downhill (alpine) skiing, there is cross-country, ski touring, ski mountaineering and snowboarding.

Heli-skiing is another attraction. In winter helicopters are used to lift skiers up to the top of long, isolated stretches of virgin snow, or even onto glaciers.

New Zealand's commercial ski areas are generally not very well endowed with chalets, lodges or hotels. Accommodation is usually in surrounding towns, but there's daily shuttles to/from the main ski areas.

Club ski areas are open to the public and much less crowded than commercial ski fields. Although nonmembers pay a slightly higher rate, they are still usually a cheaper alternative. Many have lodges you can stay at, subject to availability. Winter holidays and weekends will be fully booked, but mid-week you'll have no trouble.

At the major ski areas, lifts cost from $32 to $60 a day and two-hour group lessons are around $39/27 for adults/children (lower at the smaller resorts). All the usual equipment can be bought or hired in NZ; rental costs from $31/21 for one day for an adult/child. Snowboard with boots hire starts at $47/37. These prices are lower if the hire is over a longer period.

The ski season is generally from June to early November, although it varies considerably from one ski area to another. Snowmaking machines assist nature at some areas.

Information centres in NZ, and the NZ Tourism Board (NZTB) internationally, have brochures on the various ski areas and packages available, and can make bookings. The *NZ Ski & Snowboard Guide* by Brown Bear is an excellent (free) annual reference.

The useful snowphone services provide prerecorded information on weather, access conditions and snow levels. On the Internet, try Brown Bear (www.snow.co.nz) for ski field reports, Web cams and virtual tours; and also Nzski.com (www.nzski.com).

North Island

Whakapapa The Whakapapa ski area (☎ 07-892 3833 snowphone, 07-892 3738 information), the largest in NZ with over 30 groomed runs, is 6km above Whakapapa Village on Mt Ruapehu in Tongariro National Park. It includes a downhill course dropping nearly 675m over 4km. There are chairlifts, T-bars, platters and rope tows, and plenty of possibilities for snowboarding,

including excellent pipes off the far western T-bar, cross-country, downhill and ski touring. Check out the cool Web site (www .whakapapa.co.nz) for more information.

For accommodation see the Central Plateau chapter. You can drive yourself up to the slopes or you can take a shuttle minibus from Whakapapa Village, National Park or Turangi; a taxi service is available from Ohakune.

Lift passes are $52/26 for adults/children (five-day specials are $233/117).

Turoa Around the other side of Mt Ruapehu from the Whakapapa ski area, the Turoa ski area (☎ 0900-99 444 snowphone, 06-385 8456 information, ✉ information@ turoa.co.nz) is the country's second-largest ski area. Quad and triple chairlifts, T-bars and platters take you up to the beginning of a 4km run. There's also a beginners' lift, snowboarding and cross-country skiing. There is no road toll or parking fee and daily ski area transport is available from Ohakune, 17km away, which has the liveliest après-ski scene in the North Island.

Lift passes are $52/29 (five-day adult specials $234).

Tukino This club-operated ski area is on the eastern side of Mt Ruapehu, 50km from Turangi. It's quite remote – 14km of gravel road from the sealed Desert Rd (SH1), and you need a 4WD vehicle to get in (or make a prior arrangement to use the club transport). Because access is so limited, the area is uncrowded, but most runs are beginner or intermediate.

Accommodation at the lodges must be arranged in advance: contact either Desert Alpine Club (☎ 09-420 5339), Christiana Club (☎ 07-855 4749) or Aorangi Club (☎ 04-478 7055). For information call the mountain manager (☎ 06-387 6294). Lift passes are $30/15.

Manganui Ski Area There's more volcano-slope skiing on the eastern slopes of Mt Taranaki in the Egmont National Park, at the Manganui club ski area (☎ 06-765 7669 snowphone, 06-765 5493 information),

22km from Stratford. For accommodation see the Taranaki chapter.

Skiing is possible off the summit of Mt Taranaki; when conditions permit, it's an invigorating two-hour climb to the crater with an exhilarating 1300m descent.

Lift passes are $30/15 for nonmembers.

South Island

Coronet Peak New Zealand's southern-most slopes, near Queenstown, are rated the best in the country.

Coronet Peak (☎ 0900-99 766 snow-phone, 03-442 4640) is the oldest ski field in this region. The season here is reliable because of a multimillion dollar snow-making system. Access is from Queens-town, 18km away, and there are shuttles in the ski season.

The treeless slopes and good snow pro-vide excellent skiing – the chairlifts run to altitudes of 1585m and 1620m. The consis-tent gradient and the many undulations make this a snowboarder's paradise.

For accommodation see the Queenstown and Arrowtown sections in the Otago chap-ter. There's a multiplicity of après-ski pos-sibilities here. Lift passes are $60/30.

The Remarkables Like Coronet Peak, The Remarkables ski area is near Queenstown (23km away), with shuttle buses running from Queenstown during the season. It, too, has beginner, intermediate and advanced runs, with chairlifts and beginners' tows. Look out for the sweeping run, Homeward Bound. Contact details are the same as for Coronet Peak. Lift passes are $57/27 per day.

Treble Cone This area, 29km from Wanaka, has been improved with the exten-sion of snow-making to the top of the De-liverance Chair. The highest of the southern lake areas, Treble Cone (☎ 0900-34 444 snowphone, 03-443 7443 information) is spectacularly situated, overlooking Lake Wanaka. Slopes are steep and best for inter-mediate to advanced skiers. It has a natural half-pipe for snowboarding. For accommo-dation, see Wanaka in the Otago chapter.

Lift passes are $58/29 and first-timer packs are $42.

Cardrona Some 25km from Wanaka, Cardrona has three chairlifts, beginners' tows and a radical half-pipe for snowboard-ers. Buses run from Wanaka during the ski season, and from Queenstown, about 1½ hours away.

Cardrona (☎ 0900-34 444 snowphone, 03-443 7411) has acquired a reputation for the services it offers to disabled skiers, and it is the first resort in the South Island to have an on-field creche. In summer it at-tracts mountain bikers. See its Web site at www.cardrona.com.

Lift passes are $58/29 in winter, $20/14 in summer.

Waiorau Nordic Area New Zealand's only commercial Nordic ski area (☎ 03-443 7542 information, @ snowfarm@xtra.co.nz) is 26km from Wanaka, on the Pisa Range, high above Lake Wanaka. There are 25km of groomed trails and thousands of hectares of open rolling country for the ski tourer. Huts with facilities are dotted along the top of the Pisa Range.

Day passes are $20/10 and executive passes, giving access to 55km of groomed trails, are $30/15.

Awakino This club ski area is on Mt St Mary in the Waitaki Valley, 11km from Kurow and 45km from Oamaru. Awakino is known to get the odd powder blast during southerly storms but essentially it is for intermediate skiers. Good cross-country touring is available nearby. There's accommodation 500m below the main rope tow or at Kurow, Oamaru or Omarama. Access to the area is by 4WD.

For information, contact the Waitaki Ski Club (☎ 03-434 5110), PO Box 191, Oamaru. Lift passes are $18/11.

South Canterbury Region There are three fields in the region; for accommoda-tion see the Canterbury and Otago chapters. The most distant field, the **Ohau** commercial ski area, is on Mt Sutton, 52km from Twizel. It has the longest T-bar

Ride the Shotover River if you're game, near Queenstown in the South Island

Hang glider – Otago Peninsula

Airborne at Treble Cone skifield

Bungy jumping – Queenstown

Hair-raising adventures on the luge – Queenstown yet again

Banana-powered bike on the Great Lake Cycle Challenge, Taupo

'Lost World' Waitomo Caves

The fastest way down a hill – 'zorbing' near Rotorua

White-water rafting on the Buller River, near Murchison

lift in NZ. It has a large percentage of intermediate and advanced runs, plus excellent terrain for snowboarding, cross-country and ski touring to Lake Dumb Bell.

Contact the Ohau Ski Area (☎ 03-438 9885 snowphone), PO Box 51, Twizel. Lift passes are $39/13 ($33/11 for lodge guests).

With a 3km-wide basin, **Mt Dobson** (☎ 03-685 8039 snowphone), a commercial ski area 26km from Fairlie, caters for learners and has NZ's largest intermediate area. From the summit of Mt Dobson, on a clear day, you can see Mt Cook and the Pacific Ocean. Check out the Web site www.dobson.co.nz. Lift passes are $39/12.

Fox Peak (☎ 03-688 0044 snowphone, 685 8539 information), a club ski area, is 29km from Fairlie in the Two Thumb Range. It has four rope tows and the learners' tow is free. There is good ski touring from the summit of Fox Peak and parapenting is also popular here. There's accommodation at Fox Lodge, 3km below the ski area. Lift passes are $30/20 for members/nonmembers.

Mt Hutt Mt Hutt is one of the highest ski areas in the southern hemisphere and is rated as one of the best in NZ. It's 118km west of Christchurch, close to Methven and can be reached by bus from Christchurch.

Mt Hutt (☎ 0900-99 766 snowphone, 03-302 8811 information) has beginner, intermediate and advanced slopes, with a quad and a triple chairlift, three T-bars, various other lifts and heli-skiing from the car park to slopes farther afield. The wide open faces are good for those learning to snowboard.

For accommodation see Methven and Ashburton in the Canterbury chapter. Lift passes are $55/27 per day.

Mt Potts The former Erewhon club ski area (☎ 03-309 0960) must be one of the best gems in NZ. It is based on Mt Potts, above the headwaters of the Rangitata River, and is about 75km from Methven. It is now the base for a snow cat and heli-skiing operation. Accommodation and meals are available from a lodge at Mt Potts, 8km from the ski area (B&B with dinner $50 per person). It has a good mix of beginner, intermediate and advanced slopes, with snowboarding and cross-country also popular here. Transport by 4WD is essential, and can be arranged through the club. See the Web site (www.mtpotts.co.nz).

A day of skiing from the snow cat is $90, and a five-run heli-ski pass costs $549 (a week 'powder pig' deal costs $990, heli-ski costs $3990).

Porter Heights The closest commercial ski area to Christchurch, Porter Heights (☎ 0900-34 444 snowphone, 03-379 7087 information, @ ski@porterheights.co.nz) is 96km away on the Arthur's Pass road. The 720m-long Big Mama is the steepest run in NZ. There's a half-pipe for snowboarders, plus good cross-country areas, and ski touring out along the ridge. There is a $6 toll on the access road. Lift passes are $44/26.

Arthur's Pass & Craigieburn Regions
There are five ski areas in the Arthur's Pass and Craigieburn regions. For accommodation see the Methven, Springfield and Arthur's Pass sections in the Canterbury chapter.

The most distant from Christchurch, **Temple Basin** (☎ 03-366 6644 ext 1104 snowphone, 377 7788) is a club area just 4km from the Arthur's Pass township. It is a 45-minute walk uphill from the car park to the lift area. At night there's floodlit skiing. There are good back-country runs for snowboarders. Lift passes are $32/23.

The **Craigieburn Valley** ski area (☎ 03-366 6644 snowphone, 379 2514 information), centred on Hamilton Peak, is 40km from Arthur's Pass. It is one of NZ's most challenging club areas, with intermediate and advanced runs and a shredder's 'soggy dream'. It is a pleasant 10-minute walk through beech forest from the car park to the ski area. Lift passes are $28/25 for adults/students. Check out the Web site (www.craigieburn.co.nz).

It is possible to ski from Craigieburn to the **Broken River** club ski area (☎ 03-366 6644 ext 111 snowphone, 318 7270 information), 50 minutes away. It will take twice that time to ski back, so plan accordingly.

Otherwise access to Broken River is unsealed for the last 6km, after which it's a 15-minute walk to the lodges and a further 10-minute walk to the ski area. Lift passes are $30/20.

Another good club area in the Craigieburn Range is **Mt Cheeseman**, 112km from Christchurch. The ski area (☎ 03-366 6644 ext 1105 snowphone, 379 5315 information), based on Mt Cockayne, is in a wide, sheltered basin. Southern Excursions (☎ 03-358 9249) has transport to Cheeseman and Porter Heights. Lift passes are $38/23.

The fifth ski area is **Mt Olympus** (☎ 03-366 6644 ext 1108 information). Hard to find, but worth the search, Mt Olympus, is 66km from Methven and 12km from Lake Ida. This club area has four tows which lead to intermediate and advanced runs. Snowboarding is allowed, there are good cross-country areas and ski-touring trails to other areas. 4WD is advisable from the bottom hut. Lift passes are $30/20.

Hanmer Springs Region There are three ski areas near Hanmer Springs. Accommodation is on-field, or you can stay in Hanmer Springs.

Hanmer Springs Ski Area (☎ 03-366 6644 snowphone, 315 7233), a field based on Mt St Patrick, is 17km from Hanmer Springs and has mostly intermediate and advanced runs. Lift passes are $28/15.

Mt Lyford (☎ 03-366 6644 snowphone, 315 6178 information) is about 60km from Hanmer Springs or Kaikoura, and 4km from Mt Lyford Village where accommodation is available. The Lake Stella field has skiing at all levels, basin and off-piste cross-country skiing, 15km of groomed trails for ski touring, and a natural pipe for snowboarding. A $5 toll applies on the access road.

The nearby **Terako Basin** ski field has advanced skiing and is linked by rope tow to Mt Lyford. Lift passes are $35/20.

Nelson Region In the north, near St Arnaud in Nelson Lakes National Park, there are two ski areas. Accommodation is available in St Arnaud or in Nelson or Blenheim.

The **Rainbow Valley** commercial ski area (☎ 0900-34 444 snowphone, 03-521 1861 information) is just outside the park. There is a double chair and a T-bar that lift skiers to the top of a spacious bowl and two learners' tows, and there's good cross-country ski touring. Lift passes are $44/24 (learners' pack $61/45).

Inside the park, 15km from St Arnaud, **Mt Robert** (☎ 03-548 8336 snowphone) is a club area, but it's a two-hour walk from the car park, 7km from St Arnaud, to reach it. This area is known for its powder and many cross-country opportunities, but only for those suitably equipped. Lift passes are $20/15.

Heli-Skiing & Glacier Skiing

New Zealand is a great place to try heli-skiing. From July to October, operators cover a wide area of off-piste all along the Southern Alps.

Heli-skiing companies (all in the South Island) include: Harris Mountains Heli-skiing (☎ 03-443 7930, @ hmhres@heliski.co.nz), 99 Ardmore St, Wanaka; Fox and Franz Heli-services (☎ 0800-800 732); Mt Hutt Heli-Ski (☎ 03-302 8401); Heli-Guides Heli-ski (☎ 03-442 7733, @ heliski@flynz.co.nz) in Queenstown; and Hanmer Heli-ski & Heliboard (☎ 0800-888 308).

The **Tasman Glacier** is a ski resort for the jetsetter – to ski 10km to 12km down from the upper reaches of the Tasman Glacier first requires a flight up from Mt Cook airfield in a ski-plane. You need to be a competent skier as well as a rich one. The lower reaches of the glacier are almost dead flat and are usually covered in surface moraine so you must either walk out – or fly once again. Count on around $650 for a flight up, the guide fee, two runs down the glacier and the flight back.

MOUNTAINEERING

New Zealand has a rich history of mountaineering (remember this is the home of Sir Edmund Hilary, the first to conquer Mt Everest), providing an ideal training ground for greater adventures overseas. The Southern Alps offer many challenging climbs, and are studded with a number of impressive

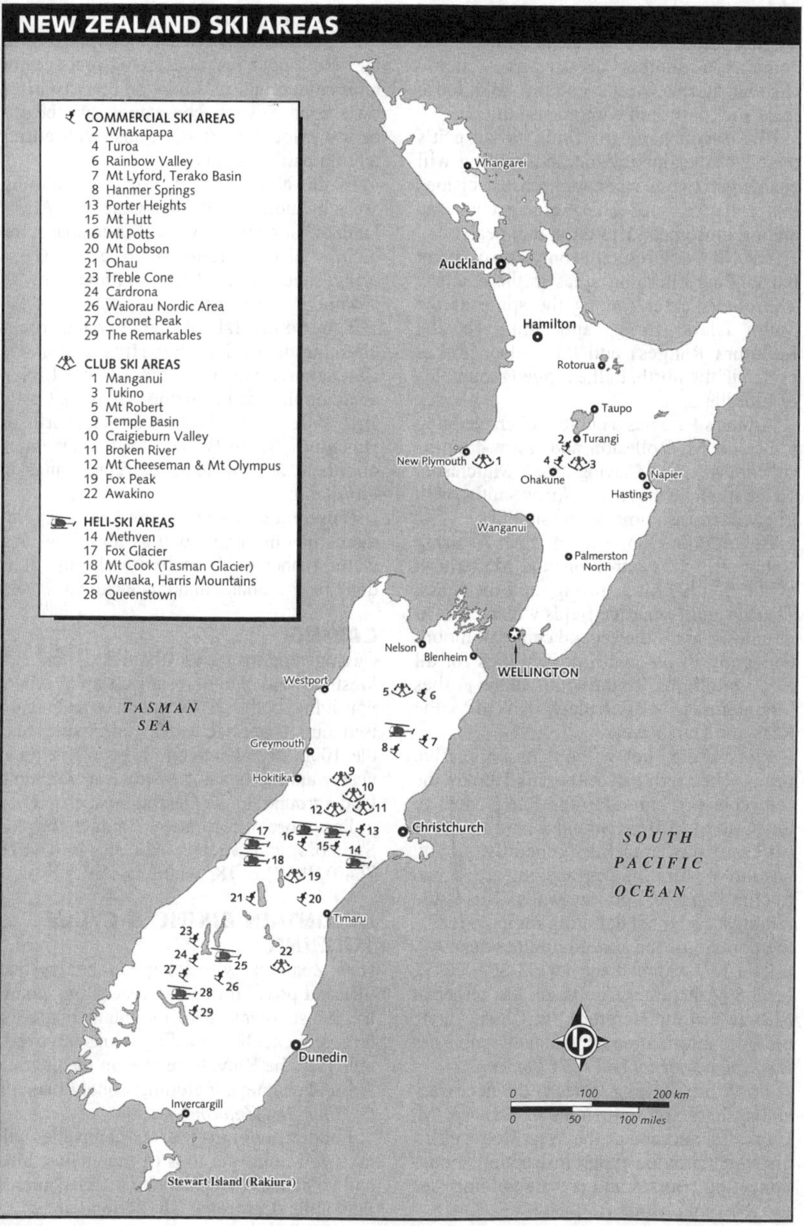

NEW ZEALAND SKI AREAS
COMMERCIAL SKI AREAS
2 Whakapapa
4 Turoa
6 Rainbow Valley
7 Mt Lyford, Terako Basin
8 Hanmer Springs
13 Porter Heights
15 Mt Hutt
16 Mt Potts
20 Mt Dobson
21 Ohau
23 Treble Cone
24 Cardrona
26 Waiorau Nordic Area
27 Coronet Peak
29 The Remarkables
CLUB SKI AREAS
1 Manganui
3 Tukino
5 Mt Robert
9 Temple Basin
10 Craigieburn Valley
11 Broken River
12 Mt Cheeseman & Mt Olympus
19 Fox Peak
22 Awakino
HELI-SKI AREAS
14 Methven
17 Fox Glacier
18 Mt Cook (Tasman Glacier)
25 Wanaka, Harris Mountains
28 Queenstown
Whangarei
Auckland
Hamilton
Rotorua
Taupo
Turangi
New Plymouth
Ohakune
Napier
Hastings
Wanganui
Palmerston North
Nelson
Blenheim
WELLINGTON
Westport
TASMAN SEA
Greymouth
Hokitika
Christchurch
SOUTH PACIFIC OCEAN
Timaru
Dunedin
Invercargill
Stewart Island (Rakiura)
0 100 200 km
0 50 100 miles

peaks. This very physical and highly challenging pursuit is not for the uninitiated, and contains a number of dangers – fickle weather, storms, winds, extreme cold, loose rock, rock falls and equipment failure.

But if you have to climb 'because it's there', proper instruction and training will enable you to make commonsense decisions that enhance your safety and get you up among those beautiful mountain peaks.

The Mt Cook region is only one of many outstanding climbing areas in the country. The others extend along the spine of the South Island from Tapuaenuku (in the Kaikoura Ranges) and the Nelson Lakes peaks, in the north, to the rugged mountains of Fiordland.

Arthur's Pass has a number of challenging routes on Mt Rolleston and 'away-from-it-all' climbs on Mts Carrington and Murchison. To the south lie the remote Arrowsmiths, with true wilderness climbing possibilities.

Beyond the Cook region is Mt Aspiring National Park, centred on 'the Matterhorn of the South', Mt Aspiring, and the Volta, Therma and Bonar ice fields which cling to its sides. This is the second centre of mountaineering in NZ, with possibilities for all levels of climbs. To the south, in the Forbes Mountains, is Mt Earnslaw, flanked by the Rees and Dart Rivers.

Fiordland is not without its impressive peaks. The mightiest of these is Tutoko, the centrepiece of the Darrans Range, just to the north of Milford Sound. There are some walks in this area but, generally, if you wish to explore the Darrans you are forced to climb up sheer granite walls. This is the remotest and most daunting region of NZ – the domain of the skilled mountaineer.

The NZ Alpine Club (☎ 03-377 7595), level 6 Manchester Courts, on the corner of Manchester and Hereford Sts, Christchurch, provides information and annually publishes *NZ Alpine Journal* and *NZ Climber*.

For those seeking to learn the necessary skills, there are companies in Wanaka, Mt Cook, Tekapo and at the West Coast glaciers which provide expert instruction, mountaineering courses and private guiding (see the relevant chapters).

ROCK CLIMBING

This sport has increased in popularity in NZ. No longer just considered practice for mountaineering, it is now an activity in its own right. Several companies take beginners out for their first climbs, with all attention paid to safety.

In the North Island, popular climbing areas include the Mt Eden Quarry in Auckland, Whanganui Bay and Motuoapa in the vicinity of Lake Taupo, Piarere near Cambridge and, about 20km south-east of Te Awamutu, Wharepapa.

The South Island has myriad rock-climbing areas. The Port Hills area above Christchurch has many climbs, and 100km away on the road to Arthur's Pass is Castle Hill with great friction climbs. North of Dunedin is Long Beach. For the adventurous there are the long, extreme routes in Fiordland.

Canyoning involves some of the elements of climbing, such as abseiling and water rushes such as hydro-sliding. It is done near Wanaka and Queenstown.

CAVING

Caving opportunities abound. Auckland, Westport and Waitomo are all areas where you'll find both active local clubs and organised tours. A spectacular caving experience is the 100m abseil into the Lost World tomo near Waitomo (see the boxed text 'Waitomo Underground' in the Central West chapter).

For more information contact the NZ Speleological Society (NZSS; ☎ 07-878 7640), PO Box 18, Waitomo Caves.

MOUNTAIN BIKING & CYCLE TOURING

New Zealand, with its great scenery and off-road possibilities, is great biking country. Most towns have mountain bikes for hire, and excellent cycling books are available (see the Bicycle section in the Getting Around chapter), including Lonely Planet's *Cycling New Zealand*.

For downhill fans, various companies will take you up to the tops of mountains, hills and volcanoes (Mt Ruapehu, Christchurch's Port Hills, Cardrona, The Remarkables) so that you can hurtle down without the usual grunt of getting uphill beforehand.

Many routes that were traditionally walked are now being cycled. One thing to remember, though, is *never* to cycle on walking tracks in national parks unless it's permitted. DOC will fine you if you're caught.

Contact the NZ Mountain Bike Association (NZMBA; ☎ 07-378 9552), PO Box 371, Taupo.

WATER ACTIVITIES
Jet-Boating
New Zealand is the home of the amazing jet-boats, invented by CWF Hamilton in 1957. An inboard engine sucks water into a tube in the bottom of the boat, and an impeller driven by the engine blows it out a nozzle at the stern in a high-speed stream. The boat is steered simply by directing the jet stream.

The boats are ideal for use in shallow water and white water because there are no propellers to damage, there is better clearance under the boat and the jet can be reversed instantly for quick braking. The instant response of the jet enables the boats to execute 360° spins almost within the length of the boat.

The Shotover and Kawarau Rivers near Queenstown and the Buller near Westport are renowned jet-boating rivers in the South Island; the Dart River is less travelled but also good.

In the North Island, the Whanganui, Manganui-a-te-Ao, Motu, Rangitaiki, Kaituna and Waikato Rivers are excellent for jet-boating. At Broadlands, Waikato, you can ride as a passenger in an exhilarating sprint jet.

Just about every riverside and lakeside town throughout NZ has a jet-boat company that runs trips, sometimes in combination with other adventure activities.

Rafting
There are almost as many white-water rafting possibilities as there are rivers in NZ. And there is no shortage of companies to take you on a heart-pounding, drenching, exhilarating and spine-tingling ride down some wild, magnificent rivers. The Shotover and

Kawarau Rivers in the South Island are popular for white-water rafting. Canterbury has the Rangitata River, considered one of the country's best.

The north of the South Island has great rafting possibilities, such as the Buller, Karamea, Mokihinui and Gowan Rivers. The West Coast has endless possibilities, including the Hokitika, Perth, Landsborough, Arnold and Waiho Rivers.

In the North Island there are plenty of rivers, such as the Rangitaiki, Wairoa, Motu, Tongariro, Rangitikei and Ngaruroro, that are just as good. There is also the Kaituna Cascades near Rotorua, with the 7m Okere Falls as its highlight.

Rivers are graded from I to VI, with VI meaning 'unraftable'. The grading of the Shotover canyon varies from III to V+, depending on the time of year, the Kawarau River is rated IV, and the Wairoa River III to V. On the rougher stretches there's usually a minimum age limit of 12 or 13 years. All safety equipment is supplied.

Rafting trips cost between about $75 and $130 per person per day, depending on whether or not helicopter access is involved. Spring and summer are the popular rafting times.

Note that there are risks in all such adventure activities, and accidents have happened.

Cave Rafting
This is a variation on the rafting theme and not true rafting at all, but it's very unusual and exciting. It's known as 'tumu tumu toobing' and 'black-water rafting' at Waitomo in the North Island, as 'underworld rafting' at Westport and as 'adventure caving' at Greymouth in the South Island.

It involves donning a wet suit, a lighted hard hat and a black inner tube and floating on underground rivers through some spectacular caves with glowworms.

Canoeing & Kayaking
An open two-person canoe is called a 'Canadian canoe' in NZ. A smaller, narrower one-person craft covered except for a hole in which the paddler sits, is often called a 'kayak' in NZ but it can also be

called a 'canoe'. Specify whether you mean a 'Canadian canoe' or a 'kayak' when talking about river trips in NZ.

Many companies offer canoeing and kayaking trips on the same rivers where rafting is popular.

Canoeing is especially popular on the Whanganui River in the North Island, where you can hire a canoe for days at a time. It's also popular on lakes, notably Lake Taupo and many lakes in the South Island.

Kayaking is a very popular sport. Commercial trips (for those without their own equipment) are offered on a number of rivers and lakes in the North and South Islands. Contact the NZ Canoeing Association (NZCA), PO Box 3768, Wellington.

Sea Kayaking Sea kayaking is very popular. Renowned areas are the Hauraki Gulf, Bay of Islands and Coromandel in the North Island and, in the South Island, the Marlborough Sounds and along the coast of Abel Tasman National Park, where sea kayaking has become a viable alternative to walking (see that section in the Marlborough & Nelson chapter for further details). Fiordland is also a great destination. Tour operators in Te Anau, Milford and Manapouri arrange spectacular trips on the lakes and fiords.

River Sledging

Discard the raft, kayak, canoe, Lilo or inflated inner tube if you think they lack manoeuvrability. Instead, grasp a responsive polystyrene sled or a modified boogy board, flippers, wet suit, helmet and a positive attitude, and go for it.

In the South Island, rivers around Queenstown and Wanaka offer this thrill (see those sections in the Otago chapter).

In Taranaki, there is a new variant called 'dam dropping', the highlight of sledging on the Waingongoro River.

Sailing

Auckland is appropriately named the City of Sails – the insular nature of NZ throws up the world's best mariners and some Kiwis have swept the world before them in international yachting races. Most recently Kiwi sailors have dominated the Whitbread Round the World Race and, in 1995 and 2000, captured and defended the America's Cup (see the boxed text 'America's Cup 2000' in the Auckland chapter).

The Bay of Islands (and Whangaroa to the north), the southern lakes (Te Anau and Wakatipu) and the cities of Auckland and Dunedin are good venues to experience the thrill of the wind in the sails.

DAVID WALL

Sea kayaking is incredibly popular in NZ; here at Abel Tasman National Park

Scuba Diving

The Bay of Islands Maritime & Historic Park and the Hauraki Gulf Maritime Park in the North Island, and the Marlborough Sounds Maritime Park in the South Island, are obvious attractions but both islands have many more diving possibilities. Even Invercargill, with its notoriously cold water, has a club!

NZ has two marine parks offering interesting diving. The Poor Knights Islands, off the coast near Whangarei, is reputed to have the best diving in NZ and the late Jacques Cousteau rated it one of the top 10 diving spots in the world. The interesting Sugar Loaf Islands reserve is off Back Beach in New Plymouth, not far from the city centre.

Fiordland in the South Island is most unusual because the extremely heavy rainfall leaves a layer of freshwater, often peaty brown, over the saltwater. You descend through this murky and cold freshwater into amazingly clear and warmer saltwater. The freshwater cuts out light, discouraging the growth of seaweed, and this provides ideal conditions for the growth of black coral *(Antipathes fiordensis)*. Fiordland also has snake stars which symbiotically live on the black coral, and brachiopods, true living fossils.

For more information contact the NZ Underwater Association (NZUA; ☎ 09-849 5896), PO Box 875, Auckland. The bimonthly *Dive NZ* ($4.95) is jam-packed with information.

Surfing

With its thousands of kilometres of coastline, NZ has excellent surfing possibilities. Swells come in from every angle and, while any specific beach will have better surfing at some times of the year than at others, there's good surfing to be found *somewhere* in NZ at any time of the year.

Raglan's 2km-long left-hander is NZ's most famous wave, but areas closer to Auckland also have great surfing. Dunedin is one of the best spots in the South Island, especially in summer and autumn, but there are hundreds of other possibilities. Among the guidebooks on surfing in NZ, look out for *The New Zealand Surfing Guide*, by Mike Bhana, and *A Guide to Surf Riding in New Zealand*, by Wayne Warwick.

A few spots in the North Island recommended by surfers are: Auckland area (Muriwai, Piha); Matakana Island and Tauranga; Whangamata, on the Coromandel; Gisborne (city beaches and Mahia Peninsula); Raglan, near Hamilton; Taranaki (Greenmeadows Point, Puniho Rd and Stent Rd); and Wellington region (Castlepoint, Palliser Bay and Titahi Bay).

South Island locations include: Dunedin (Lobsters, near Akatore River, Long Point and Sandfly Bay); Greymouth (Blaketown and Cobden breakwater); Kaikoura (Mangamanu Reef, Mangawhau Point and Meatworks); and Westport (local beaches and Tauranga Bay).

Windsurfing

Windsurfing has thousands of Kiwi adherents and plenty of popular spots to catch the wind. The lakes of both main islands are popular.

Auckland harbour and the Hauraki Gulf, the Bay of Islands, Oakura near New Plymouth and 'windy' Wellington are just some outstanding coastal locations. There are many places from where you can hire boards and receive NZ Windsurfing Association-approved instruction.

Fishing

New Zealand is renowned as one of the great sportfishing countries of the world, thanks largely to the introduction of exotic rainbow trout, brown trout, quinnat salmon, Atlantic salmon, perch, char and a few other fish.

The lakes and rivers of central North Island are famous for trout fishing, especially Lake Taupo and the rivers that feed it. (See the boxed text 'It's a Trout's Life' in the Central Plateau chapter.) The rivers and lakes of the South Island are also good for trout, notably the Mataura River, Southland. The rivers of Otago and Southland also have some of the best salmon fishing in the world.

Saltwater fishing is also a big attraction for Kiwi anglers, especially in the warmer waters around the North Island where surfcasting or fishing from boats can produce big catches of grey mullet, trevally, mao mao, porae, John Dory, gurnard, flounder, mackerel, hapuku, tarakihi, moki and kahawai.

The Ninety Mile Beach and the beaches of the Hauraki Gulf are good for surfcasting. The Bay of Islands and Whangaroa in Northland, Tutukaka near Whangarei, Whitianga on the Coromandel and Mayor Island in the Bay of Plenty are noted big game fishing areas.

The colder waters of the South Island, especially around Marlborough Sounds, are good for snapper, hake, hapuku (groper), trumpeter, butterfish, ling, barracouta and blue cod. The Kaikoura Peninsula is great for surfcasting.

Fishing gear can be hired in areas such as Taupo and Rotorua, and at a few sports outlets in other towns, but serious enthusiasts may wish to bring their own. Rods and tackle may have to be treated by NZ quarantine officials, especially if they are made with natural materials such as cane or feathers.

A fishing permit is required to fish on inland waters. They cover particular regions and are available for a day, a month or a season; these are sold at sport shops. Local visitor information centres and DOC offices have more information about fishing licences and regulations.

Many books have been written about fishing in NZ. John Kent has written the *North Island Trout Fishing Guide* and the *South Island Trout Fishing Guide*. Tony Orman, a renowned NZ fisherman and author, has written *21 Great New Zealand Trout Waters* as well as *Fishing the Wild Places of New Zealand*, telling not only how to catch fish but also relating some of the author's adventures fishing in many of NZ's wilderness areas. For surfcasting, check out *Surfcasting – A New Zealand Guide*, by Gil Henderson.

Marine-Mammal Watching

Kaikoura, on the north-eastern coast of the South Island, is the country's centre for marine-mammal watching. The main attraction is whale-watching tours, plus swimming with dolphins and seals (see the boxed text under Kaikoura in the Canterbury chapter). The sperm whale, the largest toothed whale, is seen from October to August. Most of the other mammals are seen year-round.

Dolphin swimming is common across NZ, with dolphins in the North Island at Whakatane, Paihia, Tauranga and Whitianga, and at Kaikoura in the South Island. You might be lucky enough to bodysurf with Hector's dolphins at Porpoise Bay in the Catlins if you're there at the right time.

Swimming with sharks (not mammals, of course) is also popular, but thankfully it is done with a protective cage.

AERIAL ACTIVITIES
Bungy Jumping

Bungy jumping was made famous by Kiwi AJ Hackett's bungy dive from the Eiffel Tower in 1986. He teamed up with NZ's champion speed skier, Henry van Asch, and looked for a way to make commercial jumping safe. This company alone has sent many thousands of people hurtling earthward from bridges over the Shotover and Kawarau Rivers near Queenstown, in Normandy, France, and even from a tower in Cairns, Australia, with nothing between them and kingdom come but a gigantic rubber bungy cord tied to their ankles.

The jump begins when you crawl into the preparation area, get your ankles strapped up with a towel for padding, and have adjustments made to the cord depending on your weight. You then hobble out to the edge of the jumping platform, stand looking out over thin air, and get ready to jump. The crew shout out 'five, four, three, two, ONE!' and you dive off and are flying, before soaring upwards again on the bungy.

After bobbing up and down like a human yo-yo, the crew down below pull you into a rubber raft or winch you back to terra firma. No doubt about it, it's a daredevil sport, and the adrenaline rush can last for days. But it's all very well organised, with every possible precaution and attention to safety.

The historic Kawarau Suspension Bridge near Queenstown, attracts the most jumpers; it's 43m above the Kawarau River. Other spectacular bungy spots are the Skippers Canyon Bridge (71m) and The Pipeline

(102m), both in canyons on the Shotover River. The Ledge (47m) is an urban jump in Queenstown, where you can also jump at night. Highest of the lot, also near Queenstown, is the 134m Nevis Highwire (see the boxed text 'Nervous on the Nevis' under Queenstown in the Otago chapter). There's another bungy jump at the Waiau River Bridge near Hanmer Springs.

Jumping is also done in the North Island at Taupo (45m), above the scenic Waikato River, and from a bridge over the Rangitikei River near Mangaweka (80m).

A new variation is the bungy rocket – zoom up and bounce around in a tandem capsule in Tauranga or Christchurch.

Parapenting & Paragliding

This is perhaps the easiest way for humans to fly. After half a day of instruction you should be able to do limited solo flights. Before you know it you could be doing flights from 300m.

The best place to learn the skills necessary to operate your parapente/paraglider is the Wanaka Paragliding School (see Wanaka and Queenstown in the Otago chapter). Initial instruction is conducted at Mt Iron, just outside the town, and the long jumps are from the road up to the Treble Cone ski field.

Tandem flights, where you are strapped to an experienced paraglider, are offered all over the country. Perhaps the most popular is from the top of the gondola hill in Queenstown or from Te Mata Peak in Hawkes Bay.

Aerial Sightseeing

All over NZ planes and helicopters offer sightseeing trips (called 'flightseeing' by the locals), a great way to see the incredible contrast in scenery and the spectacular mountain ranges.

Some of the best trips are around the Bay of Islands, the Bay of Plenty, Tongariro National Park and Mt Taranaki in the North Island, and Mt Cook and the West Coast glaciers and fiords in the South Island.

Aerial sightseeing companies operate from local aerodromes, and a flight can often be arranged on the spot. Ask at the local tourist office for information.

A far more sedate way to see the countryside is from a hot-air balloon. A company operating from near Methven takes you up to an altitude where you get spectacular views of the Southern Alps.

Skydiving

A lot of the aerial sightseeing companies also operate skydiving courses and trips. Many visitors jump in tandem with a fully qualified instructor. It is not cheap, usually around $200, but the thrill is worth every dollar.

Tandem skydiving can be tried in the North Island at Taupo, Rotorua, at Parakai near Auckland, Paraparaumu near Wellington and Hastings near Napier. In the South Island there's tandem skydiving at Nelson, Christchurch, Fox Glacier, Wanaka and Queenstown.

A bonus is that you also get in some great aerial sightseeing, so pick the views you really want to see.

OTHER ACTIVITIES

New Zealand is the home of invention when it comes to activities, for example, Zorbing (rolling downhill in a transparent plastic ball – see Rotorua in the Bay of Plenty chapter) and Fly By Wire (a self-drive flying machine dangling from a wire – see Paekakariki in the Wellington chapter).

A variation on a traditional theme, quad bikes (four-wheel farm bikes) are a fun way to traverse the countryside and are popping up everywhere (see Rotorua, Taupo, Nelson, Queenstown and Hanmer Springs sections).

Mazes are another thing that Kiwis do with a different slant. The original three-dimensional maze at Wanaka, in the South Island, can take hours to work through (see also Rotorua), and the idea has been exported to Japan.

Horse Riding

Horse riding is offered almost everywhere, and unlike some other parts of the world where beginners only get led around a paddock, in NZ you can get out into the countryside. Horse rides range from half-hour rides to 12-day treks. In the South Island, all-day adventure rides on horseback are a great way to see the surrounding country in Kaikoura, around Mt Cook, Queenstown and Dunedin. There are many treks offered in West Coast national parks, from all-day rides at Punakaiki, and excursions up to two weeks long elsewhere.

In the North Island, Taupo has options for wilderness horse trekking and for rides in the hills overlooking the thermal regions. The Coromandel Peninsula, Waitomo, South Kaipara and Pakiri are also good places for horse trekking.

The informative *Where to Ride In New Zealand* pamphlet, produced by the International League for the Protection of Horses (ILPH; ☎ 07-849 0678), PO Box 10-368, Pukete Rd, Te Rapa, is available from information centres. Hamilton has Riding for the Disabled (☎ 07-849 4727).

Bird-watching

New Zealand is a bird-watcher's paradise – in a relatively small area it has many unique endemic species, interesting residents and wave upon wave of visitors. Sadly, NZ is as famous for extinct and point-of-extinction species as it is for common species.

The extinct species can't of course be 'watched' but a tour through museums, into caves where their bones are found and into former habitats is fascinating. These were the islands of the giant 4m-tall moa and the Haast's eagle, which was large enough to have preyed upon the moa. They were also home to the remarkable huia, with its vastly different male and female beaks. A number of species are on the point of extinction and the frenzied efforts to rebuild their populations is a captivating story.

The kiwi is probably the species most sought after by bird-watchers and you are almost guaranteed to see the Stewart Island subspecies at all times of the year. Other sought-after birds are the royal albatross, white heron, Fiordland crested penguin, yellow-eyed penguin, Australasian gannet and wrybill. For more information, see the colour 'Fauna & Flora' section – it lists locations where species are likely to be seen.

Two good guides are *A Field Guide to New Zealand Birds,* by Geoff Moon, and *Birds of New Zealand – Locality Guide,* by Stuart Chambers. Both have excellent colour photos of the birds in their natural environments and lots of good information.

Golf

New Zealand has more golf courses per capita than any other country. Included among the more than 400 courses are some in spectacular settings – Formosa and Gulf Harbour in Auckland, Wairakei near Taupo, Paraparaumu near Wellington, and Arrowtown and Millbrook near Queenstown. The *HANZ on Golfing* lists concessional green-fee rates, places to get equipment and nearby accommodation.

The average green fee varies from $25 to $30.

Vineyards

Many regions have clusters of wineries, and those of Central Otago are the most southerly in the world (45°S). North to south you can cycle or drive and taste at the cellar door. Try a Stonyridge Larose on Waiheke Island, chardonnays in Gisborne, pinot noirs in Martinborough Wine Village in the Wairarapa, cabernets in Hawke's Bay, sauvignon blancs in Marlborough (the largest region) and several varieties at the impressive Canterbury House Vineyard in Waipara Valley.

There are several tour operators listed in the relevant chapters.

MAORI
CULTURE & ARTS

S. Parkinson del.   T. Chambers Sc.

The Head of a Chief of New Zealand, the face curiously tattowd, or markd, according to their Manner.

CULTURE

'Maoridom' is a complex cosmos, and it is only possible to describe an infinitesimal speck of its depth in such a short section. For a description of the coming of the Maori to New Zealand (both popular myth and substantiated theory) see History in the Facts about New Zealand chapter.

Mythology
In the Beginning ...

In the Beginning there was Te Kore – nothingness, and after nine periods of nothingness came Te Ata – the Dawn. And from the womb of the darkness came Ranginui, the Sky Father, and Papatuanuku, the Earth Mother. The two were united and bore many children.

The six most important children of Ranginui and Papatuanuku were Tawhiri-matea, god of winds and storms; Tangaroa, god of the ocean; Tane-mahuta, god of the forest; Haumia-tike-tike, god of wild food such as fern roots and berries; Rongo-matane, god of peace and cultivated food such as the kumara; and Tu-matauenga, the god of war and humans.

After aeons of living in darkness because their parents were joined together and no light came between them, the children of Ranginui and Papatuanuku could take it no longer; they wanted light. They

Left: Traditional Maori carving at the Otago Museum (photographer David Wall)

Title Page: *The Head of a chief of New Zealand, the face is curiously tataoud [ie tattooed], or marked, according to their Manner* (Thomas Chambers, circa 1770)

Left: *Maui Fishing New Zealand out of the Ocean* (Wilhelm Dittmer, 1907)

Right: *Hawaiki* (Wilhelm Dittmer, 1907)

debated what they should do. Eventually they decided that they should separate their parents, so that light could enter the world.

They each tried, and failed, to separate Ranginui and Papatuanuku. Finally it was Tane-mahuta's turn to try, and he pushed and strained, his shoulders to the ground and his feet to the sky, and finally succeeded in forcing his parents apart. Light flooded into the world.

But all the six gods were male, and for the earth, Papa, to be inhabited Tane-mahuta had to procreate with a woman. After unsuccessful tries with immortals he created a woman out of soil and gave her the breath of life. The Earth-formed maid Hine-ahuone had a daughter, Hine-titama, the Dawn Maid, and Tane-mahuta procreated with her, ensuring the birth of humanity.

And Then Came Aotearoa ...

A long time after the creation of the world – after Tane-mahuta had a daughter, who also became his wife and bore him other daughters, and after many other things had happened – the demigod Maui, who lived in Hawaiki, went out fishing with his five brothers.

They went further and further out to sea. When they were a long way out, Maui took out his magic fish-hook (the jaw of his sorcerer grandmother), tied it to a strong rope, then dropped it over the side of the canoe. Soon he caught an immense fish and, struggling mightily, pulled it up to the surface. He leapt into the water and beat the fish with his greenstone *mere* (club). This fish became the North Island of NZ, called Te Ika a Maui (The Fish of Maui) by the ancient Maori. Wellington Harbour is the fish's mouth, the Taranaki and East Cape regions are its two fins, Lake Taupo is its heart and the Northland peninsula is its tail. Mahia Peninsula in Hawke Bay is Te Matau a Maui (The Fish-hook of Maui) – the hook with which the demigod caught the giant fish. Maui's mere created the mountains and valleys when the fish was clubbed.

The South Island, known as Te Waka o Maui (The Canoe of Maui), was the canoe in which he went fishing. Kaikoura Peninsula was where he braced his foot while hauling up the fish – the peninsula was called Te Taumanu o te Waka o Maui (The Thwart of Maui's Canoe).

Finally, Stewart Island, south of the South Island, was known as Te Punga a Maui (The Anchor of Maui) – the anchor that held the canoe as Maui hauled in the giant fish.

Many years later people came to these islands, sailing thousands of kilometres from the Polynesian homeland, Hawaiki. First, in about AD 800, was the navigator Kupe, accompanied by his wife Hine-te-aparangi and slave Ngahue. After exploring the new land and naming it 'Aotearoa' (Land of the Long White Cloud), they returned to Hawaiki to tell people of their find. A hundred years later others from Hawaiki followed Kupe's instructions to find Aotearoa and settled there permanently. See History in the Facts about New Zealand chapter for the story of the waves of migration from Hawaiki to Aotearoa.

Tribal Society

Maori society was (and to a large degree still is) tribal – the Maori refer to themselves in terms of their *iwi* (tribe), with the tribe often named after an ancestor, for example Ngati Kahungunu (The Descendants of Kahungunu) or Ngapuhi (The Descendants of Puhi). The Ngapuhi, of Northland, is the largest iwi in the country, with nearly 100,000 members; next are Ngati Porou (55,000), Ngati Kahungunu (45,000) and Ngai Tahu, the main South Island iwi, with 30,000 members.

Many different iwi are related by their descent from one *waka*, or migratory canoe. These are the canoes that sailed from Hawaiki to NZ up to a thousand years ago, however such relationships are still re-membered and have always been important in inter-tribal politics. For example, the Waikato and Ngati Maniapoto tribes were historically allied because of their common descent from the *Tainui* canoe.

Often of more relevance than the iwi was the *hapu* (the sub-tribe), and the village structure based around *whanau* (extended family groups). Whanau combined to form communal villages centred around the *marae* (the sacred ground in front of the *whare whakairo*, the carved meeting house where the tribe's ancestral spirits live). The marae was the focus of Maori culture because it was where the tribe gathered. It was on the marae and in the whare whakairo that ceremonies were held, and elders and others of authority addressed the community.

Within each hapu there were clear lines of responsibility between chiefs, men, women and slaves as to which daily tasks they would

Below: *Pirogue de Guerre de la Nouvelle Zelande* (War Canoe of New Zealand; Louis Auguste de Sainson, 1839)

perform. Men prepared the agricultural plots (chiefs participated in this also) but women did the planting; men fished in the open sea and dove for shellfish and the women were allowed to bring food out to them; only slaves and women were allowed to cook, weave and make cloaks; and only men were allowed to go to war, build canoes, tattoo or carve. The delineation of responsibility was ruled by complex laws of *tapu,* which is literally translated as 'taboo' but was very complex; see later in this special section.

Key Values

The four essential pillars of Maori society were spirituality, the land, hospitality and ancestors.

Spirituality (Wairua) Maori religion, like that of other Polynesian cultures, was complex, with a pantheon of gods representing the sea, sky, war, agriculture and other departments. Spirituality was expressed in all aspects of the daily lives of the Maori.

The *tohunga atua* (priests) could communicate with the gods and knew the rituals associated with offerings, and were also responsible for maintaining the history, genealogy, stories and songs of the tribe. The tohunga were not just priests but included many different experts: *tohunga ta moko* (expert tattooists), *tohunga whakairo* (master wood-carvers) and *tohunga tarai waka* (shipwrights).

The tohunga would request that a god come to rest in his *toko* (god stick) during consultation. Symbols such as the toko did not have the same religious significance as, say, the crucifix in Christianity, but were merely temporary resting places *(taumata atua)* for the gods.

Essential to Maori beliefs and society were the notions of *mauri* (active life force) and *wairua* (soul or spirit) that reside in all things, and *mana* (personal spiritual power or prestige). All things were imbued with mauri, but upon death it was the wairua which went to the spirit world. If a stone used to signify the mauri of a particular river was removed, then it was believed that its inhabitants (fish, eels, birds) would go elsewhere.

Mana, or personal spiritual power, was possessed by chiefs and from them it flowed through to their tribe. Gods had mana, and it was inherent in the *karakia* (prayers or chants) that the tohunga made to them. The chanting tohunga invariably had mana. It could be lost – a chief captured in battle would lose his, and that of his tribe. A warrior who killed the *mata ika* or 'first fish' – the first enemy killed – in a battle would attain considerable mana.

Tapu applied to forbidden objects, such as sacred ground or a chief's possessions, and also to actions prohibited by the tribe. Its application could be temporary or permanent; canoe builders would be given tapu in a ceremony prior to commencing work, and war parties a blood tapu which was removed when they returned to their families. *Noa* was the quality of 'ordinariness', the opposite of tapu, and applied to everyday objects, cooked food, women, and captured male slaves.

Ko Tongariro te Maunga

In this famous quote in 1856 Te Heuheu Iwikau, the hereditary *ariki* (high chief) of the Tuwharetoa tribe, established his credentials by identifying himself and his tribe with his mountain and his 'sea':

Ko Tongariro te maunga, ko Taupo te moana, ko Ngati Tuwharetoa te iwi, ko Te Heuheu te tangata

(Tongariro is the mountain, Taupo is the sea, Ngati Tuwharetoa is the tribe, Te Heuheu is the person)

Land (Whenua) Geographical features such as *maunga* (mountains) and *awa* (rivers) often delineated tribal boundaries, and were an important genealogical indicator.

Many mountains were personified, featuring in intricate myths and stories (for example, see the story of the mountain Taranaki in that chapter). Even today, each tribe of the 160 tribal and sub-tribal groups has one or more sacred *maunga*. Tribal *whakapapa* (genealogies) always refer to the names of mountains, as they were an important part of the social grid (see the boxed text 'Ko Tongariro te Maunga').

Following European settlement, many mountains were given English names in an almost deliberate attempt to tame the 'wilderness'. This practice was more prevalent in areas with small Maori populations (such as the colonised towns of the South Island), but regions like Taupo retained their original names.

Hospitality (Manaaki) This is an extremely important pillar of Maori society, based on the principle that people are the most important thing in the world (see The Marae later).

Ancestors (Tipuna) Ancestor worship was important and, in the absence of a written language, long whakapapa, stretching back hundreds of years to people who arrived by waka from Hawaiki, were committed to memory. Whakapapa defined ancestral and family ties and determined everyone's place in the tribe. The Maori saw themselves not as individuals but as part of the collective knowledge and experience of all of their ancestors.

Burial practices differed between tribes but the *tangi* (funeral) was similar. The wairua of the departed was told to *haere ki te Po* (go to the Underworld). At Te Rerenga-Wairua, Cape Reinga in the far north, the soul slid down the roots of a lone pohutakawa tree (which still stands), took a last look at Aotearoa from the summit of Ohau in the Three Kings Islands, and then rejoined the ancestral spirits in Hawaiki (simultaneously the name for the Underworld and the ancestral homeland).

Heru – ornamental comb

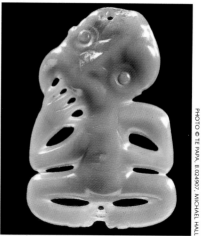

Pounamu hei tiki – greenstone ornament

Poi made from lace bark

Kahu huruhuru – feather cloak

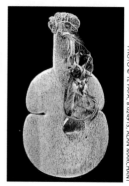

Kotiate – bone fighting club

Traditional Maori carving at the Otago Museum

Wakahuia – small carved box for storing treasures

Carved face with *moko*, Otago Museum

Inside a *whare whakairo* (carved Maori meeting house), Whakarewarewa in Rotorua, Bay of Plenty

The Marae

Strictly, the 'marae' is the open area in front of the whare whakairo (the carved meeting house), but today the term is most-often used to describe the entire complex of buildings – meeting house, eating house etc.

Today, many Maori are re-establishing contact with the marae of their tribe. But even the marae are subject to the winds of change. Traditional tribal leadership has evolved into today's trust boards, whose power bases are the marae in rural areas. The trust boards are under increasing attack from young, urban Maori who see the old leaders as too conservative and exclusive. With elders' adherence to traditional etiquette and Maori language, many urban Maori not brought up on the marae feel excluded and want a greater say in tribal affairs and negotiations with the government.

Recent census figures show that a quarter of all Maori cannot name their iwi, but the number who can has risen since the previous census. Many Maori are now attempting to trace their whakapapa.

Visiting a Marae The best way to gain some understanding of *Maoritanga* (Maori culture) is by visiting a marae. It is a place which is sacred to the Maori and should be treated with great respect.

A welcoming ritual called *te powhiri ki te manuhiri* is followed every time *manuhiri* (visitors) come onto the marae. The manuhiri and the *tangata whenua* (hosts) bring with them the memories of their

Below: A *tangi* (funeral ceremony) at Takapuwahia Marae (JN Taylor, circa 1920)

ALEXANDER TURNBULL LIBRARY, WELLINGTON NZ

dead, and both groups pay their respects to one another's deceased. The ceremony removes the tapu and permits the manuhiri and tangata whenua to interact. The practice varies from marae to marae. Note that shoes must be removed before entering a whare whakairo.

Te powhiri ki te manuhiri may proceed as follows: a *karanga* (welcoming call) is made by women of the tangata whenua to the manuhiri. It could also include a *taki* or *wero* (ceremonial challenge). The manuhiri reply to the karanga and proceed on to the marae. They pay their respects and sit where indicated, generally to the left (if facing outwards) of the whare whakairo.

Mihi (welcoming speeches) are given by the tangata whenua from the *taumata tapu* (threshold) in front of the meeting house. Each speech is generally supported by a *waiata* (song), generally led by the women. When the mihi is finished the manuhiri reply. (It is important to mention the iwi, hapu, maunga and awa of respective ancestors.) The tapu is deemed to have been lifted from the manuhiri when the replies are finished. The manuhiri then greet the tangata whenua with handshakes and the *hongi* (pressing of noses). In some places the hongi, a sharing of life breath, is a single press, in others it is press, release, press. It is never a rubbing together of noses (a popular misconception).

Before the manuhiri leave the marae they make *poroporoaki* (farewell speeches), which take the form of thanks and prayer.

As a visitor, once invited you are extremely welcome on the marae, as hospitality is a cornerstone of Maori culture. Once protocol has been satisfied, your welfare is the primary concern of the tangata whenua. They want to see you fed and looked after, almost spoiled, because you are a guest. Such hospitality is fantastic and lucky visitors to NZ are increasingly being given the opportunity to enjoy it, often on one of the marae tours that are becoming popular.

If you do receive hospitality such as food and lodging, it's customary to offer a *koha* (donation) to help cover costs. When the roles are reversed and you are the tangata whenua, remember that the care of your guests becomes your first concern. See Maori Culture under Books in the Facts for the Visitor chapter for some guides to marae protocol. Some of the customs and conventions of the marae include:

• The marae is a place of kinship *(whanaungatanga)*, friendship *(manaakitanga)*, love *(aroha)*, spirituality *(wairua)* and the life force *(mauri)*
• Respect for elders *(whakarongo ki nga kaumatua)*
• The marae is a place where life and death merge, where the living *(nga hunga ora)* give great honour to the dead *(nga hunga mate)*
• The preservation and use of the Maori language *(te reo Maori)*

The term *hui* you often hear refers to a meeting or congregation. It is usually a large group gathering to discuss important issues, or to engage in cultural competitions (eg, action songs).

War (Pakanga)

Perhaps the greatest social change in Maori culture was the progression from a peaceful hunter-gatherer society to a warlike society as land pressures increased. Associated with this was the migration from open *kainga* (unfortified settlements) to *pa tuwatawata* (fortified enclosures), especially in the richer northern region where kumara and fern root thrived.

One of the best ways to promote the mana of a tribe was through battle, so the Maori had a highly developed warrior society. War had its own worship, sacrifices, rituals, dances and art forms.

Weapons used in war included the wooden long clubs *(taiaha, pouwhenua* and *tewhatewha)* and short clubs known as *patu,* including the greenstone mere (club). Although the long clubs resembled spears, they were never thrown.

Below: Bludgeons, used as weapons by the New Zealanders, and called patoo-patoos, as seen on the side, the edge and the end (John Record, 1773)

Tribes engaged in numerous battles over territory, for *utu* (revenge or payment) or for other reasons, with the losers often becoming slaves or food. Cooking and eating an enemy not only delivered the ultimate insult, by removing a warrior's tapu status, but also passed on the enemy's life force or power. Usually a *taua muru* (plundering raid) rather than a pitched battle was enough to settle a matter. But reprisal

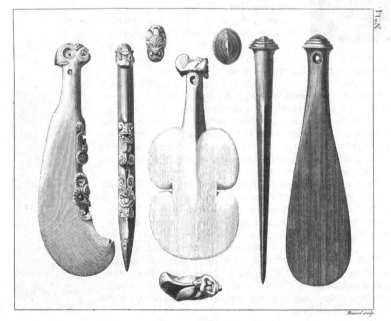

raids were demanded often as a matter of utu or restoration of a hapu's mana, leading to an almost constant state of warfare.

The defensive villages, or *pa*, to which the Maori retreated when attacked, were built on terraced hill tops with concentric defensive walls and elaborate earth defences. If the outer wall was breached the defenders could retreat to the next fortified inner terrace. Many of these earthworks are still visible, for example on the sculptured hills that dot the city of Auckland.

These defensive earthworks were successfully adapted to deal with cannon and musket fire during the Land Wars against the government in the 1840s and 1860s – the world's first trench warfare. Some of these earthworks were incredibly complex and effective: at Gate Pa near Tauranga, in 1864, a defending force of only 200 Ngai-te-rangi warriors managed to repel an attack by almost 1700 government soldiers, routing the attacking party even after hours of artillery bombardment.

ARTS

Maori arts are dramatic and include various arts that people of European backgrounds might not be familiar with.

Song (Waiata) & Dance (Haka)

Traditionally the Maori did not keep a written history; their history was kept in long, specific and stylised songs and chants. As in many parts of the world where oral history has been practised, oratory, song and chant developed to become a magnificent art in Maori culture.

The Maori arts of song *(waiata)* and dance *(haka,* see the boxed text) include some special features, such as the *poi* dance, hand games *(mahi ringaringa)* and other action songs *(waiata kori).*

The highly expressive action song is perhaps the most beloved tradition, and a highlight of a visit to NZ could be learning some songs with members of a Maori cultural group. Usually the men performed with vigorous actions, whereas the movements of women were graceful and flowing, reflecting some of the artistic forms of Asia.

The poi dance *(haka poi)* is distinctive to the NZ Maori. Originally the poi, small balls whirled around on the end of a string, were made of flax but many types of material are now used. There are long- and short-stringed poi, with the long poi being easier to dance with. The most famous dance is the *waka poi,* with the women sitting in a row as if in a canoe; normally the poi dance is performed standing.

Musical instruments included two forms of flute – the *putorino* played with the mouth, and the *koauau,* a nose flute; and the trumpet *(pu),* of which the best known is the shell version with a wooden mouthpiece. There was no drum to provide a beat, this being provided by rhythmical stamping.

Haka

The word *haka* is Maori for any form of dance but it has come to be associated with the war chant *(haka taparahi)* that preceded a battle or challenged suspicious visitors.

Delivered with fierce shouting, flexing arm movements that resemble fists pummelling the side of someone's head, and thunderous stamping to grind whatever is left into the dust, it is indeed a frightening sight.

Each tribe had its own haka, but the most famous and widely used comes from Te Rauparaha (1768–1849), chief of the Ngati Toa tribe. He was one of the last great warrior chiefs, carving a course of mayhem and slaughter from Kapiti, near Wellington, to the South Island. Made famous by the All Blacks, NZ's national rugby team, Te Rauparaha's haka is:

Ka mate, ka mate. Ka ora, ka ora (I die, I die. I live, I live)
Ka mate, ka mate. Ka ora, ka ora (I die, I die. I live, I live)
Tenei te tangata puhuruhuru (Behold the hairy man)
Nana nei i tiki mai (Who fetched the sun)
Whakawhiti te ra (And caused it to shine again)
A upane, ka upane (An upward step, another upward step)
A upane, ka upane. Whiti te ra (An upward step, another upward step. The sun shines again)
Hi!

It is said to have originated when Te Rauparaha was fleeing from his enemies. A local chief hid him in an underground kumara store, where Te Rauparaha waited in the dark, expecting to be found and killed. When the store was opened and the sun shone in, it was not his enemies but the hairy local chief telling him they had gone. Te Rauparaha climbed the ladder to perform this victorious haka.

Sir Apirana Ngata (1874–1950) takes the lead in a *haka* at the Waitangi celebrations (B Snowdon, 1940)

MAORI CULTURE & ARTS

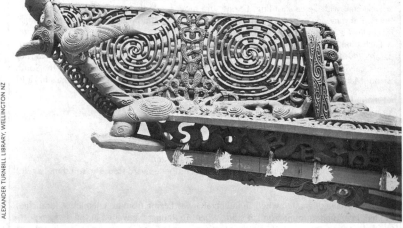

Carving (Whakairo)

Despite remaining a stone age culture (it would have been difficult to get beyond that stage in NZ, since there are few metals apart from gold) the Maori evolved elaborate artistic traditions. The chisels *(whao)* used were of basalt or greenstone, and cord drills were used for making holes.

Woodcarving *(whakairo rakau)* became increasingly refined, peaking in the period immediately before European arrival. Facing the marae, ornate whare whakairo were built with powerful wooden carvings depicting ancestors, as well as *tukutuku* (wall panelling) and symbolic paintings on rafters and other parts of buildings.

The human figure was the central motif, usually shown with enlarged head, mouth and eyes. To imitate exactly the human form, a creation of the gods, would be a form of insult. Another prevalent feature, often seen in window lintels and along canoes' barge boards, is the *manaia*, a 'bird-headed man' identifiable by a human-shaped head with a beak.

Beautifully carved *waka taua* (war canoes) were a source of great mana for a tribe and were protected by tapu. Built of kauri or totara, they were up to 25m (80 feet) in length and the bow and stern pieces were elaborately fashioned and carved by tohunga tarai waka. Because these canoes were tapu, women were not allowed to travel in them and cooked food could not be carried.

A variety of household items were also intricately carved, such as feather boxes to hold huia feathers *(a waka huia)* and other treasures *(taonga)*; the handle of adzes *(toki)*; funnels for feeding people that were temporarily too tapu to touch cooked food; and digging sticks *(ko)*.

Above: Carved prow of a *waka* (photographer unknown, circa 1910)

Tattoos (Moko)

The higher classes were decorated with intricate *moko*, or tattoos – women only had moko on their chins and lips, while high-ranking men not only had tattoos over their entire face but also over other parts of their body (especially their buttocks). The tattoos were created using bone chisels, a mallet and blue pigment.

Clothing (Kakahu)

The Maori made clothing from dog fur, flax, feathers and other materials. The two principal items of clothing were the kilt and the cloak.

The *maro* (male kilt) was scanty, designed to cover the penis, whereas the *rapaki* (female kilt) was much larger. At times men wore a *whitiki* or *tatua* (belt of dried flax). A woman's flaxen belt was called a *tu*.

The *piupiu* (skirt) worn in cultural performances is a modern innovation, as is the colourful *pari* (bodice).

The usual *kahu* (cloaks) were made of flax but some were of dog skin or bird skins sewn together. The most prized of the cloaks, used for ceremonial purposes, were the *kahu huruhuru* (feather cloaks), often using huia or kiwi feathers and fringed with *taniko* (dog fur). Other feathers used were from the tui, kaka, pukeko, takahe and wood pigeon *(kereru)*.

Right: Portrait of unidentified woman (Samuel Carnell, circa 1870)

S CARNELL COLLECTION; ALEXANDER TURNBULL LIBRARY, WELLINGTON NZ

Greenstone (Pounamu)

Greenstone (jade or nephrite, called *pounamu* in Maori) was highly prized by the Maori. The South Island, where pounamu was found, was called Te Wahi Pounamu (The Place of Greenstone) or Te Wai Pounamu (The Water of Greenstone). Since greenstone is found predominantly on the West Coast, expeditions undertaken by the Maori to collect it often took months, following treacherous transalpine trails.

Working the stone with their primitive equipment was no easy task either, but they managed to produce some exquisite items.

Pounamu ornaments and mere (war clubs) were great treasures. The *heitiki* is one of the most popular greenstone mementos purchased in NZ. Its name literally means 'hanging human form', as Tiki was the first man created and *hei* is 'to hang'. Heitiki were passed on through generations – it was believed that each ancestor who wore it added something to its value. Other popular motifs are the manaia, the *taniwha* (monster) and the *marakihau* (sea monster).

The best places to buy greenstone items are Hokitika and Greymouth in the South Island. Collections of both ancient and modern pieces are held at Te Papa Museum in Wellington, and at the Otago (Dunedin), Canterbury (Christchurch) and Auckland Museums. Traditionally, greenstone is bought as a gift for another person, not for yourself.

Tama & the Greenstone

The legend of Tama explains why there are differing types of greenstone in the South Island. Tama's three wives (Hine-kawakawa, Hine-kahurangi and Hine-pounamu) were abducted by the taniwha Poutini. At Anita Bay near Milford Sound he found one wife, Hine-pounamu, turned into greenstone, and when he wept his tears gave the stone a flecked appearance, hence the name of *tangiwai* (water of weeping) given to that type of stone. Tama's companion, Tumu-aki, breached *tapu* by putting his burnt fingers in his mouth while cooking some birds, so Tama was not able to find his other wives. Like the first discovered, they were turned into greenstone – *kawakawa* and *kahurangi*. The careless Tumu-aki was turned into a mountain and *tutaekoka*, a fourth form of greenstone, was named to remember the birds they had eaten.

Getting There & Away

The overwhelming majority of visitors to New Zealand arrive by air. Apart from cruise ships, there are no regular sea services to New Zealand.

AIR

Airports & Airlines

New Zealand has six airports that handle international flights: Auckland, Wellington, Palmerston North and Hamilton in the North Island, and Christchurch and Dunedin in the South Island. Most international flights go through Auckland. Wellington airport has limited runway capacity and international flights are mainly to Australia, as they are from Christchurch, although there are some connections from Christchurch to other countries. Contact numbers of the major airlines (and overseas links) include:

Aerolineas Argentinas (☎ 09-379 3675) 15th floor, ASB Centre, 135 Albert St, Auckland
Air New Zealand (☎ 0800-737 000)
Auckland: (☎ 09-377 7999) 29 Custom St West
Christchurch: (☎ 03-353 2800) 702 Colombo St
Wellington: (☎ 04-474 8950) 41 Panama St;
Web site: www.airnz.co.nz
Ansett Australia (☎ 09-357 2146) Level 5, Downtown House, Queen Elizabeth Square, Auckland; Web site: www.ansett.com.au
British Airways
Auckland: (☎ 09-366 3200) 191 Queen St
Christchurch: (☎ 03-379 2503)
Wellington: (☎ 04-472 7334);
Web site: www.british-airways.com
Cathay Pacific (☎ 09-379 0861) 11th floor, Arthur Andersen Tower, National Bank Centre, 205–209 Queen St, Auckland
Freedom Air (☎ 0800-600 500) Dunedin, Hamilton and Palmerston North;
Web site: www.freedomair.co.nz
Polynesian Airlines (☎ 0800-800 993) Samoa House, 283 Karangahape Rd, Auckland;
Web site: www.polynesianairlines.co.nz
Qantas Airways (☎ 0800-808 767)
Auckland: (☎ 09-357 8700) 19 Queen St
Christchurch: (☎ 03-379 6504) 119 Armagh St;
Wellington: (☎ 04-472 1100) ASB Bank, 2 Hunter St
Web site: www.qantas.com.au

Singapore Airlines (☎ 0800-808 909)
Auckland: (☎ 09-303 2129) 10th floor, West Plaza Bldg, cnr Fanshawe & Albert Sts
Wellington: (☎ 04-499 0271) Microsoft House, 3/11 Hunter Street
Christchurch: (☎ 03-365 2039) Level 13, Forsyth-Barr House;
Web site: www.singaporeair.com
Thai Airways International (☎ 09-379 6455) 22 Fanshawe St, Auckland
United Airlines
Auckland: (☎ 09-379 3800) 5–7 City Rd
Wellington: (☎ 04-472 0470) Castrol House, 36 Customhouse Quay;
Web site: www.ual.com

Buying Tickets

As in Australia, STA Travel and Flight Centre are popular travel agents specialising in discount fares. Flight Centre, which has a Web site at www.flightcentre.com.au, has some of the cheapest fares and there are branches throughout NZ.

STA, which has a Web site at www .statravel.com, has numerous offices around the country; in Auckland (☎ 09-356 1550), Hamilton (☎ 07-839 1833), Palmerston North (☎ 06-354 5670), Wellington (☎ 04-472 8510), Christchurch (☎ 03-379 9098) and Dunedin (☎ 03-474 0146).

Some sample discount fares offered from Auckland are listed below – all prices are quoted in NZ dollars:

destination	one way	return
Bangkok/Hong Kong	1120	1550
Buenos Aires	3000	2200
Cairns	810	960
Fiji	750	820
Frankfurt	1570	2870
Honolulu	1080	1400
London	1570	2870
Los Angeles/San Francisco/Vancouver	1400	2000
New York	1900	2600
Singapore	1020	1380
Sydney/Melbourne/ Brisbane	560	560
Tokyo	2580	1780

Price Warning

Use the fares quoted in this book as a guide only. They are approximate and based on the rates advertised by travel agents at the time of going to press.

Round-the-World & Circle Pacific Tickets Round-the-World (RTW) tickets are often real bargains. They are usually put together by a combination of two airlines and permit you to fly anywhere you want on their route systems so long as you do not backtrack. There are restrictions on how many stops you are permitted and usually the tickets are valid for 90 days up to a year. An alternative type of RTW ticket is one put together by a travel agent using a combination of discounted tickets.

Circle Pacific tickets use a combination of airlines to circle the Pacific – combining Australia, NZ, North America and Asia. As with RTW tickets, there are advance purchase restrictions and limits to how many stopovers you can take. These fares are likely to be around 15% cheaper than RTW tickets.

Departure Tax

There's a $20 departure tax from Auckland, Wellington and Dunedin airports, and a $25 tax from Christchurch, Hamilton and Palmerston North, payable at the airport.

The USA

Most flights between the USA and NZ are to/from the USA's west coast. Most travel through Los Angeles but some are through San Francisco. If you're coming from some other part of the USA, your travel agent can arrange a discounted 'add-on' fare to get you to the city of departure.

Excursion (round-trip) fares are available from various airlines but are more expensive than those from travel agents. Cheaper 'short life' fares are frequently offered for limited periods. The easiest way to get a cheap air fare from the USA is through a travel agency selling discounted fares; these fares can be about US$650 return from Los Angeles or about US$1050 return from New York. For as little as US$100 extra you can fly from Los Angeles to Australia with a stopover in New Zealand.

The *New York Times,* the *Los Angeles Times,* the *Chicago Tribune* and the *San Francisco Examiner* all produce weekly travel sections in which you'll find any number of travel agents' ads. Council Travel and STA Travel have offices in major cities nationwide. The magazine *Travel Unlimited* (PO Box 1058, Allston, MA 02134) publishes details of the cheapest air fares and courier possibilities for destinations all over the world from the USA.

If you want to visit other Pacific destinations on your way to or from NZ, compare carefully the stopover possibilities offered by each airline. Air New Zealand offers an excellent variety of stopover options on its route between Los Angeles and Auckland. You can tack on stopovers in Honolulu, Tahiti, Rarotonga, Western Samoa, Tonga and Fiji quite cheaply. Other airlines fly to NZ for the same price, or sometimes cheaper, but with more limited stopover options.

Canada

Travel CUTS has offices in all major cities. It has a Web site at www.travelcuts.com. The *Toronto Globe* and *Mail* and the *Vancouver Sun* carry travel agents' ads. The magazine *Great Expeditions* (PO Box 8000-411, Abbotsford, BC V2S 6H1) is useful.

Australia

New Zealand cities with flights to Australia are Auckland, Christchurch, Wellington, Dunedin, Palmerston North and Hamilton (the last three have Freedom Air flights only). Australian cities with flights to NZ are Brisbane, Cairns, Melbourne, Perth and Sydney. Air New Zealand, Qantas Airways and United Airlines (Sydney and Melbourne only) are the main carriers. Smaller carriers include Garuda Indonesia and EVA Air (Taiwan) from Brisbane and Aerolineas Argentinas, Thai Airways International,

Royal Tongan Airlines and Polynesian Airlines from Sydney.

The fare depends on the day you fly out as well as where you fly to and from. The year is divided into peak and off-peak (low) times, which can vary between airlines. The main peak season is over the summer school holidays (10 December to 15 January). Typical low-season, rock-bottom fares from a travel agent specialising in discount tickets from Sydney cost around A$515/550 one-way/return to Auckland, Christchurch or Wellington with the main carriers, or A$420/470 return from Sydney/Brisbane to Hamilton, Palmerston North and Dunedin in K Class (a no-frills version of economy class) with Freedom Air. From Melbourne the equivalent fare is around A$580/620 to Auckland, Christchurch or Wellington. Return fares in the high season cost around A$200 more, while tickets valid for two months or longer are also more expensive.

If you're travelling from Australia to the US west coast via NZ, the high season varies but is generally during the northern hemisphere summer (June, July and August). Low-season fares start at around A$1400/2000 one-way/return; high-season fares are more like A$2400 return.

RTW fares departing from Australia, which can include a stopover in NZ, vary with the season. The northern hemisphere summer is usually the high season for RTW fares; tickets cost around A$2300 (with Philippine Airlines) to A$3000 (with Air New Zealand) in the high season, but can be around A$1800 in the low season.

STA Travel and Flight Centre are major dealers in cheap air fares. Check the travel agents' ads in the *Yellow Pages* and ring around.

The UK

London-Auckland return tickets can be found in London bucket shops for around £800. Some stopovers are permitted on this sort of ticket. Depending on which airline you travel with, you may fly across Asia or across the USA. If you come across Asia you can often make stopovers in countries like India, Thailand, Singapore and Australia; in the other direction, stopover possibilities include New York, Los Angeles, Honolulu or a variety of Pacific islands. Stopover options vary depending on the airline you use.

Since NZ is about as far from Europe as you can get, it's not much more expensive to continue round the world rather than backtracking. Agents can organise you a RTW route through the South Pacific from around £750.

Trailfinders in west London produces a lavishly illustrated brochure which includes air fare details. STA Travel also has branches in the UK. Look in the Sunday papers and *Exchange* and *Mart* for ads. Also look out for the free magazines widely available in London – start by looking outside the main train stations.

Most British travel agents are registered with the Association of British Travel Agents (ABTA). If you have paid for your flight to an ABTA-registered agent which then goes out of business, ABTA will guarantee a refund or an alternative. Unregistered bucket shops are riskier but also sometimes cheaper.

There has been cut-throat competition between London's many bucket shops; London is an important European centre for cheap fares. Although there are some untrustworthy operators most of them are fine.

The Globetrotters Club (BCM/Roving, London WC1N 3XX) publishes a newsletter called *Globe,* which covers obscure destinations and can help in finding travelling companions.

Continental Europe

Frankfurt is the major arrival and departure point for NZ flights, with connections to other European centres.

There are many bucket shops on mainland Europe where you can buy discounted air tickets. The international student and discount travel agencies STA and Council Travel also have a number of offices in various European countries. Any of their offices can give you the details on which office might be nearest you.

In Amsterdam, NBBS is a popular travel agent.

Air Travel Glossary

Cancellation Penalties If you have to cancel or change a discounted ticket, there are often heavy penalties involved; insurance can sometimes be taken out against these penalties. Some airlines impose penalties on regular tickets as well, particularly against 'no-show' passengers.

Courier Fares Businesses often need to send urgent documents or freight securely and quickly. Courier companies hire people to accompany the package through customs and, in return, offer a discount ticket which is sometimes a phenomenal bargain. However, you may have to surrender all your baggage allowance and take only carry-on luggage.

Full Fares Airlines traditionally offer 1st class (coded F), business class (coded J) and economy class (coded Y) tickets. These days there are so many promotional and discounted fares available that few passengers pay full economy fare.

Lost Tickets If you lose your airline ticket an airline will usually treat it like a travellers cheque and, after inquiries, issue you with another one. Legally, however, an airline is entitled to treat it like cash and if you lose it then it's gone forever. Take good care of your tickets.

Onward Tickets An entry requirement for many countries is that you have a ticket out of the country. If you're unsure of your next move, the easiest solution is to buy the cheapest onward ticket to a neighbouring country or a ticket from a reliable airline which can later be refunded if you do not use it.

Open-Jaw Tickets These are return tickets where you fly out to one place but return from another. If available, this can save you backtracking to your arrival point.

Overbooking Since every flight has some passengers who fail to show up, airlines often book more passengers than they have seats. Usually excess passengers make up for the no-shows, but occasionally somebody gets 'bumped' onto the next available flight. Guess who it is most likely to be? The passengers who check in late.

Promotional Fares These are officially discounted fares, available from travel agencies or direct from the airline.

Reconfirmation If you don't reconfirm your flight at least 72 hours prior to departure, the airline may delete your name from the passenger list. Ring to find out if your airline requires reconfirmation.

Restrictions Discounted tickets often have various restrictions on them – such as needing to be paid for in advance and incurring a penalty to be altered. Others are restrictions on the minimum and maximum period you must be away.

Round-the-World Tickets RTW tickets give you a limited period (usually a year) in which to circumnavigate the globe. You can go anywhere the carrying airlines go, as long as you don't backtrack. The number of stopovers or total number of separate flights is decided before you set off and they usually cost a bit more than a basic return flight.

Transferred Tickets Airline tickets cannot be transferred from one person to another. Travellers sometimes try to sell the return half of their ticket, but officials can ask you to prove that you are the person named on the ticket. On an international flight tickets are compared with passports.

Travel Periods Ticket prices vary with the time of year. There is a low (off-peak) season and a high (peak) season, and often a low-shoulder season and a high-shoulder season as well. Usually the fare depends on your outward flight – if you depart in the high season and return in the low season, you pay the high-season fare.

Asia & Africa

There are far more flights to NZ from Asia than there were only a few years ago, with direct flights to Auckland from Tokyo, Hong Kong, Singapore, Denpasar/Bali and Taipei, and connecting flights to most other places. Many of the connecting flights have stopovers in Australia. There are also a few direct flights to Christchurch including flights from Tokyo and Singapore.

Hong Kong is the discount air fares capital of the region. Its bucket shops are at least as unreliable as those of other cities. Seek advice from other travellers before buying a ticket.

STA Travel has branches in Hong Kong, Tokyo, Singapore, Bangkok and Kuala Lumpur.

Flights to South Africa pass through Australia. Air New Zealand has regular connections with South African Airways via Sydney and Perth.

SEA

Cruise ships aside, there are no longer any regular passenger ship services to NZ. Even arranging to work your way across the Pacific as crew on a yacht is much more difficult than it used to be. There are many yachts sailing around the Pacific but nowadays they're usually only willing to take on experienced yachties as crew.

To try your luck finding a yacht, you have to go to the appropriate port at the appropriate time. There are lots of favourite islands, ports and harbours where you're likely to find yachts, such as: Sydney and Cairns in Australia; Bali in Indonesia; various ports in Fiji or Tahiti; and Hawai'i, San Diego or San Francisco in the USA. In NZ, popular yachting harbours include the Bay of Islands and Whangarei (both in Northland), Auckland and Wellington.

There are certain times when you're more likely to find yachts. From Fiji, October to November is a peak departure season as cyclones are on their way. March-April is the main departure season for yachts heading to Australia; be prepared for rough seas and storms when crossing the Tasman Sea.

ORGANISED TOURS

As well as the host of tours you can arrange in NZ, many can be arranged from outside the country. The New Zealand Tourism Board can provide details of tour companies; its offices around the world are listed in the Tourist Offices section in the Facts for the Visitor chapter. If you just want to add accommodation or car or campervan hire to your air ticket, travel agents can often get better deals than those available on arrival.

WARNING

The information in this chapter is particularly vulnerable to change: prices for international travel are volatile, routes are introduced and cancelled, schedules change, special deals come and go, and rules and visa requirements are amended. Airlines and governments seem to take a perverse pleasure in making price structures and regulations as complicated as possible. You should check directly with the airline or a travel agent to make sure you understand how a fare (and ticket you may buy) works. In addition, the travel industry is highly competitive and there are many lurks and perks.

The upshot of this is that you should get opinions, quotes and advice from as many airlines and travel agents as possible before you part with your hard-earned cash. The details given in this chapter should be regarded as pointers and are not a substitute for your own careful, up-to-date research.

Getting Around

New Zealand has an extensive air service, reasonable bus networks and a limited, but useful, train service. The main cities and tourist areas are well covered and easy to reach. Smaller communities and many interesting out-of-the-way places are not so easy, or often impossible, to reach by public transport.

Private competition has thrown up some useful services, such as the many small shuttle buses which often pick up and drop off travellers at their accommodation.

Transport can be expensive, but discounts are almost always available. The rules for cheaper travel are: always assume a discount is available, book as far in advance as possible, and get yourself a discount card.

The most readily available discounts are for backpackers. Cards issued by backpacker associations, such as Youth Hostel Association (YHA), International Student Identity Cards (ISIC), VIP Backpackers Resorts International (VIP) and Budget Backpackers Hostels (BBH) cards, can bring reductions of around 30% to 50% on some services without prebooking.

This discount system disadvantages independent travellers. If you are not on a fixed schedule and don't want to be tied down by bookings, you'll end up paying more for transport. But flexibility has its advantages, and prebooked discount fares often have nasty penalty or no-refund clauses if you change your mind.

Flexibility and the ability to reach so many delightful places away from the tourist hordes make car travel the best way to see NZ. Competition between the many small rental car operators makes for cheap car hire, but beware of insurance policies. For stays of a couple of months or more, it is worth considering buying a car and reselling it when you leave. NZ is also very well set up for cyclists.

AIR

Flying can be a good option, particularly if you've already done the same journey by land. There are great views to be had, particularly over the mountains or volcanoes. And discounted flights can make flying in NZ quite economical.

Domestic Air Services

New Zealand's major domestic airlines are Air New Zealand (☎ 0800-737 000) and Ansett New Zealand (☎ 0800-803 146). With a host of connecting flights, the Air New Zealand network just about covers the country. Ansett's coverage is more limited but it, too, has many useful flights. Smaller airlines, such as Mt Cook Airline, Eagle Air and Air Nelson, are partly owned or booked by Air New Zealand and come under its 'Air New Zealand Link' umbrella.

Origin Pacific (☎ 0800-302 302) is a newcomer, with services to all major centres between Auckland and Christchurch. The company's comprehensive Web site is at www.originpacific.co.nz.

Apart from the major operators, there are many local and feeder airlines, such as Southern Air (between Invercargill and Stewart Island), Great Barrier Airlines and Air Chathams. Flights between the North and South Islands are a popular alternative to the ferry services (see under Getting There & Away for Wellington in the Wellington Region chapter).

Discount Fares

Air New Zealand, Ansett New Zealand and Origin Pacific have regular listed economy fares, but also discounts which make it virtually unnecessary to ever pay the full fare.

Some discounts apply for domestic tickets bought before arrival in NZ. Air New Zealand's Visit New Zealand fares, which can only be bought outside the country, offer a 15% discount from 1 October to 30 April and 25% during the other months. However, better discounts often apply to tickets bought in conjunction with an international flight (on any airline), depending on the country you are flying from; consult your travel agent.

AIR, BUS & TRAIN ROUTES

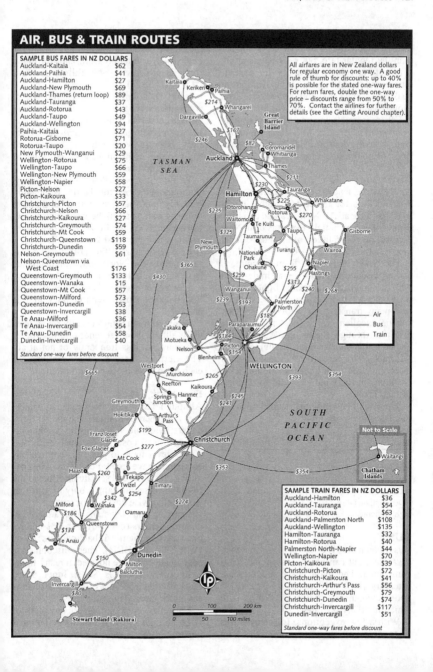

SAMPLE BUS FARES IN NZ DOLLARS

Auckland-Kaitaia	$62
Auckland-Paihia	$41
Auckland-Hamilton	$27
Auckland-New Plymouth	$69
Auckland-Thames (return loop)	$89
Auckland-Tauranga	$37
Auckland-Rotorua	$43
Auckland-Taupo	$49
Auckland-Wellington	$94
Paihia-Kaitaia	$27
Rotorua-Gisborne	$71
Rotorua-Taupo	$20
New Plymouth-Wanganui	$29
Wellington-Rotorua	$75
Wellington-Taupo	$66
Wellington-New Plymouth	$59
Wellington-Napier	$58
Picton-Nelson	$27
Picton-Kaikoura	$33
Christchurch-Picton	$57
Christchurch-Nelson	$66
Christchurch-Kaikoura	$27
Christchurch-Greymouth	$74
Christchurch-Mt Cook	$59
Christchurch-Queenstown	$118
Christchurch-Dunedin	$59
Nelson-Greymouth	$61
Nelson-Queenstown via West Coast	$176
Queenstown-Greymouth	$133
Queenstown-Wanaka	$15
Queenstown-Mt Cook	$57
Queenstown-Milford	$73
Queenstown-Dunedin	$53
Queenstown-Invercargill	$38
Te Anau-Milford	$36
Te Anau-Invercargill	$54
Te Anau-Dunedin	$58
Dunedin-Invercargill	$40

Standard one-way fares before discount

All airfares are in New Zealand dollars for regular economy one way. A good rule of thumb for discounts: up to 40% is possible for the stated one-way fares. For return fares, double the one-way price – discounts range from 50% to 70%. Contact the airlines for further details (see the Getting Around chapter).

Air
Bus
Train

SAMPLE TRAIN FARES IN NZ DOLLARS

Auckland-Hamilton	$36
Auckland-Tauranga	$54
Auckland-Rotorua	$63
Auckland-Palmerston North	$108
Auckland-Wellington	$135
Hamilton-Tauranga	$32
Hamilton-Rotorua	$40
Palmerston North-Napier	$44
Wellington-Napier	$70
Picton-Kaikoura	$39
Christchurch-Picton	$72
Christchurch-Kaikoura	$41
Christchurch-Arthur's Pass	$56
Christchurch-Greymouth	$79
Christchurch-Dunedin	$74
Christchurch-Invercargill	$117
Dunedin-Invercargill	$51

Standard one-way fares before discount

On the other hand, the various discount fares available in NZ are up to 50% cheaper than the regular fare, but restrictions apply – no-refund rules may apply for cancellations and the fares may not be available at peak times, such as school holidays, and on Monday morning commuter flights.

Other discounts and one-off specials may be available. Always ask about discounts when booking domestic tickets at airline offices, or go through a travel agent.

Air Passes

Air New Zealand offers an Explore New Zealand Pass for residents of other countries. Valid for all Air New Zealand and Link flights, it can be bought overseas or in New Zealand on presentation of an international ticket, but in NZ a 12.5% GST is added.

The tickets are in the form of coupons and represent one sector (ie, a single flight with just one flight number). Flights use between one and three coupons, depending on how many transfers are involved. The pass can be excellent value for long-distance, direct or through flights, eg, Auckland to Dunedin, but shorter hops involving transfers make it less attractive. Passes are issued in conjunction with an international ticket (with any airline) and are valid for the life of that ticket.

The cost of passes varies according to the number of coupons involved:

pass	price (NZ$)
three coupons	515
four coupons	686
five coupons	858
six coupons	1030
seven coupons	1201
eight coupons	1373

BUS

Bus travel in NZ is relatively easy and well organised, but can be expensive and time-consuming. The main bus companies are InterCity (☎ 09-913 6100, 03-379 9020) and Newmans (☎ 0800-777 707), with which InterCity operates.

With a few exceptions, InterCity buses go to almost all bigger towns and the main

tourist areas. Newmans operates only in the North Island, and schedules do not include the Northland region. The Northland route is covered by Northliner Express (☎ 09-307 5873).

InterCity's comprehensive Web site at www.intercitycoach.co.nz has information on fares and routes. Newmans' Web site at www.newmanscoach.co.nz and the Northliner Express Web site at www.nzinfo.com/northliner also have good coverage of timetables and fares.

White Star (☎ 06-358 8777) runs Wellington–Palmerston North–Wanganui–New Plymouth services with other connections, as well as a link between Nelson and Christchurch via the Lewis Pass, with connections to Picton and Westport.

Local operators offer more limited services. Both the North and South Islands have small shuttle services and there's also a network of backpackers buses (see the Backpackers Buses section later in this chapter).

Buses on main routes usually run at least daily, although on weekends on some routes they may run less frequently or not at all. The Getting There & Away sections for each town have more bus information.

Discount Fares

Although fares vary between companies, they are generally similar. Knowing the discounts available from various companies can cut travel costs by as much as 50% – you'll never have to pay full fare. All bus companies have free timetable booklets detailing discounts and schedules. Most of the following discounts apply only to trips that would otherwise cost $20 or more.

InterCity and Newmans offer a 30% discount to seniors (over 60) and 20% to anyone with recognised backpackers cards (VIP, YHA and BBH). These discounts are easy to get and have no special restrictions.

InterCity also has Saver/Super Saver fares offering a 30/50% discount. Discounts for return fares are usually 20%.

Cancellation penalties on any sort of fares are high – 50% if within two hours of departure time.

Travel Passes

The major bus lines offer discount travel passes valid from around 14 days to three months. InterCity, with the biggest network, has the most options. As with any unlimited travel passes, you have to do lots of travelling to make them pay. Book ahead on the buses to be sure of a seat.

InterCity, in conjunction with the Tranz Scenic rail network and the *Interislander* ferry (or the *Lynx* high-speed ferry at certain times), offers a Best of NZ pass covering bus/train/ferry travel. You have three points options (600 points for \$420/280 adults/children, 800 for \$544/365 and 1000 for \$659/442) and can purchase top-up points when you need them (100 points costs \$70/47).

A 1000-point ticket could include Auckland to Wellington by train and coach, the *Interislander* and a fair whack of the South Island by train (including the TransAlpine) and coach.

Air New Zealand offers a Best of NZ Plus Air option allowing one sector of air travel (it adds about \$250 to the costs given above).

The main travel passes (available at visitor information centres and bus depots) include:

InterCity Passes InterCity has numerous North Island passes including: Auckland–Wellington and all points between (\$99, children \$66); Auckland–Napier via Rotorua and the east coast (\$149/99); Auckland, Northland, Great Barrier Island, Rotorua, Taupo, Wellington (or Waitomo with return to Auckland, \$275/184); and Coromandel Busplan from Auckland with onward travel to Rotorua or return to Auckland (\$89/60). Its South Island passes include: Picton–Invercargill, or Queenstown and Te Anau (\$132/88); Queenstown to Nelson via the West Coast (\$125/84), and Christchurch to Milford via Queenstown and Mt Cook (\$132/88). Combo passes combine the various options for either island. Passes are usually valid for three months and reservations cost \$3 per sector (or check to see if stand-by seats are available).

Newmans Stopover Passes The North Island Auckland to Wellington or return pass (\$95) and South Island Christchurch to Queenstown via Milford Sound pass (\$129) do not allow backtracking.

Northliner Express This company offers discount backpackers passes for Northland which provide unlimited travel on various routes. The Bay of Islands (\$49), Northland Freedom (\$109) and Loop (\$79) passes are valid for one month from date of purchase.

Shuttle Buses

Small shuttle-bus companies offer useful services throughout the country. Typically these buses are smaller, cheaper and have a friendlier atmosphere than the regular large buses.

Some of these services are designed with foreign travellers and/or backpackers in mind and have lots of little extras that make them attractive: some will pick up and drop off at your accommodation or leave from central destinations.

Following are a few examples of the more useful or extensive services in New Zealand. North Island services are listed first:

Alpine Scenic Tours (☎ 07-386 8918) Services between Turangi and National Park, with useful stops for trampers in Tongariro National Park and extension services up to Taupo and Rotorua

Awesome Adventures & Top Bit (☎ 09-366 9830, ✉ enquires@kiwiex.co.nz) An opportunity to go right to the top of Northland from Auckland if you have limited time

Call-a-Bus (☎ 0800-100 550) From Auckland to Rotorua

Hot Water Beach Conxtions (☎ 06-866 2478) Whitianga to Hahei and Hot Water Beach on the Coromandel Peninsula

Little Kiwi Bus Co (☎ 0800-759 999) Auckland to Hamilton

Slim's East Cape Escape (☎ 09-366 9830, ✉ enquires@kiwiex.co.nz) A long-needed service which goes from Rotorua around East Cape (Monday, Wednesday and Friday)

Thermal Connection (aka Pink Bus; ☎ 0800-222 231) Taupo to Rotorua via Waimangu and Waiotapu thermal areas

Tranzit (☎ 06-355 5633) Palmerston North to Wellington via the Wairarapa

Waitomo Adventure Shuttle (☎ 0800-924 866) Auckland to Waitomo, Thursday to Monday

Waitomo Shuttle (☎ 0800-808 279) Otorohanga to Waitomo

Waitomo Wanderer (☎ 07-873 7559) Loops between Waitomo–Rotorua–Taupo

South Island shuttle bus companies include:

Alpine Coaches (☎ 0800-274 888) Christchurch–Hokitika/Greymouth via Arthur's Pass

Alpine Shuttles (☎ 03-443 7966) Services from Wanaka to Cardrona and Treble Cone skifields

Atomic Shuttles (☎ 03-322 8883) Daily services between Christchurch, Dunedin, Invercargill, Picton, Greymouth and Queenstown/Wanaka

Bottom Bus (☎ 03-442 7038) Dunedin to Invercargill via the scenic Catlins route, then on to Te Anau (with an option for Milford Sound), Queenstown and back to Dunedin

Catlins Coastal Link (☎ 03-474 3300, 03-214 6243) Follows the scenic route between Invercargill and Dunedin

Coast to Coast (☎ 0800-800 847) Christchurch–Hokitika/Greymouth via Arthur's Pass

Cook Connection (☎ 025-583 211) Mt Cook to Timaru and return on Monday, Wednesday and Saturday, and Mt Cook to Oamaru on Sunday, Tuesday and Friday

East Coast (☎ 0508-830 900) Christchurch to Picton and return daily

Hanmer Connection (☎ 0800-377 378) Daily from Hanmer to Christchurch and Kaikoura

High Country Shuttles (☎ 0800-435 050) Twizel to Mt Cook three times daily

Kahurangi Bus (☎ 0800-173 371) Services all the towns between Nelson and Collingwood, and the Abel Tasman and Heaphy Tracks

Karamea Express (☎ 03-782 6617) Westport to Karamea for the southern end of the Heaphy Track

Kiwi Discovery (☎ 0800-505 504) Queenstown to Milford and Fiordland/Aspiring walking tracks; also to Christchurch

Knightrider (☎ 03-217 0575) Dunedin to Invercargill via Gore

Lazerline (☎ 0800-220 001) Christchurch to Nelson via Lewis Pass daily

Nelson Lakes Transport (☎ 03-547 5912) Nelson to St Arnaud (for Nelson Lakes National Park)

Sounds to Coast (☎ 0800-802 225) Picton to Greymouth via St Arnaud (Monday, Wednesday and Friday)

Southern Link Shuttles (☎ 03-358 8355) Christchurch to Queenstown, Picton and Dunedin

Backpackers Buses

Bus companies which cater for backpackers sell passes lasting from several days to weeks for various parts of the country. In some places, notably the west coast of the South Island, these passes can be the best way to see the area, as hitchhiking is difficult and the more conventional bus services simply whiz past many of the most attractive spots. The passes offer a degree of flexibility, some more than others, allowing you to get off the bus for independent travel and then catch the next bus. In summer it can be difficult to get a seat on a crowded bus, so advance bookings are necessary.

The buses are comfortably fitted, their atmosphere is casual and there are plenty of sightseeing stops along the way, plus stops for walks, picnics, shopping and activities such as skydiving, bungy jumping and white-water rafting. The bus companies often get good discounts on activities for their passengers.

If you have limited time, can't be bothered arranging transport connections, want to see a number of spots en route and sample a wide variety of activities, these buses may be ideal. They are also a great way to meet like-minded people. Some travellers have come away disappointed because they mistakenly thought the backpackers buses were normal buses with just a few stops at scenic spots on the way.

Accommodation costs are extra; low-cost overnight accommodation is prebooked, usually at backpackers, with an option to camp if you have a tent.

The main companies are Kiwi Experience and Magic Bus. A few others run specialised routes with varying degrees of flexibility.

All companies have pamphlets detailing itineraries, departure times and costs; they require advance booking and usually a deposit. Be sure you understand the refund policy in case you decide to cancel. The main companies (and their routes, prices and details) include:

Flying Kiwi (☎ 0800-693 296, ✉ flying .kiwi@xtra.co.nz) Specialising in outdoor tours, Flying Kiwi's 'rolling travellers home' includes bunks, tents, hot shower and kitchen and carries mountain bikes, a Canadian canoe, a windsurfer, fishing gear and more. South Island trips include eight-day ($395) and 20-day ($890) trips. North Island options include nine-day comprehensive ($445) and two-day Northern Express ($99) trips. A 27-day, all-NZ tour costs from $1125.

Kiwi Experience This comprehensive service operates on the North and South Islands, offering 17 routes, with from one to 25 days being the minimum period allowed to complete a particular route; most passes are valid for six months. Trips include: North Island Loop ($265, seven-day minimum) or South Island Loop ($360, eight-day minimum); all-NZ tours ($470 to $615, from a minimum 12 to 18 days); and the Whole Kit & Caboodle trip ($925, minimum 25 days). Useful small loops where other services are limited include Awesome Adventures & Top Bit around Northland, the Bottom Bus along the Catlins and Southern Scenic Route, East Cape Escape, Milford Sound Overland Adventure and the Ghost Train which includes the *Tranz-Alpine* ($310). For reservations contact Auckland (☎ 09-366 9830, ✉ enquires@kiwiex.co.nz) or Sydney, Australia (☎ 02-9368 1766).

Magic Bus (☎ 09-358 5600, ✉ info@magicbus .co.nz) Affiliated with InterCity buses, Magic Bus operates on the North and South Islands. Its network is extensive but does not include Northland. It has all-NZ tours for 12/14/16-day minimums ($419/423/529).

West Coast Express (☎ 03-546 5007) A six-day Nelson to Queenstown route via the West Coast costs $115; you can depart from either end of the line. West Coast has a Web site at www .WestCoastExpress.co.nz.

TRAIN

New Zealand's privately owned rail network covers just a few main routes: Auckland–Rotorua/Tauranga/Wellington, Wellington–Napier, Picton–Christchurch and Christchurch–Greymouth/Invercargill. There are more details on these routes in the relevant regional chapters. The Tranz Scenic fares and timetables booklet is available at most train stations and visitor centres.

New Zealand trains are modern and comfortable, and the elimination of many smaller halts has made train travel reasonably speedy, usually a little quicker than the buses. Some routes are scenic and trains are certainly more comfortable than buses, but train travel is expensive unless you can get a big discount.

Tranz Scenic has a nationwide central reservations centre (☎ 0800-802 802) which is open from 7 am to 9 pm daily (from overseas call ☎ 64-4-498 3303). Reservations can also be made at most train stations, travel agents and information centres. Its Web site is at www.tranzrail.co.nz.

As with the buses, there are discounts for trains. YHA and VIP card holders get a 30% discount, students 20%, seniors 30% and disabled travellers 50%. A limited number of other discounted seats are set aside on each train – advance booking is required. Discount fares are: Super Saver (50% discount), Saver (30%) and Economy Fare (15%).

For information on the three-in-one Best of NZ travel pass (rail/ferry/bus), see the Bus section earlier in this chapter.

CAR & MOTORCYCLE

Driving around NZ is quite easy: distances between towns are short, traffic is light and the roads are usually in good condition. Petrol (gasoline) is expensive at about $0.95 a litre (around $4 a US gallon); prices vary slightly from station to station and from city to countryside, but only by a few cents.

Driver courtesy is reasonably good in the towns, except for perhaps Auckland, but the highways are full of cowboys. Driving 20km/h over the speed limit and aggressive tailgating are common, despite the forever twisting and narrow roads. Autobahns don't exist: apart from the occasional overtaking lane, highways are single lane in either direction and pass through the towns. Traffic is generally light, but it is easy to get stuck behind a truck or campervan. Count on covering about 80km for every hour of driving on the highways.

Unsealed, backcountry roads are another hazard for the uninitiated. Many visitors lose control by moving onto the loose gravel verges and skidding into ditches.

Kiwis drive on the left, as in the UK, Australia, Japan and much of Asia. For those used to driving on the right – take care. Every year almost 100 serious or fatal accidents involve foreign drivers, many of them driving on the wrong side of the road.

A 'give way to the right' rule applies. This is interpreted in a rather strange fashion when you're turning left and an oncoming vehicle is turning right into the same street. Since the oncoming vehicle is then on your right you have to give way to it.

Speed limits on the open road are generally 100km/h; in built-up areas the limit is usually 50km/h. An LSZ sign stands for Limited Speed Zone, which means that the speed limit is 50km/h (although the speed limit in that zone is normally 100km/h) when conditions are unsafe due to bad weather, limited visibility, pedestrians, cyclists or animals on the road, excessive traffic, or poor road conditions. At one-way bridges, a red arrow pointing in your direction of travel means that *you* give way.

Pick up a copy of *The Road Code,* a wise investment that will tell you all you need to know. It's available at NZ Automobile Association (AA; ☎ 0800-500 444) offices and bookshops. There is a similar book for motorcyclists.

A valid, unrestricted driver's licence from your home country is required to rent and drive a car in NZ. The AA staff can advise if you wish to obtain an NZ driver's licence. To drive a motorcycle you must have a motorcycle licence or special endorsement on your home-country driver's licence.

Excellent road maps are readily available in NZ, and good maps are essential for exploring off the highways where signposting is not always good. The best of the lot are AA's 1:350,000 district maps ($3.50, free to members).

Members of an equivalent automobile association overseas may qualify for reciprocal benefits from the AA in NZ; remember to bring your card. Otherwise AA membership is good insurance if you buy a car. Apart from free maps and publications, membership entitles you to free emergency breakdown service, free advice on traffic tickets and accidents, and discounts on services/accommodation.

Theft from cars is a problem in NZ, particularly at isolated parking areas at scenic spots and walks. The North Island tends to be worse than the South Island, but wherever you park, don't leave valuables in the car and hide your gear if you can't take it with you.

House Trucks

When you're travelling around NZ, watch out for colourful and exotic house trucks. These individually built constructions look like a collision between an elderly truck and a timber cottage, sometimes complete with shingle roof and bay windows. Many of these uniquely Kiwi contraptions look far too fragile for road use, but seem to travel all over the country and are often parked for days or even months in the most idyllic settings.

Rental

Car Usually you must be at least 21 years old to rent a car in NZ (sometimes 25) and under 25s often incur a larger insurance excess.

The major car hire companies offer new cars, countrywide networks, more reliability, better insurance and high prices. The many smaller companies are much cheaper, have mostly older cars, and contracts and insurance policies have to be looked at closely.

Because rental car accidents (usually minor) are so common in NZ, insurance premiums are very high. Bigger companies will remove the excess for around $10 a day extra, but smaller operators offering cheap rates often have a compulsory insurance excess of around $700. Insurance coverage for all hire cars is invalid on certain roads, typically beaches and unsealed roads in major tourist areas.

The big operators – Avis, Budget, Hertz – have extensive fleets of cars with offices in most towns and at major airports, and current contact details can be found in the *Yellow Pages.* Unlimited kilometres rental of a small car (a late-model Japanese car of 1600cc or less) starts at around $70 per day, more for rental of only a few days. For driving around town without an unlimited kilometres option, expect to pay about $0.30 a kilometre. Medium-sized cars are typically around $100 per day with unlimited kilometres. A drop-off fee applies if you're not returning the car to the city of hire. Overseas travel agents can often get better deals in hiring new cars through major operators than you can hunt out yourself in NZ.

A huge number of smaller companies undercut the big operators, but there may be more restrictions on use and one-way rentals may not always be possible. Some budget operators, such as Pegasus (☎ 0800-803 580) and Shoestring (☎ 0800-746 378) have national networks. Pegasus has a Web site at www.rentalcars.co.nz.

Car rental is competitive in the major cities, but Auckland is the cheapest place to rent a car. The surplus of operators means that you can often get special deals for longer rentals, especially outside the peak summer months. Shop around by phone – quoting a competitor's rates may bring a reduction, even from the major companies. In peak season you may get a good, reasonably current model for $55 a day (all inclusive) for rentals of more than four days, while in off-peak periods the cost may drop to $45.

Many smaller operators have old second-hand cars, advertised for as little as $25 per day, but you get what you pay for. Advertised rates (and even quotes over the phone) are often misleading, and business practices can leave a lot to be desired. Always check kilometre rates, if the price includes GST, minimum hire periods, the age of the car, bonds and insurance coverage. Always read the rental agreement before you sign.

Rock-bottom rates usually apply to minimum one-month hire in the off season for a beat-up car over 10 years old with limited or even no insurance. Full payment in advance and a credit-card bond is usually required. Insurance from the cheaper rental agencies is usually subject to a $700 excess for any accident or damage to the car (some even include tyre replacement and puncture repairs), even if it is not your fault. Most, however, will cash your bond but refund it later if the other driver's blame can be proved and they have insurance (don't count on it).

If you are prepared to risk the insurance excess, second-hand car hire can be good value. By shopping around, you can hire a 10-year-old Japanese import for a month in the off season for as little as $30 a day or a more recent model for $40 a day (sometimes less). Prices are up to 50% higher in the peak season and also higher outside Auckland.

Smaller operators include A2B Rentals (☎ 0800-222 929), 11 Stanley St, Parnell, Auckland; Ace Tourist Rentals (☎ 0800-422 771) in Auckland and Christchurch; About New Zealand Rental Cars (☎ 0800-455 565); ARF (☎ 0508-112 233, @ arf@world-net .co.nz); Rent-a-Dent (☎ 0800-736 823) in Auckland and Christchurch; Avon Percy (☎ 0800-7368 2866) in Christchurch and Auckland; Scotties (☎ 0800-736 825) in Christchurch; and Dollar Save (☎ 0800-127 231) in Auckland.

Campervan Campervans (also known as mobile homes, motor homes or, in US parlance, Winnebago's or RVs) are an enormously popular way of getting around NZ. In tourist areas of the South Island almost every other vehicle seems to be a campervan. Campervans combine transport and accommodation in one neat package and you've also got your own kitchen on wheels.

Many companies rent out campervans and their costs vary with the type of vehicle and the time of year. A small van, suitable for two people, typically has a sink, hot and cold water, gas cooker, 12V fridge and 240V heater. The dining table and seats fold down to form a double bed. Usually they are of minivan size with a 2L unleaded petrol engine, and are easy to drive, manoeuvrable around town and have enough pep for the hills. Slightly larger varieties may have their own toilets and showers. Others may be kitted-out kombi vans or 4WDs, or even station wagons with pop-up tents fitted on top.

Four- to six-berth campervans are of light-truck size and usually contain the works. They are very comfortable, with an extra double sleeping cabin at the front, microwave, toilet, shower etc. Fuel consumption is about the same as for the smaller vans but they may run on much cheaper diesel fuel. The only drawback is their size – they're not much fun to drive in the cities and sluggish on the hills. They are high (around 3.3m), so the top is easily scraped by the inexperienced, especially on signs or verandas when parking on the camber of a road.

Campervans usually have 240V AC power systems (just plug them in at a motor camp) with backup 12V DC systems, so you can still camp in luxury out in the wild or at basic camp sites. Dispose of waste water properly; toilets must be emptied at designated dumping stations, found at motor camps or provided by some councils.

Usual rates through the main companies for two/four/six-berth vans are around $150/220/250 a day, dropping to $90/130/150 in winter (May to September) and slightly less again for more than three weeks' hire. But price wars have seen rates drop to as low as $65 a day for a four-berth van. Overseas travel agents can also get good discounts.

Maui (☎ 0800-651 080) and Britz (☎ 0800-831 900) are two of the biggest operators. Others include Kea Campers (☎ 0800-404 888) and Adventure Rentals (☎ 09-256 0255) in Auckland, and Avon Campervans (☎ 03-379 3822, 09-275 3034) and Backpacker Campervans (☎ 03-358 8300, 09-275 0200) in Christchurch and Auckland. Smaller operators' rates start at around $40 per day for kitted-out minivans.

Motorcycle It's also possible to hire a motorcycle for touring in NZ. Most of the country's motorcycle hire shops are in Auckland, but Christchurch has a few too. You can hire anything from a little 50cc moped (nifty-fifty) for zipping around town to a big 750cc touring motorcycle.

Remember you will need a motorcycle licence; a car licence will get you by if you want to tootle around on a moped, but to hire a regular motorcycle (rental bikes are usually from 250cc to 750cc) you need a motorcycle licence.

NZ Motorcycle Rentals (☎ 09-377 2005, @ info@nzbike.com), 31 Beach Rd, Auckland, has Yamahas, BMWs, touring and enduro bikes. It also has a buy-back option. Other possibilities are Bike Adventure (☎ 0800-498 600, @ info@banz.co.nz) and Crosby Red Baron Motorcycles (☎ 09-376 3320), 299 Great North Rd, Grey Lynn.

Purchase

Car For a longer stay and/or for groups, buying a car and then selling it at the end of your travels can be one of the cheapest and best ways to see NZ: you're not tied to the bus schedules or forced to wait on the side of the road for a lift.

Auckland, as the largest city and main gateway to NZ, is the easiest place to buy a car. Christchurch is the next best for overseas visitors. One of the easiest ways to buy a cheap car is to scour the notice boards of backpackers places, where other travellers sell their cars before moving on. You can pick up an old car for only a few hundred dollars. Some backpackers specials are so cheap it may be worth taking the risk that they will finally die on you.

Otherwise, cars are advertised in the newspapers just like anywhere else in the world. Auckland also has a number of popular auctions and car fairs, where people bring their cars to sell (see the Auckland chapter). These events have lots of cars from around $1000 to $4500. The cars sold at these are older, cheap cars. A good, later model used car from a dealer may start at around $8000. Cheap, Japanese secondhand imports, shipped to NZ, are numerous and getting spares is not a problem. The cheapest prices are generally at the auctions and the next-cheapest prices are at the car fairs, where you have more time to browse.

Another option is the 'buy-back system', where the dealer guarantees to buy the car back from you at the end of your travels. The buy-back amount varies, but may be 50% less than the purchase price. Hiring or buying and selling it yourself is usually much better value.

Make sure any car you buy has a WOF (Warrant of Fitness) and that the registration lasts for a reasonable period. A WOF certificate, proving that the car is roadworthy, is valid for six months but must be less than 28 days old when you buy a car. To transfer registration, both you and the seller fill out a form which can be filed at any post office. Papers are sent by mail within 10 days. It is the seller's responsibility to transfer ownership and pay the costs involved. If needed, registration can be purchased for either six months or a year (around $200 per year). Third-party insurance, covering the cost of repairs to another vehicle in an accident that is your fault, is also a wise investment.

Car inspections are highly recommended and the cost may well save you in repair bills later. Various car inspection services will check any car you intend to buy for around $85. They stand by at car fairs and auctions for on-the-spot inspections, or will come to you. The AA also offers a mobile inspection service – it is slightly cheaper if you bring the car to an AA-approved mechanic. AA checks are thorough, but most garages will look over the car for less.

Another wise precaution before you buy a car is to ring for a credit check (☎ 0800-658 934). With the licence plate and chassis numbers, the ownership of the car can be confirmed and you can find out if any outstanding debts are owed on it.

BICYCLE

Touring cyclists are almost everywhere in NZ, especially in summer. Hills make for hard going at times, but it's a compact country with plenty of variety. Many cyclists call NZ a cyclists' paradise – it's clean, green, uncrowded, friendly, there are numerous camping options and cheap accommodation, plenty of fresh water, the climate is not too hot or too cold, the roads are good, and bikes and cycling gear (to rent or buy) are readily available, as are bicycle repair services.

And remember, the law states that you must wear an approved safety helmet (or risk a fine).

Lonely Planet's up-to-date *Cycling New Zealand Guide* has all the tips and route descriptions a cyclist needs. The excellent *Pedallers' Paradise* booklets by Nigel Rushton cover the North and South Islands, and include city maps and elevation profiles of the routes.

Classic New Zealand Mountain Bike Rides by the Kennett brothers, Paul, Simon and Jonathan, suggests a wide variety of short and long rides all over NZ.

Occasionally a cyclist may resort to public transport. The major bus lines and trains only take bicycles on a 'space available' basis (meaning bikes may not be allowed on) and charge up to $10. Some of the shuttle or backpackers buses, on the other hand, make sure they always have storage space for bikes and often carry them for free.

Many international airlines will carry your bicycle at no additional cost as 'sporting equipment'. Except on the smallest planes, domestic airlines take bicycles for $20.

Adventure South (☎ 03-332 1222) has back-road cycle tours in the South Island.

Pedaltours NZ (☎ 09-302 0968, ✉ info@pedaltours.co.nz) has a variety of guided bicycle tours throughout NZ.

Rental

Many bicycle rental operators offer daily and weekly bicycle hire, with negotiable monthly rates. Bicycle rental is listed in the Getting Around sections of cities and towns in this book. Costs vary widely – rates can be anywhere from around $12 to $25 a day, from $55 to $125 a week and from around $135 to $350 a month. They depend on what kind of bike you get and where you get it from. Most rental companies also offer bicycle touring gear and repair kits.

Purchase

Bicycles can be readily bought in NZ, but prices are high for new bikes. You're better off bringing one with you or buying a used one. Backpackers notice boards frequently have signs offering mountain bikes for sale, or check newspaper ads.

HITCHING

Hitching is never entirely safe in any country in the world, and we cannot recommend it. Travellers who decide to hitch should understand that they are taking a small but potentially serious risk. People who do choose to hitch will be safer if they travel in pairs and let someone know where they are planning to go. The well-publicised murder of two Swedish hitchhikers a few years ago highlights the fact that even in relatively safe NZ hitchhiking can be a risky undertaking.

That said, NZ is a great place for hitching, and although almost anybody who does a fair amount of hitching will get stuck somewhere uncomfortable for an uncomfortably long time, most travellers rate it highly. It's pretty safe and the roads are not crowded, but there are just enough cars to make things fairly easy and the locals are well disposed towards hitchhikers.

Hitching on the main North Island routes is generally good. In the South Island hitching down the east coast from Picton through Christchurch to Invercargill is mostly good. Elsewhere in the South Island, hundreds of kilometres of main roads have very little traffic. Expect long waits – even days – in some places. If it gets too much (eg, you find yourself hurling abuse at drivers who don't stop), catch a bus, but you may have to get into the next town first.

It's easier hitching alone if you are male. Unfortunately, even though NZ is basically a safe country for women, a woman on her own may experience some tricky – if not dangerous – situations. It is better to hitch with someone else if possible. Many backpackers places have local hints for hitching (such as what bus to get out of town and where to hitch from) on their notice boards. We have added tips where they are relevant.

BOAT
Inter-island Ferries
The *Interislander, Lynx* and *Top Cat* services, operating between Wellington in the North Island and Picton in the South Island, are covered in the Wellington Region chapter.

Other regularly scheduled inter-island ferry services include those to the various islands off Auckland (see the Auckland chapter). A ferry also connects Stewart Island with the South Island at Bluff, near Invercargill.

Other Water Transport
Transport can be more convenient by water than by land, especially in the Marlborough Sounds where many places to stay can only be reached by water. Regular launch and water-taxi services also operate along the coast of Abel Tasman National Park.

Other convenient ferry services include the ferries in the Bay of Islands, such as the Russell-Paihia passenger ferry and the car ferry crossing over from Opua. On the west side of Northland is the convenient car ferry from Rawene to Kohukohu.

In other places, such as Wakatipu, Taupo and Waikaremoana, transport over lakes is a good way to get around and see things. Sometimes the most interesting sights are reached by water rather than by land; cruises on Milford and Doubtful Sounds in Fiordland in the South Island and on the Bay of Islands in Northland are especially popular.

LOCAL TRANSPORT
Bus & Train
Most of the urban buses have been privatised and only operate on profitable runs, ie, hardly at all. Larger cities have bus services but, with a few honourable exceptions, they are mainly daytime, weekday operations and departures are infrequent. On weekends, particularly on Sunday, bus services can be hard to find or stop altogether.

The only city with a good suburban train service is Wellington.

Taxi
The main cities have plenty of taxis and even small towns may have a local service. Taxis cruise the busy areas in Auckland, Wellington and Christchurch, but otherwise you usually either have to phone for one or go to a taxi rank.

ORGANISED TOURS
Tours can sometimes be a useful way of getting around, especially in otherwise hard-to-reach areas, when your time is limited or when you want the benefit of commentary.

Backpackers often use the 'alternative' buses as a sort of informal tour (see Backpackers Buses under Bus earlier in this chapter).

New Zealand Nature Safaris (☎ 0800-697 232) has tours with an emphasis on wildlife, wilderness areas, walks and small groups. A North Island safari, the West Coast Wilderness and Secret South tours are all 10 days and cost $850. Food and accommodation (camping, cabins etc) cost extra. For more information go to the Web site at www.nzsafaris.co.nz.

Otherwise there is a variety of more conventional tours. Thrifty Tours (☎ 09-478 3550) is indeed thrifty, using a combination of tour buses and public transport to create a variety of short and long tours all over NZ. Its Web site is at www.tourmasters.co.nz.

Great Sights (☎ 0800-744 487) and Best Deal Sights (☎ 09-836 6337, ✆ nzsights @pop.ihug.co.nz) are other major tour operators, offering different one-day tours in various cities and towns, plus intercity tours. Great Sights has a Web site at www.new-zealand.com/GreatSights. All of these are major companies which can be contacted through virtually any travel agent or visitor information centre in NZ, or through travel agents or the New Zealand Tourism Board (NZTB) before you arrive in the country.

Specific, worthy and interesting tours (some several days long) are listed in the regional chapters under the towns from where they depart.

Bushwise Women (☎ 03-332 4952) specialises in trips for women only. The trips range from working on conservation projects to tramping and kayaking, but all provide a good opportunity to meet other women travellers. There's a Web site at www.bushwise.co.nz.

NORTH ISLAND

Auckland

☎ 09 • pop 1.1 million

The name Auckland (in Maori: 'Tamaki Makaurau') refers both to a region, stretching roughly from the Bombay Hills in the south to the towns of Wellsford and Warkworth in the north, and to a city, nestled between the Waitemata and Manukau Harbours.

Administratively, Auckland city consists of four cities and three districts, which form one vast urban sprawl. Auckland City proper lies between Waitemata and Manukau Harbours. North Shore City, centred on Takapuna, is just over the harbour bridge. Manukau City is to the south of Auckland, around the airport, and Waitakere City is to the west. Rodney District is on the North Shore and borders the Kaipara Harbour; Papakura and Franklin Districts are south of Manukau City. Some 30% of New Zealand's population calls the Auckland region home.

Auckland is one of the world's most exciting waterside cities. A mere stroll down its main artery, Queen St, is not enough. You have to explore its heart – the magnificent harbour. Auckland has lots of enthusiastic yachties; it's very much the 'the City of Sails' and was the site of the America's Cup defence in 2000, which breathed new life into the viaduct area.

Auckland is surrounded by water and covered in volcanic hills, replete with *pa* (fortified Maori villages). So many islanders from NZ's Pacific neighbours have moved to Auckland that it now has the largest concentration of Polynesians in the world. More recently it has attracted immigrants from Asia. These foreign influences help give Auckland a much more cosmopolitan feel than other NZ cities.

The main entry point for international visitors, Auckland also has a wide range of accommodation and entertainment.

History

Maori settlement in the Auckland area dates back at least 800 years. Initial settlements were concentrated on the coastal regions of

HIGHLIGHTS

- Cruising the Waitemata Harbour
- Exploring the cultural, historical and natural exhibitions at Auckland War Memorial Museum
- Strolling and dining in inner-city suburbs
- Tripping to historical Devonport on the ferry
- Discovering the islands of the Hauraki Gulf, particularly volcanic Rangitoto, island-suburb Waiheke and the wild Great Barrier
- Walking through the rugged forest of the Waitakeres
- Touring and tasting at West Auckland wineries

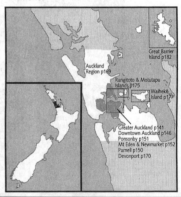

Great Barrier Island p182
Auckland Region p169
Rangitoto & Motutapu Islands p175
Waiheke Island p177
Greater Auckland p141
Downtown Auckland p146
Ponsonby p151
Mt Eden & Newmarket p152
Parnell p150
Devonport p170

the Hauraki Gulf islands, but gradually the fertile isthmus became settled and land was cleared for gardens. From the 17th century tribes from outside the region challenged the local Ngati Whatua tribe for this desirable place. The locals in response built fortified villages or pa on Auckland's numerous volcanic cones. But when the first Europeans arrived in the area in the 1830s they reported a land largely devoid of inhabitants. The Auckland isthmus (Tamaki Makaurau – literally, 'Tamaki Desired by

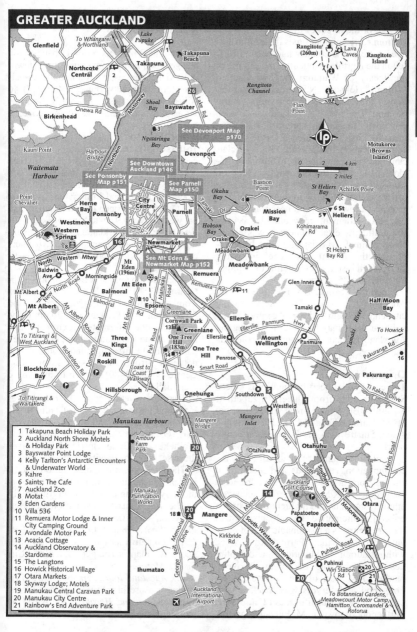

GREATER AUCKLAND

1 Takapuna Beach Holiday Park
2 Auckland North Shore Motels & Holiday Park
3 Bayswater Point Lodge
4 Kelly Tarlton's Antarctic Encounters & Underwater World
5 Kahre
6 Saints; The Cafe
7 Auckland Zoo
8 Motat
9 Eden Gardens
10 Villa 536
11 Remuera Motor Lodge & Inner City Camping Ground
12 Avondale Motor Park
13 Acacia Cottage
14 Auckland Observatory & Stardome
15 The Langtons
16 Howick Historical Village
17 Otara Markets
18 Skyway Lodge; Motels
19 Manukau Central Caravan Park
20 Manukau City Centre
21 Rainbow's End Adventure Park

Many') had largely been forsaken, ravaged by war, or the threat of it.

From early colonial times the administrative centre of the country had been at Russell in the Northland, but after the signing of the Treaty of Waitangi in 1840 Captain William Hobson, NZ's first governor, moved the capital south to a more central position. The site of Auckland was chosen principally for its fine harbour (Waitemata, meaning 'Sparkling Waters'), fertile soil and central location. In September 1840 officials came down from Russell to formally proclaim Auckland the NZ capital. Hobson named the settlement after his commanding officer George Eden (Lord Auckland). At first just a few tents on a beach at Official Bay, the settlement grew quickly. Twenty years after its establishment it was extensively farmed, with its port kept busy exporting the region's produce, including kauri. Yet it lost its capital status to Wellington after just 25 years.

Since the beginning of the 20th century Auckland has been NZ's fastest-growing city and its main industrial centre. While political deals may be done in Wellington, Auckland remains the dominant commercial centre.

Orientation

The commercial heart of the city is Queen St, which runs from Queen Elizabeth II Square (QEII Square) near the waterfront up to Karangahape Rd (K Rd), passing Aotea Square with the information centre nearby.

While the commercial district has accommodation, restaurants and nightlife, it suffers from the 'dead heart' syndrome of many cities. K Rd, with its artists' enclaves, ethnic restaurants and nightclubs is a lively, bohemian alternative. Parnell, just east of the city centre, is a fashionable area of renovated wooden villas. Parnell Rd is lined with restaurants and boutiques, and continues to fashionable Broadway in Newmarket. Just west of the city centre are Ponsonby and Jervois Rds, packed with cafes and bars. But life doesn't stop here. Further out of town, in Mt Eden, Kingsland,

Takapuna and the eastern beaches, are more restaurants and cafes.

Maps The Minimap series is handy. You can get good maps from either of the downtown visitor centres, the Automobile Association (AA), Specialty Maps (☎ 307 2217), 46 Albert St, and bookshops. Jason's has a free series of *Official Auckland Region* guides.

Information

Tourist Offices There are two visitor centres in downtown Auckland: Tourism Auckland (☎ 979 2333, fax 979 2334, ✉ visitor@auckland.tourism.co.nz) is at the Auckland Travel and Information Centre at 287 Queen St. It's open from 8.30 am to 5.30 pm weekdays and 9 am to 5 pm weekends. Its Web site is www.aucklandnz.com and bookings for transport, accommodation or tours can be made via email (✉ reservations@aucklandnz.com).

Also downtown, the New Zealand Visitor Centre (☎ 979 7005, ✉ nzvc@aucklandnz.com), near the corner of Quay and Hobson Sts, is open from 9.30 am to 5.30 pm daily.

The Visitor Information Centre (☎ 275 6467), at the international airport, is open daily from the first flight to the last. At the domestic airport, the Visitor Information Centre (☎ 256 8480) is open from 7 am to 7 pm daily.

There are several regional tourism offices including the Arataki Visitor Centre in the Waitakere Ranges, and centres at Devonport, Orewa on the Hibiscus Coast, and Waiheke and Great Barrier Islands (see those sections for details).

The Department of Conservation (DOC) has an information centre (☎ 379 6476) at the ferry building in downtown Auckland.

The free tourist information booklets *Auckland A-Z Visitors Guide,* Jason's *Auckland – What's On* and *Auckland Great Time Guide* contain maps of the city. Another good free map is Budget's *Auckland City Visitor Map.*

The *Auckland Tourist Times: What's Happening* is a useful free weekly for visitors. The *New Zealand Herald* is the Auckland morning daily.

The Automobile Association (AA; ☎ 377 4660) is at 99 Albert St. Members of an overseas auto club have reciprocal rights, and it has accommodation directories and excellent maps. The office is open from 8.30 am to 5 pm on weekdays and 9 am to 3 pm Saturday.

Money The Bank of New Zealand branch at the airport is open for all international arrivals and departures.

Queen St has plenty of moneychangers, and banks open from around 9 am to 4.30 pm weekdays. The exchange rates offered are similar but it pays to shop around. Thomas Cook has bureaux de change on Queen St, near Customs St and near Shortland St. The Amex Travel Services office (☎ 379 8286) is at 105 Queen St. For after-hours transactions, a Thomas Cook automatic note-changing machine operates 24 hours outside the Downtown Airline Terminal on Quay St. Inforex (☎ 302 3066), at the ferry building on Quay St, changes money from 8 am to 8 pm daily, but its rates are not as good as those offered at banks.

Post Poste restante (general delivery) is held at the main post shop in the Bledisloe building on Wellesley St West, near the corner of Queen St. There are several NZ post shops throughout the city – office hours are from 9 am to 5 pm weekdays.

Email & Internet Access Rates vary slightly from place to place, but generally expect to pay from $10 an hour. Internet cafes include:

Citinet Cybercafe (☎ 377 3674) Shop 4, 115 Queen St
Cybercafe@MacJava (☎ 377 8082) 268 K Rd
Cyber City (☎ 303 3009) 29 Victoria St
Live Wire (☎ 356 0999) Level 1, Mid City, 239 Queen St
Login 1 (☎ 522 9303) 1st floor, Rialto Centre, 153 Broadway, Newmarket
Netcafe (☎ 358 4874) Auckland Central Backpackers, 9 Fort St
Net Central Cafe (☎ 373 5186) 4 Lorne St
NZ Phone & Email Centre (☎ 358 3000) 1 Queen St (QEII Square)

Internet Resources The following sites are useful for tracking down information about Auckland:

Auckland City Council A guide to Auckland City proper
www.akcity.govt.nz
Auckland Live Gig guide, events guide, activities and exhibitions
www.aucklandlive.co.nz
Auckland Regional Council Facts and information about Auckland's environment parks and transport
www.arc.govt.nz
Manukau City
www.manukau.govt.nz
North Shore City
www.nscc.govt.nz
Out & About For restaurant listings, what to do and local events
www.outandabout.co.nz
Tourism Auckland An excellent site for anything to do with Auckland
www.aucklandnz.com
Waitakere City
www.waitakere.govt.nz

Travel Agencies For international air tickets, try STA Travel (☎ 309 0458), 10 High St, and Flight Centre (☎ 309 6171, 377 4655). Both have several offices in Auckland.

Backpacker travel centres offer good deals and discounts on activities, but remember if activities are cancelled you may have to return to Auckland to collect your refund. The biggest is Auckland Central Travel (☎ 358 4874) in Auckland Central Backpackers, 9 Fort St. Others include USIT Beyond Travel (☎ 379 3280), at 18 Shortland St, and Independent Travel Services (☎ 303 3442), in the Central City Backpackers at 26 Lorne St.

Bookshops Whitcoulls on the corner of Queen and Victoria Sts is a huge bookshop with good sections on NZ, travel and fiction. The US chain Borders has a store next to the Force Entertainment Centre in Queen St. Unity Books at 19 High St has an excellent selection of fiction and nonfiction. Parsons Bookshop, on the corner of Lorne and Wellesley Sts, specialises in books on art and culture.

Auckland has many second-hand book-shops (look in the *Yellow Pages* directory). Among the best is the Hard to Find (But Worth the Effort) Secondhand Bookshop at 171–73 The Mall, Onehunga. There's a branch in Victoria Rd, Devonport.

Libraries The Central City Library(☎ 377 0209) is at 44–46 Lorne St. It's open from 9.30 am to 8 pm Monday to Thursday, until 9 pm Friday and from 10 am to 4 pm Saturday.

Cultural Centres Alliance Française d'Auckland (☎ 376 009) is at 9 Kirk St, Grey Lynn.

Laundry Most hostels and of course all hotels have laundry services. However, a convenient laundry at 18 Fort St is open from 8.30 am to 7 pm Monday to Friday and 9 am to 5 pm Saturday.

Medical Services Vaccinations for on-ward travel are available at the Traveller's Medical and Vaccination Centre (TMVC; ☎ 373 3531, fax 373 3732), Level 1, Canterbury Arcade (off Queen St); Travel-care (☎ 373 4621), 5th floor, Dingwall building, 87 Queen St; and Traveller's Health & Vaccination Centre (☎ 520 5830), 21 Remuera Rd, Newmarket.

Public hospitals, such as Auckland Hospital (☎ 379 7440), Park Rd, Grafton, Middlemore Hospital (☎ 270 4799), Hospital Rd, Otahuhu, and North Shore Hospital (☎ 486 1491), Shakespeare Rd, Takapuna, have accident and emergency clinics. There are also many private accident and emergency clinics. See the *White Pages* telephone directory under 'Hospitals' and other health service providers for contact details.

For information on HIV/AIDS call the AIDS hotline on ☎ 358 0099.

Gay & Lesbian The Out! Bookshop (☎ 377 7770) at 45 Anzac Ave and the Pride Centre (☎ 302 0590) at 33 Wyndham St are good contact points for the gay and lesbian community. *Out!* is NZ's leading gay magazine, with a complete guide to gay Auckland.

Auckland hosts the very popular HERO Festival every February.

See Entertainment later in this chapter for gay-friendly venues and see the Facts for the Visitor chapter for gay and lesbian organisations in NZ.

Emergency In the case of an emergency, the police can be contacted on ☎ 111. For medical emergencies see the Medical Services section earlier.

Skytower

The imposing Skytower on the corner of Federal and Victoria Sts is part of the Sky City complex – a 24-hour casino with revolving restaurant, cafes, bars and its own Web site at www.skycity.co.nz. It is NZ's tallest structure at 328m (and bigger than the Eiffel Tower). A lift takes you from the ground up to the observation decks in 40 seconds and in a 200km/h wind the top of the building sways up to 1m. Catching the skyway lift costs $15 ($3 extra to go to the ultimate viewing level); the spectacular views are well worth the extra $3.

New Zealand National Maritime Museum

This museum (☎ 373 0800) on the downtown waterfront is dedicated to one of NZ's national obsessions – sailing. This extensive museum explores 1000 years of NZ's seafaring history. Dozens of sailing craft and displays are exhibited, including the huge 25m (76ft) outrigger canoe *Taratai* that navigator Jim Siers constructed using 1000-year-old methods and sailed across the Pacific. Outside is *KZ1*, the 1988 America's Cup challenger.

Other exhibits illuminate the Maori and European discoveries of and migrations to NZ. There's even a re-creation of an old immigrant ship, complete with swaying movement and creaking floorboards. There are exhibits on navigation, fishing, oral history and even a NZ seaside dairy, not to mention the Hall of NZ Yachting, and the world's first jet-boat (the Hamilton

A bird's-eye view from the Skytower over Auckland Harbour with volcanic Rangitoto in the distance

Auckland War Memorial Museum

Beer in the sun at Devonport

City of Sails – Westhaven Marina and the famous Harbour Bridge over Auckland Harbour

Cape Maria van Dieman, south of Cape Reinga

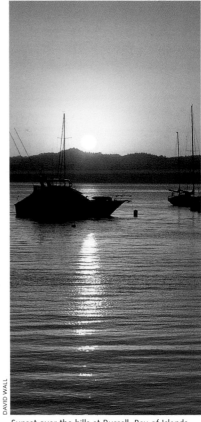

Sunset over the hills at Russell, Bay of Islands

The historic Stone Store in Kerikei – the oldest stone building in the country

Jet) invented in NZ in 1957. The most recent exhibition centres on the history of the America's Cup.

Auckland War Memorial Museum (Te Papa Whakahiku)

The museum sits at the apex of a sweeping expanse of lawn that forms part of the Auckland Domain, one of Auckland's oldest parks. Completely refurbished, the museum has an excellent display on Pacific Island and Maori cultures on the ground floor, including the historic 25m-long war canoe *Te Toki a Tapiri*. The 1st floor is dedicated to the natural world. There is a first-class activities centre here for children. The 2nd floor focuses on New Zealanders at war – from the 19th century to the peacekeeping assignments of today.

Pounamu Ventures runs a regular program of **Maori music and dance**, which is a good introduction to Maori culture. The shows are at 11 am and 1.30 pm daily ($8, children $5).

The museum is open from 10 am to 5 pm daily; a donation of $5 per adult is encouraged. The Explorer Bus passes the museum's front door every 30 minutes. It's about a 25-minute walk from Queen St through the domain or you can catch either the Link or Explorer bus to Parnell Rd, from where it's a short walk.

It is open from 9 am to 5 pm daily (to 6 pm in summer) and entry is $12 (children $6, family $28). Guided tours are usually conducted at 11 am or 2 pm, as are sailing trips, weather permitting (check for times).

During summer, a one-hour luncheon cruise on Waitemata Harbour on the *Ted Ashby* departs at noon ($30/20 for adults/children, including lunch and museum entry). At other times of the year harbour cruises cost $10/7 (cruise only).

Kelly Tarlton's Antarctic Encounter & Underwater World

On Tamaki Drive, 6km east of downtown Auckland, this unique aquarium is housed in old stormwater holding tanks. A transparent acrylic tunnel runs through the centre of the aquarium, through which you travel on a moving footpath – the fish swimming all around you. You can step off at any time to take a better look – it is designed to re-create the experience of scuba diving around the NZ coast. The aquarium was the inspiration of the late Kelly Tarlton, himself a diver.

The big attraction now is the Antarctic Encounter. It includes a walk through a replica of Scott's 1911 Antarctic hut; a ride aboard a heated Snow Cat through an environment where a penguin colony lives at -7°C; a simulated attack by an orca; and a very cold below-the-ice aquarium. There's also a visit

Auckland War Memorial Museum

DENNIS JOHNSON

AUCKLAND

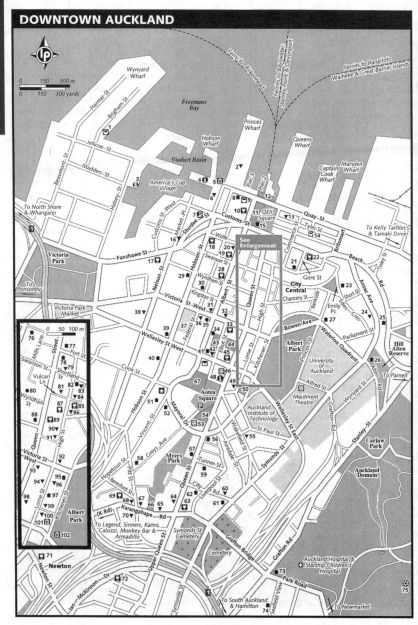

DOWNTOWN AUCKLAND

DOWNTOWN AUCKLAND

PLACES TO STAY
8 Copthorne Harbour City
15 Novotel Hotel
21 Nomads City Backpackers
   Hotel; Third Rock Cafe & Bar
23 Aspen Lodge
25 Harbourview Station Hotel
26 Bay City Backpackers
27 Hyatt Regency Hotel
29 The Heritage Auckland
30 Rydges Auckland; Circa
34 Centra Hotel
39 Albion Hotel
40 First Imperial Hotel &
   Apartments
41 City Central Hotel
51 YWCA
52 Carlton Hotel
56 Kiwi Backpackers
57 Quest Auckland
58 YMCA
59 Auckland International YHA
61 Sheraton
62 Auckland City YHA
73 Huia Residence Hostel
74 Grafton Hall of Residence
76 Stamford Plaza Hotel; Tabac
77 Queen St Backpackers
78 Auckland Central Backpackers; Net Cafe; Rat's Bar;
   Auckland Central Travel
82 Hotel De Brett
88 City Life Auckland; Zest
95 Albert Park Backpackers
97 Central City Backpackers;
   Embargo

PLACES TO EAT
2 Euro Restaurant & Bar;
   Wildfire; Lenin Bar; Leftfield;
   Cafe Hoegaarden
6 Kermadec; Viaduct Central;
   Loaded Hog; Watertours
13 Daikoku; Daikoku Ramen;
   Quest Auckland

16 Seamart
20 Food Alley
24 Gloria
31 Mai Thai; Mexican Cafe;
   Cafe Midnight Express
32 A Little Italy
36 Sultans's Table
38 Toto
42 Middle East Restaurant;
   Tony's Steak & Seafood;
   Okonomi-yaki Japanese
49 Pizza Pizza
55 Sun World
60 Five City Restaurant
64 Food for Life
65 Verona; Wagamama
67 Rasoi; Little Turkish Cafe
68 Habanero
70 Brazil
79 Whitelady
81 Khymer; Raw Power; Equinox
83 O'Connell St Bistro
84 Melba
86 D-72
90 Colombus
91 Jolt
92 Foodoo; Paneton; Simple
   Cottage; High Street
   Suprette; Wofem Bros
   Bagelry
93 Victoria Yeeros
94 Alba
96 Sierra; City
98 Countrywide Plazas
   International Food Hall
99 Tony's Steak & Seafood
100 Paramount Restaurant & Bar

PUBS & BARS
10 Stars & Stripes
17 The Immigrant
18 Soho Kitchen & Bar
19 The Ministry
22 Rose & Crown
28 Shakespeare Tavern

33 Margarita's
45 Murphy's; London Bar
63 The Khuja Lounge
69 Club Havana
71 Dogs Bollix
72 The Kings Arms Tavern
85 Bacchus; The Factory
87 Cause Celebre/The Box;
   Rakinos; Deschlers
89 Fu Bar

OTHER
1 Subritsky Ferry Terminal
3 American Express
4 NZ Visitor Centre
5 NZ National Maritime Museum
7 Tepid Baths
9 Downtown Airline Terminal
11 Downtown Shopping Centre
12 Ferry Building; DOC; Fullers;
   Cin Cin; Harbourside
14 Downtown Bus Terminal
35 Automobile Association
37 Skytower; Sky City Hotel;
   Sky City Coach Terminal;
   Tamarind; Orbit; SkyV
   Theatre (City)
43 Atrium on Elliot
44 Mid City Plaza
46 Civic Theatre
47 Aotea Centre
48 Auckland Travel & Information Centre Force Entertainment Centre; Planet
   Hollywood, Borders
50 Central City Library;
   Academy Cinema
53 Silo Theatre
54 Auckland Town Hall
66 St Kevins Arcade; Alleluya;
   Calibre
75 Wintergardens
80 Pride Centre
101 New Gallery; New Cafe
102 Auckland Art Gallery

to an Antarctic scientific base of the future and exhibits on the history of Antarctica.

One ticket gives you entry to all parts of the complex ($20, children $10). It's open from 9 am to 9 pm daily in summer (to 6 pm in winter). Check (☎ 528 0603) for the shark feeding times. Get there on bus Nos 746, 750, 755–57 or 767–69 from the Downtown Bus Terminal, or on the Explorer bus. The *Harbour Explorer* ferry also stops here.

Auckland Art Gallery Toi o Tamaki

The Auckland Art Gallery is in two parts. The original building is two blocks east of Queen St, on the corner of Wellesley St East and Kitchener St, below Albert Park. The art gallery has an extensive collection of NZ art, including many works by Colin McCahon and Frances Hodgkins (entry to the art gallery is free, except for special

America's Cup 2000

The America's Cup (affectionately known as the 'Auld Mug') has a long and illustrious history. In 1851 the *America* sailed to England, participated in and won the Round the Isle of Wight Race. A silver pitcher was presented to the skipper of *America,* taken back to the USA and, in 1857, entrusted to the New York Yacht Club (NYYC). It was first challenged for (unsuccessfully) in 1870–71 by the British.

Challenge after challenge was mounted but the cup seemed to be cemented safely in its case at the NYYC. The Australians had been peppering away with challenges and in 1983 *Australia II,* with its now legendary winged keel, beat the NYYC's *Liberty* 4-3, taking the cup out of the USA for the first time. US defence stalwart Dennis Conner, skipper of the unsuccessful defender, was flabbergasted and vowed to get it back. In 1987 he wrested the cup from the Aussies off Fremantle, Western Australia.

New Zealand's first real challenge was mounted in 1988 in San Diego. Amid legal wrangling, the defender's *Stars and Stripes* beat challenger *KZ1*. In 1992 the cup was again successfully defended by the San Diego Yacht Club.

ANN JEFFREE

On 14 May 1995 NZ's *Black Magic,* skippered by Russell Coutts, won the fifth straight race against *Young America,* skippered by Conner. The 5-0 victory in this final challenge series off San Diego entitled the Kiwis to take the America's Cup out of the USA for only the second time in 144 years. And it was only NZ's third cup challenge.

After Black Magic's 1995 win, the defence of the cup fell to Team New Zealand/Royal NZ Yacht Squadron. After some indecision, Auckland and the Hauraki Gulf were chosen as the defence site, and regatta courses were sited in the East Coast Bays between Rangitoto Island and the Whangaparaoa Peninsula.

In 1997 a protester walked into a room where the cup was displayed and smashed it with a sledgehammer. It has since been repaired.

The Viaduct Basin was totally redeveloped and 12 challenger syndicates settled into the Cup Village in 1999. Many new bars and restaurants opened up to cater for the influx of spectators and accommodation prices went skyhigh.

Challenging syndicates from Spain, Japan, Italy, Switzerland, France and Australia sailed in the Louis Vuitton Challenger Series from October 1999 to February 2000 to earn the right to challenge the defending Team New Zealand. Italy's *Luna Rossa* eventually won and went through to compete against NZ's *Black Magic* (the first time in history that the USA was not involved in the finals).

The Italian and New Zealand boats raced in February and March 2000. *Black Magic,* skippered by Russell Coutts and buoyed along by a nation clad in red socks, trounced *Luna Rossa* conclusively, five to nil in a possible nine race series. Auckland went bonkers knowing that the party would recommence in four years time – harbourside investors rubbed their hands in glee!

---

exhibitions). **The New Gallery** across Kitchener St is for contemporary art and special exhibitions. The entry fee ($4, children $2) is waived on Monday, and on Monday for special exhibitions at the main gallery. Both galleries are open from 10 am to 5 pm daily.

Museum of Transport & Technology

This museum (known as Motat) is at Western Springs near the zoo, just off the Great North Rd. Motat is in two sections. **Motat I** has exhibits on transport, communications and energy, including one about pioneer aviator

Richard Pearse. This eccentric South Island farmer may have even flown before the Wright brothers, and during his life he produced a steady stream of inventions and devices. Also at Motat I is the infotainment Science Centre, with hands-on exhibits.

Motat II, at nearby Sir Keith Park Memorial Airfield, features displays of rare and historic aircraft. Exhibits include a V1 flying bomb and Lancaster bomber from WWII, but pride of place goes to the huge Solent flying boat that ran a Pacific islands loop in the luxury days of flying.

Motat is open from 10 am to 5 pm daily and entry is $10 (children $5). Electric trams run regularly from Motat I to the zoo and Motat II.

Motat is signposted just off the North-Western Motorway. For bus details, see the Auckland Zoo section.

Auckland Zoo

The Auckland Zoo is on Motions Rd off Great North Rd, in the same area as Motat. Though not a large zoo, it is beautifully landscaped and a continuing renovation program has replaced many of the old animal houses with more spacious, naturalistic compounds. The **primate exhibit** is particularly well done, and the African animals' enclosure, **Pridelands**, is also excellent, as is the meerkat enclosure which can be explored through tunnels.

The zoo is open from 9.30 am to 5.30 pm daily (last admission 4.15 pm) and entry is $12 (children $7). The Explorer bus or the Pt Chevalier bus (No 045) from Customs St East will get you to both Motat and the zoo.

Historic Buildings

There are numerous restored and preserved colonial-era buildings in the city. The oldest of these is **Acacia Cottage** in Cornwall Park at the foot of One Tree Hill. Built in 1841, the cottage was originally where Shortland St is today.

Highwic (1862), at 40 Gillies Ave, Epsom, and **Alberton**, at 1 Kerr-Taylor Ave, Mt Albert, were both large houses of wealthy Victorian New Zealanders. Each house is open from 10.30 am to noon and

from 1 to 4.30 pm Wednesday to Sunday. Entry is $5 (accompanied children free).

In Parnell, **Ewelme Cottage** at 14 Ayr St was built from fine native kauri by a clergyman in the 1860s. Opening hours are the same as for Highwic and Alberton, entry is $3 (accompanied children free). Just five doors from Ewelme, **Kinder House** (1857) at 2 Ayr St is a fine example of early architecture and contains two galleries of the artwork and memorabilia of the Rev Dr John Kinder. The restored home is open from 11 am to 3 pm Monday to Saturday ($2).

Parnell is an old inner suburb, only 2km from the centre, where there was a concerted effort to stave off the office developers and restore the old houses and shops, many of them with a decidedly eccentric touch. **Parnell Village** is an interesting area – a unified cluster of restored shops and houses, linked by paved alleyways, courtyards and boardwalks. Browse in the exclusive shops even if you can't afford to buy. The handy Link bus stops in Parnell.

Renall St, off Ponsonby Rd, has been declared a conservation area and is registered as a historic place of interest for its 19th-century atmosphere. The houses along this block are not open to the public, but you can stroll along and admire the 20 or so early artisans' houses.

In south-east Auckland, **Howick Historical Village** (☎ 576 9506) in Lloyd Elsmore Park on Bells Rd, Pakuranga, is a restored village from 1840 to 1880, on the old military settlement of Howick. The restored buildings include a thatched sod cottage, forge, village store and settlers' houses. It's open from 10 am to 5 pm daily ($9, children $7).

Mt Eden & One Tree Hill

Auckland is punctuated by some 48 volcanoes, many of which provide parkland retreats and great views.

The view from Mt Eden (Maungawhau), the highest volcanic cone in the area at 196m, is superb. You can see the entire Auckland area – all the bays and both sides of the isthmus – and look 50m down into the volcano's crater. The summit crater is sacred to the Maori and known as Te Ipu a

AUCKLAND

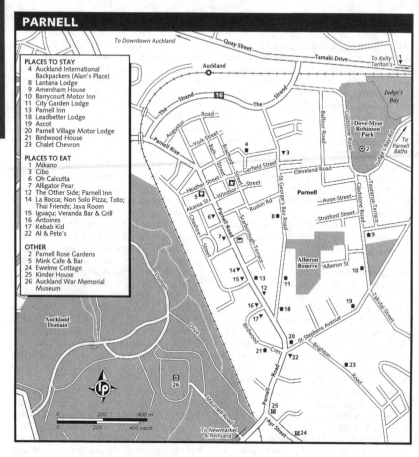

PARNELL

To Downtown Auckland
Quay Street
Tamaki Drive
To Kelly
Tarlton's
Auckland
Judge's
Bay
The Strand
The Strand
16
Balfour Road
Gladstone Road
Dove-Myer
Robinson
Park
To
Parnell
Baths
Road
Augustus
Judge's Bay Road
2
Parnell Rise
York Street
Bradford Street
Bath Street
Garfield Street
Cleveland Road
Gladstone Road
4
3
Parnell Rise
Heather Street
Windsor Street
Garfield Street
Parnell
Avon Street
Tauranga Terrace
5
Akaroa St
Ruskin Rd
St George's Bay Road
Stratford Street
Iguaçu Street
6
Parnell Road
Scarborough Terrace
8
9
Cheshire Street
7
Alberon
Reserve
Alberon St
10
Domain
14
15
13
11
12
18
19
Takutai Street
16
17
Birdwood Road
St Stephens Avenue
Auckland
Domain
Drive
20
Cres
St Stephens Avenue
Brighton Road
21
22
23
Parnell Road
26
0   200   400 m
0   200   400 yards
Maunsell Road
St Ayr Street
25
24
To Newmarket
& Remuera

PLACES TO STAY
4 Auckland International
   Backpackers (Alan's Place)
8 Lantana Lodge
9 Amersham House
10 Barrycourt Motor Inn
11 City Garden Lodge
13 Parnell Inn
18 Leadbetter Lodge
19 Ascot
20 Parnell Village Motor Lodge
21 Birdwood House
23 Chalet Chevron

PLACES TO EAT
1 Mikano
3 Cibo
6 Oh Calcutta
7 Alligator Pear
12 The Other Side; Parnell Inn
14 La Bocca; Non Solo Pizza; Toto;
   Thai Friends; Java Room
15 Iguaçu; Veranda Bar & Grill
16 Antoines
17 Kebab Kid
22 Al & Pete's

OTHER
2 Parnell Rose Gardens
5 Mink Cafe & Bar
24 Ewelme Cottage
25 Kinder House
26 Auckland War Memorial
   Museum

Mataaho (meaning 'The Bowl of Mataaho') after the god of volcanoes. You can drive to the top or take bus Nos 274–77 from Customs St East and then walk.

Maungakiekie ('Mountain of the Kiekie Tree') or One Tree Hill (183m) is a distinctive bald hill, topped only by a lone pine tree and a huge obelisk. It was the largest and most populous of the Maori pa, and the terracing and dugout storage pits are still visible. It was named after a sacred totara tree which stood here until 1876 and was since replaced by the (now huge) pine tree. The pine was braced with steel cables after

a Maori protester attempted to fell it a few years back in retribution for the felling of the original tree. In September 1999 it was attacked again with a chainsaw and at the time of writing a replacement was being sought. Cornwall Park, which has an information centre at Huia Lodge, occupies the lower slopes of One Tree Hill.

Auckland Observatory & Stardome

The Auckland Observatory (☎ 625 6945) is in the One Tree Hill Domain, off Manukau Rd. The **Stardome Show** is held Tuesday to

Sunday and costs $10/5 for adults/children. Phone the observatory for times.

After the evening Stardome Show on Wednesday, Thursday and Saturday (clear nights only) you can view the night sky for $5/3 – discounted if you already hold a Stardome ticket.

Markets

On Victoria St West, opposite Victoria Park, is the large **Victoria Park Market**, open from 9 am to 7 pm on weekends. It mostly sells crafts, souvenirs and clothes, but also has outdoor cafes, entertainers and a concentration of eclectic New Age goods. It's a 20-minute walk west from the city centre, or you can take the Link or Explorer buses.

Auckland also has traditional markets that sell fruit, vegetables and everyday goods. The biggest and most interesting are the **Otara Market**, held from around 6 am to noon every Saturday in the car park between the Manukau Polytech and the Otara town centre on Newbury St, and the **Avondale Market**, held every Sunday at the Avondale Jockey Club raceway.

There are other markets selling food, art and craft, antiques and clothing in the city

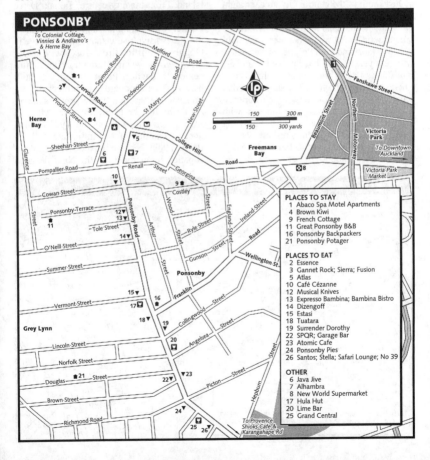

PONSONBY

PLACES TO STAY
1 Abaco Spa Motel Apartments
4 Brown Kiwi
9 French Cottage
11 Great Ponsonby B&B
16 Ponsonby Backpackers
21 Ponsonby Potager

PLACES TO EAT
2 Essence
3 Gannet Rock; Sierra; Fusion
5 Atlas
10 Café Cézanne
12 Musical Knives
13 Expresso Bambina; Bambina Bistro
14 Dizengoff
15 Estasi
18 Tuatara
19 Surrender Dorothy
22 SPQR; Garage Bar
23 Atomic Cafe
24 Ponsonby Pies
26 Santos; Stella; Safari Lounge; No 39

OTHER
6 Java Jive
7 Alhambra
8 New World Supermarket
17 Hula Hut
20 Lime Bar
25 Grand Central

and surrounding suburbs; the visitor centre keeps a current list.

Auckland Suburbs

The suburban sprawl stretches almost 60km north to south and 30km east to west. Like many cities, much of it is suburban conformity, but parts are interesting for their history, vistas or character.

Auckland's most prestigious and historical real estate is found around the city's delightful bays and beaches. For architecture buffs, the older suburbs have fine, 19th-century wooden villas, built mostly of durable kauri.

Just south of the central city area, straight up the hill from Queen St, is **K Rd** (see the Downtown Auckland map). After WWII, the area around K Rd was a popular inner suburb for Maori and then Polynesian residents. In recent years artists have moved in and established studios, and the street has a distinctly bohemian flavour. The strip clubs that gave the street its notoriety are clustered in the western end, towards the junction with Ponsonby Rd. The eastern end has a growing numbers of cafes and ethnic restaurants.

K Rd runs south-west to Ponsonby Rd in the fashionable suburb of **Ponsonby**. Behind historic shopfronts, Ponsonby Rd's many restaurants are abuzz with the chatter of diners, the hiss of cappuccino machines and the bleep of mobile phones. Ponsonby has many fine old houses, and the adjoining **Herne Bay**, right on the harbour, has some of Auckland's best Victorian homes.

Just south of Parnell is **Newmarket**, a lively and trendy shopping area along Broadway, with an indoor swimming centre and two theatre complexes.

Tamaki Drive starts at the Auckland train station and runs east past sheltered bays to several wealthy suburbs facing Rangitoto Island. From the city centre, Tamaki Drive crosses Hobson Bay and first reaches **Orakei**, which contains some of Auckland's most expensive real estate. Paratai Drive in Orakei is millionaires' row, with great views across the city. Tamaki Drive continues on to **Bastion Point**. A fort was built here in the 19th century to protect the entrance to the harbour. It now protects the remains of former prime minister Michael Joseph Savage, who in the 1930s introduced the notion of a welfare state. In 1978 Bastion Point became the focus of a land occupation by members of the Ngati Whatua

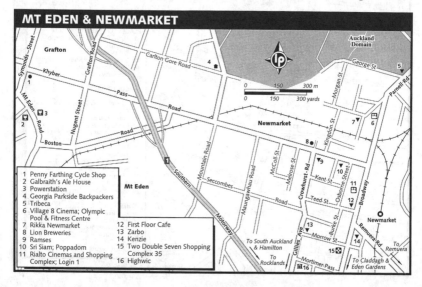

MT EDEN & NEWMARKET

1 Penny Farthing Cycle Shop
2 Galbraith's Ale House
3 Powerstation
4 Georgia Parkside Backpackers
5 Tribeca
6 Village 8 Cinema; Olympic Pool & Fitness Centre
7 Rikka Newmarket
8 Lion Breweries
9 Ramses
10 Sri Siam; Poppadom
11 Rialto Cinemas and Shopping Complex; Login 1
12 First Floor Cafe
13 Zarbo
14 Kenzie
15 Two Double Seven Shopping Complex 35
16 Highwic

tribe in protest to a proposed development. The protesters were eventually evicted in a huge police operation.

Tamaki Drive leads further around to **Mission Bay**, where there is a park by the beach with an attractive fountain (floodlit at night), and plenty of sidewalk cafes. Further on, **St Heliers Bay** is smaller and more relaxed, with good dining right across the road from the beach. Further east along Cliff Rd, the **Achilles Point lookout** has dramatic views of the city, harbour and Hauraki Gulf.

Rainbow's End Adventure Park

This large amusement park on the Great South Rd (corner of Wiri Station Rd) at Manukau is open from 10 am to 5 pm daily. Super passes for $30 (children $20) allow unlimited rides all day; otherwise, $15 entry will buy you three rides.

Lion Breweries

Lion Breweries (☎ 377 8840) is NZ's largest multinational brewery and gives free tours of the plant at 368 Khyber Pass Rd in Newmarket. See the process, guzzle a Steinie and try other popular commercial beers. Free tours are held on request at 10.30 am and 2 pm; bookings are essential.

Parks & Gardens

Covering about 80 hectares, the **Auckland Domain**, right near the centre of the city, is a lovely public park that contains the museum and the **Wintergarden** with its hothouse and fernery.

On Gladstone Rd in Parnell is the **Parnell Rose Gardens**. There are harbour views and the roses are in bloom from November to March.

Popular for jogging, picnics and walks, **Cornwall Park** adjoins One Tree Hill on Greenlane Rd and is an extensive pastoral retreat only 6km south of the city centre. It has sportsgrounds, fields of grazing sheep, a visitor centre (Huia Lodge), Acacia Cottage (see Historic Buildings earlier) and a restaurant.

Eden Gardens, on the slopes of Mt Eden, is noted for its camellias, rhododendrons and azaleas – July and August are the best

months for viewing camellias. Entry is via Omana Ave and costs $4 (seniors $2).

The extensive **Auckland Regional Council Botanical Gardens** are 27km south of the city. Take the Southern Motorway to the Manurewa turn-off (the one past Rainbow's End). The country's most important horticultural fair, the Ellerslie Flower Show, is held here annually in mid-November.

Get the Auckland Regional Parks guide from the Auckland Travel and Information Centre or the DOC office at the ferry building.

Walking

The Auckland Travel and Information Centre and the DOC office have pamphlets on walks in and around Auckland. DOC's *Auckland Walkways* pamphlet has a good selection of forest and coastal day walks outside the metropolitan area.

The *Coast to Coast Walkway* pamphlet covers the walk we've marked on the Greater Auckland map between Waitemata and Manukau Harbours. The four-hour walk encompasses Albert Park, the university, the domain, Mt Eden, One Tree Hill and other points of interest, keeping as much as possible to reserves rather than city streets.

Swimming & Surfing

Auckland is known for its fine and varied beaches dotted around its harbours and the coast.

The east coast beaches along Tamaki Drive, including Mission and St Heliers Bays, are very popular. At most east coast and harbour beaches, swimming is best at high tide. Popular North Shore beaches include Takapuna, Cheltenham and Milford.

For good surf less than 50km from the city, try Te Henga (Bethells Beach) on the west coast where the water is often very rough, Piha or Muriwai. Most of the surfing beaches have surf clubs and lifeguards. Further afield Tawharanui and Pakiri, near Warkworth, have some of NZ's best waves.

City swimming pools include Tepid Baths; the Olympic Pool in Newmarket; Parnell Baths on Judges Bay Rd, with a saltwater pool on the waterfront (closed in winter); Point Erin pool on Shelly Beach Rd, Herne Bay; and Takapuna Pools on Killarney St, Takapuna. A good all-weather venue is the Philips Aquatic Centre in Mt Albert, which has a wave pool and slides.

The Tepid Baths (☎ 379 4794) at 100 Customs St has two undercover pools, a gym, sauna, spa and steam rooms. The Teps is open from 6 am to 9 pm (7 am to 7 pm on weekends). Entry costs $4.50/3.50 for adults/children.

Outside the city, hot pool and swimming complexes include the **Aquatic Park** at Parakai near Helensville (see the Around Auckland section), and Waiwera Thermal Pools, 48km to the north.

Sea Kayaking

Fergs Kayaks (☎/fax 529 2230), 12 Tamaki Drive, at Okahu Bay, hires out a variety of kayaks for $7 to $15 an hour ($30 to $60 a half-day). Auckland Wilderness Kayaking (☎ 630 7782) has half- and full-day tours out to the gulf islands, and an overnight trip to Mahurangi Regional Park north of Auckland (from $50 for half-day tours).

Other Activities

The Auckland Travel and Information Centre lists activities and operators.

Scuba-diving trips are organised by the Dive Centre (☎ 444 7698) in Takapuna, Orakei Scuba Centre (☎ 524 2117) and other operators.

Horse riding is available at Ambury Park in South Auckland (contact Ride the Parks ☎ 0800-743 384). Further out are South Kaipara Horsetreks (☎ 420 2835) for experienced riders, and Pakiri (☎ 420 7269) near Wellsford.

Mountain bike rentals and tours abound. Trails range from the very easy at Cornwall Park in the city to the very strenuous at Dome Valley, near Warkworth. Auckland Adventures (☎ 379 4545) has a full-day mountain-biking experience near Muriwai Beach for $75.

Cliffhanger Adventures (☎ 021-661 851) has an **abseiling** trip to the Waitakere Ranges; ring for costs. Balloon Safaris (☎ 415 8289) and Balloon Expedition

Company of NZ (☎ 416 8590) do **hot-air balloon** flights for around $200. There are also many possibilities for fishing, tennis, golf and other sports in and near Auckland. The information centre will have details.

Language Courses

People from around the world, especially Asia and the Pacific, come to NZ to study English. Auckland has the highest concentration of language schools, and the visitor centre keeps a complete, up-to-date list (check also in *Auckland A-Z*).

Organised Tours

You can tour the major Auckland attractions in the United Airlines Explorer Bus (☎ 571 3119) for $20 – all day. It departs daily from the ferry building on the hour every hour from 10 am to 4 pm in winter and every half-hour from 9 am to 4 pm in summer (October to April). It goes to Mission Bay, Kelly Tarlton's, Parnell Rose Gardens, Auckland Museum, Parnell Village, Victoria Park Market and back to the ferry building. At the museum you can pick up its Satellite Link (summer only) to Mt Eden, St Lukes Shopping Mall, Auckland Zoo, Motat, Auckland Art Gallery, the America's Cup Village and Sky Casino.

Auckland has many tour operators. Three-hour tours will typically drive around the city centre, over the harbour bridge and out along Tamaki Drive, including stops at Mt Eden, the Auckland Museum and Parnell, for about $38. Other tours (eg, Sea City Tours ☎ 0800-732 2489) do the above and include a harbour cruise for $98. ABC Tours (☎ 0800-222 868), Scenic Tours (☎ 634 2266) and Great Sights (☎ 0800-744 487) are all reputable companies. Hotel pick-up and drop-off is usually included in the price. The Devonport Tour Company (☎ 357 6366, 0800-868 774) runs daily trips in a minibus that meets the ferry from Auckland city. For $22 (children $11) you get a one-hour tour of Devonport's volcanic cones plus a bit of history (includes return ferry fare).

Auckland Adventures (☎ 379 4545) has a tour that includes a Maori cultural show at Auckland War Memorial Museum, a trip up

Mt Eden, visits to a winery, orchards and farms and to the gannet colony at Muriwai ($55). Its Wilderness Adventure tour ($75) provides a more extensive trip through the West Coast region.

Other possibilities include a tour of Auckland's volcanic cones and other geological features as well as flora and fauna with Geotours (☎ 525 3991). There are also garden tours with Mike's Garden Tours (☎ 846 5350).

Numerous companies take trips to West Auckland. Most, such as Bush & Beach Nature Tours, will pick up and drop off in the city centre. (You can see where the movie *The Piano* and episodes of the cult TV classic *Xena: Warrior Princess* were filmed.)

Scenic Flights

Flight 2000 (☎ 422 6334), based at Ardmore Airport in South Auckland, has biplane trips ($99 per person, seats two passengers, 20 minutes), Cessna 172 flights ($200 for the craft, seats up to three, one hour) and trips with the Warbird Dakota DC3 ($45 per adult). The Warbird flights last about half an hour and leave at 1 pm on Sunday.

For helicopter flights try Helilink (☎ 377 4406), which has flights starting at $130 per person for 12 minutes, which takes you over the city centre, One Tree Hill, the Harbour Bridge and Rangitoto. The flights leave from Mechanics Bay in the city.

Harbour Cruises

The best way to appreciate the City of Sails is to take to the water. Fullers Cruises (☎ 367 9111) has the largest selection of cruises and operates almost all the ferries.

The cheapest option is to take the 12-minute ferry ride to picturesque Devonport. Ferries also go to many of the nearby islands in the gulf. Rangitoto and Waiheke are easy to reach and make good day or half-day trips from Auckland. Pacific Ferries (☎ 303 1741) also has trips to Waiheke.

Fullers has popular tours around the inner harbour, including a daily two-hour coffee cruise ($20) which stops at Devonport, Rangitoto and Kelly Tarlton's.

Pride of Auckland (☎ 373 4557), which is based at the NZ National Maritime Museum, operates a fleet of four monohulls and a catamaran (all with distinctive blue and white sails). Cruises include Experience Sailing.

The NZ National Maritime Museum (☎ 373 0800) has a sailing Scow, the *Ted Ashby,* which departs at noon daily for lunch and harbour cruises. (See also the NZ National Maritime Museum section earlier.)

For one of the best experiences on the water take a trip on the tall ship *Soren Larsen,* a square-rigged, 19th-century brigantine beauty with 12 sails. The *Soren Larsen* was built out of oak in Nykøbing Mors in Denmark and achieved fame as the star of the TV series *The Onedin Line*. For details contact ☎ 411 8755.

Watertours (☎ 357 0700) runs 15-minute boat tours of the America's Cup Village, departing from the Viaduct Harbour every 10 to 15 minutes and costing $10/5 for adults/children.

Plenty of other companies offer cruises; the visitor centre has details. If you're a sailor yourself, most charter companies offer skippered, skippered and crewed, or bareboat (skipper the boat yourself) charters, as well as instruction. Fishing charters are also available. Penny Whiting Sailing (☎ 376 1322) has well-run courses for those who want to learn to sail.

Special Events

The visitor centre keeps a list of the many annual events held in Auckland and will provide precise dates. Some of these events follow:

January
Open Tennis Championships; Opera in the Park; Auckland Anniversary Day Regatta

February
Symphony Under the Stars; Devonport Food & Wine Festival; HERO Festival, Parade & Party; Dragon-Boat Races

March/April
Around the Bays Fun Run; Pasifika Polynesian Festival; Royal NZ Easter Show; Sky Show (Waitemata Harbour)

June
NZ Boat Show

October
Auckland to Russell Yacht Race; Wine Wai-takere (food and wine festival); BMW Marathon and wheelchair marathon (Tamaki Drive)
November
Ellerslie Flower Show (at the ARC Botanical Gardens)
December
Auckland Cup horse racing

Places to Stay

Camping & Cabins North of the city is the four-star *Auckland North Shore Motels & Holiday Park* (☎ 418 2578, 52 Northcote Rd, Takapuna), 4km north of the Harbour Bridge. Camp sites are $30 for two, cabins start at $55, motels at $96.

The *Takapuna Beach Holiday Park* (☎ 489 7909, 22 The Promenade, Takapuna) is 8km north of the city centre and right on the beach, with a view of Rangitoto. It's an easy walk to the shops and central Takapuna, and a 10-minute ride into downtown Auckland. Tent/powered sites are $24/26 for two, cabins are $38 and on-site vans $48.

Further north of Auckland, the *Tui Glen Motor Camp* (☎ 838 8978) is beside the swimming pool complex at Henderson, 13km north-west of Auckland. Tent/powered sites are $15/20, cabins are $38 and tourist flats $48 (prices for two).

The closest camping ground to the city is the quiet and secure *Remuera Motor Lodge & Inner City Camping Ground* (☎ 524 5126, 16 Minto Rd), 8km south-east of downtown Auckland. Take bus No 64 or 65 from the Downtown Bus Terminal. It has a large pool and is just 100m from shops and the bus stop. Tent/powered sites are $13.50/15 per person, a self-contained bunkroom costs $50 for one or two people and tourist flats start at $75 for two.

The *Avondale Motor Park* (☎ 828 7228, 46 Bollard Ave), off New North Rd, is 9km south-west of central Auckland and close to Motat and the zoo. Tent/powered sites are $9/10, on-site vans are $40 for two, cabins with en suite are $55 for two and tourist flats are $60.

South Auckland has many caravan parks, such as the *Manukau Central Caravan* *Park* (☎ 266 8016, 902 Great South Rd, Manukau), and *Meadowcourt Motor Camp* (☎ 278 5612, 630 Great South Rd), close to Manukau city and the airport.

Auckland Regional Council has camping grounds in the regional parks around Auckland, many in coastal areas. Some are accessible by vehicle, others are reached by tramping. Contact Parksline (☎ 303 1530) for information and bookings.

Hostels Auckland has plenty of hostels in the city centre and inner suburbs. Prices given here are for summer. All hostels have kitchens; some have cafes and even bars.

City Centre The *Auckland Central Backpackers* (☎ 358 4877, ❷ backpackers@acb .co.nz, 9 Fort St) is Auckland's, indeed NZ's, largest hostel, with room for 300 people. Amenities include made-up beds, two cafes, a lively rooftop bar (The Hard Rat), a dairy (grocery store) downstairs, 24-hour Internet access and an excellent backpackers travel agency. Dorm beds are $18, multishare rooms for three or more are $19, singles $24, doubles and twins $23 (all prices per person). The hostel's Web site is www.acb .co.nz.

Queen St Backpackers (☎ 373 3471, 4 Fort St) is rather more basic. It has three- and four-bed dorms for $16, singles/doubles/twins for $29/39/38.

The 200-bed *Nomads City Backpackers Hotel* (☎ 0800-220 198, ❷ reservations@ city-backpacker-hotel.co.nz) on the corner of Gore and Fort Sts provides apartment-style accommodation. Dorm beds are $17, a single room is $35, a twin $40, doubles are from $40 to $50 and a deluxe double $65. The rooms open onto a kitchen and lounge area. The Third Rock Cafe & Bar is next door.

Hotel De Brett (☎ 377 2389, ❷ debrett@ acb.co.nz) is an Art Deco building on the corner of High and Shortland Sts. Recently renovated, it's looking smart. A continental breakfast and complimentary glass of champagne are included in the price of $60/75 for a single/twin or double, $90/120 for a triple/family. There's a small house bar, a lounge and TV area and a breakfast room, as well as a laundry.

The *Auckland City YHA Hostel* (☎ 309 2802, ✆ yhaauck@yha.org.nz) on the corner of City Rd and Liverpool St is one of Auckland's biggest hostels. Comfortable, multishare rooms cost $19 per person and double and twin rooms are $46. It is open 24 hours and has a shop and luggage safes.

The sparkling new *Auckland International YHA* (☎ 302 8200, 5 Turner St) is nearby. Prices are the same as at the Auckland City, although it also has en suite rooms. There is an excellent kitchen and dining area.

Also known as Kiwi Hilton, the basic *Kiwi Backpackers* (☎ 358 3999, 430 Queen St) has dorm beds starting at $13, doubles and twins for $38 and singles for $25.

Albert Park Backpackers (☎ 309 0336, ✆ bakpak@albertpark.co.nz, 27–31 Victoria St East) will store luggage and make bookings for activities. There's a rooftop garden with barbecue facilities. A bed in a 12-bed dorm is $17 and in a six-bed share room is $18. A twin/double is $40/45 and there's one single for $30.

Another good, large hostel is *Central City Backpackers* (☎ 358 5685, ✆ ccbnz@xtra .co.nz, 26 Lorne St). Though large, it manages to maintain a homey feel and the rooms are spotless, if a little dark. It sleeps 160 and has all the usual amenities, including a travel agency. Dorms start at $18, and doubles and twins at $23 per person. Downstairs is the popular Embargo bar.

The smaller but conveniently located *Bay City Backpackers* (☎ 303 4768, 6 Constitution Hill) is near the university. It has a good atmosphere and parking is available. It is $12 to $17 in a dorm and $45 in a double with private shower ($40 with shared facilities).

Huia Residence Hostel (☎ 377 1345, fax 377 4871, 110 Grafton Rd) has quality single rooms for $35, twins and doubles for $50. Friendly, safe and highly organised, the hostel's reception is open 24 hours and facilities include laundry and Internet access.

Georgia Parkside Backpackers (☎ 0508-436 744, ✆ bacpacgeorgia@xtra.co.nz, 189 Park Rd) is on the corner of Park and

Carlton Gore Rds in Grafton, overlooking the domain. This rambling old place has a variety of rooms. Dorms start at $18, doubles and twins at $21 per person. Tent sites are also available for $12 per person. Weekly rates are available.

The *Grafton Hall of Residence* (☎ 373 3994, 40 Seafield View Rd) is a large, well-equipped hostel that services students during term time. Its doors open to travellers from mid-June to the second week of July and from 20 November to 20 February. B&B costs $32 per person.

The YWCA and YMCA have beds, and often have rooms in summer when everything else is full. The *YWCA* (☎ 377 8763, fax 375 3093, 67 Vincent St) relocated from Grafton to its current inner-city location in February 2000. It takes men and women, and has a friendly, relaxed atmosphere. There is a fully equipped kitchen, a cafe and laundry. Linen is included in the cost of accommodation: $30/25 per person for singles/twins, and $40 for a double room.

The *YMCA* (☎ 303 2068), on the corner of Pitt St and Greys Ave, takes both sexes; singles/twins are $35/55 (linen included).

Parnell From the city, stylish Parnell is a 20-minute walk or you can take the Link bus.

Auckland International Backpackers (☎ 358 4584, ✆ international.bp@xtra.co .nz, 2 Churton St), also known as Alan's Place, is in the former Parnell YHA. It's a comfortable place in a quiet location. Dorms are $19, singles are $44 and twins and doubles are $23 per person.

There are a few backpackers on St Georges Bay Rd. The *City Garden Lodge* (☎ 302 0880) at No 25 is a fine hostel in a large, elegant old home originally built for the queen of Tonga. Dorm beds/singles/doubles/twins start at $18/35/44/42.

Lantana Lodge (☎ 373 4546), further down the hill at No 60, is a friendly, neat and well-run place; the cost is $18 in dorms, $44 for doubles and twins (duvets provided) and $54 for triples. There are good views of the city from the rear of the lodge. *Leadbetter Lodge* (☎ 358 0665), at No 17, has basic dorms at $13 and doubles for $30 to $35.

Mt Eden & Epsom Mt Eden, a pleasant residential area 4km south of the city centre, has hostels which tend to be the last to fill up in summer. Bus Nos 274 and 275 run from the Downtown Bus Terminal to Mt Eden Rd.

Formerly Eden Lodge, **Bamber House** (☎ 623 4267, ✉ bamber@ihug.co.nz, 22 View Rd) is in a huge colonial-era home surrounded by gardens. The rooms are comfortable, the house has large and pleasant communal areas and there is a swimming pool. Children are welcome. Dorms cost from $14 to $17, double and twin rooms are $44 and family rooms are $44 for two plus $10 for each extra person. Buses stop on the corner of Mt Eden and View Rds.

Oaklands Lodge (☎ 0800-222 725, ✉ backpacker@ak.planet.gen.nz, 5A Oaklands Rd) is in a quiet tree-lined street at the foot of Mt Eden – the bus stops at the Mt Eden shops, 100m away. Oaklands charges from $15 to $17 for dorms, $30 for singles and $42 for twins and doubles.

Rocklands (☎ 630 0836, 187 Gillies Ave, Epsom) is a YWCA-run hostel that accepts men and women. Situated in a once-grand mansion, it is popular with students from the nearby teachers training college. It has 160 beds and charges $25/40 for a single/double (linen included).

Ponsonby Like Parnell, Ponsonby is another happening area close to the city. The **Brown Kiwi** (☎ 378 019, ✉ bookings@brownkiwi.co.nz, 7 Prosford St) is a homey, friendly, well-run hostel with all the requisite facilities. Dorm beds start at $18, doubles are $45.

Ponsonby Backpackers (☎ 360 1311, ✉ booking@ponsonby-backpackers.co.nz, 2 Franklin Rd) is in a historic house, only a street from Ponsonby Rd. Dorms cost $15, singles start at $25 and doubles and twins at $40. The rooms vary in quality.

Airport For budget accommodation near the airport try **Skyway Lodge** (☎ 275 4443, ✉ skyway@ihug.co.nz, 30 Kirkbride Rd, Mangere). It has bunk beds for $18, singles

for $45 and doubles for $55. You can get a shuttle to the airport from here.

There is a cluster of motels in this area.

B&Bs & Guesthouses B&Bs and guesthouses are popular. Those mentioned here are reliable, with a 'home away from home' feeling and all include breakfast in the rate.

In the city centre, **Aspen Lodge** (☎ 379 6698, 63 Emily Place) looks out on a delightful little park and is about a five-minute walk from Queen St. It has a convivial dining/common area and singles/doubles are $54/78.

The fashionable Parnell district has several excellent guesthouses. The **Ascot** (☎ 309 9012, 36 St Stephens Ave), off Parnell Rd, is a long-standing favourite, with 11 guest rooms in a restored historic home. It charges $95/117 to $185 for singles/doubles. Nearby, **Chalet Chevron** (☎ 309 0291, 14 Brighton Rd) has beautiful harbour views. It charges $78 for singles and $150 for doubles and twins.

Also at the southern end of Parnell is **Birdwood House** (☎ 306 5900, 41 Birdwood Crescent), a quiet, carefully restored house with prices starting at $130 for a single and $145 for a double. **Amersham House** (☎ 303 0321, 1 Canterbury Place) is a luxurious place with a heated pool and spa. Prices start at $200.

Mt Eden also has attractive guesthouses. **Villa 536** (☎ 630 5258, 536 Mt Eden Rd) has three attractive rooms in a restored kauri villa. Prices start at $85/95 for singles/doubles.

The **Great Ponsonby B&B** (☎ 376 5989, 30 Ponsonby Terrace), a tastefully decorated old villa, has five en suite rooms and six studios. Prices start at $135 for two. Other good places in Ponsonby include: the **Ponsonby Potager** (☎ 378 7237, 43 Douglas St), which has rooms from $90 for a single and $120 for a double; **Colonial Cottage** (☎ 360 2820, 35 Clarence St), a restored kauri villa off Jervois Rd with rooms for $80/100; and the **French Cottage** (☎ 376 6046, 7 Georgina St, Freemans Bay), a place built in French provincial style which goes for $150 a night ($500 weekly).

Right next door to Cornwall Park and One Tree Hill is **The Langtons** (☎ 625 7520, 29 Haydn Ave, One Tree Hill), a lovely two-storey home with a swimming pool and en suite rooms. Prices start at $185 for two.

Top places in Remuera, one of Auckland's most exclusive suburbs, include **Aachen House Boutique Hotel** (☎ 520 2329, 3 Market Rd), a restored Edwardian home nestled at the foot of Mt Hobson; **Omahu House** (☎ 524 9697, 35 Omahu Ave), beautifully renovated with lovely gardens; and **The Devereux** (☎ 524 5044, 267 Remuera Rd), a large place set back from the road, with each guest room individually themed.

Motels Auckland has over 100 motels and costs start at around $80/95 for singles/doubles. Several areas reasonably close to the city have a good selection of motels.

Parnell Village Motor Lodge (☎ 377 1463, 2 St Stephens Ave), on the corner of Parnell Rd, has studio units from $85, and a range of units with kitchens for $140 for two. All are self-contained, and reasonably priced for the good location. The **Parnell Inn** (☎ 358 0642, 320 Parnell Rd) is another reasonably priced motel with studio units from $75/110 a single/double. **Barrycourt Motor Inn** (☎ 303 3789, 10–20 Gladstone Rd) has a wide selection, with double or twin rooms, studio apartments and suites. Prices start at $86 and range up to $300.

Another alternative is Jervois Rd in Herne Bay, beyond the junction with Ponsonby Rd. A number of motels are on, or just off, Jervois and Shelly Beach Rds, close to the southern end of the Harbour Bridge.

In Herne Bay, **Sea Breeze Motel** (☎ 376 2139, 213 Jervois Rd) is near beaches, fishing areas, restaurants and shops. Studio units are $95 and one-bedroom units are $98. The **Abaco Spa Motel Apartments** (☎ 376 0119, 59 Jervois Rd) has units from $99 to $16, six with private spas.

Remuera just past Newmarket, 5km from the city, has a motel row along Great South Rd, starting at around No 70. Most charge from around $80 for a studio.

Hansen's (☎ 520 2804) at No 96 and the **Tudor Court** (☎ 523 1069) at No 108 are two of the cheapest, with units from $60 and $70 respectively.

Across the Harbour Bridge, Takapuna and Birkenhead have plenty of motels. Out near the airport, Mangere has dozens, particularly along Kirkbride and McKenzie Rds. **Pacific Inn** (☎ 275 1129, 210 Kirkbride Rd) and **Gateway Hotel** (☎ 275 4079, 206 Kirkbride Rd) charge around $89 for a double and provide free shuttles to the airport. More expensive are the **Centra** (☎ 275 1059) and the **Grand Chancellor** (☎ 275 7029), which are opposite one another at the junction of Ascot and Kirkbride Rds.

Hotels Several hotels are conveniently situated in the city. The **Albion Hotel** (☎ 379 4900) on the corner of Hobson and Wellesley Sts has 20 rooms in an old restored building. Doubles with private bathrooms are $65. On the corner of Albert and Wellesley Sts, **City Central Hotel** (☎ 307 3388) is close to the information centre and Skytower. The clean rooms are a little cell-like, especially those beside the internal lightwell. Doubles with their own bathrooms cost $79.

More expensive, but an excellent place to stay, the **First Imperial Hotel & Apartments** (☎ 357 6770, 131–39 Hobson St) has 61 rooms, with private bathrooms and other amenities, priced from $185.

Directly opposite the train station, the **Harbourview Station Hotel** (☎ 303 2463, 131 Beach Rd) looks a bit decrepit on the outside but the interior has been renovated. Standard rooms with private bathrooms and telephones cost $50/70; superior rooms cost $70/80.

Auckland's best business hotels charge from around $200 per room, but substantial discounts are usually available. The **Copthorne Harbour City** (☎ 377 0349, 96–100 Quay St West) and the **Novotel Hotel** (☎ 377 8920, 8 Customs St East) are older luxury hotels and, hence, cheaper.

Next rung up the price ladder are the **Hyatt Regency Hotel** (☎ 366 1234), on the corner of Princes St and Waterloo Quadrant, **Centra Hotel** (☎ 302 1111, 128 Albert St),

Rydges Auckland (☎ 359 9100) on the corner of Kingston and Federal Sts, where you'll also find the excellent Circa bar and restaurant, and *Sky City Hotel* (☎ 0800-759 2489). *City Life Auckland* (☎ 379 9222, 171 Queen St) is right in the centre of town, and has the good Zest restaurant on the 1st floor.

Auckland's best hotels include the *Sheraton* (☎ 379 5132, 83 Symonds St); the *Stamford Plaza Hotel* (☎ 309 8888) on Al-bert St; the *Carlton Hotel* (☎ 366 3000) on the corner of Mayoral Drive and Vincent St; and *The Heritage Auckland* (☎ 379 8553, 35 Hobson St).

There are a growing number of self-contained, upmarket apartments in Auckland. Expect to pay around $200 or more for two. They include *Quest Auckland* (☎ 366 5190, 363 Queen St).

Places to Eat

Because of its size and ethnic diversity, Auckland has the best range of dining options in the country. In downtown Auckland a plethora of sushi and kebab places cater to those who want something fast and inexpensive.

Aucklanders have really taken to cafe culture, and there is a huge choice of places. In the city, Lorne St, High St and Vulcan Lane are lined with cafes of all shapes, sizes and philosophies. The highest concentrations of cafes and restaurants are in Ponsonby and Parnell. Other inner-suburbs, such as Newmarket, Mt Eden and Herne Bay, have smaller clusters. Devonport (see the Around Auckland section), which is replete with cafes and bars, is only a short ferry ride from the city centre.

City Centre *Tony's Steak & Seafood* (27 Wellesley St West and 32 Lorne St) must be doing something right because it has continued unchanged while other places have come and gone. It has a basic steakhouse menu which also features lamb and pasta dishes. Steaks cost around $24 for dinner, but are less for lunch.

For cheap Italian food, *A Little Italy* (43 Victoria St West) has good pizza and pasta.

The *Mexican Cafe* (67 Victoria St West), upstairs, has a fun, casual atmosphere.

Victoria Yeeros (15 Victoria St) may not have flash decor, but its Middle Eastern fare is reliable and inexpensive. The *Middle East Restaurant* (23A Wellesley St West) is tiny and often crowded, and the food is excellent and reasonably priced. For authentic Turkish food, try the similarly priced *Cafe Midnight Express* (59 Victoria St West), near the Mexican Cafe; it's open until 11 pm. Another good Turkish place is the *Sultan's Table* (68 Victoria St West).

Pizza Pizza in Lorne St, opposite the public library, is popular with students from the nearby university. It has pizzas and snacks plus an interesting range of local and imported beer.

For vegetarian meals try *Food for Life*, run by the Hare Krishnas at the top of Queen St. For $3 you get a plate heaped with rice, dhal and a pappadam, and for $6 you get all you can eat. It's open from noon to 3 pm Monday to Friday.

Raw Power in Vulcan Lane serves healthy food from free-range eggs to tofu, soups, salads and fresh juices. Downstairs, *Khymer* dishes up steaming bowls of Cambodian-style noodle soup for $5, satay and fried noodles.

For tasty soups, salads and light lunches for under $10, try *Foodoo* on the corner of Victoria and High Sts. *Simple Cottage* (50 High St) is sleek and modern in its new abode, and still serving good wholesome vegetarian food.

Auckland has many Japanese restaurants. They include *Daikoku* (148 Quay St); *Daikoku Ramen* in Tyler St, behind the main restaurant, where you can get a steaming bowl of ramen noodles for $10; and *Okonomi-yaki Japanese*, on Wellesley St West, where you sit around a teppan (hot plate) with a spatula and chopsticks while the meal is cooked in front of you.

There are many choices for Thai in Auckland. One of the longest-running is the reliable *Mai Thai* on the corner of Albert St and Victoria St West.

For Chinese try *Sun World* (56 Wakefield St). Chicken, duck and vegetarian are all on the menu, plus things like chicken feet for the adventurous. Prices are very reasonable.

If you are not on a really tight budget there are many more upmarket places to try. For seafood try *Seamart* on the corner of Fanshawe St and Market Place. It's right next to the fish market, so you know the seafood is really fresh. There are daily specials.

O'Connell St Bistro (30 O'Connell St) is a bar and restaurant with fresh, simple food and a pleasantly intimate environment. *Toto (53 Nelson St)* has good Italian food and a great atmosphere, plus live opera on Saturday and Thursday.

Paramount Restaurant & Bar is near the corner of Lorne and Wellesley Sts, near the New Gallery.

For fine dining try *Five City Restaurant (5 City Rd)*, which charges $75 for a three-course menu. For the best views of the city try *Orbit* at Skytower; also at Skytower, *Tamarind* is excellent.

For fine views of the ferries and harbour, *Cin Cin on Quay (99 Quay St)* in the ferry building and *Harbourside* on the floor above, are stylish, albeit expensive. Nearby, opposite Princes Wharf, are *Kermadec* and *Viaduct Central*. The America's Cup has left a legacy of great pubs and eateries on Princes Wharf, including the stylish *Euro Restaurant & Bar*, *Wildfire* and *Cafe Hoegaarden*.

Most cafes in the downtown area are along Lorne and High Sts, and on Vulcan Lane. The *New Cafe*, on the corner of Lorne and Wellesley Sts, is right next to the gallery and its culinary offerings are suitably artistically presented. Other good places in Lorne St include the understated *City*, easy to miss but popular among those who have discovered it (courtyard dining in summer), *Sierra* and the stylish *Alba*, which is open until 10 pm most nights. High St is virtually lined with cafes, starting with the ever-reliable *Paneton*, the very modern *Wofem Bros Bagelry*, the hip little *Jolt*, the seriously-dedicated-to-coffee *Colombus*, and the sleek *D-72*, which is open late.

Gloria (97 Anzac St) is a trendy spot with a good blackboard menu and lots of tasty cakes and muffins – and of course good coffee. *Melba (33 Vulcan Lane)* is always busy.

Last but not least, the cheap eats and late nights quandary can be solved by the *White Lady* mobile hamburger stand, an Auckland institution. It's on Shortland St just off Queen St and is open in the evenings, until around 3 am during the week and 24 hours on weekends and holidays.

Central Food Halls & Supermarkets Food halls in central Auckland are mostly open during shopping hours only. The Downtown shopping centre on QEII Square, on the corner of Queen St and Customs St West, has the *Downtown Food Court*.

Other *food halls* are on the lower ground floor of the BNZ Tower, on the corner of Queen and Swanson Sts, and on the 4th floor of the Finance Plaza, on the corner of Queen and Durham Sts. At the Countrywide shopping plaza at 280 Queen St, down from Wellesley St, there's an *international food hall* with kebabs, fish and chips, Chinese, Japanese and traditional cafes. *Atrium on Elliot*, on Elliot St, also has seven international outlets.

For Asian fare, you can't beat *Food Alley*, in Albert St opposite the Stamford Plaza Hotel. Thai, Chinese, Malay, Korean and Japanese meals mostly cost under $10. It's open from 10.30 am to 10 pm daily.

There is a *New World supermarket (College Hill Rd)* near Victoria Park Market, open from 8 am to 10 pm daily, and a *mini supermarket* in the basement of Deka (48 Queen St). There's also the *Mid Town mini supermarket*, on the ground floor of the Landmark building on the corner of Durham St West and Queen St, and the *High St Superette (50 High St)*.

K Rd One of Auckland's most interesting and culturally diverse streets, K Rd offers some unusual dining options. The following is a small sample.

Rasoi at No 211 specialises in authentic thalis and Indian sweets; eat till you burst for under $10. The *Little Turkish Cafe* at No 217 is brisk and bright and has inexpensive food, such as kebabs and moussaka.

Wagamama at No 173 has tasty Italian dishes plus DJ nights on Friday and Saturday;

AUCKLAND

Verona at No 169 uses organic fare and has a good vegetarian selection, but it's also a pleasant low-key place for a drink.

One of the trendiest places is *Armadillo;* good for a drink and/or a meal in very pleasant surroundings. The *Monkey Bar* nearby is also a classy place. *Brazil* is a cafe with a uniquely urban interior, and an interesting barrel-shaped roof that arcs over the sitting area upstairs.

Habanero (65 Pitt St), just off K Rd, has fresh, innovative food and is busy at lunchtime.

For atmosphere it's hard to beat *Alleluya* which is tucked away beside the big windows at the end of St Kevins Arcade in K Rd.

Parnell East of the city centre, Parnell Rd heads uphill and is lined with bars, cafes and restaurants. Parnell Village, a labyrinth of shops near the top of the rise, has some good medium-priced restaurants, several with tables in open courtyards. They include *Thai Friends* for good Thai food (mains from $15.80); *Asahi,* with tempura from $15, rice meals from $10; and the *Java Room,* which has Indonesian and Thai (mains from $16.50). The *Chocolate Cafe* is a great place for chocaholics, and it has a wide selection of coffees, snacks and desserts.

Verve (☎ 379 2860) has an imaginative and appealing menu and a pleasant outdoor eating area. The *Kebab Kid* at No 363 does great doner kebabs and shwarmas (including vegetarian) starting at $6.50.

Oh Calcutta at No 131 specialises in tandoori. The prices are very reasonable with mains under $15. *Alligator Pear,* tucked downstairs between the shop fronts, has pasta, salads, chicken, fish and so on.

La Bocca at No 251 is a small place that serves delicious Italian food. Nearby, *Non Solo Pizza* at No 259 has some 20 toppings to choose from. Prices start at $18.50 for a classic pizza. Next door is *Toto,* a small, licensed place that's a pleasant spot for panini, bagels and bruschetta.

Iguaçu at No 269 is a perennially popular place with a regular live jazz slot on Sunday. The nearby *Veranda Bar & Grill (VBG)* has a busy bar and a restaurant that serves good, uncomplicated food. *The Mink Cafe & Bar (99 Parnell Rd)* is a relatively new, trendy place with wood-fired pizzas.

The Other Side (☎ 366 4426) has a selection of Continental food, as well as steaks, fish and venison, with mains from $32.

For fine dining, *Antoines* (☎ 379 8756, 333 Parnell Rd) is one of Auckland's best. In a renovated house, it's one of those silver service, gold credit-card places where the best local produce is tantalisingly presented in the French way. Bookings are essential.

Cibo (☎ 309 2255, 91 St Georges Bay Rd) serves great food and has courtyard dining in summer.

Tribeca (☎ 379 6359, 8 George St) is halfway to Newmarket. There is a wide choice of entrees and mains, and the desserts are especially enticing. You can dine outdoors under umbrellas on the lawn or in the courtyard.

Locals swear by the hamburgers from *Al & Pete's* on Parnell Rd, opposite Domain Drive. The Indian takeaway *Bombay Junction* next door is also recommended.

Mikano (☎ 309 9514, 1 Solent St) is in a great spot at Mechanics Bay, right on the water's edge. It's open for lunch daily except Saturday, and for dinner every night. There is a bar area behind the main dining space.

Ponsonby This is Auckland's busiest restaurant district, strung out over many blocks along Ponsonby Rd. You can walk along and see what captures your fancy, but on Saturday nights get here early or else book.

Café Cézanne (296 Ponsonby Rd) is a small, casual place that's always busy. *Tuatara* at No 198 has straightforward, well-prepared food and serves good coffee. The tables outside are popular during the day, but this place also packs them in until late at night.

The smaller *SPQR* at No 150 is similar, with stylish decor, hearty breakfasts and a good range of moderately priced snacks and light meals. The food is really an accompaniment to the wine quaffing, which goes on into the early hours. Opposite SPQR, the *Atomic Cafe,* at No 121, is a breakfast and daytime hang-out. Some other popular cafes include *No 39*, *Santos* (No 114), and the gay-friendly cafes *Atlas* (No 285) and *Surrender Dorothy* (No 175). *Stella* (No 118) is a popular place with a brasserie-style menu.

Musical Knives at No 272 has stylish although not cheap vegetarian, including organic soba and organic vegetables with tofu. *Dizengoff* at No 256 has food with a Jewish emphasis and interesting breakfasts. *Expresso Bambina* at No 266 is a great place for coffee and all that goes with it; *Bambina Bistro* (☎ 378 7766) next door is classy, with good food.

Estasi (☎ 378 7888, 222 Ponsonby Rd) specialises in Pacific Rim cuisine, including oven-baked salmon and pumpkin gnocchi. *Ponsonby Pies*, at No 134, has many imaginative fillings on offer, such as smoked fish or Thai chicken curry, as well as more traditional fare. *Provence* (☎ 376 8147) at No 44 is an atmospheric, classy place with good French food. For Malaysian food try *Shioks Cafe* at No 6.

There are numerous cafes and restaurants along Jervois Rd, at the north-western end of Ponsonby Rd. Award-winning restaurants here are *Vinnies* (☎ 376 5597) at No 166 and *Essence* (☎ 376 2049) at No 70–72. One of the most popular places for breakfast, brunch and lunch is *Andiamo* at No 194, although *Fusion* and *Sierra* are also great. Try *Gannet Rock* for seafood.

Other Suburbs The busy Newmarket shopping district has numerous restaurants and cafes. Right in the heart of Newmarket is *Zarbo (24 Morrow St)*, an excellent deli and fine food outlet. *Kenzie*, on Remuera Rd, is a longtime favourite for espresso, cake and light meals. *First Floor Cafe (1 Teed St)* is consistently good, and is a pleasant spot to linger over lunch. *Poppadom (471 Khyber Pass Rd)* always has good and reasonably priced Indian food. *Sri Siam* at No 473 has inexpensive Thai food. *Ramses* at No 435 has a long-standing reputation for quality, with fish a speciality. *Rikka Newmarket (73 Davis Crescent)* is a smart Japanese restaurant.

For fine French food try *The French Café (210 Symonds St)*.

Along Tamaki Drive there are plenty of places to recharge on caffeine or idle away a summer evening over a drink and a meal. At Okahu Bay, not far from Kelly Tarlton's, is *Hammerheads*, which has an expansive deck for outdoor dining and where seafood is a speciality.

At Mission Bay there is a string of cafes with outdoor seating – stroll along and take your pick. Recommended is *Bluefins* on the corner of Tamaki Drive and Atkin Ave, and *Cafe on Kohi* at Kohimaramara Beach.

Another pleasant spot for dining by the sea is St Heliers, where you'll find the excellent *Saints* and *Kahve* among others. *The Cafe*, next to Saints, has live jazz on Sunday afternoon.

Entertainment

To find out what's happening in the city try the *NZ Herald*'s entertainment pages and Saturday 'What's On' supplement, and *7 Days* which comes out on Thursday. *What's Happening* is a free monthly magazine that lists major events. It's available from visitor centres and other places.

The weekly *Alive & Happening* from the Auckland Travel and Information Centre lists the latest events, music, concerts, theatre, opera, dance and sports. Gig guides tend to come and go.

The giveaway events calendar *The Fix* is available at record and music shops (try Real Groovy Records at 438 Queen St). It comes out on Thursday. *Re-Mix* (free) and *Lava* ($2.50 from bookshops) also have gig guides.

Nightclubs & Pubs Nightlife tends to be quiet during the week. On weekends the popular spots are full to overflowing and dress standards apply at many of the fancier bars.

Among the most popular clubs is *Calibre (St Kevins Arcade, 179 K Rd)*, which has dance and house music from 11 pm to 8 am Thursday to Saturday.

The Khuja Lounge on the corner of Queen St and K Rd (above Westpac) is a popular venue with plenty of variety in musical style, and a mix of DJ and live music. It's open Tuesday to Saturday from 7 pm.

The Dogs Bollix (582 K Rd) is a lively Irish Pub with live music nightly, except for Monday when it's quiz night.

Club Havana, in Beresford St off K Rd, pulsates to Latin rhythm; tango lessons are available.

In the downtown area, in High St, you'll find *Deschlers*, a trendy bar that has consistently good live jazz, and *Cause Celebre/The Box*, a popular late-night venue with techno, house and live. The High St cafe *Rakinos* has live jazz from Thursday to Saturday. In O'Connell St are *Bacchus* and *Factory*, both of which have DJ and live music. *The Ministry* on Albert St has a regular drum and base night on Thursday, and DJ and house at other times. In Vulcan Lane *Papa Jack's Voodoo Lounge* turns up the volume, attracting a mixed crowd. *Fu Bar (168 Queen St)*, downstairs, has house and techno with some drum and base and hip-hop, plus pool tables (open Tuesday to Saturday).

The Temple (486 Queen St) has a small cafe, pool tables, and everything from solo acoustic to fully plugged bands. Singer-songwriters come here to perform, and so can you; Monday is open mike night.

Manifesto (315 Queen St) has regular wine tastings and jazz evenings.

Along Ponsonby Rd there's the long-running *Java Jive*, which has a mix of most things. Also on Ponsonby Rd and featuring live music are *Grand Central*, the *Safari Lounge* and *Alhambra*.

The *Garage Bar (152 Ponsonby Rd)*, next to SPQR, has a peculiar glass floor and a good selection of drinks.

Out in Newmarket, *Claddagh (372 Broadway)* combines a cosy Irish-pub atmosphere with traditional Irish music on weekends.

For hearty pub food and a terrific selection of beer, try *Galbraith's Ale House (2 Mt Eden Rd)*.

The America's Cup stimulated a flurry of pub and restaurant activity on the waterfront. New places to drink here include *Euro Restaurant & Bar Leftfield*, *Cafe Hoegaarden* and the *Lenin Bar* at Princes Wharf, and *Stars & Stripes* on the corner of Quay and Albert Sts. Other waterfront watering holes are *Viaduct Central*, and the microbrewery *Loaded Hog*.

Other options in the downtown area include the *Rose & Crown (104 Fanshawe St)*, *Shakespeare Tavern (61 Albert St)*, a microbrewery, and the *London Bar* and *Murphy's* on the corner of Queen and Wellesley Sts.

The Immigrant (104 Fanshawe St) is a good traditional Irish bar with live northern-hemisphere sports telecasts and bands on Friday and Saturday. *Soho Kitchen & Bar (2 Hobson St)* is also good for a night out.

Margarita's (18 Elliot St) is a popular bar with backpackers, and other backpacker haunts include the *Embargo* bar below Central City Backpackers and *The Hard Rat* at Auckland Central Backpackers.

In trendy Vulcan Lane are the popular *Occidental Belgium Bar* and the *Equinox* next door. Hidden behind the Stamford Plaza Hotel is trendy little *Tabac (6 Mills Lane)*.

Among the hottest places at the time of writing were the tiny *Lime Bar* and the tropically themed *Hula Hut*, both in Ponsonby Rd.

Skytower Casino on the corner of Victoria and Hobson Sts is one of the biggest entertainment venues. The main attraction here is, of course, gambling, but it also has a 700-seat theatre, restaurants, bars, a hotel and observation decks.

Gay & Lesbian Venues Auckland's gay and lesbian scene is fairly low-key. Cafes and clubs with a gay and lesbian following are mainly found in Ponsonby and the western end of K Rd. They include the cafes *Atlas* and *Surrender Dorothy* on Ponsonby Rd (see Places to Eat), *Kamo (382–386 K Rd)*, which won the 1999 Monteith's Wild Food Challenge, and *Caluzzi (461 K Rd)*, which has good food and a lively atmosphere.

K Rd clubs which have a gay and lesbian following include *Sinners* at No 373 and *Legend* at No 335.

Cinema, Performing Arts & Popular Music The newest cinema complex in town is the *Force Entertainment Centre* on Aotea

Square. It boasts a giant Imax screen as well as several conventional screens. For details on suburban cinemas see the *NZ Herald*. The main venue for dance and theatre is the *Aotea Centre*. Other venues include the *Maidment Theatre* at the University of Auckland and the *Sky City Theatre* at Sky City. *Silo Theatre* on Lower Greys Ave specialises in fringe theatre. Musical performances are held at the *Auckland Town Hall* and the Aotea Centre. The Auckland Theatre Company, Auckland's only professional theatre company, performs mainly at the Aotea Centre, Sky City Theatre and Maidment Theatre.

The renovated *Civic Theatre* with its eastern fantasy interior reopened in early 2000. Situated on the corner of Queen St and Wellesley St West, it is now the venue for major productions including opera, musicals, film and live theatre.

For big international bands and major local bands, the main venues in Auckland are the *Powerstation (33 Mt Eden Rd)*, and the *North Shore Events Centre* on Torana Rd, Glenfield. Big dance venues are at Alexandra Park and Ellerslie Racecourse.

The most popular small venue currently is *The Kings Arms Tavern (☎ 373 3240, 59 France St, Newton)*, which has emerging bands, rock and alternative rock. You can hear live music Thursday to Sunday and on the second Wednesday of each month.

For comedy, Auckland's top venue is *The Classic Comedy Club (321 Queen St);* a bi-monthly calendar of events is available at the door.

The *NZ Herald* carries listings of what's on. Most theatrical and major musical events can be booked through Ticketek (☎ 307 5000).

Getting There & Away

Air Auckland is a major gateway to NZ. See the Getting There & Away chapter in the front of this book for information on international airlines represented in Auckland.

Domestic airlines operating to/from Auckland include:

Air New Zealand (☎ 357 3000) cnr Customs and Queen Sts

Ansett New Zealand (☎ 0800-267 388) 75 Queen St; 50 Grafton Rd
Great Barrier Airlines (☎ 256 6500, 0800-900 600) Auckland Domestic Terminal
Mountain Air – Great Barrier Xpress (☎ 256 7025) Auckland Domestic Terminal
Origin Pacific (☎ 0800-302 302) Trent Drive, Nelson Airport, Nelson
Waiheke Air Services (☎ 372 5001) Ostend, Waiheke Island

At the international terminal a bank is open to change money with all arriving and departing flights, but charges a transaction fee.

Bus The main bus company in Auckland, as for the rest of NZ, is InterCity, in combination with Newmans. With a few exceptions, these buses go to almost all bigger towns and the main tourist areas.

There are services from Auckland to just about everywhere in NZ, and these operate from the Sky City Coach Terminal at 102 Hobson St (reservations ☎ 913 6100, 0800-777 707). Note that Newmans does not operate in Northland.

Northliner Express (☎ 307 5873) buses operate from the Downtown Airline Terminal, with services heading north from Auckland to Whangarei, the Bay of Islands and Kaitaia.

Smaller services include the Little Kiwi Bus (☎ 309 0905, 0800-759 999), which goes to Hamilton and has connections to Rotorua.

Backpacker buses operate in and from Auckland; both Kiwi Experience (☎ 366 9830) and Magic Travellers Network (☎ 358 5600) offer a door-to-door service, pick-ups and drop-offs at any Auckland hostel.

Train Trains arrive at and depart from the Auckland Station (☎ 0800-802 802) on Beach Rd, about 1km east of the city centre. Several readers have written saying they felt intimidated at the station at night. You can check reservations and information from 7 am to 9 pm daily.

Two trains operate between Auckland and Wellington. The *Overlander* runs daily, departing from both cities in the morning and arriving around dinner time. The *Northerner* is an overnight train operating Sunday to Friday, departing from both cities in the evening and arriving early in the morning.

The *Geyserland* operates daily between Auckland and Rotorua and the *Kaimai Express* operates daily between Auckland and Tauranga; both stop in Hamilton on the way.

Hitching Getting out of Auckland by thumb can be hard work. The only legal ways to hitch out of town are either to stand by the motorway on-ramps or take a bus to Mercer or Albany and start from there.

Getting Around

To/From the Airport Auckland airport (☎ 256 8899) is 21km south-west of the city centre. It has an international terminal and two domestic terminals (Ansett and Air New Zealand), each with a tourist information centre. A free shuttle service operates between the terminals and there's also a signposted footpath between them.

At the international terminal there's a freephone for accommodation bookings, and many places to stay also provide a free shuttle to/from the airport. Both terminals have left-luggage facilities and car-rental desks, though you get better rates from companies in town.

The AirBus shuttle (☎ 272 9396) runs every 20 minutes between the international and domestic terminals and the Downtown Airline Terminal; reservations are not required, you buy a ticket from the driver. The trip takes about 50 minutes one way (longer during rush hour) and costs $10 one way, $16 return.

Door-to-door shuttles run to and from the airport, and competition is cut-throat. The two main operators are Super Shuttle (☎ 307 5210) and Johnston's Shuttle Link (☎ 275 1234). The cost between the airport and the city centre is around $15 for one person and $20 for two; all sorts of deals are available.

A taxi to the airport from the city will cost around $38 one way.

Bus The Downtown Bus Terminal is on Commerce St, between Quay St and Customs St East, but not all buses leave from here. Local bus route timetables are available from the bus terminal, newsagents and the information centre, or you can phone Rideline (☎ 366 6400) for information and schedules. Inner-city fares are $0.50/0.30 for an adult/child or senior citizen (you pay the driver when you board).

The Link is an excellent bus service that travels clockwise and anticlockwise around a loop which includes Queen St, the casino, Ponsonby Rd, K Rd, the university, Newmarket, Parnell, the train station and QEII Square. It's $1 to most places; the bus runs every 10 minutes.

A free bus service that does a continuous loop around the downtown area was introduced during the America's Cup. It passes the Cup Village and travels down Queen St. The Auckland Travel and Information Centre has details on its exact routing. It's easy to spot this bus: it's a colourfully painted double-decker with 'Get Into It' emblazoned on its sides.

Train There's a limited Tranz Metro (Rideline; ☎ 366 6400) train service, with just two main lines running west to Waitakere and south to Papakura. The Auckland Station is on Beach Rd, behind the imposing former Auckland central railway station.

Car & Motorcycle Auckland is crawling with car hire operators and is the best city in which to hire a vehicle for touring NZ. Some good deals can be had for long-term hire, but be warned that cheapest is not necessarily the best.

The major companies – Avis, Budget, Hertz and Thrifty – are the most reliable, offer full insurance and have offices at the airport and all over the country. They are expensive, but rates are often negotiable for longer rentals.

If you are prepared to take limited insurance and risk losing an excess of around $700, then the cheaper operators offer some pretty good deals. Prices vary with the season, the age of the car and length of rental.

In the off season, for rental of a month or more, a good 1990 model car costs as little as $30 a day. For shorter rentals in the high season expect to pay $50 or more a day. A campervan or kitted-out minibus starts at around $70 per day.

Ignore prices quoted in brochures and shop around by phone. Always read the rental agreement thoroughly before you sign.

Auckland has more than 60 rental operators. They include:

A2B	☎ 377 0825, 800-222 929
Ace*	☎ 0800-502 277
Alternative Rental Cars	☎ 373 3822
Avis	☎ 526 2800
Britz NZ*	☎ 0800-831 900
Budget*	☎ 375 2270, 800-652 227
Hertz	☎ 309 0989, 800-654 321
Maui*	☎ 275 3013, 800-651 080
Thrifty	☎ 309 0111, 800-737 070

* Rents out sleepervans or campervans as well as cars

You can rent a small scooter for $24 for 24 hours; only a car driving licence is needed. New Zealand Motorcycle Rentals (☎ 377 2005), 31 Beach Rd, has one-day hire starting at $90.

Buying a Car For stays of two months or more many people look at buying a car. You can buy through dealers on the buy-back scheme at car fairs or through ads in the newspapers. Backpacker hostels in Auckland also have notice boards where travellers leaving the country advertise the sale of their cars.

For newspaper listings, cars are advertised in the *NZ Herald* on Wednesday, the *Trade & Exchange* on Monday and Thursday, and the *Auto Trader* magazine.

Buy-backs, where the dealer agrees to buy back your car for an agreed price, are not usually a great deal but are an easier option. Dealers who work on this system include:

Budget Car Sales	☎ 379 4120
Downtown Rentals	☎ 303 1847
Geraghty McGregor Motors	☎ 307 6700
Rex Swinburne Motors	☎ 620 6587
Rock Bottom Rentals	☎ 622 1592

The most popular way to buy a car is through the car fairs, where people bring their cars to sell them. Manukau is the biggest and the best, but the Ellerslie Racecourse car fair is also good. Arrive between 8.30 and 9.30 am for the best choice; car fairs are over by about noon. For a credit check (☎ 0800-658 934) quote chassis and licence-plate numbers. Mechanical inspection services, credit agencies and Auto Check details are all on hand at the car fairs, which are listed below:

Ellerslie Racecourse (☎ 810 9212) Near the Greenlane roundabout, from 9 am to noon on Sunday

Manukau (☎ 358 5000) In the car park of the giant shopping mall of the Manukau City Centre near the Manukau motorway off ramp (Manukau City, South Auckland), from 8.30 am to 1 pm on Sunday

Old Oriental Markets (☎ 524 9183) On Beach Rd in the city centre, from 9 am to noon on Saturday

Alternatively, you could try the car auctions. Two of the best known are:

Hammer Auctions (☎ 579 2344) 830 Great South Rd, Penrose. Auctions are held several times a week – 6 pm Monday, Wednesday and Friday for budget vehicles.

Turner's Car Auction (☎ 525 1920) McNab St, Penrose. Auctions several times a week – 11.30 am Wednesday for budget vehicles.

Taxi Auckland's many taxis usually work from ranks but also cruise popular areas. You often have to phone for a taxi; Auckland Taxi Co-Op (☎ 300 3000) is one of the biggest.

Taxi companies are listed in the *Yellow Pages*. Flagfall is $2 and then around $1.60 per kilometre.

Bicycle Adventure Cycles (☎ 309 5566) is at 1 Fort Lane, just off Fort St. The Penny Farthing Cycle Shop (☎ 379 2524) is on the corner of Symonds St and Khyber Pass Rd. Both hire mountain bikes for around $25 a day.

Tuk Tuk Located on the city side of the harbour bridge Auckland City Tuk Tuks

(☎ 360 1988) will take you on short trips around the city centre for $3, or for longer trips (eg, along Tamaki Drive, to Auckland Museum etc). Auckland City Tuk Tuks can generally be found outside the ferry building. In Devonport contact Ultimate Tours (☎ 482 0025).

Boat Fullers Auckland (☎ 367 9111) operates ferries between the city and Devonport, Stanley Bay, Birkenhead and Bayswater on the North Shore, the gulf islands and, most recently, Half Moon Bay near Howick. Fullers' Web site at www.fullers.co.nz lists timetables. Ferries to Devonport (12 minutes one way) run frequently.

Pacific Ferries (☎ 303 1741), whose Web site is at www.pacificferries.co.nz, has a 'fast ferry' service to Waiheke. See the Waiheke section later in this chapter for details.

For ferries to Kawau Island see the Northland chapter.

Around Auckland

REGIONAL PARKS

The Auckland Regional Council (ARC) administers 21 regional parks around the Auckland region, all within 15km to 90km of the city. There are several coastal and beach parks with swimming and surfing beaches, plus bush parks, a kauri park, the Waitakere Ranges west of Auckland, the Hunua catchment south-east of Auckland and a gannet colony at Muriwai. The parks have good walking and tramping tracks, ranging from 20 minutes to several hours to walk, and camping is allowed in several parks.

An Auckland Regional Parks pamphlet, with a list of facilities in each park, is available from the visitor centre, or the DOC office in the ferry building in Auckland.

DEVONPORT

Devonport is an attractive suburb on the tip of Auckland's North Shore peninsula. One of the earliest areas of European settlement, it retains a 19th-century atmosphere with many well-preserved Victorian and Edwardian

buildings. It's touristy, only 15 minutes from the city by ferry and has lots of small shops, art and craft galleries and cafes.

The helpful Devonport Information Centre (☎ 446 0677, @ visitorinfo@nthshore.govt .nz) on Windsor Reserve is open from 10 am to 4 pm daily. Get a copy of *Old Devonport Walk*, a pamphlet outlining the many historic buildings in this antique port, or check the Web site (www.devonport.co.nz).

Things to See

Devonport has several points of interest. Two volcanic cones, Mt Victoria and North Head, were once Maori pa – you can see the terracing on the sides of the cones. **Mt Victoria** is the higher of the two, with a great 360° view and a map at the top pointing out all the landmarks and giving the names of the many islands you can see. You can walk or drive to the summit of Mt Victoria; the road is open at all times except from 6 pm to 7 am on Thursday, Friday and Saturday.

North Head, on the other cone, is a historic reserve riddled with old tunnels built at the end of the 19th century in response to fears of a Russian invasion. The fortifications were extended and enlarged during WWI and WWII, but dismantled after the latter. Some of the old guns are still here. The reserve is open to vehicles from 6 am to 6 pm daily and to pedestrians until 10 pm.

The **waterfront promenade**, with a fine view across the harbour to the city, makes a good stroll. Near the ferry wharf is a childrens playground and a large lawn area where families picnic on sunny days.

Walk west from the wharf along the promenade (left as you exit the wharf building) for about five blocks, until you reach the navy base, then turn right into Spring St. At the end of the street is the small **Naval Museum**, open from 10 am to 4.30 pm daily (entry is free).

The **Devonport Museum**, on Mt Cambria Reserve, just east of Mt Victoria, chronicles Devonport's history and is open from 2 to 4 pm on weekends.

Just north of the foot of North Head, **Cheltenham Beach** is a lovely little beach with a superb view of Rangitoto.

AUCKLAND REGION

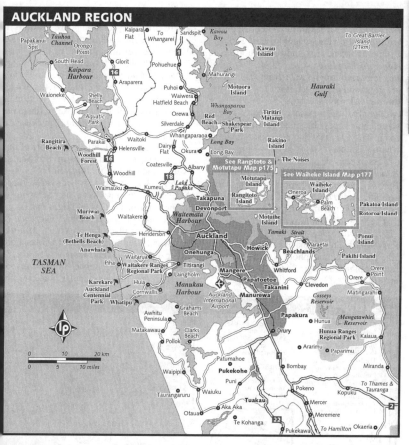

Places to Stay

Devonport has more B&Bs than any other Auckland suburb, many of them lovingly restored Victorian or Edwardian villas. The information centre has a list of all accommodation in the area.

Facing the water, on Flagstaff Terrace, are *Hyland House* (☎ 445 9917) at No 4 and the *Peace & Plenty Inn* (☎ 445 2925) at No 6, both beautiful houses with excellent accommodation from $200 for two. *Jeong-K Place by the Sea* (☎ 445 1358, 4 King Edward Parade) is another carefully restored place with similarly priced quality accommodation.

Other top places in Devonport include *Villa Cambria* (☎ 445 7899, 71 Vauxhall Rd), with doubles from $130 and *Devonport Villa Inn* (☎ 445 8397, 46 Tainui Rd), with doubles from $185. *Badger's of Devonport* (☎ 445 2099, 30 Summer St) has doubles from $119, *Karin's Garden Villa* (☎ 445 8689, 14 Sinclair St) has doubles from $125 and *Cheltenham by the Sea* (☎ 445 9437, 2 Grove St) costs $65/90/100 for a single/twin/double room ($120 for double with en suite).

At Bayswater, on a narrow finger of land jutting out into the Waitemata Harbour, is

Bayswater Point Lodge (☎ 445 7163, 27 Norwood Rd), a beautifully kept mansion with fantastic views. Doubles cost $165.

One of the newest and nicest options is *Admirals Landing* (☎ 445 4394, 11 Queens Parade), right on the waterfront. The views are great and the garden is lovely. There are three guest rooms costing about $130 for two, including breakfast. There is also a wheelchair-accessible guest room and bathroom. The owners will meet you at the ferry if you wish.

Less expensive options include *Parituhu Beach Stay* (☎ 445 6559, 3 King Edward Parade), where single/double rooms cost $60/80, and *The Secret Garden* (☎ 445 3605, 18 Eton Ave), which costs $55/75.

The historic *Esplanade Hotel* (☎ 455 1291, 1 Victoria Rd) is directly opposite the ferry wharf. The rooms are simple but stylish, with TVs and phones, and the bathrooms range from big to huge. Doubles start at $106.

Places to Eat

There are many cafes and restaurants in Devonport, most of them on Victoria Rd. There are restaurants as well as fast-food/snack places at the Devonport Wharf.

Port-O-Call is in a great spot overlooking the harbour at the end of the wharf. There is a reasonably wide selection of dishes from which to choose, with mains starting at $20. The *Torpedo Bay Tavern & Grill* is upstairs.

The Esplanade Hotel has a couple of dining rooms, *LIC* and *Pasta by the Sea*, as well as the *Grapevine Wine Bar*.

Java House tucked away down WJ Scott Mall off Victoria Rd has a tasty selection of scones, muffins, cakes and light meals.

The Stone Oven Bakery (5 Clarence St) is the perfect place for breakfast. *Manuka* has wood-fired pizza, as well as pasta and other dishes. *Bankers Arms* is a nonsmoking pub with seating outside or in. *Monsoon* (71 Victoria Rd) is a popular place serving

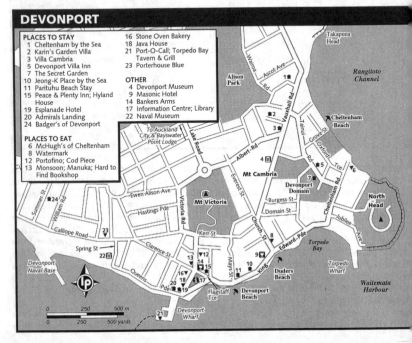

DEVONPORT

PLACES TO STAY
1 Cheltenham by the Sea
2 Karin's Garden Villa
3 Villa Cambria
5 Devonport Villa Inn
7 The Secret Garden
10 Jeong-K Place by the Sea
11 Parituhu Beach Stay
15 Peace & Plenty Inn; Hyland House
19 Esplanade Hotel
20 Admirals Landing
24 Badger's of Devonport

PLACES TO EAT
6 McHugh's of Cheltenham
8 Watermark
12 Portofino; Cod Piece
13 Monsoon; Manuka; Hard to Find Bookshop

16 Stone Oven Bakery
18 Java House
21 Port-O-Call; Torpedo Bay Tavern & Grill
23 Porterhouse Blue

OTHER
4 Devonport Museum
9 Masonic Hotel
14 Bankers Arms
17 Information Centre; Library
22 Naval Museum

good Thai and Malay food, with mains starting at $14.50. It's open from 5 pm daily.

Portofino has a selection of Italian food, with mains starting at $17. It's open for dinner weekdays and from 11 am until late on weekends. Nearby, the **Cod Piece (26 Victoria Rd)** is a good place for fish and chips and hamburgers.

Porterhouse Blue has an interesting menu that includes venison, kangaroo and hare, with mains starting at $25.50. You should book two to three weeks in advance to ensure a table here.

Watermark (33 King Edward Parade) has a $25 buffet dinner from Wednesday to Sunday and a $15 brunch buffet from 9.30 to 11.30 am on Sunday; a set lunch starts at noon. **McHugh's of Cheltenham (46 Cheltenham Rd)** is in a great location overlooking the beach. The popular $20 lunchtime buffet is from noon to 2 pm.

The **Masonic Tavern (☎ 445 0484, 29 King Edward Parade)** has inexpensive counter meals. It has a pool playing area upstairs, and sometimes a band.

Getting There & Away

Bus Buses to Devonport run regularly from the Downtown Bus Terminal in Auckland, but you have to pass through Takapuna and traffic can be slow. The ferry crossing is quicker and more enjoyable.

Boat The Devonport ferry departs from the Auckland ferry building every 30 minutes during the day and hourly in the evening. The last ferry is at 11 pm weekdays and 1 am on weekends ($7, children $3.50).

Fullers' **Harbour Explorer** departs from pier 3 near the ferry building and stops at Devonport, Kelly Tarlton's and Rangitoto; an all-day pass entitles you to get on and off the boat wherever you like. Ring Fullers (☎ 367 9111) for information.

WEST OF AUCKLAND

No more than an hour's drive from the city, West Auckland has a dramatic, rugged coastline with iron-sand beaches backed by regenerating bush. There are excellent surf beaches and more than 130 bushwalks,

making this an important recreational zone for Auckland city.

West Auckland is also the place to go for vineyards and craft outlets. Enterprise Waitakere (☎ 837 1855) puts out a map called **Art out West**, available from the Auckland and Arataki visitor centres, which provides information on galleries and studios. **Lopdell House Gallery** (☎ 817 8087) on the corner of Titirangi and South Titirangi Rds is an exhibition space that showcases local artists.

The Waitakere Tramline Society (☎ 832 3300) has weekend trips leaving from East Portal (near Titirangi), which pass through tunnels filled with glowworms ($8).

Watercare's **Rain Forest Express** (☎ 634 4809) departs from Jacobsons' Depot (off Scenic Drive) at 2 pm on Sunday, and there's a glowworm special trip at 5.30 pm ($12, children $6). You may catch a glimpse of long-legged cave weta in the tunnels. Bookings are essential for both trips.

Vineyards

New Zealand wine has a worldwide reputation and there are numerous vineyards in the West Auckland area. The glossy map **Winemakers of Auckland**, available from all Auckland visitor centres, details the vineyards, their addresses and opening hours.

Some places, such as Delegat's and Corbans, are within walking distance of Henderson, which can be reached by bus or the Tranz Metro train from downtown Auckland. Other large and well-known vineyards, such as Matua Valley, House of Nobilo and Coopers Creek, are further out near Kumeu. There are also a couple of vineyards as far afield as Matakana, near Warkworth.

Some of the wineries have excellent restaurants. For fine dining in a beautiful setting, the **Hunting Lodge (☎ 411 8259)** at Matua Valley is open from Friday to Sunday for lunch and dinner. Other restaurants are **de Vines** at Lincoln Vineyards, the **cafe** at Pleasant Valley Wines and **Allely House** at Selaks Wines.

There are a couple of regular festivals out this way – Vintage Alfresco (mid-March) and Wine Waitakere (October). Visitor information centres will have details.

Waitakere Ranges

These scenic ranges once supported important kauri forests, but these were logged almost to extinction in the 19th century. A few stands of kauri and other mature trees such as rimu survive.

The **Centennial Memorial Park** now protects many native plants in the regenerating forest. Bordered to the west by the beaches on the Tasman Sea, the park's sometimes rugged terrain with steep-sided valleys is the most significant forest area close to Auckland. It is popular for picnics and walks (there are some 143 tracks).

The **Arataki Visitor Centre** (☎ 817 7134) is 6km north-west of Titirangi on **Scenic Drive** (SH24), which goes from Titirangi to Swanson. It is a good starting point for exploring the ranges and is open from 9 am to 5 pm daily. As well as providing a host of information on the area, this impressive centre with its Maori carvings and spectacular views is an attraction in its own right. The nature trail opposite the centre takes you past labelled native species, including mature kauri.

Huge Maori carving at the Arataki Visitor Centre

The centre has numerous pamphlets and maps for walking over 200km of trails in the ranges. Noted walks are the **Karamatura Loop Walk** (one hour return) near Huia, leading to the waterfalls and northern rata forest, and the Cascade/Kauri area to the north, which has three good walks: **Auckland City Walk**, the **Upper Kauri Track** and **Pukematekeo Track**.

Whatipu & Karekare

In the 19th century steam trains hauled huge kauri logs from Karekare along the surf-pounded coast to the wharf at Paratutai Island, just off Whatipu. Many ships have foundered on the treacherous sand bars near here, the most famous and tragic being the *Orpheus,* which went down in 1863 with the loss of 189 lives. Scenes from Jane Campion's *The Piano* were filmed at Karekare.

Piha & Te Henga (Bethells Beach)

Piha, with its wave-pounded, iron-sand beach, has long been a favourite with Auckland holiday-makers as well as with artists and alternative types. The distinctive **Lion Rock** (101m) sits just off the beach.

Piha comes alive in summer with hundreds of beach-goers, holiday-makers and surfers. In summer, in addition to the beach life, there's tennis, lawn bowls, live bands at the surf club on weekends, and lots of partying. Surfing competitions are held at Piha and there are horse races along the beach towards the end of summer.

Some 8km north of Piha is Te Henga, or Bethells Beach, with its windswept sand dunes. Although much less visited than Piha, Te Henga has a surf club and there's a walkway (part of the NZ Walkway system) that starts at the freshwater Lake Wainamu.

Places to Stay The *Piha Domain Motor Camp* (☎ 812 8815) is right on the beach and has tent sites for $10 per person ($6 per child), caravans for $38 per couple, $25 per single and $8 per child.

Much more upmarket is *Grenvilles* (☎ 812 8870, 136 Garden Rd, Piha),* which has one double/twin bedroom with its own

Warning

The West Coast beaches have powerful currents and heavy surf. Lifesaving clubs have been established to patrol the beaches to protect swimmers and surfers. You should always swim between the flags planted on the beach by lifeguards. Remember that currents change and a place that's OK one day may not be the next. If you have been warned not to swim at a particular place, take heed. If in doubt, ask. The lifeguards will be happy to advise on conditions and explain which places are safe. You should never go out of your depth and, of course, children should be supervised at *all* times. Drownings along this coast are not uncommon.

bathroom and wood burner, and one queen-size bedroom which shares a bathroom. This attractive two-storey cottage is made of adobe brick. Breakfast is included in the price of $95/140 to $160 per single/double.

Bethells Beach Cottages (☎ 810 9581, fax 810 8677, 267 Bethells Rd) comprises two lovely, self-contained cottages for $126 (Turehu Cottage) or $195 (Te Koinga Cottage) a double. Meals are available for an extra cost.

The Barn (☎ 818 9431, 3 Cochran Rd) in Oratia is a good base from which to explore the Waitakere Ranges. Accommodation (one double bed, two single) is in a large comfortable barn, complete with open fireplace, pool table, kitchen (barbecue outside) and laundry. Organic fruit and free-range eggs are available in season. It costs $20 per person. It's off Carter Rd, which is off the West Coast Rd. The owners will pick up guests from Glen Eden train station (there are frequent trains here from Richmond station).

Muriwai Beach & Gannet Colony

The road to Muriwai Beach is well signposted at Waimauku on SH16. Apart from the renowned **surf beach**, the main attraction is the colony of Australasian gannets. The colony was once confined to a nearby rock stack but has now overflowed to the shore cliffs, even past the barriers erected to keep observers out. If you haven't seen these beautiful birds at close range before, take the opportunity to see them here.

Helensville

This town is less than an hour's drive from Auckland, 4km inland from the southern end of Kaipara, NZ's biggest harbour.

Helensville itself is no great attraction, but you can take interesting **harbour cruises** on the MV *Kewpie Two* (☎ 420 8466) – advance bookings are essential. There are three-hour trips at 1 pm on Saturday, Sunday and Monday ($12, children $6), as well as day trips and three-day trips. The **Pioneer Museum** on Porter Crescent is open from 1 to 3.30 pm daily.

Four kilometres north-west of Helensville, at Parakai, **Aquatic Park** is a huge hot pool/swimming complex with indoor and outdoor hot mineral pools and various waterslides. The centre is open from 10 am to 10 pm daily ($10, children $6).

Tandem skydiving (☎420 8064, fax 420 8010, ☻ c.pine@xtra.co.nz) at Parakai Parachute Centre is also popular. Jumps take place daily in summer and weather permitting in winter, and cost $195 or $225 per jump depending on height. You can arrange in advance to be picked up from Auckland city ($15 per person).

Places to Stay & Eat The small Helensville Visitor Information Centre (☎ 420 7468) in the main street has details on B&Bs and other accommodation, as well as on things to see and do.

Malolo House (☎ 420 7262, 110 Commercial Rd) is a friendly place. It's a late 19th-century kauri villa with dorms for $17, twins and doubles for $22 and singles $30 (prices per person). The B&B, in a separate part of the house, costs $70/85 a single/double. Breakfast is $10 extra.

The *Point of View Backpackers (☎ 420 7331, 160 Wishart Rd)* is a small place overlooking the Kaipara harbour. There are bushwalks on the property, which has kauri trees and plenty of native birds. A bed costs $15 per person.

Kaipara House B&B (☎ *420 7462),* on the corner of SH16 and Parkhurst Rd, is an 1890 villa with three guest rooms starting at $45/70 a single/double.

A good place to eat is *No 88 Bar & Restaurant* on Commercial Rd, which has steaks, chicken, seafood and pasta. Other options include *Da Gina* on the corner of Rata St, a BYO place serving pizza, pasta and other Italian dishes; *Golden River Chinese,* a takeaway on the main road; and the nearby *Fish Country Cafe* for fish and chips and seafood.

The *Kaipara Tavern,* next to Parakai Springs, has mains from $7.

Hauraki Gulf Islands

The Hauraki Gulf off Auckland is dotted with islands (Maori: *motu).* Some are within minutes of the city and are popular as day trips. Waiheke, a favourite weekend escape, has become almost a dormitory suburb. It also has some fine beaches and hostels, so it's a popular backpacker destination. There is plenty of choice if you are seeking something more upmarket.

Great Barrier, once a remote and little-visited island, is also becoming a popular destination, and it can be used as a stepping stone to the Coromandel. The islands are generally accessible by ferry or light aircraft.

There are 47 islands in the Hauraki Gulf Maritime Park, administered by DOC. Some are good-sized islands, others are simply rocks jutting out of the sea. The islands are loosely put into two categories: recreation and conservation. The recreation islands can be visited; transport to them is available, and their harbours are dotted with yachts in summer. The conservation islands, however, have restricted access. Special permits are required to visit some and others cannot be visited at all, as these islands are refuges for the preservation of plants and animals, especially birds, that are often extremely rare or even endangered species. For information on Kawau Island and Goat

Island, see the Kawau Island & Warkworth to Bream Bay sections of the Northland chapter.

Information

The DOC information centre in Auckland's ferry building has the best information about natural features, walkways and camping. The Auckland Travel and Information Centre is where you can find out about the more commercial aspects of the islands, such as hotels, ferry services etc. Trampers should get hold of the 1:50,000 Topomaps for Waiheke and Great Barrier. For information on the islands, visit www.islands.co.nz.

RANGITOTO & MOTUTAPU ISLANDS

About 600 years ago, Rangitoto (260m) erupted from the sea and was probably active for several years before settling down. It's now believed to be extinct. Maori living on nearby Motutapu Island, to which Rangitoto is now joined by a causeway, certainly witnessed the eruptions. Human footprints have been found here, embedded in the ash thrown out during the course of the mountain's creation. It is the largest and youngest of Auckland's volcanic cones.

Rangitoto literally means 'Blood Red Sky', although this is generally thought to allude not to the eruptions but to a battle in which the commander of the *Awara* canoe, Tamatekapua, was badly wounded. Rangitoto is an abbreviation of Nga Rangi i Totongia a Tamatekapua, meaning 'The Days of Tamatekapua's Bleeding'.

Ten kilometres north-east of downtown Auckland, Rangitoto is a good place for a picnic. It has many pleasant walks, barbecues and a great view from the summit of the cone. There's an information board at the wharf with maps of the walks and a shop which opens for the ferries. The DOC pamphlet *Rangitoto* ($1) has a useful map and descriptions of good walks.

The hike from the wharf to the summit takes about an hour. Up at the top, a loop walk goes around the crater's rim. The walk to the lava caves branches off the summit walk and takes 30 minutes return.

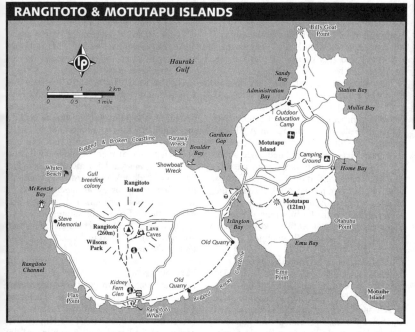

RANGITOTO & MOTUTAPU ISLANDS

There are other walks, some easy enough for kids. Bring water – on sunny days the black basalt gets pretty hot – and sturdy footwear.

Motutapu (1508 hectares), in contrast, is mainly covered in grassland grazed by sheep and cattle. Archaeologically, this is a very significant island – the traces of some 500 years of continuous human habitation are etched into its landscape.

There's an interesting three-hour round-trip walk between the wharf at Islington Bay and the wharf at Home Bay. Islington, the inlet between the islands, was once known as Drunken Bay because sailing ships would stop here to sober up crews who had overindulged in Auckland.

There's a **DOC camping ground** at Home Bay on Motutapu Island. Facilities are basic, with only a water tap and toilet provided. Bring cooking equipment, as open fires aren't permitted. Camping fees are $5 per night (children $2); for information contact the senior ranger (☎ 372 7348) or DOC in Auckland.

Getting There & Away

The ferry trip to Rangitoto Island from the ferry building in Auckland takes about half an hour. Fullers (☎ 367 9120) has ferries leaving at 9.30 and 11.45 am daily with an additional sailing at 2 pm during summer and weekends.

Ferries depart Rangitoto for Auckland at 12.30 and 3 pm, with an extra boat leaving the island at 5 pm in summer and weekends. The return fare is $18 (children $9).

Fullers has one-day tours to Rangitoto. On the Volcanic Explorer you ride in a canopied trailer, towed by a 4WD tractor, to a 900m boardwalk leading to the summit. The trips depart from Auckland's pier 3 at 9.30 and 11.45 am daily and there's a 2 pm sailing in summer and weekends; bookings are essential. It costs $35/17.50 for adults/children ($8.50 children under five).

WAIHEKE ISLAND

Waiheke is the most visited of the gulf islands and at 93 sq km is one of the largest. It's reputed to be sunnier and warmer than Auckland and has plenty of picturesque bays and beaches.

The island attracts all kinds of artistic folk, who exhibit their work in galleries and craft shops on the island. There is also an increasing number of retirees and commuters. While it is slowly becoming an Auckland suburb, it is still a relaxed, rural retreat.

Waiheke has been populated since about AD 950; legends relate that one of the pioneering canoes landed on the island. Traces of an old fortified pa can still be seen on the headland overlooking Putiki Bay. Europeans arrived with the missionary Samuel Marsden in the early 1800s and the island was soon stripped of its kauri forest.

Orientation & Information

The island's main settlement is Oneroa, at the western end of the island. From there the island is fairly built-up through to Palm Beach and Onetangi in its middle. Beyond Onetangi the eastern end of the island is lightly inhabited. The coastline is a picturesque mixture of coves, inlets and private beaches.

The Waiheke Island Visitor Information Office (☎ 372 9999) is at the Artworks complex on Ocean View Rd (the main road) in Oneroa, 1km from the ferry wharf. Its Web site, at www.ki-wi.co.nz, lists selected businesses and services and the office is open from 9 am to 5 pm daily (it closes earlier in winter).

Oneroa has a post office, banks and 24-hour ATMs. You can access the Internet at Waiheke Commercial Stationers.

Things to See

The **Artworks** centre is home to a variety of art and craft galleries, and other businesses and community groups. Artworks is on Ocean View Rd on the corner of Kororoa Rd, between Oneroa and Matiatia Wharf; it's open from 10 am to 4 pm daily.

Whittaker's Musical Experience, in the Artworks centre, is your chance to savour antique instruments; entry to the 1½-hour show (1 pm) is $7 ($5 children and seniors). It's open 10 am to noon and 2.30 to 4 pm.

At **Waiheke Potteries** at the Matiatia end of Oneroa's main shopping street, you can paint your own pots. Prices start at $10.

On the road to Onetangi, between the airstrip and the golf club, is the small **Historic Village** and **Waiheke Island Museum**, open from 1 to 4 pm daily in summer and on weekends in winter and on school holidays.

Waiheke has 22 **vineyards**, but you can only visit four of them (Goldwater Estate, Stonyridge Vineyard & Cafe, Peninsula Estate and Mudbrick Vineyard & Restaurant) on either a tour or by arrangement. Some will charge you for tours and tastings. The information office has brochures.

The annual Waiheke Jazz Festival is held at Easter, and the Waiheke Arts & Crafts Fair in October.

Water Sports

Popular beaches with good sand and swimming include Oneroa Beach and the adjacent Little Oneroa Beach. Palm Beach is in a lovely little cove, and there's a long stretch of sand at Onetangi Bay. A number of the beaches have shady pohutukawa trees.

There are nudist beaches at Palm Beach and on the west end of Onetangi Bay. Surf Skis and boogy boards can be hired on Onetangi and there's snorkelling at Hekerua Bay.

Sea Kayaking Waiheke's many bays and central position in the Hauraki Gulf make it an ideal spot for sea kayaking. Operators include Kayak Waiheke (☎ 372 7262) and Ross Adventures (☎ 372 5550), which is based at Matiatia. Ross Adventures offers trips from half-day (four-hour) sessions to four-day camping excursions. Kayak Waiheke has daily guided tours.

Walking

Waiheke has a system of walkways outlined in the *Waiheke Islands Walkways* pamphlet, available on the island or at the DOC office in Auckland.

In Onetangi there's a forest and bird reserve with several good walks, one of them

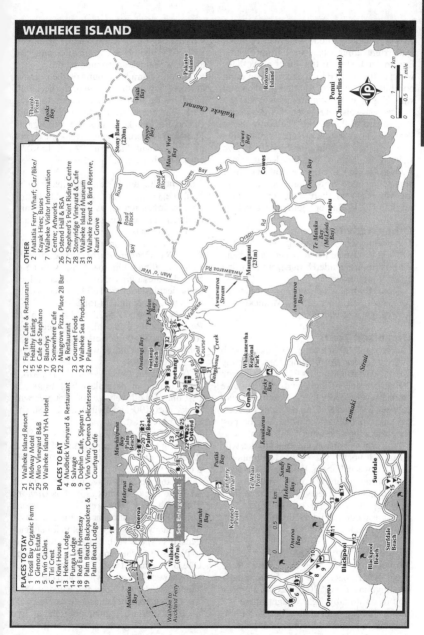

WAIHEKE ISLAND

PLACES TO STAY
1 Fossil Bay Organic Farm
3 Glenora Estate
5 Twin Gables
6 Tin Crest
11 Kiwi House
13 Hekerua Lodge
14 Punga Lodge
18 Red Earth Homestay
19 Palm Beach Backpackers &
   Palm Beach Lodge
21 Waiheke Island Resort
25 Midway Motel
29 Miro Vineyard B&B
30 Waiheke Island YHA Hostel

PLACES TO EAT
4 Mudbrick Vineyard & Restaurant
8 Salvage
9 Dolphin Cafe, Stjepan's
10 Vino Vino, Oneroa Delicatessen
   Courtyard Cafe
12 Fig Tree Cafe & Restaurant
15 Healthy Eating
16 Cafe de Stephano
17 Blanchys
20 Somewhere Cafe
22 Mangrove Pizza, Place 2B Bar
   & Restaurant
23 Gourmet Foods
24 Waiheke Sea Products
32 Palaver

OTHER
2 Matiatia Ferry Wharf; Car/Bike/
   Kayak Hires; Buses
7 Waiheke Visitor Information
   Centre; Artworks
26 Ostend Hall & RSA
27 Shepherd's Point Riding Centre
28 Stonyridge Vineyard & Cafe
31 Waiheke Island Museum
33 Waiheke Forest & Bird Reserve,
   Kauri Grove

going up to three large kauri trees. For coastal walks, a good, well-marked track leads right around the coast from Oneroa Bay to Palm Beach. It's about a two-hour walk; at the Palm Beach end you can jump on a bus back to town. Another good coastal walk begins at the Matiatia ferry wharf.

The best walks are in the less-developed eastern part of the island. The **Stony Batter Walk**, leading through private farmland, derives its name from the boulder-strewn fields. From Man o' War Bay Rd, the track leads to the old gun emplacements with their connecting underground tunnels and sweeping views. From there you can continue north to Hooks Bay or south to Opopo Bay.

Other Activities

The Shepherd's Point Riding Centre (☎ 372 8104) at 91 Ostend Rd, between Ostend and the airstrip, has guided **horse riding** starting at $25 for an hour.

Scenic flights, which cost upwards of $15 per person, are operated by Waiheke Airservices (☎ 372 5000).

Organised Tours

Fullers has a host of tours in conjunction with its ferry service. See Getting There & Away later. The 'Postie Run' (☎ 372 9166) goes to the eastern end of the island, and can take around seven people for $15 each. It leaves between 8.15 and 8.30 am on Monday, Tuesday and Wednesday from the Oneroa post shop and returns between 1 and 2 pm.

You can visit artists and their studios with Ananda Tours (☎ 372 7530). The tours run daily between Labour Weekend (October) and Easter (March/April). You can be picked up from the ferry at Matiatia or from your accommodation on Waiheke. The tours are about four hours' duration and cost $40 per person.

Places to Stay & Eat

Waiheke has some 100 homestays, farmstays, B&Bs, baches or flats for rent, costing anything from $20 to $200 a night. If you're on a really tight budget, there is a reasonable degree of choice, but if you want to splash out, there are some real treats.

Staff at the information office in Oneroa will match you with the type of place you seek. The visitor centre in Auckland city also lists Waiheke accommodation.

The only camping ground on the island is at Rocky Bay, at the far end of the beach off Gordon's Rd in the Whakanewha Regional Park (and there are limited sites at Palm Beach Backpackers, Fossil Bay Organic Farm and Hekerua Lodge). Book the camping ground with Parksline (☎ 303 1530). It costs $6 (children $3).

Oneroa Although it's the principal town of Waiheke, Oneroa is not very big. Straddling a ridge, it has sea views on both sides and contains most of the island's services and good restaurants.

To get away from it all, call in at the *Fossil Bay Organic Farm (☎ 372 7569, 58 Korora Rd)* near Oneroa. Singles cost $20 and doubles/twins $38. Self-contained units sleeping four are $60 for three people, and you can camp here for $10.

Tiri Crest (☎ 372 5423, 528 4794, 16 Tiri Rd) has a neatly kept, fully furnished house for rent for $140, as well as a flat for $85 and a cute little cottage with polished floorboards for $110.

Twin Gables (☎ 372 9877, 17 Tiri Rd) is a welcoming, modern place built to get the best out of the lovely views. Doubles with decks cost $90 and twinshare is $80, including breakfast.

Kiwi House (☎ 372 9123, 23 Kiwi St) is a pleasant, modern place that sleeps 12. Rates start at $35 to $40 per person (at $70 a double).

The top place to stay in pretty Church Bay, and one of Waiheke's best, is *Glenora Estate (☎ 372 5082)* on Nick Johnstone Drive. This romantic place, built in the style of a Brittany farmhouse, is set in lovely gardens. It's expensive, but an excellent choice.

Places to eat are clustered around Oneroa's main street. They include *Salvage*, a popular venue where you can sit inside or out. *Vino Vino* is at the end of View Mall. It's a popular licensed restaurant with good food and a regular program of live music. You get great views from the deck (book to ensure a place). The little *Courtyard Cafe*, tucked away one floor below, is a quiet place for a cold drink or a coffee.

The *Oneroa Delicatessen*, at the mall entrance, serves good coffee, salads, sandwiches and soups. *Stjepan's*, across the road, has pizzas and seafood ($18 for mains). It's open from morning till late daily.

The *Dolphin Cafe (147 Ocean View Rd)* is one of the best places for inexpensive burgers and snacks.

The *Fig Tree Cafe & Restaurant (46 Moa Ave, Blackpool)* is near the waterfront, between Surfdale and Oneroa. Meat, seafood and vegetarian dishes start at about $15.

Blanchys at Surfdale, one beach along from Blackpool, has good steaks as well as chicken, seafood and so on. Blanchys will pick you up and drop you off anywhere on the island. Also at Surfdale are *Caffe de Stefano*, where you can get Italian pizza (from $10 to $14), antipasto, focaccia and so on, and *Healthy Eating*, which has pita kebabs and burgers, burritos, salads, sandwiches and more (all under $10).

The *Mudbrick Vineyard & Restaurant*, on Church Bay Rd, is a top dining spot on Waiheke. From the patio you look across the rows of vines towards that harbour and Auckland city. It's open daily for lunch and dinner. The menu is seasonal, but always good, with mains starting at around $25. Another good venue is the *Stonyridge Cafe (80 Onetangi Rd)* at the vineyard.

Little Oneroa Just east of Oneroa, Little Oneroa has a reasonable beach and one of the island's few areas of native bush. *Punga Lodge (℡/fax 372 6675, 223 Ocean View Rd)* is set in tranquil bush surroundings. B&B en suite rooms and apartments are available and start at $95 per room.

Nestled in bush is *Hekerua Lodge (℡ 372 2556, @ collrich@clear.net.nz, 11 Hekerua Rd)*. Doubles start at $50 and shared rooms at $17. Tent sites are available for $12 per person. It also has a swimming pool.

Palm Beach In a beautiful little cove with a pleasant beach is Palm Beach. *Waiheke Island Resort (℡ 0800-924 4353)* is at the top of Palm Rd, which leads to the beach. There is a variety of accommodation; in the high season chalets are $149 and villas $199.

Palm Beach Lodge (℡ 372 7763, 23 Tiri View Rd), which is a few streets up from the beach, has three modern, self-contained apartments with decks, sea views and barbecues. Each apartment has two double bedrooms and they cost $180 to $240 a night.

Palm Beach Backpackers (℡ 372 8662, 54 Palm Rd) is a sprawling place right across from the beach, with a school camp feel. Dorm beds start at $16, doubles at $40 and camping is $12 per person.

Right by the beach, the *Somewhere Cafe (39 Palm Rd)* has inexpensive cafe food. Next door the *general store* sells takeaways and groceries.

Ostend This village has shops and a couple of places to eat, but it is a fair way from the beach. There is a colourful local market at the RSA hall from 8 am to 3 pm Saturday in summer (closing earlier in winter), where you can find local preserves and jams, second-hand books and clothes, handicrafts, plants and more.

On the main road, the *Midway Motel (℡ 372 8023, 1 Whakarite Rd)* has units from $75 to $120 for two. There's a heated swimming pool.

In the centre of Ostend, the *RSA* serves good, cheap pub food and the cheapest beer on the island. Opposite this are several takeaways, some serving Chinese food.

Gourmet Foods serves a variety of good dishes – salads, focaccia, pancakes, cooked breakfasts – for less than $10. Right at the opposite end of the street are *Mangrove Pizza* (large pizza $16) and *The Place2B Bar & Restaurant (3 Belgium St)*, which has steaks, fish, chicken and nachos. The fish and chips from *Waiheke Sea Products* are also pretty good.

Surfdale & Kennedy Point *Red Earth Homestay (℡ 372 9975, 6 Kennedy Rd)*, off Michell Rd, is a cosy little five-bed backpackers. Dorm beds cost $17, and a twin is $17 per person. The Surfdale-bound bus from Matiatia will take you to the start of

Kennedy Rd from where it's a short walk. You can hire bikes for $5 per day.

Onetangi The long, sandy beach at Onetangi is one of the best on the island – it's popular in summer for swimming, surfing, windsurfing and other activities. Surf-skis, surfboards and boogy boards can be hired at the store or on the beach in summer.

The popular *Waiheke Island YHA* (☎ 372 8971, ✉ robb.meg@bigfoot.com, 419 Seaview Rd) is on a hill overlooking the bay. It's $15 in a dorm, and $19/17 per person in a double/twin room.

The *Onetangi Beachfront Apartments* (☎ 372 7051, 27 The Strand) has a variety of rooms. Modern beachfront apartments are about $245 a night for two. Motel rooms start at $85.

Above the beach and set in vineyards, is the swish *Miro Vineyard B&B* (☎ 0800-168 007, Browns Rd), a self-contained luxury villa with decks and sea views. Rates depend on the season, but prices are about $150 for two.

The *Palaver* (☎ 372 7583) bar and restaurant is the place to see the many bands that visit in summer. Next door is the *Strand Bar*. At *Onetangi Beach Store* you can get takeaways or sit-down and eat meals inside or out.

Getting There & Away

Air Waiheke Airservices (☎ 372 5000, ✉ flingwing@hotmail.com) has on-demand flights between Auckland's domestic terminal and Waiheke ($65 per person for two or more people one way; 12 minutes).

Sea Pacific Ferries (☎ 303 1741) and Fullers (☎ 367 9111) both have frequent daily ferries running between downtown Auckland and Matiatia on Waiheke. Pacific Ferries' fast ferry service is $17 return ($14 on some sailings; check with the company for details) and Fullers is $23 ($17 if you go via Devonport – an extra five minutes). Auckland to Matiatia takes about 35 minutes.

You can take your car over to Waiheke on the Subritzky vehicle ferry, which departs daily from Half Moon Bay in Pakuranga for Kennedy Point on Waiheke, and on Friday at 5.30 pm and Monday at 10 am from Wynyard Wharf in downtown Auckland. Ferries ply between Half Moon Bay and Kennedy Point every three hours between 7 am and 4 pm. The trip takes an hour one way and bookings are essential. The return trip costs $110 for a car and driver; passengers $20 each.

Getting Around

Bus Two bus routes operate on the island, both connecting with the arriving and departing ferries. The Onetangi bus goes from Matiatia Wharf, through Oneroa, Surfdale and Ostend to Onetangi. The Palm Beach bus goes from Matiatia through Oneroa, Blackpool, Little Oneroa, Palm Beach and Ostend to Rocky Bay.

Car, Scooter & Bicycle Waiheke Rental Cars (☎ 372 8635) has an office at Matiatia Wharf and at Artworks, in Oneroa. Cars, motorbikes and nifty-fifty scooters can be rented. Waiheke Auto Rentals (373 8998) will deliver a car to you anywhere on the island.

Waiheke Shuttles (☎ 372 7756) charges per person per trip. From Matiatia to Oneroa it is $2 and to Onetangi $7.

Attitude Rentals (☎ 372 7897) has motor-assisted mountain bikes for hire (minimum two hours). You will need to pick up the bike from Waiheke Island Resort, Palm Beach.

Ordinary bicycles can be rented at various places, including the visitor information office. Get a copy of the *Bike Waiheke* pamphlet; the route takes you past most of the sights and usually takes four to six hours to complete – although at least one speed freak's done it in just over two hours.

Taxi For taxi service on the island ring Waiheke Taxis (☎ 372 8038), Dial-a-Cab (☎ 372 9666) or Waiheke Island Shuttle Service (☎ 372 7756).

PAKATOA ISLAND

Pakatoa is a small tourist resort 36km from Auckland and just off the east coast of Waiheke. The resort was sold early in 2000 and closed its doors at Easter (April). At the time of writing it was not known if the new owners planned to reopen the resort. To find out the latest information contact the Auckland Travel and Information Centre (☎ 979 2333) at 287 Queen St, Auckland.

GREAT BARRIER ISLAND

pop 1200

Great Barrier, 88km from the mainland, is the largest island in the gulf. It is a rugged scenic island, resembling the Coromandel Peninsula to which it was once joined.

Great Barrier has hot springs, historic kauri dams, a forest sanctuary and myriad tramping tracks. Because there are no possums on the island, the native bush is lush.

The island's main attractions are its beautiful beaches and its fine tramping. The west coast has safe sandy beaches; the east coast beaches are good for surfing. The best tramping trails are in the Great Barrier Forest between Whangaparapara and Port Fitzroy, where there has been much reforestation. Cycling, swimming, fishing, scuba diving, boating, sea kayaking and just relaxing are the other popular activities on the island.

Named by James Cook, Great Barrier Island later became a whaling centre. The island implemented the world's first airmail postal service in 1897 (using pigeons). The centenary of the service was celebrated with the release of hundreds of birds. Great Barrier has also been the site of some spectacular shipwrecks, including the SS *Wairarapa* in 1894 and the *Wiltshire* in 1922. There's a cemetery at Katherine Bay, where victims of the *Wairarapa* wreck were buried. There is a signposted NZ Walkways track from Whangapoua Beach (20 minutes from Port Fitzroy by taxi) to the mass graves on the Tapuwai headland.

Great Barrier Island is decidedly isolated. Only two hours by ferry from Auckland, the Barrier (as it is called locally) is 20 years away. The island has no electricity supply (only private generators), most roads are unpaved and it has only a few shops.

Tryphena is the main settlement and arrival point for the ferries. It consists of a few dozen houses, a cardphone, toilets, a school,

Pigeon Post

Great Barrier's first pigeon postal service took flight in 1897, a year after an enterprising Auckland newspaper reporter had used a pigeon to file a report from Great Barrier Island. From small beginnings the service expanded to include a good part of the Hauraki Gulf: shopping lists, election results, mine claims and important pieces of news winged their way across land and sea bound to the legs of the canny birds. The arrival of the telegraph in 1908 grounded the service, but it was resurrected in 1993 as a novelty for visitors. Twenty dollars buys a pigeon pack, which includes a leaflet on the history of the service, a pigeon-gram form and a triangular stamp. (The original stamps used are now worth a small fortune.)

Your message will be flown by pigeon to Auckland and forwarded to you by more conventional means. Postal centres in Tryphena, Claris and Port Fitzroy all sell the packs.

Postscript: Our carrier pigeon had a delayed take-off due to bad weather. But, for the record, it was released one fine afternoon at 2 pm and touched down at its home loft in North Auckland safe and sound some 2¼ hours later. Message intact. Mission accomplished.

Christine Niven

a ferry wharf and a handful of accommodation places dotted around the harbour. From the wharf it is a couple of kilometres to Mulberry Grove, and then another 1km over the headland to Pa Beach and the Stonewall Store.

The airport is at **Claris**, a small settlement with a small shopping centre (including a laundry, cafe and fuel) and a community health centre. **Whangaparapara** is an old timber town and the site of the island's 19th-century whaling activities. **Port Fitzroy** is the other main town; it is also very small.

From around mid-November to Easter the island is a busy holiday destination, especially during the Christmas holidays until the end of January, Easter and the Labour

GREAT BARRIER ISLAND

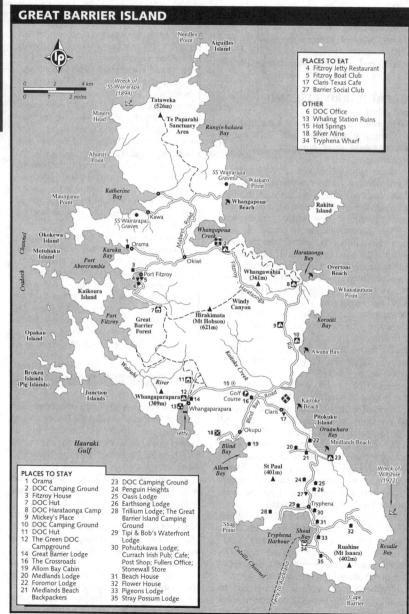

PLACES TO EAT
4 Fitzroy Jetty Restaurant
5 Fitzroy Boat Club
17 Claris Texas Cafe
27 Barrier Social Club

OTHER
6 DOC Office
13 Whaling Station Ruins
15 Hot Springs
18 Silver Mine
34 Tryphena Wharf

PLACES TO STAY
1 Orama
2 DOC Camping Ground
3 Fitzroy House
7 DOC Hut
8 DOC Harataonga Camp
9 Mickey's Place
10 DOC Camping Ground
11 DOC Hut
12 The Green DOC Campground
14 Great Barrier Lodge
16 The Crossroads
19 Allom Bay Cabin
20 Medlands Lodge
22 Foromor Lodge
21 Medlands Beach Backpackers
23 DOC Camping Ground
24 Penguin Heights
25 Oasis Lodge
26 Earthsong Lodge
28 Trillium Lodge; The Great Barrier Island Camping Ground
29 Tipi & Bob's Waterfront Lodge
30 Pohutukawa Lodge; Currach Irish Pub; Cafe; Post Shop; Fullers Office; Stonewall Store
31 Beach House
32 Flower House
33 Pigeons Lodge
35 Stray Possum Lodge

Day long weekend. At these times make sure you book transport, accommodation and activities in advance.

Information

In Tryphena, the Fullers office (☎ 429 0004), next to the Stonewall Store, is a mine of information. The office maintains an extensive list of homestays and lodges. It's open from 8 am to 5 pm daily in summer and 9.30 am to 3.30 pm except Tuesday in winter.

On the island, the main DOC office (☎ 429 0044) is in Port Fitzroy, a 15-minute walk from the Port Fitzroy ferry landing. It has information and maps on the island, collects fees and sells hut tickets and has a good camping ground. It's open from 8 am to 4.30 pm weekdays. (There is a NZ Walkway track that goes along the coast from Okiwi to Harataonga, where there is an historic homestead – get a pamphlet from DOC).

Because there's no power on the island, make sure you bring a torch (flashlight). Most people on the island generate their own power by using solar, wind or diesel energy, but there are no street lights anywhere. Great Barrier has an automatic telephone service and cardphones are dotted around the island. See the Places to Eat section for information on buying groceries.

Things to See & Do

Medlands, with its wide sweep of white sand, is one of the best **beaches** on the island and is easily accessible from Tryphena. Whangapoua is a fine surfing beach, while Kaitoke, Awana Bay and Harataonga are also good. Whangapoua has an excellent right-hand break, while Awana has both left- and right-hand breaks. Tryphena's bay, lined with pohutukawa, has sheltered beaches.

Many people come just for the **walks** – be aware they are often not well signposted. The Great Barrier Forest walks are most easily reached from Whangaparapara or Port Fitzroy. You can take the ferry to either of these destinations from Auckland or Tryphena and walk 45 minutes to one of the two huts that can be used as bases for exploring the forest.

The most spectacular short walk is from Windy Canyon to Hirakimata (Mt Hobson). **Windy Canyon**, only a 15-minute walk from the main Port Fitzroy-Harataonga road, has spectacular rock outcrops and affords great views of the island. From Windy Canyon, an excellent trail continues for another 1½ hours through scrubby forest to **Hirakimata** (621m), the highest point on the island with views across to the Coromandel Peninsula and Auckland on a fine day. Near the top of the mountain are lush forests and a few mature kauri that survived the logging days. From Hirakimata it is two hours through forest to the hut closest to Port Fitzroy and then 45 minutes to Port Fitzroy itself.

Many other trails traverse the forest. From the road outside Whangaparapara you can also walk to the **hot springs**. There is also a good, four-hour walk west from Tryphena to Okupu Bay that eventually joins the Blind Bay Rd.

Mountain biking is popular on the island. There is diverse scenery, and biking is not too difficult here, even though the roads are unsealed. A popular ride is from Tryphena to Whangaparapara: cycle about an hour to Medlands Beach where you can stop for a swim, then cycle another hour to the hot springs, from where it's another half-hour to accommodation in Whangaparapara. You could catch the ferry out from Whangaparapara, or spend another day cycling through the forest up to Port Fitzroy, stopping on the way for a hike up to the kauri dams on a good, well-marked 4WD track.

Great Barrier provides some of the most varied **scuba diving** in NZ. There's pinnacle diving, shipwreck diving, lots of fish and over 33m visibility at some times of the year; February to April is probably the best time. There are no scuba operators on the island (although there are facilities for filling tanks).

Sea kayaking is a good way of experiencing Great Barrier from the water. Great Barrier Island Kayak Hire and Adventure Tours (☎ 429 0551) has a twilight mystery tour with a barbecue afterwards ($45; without the barbecue it's $25). You can also rent kayaks from this company, which is next to the Stonewall Store in Tryphena, for $10 an hour, or go on a coastal foray for $45 per day. Aotea Sea Kayak Adventures (☎ 429 0664) hires out kayaks for $40 for a half-day with snorkelling. There is an evening twilight paddle to the Colville Channel. Some of the accommodation places also rent out kayaks, eg, Fitzroy House (☎ 429 0091).

Horse Treks can be arranged through Adventure Horse Treks (☎ 429 0274) and Nagle Cove Horse Treks (☎ 429 0212). Prices start at about $25 for an hour.

Boat and fishing trips can be organised through Stanley Marine Charters (☎ 429 0570), Puriri Bay Fishing Charters (☎ 429 0485) and Tipi & Bob's (☎ 429 0550).

Fitzroy House (☎ 429 0091) will take you to the beginning of a walking track in a 4WD unimog and pick you up at the other end, usually at the beach, in a yacht and sail back. This costs about $50 per person.

Places to Stay

Most accommodation is in Tryphena, but places are scattered all over the island. Prices are steep in summer, but rates drop dramatically outside the peak period. Summer prices are quoted here.

Camping & Huts There are *DOC camping grounds* at Harataonga Bay, Medlands Beach, Akapoua Bay, Whangapoua, The Green (Whangaparapara) and Awana Bay, all with basic facilities, including water and pit toilets. Only Akapoua Bay has a barbecue; you are not allowed to light fires elsewhere. Camping is not allowed outside the camping grounds without a permit. Camping costs $7 for adults (children $3.50).

As well as the camping grounds, DOC has one hut in the Great Barrier Forest, near Port Fitzroy, a 45-minute walk from Port Fitzroy wharf. The hut sleeps up to 24 in bunkrooms and facilities include cold water, pit toilets and a kitchen with a wood stove. Bring your own sleeping bag and cooking equipment. The cost is $10 for adults (children $5). From November to January the hut and camping grounds are very busy. Bookings are essential at all DOC camp sites (☎ 429 0044). The hut is on a first-come, first-served basis.

There are two camping grounds on private property. There's one at Awana Bay called *Mickey's Place* (☎/fax 429 0170), costing $4 for adults (children $2). The other is at Puriri Bay, Tryphena; *The Great Barrier Island Campground* (☎ 429 0184) charges $8.50 per person and facilities include toilets, barbecue sites and cold-water showers.

Hostels The *Stray Possum Lodge* (☎ 0800-767 786, @ straypossum@acb.co.nz) in Tryphena provides quality accommodation in a lovely bush setting. Dorms cost $18, a bed in a four-bed room is $20 and twins and doubles cost $50. There is also limited camping space for $12 per person. Two great, self-contained chalets sleeping up to six are also available for $95 for the first two people and $15 for each additional person. Each chalet has a spiral staircase leading to a mezzanine sleeping space.

Stray Possum has a bus for transport around the island. For $45 you can use the pass as frequently as you wish, and it includes the use of mountain bikes, boogy boards and snorkelling gear.

The Crossroads (☎ 429 0889, @ pfl@ ihug.co.nz), a new, purpose-built backpackers at the junction of the Claris and Blind Bay roads, has a bar and Internet access. A dorm/single/double costs $20/30/50. The golf club and the Sports and Social Club are 100m away (the hostel provides golf clubs).

Penguin Heights (☎ 429 0628, 41 Medland Rd) is another, albeit smaller, new purpose-built place with backpacker accommodation and a self-contained unit. The backpacker section sleeps six (two in the loft, four in bunk beds) and has a kitchen and bathroom attached. A bed costs $15 (with linen $20). The unit sleeps six and has a kitchen and sitting/dining area. It costs $115 for two. Penguin will pick up from the airport or ferry, but call first.

Pohutukawa Lodge (☎ 429 0211, @ plodge@xtra.co.nz) in Tryphena has three modern en suite rooms for $95 for two ($10 for each extra person), and bunkrooms for $17 a person. The lodge welcomes children, and it has a big back garden.

Medlands Beach Backpackers (☎ 429 0320) is on Mason Rd, just inland from the main road at Medlands Beach. It's fairly basic, but close to the superb beach ($20 for a dorm bed). Boogy boards, bikes and snorkelling gear are available.

Great Barrier Lodge at Whangaparapara has backpacker accommodation as does *Orama* at Karaka Bay (see below).

Guesthouses, Lodges & Motels Tryphena has several great upmarket places. *Earthsong Lodge (☎ 429 0030)* is a stunning place with wonderful sea and bush views. Made of adobe, with polished eucalypt floors, it's spacious and comfortable. There are three guest suites, all with balconies that look out over a small olive grove and beyond that to the bush and the sea. A courtyard garden separates the suites from the lounge and dining area – from which you get more great views. It costs $295 per person (double occupancy) and $395 (single occupancy). This includes pre-dinner cocktails, a fine four-course dinner, a full breakfast and transfers.

Oasis Lodge (☎ 429 0021) is nearby and has modern, luxury accommodation on a property that includes a vineyard. There are three double en suite rooms and a self-contained unit. It costs $95 per person for B&B and $140 for full board. There is a great licensed restaurant here as well (see Places to Eat).

Trillium Lodge (☎ 4290 454) at Puriri Bay is built in the style of a traditional Canadian log cabin, and is named for Ontario's provincial floral emblem. There are three log-style rooms downstairs and three conventional rooms upstairs (each room has its own heating and is individually styled). It's $295 plus GST per day per person, including meals and transfers.

On a more modest scale is the pleasant self-contained cottage *Beach House (☎ 429 0483)* overlooking the sea just a minute's walk from the Stonewall Store. It costs $100 for two ($20 for each extra person; it sleeps six).

Pigeons Lodge (☎ 429 0437), on the beachfront at Shoal Bay, is in a bush setting and has a licensed restaurant and bar. It charges from $95 to $120 for double/twin rooms with en suites.

Tipi & Bob's Waterfront Lodge (☎ 429 0550) has motel-style accommodation 50m from the sea, and has a garden bar and restaurant. There are five self-contained en suite units, most with great sea views, starting at $120. There's also a self-contained cottage that sleeps six for $250.

For a spot of luxury at Medlands Beach try *Foromor Lodge (☎ 429 0335)* where, for $300 per day, you can enjoy great food and activities such as fishing, hiking, horse trekking, golf and scuba diving. A 4WD is included.

Medlands Lodge (☎ 429 0352) on Mason Rd, Medlands Beach, is set on four hectares of park-like grounds at the foot of the hills inland from the beach. Excellent self-contained units sleeping four cost $120 for two (each additional adult $15) and there's also a five-bed bunkroom. You can cook or order meals.

At Whangaparapara, the *Great Barrier Lodge (☎ 429 0488)* is a big place on the water's edge overlooking the inlet. Ferries from Auckland will drop off/pick up here. It has a restaurant and bar, and there is a general store. Prices range from $90 for a double/twin room to $125 in the colonial cottage. There are also backpacker beds for $25 (including linen).

Fitzroy House (☎ 429 0091) is on the other side of the bay from the ferry wharf at Port Fitzroy. This old homestead, set in lovely gardens, offers fine views of the bay and two self-contained cottages: Seaview Cottage is $300 per night in the peak season and Lavender Cottage is $250.

At Karaka Bay, just north of Port Fitzroy, *Orama (☎ 429 0063)* is a Christian community where there are self-contained flats starting at $100 in summer and backpacker beds from $15. It has good facilities, including a swimming pool (open in summer) and a general store. Orama will pick up from the Port Fitzroy ferry wharf.

More remote possibilities abound. The secluded *Allom Bay Cabin (☎ 429 0025)* can be accessed by boat or walking track. It's fully self-contained and right on the beach ($120). The *Flower House* (☎ 429 0464), off Rosalie Bay Rd and via a private road, is a very private place nestled in native bush. It's $140 for two (including all meals) or $100 a single.

Baches Great Barrier Island has a big array of baches (holiday homes), all privately owned and maintained. The going rate is $80-plus a double, and many sleep four or more.

Fullers (☎ 372 9122) keeps a list and will mark them on the map, and will fax you a list upon request.

Places to Eat
The Claris Centre near the airport has the good BYO *Claris Texas Cafe*, which is open seven days, and until 10 pm Thursday to Saturday. Espresso, nachos, big breakfasts, panini, soup, cakes and sandwiches are available. Other possibilities are *Tipi & Bob's*, *Medlands Lodge* and *Pigeons Lodge* (bookings essential for the last two).

The *Currach Irish Pub* at Tryphena is a lively spot with a good atmosphere. In summer you can sit out in the garden; in winter an open fire will keep you warm. Seafood chowder, fish of the day, steaks and Thai curry are all on the menu. Drinks include the locally produced John Mellars red wine and Island Mead. A regular jam session on Thursday attracts local talent – and you can try your hand too if you wish. The gallery room features work by local artists. The family who built the original homestead some 100 years ago were emigrants from Tipperary.

For fine dining try the restaurant (☎ 429 0034) at *Oasis Lodge*; fresh, local seafood is a speciality. It's open for lunch and dinner daily and bookings are essential.

For a vegetarian, organic lunch in a lovely setting try the *Flower House* (☎ 429 0464); see Places to Stay earlier. The meal includes home-made organic bread, freshly picked salad, home-made cheeses, pickles, chutneys and jams – plus dessert ($20 per person, including a garden tour). Bookings are essential.

The *Barrier Social Club* (☎ 429 0421) in Tryphena has good-value meals and cheap bar prices. It is open from 4 pm Saturday to Wednesday in winter and daily in summer.

The *Great Barrier Island Sports & Social Club* at Claris has meals available in winter from 4 pm on Wednesday, Friday and Saturday and daily in summer.

In summer the *Port Fitzroy Jetty restaurant* is open daily, as is the *Port Fitzroy Boat Club* (lunch and dinner; in winter it's open on Saturday evening only).

There is a well-stocked *grocery store* at the Claris Centre, near the airport. The *Stonewall Store* at Tryphena is also good, and there are *general stores* at Port Fitzroy, Great Barrier Lodge and Orama.

Getting There & Away
Air Two airlines currently service the island: Great Barrier Airlines (☎ 0800-900 600) and Mountain Air (Great Barrier Xpress; ☎ 0800-222 123). It takes about 35 minutes to reach Great Barrier from Auckland's domestic airport at Mangere. The standard return fare is around $169. You can also go by Fullers ferry one way and with Mountain Air the other way; check with Fullers for details of prices and times. Heletranz (☎ 479 1991) offers helicopter flights between Auckland and Great Barrier.

Boat There are two main services: Fullers (☎ 367 9111) and Gulf Tranz (Sealink; ☎ 373 4036). Fullers is a passenger service; Gulf Tranz takes passengers and freight, including cars. Both operate daily between Auckland and the Barrier in summer. Fullers departs from the downtown ferry building in Auckland and Sealink operates from Subritzky's terminal at Wynyard wharf. Bookings are essential in summer.

Travel Passes There are various passes (handy for backpackers) that enable you to take in the Great Barrier and other destinations at a reasonable cost. One is the Forests, Islands & Geysers pass offered by InterCity (☎ 913 6100). This pass enables you to travel by bus to the Bay of Islands via Waipoua Kauri Forest, then fly to Great Barrier and on to Whitianga, from where you travel by bus to Rotorua. Here you can choose to either continue to Taupo and Wellington or head to Auckland via Waitomo ($275, children $184).

For more options get hold of the *Top 3* travel passes brochure available from visitor centres and the Stray Possum on Great Barrier (☎ 0800-767 786 for details).

Getting Around

From Tryphena in the south to Port Fitzroy in the north is 47km by (mostly) unsealed road, or 40km via Whangaparapara using the walking tracks. The roads are graded but rough.

Great Barrier Travel (☎ 429 0568) has a bus that meets the ferry and takes passengers into Tryphena for $5. In theory it continues through Medlands Beach and Claris to Port Fitzroy, but unless enough passengers want to go you will have to charter. In summer Safari Tours (☎ 429 0448) runs a beach bus and hot spring shuttle.

Great Barrier Airlines (☎ 0800-900 600) has a shuttle (the Airporter) that meets flights. Okupu Coaches (☎ 429 0270) does transfers to Okupu, and tours.

Many of the accommodation places will pick you up if notified in advance; the Stray Possum has a bus for its guests. In summer the best option for getting between Port Fitzroy and Tryphena is the daily Fullers boat.

You can hire cars and 4WDs:

Aotea Tours	☎ 429 0055
Bob's Rentals	☎ 429 0988
Great Barrier Lodge	☎ 429 0488
Wheels Down Under	☎ 429 0110

Most of these places offer taxi services, as does Barrier Taxis (☎ 429 0527).

MOTUIHE ISLAND

Named for an ancestor of the Arawa tribe, Motuihe contains much evidence of pre-European occupation: pa, storage pits and gardens. There are picnic grounds, barbecue sites, changing sheds and toilets on the northern end of the island where the old wharf is. Also in this area is a kiosk where you can get food, fishing supplies and information. It's open daily in summer and whenever there is a demand in winter. *Camping* (☎ 534 5419) costs $5 (children $2). The DOC pamphlet *Motuihe* has a map of the island, and a description of three walks.

Fullers (☎ 367 9111) runs ferries to Motuihe three times weekly in summer.

TIRITIRI MATANGI ISLAND

Tiritiri Matangi was at one time occupied by Maori; there are remains of a pa site here. In 1841 it was bought by the Crown and eventually leased and farmed; its forests were mostly cleared. The historic and well-preserved 30m-high lighthouse was completed in 1865 and donated to Auckland city by the wealthy brewer Sir Ernest Davis. The island has been part of the Hauraki Gulf Maritime Park since 1971. Since 1984 volunteers have planted many thousands of native trees, and as the forest has regenerated, endangered native birds have been reintroduced. Book for trips to the island with Fullers (☎ 367 9111).

OTHER ISLANDS

Dotted around Rangitoto, Motutapu and Waiheke, and further north, are many smaller islands.

South of Rangitoto is the small island of **Motukorea** (Island of the Oystercatcher), also known as Browns Island. The island had three fortified Maori pa on the volcanic cones in 1820; it was purchased from Maori by John Logan Campbell and William Brown in 1839, before the founding of Auckland, and used as a pig farm. It's now part of the Hauraki Gulf Maritime Park; access is unrestricted.

Rotoroa, a Salvation Army alcohol rehabilitation clinic, is just south of Pakatoa. **Ponui**, also known as Chamberlins Island, is a larger island just south of Rotoroa. It has been farmed by the Chamberlin family ever since they purchased it from Maori in 1854. Further south is **Pakihi**, or Sandspit Island, and tiny Karamuramu Island.

Little Barrier, 25km north-east of Kawau Island, is one of NZ's prime nature reserves, and the only area of NZ rainforest unaffected by humans, deer or possums. Several rare species of birds, reptiles and plants live in the varied habitats on the volcanic island. Access to the island is highly restricted and a DOC permit, which is very difficult to obtain, is required before landing can be made on this closely guarded sanctuary.

Motuora Island is halfway between Tiritiri Matangi and Kawau. There is a wharf and *camping ground* on the west coast of the island, but there is no regular ferry service. Get

a camping permit from the ranger (☎ 422 8882) on Kawau, or from the caretaker on Motuora.

The most remote islands of the Hauraki Gulf Maritime Park are the **Mokohinau Islands**, 23km north-west of Great Barrier. They are all protected nature reserves and visitors require landing permits.

See the Northland chapter for details of Kawau Island.

Northland

☎ 09 • pop 141,900

Geographically, this region is shaped like a finger pointing north from Auckland. Northland is the cradle of modern New Zealand: it was one of the first regions settled from eastern Polynesia, and was where Europeans first made permanent contact with the Maori; the first squalid sealers' and whalers' settlements were formed; and the Treaty of Waitangi between the settlers and the Maori was signed. To this day Northland has a greater proportion of Maori in its population than almost anywhere else in NZ.

The big attraction of Northland is the beautiful Bay of Islands. Although far less touristy, there are scenic, sheltered bays and beaches all along the east coast.

The west coast is a long stretch of sand pounded by the surf of the Tasman Sea. It also has scenic harbours, such as Hokianga, but the main attraction is the Kauri Coast, where the best remaining stands of NZ's once mighty kauri forests can be seen.

Kaitaia and the Far North feature some great beaches and are home to Maori communities, offering travellers the chance to learn about Maori lifestyle and culture.

Getting Around

There are two main routes – east and west – through Northland to the top of New Zealand. To reach Northland, go through Helensville or Warkworth to Wellsford and then on to Brynderwyn, 112km north of Auckland. From here, the simplest and fastest route is to head straight up through Whangarei on the eastern side of the peninsula and through the Bay of Islands to Kaitaia.

The west coast route is longer and slower, though the road is now sealed virtually all the way. It goes along the Kauri Coast through Matakohe, Dargaville, the Waipoua Kauri Forest and the remote and scenic Hokianga Harbour.

Look for the free Jasons Routeplanner *Twin Coast Discovery Highway,* which provides a clear description of the east and

HIGHLIGHTS

- Exploring the Bay of Islands, with the most beautiful of Northland's wonderful coastal scenery
- Visiting the ancient kauri forests of the Kauri Coast
- Travelling through the desolate landscapes of Ninety Mile Beach and Cape Reinga
- Swimming at the beaches near Whangarei, Doubtless Bay and the Hokianga Harbour
- Deep-sea fishing anywhere on the coast, but especially Tutukaka, the Bay of Islands and Whangaroa

west coast routes. It's available from visitor centres. The route is signposted.

The two main bus lines serving Northland are Northliner Express (☎ 09-307 5873 in Auckland), leaving from Auckland's Downtown Airline Terminal, and InterCity (☎ 09-913 6100), leaving from the Sky City Coach Terminal, Auckland. These services follow the east coast from Auckland to Whangarei, Bay of Islands and Kaitaia, but connect with the West Coaster service for the west coast.

Northliner has bus passes for backpackers with ID (YHA, VIP or BBH card).

The West Coaster/Pioneer (☎ 438 3206), in Whangarei, links Paihia with Dargaville via Kaikohe, Rawene, Opononi and the Waipoua forests, allowing time for photo stops. It leaves Paihia at 9 am for Auckland, Monday, Wednesday and Friday, arriving in Auckland at 5.30 pm. On weekdays it also leaves from Dargaville at 9 am, arriving in Auckland at 12.45 pm.

The main backpacker connection running through Northland is Kiwi Experience's Awesome & Top Bit (☎ 366 9830).

Auckland to Whangarei

While many visitors do this trip along SH1 in just a few hours in their haste to get to the Bay of Islands, the east coast between Auckland and Whangarei has many delightful bays and beaches. The Hibiscus Coast between Whangaparaoa and Warkworth, always a popular holiday spot, is now becoming an extension of the city. Heading further north, the coast is less developed but no less beautiful.

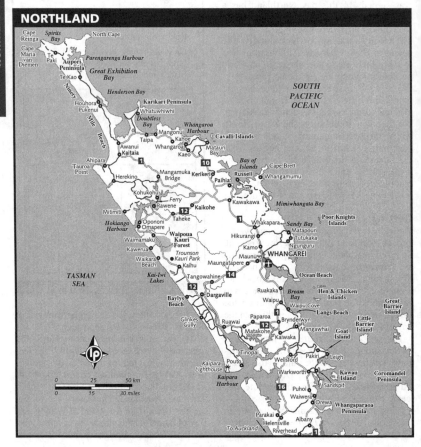

NORTHLAND

WHANGAPARAOA PENINSULA

Now virtually a suburb of Auckland, the Whangaparaoa (pronounced 'fa-nga-pa-ro-a') Peninsula – just north of Auckland off SH1 – is good for water-based activities; windsurfers flock to Manly Beach, boaties leave from the Weiti River and Gulf Harbour and swimmers find great beaches around the tip of the peninsula at **Shakespear Regional Park**. Many native bush birds and waders can be seen, and the native forests of the park contain karaka, kowhai and old puriri trees. A number of walking tracks traverse the park. The park is just beyond the huge Gulf Harbour Marina development, which boasts a golf course and country club. Gulf Harbour Ferries (☎ 424 5561) stops here to and from Tiritiri Matangi Island, and there is a regular service from the ferry building in central Auckland.

Whangaparaoa has a small **narrow gauge railway** (☎ 424 5018), with steam trains offering rides from 10 am to 5 pm on weekends ($5/2.50/12 for adults/children/family). It's at 400 Whangaparaoa Rd, east of Silverdale.

OREWA

pop 4900

Orewa's main attraction is the great beach that runs next to the highway. The town also has a statue of Sir Edmund Hillary, one of the first two people to stand on top of Mt Everest (the other was Tenzing Norgay).

The Hibiscus Coast Information Centre (☎ 426 0076) is on the highway south of town, next to KFC. The free *Let's go Walking on the Hibiscus Coast* outlines good walks in the area.

Orewa Cycle Works (☎ 426 6958), 278 Main Rd, has proved indispensable for travellers; staff hire out bikes ($12 per day), do repairs and sell parts.

Places to Stay

There are two excellent backpacker places in Orewa. *Pillows Travellers Lodge* (☎ 426 6338, @ pillows.lodge@xtra.co.nz, 412 Hibiscus Coast Highway) costs $15 in a dorm, $32/36 for singles/twins and doubles, and $49 with en suite. There's also a spa, camp site ($10), bone carving and cooking lessons and Internet access. Excursions can be arranged.

The *Marco Polo Backpackers Inn* (☎ 426 8455, @ marcopolo@clear.net.nz, 2a Hammond Ave, Hatfields Beach) is just off the highway on the northern outskirts of Orewa. Take Bus No 884, 894 or 895 from Auckland city; the owners will pick up from Orewa. At this very peaceful, spotless purpose-built hostel, nestled into hillside greenery, tent sites are $10, dorm beds are $15, and singles/doubles are $28/36. Staff can arrange a variety of trips, including snorkelling trips to Goat Island ($25).

Orewa has a dozen motels and three camping grounds/motor camps. *Puriri Park* (☎ 426 4648) on Puriri Ave is a well-equipped motor camp with a pool in a quiet setting. Camp sites are $10 per adult (minimum $20; children half-price), cabins are $59 for two, and tourist flats are $76 for two.

Motels (all on Hibiscus Coast Highway) include the *Orewa Motor Lodge* (☎ 426 4027, 0800-267 392, 290 Hibiscus Coast Highway), with studio units and one- or two-bedroom Lockwood units. On the beachfront are the *Best Western Golden Sands* (☎ 426 5177, 381 Main Rd), which has 25 units, some with spas, and *Edgewater* (☎ 426 5260, 387–389 Main Rd), with 14 units. Expect to pay about $100 a night for two people during summer; prices drop in the low season and there are always specials and discounts, so it's worth checking.

There are also several good B&Bs in the area. The information centre at Orewa has details.

Places to Eat

Creole Bar & Brasserie (☎ 426 6250, 310 Main Rd) usually has some sort of live entertainment at weekends. *Thai Orewa* (☎ 426 9711) at No 328 is a licensed eatery where rice and noodle dishes start at about $12. *Double Three Six Cafe & Bar* (☎ 426 9499) is open till late daily. Mains (steak and seafood) are about $18. *Rock Salt* in the main shopping area is also good.

The *Walnut Cottage* (☎ 426 6523, 498 Main Rd) is tucked away off the main road,

NORTHLAND

beside Orewa's oldest house. The cottage is open for lunch from noon Thursday to Sunday, and dinner from 6.30 pm Wednesday to Sunday.

Il Veneziano (☎ *426 5444)* at the Red Beach shopping centre (about 2km south of Orewa) is one of the best places, with good Italian food and plenty of atmosphere. It's licensed.

Getting There & Away
Stagecoach buses (Nos 893, 894, 895 and 897) run between Auckland and Orewa/ Waiwera via Takapuna, Albany and Silverdale. There are local Hibiscus Coast buses between Orewa and Army Bay at the end of the Whangaparaoa Peninsula via Red Beach approximately every hour.

WAIWERA
pop 305
The coastal village of Waiwera (literally 'Warm Waters'), 48km north of Auckland (bus No 895 from the Downtown Bus Terminal), is noted for its thermal pools. This huge complex of hot pools, spa pools, waterslides (plus a luxury private spa and gym) is open from 9 am to 10 pm daily (to 10.30 pm on Friday and Saturday). Entry is $14/8 for adults/children; the spa and gym cost extra.

Horse riding is offering by Ti Tree (☎ 426 7003) for $20/35 for one/two hours.

Mountain bikes can be hired from Pedal Adventures (☎ 025-276 3835, 025-296 2610), Waiwera Holiday Park ($10 an hour, $35 a day). It's possible to cycle to Puhoi and back.

Another possibility is kayaking to Warkworth and back on the Mahurangi River with Auckland Canoe Centre Adventures (☎ 426 5369); you can book at the Wairewa thermal pools.

Just north of Waiwera is **Wenderholm Regional Park**, a coastal farmland park with a good beach, estuary and walks. Couldrey House, the original homestead, is now a museum. It's open from 1 to 4 pm Saturday (Labour weekend to Easter) and from 1 to 4 pm Sunday year-round ($1.50, $0.50 for children).

Places to Stay & Eat
All the accommodation at Waiwera is within walking distance of the pools.

The *Waiwera Resort Hotel* (☎ *426 4089, 15 Waiwera Rd)* has 22 motel-style units for $75 a double. The restaurant opens at 6 pm; bar meals are available during the day.

The *Waiwera Motel* (☎/fax *426 5153, 25 Weranui Rd)* has five ground-floor family and studio units (self-contained), with dinghies and kayaks for rent. Doubles cost $85 to $90 (each extra adult $15).

The *Coach Trail Lodge* (☎ *426 4792, 1 Waiwera Rd)* has 15 studio and family units and a licensed restaurant. Prices range from $100 to $150 for two. Self-contained cottages, at 14 The Strand, are also available from $110 for two.

The *Waiwera Thermal Resort Holiday Park* (☎ *426 5270, 37 Waiwera Place)* has 90 tent/campervan sites. It costs $13 per adult for a powered site and $9 per child, and $11 for a tent site.

Getting There & Away
The Stagecoach buses that pass by Orewa (see that section earlier) also take you to Waiwera.

PUHOI
North of Waiwera, 1km west off SH1, Puhoi is a picturesque historic village that claims to be NZ's first Bohemian settlement. The small **Puhoi Bohemian Museum** is open from 1 to 4 pm on weekends (entry free but a donation of $1 is appreciated). However, the main point of interest is the historic pub, crammed with old artefacts (open from 11 am to 10 pm daily).

Puhoi Cottage, 500m past the Puhoi Store, has delicious Devonshire teas and home-cooked goodies. It's open daily except Wednesday.

At Puhoi you can hire canoes (☎ 422 0891) or go mountain biking with Puhoi Adventure Bike Tours (☎ 025-905 227).

WARKWORTH
pop 2450
Just off the main highway, beside the Mahurangi River, this pretty town was

once connected to Auckland by steamships that docked at the town's old wharf. Today Warkworth has cafes, galleries and arts and crafts shops; wineries, galleries and more arts and crafts places can be found a little to the north.

The Warkworth Visitor Information Centre (☎ 425 9081), 1 Baxter St, is near the river and bus station. Get the brochure *Warkworth, The Kowhai Town* which marks out a heritage trail taking you past Warkworth's most historic sites.

On the outskirts of town, the **Parry Kauri Park** has short forest walks and a couple of monstrous old kauri, including the 800-year-old McKinney kauri. Also at the park, the small **Warkworth Museum** (☎ 425 7093), open from 9 am to 4 pm daily, has well-preserved pioneer-era exhibits ($4, children $0.50).

Places to Stay & Eat

There are numerous B&Bs in Warkworth and several wonderful upmarket guesthouses and lodges. The information centre has details.

Warkworth's historic pub, the *Warkworth Inn* (☎ 425 7569) on Queen St has typical old pub rooms with shared facilities for $40/60 a single/double.

Bridge House Lodge (☎ 425 83510) is on Elizabeth St next to the river. Rooms with attached bathroom start at $65.

Homewood Cottage (☎ 425 8667, 17 View Rd) has doubles and twins for $70 including breakfast.

On Neville St you'll find *The Art's Cafe* and next door, the *Gallery & Tea House*, the latter with an upstairs veranda; soup, panini, bagels and so on.

The *Seafood Cafe* next to the Gallery has good fish and chips. On the corner of Queen and Neville Sts is the *Queen St Cafe & Bookshop*, another pleasant cafe. Further along Queen St, next to the Bridge House Lodge, is the *Bombay India Restaurant*.

The licensed *Riverbank Cafe* on Wharf St, with a fine selection of wines, and *Ducks Crossing* in Riverview Plaza, both have fine outlooks over the river and the old wharf.

Getting There & Away

Gubbs Motors (☎ 425 8348) has three daily buses on weekdays to Silverdale (which connect with Stagecoach buses to Auckland). The only way of getting to/from Warkworth by bus on weekends is on an InterCity bus (☎ 357 8400). There is no bus from Warkworth to Sandspit for Kawau Island; the only option is a taxi which will cost you $14 one way.

AROUND WARKWORTH

Take the road towards Matakana, heading towards Leigh, and you'll find numerous art and craft places, good cafes and a couple of wineries. The Warkworth Visitor Information Centre has maps and details. Gallery/collectibles places include Hugh Brading's gallery, The Red Barn Antiques, D'vine Arts (textiles and ceramics), and the Matakana Market Co-op.

Good cafes include *Morris & James Cafe & Bar*, which is open daily. There's a pleasant courtyard for summer dining. But equally, there's a large showroom for the pottery; bright, attractive ceramics are for sale and you can also see potters and artists at work. Morris & James is on Tongue Farm Rd; continue a little further along this road and you come to **Hyperion Wines** (winery hours are 11 am to 6 pm weekends and public holidays).

You can also visit **Heron's Flight**, further north at 49 Sharp's Rd (open from 10 am to 6 pm daily). There's a cafe here. A detour down Ti Point Rd takes you to the **Ti Point Reptile Park**, open from 10 am to 5 pm daily ($7, children $3).

There are a couple of backpacker places in this area: *Matakana Backpackers* (☎ 422 9264, 19 Matakana Valley Rd), which has dorms and twin shares for $15 per person, and *Omaha Backpackers* (☎ 422 9405, 1 Takatu Rd), which is about the same. Both cater for people who come to harvest the capsicum and courgette crops from November to March.

There are also some interesting upmarket places. These include *The Castle* (☎ 422 9288, 378 Whitmore Rd), and *Hurstmere House* (☎ 422 9220) on Tongue Farm Rd.

NORTHLAND

The biggest unabashedly touristy attraction is 4km north of Warkworth on SH1. **Sheepworld** (☎ 425 7444, 0800-227 433) demonstrates many aspects of NZ sheep farming – shearing and things you can try for yourself, such as carding, spinning and feeding tame sheep and lambs. Recent additions include an adventure playground and an arts and crafts cooperative. It's open from 9 am to 5 pm daily, with shows at 11 am and 1 pm (Saturday and Sunday). It costs $10/5 for adults/children. There is a caravan park and camping ground (☎/fax 425 9962) nearby.

The **Dome Forest**, 10km north of Warkworth on SH1, is a regenerating forest which was logged about 90 years ago. A walking track to the Dome summit (336m) and its great views across the Mahurangi Peninsula leads from the car park and takes about 1½ hours return. A three-hour (return) walk leads beyond the Dome summit to the **Waiwhiu Kauri Grove**, a stand of about 20 mature kauri trees. The start of the walkway is some 6km north of Warkworth on SH1.

Six kilometres south of Warkworth, the **Earth Satellite Station** has an information centre with hands-on exhibits explaining satellite communications; it was a Kiwi astrophysicist from Warkworth who in 1970 picked the location of the disabled Apollo 13 in outer space, enabling NASA ground crew to bring it home. The station is open to the public from 9 am to 3 pm.

Near the main-road turn-off for the satellite station is the **Honey Centre & Cafe** where you can see bees at work. The shop sells all manner of bee-related products. Nearby is **Greg's Sheep-n-Show** which has sheep and dog shows at 11 am and 1.30 pm daily.

To the east of Warkworth on the scenic Mahurangi Peninsula is **Sandspit**, from where the ferry departs for beautiful Kawau Island. To the south of Sandspit are the beach suburbs of **Snells Beach** and **Algies Bay**. These shallow bays are pleasant enough, but 3km further, **Martins Bay** is the pick of the beaches and has a motor camp.

KAWAU ISLAND
pop 175

Directly east of Warkworth, Kawau Island's main point of interest is **Mansion House** (☎ 422 8882), an impressive historic house built in 1846 by Sir George Grey, NZ's third governor and 17th prime minister. It was a hotel for many years before being restored and turned into a museum. It's open from 9.30 am to 3.30 pm daily; entry is $4/2 for adults/children. Inside is a collection of Victorian memorabilia including some items once owned by Sir George.

Kawau has many beautiful walks, starting from Mansion House and leading to beaches, the old copper mine and a lookout. The *Kawau Island Historic Reserve* pamphlet ($1) published by DOC has a map of walking tracks. You can get it from the DOC office at the Auckland ferry terminal. Numerous wallabies, introduced from Australia, are housed in an enclosure on Pah Farm in Bon Accord Harbour.

Every year, in the last week of February, the four-day Furuno fishing competition, one of the world's biggest, is held off Pah Farm's stretch of coast.

Vivian Bay is the only sandy bay with accommodation on the island; attractions include a white, sandy beach, swimming, fishing, snorkelling and bush walks.

Places to Stay

There are a couple of places to stay at *Vivian Bay*, on the north side of Kawau Island, and a *camp site* and a couple of *cottages* on Bon Accord Harbour.

Heavenly Homestay (☎ 422 8887) at North Cove is a new, self-contained place right on the beach with a generous deck. The cost is $100 for two people including breakfast. Other meals are available; dinner is $20.

St Clair Lodge (☎ 422 8850) is another upmarket B&B charging from $250 (all meals inclusive) for two. The St Clair beachfront units cost $190 and there is a chalet costing $180 for two. Meals are extra.

There is one self-contained *DOC cottage* at Sandy Bay for rent (contact Mansion House on ☎ 422 8882). It sleeps five and costs $60 per night.

At Swansea Bay there is a *cottage* for rent for $120 for two. All food is included. This place has its own jetty and a dinghy that you can use to row out to the Pah Farm bar and restaurant. Expect visits from Sally the friendly Labrador-cross. For bookings call ☎ 422 8816.

For a meal or a drink try the *Kawau Island Yacht Club* (☎ 422 8845), open from 9 am to noon and again from 4 pm daily – check to see what time it's closing on any particular day; or the *Pah Farm Restaurant & Lodge* (☎ 422 8765), open from about 9 am until late daily. Both are in Bon Accord Harbour. Pah Farm also has accommodation. A bunk in a four-bunk room (there are 12 bunk rooms) costs $15 and a room in the house is $40. You can camp here; it costs $7.50/5 per adult/child.

Getting There & Away

Two ferry companies operate trips to Kawau from Sandspit (one hour) year-round. Departures from central Auckland run between October and April only.

The Kawau Kat (☎ 0800-888 006), Web site: www.kawaukat.co.nz, has a Royal Mail Run daily at 10.30 am which stops at Mansion House and many coves, bays and inlets ($39/15 for adults/children). The Paradise Cruise departs from central Auckland on weekends at 10 am, visiting the *Rewa* shipwreck en route ($39/15).

Matata Cruises (☎ 0800-225 292, ✉ matata.cruises@xtra.co.nz) has a coffee cruise to Kawau for $25 (children $10). It leaves at 10 am daily (returning 2 pm). It also offers a combined three-hour Mansion House lunch cruise ($35, children $22). Phone ahead to book.

Ship 'n' Shore Tours & Cruises (☎ 478 1462) does weekend trips from central Auckland to Kawau Island costing $39/15 return.

WARKWORTH TO BREAM BAY

Less frequented than the main road to Whangarei is the scenic route from Warkworth out to Leigh on the east coast, and then north via Mangawhai and Waipu to Bream Bay. This route has a number of places where you can relax off the not-so-beaten track.

The first good beach, **Omaha**, a short detour from the Leigh Road, has a sweeping stretch of white sand, good surf and lifesaving club. For a pleasant, sheltered beach try **Mathesons Bay** just before you enter the small town of Leigh. **Leigh** sits above a picturesque harbour dotted with fishing boats.

There is the *Leigh Motel* (☎ 422 6179, 15 Hill St), from $75 for two; and the excellent *Leigh Sawmill Cafe*, on Pakiri Rd, open from 6 pm Friday and from 10 am on weekends. At the cafe you can hear live music, and there are occasional wine tastings and art exhibitions.

Further north, around the cape from Leigh, **Goat Island** is the site of the Cape Rodney-Okakari Point Marine Reserve. The reserve is teeming with fish that can be handfed in the water or viewed from a glass-bottomed boat, the *Habitat Explorer* (☎ 422 6334). The trips run year-round, weather permitting. The popular 45-minute round-the-island trip costs $15/10 for adults/children.

Snorkelling and diving gear can be hired at *Seafriends* (☎ 422 6212), 1km before the beach. Seafriends has a good, inexpensive restaurant and a small aquarium. There is also a marine education centre here.

Accommodation can be found at *Goat Island Backpackers* (☎ 422 6185) down the road from Seafriends. Tent/powered sites costs $10/12 per person, a bed in the bunkhouse costs $12, cabins are $50 for two and caravans are $40. There are two kitchens, and showerblocks.

There's also *Fantail Farm Backpackers* (☎ 422 6123) next to the main road, just before Seafriends. A bed costs $15.

Continuing along the coast, a gravel road leads to **Pakiri**, a tiny rural settlement with a white-sand beach. A good way of seeing the unspoilt beach and the forests behind is on horseback. Pakiri Beach Horse Rides (☎ 422 6275) has popular rides along the beach; these cost from $30 for a one-hour ride to $120 for a full day (including lunch).

From Pakiri, the gravel road via Tomatara eventually meets up with the sealed road to

Mangawhai. You rejoin the coast at **Manga-whai Heads**, a growing summer resort town with a great surf beach and a lifesaving club. The **Mangawhai Cliffs Walkway** (1½ to two hours one way) starts at the beach and affords extensive views inland and out to the Hauraki Gulf islands. Mangawhai has motels, caravan parks and some lovely guesthouses. These include *Lake View Chalets* (☎ 431 4086, 622 Ocean View Rd), with six self-contained two-bedroom chalets for $120 for two; and *Hidden Valley Chalets* (☎ 431 5332) on the corner of Te Arai Point and Mangawhai Rds, with four self-contained chalets from $95 for two.

At Mangawhai Heads is *Milestone Cottages* (☎ 431 4018, 27 Moir Rd), which has self-contained accommodation set in lovely gardens (there are kayaks available to guests, and a pool). Prices start at $95 for studio apartments, and range up to $175.

Not far away is *Mangawhai Lodge* (☎ 431 5311, 4 Heather St), a boutique B&B with a commanding position and great views. Rooms start at $60/90 a single/double, including breakfast.

A couple of minutes' walk from here, on Molesworth Drive, is the pleasant *Naja Cafe* (open daily), which is set in one of NZ's best garden centres. If you are travelling with children, **Penrose Farm** on Old Waipu Rd has donkeys they can ride, kune kune pigs (the tamer of NZ's two breeds of pig), sheep and goats, doves and ducks. You need to book ahead (☎ 431 4711).

For an insight into local history there's the **Mangawhai District Museum** on Moir Rd (open from 10 am to noon on Saturday).

A particularly scenic part of the road goes over the headland to Langs Beach and then on to Waipu.

WAIPU & BREAM BAY
pop 1980

Near the mouth of the Waipu River is an estuary which provides a home for many species of wader birds, including the rare NZ dotterel, variable oyster-catchers and fairy terns.

The *Ebb & Flow Backpackers* (☎ 432 0217, fax 432 0338) is well situated – it overlooks the Waipu River estuary on Johnson Point Rd. A bed in a dorm costs $14, and twins and doubles cost $36.

A new backpackers (still being finished at the time of writing) is the *Waipu Wanderer Backpackers Hut* (☎ 432 0532, 25 St Marys Rd), right in town. This is a small, purpose-built place with two four-bed rooms and one double room ($15 per person). It's situated behind the main house. Muffins and hot bread are available free in the evening.

Also in town is the *Waipu Clansmen Motel* (☎ 432 0424), Cove Rd, which has doubles from $70 and budget rooms (shared bathrooms) from $45.

At Waipu Cove you'll find the *Cove Beach Motel* (☎ 432 0348), on Cove Rd, with one-bedroom units from $75 and two-bedroom units from $120.

There are several lovely guesthouses out here. *The Stone House* (☎ 432 0432) is built in the style of a Cornish cottage. The delightful guest accommodation here has a pretty lounge area with a patio. A little way from the main house, overlooking a lagoon rich in bird life, is another self-contained cottage. Prices range from $80 to $100 for two, including breakfast. Adjacent to the main cottage is an outdoor loft with backpacker accommodation ($10 per person with your own linen, $20 without; no kitchen).

Waipu Cove Cottages (☎ 432 0851), Cove Rd, has three self-contained two-bedroom cottages from $80 to $110.

There are more lovely places; the information centre at the museum in Waipu has details. The *Waipu Cove Reserve Camp* (☎ 432 0410) has tent and powered sites for $16 for two.

If you want to splash out there's *Wychwood Lodge* (☎ 432 0757), Cove Rd, Langs Beach, a stylish place with a lovely conservatory. Prices start at $135 for two (includes breakfast).

At Uretiti, DOC has a *camping ground* ($6); book on ☎ 430 2133. You can buy groceries and other supplies from the Waipu Four Square supermarket.

In Waipu there's an unusual, small museum, the **House of Memories** (☎ 432 0746), which has displays relating to the

Nova Scotian settlers of Waipu and the surrounding district; it is open from 9.30 am to 4 pm daily (entry $4). There is a small visitor information service here as well. A visit to the **Old Waipu Firehouse Gallery** (open from 10 am to 4 pm daily) is also worthwhile, especially to see the acclaimed Waipu tiles. There's also ceramics, glasswork, pottery, limited edition prints, and more. The **Waipu Herbal Apothecary** at 43 The Centre has an intriguing collection of tonics, lotions, balms and salves. Internet access is available at the Waipu off-licence at 15-17 The Centre.

For great pizzas, light meals and snacks – or just a pleasant place to have a drink – try the *Pizza Barn 'n' Bar (3 Cove Rd)*.

The biggest annual event in Waipu is the Highland Games held at Caledonian Park in town on 1 January (or the 2nd if the 1st falls on a Sunday). Come and see the lads toss the caber, and throw the Caledonian hammer. There's also highland dancing and piping.

About 10 minutes' drive west of Waipu is North River Treks (☎ 432 0565), offering a variety of rides along rivers, through farmland and on beaches. Other things to do in the area include caving, abseiling and climbing (☎ 432 0858), dolphin and whale-watching (contact Bream Bay Charters on ☎ 432 7484) and golf – the Waipu Golf Club (☎ 432 0259) has an 18-hole course; visitors are welcome.

There are many **walks** including the McKenzie Walking track (starts near Waipu Caves), the Brynderwyn Walkway and the Mangawhai Coastal Walkway. All these walks are outlined in the pamphlet *Bream Bay Northland,* available from the visitor centre and from most places to stay.

Kauri Coast

Heading towards Whangarei, you can turn off SH1 past Wellsford and travel along SH12 to the area known as the Kauri Coast. From the northern end of Kaipara Harbour, extending along the west coast to Hokianga, the Kauri Coast is so-called because of the Kauri timber and gum industry that flourished here in the 19th century, generating much of NZ's wealth. The massive kauri forests are all but gone; however, the Waipoua Kauri Forest has untouched kauri forest and is the best place in NZ to see these magnificent trees. A prior visit to Matakohe is worthwhile for an understanding of kauri and the kauri industry.

MATAKOHE

Turning off at Brynderwyn for Dargaville, you pass through Matakohe, where the **Matakohe Kauri Museum** (☎ 431 7417) has a strange and wonderful collection of kauri gum. It also has lifelike displays of various aspects of the life of the kauri bushpeople and an extensive photographic collection.

The museum shop has some excellent items crafted from kauri wood. The museum is open from 8.30 am to 5.30 pm daily (until 5 pm in winter); $7, $2.50 for children.

Kauri Country Safaris (☎ 0800-246 528) runs three-hour tours (guided by a descendant of one of the original pioneering families in the area) that explain the history of kauri logging (there is even a bullock team) and provide an insight into conservation efforts today. The trips ($45/30 for adults/children) leave from the museum daily (10 am to 1.30 pm, winter 12.30 pm. It's best to book ahead.

Facing the museum is the **Matakohe Pioneer Church**, built in 1867 of local kauri. The tiny church served both Methodists and Anglicans, and also acted as the town hall and school for the pioneer community.

Back on the main road is **Tui Park Car & Collectibles**, a museum with vintage Austins, Rileys, Minis, Morris and Holdens on show. It's open from 9 am to 5 pm daily ($3/1).

Places to Stay

At Paparoa, 7km from Matakohe, the *Old Post Office Guesthouse (☎/fax 431 6444)* is a very pleasant hostel with all the facilities; a double or twin room is $35 per person and a dorm bed $18/23 with/without your own linen.

A short walk from the museum, *Matakohe House (☎ 431 7091, @ mathouse@xtra.co .nz)* is purpose-built in colonial style; it has en suite singles/doubles for $70/85 (including breakfast). There are decks, plenty of land and a little artist's cottage tucked away in a corner of the garden. The licensed restaurant is a good spot for a meal.

There is a *homestay (☎ 431 7288)* in Barlow Lane, 1km from the museum.

The *Matakohe Motor Camp (☎ 431 6431),* which is only about 350m from the museum, has tent and powered sites for $10 per person, a cabin for $38 for two, and a tourist flat for $60. On-site caravans are $36.

At Ruawai, west of Matakohe on the main road to Dargaville, is the small *Ruawai Travellers Lodge (☎ 439 2283).* All beds cost $15 in this clean place.

DARGAVILLE
pop 4530
Founded in 1872 by Joseph McMullen Dargaville, this once-important river port thrived on the export of kauri timber and gum. As the kauri forests were decimated, Dargaville declined, and today it is a quiet backwater servicing the agricultural Northern Wairoa area.

Dargaville is the main town on the Kauri Coast and the access point for the Waipoua kauri forests to the north. Dargaville's only other claim to fame is its title as the Kumara Capital of NZ (the winner of the local beauty competition is named the Kumara Queen).

The helpful information centre (☎ 439 8360, @ info@kauricoast.co.nz) on Normanby St is also the AA office. See its Web site: www.kauricoast.co.nz.

Harding Park & Maritime Museum
On a hill overlooking the town and the sweeping Wairoa River, Harding Park is the site of an old Maori *pa,* Po-tu-Oterangi. Tucked into the bottom of the hill is an early European cemetery.

On top of the hill, the small **Maritime Museum** (☎ 439 7555) has an eccentric collection of anything over 50 years old,

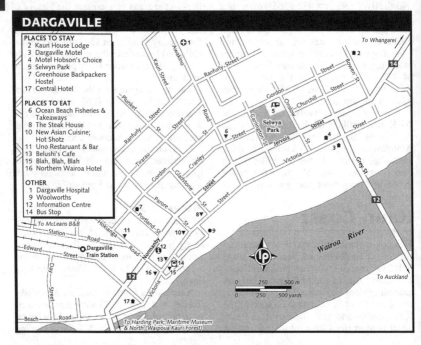

DARGAVILLE

PLACES TO STAY
2 Kauri House Lodge
3 Dargaville Motel
4 Motel Hobson's Choice
5 Selwyn Park
7 Greenhouse Backpackers Hostel
17 Central Hotel

PLACES TO EAT
6 Ocean Beach Fisheries & Takeaways
8 The Steak House
10 New Asian Cuisine; Hot Shotz
11 Uno Restaurant & Bar
13 Belushi's Cafe
15 Blah, Blah, Blah
16 Northern Wairoa Hotel

OTHER
1 Dargaville Hospital
9 Woolworths
12 Information Centre
14 Bus Stop

To Whangarei
To Auckland
Wairoa River
Selwyn Park
To McLeans B&B
Dargaville Train Station
To Harding Park; Maritime Museum & North (Waipoua Kauri Forest)

0   250   500 m
0   250   500 yards

The *Rainbow Warrior* Trail

With a population of 3.5 million and relatively isolated, New Zealand is seldom mentioned on the world stage. However, in 1985, an explosion in Auckland Harbour made world headlines and put NZ on the map.

The Greenpeace flagship *Rainbow Warrior* lay anchored in Auckland Harbour, preparing to sail to Moruroa near Tahiti to protest against French nuclear testing.

The *Rainbow Warrior* never left Auckland. French saboteurs, in the employ of the French government, attached explosives to the side of the ship and sank her, killing one green campaigner, Fernando Pereira.

It took some time to find out exactly what had happened, but in inquisitive, rural NZ the comings and goings of foreigners are not easily forgotten. Two of the saboteurs were captured, tried and found guilty, while the others have never been brought to justice.

The incident caused an uproar in France – not because the French government had conducted a wilful and lethal act of terrorism on the soil of a friendly nation, but because the French secret service had bungled the operation and been caught. The French used all their political and economic might to force NZ to release the two saboteurs, and in a farcical turn of events the agents were imprisoned on a French Pacific island as if they had just won a trip to Club Med. Within two years, and well before the end of their sentence, they returned to France to receive a hero's welcome.

Northland was the stage for this deadly mission involving several secret service agents. Explosives for the sabotage were delivered by a yacht (which had picked them up from a submarine) from Parengarenga Harbour in the far north. They were driven to Auckland in a Kombi van, by French agents posing as tourists. Bang! An innocent man dead, and international outrage – Auckland Harbour was in the news.

The skeletal remains of the *Rainbow Warrior* were taken to the waters of Northland's beautiful Cavalli Islands (the site has become a popular destination for divers). The masts of this oceanic crusader were sent to the Maritime Museum in Dargaville. The memory of the Portuguese photographer and campaigner who died endures in a peaceful bird sanctuary in Thames. A haunting memorial to the once-proud boat sits atop a Maori *pa* site at Matauri Bay, Bay of Islands.

Attention again focused on the *Rainbow Warrior* in 1995. Ten years after the sinking the French announced they were resuming nuclear testing in the Pacific, and Greenpeace's new flagship bearing the name of its ill-fated predecessor set sail for the Moruroa test site. It entered the exclusion zone and was stormed by French marines.

DAVID WALL

Rainbow Warrior memorial – Matauri Bay

including settlers' items, kauri gum samples and a huge slab of kauri. The maritime section has models of ships built or repaired in Kaipara Harbour, notorious for its shipwrecks, and a massive Maori war canoe. Nearly 18m long, the 18th-century canoe is the only surviving example from pre-European times. In front of the museum are the masts from the *Rainbow Warrior,* the Greenpeace flagship bombed by the French in 1985. The museum is open from 9 am to 4 pm daily ($5/1 for adults/children).

Te Aroha

The historic 90-year-old kauri schooner, *Te Aroha,* which used to take people out to visit the islands on the Hauraki Gulf in Auckland, now plies Kaipara Harbour and its surrounds. You can go out on a 2½-hour cruise or one that lasts several days. A three-day cruise, all inclusive, costs about $225 per person. Contact ☎ 025-948 166.

Organised Tours & Jet-Boat Tours

The information centre has details on tours to Waipoua Kauri Forest, Trounson Kauri Park, Kai-Iwi Lakes, and 4WD tours along the beach to Kaipara Lighthouse, returning to Dargaville or connecting with a boat ride south to Shelley Beach. Kaipara Kapers (☎ 431 7493) takes jet-boat trips down the northern Wairoa River to Kaipara Harbour, and organises quad-bike safaris. The information centre has details.

Places to Stay

Selwyn Park (☎ *439 8296, 10 Onslow St*) has tent/powered sites for $18/19, simple cabins for $30 and fully equipped tourist cabins for $42 for two.

The *Greenhouse Backpackers Hostel* (☎ *439 6342,* ✉ *greenhousenz@hotmail .com, 13 Portland St)*, a YHA associate, charges $15 for dorms and $18 per person for twins or doubles. It has a pool table, rents out bicycles and arranges Baylys Beach horse rides and walks in Waipoua Kauri Forest.

The *Central Hotel* (☎ *439 8034, 18–22 Victoria St)* is an old kauri building with singles/doubles from $20/40.

Local motels range from the straight-forward *Dargaville Motel* (☎ *439 7734, 217 Victoria St)*, with doubles from $70, to the well-appointed *Motel Hobson's Choice* (☎ *439 8551, 212 Victoria St)*, with a pool and a variety of studios, plus one- and two-bedroom units starting at $85 a double.

The delightful *Kauri House Lodge* (☎/fax *439 8082)* on Bowen St is a rambling colonial homestead furnished with antiques. This fine B&B, set on 40 hectares, has only two double rooms (bookings essential) for $130 to $150, and a pool.

Another option is *McLeans B&B* (☎ *439 5915, 136 Hokianga Rd)*, originally built for one of Dargaville's mayors. It has three

guest bedrooms and a large lounge on the top floor. Singles/doubles cost $35/65.

Places to Eat

Ocean Beach Fisheries & Takeaways (164 Victoria St) is the place to come for fish and chips. For moderately priced Chinese food, try the *New Asian Cuisine (14 Victoria St)*, open daily from 10 am to 10 pm. Nearby, *Hot Shotz* dishes up hearty pizzas.

Belushi's Cafe (102 Victoria St), *Blah, Blah, Blah*, opposite and *Uno Restaurant & Bar (17 Hokianga Rd)* offer good food, and the latter two are congenial places for a drink as well.

The *Northern Wairoa Hotel* has pub food, a Sunday smorgasbord (5 to 8 pm) and a Monday 'cheap and cheerful' spread; both cost $10 a head.

The *Steak House & Bar* on the corner of Victoria and Gladstone Sts, opposite Woolworth, is open daily.

Getting There & Away

The bus stop is on Kapia St. Main Coach-lines has a bus to/from Auckland via Matakohe every day except Saturday. Inter-City also does this run.

The West Coaster bus service runs from Paihia to Dargaville on Monday, Wednesday and Friday, and from Dargaville to Paihia on Tuesday, Thursday and Sunday. The route goes via Kaikohe. On Monday, Wednesday and Friday it goes from Dargaville to Whangarei and Paihia, looping back to Dargaville and then on to Matakohe, Brynderwyn and return.

AROUND DARGAVILLE
Kaipara Lighthouse

A worthwhile trip from Dargaville, if you can find a way to get there, is the 71km run south-east to Kaipara Lighthouse (built 1884); the last 6.5km is on foot along the foreshore.

Baylys Beach & Ripiro Ocean Beach

Only a 15-minute drive from Dargaville is Baylys Beach, lying on the 100km-long Ripiro Ocean Beach which is backed by high, yellow sand dunes. This stretch of surf-pounded coast is the site of many shipwrecks, including a French man o' war and an ancient Portuguese ship.

Ripiro Ocean Beach is a gazetted highway and you can drive along its hard sands at low tide, although it is primarily for 4WD vehicles. Ask locals about conditions before venturing out onto the sands. There is also access at Glinks Gully, Mahuta Gorge and Omamari.

Horse rides on Baylys Beach are popular. Baylys Beach Horse Treks (☎ 439 6342) offers regular half-day beach rides for $30.

The *Baylys Beach Motor Camp* (☎/fax *439 6349)* at Baylys Beach, 13km west of Dargaville, has powered and nonpowered sites for $18 and cabins from $30 for two.

The *Oceanview Bed & Breakfast* (☎ *439 6256, 7 Oceanview Terrace)* is a small, simple bach-turned-B&B for $40/70 a single/double.

DARGAVILLE TO HOKIANGA

En route to the big trees from Dargaville you can make a number of excursions. There are many walks you can undertake in Waipoua Kauri Forest and the smaller reserves. Any visit to this area should be preceded by a visit to the kauri museum in Matakohe. Get the DOC brochure *Waipoua Kauri Forests* from the Dargaville information centre.

Kai-Iwi Lakes

Only 34km north of Dargaville are three freshwater lakes called Kai-Iwi Lakes (Taharoa Domain), which are popular for swimming, trout fishing and boating. The lakes are Kai-Iwi, Taharoa and Waikere. The largest, Taharoa, has deep-blue water fringed with gleaming white-sand beaches and pine groves. Activities are outlined in the *Taharoa Domain: Kai-Iwi Lakes* pamphlet available from information centres throughout Northland. You can rent kayaks at Lake Taharoa.

A three-hour return **walk** from the lakes leads to the coast, then north along the beach to the base of Maunganui Bluff. You can also climb the summit (three hours return) or continue north for the three-day walk to Omapere (see the Omapere & Oponomi section).

Places to Stay There are two rustic camping grounds at Kai-Iwi Lakes, one at *Pine Beach* right on the main lake and another at *Promenade Point* (book these at Kai-Iwi Lakes or at Dargaville's information centre). They have toilets, cold showers, fireplaces, but no power, and cost $7 (children $5).

Waterlea (☎ *439 0727)* is a farm with self-contained accommodation right at the entrance to the lakes, and costs from $60 to $80 for two, depending on the season. The owners organise trout fishing tours (from $40 per hour for two).

Trounson Kauri Park

Heading north from Dargaville you can take a route passing by the 573-hectare Trounson Kauri Park, 40km north of Dargaville. There's an easy half-hour walk leading from the parking and picnic area by the road, passing through beautiful forest with streams and some fine kauri stands, a couple of fallen kauri trees and the Four Sisters – two trees each with two trunks. There's a ranger station and camp sites.

Guided night-time **nature walks** are organised through the Kauri Coast Holiday Park. These excellent, informative walks cost $15 per adult ($9 children) and explain the flora and nightlife. Trounson is a mainland refuge for threatened bird species.

Places to Stay The turn-off for Trounson Kauri Park is 32km north of Dargaville. Just after the turn-off, the *Kauri Coast Holiday Park* (☎ *439 0621)* is in a lovely riverside spot central to the lakes and the kauri forest. Bushwalks, pony rides, river, lake and sea fishing can be organised. Tent or powered sites cost $19, cabins are $30 and a tourist cabin is $42. Motel units are $75.

The *camping ground* (☎ *439 0605)* at Trounson Kauri Park is run by DOC and is only open in summer. It's a beautiful place, ringed by superb kauri trees. Sites are $7 per person, with or without power.

On SH12, 2km north of the Trounson turn-off, the *Kaihu Farm Hostel* (☎ *439 4004)* has dorms for $15, twins and doubles for $18 per person, and a single for $25. Tent sites are $10. Breakfast/dinner costs $7/12. You can rent a mountain bike for $12 per day, go horse riding ($18 per hour) or take a walk down the secret glowworm trail.

Waipoua Kauri Forest

The highlight of the west coast, this superb forest sanctuary – proclaimed in 1952 after much public pressure and antagonism at continued milling – is the largest remnant of the once extensive kauri forests of northern NZ.

The road through the forest passes by some splendid huge kauri trees. Turn off to the forest lookout just after you enter the park – it was once a fire lookout and offers a spectacular view. A little further north, the park visitor centre (☎ 439 0605) has plenty of information and excellent exhibits on kauri trees, native birds and wildlife. A fully grown kauri can reach 60m and have a trunk 5m or more in diameter.

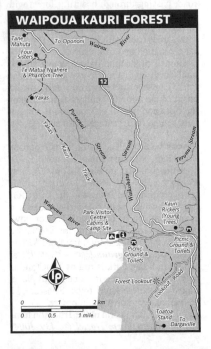

Several huge trees are easily reached from the road. **Te Matua Ngahere** (The Father of the Forest) has a trunk over 5m in diameter, believed to be the widest girth of any kauri tree in NZ, and is currently believed to be the oldest in NZ (possibly 4000 years). This massive tree is a short drive, then a 20-minute walk from the car park. Close by are the **Four Sisters** (not to be confused with the kauri siblings of the same name in Trounson Kauri Park), a graceful collection of four tall trees in close proximity. Also near Te Matua Ngahere is the **Phantom Tree**, believed to be the second largest in the forest.

In the past, theft from cars has been a problem – the car park is guarded voluntarily (a $2 donation is appreciated).

From the same access path you can follow a half-hour walking track to the large **Yakas Tree** and continue on the full two-hour trek to the park information centre.

Further up the road is **Tane Mahuta**, named for the Maori god of the forests, the largest kauri tree in NZ, standing close to the road and estimated to be between 1200 and 2000 years old. At 51m, it's much taller than Te Matua Ngahere but doesn't have the same impressive girth – although its volume is greater.

Places to Stay Right in the heart of the forest, next to the Waipoua River and just past the visitor centre, are *camp sites* costing $7. In addition there are caravan sites (nonpowered) for $7 per adult, single cabins for $8 per adult, two-berth cabins for $14 per adult and four-berth cabins for $10. There is a kitchen, showers and toilets. To book call the visitor centre (☎ 439 0605). Bookings aren't required for camping, but it's advisable during summer for cabins.

On SH12 at the southern edge of the forest, 48km north of Dargaville, *Waipoua Lodge* (☎ 439 0422) is a fine old homestead with B&B from $110 to $125 for two.

In Waimamaku, just north of the forest, the pleasant *Solitaire Homestay* (☎ 405 4891), a well-restored old kauri house set in a pretty garden, charges $45/70 for singles/doubles (dinner is $20).

Hokianga

Further north from the Kauri Coast, the road winds down to Hokianga Harbour and the tiny twin townships of Omapere and Opononi. Hokianga is a depressed rural area with no industry and little development, but the harbour is beautiful, and the area is unspoilt – much less commercial than the Bay of Islands. It is a good place to take time-out and drift for a while, as plenty of alternative lifestylers have discovered.

As you come up over the hill from the south, the rest stop on **Pakia Hill** has a great view of the harbour and is worth a stop.

Further down the hill, 2km west of Omapere, Signal Station Rd leads out to **Arai-Te-Uru Recreation Reserve**, on the South Head of Hokianga Harbour. It's about a 30-minute walk from Omapere or, if you're driving, a five-minute walk from the car park to Signal Station Point. This overlooks the harbour entrance, the massive sand dunes of North Head and the turbulent confluence of the harbour and the open sea. There's a swimming beach, people fish off the rocks and it's also the northern end of the superb Hokianga-Waipoua Coastal Track.

OMAPERE & OPONONI
pop 630

These two sleepy towns, on the southern shore of the Hokianga Harbour, almost run into one another.

Omapere has a tiny museum, on the main road through town, which also houses the Hokianga Information Centre (☎ 405 8869). It's open from 8.30 am to 5 pm daily. There's a small art and craft shop which sells locally made items including bone carvings, printed and painted textiles, flax kits and ceramics.

Only 3.5km past Omapere the road passes through the tiny settlement of Opononi. The stone walls along Opononi's seafront were constructed from rock ballast used in timber ships which were sailed out from Sydney by convicts.

Back in 1955 a dolphin paid so many regular, friendly visits to the town that it became a national attraction. Opo, as the dolphin was named, played with children and learned to perform numerous tricks with beach balls. The nation almost went into mourning when Opo was found dead – probably killed accidentally by illegal dynamite fishers. A **sculpture of Opo** marks the dolphin's grave outside Opononi's pub and you can see a video of Opo at the information centre in Omapere.

Walking
The **Hokianga-Waipoua Coastal Track** leads south from South Head at the entrance of Hokianga Harbour along the coast: it's four hours to the Waimamaku Beach exit; six hours to the Kawerua exit, which has a camping ground and hut; 12 hours to the Kerr Rd exit, where there's a camping ground at Waikara Beach; or you could continue the entire 16 hours (allow about three days) to Kai-Iwi Lakes. Pick up a brochure from any local information centre or DOC office.

From Cemetery Rd on the eastern outskirts of Opononi, a half-hour climb leads up **Mt Whiria**, one of the oldest unexcavated pa sites, with a splendid view of the harbour.

Two kilometres east of Opononi the Waiotemarama Gorge road turns south for 6km to the **Waiotemarama bush track**, the best short walk from Opononi. This track climbs to Mt Hauturu (680m). It's a four-hour walk to the summit (six hours return), but there's a shorter loop walk starting from the same place which takes only about two hours and passes kauri trees and a picturesque waterfall.

Between Waima and Taheke the **old Waoku coach road** runs off to the south. Once the sole route to Dargaville, the road is only open during summer. This is a more adventurous walk, muddy and not well marked, so proper gear and preparation are required. Get information from DOC.

The **Six Foot Track** at the end of Mountain Rd (near Okopako Lodge) gives access to many Waima Range walks.

Other Activities
Fishing and shellfishing are excellent around Hokianga Harbour. Trips are easily

arranged. The *Alma* (☎ 405 7704) is an 78-foot, solid kauri boat built in 1902. Originally a twin-masted scow, she's now powered by twin diesel motors. Regular fishing trips on this working museum are run between December and April on Friday ($25 a head for four hours), and there's a cruise from Rawene during summer (Thursday at 10 am). At other times the *Alma* goes when there is sufficient demand (a minimum of 10 people required for fishing trips; gear can be hired). Charters an also be arranged through Hokianga Express (☎ 405 8872).

Okopako Pony Trekking (☎ 405 8815) at Okopako Lodge has two-hour horse treks ($30) and longer rides through the bush of the Waima Hills.

You can hire boogy boards and slide down the North Head sand dunes. The ferry there leaves hourly from the wharf opposite the Opononi Resort Hotel. It costs $15 for board hire and the return fare.

Places to Stay & Eat

Omapere *Globe Trekkers* (☎ 405 8183, @ shirley@xtra.co.nz) is a good, well-run backpackers on the main road in Omapere overlooking the harbour. Dorm beds cost $16, twins and doubles are $40. There is a self-contained unit (kitchenette, bathroom, double bed and single bed) for $50 for two. There is ample space for tents. It offers a variety of activities and the Northland hostel special – bone-carving courses.

The oft-empty *Green Cafe Guest House* (☎ 405 8193) is across from the beach; a dorm bed is $16 and twins and doubles cost $19 per person.

The *Omapere Tourist Hotel & Motel* (☎ 405 8737) has a variety of accommodation, ranging from camp sites for $9 per person to motel units from $90 a double.

Whaley B&B (☎ 405 8641) is on the way to the heads on Signal Station Rd; it is reasonably priced at $35/70 for singles/doubles. *Baxters B&B* (☎ 405 8727, 255 SH12) is near the information centre. It costs $30/55. *Dawn Homestay* (☎/fax 405 8773), also on Signal Station Rd, has good views and two guest rooms (from $80 for a double). You can arrange a yacht charter here.

Opononi The *Opononi Holiday Park* (☎/fax 405 8791) has powered and non-powered sites for $10 per adult, tourist cabins from $40 for two, and standard cabins from $30 to $45 for two (up to $55 in summer and on public holidays).

The *House of Harmony* (Te Rangimarie; ☎/fax 405 8778, @ harmony@igrin.co.nz) is conveniently located and charges $15 per person in dorms or $16 per person in twin and double rooms. There are tent sites for $10. It's in the centre of Opononi.

The *Opononi Resort Hotel* (☎ 405 8858) opposite the wharf has units from $45 for two and backpacker beds for $15. Next door the new *Taha Moana Motel* (☎ 405 8824) has one-bedroom units from $60 and two-bedroom units from $90.

Five kilometres east of Opononi, off the highway just before Whirinaki on Mountain Rd, is *Okopako* (☎/fax 405 8815), a YHA associate and B&B. It's a peaceful farm with good views. Dorm beds cost $16 per person, and doubles and twins are $40. Tent sites are available. You can go horse trekking, walking (eg, along the Six Foot Track) or join in farm activities.

In central Opononi, the *Opononi Resort Hotel* (☎ 405 8858) has budget rooms ($45), through to deluxe units for $120.

The *Dunes Motel* (☎/fax 405 8824) has 10 units from $60 to $90 for one-bedroom units and $90 to $120 for two-bedroom units.

Places to Eat

Omapere For a splurge the fancy *Harbourmaster's Restaurant* is at the Omapere Tourist Hotel & Motel, where you can eat outside, watching the boats. The *Omapere Tearooms* next to Four Square has homemade cakes and biscuits, sandwiches and savouries. There's also a fish and chips place. The *Panorama Tearooms* up the hill, heading towards Dargaville, has great views.

Opononi Opononi has *cafes* and *takeaways*, and the restaurant at the *Opononi Resort Hotel* provides basic food at moderate prices. You can also try *Opononi Takeaways* or the *South Hokianga RSA* for cheap beer and a kitbag of reminiscences.

Getting There & Away
West Coaster buses stop at Omapere and Opononi on their Sunday to Friday run from Paihia to Dargaville. From Dargaville to Paihia, InterCity buses only go on Tuesday, Thursday and Sunday.

RAWENE
pop 515
Rawene is a tiny settlement on a point on Hokianga Harbour, from where ferries cross to Kohukohu for the pleasant back route to Kaitaia. The shallow waters around Rawene become mudflats at low tide but, while it lacks beaches, Rawene is full of history. Notable structures include **Clendon House**, built in the late 1860s by James Clendon, the resident magistrate. It is open from 10 am to 4 pm Saturday to Monday from November to April. Entry is $2/1 for adults/children.

The **Wharfhouse** (formerly the Harp of Erin Hotel) is the oldest building in Rawene. (The intriguing, musical public toilets are opposite.) Rawene's **hotel** dates from the 1870s.

Further up Hokianga Harbour, 3km west of Horeke, **Mangungu Mission** dates from 1839. The Hokianga chiefs signed the Treaty of Waitangi here in 1840.

Places to Stay & Eat
Rawene has a *motor camp* (☎ 405 7720, 1 Marmon St) just off Manning St with tent/powered sites at $8/9 per person, on-site caravans for $12 per person, cabins with kitchenettes for $15 per person and four new chalets for $18 per person.

The *Masonic Hotel* (☎ 405 7822), just a few steps up from the ferry landing, has rooms from $30/40 for singles/doubles.

There are several guesthouses. The *Old Lane's Store Homestay* (☎ 405 7554, 9 Clendon Esplanade) is a delightful new, self-contained extension of an historic 1885 villa right on the harbourfront next to Clendon House. It has a large lounge area, plus a patio. To find it, take the harbour road past the cafe; it's on your right. It costs $110 for two, including breakfast.

Hokiangamai (☎ 405 7782) on Bundry St has singles/doubles for $35/70. On

Nimmo St, *Searell Homestay* (☎ 405 7835) has guestrooms for $35/65.

About 2km south of Rawene, on the road to Opononi, is *Senace Backpackers* (☎ 405 7787), which has simple units in a separate block for $18 per person.

East of Rawene are two historic homes: *Riverhead* (☎ 401 9610) at Horeke (43km east of Rawene) is a restored kauri house built in 1871. *Lewood Park* (☎ 401 9290) is further east again, on Mangataraire Rd, Okaihau. The home is set in a working farm and you can take part in farming activities. Both places are within easy reach of the Bay of Islands, as well as the Hokianga.

For good coffee, panini, quiche, pizza, cake, muffins and other nice things head for the *Boatshed Cafe* right on the waterfront. There's also a gallery here, featuring flax kits, colourful textiles, jewellery, bone carving, paintings and more – all done by local artists.

You can also stock up on locally grown organic fruit and vegies at the *Hokianga Wholefood* store, which also has cheese, yoghurt, dried fruits, essential oils, soaps and so on.

Getting There & Away
Ferries run daily between Rawene and the Narrows on the north side of the harbour. Ferries run about every hour from 7.30 am to 7.30 pm; the crossing takes 15 minutes, and fares are $13/1.50 for cars/passengers ($18/3 return). Visitor centres have timetables or you can call ☎ 401 2101. You buy your ticket on board. The InterCity bus stops outside the Wharf Cafe.

KOHUKOHU
pop 220
This pleasant town is in a very quiet backwater on the north side of Hokianga Harbour. It is a beautifully preserved town with a number of historic kauri villas over 100 years old and other fine buildings including the Masonic Lodge, the Anglican Church and an old school.

Travellers are spoilt at the *Kohukohu Tree House* (☎ 405 5855, fax 405 5857), one of the finest backpackers in the country. Constructed of wood and stained glass, it is nestled in the hills 2km from the northern ferry terminus (turn sharp left as you come off the ferry). Dorms cost from $16 per person, and doubles and twins are $40. This is a good place to relax.

Harbour Views Guest House (☎ 405 5815) is a restored kauri home on Rakautapu Rd. There are two rooms (one with a queen-sized bed, one twin), and a large guest bathroom (with bath as well as shower). Both guestrooms open onto a veranda from which there are expansive harbour views. B&B costs $40 per person (dinner is $18 extra).

Plans are afoot to open a cafe right on the waterfront.

MITIMITI
About 45km west of Kohukohu, via Panguru on a rugged, wild stretch of coast, is the isolated settlement of Mitimiti. Here you'll find *Manaia Hostel & Treks* (☎ 409 5347). A bed is $20, or you can hire the entire house for $100 a night (it sleeps six). You can arrange trips over the North Head sand dunes on an all-terrain vehicle (1½ hours on the dunes; $45 per person plus the water taxi fare of $15 if you go from Opononi, or $60 from Mitimiti). You can also do horse trekking, fishing off the rocks, and drag netting. There is lots of scope for great walks, including Warawara Forest (NZ's second-largest kauri forest).

KAIKOHE
pop 3950
Kaikohe is the main town of central Northland. A centre for the Ngapuhi tribe, it was the scene of bloody battles during the Northland Land War (1844–46). Hone Heke eventually settled in Kaikohe and died here in 1850. His nephew (a prominent member of the Young Maori Party and local MP 1892–1909), also known as Hone Heke, lived in Kaikohe. A monument to him lies on the western outskirts of town on **Kaihoke Hill**, with fine views across Hokianga Harbour. He is credited with having introduced rugby to Northland.

The **Pioneer Village** (☎ 401 0816) is on the back road through town. The village houses a historic court house, cottage, school, jail, general store, fire station and sawmill, and features various memorabilia, farm machinery and steam engines. It is open from 10 am to 4 pm (Sunday from 1 pm). Admission of $5 (children $1) includes a guided tour.

The Kaikohe Information Centre (☎ 401 1911) is at the Curly Rock Cafe at 112 Broadway. It's open from 9 am to 5 pm Monday to Friday.

The *Mid North Motor Inn* (☎ 401 0149, 158 Broadway) has singles/doubles for $55/75 and camp sites (summer only) for $15.

The *New Haven Motel* (☎ 401 1859, 36 Raihara St) has studios ($55/60), and self-contained two-bedroom units ($75/80).

The *Kaikohe Hotel* on the main street has backpacker beds for $17.

For good coffee and a cafe culture ambience try the *Curly Rock Cafe* which is on Broadway, right in the centre of town. Also recommended is the eclectic fare at *ET's Maori Food and Chinese Restaurant* on Lower Broadway.

The Mid North Motor Inn has a *restaurant* with mains for about $20 and a Saturday night buffet for $25 a head (book ahead).

PUKETI & OMAHUTA FORESTS
North of Kaikohe, the Puketi and Omahuta Forests consist of one large forest area with kauri sanctuaries and other native trees, camping and picnic areas, streams and pools. Kauri milling in Puketi was stopped some years back to protect not only the kauri trees but also the rare kokako bird.

The two forests are reached by several entrances and contain a network of walking tracks varying in length from 15 minutes (the Manginangina Kauri Walk) to two days (the Waipapa River Track). A pamphlet detailing the tracks and features of the forests is available from any DOC office. Camping is permitted and there are basic trampers huts and a *camping ground* at Puketi Recreation Area on Waiare Rd, 28km north of Kaikohe. Book at DOC in Kerikeri (☎ 407 8474); a camp site is $6.

The Far North

KAITAIA

pop 5630

Kaitaia is the jumping-off point for trips up Ninety Mile Beach to Cape Reinga and offers a good chance to participate in aspects of Maori culture.

Entering Kaitaia you'll see a welcome sign in three languages – welcome, *haere mai* (Maori) and *dobro dosli* (Dalmatian) – as many Maoris and Dalmatians live in the area. Both groups are culturally active, with a Maori *marae* and a Yugoslav Cultural Club the focus of activities.

Every year a special marathon is conducted along the length of Ninety Mile Beach, celebrating the legend of Te Houtaewa. This great runner ran the length of the beach from Te Kao to Ahipara to steal kumara (sweet potatoes) from the Te Rarawa people, returning with two full baskets after being angrily pursued. The marathon celebrates the return of the kumara – reconciliation for a past deed.

Information

The Northland Information Centre (☎ 408 0879, ℮ visitorinfo@fndc.govt.nz) in Jaycee Park on South Rd has information on Kaitaia and all the Far North, and books accommodation, tours and activities. It is open from 8.30 am to 5 pm (to 1 pm on winter weekends).

Far North Regional Museum

This museum, near the information centre, houses an interesting collection, including a giant moa skeleton, various bits and pieces from shipwrecks and the Northwood Collection – photographs taken around 1900. The giant 1769 de Surville anchor, one of three the explorer lost in Doubtless Bay, is one of the museum's prizes. It's open from 10 am to 5 pm on weekdays, with extended summer hours ($2.50, children $0.50).

Te Wero Nui

The locals in Kaitaia have banded together to build an excellent cultural centre in the heart of this very Maori town. Entitled Te

Wero Nui (The Ultimate Challenge), this is a tourist-focused learning centre offering cultural activities and practical crafts such as herbal medicines, weaving, bone and woodcarving.

The centre (☎/fax 408 4884) is behind KFC on Commerce St. It's possible to stay on the marae and to participate in all activities. Accommodation can be arranged for groups and individuals; prices on application. There is an arts and crafts shop which sells authentic items crafted on the premises. An arts and crafts festival is held in March, four days before the annual

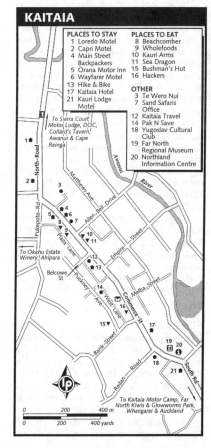

KAITAIA

PLACES TO STAY	PLACES TO EAT
1 Loredo Motel	8 Beachcomber
2 Capri Motel	9 Wholefoods
4 Main Street Backpackers	10 Kauri Arms
5 Orana Motor Inn	11 Sea Dragon
6 Wayfarer Motel	15 Bushman's Hut
13 Hike & Bike	16 Hackers
17 Kaitaia Hotel	
21 Kauri Lodge Motel	**OTHER**
	3 Te Wero Nui
	7 Sand Safaris Office
	12 Kaitaia Travel
	14 Pak N Save
	18 Yugoslav Cultural Club
	19 Far North Regional Museum
	20 Northland Information Centre

NORTHLAND

Ninety Mile Beach Te Houtawea Challenge (half, full and ultra marathon).

The Aero Club (☎ 406 7320) operates scenic flights to Cape Reinga. Sailing and fishing trips can be arranged from Kaitaia.

Jayar Horse Treks (☎ 409 4888) and Heather's Horse Treks (☎ 406 7133) do rides along Ninety Mile Beach, farmland and sand hills (around $40 for two hours).

Kaitaia is a centre for tours to surrounding areas, notably Cape Reinga and the gumfields of Ahipara (see Around Kaitaia and Cape Reinga & Ninety Mile Beach later in the chapter).

The **Ancient Kauri Kingdom** in Awanui is worth a visit. Here 30,000- to 50,000-year-old kauri stumps, which have been dragged from swamps, are fashioned into furniture and woodcraft products; the factory is open from 9 am to 5 pm daily (entry is free). For other arts and crafts try Crafty Jacks at Awanui, and The Wood Weta at Ahipara. Wildwood Creations of Kaitaia has products for sale at the Saturday market.

Okahu Estate (☎ 408 0888), 3.5km south of Kaitaia, is NZ's most northerly winery. Enjoy its great selection from 10 am to 6 pm weekdays (daily in summer).

There is a market day in Kaitaia's main street every Saturday from 7 am to noon; wholefoods, organic vegetables, arts and crafts and more.

If you are interested in exotic and subtropical plants you may find the nursery on Larmers Rd, just south of Kaitaia, worth a visit (open from 8 am to 5 pm Monday to Saturday; entry $4).

Based at Ahipara, Wildcat Charters (☎ 409 4729) does full-day fishing charters, with all gear supplied.

Places to Stay
Camping, Cabins & Hostels The *Kaitaia Motor Camp* (☎ 408 1212, 67 South Rd) is at the southern end of town (camp sites $10), and the basic *Pine Tree Lodge Motor Camp* (☎ 409 2108) on Takahe St, Ahipara, has nonpowered and powered sites for $9 per person and cabins for $28 for two.

The *Park Ninety Mile Beach* (☎ 406 7298) is 18km north on the Cape Reinga

road at Waipapakauri Ramp and has tent and powered sites for $22, cabins for $45 and self-contained cabins for $60 (prices are for two). There's a licensed restaurant.

Main Street Backpackers (☎ 408 1275, 235 Commerce St) is a good backpackers that organises many activities. The live-in owner, Peter, is active in the Maori community and takes visitors to see the local marae. Its rates are $13 to $16 (dorms and shared rooms), doubles and twins are $34, singles $30 and camp sites $10 per person. You can do your own bone carving; equipment supplied.

The *Hike & Bike* (☎ 408 1840, 160 Commerce St), a YHA associate, has tent sites for $10 per person, dorms for $15, twins for $34 and doubles for $40. Trips to Cape Reinga can be arranged for guests. Bookings are essential in summer.

Motels, Hotels & Lodges Motels include the *Sierra Court Motor Lodge* (☎ 408 1461, 65 North Rd), which has 16 self-contained studio one- and two-bedroom units from $70/80 a single/double, and the *Orana Motor Inn* (☎ 408 1510, 238 Commerce St), which has studio, suites and two-bedroom units from $75 (two people).

In Ahipara, there's *Baylinks* (☎ 409 4694, 115 Takahe St), with seven units from $50 for two people depending on the season; and *Adriaan Lodge* (☎ 409 4888) on Reefview Rd, which has backpackers beds for $20 per person and units from $50 for two.

Taharangi Marie Lodge (☎ 408 6282) between Ahipara and Waipapakauri Ramp has rooms from $195 for two (including breakfast).

Awanui, 6km north of Kaitaia, has the *Norfolk Motel* (☎ 406 7515), with units from $70.

The *Kaitaia Hotel* (☎ 408 0360, 15-33 Commerce St) is a venerable hotel (established 1837) with 35 rooms at $38/52, all with bathroom. Right in the centre of town, the hotel is a Kaitaia institution.

Places to Eat
The *Kauri Arms, Collard's Tavern* and the *Kaitaia Hotel* serve pub food and have live bands on weekends.

The *Sea Dragon* on Commerce St is a reasonable BYO Chinese restaurant; smorgasbords are $10 per diner. Kaitaia's top restaurant by far is the licensed *Beachcomber* on Commerce St, featuring good seafood.

The *Bushman's Hut*, featuring cook-your-own steaks, was due to open when we visited. For reasonable espresso try the *Hackers* Internet cafe *(84 Commerce St)*.

At Awanui to the north, and opposite Crafty Jacks, is *Kooldowns* where you can get good espresso, muffins, cakes, light meals and delicious ice cream.

The gigantic *Pak N Save* on West Lane is the cheapest place for self-caterers. For organic fruit and vegies as well as health foods try *Wholefoods* in the shopping mall near the Beachcomber restaurant.

Getting There & Away
Air New Zealand Link (☎ 408 0540) has flights between Kaitaia and Auckland, and the Bay of Islands, daily except Saturday.

InterCity (☎ 408 0540) and Northliner (☎ 408 0540) leave from Kaitaia Travel on Blencowe St. Buses go daily to Auckland via Paihia and Whangarei.

Getting Around
Major car rental companies have agents in Kaitaia: Budget (☎ 408 0540) is at Kaitaia Travel, 170 Commerce St and Hertz (☎ 408 2920) is at Rod Knight Automotive, 9 Allen Bell Drive. Nationwide Rental (☎ 408 0265) is at Matthews Ave.

AROUND KAITAIA
Ahipara
It's easy hitching a ride out to the beach at Ahipara, 14km south-west of Kaitaia. Ahipara is the southernmost section of Ninety Mile Beach and is popular with locals and visitors. It offers fishing, surfing, horse riding, a motor camp and picnic grounds.

Ahipara is best known for the massive gumfields sand dunes. Sand tobogganing, beach safaris and quad-bike rides are popular activities on the dunes above Ahipara and further around the Tauroa Peninsula.

Tua Tua Tours (☎ 409 4875) in Ahipara operates **quad-bike trips** along and around the gumfields and Ninety Mile Beach; a 90-minute tour is $70 per bike (or $85 with a passenger), and three hours is $115 (or $150). You can go alone by hiring a quad bike from Adriaan Lodge (☎/fax 409 4888); it's $50 for one hour and $30 for each subsequent hour. To minimise damage to the environment, stay below the high tide line and formal tracks.

A **walk** through the Ahipara gumfields gives you the chance to find ancient moa crop stones, to search for pieces of kauri gum in the sand and to gaze out to Ninety Mile Beach stretching far to the north. Get a good 'mud map' ($1) from Main Street Backpackers in Kaitaia.

Herekino
This remote spot, 29km south of Kaitaia, is a great getaway. Its attractions are its isolation and country pub (known for drinkin', and talkin' of shearin', crutchin' and dockin').

The *Tui Inn (☎ 409 3883)* on Puhata Rd (past the pub) is not flash (yeah, basic) but is a great place to stay and learn about the 'bush', real 'Kiwis', ridin', huntin', fishin' and shootin'. A bed is $12 per person and it's likely you will be cookin' and eatin' somethin' you have caught or shot (and gutted, filleted or skinned) yourself.

Kaitaia Region Walks
The **Kaitaia Walkway**, on the edge of the Herekino Forest, makes a good day trip and has excellent views. The track has a gentle gradient along its 9km and you should allow four hours to walk it. To get there head south from Kaitaia on SH1 for 3km, then turn right into Larmers Rd and follow it to the end.

More challenging is the **Mangamuka Walkway** which connects the Takahue Valley south of Kaitaia with the Mangamuka Gorge. The 9km track through the Raetea and Maungataniwha Forests requires good bush skills to negotiate and could take up to six hours. You can best reach the walk from SH1 at the Top of the Range picnic area.

There are many tough **mountain-biking** trips in the region. Get information on walks from the local DOC office (☎ 408 2100), 127 North Rd, Kaitaia.

Far North Kiwi & Glowworms Park

In Fairburn, about 30 minutes' drive east of Kaitaia, this nocturnal park (☎ 408 4100) is open from 9 am till dusk daily. The main attraction is a glowworm grotto beside a waterfall; at night there are trips to see the glowworms in their natural habitat. There's also a nocturnal kiwi house and areas for daytime picnics ($10, children $3).

To reach the park from Kaitaia, travel 8km south-east on SH1, turn left at the Fairburn signpost and continue for 9km along the gravel road.

CAPE REINGA & NINETY MILE BEACH

At the tip of the long Aupouri Peninsula, Cape Reinga is at the northern tip of NZ. As such it is a pilgrimage site for those who want to travel from one end of the country to the other. Contrary to popular belief, Cape Reinga is not the northernmost point of the country – that's Surville Cliffs on North Cape, 30km to the east. Nor is it the most western part of the North Island – Cape Maria van Diemen, just one bay around, claims that title. But standing at the windswept **Cape Reinga lighthouse** and looking out over the endless sea certainly has an end-of-the-world feel to it. Directly below the lighthouse is the Columbia Bank maelstrom, where the waters of the Tasman Sea and Pacific Ocean meet, generating waves up to 10m high in stormy weather.

Still visible on the very tip of Cape Reinga is the 800-year-old pohutukawa tree whose roots hide the entrance to the mythical Maori Underworld; see Ancestors (Tipuna) in the 'Maori Culture & Arts' special section.

The Aupouri Peninsula is known to the Maori as Te Hiku o te Ika a Maui (The Tail of Maui's Fish) from the creation legend that tells of how Maui hauled a great fish from the sea, which became the North Island (see And Then Came Aotearoa... in 'Maori Arts & Culture'). The peninsula is a rugged, desolate landscape dominated by high sand dunes and flanked by Ninety Mile Beach. If they metricate it to Ninety Kilometre Beach the name will be a lot more accurate.

The **Aupouri Forest**, about 75km long and 5km wide, covers two-thirds of the western side of the peninsula. It's an exotic forest, mostly pine, planted for timber. Kauri forest used to cover the area; in fact, traces have been found of three separate growths of kauri which were buried and then grew up again. This was a fruitful area for gumdiggers. On the northern edge of the Aupouri Forest, a volcanic rock formation called **The Bluff** is part of a private reserve used for fishing by the Aupori tribe living in nearby Te Kao. A colony of white-fronted terns can be seen just past The Bluff on a prominent sandspit.

North of The Bluff, Te Paki Reserves are public land with free access; just leave the gates as you found them and don't disturb the animals. There are about seven sq km of giant sand dunes on either side of where Te Paki Stream meets the sea; a stop to take flying leaps off the dunes is a highlight of locally operated tours.

Bus tours travel along the hard sands of Ninety Mile Beach on their way from Kaitaia to Cape Reinga, or vice versa, depending on the tides. Private vehicles can also do the beach trip but all hire-car agreements prohibit use on the beach. The usual access point for vehicles is Waipapakauri, just north of Kaitaia. Tours go as far as Te Paki Stream, though most cars only go as far as The Bluff. The beach 'road' is only for the well prepared with rugged vehicles. Cars have hit soft sand and been swallowed by the tides – you may see the roof of an unfortunate vehicle poking through the sands.

Motorcycling on the beach is OK, but take it slow and be extra careful – a few bikers have been killed by riding into washouts or soft sand.

Surprisingly, this tiny outpost even has a post shop.

Wagener Museum

This museum at Houhora houses an unrelated collection of oddities but the sheer number of items makes it astonishing. Exhibits include stuffed animals and birds, Maori artefacts, antique gramophones and washing machines, a commode collection, pianolas and other musical instruments that the guide will play for you.

The museum has a cafe and is open from 8.30 am to 6 pm daily (to 4.30 pm in winter; $6/2 for adults/children). All Cape Reinga tours stop here. For an extra $3 (children $1.50) you can also visit the **Subritzky Homestead** next door. Dating from 1862, the homestead is constructed of local swamp kauri, and is set in a pretty cottage garden.

Walking

The coastline is scattered with beautiful beaches, connected by a network of tracks. You can walk the **Ninety Mile Beach** but you'll need to be prepared as there are no huts.

From Cape Reinga you can walk along Te Werahi Beach to **Cape Maria van Diemen** in about five hours return. Beautiful **Tapotupotu Bay** is a two-hour walk east of Cape Reinga, via Sandy Bay and the cliffs. From Tapotupotu Bay it is about an eight-hour walk to **Kapowairua** at the eastern end of Spirits Bay. Both Tapotupotu Bay and Kapowairua have camping grounds and road access. For details of walking tracks in the area, inquire at the information centre in Kaitaia.

Organised Tours

Bus tours go from Kaitaia, Mangonui (Doubtless Bay) and the Bay of Islands. Tours from Kaitaia or Doubtless Bay are preferable since they're much closer to Cape Reinga. Tours from the Bay of Islands are larger, more commercial, and involve considerably more travel at each end of the day.

From Kaitaia, Sand Safaris (☎ 408 1778), 221 Commerce St, and Harrison's Cape Runner (☎ 408 1033), 123 North Rd, have small buses for day trips taking in the main features of the cape and sand tobogganing. The cost is $40 (children $20), including a picnic lunch. Paradise Connexion (☎ 406 0460) operates from Mangonui for $55 per adult ($20 children under 15); lunch is included.

Fullers, King's Tours & Cruises, DuneRider and Northern Exposure tours operate from the Bay of Islands (see that section later in this chapter for details).

The northern beaches are great for horse riding; contact Manuka Treks (☎ 409 8848) or Puketutu Pony Rides & Bushwalks (☎ 408 0979). Expect to pay about $35 per hour.

Places to Stay & Eat

There are several DOC camping grounds in the Cape Reinga area. There's a site at **Kapowairua** on Spirits Bay ($5 per person), with cold water and limited toilet facilities, and another at **Tapotupotu Bay** ($6), with toilets and showers; neither has electricity. Bring a cooker as fires are not allowed. Both bays have mosquitoes and biting sandflies, so come prepared with repellent. The Rarawa Beach *camping ground* ($6), 10km south of Te Kao, has water and toilet facilities only (no prior bookings, no open fires; closed from May to August).

At Waitiki Landing, the last settlement before the cape, *Waitiki Landing Complex (☎ 409 7508)* is the northernmost accommodation in NZ. A tent site costs $7 per person, a dorm costs $13 and a cabin is $55 (for two). There is a camp kitchen, laundrette and hot (metered) showers. Waitiki Landing has a shop and a restaurant which makes great pizzas and ostrich burgers. Sea kayaking, fishing and 4WD trips across tribal land can be organised here (Salt Air flies from Paihia to a nearby airstrip; you can take a three-hour tour with Waitiki Landing and return the same day).

North Wind Lodge Backpackers (☎ 409 8515) is on Otaipango Rd, 6km down an unsealed road at Henderson Bay on the peninsula's east side. It is spacious and modern, quiet and friendly, and near a great stretch of beach. There are two shared rooms ($15 per person) and one twin for $32. Boogy boards and sand toboggans are available to guests.

At Pukenui, the *Pukenui Lodge Motel & Youth Hostel (☎ 409 8837)* is in a lovely setting overlooking Houhora Harbour. Motel units cost from $59 to $99 for two people, depending on the season; there's one wheelchair-accessible unit. There is backpacker accommodation in historic Thomson House (built in 1891): dorm beds cost $15.50 per person, doubles and twins cost $20 per person. There are also two studio units from $59 (for two people). There's a pool and a spa. See the lodge's Web site (www.pukenuilodge.co.nz) for more information.

Across the road is *The Ranch House B&B*. Follow Lambs Rd west for about 500m to the *Pukenui Holiday Camp* (☎ 409 8803), with camp sites at $10 per person, backpackers beds at $15 per person and cabins from $30 to $60 for two.

Further on, almost at the end of Lambs Rd, is the *Pukenui Farmstay* (☎ 409 7863), a delightful cottage with all the amenities and a veranda from which you see memorable sunsets. It charges $13 per dorm bed, from $15 to $17 per person a double; camping is $8. Staff will pick up from the Pukenui shop and let visitors collect their own eggs and vegetables.

The *Houhora Heads Motor Camp* (☎ 409 8564) is next to the Wagener Museum. It has limited facilities but tent/powered sites are $14/18 for two, on-site vans $15 to $20, and there are discounts for long stays.

At the turn-off to the museum, on the highway, the *Houhora Chalets Motel* (☎ 409 8860) has six self-contained A-frame units from $60 to $80 a double, depending on the season.

KARIKARI PENINSULA

Remote Karikari Peninsula forms the western end of Doubtless Bay. Roads are mostly unsealed and facilities are limited, but the peninsula's beaches are among Northland's finest.

Rangiputa has lovely white-sand beaches that are easy to reach. A turn-off on the road to Rangiputa takes you to remote **Puheke Beach** with white sand dunes and long, lonely windswept beaches.

On the east coast of the peninsula, **Tokerau Beach** is a depressed place, while further north, **Whatuwhiwhi** is more attractive. But loveliest of all is **Matai Bay** with its tiny 'twin coves'.

Places to Stay

At Rangiputa the *White Sands Motor Lodge* (☎ 408 7080) has an attached shop; pleasant, modern units cost $125/65 for two in summer/winter. *Reef Lodge* (☎ 408 7100) has studios and one- and two-bedroom units on the beachfront from $70 for two people (up to $180 in season). *Rangiputa Beach B&B* (☎ 406 7997) is right on the beach and worth considering.

There is a DOC *camping ground* (☎ 408 6014) at Matai Bay. During the Christmas holidays it is popular, but at other times is usually not full ($6). A good walking track goes from the end of the beach up onto the southern peninsula.

The *Whatuwhiwhi Holiday Park* (☎ 408 7202) is at the end of Whatuwhiwhi Rd. A camp site is $20 for two, cabins are $40 to $50, tourist flats are $65 to $70 and the motel unit is $85.

DOUBTLESS BAY

The bay gets its unusual name from an entry in Captain Cook's logbook, where he wrote that the body of water was 'doubtless a bay'. Lying between the Bay of Islands and Kaitaia, Doubtless Bay has picturesque bays, coves and beaches. The whole area is great for fishing and shellfishing, boating, swimming and other water sports.

The principal town, Mangonui, is a charming historic village. Stretching west around the bay are the modern, popular beach resorts of Coopers Beach, Cable Bay and Taipa. With its glorious climate and beautiful beaches, Doubtless Bay is a go-ahead area, attracting moneyed retirees and other rat race escapees.

Doubtless Bay competes with Kaitaia as a good base for exploring the Far North. Paradise Connexions (☎ 406 0460) in Mangonui has tours to Cape Reinga; see that section.

Mangonui

Mangonui is a small, picturesque fishing village – the name means 'Great Shark' – with numerous old kauri buildings lining the shallow Mangonui harbour. It has all the basic services. If you need to make bookings or are after information about the area, the Wharf Store (☎ 406 0009), opposite the wharf, is the best option.

The surrounding area attracts many craftspeople and Doubtless Bay has plenty of craft outlets. In Mangonui you'll find the Flax Bush Sea Sheel Shop, the Wharf Store, and Arterior. The **Mangonui Courthouse** is a historic reserve.

Also at Mangonui is attractive **Mill Bay**, dotted with tiny boats; you can take Silver Egg Rd out to Mill Bay's Mangonui Cruising Club and an assortment of historical markers. This was the spot where Mangonui's first European settler made his base, and whaling ships replenished their water from the stream.

Between Mangonui and Coopers Beach is the **Rangikapiti Pa Historic Reserve**, with ancient Maori terracing and a spectacular, sweeping view of Doubtless Bay. There's a walkway from Mill Bay, west of Mangonui, to the top of the pa.

At Hihi, about 10 minutes' drive from Mangonui, is **Butler Point**, site of an 1847 homestead built by whaler turned MP, Captain William Butler. Near the house is a museum dedicated to whaling. On the other side of the point are the remains of a Maori pa. You can only visit by appointment: phone ☎ 406 0006. It costs $5 to enter the grounds (or $7.50 including the museum).

Beaches
The first beach west of Mangonui is **Coopers Beach**, a fine sweep of sand lined with pohutukawa trees. Coopers Beach is quite developed and has a small shopping centre. The next bay along, less-developed **Cable Bay**, was once a terminus of the longest cable in the world: a cable stretched 3500 nautical miles from here to Queensland, Australia, and was used from 1902 to 1912 when another cable was laid between Sydney and Auckland.

Across the river from Cable Bay, **Taipa** is another popular summer destination. According to local legend, Taipa is the place where Kupe first set foot on the mainland. Today it has a fine beach, a harbour where the Taipa River meets the sea, and several motels and motor camps.

Dolphin Swimming
Dolphin Rendezvous (☎ 406 0914) runs two trips daily out to the dolphins (weather permitting) from Mangonui. The trips are four hours long and leave at 8 am and 1 pm; the cost is $70/50 for adults/children and all equipment is provided. The trip includes commentary on the flora, fauna and history of the Karikari Peninsula and Doubtless Bay.

Fishing & Diving
Hooked on Fishing (☎ 0800-466 533) has a catamaran *(Happy Hooker)* for full or half-day charters. Far North Charters Seabed Safaris (☎ 408 5885) does dives in Doubtless Bay, including to the *Rainbow Warrior*.

Places to Stay
Camping & Cabins The closest place to Mangonui is the *Hihi Beach Holiday Camp (☎ 406 0307)*, with tent/powered sites from $10/12 for two, and cabins from $30.

Taipa is a more attractive destination than Hihi. The *Taipa Caravan Park (☎ 406 0995)* on the river close to the beach has camp sites from $10 per person and on-site caravans from $25.

Guesthouses & Apartments There are numerous B&Bs and homestays, plus a few self-contained apartments. The information centre in Mangonui has details.

The *Old Oak Inn (☎ 406 0665, 66 The Waterfront)* in Mangonui is a pleasant 1861 kauri house. Dorms cost $17, four-bed rooms are $20 and doubles are $45. Cute rooms upstairs cost $60 for a twin, $70 for a double and $80 for a double with bathroom. There's also a bar and restaurant.

Waterfront Apartments (☎ 406 0347) has self-contained apartments looking right over the water from $80 for two.

Mac 'n' Mo's (☎ 406 0538), on the highway in Coopers Beach, has singles for $40 and doubles for $65 to $70.

Time Out (☎ 406 0101, 6 Heretaunga Crescent) has a self-contained unit facing a beach at Cable Bay. It costs $20 for two.

Macrocarpa Cottage (☎ 406 1245, 2 Bush Point Rd) in Taipa has a self-contained unit that sleeps four near the water's edge.

Just off the road to Hihi, 2km from the highway, *Abraham Lincoln's B&B (☎ 406 0090)* is a pleasant farmstay high on a hill with expansive views across Mangonui Bay; singles/doubles are $35/70.

Motels & Hotels There are many motels in the area costing around $60 to $80 a double, but most charge $100 or more from Christmas to the end of January. Motels include the *Mangonui Motel (☎ 406 0346)* in Mangonui, with self-contained one-bedroom units from $75 for two ($150 in the high season), and the similarly priced *Taipa Sands Motel (☎ 406 0446)* on the beach in Taipa. The *Taipa Resort Hotel (☎ 406 0656, 22 Taipa Point Rd)* is superbly situated. The *Driftwood Lodge (☎ 406 0418)* in Cable Bay is a standard motel but right on the beach.

In Mangonui the historic *Mangonui Hotel (☎ 406 0003)* has comfortable singles/doubles for $40/80.

Places to Eat

In Mangonui the licensed *Waterfront Cafe* is a cosy little cafe with good pizzas and seafood; it's open until 1 am Tuesday to Sunday. The *Bayside Cafe* nearby has espressos, snacks and light meals.

The *Slung Anchor* is opposite the local supermarket. There's courtyard dining; snacks, drinks and meals are available.

The popular, licensed *Mangonui Fish Shop*, near the wharf, is on stilts over the water. You can eat your fish and chips (and shellfish, seafood salads and smoked fish) on tables overlooking the bay.

The *Mangonui Hotel* has a restaurant with a pleasant outdoor garden area to one side; the hotel has bands on the occasional weekend.

At the Taipa Resort Hotel (see Places to Stay) is the *Flame Tree Restaurant & Bar*, which has fresh local seafood.

Getting There & Away

InterCity buses pass through Mangonui once a day on the Bay of Islands–Kaitaia route. Northliner buses do the same run, stopping at Mangonui, Coopers Beach and Taipa, daily except Saturday.

WHANGAROA

Whangaroa Harbour is a picturesque inlet of small bays and bright green water, surrounded by high, rugged cliffs. The area was once well known for its kauri forests (now gone).

The small town of Whangaroa, 6km off the main road (SH10), is a popular game-fishing centre. This is a very quiet town but good tours and activities are available. Totara North, on the other side of the bay, is even sleepier and has an old timber mill.

The Boyd Gallery (☎ 405 0230), the general store in Whangaroa, is also an informal tourist information office.

Walking

For walks, the domed, bald summit of St Paul's offers fine views. It is a half-hour walk above Whangaroa to the south. The Wairakau track north to Pekapeka Bay (90 minutes) begins near the church hall on Campbell Rd in Totara North and passes through farmland, hills and shoreline before arriving at DOC's Lane Cove Cottage.

Organised Tours

The yacht *Snow Cloud* (☎ 405 0523) operates out of Whangaroa Harbour to the Cavalli Islands, where there are excellent beaches, diving spots (including the wreck of the *Rainbow Warrior*), snorkelling and walks. It costs $65 per person (minimum two) for this excellent day trip.

Several other boats are available for deep-sea fishing, water-skiing and diving. Book boats through the Boyd Gallery or Marlin Hotel.

The area around Whangaroa Harbour is ideal for sea kayaking. Northland Sea Kayaking (☎ 405 0381) is located east on the coast, past Tauranga Bay (pick-up from Kaeo can be arranged). This coast is magical, with bays, beaches, sea caves, tunnels and islands to explore. The kayak tours 'comb' the coast for a very reasonable $60 per day, including accommodation.

Places to Stay

Camping & Cabins The *Whangaroa Harbour Retreat (☎ 405 0306)* charges $10/13 per person for tent/powered sites and from $35 for cabins. The camp is about 2.5km before the wharf.

Lane Cove Cottage, run by DOC, is reached by the Wairakau track or by boat. It charges $8 per night (it sleeps 16) and has showers and flush toilets, but you have to bring your own cooker. Book through DOC (☎ 407 8474) in Kerikeri.

Backpackers The *Sunseeker Lodge* (☎ 405 0496) is up on a hill about 500m beyond the wharf, with a great view of the harbour. It charges $16 for dorms and $38 for twins or doubles. Motel units are $65 to $90 for two.

Just west of the Totara North turn-off, the pleasant *Kahoe Farm Hostel* (☎ 405 1804, ✉ mjoh@igrin.co.nz) has dorm beds for $17, and doubles or twins for $40. It is run by fifth-generation Kiwis – although the Italian chef doesn't qualify for this status (yet!). The enthusiastic owners organise activities like walks to kauri dams, kayaking, sailing and soccer competitions. Meals include genuine Italian pizza.

Motels & Hotels The *Whangaroa Motel* (☎ 405 0022) and the *Truant Lodge Motel* (☎ 405 0133) have motel rooms from $75 to $125 depending on the season.

At the exclusive *Kingfish Lodge* (☎ 405 0164), reached by boat, the cost is $200/250 a single/double including transfers in the high season.

Right by the wharf the *Marlin Hotel* (☎ 405 0347) has share-facility rooms at $45 for singles, $50 to $55 for doubles and twins; the hotel is the social centre of the town.

Places to Eat
The *Marlin Hotel* does dinner, breakfast and lunch, or visitors can gain temporary membership at the *Big Gamefish Club*, opposite the pub, where fish, of course, features heavily on the menu. Come during the summer and see them weigh in the marlin.

AROUND WHANGAROA
For a scenic drive, you can visit the many beautiful bays and fine beaches east of Whangaroa. From the SH10, just south-east of Kaeo, the road via Otoroa is sealed almost all the way to Matauri Bay, except for the final descent to the beach. From Matauri Bay through to Whangaroa the road is unsealed almost all the way, but the great scenery makes the strain on the nerves worthwhile!

The trip out to **Matauri Bay** is one of *the* surprises of Northland. Matauri Bay is owned by the Ngati Kura tribe, and this superb stretch of beach sees few tourists. The view from the ridge above the bay is spectacular with the beach, Cavalli Islands and headland way down below. At the top of the headland in Matauri Bay is a monument to the *Rainbow Warrior*. The boat itself lies offshore in the waters of the Cavalli Islands and dives can be arranged at Matauri Bay Holiday Park or in Paihia – for background information see the boxed text 'The *Rainbow Warrior* Trail' under Dargaville, earlier in this chapter.

Heading north-west from Matauri Bay, the road leads to **Te Ngaire**, a small settlement with a lovely quiet beach, then on to nearby **Wainui Bay** which is great for cast fishing. You can then detour to **Mahinepua Bay** or continue on to **Tauranga Bay**, another fine sweeping beach with good surf and accommodation.

Places to Stay
The *Matauri Bay Holiday Park* (☎ 405 0525) has sites for $20 (two people) and on-site caravans for $45.

The *Oceans Beachfront Holiday Village* (☎ 405 0417) at the end of the road has comfortable units from $80 a double; it also has a licensed restaurant.

There is a very basic DOC *hut* (sleeps eight) at Papatara Bay on Motukawanui Island, one of the Cavallis; book through DOC in Kerikeri.

The *Tauranga Bay Holiday Park* (☎ 405 0436), on the beach at Tauranga Bay, has camp sites for $11, cabins for $30 to $80 for two, and tourist flats for $50 to $100.

The *Tauranga Bay Motel* (☎ 405 0222) is a plain but comfortable motel for $100 a double in summer.

Bay of Islands

Long famed for its stunning coastal scenery, the Bay of Islands is one of NZ's major attractions. The bay is punctuated by dozens of coves and its clear waters range in hue from turquoise to deep blue. Dotted with nearly 150 islands, the Bay of Islands is aptly named. The islands have escaped development; townships are all on the mainland.

The Bay of Islands is also of enormous historical significance. As the site of NZ's first permanent English settlement, it is the cradle of European colonisation. It is here that the Treaty of Waitangi was drawn up and first signed by 46 Maori chiefs in 1840; the treaty remains the linchpin of race relations in modern-day NZ (see History in the Facts about New Zealand chapter).

Paihia is the centre of the Bay of Islands. Though only a small town, its population swells dramatically in summer. Waitangi Reserve is within walking distance.

Only a short passenger ferry ride away, Russell has all the character that Paihia lacks. Though also a popular tourist destination, historic Russell is a smaller, sleepier town with many fine old buildings and a delightful waterfront.

To the north is Kerikeri, more like a real town and much less touristy.

Organised Tours & Activities

As a major tourist centre, the Bay of Islands has a mind-boggling array of activities and tours. Many are water-based to make the most of the natural surroundings. Backpacker discounts are available for many activities and tours, and the hostels arrange cheap deals.

Cruises One of the best introductions to the area is a cruise. Fullers (☎ 402 7422), Web site: www.fullers-bay-of-islands.co.nz, and King's Tours & Cruises (☎ 402 8288), Web site: www.kings-tours.co.nz, operate

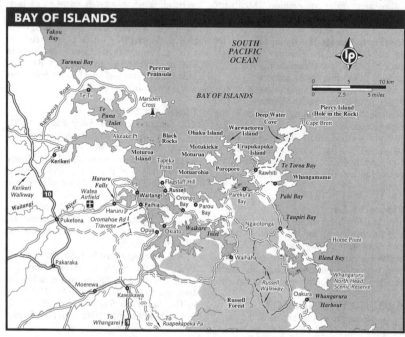

BAY OF ISLANDS

popular regular cruises. There are also smaller operators.

Best known is Fullers' 'Cream Trip', which started back in 1920 when one Captain Lane picked up dairy products from the many farms around the bay. As more roads were built and the small dairy farms closed, the service became more of a tourist trip. The trip takes about five hours ($65, children $33), incorporating the Hole in the Rock, Urupukapuka Island and views of dolphins, seals and birds. It leaves Paihia at 10 am daily in the main season, stopping at Russell 10 minutes later. From June to September it runs on Monday, Wednesday, Thursday and Saturday.

Other Fullers cruises include the Hole in the Rock (passing through it) off Cape Brett ($58/29 for adults/children) and the *R Tucker Thompson* tall sailing ship cruise ($85/45). Most tours stop at Otehei Bay on Urupukapuka Island, where Westerns writer Zane Grey went big game fishing, and a tourist submarine, the *Nautilus*, is submerged. To go underwater costs $12 (children $6).

Kings has a Day in the Bay cruise for $79/45 with a stopover on either Waewaetorea or Urupukapuka Islands. It also has a Hole in the Rock cruise for $50/25.

Also very popular are the high-speed Hole in the Rock trips, which are a neck-snapping jet-boat ride of the adrenaline-pumping, rather than the camera-priming, kind. Exitor (☎ 402 7020) and Kings run trips for $60/30.

All cruises depart first from Paihia and then from Russell about 15 minutes later.

Sailing A very pleasant way to explore the Bay of Islands is on a sailing trip. There are numerous operators and the information centre at Paihia has details. Expect to pay about $40 for a half-day and $65 for a full day.

Dolphin Swimming Although Kaikoura in the South Island is still the premier destination for swimming with dolphins, trips from the Bay of Islands are becoming increasingly popular. The big plus for Bay of Islands trips is that they also operate in winter.

The Bay of Islands trips have a high success rate, and operators have offered another, free trip if dolphins are not sighted. Dolphin swims are subject to weather and sea conditions. Dolphin Discoveries (☎ 402 8234) operates with small groups and provides all necessary equipment ($85/45 for adults/children).

NORTHLAND

The destination for many tour boats – Hole in the Rock, Bay of Islands

DAVID WALL

Heritage Trails (☎ 402 6288) has trips in which Maori culture, myths and legends are explained. Fullers, the big tour conglomerate, is not to be outdone and also runs Dolphin Encounters for $85/45.

Sea Kayaking Coastal Kayakers (☎ 402 8105) and New Zealand Sea Kayak Adventures (☎ 402 8596) both have trips ranging from half a day to longer expeditions. A half-day guided tour with Coastal Kayakers costs $43 per person ($65 for a full day), and a two-day budget harbour wilderness tour is $110 (minimum two people).

There are three-day 'outer island' trips, and rates for independent hire. Sea Kayak Adventures runs day trips ($40 half-day, full day $60) as well as multiday trips where you camp out in little-visited spots in the Bay ($125 per day), or go along the north-east coast. There is a backpackers special ($175 to $250 for two or three days).

Scuba Diving Paihia Dive Hire (☎ 402 7551) on Williams Rd hires full sets of scuba gear to qualified divers. It also offers scuba and snorkelling courses, tank filling, scuba gear servicing, and diving trips, including expeditions to the sunken *Rainbow Warrior* ($145; two tanks, all gear included). Dive North (☎ 401 1777; bookings at the information centre or Kings) has trips to the *Rainbow Warrior* for $135 (all gear, two tanks), as well as other trips, on the 6m aluminium *Diversion*. Matauri Cat Charters (☎ 405 0525), near the Oceans Motel at Matauri Bay, arranges dives to the *Rainbow Warrior* for $135 (two tanks, all gear included).

Other Activities The Bay of Islands is noted for its **fishing**, particularly snapper and kingfish. Fishing charter boats abound and can be booked at the Maritime Building in Paihia or at Russell wharf.

Surprisingly inexpensive are the **scenic flights**: you can take a short aerial tour (about 15 minutes) for around $45. Bay of Islands Aero Club (☎ 407 8400) at Kerikeri has scenic flights or you can take seaplane flights ($95) from the Paihia wharf (for details phone ☎ 402 8338).

Sky-Hi Tandem Skydive (☎ 025-756 758) operates from the Watea (Haruru Falls) airport; the cost is $185 (30 seconds of free fall).

Flying Kiwi Parasail (☎ 402 6078, after hours 402 7905) does one-hour trips leaving from Paihia wharf hourly during summer. A 400-foot (ie, 400-foot rope) flight costs $50 per person and an 800-foot one $60 (you're in the air for about seven minutes in the first, and 10 minutes in the second). You should book ahead.

There is an excellent barbecue cruise (☎ 402 7848) up the Waitangi River; fresh pan-fried fish and T-bone steak are served ($35).

There are a couple of **horse riding** operators – with Big Rock Springs Trail Rides (☎ 405 9999) you swim the horses; a full-day trip, including pick-up from Paihia, is $65.

Organised Tours It's easier to make trips to Cape Reinga and Ninety Mile Beach from Kaitaia or Doubtless Bay. However, a few trips leave from the Bay of Islands.

King's Tours & Cruises (☎ 402 8288) has trips departing from Paihia with pick-ups in Kerikeri daily at 7.30 am, returning at 6.30 pm. The tour also stops at the Puketi kauri forest and Wagener Museum ($77, children $40). Fullers (☎ (402 7421) charges $89/50 for a similar trip with lunch thrown in.

A popular tour with the younger set is the 4WD Dune Rider (☎ 402 8681), which costs $75/55 ex-Paihia. Kiwi Experience's (☎ 09-366 9830) Awesome & Top Bit Pass (minimum three days; $135) includes a trip to the cape – it is well recommended.

Getting There & Away

Air Air New Zealand Link (☎ 407 8419) has daily flights to Kerikeri from Auckland.

Bus All buses serving Paihia arrive at and depart from the Maritime Building by the wharf.

InterCity has buses daily from Auckland to the Bay of Islands, via Whangarei and Opua. The trip takes about four hours to Paihia and goes to Kerikeri before continuing north to Kaitaia.

Northliner has an Auckland–Whangarei–Bay of Islands–Kaitaia bus service. It departs from the Downtown Airline Terminal in Auckland and stops in Paihia, Haruru Falls and Kerikeri. There's a connecting service to Russell and also a direct Whangarei–Russell service.

Getting Around

Passenger ferries connect Paihia with Russell, running from around 7 am to 7 pm (to 10 pm from October to June). Three ferries, the large Fullers ferry and two local services, operate on average every 20 minutes from Russell to Paihia in summer. The fare is $3 one way, $6 return.

To get to Russell with your car, cross from Opua to Okiato Point using the car ferry (see Getting There & Away under Russell later in this chapter).

There's also a water taxi (☎ 403 7123) for getting around the bay islands.

BAY OF ISLANDS MARITIME & HISTORIC PARK

The park consists of some 40 different sites extending all the way from Mimiwhangata Bay in the south to Whangaroa Harbour in the north. Marked walks of varying levels of difficulty (many very easy) take anywhere from 10 minutes to 10 hours and include tramps around islands, pa sites and other historical sites, scenic, historic and recreational reserves, and the Mimiwhangata Marine Park.

The Bay of Islands Maritime & Historic Park Visitor Centre (☎ 403 7685) is at Russell. The Kerikeri DOC office (☎ 407 8474), 34 Landing Rd, can also help with information. *The Story of the Bay of Islands Maritime & Historic Park* published by DOC is indispensable and has a haunting frontispiece: *Whatungarongaro te tangata toitu te whenua* (People are perishable but the land endures). You can also get the useful *Urupukapuka Island Archaeological Walk* and *Bay of Islands Walks* pamphlets from the DOC visitor centre.

Development of islands in the Bay of Islands is limited, though **Urupukapuka Island** has camping facilities.

Places to Stay

The DOC office in Russell (☎ 403 7685) has details of accommodation in the park. The *Cape Brett Hut* is a very popular destination. You can arrange to walk there and stay in the hut by ringing DOC in Russell (bookings essential). It costs $8 per adult per night.

Camping is only permitted at two bays on Urupukapuka Island. Cable and Urupukapuka Bays have water supplies and cold showers but you need food, a stove, fuel, and a chemical toilet; the cost is $6 per person. To get to Urupukapuka Island, take a Fullers tour, get off at Otehei Bay and arrange to catch the tour on another day.

Also popular is *Mimiwhangata Cottage & Lodge* in Mimiwhangata Coastal Park ($5); book through DOC in Russell.

PAIHIA & WAITANGI
pop 7250

The main town in the area, Paihia was settled by Europeans as a mission station in 1823 when the first raupo (bullrush) hut was built for the Reverend Henry Williams. Paihia still has a very pretty setting but the missionary zeal has been replaced with an equally fervent tourist industry. It's basically an accommodation, eating and tours centre.

Adjoining Paihia to the north is Waitangi, the site of the historic signing on 6 February 1840 of the treaty between the Maori people and the representatives of Queen Victoria's government.

The Treaty of Waitangi is a momentous document that on the one hand saw the Maori tribes accept British governorship, but on the other granted the Maori citizenship and land rights. See History in the Facts about New Zealand chapter for more on the treaty.

Information

Most of the information places are conveniently grouped together in the Maritime Building right by the Paihia wharf on Marsden Rd. Here you'll find the Bay of Islands Visitor Information Centre (☎ 402 7345, ✆ visitorinfo@fndc.govt.nz). The offices are open from 8 am to 5 pm daily (to 8 pm in peak times). Also here are the Fullers,

NORTHLAND

King's and other offices for cruises and tours, fishing boat bookings, the bus station, and terminal for the ferry to Russell.

Close by is Aquatic World (☎ 402 6220), which struggles to make an ordinary aquarium interesting. It is open from 9 am to 5.30 pm daily ($7, children $3.50).

Waitangi National Reserve

The **Treaty House** in Waitangi has special significance in NZ's European history. Built in 1832 as the home of British resident James Busby, it was eight years later the setting for the signing of the Waitangi

treaty. The house, with its beautiful sweep of lawn running down to the bay, is preserved as a memorial and museum.

Just across the lawn, the magnificently detailed Maori **Whare Runanga** (meeting house) was completed in 1940 to mark the centenary of the treaty. The carvings represent the major Maori tribes.

Down by the cove is the largest war canoe in the world – the Maori canoe *Ngatokimatawhaorua,* named after the canoe in which the legendary Polynesian navigator Kupe discovered NZ. It too was built for the centenary, and a photographic exhibit details

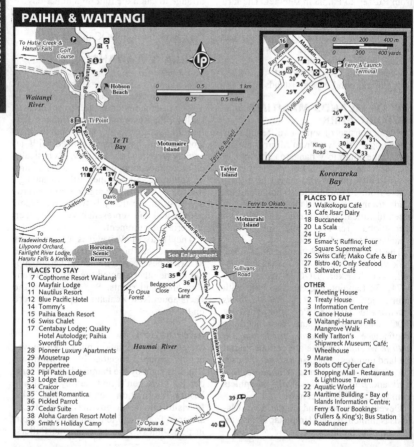

PAIHIA & WAITANGI

PLACES TO STAY
7 Copthorne Resort Waitangi
10 Mayfair Lodge
11 Nautilus Resort
12 Blue Pacific Hotel
14 Tommy's
15 Paihia Beach Resort
16 Swiss Chalet
17 Centabay Lodge; Quality Hotel Autolodge; Paihia Swordfish Club
28 Pioneer Luxury Apartments
29 Mousetrap
30 Peppertree
32 Pipi Patch Lodge
33 Lodge Eleven
34 Craicor
35 Chalet Romantica
36 Pickled Parrot
37 Cedar Suite
38 Aloha Garden Resort Motel
39 Smith's Holiday Camp

PLACES TO EAT
5 Waikokopu Café
13 Cafe Jisar; Dairy
18 Buccaneer
20 La Scala
24 Lips
25 Esmae's; Ruffino; Four Square Supermarket
26 Swiss Café; Mako Cafe & Bar
27 Bistro 40; Only Seafood
31 Saltwater Café

OTHER
1 Meeting House
2 Treaty House
3 Information Centre
4 Canoe House
6 Waitangi-Haruru Falls Mangrove Walk
8 Kelly Tarlton's Shipwreck Museum; Café; Wheelhouse
9 Marae
19 Boots Off Cyber Cafe
21 Shopping Mall - Restaurants & Lighthouse Tavern
22 Aquatic World
23 Maritime Building - Bay of Islands Information Centre; Ferry & Tour Bookings (Fullers & King's); Bus Station
40 Roadrunner

how the canoe was made from two gigantic kauri logs. Traditionally the canoe was launched every year on 6 February (New Zealand Day) for the annual treaty-signing commemoration ceremonies.

Beyond the Treaty House a road climbs Mt Bledisloe, from where there are commanding views. Beginning from the visitor centre, a **walking track** takes off through the reserve, passing through the mangrove forest around Hutia Creek and on to Haruru Falls. The walkway has a boardwalk among the mangroves so you can explore them without getting wet feet. The walk to the falls takes about 1½ hours each way.

Entry to Waitangi Reserve is $8 (children under 12 free); it's open from 9 am to 5 pm daily. At the visitor centre an audiovisual presentation relating the history of the signing of the treaty begins every half-hour.

Kelly Tarlton's Shipwreck Museum

Beached beside the bridge over the Waitangi River is the barque *Tui,* an old sailing ship imaginatively fitted out as a museum of shipwrecks. It's open from 9 am to 5.30 pm daily, longer during holidays ($7, $2.50 for children under 16). Recorded sea chants, creaking timbers and swaying lights accompany the collection of over 1000 bits and pieces that the late Kelly Tarlton dragged up from wrecks.

Haruru Falls

A few kilometres upstream from Waitangi are the attractive Haruru Falls, also accessible via the walkway through Waitangi National Reserve. At the foot of the falls there's good swimming, several motor camps, a licensed restaurant and a tavern. If you wish to kayak to the base of the falls, this can be arranged through the companies listed under Sea Kayaking in Organised Tours & Activities earlier in this section.

Walking

Just behind Paihia is **Opua Forest**, a regenerating forest with a small stand of kauri trees and a number of walking tracks ranging from 10 minutes to three hours. There are

lookouts up graded tracks from the access roads and a few large trees have escaped axe and fire, including some fairly big kauri trees. If you walk up from School Rd for about 20 minutes, you'll find a couple of good lookouts. Pamphlets with details on all the Opua Forest walks are published by DOC. You can also drive into the forest by taking the Oromahoe Rd west from Opua. The visitor information centre in Paihia has leaflets.

There is a variety of good short and long walks around the Bay of Islands and on the islands themselves. The park information centre in Russell and DOC Kerikeri have lots of information on walks.

Special Events

This region celebrates many special events. In January there is a Tall Ships Race at Russell. February has Waitangi Day on the 6th and a 10-day arts festival, with exhibits of touchable art, plays, music, comedy and dance.

There is a Country Music Festival in early May and a Jazz & Blues Festival in mid-August. September is 'foodies' month, with Russell's Oyster Festival and the very popular Wine & Food Festival in Paihia, on the Waitangi foreshore.

In October, the Auckland to Bay of Islands Weekend Coastal Classic – NZ's largest yacht race – is held.

Places to Stay

Camping & Cabins There are many camping grounds around Paihia and Waitangi, most of them near pretty Haruru Falls. The *Haruru Falls Resort (☎ 402 7525),* beside the falls, has tent or powered sites at $15 per person, cabins with bathrooms for $60 (two people) and motel units with/without kitchen for $110/95 for two. The camp is well equipped with a pool, bar and restaurant.

The *Bay of Islands Holiday Park (☎ 402 7646),* 3km from the falls and 6.5km from Paihia on Puketona Rd, has tent and powered sites for $10 per person, cabins/tourist flats from $37/50 for two and on-site caravans from $37.

Smith's Holiday Camp (☎ 402 7678) is a lovely spot right at the waterside, 2.5km south of Paihia towards Opua. Powered sites are $10 per person, cabins/tourist flats/motel units are from $45/65/75 for two.

Backpackers Paihia has a good selection of backpacker accommodation; all make bookings for activities at discounted prices.

There are several on Kings Rd, Paihia's 'hostel row'. The *Pipi Patch Lodge* (☎ 402 7111, @ pipipatch@acb.co.nz) at No 18 charges $18 for dorm beds, and $45 to $55 for doubles or twins. Each room has kitchen and bathroom facilities. There is also a pool, spa and bar with an outdoor patio.

The *Mousetrap* (☎ 402 8182) at No 11 is comfortable and laid-back with spacious meeting areas and a veranda shaped like a ship's bridge. It costs from $15 for dorms, and doubles and twins are $40.

Another good backpackers, the *Peppertree* (☎ 402 6122, @ peppertree.lodge@xtra.co.nz) at No 15 is a sparkling, well-equipped place with good communal areas, pool table and kayaks. Dorm beds cost $19 in rooms with attached bathroom; doubles with bathroom cost $49.

Lodge Eleven (☎ 402 7487), a YHA associate hostel on the corner of Kings and MacMurray Rds, charges from $16 in dorms, and from $40 to $48 for twins and doubles. Each room has a toilet and shower.

Just around the corner from Kings Rd, the *Pickled Parrot* (☎ 402 6222, @ parrot@igrin.co.nz) on Greys Lane is a good place in a nice setting with a pleasant outdoor area (and a 'pickled parrot'). Dorms are $16 and twins and doubles $38; breakfast is included.

The *Centabay Lodge* (☎ 402 7466, 27 Selwyn Rd), Web site: www.centabay.co.nz, just behind the shops, is part-backpacker, part-tourist lodge. The standards of accommodation remain high and reasonably priced. Bunkrooms cost from $16 per person, doubles are $39, twin units with bathroom are $49, and self-contained studios are from $50 to $75 (prices are seasonal).

Tommy's (☎/fax 402 8668, @ tommys@xtra.co.nz, 44 Davis Crescent), down at the Waitangi end of Paihia, has tidy dorm rooms for $16 per person ($18 in peak season), twins and doubles for $40 ($44 peak) and a unit for $45 ($70 peak). The *Mayfair Lodge* (☎ 402 7471, @ mayfair.lodge@xtra.co.nz, 7 Puketona Rd) has dorms from $16, and twins/doubles for $36/39. It's well equipped, including a spa.

B&Bs, Guesthouses & Apartments Several B&Bs are found around Paihia and the Bay of Islands; the information centre makes referrals and bookings. The *Cedar Suite* (☎ 402 8516, 5 Sullivans Rd) is a relaxing, pleasant place. The self-contained suite with spa is $110, the cottage with sea views is $125 and the studio suite is from $75 (B&B is $95).

At *Craicor* (☎ 402 7882, 49 Kings Rd), the Garden Room (double $80) and the Tree House (double $95) have decks and views. *Chalet Romantica* (☎ 402 8270, 6 Bedggood Close) has a Swiss touch and great views (from $80 to $190 depending on the season).

Fairlight River Lodge (☎ 402 8005, 107b Yorke Rd) is at Haruru Falls. Singles/doubles are $70/80. *Pioneer Luxury Apartments* (☎ 402 7924) on Marsden Rd has self-contained apartments from $175.

Motels & Hotels In Paihia motels stand shoulder to shoulder along the waterfront; doubles are around $120 during the peak summer season, dropping to $80 or so during the low season.

The *Quality Hotel AutoLodge* (☎ 402 7416) on Marsden Rd has 72 rooms and four suites; standard rooms start at $135. There is a pool and spa.

Aloha Garden Resort Motel (☎ 402 7540, 32-36 Seaview Rd) has one- and two-bedroom self-contained apartments, a pool and spa (from $95 a double, from $145 for a two-bedroom).

Swiss Chalet (☎ 402 7615, 3 Bayview Rd) has a variety of units (studio, one/two-bedroom, executive) from $95 to $160. There is a spa.

Nautilus Resort (☎ 402 8604) on Puketona Rd has studio units from $90 and two-bedroom self-contained apartments from

$120. There is a swimming pool and tennis court.

Paihia Beach Resort (☎ 402 6140, 116 Marsden Rd) has 22 apartments, all with harbour views. Prices range from $175 to over $600 depending on the season.

The **Copthorne Resort Waitangi** (☎ 402 7411) is in a nice setting, north across the bridge, with an excellent restaurant, bar and heated pool; standard rooms start at $166.

Places to Eat

The lane that runs through the shopping mall has several places to choose from.

The **Sidewalk Cafe & Bar** is a popular meeting place and serves a variety of light meals and snacks. Virtually opposite is the **Jazz Cafe**, which also has snacks and light meals (burgers from $7, steak, fish).

King Wah is a licensed Chinese restaurant with dark decor and reasonably priced banquets and buffets, and next door the **Orient Express** does Chinese takeaways.

The Carvery dishes up hot roast-meat rolls ($5). Next door **The Vienna Inn** has Austrian food, including schnitzel ($18.50), Vienna Inn specials (eg, Zurich stirred meat, Berner Wurstel) and crepes.

Opposite, **Basrah** does Middle Eastern food: kebabs ($7), falafel ($6), breads and dips. On the harbourside of the mall, up a flight of stairs, is **Caffé Over the Bay** which has espresso, cakes, desserts and light meals (nachos, pizza, quiche, bagels and so on), and a pleasant balcony to sit out on.

The licensed **La Scala** restaurant on Selwyn Rd specialises in seafood: fish of the day is $17.50. There is also lamb, steak and pasta, and children's meals ($5). The **Buccaneer**, to the north on Selwyn Rd, has seafood, including a seafood platter for $28, roasts, lamb, chicken and pasta. **Lips**, a few doors down, is a cosy cafe with espresso, light meals and filling cooked breakfasts.

Esmae's (41 Williams Rd) is a fancy, licensed restaurant with interesting nouvelle Kiwi cuisine from around $18 for a main dish. Upstairs at 39 Williams Rd, **Ruffino** is a little pizza cafe with cheap meals.

Bistro 40 and **Only Seafood** (40 Marsden Rd) are in a converted old home with attractive decor and areas indoors and out overlooking the sea. Both have good seafood, with Bistro 40 also serving venison, chicken and steak. Mains are around $22. At No 48 is **Swiss Café & Grill**, which has an eclectic menu that includes a hearty Swiss farmhouse plate ($15.90), pizza (about $14), pasta, Asian dishes, soups and salads. Next door is the new **Mako Cafe & Bar**, which has a large deck to sit out on.

The **Saltwater Cafe** (14 Kings Rd) is licensed and BYO, and open daily. It has an innovative blackboard menu; a main meal, corkage and coffee costs about $25.

Cafe Jisar, on the corner of Marsden Rd and Davis Crescent, has seafood chowder, fish of the day, and meat dishes for reasonable prices.

There are two places to eat at Kelly Tarlton's **Tui** – a simple **cafe** and the more stylish **Wheelhouse**.

At Waitangi, a hop, skip and a jump from the information centre's car park, is the excellent **Waikokopu Cafe**. You can sit inside or out – outside has a deck that borders a little pond – and enjoy the good coffee (Roasted Addiqtion), a snack or something more substantial (eg, Moo! – eye fillet, chilli roast onions and radish cakes; $14.50). The Whalers breakfast ($11.50) is hearty, and generally the food is first class.

Entertainment

The **Lighthouse Tavern** upstairs in the shopping mall on Marsden Rd has a restaurant and a pub, and features live bands (a small cover charge usually applies). At Haruru Falls the **Twin Pines** has a tavern with house brews on tap and entertainment on weekends. The **Roadrunner** pub is a five-minute drive south of Paihia.

The barn-like **Paihia Swordfish Club** on Marsden Rd allows nonmembers when it suits them.

RUSSELL
pop 1140

Russell is a short ferry ride across the bay from Paihia/Waitangi. It was originally a fortified Maori settlement which spread over the entire valley, then known as Kororareka.

Russell's early European history was turbulent. In 1830 it was the scene of the War of the Girls, when two Maori girls from different tribes each thought they were the favourite of a whaling captain. This resulted in conflict between the tribes, which the Maori leader, Titore, who was recognised as the *ariki* (high chief) of the area, resolved by separating the two tribes and making the border at the base of the Tapeka Peninsula. A European settlement quickly sprang up in place of the abandoned Maori village.

In 1845, during the Northland Land War, government soldiers and marines garrisoned the town after the Ngapuhi leader Hone Heke threatened to chop down the flagstaff, a symbol of Pakeha authority, again – he had already chopped it down three times. On 11 March 1845 the Ngapuhi staged a diversionary siege of Russell. It was a great tactical success, with Chief Kawiti attacking from the south and another Ngapuhi war party attacking from Long Beach. While the troops rushed off to protect the township, Hone Heke felled the hated symbol of European authority on Maiki (Flagstaff Hill) for the fourth and final time. The Pakeha were forced to evacuate to ships lying at anchor off the settlement. The captain of HMS *Hazard* was wounded severely in the battle and his replacement ordered the ships' cannons to be fired on the town – most of the buildings were razed.

Russell today is a peaceful and pretty little place which justifiably features 'romantic' in its self-promotion. It's a marked contrast to the hustle of Paihia across the bay.

Information

There is no information office. Fullers (☎ 403 7866) near the pier may proffer information. Get a copy of *Russell: Kororareka* from the information centre in Paihia.

The excellent Bay of Islands Maritime & Historic Park Visitor Centre (☎ 403 7685) is in Russell – see under the Bay of Islands Maritime & Historic Park heading earlier in the Bay of Islands section. The *Russell Heritage Trails* pamphlet ($1) includes walking and driving tours.

Russell Museum

The Russell Museum was built for the bicentenary of Cook's Bay of Islands visit in 1769. It's small but it houses maritime exhibits, displays relating to Cook and his voyages, and a fine 1:5 scale model of his barque *Endeavour* – a real working model – in addition to a collection of early settlers' relics. The museum is open from 10 am to 4 pm daily ($2.50, children $0.50).

Pompallier House

Close by, and on a lovely waterfront site, is Pompallier House, built to house the printing works for the Roman Catholic mission founded by the French missionary Bishop Pompallier in 1841. In the 1870s it was converted to a private home. One of the oldest houses in NZ, it has been restored and is now true to its original state. It is open from 10 am to 5 pm daily, but is closed on weekends from June to October ($5). In winter guided tours are taken several times a day. Call ☎ 403 7861 for times.

Maiki

Overlooking Russell is Maiki (Flagstaff Hill), where Hone Heke made his attacks – this, the fifth flagpole, has stood for a lot longer than the first four. The view is well worth the trouble to get up there, and there are several routes to the top. By car take Tapeka Rd, or on foot take the track west from the boat ramp along the beach at low tide, or up Wellington St at high tide. Alternatively, simply walk to the end of Wellington St and take the short track up the hill, about a 30-minute climb.

Long Beach

About 1km behind Russell to the east is Oneroa Bay, with a beautiful beach known variously as Oneroa Bay Beach, Donkey Bay Beach or Long Beach. There is an interesting adobe house here. It's about a 15-minute walk from the Russell wharf, heading over the hill on Long Beach Rd. When you reach the hill's summit, at the intersection with Queen's View Rd, there's a tiny graveyard with benches and a good view of Oneroa Bay. Turn right here and

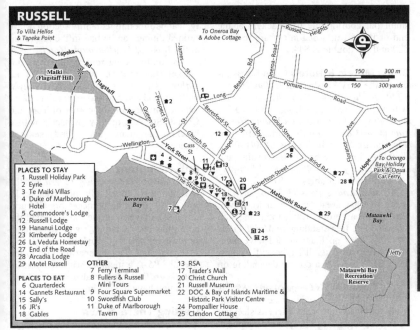

RUSSELL

To Villa Hellos & Tapeka Point

To Oneroa Bay & Adobe Cottage

Maiki (Flagstaff Hill)

Kororareka Bay

Matauwhi Bay

To Orongo Bay Holiday Park & Opua Car Ferry

Matauwhi Bay Recreation Reserve

Jetty

NORTHLAND

PLACES TO STAY
1 Russell Holiday Park
2 Eyrie
3 Te Maiki Villas
4 Duke of Marlborough Hotel
5 Commodore's Lodge
12 Russell Lodge
19 Hananui Lodge
23 Kimberley Lodge
26 La Veduta Homestay
27 End of the Road
28 Arcadia Lodge
29 Motel Russell

PLACES TO EAT
6 Quarterdeck
14 Gannets Restaurant
15 Sally's
16 JR's
18 Gables

OTHER
7 Ferry Terminal
8 Fullers & Russell Mini Tours
9 Four Square Supermarket
10 Swordfish Club
11 Duke of Marlborough Tavern
13 RSA
17 Trader's Mall
20 Christ Church
21 Russell Museum
22 DOC & Bay of Islands Maritime & Historic Park Visitor Centre
24 Pompallier House
25 Clendon Cottage

go about one block up Queen's View Rd to where it meets Oneroa Rd and the view is even better – a sweeping vista of the peninsula. There's an unofficial nudist beach past the rocky outcrops at the beach's northern end.

Other Attractions
Christ Church on Robertson St is the oldest church in NZ. Built in 1835, it is suitably scarred with musket and cannonball holes, and has an interesting graveyard.

Clendon Cottage was built by James Clendon, US Consul in 1839, who later moved to Rawene (see that section under Hokianga earlier in this chapter) as resident magistrate.

Organised Tours
Russell Mini Tours (☎ 403 7866) departs from Fullers, fronting the pier, several times daily and charges $12 (children $6) for a one-hour tour. Many of the cruises out of

Paihia pick up passengers at Russell about 15 minutes after their Paihia departure.

Places to Stay
Camping, Cabins & Hostels The *Russell Holiday Park* (☎ 403 7826) on Long Beach Rd has tent and powered sites from $10 per person and cabins/tourist flats/motel units from $30/50/60. There are backpacker beds from $14.

The *Orongo Bay Holiday Park* (☎ 403 7704) is 3km south of Russell on the road to the Opua car ferry. Orongo Bay has cabins from $25 for two people, and camp sites from $8 per person. There's a pool and a TV/games room.

Centrally located on the corner of Beresford and Chapel Sts, *Russell Lodge* (☎ 403 7640, 0800-478 773) has 10 studio and motel units from $60 per person and backpackers cabins from $18 per person. There's a fully equipped kitchen, a pool table and TV lounge.

The *End of the Road* (☎ 403 7632) is a small but comfortable backpackers at the end of Brind Rd; a bed in a share room is $20 and the double is $44.

B&Bs, Motels & Hotels Good B&Bs include: the very swish *Villa Hellos* (☎ 403 7229, 44 du Fresne Place, Tapeka Point), with self-catered villas from $150 to $250 depending on the season; *La Veduta Homestay* (☎ 403 8299), on the corner of Gould and Hazard Sts, which costs $100/130 for doubles with share bathroom/en suite; and the modern *Eyrie* (☎ 403 7306, 7 Prospect St) with singles/doubles for $75/95.

Arcadia Lodge (☎ 403 7756) on Florance Ave has great views over Matauwhi Bay; rooms are from $120 ($155 in the high season). The free-standing *Te Maiki Villas* (☎ 403 7046) on Flagstaff Rd have awesome views of Russell Harbour; they cost from $149 to $199 a double depending on the season.

The *Commodore's Lodge* (☎ 403 7899) is a stylish old building right on the waterfront. Well-equipped units with kitchens sleeping up to six people cost $75 ($190 in summer).

Similar, though more modern, is the *Hananui Lodge* (☎ 403 7875), which backs onto the waterfront. Self-contained motel units cost from $85 and up to $195 in the peak season.

The *Motel Russell* (☎ 403 7854) has doubles from $60 in the off season, $185 in the high season.

The top place in town (with a price to match) is *Kimberley Lodge* (☎ 403 7090) on Pitt St.

The fine old *Duke of Marlborough Hotel* (☎ 403 7829), right on the waterfront, has real old-fashioned charm. Rooms cost from $110 to $250 for two depending on the season.

Places to Eat

Russell has several cafes and takeaways, including *JR's*, where you can get excellent lamb pitta bread rolls.

In the Traders Mall, *York St Cafe* is a licensed cafe and takeaway with Asian food, pasta and seafood.

The *Duke of Marlborough Tavern* has typical pub food in its family section. More refined dining can be had in the restaurant at the *Duke of Marlborough Hotel*.

Also on the waterfront are the more up-market *Quarterdeck*, with local seafood, *Gables*, with mains from $21, and *Sally's*, with seafood and blackboard specials. *Gannets Restaurant* on the corner of York and Chapel Sts is a quality brasserie with a blackboard menu and good seafood choices.

Entertainment

The *Duke of Marlborough Tavern* was the first pub in NZ to get a licence, back on 14 July 1840. Its three predecessors all burnt down. The tavern, in the block behind the hotel, has both a family room and a more serious, perhaps 'rougher', bar.

If you want cheaper beer then go to the friendly *RSA;* a member will sign you in. The *Swordfish Club* is also worth a visit; again you have to sign in.

Getting There & Away

Your choices are to come on the passenger ferry from Paihia ($3 each way), to drive or hitch in via the Opua car ferry, or take the Northliner bus.

Fullers runs a continuous shuttle service during the day from Opua to Okiato Point, still some distance from Russell. This ferry operates from 6.50 am to 9 pm (10 pm on Friday). The one-way fare is $7 for a car and driver, $12 for a campervan and driver, $3.50 for a motorcycle and rider, plus $1 for each additional adult passenger. There's a much longer dirt road which avoids the Opua ferry, but it's a very long haul.

OPUA

pop 590
As well as being the car ferry terminus, Opua is a deep-sea port from which meat, wool and butter are exported. The town was established as a coaling port in the 1870s, when the railway line was constructed. Before the wharf was built, after WWI, the coal was transported out to ships on lighters (flat-bottomed barges). Today, the occasional

cruise ship may be seen alongside the wharf, as well as many local and foreign yachts during summer.

See Walking under Paihia earlier for information about the **Opua Forest**.

The *Ferrymans Restaurant & Bistro* by the car ferry is a great place to sit out by the waterside and enjoy a light meal. *Opua General Stores* has ice creams and snacks.

Vintage Railway

There's a historic steam train service that operates from Opua to Kawakawa, running from Saturday to Tuesday in winter and daily except Friday in summer. The trip takes 45 minutes each way and a one-way/return ticket costs $10/16 (children $6/10). The train goes through Kawakawa's main street; while in the town keep an eye out for the unusual, earth-canopied public toilets, designed by the late Austrian-born artist Frederick Hundertwasser. You can contemplate their exterior at your leisure from the vantage point of a sidewalk table at the good *Trainspotter Cafe* across the road. Sadly, Hundertwasser died in February 2000. He is buried near Kawakawa where he lived and worked for many years.

KERIKERI
pop 4290

At the northern end of the Bay of Islands, Kerikeri is a laid-back provincial town. It has plenty of accommodation and can be used as a base for exploring the region, but is primarily a service town for the surrounding agricultural district.

The word *kerikeri* means 'to dig'; the Maori grew large crops of kumara here before the Pakeha arrived, and it was here, in 1820, that the first agricultural plough was introduced to NZ. Today it is still primarily an agricultural region, with kiwi fruit, citrus and other orchards. Large numbers of itinerant farm workers congregate in Kerikeri for the six-week kiwi fruit harvest beginning in early May, but orchard work of one kind or another is usually available year-round.

Kerikeri is significant in NZ history. It became the site of the country's second mission station when the Reverend Samuel Marsden chose the site at the head of the Kerikeri inlet under the protection of the Ngapuhi chief, Hongi Hika. In November 1819 the Reverend John Butler arrived at the site and set up the mission headquarters. New Zealand's oldest wooden building, Kemp House, and its oldest stone building, the Stone Store, were established as part of this mission.

The visitor centre at Rewa's Maori Village has pamphlets, and a Web site (www.kerikeri.co.nz) provides more information. Get information on walks in the area from DOC (☎ 407 8474) on Landing Rd.

Stone Store & Kemp House

The Stone Store is the oldest stone building in NZ; construction began in 1833 and was completed in 1836. It was recently re-opened after extensive renovation. It's open from 9.30 am to 5.30 pm (free; access to the attic is $2).

Kemp House is NZ's oldest surviving building, a remarkable fact given that it is made of wood. It was erected in 1821 by Reverend Butler. Complete with original fittings and chattels, it's open from 9.30 am to 5.30 pm daily ($5).

Rewa's Maori Village

Just across the river from the Stone Store, Rewa's Maori Village is built on a site thought to have been occupied at one time by Chief Rewa. The various buildings are part of an authentic reproduction of a *kainga*, a pre-European unfortified Maori village, with various dwellings, kitchen buildings, storerooms and so on, and exhibits of the many plants the Maori used. It's open from 9 am to 5 pm in summer and 10 am to 4 pm in winter, daily ($2.50, children $0.50).

Arts, Crafts, Food & Wine

The Kerikeri area is home to many artists and artisans. Several shops display their work, and in most you can see work in progress, especially pottery.

On SH10 there are several good shops, including the Origin Art & Craft Cooperative with many kinds of craft, Akatere Wool

NORTHLAND

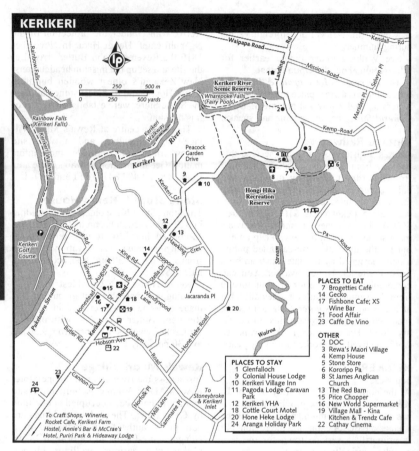

KERIKERI

0   250   500 m
0   250   500 yards

Kerikeri River Scenic Reserve
Wharepoke Falls (Fairy Pools)

Rainbow Falls Road
Rainbow Falls (Kerikeri Falls)
Kerikeri Walkway
Kerikeri River
Peacock Garden Drive
Kerikeri-Gr
Golf-View-Rd
Kerikeri Golf Course
Fairway
Augusta Pl
Clark-Rd
King-Rd
Stella Dr
Support St
Hawking Cres
Kerikeri Rd
Homestead Dr
Butler Rd
Wendywood Lane
Jacaranda Pl
Pukeawara Stream
Hobson Ave
Cobham Road
Hone Heke Road
Cannon Dr
Norfolk Pl
Mill Lane
Sammaree Pl

Waipapa Road
Landing Rd
Mission Road
Kendall Rd
Kemp Road
Marsden Pl
Selwyn Pl
Hongi Hika Recreation Reserve
Pa Road
Wairoa Stream

To Stoneybroke & Kerikeri Inlet

To Craft Shops, Wineries, Rocket Cafe, Kerikeri Farm Hostel, Annie's Bar & McCrae's Hotel, Puriri Park & Hideaway Lodge

PLACES TO EAT
7   Brogetties Café
14 Gecko
17 Fishbone Cafe; XS Wine Bar
21 Food Affair
23 Caffe De Vino

OTHER
2   DOC
3   Rewa's Maori Village
4   Kemp House
5   Stone Store
6   Kororipo Pa
8   St James Anglican Church
13 The Red Barn
15 Price Chopper
16 New World Supermarket
19 Village Mall – Kina Kitchen & Trendz Cafe
22 Cathay Cinema

PLACES TO STAY
1   Glenfalloch
9   Colonial House Lodge
10 Kerikeri Village Inn
11 Pagoda Lodge Caravan Park
12 Kerikeri YHA
18 Cottle Court Motel
20 Hone Heke Lodge
24 Aranga Holiday Park

Craft, Country Treasures, Blue Gum Pottery, Redwoods (pottery, ceramics), Cottle Hill Winery and Marsden Estate Winery.

Turning onto Kerikeri Rd towards town, you pass Robbs Winery, The Kauri Workshop, Makana (handmade chocolates) and Keriblue Ceramics on the north side of Kerikeri Rd, and The Red Shed on the south side.

Closer in to town are The Red Barn, at 127 Kerikeri Rd, and Spectrum Glass.

Walking
Just up the hill behind the Stone Store is a marked Historical Walk which takes about 10 minutes and leads to **Kororipo Pa**, the fortress of the famous Ngapuhi chief Hongi Hika. Huge Ngapuhi warfaring parties led by Hika once departed from here on raids, terrorising much of the North Island (see History in the Facts about New Zealand chapter). The walk emerges near the St James Anglican church, built in 1878.

Across the river from the Stone Store is a scenic reserve with several marked tracks. There's a 4km Kerikeri River track leading to Rainbow Falls, passing by the Wharepoke Falls (Fairy Pools) along the way. Alternatively, you can reach the Rainbow

Falls from Waipapa Rd, in which case it's only a 10-minute walk to the falls. The Fairy Pools are great for swimming and picnics and can be reached from the dirt road beside the YHA hostel if you aren't up to the hike along the river. Get the free *Kerikeri Basin Walks* from the information centre in Paihia.

Places to Stay
Camping & Cabins The *Pagoda Lodge Caravan Park* (☎ 407 8617) is on Pa Rd at the inlet near the Stone Store. Powered sites are $10 per person and tourist flats are $60 for two.

The *Aranga Holiday Park* (☎ 407 9326) is on Kerikeri Rd in a lovely setting beside the Puketotara Stream, only five minutes' walk from town. Tent/powered sites are $9/10 per person, cabins are from $30 for two and a tourist flat with private facilities is $56 for two. There is a backpackers dorm ($13).

The *Hideaway Lodge* (☎ 407 9773) on Wiroa Rd, west of the SH10 junction, has tent sites for $8 per person, dorms for $14 and twin or double rooms for $45. It's 4km out but offers free rides to town. It has a pool and games room.

Backpackers Kerikeri's backpacker places attract both tourists and itinerant workers, catered for in large dorms; some will help to find orchard work.

The *Kerikeri Farm Hostel* (☎ 407 6989, ✉ kkfarmhostel@xtra.co.nz), 1.5km north of the Kerikeri turn-off on SH10, is a pleasant farm and the friendly owners encourage you to participate in farm activities – squeeze your own organic orange juice or crack a bowl of macadamia nuts. Dorms are $15, twins and doubles are $18 per person, singles are $25 and a self-contained unit is $65.

The *Kerikeri YHA* (☎ 407 9391) on Kerikeri Rd charges $15 for a dorm or $18 per person for doubles.

The *Hone Heke Lodge* (☎/fax 407 8170, ✉ honeheke@xtra.co.nz, 65 Hone Heke Rd), an itinerant picker's haven, is in a quiet residential area; the cost is $15 for a dorm and

$18 per person for a double ($21 per person for a double with its own bathroom) and there is an en suite single for $37.50.

B&Bs & Guesthouses The information centre in Paihia has details on B&Bs in the area.

Stoneybroke (☎ 407 7371) on Edmonds Rd, 12km east of Kerikeri near Kerikeri Inlet, has singles/doubles for $40/70; the owners cultivate macadamia and almonds.

Puriri Park (☎ 407 9818) on SH10 is a comfortable cottage offering double B&B for $75. It also has two-bedroom self-contained units from $75.

Glenfalloch (☎ 407 5471) on Landing Rd charges $55 for singles and $75 to $85 for doubles.

The *Kerikeri Village Inn* (☎ 407 4666, 165 Kerikeri Rd) is a contemporary place.

Motels The *Colonial House Lodge* (☎ 407 9106, 178 Kerikeri Rd) is a spic-and-span place with one- and two-bedroom cottages, apartments and family units. Prices range from $85 to $160 per unit, depending on the season.

The *Cottle Court Motel* (☎ 407 8867) on Kerikeri Rd is reasonably priced, charging from $75/85 a single/double. It has a heated outdoor pool.

Places to Eat
There are several cafes and restaurants. The *Fishbone Cafe* is a great place for good espresso, light meals (eg, gado gado, pizza, panini), soups and salads. Behind it is the *XS Wine Bar*. The *Food Affair* has medium/large gourmet pizzas, espresso and other cafe fare.

In Village Mall are *Kina Kitchen* ('we serve large meals'), which has pasta, *cervena* (venison) and seafood; mains cost about $19. Nearby is *Trendz Cafe* which has all-day breakfasts, soups, salad, pasta, chicken and so on. It's closed Wednesday.

Gecko has wood-fired pizzas. *Caffe di Vino* on Kerikeri Rd is set in a farmlike, peaceful place. It's open for lunch and dinner. Towards the intersection of Kerikeri Rd and SH10 is the excellent *Rocket Cafe*.

NORTHLAND

Across from the Stone Store *Brogetties Café* is open daily. It's a lovely spot to eat indoors or out on the veranda overlooking the inlet.

If you are after a drink, *Annie's Bar* in McCrae's Hotel on SH10 is a good choice; relax next to the big open fire.

Getting There & Away

InterCity and Northliner Express buses come and go from Cobham Rd, just off Kerikeri Rd in the town centre; see the Getting Around section at the start of this chapter. Both companies have buses departing from Kerikeri in the morning for the half-hour trip to Paihia, returning in the evening.

Paihia to Whangarei

There are two very scenic routes out on the east coast: the back road from Russell to SH1, and the drive out to Tutukaka from Hikurangi on SH1, which loops around to Whangarei. Out to sea are the Poor Knights Islands.

RUSSELL ROAD

The back road from Russell skirts around the coast before joining SH1 at Whakapara. The road is long, unsealed and rough for most of the way, but it's scenic. It is for those with their own transport, plenty of time and a desire to get off the beaten track.

From Russell, the road starts near Orango Bay and skirts along the Waikare Inlet before reaching the Waikare Rd to Waihaha. This turn-off eventually leads back to the highway and Paihia, about a 90-minute drive all up from Russell.

Continuing along the Russell Road past the Waihaha turn-off, there's access to the **Ngaiotonga Scenic Reserve**, which preserves the mixed forest that was once predominant throughout Northland. There are two short walks, suitable for families. The 20-minute **Kauri Grove Nature Walk** and the 10-minute **Twin Bole Kauri Walk** both provide opportunities to see these majestic trees.

Another side trip from the Russell Road is to take the northern Manawaora Rd, which passes many small bays, including **Parekura Bay**, where there is accommodation and boat rental. Further on is the turn-off to isolated **Rawhiti**, a small Ngapuhi settlement where life still revolves around the marae. Past the marae on the headland is the *Rawhiti Motor Camp*, which has a small shop, camp sites, some on-site vans and stunning views of the Bay of Islands.

Rawhiti is also the starting point for the trek to **Cape Brett**, a hard 7½-hour walk to the top of the peninsula, where overnight stays are possible in the Cape Brett Hut. You can book the hut and get information on the walk at the Bay of Islands Maritime & Historic Park Visitor Centre (☎ 403 7685) in Russell.

Closer to the Rawhiti turn-off, a shorter one-hour walk leads through tribal land and over the headland to Whangamumu Harbour. At the main beach on the harbour, the **Whangamumu Scenic Reserve** has a 'back to nature' camping ground. There are over 40 prehistoric sites on the peninsula and the remains of an unusual whaling station. A net, fastened between the mainland and Net Rock, was used to ensnare or slow down whales so the harpooners could get an easy shot in. The whales taken were mainly humpbacks; in 1927 over 70 whales were trapped in this fashion.

Further south, another side road leads to the **Whangaruru North Head Scenic Reserve**, which has beaches, camping grounds, walks and fine coastal scenery in a farmland park setting; camping is $6 per person. Pohutukawa, puriri and kowhai abound and many bird species can be seen in the area. The small settlement of Whangaruru North, just before the reserve, also has a motor camp, as does Oakura on the other side of the harbour.

Backpackers Beach House (☎/fax 433 6806) gives the budget-conscious the option to stop in this magnificent isolated region; the cost is $15 per person. You can also do kayaking here.

At the adjacent *Whangaruru Beach Camp* (☎ 433 6806) there are tent & powered sites ($17 to $19.50), cabins from $30 to $45 for two, and motel units from $70 for two.

At Oakura is the **Oakura Motels and Caravan Park** (☎ 433 6803), which has camp sites from $18, cabins and on-site vans from $35, and motel units from $55.

At Helena Bay, Russell Road returns to tarseal and leads back to SH1. About 8km from Helena Bay along a rough, winding side road is the **Mimiwhangata Coastal Park**. This is a truly scenic part of the coastline, with coastal dunes, pohutukawa, jutting headlands and picturesque beaches. There is a luxurious lodge run by DOC, and a simpler but comfortable cottage; both sleep eight people. Camping is also possible and much cheaper ($5). Book and inquire about fees with DOC (☎ 403 7685) in Russell.

TUTUKAKA COAST

At Hikurangi on SH1 you can turn off and take a very scenic route to Whangarei. At **Hikurangi** there is a small museum, open from 9.30 to 11 am Tuesday to Thursday and Saturday and 1 to 2.30 pm on Wednesday (gold coin donation). From Hikurangi, the first place on the coast is Sandy Bay surf beach, where you can horse trek on a little-frequented piece of the east coast. There is a succession of idyllic bays from here on – all have scope for walking, boating, swimming and, most popularly, fishing.

Small, exclusive **Tutukaka** is the home of the Whangarei Deep Sea Anglers Club and the beautiful harbour is cluttered with yachts and fishing boats. The tiny yacht club here launched a multimillion dollar challenge for the 1995 America's Cup, eventually won by Auckland-based *Black Magic*.

Tutukaka is best known as a premier game-fishing destination, and late in the day marlin and other catch are weighed in. The well-organised Tutukaka Charter Boat Association (☎ 434 3818) at the marina handles fishing, diving and cruise charters.

Ngunguru, a few kilometres south of Tutukaka, has food outlets, accommodation, petrol, a laundrette and a sports complex. You can get from Whangarei to Ngunguru ($6) and Tutukaka ($7) on weekdays with Tuatara Transit (☎ 025-529 722).

Places to Stay & Eat

At Sandy Bay, **Whananaki Trail Rides** (☎ 433 8299) has backpackers farmhouse beds for $15, a three-berth caravan for $25 and camping for free. Horse trekking is $30 for two hours, or a two-day trek is $150.

Pacific Rendezvous (☎ 434 3847) is an exclusive resort on its own headland just south of Tutukaka; one- to three-bedroom, self-contained chalets are from $170 in summer ($90 in winter).

At Ngunguru, the **motor camp** (☎ 434 3851) on Papaka Rd has camp sites at $25 for two and cabins and on-site vans from $35. The **Chalet Court Motel** (☎ 434 3786) charges from $60/$85 a single/double, while the well-situated **Sea Breeze Motel** (☎ 434 3844) on Ngunguru Rd charges from $60 to $100 depending on the unit's size.

If you love seafood, Tutukaka is paradise. The places to go for a meal are **Scnappa Rock** and the **Blue Marlin** (☎ 434 3909) at the Whangarei Deep Sea Anglers Club.

POOR KNIGHTS ISLANDS MARINE RESERVE

This marine reserve, 24km off Northland's east coast near Tutukaka, was established in 1981. It is reputed to have the best scuba diving in NZ and has been rated as one of the top diving spots in the world.

The two large islands, Tawhiti Rahi and Aorangi, were once home to members of the Ngati Wai tribe but, since a massacre in the early 1800s by a raiding party, the islands have been *tapu* (sacred). You're *not* allowed to land on the islands but you can swim near them.

Since the northern islands are bathed in a subtropical current, varieties of tropical and subtropical fish not seen in other coastal waters are observed. The waters are clear and there are no problems with sediment. The underwater cliffs drop steeply (about 70m) to a sandy bottom, where there is a labyrinth of archways, caves and tunnels, packed with a bewildering variety of fish.

As the islands are relatively isolated from the mainland they have acted as a sanctuary for flora and fauna – the most famous example is the prehistoric tuatara

NORTHLAND

(see Other Fauna in the 'Fauna & Flora' colour section).

Diving trips depart from Whangarei, Tutukaka and elsewhere. A sightseeing day trip on the boats costs around $80 (children $40). Divers should count on about $150 for full diving equipment and two dives.

Operators in Tutukaka are Knight Line (☎ 434 3733), the Tutukaka Charter Boat Association (☎ 434 3818), Pacific Hideaway (☎ 434 3675), Action Adventures (☎ 434 3867) and Knight Diver Tours (☎ 0800-766 756). In Whangarei, contact the Dive Shop (☎ 438 3521) on Water St, the Dive Connection (☎ 430 0818) at 140 Lower Cameron St and Sub Aqua Dive (☎ 438 1075) at 41 Clyde St.

The MV *Wairangi* (☎ 434 3350) has interesting ecotourism trips along the coast and to the islands; ring for costs and itineraries.

WHANGAREI
pop 45,800

Whangarei is the major city of Northland and a haven for yachts. It is a pleasant city with an equable climate, though its main attractions are in the surrounding area. The beaches at Whangarei Heads, about 35km east of town, are incredibly scenic and have many tiny bays and inlets.

The climate and soil combine to make Whangarei a gardener's paradise – many parks and gardens thrive in this city; there's an interesting collection of dry-stone walls just north of the city.

Information

The helpful and friendly Whangarei Visitors Bureau (☎ 438 1079, ✉ whangarei@clear .net.nz) is at Tarewa Park on Otaika Rd, on SH1 at the southern entrance to town. It's open from 8.30 am to 5 pm on weekdays and 10 am to 4 pm weekends (8.30 am to 6.30 pm daily in January). There is a cafe which overlooks a 'kid-friendly' park.

The AA office (☎ 438 4848) is on the corner of Robert and John Sts. Next door to the visitors bureau is DOC (☎ 438 0299), with information on camping, recreational activities, maps and hut tickets, as well as an environmental shop with souvenirs.

Things to See & Do

Boats from around the world are moored in the **Town Basin**, an attractive area right on the edge of the town centre along Quay St. The waterfront along the river has been renovated and includes the **Clapham Clock Museum** (☎ 438 3993), which has an awesome 1300 timepieces, all ticking away furiously. It is open from 9 am to 5 pm daily ($5, children $3, including a guided tour).

Also at the Town Basin is the **Museum of Fishes**, open from 10 am to 4 pm daily ($5, children $2). Fishing enthusiasts will appreciate the stuffed game fish – otherwise forget it. Shops here include the Vortex complex which has a bookshop (Chapter 1) with Internet access, as well as textiles, photographs and the Bliss espresso bar.

Spanning a stream in the centre of town, **Cafler Park** has well-tended flowerbeds, and the Margie Maddren Fernery & Snow Conservatory, an all-native fernery. Both are open from 10 am to 4 pm daily (entry is free). Also here is the **Whangarei Art Museum** which showcases arts and crafts from Northland; open from 10 am to 4.30 pm Tuesday to Friday and from noon on weekends. Entry is by *koha* (donation).

The Northland Craft Trust, known simply as **The Quarry**, is about 500m west of town in an old quarry. This artists' cooperative has studios where you can observe work in progress or buy craft at the showroom. It is open from 10 am to 4 pm daily.

West of Whangarei, 5km out on the Dargaville Road at Maunu, is the **Whangarei Museum**, open from 10 am to 4 pm daily. The museum includes a kiwi house, the 1885 Clarke Homestead and the Exhibition Centre museum, which houses European relics and an impressive collection of Maori artefacts (including superb feather cloaks). The museum park also has an old locomotive, which runs in summer, and an abandoned mercury mine ($7, children $3.50), or $3 for any one of the venues.

Nearby is the **Native Bird Recovery Centre**, which nurses sick and injured birds back to health. It's open from 10 am to 4 pm weekdays, afternoons only on weekends. Entry is by donation.

Scenic Reserves & Walks The 26m-high **Whangarei Falls** are very photogenic, with water cascading over the edge of an old basalt lava flow. Next to Ngunguru Rd, in the suburb of Tikipunga, 5km north of the town centre, the falls can be reached by Tikipunga bus (weekdays only). The surrounding domain has three natural pools in the river and numerous picnic spots.

About 5km north-east of town, out on Whareora Rd, the **AH Reed Memorial Kauri Park** spans a pretty stream and has a waterfall, several easy walkways and over 50 kinds of native trees including punga, totara and large kauri (some of them up to 3m in diameter).

South-east of Whangarei, the **Waimahanga Walkway** in Onerahi is an easy walk along an old railway embankment. It takes two hours and passes through mangrove swamps and over a 300m-long timber truss harbour bridge. The free *Whangarei Walks* describes more walks.

Activities

The visitors bureau provides a leaflet on activities and attractions. Whangarei is a popular centre for diving and fishing, mostly

NORTHLAND

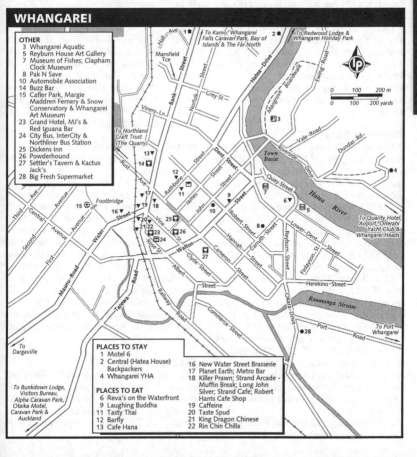

WHANGAREI

OTHER
3 Whangarei Aquatic
5 Reyburn House Art Gallery
7 Museum of Fishes; Clapham Clock Museum
8 Pak N Save
10 Automobile Association
14 Buzz Bar
15 Cafler Park, Margie Maddren Fernery & Snow Conservatory & Whangarei Art Museum
23 Grand Hotel, MJ's & Red Iguana Bar
24 City Bus, InterCity & Northliner Bus Station
25 Dickens Inn
26 Powderhound
27 Settler's Tavern & Kactus Jack's
28 Big Fresh Supermarket

To Kamo, Whangarei Falls Caravan Park, Bay of Islands & The Far North

To Redwood Lodge & Whangarei Holiday Park

To Northland Craft Trust (The Quarry)

Town Basin

To Quality Hotel, Airport, Onerahi Yacht Club & Whangarei Heads

To Dargaville

To Bunkdown Lodge, Visitors Bureau, Alpha Caravan Park, Otaika Motel, Caravan Park & Auckland

To Port Whangarei

PLACES TO STAY	PLACES TO EAT
1 Motel 6	16 New Water Street Brasserie
2 Central (Hatea House) Backpackers	17 Planet Earth; Metro Bar
4 Whangarei YHA	18 Killer Prawn; Strand Arcade - Muffin Break; Long John Silver; Strand Cafe; Robert Harris Cafe Shop
	19 Caffeine
PLACES TO EAT	20 Taste Spud
6 Reva's on the Waterfront	21 King Dragon Chinese
9 Laughing Buddha	22 Rin Chin Chilla
11 Tasty Thai	
12 Barfly	
13 Cafe Hana	

organised out of Tutukaka. The Whangarei Tramping Club (☎ 436 1441) welcomes visitors. Northland Districts Aero Club (☎ 436 0890) has scenic flights; Takumana Riding Centre (☎ 437 5710) runs horse treks; Northland Coastal Adventures (☎ 436 0139) has a variety of trips – beach and bushwalks, kayaking, fishing and snorkelling included; and Farm Safaris (☎ 432 3794) has quadbike trips through a working farm at Maungakaramea ($50 per person; one hour).

Whangarei Aquatic on Ewing Rd has indoor and outdoor pools, saunas and spas. It's open from 6.30 am to 8 pm Monday to Saturday, and from 8 am on Sunday ($3.50, children $2).

There's an indoor climbing wall northwest of the city centre at the Kensington Stadium; the visitors bureau has details.

Readers have recommended the Bushwacka Experience tours (☎ 434 7839), which involve 4WD bush and farm trips, abseiling, glowworms and more – with billy tea thrown in.

Places to Stay

Camping & Cabins The *Alpha Caravan Park* (☎ 438 9867, 34 Tarewa Rd) is centrally located, less than 1km from town. Tent and powered sites are $18 for two and self-contained motel units are $59 for two.

The *Whangarei Holiday Park & Cabins* (☎ 437 6856) on Mair St, 2.5km north of the town centre beside Mair Park, has tent or powered sites at $8 per person and cabins at $32 for two (en suite cabins $42), and backpacker cabins at $15 per person.

The *Otaika Motel & Caravan Park* (☎ 438 1459, 136 Otaika Rd), at the southern entrance to Whangarei, has tent and powered sites at $9 per person, tourist flats from $50 and motel units from $65 to $85.

The *Whangarei Falls Caravan Park* (☎ 437 0609, 0800-227 222), 5km north of town, is a good place with swimming and spa pools and cheap backpacker accommodation. There are tent and caravan sites at $9 per person, bunk beds at $14 and cabins at $34 for two.

Other camping and caravan sites include *Kamo Springs Caravan Park* (☎ 435 1208,

55 Great North Rd, Kamo) to the north and the *Blue Heron Holiday Park* (☎ 436 2293), south-east on Tamaterau Beach.

Backpackers South of the city centre, the popular *Bunkdown Lodge* (☎ 438 8886, ✉ bunkdown@ihug.co.nz, 23 Otaika Rd) has comfortable, well-equipped communal areas and a homely atmosphere. There are mountain bikes for rent ($10 per day), bushwalks and free pick-up from the visitors bureau or the bus station. Dorm beds are $15, twins $20 per person and doubles $45.

The *Whangarei YHA* (☎ 438 8954, ✉ yhawhangarei@hotmail.com, 52 Punga Grove Ave) is a small, easy-going hostel with fine views. A bed costs $15 in a dorm or $19 in a twin or double room. It's a short walk from town, but the final climb is up a steep hill – take the signposted short cut from Dundas Rd if walking.

Central (Hatea House) Backpackers (☎ 437 6174, 67 Hatea Drive) has bunk beds for $15 and twins/doubles for $17.50/20 per person, and singles for $30 to $35.

Motels & Hotels Whangarei's budget motels generally charge from around $60 to $80 a double.

The following are good: *Motel Six* (☎ 438 9219, 153 Bank St), five minutes from the city centre; *Burgundy Rose* (☎ 437 3500, 100 Kamo Rd), with indoor spa; *Redwood Lodge* (☎ 437 6843) on the corner of Hatea Drive and Drummond St; *San Jose* (☎ 438 7459, 10 Cross St); *Cypress Court* (☎ 437 6193, 29 Kamo Rd); the *Continental Motel* (☎ 437 6359, 67 Kamo Rd), with heated pool; and the colonial-style *Stonehaven* (☎ 0800-336 655, 30 Mill Rd).

The *Quality Hotel* (☎ 438 0284) is 500m from the city on Riverside Drive; a standard double is $115.

Places to Eat

The *Eating Out* guide, available from the visitors bureau, has a comprehensive rundown on Whangarei's many restaurants. *Reva's on the Waterfront* in the Town Basin has a Tex-Mex and seafood menu. It often has live music.

King Dragon Chinese (11-13 Lower Bank St) is good for Cantonese banquets and does lunch buffets on weekdays. The *Laughing Buddha (79 Walton St)* is a gourmet vegetarian cafe, open daily for lunch and from Thursday to Saturday for dinner.

The *New Water Street Brasserie (24 Water St)* has a typical lamb/fish/venison/steak menu and a reputation as one of Whangarei's best restaurants. *MJ's* in the Grand Hotel at 2 Bank St is also pretty reliable.

The *Topsail Cafe (☎ 436 0529)* on the 1st floor of the Onerahi Yacht Club is a must for crayfish.

The *Killer Prawn* on Bank St is a seafood place (sashimi, chowder and, of course, prawns), although you can also get steak. Mains are around $12.

Nearby, inside Strand Arcade, are a few more places including *Muffin Break* ('Proud to be a Kiwi'), *Long John Silver* which is good for fish and chips, and the *Strand Cafe* and *Robert Harris Cafe Shop* upstairs.

Tasty Thai in Rathbone St has, well, Thai food. Virtually opposite is *Barfly*, a trendy bar with pizza and other light meals.

Cafe Hana (77 Bank St) has Japanese food: teriyaki chicken ($12), sushi and tempura ($12), udon, soba and so on.

For yummy cafe fare in a good atmosphere try *Caffeine* near the corner of Water and Bank Sts. *Taste Spud* further down Water St has about 20 different kinds of baked potatoes and a few Mexican and Indian snacks. Around the corner from Caffeine, on Bank St, are *Planet Earth* and *Metro Bar* where you can get pizzas, beasty burgers, 'smiles, free stuff, and shitloads of beer'. If you're in town on a Tuesday night why not drop in on the 'clever bastards quiz nite' (kicks off at 7.30 pm).

Rin Chin Chilla on Vine St is all orange and black with a good selection of magazines. You can get soups, nachos, burritos and kebabs for under $10 – plus good, strong espresso.

The Settler's Tavern in the town centre has a number of bars, of which *Kactus Jack's* is the best. Steak and fish dishes cost under $15.

The restaurant in the *Stage Coach Hotel (567 Kamo Rd)*, about 2km north of the town

centre, has a family menu. The *Dickens Inn* on Cameron St is open daily for all meals.

Entertainment

The *Buzz Bar* on Bank St has live bands and DJs. *Kactus Jack's*, behind the Settler's Tavern, is always popular with the locals and features local bands.

The *Red Iguana Bar* in the Grand Hotel has live music on weekends. *Reva's on the Waterfront* is another restaurant with live music on most weekdays.

The *Powderhound* on Vine St is a popular local nightclub.

Out of town, the *Tutukaka Hotel* on the north-east coast and the *Parua Bay Hotel*, south-east of town at Whangarei Heads, are popular on weekends.

Getting There & Away

Air Air New Zealand Link and Ansett have flights between Auckland and Whangarei daily, with onward connections. Great Barrier Airlines (☎ 0800-900 600) flies three times a week between Whangarei and Great Barrier Island.

Bus The InterCity bus depot (☎ 438 2653) is on Rose St. InterCity has frequent buses between Auckland and Whangarei, continuing north to Paihia, Hokianga Harbour and Kaitaia, with another route to Dargaville.

Northliner has an Auckland-Whangarei-Bay of Islands service daily, with a route to Kerikeri via Paihia or directly to Russell on the Opua ferry. It operates from the Northliner Terminal (☎ 438 3206), 11 Rose St.

Hitching Whangarei is a very busy spot for hitchhikers going north and south. Heading north, the best hitching spot is on SH1 just after the Three Mile Bush Rd intersection, in Kamo, 5km north of town; any Kamo bus will drop you there. Heading south, the best spot is on SH1 opposite Tarewa Park or about 500m further south, by the supermarket.

Getting Around

The Whangarei Airport Shuttle (☎ 437 0666) has a door-to-door service for $8.

JB City Bus Services (☎ 437 5261) runs on Tuesday and Thursday.

Avis (☎ 438 2929), Budget (☎ 438 7292) and Rent-a-Cheepy (☎ 438 7373) are represented. There are plenty of taxis. Pro Drive (☎ 438 7977) returns you and your car home safe after a night out drinking.

AROUND WHANGAREI
Whangarei Heads

From Whangarei, Heads Rd winds its way around the northern shore of Whangarei Harbour, passing picturesque coves and bays on its way to the heads at the harbour entrance. This drive (there is no bus) has magnificent scenery and passes small settlements such as Parua Bay, McLeod Bay and McKenzie Bay. There are great views from the top of 419m **Mt Manaia**, a sheer rock outcrop above McLeod Bay, but it is a hard, steep climb.

Urquharts Bay near the heads has good views (somewhat blighted by the oil refinery on the other side), and from adjoining Woolshed Bay it is a 30-minute walk over the headland to the delightful beach at Smugglers Bay.

You can also make a detour from Parua Bay to beautiful **Pataua**, a sleepy fishing settlement that lies on a shallow inlet. A footbridge leads to the small offshore island, which has a surf beach.

Marsden Point Refinery Model

New Zealand's only oil refinery is at Marsden Point, across the harbour from Whangarei Heads.

At the information centre (☎ 432 8194) there is a 130-sq-m scale model of the refinery, accurate down to the last valve and pump. The centre, on Marsden Point Rd, Ruakaka, is open from 10 am to 5 pm daily.

The Central West

The Central West, predominantly the Waikato and King Country regions, lies to the south of Auckland.

The Waikato, one of the world's richest dairy, thoroughbred and agricultural areas, is about one hour's drive from central Auckland. It includes four fertile plains and Hamilton, New Zealand's fifth-largest city, as its major centre. The region also encompasses the central and lower reaches of New Zealand's longest river, the Waikato, which starts in central North Island, flows out from Lake Taupo and meets the sea on the west coast.

Further south is a historic region known as the King Country, extending roughly from the towns of Otorohanga in the north to Taumarunui in the south, and from Lake Taupo west to the coast.

Waikato

☎ 07 • pop 236,200

The Waikato region was cultivated by the Maori in pre-European times; archaeological evidence shows that thousands of hectares were under cultivation with kumara (sweet potatoes) and other crops.

When the Europeans settled in Auckland in 1840, relations with the local Maori were peaceful at first; missionaries in the 1830s introduced European crops and farming methods to the Waikato region, and by the 1840s the Maori were trading their agricultural produce with the European settlers in Auckland.

Relations between the two cultures soured during the 1850s, largely due to the Europeans' eyeing of Maori land for settlement. By the early 1860s the Waikato Maori had formed a 'King Movement' and united to elect a king. The movement probably stemmed both from a need for greater organisation of Maori tribes against the Pakeha and from a desire to have a Maori leader equivalent to the British queen when dealing with the Pakeha.

- Experiencing adventure activities at Waitomo Caves
- Surfing at Raglan beaches
- Exploring the coastal backwaters of Kawhia and Mokau
- Enjoying the rich agricultural lands of the Waikato, the English-style settlements of Cambridge and Te Aroha and the secluded reaches of the Waikato River

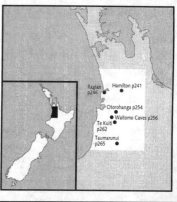

THE CENTRAL WEST

Potatau Te Wherowhero was a paramount high chief of the Waikato tribes when he was made the first Maori king in 1858. He died in 1860 aged about 85 and was succeeded by his son, the second and most widely known Maori king, Matutaera Te Wherowhero – known as King Tawhiao – who ruled for the next 34 years until his death.

The King Movement was a nationalistic step for the Maori, who were unwilling to sell or otherwise lose their homeland to the Europeans. The Europeans, however, were equally unwilling to take no for an answer. In July 1863 they sent a fleet of gunboats and small craft up the Waikato River to put down what they regarded as the 'open rebellion' of

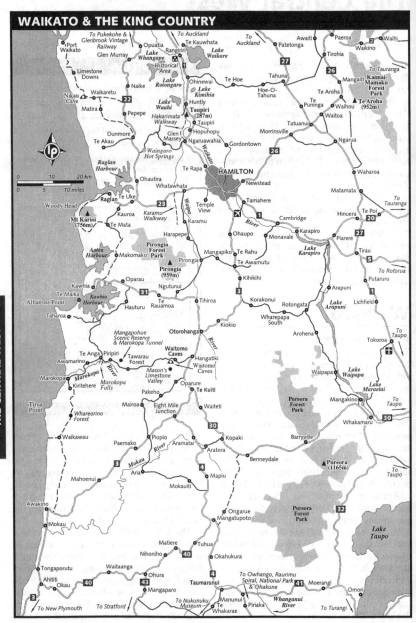

WAIKATO & THE KING COUNTRY

Te Arikinui Dame Te Atairangikaahu

The Maori King Movement, in which local chief Te Wherowhero was elected as the first Maori king in 1859, is still very much alive among the Waikato tribe. Te Arikinui Dame Te Atairangikaahu, 'the Maori queen', is sixth in the line of succession.

Her father, Koroki Mahuta, was the fifth Maori king. When he died in 1966, there was widespread concern over his successor, since he had no sons but two daughters, Tura and Piki, and there had never been a Maori queen.

According to Tainui tradition, if an *ariki* (first-born of a noble family) died and had no sons, office would be passed on to a close male relation. This posed a major question: should it be passed on to one of Koroki Mahuta's female descendants or bestowed upon someone else?

After much discussion and debate, the Waikato chiefs and elders decided that the office should pass to his daughter Piki. Princess Piki became the first Maori queen on 23 May 1966. In 1970 Queen Elizabeth II gave her the title of Dame Commander of the British Empire, and her official title became Te Arikinui Dame Te Atairangikaahu.

Many westerners misunderstand her position, believing her to be queen of all New Zealand Maori; in fact Te Arikinui Dame Te Atairangikaahu is queen only of the tribes who united to form the Maori King Movement in the 1850s. She is head of the Tainui tribal confederation, which consists of four major tribes: the Waikato, Maniapoto, Hauraki and Raukawa – all descended from those who arrived in NZ on the *Tainui* canoe (see the boxed text elsewhere in this chapter). Tainui is one of NZ's largest Maori confederations.

Te Arikinui Dame Te Atairangikaahu's marae is the magnificent Turangawaewae Marae, beside the Waikato River in Ngaruawahia. If you are travelling through Ngaruawahia on SH1, you can see the marae as you cross the bridge over the river. The queen has houses in various places significant to her people – for example, there is a house for the Maori queen beside the Maketu Marae in Kawhia, where the *Tainui* canoe is buried.

the Maori King Movement. After almost a year of warfare, known as the Waikato Land War and involving many historic battles, the Pakeha finally won in April 1864 and the Kingites retreated south to what became known as the King Country, where Europeans dared not venture for several more decades.

AUCKLAND TO HAMILTON

The trip to Hamilton by road from Auckland takes about 1½ hours and there are a few points of interest along the way. Steam train enthusiasts can pause at the **Glenbrook Vintage Railway**, where 12km steam train rides for $9 (children $4) run on Sunday and public holidays between October and July. To get there follow the yellow signs west after leaving the Southern Motorway at Drury, 31km south of Auckland, and head for Waiuku.

The Waiuku Visitor Information Centre (☎ 235 8924) at 2 Queen St has information

on the sailing scow *Jane Gifford* (undergoing maintenance at the time of writing) and other attractions in the Waiuku area.

Te Kauwhata, 67km south of Auckland and just off SH1, is a good place for wine tasting. Of particular interest here is the **Rangiriri Battle Site Heritage Centre** (☎ 826 3663), open from 9 am to 5 pm daily. New Zealand is a little bereft in representing the history of the land wars between European and Maori – this is a small attempt to redress the imbalance. Wander over the battleground, including cemetery and redoubts, where a small group of warriors made a stand against the British forces in November 1863.

At Mercer, north of Te Kauwhata, is a good petrol/food stop where you can buy bacon and pork produced locally at Pokeno, and locally produced cheese and wine.

From Rangiriri the road follows the Waikato River all the way to Hamilton.

Along the way is **Huntly,** a coal-mining town with the large Huntly Power Station. There is an information centre (☎ 828 6406) at 160 Great South Rd. The **Huntly Mining & Cultural Museum** at 26 Harlock Place is open from 10 am to 3 pm Monday to Friday and 1 to 3 pm on Saturday. Entry is $3/1 for adults/children.

South of Huntly the road enters Taupiri Gorge, a gap through the ranges. On the left, as you emerge from the gorge, is the sacred mountain Taupiri, and a Maori cemetery on the hillside where past Maori kings are buried.

Ngaruawahia, 19km north of Hamilton on SH1, is an important centre for the Waikato Maori people and the home of the present Maori queen, Te Arikinui Dame Te Atairangikaahu. The Ngaruawahia Regatta is held here every March. About 300m east of SH1, beside the river on River Rd, is the impressive **Turangawaewae Marae**.

If you're fit, the top of Taupiri Mountain has excellent views (a sign on the track explains the appropriate etiquette near graves), and the **Hakarimata Walkway** on the opposite side of the river also has good views. The northern end leads off Parker Rd, which can be reached by crossing the river at Huntly and following the Ngaruawahia–Huntly West Road. The southern end meets the Ngaruawahia–Waingaro Road just out of Ngaruawahia. To walk the length of the track takes seven hours.

A shorter walk, and easier to get to if you have no transport, is the three-hour return trek from Brownlee Ave, Ngaruawahia, to Hakarimata Trig (371m). The top part of this is fairly steep but the view is rewarding. Tracks from each access point meet at the trig.

If you detour west, off SH22, you'll find **Nikau Cave**, where you can see glow-worms, limestone formations and subterranean streams. The cave lies beneath a farm and the farm owners will happily take you on tours (1½ hours; $20/10/60 for adults/children/family). Hats and torches are supplied, just bring sturdy shoes with a decent tread (trainers are OK). Nikau Cave (☎ 09-233 3199 to book) is at 1779 Waikaretu Rd, RD5 Tuakau.

HAMILTON
pop 132,100

New Zealand's largest inland city, Hamilton is 129km south of Auckland. Built on the banks of the Waikato River, it is the Waikato region's major centre and in the past few decades has undergone spectacular growth.

Archaeological evidence shows that the Maori had long been settled around the Hamilton area but, when the Europeans arrived, the site was deserted. European settlement was initiated by the 4th Regiment of the Waikato Militia, who were persuaded to enlist with promises of an acre (less than half a hectare) in town and another 50 in the country. The advance party, led by Captain William Steele, travelled up the Waikato River on a barge drawn by a gunboat and on 24 August 1864 went ashore at the deserted Maori village of Kirikirioa. The township built on that site was named after John Fane

DAVID WALL

THE CENTRAL WEST

Carved *tekoteko* and *taurapa* at the stern of a Maori canoe – Ngaruawahia Regatta

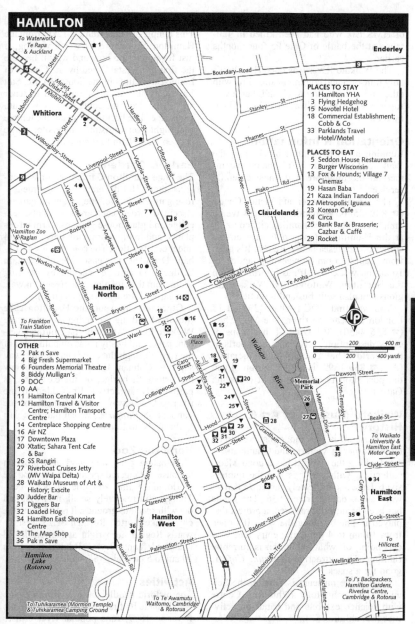

HAMILTON

To Waterworld
Te Rapa
& Auckland

Enderley

Boundary Road

Whitiora

Claudelands

Hamilton
North

Hamilton
West

Hamilton
East

Hamilton
Lake
(Rotoroa)

PLACES TO STAY
1 Hamilton YHA
3 Flying Hedgehog
15 Novotel Hotel
18 Commercial Establishment;
  Cobb & Co
33 Parklands Travel
  Hotel/Motel

PLACES TO EAT
5 Seddon House Restaurant
7 Burger Wisconsin
13 Fox & Hounds; Village 7
  Cinemas
19 Hasan Baba
21 Kaza Indian Tandoori
22 Metropolis; Iguana
23 Korean Cafe
24 Circa
25 Bank Bar & Brasserie;
  Cazbar & Caffé
29 Rocket

OTHER
2 Pak n Save
4 Big Fresh Supermarket
6 Founders Memorial Theatre
8 Biddy Mulligan's
9 DOC
10 AA
11 Hamilton Central Kmart
12 Hamilton Travel & Visitor
  Centre; Hamilton Transport
  Centre
14 Centreplace Shopping Centre
16 Air NZ
17 Downtown Plaza
20 Xtatic; Sahara Tent Cafe
  & Bar
26 SS Rangiri
27 Riverboat Cruises Jetty
  (MV Waipa Delta)
28 Waikato Museum of Art &
  History; Exscite
30 Judder Bar
31 Diggers Bar
32 Loaded Hog
34 Hamilton East Shopping
  Centre
35 The Map Shop
36 Pak n Save

To Frankton
Train Station

To Hamilton Zoo
& Raglan

Garden
Place

Waikato
River

Memorial
Park

To Waikato
University &
Hamilton East
Motor Camp

To Hillcrest

To J's Backpackers,
Hamilton Gardens,
Riverlea Centre,
Cambridge & Rotorua

To Tuhikaramea (Mormon Temple)
& Tuhikaramea Camping Ground

To Te Awamutu
Waitomo, Cambridge
& Rotorua

0   200   400 m
0   200   400 yards

THE CENTRAL WEST

Charles Hamilton, the popular commander of HMS *Esk* who had been killed in Tauranga at the battle of Gate Pa four months earlier.

The Waikato River was once Hamilton's only transport and communication link with other towns including Auckland, but it was superseded by the railway in 1878 and later by roads.

Orientation & Information

Running north to south a block from the Waikato River, Victoria St is the main commercial thoroughfare with most essential services.

The Hamilton Travel and Visitor Centre (☎ 839 3580, @ hamiltoninfo@wave.co .nz), Web site: www.hamiltoncity.co.nz, is at the Hamilton Transport Centre on the corner of Anglesea and Ward Sts. It's open from 9 am to 5 pm on weekdays and from 10 am on weekends. It has information on the Hamilton, Waitomo and Waikato regions and also sells bus and train tickets.

You will find DOC (☎ 839 1393) at 18 London St near the river. The Map Shop (☎ 856 4450), 361 Grey St, has maps of every description on NZ and most parts of the world. The Automobile Association (AA; ☎ 839 1397) is at 295 Barton St and the post shop is on Victoria St (opposite Garden Place).

Waikato Museum of Art & History

This museum is in a modernistic building on the corner of Victoria and Grantham Sts overlooking the river. It has a good Maori collection, with carvings and the impressively large and intricately carved *Te Winika* war canoe, dating from 1836. The canoe has been beautifully restored, a project displayed in photos along the wall. It's open from 10 am to 4 pm daily; entry fees vary depending on what exhibition is currently running. The attractive *Museum Cafe* is good for a snack.

Also at the museum is **Exscite**, the Science and Technology Exhibition Centre with science exhibits and hands-on activities ($5, children $3).

Mormon Temple

This temple at Tuhikaramea, 12km from the Hamilton city centre, is worth visiting, if just for pondering how and why it became the first to be established by the Church of Latter-Day Saints in the South Pacific. Salt Lake City, USA, is far removed in tenor and texture from the contemporary Waikato landscape. The best time to visit the temple is at night over Christmas; its visitor centre is open from 9 am to 9 pm daily.

Parks & Gardens

The huge **Hamilton Gardens** complex contains about 100 different theme gardens – rose gardens, a riverside magnolia garden, a scented garden, cacti and succulents, vegetable and glasshouse gardens, carnivorous plants, and many more, with new ones still under construction. The complex is on Cobham Drive on the east side of Cobham Bridge, and can be reached by walking south from the city along the river walkway. The gardens are always open (free).

Other relaxing spots are **Hamilton Lake (Rotoroa)** and the green domains along the **Waikato River**. Walkways pass through verdant parks and bushy areas on both sides of the river through the city centre all the way south to Cobham Bridge. The area below the Bridge St bridge, on the east bank, is particularly attractive. Embedded in the riverbank walkway are the remains of the gunboat SS *Rangiriri*, which played a part in the Waikato Land War.

Hamilton Zoo

More-natural pens, walkways and a program to house endangered species from around the world make this zoo one of NZ's best. Though still relatively small, it is well laid out with spacious grounds. It is 8km from the city – take Norton Rd then SH23 west towards Raglan, turn right at Newcastle Rd and then left onto Brymer Rd. It is open from 10 am to 5 pm daily ($7, children $3.50).

Activities

The historic paddleboat MV *Waipa Delta,* which made its first voyage on the Waikato River in 1877, runs popular river cruises from Memorial Park, on the riverbank opposite the town centre. Cruises range from afternoon tea ($20) to dinner cruises ($45, children $22.50). Reservations are recommended (☎ 0800-472 335).

The visitor centre supplies a free map of the walkways around the lake, along the river and down to Hamilton Gardens. Information on other walks in and around Hamilton can be obtained from DOC.

Waterworld Te Rapa (☎ 849 4389) on Garnett Ave in Te Rapa, 4km north of the centre, is a large place with several indoor and outdoor pools and waterslides.

Skivys Tours (☎ 856 2005) has good half-day tours of Hamilton ($30 includes admissions) and day tours to Waitomo ($85, includes lunch and admissions).

Places to Stay

Camping & Cabins Hamilton has a couple of camping grounds on the eastern side of the river, 2km or 3km from the city centre. The *Municipal Motor Camp* (☎ 855 8255) on Ruakura Rd in Claudelands, 2km east, has tent/powered sites for $14/17 for two, standard cabins at $24 and family/tourist cabins at $34/42.

The *Hamilton East Motor Camp* (☎ 856 6220) on Cameron Rd, 3km east, has tent/powered sites at $14/17 for two and cabins from $30 for two.

Backpackers The *Flying Hedgehog* (☎/fax 839 3906, 8 Liverpool St) is a large two-storey house with bright rooms for $17 in the dorms, and $19 per person for doubles and twins. It even boasts a petanque court in the landscaped garden. It provides a good, simple, free city map.

The plain *Hamilton YHA* (☎ 838 0009, 1190 Victoria St) is beside the river a few blocks north of the centre, a pleasant 15-minute walk along the river. It charges $15/18 in dorms/doubles.

About 1.5km south of the Hamilton East shops is *J's Backpackers* (☎ 0800-800 2818, ✉ admin@jsbackpackers.co.nz, 8 Grey St). This cosy hostel in a suburban house has dorm beds for $17 or twins for $20 per person.

Farmstays, Homestays & B&Bs The visitor centre lists farmstays, homestays and B&Bs in the Waikato region.

Motels There are many motels, particularly along Ulster St, the main road from the north.

They include the *Aquarius Motor Inn* (☎ 839 2447, 230 Ulster St), which has units starting at $90 for two, *Chloe's Motor Inn* (☎ 839 3410, 181 Ulster St), which has units from $79, and the *Cedar Lodge* (☎ 839 5569, 174 Ulster St), which has units from $65 for two.

Hotels The *Parklands Travel Hotel/Motel* (☎ 838 2461, 24 Bridge St), just across the river, has hotel rooms at $25 a single or $50 a double with bathroom. The motel has studio units from $67 a double with kitchen. Backpacker singles cost $18.

Right in the city centre on Victoria St near the corner of Collingwood St, the *Commercial Establishment* (☎ 839 4993) has private-facility rooms at $79/89 for a twin/double as well as shared-facility rooms at $44/55 for singles/doubles.

One of the newest hotels in Hamilton is the *Novotel* (☎ 838 1366, 7 Alma St), which has 176 rooms and a health club; it's fairly expensive (from $156 a double), but specials often apply.

Places to Eat

Restaurants & Cafes Hamilton has plenty of good places to eat, with a wealth of choice along Victoria St. Here you'll find that *Kaza Indian Tandoori* has a good range, plus lunch specials from $10. Opposite, *Hasan Baba* has Turkish, Greek and Middle Eastern food.

The *Sahara Tent Cafe & Bar (254 Victoria St)* is a real surprise – it is not really 'Saharan' but you could be forgiven for thinking that you had just drifted into a backstreet place in Istanbul.

The excellent *Metropolis* with its distinctive black-and-white tiled entrance, artwork and upstairs dining area, is a good place for a glass of wine with your pasta or whatever.

Iguana has a classy, spacious dining area and specialises in gourmet pizzas. Further along is the cafe *Circa*, with espressos and food, and the *Bank Bar and Brasserie*, a pleasant spot for a drink and reasonably priced food. Heading round the corner into Hood St you'll find the retro cafe *Rocket*.

The *Korean Cafe* on Collingwood St serves an unusual mix of cheap Mexican snacks and Korean food.

Pub Food There's a popular *Cobb & Co* in the Commercial Establishment on the corner of Victoria and Collingwood Sts. The friendly, English-style *Fox & Hounds* on Ward St does pub lunches and ploughman's platters.

Food Halls The modern Centreplace shopping centre is good for a quick and cheap meal. On the ground floor is an *international food hall* with a variety of cuisines, including Italian, Chinese and Singaporean. The Downtown Plaza also has a busy *food hall* with a variety of foods.

Entertainment

Music, Dancing & Pubs Hamilton has plenty of lively nightspots on weekends. Most have DJs and a few have bands.

Down on Hood St, the *Bank* is a trendy bar in a renovated historic building and is always a popular place for a drink. The dance floor gets active.

Next door, the *Outback Inn* is popular with students and also has a lounge dance floor. Opposite is the *Judder Bar* (a familiar name if you've been in Auckland, where there are two), the *Diggers Bar* which has Mac's Ales on tap and occasional bands, and the *Loaded Hog*.

Biddy Mulligan's (742 Victoria St) is an Irish pub and one of the town's most popular places. Live bands play regularly.

The *Cazbar & Caffé* in Market Place on Hood St is another pleasant spot to enjoy a meal with a drink (before its metamorphosis into a late-night venue). *Xtatic* on Victoria St has techno.

The *Fox & Hounds* on Ward St is a popular English-style pub with 27 varieties of imported beer, as well as Newcastle Brown, Guinness and cider on tap. It has live entertainment on Thursday and Saturday nights.

The ubiquitous and popular drinking venue *Loaded Hog* can be found at 27 Hood St.

Cinema & Theatre The *Village 7 Showcase*, upstairs on Ward St, has 10 movie theatres showing latest releases.

Live theatre venues in the city include the *Founders Memorial Theatre (☎ 838 6600)* on Tristram St, and the *Riverlea Centre (☎ 856 5450)* on Riverlea Rd off Cambridge Rd.

Getting There & Away

Air Air New Zealand (☎ 839 9835), 33-35 Ward St near Victoria St, has direct flights to Auckland, Christchurch, Dunedin, Palmerston North and Wellington, with onward connections. Origin Pacific (☎ 0800-302 302) has direct flights from Hamilton to Auckland and Nelson with connections to Wellington, Christchurch and other cities. Freedom Air (see the Getting There & Away chapter) flies from Hamilton to Australia.

Bus All local and long-distance buses arrive at and depart from the Hamilton Transport Centre on the corner of Anglesea and Ward Sts. InterCity (☎ 834 3457) and Newmans (☎ 838 3114) are both represented.

Frequent buses make the connection between Hamilton and Auckland and Hamilton and Rotorua. Buses also leave for Thames, Tauranga, Whakatane, Opotiki, Gisborne, Rotorua, Taupo, New Plymouth and Wellington. The Little Kiwi Bus Co (☎ 0800-759 999) runs between Hamilton and Auckland.

A number of local bus operators run regular services to nearby towns including Raglan, Huntly, Te Awamutu, Morrinsville, Te Aroha and Thames. Kiwi Experience and Magic Bus stop at Hamilton.

Train Hamilton is on the main rail line and all trains between Auckland and Wellington, Rotorua and Tauranga stop at Hamilton's Frankton train station on Queens Ave, west of the city centre. Tickets can be bought at the Frankton train station, or conveniently at the Hamilton Transport Centre or the visitor centre.

Hitching Hamilton is spread out and it's a long walk to good hitching spots in any direction on the outskirts of town.

Heading south to Waitomo or New Plymouth, catch a Glenview bus to the outskirts. For hitching to Rotorua, Taupo, Tauranga or Wellington, catch a Hillcrest bus and get off by the Hillcrest School. Hitching north to Auckland is easiest if you take a Huntly bus to the outskirts.

Getting Around
To/From the Airport Hamilton Airport is surrounded by farmland, 12km south of the city. The Airport Shuttle (☎ 847 5618) offers a door-to-door service to/from the airport for $7 per person (the more people, the less the amount per person).

Bus Hamilton's city bus system operates on weekdays with a limited service on Saturday; services start around 7 am and finish around 5.45 pm (until 8.45 pm on Friday). All local buses arrive at and depart from the Hamilton Transport Centre.

For information and timetables of local city bus routes and local buses travelling further afield (to Huntly, Te Aroha, Thames, Raglan – see Getting There & Away in the Raglan section) consult the Hamilton Transport Centre or the visitor centre. For bus information, ring the Hamilton Travel and Visitor Centre (☎ 839 3580) or Busline (☎ 856 4579).

Car The many car rental agencies include:

Waikato Car Rentals (☎ 856 9908)
Rent-a-Dent (☎ 839 1049)
Cambridge Car Rentals (☎ 0800 278 333)

WAINGARO HOT SPRINGS
A popular day trip from Hamilton, Waingaro Hot Springs has three thermal mineral pools, private spa pools, giant waterslides, children's play areas and bar-

becues. The complex is open from 9.30 am to 9.45 pm daily ($6, children $3).

You can stay nearby in the *Waingaro Hot Springs Motel & Caravan Park* (☎ 825 4761). Camp sites with power cost from $24 for two, on-site vans are $44 for two and motel units are $80. To get there, turn west at Ngaruawahia, 19km north of Hamilton, and travel for 23km; it is clearly signposted.

RAGLAN
pop 2700
On the coast 48km west of Hamilton, Raglan is Hamilton's closest and most popular beach. Raglan is world famous for its surfing, attracting top surfers from around the world to Manu Bay and Whale Bay, especially in summer when surfing competitions are held. It is named after Lord Raglan, a British officer who 'wiped out' seriously at the Charge of the Light Brigade.

Relaxed little Raglan, with its art and craft shops and cafes, lies on a beautiful sheltered harbour, good for windsurfing, boating and swimming. The famous black-sand surfing beaches are west of town.

There is a small, interesting **museum** on Wainui Rd; inquire at the information centre for opening times.

Information
The Raglan Information Centre (☎ 825 0556) on Bow St is open from 10 am to 4 pm daily, usually closing for an hour at lunch.

Beaches
The beach at the **Kopua Recreational Reserve** near the camping ground, a five-minute walk over the footbridge from town, is a safe, calm estuary beach popular with families. On the other side of the tiny peninsula is a popular windsurfing beach, reached via the camping ground (a $2 day-use fee is charged).

Other sheltered inner-harbour beaches close to town include **Cox's Bay**, reached by a walkway from Government Rd or from Bayview Rd, and **Puriri Park**, towards the end of Wallis St, a safe swimming spot at high tide.

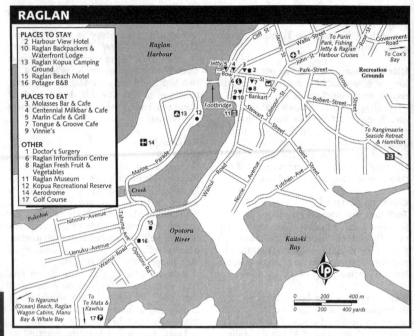

RAGLAN

PLACES TO STAY
2 Harbour View Hotel
10 Raglan Backpackers &
   Waterfront Lodge
13 Raglan Kopua Camping
   Ground
15 Raglan Beach Motel
16 Potager B&B

PLACES TO EAT
3 Molasses Bar & Cafe
4 Centennial Milkbar & Cafe
5 Marlin Cafe & Grill
7 Tongue & Groove Cafe
9 Vinnie's

OTHER
1 Doctor's Surgery
6 Raglan Information Centre
8 Raglan Fresh Fruit &
   Vegetables
11 Raglan Museum
12 Kopua Recreational Reserve
14 Aerodrome
17 Golf Course

*Raglan
Harbour*

To Puriri
Park, Fishing
Jetty & Raglan
Harbour Cruises

Government
Road

To Cox's
Bay

Cliff St

Wallis Street

James St

Rose St

Jetty
Bow

John St

Park Street

Recreation
Grounds

Footbridge

Bankart

Stewart Street

Gilmour St

Cross Street

Robert Street

Street

To Rangimaarie
Seaside Retreat
& Hamilton

Marine Parade

Creek

Wainui Road

Norrie Avenue

Point Street

Tutchen Ave

23

Pokohui

Nihinihi Avenue

Lahuna Ave

Opotoru Rd

Uenuku Avenue

Wainui Road

*Opotoru
River*

*Kaitoki
Bay*

To Ngarunui
(Ocean) Beach, Raglan
Wagon Cabins, Manu
Bay & Whale Bay

To
Te Mata &
Kawhia

17

0   200   400 m
0   200   400 yards

THE CENTRAL WEST

Ngarunui (Ocean) Beach, about 5km west of town, is a popular surf swimming beach. Swim on the left side, away from the riptides, where lifeguards are posted in summer.

Manu Bay, 8km west of Raglan, is a world-famous surfing beach, said to have the longest left-hand break in the world. Featured in the 1966 cult surfing film *Endless Summer*, this beach was where a surfer rode a wave for 10 minutes. The very long, uniform waves at Manu Bay are created by the angle at which the ocean swell from the Tasman Sea meets the coastline. Whale Bay, a couple of kilometres further west, is another excellent surfing spot. There are some tattooed rock faces nearby; they are difficult to find so ask for directions.

Ruapuke Beach, a rugged stretch of coastline still further past Whale Bay, is good for surfcasting but not so good for swimming, due to treacherous crosscurrents; it can be reached from Ruapuke Rd.

Activities

It's always pleasant to walk down to the fishing jetty around sunset and meet the trawlers returning from the day's fishing. A few locals are often hanging around to inspect the day's catch. The jetty is four blocks east of the town centre along Wallis St.

Midway between Hamilton and Raglan, the Karamu Walkway goes through the Four Brothers Scenic Reserve. Other walking possibilities are in Pirongia Forest Park, south of Raglan.

Raglan Harbour Cruises (☎ 825 0300) has 1½-hour cruises in summer for $15 (children $7.50). It also arranges fishing charters. The information centre can give information on canoeing and mountain-biking possibilities.

Places to Stay

Camping, Cabins & Hostels The beachside *Raglan Kopua Holiday Park (☎ 825 8283)* is on a sheltered, sandy inner-harbour beach across the estuary from town, popular for swimming and windsurfing. It has tent sites at $8 per person, caravan sites for $9 per person, cabins at $40 and tourist flats at $50 a double.

Raglan Wagon Cabins (☎ *825 8268)* on Wainui Rd is 6km west of Raglan, on a hill with magnificent views of the coast. Comfortable cabins, imaginatively constructed from restored railway carriages, cost $20 per person. Self-contained units cost $80 a double and tent sites are $9 per person. There's a kitchen and TV lounge. The friendly owner has a video copy of *Endless Summer*.

The *Raglan Backpackers & Waterfront Lodge* (☎ *825 0515, 6 Nero St)* is on the edge of the water and has fine views. This purpose-built hostel, with its central outdoor recreation area, provides excellent standards for $14 in dorms or $16 per person in doubles and twins (prices inclusive of linen). Kayaks are free for guests.

B&Bs, Motels & Hotels The *Potager B&B* (☎ *825 8722, 78 Wainui Rd)* has comfortable singles/doubles for $30/55. About five minutes' drive from town, the *Rangimaarie Seaside Retreat* (☎ *825 7567)* on Greenslade Rd charges $45/68 a single/double and $78 for two people in the self-contained flat.

The *Harbour View Hotel* (☎ *825 8010)* on Bow St has rooms at $35/50.

Across the bridge on the west side of town, the peaceful *Raglan Beach Motel* (☎ *825 8153, 50 Wainui Rd)* is right on the shore of the estuary, with rooms from $70 for two.

Places to Eat

Vinnie's on Wainui Rd serves great pizzas as well as kumara chips, tacos, steaks and much more. Also on Wainui Rd, on the corner of Bow St, is the excellent *Tongue & Groove Cafe* which serves soups, salads, panini, pasta, burgers, wedges and other scrumptious fare.

The *Molasses Bar & Cafe* on Bow St is also good for coffee, snacks and light meals. The *Centennial Milkbar & Cafe*, near the corner of Cliff St, has all-day

breakfasts, *kai moana* (seafood) and burgers. All these places have occasional live music.

The Harbour View Hotel on Bow St has the *Verandabah* serving snacks, drinks and light meals with dining inside or outside. It also has bands – the well-known blues musician Midge Marsden and his band are regulars.

Getting There & Away

Pavlovich Coachlines (☎ 847 5545) operates a return service to Hamilton four times daily on weekdays; the cost is $5 (children $3) one way. It departs from the Raglan Information Centre.

RAGLAN TO KAWHIA

The back roads between Raglan and Kawhia, 55km south on the coast, are slow and winding, but scenic, enjoyable and off the beaten track. The gravel roads take at least 1½ hours of driving time, not counting stops. Traffic is light.

There are two routes between Raglan and Kawhia. From Raglan you can head west along the coast, out past Ngarunui Beach, Manu Bay and Whale Bay, and keep following the coast road until it turns inland and meets the interior road at Te Mata, 20km south of Raglan. Along the way is the *Ruapuke Motor Camp* near the beach at Ruapuke. Alternatively, from Raglan head towards Hamilton and take the signposted Te Mata–Kawhia turn-off.

Near Te Mata, 20km south of Raglan, are the **Bridal Veil Falls**. From the car park it's an easy 10-minute walk through native bush to the top of the falls, with a further 10-minute walk leading down to the pool at the bottom, where it's possible to swim.

Magic Mountain Farmstay (☎ *825 6892)* is a sheep and cattle farm, high on a hill with stunning views. B&B in a self-contained house costs $80 for two. The farm is at the end of Houchen Rd, 4km off the main road just north of Te Mata.

About 12km south-west of Raglan is **Mt Karioi**. You can take a good round-the-mountain drive, over mostly gravel roads, in a couple of hours from Raglan. Along this

The *Tainui* Canoe

Though it's only a small town, Kawhia has an illustrious history. It was here that the *Tainui* canoe – one of the ancestral canoes that arrived here in the 14th century from Hawaiki, the Maori homeland – made its final landing.

Before the *Tainui* canoe departed from Hawaiki, the priests there prophesied that the departing canoe would eventually come to a favourable place where its people would make a new home, have a good life and prosper. The priests told the leaders of the *Tainui* canoe which landmarks to look for so they would know they had arrived at the new home they were destined to find.

The *Tainui* canoe left Hawaiki, stopping at Rarotonga in the Cook Islands as it crossed the Pacific. It landed in NZ at Maketu in the Bay of Plenty, accompanied by the *Arawa* canoe. The *Arawa* canoe stopped there, its people becoming the Arawa people, a large Maori tribe that still lives in the Bay of Plenty and Rotorua areas today.

The leaders of the *Tainui* canoe – Hoturoa, the captain, and Rakataura, the *tohunga* or high priest – knew that the *Tainui's* home was destined to be on the west coast. So they continued on, seeking a way to get to the west coast. They finally dragged their canoe overland at Manukau Harbour, near Auckland. Setting off southwards in search of the prophesied landmarks, they journeyed all the way to the South Island. They turned around and came north again, still searching, and finally recognised their prophesied new home at Kawhia Harbour.

When they landed the canoe, they tied it to a pohutukawa tree on the shore, naming the tree Tangi te Korowhiti. Though the tree is not marked, it still grows with a few other pohutukawa trees on the shoreline between Kawhia town and the Maketu Marae; you can easily see them. At the end of its long voyage, the *Tainui* canoe was dragged up onto a hill and buried. Hoturoa and Rakataura placed sacred stones at either end to mark its resting place. Hani, on higher ground, is the stone marking the bow of the canoe, and Puna, the lower stone, marks the stern. You can walk up behind the marae and see the stones behind a wooden fence.

The prophecy that this canoe would be a good home for the long-journeying Tainui people did come true. Kawhia Harbour was abundant with shellfish, fish and food. Today the Tainui tribes extend over the entire Waikato region, over the Coromandel Peninsula, north to Auckland and south to Lake Taupo and south past Mokau on the coast. Kawhia, the Maketu Marae and the burial place of the *Tainui* canoe are supremely sacred to all the Tainui people.

Another point of historical significance for Kawhia is that it was once the home of Te Rauparaha, the great warrior of the Ngati Toa tribe. When pushed out of Kawhia by warring Waikato tribes in 1821, Te Rauparaha moved southwards, making his base on Kapiti Island off the west coast near Wellington, from there making raids all the way down to the South Island. For more on Te Rauparaha, see Kapiti Coast in the Wellington chapter and also the boxed text 'Haka' in the 'Maori Culture & Arts' special section.

route **Te Toto Track**, starting from Te Toto car park on Whaanga Rd (the coast road) on the western side of Mt Karioi, is strenuous but scenic, ascending steeply to a lookout point (two hours) followed by an easier stretch up to Karioi summit (one hour). From the east side of the mountain, the **Wairake Track** is a steeper two-hour climb to the summit and meets the Te Toto Track.

Mt Karioi is in one part of the Pirongia Forest Park; a much larger part lies within the triangle formed by the towns of Raglan, Kawhia and Te Awamutu, with the 959m summit of **Mt Pirongia** clearly visible from much of the Waikato region. Tracks going through the forest park lead to the summit of Mt Pirongia – the mountain is usually climbed from Corcoran Rd on the Hamilton side. There's a hut near the summit if you want to spend the night. Maps and information about Pirongia Forest Park are available from DOC in Hamilton. The township of **Pirongia** is 32km south-west of Hamilton.

You can go horse riding on the slopes of the mountain with Mt Pirongia Horse Treks (☎ 07-871 9960) – a one-hour ride is $20.

KAWHIA
pop 670

Kawhia is a sleepy, crumbling little port on Kawhia Harbour. The harbour is large, with many extensions, but its entrance is narrow – the occupants of the *Tainui* canoe missed it on their first trip down the coast in the 14th century and Captain Cook also missed it when he sailed past in 1770, naming Albatross Point on the southern side of the harbour but failing to note the harbour itself.

Today Kawhia (pronounced 'kar-fee-a') is still easy to miss, though it gets a few fishing enthusiasts and bathers during summer.

Things to See & Do

The **Kawhia Museum** (☎ 870 0161) is in the historic former Kawhia County Building right near the wharf. It has interesting exhibits as well as pamphlets and information on the town. The museum is open from noon to 4 pm Saturday and Sunday (free).

From the museum and the wharf, a pleasant **walk** extends along the coast to the **Maketu Marae** with its impressively carved meeting house, Auaukiterangi. Through the marae grounds and behind the wooden fence, two stones, Hani and Puna, mark the burial place of the *Tainui*. You need permission from a Maori elder to visit this marae.

Three kilometres behind the town and through the Tainui Kawhia Pine Forest is windswept **Ocean Beach** and its black dunes; swimming can be dangerous. Two hours either side of low tide you can find the **Puia Hot Springs** in the sands – just dig a hole for your own little natural spa. It is a lot less crowded than Hot Water Beach near Hahei on the Coromandel. There's a driveable track over the dunes.

Places to Stay & Eat

Kawhia's camping grounds fill up at busy periods in summer, so plan ahead. The *Forest View Motor Camp* (☎ 871 0858) on Waiwera St has tent sites, van sites and cabins, as does the *Beachside Motor Camp* (☎ 871 0727) on the beachfront. The *Kawhia Motor Camp* (☎ 871 0863) on Moke St is smaller and simpler, with just tent and van sites.

The *Kawhia Motel* (☎ 871 0865) is a friendly place on the corner of Jervois and Tainui Sts; units cost $57/67 for singles/doubles. Historic *Rosamond House* (☎ 871 0681) on Rosamond Terrace has B&B for $40/60.

Kawhia has a general store, a *pub*, a *fish and chip shop* and *Annie's Cafe & Restaurant* – which is next door to the *Wee Knot Inn* watering hole.

Getting There & Away

Kawhia Bus & Freight (☎ 871 0701) takes passengers on the freight run to Te Awamutu daily except Sunday.

The 50-minute drive to Kawhia from Te Awamutu or Otorohanga is a scenic route offering fine views of the harbour. Along the way is Te Kauri Park Nature Reserve, with a one-hour walk from the road to a kauri grove – the harbour probably marks the southernmost 'boundary' of where kauri grow naturally.

You can drive or cycle down the mostly unsealed coastal back roads all the way from Raglan in the north to Awakino and Mokau in the south, finally coming to New Plymouth (or vice versa). It's slow going but scenic.

TE AWAMUTU
pop 9340

Te Awamutu is a service town for the local dairy-farming community. It is noted for its rose gardens, hence its title 'the Rose Town of New Zealand'. Brothers Tim and Neil Finn of the popular band Split Enz (and later of Crowded House) came from here (see the boxed text 'A Blind Date with Destiny').

Te Awamutu was an important site in the Waikato Land War – you can still see the flat-topped hill where there was a fort. After the war, it became a frontier town. The name Te Awamutu means 'The River Cut Short', since the river above this point was unsuitable for canoes.

THE CENTRAL WEST

Te Awamutu Information Centre (☎ 871 3259, ✉ ta.info@xtra.co.nz) on the corner of Gorst Ave and SH3, opposite the Rose Garden, is open from 9 am to 4.30 pm on weekdays and 10 am to 3 pm on weekends.

Things to See & Do

Te Awamutu Rose Garden has over 2000 rosebushes. The garden is on the main road, opposite the information centre. The roses are at their best from November to April; a rose show is held every November.

Beginning behind the Rose Garden, the Pioneer Walk goes beside the river for about 1.5km to Memorial Park and the **Aotearoa Centre**, where there's a Maori carving and weaving institute.

Te Awamutu Museum in the Civic Centre on Roche St houses a fine collection of Maori *taonga* (treasures), the centrepiece of which is Uenuku, a totara carving that once housed a tribal god said to have been brought to NZ on the *Tainui* canoe from Hawaiki. It's open from 10 am to 4 pm (weekends to 1 pm) and entry is free. There is now a small exhibit of Finn brothers memorabilia.

On Thursdays from around 10 am to 3 pm, farm animals are auctioned off at the **Te Awamutu Sale**, held at the saleyard on Gorst Ave, near the information centre. Check the local paper or with the information centre for dates. Urban visitors find this rural event fascinating.

The **Wharepapa Rock Climbing Field**, with over 50 rock climbs ranging from beginner to advanced, is 22km south-east of Te Awamutu.

Places to Stay & Eat

The *Road Runner Motel & Holiday Park* (☎ *871 7420, 141 Bond Rd*) has tent and powered sites for $9 per person and cabins for $35 for two.

The *Farmstay Foxhill* (☎ *870 2266, 106 Herbert St, Kihikihi*) has singles/doubles for $30/60 – the owners speak German, English and French.

Te Awamutu's newest motel is the *Albert Park Motor Lodge* (☎ *870 2995, 299 Albert Park Drive*), which has double rooms with spa baths and two wheelchair-accessible units. Prices start at $85 for two.

Rosetown Motel (☎ *871 5779, 844 Kihikihi Rd*) has rooms from $72 for two.

Te Awamutu has a selection of eateries on Alexandra St, the town's main commercial street. Next to the Woolworths supermarket is *Daddio's Take-n-bake* which has pizza and Mexican. Across the road are *KFC* and *Ruang Thai*. The *Gold Star* has Chinese food.

A popular place for good, cheap grills is the *Rose & Thorn (32 Arawata St)*. Nearby,

Members of the Te Awamutu cavalry volunteers on horseback at the opening of the main trunk railway at Puniu (DM Beere, 1885) – this image has been cropped.

at No 39, is the ***Robert Harris Coffee Shop***, open daily.

One of the newest culinary additions in town is ***The Redoubt Bar & Eatery*** on the corner of Rewi and College Sts.

Getting There & Away

Buses and trains between Auckland and Wellington stop at Te Awamutu. There are local buses between Te Awamutu and Hamilton.

CAMBRIDGE

pop 11,300

On the Waikato River 20km south-east of Hamilton, Cambridge is a small, peaceful town with a charming rural English atmosphere. Cricket is played on the village green in the centre of town and the avenues are lined with broad, shady European trees, at their best in autumn. The Cambridge region is famous for the breeding and training of thoroughbred horses. One well-known Cambridge-bred horse is Charisma, winner of the Olympic three-day event in both 1984 and 1988, ridden by New Zealander Mark Todd.

Information

The Cambridge Visitors Centre (☎ 823 3456) on the corner of Victoria and Queen Sts is open from 9 am to 4 pm weekdays and 10 am to 4 pm weekends. Get the free *Cambridge Welcomes You* and *Cambridge and Heritage Tree Trails* pamphlets.

Things to See

Cambridge has a number of arts and crafts and antiques shops, adding to the town's twee atmosphere. Best known is the award-winning **Cambridge Country Store**, in an old church on SH1.

Another old church worth seeing, also on SH1, is the 100-year-old **St Andrew's Anglican Church**, a white church with a beautiful wooden interior, fine stained-glass windows and a high steeple sheathed in copper. The outside is beautiful but it's still a surprise to see the beauty of the interior.

The **Cambridge Museum**, occupying the former Cambridge Courthouse building

'A Blind Date with Destiny'

Fans of Split Enz or Crowded House, NZ's two most famous pop music exports, can trace the early lives of the bands' best-known members – the Finn brothers, Neil and Tim. They allude to their beginnings in this humble NZ town in songs such as Crowded House's *Mean to Me* and keen fans of the bands can analyse the brothers' roots by taking a walk through Te Awamutu (the information centre even provides a keyed map!).

Included on the walk is 588 Teasdale St where the brothers lived when they were young; St Patrick's School, which both attended; Te Awamutu College, which Neil attended from Form 4; Martins Electrical Store, where Neil worked (and played piano outside on Friday nights); Craft Shop Pot Pourri (now Trade Aid Shop), where Neil often played guitar; Hammond, Finn & Chaplin, the firm in which their father Dick was a partner (he and his wife now live in Cambridge); and Albert Park, where the brothers performed for the Te Awamutu Centennial in 1984.

(built in 1909) on Victoria St, is open from 10 am to 4 pm Tuesday to Saturday and 2 to 4 pm on Sunday (summer only).

Te Koutu Lake in the centre of town is a peaceful bird sanctuary.

The **Cambridge Thoroughbred Lodge**, ideal for horse lovers, is 3km south of town on SH1. It's a magnificent horse stud that has tours daily except Monday at 10.30 am ($12, children $5). The thoroughbreds are brought out on show with commentaries and there are show-jumping and dressage exhibitions.

Activities

Other attractions in Cambridge include jet-boat rides and canoeing on the Waikato River and walking on tracks along both sides of the river and around Te Koutu Lake.

There are also walks further afield. From SH1 take the turn-off north at Cambridge and after about a five-minute drive you'll

THE CENTRAL WEST

reach the Maungakawa Scenic Reserve, a regenerating forest with some exotic timber species and a fairly easy short bush walk. From the eastern side of Mt Maungakawa, a track suitable for experienced trampers ascends from Tapui Rd; it takes half a day to walk there and back.

Also about a five-minute drive south from town, Mt Maungatautiri is another good walking spot; it takes about 1½ hours to climb to the summit.

Places to Stay

The *Cambridge Motor Camp* (☎ 827 5649, 32 Scott St, Leamington), about 1.5km from town, has tent and powered sites at $9 per person and cabins at $28 for two.

The *Cambridge Country Lodge Backpackers* (☎ 827 8373) is a pleasant hostel in a rural setting on a small farm 100m down Peake Rd, a turn-off from the SH1 1km north of Cambridge. It provides courtesy transport and bicycles. You can do your own cooking, or home-prepared meals are available. It's $16 in dorms, $35 per person for twins and doubles. Self-contained units are $50 for two.

Motels include the *Cambrian Lodge Motel* (☎ 827 7766, 63 Hamilton Rd), which has a variety of units from $70 a double, and the *Mews Motor Inn* (☎ 827 7166, 20 Hamilton Rd), which has 12 studio units and one- and two-bedroom units with spa baths. Prices start at $115 for two.

Cambridge also has good B&Bs and farmstays; the visitor centre has details.

Places to Eat

Cambridge is a popular lunch spot. *The Gallery* (69 Victoria St) has nachos, filo parcels, lamb pie and coffee. A trendy place is the *Alphaz Restaurant & Wine Bar* (72 Alpha St).

For an elegant dinner there is the *Interlude Restaurant* (19 Victoria St). The *All Saints Cafe* (92 Victoria St) is in a former church and is busy and atmospheric.

The *Prince Albert Tavern* in the Victoria Plaza, Halley's Lane (off Duke St), is an old English-style pub with open fires and an outdoor garden area, and serves pub meals.

The *Masonic hotel* (72 Duke St) serves inexpensive meals.

Getting There & Away

Lying on SH1, Cambridge is well connected by bus. Most long-distance buses from Hamilton to Rotorua or the Bay of Plenty stop in Cambridge.

Cambridge Travel Lines (☎ 827 7363) and Cresswell Motors (☎ 827 7789) both have weekday services between Cambridge and the Hamilton Transport Centre.

MATAMATA

pop 7800

This town, 23km north-east of Cambridge and nestled beneath the Kaimai-Mamaku Ranges, is the apotheosis of NZ rural living. It is one of the premier thoroughbred training and breeding centres in the world, producing many great champions.

The information centre (☎ 888 7260, ✉ matvin1@xtra.co.nz), at 45 Broadway, is open from 8.30 am to 5 pm on weekdays and 10 am to 3 pm on weekends. It provides a list of places to stay (especially homestays and farmstays). You can also access the Internet here.

Things to See & Do

Of particular interest in town is the **Firth Tower**, Tower Rd, built in 1882 by Yorkshireman Josiah Clifton Firth. Firth spoke Maori fluently and was respected by the regional Maori leaders with whom he negotiated during the Waikato Land War. He must have had some doubts about his standing, however, as the tower, with its 24-rifle loopholes and 45cm-thick walls, was built long after the war had ended. It's open from 10 am to 4 pm daily ($3, children $0.60).

Opal Hot Springs, 6km from the town centre, has private mineral pools and a public swimming pool. You can tour the **Oraka Wapiti Deer Park** (☎ 883 1382) or learn all about racing pigeons at **Keola Lofts** (☎ 888 1728), 428 Hinuera Rd.

Groups can find out how a real working dairy farm operates at **Longlands** (☎ 888 6588). The information centre has details on parachuting, gliding, jet-boating and the many **walking tracks** through the Kaimai-Mamaku Ranges.

Places to Stay & Eat

A pleasant place to stay, right in town, is the *Southern Belle B&B (☎ 0800-244 233, 101 Firth St)*, built in 1936. There are three guestrooms: single/twins/double for $50/60/70. There's a separate guest lounge and bathroom facilities. Surprisingly, breakfast is extra.

Motels include *Maple Lodge (☎ 888 8764, 11 Mangawhero Rd)* and *Tower Lodge Motel (☎ 0800-656 112)* on Tower Rd.

In town are numerous places to eat including the good *Vault Bar and Restaurant*, in a stately former bank building. You can get steaks, seafood, soups and so on.

KARAPIRO

Karapiro, the furthest downstream of a chain of hydroelectric power stations and dams on the Waikato River, is 28km southeast of Hamilton, 8km past Cambridge, just off SH1. The side road passes over the dam and the lake is popular for aquatic sports.

For camping at the lake, the *Karapiro Lake Domain (☎ 827 4178)* beside the lake has tent sites ($5.50 per person), powered sites ($6.50) and bunkrooms ($7).

The King Country

☎ 07 and 06 • pop 53,000

The King Country is named for the Maori King Movement, which developed in the Waikato region in the late 1850s and early 1860s. When King Tawhiao and his people were forced to move from their Waikato land after the Waikato Land War of 1863 to 1864 against British troops, they came south to this region, which was as yet unaffected by European encroachment. Legend has it that King Tawhiao placed his white top hat, symbol of the kingship, on a large map of NZ and declared that all the land it covered would be under his *mana*, or authority.

The area coincided roughly with the present-day districts of Otorohanga, Waitomo and Taumarunui, extending west to the coast and eastwards as far as Lake Taupo.

For several decades the King Country remained the stronghold of King Tawhiao and other Maori chiefs, who held out against the Europeans longer than other Maori elsewhere in NZ. This area was forbidden to the Europeans by Maori law until the 1880s, and was even then not much penetrated by Europeans until, with the consent of the Maori chiefs, the Auckland-Wellington Main Trunk Railway line entered the region in 1891. The earliest Europeans to settle in Otorohanga were timber millers, the first of them arriving in 1890. The laying of the railway to form a continuous line from Auckland to Wellington in 1908 marked the end of the region's isolation, though even today a powerful Maori influence pervades.

From 1884, when Pakeha were allowed into the district, until 1955, the King Country was 'dry' (alcohol was prohibited). This condition was apparently imposed by Maori chiefs when they agreed to the Europeans building the railway through their country, opening it up even more to the outside world. Needless to say there are now hotels everywhere, so you won't go thirsty.

OTOROHANGA
pop 2590

Otorohanga, in the upper Waipa basin, is on SH3, 59km south of Hamilton and 16km from Waitomo. A dairy and sheep-farming community, it is the northernmost township of the King Country. Otorohanga's only real tourist attraction is its impressive kiwi house.

For rural atmosphere, the local stock and farm auction, the Otorohanga Sale – the biggest in the King Country – is held every Wednesday at the saleyards from around 10 am to 2 pm. The Otorohanga County Fair is held on the second Saturday in February.

The Visitor Information Centre (☎ 07-873 8951, fax 873 8398) on the corner of Maniapoto and Tuhoro Sts is open from 8.30 am to 5.30 pm Monday to Thursday, 9 am to 5.30 pm on Friday and 10 am to 4 pm on weekends. It is also the AA agent, is home to the post shop and sells bus, ferry and train tickets. There is a small museum on Kakamutu Rd.

Otorohanga Kiwi House

'Not another kiwi house,' you may groan – but this one is worth a visit. In a kiwi house night and day are reversed, so you can watch the nocurnal kiwi in daytime under artificial moonlight. There are also various other native birds, including some kea, which more than live up to their reputation for being inquisitive. The walk-in aviary is the largest in NZ. Other birds include morepork owls, hawks and weka. Tuatara are also on display.

The kiwi house is open from 9 am to 5 pm daily. The last entry is half an hour before closing time ($8, children $3).

Places to Stay

The *Otorohanga Kiwitown Caravan Park* (☎ 07-873 8214) is on Domain Drive, adjacent to the kiwi house – you can hear the kiwi calling at night. There's a barbecue area, with free wood; tent sites are $6.50 per person and on-site vans $27.

Also near the kiwi house, *Oto-Kiwi Lodge* (☎ 07-873 6022, @ oto-kiwi@xtra.co .nz, 1 Sangro Crescent) is a well-equipped backpackers. It has four-bed shared rooms at $15 per person, and twins and doubles for $37. It operates day bushwalking trips near Waitomo and fishing trips near Kawhia – these are both $40 – as well as river kayaking trips ($30).

The *Royal Hotel* (☎ 07-873 8129) on Te Kanawa St has singles/doubles at $35/55.

The *Waitomo Colonial & Otorohanga Motels* (☎ 0800-828 289) on Main North Rd about 1km from town has rooms from $65/69.

The visitor information centre keeps a list of B&Bs and farmstays in the area.

Places to Eat

Maniapoto St has many takeaways and coffee shops. The *Regent Cafe & Bar* is a pleasant place open during the day.

Other possibilities include the *Flying Horse Chinese Restaurant* and *Toni's*.

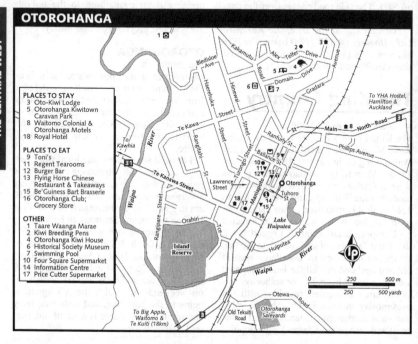

OTOROHANGA

THE CENTRAL WEST

PLACES TO STAY
3   Oto-Kiwi Lodge
5   Otorohanga Kiwitown Caravan Park
8   Waitomo Colonial & Otorohanga Motels
18 Royal Hotel

PLACES TO EAT
9   Toni's
11 Regent Tearooms
12 Burger Bar
13 Flying Horse Chinese Restaurant & Takeaways
15 Be'Guiness Bart Brasserie
16 Otorohanga Club; Grocery Store

OTHER
1   Taare Waanga Marae
2   Kiwi Breeding Pens
4   Otorohanga Kiwi House
6   Historical Society Museum
7   Swimming Pool
10 Four Square Supermarket
14 Information Centre
17 Price Cutter Supermarket

To YHA Hostel, Hamilton & Auckland

To Kawhia

To Big Apple, Waitomo & Te Kuiti (18km)

Old Tekuiti Road

Otorohanga Saleyards

0   250   500 m
0   250   500 yards

One of the best places is the restaurant at the *Otorohanga Club*, which is good value for money. Another option is *Be'Guiness Bar & Brasserie*.

The *Royal Hotel* on Te Kanawa St has bistro meals, a licensed restaurant, a pub and a lounge bar with entertainment on weekends.

The *Big Apple*, a barn-like complex with a large restaurant, is on the highway south of town just before the Waitomo turn-off.

Getting There & Away

InterCity buses arrive at and depart from the visitor information centre, which sells tickets. There are several buses a day in each direction (via Hamilton there are connecting services to Rotorua and Tauranga).

To get to Waitomo, change buses in Otorohanga. The Waitomo Shuttle (☎ 0800-808 279) runs to and from Waitomo for $7; book through the information centre. For more information see Getting There & Away under Waitomo.

The train station is in the centre of town. The day and evening Auckland-Wellington trains stop at Otorohanga.

WAITOMO

Waitomo is famous for its limestone caves, and the whole region is riddled with caves and limestone formations. Tours through the Waitomo Cave (more commonly known as the Glowworm Cave) and the Aranui Cave have been feature attractions for decades and are still one of the North Island's main tourist attractions. Eight kilometres west of SH3, it is a great place to chill out.

Visitors used to stop for an hour or a day, just to see the caves; now there's plenty to do during a longer stay. Waitomo has a host of activities – organised caving expeditions, rafting through caves, abseiling, horse trekking, canoeing and more.

The name Waitomo comes from *wai* (water) and *tomo* (hole or shaft). It's aptly named: dotted throughout the countryside are a number of shafts dropping abruptly through the surface of the ground into underground cave systems.

Information

The information centre, which is located at the Museum of Caves (☎ 07-878 7640, ✉ waitomomuseum@xtra.co.nz), has Internet access and is also a post shop and a booking agent for most activities. It's open from 8.30 am to 5.30 pm daily (until 5 pm in winter from Easter to the end of October, and until around 8 pm in January and February).

Serious cavers can get more information from the Tomo Group Lodge (see Places to Stay).

Groceries are available at the store next to Cavelands Cafe, but the choice is wider at nearby Otorohanga or Te Kuiti.

Waitomo Caves

Glowworm Cave had been known to the local Maori for a long time, but the first European to explore it was English surveyor Fred Mace, who was shown the cave in December 1887 by Maori chief Tane Tinorau. Mace prepared an account of the expedition, a map was made and photographs given to the government, and before long Tane Tinorau was operating tours of the cave.

The Glowworm Cave is just a big cave with the usual assortment of stalactites and stalagmites – until you board a boat and swing off onto the river. As your eyes grow accustomed to the dark you'll see a Milky Way of little lights surrounding you – these are the glowworms. You can see them in other caves and in other places around Waitomo, and in other parts of NZ, but the ones in this cave are something special; conditions for their growth here are just about perfect, so there is a remarkable number of them.

The Glowworm Cave is the most popular cave, crammed with tourists being shuttled through, one tour after the other. The big tour buses peak at around lunchtime; try to go on the first tour of the day.

Aranui Cave is 3km further up the road from the Glowworm Cave. The cave has no river running through it and hence no glowworms. It is a large cave with thousands of tiny, hollow 'straw' stalactites hanging from the ceiling. Various scenes in the formations are pointed out and photography is permitted. Transport to the cave is not included with the tour ticket.

Nearby **Ruakuri Cave** is open only for black-water rafting (see the boxed text 'Waitomo Underground').

Tours & Tickets The Waitomo and Aranui Caves can be visited individually or with a combined ticket. Tickets are sold at the entrance to the Glowworm Cave. Entry to the Glowworm Cave is $20 (children under 13 cost $10), the Aranui Cave costs $20 ($10 for kids) or a combined two-cave ticket is $30 ($15).

The 'museum-cave special' includes the Glowworm Cave tour and the Museum of Caves for $22 ($10).

The 45-minute tours of the Glowworm Cave leave daily on the half-hour from 9 am to 5 pm. From late October to Easter there's also a 5.30 pm tour, with more at the height of the summer season. Aranui Cave tours go at 10 and 11 am, 1, 2 and 3 pm, and also take about 45 minutes.

Museum of Caves
This museum has excellent exhibits about how caves are formed, the flora and fauna that live in them, the history of the caves and cave exploration.

Displays include a cave model, fossils of extinct birds and animals that have been discovered in caves, and a cave crawl for the adventurous. There are also audiovisual presentations about caving, glowworms and the many other natural attractions in the Waitomo area.

It is open from 8.15 am to 5 pm daily (until 5.30 pm in summer). Entry is $4 (children free); free entry is often included with various activities or you can get a 'museum-cave special' (see Tours & Tickets under Waitomo Caves earlier).

Other Attractions
Woodlyn Park (☎ 07-878 6666) is the realisation of a dinkum Kiwi's dream. Barry Woods, ex-shearer, puts on a helluva show, in which he cleverly integrates a history lesson into his inimitable humorous piece of theatre.

It is a New Zealand farm show with a difference, with many introduced, trained animals. A sheepdog, cows, bulls, sheep, pigs (including Trev the Captain Cooker and Sam the kune kune – one of each of NZ's

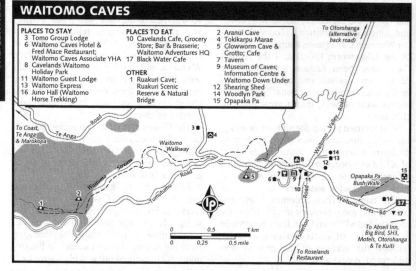

WAITOMO CAVES

PLACES TO STAY
3 Tomo Group Lodge
6 Waitomo Caves Hotel &
   Fred Mace Restaurant;
   Waitomo Caves Associate YHA
8 Cavelands Waitomo
   Holiday Park
11 Waitomo Guest Lodge
13 Waitomo Express
16 Juno Hall (Waitomo
   Horse Trekking)

PLACES TO EAT
10 Cavelands Cafe, Grocery
   Store; Bar & Brasserie;
   Waitomo Adventures HQ
17 Black Water Cafe

OTHER
1 Ruakuri Cave;
   Ruakuri Scenic
   Reserve & Natural
   Bridge

2 Aranui Cave
4 Tokikarpu Marae
5 Glowworm Cave &
   Grotto; Cafe
7 Tavern
9 Museum of Caves;
   Information Centre &
   Waitomo Down Under
12 Shearing Shed
14 Woodlyn Park
15 Opapaka Pa

DAVID WALL

Performing in a *poi* dance at the annual Ngaruawahia Regatta

CHRIS MELLOR

Cattle graze beneath mighty Taranaki (Mt Egmont), a dormant volcano in the North Island

TIM UDEN

Auckland's Victoria Park Market

CHRISTINE NIVEN

Catching the ferry to Waiheke, Hauraki Gulf

CHRISTINE NIVEN

MOTAT mural

DENNIS JOHNSON

Mural at the Old Oriental Markets, Auckland

DAVID WALL

International Cultural Festival, Auckland

Glowworms

Glowworms are the larvae of the fungus gnat, which looks much like a large mosquito without mouth parts. The larvae glowworms have luminescent organs which produce a soft, greenish light. Living in a sort of 'hammock' suspended from an overhang, they weave sticky threads which trail down and catch unwary insects attracted by their lights. When an insect flies towards the light, it gets stuck in the threads and becomes paralysed – the glowworm reels in the thread and eats the insect.

The larval stage lasts for six to nine months, depending on how much food the glowworm gets. When the glowworm has grown to about the size of a matchstick it goes into a pupa stage, much like a cocoon. The adult fungus gnat emerges about two weeks later.

The adult insect does not live very long because it does not have a mouth; it emerges, mates, lays eggs and dies, all within about two or three days. The sticky eggs, laid in groups of 40 or 50, hatch in about three weeks to become larval glowworms.

Glowworms thrive in moist, dark caves, but they can survive anywhere if they have the requisites of moisture, an overhang to suspend from, and insects to eat. Waitomo is famous for its glowworms but you can see them in many other places around NZ, both in caves and outdoors.

When you come upon glowworms, don't touch their hammocks or hanging threads, try not to make loud noises and don't shine a light right on them. In daylight their lights fade out, and if you shine a torch right on them they will dim their lights. It takes the lights a few hours to become bright again, during which time the glowworm will catch no food. The glowworms that shine most brightly are the hungriest.

two types of pig) and a 'Kiwi bear' (possum) work in cohorts with Barry and his simple, manual 'virus-free' computer to explain the country's early European heritage. The shows are riotous fun and the audience are deliberately involved. It is well worth the entry fee of $10 (children $5).

You can also take part in the Pink Gumboot experience, a treasure hunt that takes you through native bush and a cave (1¾ hours). The goal is to discover the treasure chest by finding the clues scattered along the route. It's something that can be enjoyed by all ages and costs $13/10 for adults/ children. If you do two activities with Woodlyn Park you can get a free pass to the Museum of Caves. Woodlyn Park is 600m up the Waitomo Valley Road.

Quad bike rides through bush and countryside lasting around two hours ($65 per person) are available with Big Red; call the information centre (☎ 07-878 7640) for details and booking.

The **Shearing Shed** exhibits products made with the fibre of Angora rabbits. It's open from 9 am to 4.30 pm daily; rabbit shearing takes place at 12.45 pm daily. It's free.

Waitomo's Moa and Glowworm Experience, operated by Black Water Rafting (☎ 0800-228 464), is a three-hour guided tour through parts of the Mangawhitikau cave system at Oparure, 12km south of Waitomo. During the tour (which involves a boat trip) you will learn all about the life cycle of glowworms, and gain an insight into other things that inhabit the caves. Moa bones were discovered in this cave back in 1849. Bookings are essential; transport from the Museum of Caves in Waitomo, tea/coffee and muffins are included in the price of $50.

Activities

For details on cave activities, see the boxed text 'Waitomo Underground'.

The Museum of Caves has free pamphlets on various walks in the area. The walk from the Aranui Cave to the Ruakuri Cave is an excellent short walk. From the Glowworm Cave ticket office, it's a 15-minute forest walk to a grove of California redwood trees. Also from here, the 5km three-hour Waitomo Walkway takes off through farmland and follows Waitomo Stream to the Ruakuri

THE CENTRAL WEST

Waitomo Underground

If it's adventure you're after, then Waitomo is the place to be. The caves offer many challenging activities, from abseiling and rock climbing to cave tubing.

Lost World

With 100m (330ft) of free-hanging abseiling to get into the Lost World Cave, it's one of the most amazing things you can do in this country. And you don't even need prior abseiling or caving experience. The first four trips described below are run by Waitomo Adventures (☎ 07-878 7788, 0800-924 866), Web site: www.wapadc.govt.nz, which is based at the Cavelands Cafe.

The principal trip to Lost World is an all-day affair. First you abseil 100m down into the cave (accompanied by your guide), then, by a combination of walking, rock climbing, spider-walking, inching along narrow rock ledges, wading and swimming through a subterranean river, you take a three-hour journey through a 30m-high cave to get back out, passing glowworms, amazing rock and cave formations, waterfalls and more. A new spin on this trip is the option of stunt jumping instead of abseiling the 100m. In a stunt jump you are harnessed to a wire; you drop 90m at which stage your fall is slowed for the last 10m to allow you to make a gentle landing. You get dinner at the end. Cost: $295.

The other option is a four-hour trip that involves a 100m abseil into the cave, with a guide right beside you on another rope. At the bottom, you walk for half an hour into the cave, and exit via another vertical cavern back to the surface, without doing the underground river trip. It takes four hours and costs $195.

Haggas Honking Holes

This four-hour caving trip includes professional abseiling instruction followed by a caving trip with four abseils, rock climbing, and going along a subterranean river with waterfalls. Along the way you see glowworms and a variety of cave formations – including stalactites, stalagmites, columns, flowstone and cave coral. It's a good experience for seeing real caving in action, using caving equipment and going through caverns of various sizes, squeezing through some tight spots and narrow passageways as well as traversing huge caverns.

The name of the adventure derives from a local farmer, 'Haggas', and characters in a Dr Seuss story, 'honking holers'. The cost is $125; or the 'Gruesome Twosome' combines this with the Lost World tandem abseil.

Tumu Tumu Toobing

Waitomo Adventures also operates a physical four-hour tubing trip for the adventurous traveller through the Tumu Tumu Cave. It costs $65. If you combine this with either the Lost World or Haggas Honking Holes adventures you get $20 off the tubing trip.

Scenic Reserve, where a half-hour return walk passes by the river, caves and a natural limestone bridge. This last section of the walk is magical at night when glowworms blaze away (bring a torch).

A one-hour return walk, the **Opapaka Pa Bush Walk** leads up to a pre-European *pa* (fort) site on a hill. Plaques along the way describe traditional Maori medicines found in the forest, traditional forest lore and the pa site itself.

Many other good walks are west of Waitomo on the Marokopa Road; see the following Marokopa Road section.

Waitomo Horse-Trekking (☎ 07-878 7649) operates from the Juno Hall hostel (see Places to Stay), with a variety of rides through Waitomo wilderness areas. The

Waitomo Underground

Cave Tubing (Rafting)

Peter Chandler and John Ash introduced the sport of cave tubing to the unsuspecting traveller in 1987. Also known as black water rafting, it soon became one of NZ's most popular adventures.

Black Water Rafting I is a three-hour trip on an inner tube floating down a subterranean river that flows through Ruakuri Cave. The high point is leaping off a small waterfall and then floating through a long, glowworm-covered passage. The trip ends with hot showers, soup and bagels. You wear a wetsuit which will keep you warm, but having something hot to eat or drink before the trip will make you feel more comfortable. Cost: $65.

Black Water Rafting II is a more recent and more adventurous trip. It involves a 30m abseil into Ruakuri Cave, more glowworms, tubing and cave climbing. The trip takes five hours. Food to be consumed in the cave is included in the cost of $125.

Both trips are run by Black Water Rafting (☎ 0800-228 464, ✉ bwr@blackwaterrafting.co.nz) and depart from the Black Water Cafe several times daily; admission to the Museum of Caves is included in the price.

Aranui Cave, Waitomo

Waitomo Down Under

Waitomo Down Under (☎ 07-878 6577), next door to the Museum of Caves, operates 'float through' caving adventures. In its main adventure, you go through Te Ana Roa (Long Cave) in inner tubes, going over *two* waterfalls (one on a slide) and getting a good close-up view of some glowworms along the way. The cost is $65. Its Adventure II is a 50m abseil down into the 'Baby Grand' *tomo* (it is also $65 – you can do it at night as well).

Long Tomo Rafting

This is the latest way to experience Waitomo's underworld. Abseil 27m into a natural cave then float along the subterranean river on an inner tube. How fast you float will depend on the season; in winter the water moves more swiftly. But whatever time you do it, one of the outstanding features of this trip is the magnificent glowworm display here. After some caving you do a belayed rock climb up a stepped 20m pitch to the surface. The trips are taken by qualified guides and cost $65 per person; phone ☎ 0800-228 372. There is a minimum of two people and a maximum of six.

cost is $30 for a one-hour ride, $40 for two hours, $70 for a half-day, $125 for a full-day ride and $200 for overnight treks.

At Woodlyn Park (see Other Attractions) you can drive a powerful jet-boat, capable of 100hp, around a specially designed course – this is the only operation of its type in NZ and a thrilling experience. Seven laps cost $35. The course is open from 9.30 am to 6.30 pm (until 5 pm from May to October).

Places to Stay

Camping, Cabins & Hostels The *Cavelands Waitomo Holiday Park* (☎ 07-878 7639) is opposite the museum. Tent/powered sites cost $20 for two, while cabins which sleep four are $35 for two. The new

THE CENTRAL WEST

chalets cost $70 for two. The owners will lend you torches for the night-time Waitomo Walkway experience.

Juno Hall (☎ 07-878 7649) is on the main road in from the highway to the caves, about 1km before the Museum of Caves. Its communal area has the feel of a ski lodge and it has good accommodation. The cost is $17 in dorms, $42 in twins or doubles with shared facilities ($52 with private facilities). You can camp for $10 per person. Activities include horse trekking, hunting and fishing trips. There's a pool.

Two kilometres further on past the Glowworm Cave, the *Tomo Group Lodge* (☎ 07-878 7442) is the clubroom of the Hamilton Tomo Group, the largest caving club in NZ. It welcomes visitors, and the cost of $12 for the first night and $10 for each successive night helps to support the club. The hut is quite 'rustic' but has good lounge and kitchen areas, even if the beds in the shared rooms are hard. Bring your own sleeping bag. The helpful caretaker can tell you about walks and free activities in the area, or if you're lucky you may be invited on a caving trip, particularly on weekends.

Guesthouses & Farmstays

Waitomo Guest Lodge (☎ 07-878 7641) is conveniently situated just 100m from the Museum of Caves. It's a pleasant, friendly B&B. Rooms, each with private bath, cost $50/70 for singles/doubles, including breakfast.

At Woodlyn Park (see Other Attractions) you can stay in the *Waitomo Express* (☎ 07-878 6666), a converted railcar which has all mod cons – kitchen, shower, toilet, three bedrooms and comfortable lounge. It is an absolute bargain at $75 for two ($10 for each extra person). A kitchen is available to picnickers for lunch in summer.

Abseil Inn (☎ 07-878 7815) on Waitomo Caves Rd has en suite accommodation for $70 single, or $90 a double including breakfast. The owners are also guides for Waitomo Adventures.

Big Bird (☎ 0800-733 244, 17 Waitomo Caves Rd) is near the turn-off to Te Kuiti and Otorohanga (7km east of the information centre). It has farmstay single/double

accommodation for $40/65 including breakfast. There's also a self-contained cottage across the road at the same rates ($80 for the entire cottage for a family of four). Free tours of the adjacent ostrich farm are available.

Motels & Hotels There are a couple of motels on SH3 at Hangatiki, at the junction of the Waitomo turn-off, 8km from Waitomo. The *Glowworm Motel* (☎ 07-873 8882), which has a swimming pool and spa, has doubles from $74. About 100m south on SH3, the *Caves Motor Inn* (☎ 07-873 8109) has a lodge at $20 per person (shared) and standard units from $55/65 for singles/doubles. There's also a bar and restaurant.

The *Waitomo Caves Hotel* (☎ 07-878 8227), high on the hill in the centre of the village, was built in 1908 and was *the* place to stay. It retains a certain charm. From here it's a five-minute walk to the glowworm caves. Rooms are about $90/130, although there are occasional specials.

Places to Eat

The store beside the Museum of Caves is open daily, with the *Cavelands Cafe, Bar & Brasserie* off to one side, where you can get inexpensive meals to take away or eat in.

The good *Black Water Cafe*, 2km from the caves out towards SH3, has both indoor and patio seating. There is also a new *cafe* at the entrance to the Glowworm Cave.

The *Tavern* near the Museum of Caves is excellent value for light meals and snacks (from $6). Drinks are reasonably priced and bands also play most weekends.

The Waitomo Caves Hotel has the *Fred Mace Restaurant*, which has set menus ($25 for dinner).

The upmarket *Roselands Restaurant* is open for lunch, with an ample barbecue of steak or fish, a salad buffet, dessert and coffee. It is in an attractive setting with garden, veranda or indoor seating. From Waitomo village, go 400m east towards SH3, then follow the signs for 3km.

Getting There & Away

The Waitomo Shuttle (☎ 0800-808 279) operates between Waitomo and Otorohanga

($7 one way). The Waitomo Adventure Shuttle (☎ 0800-924 866) runs Thursday to Monday between the Auckland Central Backpackers and Waitomo via Hamilton, Te Awamutu, Otorohanga and Te Kuiti. It departs Auckland at 7.45 am and arrives in Waitomo at 10.45 am. It leaves Waitomo at 4 pm and arrives back in Auckland at 6.30 pm. The cost is $31 one way.

InterCity (☎ 09-913 6100) has round-trip bus services to the Glowworm Cave from Auckland and Rotorua ($136). You only get to spend an hour at the caves so it's a very rushed trip. Magic Bus and Kiwi Experience also come to Waitomo.

The Waitomo Wanderer (in Waitomo ☎ 07-873 7559; in Rotorua ☎ 07-348 5179) operates a useful daily loop around central North Island. It departs from Waitomo at 4 pm, and Rotorua at 6 pm. It will continue to Taupo and return to Waitomo if there are at least two people. Otherwise there is an overnight stop at Rotorua and you can pick up the bus again at 7.30 am for the trip back to Waitomo (arriving 9.30 am). It costs $30 if Taupo is included in the loop; otherwise $25.

Hitching to Waitomo from the turn-off on SH3 is usually pretty easy, as is hitching around Waitomo once you're there. Hitching out towards Te Anga and Marokopa can be more difficult because there's so little traffic.

MAROKOPA ROAD

Heading west from Waitomo, Te Anga Road becomes Marokopa Road and follows a rewarding and scenic route with a couple of natural beauties worth visiting. The useful *West to Marokopa* pamphlet is produced DOC; or get a copy of *A Trip Through Time* by Peter Chandler, available from the Waitomo Museum of Caves, which outlines a geological driving tour of the 53km road from Waitomo to Kiritehere on the coast, with suggestions for walks.

On weekdays Perry's Bus (☎ 07-876 7595) runs from Taharoa on the coast along the Marokopa Road to Te Kuiti via Te Anga and Waitomo. It departs from the Te Kuiti train station at 1 pm for the return trip.

The **Tawarau Forest**, about 20km west of Waitomo village, has various walks outlined in a DOC pamphlet, including a one-hour walk to the Tawarau Falls from the end of Appletree Rd.

The **Mangapohue Natural Bridge Scenic Reserve**, 26km west of Waitomo, is a 5½-hectare reserve with a giant natural limestone bridge formation; this is a 20-minute walk from the road on a wheelchair-accessible pathway. You can easily walk to the summit. On the far side, big rocks full of oyster fossils jut up from the grass. At night you'll see glowworms.

Not far from Natural Bridge, the **Marokopa Tunnel** is another massive limestone formation – a natural tunnel 270m long and 50m high at its highest point, going through a limestone hill. Limestone formations, fossils and glowworms can be seen.

About 4km further west is **Piripiri Caves Scenic Reserve**, where a 30-minute track leads to a large cave containing fossils of giant oysters. Bring a torch.

The impressive 36m **Marokopa Falls** are 32km west of Waitomo. You can view them from the road above, or walk to the bottom on a track starting just downhill from the roadside vantage point.

The falls are near **Te Anga**, where you can stop for a drink at the pleasant Te Anga Tavern. From Te Anga you can turn north to Taharoa or Kawhia, 53km away, or southwest to **Marokopa**, a small village on the coast, 48km from Waitomo. The whole Te Anga-Marokopa area is riddled with caves. The bitumen ends just past Marokopa at Kiritehere, but it is possible to continue, on a difficult but scenic road, 60km further south until you meet SH3 at Awakino (see Te Kuiti to Mokau). About 20km south of Marokopa is the **Whareorino Forest**, which has forest walks and overnight accommodation at Leitch's Hut (inquire at DOC in Te Kuiti).

Places to Stay

In Te Anga, the *Bike 'n' Hike* (☎ 07-876 7362) is a small backpackers operated by an outdoorsy fellow knowledgeable about caving, geology and fossils; he organises activities and has a couple of bikes for rent.

About 10km south of Te Anga on the road to Marokopa, *Hepipi Farm* (☎ 07-876 7861)

THE CENTRAL WEST

is a B&B and also has three self-contained units at the beach in Marokopa for $40 per unit, each sleeping four or five people.

TE KUITI
pop 4540

This small, provincial town, south of Otorohanga, is another base for visiting Waitomo, 19km away. Te Kuiti probably comes from Te Kuititanga, meaning 'the narrowing in', referring not only to the narrowing of the Mangaokewa Valley here but also to the confiscation of Maori property after the Waikato Land War. Locals will proudly tell you, however, that the town is named for Te Kooti, a prominent Maori rebellion leader who settled here in 1872, seeking refuge from the Pakeha, and stayed for a number of years (see the boxed text about Te Kooti in the East Coast chapter).

The magnificently carved Te Tokanganui-o-noho Marae, overlooking the south end of Rora St, was Te Kooti's grateful gift to his hosts, the Ngati Maniapoto people, once he had accepted the Maori king's creed of pacifism.

Te Kuiti, home to many champion sheep shearers, is known as 'the Shearing Capital of the World'. A 'big shearer' statue is the most prominent feature of the town.

Information
The Te Kuiti Visitor Information Centre (☎ 07-878 8077, ✉ tkinfo@voyager.co.nz) on the main drag, Rora St, is open from 9 am to 5 pm daily (from 10 am to 4 pm on weekends in winter). It has information on homestays and farmstays and does bus and train bookings.

The DOC office (☎ 07-878 7297) is at 78 Taupiri St.

Things to See & Do
Apart from the big shearer, Te Kuiti's main attraction is the **Te Kuiti Muster**, held on the first weekend in April (or the following weekend, if Easter falls then). This popular event has all kinds of entertainment including sheep and goat-shearing championships, a country parade, arts and crafts, live music, sheep races, Maori culture groups, barbecues and *hangi*, a duathlon and a town-wide bargain day.

Te Kuiti has some fine gardens and parks. If you're a garden fan, ask at the information centre for its King Country Gardens

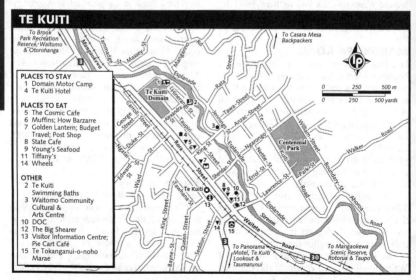

TE KUITI

PLACES TO STAY
1 Domain Motor Camp
4 Te Kuiti Hotel

PLACES TO EAT
5 The Cosmic Cafe
6 Muffins; How Barzarre
7 Golden Lantern; Budget
  Travel; Post Shop
8 State Cafe
9 Young's Seafood
11 Tiffany's
14 Wheels

OTHER
2 Te Kuiti
  Swimming Baths
3 Waitomo Community
  Cultural &
  Arts Centre
10 DOC
12 The Big Shearer
13 Visitor Information Centre;
  Pie Cart Café
15 Te Tokanganui-o-noho
  Marae

To Brook Park Recreation Reserve, Waitomo & Otorohanga

To Casara Mesa Backpackers

0   250   500 m
0   250   500 yards

Te Kuiti Domain

Centennial Park

To Panorama Motel, Te Kuiti Lookout & Taumarunui

To Mangaokewa Scenic Reserve, Rotorua & Taupo

brochure, which gives details on 20 private gardens you can visit in the region.

The **Mangaokewa Stream** winds through the town, with a pleasant riverside walkway. Beside the stream, the **Mangaokewa Scenic Reserve**, 3km south of town on SH30, has picnic and barbecue areas, a waterhole for safe swimming and overnight camping.

On the north-western boundary of Te Kuiti, the attractive **Brook Park Recreation Reserve** has walking tracks leading to the summit of the Ben Lomond Hill. Besides affording a fine view, the hill is the site of the historic Matakiora Pa, constructed in the 17th century by Rora, son of Maniapoto. Camping is permitted.

Te Kuiti Lookout, on Awakino Rd (SH3) as it climbs out of town heading south, provides a great view over the town, especially at night with the sparkling lights stretching out below.

Places to Stay & Eat

The ***Domain Motor Camp*** (☎ 07-878 8966) on Hinerangi St on the north side of town beside the Mangaokewa Stream, about 800m north of the information centre, is a peaceful camping ground with tent/powered sites at $11/13 for two, on-site vans at $20 and cabins at $25 for two.

Camping is also permitted at the ***Brook Park Recreation Reserve*** on the north-western boundary of Te Kuiti, and at the ***Mangaokewa Scenic Reserve*** beside the stream (see Things to See & Do); both have barbecues, picnic areas and toilets, but no other facilities. Payment is by donation.

On Mangarino Rd, just north of town, is the ***Casara Mesa Backpackers*** (☎ 07-878 6697). This farmstay has great views over the town from its veranda and is well worth the $15 per person for a bed with linen (breakfast is extra). The owner picks up and drops off in Te Kuiti.

On Rora St in the town centre, ***Te Kuiti Hotel*** (☎ 07-878 8172) has singles/doubles with private facilities costing $35/50.

The ***Panorama Motel*** (☎ 07-878 8051, 59 Awakino Rd), on SH3 about 1.5km south of town, has a pool and units from $60/70.

Te Kuiti – 'Shearing Capital of the World'

CHRISTINE NIVEN

Te Kuiti has daytime cafes on Rora St, or the ***State Cafe*** is open until 8 pm for standard takeaways and the ***Pie Cart Cafe*** is open until very late.

Also on Rora St, ***Tiffany's Restaurant*** is open late or ***Wheels Restaurant***, beside the BP petrol station, is a friendly, casual restaurant. It has both Continental and Chinese food, with a restaurant and a takeaway section.

The Cosmic C@fe has food, espresso and Internet access. ***Muffins*** on King St has snacks and light meals. The ***Golden Lantern*** serves Chinese food.

Te Kuiti's one nightspot, ***How Barzarre*** on the corner of King and Taupiri Sts, serves snacks such as nachos before it transforms into a late-night venue.

Getting There & Away

InterCity buses arrive at and depart from Tiffany's Restaurant at the south end of Rora St; book and buy your tickets from the information centre. Long-distance buses include those to New Plymouth, Taumarunui or north to Hamilton and on to Auckland.

THE CENTRAL WEST

Buses also operate in the local region. On weekdays the Perry's bus runs between Taharoa on the coast and Te Kuiti, passing through Waitomo, Te Anga and the other scenic attractions along the Waitomo–Marokopa Road. Call Perry's on ☎ 07-876 7596 for details. The Waitomo Wanderer (see Waitomo earlier in this chapter) operates a loop between Rotorua and Waitomo via Te Kuiti.

The Auckland–Wellington trains stops in Te Kuiti at the Rora St station. Get tickets from the information centre or Budget Travel (☎ 07-878 8184).

TE KUITI TO MOKAU

From Te Kuiti, SH3 runs south-west to Mokau on the rugged west coast before continuing on to New Plymouth in Taranaki. The road runs through a lightly populated farming area and is very scenic in parts. InterCity buses between Hamilton and New Plymouth take this route. The telephone area code in this area is ☎ 06.

The road passes through the small town of **Piopio**, which has a small museum, and then tiny **Mahoenui**, from where the road follows the Awakino River. The road along the river is the most spectacular part of the route. Through a short road tunnel you enter the steep **Awakino Gorge**, lined with dense bush and giant ponga.

The road follows the river all the way to **Awakino**, a small settlement on the coast where boats shelter on the river estuary away from the windswept coast. Awakino can also be reached via the Marokopa Road from Waitomo. Just south of Awakino is the **Manioroa Marae**, which contains the anchor stone of the *Tainui* canoe, whose descendants populated Waikato and the King Country. Ask at the organic farm opposite the marae on SH3 for permission to enter. Marae protocol should be observed (see Visiting a Marae in the 'Maori Culture & Arts' special section).

Five kilometres further south, the little town of **Mokau** is at the border of King Country and Taranaki. The town's Tainui Museum, open from 10 am to 4 pm, has a fascinating collection of old photographs from the time when this once-isolated outpost was a coal and lumber shipping port for Pakeha pioneer settlements along the Mokau River.

Mokau River Cruises (☎ 06-752 9775) has good three-hour trips up the river in the historic *Cygnet* for $30 in summer.

Mokau is otherwise just a speck on the map, but it does have a fine stretch of wild beach and good fishing. The river mouth hides some of the best whitebait in the North Island.

Places to Stay & Eat

The *Awakino Hotel* (☎ 06-752 9815) has singles/doubles for $40/70 and offers backpackers accommodation for $13 per person.

The *Palm House* (☎ 06-752 9081, @ palmhouse@taranaki-bakpak.co.nz) in Mokau is a good little backpackers on SH3 and close to the beach. Dorms are from $16, and a double is $40. Inquire at the house next door if no-one is around.

Mokau also has two motor camps and the *Mokau Inn Motel* (☎ 06-752 9725), which charges from $50/65.

There are a couple of little stores selling a limited range of goods, and a butcher. The *Whitebait Inn* has takeaway and sit-down meals, with the area's famous whitebait on the menu in various forms.

TAUMARUNUI
pop 4500

Taumarunui is a quiet little town on SH4, 82km south of Te Kuiti and 43km north of National Park. Its name, meaning 'Big Screen', comes from an episode in the town's history when a Maori chief, Pehi Taroa, was dying and asked for a screen *(taumaru)* to shade him from the sun. They say that he died before the screen was in place, still asking for it with his final words – *'taumaru nui'*.

In winter Taumarunui operates as a ski town, but is really too far from the snow to be convenient. In summer it is one of the main access points for canoeing on the Whanganui River (see Whanganui National Park in the Wanganui & Manawatu chapter for details).

History

At the confluence of the Whanganui and Ongarue Rivers, both major transport waterways, Taumarunui was already an important settlement in pre-European days. It was also significant as the historical meeting place of three important Maori tribes: Whanganui, Tuwharetoa and Maniapoto.

Pakeha did not settle in the area until the 1880s, but even then their influence was minimal until the Main Trunk Railway Line came south from Te Kuiti in 1903. In the same year, the riverboat service coming from the coast at Wanganui was extended up the Whanganui River to Taumarunui. Taumarunui flourished as the rail link, running all the way to Auckland, became a much-travelled route and timber from the area's sawmills was freighted out.

Information

The Taumarunui Visitor Centre (☎ 07-895 7494, ✉ tauvin@ruapehudc.govt.nz), Web site: www.middle-of-everywhere.co.nz, is at the train station on Hakiaha St in the town centre. It's open from 9 am to 4.30 pm on weekdays and 10 am to 4 pm on weekends. It's the agent for AA and for InterCity bus and train tickets. It's worth a stop just for a look at the operating model of the Raurimu Spiral.

The DOC office (☎ 895 8201) at Cherry Grove, beside the river, is the place to go for information on the Whanganui National Park and canoeing the river.

Taumarunui's telephone area code is ☎ 07.

Raurimu Spiral

The Raurimu Spiral is a feat of rail engineering that was declared a 'wonder of the world' when it was completed in 1908. The spiral's three horseshoe curves, one complete circle and two short tunnels, allowed the Main Trunk Railway coming south from Auckland and north from Wellington to finally be joined (at Horopito). The information centre has an excellent working model of the spiral and pamphlets explaining its construction. At Raurimu, 37km south of Taumarunui, you can see the real thing from a lookout just off the highway.

Rail buffs can experience the spiral on any train between Wellington and Auckland. For a day trip, you can take the train from Taumarunui to National Park and return to Taumarunui the same day – the information office has all the relevant schedules.

THE CENTRAL WEST

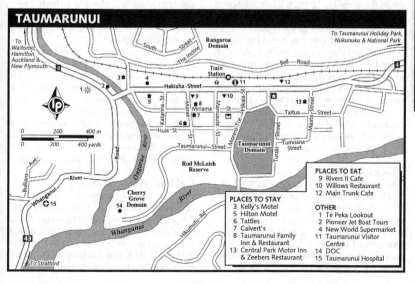

TAUMARUNUI

PLACES TO STAY
3 Kelly's Motel
5 Hilton Motel
6 Tattles
7 Calvert's
8 Taumarunui Family Inn & Restaurant
13 Central Park Motor Inn & Zeebers Restaurant

PLACES TO EAT
9 Rivers II Cafe
10 Willows Restaurant
12 Main Trunk Cafe

OTHER
1 Te Peka Lookout
2 Pioneer Jet Boat Tours
4 New World Supermarket
11 Taumarunui Visitor Centre
14 DOC
15 Taumarunui Hospital

Nukunuku Museum

This private museum (☎ 07-896 6365) is devoted to the Whanganui River and the area around it, with Maori and pioneer artefacts, and pioneer buildings. The museum is at Nukunuku, 17km down the Whanganui River from Taumarunui. It can visited by river or via Saddlers Rd, off the Whanganui River Road. It is open by appointment only (entry by donation).

Stratford–Taumarunui Heritage Trail

See the Taranaki chapter for details on this route between Taumarunui and Stratford (note that 25km of this is unsealed).

Walking

The visitor centre has suggestions for several enjoyable walks around Taumarunui. A pleasant walkway extends east along the Whanganui River from Cherry Grove Domain to the Taumarunui Holiday Park, about 3km away. Another track leads to the Rangaroa Domain with a good view over the town, its rivers and mountains; go over the train line, up The Incline and through the native bush behind the scout den to reach the domain. Te Peka Lookout across the Ongarue River on the western side of town is another good vantage point.

For even better views extending to Tongariro National Park in the south, climb flat-topped Mt Hikurangi (770m), north of the town. This curious hill can be seen from far and wide. Before climbing, you must ask permission from the owner (☎ 07-895 3031).

The Ohinetonga Scenic Reserve on the banks of the Whakapapa River, 26km south of town at Owhango, has bush walks lasting from one to three hours.

Places to Stay

The *Taumarunui Holiday Park* (☎ 07-895 9345) is on the banks of the Whanganui River near SH4, 3km east of town. Tent/powered sites are $8/9 per person, cabins are $29 a double and a family unit is $45. Features of the camp include kayaks and bicycles for hire, bush walks, overnight tramping and guided tours. For those who

have just finished a river journey, there is a laundry.

The *Taumarunui Family Inn* (☎ 07-895 3478) on the corner of Marae and Miriama Sts is basically a large pub. Twin share costs $20 per person, and doubles (with en suite) cost $56. There are backpacker singles for $16 ($18 with linen provided). There's a small kitchen.

The motel across the road, *Calvert's* (☎ 07-895 8500), has good units for $64/74; a light breakfast is included.

At the west end of town, *Kelly's Motel* (☎ 07-895 8175) has studio singles/doubles at $48/70, plus two-bedroom family units.

The more luxurious *Central Park Motor Inn* (☎ 07-895 7132) on Maata St has a pool and singles/doubles from $65/75. Other motels include the *Hilton Motel* (☎ 07-895 7181) on Hakiaha St (from $55/66) and *Tattles* (☎ 07-895 8063, 23 Marae St), from $55 a double.

The visitor centre has a list of B&Bs.

Places to Eat

The *Main Trunk Cafe* on Hakiaha St at the east end of town is in a brightly painted red, 1913 railway passenger car, now restored and converted to a cheerful cafe. It's open from 10 am to 10 pm Wednesday to Sunday, with a menu including fish and chips, burgers and sandwiches.

There are other tearooms, takeaways and cafes along Hakiaha St and down the side streets, including two Chinese restaurants and the *Rivers II Cafe* on the corner of Marae St – the latter has good coffee, cakes, sandwiches and light meals.

The *Taumarunui Family Inn Restaurant & Bar* has reasonably priced meals. The *Willows Restaurant* upstairs on Hakiaha St opposite the train station is also licensed.

Getting There & Away

Buses and trains travelling between Auckland and Wellington all stop at the train station at Taumarunui. The station also houses the visitor centre, where you can buy tickets.

Hitching is easy heading north or south on SH4. It's a lot harder hitching on the lightly trafficked Stratford–Taumarunui Road.

Taranaki

☎ 06 • pop 107,600

The Taranaki region juts out into the Tasman Sea on the west coast of the North Island, about halfway between Auckland and Wellington. The region is named after the Mt Taranaki volcano, also called Mt Egmont, the massive cone of which dominates the landscape. Conditions are excellent for agriculture, with rich volcanic soil and abundant rainfall.

The names Taranaki and Egmont are both widely used in the region. Taranaki is the Maori name for the volcano and Egmont is the name James Cook gave it in 1770, after the Earl of Egmont, who had encouraged his expedition. Today the region is called Taranaki, the cape is called Cape Egmont, and the waters on either side of the cape are called the North and South Taranaki Bights. Egmont National Park retains the name of the national park but Taranaki and Egmont are *both* official names for the volcano.

In addition to the obvious attraction of Taranaki – the 'most climbed' mountain in NZ – the region is popular for its world-class surfing and windsurfing beaches.

NEW PLYMOUTH
pop 49,100

The principal centre of the Taranaki region, New Plymouth is roughly equidistant from Auckland (373km) and Wellington (357km). A coastal city backed by towering Mt Taranaki and surrounded by rich agricultural and dairy lands, New Plymouth is a good base for visiting Egmont National Park. It has some fine parks and the spectacular backdrop of Mt Taranaki, but near the sea the city's industrial installations blight the landscape.

History

Archaeological evidence shows that the region was settled by the Maori from early times. In the 1820s the Taranaki Maori fled in droves to the Cook Strait region to avoid

HIGHLIGHTS

• Walking, mountain climbing or skiing on the awe-inspiring Mt Taranaki volcano

• Visiting Maori and European historical sites

• Windsurfing or surfing the beaches of Oakura, Opunake and New Plymouth

• Driving along the Stratford–Taumarunui Heritage Trail

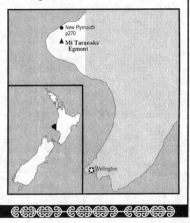

a threatened attack by the Waikato tribes, but it was not until 1832 that the Waikato attacked and subdued the remaining Te Ati-awa tribe. The Te Ati-awa remained only at Okoki Pa (New Plymouth), where whalers had joined in the battle. Thus when the first European settlers arrived in the district in 1841 the coast of Taranaki was almost deserted. Initially it seemed there would be no opposition to land claims, so the New Zealand Company managed to buy extensive tracts from the Te Ati-awa who had stayed.

When other members of Te Ati-awa and other tribes returned after years of exile and slavery they objected strongly to the sale of their land. Their claims were substantially

TARANAKI

TARANAKI

TASMAN
SEA

0   10   20 km
0   5   10 miles

North Taranaki
Bight

To Auckland
& Waitomo

Awakino

Mokau

Tongaporutu

White
Cliffs

Ahititi

Okau

Pukearuhe

Uruti

To
Taumarunui

Waitara

Onaero

Bell
Block

Brixton

Motonui

Urenui

Okoki

Tahora

FITZROY
BEACH

Huirangi

Waitui

Kohuratahi

NEW
PLYMOUTH

Pukerangiora Pa
Lake
Mangamahoe

Egmont
Village

Whangamomona

Oakura

Hurworth
Huatoki
Stream

Carrington Rd

Inglewood

Kaimata

Matau

Lucy's Gully

Tataraimaka

Okato

Pukeiti
Rhododendron
Trust

Kaimiro

Tariki

Manganui
River

Te Wera

Huiakama

Cape
Egmont
Lighthouse

Stony River

EGMONT
NATIONAL
PARK

The
Camphouse
North
Egmont

Midhurst

Wharehuia

Douglas

Makahu

Pungarehu

Mt Taranaki/
Egmont
(2518m)

East Egmont

Pembroke

Tututawa

Puniwhakau

Parihaka Pa

Dawson
Falls

Dawson
Falls

Stratford

Rahotu

Waiau River

Mahoe

Cardiff

Ngaere

Mangamingi

Omoana

Oaonui

Rowan

Kaponga

Eltham

Rukumoana
Lake
Rotorangi

Moeroa

Te Kiri

Awatuna

Riverlea

Mangatoki

Opunake

Kapuni

Lake
Rotokare

Pihama

Auroa

Oeo

Otakeho

Normanby

Tarere
State
Forest

Rimunui
State
Forest

Manaia

Tawhiti

Hawera

Ohawe Beach

Dairyland
Visitor
Centre

Mokoia

Hurleyville

TASMAN
SEA

Manutahi

Alton

Kakaramea

Whenuakura

Waverley

South Taranaki
Bight

Patea

Waitotara

To Wanganui

Waitara River

Waiwakaiho River

Kapuni Stream

Whenuakura River

TARANAKI

upheld when Governor Fitzroy ruled that the NZ Company was only allowed to retain just over 10 sq km around New Plymouth of the 250 sq km it had claimed. The Crown slowly acquired more land from the Maori, but the Maori became increasingly reluctant to sell. At the same time the European settlers became increasingly greedy for the fertile land around Waitara, just north of New Plymouth.

The settlers' determination finally forced the government to abandon its policy of negotiation, and in 1860 war broke out. For 10 years the Maori kept the military engaged in guerrilla warfare. During this time, settlers moved in on Waitara and took control there, but the Maori came and went as they pleased throughout the rest of the province. The Taranaki chiefs had not signed the Treaty of Waitangi and did not recognise the sovereignty of the British queen, so they were treated as rebels. By 1870 over 500 hectares of their land had been confiscated and much of the rest acquired through dubious transactions.

The Taranaki province experienced an economic boom with the discovery of natural gas and oil at Kapuni in 1959 and more recently at the Maui natural gas field off the coast of South Taranaki.

Orientation & Information

Devon St (East and West) is the main street; its central section is a mall.

The New Plymouth Information Centre (☎ 759 6080, ✉ info@newplymouth.govt .nz), on the corner of Liardet and Leach Sts, is open from 8.30 am to 5 pm on weekdays and 10 am to 3 pm on weekends (longer in summer). The staff are helpful and the informative brochure *Options* is good. The centre also has a Web site (www.newplymouthNZ.com) with general information and a comprehensive coverage of accommodation options.

The Department of Conservation (DOC) office (☎ 758 0433), 220 Devon St West, is open from 8 am to 4.30 pm on weekdays.

The Automobile Association (AA) office (☎ 757 5646) is at 49–55 Powderham St and the main post shop is on Currie St.

Museums & Galleries

The **Taranaki Museum** on Ariki St, between Brougham and Egmont Sts, has a collection of Maori artefacts, wildlife exhibits including moa and whale skeletons, and an early colonists' exhibition. It is open from 9.30 am to 4.30 pm on weekdays and 1 to 5 pm on weekends (entry is free, but donations are welcome).

The **Govett-Brewster Art Gallery**, on the corner of Queen and King Sts, is a renowned contemporary art gallery with a good reputation for its adventurous shows. Fans of abstract animation on film should seek out the films of Len Lye, pioneer animator of the 1930s, whose works are held here and shown from time to time. It's open from 10.30 am to 5 pm daily (entry is free, except during special exhibitions).

Historic Places

The free *Heritage Walkway* leaflet, obtainable from the information centre, outlines a self-guided tour of 30 historic sites around the city.

Richmond Cottage, on the corner of Ariki and Brougham Sts, was built in 1853. Unlike most early cottages, which were made of timber, Richmond Cottage was sturdily built of stone. From June to October it's open from 2 to 4 pm on Friday and 1 to 4 pm on weekends ($1, children $0.20).

St Mary's Church on Vivian St between Brougham and Robe Sts, built in 1846, is the oldest stone church in NZ. Its graveyard has headstones of early settlers and of soldiers who died during the Taranaki Land Wars (1860–61 and 1865–69). Impressed by their bravery, the British also buried several Maori chiefs here.

On Devon St at the eastern end of the city is the **Fitzroy Pole**, erected by the Maori in 1844 to mark the point beyond which Governor Fitzroy had forbidden settlers to acquire land. The carving on the bottom of the pole depicts a sorrowful Pakeha topped by a cheerfully triumphant Maori.

Marsland Hill & Observatory

The New Plymouth Observatory is on Marsland Hill off Robe St. Public nights are

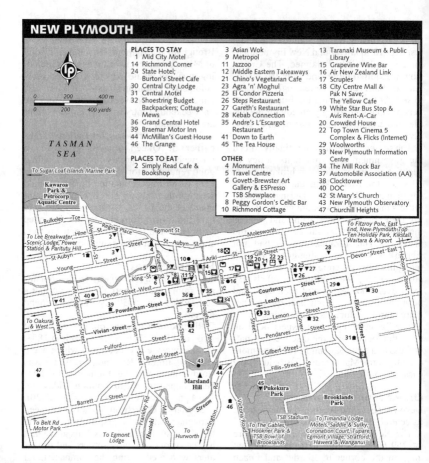

NEW PLYMOUTH

PLACES TO STAY
1 Mid City Motel
14 Richmond Corner
24 State Hotel;
   Burton's Street Cafe
30 Central City Lodge
31 Central Motel
32 Shoestring Budget
   Backpackers; Cottage
   Mews
36 Grand Central Hotel
39 Braemar Motor Inn
44 McMillan's Guest House
46 The Grange

PLACES TO EAT
2 Simply Read Cafe &
   Bookshop

3 Asian Wok
9 Metropol
11 Jazzoo
12 Middle Eastern Takeaways
21 Chino's Vegetarian Cafe
23 Agra 'n' Moghul
25 El Condor Pizzeria
26 Steps Restaurant
27 Gareth's Restaurant
28 Kebab Connection
35 Andre's L'Escargot
   Restaurant
45 The Tea House

OTHER
4 Monument
5 Travel Centre
6 Govett-Brewster Art
   Gallery & ESPresso
7 TSB Showplace
8 Peggy Gordon's Celtic Bar
10 Richmond Cottage

13 Taranaki Museum & Public
   Library
15 Grapevine Wine Bar
16 Air New Zealand Link
17 Scruples
18 City Centre Mall &
   Pak N Save;
   The Yellow Cafe
19 White Star Bus Stop &
   Avis Rent-A-Car
20 Crowded House
22 Top Town Cinema 5
   Complex & Flicks (Internet)
29 Woolworths
33 New Plymouth Information
   Centre
34 The Mill Rock Bar
37 Automobile Association (AA)
38 Clocktower
40 DOC
42 St Mary's Church
43 New Plymouth Observatory
47 Churchill Heights

held every Tuesday and include a planetarium program and viewing through a 6-inch refractor telescope if the weather is clear. Opening times are 7.30 to 9 pm from March to October and 8 to 10 pm from November to March. A donation is appreciated.

Paritutu & Other Viewpoints

Above the power station is Paritutu, a steep hill with a magnificent view from the top. The name means 'rising precipice' and it's worth the tiring but quick scramble to the summit. Not only do you look down on the station but also out over the city and the rocky Sugar Loaf Islands rising just offshore.

Another good viewpoint is Churchill Heights, with a trig marker on top showing directions and distances to places near and far. You can walk up from Morley St or drive up from the entrance on Cutfield St.

Parks

New Plymouth is renowned for its superb parks. **Pukekura Park**, a 10-minute walk from the city centre, is worth a visit, with 49 hectares of gardens, bushwalks, streams, waterfalls, ponds and a kiosk cafe. Display houses with orchids and other exotic plants are open from 8.30 am to 4 pm daily. Rowing boats on the lake can be hired on weekends, holidays and summer evenings. The lights and decorations in Pukekura Park from mid-December to early February are worth making a special trip to see. The park also has a delightful cricket oval in the English tradition.

Adjoining Pukekura is the lovely **Brooklands Park** and, between the two, the Bowl of Brooklands, an outdoor sound-shell in a bush and lake setting. Brooklands Park was once the land around an important early settler's home; the fireplace and chimney are all that remain of the house after the Maori burnt it down. Highlights include a 2000-year-old puriri tree, a rhododendron dell with over 300 varieties, and a children's zoo open from 9 am to 6 pm daily.

On the waterfront is **Kawaroa Park**, with green areas, squash courts and the Petrocorp Aquatic Centre, which has a waterslide, an outdoor pool and an indoor pool (open all year). Also on the waterfront in the central city area is **Pukeariki Landing**, an historic area with sculptures.

Sugar Loaf Islands Marine Park

This marine park, established in 1986, includes the rocky islets offshore from the power station, Back Beach on the west side of Paritutu, and the waters up to about 1km offshore. The islands, eroded volcanic remnants, are a refuge for seabirds, NZ fur seals and marine life; the greatest number of seals is from June to October but some are there all year round.

Activities in the park include boating and sailing, diving, bird-watching, pole fishing, surfing and beach walks. Boat trips to the islands are popular in summer. Happy Chaddy's Charters (☎ 758 9133) has boats departing from Lee Breakwater, tide and weather permitting ($20, children $10).

Walking

The information centre has leaflets on good walks around New Plymouth, including coastal walks and others through local reserves and parks, in addition to the Heritage Walkway already mentioned. Te Henui Walkway, extending from the coast at East End Reserve to the city's southern boundary, is one of the most interesting and varied walks.

Huatoki Valley Walkway, following Huatoki Stream, makes an attractive walk to the city centre.

There are many walks on Mt Taranaki; the New Plymouth Tramping Club (☎ 757 9622) may help visiting walkers.

Surfing & Windsurfing

Besides being beautiful to look at, the Taranaki coastline is a world-class surfing and windsurfing area. In the New Plymouth area, Fitzroy and East End beaches are at the eastern end of the city. Fitzroy is a surfing beach and can be reached by bus from New Plymouth. There's also good surf at Back Beach, by Paritutu at the western end of the city, and at Oakura, 15km west of New Plymouth. There are no buses to Oakura but hitchhiking is easy.

The Sirocco Windsurfing Shop & School, also called the Coastal Surf Shop (☎ 752 7363), on SH45 just before Oakura, hires out surfboards and sailboards and offers instruction. Vertigo Total Surf (☎ 752 7363) is also on the Main Rd in Oakura. Both are good sources of up-to-the-minute information on wind and surf conditions.

Aerial Sightseeing

Several operators offer scenic flights around the area including flights over the snow-capped summit of Mt Taranaki – superb if the weather's clear. Operators include Air Taranaki (☎ 754 4375), Taranaki Scenic Flights (☎ 755 0500) and the Stratford Aero Club (☎ 765 6628).

Organised Tours

Cruise NZ Tours (☎ 758 3222), 8 Baring Terrace, is highly recommended; its city tour is $38. Neuman's Sightseeing Tours (☎ 758 4622), at 78–80 Gill St, has a variety of tours, ranging from a $30 half-day scenic city tour to a three-quarter day tour around Mt Taranaki ($45) or down the Stratford-Taumarunui Heritage Trail ($60). Minimum numbers apply on some tours.

TARANAKI

Carter Travel (☎ 759 9039) operates a shuttle service to Mt Taranaki, from $30 for one person or $20 each for two or more.

Places to Stay

Camping & Cabins The *Belt Rd Holiday Park* (☎ 758 0228, 2 Belt Rd) is on a bluff overlooking the port, 1.5km west of the town centre. Tent and powered sites are $17 for two, backpackers cabins are $22 per person and other cabins range from $25 to $50 for two, depending on facilities.

In Fitzroy, 3.5km east of the centre, the *New Plymouth Top Ten Holiday Park* (☎ 758 2566, 29 Princes St) has motel units ($60 to $65 for two), tourist flats from $50 for two, cabins for $35, tent sites for $18, and backpacker accommodation ($30 for two).

Heading around the coast in the other direction, the *Oakura Beach Motor Camp* (☎ 752 7861) is an attractive camping ground right on Oakura, a beautiful beach for surfing and windsurfing. The turn-off to the beach is 1km west of Oakura, which is 15km west of New Plymouth. The cost for two is $15/17 for tent/powered sites.

Hookner Park (☎ 753 6945, 885 Carrington Rd) is a quiet, peaceful camp on a commercial dairy farm 10km south of the town centre. Campers are welcome to join in the farm life. The cost for powered/tent sites is $8 per person, on-site vans are $18 per person and cabins $30 ($40 with en suite).

Backpackers The *Egmont Lodge* (☎ 753 5720, ✉ egmontlodge@taranaki-bakpak .co.nz, 12 Clawton St), a YHA Associate, is a tranquil hostel in large, parklike grounds with a stream running through them. It's a fair way from town – a 15-minute walk on a pleasant streamside walkway or phone for free pick-up from the bus station. It's well set up for information on walks and other activities. The cost is $16 in dorms, $25 in singles; twins and doubles are $36, or you can pitch a tent ($10).

More central, the *Shoestring Budget Backpackers* (☎/fax 758 0404, 48 Lemon St) is in a large, stately old home; it charges $14 in dorms, $22 in singles and doubles or from $32 for twins. It's a well-equipped, friendly place with an outside patio, and the rooms are excellent.

The *Central City Lodge* (☎ 758 0473, 104 Leach St) is on a busy road but has off-street parking. Singles/twins are $30/40, backpackers beds $15 (linen $5 extra).

The *Richmond Corner* (☎ 759 0050, ✉ jrsanders@xtra.co.nz, 25 Ariki St) is an old converted hotel with a great barbecue area, central location and sea views. Backpackers beds are $15 (in a five-bed dorm), singles are $30, twin share $25 per person and doubles $45.

The *Scenic Lodge* (☎ 751 3310, 199 Centennial Drive) is the former quarters for the power station; singles/doubles are $20/40 (there are weekly rates) and backpackers beds are $10.

B&Bs The *Grange* (☎ 758 1540, 44b Victoria St) is a lovely, welcoming, contemporary home with decks and bush views. It's also opposite beautiful Pukekura Park. Each room has an en suite ($70 single, $90 double; including breakfast).

Henwood House (☎ 755 1212, 314 Henwood Rd) is 5km north of Bell Block. This restored Victorian home with lovely grounds has rooms (three en suites) costing from $95 with breakfast.

The information centre has details on numerous other homestays and B&Bs.

Motels & Hotels New Plymouth has plenty of motels, charging from around $70/80 for singles/doubles.

The *Mid City Motel* (☎ 758 6109) on the corner of St Aubyn and Weymouth Sts is reasonably central, with doubles for $70.

The *Central Motel* (☎ 758 6444, 86 Eliot St), a few blocks east of the centre, is small but convenient, with units at $60 to $80.

The *Timandra Lodge Motels* (☎ 758 6006, 31B Timandra St) off Coronation Ave, the extension of Eliot St, charges from $60/70.

The *Cottage Mews* (☎ 758 0404, 50 Lemon St), next door to the Shoestring Budget Backpackers, is good value, with tidy rooms from $60.

Other motel choices are **Coronation Court** (☎ 757 9125, 226 Coronation Ave), with rooms at $67/70 and the clean, friendly **Saddle & Sulky** (☎ 757 5763, 188 Coronation Ave), with rooms at $70/74.

There are several old-style hotels around central New Plymouth. The **State Hotel** (☎ 758 5373), on the corner of Devon St East and Gover St, has rooms for $48/60 and a family restaurant. More modern, **Braemar Motor Inn** (☎ 758 0859, 157 Powderham St) has rooms from $69/79.

The **Grand Central Hotel** (☎ 758 7495, 42 Powderham St), a new place, has 60 rooms ranging from $85 to $160.

Places to Eat
Restaurants The popular **Jazzoo** is upstairs on the corner of Egmont St and Devon St West. There's an outdoor balcony, an innovative and tempting menu and a bar. On weekends there's live music.

The BYO **Steps Restaurant** (37 Gover St) is a popular Mediterranean place offering good lunches and dinners and a pleasant atmosphere.

The cosy **Yellow Cafe** in the City Centre Mall on Ariki St has good espresso, cakes, sandwiches and soup.

The **Asian Wok** on the corner of St Aubyn and Dawson Sts has great-value smorgasbords of Chinese, Thai and Indonesian food. It's a pleasant little cafe, open evenings only.

For authentic, good Indian food try the **Agra 'n' Moghul** (103 Devon St East).

Chino's Vegetarian Cafe (117 Devon St) is a trendy BYO with blackboard menu (also featuring meat and fish dishes) which is open daily from 7 am to midnight.

The **Metropol** on the corner of King and Egmont Sts is the place to taste NZ and Pacific Rim dishes.

Quality licensed restaurants include **Gareth's Restaurant** (182 Devon St East) and the 'genuinely French' **Andre's L'Escargot** (37–39 Brougham St), in a historical building.

Pub Food The **Mill Rock Bar** on the corner of Currie and Courtenay/Powderham

Sts, is popular for its evening entertainment. It has a dining area with bar meals always available and is open from 11 am until late daily except Sunday.

The licensed **Burton's Street Cafe** in the State Hotel (see Places to Stay) is open daily for all meals.

Fast Food There are plenty of **Chinese takeaways** around the centre, especially on Devon St, as well as fast food.

El Condor Pizzeria on Devon St East near the corner of Gover St is a trendy little pizza and pasta place with a difference – it's Argentinian. It opens from Tuesday to Sunday for dinner. In the same block, the **Kebab Connection** at No 211A features doner kebab and other Middle Eastern fare.

On Devon St West, between Egmont and Brougham Sts, is the ever-reliable **Middle Eastern Takeaways**.

In the City Centre shopping mall on Gill St there's a **food hall** with Chinese and Italian food, seafood, wholefood, sandwich and dessert counters, and a **Robert Harris Coffee Shop** upstairs (with superb sea views). Also in the City Centre shopping mall is the large **Pak N Save** supermarket for groceries. **Woolworth** is on Leach St between Eliot and Cameron Sts.

Down to Earth is a bulk wholefood grocery on the corner of Devon St West and Morley St with 'healthy takeaways'.

Simply Read Cafe & Bookshop on the corner of Dawson and Hine Sts is a bookshop cafe and an ideal place for a coffee and snack during the day with views across the sea. Other good cafes are **ESPresso** in the Govett-Brewster Art Gallery, **Flicks** in the Top Town Cinema 5 Complex on Devon St East (it also has Internet access), and the **Kiosk** (aka The Tea House) in Pukekura Park.

Entertainment
Jazzoo has live music on weekends including acid jazz, drum and base and acoustic. **Peggy Gordon's Celtic Bar** on the corner of Devon St West and Egmont St has bands on weekends.

The Mill Rock Bar (see Places to Eat) is a popular place for a night out, with a section

TARANAKI

for bands from Wednesday to Saturday night and a separate disco. Bar meals are available and it's known for having something enjoyable for all ages.

Some other popular nightspots include *Crowded House* and *Scruples*, both on Devon St, and the *Grapevine Wine Bar* on the corner of Currie and Devon Sts.

The *TSB Bowl of Brooklands*, at the entrance to Brooklands Park, is a large outdoor theatre; the information centre will have current concert schedules and prices. The *TSB Showplace* on Devon St West stages a variety of performances.

Getting There & Away

Air Air New Zealand Link (☎ 737 3300), 12-14 Devon St East, has direct flights to Auckland, Hamilton, Nelson, Wanganui and Wellington, with onward connections. Origin Pacific (☎ 0800-302 302) has direct flights to Nelson, Wellington and Auckland with onward connections.

Bus InterCity (☎ 759 9039) stops at the Travel Centre on the corner of Queen and King Sts. It has several buses daily heading north to Hamilton and Auckland, and southeast to Wanganui and Palmerston North, from where buses proceed south to Wellington or east to Napier and Gisborne.

White Star (☎ 758 3338) buses depart from the Avis Rent-A-Car office at 25 Liardet St. They operate daily, with two buses a day on weekdays and one daily on weekends heading to Wellington ($41 one way) via Wanganui and Palmerston North.

Bookings and ticketing for InterCity can be done at the visitor centre.

Hitching A good spot to hitch north from is on Courtenay St, about 1.5km east of the town centre; anywhere from about Hobson St eastwards is good, the further out the better.

A good hitching spot for south towards Wanganui is on the corner of Coronation Ave and Cumberland St, about 1.5km south of the town centre.

To hitch west around the Taranaki coast towards Oakura, head west out of town on Devon St West, which becomes South Rd.

Getting Around

New Plymouth's airport is 11km east of the centre. Withers (☎ 751 1777) operates a door-to-door shuttle to and from the airport ($10).

City buses operate daily except Sunday. The information centre has timetables.

For details of shuttle services from New Plymouth to Mt Taranaki see the Mt Taranaki/Egmont section later.

AROUND NEW PLYMOUTH

Egmont National Park, of course, is the primary attraction of the New Plymouth area, but there are several other places of interest, all within about 20km of New Plymouth. Hurworth, the Pouakai Zoo Park and the Pukeiti Rhododendron Trust can all be reached by heading south from the centre on Carrington Rd.

Tupare

Tupare, 7km south of New Plymouth, is a fine three-storey Tudor-style house surrounded by 3.6 hectares of lush English garden. It's part of the National Trust; look for it at 487 Mangorei Rd on the Waiwhakaiho River. The garden is open from 9 am to 5 pm daily from 1 September to 31 March ($5, children free).

Hurworth

This early homestead at 552 Carrington Rd, about 8km south of New Plymouth, dates from 1856. Its pioneer builder and first occupant, Harry Atkinson, was later to become New Zealand premier four times. The house was the only one at this site to survive the Taranaki Land Wars and is today owned by the Historic Places Trust. It's open on request (☎ 753 3593 or 758 3407).

Pukeiti Rhododendron Trust

This is a four-sq-km garden surrounded by native bush and internationally renowned for its collection of rhododendrons and azaleas. Peak flowering of rhododendrons generally takes place from September to November, though the garden is worth seeing at any time of year.

Pukeiti is 20km south of New Plymouth. To get there, just keep following Carrington

Rd all the way from town. The road passes between the Pouakai and Kaitake Ranges, both part of Egmont National Park, but separated by the trust. Pukeiti is open from 9 am to 5 pm daily ($8, children free).

Lake Mangamahoe & TATATM

If you're heading out towards Stratford or North Egmont on SH3, stop at Lake Mangamahoe, 9.5km south of New Plymouth. It's a great setting for photographs of Mt Taranaki, reflected in the waters of the lake.

Opposite the lake, on the corner of SH3 and Kent Rd, is the Taranaki Aviation, Transport & Technology Museum (TATATM), with vehicles, railway and aviation exhibits, farm equipment and household items. The museum is open from 10.30 am to 4 pm on Sunday and public holidays ($4, children $0.50).

Inglewood

pop 3145

This small village, 13km south-east of New Plymouth, is worth a stop to visit *Macfarlanes Caffé* (☎ 756 6665) on Matai St. There is seating inside or outdoors.

The *Forrestal Lodge* (☎ 756 7242, 23 Rimu St) has backpackers beds for $15, and single/twin B&B for $25/45.

Waitara

Waitara is 13km east of New Plymouth on SH3. If you turn off SH3 at Brixton, just before Waitara, and head 7km south, you'll reach the site of the Pukerangiora Pa. It's beautifully situated on a high cliff by the Waitara River, but historically it was a particularly bloody battle site.

Rafting and canoeing on the Waitara and Mokau Rivers are popular local activities. For details of times and costs, phone Camp 'n' Canoe (☎ 764 6738).

Just beyond Waitara on SH3 heading east from New Plymouth is the Methanex NZ's Motunui Plant (☎ 754 8009). Opened in 1986, it was the world's first plant to convert natural gas to petrol (gasoline) and remains the world's largest methanol production facility. Natural gas is piped here from the

Maui natural gas field, 34km offshore from Cape Egmont. The synthetic fuel produced here meets a third of NZ's petrol needs. You can stop by the visitor centre near the plant's main entrance to see exhibits; it's open from 8 am to 5 pm daily (free).

North via SH3

Heading north towards Waikato from New Plymouth, SH3 is a scenic route. This is the route to take for Waitomo, and buses heading north go this way to Hamilton. Get the free *Scenic 3 Highway* pamphlet from the Otorohanga or New Plymouth visitor centre.

Heading past Waitara the highway follows the west coast with its high sand dunes and surf beaches. **Urenui**, 16km past Waitara, is a popular beach destination in summer. *Urenui Beach Motor Camp (☎ 752 3838)* has a variety of accommodation options right next to the beach and sand dunes. About 5km past Urenui, you can sample natural beers at the **White Cliffs Brewing Company**, a boutique brewery open from 9.30 am to 6 pm Monday to Saturday.

The brewery is near the turn-off to Pukearuhe and the **White Cliffs**, huge cliffs resembling their namesake in Dover. The cliffs dominate the coastal landscape and contain two-million-year-old marine sediments. A walkway along the cliffs leads from Pukearuhe to Tongaporutu via a tunnel from the beach, accessible only at low tide. On a fine day the full-day walk has superb views of the coastline and of Mts Taranaki and Ruapehu.

SH3 continues further north from Tongaporutu to Mokau, on the border of Taranaki and Waikato. Mokau has backpackers and other accommodation (see The Central West chapter).

MT TARANAKI/EGMONT

The Taranaki region is dominated by the massive cone of 2518m Taranaki, a dormant volcano that looks remarkably like Japan's Mt Fuji or the Philippines' Mayon.

Geologically, Mt Taranaki is the youngest of a series of three large volcanoes on one fault line, the others being Kaitake and Pouakai. Mt Taranaki last erupted 350 years ago, and is considered dormant rather than extinct. The top 1400m is covered in lava flows and a few descend to 800m above sea level. An interesting feature is the small subsidiary cone on the flank of the main cone and 2km south of the main crater, called Fantham's Peak (1962m).

There's a saying in Taranaki that if you can see the mountain it's going to rain and if you can't see the mountain it's already raining! The mountain is one of the wettest spots in NZ, with about 7000mm of rain recorded annually at North Egmont (compared with 1584mm in New Plymouth), as it catches the moisture-laden winds coming in from the Tasman Sea and sweeps them up to freezing heights. Still, it doesn't *always* rain there and the volcano is a spectacular sight on a clear day.

History

Mt Taranaki was supremely sacred to the Maori, both as a burial site for chiefs and as a hide-out in times of danger.

According to legend, Taranaki was once a part of the group of volcanoes at Tongariro. He was forced to leave rather hurriedly when Tongariro caught him with the beautiful Pihanga, the volcano near Lake Taupo who was Tongariro's lover.

So angry was Tongariro at this betrayal that he blew his top (as only volcanoes can) and Taranaki took off for the coast. The defeated Taranaki gouged a wide scar (the Wanganui River) in the earth as he fled south in anger, pain and shame, meeting the sea at Wanganui and then moving still further west to his current position, where he's remained in majestic isolation ever since, hiding his face behind a cloud of tears.

The Maori did not settle the area between Taranaki and Pihanga very heavily, perhaps because they feared the lovers might be reunited, with dire consequences. Most of the Maori settlements in this district were clustered along the coast between Mokau and Patea, concentrated particularly around Urenui and Waitara.

Egmont National Park was created in 1900 and is the second-oldest national park in the country.

Information

If you plan to tramp in Egmont National Park, get hold of local information about current track and weather conditions before you set off. Two visitor information centres are operated by DOC on the mountain, offering maps and advice on weather and track conditions. The North Egmont Visitor Centre (☎ 756 0990, fax 756 0991) is the closest to New Plymouth and therefore the most visited. It is open from 9 am to 5 pm daily from December to April. Otherwise it's open to 4 pm on weekdays (except Tuesday, when it is closed) and to 5 pm on weekends. On the other side of the mountain, the Dawson Falls Visitor Centre (☎ 025-430 248) is open from 8 am to 4.30 pm Wednesday to Sunday (daily in December and January).

Other places for maps and information on the mountain include DOC's Stratford Area Office (☎ 765 5144) on Pembroke Rd, coming up the mountain from Stratford, and the DOC office in New Plymouth (☎ 758 0433). There are also information centres around the mountain in New Plymouth (☎ 759 6080), Stratford (☎ 765 6708) and Hawera (☎ 278 8599).

Tramping & Skiing

In winter the mountain is popular with skiers, while in summer it can be climbed in one day. There are a number of excellent tramping possibilities, including hikes to the summit or right round the mountain. Shorter tracks ranging from easy to difficult and in length from 30 minutes to several hours start off from the three roads heading up the mountain.

Due to its easy accessibility, Mt Taranaki ranks as the 'most climbed' mountain in NZ. Nevertheless, tramping on this mountain holds definite dangers and should not be undertaken lightly.

The principal hazard is the erratic weather, which can change from warm and sunny to raging gales and white-out conditions unexpectedly quickly; snow can come at any time of year on the mountain, even in summer. There are also precipitous bluffs and steep icy slopes. In good conditions tramping around the mountain, or even to the summit, can be reasonably easy, but the mountain has claimed over 50 lives. Don't be put off, but don't be deceived.

If you intend to go tramping, get a map and consult a conservation officer for current weather and track conditions before you set off. Ensure that you have up-to-date maps. Be sure to register your tramping intentions and some emergency contact numbers with a DOC office. Read and heed its pamphlet *Taranaki: The Mountain*.

If you intend to walk or climb for any distance or height then get the relevant Infomap (No 273-09).

A trip to the North Egmont and Dawson Falls visitor and display centres is worthwhile for the views, and there are numerous long and short tracks and bushwalks as well. The Dawson Falls centre has interesting displays on the park and mountain, and screens an audiovisual.

The roads to the Stratford Mountain House Motor Lodge, East Egmont and Dawson Falls also have many worthwhile tracks and bushwalks. From the Mountain House Motor Lodge, Pembroke Rd continues 3km to the Stratford Plateau and from there a 1.5km walk takes you to the Manganui ski area. Skiing equipment can be hired at the Mountain Lodge in Stratford (see Places to Stay later).

There are two main routes to the summit. The safest and most direct route goes from the North Egmont Visitor Centre; allow about six to eight hours for the return trip. This route on the north side of the mountain loses its snow and ice earliest in the year. Another route to the summit, taking off from the Dawson Falls Visitor Centre, requires more technical skill and keeps its ice longer; if you go up this way, allow seven to 10 hours for the return trip.

The round-the-mountain track, accessible from all three mountain roads, goes 55km around the mountain and takes from three to five days to complete. You can start or finish this track at any park entrance and there are a number of huts on the mountain. You must purchase a hut ticket at visitor centres or through DOC.

If you are an inexperienced climber or want other people to climb or tramp with, DOC can put you in contact with tramping clubs and guides in the area. MacAlpine Guides (☎ 751 3542) provides guided trips to the summit year-round. Another reliable operator is Chris Prudden (☎ 758 8261).

Places to Stay

Camping, Cabins & Backpackers There are many tramping huts scattered about the mountain, administered by DOC and reached only by trails. Most cost $10 a night (for two tickets, purchased from DOC offices), but some cost $5 (one ticket). You provide your own cooking, eating and sleeping gear, they provide bunks and mattresses, and no bookings are necessary – it's all on a first-come, first-served basis.

By the Dawson Falls Visitor Centre (☎ 025-430 248), *Konini Lodge* has bunkhouse accommodation at $15/7.50 for adults/children. At North Egmont the *The Camphouse* (☎ 756 0990) has bunks for $15/7.50. If you intend staying at either place you must bring your own sleeping bag, food and cooking utensils. Bookings are essential, and you must carry out *all* your rubbish.

There are motor camps at New Plymouth, Stratford, Eltham, Hawera, Opunake, Waitara and Oakura, but camping is not encouraged within the park itself – you're supposed to use the tramping huts.

The *Missing Leg* (☎ 752 2570, 1082 Junction Rd) in Egmont Village has dorm beds for $14 and doubles for $35 and there's a swimming hole.

Guesthouses The *Dawson Falls Holiday Lodge* (☎ 765 5457), beside the visitor centre, is an attractive alpine-style lodge with lots of carved wood and painted decorations, good views, comfortable rooms and sitting rooms and a spacious dining room. Doubles cost from $110 to $130. There is fine dining (five courses) for $37.50. A courtesy car will meet public transport in Stratford.

On the east side of the mountain, *Mountain Lodge* (☎ 765 6100), on Pembroke Rd about 15km from Stratford, has rooms and chalets with kitchens from $95. You can

TARANAKI

hire skis in winter for use at the Manganui ski area. The same management also runs **Andersons Alpine Lodge** (☎ 765 6620), further down the mountain not far from the DOC office. It's a modern place in pleasant surroundings. There's one en suite double ($120) and a double and twin ($95 each).

Getting There & Away
There are several points of access to the park, but three roads lead almost right up to where the heavy bush ends. Closest to New Plymouth is Egmont Rd, turning off SH3 at Egmont Village, 12km south of New Plymouth, and heading another 16km up the mountain to the North Egmont Visitor Centre. Pembroke Rd enters the park from the east at Stratford and ascends 18km to East Egmont, Stratford Mountain House, the Plateau car park and Manganui ski area. From the south-east, Manaia Rd leads up to Dawson Falls, 23km from Stratford.

Public buses don't go to Egmont National Park but shuttle buses from New Plymouth to the mountain include Carter Travel (☎ 759 9039), Cruise NZ Tours (☎ 758 3222) and Withers (☎ 751 1777).

AROUND MT TARANAKI
Mt Taranaki is the main attraction but there are also other places of interest around the Taranaki region.

There are two principal highways around the mountain. SH3, on the inland side of the mountain, is the most travelled route, heading south from New Plymouth for 70km until it meets the coast again at Hawera. The coast road, SH45, heads 105km around the coast from New Plymouth to Hawera, where it meets up again with SH3. A round-the-mountain trip on both highways is 175km, although short cuts can be taken. Get a *Taranaki Heritage Trails* booklet, available free from information centres and DOC offices.

Stratford
pop 9730
Stratford, 40km south-east of New Plymouth on SH3, is named after Stratford-upon-Avon in England, Shakespeare's birthplace, and almost all of its streets are named after Shakespearian characters.

The town has an excellent visitor information centre (☎ 765 6708, ✉ stratford@info.stratford.govt.nz) on Broadway, the main street (it's also the AA agent), and a DOC field centre (☎ 765 5144) on Pembroke Rd, heading up to Mt Taranaki.

On SH3, 1km south of the centre, the **Taranaki Pioneer Village** is a four-hectare outdoor museum with 50 historic buildings. It's open from 10 am to 4 pm daily (entrance is $7, children $3).

At Stratford is the turn-off for Pembroke Rd, heading up the mountain for 18km to East Egmont, the Stratford Mountain House and the Manganui ski area. It is also the southern end of the Stratford–Taumarunui Heritage Trail.

Places to Stay & Eat Beside the King Edward Park, the **Stratford Top 10 Holiday Park** (☎ 765 6440, ✉ stratfordholpark@hotmail.com, 10 Page St), has tent sites, powered sites, cabins, tourist flats, a backpackers bunkhouse with dorms for $16 per person and an indoor heated pool. The same management runs the **Taranaki Accommodation Lodge** (☎ 765 5444, 7 Romeo St) near the information centre. This big, pink building used to be a home for trainee nurses. A bed in one of the rooms here costs $18.

The main street has numerous fast-food/takeaway places. Good cafes include **Urban Attitude** and the excellent **Backstage Cafe**, both on the main street.

Stratford-Taumarunui Heritage Trail
From Stratford, the Whangamomona–Tangarakau Gorge route (SH43) heads off towards Taumarunui in central North Island. The route has been designated a Heritage Trail, passing by many historic sites, including historic **Whangamomona village**, **Maori pa sites**, **small villages**, **waterfalls**, **abandoned coal mines** and small **museums**. You can pick up a free Heritage Trails booklet from information centres or DOC offices in Stratford, Taumarunui or New Plymouth that give details of places of interest along

the route; keep an eye out for the blue-and-yellow Heritage Trail signs along the way, with explanatory plaques.

It takes a minimum of 2½ to three hours to drive the 150km from Stratford to Taumarunui (or vice versa), as the road winds through hilly bush country and 30km of it is unsealed. Nevertheless it's a good trip if you can put up with the road. It's best to start early in the day; allow at least five hours for the trip if you plan to make stops to see the historic sites. Fill up with petrol from the Stratford or Taumarunui ends, as petrol stations are limited once you're on the road. This road is definitely off the beaten track.

Eltham & the Lakes
About 10km south of Stratford is Eltham, well known for its cheeses. You can get information from the Eltham Public Library (☎ 764 8838) on High St; it is open from 9.30 am to 5.30 pm on weekdays (till 6.30 pm Thursday).

Eleven kilometres south-east down the Rawhitiroa Rd is **Lake Rotokare** (Rippling Lake), the largest stretch of inland water in Taranaki. There's a 1½- to two-hour walk around the lake through native bush.

The nearby artificial **Lake Rotorangi**, 46km long, is popular for boating and fishing.

On Manaia Rd 4km north of Kaponga, which is about 13km west of Eltham on the road to Opunake, is **Hollard Gardens**, administered by the National Trust. It's most colourful from September to November when the rhododendrons bloom but many other plants provide colour year-round. The vast array of rare plants makes it a horticulturist's delight, with posted half and one-hour walks through various gardens. It's open from 9 am until 5 pm daily ($5, children free).

Hawera
pop 8740
Hawera is on the coast 70km south of New Plymouth and 90km from Wanganui. In the town is Information South Taranaki (☎ 278 8599, ✉ visitorinfo@stdc.govt.nz) at 55 High St, beside the dominating water tower. The AA office (☎ 278 5095) is at 121 Princes St.

Things to See & Do Elvis fans might be interested in visiting the **Kevin Wasley Elvis Presley Memorial Room** (☎ 278 7624, 025-982 942), 51 Argyle St, which has a collection of Elvis records (over 2000) and souvenirs. Please phone before you arrive (entry by donation).

The excellent **Tawhiti Museum** houses a private collection of remarkable exhibits, models and dioramas covering many aspects of Taranaki heritage. The lifelike human figures were modelled on real people around the region; it's quite an unusual museum.

A **bush railway** operates on the first Sunday of each month and every Sunday during school holidays. It is on Ohangai Rd near the corner of Tawhiti Rd, 4km from town. It's open from 10 am to 4 pm Friday to Monday but on Sunday only from June to August ($5, children $1.50).

One of the newest and most exciting activities is **dam dropping and white-water sledging** with Kaitiaki Adventures (☎ 0800-338 736, 025-249 9481). The trips, which centre on the Waingongoro River, take three hours ($80 per person) and include sliding down a dam on a board, and then sledging a further 4km on the river (Grade II to III). Also included is a journey past Okahutiti Pa, birthplace of the Maori prophet Tohu Kakahi, an advocate of passive resistance following the Taranaki Land Wars of the 1860s (see Parihaka later in this chapter). All gear is provided. Kaitiaki Adventures also does river trips in Tauranga and Rotorua (see those sections in the Bay of Plenty chapter for details).

Two kilometres north of Hawera on Turuturu Rd are the remains of the pre-European **Turuturumokai Pa**. The reserve is open to the public daily. The Tawhiti Museum has a model of the pa.

Dairyland (☎ 278 4537) is on the corner of SH3 and Whareroa Rd, 2km south of Hawera. It has interactive and audiovisual displays (including a dairy tanker on its collection route) covering all aspects of the dairy industry ($5). The licensed *cafe* revolves, simulating a rotary cowshed floor. It's open from 9 am to 5 pm daily, plus evenings from Thursday to Sunday.

TARANAKI

Places to Stay & Eat The *King Edward Park Motor Camp* (☎ 278 8544) on Waihi Rd, adjacent to the park, gardens and municipal pool, has tent ($8) and powered sites ($9), cabins and on-site vans.

Hawera has two farm backpackers beyond the Tawhiti Museum. *Ohangai Farm Backpacker* (☎ 272 2878), on the Urupa Rd in Ohangai, is a 360-cow dairy farm with a well-equipped backpackers in the paddocks. The cost is $14 in good four-bed rooms or $30 for twin rooms. German and French are spoken. Free pick-up from Hawera is offered, or take the Tawhiti Rd from Hawera, turn right in front of the museum and follow the signs for 5km.

Another good farmstay backpackers in the area is *Wheatly Downs* (☎ 278 6523, ⓔ wheatlydowns@taranaki-bakpak.co.nz), also past the Tawhiti Museum – don't turn right but keep going straight on the Ararata Rd (the extension of Tawhiti Rd) for 4km beyond the museum. Dorm beds are $16 and twins/doubles are $36/40. There is free pick-up from Hawera.

Oakura

If you're starting round the mountain from New Plymouth on the coast road, SH45, the first settlement you'll come to is tiny Oakura, 15km west of New Plymouth, known for its beautiful beach, which is great for swimming, surfing and windsurfing. Oakura has a craft shop called the Crafty Fox which is open daily, and a surfing and windsurfing shop.

The *Wave Haven* (☎ 752 7800, 1518 Main Rd), a comfortable place with a deck on the corner of Ahuahu and Main South Rds, isn't far from the beach and is extremely popular with wave riders. Dorms are $15 and there are single and double rooms.

The *Oakura Beach Motel* (☎ 752 7680, 53 Wairau Rd) charges from $69 for two.

The local pub has an attractive beer garden. The popular, upbeat *Burnt Toast* is licensed and has a good, varied menu.

The Carriage Theatre Restaurant & Cafe is housed in a former railway carriage behind the Crafty Fox.

Lucy's Gully

Lucy's Gully, 23km from New Plymouth on SH45, is one of the few places where exotic trees are being maintained in a national park. A pleasant picnic area, it is also the start of a couple of tracks into the Kaitake Ranges. Further along SH45, turn west at Pungarehu onto Cape Rd to reach **Cape Egmont Lighthouse** – it's closed to visitors.

Parihaka

Inland 2km from Pungarehu is the Maori village of Parihaka, formerly the stronghold of the prophets Te Whiti and Tohu, and once one of the largest and most-successful Maori villages in NZ.

Te Whiti and Tohu led a passive resistance campaign against the government's confiscation of land after the Taranaki Land Wars, but the two were jailed in 1881 (without trial) and Parihaka was razed. The heavily armed troops were opposed only by dancing children.

The spirit of Te Whiti lives on; his descendants and followers meet at Parihaka annually. Parihaka is not open to the public.

Opunake

Opunake is the largest town on the west side of the mountain. There's a fine beach in the small Opunake Bay, a peaceful place good for swimming and surfing.

The information office (☎ 761 8663) is in the Egmont Public Library & Cultural Centre on Tasman St.

Right on the beach, the *Opunake Beach Camp Resort* (☎ 761 8235) has tent/powered sites for $8/9 per person, and on-site caravans ($15 per backpacker).

In town, the *Opunake Motel & Backpackers Lodge* (☎ 761 8330, 36 Heaphy Rd) has motel units from $55, a cottage ($20 per person) and a lodge ($15 per person).

The Coromandel

The Coromandel is a rugged, densely forested peninsula where rivers force their way through gorges and pour down steep cliffs to the sea. The peninsula, with its beautiful coastal scenery and fine beaches, gets very busy in summer, and small towns and holiday resorts are scattered up and down the coast on both sides of it. The Coromandel Forest Park stretches almost the entire length of the peninsula and the landscape gets more rugged and more isolated further north. The peninsula is one of the best parts of the scenic Pacific Coast Highway, which links Auckland with Napier.

South of the Coromandel Peninsula are the pancake-flat Hauraki Plains and, to the west, the bird-watchers' heaven, the Firth of Thames.

Getting There & Away

Air Great Barrier Airlines (☎ 09-256 6500, 0800-900 600) services the Coromandel Peninsula. Flights operate between Whitianga and Great Barrier Island (Claris) via Pauanui and Matarangi. In summer there are departures from Whitianga on Wednesday, Friday and Sunday at 11 am and from Great Barrier on these days at 1 pm.

There are also flights to Auckland from Whitianga via Pauanui and Matarangi. In summer these depart both Whitianga and Auckland twice daily. There are various concessions for families, frequent fliers and groups. A student fare is $74/139 one way/return.

Bus Thames is the transport hub of the Coromandel. InterCity (☎ 09-913 6100) has daily buses from Auckland to Thames ($20; two hours). You can continue on to Paeroa, Waihi and Tauranga.

There are three InterCity bus passes that allow you to travel around the peninsula. With the Coromandel Busplan you can travel from Auckland to Thames and travel around the peninsula via Coromandel Town and Whitianga – from there returning to

HIGHLIGHTS

- Discovering Hahei, Hot Water, Matarangi and Whangamata, among NZ's finest beaches
- Driving through the dramatic coastal scenery
- Exploring the peninsula's isolated, rugged north
- Walking in the stunning Coromandel Forest Park
- Walking though history at Thames
- Bird-watching at the Firth of Thames

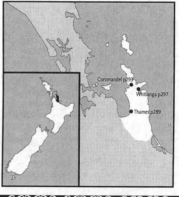

Coromandel p293
Whitianga p297
Thames p289

Thames. At this point you have a choice: to travel back to Auckland or to go to Rotorua. It's $89/60 for adults/children.

The Coromandel Loop pass ($47/31) goes from Thames to Coromandel and Whitianga, then back to Thames.

The third pass is called Forests, Islands and Geysers. With this you can travel north from Auckland to Waipoua Kauri Forest and the Bay of Islands. From here you go to Great Barrier Island with Great Barrier Airlines, and then on to Whitianga by air before bussing on to Rotorua. From Rotorua you can go to either Taupo and Wellington or to

THE COROMANDEL

THE COROMANDEL

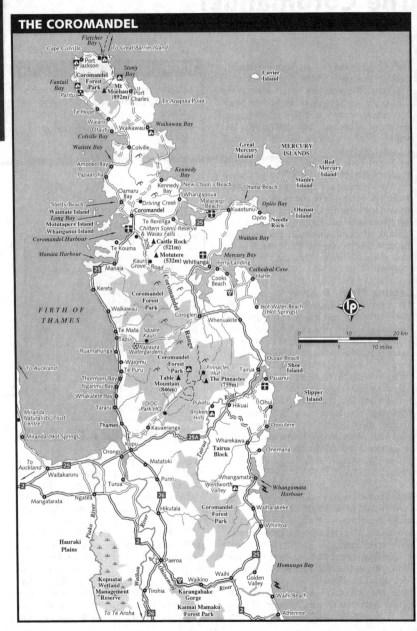

Auckland via the Waitomo Caves. This pass costs $275 (children $184).

A local bus operates daily except Saturday between Whangamata, Opoutere and Hikuai, south of Tairua.

Go Kiwi Shuttles (☎ 07-866 0336) operates a door-to-door service between Whitianga/Tairua and Auckland ($52), between Thames and Auckland ($42; one hour) and between Whitianga/Tairua and Thames ($28). There are discounts from 15% for backpackers.

It can take a surprisingly long time to get around the Coromandel. It takes about one hour and 10 minutes to get from Thames to Coromandel town, another hour from Coromandel to Whitianga, another hour from Whitianga to Tairua and 40 minutes from Tairua back to Thames.

Hitching Hitching is good on most of the peninsula but be prepared for long waits from Coromandel Town to Colville or across to Whitianga. Traffic on the east coast is busy during holiday periods, but otherwise light.

Hauraki Plains

☎ 07 • pop 21,100

The pancake-flat Hauraki Plains are drained by the Piako and Waihou Rivers, which flow into the Firth of Thames.

Bird-watching on the firth at Miranda, and hot springs at Miranda and Te Aroha help slow the traveller down. To the east of the rural centre of Paeroa is the historic Karangahake Gorge and the mining town of Waihi.

MIRANDA

Avid bird-watchers will love this area, one of the most accessible for studying birds. It's off the Thames-Pokeno road, only an hour's drive from Auckland. The vast mudflat on the western side of the Firth of Thames is teeming with aquatic worms and crustacea, which attract thousands of Arctic-nesting shore birds over the Arctic winter.

The two main species seen are the bar-tailed godwit and the lesser knot, but it isn't

---

Plant a Kauri

Coromandel Peninsula once supported magnificent stands of the long-lived kauri tree, but after logging in the 19th and early 20th centuries, little remains. In 1999 Kauri 2000 was launched to organise and encourage replanting. For $10 you can have a kauri seedling planted on your behalf by Kauri 2000 volunteers. You receive a voucher, explaining the project's vision and operation and, after the seedling is planted (June/July), a certificate indicating its exact location. If you were to return to the Coromandel, you could check on your little kauri tree.

For more information contact the secretary of Kauri 2000 Trust (☎/fax 07-866 2656), Box 174, Whitianga, New Zealand.

---

unusual to see turnstones, curlew sandpipers, sharp-tailed sandpipers and the odd vagrant red-necked stint and terek sandpiper.

Miranda also attracts internal migrants after the godwits and knots have departed, including the pied oystercatcher and the wrybill from the South Island, and banded dotterels and pied stilts from both main islands. For more information, visit the Miranda Naturalists' Trust Centre and pick up a copy of *Shore Bird Migration to and from Miranda*.

The **Miranda Hot Springs** complex (☎ 867 3055) has open and covered hot pools, private spas, play areas and powered camp sites. It's open from 9 am to 9 pm daily and entry is $7 (children $4).

Places to Stay & Eat

The **Miranda Naturalists' Trust Centre** (☎ 09-232 2781) has clean and modern rooms at its education centre. A bunk bed is a reasonable $15 for nonmembers ($10 for members); a self-contained unit costs $45 for two. Membership of the trust is $25 per year. About five minutes' drive north of the centre is the popular **Kaiaua fish and chip shop** (there's also a restaurant). The local **hotel** next door has meals as well.

Not far south of the centre, next to the hot springs, is the tidy **Miranda Holiday Park**

THE COROMANDEL

(☎ 07-867 3205), where bunk beds are $20 per person, motel units $80 and camp sites $12 for the first night and $10 a night thereafter. Guests get into the hot pools for free.

PAEROA
pop 4000

The Maori name for the Coromandel range was Te Paeroa-o-Toi (The Long Range of Toi) and local Maori are descendants of the *Arawa* and *Tainui* canoes. In the early colonial period, before the plains were drained, Paeroa was a thriving port, and evidence of this can be seen at the Paeroa Historical Maritime Park. The double-paddle steamer, *Kopu,* once operated between Paeroa and Auckland.

New Zealand's own 'internationally famous in NZ' soft drink had its beginnings in this town. But all that remains of Lemon & Paeroa is one giant bottle (left here after Gulliver's travels?).

The Paeroa Information Centre (☎/fax 862 8636) is on Belmont Rd (SH2)

A big bottle for a big thirst!

CHRISTINE NIVEN

and is open from 9 am to 5 pm weekdays and 10 am to 3 pm on weekends during summer. The town has a small museum, open from 10 am to 3 pm weekdays.

Karangahake Gorge

The Karangahake Gorge Historic Walkway, along the Ohinemuri River, was created when the Paeroa to Waihi railway line was closed in 1979. Waikino is at the eastern end of the gorge. After floods in 1981 the only building left standing was the Waikino Hotel.

The visitor centre in Waikino, now the terminus of the 6km Waihi to Waikino vintage railway, has information on the history and walks of the area. The Department of Conservation (DOC) pamphlet *Karangahake Gorge Historic Walkway* ($1.50) outlines several easy walks and suggests harder ones.

Three highlights of the walkway are the **Owharoa Falls** and the Talisman and Victoria **gold battery sites**. There's a small museum and a craft shop in Waikino. A big attraction here, especially for kids, is the **goldfield train** (using steam and diesel) that runs between Waikino and Waihi. The train departs Waihi at 11 am and 12.30 and 2 pm daily and returns from Waikino at 11.45 am and 1.15 and 2.45 pm. It costs $7/10 one way/return (children $2.50/4).

The **Ohinemuri Estate Winery & Cafe** (☎ 862 8874), on Moresby St, Karangahake (on SH2 about 6km east of Paeroa, towards Waikino), serves Mediterranean-style food and, of course, its own wines. It's open daily in summer and Friday to Sunday in winter.

Places to Stay & Eat

Singles/doubles with shared bathrooms at the *Paeroa Hotel (☎ 862 7099)* cost $25/45, while units at *Casa Mexicana (☎ 862 8216)* cost $58/70 including free spa. The *Racecourse Motel (☎ 862 7145),* with rooms for $50/60, and the refurbished *Paeroa Motel (☎ 862 8475),* $49 for singles, are other accommodation options.

On Belmont Rd, you'll find the *Colonial Cafe* opposite the information centre, *Belmont Bakery* at No 15, *Tui Coffee Lounge* at No 18 and the *Four Seasons Chinese* at No 70. The *Talisman Cafe & Crafts* is near the Ohinemuri Estate Winery.

TE AROHA
pop 3800

Te Aroha, 55km north-east of Hamilton on SH26, is at the foot of the mountain of the same name. The name (literally 'The Love') comes from a story of a chief who sat here filled with love for his people and the land. It's well worth the climb.

In European times, Te Aroha became a favourite spa resort and the hot mineral and soda pools in the domain are still a favourite place to relax after a walk in the area.

Orientation & Information

Te Aroha Domain, a large park on Whitaker St, a block or two south of the clock tower, has most of the town's attractions, including Te Aroha Museum, the spa baths, a geyser, walking tracks to Mt Te Aroha, a restaurant and the information centre and DOC office.

The Te Aroha Information Centre (☎ 884 8052, ☎ infotearoha@xtra.co.nz), 102 Whitaker St, is open from 9 am to 5 pm weekdays and 10 am to 3 pm weekends. It also serves as the town's Automobile Association (AA) agent, sells maps and provides information on Mt Te Aroha and the Kaimai-Mamaku Forest Park (on behalf of DOC).

Things to See & Do

Te Aroha Museum, in the Cadman building in the domain, occupies the town's original bathhouse building and has exhibits on the mining and agricultural development of the town. It's open from 11 am to 4 pm daily from 26 December to the end of March, and from 1 pm to 3 or 4 pm on Saturday, Sunday and public holidays for the rest of the year (entry by donation).

History buffs might also like to see NZ's oldest organ, the 1712 **Renatus Harris pipe organ** in St Mark's Church.

The **Hot Soda Water Baths** (☎ 884 8717) in the domain have two types of thermal water: soda and mineral. All the baths are in private hot-tub pools and are $7 for half an hour ($3 children). The baths are open from 10 am to 10 pm daily and are popular, so book in advance on the weekend.

Behind the pools is the 3.5m-spouting **Mokena Geyser**, said to be the only soda-water geyser in the world. It's quite active, going off every half-hour or so.

Walking

The walking tracks up Mt Te Aroha start at the rear of the domain, from behind the hot pools. It takes about an hour on a relatively easy track to ascend to the Bald Spur Lookout (350m), also called the Whakapipi Lookout; it's a further two hours' steep climbing to reach Te Aroha's summit (950m). The view is magnificent.

The **Wairere Falls**, two waterfalls at 73m and 80m high, are 26km south of Te Aroha.

Places to Stay & Eat

Te Aroha Holiday Park (☎ 884 9567), about 2km west of Te Aroha on Stanley Rd, has a pool and tennis courts. Tent sites are $7 per person, powered sites $8, cabins start at $30 for two, tourist flats at $52 and on-site caravans are $30. There are also backpacker bunks for $13 per person.

Te Aroha YHA (☎ 884 8739), on Miro St, is a pleasant small cottage and charges $12/14 per person for dorms/doubles. Bicycles (free) are available. Another budget option is *4 Seasons Backpackers Lodge* (☎ 884 9306, 21 Waihou Rd), with tent sites and a lodge that sleeps 10 ($15 per person).

Te Aroha Motel (☎ 884 9417, 108 Whitaker St) has units at $58/70 for singles/doubles.

The information centre can provide referrals for farmstays and B&Bs in the area.

At the surprisingly trendy and licensed *Caffè Banco (174 Whitaker St)*, open for lunch Tuesday to Sunday and dinner Thursday to Sunday, you can shop for collectibles while dining. Housed in a heritage building, *Domain House Restaurant (1 Wilson St)* is more formal but a perfect spot for lunch.

Getting There & Away

Turley-Murphy Connections (InterCity ☎ 834 3457) has buses travelling between Hamilton and Te Aroha ($9; one hour) and from Te Aroha to Thames ($9; 40 minutes), daily except Saturday. These connect with InterCity services in Hamilton.

WAIHI
pop 4700

Waihi, once a booming gold-mining town, has a number of architectural reminders of its heyday. Gold was first discovered in 1878 and the Martha Mine became the richest gold mine in the country and was worked until 1952. It has since been reopened. There is a lookout over part of it from the pumphouse next to the Waihi Information Centre (☎ 863 6715) on Seddon St.

Things to See & Do

The interesting **Waihi Gold Mining Museum & Art Gallery** on Kenny St has superb models of and displays about the local Martha Mine. It's open from 10 am to 4 pm weekdays (closed on Friday in winter) and 1.30 to 4 pm weekends ($2, children $1).

Tours of the **Martha Mine** are available on weekdays. There is no charge, but a donation is appreciated; the money is given to nonprofit community organisations. Bookings are essential; phone ☎ 863 9880.

Railway buffs have repaired 8km of track between Waihi and Waikino and run the **Goldfields Vintage Train** between the towns. To get to Waihi train station turn off SH2 at Wrigley St and proceed to the end. (See also the earlier section on the Karangahake Gorge.)

Garden lovers should head for the **Waihi Waterlily Gardens** at Pukekauri Rd. It's a relaxing place and there's a cafe in the gardens. It's open from 10 am to 4 pm daily from November to April. There is a small entry fee and waterlilies are also sold here.

Waihi Beach, 11km east, is a small, expanding town with a fine surf beach that is popular in summer.

Places to Stay

The **Waihi Motor Camp** (☎ 863 7654, 6 Waitete Rd), in Waihi town, has tent and caravan sites, as well as cabins starting at $30 for two, en suite cabins at $40 and two tourist flats at $50.

Waihi Beach has several options. **Waihi Beach Holiday Park** (☎ 863 5504, 15 Main Rd) has powered sites starting at $18, tourist cabins at $36, deluxe tourist cabins at $45 and on-site caravans at $36 (all prices are for two). Additionally there are backpacker cabins for $15 per person. **Athenree Hot Springs & Holiday Park** (☎ 863 5600), on Athenree Rd, has powered sites for $20, cabins starting at $35 and tourist cabins at $40. **Beachhaven Holiday Park** (☎ 863 5505, 21 Leo St) has powered sites for $10 per adult, tourist cabins starting at $40 for two and tourist flats at $60. The **Bowentown Motor Camp** (☎ 863 5381), on Seaforth Rd at Waihi Beach south, has powered sites starting at $20 for two, tourist cabins at $42, tourist flats at $55 and a motel unit at $60.

The **Golden Cross** (☎ 863 6306), on the corner of Rosemount and Kenny Sts, is an old pub offering backpacker beds for $15 in shared rooms, as well as singles, doubles and twin rooms for $20 per person. The **Palm Motel** (☎ 863 8461), on Parry Palm Ave, and **Waihi Motel** (☎ 863 8094), on SH2, both have single/double rooms starting at $60/70. The **Rob Roy Hotel** (☎ 863 7025), on the corner of Seddon and Rosemount Rds, has rooms for $22/45 as well as twin rooms with private bathrooms for $50. The **Waihi Beach Hotel** (☎ 863 5402) is a modern, beer barn-style pub with rooms with private facilities starting at $60. The **Shalimar Motel** (☎ 863 5439, 40 Seaforth Rd) has units starting at $85. The **Sea Air Motel & Motor Home Park** (☎ 863 5655), on Emerton Rd, has eight self-contained units and eight motor-home sites; units start at $60/70.

The information centre has an up-to-date list of B&Bs and homestays in the area. At Waihi is **Westwind B&B** (☎ 863 7208, 22 Roycroft St), which has singles/doubles for $30/60.

There are several places at Waihi Beach, including **Chestnut Lodge** (☎ 549 2495, 25 Ross Ware Drive), near Athenree Forest, with singles/doubles for $40/65, and **Spindrift Beachstay** (☎ 863 5136, 287 Seaforth Rd), where rooms are $50/75.

For a top-end experience try the *French Provincial Country House* (☎ 863 7339) at Golden Valley Trig Rd N, 5km from Waihi. Singles/doubles cost from $100/130, including breakfast.

Places to Eat

Good places to eat in Waihi include *Chambers Wine Bar & Restaurant (22 Haszard St)*, a classy licensed place in the former council chambers. For a cafe with lots of character try the *Miners Arms (22 Seddon St)*. It's licensed and you can get burgers, wedges, salads, quiche and good coffee. *The Farmhouse Cafe (14 Haszard St)* has a selection of home-made pies ($2.25). *Grandpa Thorn's (4 Waitete Rd)*, in a rural setting, is open Tuesday to Sunday and seafood is its speciality.

At Waihi Beach is the intriguingly named *Jellyfish & Custard Restaurant & Bar*, on the corner of Elizabeth St and Shaw Rd (lunches and dinners). *Cactus Jack's Family Restaurant (31 Wilson Rd)* and the *Waihi Beach RSA* also serve meals.

The *Waitete Orchard*, which is home to all sorts of organic delights and fruit wines, is on Waitete Rd.

Coromandel Peninsula

☎ 07 • pop 27,700

The Coromandel Peninsula has some of the North Island's finest coastal scenery and beaches. It is very much a bastion for those seeking an alternative lifestyle away from the bustle of Auckland, a serenity only briefly punctuated by the hordes of Christmas holiday-makers.

The west coast of the peninsula, bounded by the shallow Firth of Thames, is scenic and contains the picturesque historical towns of Thames and Coromandel. However, the most spectacular coastal scenery is on the east coast, which is the main resort area.

The backdrop to this beautiful coastline is a rugged, forest-clad mountain range that runs along the peninsula's spine and offers many good opportunities for tramping.

History

Maori have lived on the peninsula since well before the first settlers arrived; the sheltered areas of the east coast supported a large population. This was one of the major moa-hunting areas of the North Island, although other subsistence practices included fishing, sealing, bird-hunting and horticulture.

The history of European colonisation of the peninsula and the plains to the south is steeped in gold-mining, logging and gumdigging. Gold was first discovered in NZ at Coromandel in 1852 by Charles Ring, but the rush was short-lived once miners found it was not alluvial gold but gold to be wrested from the ground by pick and shovel. More gold was discovered around Thames in 1867, and over the next few years other fields were proclaimed at Coromandel, Kuaotunu and Karangahake. In 1892 the Martha Mine at Waihi began production and by the time it closed in 1952 around $60 million worth of gold had been extracted. The area is rich in semiprecious gemstones such as quartz, agate, amethyst, jasper, chalcedony and carnelian.

Kauri logging was big business on the peninsula for around 100 years. Allied to the timber trade was shipbuilding, which took off after 1832 when a mill was established at Mercury Bay. By the 1880s Kauaeranga, Coroglen (Gumtown) and Tairua were the main suppliers of kauri to Auckland mills. Things got tougher once the kauri around the coast became scarce due to indiscriminate felling, and loggers had to penetrate deeper into the bush for the timber. Getting the logs out became more and more difficult; some logs were pulled out by bullock teams, others had to be hauled to rivers and floated out after dams were built and tramways constructed on the west coast. By the 1930s the logging of kauri on the peninsula had all but finished.

A useful brochure entitled *Coromandel Peninsula – Heritage Trails* outlines urban heritage trails in Thames, Coromandel and Whitianga.

THAMES
pop 6810

Thames is the gateway to and main town of the Coromandel, lying on the shallow Firth of Thames. Its streets are lined with old wooden houses and pubs dating from the 19th century, when the gold rush and kauri trade made it one of the biggest towns in NZ.

Most visitors merely pass through Thames on their way to the scenic bays and beaches to the north and east.

Information

The Thames Information Centre (☎ 868 7284, ✉ thames@ihug.co.nz) is at 206 Pollen St. It's open from 8.30 am to 5 pm weekdays and 9 am to 4 pm weekends. It provides copies of the *Thames Heritage Trail* and *Coromandel Craft Trail* pamphlets, and is also an agent for AA, InterCity and Tranz Rail – you can book tickets here.

The DOC office (☎ 868 6381, 867 9080) in the Kauaeranga Valley (the main office for the Coromandel region) is open from 8 am to 4 pm daily.

Things to See & Do

At the northern end of Pollen St visit the **gold mine and stamper battery** for a look at the town's gold-mining history. The Hauraki Prospectors' Association has set up a working stamper battery, has displays and photographs, and regularly conducts tours of the mine. It is open from 10 am to 4 pm daily ($6).

The **School of Mines and Mineralogical Museum** on the corner of Brown and Cochrane Sts has a full collection of NZ rocks, minerals and fossils. It's open from 11 am to 3 pm daily. The local **historical museum**, on the corner of Cochrane and Pollen Sts, has pioneer relics, rocks and old photographs of the town. It is open from 1 to 4 pm daily ($2.50, children $1).

Kids might enjoy riding on the little train that is run on Sunday (1 to 4 pm from October to March and 1 to 3 pm from April to September) by the Thames Small Gauge Railway Society. It costs $1 to take the trip between the little station near the School of Mines, and the Goldfields shopping centre.

There is an interesting **market** every Saturday morning at Pollen St, Grahamstown, but get there by 9 am. Fruit and produce (including organic), handicrafts and clothing are on sale, and local musicians serenade shoppers.

Guided treks in the Kauaeranga Valley and further afield are available through Back Country Trekking, starting at $40 per person (half-day) all inclusive. Contact Jason Donald on ☎ 868 7597.

The large concrete phallus overlooking the town on Monument Hill is in fact the **WWI Peace Memorial**, with good views of Thames and the surrounding countryside. Another good vantage point is the former **Totara Pa**, once occupied by the Ngati Maru tribe until its defeat by Hongi Hika in 1821. It is now a cemetery, but careful observation will reveal the remains of fortifications and deep trenches.

The **Kakara Hide** is an excellent birdwatching hide at the edge of the mangroves just off Brown St.

Bicycles and kayaks can be rented in Thames, the aero club offers scenic flights and there is horse trekking in the Kauaeranga Valley. The information centre has details.

Places to Stay

Camping & Cabins The *Dickson Holiday Park* (☎ 868 7308) is 3km north of Thames in an attractive, quiet valley beside a stream. Tent sites cost $10 per person, powered sites $20, tourist cabins and vans $38 and tourist flats $58. The backpacker bunkroom (a YHA associate) costs $15 per person. There's a garden with tropical butterflies and orchids and a cafe.

See the North of Thames section for camp sites on the coast north of Thames.

Hostels *Sunkist Lodge* (☎ 868 8808, 0800-767 786, 506 Brown St) is a relaxed place in a historic building, which was the Lady Bowen Hotel from 1868 to 1952. It's said to have a resident ghost though we haven't been lucky enough to see it. Dorm beds cost $14 and $16 and twin and double rooms are $34. The upstairs veranda is a

Forested islands and clear blue seas in Northland's Bay of Islands

Kawakawa's famous toilets in the making

Waipoua Kauri Forest, Northland's west coast

Paeroa's old post office, Coromandel Peninsula

Build your own spa on Hot Water Beach

Beautiful Hahei Beach on the Coromandel

Cathedral Cove, Coromandel Peninsula

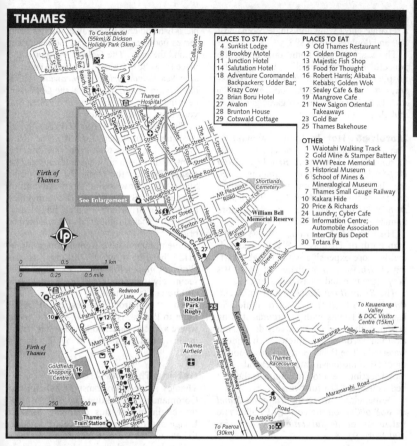

THAMES

PLACES TO STAY
4 Sunkist Lodge
8 Brookby Motel
11 Junction Hotel
14 Salutation Hotel
18 Adventure Coromandel
Backpackers; Udder Bar;
Krazy Cow
22 Brian Boru Hotel
27 Avalon
28 Brunton House
29 Cotswald Cottage

PLACES TO EAT
9 Old Thames Restaurant
12 Golden Dragon
13 Majestic Fish Shop
15 Food for Thought
16 Robert Harris; Alibaba
Kebabs; Golden Wok
17 Sealey Cafe & Bar
19 Mangrove Cafe
21 New Saigon Oriental
Takeaways
23 Gold Bar
25 Thames Bakehouse

OTHER
1 Waiotahi Walking Track
2 Gold Mine & Stamper Battery
3 WWI Peace Memorial
5 Historical Museum
6 School of Mines &
Mineralogical Museum
7 Thames Small Gauge Railway
10 Kakara Hide
20 Price & Richards
24 Laundry; Cyber Cafe
26 Information Centre;
Automobile Association
InterCity Bus Depot
30 Totara Pa

fine place to laze and watch the sun set over the placid Firth of Thames, and there's a pool table in the lounge downstairs. The manager, Geoff, is a mine of information on the Coromandel. Obtain a copy of the useful *Coromandel Backpackers' Guide* here or from the information centre.

Adventure Coromandel Backpackers (☎ 868 6200, 476 Pollen St) is situated in the Art Deco former Imperial Hotel, and was undergoing renovation at the time of writing. Dorms cost $13 to $15, twins $16 per person, doubles with en suite $40 and singles with shared bathroom $22. There's a laundry and

a little kitchen. Downstairs is the *Krazy Cow* bar and nightspot, open Friday and Saturday; the music goes on till around 1.30 am, so ask for a room as far out of earshot as possible. There are bands once a month.

B&Bs & Guesthouses The information centre keeps a list of B&Bs and homestays. Of note for its historical charm is *Brunton House* (☎ 868 5160, 210 Parawai Rd), a large place with verandas and a pool. Singles/ doubles are $50/85.

Cotswold Cottage (☎ 868 6306), on Maramarahi Rd, is a villa that has been moved here

THE COROMANDEL

all the way from Epsom, Auckland. There is a separate guest wing and single rooms cost $50 and doubles $75 to $95.

There are several homestays down the peaceful Kauaeranga Valley, including the hospitable and spotless *Valley View Homestay (☎ 868 7213, 53 Kauaeranga Valley Rd)*. The owners are keen organic gardeners and charge $70 for B&B for two.

Motels & Hotels Motels abound in Thames and north along the coast towards Coromandel. The plain *Brookby Motel (☎ 868 6663, 102 Redwood Lane)* is one of the cheapest with accommodation starting at $50/60 for singles/doubles. The *Avalon (☎ 868 7755)*, on Jellicoe Crescent, is more upmarket and charges $85 a double.

The *Coastal Motor Lodge (☎ 868 6843)*, 3km north of Thames on SH25, is considerably more expensive with cottages starting at $96 for two or chalets at $118. It's very attractive and pleasantly situated.

The *Brian Boru Hotel (☎ 868 6523, 200 Richmond St)*, on the corner of Pollen St, has double rooms with bathrooms starting at $66, with some imaginatively decked out as theme rooms complete with indoor waterfalls. The Brian Boru is known for its innovative murder-mystery weekends. The motel section, next to the hotel, has the best beds, costing $125 for two.

Desperados can try the *Junction Hotel (☎ 868 6008)*, on the corner of Pollen and Pahau Sts, or the *Salutation (☎ 868 6488, 400 Mary St)*.

Places to Eat

Pollen St, one of the longest straight shopping streets in NZ, has plenty of takeaways and coffee lounges. Try *Thames Bakehouse* at No 326 for baked goodies, *Food for Thought* for cake, quiche and sandwiches, and *Mangrove Cafe* at No 442 for good coffee.

In the Goldfields shopping centre is a *Robert Harris Coffee Shop*, the *Golden Wok* and *Alibaba Kebabs*. For value, the licensed *Old Thames Restaurant* on Pollen St is popular for moderately priced steaks, seafood and pizzas.

The *Majestic Fish Shop (640 Pollen St)* has a fish and chip takeaway at the front and serves good seafood meals in the restaurant around the back. The *Golden Dragon* is the place for a cheap Chinese meal or takeaways, as is *New Saigon Oriental Takeaways*, which has a smorgasbord. Nearby, at the *Gold Bar*, near the corner of Richmond and Pollen Sts, you can get good Tex-Mex meals.

The *Sealey Cafe & Bar (109 Sealey St)* is a fine establishment for a meal or just a drink. It has a pleasant courtyard out the front, and occasionally has live music. The *Udder Bar*, on the corner of Pollen and Sealey Sts, downstairs from Adventure Coromandel Backpackers, is a congenial place for a drink and meal. It has steaks, chicken, fish and light meals for reasonable prices.

Five minutes' drive from Thames, along SH25 heading towards Miranda, is the *Pipiroa Country Kitchen*, an excellent cafe, seemingly in the middle of nowhere, with a children's playground.

About 8km from Thames, on SH26 en route to Paeroa, is *Matatoki Farm Cheese* where you can taste and buy cheeses handmade from milk produced by the farm's cows.

Getting There & Around

Thames is the main transport hub for the Coromandel (see Getting There & Away at the beginning of this chapter). Sunkist Lodge and the information centre sell bus tickets and the Coromandel Busplan.

For local exploration, hire mountain bikes from Price & Richards on Pollen St ($20 per day).

COROMANDEL FOREST PARK

There are over 30 walks and tramps through Coromandel Forest Park, covering the area from the Maratoto Forest, near Paeroa, to Cape Colville. The most popular region is the Kauaeranga Valley, which cuts into the Colville Range behind Thames. There are old kauri dams in the valley, including the Tarawaere Waterfalls, Dancing Camp, Kauaeranga Main, Moss Creek and Waterfalls Creek Dams. Do not climb on them!

Walks in the Kauaeranga Valley, especially on weekends, have become so popular that DOC has built an 80-bed hut at the Pinnacles to accommodate trampers. Hut tickets ($15 per night) *must* be prebooked via the DOC Visitor Centre in Kauaeranga. One of the best, most accessible walks is through the valley to the Pinnacles. The three- to four-hour hike through regenerating forest to the jagged limestone outcrop is rewarded with great views. Other walks can be done in the area, though some trails are hazardous and have been closed – check with DOC.

Information
The DOC Visitor Centre (☎ 868 6381, 867 9080) is in the Kauaeranga Valley about 15km from Thames. It is open from 8 am to 4 pm daily. A pamphlet outlining the peninsula's mountain-biking tracks can be obtained here.

Places to Stay
There are *DOC camping grounds* scattered throughout Coromandel Forest Park. You'll find them around the northern tip of the peninsula at Fantail Bay, Port Jackson, Fletcher Bay, Stony Bay and Waikawau Bay. In southern Coromandel there are camp sites at Broken Hills and Wentworth Valley. Fees are $7 per night and bookings are required for Waikawau Bay over Christmas and New Year (☎ 866 1106). Elsewhere sites are available on a first-come first-served basis. There are resident site managers during summer.

Remote camping spots include those at Moss Creek, the Pinnacles Hut and Billygoat Clearing (all $7.50 per night). Pinnacles Hut ($15) must be prebooked through DOC (see earlier).

Getting There & Away
The headquarters and main entrance to the park are reached from the southern edge of Thames, along Kauaeranga Valley Rd. Sunkist Lodge in Thames has a bus going on demand to the end of the Kauaeranga Valley Rd for $10/20 one way/return. Jason Donald (☎ 868 7597) will also take you there ($15/25 per person one way/return;

$10/20 if there are two of you). Hitching in and out is reputed to be easy.

NORTH OF THAMES
As you travel north from Thames, SH25 snakes along the coast for 32km past lots of pretty little bays and calm beaches. Fishing and shellfishing are excellent all the way up the coast and the landscape turns crimson when the pohutukawa blooms in summer.

Along the way you pass through Whakatete Bay, Ngarimu Bay, Te Puru, Tapu and other small settlements. The **Rapaura Watergardens**, 6km inland from Tapu on the Tapu-Coroglen road, are open from 10 am to 5 pm daily in summer ($5, children $1) and there are tearooms here. Also on this road is the huge 'square' kauri, estimated to be 1200 years old.

Places to Stay
The *Boomerang Motor Camp (☎ 867 8879)* in Te Puru, 11km north of Thames, has camping, cabins and on-site vans. Nearby is the *Puru Park Motel (☎ 868 2686)* and the luxurious *Te Puru Coast View Lodge (☎ 868 2326),* a Mediterranean-style villa with rooms starting at $110.

A few kilometres north is the *Waiomu Bay Holiday Park & Motel (☎ 868 2777),* which has camping, cabins, tourist flats and motel units. The *Seaspray Motel (☎ 868 2863)* is also in Waiomu and charges $65/88 a single/double.

At Tapu, 22km north of Thames, the *Tapu Motor Camp (☎ 868 4837)* has camp sites, on-site vans and cabins. The backpacker rate is $12 per person in bunkrooms and cabins, and caravans are $31 for two. Also in Tapu, the *Te Mata Lodge (☎ 868 4834)* has a variety of accommodation in a quiet, idyllic bush setting. Backpacker beds are $10, and tourist flats are $58. There's an enormous kitchen and communal seating/recreation area. There are plenty of bushwalks from here, including one to the beach, and a pleasant swimming hole where the river meanders around the grounds. To reach Te Mata Lodge, go 1.5km past Tapu on the coast road, turn inland past the concrete bridge down Te Mata Creek Rd, and follow the road to the end.

COROMANDEL

pop 1620

At Wilsons Bay the road leaves the coast and cuts through hills and valleys until it reaches the next major town, Coromandel, 55km north of Thames. It was named after HMS *Coromandel*, which visited in 1820 to pick up a load of kauri spars for the navy. It was here, on Driving Creek, 3km north of the township, that Charles Ring discovered gold in 1852. At the height of the gold rush the town's population rose to over 10,000, but today it's a soporific little township noted for its crafts and alternative lifestylers.

Information

The Coromandel Information Centre (☎ 866 8598) is in the District Council building at 355 Kapanga Rd. It's open from 9 am to 5 pm daily (11 am to 3 pm on weekends in winter). The centre has many useful leaflets on the surrounding area and takes bookings for accommodation.

The DOC field centre is also in this building and has information on parks and walks.

Things to See

The small **Coromandel Mining & Historic Museum** on Rings Rd provides a glimpse of life in the old, gold days. Behind the main hall is the century-old solid kauri jailhouse (transferred here about 1990). The cell now on display was declared *tapu* (taboo) after a man asphyxiated in it in 1913 when he set his mattress on fire. The charred bit of floor where the gruesome incident occurred can still be seen. It's open from 10 am to 1 pm daily in summer, from 1.30 to 4 pm on weekends in winter ($2, children $0.50).

The **Coromandel Stamper Battery** (☎ 025-246 4898) on Buffalo Rd demonstrates the process of crushing ore, the first step in extracting gold, and shows various amalgamation processes. It is open from 10 am to 5 pm daily in summer and on weekends or by appointment in winter ($5, children $3).

Driving Creek (☎ 866 8703), 3km north of Coromandel, is the site of various fascinating enterprises masterminded by one of

Coromandel's leading artists, Barry Brickell. A potter who discovered excellent clay on his land, Brickell had to work out a way of moving it down the hill to his kiln. So he built his own railway to do it! The **Driving Creek Railway** travels up steep grades, across four high trestle bridges, along two spirals and a double switchback, and through two tunnels. It's an hour-long round trip starting at 10 am and 2 pm daily, with extra runs in summer ($12, children $6, family $30). A shop at the 'station' sells ceramics.

There are some lovely gardens in the area, including **Harmony Gardens**, 6km from town, and **Waiau Waterworks**, 9km from town, both on the 309 Rd. There's also **Waitati Gardens** on Buffalo Rd.

For crafts, Coromandel has interesting **craft shops** along Kapanga Rd. If you want to explore further afield, pick up a copy of the *Coromandel Craft Trail* pamphlet from the information centre.

Walking

Coromandel is in the middle of a region abounding in natural beauty, scenic reserves and attractive bushwalks. The information centre has a big map on the wall showing all the scenic reserves and the two farm-park recreation reserves with camping (Cape Colville and Waikawau Bay).

Two of the more notable walks are a 3km walk from Coromandel to Long Bay through a grove of large kauri and a climb through Whangapoua State Forest to the 521m Castle Rock off the 309 Rd. Get a copy of the DOC pamphlet *Coromandel Recreation Information*.

Places to Stay

Camping & Cabins The *Coromandel Motels & Holiday Park* (☎ 866 8830, 636 Rings Rd), 400m north-east of the post office, has tent/powered sites at $9/10 per person. Cabins cost $40 for two people and motel units $80. Off-season and family tariffs are available.

On the beachfront, 3km west of Coromandel, *Long Bay Motor Camp* (☎ 866 8720) has sites starting at $9 per person and on-site caravans from $40 for two.

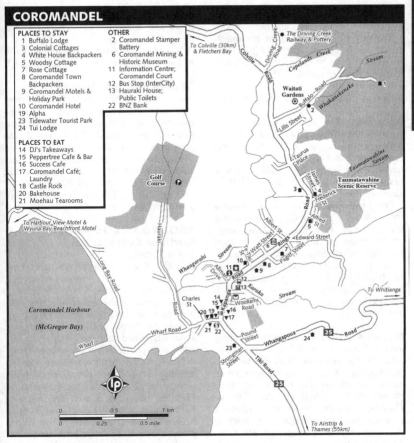

COROMANDEL

PLACES TO STAY
1 Buffalo Lodge
3 Colonial Cottages
4 White House Backpackers
5 Woodsy Cottage
7 Rose Cottage
8 Coromandel Town Backpackers
9 Coromandel Motels & Holiday Park
10 Coromandel Hotel
19 Alpha
23 Tidewater Tourist Park
24 Tui Lodge

PLACES TO EAT
14 DJ's Takeaways
15 Peppertree Cafe & Bar
16 Success Cafe
17 Coromandel Café; Laundry
18 Castle Rock
20 Bakehouse
21 Moehau Tearooms

OTHER
2 Coromandel Stamper Battery
6 Coromandel Mining & Historic Museum
11 Information Centre; Coromandel Court
12 Bus Stop (InterCity)
13 Hauraki House; Public Toilets
22 BNZ Bank

The **Shelly Beach Motor Camp** (☎ 866 8988), 5km north of Coromandel, has tent sites for $9, on-site vans for $35 and lodge units for $35. Also north of Coromandel are the **Oamaru Bay Tourist Flats & Caravan Park** (☎ 866 8735) on Oamaru Bay (7km north); **Papaaroha Motor Camp** (☎ 866 8818) at Papaaroha (12km); and **Angler's Lodge & Motor Park** (☎ 866 8584) at Amodeo Bay (18km).

Hostels The **Tidewater Tourist Park** (☎ 866 8888, 270 Tiki Rd), near the harbour, is a YHA-associate hostel. This friendly,

spotless place has cabins and tourist flats. Dorms, twins and doubles are $18 per person; self-contained two-person tourist flats are $70 and studio units $80. Bicycles can be hired for $10 per day.

Tui Lodge (☎ 866 8237, 600 Whangapoua Rd) is 10 minutes' walk from town. The Whitianga bus will stop at the gate or there's free pick-up on request. The backpacker house has a variety of accommodation and charges $16 in the dorms or $34 for twin and double rooms. Bikes are free to guests.

The **White House Backpackers** (☎ 866 8468), on the corner of Frederick St and

Rings Rd, is actually three houses. Dorm rooms are $14 and twins and doubles $35.

The tidy *Coromandel Town Backpackers* (☎ 866 8327, 732 Rings Rd) is a small hostel with dorm beds for $15 and a double room for $16 per person.

B&Bs & Guesthouses *Rose Cottage* (☎ 866 7047) is on Pagitt St, near the mining museum. This simple guesthouse in a private home charges $30/50 a single/double with a separate guest bathroom. *Woodsy Cottage* (☎ 866 8111), tucked away off Alfred St, is a delightful self-contained cottage nestled in bush. It is $75 for two ($10 for each extra person).

Other recommended places are *Allambee* (☎ 866 8011, 1720 Tiki Rd) at $70 a double, and the well-appointed *Buffalo Lodge* (☎ 866 8960) on Buffalo Rd, open in summer only and starting at $180 a double.

The peaceful *Jacaranda Lodge* (☎ 866 8002) on Tiki Rd is an imposing house set back off the highway 3km south of town. It has B&B starting at $45/75 a single/double and dinner is $25.

Motels & Hotels Coromandel has many motels charging from $65 to $95 a double, including *Coromandel Court* (☎ 866 8402, 365 Kapanga Rd), next to the information centre; the *Wyuna Bay Beachfront Motel* (☎ 866 8507, 2640 Wyuna Bay Rd); the *Harbour View* (☎ 866 8690, 25 Harbour View Rd); the *Alpha* (☎ 866 8709, 50 Wharf Rd); and *Colonial Cottages* (☎ 866 8856, 1737 Rings Rd).

The *Coromandel Hotel* (☎ 866 8760, 611 Kapanga Rd) has rooms for $50 for two.

Places to Eat

For cheap meals, try the *Bakehouse* on Wharf Rd, the bistro bar at the *Coromandel Hotel*, the *Moehau Tearooms*, *DJ's Takeaways*, *Castle Rock* (pizza, kebabs) and the *Coromandel Cafe*.

On Kapanga Rd, the *Success Cafe* has good food, including seafood (Coromandel mussels), pasta, nachos and more.

The *Peppertree Cafe & Bar* has great dishes using fresh local produce. It also offers 'helpful' breakfast items such as Berocca and mineral water. There's a kids menu as well.

You can't buy provisions beyond Colville so stock up before you leave Coromandel.

Getting There & Around

InterCity (☎ 09-913 6100) has daily buses between Coromandel, Thames, Whitianga and other places on the peninsula. The information centre has details and you should book tickets in advance.

You can get to Fletcher Bay with Carters Tours (☎ 866 8045), which also runs the town's sole taxi service (☎ 025-261 8975). See also Getting There & Away at the beginning of this chapter.

AROUND COROMANDEL
North of Coromandel

The road north is sealed up to the town of **Colville**, 85km north of Thames. Tiny Colville was formerly known as Cabbage Bay, named by Captain Cook who insisted that his crew eat the leaves of native cabbage trees to guard against scurvy. Now it is home to alternative lifestylers; there is a small wholefood cafe and a quaint cooperative store that sells just about everything.

North of Colville the roads are rough and hitching may not be so easy. From Colville you can head north along the west coast to Fletchers Bay or head over the ranges to **Port Charles**, a small collection of holiday baches (cottages) on a scenic bay with a pleasant beach. The road leads to another small bay with more holiday houses and then over a headland affording fine views to **Stony Bay** with its pebble beach and DOC camping ground. From Stony Bay, walking tracks lead to Fletcher Bay and Mt Moehau.

Following the west coast road, 12km north of Colville, you will find Te Hope and the start of the walk to **Mt Moehau** (892m), the peninsula's highest peak. This is a demanding three- to four-hour walk but you'll be rewarded with fine views of Coromandel and the Hauraki Gulf. The trail used to continue to Stony Bay, but walkers are no longer permitted to cross over the peak as it is a culturally and ecologically sensitive area.

The west coast road leads eventually to **Fletcher Bay** – a real land's end. This is a magical place with deserted beaches, forest and coastal walks and splendid views across to Great Barrier, Little Barrier and Cuvier Islands.

From Fletcher Bay, it's about a three-hour walk to Stony Bay on the east coast. Carters Tours (☎ 866 8045) will take you from Coromandel to Fletcher Bay from where you walk to Stony Bay. It will pick you up from Stony Bay and return you to Coromandel ($60). You can also arrange to do this trip from Whitianga. A lot of people elect to walk both ways. It is an easy, pleasant walk with great coastal views and an ambling section across open farmland.

Mountain bikers must use the longer and tougher marked stock route that runs along the flank of Mt Moehau.

Places to Stay There are DOC *camping grounds* at Fletcher Bay, Waikawau Bay and Stony Bay, on the eastern side of the peninsula, and at Port Jackson and Fantail Bay on the western side.

Colville Farm (☎ 866 6820, 866 6712), near Colville Town, is a place where you can join in with the activities. There's horse riding, starting at $15 per hour for guests, and interesting bushwalks to explore. A bed in the backpacker cottage is $13 to $14 per person, double rooms are $32, the bush lodge is $13 per person or it's $55 for the whole place. Camping is from $5 to $9.

The *Mahamudra Centre* (☎ 866 6851) across the road runs courses and provides accommodation for people interested in Buddhism.

Fletcher Bay Backpackers (☎ 866 6712, @ js.lourie@xtra.co.nz) is a small, comfortable 16-bed place perched up on a hill overlooking a farm and beach. It has all facilities but you must bring food (a mobile store visits daily between Christmas and about the second week of January). It charges $13 per person and is run year-round by the farm managers, Sue and Jim Lourie. Two sea kayaks and snorkelling gear are available for guests. You can also go on walks over the farmland. Fishing is good (for snapper and kingfish particularly), but you must bring your own gear. A smokehouse is also available.

You can pitch a tent in the adjacent *DOC camping ground* for $7 per night.

SH25 to Whitianga

There are two possible routes from Coromandel south-east to Whitianga. Of the two, SH25 is the longer (46km; 1¼ hours) and much of it is still gravel, but it's the more scenic route, following the coast and offering exquisite beach views. The other road is the unsealed 309 Rd.

If you continue on the much improved SH25 east of Coromandel you come to Te Rerenga, almost on the shore of Whangapoua Harbour. The road has sections of dirt and tight corners on which you have to take care. It forks at the harbour; if you head north you come to the end of the road at Whangapoua. From Whangapoua you can walk along the rocky foreshore to the isolated and pristine **New Chum's Beach**. The walk takes about 30 minutes and starts by the picnic area at the end of the road.

Continuing east you can visit the beach-side towns of Matarangi, Kuaotunu, Otama and Opito before heading south to Whitianga. This whole stretch has beautiful beaches. **Matarangi** has a good beach but it is a dull real-estate development, which seems to be the fate of parts of the Coromandel. **Kuaotunu** is a small settlement with a delightful beach and a camping ground. Off Opito Bay is the spectacular **Needle Rock**, so named because the hole through the rock is tapered like the eye of a needle.

Highway 309

Highway 309 (known locally as the 309 Rd) is the shorter route to Whitianga (32km, 45 minutes), but it's rather rough going as the road is unsealed. It's a bush road and is generally not as scenic as SH25, unless you want to get out and do some walking. It does have some excellent spots, including the **Chiltern Scenic Reserve**, **Waiau Falls**, a grove of large kauri trees and a two-hour return walking track to the summit of **Castle**

Rock (521m). The **kauri grove** is particularly interesting as there is a Siamese kauri, which forks just above the ground. The roots of the kauri are protected by a system of boardwalks.

The *309 Honey Cottage (☎ 866 5151)* is about 12km from Whitianga on the 309 Rd. It's a lovely place, relaxing and scenic, with farmland and bush. The cost is $15 per person in an old kauri cottage beside a river, or you can camp for $5 ($10 if you use cottage facilities).

WHITIANGA
pop 3540
The pleasant Whitianga area of Mercury Bay has a long history by NZ standards. The Polynesian explorer Kupe landed near here around AD 800 and the area was called Te Whitianga-a-Kupe (The Crossing Place of Kupe). At that time the land was abundant with moa but subsequent settlers soon whittled them down.

Mercury Bay was given its modern name by Captain Cook when he observed the transit of Mercury across the face of the sun while the *Endeavour* anchored in the bay in November 1769.

Whitianga is the main town on Mercury Bay. Buffalo Beach, the principal frontage onto the attractive bay, takes its name from HMS *Buffalo*, wrecked there in 1840. The beach itself is reasonable and there are seven good beaches all within easy reach of town.

The town is a big game-fishing base for tuna, marlin, mako (blue pointer shark), thresher shark and kingfish. It is very much a tourist town and its small population swells to mammoth proportions during the January holidays.

The Whitianga Information Centre (☎ 866 5555, ☒ whitvin@ihug.co.nz), 66 Albert St, is open from 8 am to 6 pm daily during the peak summer season. At other times it opens from 9 am to 5 pm weekdays, 9 am to 1 pm weekends. Also see www.whitianga.co.nz.

Museum
The little museum opposite the ferry wharf has many historical photos of Mercury Bay and the kauri-logging era, and exhibits on mining, blacksmithing, the colonial era, Maori carvings, the HMS *Buffalo* and other shipwrecks. The jaws of a 1350kg white pointer shark caught in the Hauraki Gulf in 1959 hang on the wall, overlooking all.

The museum is open from 10 am to 4 pm daily in summer, 11 am to 2 pm Sunday, Tuesday and Thursday in winter ($3, children $1.50).

Ferry Landing
From the Narrows, on the southern side of town, a passenger ferry crosses over to Ferry Landing, site of the original township on the southern side of Mercury Bay. The wharf at Ferry Landing was built in 1837 and the stone from which it is constructed came from Whitianga Rock, a *pa* (fortified Maori village) site of which Captain Cook said 'the best engineers in Europe could not have chosen a better site for a small band of men to defend against a greater number'. The view from **Shakespeare's Lookout**, on top of the white cliffs above Ferry Landing, is lovely and a great spot to see all of Mercury Bay with its many beaches and coves.

The five-minute ferry crossing costs $1 (children and bicycles $0.50). The ferry does not take cars, which have to take the circuitous route around the bay to the south, via Coroglen. The ferry runs continuously from 7.30 am to 10.30 pm in summer, from 7.30 am to noon and 1 to 6.30 pm in winter.

Bicycles can be hired from beside the store in Ferry Landing. You can walk, cycle or drive to excellent spots on this side, including the town of Cook's Beach, Lonely Bay, Front Beach and Flaxmill Bay (where Cook is believed to have careened the *Endeavour*), and further on to Hahei. A bus service also runs from Ferry Landing (see Getting There & Around later).

Purangi Winery (☎ 866 3724), 6km south, has wine tasting, including kiwi-fruit wine, and it operates cruises on the Purangi River.

At Wilderlands Trust on SH25, 14km south of Whitianga, you can buy organic produce. This place is popular with WWOOFers (see Accommodation in the Facts for the Visitor chapter). There's a children's play area here too.

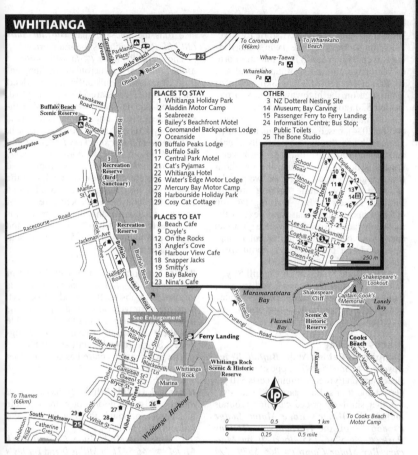

WHITIANGA

PLACES TO STAY
1 Whitianga Holiday Park
2 Aladdin Motor Camp
4 Seabreeze
5 Bailey's Beachfront Motel
6 Coromandel Backpackers Lodge
7 Oceanside
10 Buffalo Peaks Lodge
11 Buffalo Sails
17 Central Park Motel
21 Cat's Pyjamas
22 Whitianga Hotel
26 Water's Edge Motor Lodge
27 Mercury Bay Motor Camp
28 Harbourside Holiday Park
29 Cosy Cat Cottage

PLACES TO EAT
8 Beach Cafe
9 Doyle's
12 On the Rocks
13 Angler's Cove
16 Harbour View Cafe
18 Snapper Jacks
19 Smitty's
20 Bay Bakery
23 Nina's Cafe

OTHER
3 NZ Dotterel Nesting Site
14 Museum; Bay Carving
15 Passenger Ferry to Ferry Landing
24 Information Centre; Bus Stop;
     Public Toilets
25 The Bone Studio

Activities

Whitianga has many activities on land and water and the information centre can supply more details.

Dolphin Quest (☎ 866 5555) organises **swims with dolphins** in summer ($85). The dolphins, once regular visitors close to shore, are now are not so common and the tours are dependent on definite sightings. Wetsuits, snorkels and flippers are supplied. The three-hour Seven Island Seafari ($70) is a popular alternative when the dolphins are not around.

You can paddle around this interesting coastline in a **sea kayak** with Coromandel

Safaris (☎ 866 2850, 025-394 597). A one-day safari with equipment and lunch included is $75. Sailors appreciate quiet time on the sailing boat *Carino;* a full day's outing starts at $70.

Mercury Bay is rich in interesting **walks**. Watch your step, though – some of the mine shafts are quite deep. One of the more popular gold mines is reached by an enjoyable two-hour walk along a stream. The track starts on Waitaia Rd, 10km north-east of Whitianga. Many other good walks are across the estuary, five minutes away by ferry. The information centre has details on local walks, including tracks in the Whitianga Rock Scenic & Historic Reserve.

For **horse trekking**, the Twin Oaks Riding Ranch (☎ 866 5388) is 10 minutes north of Whitianga on the Kuaotunu Rd and Ace Hi Ranch (☎ 866 4897) is 8km south of Whitianga on the highway. Expect to pay around $30 (adults) for two hours.

Coromandel Four Wheel Bike Safaris (☎ 866 2034), based at Kuaotunu, takes trips in **quad bikes** through some really scenic and adventurous bush trails. If you haven't done this before it's a must; the four-hour trips are good value at $120 for two people.

There are two **bone carving** studios. Maurice Aukett of Bay Carving (☎ 866 4021), opposite the wharf and next to the museum, has a workshop where you can carve your own piece. Equipment is supplied and the process takes about three hours, costing from $25 to $50.

At the Bone Studio at 16 Coghill St you can see craftspeople at work and try your hand at it. It's open daily except Sunday and is $60 per day, including tuition and materials.

Places to Stay

Camping & Cabins At the *Buffalo Beach Resort (☎ 866 5854)*, opposite Buffalo Beach and on Eyre St, camping costs $10 per person and tourist flats start at $55 for two.

Other similarly priced camping grounds include the *Water's Edge Motor Lodge (☎ 866 5760)*, the *Harbourside Holiday Park (☎ 866 5746, 135 Albert St)*, the *Mercury Bay Motor Camp (☎ 866 5579, 121 Albert St)*; the *Whitianga Holiday Park (☎ 866 5896)*, at the northern end of Buffalo Beach; the *Aladdin Motor Camp (☎ 866 5834)*, on Bongard Rd; and the *Cooks Beach Motor Camp (☎ 866 5469)*.

Hostels *Buffalo Peaks Lodge (☎ 866 2933, @ buffalopeakslodge@xtra.co.nz, 12 Albert St)* is a friendly place with a spa and patio. It also sports an interesting mural of kiwi icons (including pavlova and a buzzy bee) and another mural around the spa depicting native birds. It is a fine backpacker lodge and charges $18 in dorms, $22 for singles

and $38 for doubles. The same management also runs the spic-and-span *Buffalo Sails (20 Mill Rd)*, which has the same prices.

The *Cat's Pyjamas (☎/fax 866 4663, 4 Monk St)* is run by an aeroplane building enthusiast (ask to see his unfinished product) and his wife. Dorms are $16, camping $10, twin and double rooms with shared bathrooms are $36 and a double with en suite is $40. They arrange trips to Hot Water Beach.

Coromandel Backpackers Lodge (☎ 866 5380, fax 866 5320, @ corobkpk@wave. co.nz, 46 Buffalo Beach Rd) is a converted seaside motel, under new ownership at the time of writing. This is a good hostel with a wonderful, sunny aspect. There's free use of kayaks, surfboards and fishing gear, plus bicycles for hire. It is $17 in a dorm, and double and twin rooms are $20 per person, linen included.

B&Bs The small and pleasant *Cosy Cat Cottage (☎ 866 4488, 41 South Highway)* is unusual – it's absolutely loaded with cat art. Cats are portrayed on everything from the sheets to the place mats at the dinner table and there are literally hundreds of cat figurines. Singles/doubles start at $50/80.

The information centre has several other B&Bs on its books.

Motels & Hotels Whitianga has about 20 motels. Most charge $70 or more a double in summer, although there are substantial reductions in winter.

Cheaper motels include *Central Park Motel (☎ 866 5471, 6 Mill Rd)* and *Bailey's Beachfront Motel (☎ 866 5500, 66 Buffalo Beach Rd)*.

Many others are along Buffalo Beach Rd, including the *Seabreeze (☎ 866 5570)* at No 71–72, and the ritzier *Oceanside (☎ 866 5766)* at No 32.

The *Whitianga Hotel (☎ 866 5818)*, on Blacksmith Lane, has double and twin rooms for $45 to $75 in the low season and from $85 to $95 in the high season.

Places to Eat

There's a range of budget places to eat. For pizza try *Bay Bakery*, for good pub food the *Whitianga Hotel*. There's a Chinese takeaway on Albert St.

Well known for its seafood and fish and chips, the popular *Snapper Jacks* on Albert St was at the time of writing being rebuilt after a fire. There's also the hard-to-find (but worth it) *Nina's Cafe*, near the intersection of Victoria and Coghill Sts. It has a Thai night on Thursday.

On the Esplanade and with sea views is *Angler's Cove*. Main meals start at $15 and there's an adjoining ice-cream parlour. There's also the *Harbour View Cafe*, which is good value. *Doyle's*, at No 21, has fancier dining in a restored, two-storey house – try a Thames flounder or a salmon steak. Mains are about $20.

At the beach end of Albert St is the licensed *Beach Cafe*, recommended for its pasta. *On the Rocks* on the Esplanade has succulent scallops and mussels. *Smitty's* on Albert St has wedges and gut-busting burgers.

Getting There & Around

Hot Water Beach Conxtions (☎ 866 2478) runs a bus from Ferry Landing at 7 and 10 am, and 12.30, 3 and 4.30 pm to Cook's Beach, Hahei and Hot Water Beach, with some services continuing to Dalmeny Corner on the highway for connections with buses to Auckland and Whitianga. It has a $20 explorer pass which allows you to get on and off along the way.

HAHEI & HOT WATER BEACH

This popular section of coast is accessible from the Stone Steps Wharf at Ferry Landing and from the highway. The offshore islands provide protection for the beaches around Hahei, which are arguably the best of the Coromandel's many fine beaches. The waters offshore and the islands have been incorporated as a **marine park** and are excellent for diving.

At the eastern end of Hahei Beach is a former Maori pa, Te Pare Point, which still has much evidence of the elaborate terracing used as fortifications. Just north of Hahei is **Cathedral Cove** (Te Whanganui a Hei), accessible only at low tide through a

gigantic arched cavern that separates it from Mares Leg Cove. This headland is also a former pa site.

To the south of Hahei is the **Hot Water Beach**, where thermal waters brew just below the sand. You can go down to the beach two hours each side of low tide, dig a hole in the sand (use a shovel as the water is hot) and sit in your own little natural spa pool; allow about 15 minutes to prepare your pool. If you want to take a cooling dip in the ocean afterwards, be very careful (see the boxed text 'Warning').

The *Hahei Explorer* (☎ 866 3910), a rigid inflatable boat, operates scenic trips to Cathedral Cove and Hot Water Beach daily from Hahei – landings are made whenever the sea allows.

Places to Stay & Eat

Sites at the *Hot Water Beach Motor Camp* (☎ 866 3735) cost $9 per person, more if you want power. On-site vans start at $30 and there's a three-bedroom house starting at $85.

The *Hahei Holiday Resort/Cathedral Cove Lodge Backpackers* (☎ 866 3889) is right on the beach and has tent/powered sites for $11/12 per person, cabins starting at $36, tourist cabins for $75 and self-contained units for $98. The backpacker lodge has beds starting at $16 and twin rooms for $38.

The *Tatahi Lodge* (☎ 866 3992) on Grange Rd behind the Hahei Store is a motel with sparkling, purpose-built backpacker accommodation. The excellent facilities cost $18 in the bunkrooms. Classy, self-contained, two-bedroom motel units cost $105 a double. The lodge lends out shovels for Hot Water Beach and arranges transport.

At the top end of the market are *Hay-Lyn Park Lodge* (☎ 866 3888, 11 Christine Terrace)*, The Church* (☎ 866 3533, 87 Beach Rd) and *Spellbound* (☎ 866 3543, 77 Grange Rd)*.

Good places to eat near the general store are *Breakers Restaurant* and *Luna Cafe*. The Church is also a great place to eat with plenty of atmosphere and terrific food. It's housed in a beautifully renovated former church, transported here from Taumarunui.

TAIRUA & PAUANUI
pop 2600

This twin-town is separated by Tairua Harbour. A passenger ferry links the two, otherwise it is a long drive. Tairua is small, older and lies on the highway; its tourist highlight is the climb to the top of **Paku** (an old pa site), which provides great views. If you climb Paku, legend has it that you will return in seven years. Most of the attractions on this side of the harbour are natural and thus free of charge.

Conversely, Pauanui is a real-estate agent's dream with canal-side homes for the rich. Pauanui has the pretty harbour on one side, a great surf beach on the other and pine-clad mountains behind. The only problem is that it's a boring, suburban development.

The area has a number of **walks**, including the Broken Hills, and activities include game fishing, canoeing and horse trekking.

The Tairua Information Centre (☎ 864 7575) on SH25 is open from 9 am to 4 pm daily (shorter hours in winter). The Pauanui Information Centre (☎ 864 7101) is at the Pauanui shopping centre.

The ferry service (☎ 864 8133 before 6 pm, 025-970 316 after hours) makes regular crossings between the two towns. It is $2/4 one way/return (children $1/2).

Places to Stay

You have the choice of five motor camps in this area. A camp site is about $10 per person and camping grounds usually have on-site vans and cabins available.

On SH25 in Tairua you'll find *The Flying Dutchman* (☎ 864 8448, 305 Main Rd)*, which had recently changed hands at the time of writing. It has a balcony area leading off the recreation room. The cost is $15 in shared rooms and $18 per person for twin and double rooms.

Closer to town, in a Spanish-style villa, is the *Tairua Backpackers Lodge* (☎ 864 8345, 200 Main Rd)*. This friendly place has people returning for the fresh fruit, vegetables and free-range eggs the owners provide for free. Dorms are $15, twins and doubles $20 per person and a single $25. Sightseeing tours to the Alderman Islands are good value. There is also a windsurfing school ($10 a session for guests), canoes and wave skis.

The *Sir George Grey Hotel* (☎ 864 8451) on Main Rd in Tairua has singles for $25.

There are at least 10 motels or lodges in Tairua and Pauanui. A good choice is the classy *Pacific Harbour Motor Lodge* (☎ 864 8581) on the main road. Doubles in this island-style resort are $140 in summer. For five-star luxury, *Puka Park Lodge* (☎ 864 8088) in snooty Pauanui is favoured by visiting dignitaries and pop stars.

Places to Eat

In Tairua, *Tyrone's Place* on the main road (near the BP station) has authentic Thai food and an interesting choice of ice cream.

The Gazebo also on the main road is popular for coffee, snacks and light meals. *Shells,* attached to the Pacific Harbour and specialising in Pacific Rim fare, is also open daily.

In the Pauanui shopping centre are *Kar-Lee's* BYO cafe and *Sweet Street*.

If you are extremely wealthy, then the *Puka Park Restaurant* and *Hunting Room Cafe* in Pauanui are probably troughs of choice.

OPOUTERE

Opoutere has a fine beach and, about a 15 minutes' walk from the road, the **Wharekawa Wildlife Refuge**, a breeding ground of the endangered NZ dotterel and the variable oystercatcher. Dogs must be kept out of here, and you must not cross into the roped-off area during the breeding season (inquire locally).

The **Opoutere YHA** (☎ 865 9072) is a fine place to get right away from it all. It's in a country setting, almost encircled by native bush and overlooking Wharekawa Harbour. You can take one of the hostel's kayaks and paddle around, and there are plenty of bushwalks in the area. Accommodation costs $15 in dorms, $18 per person in doubles, or you can camp on the extensive lawn. The management is friendly and informative.

Just down the road from the Opoutere hostel is **Opoutere Park Beach Resort** (☎ 865 9152), with camp sites starting at $19, powered sites for $21 and cabins for $27 (prices are for two).

WHANGAMATA

pop 3880

Whangamata (pronounced 'fa-nga-ma-ta') has a great 4km surf beach with an excellent break by the bar, and attracts a big influx of holiday-makers in summer. The Whangamata Information Centre (☎ 865 8340) on Port Rd, the main street, is open from 9 am to 5 pm daily in summer, with shorter weekend hours in winter.

Whangamata has a number of **craft** outlets outlined in a pamphlet available from the information centre. The area has some excellent walks. The most popular is the **Wentworth Falls walk**, which takes one hour (one way) through beautiful bush. To get to the track, take the highway south for 3km to the turn-off and then 4km to the camping ground. From the falls, a harder trail (get advice at the camping ground) leads to the top of the ranges and on to Marakopa Rd.

Horse riding, game fishing, kayaking, windsurfing and mountain biking can be arranged. The information centre has details.

Places to Stay

The **Pinefield Holiday Park** (☎ 865 8791) on Port Rd has powered and tent sites for $22 for two, standard cabins starting at $30, tourist cabins at $45 and tourist flats at $45. Similarly, the **Whangamata Motor Camp** (☎ 865 9128) on Barbara Ave has sites for $8 per person, powered sites for $18, on-site vans for $30 and tourist cabins starting at $35.

The DOC-owned **Wentworth Valley Campground** (☎ 865 7032) is in a beautiful valley setting at the start of the trek to Wentworth Falls, 7km from Whangamata. It has gas barbecues and cold showers, and camping is $7. Also in Wentworth Valley is the upmarket **Bushland Park Lodge** (☎ 865 7468). This get-away-from-it-all retreat has saunas, spas and massages available as well as a winery-style restaurant. Prices start at $145 for two.

The **Garden Lodge** (☎/fax 865 9580), on the corner of Port Rd and Mayfair Ave, is about 1km south of the shopping centre. It's spotless and well run. There are dorm bunks starting at $18, twins/doubles with shared bathrooms at $45 and motel units at $75. These prices increase during the peak season. It has all the facilities you need, including a kitchen and laundry.

Whangamata Backpackers Hostel (☎/fax 865 8323, 227 Beverley Terrace) is popular with surfers and has basic accommodation for $15.

There are numerous homestays and B&Bs; the information centre has details.

Places to Eat

Cafe culture has arrived in Whangamata, although there are also plenty of takeaways.

Vibes Cafe (638 Port Rd) is a trendy place with fresh, interesting food. **Gingers Health Food & Cafe** (601 Port Rd) is the best option for vegetarians and bakes great breads. **Pinky's** (703 Port Rd) is an unpretentious place with moderately priced meals, and is open daily. **Neros**, nearby, specialises in wood-fired pizzas.

Cafe 101, on Casement Rd (off Port Rd), has a musical theme and regular live performances. It's open Thursday to Sunday.

Bay of Plenty

☎ 07 • pop 230,500

The sweeping Bay of Plenty is blessed with a good climate and fine beaches, and is a thriving agricultural district most noted for kiwi fruit. The bay stretches from the main city of Tauranga in the west to Whakatane and Opotiki, the main focal points of the Eastern Bay.

Just inland in this region is one of NZ's premier tourist attractions, Rotorua. The Rotorua region is famous around the world for its geysers, hot springs, mud pools, shimmering lakes, trout fishing, tramping and a host of other activities.

The region is also of great significance to the Maori, whose presence dates back to their discovery and exploration of the area in the 14th century.

Rotorua

pop 56,900

Rotorua is the most popular tourist area of the North Island. Nicknamed 'Sulphur City', it has the most energetic thermal activity in the country with bubbling mud pools, gurgling hot springs, gushing geysers and evil smells. Rotorua also has a large Maori population whose cultural activities are among the most interesting and accessible in NZ.

The city itself is thriving, buoyed by the huge influx of tourism (earning it another local nickname: 'Roto-Vegas'). It's scenically located 280m above sea level on the shores of Lake Rotorua, which teems with trout. The area has some interesting trout springs and wildlife parks.

History

The Rotorua district was first settled in the 14th century when the canoe *Te Arawa,* captained by Tamatekapua, arrived from Hawaiki at Maketu in the central Bay of Plenty. The settlers took the tribal name Te Arawa to commemorate the vessel that had

HIGHLIGHTS

- Visiting the geysers and boiling mud pools and the Maori Arts & Crafts Institute at Whakarewarewa, Rotorua
- Cruising the lakes around Rotorua – Rotomahana, Rotorua and Tarawera
- Strolling and dining in an inner-city suburb
- Feasting at a Maori *hangi* and concert at Rotorua
- Visiting Whakaari (White Island), NZ's most active marine volcano
- Exploring the coastline of the eastern Bay of Plenty

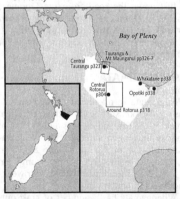

brought them safely so far. Much of the inland forest was explored by Tamatekapua's grandson, Ihenga, who also named many geographical features of the area. The name Rotorua means 'The Second Lake' (*roto* means 'lake' and *rua* 'two') as it was the second lake that Ihenga discovered.

In the next few hundred years, various sub-tribes spread through the area and, as they grew in number, they split into more sub-tribes and conflicts broke out over territory. In 1823 the Arawa lands were

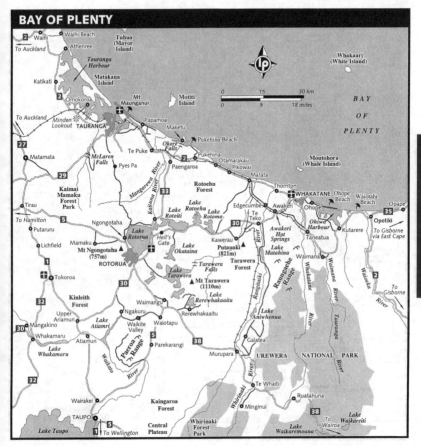

BAY OF PLENTY

invaded by the Ngapuhi chief, Hongi Hika, of Northland, in the so-called Musket Wars. Both the Arawa and the Northlanders suffered heavy losses and the Ngapuhi eventually withdrew.

During the Waikato Land War (1863–67) the Arawa tribe threw in their lot with the government against their traditional enemies in the Waikato, gaining the backing of its troops and preventing East Coast reinforcements getting through to support the Maori King Movement.

With the wars virtually over in the early 1870s, European settlement around Rotorua took off with a rush. The army and government personnel involved in the struggle helped broadcast the scenic wonders of the place. People came to take the waters in the hope of cures for all sorts of diseases, and Rotorua's tourist industry was thus founded. The town's main attraction was the fabulous Pink and White Terraces, formed by the sinter deposits of silica from volcanic activity. Touted at the time as the eighth natural wonder of the world, they were destroyed in the 1886 Mt Tarawera eruption (see the boxed text later in this chapter).

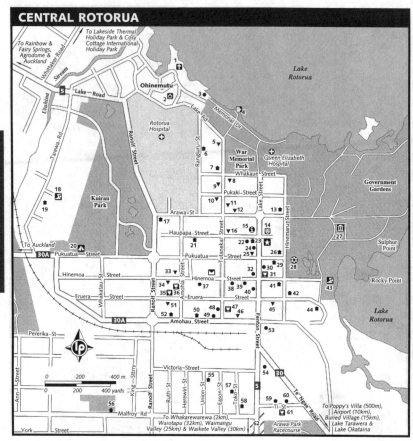

CENTRAL ROTORUA

Orientation & Information

The main shopping area is down Tutanekai St, the central part of which is a parking area and pedestrian mall. Running parallel, Fenton St starts by the Government Gardens near the lake and runs all the way to the Whakarewarewa ('Whaka') thermal area 2km away. It's lined with motels for much of its length.

The office of Tourism Rotorua (☎ 348 5179, ✉ marketing@tourism.rdc.govt.nz) is at 67 Fenton St, on the corner of Haupapa St, and is open from 8 am to 6 pm daily. The Web site is at www.rotoruanz.com. It makes bookings for everything around Rotorua and has a travel agency. There is also a money changing bureau (open 8.30 am to 5.30 pm daily), a cafe and other services for travellers, including showers, luggage storage and public telephones (buy your phonecard from the money changing bureau).

The Automobile Association (AA; ☎ 348 3069) is on Amohau St. The American Express agent is Blackmore's Galaxy Travel (☎ 347 9444), at 1315 Tutanekai St. Thomas Cook has a forex desk in the Air New Zealand office and there are plenty of banks that will change foreign currencies.

CENTRAL ROTORUA

PLACES TO STAY
6   Dudley House B&B
7   Novotel Royal Lakeside Hotel;
    Clarke's Bar
13 Princes Gate Hotel
17 Hot Rock; Lava Bar
19 Kiwi Paka YHA
20 Acacia Park
21 Cactus Jacks Downtown Backpackers
23 Rotorua Downtown Backpackers
26 Good Sports Hotel; Dobbo's Bar
29 Rotorua Central Backpackers
41 Eaton Hall
42 Millennium; Bar Zazu
44 Lake Plaza Rotorua
50 Spa Lodge
52 Backpackers Rotorua
55 Funky Green Voyager
56 Ann's Volcanic Rotorua
57 Tresco International
58 Morihana Guest House
62 Motel & Hotel Area

PLACES TO EAT
5   Pizza Hut
8   Lady Jane's Ice Cream Parlour
9   Lewisham's Austrian Restaurant; Zambique; Freos
10 Thai Restaurant
11 Japanese Sushi Bar
12 Fat Dog
16 Pig & Whistle Pub
25 Cameron's Bar & Grill
33 Zanelli's
34 Rendevous Restaurant
45 Korea House Restaurant
46 Mr India
51 Sirocco; Finally Found It

OTHER
1   St Faith's Anglican Church
2   Tamatekapua Meeting House
3   Soundshell
4   Rotorua Lakefront Jetty & Lakefront Cruises
14 Civic Theatre
15 Tourism Rotorua; Map & Track Shop; Bus Depot
18 Aquatic Centre
22 Carey's Sightseeing Tours
24 Laundry; Nomad Cyber Cafe
27 Rotorua Museum of Art & History
28 Orchid Gardens
30 Link Rent-a-Car
31 Wild Willy's
32 Air New Zealand; Mt Cook Airline; Thomas Cook
35 O'Malley's
36 Monkey Jo's
37 Ansett New Zealand
38 Indoor climbing wall
39 Rotorua Cycle Centre
40 Pins Cycles
43 Polynesian Spa
47 Churchhill's Bar
48 Blackmore's Galaxy Travel & American Express Agent
49 Automobile Association
53 Pak N Save
54 Big Fresh Supermarket
59 Budget Rent-a-Car
60 Rent-a-Dent
61 Ace of Spades

The post shop is on Hinemoa St, between Tutanekai and Amohia Sts, and a laundry is on Fenton St, opposite the police station.

A transport service for the disabled (wheelchairs) is available on the hour or by arrangement (depot at Allison's Unichem Pharmacy in the City Plaza, opposite DEKA supermarket). For inquiries contact the Arthritis Centre (☎ 348 5121) between 10 am and 3 pm Monday to Friday. Rotorua's two taxi companies can arrange taxis with wheelchair hoists (see Getting Around later in the Rotorua section).

Thermal Air is a useful free weekly tourist publication and the annual free *Rotorua Visitors Guide* is indispensable. Tourism Rotorua sells a good map *(Gateway to Geyserland)* of the city and surrounding area for just $2.

Lake Rotorua

Lake Rotorua is the largest of 12 lakes in the Rotorua district. It was formed by an eruption and subsequent subsidence of the area. Two cruises on the lake depart from the Rotorua lakefront jetty, at the northern end of Tutanekai St.

The *Lakeland Queen* paddle steamer (☎ 348 6634) does one-hour breakfast cruises ($26), luncheon cruises ($28/18 buffet/cruise only) and dinner cruises ($40 to $45, depending on the length of the cruise) on the lake. Children are half-price. The *Scatcat* motorised catamaran (☎ 347 9852) does a one-hour circuit of Mokoia Island ($25, children free).

Self-drive speedboats from Lake Front Boat Hire (☎ 025-813 209) during summer are $35 for 15 minutes and $60 for 25 minutes. Kayaks from the same firm cost $15 per hour.

Ohinemutu

Ohinemutu is a lakeside Maori village. Its name means 'Place of the Young Woman who was Killed' and was given by Ihenga in memory of his daughter.

The historic Maori **St Faith's Anglican Church** by the lakefront has a beautiful interior decorated with Maori carvings, *tukutuku* (weaved panels), painted scrollwork and stained-glass windows. An image of Christ wearing a Maori cloak is etched on a window so that he appears to be walking on the waters of Lake Rotorua. Seen from this window, it's surprising how much Lake Rotorua does resemble the Sea of Galilee. The church is open from 8 am to 5 pm daily.

Opposite the church is the impressive **Tamatekapua Meeting House**, built in 1887. Named for the captain of the *Arawa* canoe, this is an important meeting house for all Arawa people. The Magic of the Maori Concert is held here (see Maori Concerts & Hangi later in this section).

A good **craft market** is held every second weekend at the Soundshell.

Rotorua Museum of Art & History

This impressive museum (☎ 349 4350, ✆ rotoruamuseum@rdc.govt.nz), better known as the Bath House, is in a Tudor-style building in the Government Gardens. The building was an elegant spa retreat, built in 1908; it also saw service as a rehabilitation centre for soldiers during WWI. You can tour through some of the reconstructed spa rooms and marvel at the seemingly odd therapies practised therein.

The museum has a very good exhibition *(Te Ohaaki O Houmaitahiti)* of the *taonga* (treasures) of the local Arawa people. Opposite is a small theatre that runs a Tarawera exhibition that includes a rousing video (every 20 minutes) on the 1886 Mt Tarawera eruption, with great sound effects and simulated quakes. Another rather less dramatic video on the eruption (running on a continuous loop) can be viewed in the main exhibition area, where there is plenty of information on Tarawera before and after the eruption. The survivors' stories have been preserved, as has the strange tale of the ominous, ghostly war canoe that appeared before a boatload of astonished tourists hours before the eruption. The museum is open from 9.30 am to 5 pm daily in winter (until 6 pm in summer), and entry is \$7.50 (children \$3). There is a pleasant cafe with good coffee.

In the **gardens** around the Bath House are typical English touches, such as croquet lawns, and rose gardens – not to mention steaming pools and a petanque ring. There's also a nine-hole golf course (☎ 348 9126). It costs \$6 for a round (seniors \$4) and you can hire trundlers, clubs and motorised golf carts; bookings are essential. A recent addition is the 27-bay driving range; \$6 for a 50-ball bucket, \$11 for 110 balls. It's open from 7.30 am to 9 pm daily.

Orchid Gardens

The Orchid Gardens on Hinemaru St contain an extensive hothouse of orchids that bloom year-round as well as a Micro-world display where you can get a microscopic view of living reptiles and insects. There is also a big **water organ**, really a huge fountain with over 800 jets. It's a magnificent 15-minute show of water that swirls, leaps and generally makes graceful, ballet-like movements up to 4m high. It plays every hour on the hour from 9 am to 5 pm. The complex is open from 8.30 am to 5.30 pm daily (\$10, children \$4).

Te Whakarewarewa

This is Rotorua's largest and best-known thermal reserve and a major Maori cultural area. It's pronounced 'fa-ka-re-wa-re-wa' – most call it simply 'Whaka'. However, even Whakarewarewa is a shortening of its full name, Te Whakarewarewatanga o te Ope Taua a Wahiao, which means 'The Gathering Together of the War Party of Wahiao'.

Whakarewarewa's most spectacular geyser is **Pohutu** (Maori for 'Big Splash' or 'Explosion'), an active geyser that usually erupts at least once an hour. Pohutu spurts hot water about 20m into the air but sometimes shoots up over 30m in brief 'shots'. The average eruption lasts about five to 10 minutes, though the longest is reputed to have lasted for 15 hours! You get an advance warning because the Prince of Wales' Feathers geyser always starts off shortly before Pohutu.

Whaka is accessible from two sides. Access to the Whaka thermal village is from Tryon St; entry is \$15 (children and seniors

Hinemoa & Tutanekai

The story of Hinemoa and Tutanekai is one of NZ's most
well-known lovers' tales. It is
not a legend but a true story,
though you may hear one or
two variations. The descendants of Hinemoa and Tu-
tanekai still live in the Rotorua
area today.

Hinemoa was a young
woman of a sub-tribe that
lived on the western shore of
Lake Rotorua. Tutanekai was
a young man of the sub-tribe
that lived on Mokoia Island,
on the lake.

The two sub-tribes some-
times visited one another;
that was how Hinemoa and

Hinemoa and Tutanekai (George Woods, circa 1940)

Tutanekai met. But though both were of high birth in their respective tribes, Tutanekai was illegiti-
mate and so, while the family of Hinemoa thought he was a fine young man and could see that the
two young people loved one another, they were not in favour of them marrying.

At night, Tutanekai would play his flute on the island, and sometimes the wind would carry his melody
across the water to Hinemoa. In his music she could hear his declaration of love for her. Her people,
meanwhile, took to tying up the canoes at night to make sure she could not take off and go to him.

Finally, one night, as she heard Tutanekai's music wafting over the waters, Hinemoa was so overcome with longing that she could stand it no more. She peeled off her clothes to rid herself of the
weight and swam the long distance from the shore to the island. In some versions of the story she
buoyed herself up with calabash gourds.

When she arrived on Mokoia, Hinemoa was in a quandary. She had to shed her clothing in order
to swim, but now on the island she could scarcely walk into the settlement naked! She sought refuge
in a hot pool to figure out what to do next.

Time passed and eventually a man came to fetch water from a cold spring beside the hot pool. In
a deep man's voice, Hinemoa called out, 'Who is it?' The man replied that he was the slave of
Tutanekai, come to fetch water. Hinemoa reached out of the darkness, seized the calabash and broke
it. This happened a few more times, until finally Tutanekai himself came to the pool and demanded
that the interloper identify himself. He was amazed when it turned out to be Hinemoa.

Tutanekai stole Hinemoa into his hut. In the morning, when Tutanekai was sleeping very late, a
slave was sent to wake him and came back reporting that someone else was also sleeping in Tutanekai's bed. The two lovers emerged, and when Hinemoa's efforts to reach Tutanekai had been
revealed, their union was celebrated.

$7.50, under four years free) and includes
the tours and the concerts. It's open from
8.30 am to 5 pm daily. There are concerts in
the meeting house at 11.15 am and 2 pm,
and regular guided tours through the village
with its souvenir shops and cafe, and the

thermal area (try sweetcorn cooked in a hot
pool for $2) between 9 am and 4 pm daily.
On weekends, usually during summer, kids
dive for coins in the river that flows beneath
the bridge leading to the village. This is an
old tradition at Whaka.

ALEXANDER TURNBULL LIBRARY, WELLINGTON NZ

BAY OF PLENTY

On the other side of Whaka is the NZ Maori Arts & Crafts Institute (☎ 348 9047) with working craftspeople, an art gallery, a replica Maori village, kiwi house, a Maori concert held daily at 12.15 pm and access to the thermal reserve. There are guided tours at 3 pm daily (free). To enter Whaka through the institute, from Hemo Rd, it costs $18 (children five to 15 years $9). The site is open from 8 am to 5 pm daily in winter (until 6 pm in summer).

Whaka is 2km south of the city centre, straight down Fenton St. City buses drop you near Tryon St, or the Sightseeing Shuttle bus will drop you at the Maori Arts & Crafts Institute.

Close to town is **Kuirau Park**, an area of volcanic activity that you can wander around for free. It has a crater lake and pools of boiling mud.

Maori Concerts & Hangi

Maori culture is a major attraction in Rotorua and, although it has been commercialised, it's worth investing in the experience. The two big activities are concerts and *hangi* (meals cooked in an earth oven). Often the two are combined.

The concerts are put on by locals. Chances are, by the evening's end you'll have been dragged up on stage, experienced a Maori *hongi* (nose-to-nose contact), have joined hands for a group sing-in, and thought about freaking out your next-door neighbour with a *haka* (war dance) when you get home. Other features of a Maori concert are *poi* dances, action songs and hand games.

Elements of the performances you are likely to see are described in the Maori Culture & Arts special section.

For a concert only, one of the best performances is presented daily (8 pm) at Tamatekapua Meeting House in Ohinemutu, opposite St Faith's Church down by the lake ($15, children $5). You can show up at the door for the Magic of the Maori Concert or book directly (☎ 349 3949) or with Tourism Rotorua.

Another option is the daily concerts at Whakarewarewa thermal village, which are

Pokarekare Ana

Pokarekare ana is NZ's most cherished traditional song. Though most people think its origin is more ancient, the song was actually adapted from a poem by Paraire Henare Tomoana (1868–1946) of the Ngati Kahungunu tribe. His original lyrics were not about Rotorua, but rather Waiapu. Nevertheless, the words seemed to fit the story of Hinemoa and Tutanekai so perfectly that in popular song the lake's name was changed to Rotorua, and the song is thought to be about the two lovers.

Almost anyone from NZ can sing this song for you. Often you will hear only the first verse and the chorus sung, but there are several verses. If you want to sing along, the first verse and chorus go like this:

Pokarekare ana nga wai o Rotorua.
Troubled are the waters of Rotorua.
Whiti atu koe, e hine, marino ana e.
If you cross them, maiden, they will be calm.

E hine e, hoki mai ra,
Come back to me, maiden,
Ka mate ahau i te aroha e.
I will die for love of you.

included in the entry fee (see that section earlier).

For a combined concert and hangi, Tamaki Tours (☎ 346 2823) does an excellent Twilight Cultural Tour to a *marae* and Maori village complex. It provides transport and along the way will explain the traditional protocol involved in visiting a marae. A 'chief' is chosen among the group to represent the visitors. The concert is followed by a hangi; it costs $58 (children $29).

Big hotels that also offer Maori concerts and hangi are listed below with prices for adults/children:

Centra (☎ 348 1189) Froude St
Concert Only: $18/9 (8 pm)
Concert & Hangi: $47/23.50 (6.30 pm)
Lake Plaza Rotorua (☎ 348 1174) Eruera St
Concert Only: $18/10 (8 pm)
Concert & Hangi: $47/21.50 (7 pm)

Millennium (☎ 347 1234) Eruera St
Concert Only: $16/8 (8 pm)
Concert & Hangi: $45/22.50 (7 pm)
NZ Maori Arts & Crafts Institute (☎ 348 9047) Hemo Rd
Concert & Hangi: $65/35
Quality Inn Hotel (☎ 348 0199) Fenton St
Concert Only: $15/7.50 (8 pm)
Concert & Hangi: $35/17.50 (7 pm)
Rotoiti Tours (☎ 348 8969) Rakeiao Marae (includes pick-up/drop-off)
Concert & Hangi: $55/27.50
Royal Lakeside Novotel Hotel (☎ 346 3888) Tutanekai St
Concert Only: $25/12.50 (7 pm)
Concert & Hangi: $52/25 (6.30 pm)
Sheraton Rotorua (☎ 349 5200) Fenton St
Concert Only: $25/15 (8 pm)
Concert & Hangi: $49/25 (7.15 pm)

Times and prices are subject to change, so check with the tourist office or with the hotel offering the service before you book.

Thermal Pools
The popular **Polynesian Spa** (☎ 348 1328), off Hinemoa St in the Government Gardens, is open from 6.30 am to 11 pm daily (last ticket sale is 10.15 pm). A bathhouse was opened at these springs in 1886 and people have been swearing by the health-giving properties of the waters ever since.

Remember to take off anything you are wearing that has silver in it; silver will instantly turn black on contact with the water. It's advisable to put all valuables in a safe-deposit box at the ticket office. The modern complex has several pools at the lake's edge that range in temperature from the high 30s°C to the low 40s°C. Entry to the main pools (adults only) is $10, private pools are $10 per half-hour (children $4), the luxury lakeside spa is $25 (adults only), and the family spa is $10/4 for adults/children.

An Aix massage (which includes entry to the luxury lakeside spa) costs $50. Aix massage (appointment required) involves a relaxing half-hour during which you lie under jets of warm water while a masseur gets to work with oil. Towels and swimsuits can be hired, and there is a licensed cafe.

The historical **Blue Baths** (heated swimming pool) in the government gardens has recently been renovated. It is open from 9.30 am to 9 pm daily and admission is $7 (children $4).

The **Waikite Valley Thermal Pool** (☎ 333 1861) is an open-air natural mineral pool (39°C) with medicinal mineral waters. To get there, go 30km south on SH5 (the highway to Taupo) to a signposted turn-off opposite the Waiotapu turn-off. The pool is another 6km down this road. It's open from 10 am to 10 pm daily ($5, children $2.50). There is a *camp site* nearby; tent and powered sites cost $10 per adult ($4 per child), including entry to the pools.

Those wishing to swim in hot water can visit **Kerosene Creek**, out on SH5. Turn left on the old Waiotapu Rd and follow it for 3km. This is one of the few places where the public can bathe in natural thermal pools for free.

Zorbing
Like the bungy, zorbing is another of those unusual Kiwi innovations. Rotorua is the only place where you can do it. The rules are simple: climb into an inflated double plastic sphere (the two spheres are held together with shock cords), strap in and then roll downhill for about 150m. You will rotate within the sphere, and eventually the sphere will come to a stop. To cure a hangover (or make it *much* worse), skip the tying in and ask for a couple of buckets of cold water to be tossed inside the sphere – you literally slip downhill. The guys who invented it were looking for a way to walk on water. They found it. A dry or wash cycle costs $40 from the top of the hill; $35 from three-quarters of the way up; and $60 for any two rides from the top (a kid's 10-minute zorb is $10). You can zorb at the Agrodome Leisure Park (☎ 332 2768), Western Rd, Ngongotaha.

White-Water Rafting
Several rafting companies make white-water rafting trips on the Rangitaiki River (grade III to IV). Day trips with a barbecue lunch cost around $89. The trips depart from the Rangitaiki River Bridge in Murupara, and operators will provide transport

from Rotorua for an extra $5. Companies include:

Great Kiwi White Water Co	☎ 348 2144
Kaituna Cascades	☎ 357 5032
Raftabout	☎ 345 4652
River Rats	☎ 347 6049
Wet & Wild Rafting	☎ 348 3191
The Whitewater Excitement Co	☎ 345 7182

Most popular are the shorter and more dramatic rafting trips on the Kaituna River, off SH33 about 16km north-east of Rotorua. Time on the river is about 40 minutes and you go over the 7m Okere Falls, then over another 3m drop and various rapids ($65). All Rotorua's rafting companies do a Kaituna trip.

Kaituna Cascades also conducts an extreme **tandem kayak** trip, in which a passenger who weighs less than 85kg and has no prior experience can negotiate a series of grade V drops on the Kaituna. You should book well ahead for this ($95).

White-water Sledging
Kaitiaki Adventures (☎ 0800-338 736, 025-249 9481) does white-water sledging on the Rangitaiki River. You zoom along on a sledge especially designed for manoeuvrability on the river. The 1½-hour, grade II to III trip costs $90 per person and the 2½-hour, grade II to IV trip on the upper section of the river costs $98. All equipment is supplied.

Fishing
You can hire guides to trout fish or go it alone but a licence is essential and there are various regulations. Guided fishing trips cost about $65 per hour per boat but you are almost guaranteed to catch a fish. Plan to spend about two to three hours on the trip. Ask at Tourism Rotorua or at the Rotorua lakefront for fishing operators.

You can wander down to the lakefront and fish if you have a licence and it's the fishing season (October to June). Get your fishing licence directly from a fishing guide or the Map & Track Shop (☎ 349 18450) at 1225 Fenton St, costing $13/25/65 per day/week/season.

Other Activities
One of the newest activities is the **indoor climbing wall** (☎ 350 1140), at 1401 Hinemoa St. It's open from 10 am to 10 pm weekdays, 9 am to 6 pm weekends. The $20 fee includes harness and shoes; it is $12 with your own gear.

You can go **tandem skydiving** from the Rotorua airport (☎ 345 7520) for $180. The initial flight includes some amazing views over the lakes and volcanoes of the region.

Adventure Kayaking (☎ 348 9451) has a half-day **kayaking** trip on Lake Rotorua starting at Hamurana Springs ($50); a full-day trip that includes 1½ hours on Lake Tarawera then a climb up the mountain ($70); a twilight lake paddle with a soak in a hot pool ($60); and two- and three-day trips starting at $160. Sunspots Go Kayaking (☎ 362 4222) offers white-water and lake kayaking. The company also rents kayaks and gear.

Operators doing **horse treks** are Paradise Treks (☎ 348 8195), Farmhouse (☎ 332 3771) and Foxwood Park (☎ 345 7003). All charge $25 per hour.

For **4WD** experiences try Hill Hoppers (☎ 533 1818) for self-drive; Mountain Action (☎ 348 8400) for tours through farm and bush; Mt Tarawera 4WD Tours (☎ 348 9929) for tours to Mt Tarawera's summit; Mountain Magic (☎ 348 6499) for cultural tours and trips to Mt Tarawera; and Off Road NZ (☎ 332 5748) for self-drive tours through bush at Amoore Rd, 20km west of Rotorua.

Extreme Limits (☎ 025-907 907), on Tarawera Rd, has a **sport luge** that you ride down a gravel track ($10 per ride, including a helmet); **rap jumping** from a 35m rocky outcrop ($50 for two jumps); and **Wild Thing**, a twist on the zorb theme – you ride downhill harnessed inside a 2m metal sphere. The gimbal inside ensures the sensation is rather like flying ($35 for two rides). Bookings are essential.

About 45km south of Rotorua, on the Waikato River, you can go **jet-boating** and sprint jet-boating with River Glen Tours (☎ 333 8165). See Around Taupo in the Central Plateau chapter. At Longridge Park,

Paengaroa, near Te Puke (40km north of Rotorua), you can jet-boat up the Kaituna River with Longridge Jetboat (☎ 533 1515) for $55/35 per adult/child.

Organised Tours

Rotorua offers a mind-boggling array of tours. Tourism Rotorua can book any tours, as can hostels and hotels.

Carey's Sightseeing Tours (☎ 347 1197), 1108 Haupapa St, has a large range. Carey's Capers visits most of Rotorua's favourite volcanic and thermal attractions, with a dip in an isolated hot-water stream along the way (from $60 for a half-day tour to the Waiotapu and Waimangu thermal areas).

Other Carey's tours take in the main attractions in a variety of combinations, including the thermal reserves, trout springs, lake cruises, Kaituna River rafting (4WD Mud & Mayhem trips, $129) and half-day 4WD tours to Mt Tarawera ($65, children $40).

Its 'world-famous' Waimangu Round Trip, well known in these parts since 1902, is one of the best. Focusing on the 1886 Mt Tarawera eruption, it includes the Waimangu Volcanic Valley, a cruise on Lake Rotomahana past the site of the Pink and White Terraces, a cruise on Lake Tarawera, a visit to the Buried Village (formerly Te Wairoa), and a dip in the Polynesian Spa ($140, children $80, full day). The budget version is $115 (children $60), but you don't get the spa, lunch or information pack.

For popular 4WD tours see Other Activities earlier.

Other tours go to the Agrodome, thermal areas etc. InterCity, Gray Line and Taylor's are three established companies; Tourism Rotorua provides details of them and other companies.

Slim's 'Uniquely Maori' East Cape Escape (☎ 345 6645, or 09-366 9830 Kiwi Experience) takes you from Rotorua and right around the East Cape, returning to Rotorua on the second day. Pick-up from Rotorua backpackers (between 7 and 7.30 am) is included in the cost of $152 (accommodation not included).

Scenic Flights Flights over the city and the lake start at around $50; Tarawera flights start at about $100. Otherwise you can fly further afield to Whakaari (White Island) and even down to Mts Ruapehu and Ngauruhoe in Tongariro National Park.

Volcanic Wunderflites (☎ 345 6077) is particularly popular for flights over the awesome chasm of Mt Tarawera. Also available are trips in the Redcat biplane. Volcanic Air Safaris (☎ 348 9984) has fixed-wing and helicopter flights, the latter landing on the crater rim of Mt Tarawera ($240 per person). Lakeside Aviation (☎ 0800-535 363) has trips over Tarawera ($95 per person), Taupo ($190) and Whakaari ($269). Adventure Aviation (☎ 345 6780) has a Boeing Stearman WWII open-cockpit biplane; trips include nice easy 'cotton wool cruises' over the lake and city, and more challenging looping, rolling, turning, stalling, 'gravity-grabber' tours for those who like to see things from all different perspectives. All four companies are based at Rotorua airport.

Helicopter tour specialists include Marine Helicopters (☎ 357 2512), which is based at Agrodome Leisure Park and Skyline Skyrides, and New Zealand Helicopters (☎ 348 1223), based at Whakarewarewa. Both do flights to Mt Tarawera (the latter lands there) and Whakaari and link up to other activities, such as 4WD tours and jet-boating.

Places to Stay

Camping & Cabins The *Acacia Park* (☎ 348 1886, 129-37 Pukuatua St) is beside Kuirau Park and has a solar-heated swimming pool. Tent and powered sites cost $10 per person, tourist flats start at $45 for two, and motel units and luxury tourist flats at $55.

Cosy Cottage International Holiday Park (☎ 348 3793, 67 Whittaker Rd) may be the only place in the world with heated tent sites – the ground warmth gradually warms your tent at night. It also has a mineral pool and a heated swimming pool, as well as canoes, bicycles and fishing tackle for hire. Tent and powered sites are $10 per

Mt Tarawera Eruption

In the mid-19th century Lake Rotomahana, near Rotorua, was a major tourist attraction. It brought visitors from around the world to see the Pink and White Terraces: two large and beautiful terraces of multilevelled pools, formed by silica deposits from thermal waters that had trickled over them for centuries. The Maori village of Te Wairoa, on the shores of nearby Lake Tarawera, was the departure point for visiting the terraces. From here a guide and rowers would take visitors by boat across Lake Tarawera to Rotomahana and the terraces. Mt Tarawera, which had not been active in the 500 years since Maori arrival in the area, towered silently over the lakes.

On 31 May 1886, the principal terrace guide, Sophia Hinerangi, took a party of tourists across Lake Tarawera to see the terraces. Two unusual events occurred that morning: as they boarded the boat a surge of water created a wave on the lake; and as they crossed Lake Tarawera a ceremonial canoe of a kind not seen on the lake for 50 years, glided across its waters. The *waka wairua* (phantom canoe) was seen by all in the tourist boat, both Maori and Pakeha.

To Te Wairoa Maori, the appearance of the canoe was an omen of impending disaster, and Tuhoto Ariki an old *tohunga* (priest) living in Te Wairoa had already told of impending calamity in the community.

In the early hours of 10 June 1886 there were earthquakes and loud sounds, and the erupting Mt Tarawera lit up the sky with exploding fireballs from its three vents. By the time the eruption finished five hours later, over 1500 sq km had been buried in ash, lava and mud. The Maori villages of Te Wairoa, Te Ariki and Moura were obliterated, 153 people were killed, the Pink and White Terraces were destroyed and Mt Tarawera was sliced open along its length as if hit with a huge cleaver. The small Lake Rotomahana swelled to many times its pre-eruption size.

Over the following days excavations were carried out at Te Wairoa to rescue survivors. Guide Sophia became a heroine, having saved many lives by providing shelter in her well-constructed *whare* (house). The old tohunga, however, was not so fortunate. He was trapped inside his buried

whare and Maori working to rescue survivors refused to dig him out. They feared he had used his magic powers to cause the eruption as he had claimed that the orientation of the villagers towards tourism and a cash economy were not traditional, and that neglect of the old traditions would anger the fire spirit inside the mountain. After four days had passed, he was dug out alive by Europeans, who took him to the Rotorua Sanatorium. He died a week later, aged around 104.

Volcanic rift in Tarawera Mountain (circa 1940)

FIRTH FAMILY PAPERS, ALEXANDER TURNBULL LIBRARY, WELLINGTON NZ

person, tourist cabins start at $42, tourist flats at $50 and motel units are $70.

Lakeside Thermal Holiday Park *(☎ 348 1693, 54 Whittaker Rd)* has hot mineral pools and spas. Powered sites are $20 for

two, tourist cabins are $40 and tourist flats start at $55.

Rotorua Thermal Holiday Park *(☎ 346 3140)*, on the southern end of the Old Taupo Rd, is a large camping ground with a heated pool and hot mineral pools. Tent sites are $18.50 for two, campervan sites $20, and cabins and tourist flats range from $34 to $68.

A little further out, *Holdens Bay Holiday Park* (☎ 345 9925, 21 Robinson Ave) is about 500m from Lake Rotorua, 6.5km from central Rotorua on SH30.

Blue Lake Holiday Park (☎ 362 8120) is on Tarawera Rd, 10km from town. Kayaks, canoes, fishing boats and bicycles are available for hire.

Other possibilities are *All Seasons Holiday Park* (☎ 345 6240), 7.5km from the city centre on Lee Rd, Hannahs Bay, off SH30; *Lake Tarawera Lodge* (☎ 362 8754), a two-minute drive from Lake Tarawera and surrounded by native bush; *Greengrove Holiday Park* (☎ 357 4429), on the corner of Hall and School Rds, Ngongotaha; *Lake Rotoiti Lakeside Holiday Park* (☎ 362 4860), 21km from Rotorua on Okere Rd, Okere Falls, on the shore of Lake Rotoiti; *Ohau Channel Lodge* (☎ 362 4761), 17.5km from Rotorua on Hamurana Rd, at the northern end of Lake Rotorua; *Rainbow Resort* (☎ 357 4289), 8km from the city centre at 22 Beaumonts Rd, Ngongotaha; *Redwood Holiday Park* (☎ 345 9380, 5 Tarawera Rd, Ngapuna), 3km from the city centre at the intersection with Te Ngae Rd; and *Waiteti Trout Stream Holiday Park* (☎ 357 5255, 14 Okona Crescent, Ngongotaha), beside Waiteti Stream.

Hostels The *Hot Rock* (☎ 347 9469, ✉ hotrock@acb.co.nz, 1286 Arawa St) is a former motel and a number of the spacious, thermally heated rooms have en suites and kitchen facilities. The friendly, efficient staff arrange sightseeing tours and trips to Maori cultural performances. There are three hot pools (indoor and outdoor) on the premises. Shared dorms start at $16, made-up rooms sleeping four are $18 per person, and twins and doubles are $40 per room ($50 with a bathroom). The popular Lava Bar is adjacent.

The *Funky Green Voyager* (☎ 346 1754, 4 Union St) is one of the smallest and nicest of Rotorua's backpackers. In a tranquil residential neighbourhood, close to the centre, the hostel is comfortable and casual with a

spacious backyard and a pleasant sunny conservatory. Dorm accommodation starts at $16 a double and twin rooms at $39.

Rotorua Downtown Backpackers (☎/fax 346 2831), on the corner of Haupapa and Fenton Sts, is a spic-and-span place near Tourism Rotorua and the bus station. The rooms are spacious, with dorm beds starting at $15, quad rooms for $17 per person, twins for $38 and doubles $40. There is a large kitchen area and guest bar. Nomads Internet Cafe is right next door.

Rotorua Central Backpackers (☎ 349 3285, 1076 Pukuatua St) has spacious, tidy rooms and a spa pool in a classic older building. Accommodation is $15 in dorms, $17 per person in a four-bed shared room, $38 in twins and $40 in doubles. It's centrally located and quiet.

Spa Lodge (☎ 348 3486, fax 346 0485, 1221 Amohau St) is old and cramped, but the rooms are thermally heated. It's $15 in dorms, $25/30 for singles/twins and doubles.

Backpackers Century 21 (☎ 0800-100 656, 105 Amohau St), a former motel, opened late in 1999. Dorm beds are $16, twin and double rooms are $40, and family units start at $50. A two-bedroom apartment sleeping six is $80; a three-bedroom apartment sleeping eight is $100.

Cactus Jacks Downtown Backpackers (☎ 348 3121, ✉ isabella.pavlova@xtra .co.nz, 54 Haupapa St), with, as its name suggests, a distinctly Mexican theme, has rooms and cabins. It charges $15.50 in dorms, and $30/37/39 for a single/twin/ double. There are spas for guest use.

The efficient, modern associate YHA hostel, *Kiwi Paka* (☎ 347 0931, ✉ stay@ kiwipaka-yha.co.nz, 60 Tarewa Rd), is 1.2km from the city centre (it runs a transfer service for travellers). It charges $17 in four-bed shared rooms and dorms, $19/20 per person for twin/double rooms and $21 for a single. En suite chalets cost $47 for twins/doubles and $63 for a triple. Linen hire is $2. There is a thermal pool here as well as a pleasant cafe and a bar (Under Canvas).

B&Bs & Guesthouses Toko St is quiet and well away from the tourist hustle of central Rotorua. At No 3 is the *Tresco International* (☎ 348 9611), which costs $45/68 for singles/doubles, including breakfast. There are sinks in the rooms and it's a neat, tidy and comfortable place. The same can be said for the *Morihana Guest House* (☎ 348 8511), a bit further down at No 20. Here singles/doubles are $50/75 to $95. Both places have hot mineral pools.

Central *Eaton Hall* (☎ 347 0366, 1255 Hinemaru St), opposite the Quality Resort, is a comfortable, homey guesthouse with B&B from $48 to $85. Book ahead in summer as this is a popular place.

The Tudor-style *Dudley House B&B* (☎ 347 9894, 6 Rangiuru St) is decorated in English country-cottage style. It's very comfortable, spotless and excellent value at $40/60 a single/double.

Tourism Rotorua has listings for nearly 50 homestays and farmstays and can make bookings.

Motels Rotorua has over 80 motels, and Fenton St, as it heads south from town past the Big Fresh supermarket, has wall-to-wall motels as far as the eye can see. In the off season they compete, with discounts displayed.

Ann's Volcanic Rotorua (☎ 347 1007, 107 Malfroy Rd) has one- and two-bedroom units, each with its own spa, from $58 to $89, depending on the season. *Ashleigh Court Motel* (☎/fax 348 7456, 337 Fenton St) has self-contained studio units for $85 for two people and self-contained, one-bedroom units for $85 to $110. All have private spas. *Baden Lodge* (☎/fax 349 0634, 301 Fenton St) has self-contained, one-bedroom units with private spas for $85 to $160 a night for two people. The *Birchwood Spa Motel* (☎ 347 1800), on the corner of Sala St and Trigg Ave, has studio, one- and two-bedroom units with private spas for $95 to $155 for two people.

Hotels Conveniently situated on the corner of Hinemaru and Pukuatua Sts, the *Good Sports Hotel* (☎ 348 1550) has single/double pub rooms for $45/55. It has a large thermal pool and the Dobbo's Sports Bar.

Princes Gate Hotel (☎ 348 1179, 1 Arawa St), on the corner of Hinemaru St, is a luxurious hotel with crystal chandeliers, canopies over the beds, an elegant restaurant and bar, a health facility and much more. It charges $123/146.

Rotorua has some big hotels. In a rough progression of price and quality are the *Regal Geyserland* (☎ 0800-881 882) and *Lake Plaza Rotorua* (☎ 348 1174). From there it's a definite jump to the *Centra* (☎ 348 1189), *Rydges* (☎ 0800-367 793), the *Sheraton* (☎ 349 5200), *Royal Lakeside Novotel Hotel* (☎ 346 3888) and the *Millennium* (☎ 347 1234). Prices range from about $80 to $130-plus for a standard double room.

If expense is no obstacle, Rotorua has a few exclusive and secluded lodges, such as *Woodlands Country Lodge* (☎ 332 2242), on Hamurana Rd, Ngongotaha; *Kawaha Point Lodge* (☎ 346 3602, 171 Kawaha Point Rd); and *Waiteti Lakeside Lodge* (☎ 357 2311, 2 Arnold St, Ngongotaha). Prices range from about $90 for a double to over $500 (Kawaha Point Lodge).

Places to Eat

Restaurants *Lewisham's Austrian Restaurant* (1099 Tutanekai St) specialises in traditional Austrian and Hungarian food. *Freos* at No 1103 does pasta, chargrills, salmon fillet, venison hotpot and other tasty things.

Zanelli's (1243a Amohia St) is a popular Italian dinner house, with good gelati. *Sirocco* (1280 Eruera St) is a popular Mediterranean-style cafe/bar, open daily for lunch and dinner. A meal costs about $18. Next door, *Finally Found It* does good, imaginative vegetarian cuisine (peanut pasta, vegetarian curry), as well as tasty seafood.

For genuine Pacific Rim cuisine, featuring innovative use of local ingredients, try the *Rendezvous Restaurant* (1282 Hinemoa St). It is open for dinner from Tuesday to Saturday. Also highly recommended for its Kiwi fare is *Poppy's Villa* (4 Marguerita St), with main courses around $25. Both of these restaurants are in atmospheric old villas.

The *Thai Restaurant* (1141 Tutanekai St) offers good Thai meals from $18. *Mr India*

(1161 Amohau St) is moderately priced and has all the authentic subcontinental favourites, such as vindaloo, korma, naan and vegetarian dishes.

Korea House Restaurant (1074 Eruera St) is a pleasant, large and fancy place serving Korean food. A yen for Japanese fare will be satisfied at the *Japanese Sushi Bar (1148 Tutanekai St)*, where a sushi main costs between $10 and $15.

Fat Dog (1161 Arawa St) is cosy and popular for breakfast, and indeed at any time for salads, soups and other light meals, as well as cake and coffee. For good espresso try *Zambique (1111 Tutanekai St)*.

Copper Criollo (1151 Arawa St) has creole-style food, including Cajun chicken and seafood gumbo, as well as a $6.50 cooked breakfast.

Pub Food *Churchill's Bar (1302 Tutanekai St)* is another good place for a meal. A comfortable English-style bar, it serves up lunches and finger food in big, satisfying portions, and food is always available.

The *Pig & Whistle* on the corner of Haupapa and Tutanekai Sts has soups and salads, burgers and generous-sized meals including fish of the day ($17), which comes with pig-tail fries.

Fast Food *Tastebuds Mexican Cantina (1213 Fenton St)*, near the corner of Pukuatua St, serves up the usual cheap and tasty Tex-Mex fare to take away or eat there. Nearby at No 1207, *Rapscallion Gourmet Burgers* has a range of tasty burgers for under $7.

The *Charcoal Chicken Joint (1214 Tutanekai St)* has chargrilled chicken and hot carvery sandwiches.

Zippy Central Cafe (1153 Pukuatua St) has good coffee, smoothies and bagels. The *Robert Harris Coffee House*, opposite at No 1205, has good coffee, pastries and cakes. *Coffee Bean (1149 Tutanekai St)* also makes good sandwiches and hearty cooked breakfasts.

The *Kebab Cafe (1159 Arawa St)* has a good selection of Middle Eastern and Indian dishes, including vegetarian selections. For fish and chips try the *Fishspot (1123 Eruera St)*. A fisherman's basket is $21.95, while oysters and scallops are about $20. *Chez Bleu*, on Fenton St near the corner of Hinemoa St, makes good burgers.

Lady Jane's Ice Cream Parlour, near the lake end of Tutanekai St, is popular with children.

Entertainment

At the *Lava Bar* in the Hot Rock backpackers (see Places to Stay) you can mix with an international and local crowd, play pool and listen to good sounds.

The popular *Pig & Whistle* on the corner of Haupapa and Tutanekai Sts is a renovated police station with a number of brews on tap, including its own Swine Lager. Guzzle a Swiney and listen to bands on weekend nights.

Monkey Jo's, on Amohia St, is a trendy bar and popular pick-up spot that packs them in most nights of the week.

Churchill's Bar (1302 Tutanekai St) is a safe, relaxed, English-style bar with plenty of different beers on tap, NZ wines and meals.

Cameron's Bar & Grill, upstairs on the corner of Fenton and Pukuatua Sts, sometimes has live music. It, too, serves food and has Guinness on tap and a huge range of whiskies.

The *Fat Dog*, a cafe and bar (see Places to Eat), is a good place to while the evening away with an espresso. In winter it has a cosy fire going.

Other good bars are *Wild Willy's (1240 Fenton St)*, a 'Wild West' bar, and *O'Malley's (1287 Eruera St)*, an Irish pub. Both have live music on Friday and Saturday nights and O'Malley's menu includes Irish stew and cottage pie for $8.

Bar Zazu, in the Millennium, *Clarke's Bar*, in the Novotel, and *Cards Bar*, in the Sheraton, are open from 4 pm until late daily. *Dobbo's Bar*, at the Good Sports Hotel on the corner of Hinemaru and Pukuatua Sts, is a sports bar with live bands on weekends.

The *Ace of Clubs*, on Ti St, attracts the nocturnals wanting to party on; it's open until 4.30 am. The rougher set will like the *Lake Tavern* on Lake Rd.

Getting There & Away

Air The Air New Zealand and Mt Cook Airline office (☎ 347 9564) on the corner of Fenton and Hinemoa Sts is open from 8.30 am to 5 pm weekdays; it also has a counter at the airport (☎ 345 6175) open daily. It offers daily direct flights to Auckland, Christchurch, Mt Cook, Queenstown, Taupo and Wellington, with onward connections.

Ansett New Zealand (☎ 347 0596) has a city office at 1200 Hinemoa St and an airport ticket counter (☎ 345 5348). Ansett offers daily direct flights to Christchurch, Queenstown, Invercargill and Wellington, with connections to other centres.

Bus All major bus companies stop at the Tourism Rotorua centre (☎ 343 1740 information and bookings) on Fenton St, which handles bookings.

InterCity has daily buses to and from Auckland, Wellington, Taupo, Tauranga, Hamilton, Whakatane and Opotiki. On the east coast routes, InterCity goes daily to Gisborne via Opotiki, and to Napier via Taupo.

Newmans' buses go from Rotorua to Taupo, Wellington, Palmerston North, Tauranga and Napier. Magic Bus and Kiwi Experience backpackers buses also stop in Rotorua.

Train The train station is on the corner of Railway and Lake Rds, about 1km northwest of the centre. The station opens only when trains are leaving or arriving. Buy train tickets at Tourism Rotorua, not the train station.

The *Geyserland* train operates daily between Auckland and Rotorua, stopping at Hamilton. It departs from Rotorua at 1.30 pm and arrives at Auckland at 5.45 pm. In the other direction, it leaves Auckland at 8.04 am and arrives at Rotorua at 12.17 pm.

Hitching Hitching to Rotorua is generally not bad, except on SH38 from Waikaremoana – past Murupara the road is unsealed and traffic is very light. The problem hitching out of Rotorua is often the sheer number of backpackers leaving town. You may have to join the queue and wait.

Getting Around

To/From the Airport The airport is about 10km out of town, on the eastern side of the lake. Airport Shuttle (☎ 346 2386) and Super Shuttle (☎ 349 3444) offer a door-to-door service to/from the airport for $8 for the first person and $2 for each additional passenger. A taxi from the city centre is about $15.

Bus Magic of the Maori shuttle (☎ 021-674 354, 0508-300 333) makes a constant loop daily, starting at Tourism Rotorua at 8.45 am (the last circuit leaving at 4.45 pm). It calls in at several hostels, including Kiwipaka and Hot Rock, plus all the major attractions, including the Agrodome, Whakarewarewa and Rainbow Springs. It is $4 for a one-way trip and $10 for an all-day pass. A timetable is available from Tourism Rotorua.

The Pink Bus (☎ 0800-222 231) has a service to the Waiotapu and Waimangu thermal areas. It picks up passengers from Tourism Rotorua and some accommodation places at about 9 am, returning at 12.30 pm. The buses to Waiotapu are $35 and to Waimangu are $40 (fares include admission). It also has an afternoon 'farm and forestry' tour for $65 and a full-day Waiotapu and Whirinaki Forest tour for $99 (including entry into Waiotapu).

Ritchies Coachlines (☎ 349 2994, ext 2904 for 24-hour information) operates suburban buses to Whakarewarewa (route 3) and Rainbow Springs (route 2; Ngongotaha), departing/arriving Rotorua on Pukuatua St. For fares and times ring the 24-hour information line; the tourist office will also have a current timetable.

Car Rotorua has a host of car rental companies. The competition is fierce and all seem to offer 'specials' to undercut the competitors. Rent-a-Dent (☎ 349 1919), on Ti St, and Link Rent-a-Car (☎ 347 8063), at 108 Fenton St, are two economical companies.

Ask about relocating cars to Auckland; you pay only for insurance and fuel.

Bicycle Rotorua is fairly spread out and public transport is not very good, so a bicycle is worthwhile. Bicycle hire places include Lady Jane's (☎ 347 9340), on the corner of Tutanekai and Whakaue Sts, the Rotorua Cycle Centre (☎ 348 6588), and Pins (☎ 347 1151) at 161 Fenton St (the latter two are also good for repairs and parts). Expect to pay about $15 per hour for a mountain bike; a full day costs around $45.

AROUND ROTORUA
Hell's Gate

Hell's Gate (Tikitere) is another highly active thermal area 16km east of Rotorua on the road to Whakatane (SH30). The reserve covers 10 hectares, with a 2.5km walking track to the various attractions, including the largest hot thermal waterfall in the southern hemisphere. An incongruous sight are the peacocks picking their way nonchalantly around the steaming vents. There is also a contingent of pigeons with a sharp eye for any food you may have with you. It's open from 8.30 am to 5 pm daily ($10, children $5).

George Bernard Shaw visited Hell's Gate in 1934 and said of it, 'I wish I had never seen the place, it reminds me too vividly of the fate theologians have promised me'.

Waimangu Volcanic Valley

This is another interesting thermal area, created during the eruption of Mt Tarawera in 1886. Walking through the valley (an easy downhill stroll) you'll first pass Waimangu Cauldron (a pale blue lake steaming quietly at 53°C) then many other interesting thermal and volcanic features. Waimangu means 'Black Water', as much of the water here was a dark, muddy colour. In this valley the Waimangu Geyser once performed actively enough to be rated the 'largest geyser in the world'. Between 1900 and its extinction in 1904 it would occasionally spout jets of black water nearly 500m high!

The walk continues down to Lake Rotomahana (meaning 'Warm Lake'), from where you can either get a lift back up to where you started or take a half-hour boat trip on the lake, past steaming cliffs and the former site of the Pink and White Terraces.

White Terraces, Rotomahana (Burton Brothers, circa 1880)

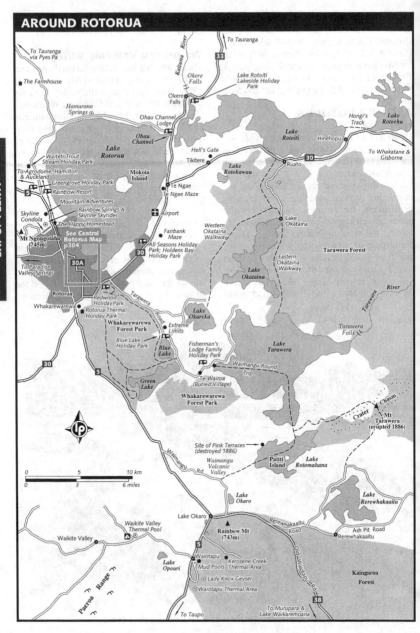

AROUND ROTORUA

To Tauranga
via Pyes Pa

The Farmhouse

Kaituna River

To Tauranga

33

Okere Falls

Lake Rotoiti Lakeside Holiday Park

Okere Falls

Hamurana Springs

Ohau Channel Lodge

Hongi's Track

Lake Rotoehu

Ohau Channel

Lake Rotoiti

Hinehopu

Waiteti Trout Stream Holiday Park

Lake Rotorua

Hell's Gate

Lake Rotokawau

Ruato

30

To Whakatane & Gisborne

To Agrodome, Hamilton & Auckland

Tikitere

5

Greengrove Holiday Park

Mokoia Island

Te Ngae

Rainbow Resort

Mountain Adventures

Te Ngae Maze

Lake Okataina

Rainbow Springs & Skyline Skyrides

Airport

Skyline Gondola

The Happy Homestead

Western Okataina Walkway

Tarawera Forest

Mt Ngongotaha (745m)

Fairbank Maze

See Central Rotorua Map p304

All Seasons Holiday Park; Holdens Bay Holiday Park

30

Eastern Okataina Walkway

Lake Okataina

30A

To Paradise Valley Springs

Lake Okareka

Rotorua

Tarawera Road

Tarawera River

Redwood Holiday Park

Whakarewarewa

Rotorua Thermal Holiday Park

Extreme Limits

Tarawera Falls

Whakarewarewa Forest Park

30

Blue Lake Holiday Park

Blue Lake

Fisherman's Lodge Family Holiday Park

Lake Tarawera

Waimangu Round Trip

5

Green Lake

Te Wairoa (Buried Village)

Crater

Chasm

Mt Tarawera (erupted 1886)

Whakarewarewa Forest Park

Waimangu Road

Site of Pink Terraces (destroyed 1886)

Patiti Island

Lake Rotomahana

Waimangu Volcanic Valley

0   5   10 km

0   3   6 miles

Lake Okaro

Lake Rerewhakaaitu

Waikite Valley Thermal Pool

Lake Okaro

Rainbow Mt (743m)

Rerewhakaaitu Road

Ash Pit Road

Rerewhakaaitu

Waikite Valley

5

Waiotapu

Mud Pools

Kerosene Creek Thermal Area

Old Waiotapu Rd

Kaingaroa Forest

Lake Opouri

Lady Knox Geyser

Waiotapu Thermal Area

38

Paeroa Range

To Taupo

To Murupara & Lake Waikaremoana

BAY OF PLENTY

The Waimangu Volcanic Valley is open from 8.30 am to 5 pm daily and costs $14.50 (children $5) for the valley walk only; it's $32.50 ($8) for both the valley walk and boat trip. Waimangu is a 20-minute drive from Rotorua, 19km south on SH5 (towards Taupo) and then 5km to 6km from the marked turn-off.

Waiotapu

Also south of Rotorua, Waiotapu (meaning 'Sacred Waters') is perhaps the best of the thermal areas to visit. It has many interesting features, including the large, boiling Champagne Pool, craters and blowholes, colourful mineral terraces and the Lady Knox Geyser, which spouts off (with a little prompting) punctually at 10.15 am and gushes for about an hour.

It's open from 8.30 am to 5 pm daily (last entry 4 pm), but is usually open later in summer ($12, children $4). It is 30km south of Rotorua on SH5 (towards Taupo), and a further 2km from the marked turn-off.

Trout Springs

Several springs run down to Lake Rotorua and the trout, lured by the feeds from tourists, swim up the streams to the springs. If you watch you may see a trout leaping the little falls to come up to the springs or returning to the lake.

The **Rainbow Springs Trout & Wildlife Sanctuary** is the best known of the trout springs. There are a number of springs (one with an underwater viewer), an aviary and a nocturnal kiwi house. It's a pleasant walk through the ponga trees and native bush to see the trout in the streams. Pick up your bag of trout feed at the entrance and watch the feeding frenzy – unless a tour bus has gone through and the trout have already pigged out. The springs also have a wildlife area with eels, wallabies, deer, birds, sheep, wild pigs and other native and introduced fauna, now all found in the wild in NZ.

Across the road, the Rainbow Farm Show is part of Rainbow Springs and has shows at 10.30 and 11.45 am, 1 and 4 pm, with sheep shearing and sheepdogs.

Performing to Schedule

How does the Lady Knox Geyser manage to perform so neatly to schedule? Simple – it's blocked up with some rags so the pressure builds up, then a couple of kilos of soap powder is shoved in to decrease the surface viscosity. And off it goes.

This scientific principle of the relation of soap powder to surface viscosity of geysers was discovered by some early settlers who thought it would be a great idea to use the hot water in the ground to wash their clothes.

Rainbow Springs is 4km north of central Rotorua, on the west side of Lake Rotorua – take SH5 towards Hamilton and Auckland, or catch the Magic of the Maori shuttle bus. It is open from 8 am to 5 pm daily ($18, children $7 – prices include the farm show as well as the springs).

Paradise Valley Springs are similar, set in an attractive 6-hectare park with various animals. The springs, 13km from Rotorua on Paradise Valley Rd, at the foot of Mt Ngongotaha, are open from 8 am to 5 pm daily ($12, children $5).

Skyline Skyrides

Skyline Skyrides is on the west side of Lake Rotorua, near the Rainbow and Fairy Springs. Here you can take a gondola ride up Mt Ngongotaha for a panoramic view of the lake area and, once there, fly 900m back down the mountain on a luge (a sort of toboggan down a long concrete pathway) or a flying fox, coming back up again on a chairlift. There is a cafe and restaurant on top of the mountain. The gondola costs $12 (children $5) for the return trip and the luge is $4.50 for one ride, less for multiple trips (eg, five rides cost $16). The gondola operates from 9 am daily. You can get a combination gondola and five-ride luge package for $22 ($17). You can also buy a ticket for a buffet lunch or dinner with a gondola ride ($29/36).

There is also a flight simulator, shooting range, minigolf course and other attractions to spend your money on at the top, and there are walking tracks around the mountain.

Agrodome

If seeing the millions of sheep in the NZ countryside has stimulated your interest in these animals, visit Agrodome. Paying to see a bunch of sheep seems a rather strange thing to do in NZ, but for $12 (children $5.50) you get an interesting educational and entertaining one-hour show at 9.30 and 11 am and 2.30 pm daily.

There are sheep-shearing and sheepdog displays, and by the time you're through you may even be able to tell the difference between some of the 19 breeds of sheep on show. There is also a dairy display, farmyard nursery and cow-milking demonstration.

You can hire horses for a guided tour or take a farm-buggy tour of the 120-hectare farm ($10, children $5). Agrodome is 7km north of Rotorua on SH1.

Mazes

Near the airport are a couple of large mazes. The **Fairbank Maze**, opposite the airport, is the largest hedge maze in NZ, with a 1.6km pathway. There are also gardens, ponds, an orchard, picnic areas, birds and animals. The maze is open from 9 am to 6 pm daily ($5, children $2.50).

Te Ngae Park, 3km beyond the airport, is a 3D, 1.7km wooden maze similar to the original Wanaka maze in the South Island. It's open from 9 am to 5 pm daily ($5, children $2.50).

Buried Village

The Buried Village is reached by a 15km scenic drive from Rotorua along Tarawera Rd, which passes the Blue and Green Lakes. There's a museum just beyond the ticket counter that has many artefacts and interesting background on the events before and after the eruption. Of particular interest is the story of the *tohunga* Tuhoto Ariki who, according to some, was blamed for the destruction. The site of his *whare* (house) has been excavated and the dwelling reconstructed. It is on display in the park along with excavations of other buildings buried

by volcanic debris, including one of the hotels. There's a peaceful bush walk through the valley to Te Wairoa Falls, which drops about 80m over a series of rocky outcrops. The last part of the track to the falls is steep and not really suitable for young children.

The village is open from 9 am to 5 pm daily in summer, and until 4.30 pm in winter ($10.50, children $3.50; discounts apply to AA and YHA members).

Lake Tarawera

About 2km past the Buried Village is Tarawera Landing on the shore of Lake Tarawera. Tarawera means 'Burnt Spear', named by a visiting hunter who left his birdspears in a hut and on returning the following season found both the spears and hut had been burnt.

Tarawera Launch Cruises (☎ 362 8595) has a cruise at 11 am crossing over Lake Tarawera towards Lake Rotomahana. It stays on the other side for about 45 minutes, long enough for people to walk across to Lake Rotomahana, then returns to the landing. The trip takes two hours and costs $27 (children $13.50).

A shorter 45-minute cruise on Lake Tarawera leaves at 1.30, 2.30 and 3.30 pm (the latter two trips operate in summer) and costs $17 (children $9.50).

Boats from Tarawera Landing can also provide transport to Mt Tarawera and to Hot Water Beach on Te Rata Bay. The beach has hot thermal waters and a basic Department of Conservation (DOC) *camping ground*.

You can relax on shore at *The Landing Cafe & Trout Bar*, near where the launch leaves. It's open for breakfast, lunch and dinner and there is a cosy open log fire.

Whirinaki Forest Park

About 50km east of Rotorua, signposted off the main road, is the 609 sq km Whirinaki Forest Park. Access is off SH38 on the way to Urewera National Park; take the turn-off at Te Whaiti to Minginui. The park is noted for the sheer majesty and density of its native podocarp forests; it has walking tracks, scenic drives, camping and huts, lookouts, waterfalls, the Whirinaki River and some pecial areas, including Oriuwaka Ecological Reserve and Arahaki Lagoon. For more nformation about this excellent forest park get a copy of the booklet *Tramping & Walking in Whirinaki Forest Park* from DOC.

There is a DOC field centre in the sawmill village of Minginui, but the park headquarters is the Ikawhenua Visitor Centre (☎ 366 5641) in Murupara.

Ask for details on the fine Whirinaki Track, an easy two-day walk. This can be combined with Te Hoe Loop Walk for a four-day walk (with seven huts) that starts in some of NZ's finest podocarp forest and proceeds along a series of river valleys.

Places to Stay Down by the Whirinaki River, at Mangamate Waterfall, there is an informal *camping area* with camp sites at $5. The forest has nine *backcountry huts* costing $4 per person. Murupara has all types of accommodation as well as food outlets.

Walking

Check in at the Map & Track Shop for pamphlets and excellent maps outlining the many fine walks in the area.

On the south-east edge of town, **Whakarewarewa State Forest Park** was planted early in the 20th century as an experiment to find the most suitable species to replace NZ's rapidly dwindling and slow-growing native trees. The Fletcher Challenge Visitor Information Centre (☎ 346 2082) in the park is open daily and has a woodcraft shop, displays and audiovisual material on the history and development of the forest. Check in here if you want to go walking. Walks range from half an hour to four hours, including some great routes to the Blue and Green Lakes. Several walks start at the visitor centre, including a half-hour walk through the **Redwood Grove**, a grove of large Californian redwood trees.

Other walks in the Rotorua area are the 22.5km **Western Okataina Walkway**, through native bush from Lake Okareka to Ruato, on the shores of Lake Rotoiti. There's public transport past the Ruato end only; the whole walk takes about six hours and you need good boots or stout shoes.

The **Eastern Okataina Walkway** goes along the eastern shoreline of Lake Okataina to Lake Tarawera – about a 2½-hour, 8km walk. A connecting track makes it possible to do a two-day walk from either Lake Okataina or Ruato to Lake Tarawera and camp overnight at a DOC camping ground ($5 per site), from where you can walk another hour to the Tarawera Falls.

To go tramping on **Mt Tarawera**, the easiest access is from Ash Pit Rd at the northern end of Lake Rerewhakaaitu, but there is no public transport. Mt Tarawera is Maori reserve land and permission should be obtained. Ask at DOC about how to arrange this in Rotorua, but in summer there is usually someone on the track to collect the $2 fee. From the parking area it is a two-hour walk along a 4WD track to the crater chasm and Ruawhaia dome. From here, most walkers return along the same route, but it is possible to follow another track leading to Lakes Rotomahana and Tarawera. You can complete a loop if you can arrange to be dropped off on Ash Pit Rd and time your return to meet the Tarawera Launch at the Tarawera outlet for transport back to Tarawera Landing.

It is essential to take water and wear good tramping shoes with ankle support – it's easy to slip on the volcanic scoria. The weather on Mt Tarawera can be very changeable, so bring warm and waterproof clothing to protect against wind and rain.

The **Okere Falls** are about 16km north-east of Rotorua on SH33 – the turn-off is well signposted. It's about a 30-minute walk through native podocarp forest to the falls. These are the 7m falls that the rafting companies take people over (see White-Water Rafting under Rotorua earlier). There are several other walks, including those up the Kaituna River to Hinemoa's Steps and to some caves.

Just north of Waiotapu on SH5, a good trail leads to **Rainbow Mountain** with its small crater lakes and fine views. It is a good, short, but fairly strenuous 1½-hour walk to the Maungakakatamea Lookout.

Other short walks can be made around Lake Okataina, Mt Ngongotaha (just north of Rotorua) and Lake Rotorua.

Western Bay of Plenty

The western Bay of Plenty extends from Katikati and Waihi Beach to Te Puke on the coast and south to the Kaimai Ranges.

Captain Cook sailed into the Bay of Plenty on the *Endeavour* in October 1769, naming it for the number of thriving settlements of friendly Maori he encountered (and the amount of supplies they gave him). It was a sharp contrast to the 'welcome' he received from the Maori of Poverty Bay several weeks earlier, when lives were lost and no food was available.

The area is not as popular with tourists as the far more commercial Bay of Islands but in summer it hums along nicely. It enjoys one of the highest proportions of sunny days in NZ, the climate is consistently mild year-round and in summer the coastal beaches are popular.

TAURANGA
pop 58,500

Tauranga is the principal city of the Bay of Plenty and one of the largest export ports in NZ – shipping out the produce of the rich surrounding region. The days of the overnight kiwifruit millionaires have gone but the area is still thriving economically and draws increasing numbers of retirees, attracted by the temperate climate and a city well endowed with facilities. Tauranga is indeed a pleasant place to live but its tourist attractions are limited mostly to the beaches and headland scenery of Mt Maunganui across the harbour.

Tauranga is Maori for 'Resting Place for Canoes', for this was where some of the first Maori arrived from Polynesian Hawaiki.

As the centre of NZ's principal kiwi-fruit region, work is available when the fruit is being picked (May and June) but you may be able to find some orchard work at almost any time. Check with the hostels for orchard work contacts.

Information

The Tauranga Information & Visitor Centre (☎ 578 8103) is at 95 Willow St; it's open from 7 am to 5.30 pm weekdays and 8 am to 4 pm on weekends. Check the Tourism Bay of Plenty Web site (www.visitplenty .co.nz) for online information.

The DOC office (☎ 578 7677) is at 253 Chadwick Rd West, Greerton (about 10 minutes' drive from the centre of Tauranga – follow Cameron Rd).

The AA office (☎ 578 2222) is on the corner of Devonport Rd and First Ave.

Things to See

The **Tauranga Community Village** (☎ 571 3700), on Seventeenth Ave, features restored period buildings (admission free), but it is mainly a location for community organisations. At the time of writing many of the artefacts usually displayed here were awaiting location in a new museum.

Te Awanui, a fine replica Maori canoe, is on display in an open-sided building at the top end of the Strand, close to the centre of town. Continue uphill beyond the canoe to **Monmouth Redoubt**, a fortified site during the Maori Wars. A little further along is **Robbins Park**, with a rose garden and hothouse.

The **Elms Mission Station House**, on Mission St, was founded in 1835 and the present house was completed in 1847 by a pioneer missionary. It is furnished in period style. The grounds contain gardens and several historic buildings. It is open from 2 to 4 pm on Sunday and public holidays ($5).

Walking

There are many walking possibilities in the region. A good number of these are outlined in the free pamphlet *Walkways of Tauranga*, available from visitor centres. Ten walks in Tauranga and Mt Maunganui (including the fascinating **Waikareao estuary**) and further afield are described. Each is accompanied by a handy map.

The backdrop to the western Bay of Plenty is the rugged 70km-long **Kaimai-Mamaku Forest Park**, with tramps for the more adventurous. More detailed information on walks in this area is available from DOC. **McLaren Falls**, in the Wairoa River valley, 11km south-west of Tauranga just off SH29, is worth a visit. There's good bushwalking, rock pools and the falls.

Sea Activities

Charter and fishing trips operate from Tauranga year-round. During the summer the place comes alive with sea activities of all kinds, including jet-skiing, swimming with the dolphins, water-skiing, windsurfing, parasailing, sea kayaking, diving, surfing, swimming, line fishing, deep-sea fishing and sailing. Ask at the visitor centre for details and see the Around Tauranga section for details of trips to Tuhua (Mayor Island).

Recommended activities include sailing on Tauranga Harbour on the *Slipstream* yacht (☎ 576 1841). Prices range from $30 for two hours to $80 for a full day, including a picnic.

Gemini Galaxsea (☎ 578 3197) runs **dolphin-swimming** experiences from a motorised yacht ($85 per day). Even if you don't meet the dolphins (they claim a high success rate) it is good value for a day cruise and you get to snorkel on the reefs.

Fishing charters are available. Get a copy of *Gateway to the Magic Triangle* from the visitor centre.

You can go on a cruise (champagne breakfast, lunch, dinner, supper) on board the *Island Princess* (☎ 025-934 703). Trips leave from Coronation Pier.

White-Water Rafting

White-water rafting is popular around Tauranga, particularly on the Wairoa River, which has some of the best falls and rafting in NZ. It's definitely a rafting trip for thrill-seekers. One highlight of the trip is a plunge over a 4m waterfall! The water level is controlled by a dam, so the Wairoa can only be rafted a few days of the year. Contact Wet 'N' Wild Rafting (☎ 348 3191) for more information. It also has trips on other rivers.

White-Water Sledging

Kaitiaki Adventures (☎ 0800-338 736, 025-249 9481) does a 1½-hour white-water sledging trip on the Wairoa River when the dam

BAY OF PLENTY

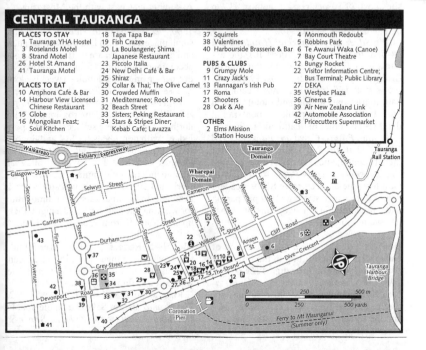

CENTRAL TAURANGA

PLACES TO STAY	18 Tapa Tapa Bar	37 Squirrels	4 Monmouth Redoubt
1 Tauranga YHA Hostel	19 Fish Crazee	38 Valentines	5 Robbins Park
3 Roselands Motel	20 La Boulangerie; Shima	40 Harbourside Brasserie & Bar	6 Te Awanui Waka (Canoe)
8 Strand Motel	Japanese Restaurant		7 Bay Court Theatre
26 Hotel St Amand	23 Piccolo Italia	PUBS & CLUBS	12 Bungy Rocket
41 Tauranga Motel	24 New Delhi Café & Bar	9 Grumpy Mole	22 Visitor Information Centre;
	25 Shiraz	11 Crazy Jack's	Bus Terminal; Public Library
PLACES TO EAT	29 Collar & Thai; The Olive Camel	13 Flannagan's Irish Pub	27 DEKA
10 Amphora Cafe & Bar	30 Crowded Muffin	17 Roma	35 Westpac Plaza
14 Harbour View Licensed	31 Mediterraneo; Rock Pool	21 Shooters	36 Cinema 5
Chinese Restaurant	32 Beach Street	28 Oak & Ale	39 Air New Zealand Link
15 Globe	33 Sisters; Peking Restaurant		42 Automobile Association
16 Mongolian Feast;	34 Stars & Stripes Diner;	OTHER	43 Pricecutters Supermarket
Soul Kitchen	Kebab Cafe; Lavazza	2 Elms Mission	
		Station House	

gates open (bookings essential). This is a grade V experience over such evocatively named rapids as 'the washing machine' and 'mother's nightmare'. It costs $80 per person.

Flying & Skydiving

The Tauranga airport at Mt Maunganui is the base for a number of air clubs. Scenic flights can be arranged at the airport. The Tauranga Glider Club (☎ 575 6768) flies every weekend, weather permitting. Tandem skydiving starts at $190 with Tandem Skydiving (☎ 576 7990); there is a $10 discount for backpackers and a free photo taken from the wing-mounted camera.

A different way to fly is on the **Bungy Rocket**. Shoot above the Strand reclamation car park for $30 per person (two at a time); it fires from 10 am until late daily.

Places to Stay

Camping & Cabins The *Mayfair Tourist Park* (☎ 578 3323, 9 Mayfair St), off Fifteenth Ave, is beside the harbour. Powered sites cost $9.50 per person, cabins $32 to $35 a double, tourist cabins $37 to $45 and on-site caravans $35 to $40.

The *Silver Birch Thermal Holiday Park* (☎ 578 4603) is at 101 Turret Rd, the extension of Fifteenth Ave, by the Hairini Bridge. Tent/powered sites cost $9/10, cabins start at $25 (double), tourist cabins at $40, tourist flats at $50 and motel units at $60. It has thermal pools, a boat ramp, dinghies and other recreational facilities.

At the *Palms Caravan Park* (☎ 578 9337, 162 Waihi Rd), about 4km south of the city centre, sites start at $10 per person. The *Bayshore Leisure Park* (☎ 544 0700), 6km from the city centre on SH29, has tent and powered sites starting at $9 per person and cabins for $31 for two. This place has its own hot mineral pools.

Hostels Tauranga has a good selection of backpackers, which fill up in the kiwi-fruit picking season. The *Tauranga YHA* (☎ 578 5064, @ yhataur@yha.org.nz, 171 Elizabeth St) is conveniently close to the city centre, next to the Waikareao expressway and the estuary. It's a cosy hostel charging

$15 per person in dorms and twin rooms, $34 for a double and $8 for a tent site. If you're coming into town by bus, ask to get off at First Ave.

Bell Lodge (☎ 578 6344, @ bell .lodge@host.co.nz, 39 Bell St), 4km west of town, is a newer, purpose-built hostel pleasantly situated on three hectares of land. This friendly hostel is well equipped, with heating in all the rooms, a big kitchen and a lounge with a fireplace. Bunk beds cost $16, a twin/double room with a private bathroom is $18/20 per person and a single $32. It also has new motel units for $50/70 and you can pitch a tent for $9 per person. It is very popular and crowded in the picking season when weekly rates are offered. Phone for a free pick-up.

The *Apple Tree Cottage* (☎ 576 7404, 47 Maxwell St), at Pillans Point, Otumoetai, is a small, friendly backpackers in a private house, with a basic bunkroom bungalow at the back with a hot spa costing $14 per person. Twins/doubles are $16/18 per person. Ask about its Coast with the Most trips.

Nearby, *Just the Ducks Nuts* (☎ 576 1366, fax 549 0336, 6 Vale St) is another small place but with a laid-back atmosphere and good communal areas. It provides good accommodation for $15 in the dorms, $18 per person in twins/doubles (weekly dorm rate $84). They will drop off and pick up.

Bracewell Lodge (☎ 552 4009, 23 Paparoa Rd) at Te Puna, approximately 9km north of Tauranga, is a self-described 'sports lodge', with dorm beds for $14 and doubles for $15 per person. It has a kitchen, two lounges with Sky TV, kayaks, volleyball equipment and a swimming pool. Between April and July kiwi-fruit industry work is available to backpackers; accommodation for working guests is only $12 a night. Pick-up and drop-off from Tauranga are free.

Motels & Hotels There are over 30 motels around Tauranga. The biggest concentrations are on Waihi Rd and Fifteenth Ave, where you'll find many older motels.

Rates at the *Strand Motel* (☎ 578 5807, 27 The Strand) start at $59/69 a single/double. *Roselands Motel* (☎ 578 2294, 21 Brown St)

is in a central, quiet location and rates start at $75/80.

Blue Water Motel (☎ 578 5420, 59 Turret Rd) has a swimming pool and prices start at $65 for two. The *Harbour View Motel (☎ 578 8621, 7 Fifth Ave)* has huge units for a very reasonable $70/80.

More upmarket and around $90 for two is the *Tauranga Motel (☎ 578 7079, 1 Second Ave)*.

Guesthouses & B&Bs *Taiparoro House (☎ 577 9607, 11 Fifteenth Ave)* is a 19th-century, two-storey house with a rather romantic ambience. It has five guestrooms and prices start at $95/140 for a single/double.

The *homestay (☎ 576 8895, 8A Vale St)*, next to Just the Ducks Nuts, is a spic-and-span modern home, which has a large room with twin beds, and a spacious bathroom. It costs $40/70.

Places to Eat
Restaurants & Cafes *Squirrels (75 Elizabeth St)* has an interesting selection of mains, including grilled emu and vegetable kebabs, with mains starting at $18.

Valentines, on the corner of Devonport and Elizabeth Sts, specialises in buffets.

Along Devonport Rd there is a good variety of places. *Mediterraneo*, at No 62, is a European-style restaurant with great cakes and coffee. *Rock Pool*, nearby, is a pleasant cafe with salads, soups, pasta and big breakfasts. Sandwiched between the Strand and Devonport Rd is *Beach St*. It has an innovative menu and is a popular place for a drink.

At the Goddards Centre (No 21) there are two good restaurants: *Collar & Thai* (Thai and European) and *The Olive Camel*, which has a Mediterranean spin to its menu. Mains at both restaurants are in the $18 to $22 range.

You can dine outside or in at the *Harbourside Brasserie & Bar*, overlooking the water at the south end of the Strand. Mains are in the $20 to $25 range and the menu includes steaks, seafood, fish and chips, and lamb. There is also a good selection of light meals for under $20.

Along the Strand are some interesting options. At *Tapa Tapa Bar* you can sample a variety of small dishes (marinated fish, raw vegies, squid rings and so on) for $4 to $5 a serve. Wash them down with sangria (Spanish red wine with fruit) for $3 a glass.

At *Fish Crazee* you can personalise your fish and chips. There's a choice of cooking styles and seasonings. The *Mongolian Feast* at No 69 has a $20 all-you-can-eat deal, or you can indulge in as many Mongolian flaps (sweet pancakes) as you can fit in for $5. At the *Harbour View Licensed Chinese Restaurant* you can sample yum cha daily. There is also a takeaway service.

Amphora Cafe & Bar, at No 43, serves Greek and Middle Eastern food, with mains mostly under $15. *Baywatch Brasserie & Bar* on the corner of the Strand and Wharf St has an innovative menu with seafood a speciality.

Shiraz (12 Wharf St) has Mediterranean and Middle Eastern food, with mains under $20. The *Shima Japanese Restaurant*, across the road, has sushi, sashimi and the like.

For Italian food try *Piccolo Italia (114 Willow St)*.

At the *Bureta Park Motor Inn restaurant*, near Just the Ducks Nuts, you can dine well for $10.

Fast Food Devonport Rd has a good mix of inexpensive places. The *Crowded Muffin* is always doing a brisk trade. The *Sisters*, further up the hill, has an eclectic mix of roasts, Japanese, Thai and fish and chips (it has daily specials).

Peking Restaurant has sit-down meals, as well as a takeaway that includes a smorgasbord option.

The Westpac Plaza at 75 Devonport Rd has the *Stars & Stripes Diner* for burgers, tortillas and other Kiwi Americana. Also in the plaza are the *Kebab Cafe* and *Lavazza*, a good place for espresso and fresh juices.

On Wharf St, the *New Delhi Cafe & Bar* has dine-in and takeaway options. For pastries try *La Boulangerie*, also on Wharf St.

Entertainment
Several hotel bars have live entertainment nightly, from Thursday to Saturday, such as

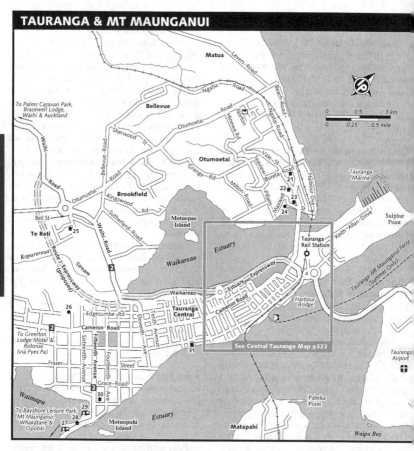

TAURANGA & MT MAUNGANUI

See Central Tauranga Map p323

the *Oak & Ale*, a pleasant English-style pub in the Mall, with a wide range of beers and occasional bands. *Flannagan's Irish Pub (14 Hamilton St)* is a similar place, and you can also get a meal here.

Places to try along the Strand include the *Grumpy Mole* for dance and live music, and *Crazy Jack's*, which has occasional jazz. For electro/techno/trance try *Roma* from Wednesday to Saturday, also on the Strand.

Shooters often has bands on weekends. The *Soul Kitchen*, on the Strand above the Mongolian Feast, has an eclectic mix of music and is open on weekends until late.

The *Bay Court Theatre* hosts an eclectic mix of highbrow entertainment.

Getting There & Away

Air Air New Zealand Link (☎ 578 0083) has an office on the corner of Devonport Rd and Elizabeth St. It has direct flights to Auckland, Rotorua and Wellington, with connections to other centres. Tauranga's airport is in Mt Maunganui.

Bus InterCity (☎ 578 7020) tickets and timetables are provided by the Tauranga Information & Visitor Centre (☎ 578 8103) at

TAURANGA & MT MAUNGANUI

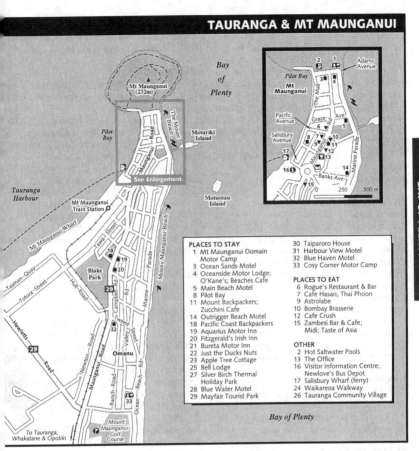

BAY OF PLENTY

PLACES TO STAY
1 Mt Maunganui Domain
  Motor Camp
3 Ocean Sands Motel
4 Oceanside Motor Lodge;
  O'Kane's; Beaches Cafe
5 Main Beach Motel
8 Pilot Bay
11 Mount Backpackers;
  Zucchini Cafe
14 Outrigger Beach Motel
18 Pacific Coast Backpackers
19 Aquarius Motor Inn
20 Fitzgerald's Irish Inn
21 Bureta Motor Inn
22 Just the Ducks Nuts
23 Apple Tree Cottage
25 Bell Lodge
27 Silver Birch Thermal
  Holiday Park
28 Blue Water Motel
29 Mayfair Tourist Park

30 Taiparoro House
31 Harbour View Motel
32 Blue Haven Motel
33 Cosy Corner Motor Camp

PLACES TO EAT
6 Rogue's Restaurant & Bar
7 Cafe Hasan; Thai Phoon
9 Astrolabe
10 Bombay Brasserie
12 Cafe Crush
15 Zambesi Bar & Cafe;
  Midi; Taste of Asia

OTHER
2 Hot Saltwater Pools
13 The Office
16 Visitor Information Centre;
  Newlove's Bus Depot
17 Salisbury Wharf (ferry)
24 Waikareoa Walkway
26 Tauranga Community Village

Bay of Plenty

95 Willow St. InterCity connects Tauranga with Auckland, Hamilton, Thames, Rotorua, Taupo and Wellington. Supa Travel (☎ 571 0583) is a local company with buses on demand to Auckland Airport ($50 one way). InterCity and Supa Travel stop at the information centre, which also handles bookings for these buses. Most buslines continue to Mt Maunganui after stopping in Tauranga.

Call-a-Bus (☎ 0800-100 550) has a door-to-door service to Auckland for $45.

Train The *Kaimai Express* to Auckland departs from Tauranga at 8.05 am. Transfers and other connections can be made in Hamilton before it goes on to Auckland. It departs from Auckland for Tauranga at 6.05 pm, arriving in Tauranga at 9.30 pm. There is a bar on board and snacks are served. The visitor information centre handles bookings.

Getting Around
The Tauranga Airport Shuttle (☎ 544 4447) charges $7 for a door-to-door airport service.

Tauranga has a local bus service that provides transport to most locations around the area, including Mt Maunganui and Papamoa.

Several car rental agencies have offices in Tauranga, including Budget, Hertz and Avis. There is also Rent-a-Dent (☎ 578 1772); the information centre has details. The harbour bridge has a $1 toll in each direction for cars, but it's free for bicycles and pedestrians.

The local taxi companies are: Citicabs (☎ 577 0999), Tauranga Taxis (☎ 578 6086), Coastline (☎ 571 8333) and Mount Taxis (☎ 574 7555).

The ferry service to Mt Maunganui, which takes about 15 minutes, operates in summer ($5).

MT MAUNGANUI
pop 16,800

The town of Mt Maunganui (the name means 'Large Mountain') stands at the foot of the 232m hill of the same name (also called 'the Mount'). It's just across the inlet from Tauranga, and its fine beaches make it a popular holiday resort for Kiwis. Like Tauranga, the town of Mt Maunganui is built on a narrow peninsula.

The downside of the drive to the Mount is the industrial area that the road goes through, reminiscent of the factory-pocked towns of the eastern US seaboard.

Information

The Mt Maunganui Information Office (☎ 575 5099) on Salisbury Ave is open from 9 am to 5 pm weekdays (until 4 pm on weekends). It is closed on Sunday in winter.

Things to See & Do

Walking trails go around Mt Maunganui and to its top for magnificent views. You can climb around the rocks on Moturiki Island, which is actually joined to the peninsula (see the *Walkways of Tauranga* pamphlet, available from the visitor centre). The beach between Moturiki and Maunganui is good for surfing and swimming.

There are excellent **heated saltwater pools** at the foot of the Mount on Adams Ave – the hot pools are open from 6 am to 10 pm daily, but from 8 am to 10 pm on Sunday ($2.50, children $1.50). Entry to the private pools is $3.50 (children $2.50).

A fun way of getting around is by tuk tuk. Phoenix Tuk Tuk Shuttle Service (☎ 025-297 1364) offers a joy ride for $2.

Places to Stay

Camping & Cabins Mt Maunganui is a popular summer resort, so there are plenty of camping grounds.

At the foot of the Mount, the *Mt Maunganui Domain Motor Camp* (☎ 575 4471) has camp sites starting at $20 for two, cabins and on-site caravans at $40.

At *Cosy Corner Motor Camp* (☎ 575 5899, 40 Ocean Beach Rd) sites are $11 per person, tourist cabins $40 and tourist flats $60.

The *Golden Grove Motor Park* (☎ 575 5821, 73 Girven Rd) has sites for $22 for two, cabins with en suites for $50, standard cabins for $35 and two-bedroom tourist flats for $60.

Hostels There are two places and both are on Maunganui Rd. The *Pacific Coast Backpackers* (☎ 574 9601) at No 432 is the larger of the two with dorms starting at $16 and twins/doubles for $21/22 per person. It runs Action Stations (☎ 0800-666 622), an adventure travel operation which organises activities such as dolphin swimming ($95 with two nights accommodation), sailing on the *Slipstream* ($25) and rafting on the Wairoa River ($69).

The *Mount Backpackers* (☎ 575 0860, 87 Maunganui Rd) has dorm beds for $18 and double rooms for $45. It's a few minutes' walk from the beach.

Motels & Apartments Mt Maunganui has fewer motels than Tauranga and prices spiral outrageously high in summer. Motels charging around $95 a double include *Pilot Bay* (☎ 575 5883, 28 The Mall) and *Blue Haven Motel* (☎ 575 6508, 10 Tweed St).

Newer places include the following. *Oceanside Motor Lodge & Twin Towers* (☎ 575 5371, 1 Maunganui Rd) has apartments, suites and studios, plus a heated pool, gym and restaurant. Prices start at $125 for a studio. *Ocean Sands Motel* (☎ 0800-726 371, 6 Maunganui Rd) has self-contained studios, one- and two-bedroom apartments and penthouse suites. Prices range from $100 for a one-bedroom unit to $250 for a penthouse suite.

Outrigger Beach Motel (☎ 575 4445, 48 Marine Parade) has 20 units and six apartments with sea views. Prices start at $108 for two. *Belle Mer* (☎ 0800-100 235, 53 Marine Parade) has a heated pool and outdoor spa. Prices start at $150 for a two-bedroom apartment. *Aquarius Motor Inn* (☎ 572 3120, 447 Maunganui Rd) is another new place. It has a swimming pool, and there are spas in most rooms. Prices start at $95 for a studio.

There are several B&Bs, including *Fitzgerald's Irish Inn* (☎ 575 4013, 463 Maunganui Rd), which is $75 for two in summer, including breakfast. Ask at the visitor centre for details of other B&Bs.

Places to Eat

Maunganui Rd has the biggest concentration of eateries.

Cafe Crush ('funky, fresh food') mostly uses organic vegetables and it serves salads, soups, sushi, fish and chips and more. There's a children's play and eating area and a courtyard.

The Office, further up the road, is a popular bar. Across the road is *Zambesi Bar & Cafe*, which serves steaks, pasta and seafood, and occasionally has live music. *Midi* is open late and serves venison, salmon, lamb, roast duck and seafood plus all-day breakfasts (mains are under $20).

Nearby is *Taste of Asia* where you can get Vietnamese noodle soup ($7.50) and a variety of Vietnamese and Thai dishes.

Astrolabe is a classy bar and restaurant with courtyard dining. For gourmet vegetarian cuisine try the *Zucchini Cafe*, which also has live music, including jazz.

Ship to Shore Takeaways dishes up good fish and chips. The *Bombay Brasserie*, near the corner of Pacific Ave and Maunganui Rd, has kebabs, and tandoori dishes for under $15.

Along Pacific Ave is *Cafe Hasan* (moussaka, kebabs etc) and *Thai Phoon*. Opposite is *Rogues Restaurant & Bar*, which has a good selection of steaks, seafood and chicken, with mains for $18 to $22.

Near the Mount itself are *O'Kane's* licensed restaurant and cafe and *Beaches Cafe*.

Getting There & Away

Tauranga airport is at Mt Maunganui (see the Tauranga section).

Newmans, Supa Travel buses and Inter-City buses serve Tauranga and also stop at Mt Maunganui, in front of the visitor centre. Newlove's buses run from Wharf St in Tauranga to the Mount, stopping outside the information centre and the hot pools.

You can reach Mt Maunganui across the harbour bridge from Tauranga ($1 toll in each direction), or from the south via Te Maunga on SH2.

There's a boat in summer from Salisbury Wharf in Mt Maunganui to Tauranga.

AROUND TAURANGA
Matakana Island

Sheltering Tauranga Harbour, this elongated island is a quiet rural retreat just across the harbour from Tauranga. Two-thirds of the island is pine forest, providing the main industry, and the rest is farmland on the western side. Matakana has 24km of pristine white-sand, surf beach on its east shore and is also good for windsurfing, kayaking and fishing. An ideal way to explore the island is by bicycle, which you can take across on the ferry. The island has a general store and social club but not much else – bring your own supplies.

Getting There & Away The main ferry (☎ 025-927 251) departs from Omokoroa daily (ring for times) for the western side of the island ($2; 15 minutes). You can also take the *Forest Lady* (☎ 025-937 426), a barge for logging trucks, that runs from the docks at Sulphur Point in central Tauranga to the south end of the island. It shuttles across every weekday, but there is no fixed schedule. The island has no public transport.

Omokoroa

This town is 22km west of Tauranga, on a promontory which protrudes well into the sheltered harbour and affords fine views of the harbour and Matakana. It is a popular summer destination and has two caravan parks. From Omokoroa you can visit Matakana on the regular ferry service.

Katikati
pop 2610
Katikati (known to many locals as 'Catty-Cat'), on the Uretara River, has become an open-air art gallery with many of its buildings adorned with **murals**. Get the *Mural Town: Katikati* brochure from the Mural Town Information Centre (☎ 549 1658) at 34 Main Rd (open from 9 am to 4 pm daily).

Morton Estate (☎ 552 0795) is one of NZ's bigger wineries, located on SH2, 8km south of Katikati. Tastings and door sales are available from 10.30 am to 5 pm daily.

Places to Stay & Eat The *Sapphire Springs Holiday Park (☎ 549 0768)* backs onto the Kaimai Ranges. Tent and powered sites are $9, cabins start at $30, tourist flats at $50, and motel rooms at $65 (all prices are for two). A bunk bed in the lodge is $12.50. The springs are free to visitors and private spas are available.

The *Katikati Naturist Park (☎ 549 2158, 149 Wharawhara Rd)* is well set up for those who prefer to remove their clothes. A day visit is $6 and an overnight stay is $10 per person for a tent or powered site, $35/40 for singles/doubles in on-site vans.

The *Katikati Motel (☎ 549 0385)* is in town and has units starting at $69 for two.

The information centre has a list of homestays and farmstays in the area. Good choices are *Jacaranda Cottage (☎ 549 0616, 230 Thompson's Track, RD2)*, which has B&B for singles/doubles at $40/65 and budget beds for $15. There is also a one-bedroom, self-contained cottage available.

At the other end of the scale is *Fantail Lodge (☎ 549 1581, 117 Rea Rd)*, a Tudor-style mansion with 12 suites and six semi-detached self-contained villas. Prices are $500-plus for two.

Good lunches are served at the *Balcony Cafe* on the main street. Also worth trying is *The Landing* licensed restaurant at the Talisman Hotel on Main St.

For elegant afternoon teas and fine dining, try the *Twickenham Homestead*, on the corner of SH2 and Mulgan St.

On the highway 6km north of Katikati is *The Country Pumpkin*, which has, yes, pumpkin soup, plus Devonshire teas and light meals.

Tuhua (Mayor Island)
Tuhua, commonly known as Mayor Island, is a dormant volcano about 40km north of Tauranga. There are walking tracks through the now overgrown crater valley and an interesting walk around the island. The north-west corner is a marine reserve, but specialist groups can ask for permission to land here.

The only place you can stay is at Opo Bay (☎ 577 0531); a camp site is $14 per person, a bunk in a cabin $20. These fees include payment for using the walking tracks. It's a good idea to book ahead, especially during summer.

Getting There & Away Ferries (☎ 578 9685) to the island operate three or four days a week from Christmas Day until mid-January. They depart from Coronation Pier in Tauranga, going via Mt Maunganui, at 7 am and returning at 4 pm. The trip takes about three hours one way and costs $60 return (children $40).

Minden Lookout
From Minden Lookout, about 10km west of Tauranga, there's a superb view back over the Bay of Plenty. To get there, take SH2 to Te Puna and turn off south on Minden Rd; the lookout is about 4km up the road.

Papamoa
pop 7460
Papamoa, 13km east of Mt Maunganui, is blessed with miles of beaches. Digging for tuatua (a type of shellfish) is popular when the tide is right. There are a couple of motor camps at Papamoa, both are along Papamoa Beach Rd.

The *Papamoa Beach Holiday Park & Motel (☎ 572 0816)* has tent sites starting at $22 for two, cabins at $38, flats at $65 and motel units at $90.

The *Pacific Palms Resort* (☎ 572 0035, 21 Gravatt Rd) has one-, two- and three-bedroom apartments starting at $100 for two.

Bent Hills Farmstays (☎ 542 0972, 1162 Welcome Bay Rd) has great sea views and horse riding. Singles/doubles cost $70/100.

Papamoa Beachfront Lodge (☎ 542 1900, 127 Karewa Parade) is a purpose-built lodge with laundry and kitchen facilities. Singles and doubles are $100-plus.

You can get takeaway food from places on Beach Rd, and the *Blue Biyou on the Beach* (559 Beach Rd) is known for fine meals and enormous Sunday brunches.

Te Puke
pop 6390

Hailed as the 'Kiwi-Fruit Capital of the World', Te Puke has native bush near the town and it is not far from several good beaches and exciting rivers. Te Puke gets busy in the kiwi-fruit picking season when there's plenty of work. The information office (☎ 573 9172) is at 72 Jellicoe St.

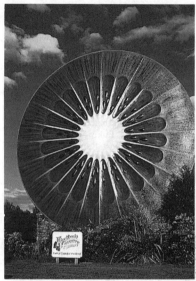

Te Puke's very big (and very tacky) kiwi fruit

Things to See & Do The Bay of Plenty is kiwi-fruit country and here you can learn a little more about the fruit that is so important to NZ's economy. Gardening enthusiasts can visit many private gardens in the area.

Kiwi Fruit Country is on SH2, 6km east of Te Puke and 36km from Tauranga. You can visit the orchards and the shop, watch a video about kiwi fruit and sample some kiwi fruit or kiwi-fruit wine. The complex is also a theme park – it's all quite tacky but the kids might enjoy it, including a 'kiwi-kart' ride through the orchards and an exhibition on how the fruit is grown and packed ($9.50, children $4.50). Kiwi Fruit Country is open from 9 am to 5 pm daily.

Next to Kiwi Fruit Country is the **Vintage Auto Barn** (☎ 573 6547), with over 50 vintage cars on display. It is open from 8.30 am to 5 pm Tuesday to Sunday ($5, children $2).

The **Comvita factory** is signposted about 2km from the turn-off to Whakatane. It uses honey and other bee products to make healthcare products, and has free guided tours (1½ hours) at 1.30 pm every second Friday. Ring ☎ 533 1987 to book.

At **Longridge Park**, Paengaroa, near Te Puke, you can take a thrilling half-hour jet-boat ride up the winding and bush-clad Kaituna River. Longridge Jetboat (☎ 533 1515) charges $55 (children $35).

Afterwards, you can 4WD over a challenging series of tracks with Hill Hoppers (☎ 533 1818). You get to drive for $50 (younger unlicensed passengers $20).

There's **horse riding** at Faraway Farms (☎ 573 5400) on No 3 Rd (signposted on Te Puke's main street). A one-hour ride costs $18. You can also do abseiling here ($25 for the first abseil).

Places to Stay The *Beacon Motel* (☎ 573 7825, 173 Jellicoe St) has singles/doubles from $55/80.

Lindenhof Homestay (☎ 573 4592, 58 Dunlop Rd), 2km north of Te Puke, has comfortable rooms for $50/90, including breakfast. Swiss French and German are spoken here and there's a spa, tennis court and pool.

De Haven (☎ 533 1025) at Paengaroa, about 8km east of Te Puke, is a small backpackers with beds for $16 per person.

BAY OF PLENTY

CHRISTINE NIVEN

Maketu

There's a Maori *pa* site overlooking the water at Town Point, near the township of Maketu, north-east of Te Puke. Maketu was the landing site of the *Arawa* canoe, more than 600 years ago, and there is a stone monument on the foreshore commemorating this. The name Maketu comes from a place in Hawaiki.

To get to Maketu from Tauranga, take SH2 through Te Puke and turn left into Maketu Rd just past Rangiuru. The information centre (☎ 533 2343) is on Maketu Rd.

The good *Bay Views Holiday Park & Motels* (☎ 533 2222, 195 Arawa Ave) is about 1.3 km from the town centre. It has a pool, and camp sites are $10 to $11 per person, tourist flats start at $55 for two and motel units at $70 for two.

The *Seaside Cafe*, near the lifesaving club on the beach, is a pleasant spot.

Eastern Bay of Plenty

The eastern Bay of Plenty extends from Maketu and Pukehina to Opotiki in the far east of the bay, taking in Whakatane and Ohope.

WHAKATANE

pop 17,700

Whakatane (pronounced 'fa-ka-ta-ne') lies on a natural harbour at the mouth of the Whakatane River. When the *Mataatua* canoe landed at the mouth of the river in the 14th century, Whakatane was already an important Maori centre. Only around the beginning of the 20th century did Europeans discover the richness of the land and settle in any numbers.

Whakatane today is the principal town for the eastern Bay of Plenty and a service centre for the Rangitaiki agricultural and milling district.

Whakatane is a pleasant town in one of the sunniest parts of the North Island. Many visitors are attracted to the nearby beaches, especially in summer. Two of its major attractions are offshore: Whakaari (White Island), NZ's most active volcano, and dolphin-swimming tours.

Information

The visitor information centre (☎/fax 308 6058, ✉ whakataneinfo@xtra.co.nz) is on Boon St, half a block off the Strand, and is open from 9 am to 5 pm weekdays, to 1 pm on Saturday and from 10 am to 2 pm on Sunday. The staff make tour bookings and also handle general inquiries for DOC. The AA office is opposite the information centre on Boon St.

Things to See

The **Whakatane Museum**, on Boon St, is one of the more interesting regional museums. It has photographic and artefact exhibits on early Maori and European settlers as well as on the natural environment, including the smoking Whakaari (White Island) volcano just offshore. It's also a centre of historical research, with an archive of historical publications. It's open from 10 am to 4.30 pm Tuesday to Friday, 11 am to 1.30 pm on Saturday and 2 to 4.30 pm on Sunday (entry by donation). Adjacent is an art gallery.

Just to one side of the traffic circle on the corner of the Strand and Commerce St is **Pohaturoa**, a large rock outcrop and important Maori sacred site (it's *tapu*). The Treaty of Waitangi was signed here by Ngati Awa chiefs in 1840. The coastline used to come right up to this point and there's a tunnel in the rock where baptisms and other rites were performed. Also here is a monument to the Ngati Awa chief Te Hurinui Apanui.

Muriwai's Cave (partially collapsed), beside Muriwai Rd, once provided shelter to an ancestress and seer who arrived on the *Mataatua*. A ceremonial *waka* (canoe), named after the original *Mataatua*, sits secure behind a grill in the reserve across the road.

The **Whakatane Astronomical Observatory** (☎ 304 9193), on Hurunui Ave in Hillcrest, opens to the public every Tuesday evening by prior arrangement, weather permitting.

WHAKATANE

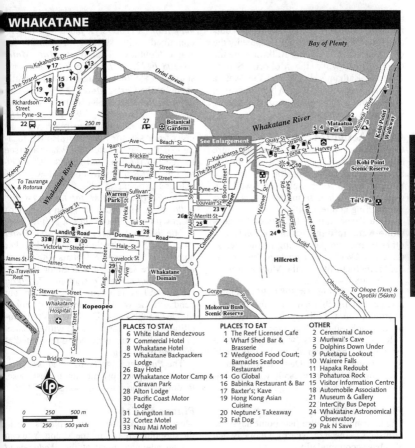

PLACES TO STAY
6 White Island Rendezvous
7 Commercial Hotel
8 Whakatane Hotel
25 Whakatane Backpackers Lodge
26 Bay Hotel
27 Whakatance Motor Camp & Caravan Park
28 Alton Lodge
30 Pacific Coast Motor Lodge
31 Livingston Inn
32 Cortez Motel
33 Nau Mai Motel

PLACES TO EAT
1 The Reef Licensed Cafe
4 Wharf Shed Bar & Brasserie
12 Wedgeood Food Court; Barnacles Seafood Restaurant
14 Go Global
16 Babinka Restaurant & Bar
17 Baxter's; Kave
19 Hong Kong Asian Cuisine
20 Neptune's Takeaway
23 Fat Dog

OTHER
2 Ceremonial Canoe
3 Muriwai's Cave
5 Dolphins Down Under
9 Puketapu Lookout
10 Wairere Falls
11 Hapaka Redoubt
13 Pohaturoa Rock
15 Visitor Information Centre
18 Automobile Association
21 Museum & Gallery
22 InterCity Bus Depot
24 Whakatane Astronomical Observatory
29 Pak N Save

The small **botanical gardens** are at the river end of McGarvey Rd, beside a children's playground.

Dolphin Swimming

Dolphins Down Under (☎ 308 4636, ✉ dolphininfo@dolphinswim.co.nz), Web site: www.dolphinswim.co.nz, at the wharf, runs popular trips year-round (subject to weather) to swim with the dolphins. It has a high success rate for dolphin spotting and in summer there are up to three trips a day ($85, children $50). All necessary equipment, including a wet suit, is supplied. (For an insight into swimming with the dolphins, see the boxed text in the Canterbury chapter.)

Walking

The information centre has lots of details on walks. An interesting 2½-hour town centre walk encompasses a number of scenic and historic spots, including Muriwai's Cave, Wairere Falls, Puketapu Lookout, Hapaka Redoubt, Pohaturoa and a big game-fishing facility.

Other notable walks include the 3½-hour **Kohi Point Walkway**, Nga Tapuwae-o-Toi (The Sacred Footsteps of Toi), which extends through the Kohi Point Scenic Reserve, passing many attractive sites including lookouts and Toi's Pa (Kapua te Rangi), reputedly the oldest pa site in NZ. Other walkways are the Ohope Bush Walk, the Mokorua Scenic Reserve, Latham's Track and the Matata Walking Track. The 300m White Pine Bush Walk, starting about 10km from Whakatane, is suitable for wheelchairs.

Other Activities

Check with the visitor information centre about the wide variety of activities in and around Whakatane. Possibilities include hunting trips, horse treks, bushwalking, trout or sea fishing, diving and kayak trips, windsurfing and jet-boating.

Motu River Rafting (☎ 308 5449) does white-water rafting trips on the Motu and other rivers, and parasailing in summer. A three-day 4WD/raft/jet-boat combination is $350. Another rafter on the Motu is Wet 'n' Wild (☎ 0800-462 723).

Pohutukawa Tours (☎ 308 6495) operates a variety of flexible half-day, full-day and overnight tours. Full-day fishing charters are available on the Charmaine.

Kiwi Jet Boat Tours (☎ 307 0663) has a 1¼-hour jet-boat trip along the Rangitaiki River from Matahina Dam to Aniwhenua Falls for $60 (children $50) with a minimum of four people.

Places to Stay

The information centre lists homestays and farmstays in the area. Nearby, Ohope Beach also has accommodation.

Camping The *Whakatane Motor Camp & Caravan Park* (☎ 308 8694), on McGarvey Rd beside the Whakatane River, has recreational facilities, including a swimming pool and a spa pool. Tent and powered sites are $18 for two, and cabins about $40.

Guesthouses & B&Bs *Travellers Rest* (☎ 307 1015, 28 Henderson St) has singles/doubles for $40/80, including breakfast.

Motels & Hotels Most motels are on, or just off, Landing and Domain Rds. The *Alton Lodge Motel* (☎ 307 1003, 76 Domain Rd) is a Tudor-style place with 11 self-contained units starting at $70/80 for singles/doubles. The *Nau Mai Motel* (☎ 308 6422, 61 Landing Rd) has rooms starting at $59/68 for singles/doubles, while rooms at the *Cortez Motel* (☎ 308 4047, 55 Landing Rd) start at $84 for two. *White Island Rendezvous* (☎ 308 9500, 15 The Strand) is a new, modern place with 10 units from $80 for two. It is also the location of Pee Jay charters to Whakaari (see that section). *Livingston Inn* (☎ 308 6400, 42 Landing Rd) has 15 units, 11 with private spas, starting at $90.

The *Pacific Coast Motor Lodge* (☎ 308 0100, 41 Landing Rd) has 14 units, eight of them with spas. Prices start at $90 for two.

The old Art Deco *Whakatane Hotel* (☎ 308 8199) on the Strand has backpacker beds for $16 per person. Rooms with private facilities are $30/55 for a single/double.

The *Commercial Hotel* (☎ 308 7399) on the Strand East is a better class of pub, but bands on the weekend can be very noisy. Singles/doubles cost $25/40 with shared facilities, and $50 for a double with en suite. (The single rooms were being renovated at the time of writing.)

The *Bay Hotel* (☎ 308 6788, 90 McAllister St) is a good private hotel/guesthouse. Rooms with private bathrooms are $40/65.

Places to Eat

Most of Whakatane's eating places are in the shopping area along the Strand. You can get an adequate meal at the *Wedgewood Food Court*.

Try *Neptune's Takeaway* in Boon St for fish and chips or burgers with the lot. *Fat Dog* on Commercial St is a good place for an espresso and a snack or for something more substantial and a drink.

Go Global where Commercial St merges with the Strand serves fish, steaks, curries and pasta (dinner mains are around $18 to $22 and there's an under-$10 lunch menu).

The *New Hong Kong Asian Cuisine*, on Richardson St, has Chinese food, with a separate counter for takeaways. Most mains are under $10 and there are regular specials.

In and around the mall that fronts onto the estuary is a cluster of places that include *Baxter's* and *Kave*. Nearby, *Babinka Restaurant & Bar* has an interesting menu that includes a variety of north and south Indian dishes (mains under $20).

The *Why Not? Cafe & Bar* and *Main Street* on the Strand have pastas, steaks and seafood.

The licensed *Barnacles Seafood Restaurant* has upmarket fish and chips. The *Harbourside Brasserie*, between Quay St and the Strand, has mains for under $15, including fish and chips, shepherds pie, roast beef and curries.

The Chambers Restaurant & Bar, opposite the Commercial Hotel on the Strand, is in the solid former council building. It's licensed and is a classy place.

The *Wharf Shed Bar & Brasserie* on Muriwai Drive has seafood and steaks, with mains under $22. At the Heads is the popular *Reef Licensed Cafe*, known for its seafood. It's open for lunch and dinner daily.

Getting There & Around
Air New Zealand Link (☎ 0800-737 000) has daily flights linking Whakatane to Auckland and Wellington, with connections to other centres.

A taxi (☎ 0800-807 038) to or from the airport costs $12. There is no bus service.

The InterCity bus depot (☎ 308 6169) is on Pyne St (Bay Coachlines). InterCity has buses connecting Whakatane with Rotorua and Gisborne, with connections to other places. All buses to Gisborne go via Opotiki. Courier services around East Cape originate in Opotiki and Gisborne (see East Cape in the East Coast chapter).

OHOPE BEACH
pop 3010
The town of Ohope with its fine beach is 7km 'over the hill' from Whakatane. It is a pleasant area in which to spend a few days, and there are a number of walks in the area.

All types of accommodation are available, including motels and guesthouses. Camping grounds include *Ohope Beach Holiday Park (☎ 312 4460)*, on Harbour Rd past Port Ohope, which has sites for $20 for two people, as well as cabins and tourist flats ranging up to $70 for two. The *Surf and Sand Holiday Park (☎ 312 4884)* is also on Harbour Rd and has 172 powered sites for $13 per person.

Cafe fans are in luck with *Julies*, which is licensed and has a courtyard. You can also access the Internet here.

For fast food try *Just Rumours*, which is nearby. On the main highway heading towards Opotiki is the *Ohiwa Oyster Farm*, a roadside takeaway place. There are tables near the water where you can consume your fish and chips, oysters (the Pacific variety; $7.50 for a half-dozen) or burgers.

WHAKAARI (WHITE ISLAND)
Whakaari, or White Island, is NZ's most active volcano, smoking and steaming away just 50km off the coast from Whakatane. It's a small island of 324 hectares, formed by three separate volcanic cones, all of different ages. Erosion has worn away most of the surface of the two older cones and the youngest cone, which rose up between the two older ones, now occupies most of the centre of the island. Hot water and steam continually escape from vents over most of the crater floor and temperatures of 600°C to 800°C have been recorded. The highest point on the island is Mt Gisborne at 321m. Geologically, Whakaari is related to Moutohora (Whale Island) and Putauaki (Mt Edgecumbe), as they all lie along the same volcanic trench.

The island is privately owned and the only way you can land on it is with a helicopter or boat tour that has arranged permission. The island has no jetty so boats have to land on the beach, which means that landings are not possible in rough seas. A visit to Whakaari is an unforgettable, if disconcerting, experience, but the constant rumblings and plumes of steam do not necessarily mean that it is about to blow up.

History
Before the arrival of Europeans, Maori caught sea birds on the island for food. In 1769 Captain Cook named it White Island because of the dense clouds of white steam hanging above it.

BAY OF PLENTY

The first European to land on the island was a missionary, the Reverend Henry Williams, in 1826. The island was acquired by Europeans in the late 1830s and changed ownership a number of times after that. Sulphur production began but was interrupted in 1885 by a minor eruption, and the following year the island was hurriedly abandoned in the wake of the Tarawera eruption. The island's sulphur industry resumed in 1898 but only continued until 1901, when production ceased altogether.

In the 1910s, further mining operations were attempted and abandoned, due to mud flows and other volcanic activity, and ownership of the island continued to change. In 1953 White Island was declared a Private Scenic Reserve.

The island was at its most active between 1976 and 1981, when two new craters were formed and 100,000 cubic metres of rock was ejected.

Getting There & Away

Trips to Whakaari include a one- or two-hour tour on foot around the island. A landing by boat is definitely weather-dependent. All trips (except for fixed-wing flightseeing) incur a $20 landing fee, which may be included in the quoted price.

Operators include:

East Bay Flight Centre (☎ 308 8446) Flightseeing tours over the island for $150 per person (minimum of two people).
Kahurangi (☎ 323 7829) Offers a six-hour boat trip for $85 per person, including lunch and a bit of dolphin spotting en route. You spend about two hours on the island. The boat used is a 44-foot keflar cat (minimum of 10 people).
Pee Jay (☎ 0800-733 529) Tours on a 60-foot monohull launch, taking six hours with two hours on the island. It costs $95 per person, lunch is included (minimum of 10 people).
White Island Volcano Adventure (☎ 0800-804 354) Has 2½-hour helicopter flights at $315 per person (minimum of five people). The pilot will land if conditions are safe. It is $635 ex-Rotorua/Tauranga (minimum of six).

MOUTOHORA

Moutohora, or Whale Island, so-called because of its shape, is 9km north off the coast of Whakatane and has an area of 414 hectares. It's another volcanic island, on the same volcanic trench as Whakaari. It's much less active, and along its shore are hot springs, which can reach 93°C. The summit is 350m high and the island has several historic sites, including an ancient pa site, an old quarry and a camp.

Whale Island was settled by Maori before the 1769 landing of Captain Cook. In 1829 there was a Maori massacre of sailors from the trading vessel *Haweis* while it was anchored at Sulphur Bay. This was followed by an unsuccessful whaling venture in the 1830s. In the 1840s the island passed into European ownership and is still privately owned, although since 1965 it has been an officially protected wildlife refuge administered by DOC.

Whale Island is principally a haven for sea and shore birds, some of which are quite rare. Some of the birds use the island only for nesting at certain times of the year, while others are present year-round. The island has a large colony of grey-faced petrels, estimated to number 10,000.

The island's protected status means landing is restricted. Contact the Whakatane DOC office and inquire about tours to the island operated at Christmas time.

WHAKATANE TO ROTORUA

Travelling along SH30 from Whakatane to Rotorua you'll come to the **Awakeri Hot Springs**, 16km from Whakatane. It has hot springs, spa pools, picnic areas and a *holiday park* (☎ 304 9117). At the latter, powered sites are $18, tourist flats $50 and motel units $70 (prices are for two).

Lying just off SH30, **Kawerau** is a timber town surrounded by pine forest and dependent on the huge Tasman Pulp & Paper Mill. Kawerau has an information centre (☎ 323 7550), on Plunket St in the centre of town, and a selection of accommodation, but the only real reason to come here is to visit the waterfalls outside town. You can visit the **mill** for a 1½-hour tour; bookings are essential (☎ 323 3999).

Tarawera Falls are a half-hour drive from Kawerau, along a well-graded road through the pine forests (watch out for the logging trucks). From the end of the road it is a 15-minute walk through native forest to the falls, which emerge from a hole in the canyon wall. The track continues another two hours up to the top of the falls and on to Lake Tarawera. This is a good walk with views of the lake and Mt Tarawera. You need a permit to visit ($2), which you can obtain from the information centre.

Also near Kawerau, **Putauaki (Mt Edgecumbe)** is a commanding volcanic cone with panoramic views of the entire Bay of Plenty from its top. You need a permit for access; contact the information centre. At the time of writing the mountain was closed to visitors. The information centre will be able to give you the latest news.

OPOTIKI
pop 7070

Opotiki, the easternmost town of the Bay of Plenty, is the gateway to the East Cape and the rugged forests and river valleys of the Raukumara and nearby ranges. The town itself is nothing special, but many visitors stop over on the way to the East Coast and there are some reasonable surf beaches nearby, such as Ohiwa and Waiotahi. Opotiki is a model of Maori tradition – the main street is lined with the works of mastercarvers.

The Opotiki area was settled from at least 1150, which was 200 years before the larger 14th century migration. In the mid-1800s Opotiki was a centre for Hauhauism, a Maori doctrine grounded in Judaeo-Christian beliefs, which advocated, among other things, an end to Maori oppression.

Known by the local Whakatohea tribe to have acted as a government spy, Reverend Carl Volkner was murdered in his church in 1865. This led to the church being employed as a fort by government troops. The murder was used as one justification for land confiscations in the area.

Information
The Opotiki Information Centre (☎ 315 8484, @ opotiki.info@xtra.co.nz), on the corner of St John and Elliot Sts, is open from 8 am to 5 pm weekdays and 10 am to 3 pm weekends during summer (there is some flexibility). The DOC office (☎ 315 6103) is in the same building. The centre does bookings for a range of activities and can organise visits to a local marae.

Things to See & Do
Just over 7km from the town centre is the fascinating **Hukutaia Domain**, which has one of the finest collections of native plants in NZ, many of the species rare and endangered. In the domain's centre a puriri tree, named Taketakerau, is estimated to be over 2000 years old. The remains of the distinguished dead of the Upokorere *hapu* (subtribe) of the Whakatohea tribe were ritually buried beneath it. The tree is no longer tapu (sacred) as the remains have been reinterred elsewhere.

The old-fashioned **Deluxe Cinema** on Church St is fun to visit. The **Historical & Agricultural Society Museum** on Church St is spilling over with historical items donated by the local community. It's open from 10 am to 3.30 pm daily ($2, children $0.50).

You can go **horse riding** along the beach with Tirohanga Beach Treks (☎ 315 7490). A two-hour ride is $40 per person.

Places to Stay
Camping & Cabins The *Opotiki Holiday Park (☎ 315 6050),* on Potts Ave, has tent and powered sites for $8 per person, on-site caravans for $30, cabins for $36 and tourist flats for $55.

There are several beachfront camping grounds near Opotiki. The *Ohiwa Family Holiday Park (☎ 315 4741, Ohiwa Harbour Rd),* 10 minutes' drive north of Opotiki, has tent sites for $20 for two, cabins from $35, flats from $60 and deluxe flats for $70.

The *Island View Family Holiday Park (☎ 315 7519),* on Appleton Rd 4km from town at Waiotahi Beach, has camp sites for $11, a cabin for $37 and tourist flats for $52.

The *Tirohanga Beach Motor Camp (☎ 315 7942),* on the East Coast Rd 6km from town, has tent/powered sites for $8/9, cabins for $35 and tourist flats for $40. Also

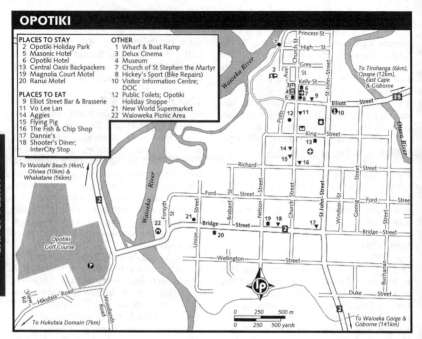

OPOTIKI

PLACES TO STAY
2 Opotiki Holiday Park
5 Masonic Hotel
6 Opotiki Hotel
13 Central Oasis Backpackers
19 Magnolia Court Motel
20 Ranui Motel

PLACES TO EAT
9 Elliot Street Bar & Brasserie
11 Vo Lee Lan
14 Aggies
15 Flying Pig
16 The Fish & Chip Shop
17 Dannie's
18 Shooter's Diner;
   InterCity Stop

OTHER
1 Wharf & Boat Ramp
3 Delux Cinema
4 Museum
7 Church of St Stephen the Martyr
8 Hickey's Sport (Bike Repairs)
10 Visitor Information Centre;
   DOC
12 Public Toilets; Opotiki
   Holiday Shoppe
21 New World Supermarket
22 Waioweka Picnic Area

on the East Coast Rd, 12km from Opotiki, the ***Opape Motor Camp*** *(☎ 315 8175)* has camp sites and an on-site caravan.

Hostels The ***Central Oasis Backpackers*** *(☎ 315 5165, 30 King St)* is in the centre of town in an old cottage. It's a delightful, friendly and small hostel with dorm beds for $12 and $14, twins and doubles for $32.

On Appleton Rd at Waiotahi Beach, about five minutes west of Opotiki, is the ***Opotiki Backpackers Beach House*** *(☎ 315 5117)*. It's a nice, small place with an adjoining kitchen and recreation room. Beds are $13 in the loft and there's a double for $30. There's also a caravan that sleeps two ($15 per person). Kayaks, surfboards and boogy boards are available to guests.

The adjoining ***Beachhouse Cafe*** is open from November to April.

Motels & Guesthouses The ***Ranui Motel*** *(☎ 315 6669, 36 Bridge St)* has units

starting at $68, and the ***Magnolia Court Motel*** *(☎ 315 8490)*, on the corner of Bridge and Nelson Sts, charges from $76 for a double.

There are a couple of historical hotels with budget accommodation: the ***Opotiki Hotel*** *(☎ 315 6078)* and the ***Masonic Hotel*** *(☎ 315 6115)*, both on Church St.

Within a reasonable distance of town there are several other options. ***Capeview Cottage*** *(☎ 315 7877, Tablelands Rd)* has two bedrooms, hot tubs and lovely views. The cost is $130 for two (weekly $750). ***Riverview Cottage*** *(☎ 315 5553)*, on SH2 heading towards Gisborne, is a small self-contained cottage nestled in bush and farmland. It costs $110 for two. Inquire at the information centre.

Places to Eat

Although not exactly the gourmet capital of the Bay, Opotiki does have a small range of places to eat.

Dannie's, near the corner of St John and Bridge Sts, is a fast-food place. The *Fish & Chip Shop* on Church St is popular and good. For a hearty breakfast go to *Shooter's Diner* on Bridge St – it also serves full meals at other times.

On Church St are two good cafes: the BYO *Aggie's* serves vegetarian quiches and lasagne and the licensed *Flying Pig* serves kebabs and other delights in pitta bread. The *Elliot Street Bar & Brasserie* on Elliot St is another possibility.

For Chinese food try *Vo Lee Lan* on Church St.

Getting There & Away

Travelling east from Opotiki there are two routes to choose from; SH2 crosses the spectacular Waioeka Gorge. There are some fine walks of one day and longer in the **Waioeka Gorge Scenic Reserve**. The gorge gets progressively steeper and narrower as you travel inland, before the route crosses typically green, rolling hills, dotted with sheep, on the descent to Gisborne.

The other route east from Opotiki is SH35 around the East Cape, described fully in the East Coast chapter.

InterCity buses pick up/drop off at Shooter's Diner on Bridge St. Tickets and bookings can be made through the Opotiki Holiday Shoppe (☎ 315 6125) at 109b Church St.

InterCity has daily buses connecting Opotiki with Whakatane, Rotorua and Auckland. Heading south, the buses connect Opotiki with Gisborne, Wairoa and Napier daily.

BAY OF PLENTY

Central Plateau

☎ 07 • pop 41,741

New Zealand's main volcanic area, the Taupo Volcanic Zone, stretches in a line from White Island, north of the Bay of Plenty, through Rotorua and down to Tongariro National Park. The Central Plateau, at the heart of the North Island, is the centre of the country's volcanic activity.

The Central Plateau was at its most active some 2000 years ago. The remaining volcanoes do not match the destructive fury of some of the world's other hot spots, but still put on spectacular shows from time to time. Since 1995 Mt Ruapehu, the tallest mountain in the North Island, has had a series of eruptions, spewing forth rock and clouds of ash and steam.

Taupo, on Lake Taupo, is the main resort town of this volcanic plateau. The plateau extends southwards to the majestic, snow-capped volcanoes in Tongariro National Park, one of NZ's premier parks with many fine walks.

Lake Taupo

New Zealand's largest lake, Lake Taupo, is in the very heart of the North Island. Some 606 sq km in area and 357m above sea level, the lake was formed by one of the greatest volcanic explosions the world has experienced (see the boxed text 'Bang!' later in this chapter). The surrounding area is still volcanically active and, like Rotorua, has thermal areas.

Today serene Lake Taupo is proclaimed as the world's trout-fishing capital. If you thought those trout in the Rotorua springs looked large and tasty, they're nothing compared to the monsters found in Lake Taupo. All NZ's rainbow trout descend from a single batch of eggs brought from California's Russian River nearly a century ago. International trout-fishing tournaments are held on Lake Taupo each year on the Anzac Day long weekend (on or around 25 April).

HIGHLIGHTS

- Visiting Tongariro National Park, dominated by smoking Mt Ruapehu
- Walking the famous Tongariro Crossing and the Northern Circuit
- Trout fishing or boating at Lake Taupo
- Exploring Wairakei Park and its thermal regions, and the Huka Falls
- Skiing at Whakapapa and Turoa
- Tandem skydiving or bungy jumping at Taupo

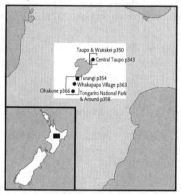

Taupo & Wairakei p350
● Central Taupo p343
■ Turangi p354
● Whakapapa Village p363
Ohakune p366 ● ■ Tongariro National Park & Around p358

TAUPO
pop 21,040

Taupo lies on the north-eastern corner of Lake Taupo and has scenic views stretching across the lake to the volcanic peaks of Tongariro National Park. This relaxed resort is the main town of the area and makes a good base from which to explore the local attractions.

Activities in Taupo range from fishing and boating on the lake to adrenaline-pumping bungy jumping and skydiving and even 'swimming with the trout'.

Lake Taupo is also the source of NZ's longest river, the Waikato, which leaves the

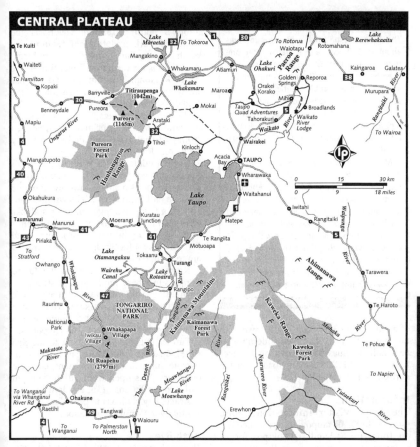

CENTRAL PLATEAU

lake at the township, flows through the Huka Falls and the Aratiatia Rapids, and then through the heart of the northern part of North Island to the west coast just south of Auckland.

History

Back in the mists of time, the Maori chief Tamatea-arikinui visited the area and, noticing that the ground felt hollow and his footsteps seemed to reverberate, called the place Tapuaeharuru (Resounding Footsteps). Another source of the name comes from the story that Tia, who discovered the lake, slept by it draped in his cloak, and it became known as Taupo-nui-a-Tia (The Great Cloak of Tia). Taupo, as it became known, was first occupied by Europeans as a military outpost during the East Coast Land War (1868–72). Colonel JM Roberts built a redoubt in 1869 and a garrison of mounted police remained there until the defeat of the rebel warrior Te Kooti (see the boxed text in the East Coast chapter) in October of that year.

In the 1870s the government bought the land from the Maori. Taupo has grown slowly and sedately from a lakeside village

Bang!

The Taupo region's *really* big eruption was about 25,000 years ago – that was the one that actually created the huge basin now filled by Lake Taupo. The eruption produced an estimated 800 cubic kilometres (km³) of ash. The North Island would have been devastated, coated with hot, poisonous ash tens of metres thick. Even the Chatham Islands (800km downwind) copped a 10cm-deep layer!

More recently, in AD 181, accounts of darkened skies and spectacular sunsets were recorded in China and Rome – the effects of another Taupo explosion. This was the world's most powerful eruption in historical times and it's bloody lucky NZ was still uninhabited: about 30km³ of ash and pumice was ejected in just a few minutes, shooting out across the land at speeds up to 900km/h and laying waste to the unfortunate fauna and flora as far away as Rotorua, Gisborne and Napier.

of about 750 in 1945 to a resort town with the population swelling considerably at peak holiday times. The town is on the lakefront where SH1, the main road from the north, first meets the lake.

Information

The Taupo Visitor Information Centre (☎ 378 9000, ✉ taupo@thinkfresh.co.nz) on Tongariro St handles bookings for all accommodation, transport and activities in the area, and exchanges currency on the weekends. It has a good, free town map as well as Department of Conservation (DOC) maps and information. The centre is open from 8.30 am to 5 pm daily. Also see its Web site (www.laketaupo.tourism .co.nz).

The Super Loo nearby is a large shower-toilet complex, with showers for $1 (for four minutes) and towels for $1.

The Automobile Association (AA; ☎ 378 6000) is at 93 Tongariro St. The post shop is on the corner of Horomatangi and Ruapehu Sts.

Things to See

Taupo's main attractions, such as the Wairakei Park and thermal regions, are north of town. But in town, on Story Place, near the visitor centre on Tongariro St, the **Taupo Regional Museum & Art Gallery** has many historical photos and mementos of the 'old days' around Lake Taupo. Exhibits also include Maori carvings, a moa skeleton and a rundown on the trout industry. It is open from 10.30 am to 4.30 pm daily (entry is by gold coin donation).

In the middle of the Waikato River, off Spa Rd and not far from the centre of town, **Cherry Island** is a small, low-key trout and wildlife park with a cafe. The wildlife consists of a few goats, pigs, pheasants, ducks etc – the kids might like it but admission is steep at $9.50 (children $4.50). The island is reached by a footbridge and open from 9 am to 5 pm daily.

Right near Cherry Island is the **Taupo Bungy** site where jumpers leap off a platform jutting 20m out over a cliff and hurtle down towards the Waikato River, 45m below. If you don't want to jump, it is a scenic spot with plenty of vantage points.

Further out, on Spa Rd next to the Spa Hotel, **Spa Dinosaur Valley** is Taupo's answer to Jurassic Park with giant, concrete dinosaurs. It is open from 10 am to 4 pm daily except Tuesday ($5, children $3).

Acacia Bay, a pleasant, peaceful beach, is a little over 5km west of Taupo.

Activities

Thermal Pools & Climbing Walls The Taupo Events Centre (☎ 378 7321) at the top of Spa Rd, about 2km east of town, has a big, heated pool with a waterslide, private mineral pools and a sauna. It's open from 8 am to 9 pm daily ($4, children $2); use of the saunas and waterslide costs $4 and $3 respectively. There is also a climbing wall, open from 5 to 9 pm Monday to Friday and noon to 7 pm weekends. The cost is $13/11 for adults/children (includes a harness and ropes).

The Taupo Hot Springs (☎ 378 0541) is on the Taupo-Napier Highway (SH5), 1km from the lake. There are also large outdoor pools, a big, hot waterslide and private

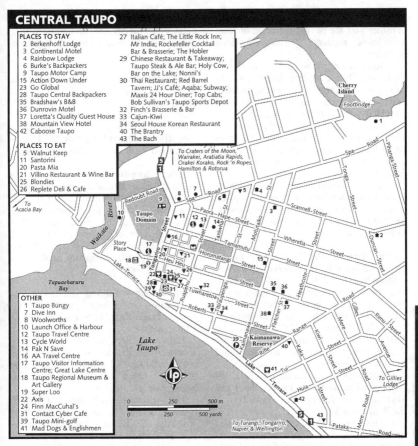

CENTRAL TAUPO

PLACES TO STAY
2 Berkenhoff Lodge
3 Continental Motel
4 Rainbow Lodge
6 Burke's Backpackers
9 Taupo Motor Camp
15 Action Down Under
23 Go Global
28 Taupo Central Backpackers
35 Bradshaw's B&B
36 Dunrovin Motel
37 Loretta's Quality Guest House
38 Mountain View Hotel
42 Caboose Taupo

PLACES TO EAT
5 Walnut Keep
11 Santorini
20 Pasta Mia
21 Villino Restaurant & Wine Bar
25 Blondies
26 Replete Deli & Cafe

27 Italian Café; The Little Rock Inn;
   Mr India; Rockefeller Cocktail
   Bar & Brasserie; The Hobler
29 Chinese Restaurant & Takeaway;
   Taupo Steak & Ale Bar; Holy Cow,
   Bar on the Lake; Nonni's
30 Thai Restaurant; Red Barrel
   Tavern; JJ's Café; Aqaba; Subway;
   Maxis 24 Hour Diner; Top Cabs;
   Bob Sullivan's Taupo Sports Depot
32 Finch's Brasserie & Bar
33 Cajun-Kiwi
34 Seoul House Korean Restaurant
40 The Brantry
43 The Bach

OTHER
1 Taupo Bungy
7 Dive Inn
8 Woolworths
10 Launch Office & Harbour
12 Taupo Travel Centre
13 Cycle World
14 Pak N Save
16 AA Travel Centre
17 Taupo Visitor Information
   Centre; Great Lake Centre
18 Taupo Regional Museum &
   Art Gallery
19 Super Loo
22 Axis
24 Finn MacCuhal's
31 Contact Cyber Cafe
39 Taupo Mini-golf
41 Mad Dogs & Englishmen

To Craters of the Moon,
Wairakei, Aratiatia Rapids,
Orakei Korako, Rock 'n Ropes,
Hamilton & Rotorua

To Acacia Bay

Taupo Domain

Story Place

Tapuaeharuru Bay

Lake Taupo

To Turangi, Tongariro,
Napier & Wellington

To Gillies Lodge

CENTRAL PLATEAU

pools. The pools are open from 7 am to 9.30 pm daily ($7, children $2.50). Private pools are $8 per person.

Fishing A number of fishing guides and charter boats operate in Taupo; check with the visitor centre. A trip costs about $60 per person on a share basis.

Boats can also be hired from the launch office (☎ 378 3444), starting at $65 per hour for a boat taking up to six people and going up to around $130 per hour for the larger boats.

The backpackers also book fishing boat trips. Count on a fishing trip lasting around two or three hours. If you go on a boat trip they'll supply all the gear and organise a fishing licence.

Taupo is world famous for its trout fly fishing. Fly fishing is the only fishing you can do on all rivers flowing into the lake, and within a 300m radius of the river mouths. Spin fishing is allowed on the Waikato River (flowing *out* of the lake) and on the Tokaanu tailrace, flowing into the lake from the Tokaanu Power Station. Both spin fishing and fly fishing are allowed on the lake. Several fly-fishing guides operate around Taupo, some of whom are very good. The price is reasonable when you consider you are paying for years of local knowledge – around $250 a day, everything included.

If you're going to do it on your own, Bob Sullivan's Taupo Sports Depot (☎ 378 5337), on Tongariro St by the waterfront, and the Fly & Gun Shop (☎ 378 4449), on Heu Heu St, have fishing tackle for hire.

Fishing licences are available from the visitor centre or the launch office. Licences for fishing on Lake Taupo and the nearby rivers cost $12/26/36/55 per day/week/month/year.

Make sure you always have your fishing licence and obey the rules listed on it when fishing – there are huge fines for violations. See the boxed text 'It's a Trout's Life' later in this chapter.

Water Sports The Acacia Bay Lodge (☎ 378 6830), at 868 Acacia Bay Rd in Acacia Bay, hires out motorboats at $24 per hour, and rowing boats, canoes and kayaks at $12 per hour. It takes an hour from there in a motorboat to reach the Maori rock carvings.

The Sail Centre (☎ 378 3299) at Two Mile Bay, south of Taupo, hires out Canadian canoes, windsurfers, catamarans and sailboats in summer.

Bruce Webber Adventures (☎ 377 1236) has a good name for its kayak school and kayaking trips. A guided two-hour trip on the Waikato is $40.

During summer there are lots of activities on Lake Taupo including **swimming, water-skiing, windsurfing, paragliding** and **sailing**. The visitor centre has details. Gear can be hired at the lakefront.

Several **white-water rafting** companies operate from Taupo and offer one-day trips on the Tongariro and Rangitaiki Rivers, and longer trips on other rivers (from grades II to IV). Book these trips through the hostels or the visitor centre. The float trips on local rivers such as the Waikato are ideal for children.

Popular and a little different is **drift diving**, which provides the chance to let the current of the Waikato River do the work, and let you swim with the trout. Contact the Dive Inn (☎ 378 1926), 26 Spa Rd, for more

details; it charges $85, including hire of gear. You need to be a certified diver to do this.

Bungy Jumping The bungy jump in Taupo is the most popular on the North Island, largely because of its scenic setting on the Waikato River. It costs $89 for a jump but there is a bewildering array of discounts. The office of Taupo Bungy (☎ 377 1135) is open from 9 am to 7 pm daily in summer.

Tandem Skydiving This is one of the popular Taupo adrenaline rushes. In addition to the skydiving itself, at the cheapest rate in NZ, you get a brilliant view over Lake Taupo and the entire region. Both Great Lake Skydive Centre (☎ 0800-373 335) and Taupo Tandems (☎ 025-428 688), at Taupo Airport, do tandem skydives for $165 (9000 feet).

Flightseeing & Gliding You can go for a scenic flight on the floatplane (☎ 378 7500) next to Taupo Boat Harbour (from $30 for 10 minutes).

Taupo Air Services (☎ 378 5325) at Taupo Airport also does scenic flights ranging from $40 for a 15-minute flight to $135 for flights across Lake Taupo, Tongariro, Ngauruhoe and Ruapehu.

The Biplane Adventure Company (☎ 0800-359 4273) at Taupo Airport will take you up in a Grumman G164A radial engine biplane (prices from $98) and can also arrange hot-air balloon trips ($225 if you book and pay in advance; otherwise $255).

Helistar Helicopters (☎ 374 8405), about 3km north-east of town on Huka Falls Rd, offers a variety of scenic helicopter flights, including a 10-minute flight over Taupo ($75).

The Taupo Gliding Club (☎ 378 5627) goes gliding on Sunday and Wednesday afternoons (when the weather is suitable) at Centennial Park on Centennial Drive, about 5km up Spa Rd from the town centre. A flight costs from $70.

Horse Trekking Taupo Horse Treks (☎ 378 0356) on Karapiti Rd (the road leading to Craters of the Moon) has a good reputation for treks, which are off-road and go through some fine forest with good views over the Craters of the Moon. An hour's ride is $25, two hours $40.

Cycling If you don't make it to Arataki (see Arataki & Pureora Forest Park later) then Taupo Quad Adventures (☎ 377 6404) has fully guided off-road mountain bike trips. It's at the turn-off to Orakei Korako on SH1 (see the Central Plateau map). A bike is $55 for 1½ hours and $75 for 2½ hours (twilight or night rides are available).

Lake Taupo is the location of NZ's most popular fun ride, the 160km Great Lake Cycle Challenge, held in November each year.

Rock 'n' Ropes The masochist from Rock 'n' Ropes (☎ 374 8111, 0800-244 508) who dreamt up this diabolical confidence course must lurk furtively in bush near Taupo – obviously he/she led a Tarzan/Jane-like existence as a kid. Enough said – leap to your death (only to be saved by a rope), swing into oblivion, be a 'flying fox' and generally have a good time. The cost depends on how daring you are. What did these guys do before kernmantel ropes? A swing is $15, an adrenaline combo (swing, high beam and trapeze) is $35 and a half-day blast is $59. You can find Rock 'n' Ropes at Crazy Catz Adventure (formerly Deerpark) on SH5, 13km north of Taupo. Free pick-up from Taupo is available.

Paintball Try out pump action paintmarkers with Topgun Paintball (☎ 025-908 964), which can be found just off the road that leads to the Craters of the Moon. You'll need a team of at least six to play, and sandshoes (overalls, masks and paintmarkers supplied). The markers fire small gelatine balls filled with coloured vegetable oil. It costs $30 a head (including 40 rounds of paintballs per person) if there are six to nine of you – more people, less cost. Bookings are essential.

Walking You can walk from Taupo to Aratiatia. From the centre of town head up Spa Rd, passing the Taupo Bungy site. Turn left at County Ave and continue through Spa Thermal Park at the end of the street, past the skateboard bowl and over the hill, following the rough roadway to the left until you hit the track.

CENTRAL PLATEAU

PETER HINES

Getting ready for the Great Lake Cycle Challenge around Lake Taupo

The track follows the river to Huka Falls, crossing a hot stream and riverside marshes en route. It's about a one- to 1½-hour walk from the centre of Taupo to Huka Falls. From the falls you continue straight ahead along the 7km Taupo Walkway to Aratiatia (another two-plus hours). There are good views of the river, Huka Falls and the power station across the river. It's easy walking. Alternatively, you can drive out to the falls and park, cross the bridge and walk out to Aratiatia.

Another walk worth mentioning is to **Mt Tauhara**, with magnificent views from the top. Take the Taupo-Napier Highway (SH5) turn-off, 2km south of the Taupo town centre. About 6km along SH5, turn left into Mountain Rd. The start of the track is signposted on the right-hand side. It will take about two hours to the top, walking slowly.

A pleasant **walkway** goes from the Taupo lakefront to Four Mile Bay. It's a flat, easy walk along public-access beaches. Heading south from Taupo, there's a hot-water beach on the way to Two Mile Bay. At Two Mile Bay the walkway connects with the Lions Walk, going from Two Mile Bay (3.2km south of Taupo) to Four Mile Bay (6.4km). Anywhere along here you can easily get back to SH1, the lakeside road.

There are plenty of other good walks and tramps in the area; the visitor centre has the relevant DOC pamphlets ($1).

Organised Tours

Walter's Backpackers Tours, run by a delightful, spry old fellow, includes three-hour tours of the local sights ($20), further afield to places like Waitomo ($75), Rotorua and Orakei Korako. Book with Walter (☎ 378 5924) at backpackers or the visitor centre.

Paradise Tours (☎ 378 9955) does 2½-hour tours to the Aratiatia Rapids, Geothermal Centre, Craters of the Moon and Huka Falls for $25 (children $12). Rapid Sensations (☎ 378 7902) does guided three-hour mountain-bike tours through the geothermal areas ($45).

Wilderness Escapes (☎ 378 3413) has a number of trips; guided walks are from $50 per hour and full-day kayak trips from $90.

Taupo Volcano Tours (☎ 378 5901, 025-2233 524) runs a variety of tours with an interesting, informed commentary on the geology and volcanology of the region. There are two half-day tours – one on the lake ($90) and the other using a 4WD to get around the lake ($70) – and two full-day tours to National Park, one using a 4WD ($145) and another in which you take to the air at Turangi ($185).

Kiwi Value Tours (☎ 378 9662), at 56 Kaimanawa St, does four-hour trips to Waiotapu ($50 including entry), three-hour trips to Orakei Korako ($40 per person) and 2½-hour tours of Taupo's sights ($20 per person). There is also a 5½-hour combo tour of Taupo and Orakei Korako for $45.

You can do a 20-minute tour of central Taupo's main sights in a 1951 Bristol double-decker bus with Discover Taupo (☎ 0800-100 679). The bus departs every half-hour from 9.30 am (bus stops behind the Super Loo and at the town end of the lakefront). It costs $5 for adults and $2.50 for children aged four to 15.

How did this bus get to Taupo? New Zealand was the last stop on a 40,000-mile world tour.

Lake Cruises & Jet-Boating Four boats specialise in cruises on the lake: the *Barbary,* the *Ernest Kemp,* the *Cruise Cat* and the *Superjet*. The *Barbary,* built in 1926, is a 15m ocean-going racing yacht once owned by actor Errol Flynn. 'Barbary Bill', the skipper, is much loved by tourists and locals and his trip is probably the most popular.

The *Ernest Kemp,* built to resemble a 1920 steamboat, is named for Alfred Ernest Kemp whose family occupied the house that still bears their name in Kerikeri, Northland. There are written commentaries for its trips in various languages. The *Superjet* is a fast, twin-jet catamaran.

All the boats offer similar trips, visiting a modern Maori rock carving beside the lake. The carving is on private land so it cannot be reached by foot; the only way to see it is by boat. All also offer morning and afternoon cruises, with the *Ernest Kemp* doing a 4.15 pm cruise in summer and the *Barbary* doing a 5 pm one in summer. There is also a Sunday bubbly brunch special on the *Cruise Cat* departing 10.30 am ($38). Trips last one to 2½ hours.

All the boats leave from the wharves at the Taupo Boat Harbour, off Redoubt St. Bookings can be made at the visitor centre or at the launch office (☎ 378 3444) by the wharves.

Places to Stay

Camping & Cabins Camping is free beside the river at *Reid's Farm* about 1.5km south of Huka Falls towards Taupo; it is popular, and colourful house trucks are often parked there.

The *Taupo Motor Camp* (☎ 377 3080, 15 Redoubt St) by the river has tent and powered sites for $10 per person, cabins for $38 and on-site caravans from $40.

The *Taupo All Seasons Holiday Park* (☎ 378 4272, 16 Rangatira St) is about 1.5km from the town centre. It has a hot thermal pool. Tent sites cost $10 per person, lodge accommodation starts at $42 for two, tourist cabins are $57 and tourist flats $72.

The *De Bretts Thermal Resort* (☎ 378 8559, **@** debrett@voyager.co.nz) is 1km from the lake on SH5. Powered sites are $10, cabins are from $40, motel units are from $70 and lodges from $75 for two.

The *Hilltop Thermal Holiday Park* (☎ 378 5247, 39 Puriri St), off Taharepa Rd, has hot mineral spas and a cold pool. Powered and tent sites are $10 per person, and cabins and caravans cost from $40 for two people.

The *Lake Taupo Holiday Park* (☎ 378 6860, 28 Centennial Drive) is opposite the Taupo Leisure Centre. It's a seven-hectare park with tent and powered sites for $10, on-site caravans for $35, tourist cabins for $45 and tourist flats for $60.

Great Lake Holiday Park (☎ 378 5159) on Acacia Bay Rd, 3km west of town, has powered and tent sites for $9, cabins for $28, on-site caravans for $35 and tourist flats for $54.

The *Windsor Motel* (☎ 378 6271) at Waitahanui, 12km south on SH1, has non-powered/powered sites at $12/15, and cabins from $25.

Backpackers *Taupo Central Backpackers* (☎ 378 3206, fax 378 0344, 7 Tuwharetoa St) is a former hotel. There is an attached bathroom in every room, a rooftop bar (named Trout's, after its ebullient owner), and a barbecue/meeting area with superb views of the lake and the Central Plateau. Dorms cost $19, and doubles and twins are $44, including breakfast.

Go Global (☎ 377 0044, **@** goglobal@ reap.org.nz), across the road on the corner of Tongariro and Tuwharetoa Sts, is a tidy place with good facilities above the popular Axis bar. Dorm beds are $18, singles $25, twins $40 and doubles with TV, bathroom and made-up beds $48.

Rainbow Lodge (☎ 378 5754, 99 Titiraupenga St) is a popular backpackers with an excellent reputation among travellers (its owners Mark and Sue are veteran travellers). It has a large communal area, a sauna and a games area, and is on the ball with activities, tours and travel information. Mountain bikes, fishing tackle and camping gear are available for hire, and there's free luggage storage. It charges $15 to $17 in dorms, $26 in singles and $18 to $19.50 per person in doubles and twins.

Action Down Under (☎ 378 3311, 56 Kaimanawa St), a YHA associate, has bright rooms, good views of the lake and roomy outside deck areas. The cost is $16 in three- and five-bed dorms, or $36 in double and twin rooms.

Sunset Lodge (☎ 378 5962, **@** sunset@ reap.co.nz, 5 Tremaine Ave), 2km south of town, is a small, friendly backpackers. It has a comfortable atmosphere and free services including pick-up and shuttles to attractions. Dorms are $14 or $15; doubles are $16 or $17 per person and twins $17 per person. To get there, turn off from Lake Terrace into Hawai St, then into Pipi St – it's on the corner.

Burke's Backpackers (☎ 378 9292, **@** burkes@reap.co.nz, 69 Spa Rd) is a converted motel and each of the former units has a dorm with a double room off it and a shared bathroom. It charges $15 in dorms, $16 in quad rooms, and from $18 per person in twins and doubles. A single costs $25. It has a landscaped garden.

CENTRAL PLATEAU

Berkenhoff Lodge (☎ 378 4909, @ bhoff@ reap.co.nz, 75 Scannell St) is a rambling old place. It has a bar/games room (named after a resident canine), dining room (with $7 steak meals) and a spa. It charges $16 in dorms; $38 in twins and doubles (including a light breakfast).

About to open at the time of writing is the 61-room *Caboose Taupo* (☎ 377 2077, 100 Lake Terrace), which has a 14-bed bunkroom ($20 per person; minimum six) and doubles with bathroom ($89).

B&Bs & Guesthouses *Bradshaw's B&B* (☎ 378 8288, 130 Heu Heu St) has a tea-room where meals are available. It charges $35 for a single with shared facilities; a double with en suite costs $65.

The pleasant *Gillies Lodge* (☎ 377 2377, 77 Gillies Ave) is a well-appointed place with B&B for $65/85.

Loretta's Quality Guest House (☎ 378 4927, 135 Heu Heu St) is good value for $67/77, including continental breakfast.

There are several top-end guesthouses around the lake where you can bask in beautiful surroundings. The visitor centre provides details on these as well as B&Bs and farmstays.

Motels & Hotels Taupo is packed with motels and the competition tends to keep prices down, though many of them have minimum rates during holiday periods.

Economical, good-value motels include the *Dunrovin* (☎ 378 7384, 140 Heu Heu St), a 1950s-style motel with a classic 50s name. It's basic but smart and singles/doubles cost from $53/66.

The *Continental Motel* (☎ 378 5836), on the corner of Scannell and Motutaiko Sts, has doubles from $75.

On the lakeside, along Lake Terrace, are numerous upmarket places. The visitor centre has details. They include *Copthorne Manuels Resort* (☎ 378 5110), at No 243; *Lane Cove Hotel* (☎ 378 7599), at No 213; and the *Boulevard Waters Motor Lodge* (☎ 377 3395), at No 215.

If money is no object and you're looking for the height of understated luxury, one of NZ's most celebrated hotels is just outside Taupo. *Huka Lodge* (☎ 378 5791, fax 378 0427), near Huka Falls, is internationally renowned for the quality of its accommodation and cuisine. Fishing, hunting, golf, boating, horse riding and sailing are some of the activities that can be arranged.

Places to Eat

Tuwharetoa St is the main dining strip. The BYO *Italian Cafe* at No 28 has a good selection of pizza and pasta.

Mr India, tucked behind the **Little Rock Inn** (30 Tuwharetoa St), has a good selection of vegetarian and meat/seafood dishes, with mains around $16.

Finch's Brasserie & Bar (64 Tuwharetoa St) is an excellent restaurant with a range of pasta, steak and seafood; the *Hobler* at No 42 is a casual place with an open fire and a good selection of NZ dishes; and *Blondies* at No 22 has inexpensive meals and a casual atmosphere.

The *Seoul House Korean Restaurant* (100 Roberts St) is the sole Korean place in Taupo and worth a visit for the authentic barbecue-style food.

Cajun-Kiwi, on the corner of Roberts and Titiraupenga Sts, serves Louisiana favourites such as jambalaya and gumbo.

Santorini (133 Tongariro St) has such favourites as moussaka, ravioli, chicken souvlaki and lamb kofta.

The Tongariro St-Lake Terrace corner has a collection of restaurants. On the Tongariro St side, upstairs at No 5, the *Bar on the Lake* has superb lake views and good food. *Nonni's* at No 3 is a good Italian place with pasta and speciality breads. The excellent *Taupo Steak & Ale Bar*, with its intimate booths and popular bar, has an eclectic menu featuring succulent steaks.

Around the corner, the *Thai Restaurant* (2 Roberts St) cooks authentic Thai favourites. *JJ's Cafe* and the Mediterranean-style brasserie *Aqaba* next door at No 10 are also popular. *Maxi's 24 Hour Diner* a few doors down is a good burger stop for night owls.

Pasta Mia (5 Horomatangi St) has fresh pasta to eat in or take out, coffee and cakes.

Along Heu Heu St is the excellent *Replete Deli & Cafe*, a great place for breakfast or brunch.

Villino Restaurant & Wine Bar (45 Horomatangi St) is excellent and extremely popular, with German and Italian cuisine (including an authentic German breakfast from 7.30 am). Other top restaurants in Taupo include *Walnut Keep (77 Spa Rd)*, *The Bach (2 Pataka St)* and *The Brantry (45 Rifle Range Rd)*.

For self-caterers, *Pak N Save* and *Woolworths* are open daily.

Entertainment

The *Holy Cow (11 Tongariro St)*, upstairs, hums till late and table dancing is permitted. You can get good counter meals at reasonable prices.

The *Axis*, on the corner of Tongariro and Tuwharetoa Sts, is also lively as is *Finn MacCuhal's* Irish pub next door.

Other good places are *Rockefeller Cocktail Bar & Brasserie*, which is also recommended for its food, and *Mad Dogs & Englishmen* on Lake Terrace between Rifle Range Rd and Tui St, which has a good range of imported English beers.

The *Red Barrel Tavern* on the lakefront near Tongariro St has live bands for dancing on weekends.

The *Great Lake Centre (☎ 377 1200)* on Tongariro St has a theatre and hall for performances, exhibitions and conventions. The visitor centre has the current schedule.

The *Starlight Cinema Centre* is on Horomatangi St.

Getting There & Away

Air Air New Zealand Link (☎ 0800-800 737) has direct flights to Auckland and Wellington, with onward connections.

In Taupo, ticketing is handled through travel agencies: AA Travel Centre (see Information), Budget Travel (☎ 378 9799) at 37 Horomatangi St and the James Holiday Shoppe (☎ 378 7065) on the same block of Horomatangi St.

Bus Taupo is about halfway between Auckland and Wellington. InterCity, Newmans

and Alpine Scenic Tours arrive at and depart from the Taupo Travel Centre (☎ 378 9032) at 16 Gascoigne St. The travel centre also sells tickets for trains, the *Interislander* ferry and Tranz Rail.

InterCity and Newmans have several daily buses to Turangi, Auckland, Hamilton, Rotorua, Tauranga, Napier, Wanganui, Palmerston North and Wellington.

Shuttle services operate year-round between Taupo, Tongariro National Park and the Whakapapa Ski Area, a 1¼-hour trip. They travel daily and may include package deals for lift tickets and ski hire. Bookings can be made at the visitor centre or at the backpackers. Central Plateau Transport (☎ 377 0435) leaves Taupo (will pick up from backpackers and so on) daily at 7.30 am for Whakapapa, returning from Whakapapa at 4.30 pm ($35 return from Taupo).

Getting Around

Taxi services are provided by Taupo Taxis (☎ 378 5100) and Top Cabs (☎ 378 9250).

Bikes are forbidden on the track from Spa Park to Huka Falls due to track damage.

AROUND TAUPO
Wairakei Park

Crossing the river at Tongariro St and heading north from town on SH1, you'll arrive at the Wairakei Park area, also known as the Huka Falls Tourist Loop. Take the first right turn after you cross the river and you'll be on Huka Falls Rd, which passes along the river. At the end, turn left, back onto the highway, and you'll pass other interesting spots on your way back to town.

There's no public transport but tours go to a few places along here; otherwise walk or hire a mountain bike for the day.

En route look out for **Honey Hive New Zealand**, for all you ever wanted to know about bees, and **New Zealand Woodcraft**, where you can buy wood-turned items made from native timbers. Both are open daily and entry is free.

Huka Falls Along Huka Falls Rd are the spectacular Huka Falls, known as Hukanui in Maori, meaning 'Great Body of Spray'.

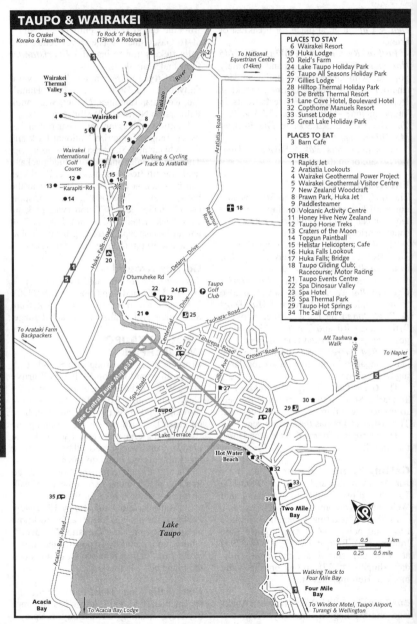

TAUPO & WAIRAKEI

PLACES TO STAY
6 Wairakei Resort
19 Huka Lodge
20 Reid's Farm
24 Lake Taupo Holiday Park
26 Taupo All Seasons Holiday Park
27 Gillies Lodge
28 Hilltop Thermal Holiday Park
30 De Bretts Thermal Resort
31 Lane Cove Hotel, Boulevard Hotel
32 Copthorne Manuels Resort
33 Sunset Lodge
35 Great Lake Holiday Park

PLACES TO EAT
3 Barn Cafe

OTHER
1 Rapids Jet
2 Aratiatia Lookouts
4 Wairakei Geothermal Power Project
5 Wairakei Geothermal Visitor Centre
7 New Zealand Woodcraft
8 Prawn Park, Huka Jet
9 Paddlesteamer
10 Volcanic Activity Centre
11 Honey Hive New Zealand
12 Taupo Horse Treks
13 Craters of the Moon
14 Topgun Paintball
15 Helistar Helicopters; Cafe
16 Huka Falls Lookout
17 Huka Falls; Bridge
18 Taupo Gliding Club;
     Racecourse; Motor Racing
21 Taupo Events Centre
22 Spa Dinosaur Valley
23 Spa Hotel
25 Spa Thermal Park
29 Taupo Hot Springs
34 The Sail Centre

CENTRAL PLATEAU

A footbridge crosses the Waikato River above the falls – a great torrent of water, more like a giant rapid that plunges through a narrow cleft in the rock. The water here is clear and turquoise, particularly on a sunny day.

Volcanic Activity Centre This is the place for budding volcanologists. The observatory monitors volcanic activity in the volatile Taupo Volcanic Zone, and the visitor centre has excellent displays on NZ's geothermal and volcanic activity.

Exhibits include a large relief map with push-button highlighters to show the volcanic regions, and old documentaries about the eruptions of Ngauruhoe and Ruapehu in 1945, the largest NZ eruptions this century. Pick up a monitoring report to tell you about recent earthquakes or to see if Ruapehu is about to erupt. The centre and bookshop (☎ 374 8375) are open from 9 am to 5 pm Monday to Friday and 10 am to 4 pm on weekends ($5, children $2.50).

Paddlesteamer Next along, 9km north of Taupo, is the paddlesteamer *Otunua* (☎ 0800-727 437). It makes one-hour cruises daily to Huka Falls, on the hour from 11 am to 4 pm; the cost is $20/10 for adults/children. The Moonlight Glowworm Cruise goes at 7.30 pm in winter and 9 pm in summer ($25/15).

The Huka Jet & Prawn Park A short distance from the paddlesteamer is Prawn Park and next door to it the office for the *Huka Jet.*

Partly inspired by the engineering of riverboats like the *Waireka,* which has a draught of only 30.5cm laden, Kiwi CWF Hamilton was inspired to invent the jet-boat. In the *Huka Jet* (☎ 374 8572) you can take a 25-minute ride down to the Aratiatia Dam and up to Huka Falls. Trips run all day ($55, children $25, including transport from Taupo).

Prawn Park (☎ 374 8474) is the world's only geothermally heated freshwater prawn farm. There are tours on the hour from 11 am to 4 pm, more frequently in summer. It costs $6 (children $1.50) for a tour. There's

a restaurant where you can try the prawns prepared various ways.

Aratiatia Rapids Two kilometres off SH5 is the Aratiatia Rapids, a spectacular part of the Waikato River until the government, in its wisdom, plonked a power house and dam down, shutting off the water. To keep the tourists happy they open the control gates at various times: in summer (1 October to 31 March) at 10 am, noon and 2 and 4 pm; in winter at 10 am, noon and 2 pm. You can see the water flow through from three good vantage points (entry is free).

Rapids Jet (☎ 378 5828) shoots up and down the lower part of the Aratiatia Rapids ($55). It's a sensational ride, rivalling the trip to Huka Falls. The jet-boats depart from the end of the access road to the Aratiatia lookouts. Go down Rapids Rd; look for the signpost to the National Equestrian Centre.

Wairakei Thermal Valley This thermal valley, like Orakei Korako, gets its name from the water having once being used as a mirror (see Orakei Korako later). It is the remains of what was once known as Geyser Valley. Before the geothermal power project started in 1959 it was one of the most active thermal areas in the world, with 22 geysers and 240 mud pools and springs. The neighbouring geothermal project has sucked off the steam, and only eight or so mud pools remain active. There's a bush-walk to the Huiata Pools but the pools are only active after a heavy rain. It's open from 9 am daily ($6, children $2). The quaint *Barn Cafe* is here. There's also a *camping ground (☎ 374 8004);* powered and non-powered sites are $9 per person.

Wairakei Geothermal Power Project New Zealand was the second country in the world to produce power from natural steam. If you dive into all that steam you will find yourself at the Wairakei Geothermal Power Project, which generates about 150MW, providing about 5% of NZ's electricity.

The visitor centre is close to the road. You can make an educational stop there between 9 am and 5 pm (4.30 pm weekends).

Information on the bore field and power house is available and an audiovisual is shown. You can drive up the road through the project and from a lookout see the long pipes, wreathed in steam. Tours of the centre and the geothermal field are available.

Just south of here is the big Wairakei Resort and its international golf course.

Craters of the Moon Craters of the Moon is an interesting and unexploited thermal area. It's run by DOC, so it is less touristy than other commercially exploited thermal areas. Don't miss the lookout just before the car park – it's the best place for photos.

This thermal area sprang up in the 1950s. The power station lowered underground water levels, reducing the pressure of the heated water, and causing more vigorous boiling and steam. New mud pools and steam vents appeared, and you can wander through them on a plank-walk.

It is open from dawn to dusk. There is a small kiosk staffed by volunteers at the car park (they will keep an eye on your car). Entry is free (donations appreciated).

Craters of the Moon is signposted on SH1 about 5km north of Taupo.

Broadlands

This beautiful and often unseen stretch of the mighty Waikato River, equidistant (40km) from Rotorua and Taupo, is worth visiting. To get there turn off SH5 onto Homestead Rd, just south of Reporoa. The stunning scenery is best seen by River Glen Tours (☎ 333 8165). You can travel by jet-boat downstream to the Orakei Korako thermal region ($75) through some magnificent steamy gorges or head upstream through the exciting Full James Rapids to Aratiatia ($90).

The brave can take a spin with one of NZ's best drivers in a V8 Group A sprint boat on the specially designed slalom course on the Waikato. This two-minute, G-force pulling adrenaline buzz is not easily forgotten and well worth the $50 per person cost.

Waikato River Lodge (☎ 333 8165) is mainly for conference groups but has a popular self-contained Lockwood chalet which sleeps six.

Arataki & Pureora Forest Park

The dominating western ramparts of Lake Taupo largely comprise the huge Pureora Forest. Logging was eventually stopped in the park in the 1980s after long campaigns by conservationists.

There are long and short forest treks, including tracks to the summits of Mt Pureora (1165m) and the rock pinnacle of Mt Titiraupenga (1042m). Pamphlets, maps and information on the park are available from the DOC offices in Taupo and Te Kuiti. The north section of the park is designated for recreational hunting, but you must obtain a permit from park headquarters.

Arataki Country Villa (☎ 882 8857, 025-819 145), nestled beside the picturesque Mangakino Stream, is one of those rare gems. There are activities galore here, including horse trekking, quad bikes, tramping, and trout fishing on a secluded section of the stream. The house, surrounded by a working farm (where you can participate in daily activities), is fully equipped with comfortable beds. On the balcony is a barbecue and heated spa pool – enjoying the sunsets from here is a pure delight. The cost is a mere $18 per person, with a minimal fee charged for the many activities. To get there take SH30 from Te Kuiti, turn south on SH32 and follow the signs. From Taupo, take the Kinloch Rd to SH30, then turn north.

Orakei Korako

Between Taupo and Rotorua, Orakei Korako receives fewer visitors than other thermal areas because of its remote location, but since the destruction of the Pink and White Terraces by the Tarawera eruption it has been possibly the best thermal area left in NZ, and one of the finest in the world. Although three-quarters of it now lies beneath the dam waters of Lake Ohakuri, the quarter that remains is the best part and still very much worth seeing.

A walking track takes you around the large, colourful silica terraces for which the park is famous, as well as geysers and Ruatapu Cave – a magnificent natural cave with a pool of jade-green water. The pool may have been used by Maori as a mirror during hairdressing ceremonies: Orakei Korako means 'the place of adorning'.

Entry is $15 (children $5), including a boat ride across Lake Ohakuri. It's open from 8 am to 5 pm daily. Canoes and dinghies are available for hire and there are two hot tubs.

Accommodation is available at *Geyserland Resort Lodge* (☎ *378 3131);* a self-contained lodge costs $60 (it sleeps up to seven people) and a bunk in the communal lodge costs $20. On weekends different rates apply.

To get to Orakei Korako from Taupo, take SH1 towards Hamilton for 23km, and then travel for 14km from the signposted turn-off. From Rotorua the turn-off is on SH5, via Mihi.

TURANGI
pop 3900

Developed for the construction of the nearby hydroelectric power station in 1973, Turangi is Taupo's smaller cousin at the southern end of Lake Taupo. The town itself is 4km inland from the lake, access to which is from nearby Tokaanu.

Turangi's main attractions are its excellent trout fishing (on the Tongariro River) and access to the northern trails of nearby Tongariro National Park.

Information

The Turangi Visitor Centre (☎ 386 8999, @ turangi@thinkfresh.co.nz), just off SH1, has a detailed relief model of Tongariro National Park and is the place to stop for information on the park, Kaimanawa Forest Park, trout fishing, walks, and snow and road conditions during the ski season. The office also issues hut tickets, ski passes and hunting and fishing licences, and acts as the AA agent. It is open from 8.30 am to 5 pm daily.

You will find DOC (☎ 386 8607) near the junction of SH1 and Ohuanga Rd. The post shop and banks are in the Turangi shopping mall, opposite the visitor centre.

Tongariro National Trout Centre

About 5km south of Turangi on SH1 is the DOC-managed trout centre, an important

hatchery. It's open from 10 am to 3 pm daily (entry is free). This landscaped centre has a self-guided walk to an underwater viewing area, keeping ponds and a picnic area. You can fish for trout in the Tongariro River, which runs close by.

Tokaanu

About 5km west of Turangi on the lake, this settlement has a collection of motels and fishing lodges.

The **Tokaanu Thermal Park** is an interesting thermal area with hot baths. A 15-minute boardwalk leads around the mud pools and thermal springs. In the park, Thermal Pools has hot pools, a sauna and exhibits. The walk is free, while entry to the public pool costs $3 (children $1.50); entry to the private pools and sauna is $5. All are open from 10 am to 9 pm daily.

Walking

The DOC *Turangi Walks* leaflet outlines notable walks such as the Tongariro River Walkway (three hours return), Tongariro River Loop Track (one hour), Hinemihi's Track near the top of Te Ponanga Saddle (15 minutes return), a walk on Mt Maunganamu (40 minutes return) and a walk around Lake Rotopounamu, which abounds in bird life (20 minutes to the lake, then 1½ hours around it).

Trout Fishing

February and March are the best months for brown trout and June to September are the best for rainbow trout, but the fishing is good most of the year. Don't forget that you need a fishing licence.

Turangi has a number of fishing guides who charge from around $45 to $50 per hour, including all gear. Or you can hire your own gear from Greig Sports (☎ 386 7713) in the shopping mall.

Boats can be hired for lake fishing; aluminium dinghies cost $15 per hour from Braxmere Lodge, just before Waihi, which also rents out fishing gear.

Other Activities

River rafting is popular, and the Tongariro River has grade III rapids or, for families,

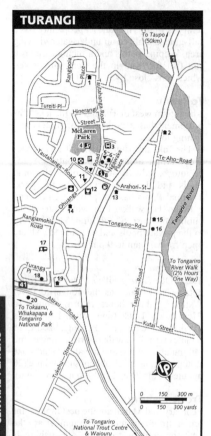

grade I on the lower reaches in summer. The Rafting Centre (☎ 0800-101 024, 386 6409) on Atirau Rd is the home of Tongariro River Rafting; its four-hour trip on grade III (half that time spent on the river) costs $75 per person. The family floats are $120 for four people.

Rock 'N' River (☎ 0800-865 2268, ☎/fax 386 0352) at 203 Puanga St, Tokaanu, has various trips. The Tongariro River trip (grade III) includes a visit to the Puketarata Falls topped off by a soak in a thermal pool. There is also a two-hour float trip (grade II) on the Lower Tongariro, a one-hour float trip down the Tokaanu Stream, and three grade V trips (the Wairoa, Kaituna and Mohaka Rivers – the latter is an overnight trip).

Rapid Sensations (☎ 0800-227 238) has trips on the Tongariro (grade III, and a more gentle trip), raft fishing, white-water rafting on the Rangitaiki, Wairoa and Mangahao Rivers, and multiday trips on the Upper and Lower Mohaka Rivers.

A highly recommended trip is the wetlands ecotour with Tongariro Eco Tours (☎ 386 6409), based at the Rafting Centre. You will have the chance to see some 40 species of bird life in the wetlands environment as you cruise around the lake edge on the *Delta Queen* ($40 per person, binoculars supplied).

Kiwi Outback Tours (☎ 386 6607) does quad-bike trips from three hours to a full day.

Tongariro Hike 'n' Bike (☎ 386 7588) at 203 Taupahi Rd has guided walks, mountain biking and scenic tours, and will arrange track transport.

It's a Trout's Life

DOC operates three trout hatcheries in NZ – one in Wanaka in the South Island, one near Rotorua and one in Turangi. The Wanaka hatchery is more for salmon than trout, while the two North Island hatcheries are almost exclusively for rainbow trout. There are other private hatcheries, some of which obtain their eggs from DOC operations.

The first brown trout eggs arrived in NZ from Tasmania in 1867. They had originally come to Australia from England. Rainbow trout eggs first arrived from California in 1883. Hatcheries were established at that time to rear the first young fish and, while many fish are hatched naturally nowadays, there is still a need for artificial hatcheries. This is because some of NZ's lakes and rivers, while ideal for adult trout, have insufficient good spawning grounds. Plus there's a lot of fishing going on (although there are tight limitations on the number of fish that can be caught).

In the wild, fully grown trout migrate each winter to suitable spawning beds. This usually means gravel beds in the upper reaches of rivers and streams. Here a female fish makes a shallow depression and deposits eggs that are quickly fertilised by an attendant male. The female then sweeps gravel over the eggs. Over two or three days this process is repeated to create a redd with several pockets of eggs. During this process the fish do not feed and a female fish may lose one-third of her body weight by the time she returns to the lake. Male fish are in even worse shape because they arrive at the spawning grounds before the females and leave afterwards.

Less than 1% of the eggs survive to become mature fish. The eggs may be damaged or destroyed by gravel movement, and once hatched the tiny fish may be eaten by other fish, birds, rats or even other trout.

Because there were only a few shipments of eggs, from which all of today's trout are descended, NZ's rainbow trout are considered to be a very pure strain. The hatchery eggs are collected by capturing fish during their spawning run. Eggs are gently squeezed from a female fish and milt from males added and stirred together in a container. Incubator trays containing about 10,000 eggs are placed in racks and washed over by a continuous flow of water.

After 15 days the embryos' eyes start to appear and by the 18th day the embryos, previously very sensitive and frail, have become quite hardy. They need to be because on that day the eggs are poured from a metre height into a wire basket. Any weak eggs are killed off by this rough treatment, ensuring that only healthy fish are hatched out. The survivors are now placed 5000 to a basket and about 10 days later the fish hatch out, wriggle through the mesh and drop to the bottom of the trough. They stay there for about 20 days, living off the yolk sac.

When they have totally absorbed their yolk sac they are known as fry and although they can be released at this stage they are normally kept until they are 10cm to 15cm long. At this time they are nine to 12 months old and are known as fingerlings. They are moved outside when they are about 4cm long and reared in ponds. Fingerlings are transported to the place where they will be released in what looks rather like a small petrol tanker, and simply pumped out the back down a large pipe!

The Rafting Centre also hires mountain bikes ($20 for two hours) and will take guided bike trips.

Places to Stay

Camping & Cabins *Turangi Cabins & Holiday Park* (☎ 386 8754) is on Ohuanga Rd off SH41. There are 96 cabins for $16 per person, on-site vans for $40 for two, and tent/powered sites for $9/10 per person.

This was once the power station construction workers' quarters, which explains all the cabins.

At Tokaanu, *Oasis Motel & Caravan Park* (☎ 386 8569) on SH41 has tent/powered sites for $9/10 per person, cabins from $16 per person and on-site vans for $40 for two. It also has hot pools and spa pools.

Other motor camps north of Turangi on the lakeside road north toward Taupo are the

Tauranga-Taupo Fishing Lodge (☎ 386 8385), 11km north, and the *Motutere Bay Caravan Park (☎ 386 8963),* 17km north.

Eivin's lodge (☎ 386 8062), on SH47 about halfway between Turangi and the Chateau (approximately 24km from either; see Tongariro National Park map), has 40 twin rooms, a kitchen, a lounge and ski hire in winter. If you have your own bedding it costs about $12.50 (linen hire is $5).

Backpackers *Extreme Backpackers (☎ 386 8949, fax 386 8946, 26 Ngawaka Place)* is an excellent, new lodge. There's a pleasant lounge with an open fire, an inner courtyard, patio, Internet access and off-street parking. A bunk bed costs $17, a double $38 (including linen), a double with bathroom $45 and a family room (four people) $55.

Bellbird Lodge (☎ 386 8281, ❸ bellbird@ reap.co.nz, 3 Rangipoia Place) is a small, friendly place with a spacious lounge area and kitchen. It costs $9 to camp, $16 in dorms, or $36 in twins and doubles. Fishing licences and tackle can be arranged. There's a freezer and you can arrange to have your catch smoked. Ask Clint where the big fish are.

Club Habitat (☎ 386 7492, fax 386 0106) on Ohuanga Rd is a huge complex (220 beds) with rooms scattered around the grounds. Camping is $7 per person, campervan sites are a minimum of $18 for two, and backpackers beds are $16 in dorms, $20 per person in twins and doubles, and $23 for singles. Rooms with bathrooms and tourist cabins are $62 for two, motel units are $72 for two and family units are $95 (four people). There is a big restaurant/bar complex, and a sauna and spa.

Motels The *Sportsman's Lodge (☎ 386 8150, 15 Taupehi Rd)* has rooms with shared kitchen and TV lounge from $40/50 a single/double.

The *Creel Lodge (☎ 386 8081, 165 Taupehi Rd)* has units from $50/67.

The *Tokaanu Lodge Motel (☎ 386 8572)* in Tokaanu has 14 self-contained units ($79 a double, two-bedroom units sleeping four

for $115), two private mineral heated pools and a heated freshwater pool.

The *Anglers Paradise Resort Motel (☎ 386 8980),* on the corner of SH41 and Ohuanga Rd, has studio or one-bedroom units from $89 for two; it also has a restaurant and heated pool and spa.

Parklands Motor Lodge (☎ 386 7515), on the corner of SH1 and Arahori St, has tent or powered sites for $10 per person and units from $70 for two.

Places to Eat

The *Hong Kong Chinese Restaurant* is in the shopping mall opposite the visitor centre. Also in the mall is the *Turangi Smokehouse & Deli* where you can get good coffee and a tasty salad, quiche, sandwich or cake.

Near the shopping mall is *Valentino's,* a good Italian restaurant and a solid reminder of the many Italian construction workers here when the power station was built.

Club Habitat has a cafeteria-style restaurant with good, cheap meals.

The restaurant in the *Anglers Paradise* specialises in seafood.

For fast food try *Grand Central Fry* next to the Civic Video; the burgers and fish and chips are good value.

Getting There & Away

InterCity and Newmans buses stop at the Turangi Bus & Travel Centre. Auckland–Wellington and Rotorua–Wellington buses running along the eastern side of the lake to/from Taupo all stop at Turangi.

Alpine Scenic Tours (☎ 386 8918) runs a shuttle several times daily between Turangi and National Park, stopping at the Ketetahi and Mangatepopo trail heads, Whakapapa and, in winter, the Whakapapa ski area – an excellent service for skiers and trampers. It also has services to/from Taupo and a service three times weekly to/from Rotorua.

Bellbird Connection, based at the Bellbird Lodge (see Backpackers in Places to Stay), provides a shuttle for the Tongariro Crossing/Whakapapa ski area.

Club Habitat (see Places to Stay) also has a shuttle ($20/10 return for adults/children) to the Tongariro Crossing.

Tongariro National Park

Established in 1887, Tongariro was NZ's first national park. The three peaks were given to the country in September 1887 by Horonuku Te Heuheu Tukino, a far-sighted paramount chief of the Ngati Tuwharetoa people who realised it was the only way to preserve an area of such spiritual significance. The name Tongariro originally covered the three mountains of the park (Tongariro, Ngauruhoe and Ruapehu) and comes from *tonga* (south wind) and *riro* (carried away). The story goes that the famous *tohunga* (priest) Ngatoro-i-rangi was stuck on the summit and had almost perished from the cold. He called to his sisters in Hawaiki for fire, saying he was being 'carried away by the south wind'. As the sisters approached they stopped at Whakaari (White Island), Tarawera, Rotorua and Taupo, igniting the fires that still burn in those places.

With its collection of mighty (and still active) volcanoes, Tongariro is one of the country's most spectacular parks. In summer it has excellent walks and tramps, most notably the Tongariro Northern Circuit and the Tongariro Crossing. In winter it's an important ski area.

Information

The Whakapapa Visitor Centre (☎ 892 3729, fax 892 3814), Web site: www.whakapapa .co.nz, in Whakapapa (pronounced 'fa-ka-pa-pa' – without giggling if you can) Village, on the north-western side of the park, is open from 8 am to 5 pm daily (till 6 pm in summer). It has maps and lots of information on the park, including walks, huts and current skiing, track and weather conditions. Audiovisuals and the many displays on the geological and human history of the park, plus a small shop, make the centre an interesting place to visit. The detailed *Tongariro National Park* map ($13.50) is worth buying before you go tramping.

There are DOC centres serving the park are in Ohakune and Turangi. In December and January, ask the park centres about their summer activities program.

Volcanoes

The long, multipeaked summit of **Mt Ruapehu** (2797m) is the highest and most active of the volcanoes. The upper slopes were showered with hot mud and water in the volcanic activity of 1969 and 1975, and in December 1988 the volcano threw out some hot rocks. These were just tame precursors to the spectacular eruptions of September 1995, when Ruapehu sprayed volcanic rock and emitted massive clouds of ash and steam. From June to September the following year the mountain rumbled, groaned and sent ash clouds high into the sky. The 1996 ski season was pretty much a write-off, and local businesses really felt the pinch. The locals in Ohakune set up deck chairs at the end of their main street and sipped wine as they observed the mountain's antics.

These eruptions were not the worst this century, however. Between 1945 and 1947 the level of Crater Lake rose dramatically when eruptions blocked the overflow. On Christmas Eve 1953 the overflow burst and the flood led to one of NZ's worst disasters. The torrent swept away a railway bridge at Tangiwai (between Ohakune and Waiouru) moments before a crowded express train arrived and 153 people lost their lives in the resulting crash.

Mt Tongariro (1968m) is another old volcano but it is still considered active – Red Crater last erupted in 1926. It has a number of coloured lakes dotting its uneven summit as well as hot springs gushing out of its side at Ketetahi. The Tongariro Crossing (see later), a magnificent walk, passes beside the lakes, right through several craters, and down through lush native forest.

Mt Ngauruhoe is much younger than the other volcanoes in the park – it's estimated to have formed in the last 2500 years and the slopes to its 2291m summit are still perfectly symmetrical. In contrast to Ruapehu and Tongariro, which have multiple vents, Ngauruhoe is a conical, single-vent volcano. It can be climbed in summer, but in winter (under snow) it is definitely only for

CENTRAL PLATEAU

TONGARIRO NATIONAL PARK & AROUND

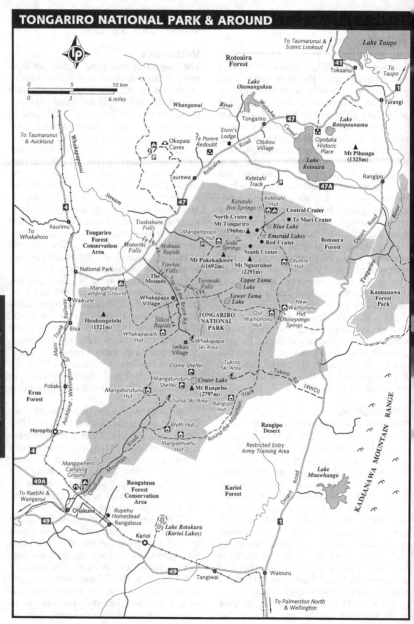

experienced mountaineers. It's a steep but rewarding climb.

Tongariro Northern Circuit

The long, circular Round-the-Mountain Track circling Ruapehu requires five to six days to complete. More popular is the shorter Northern Circuit, normally done in three to four days, and embracing Ngauruhoe and Tongariro. One of NZ's Great Walks (see The Great Walks in the Activities chapter), it has several possibilities for shorter walks taking from a few hours to overnight, and includes the famous one-day Tongariro Crossing.

Highlights of the Northern Circuit include tramping through several volcanic craters, including the **South Crater**, **Central Crater** and **Red Crater**; brilliantly colourful volcanic lakes including the **Emerald Lakes**, **Blue Lake** and the **Upper** and **Lower Tama Lakes**; the cold **Soda Springs** and **Ohinepango Springs**; and various other volcanic formations including **cones**, **lava flows** and **glacial valleys**.

The most popular side trip from the main track is to Ngauruhoe summit, but it is also possible to climb Tongariro from Red Crater (1½ hours) or walk to Ohinepango Springs from New Waihohonu Hut (30 minutes).

Walking the Track The track is served by the Mangatepopo, Ketetahi, Oturere and New Waihohonu Huts. These have mattresses, gas heating (cookers in summer), toilets and water. Camping is allowed near all the huts.

During the full summer season (from late October to early June) a Great Walks Pass is required and must be bought in advance, whether you stay in the huts or camp beside them. Ordinary backcountry hut tickets and annual passes (see Hut & Camping Fees in the Activities chapter) cannot be used during these months. All park visitor centres sell passes. You can also book by email (✆ greatwalksbookings@doc.govt.nz). A pass is $12/15 per night for prebooking/paying on the track; it's $8/6 for camping.

At other times, ordinary backcountry hut passes or annual passes may be used ($8 per night for huts and camping). However, this track is quite different in winter, when it is covered in snow and becomes a tough alpine trek.

Estimated walking times are:

Mangatepopo car park to Mangatepopo Hut	15 minutes
Mangatepopo Hut to Emerald Lakes	three to four hours
Emerald Lakes to Ketetahi Hut	two to three hours
Emerald Lakes to Oturere Hut	one to two hours
Oturere Hut to New Waihohonu Hut	two to three hours
New Waihohonu Hut to Whakapapa Village	five to six hours

Track Safety Check with one of the DOC offices for current track and weather conditions before you set out. The weather on the mountains is extremely capricious – it can change from warm brilliant sunshine to snow, hail or wind within a few minutes. Bring a raincoat and warm, woollen clothing.

Accidents occur on this track when people misjudge loose rocks or go sliding down the volcanic slopes – watch your step!

On Ngauruhoe, watch out for loose scoria, and be careful not to dislodge rocks onto people coming up behind.

In winter, alpine or mountaineering experience is essential, especially to climb the peaks. If you don't know how to use ice axes, crampons and avalanche gear, do not attempt the summit.

Tongariro Crossing

Often called 'the finest one-day walk in NZ', the Tongariro Crossing covers many of the most spectacular features of the Tongariro Northern Circuit between the Mangatepopo and Ketetahi Huts. On a clear day the views are magnificent. This is what many trampers do as day two of the Northern Circuit, with the extra walk along the Ketetahi track. Because of its popularity, shuttles are available to both ends of the track.

There are a couple of steep spots, but most of the track is not terribly difficult. However, it is a long, exhausting day's walk.

CENTRAL PLATEAU

Mt Ruapehu's Crater Lake

It's billed as a six- to seven-hour walk, but expect it to take longer if you're not in top condition. Some prefer to do it as a two-day walk, especially if side trips are included.

The track passes through vegetation zones ranging from alpine scrub and tussock to places where there is no vegetation at all on the higher altitudes and to the lush podocarp forest as you descend from Ketetahi Hut to the end of the track.

Worthwhile side trips from the main track include ascents to the summits of Mt Ngauruhoe and Mt Tongariro. Mt Ngauruhoe can be ascended most easily from the Mangatepopo Saddle, reached near the beginning of the track after the first steep climb. The summit of Tongariro is reached by a poled route from Red Crater.

Walking the Track The Mangatepopo Hut, accessed by Mangatepopo Rd, is near the start of the track and the Ketetahi Hut is a couple of hours before the end of the track. To stay at or camp beside either hut in summer

you must have a Great Walks Pass, purchased in advance and valid from the end of October until the Queen's Birthday weekend.

The Ketetahi Hut is the most popular in the park. It has bunks to sleep 24 people, but regularly has 50 to 60 people trying to stay there on Saturday night and at the busiest times of year (summer and school holidays). As bunks are claimed on a first-come, first-served basis, it's not a bad idea to bring camping gear, just in case. Campers can use all the hut facilities – except for bunks – which can make the kitchen crowded, especially at peak times.

Estimated walking times are:

Mangatepopo Rd end to Mangatepopo Hut	15 minutes
Mangatepopo Hut to Mangatepopo Saddle	1½ hours
(Side trip) Mangatepopo Saddle to summit of Mt Ngauruhoe	three hours return
(Side trip) Red Crater to Tongariro summit	1½ hours return

Mangatepopo Saddle to	
Emerald Lakes	1½ to two hours
Emerald Lakes to	
Ketetahi Hut	two hours
Ketetahi Hut to road end	two hours

Crater Lake

When Ruapehu is volcanically active the area within 1.5km around Crater Lake is off limits; check with DOC park offices for the latest information.

The walk to Crater Lake in the crater of Ruapehu begins at Iwikau Village, at the end of the Top of the Bruce Rd above Whakapapa Village, and takes about seven hours return (four hours up, three hours down). It's definitely not an easy stroll and the track isn't marked. Even in summer there may be ice and snow to get through; in winter, forget it unless you are an experienced mountaineer. Check with the Whakapapa Visitor Centre for current weather conditions before you set off. Boots, sunglasses and windproofs are always essential, while ice axes and crampons may be needed.

From December to April you can use the chair lift at the Whakapapa Ski Area to get you up the mountain, cutting about three hours off the walk. Guided walks to Crater Lake go from the chair lift (☎ 892 3738 for reservations) for $55 (children $35).

You can reach Crater Lake from the Ohakune side, but the track is steeper and ice axes and crampons are always necessary (to ascend a steep glacier). From this side, allow five hours to go up and three to come down.

Other Walks

The visitor centres at Whakapapa, Ohakune and Turangi have maps and information on interesting short and long walks in the park as well as track and weather conditions.

Keen trampers can do the entire Round-the-Mountain Track (five to six days). Be sure to get a good map (such as Parkmaps No 273-04) before walking this track.

Both the Tongariro Northern Circuit and Tongariro Crossing can be reached from Mangatepopo Road off SH47.

South & West A number of fine walks begin at or near the Whakapapa Visitor Centre and from the road leading up to it. Several other good walks take off from the road leading from Ohakune to the Turoa Ski Area (see Ohakune later). *Whakapapa Walks* published by DOC lists walks from the visitor centre, including:

Ridge Track A 30-minute return walk, which climbs through beech forest to alpine shrub lands for views of Ruapehu and Ngauruhoe.

Silica Rapids A 2½-hour, 8km loop track to the Silica Rapids, named for the silica mineral deposits formed here by the rapids on Waikare Stream. The track passes interesting alpine features and, in the final 2km, back down the Top of the Bruce Rd above Whakapapa Village.

Tama Lakes A 16km track to the Tama Lakes (five to six hours return). On the Tama Saddle between Ruapehu and Ngauruhoe, the Tama Lakes are great for a refreshing swim. The upper lake affords fine views of Ngauruhoe and Tongariro (beware of winds on the saddle).

Taranaki Falls A two-hour, 6km loop track to the 20m Taranaki Falls on Wairere Stream.

Whakapapa Nature Walk A 15-minute loop track suitable for wheelchairs, beginning about 200m above the visitor centre and passing through beech forest and gardens indicating the park's vegetation zones.

North Still more tracks take off from SH47, on the national park's north side, including:

Lake Rotoaira On the shores of Lake Rotoaira, on the northern side of the park, are excavations of a pre-European Maori village site.

Lake Rotopounamu A beautiful, secluded lake set in podocarp forest on the saddle between Lakes Rotoaira and Taupo, Rotopounamu can be reached by a 20-minute walk from SH47. The lake is on the western side of Mt Pihanga. To walk around the lake takes two hours.

Mahuia Rapids About 2km north of the SH48 turn-off leading to Whakapapa, SH47 crosses the Whakapapanui Stream just below the rapids.

Matariki Falls A 20-minute return track to the falls takes off from SH47 about 200m from the Mahuia Rapids car park.

Skiing

The two main ski areas are the Whakapapa Ski Area, above Whakapapa Village, and

CENTRAL PLATEAU

the Turoa Ski Area, to the south near Ohakune. The Tukino Ski Area is on the eastern side of Ruapehu. The only accommodation at the skifields is in private lodges, so most skiers stay at Whakapapa Village, National Park or Ohakune. (See Skiing in the Activities chapter.)

Other Activities

The most popular activities in the park are tramping, over the summer, and skiing over winter, but there are several other interesting activities.

The Grand Chateau in Whakapapa has a public nine-hole golf course and tennis courts and hires out golf clubs, tennis rackets etc. Even if you can't afford to stay at the hotel, stop in for a drink in the lobby just to savour the atmosphere.

The ski lifts at Whakapapa Ski Area (☎ 892 3738) also operate for sightseeing and for trampers' transport up the mountain from December to April (subject to weather).

Mountain Air (☎ 892 2812), with an office on SH47 near the SH48 turn-off to Whakapapa, has flights over the volcanoes (from $65 per person).

Plateau Outdoor Adventure Guides (☎ 892 2740), based at Raurimu 6km north of National Park township, offers a wide variety of activities around Tongariro and the Whanganui River. These include canoeing, white-water rafting, horse riding, mountaineering, tramping and ski-touring.

Places to Stay

Within the park itself, Whakapapa Village has an expensive hotel, a motel and a motor camp. Also in the park are two DOC camping grounds (near National Park and Ohakune) and the huts, accessible only by walking tracks. Prices quoted here are for summer; rates are much higher in winter. Towns near the park include National Park, Ohakune and Turangi (see those sections).

Camping & Cabins There are two basic DOC camping grounds in the park with cold water and pit toilets; the cost is low ($4) and you place your money in an honesty box.

The *Mangahuia Camping Ground* is on SH47, between National Park and the SH48 turn-off heading to Whakapapa. The *Mangawhero Camping Ground* is near Ohakune, on Ohakune Mountain Rd.

The popular *Whakapapa Holiday Park* (☎ 892 3897) is up the road from the Grand Chateau, opposite the visitor centre. It's in a pretty spot and couldn't be more conveniently located. Tent/powered sites cost $8/10 per person, cabins are $35 for two and tourist flats are $55 for two, with prices the same all year. From December to June there's also a special backpackers share rate of $14 in cabins.

Scattered around the park's tramping tracks are nine huts, with foot access only. The cost is $8 in huts, $4 for camping beside the huts, with backcountry hut tickets and annual hut passes both acceptable. However, in the summer season a Great Walks Pass is required for the four Tongariro Northern Circuit huts: Ketetahi, Mangatepopo, New Waihohonu and Oturere. It is $15 in huts, and $8 for camping.

All park visitor centres have information on huts and can sell hut tickets or Great Walks Passes. Howard's Lodge at National Park sells DOC hut tickets.

Motels & Hotels At Whakapapa Village, *Grand Chateau Hotel* (☎ 892 3809) is indeed a grand hotel, with 63 rooms, an executive suite and nine villas. Apart from the Hermitage at Mt Cook, it is the best-known hotel in NZ. Built in 1929 in an opulent style, it has been well preserved and is priced accordingly. In summer, economy rooms cost $125, standard rooms $147 and premium rooms $186. Top of the range is the executive suite for $450 with the premium king next down at $211. Discount packages are sometimes available.

Behind the Chateau is the *Skotel Alpine Resort* (☎ 892 3719). There's a communal kitchen for the regular rooms (you provide crockery and cutlery), as well as a sauna, spa pool, gym, games room and a licensed restaurant and bar. Standard rooms cost $84, deluxe rooms $124 and a bed in a hostel room $36. Chalets cost $110.

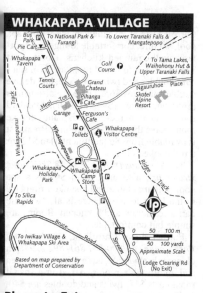

WHAKAPAPA VILLAGE

Based on map prepared by Department of Conservation

Places to Eat

The *Whakapapa Camp Store* sells takeaway snacks and food for self-catering – as usual it's more expensive than elsewhere. During the ski season, there's a *pie cart* (takeaway food van) at Whakapapa Village. The *restaurant* at the Top of the Bruce, where the lifts start, is for hungry skiers and sightseers over summer.

Ferguson's Cafe is reasonably priced for snacks, light meals and coffee, and its cakes are superb. The *Skotel* has a licensed restaurant and bar.

The restaurant at the *Whakapapa Tavern* may be open only in winter. Tucked away in the side of the Grand Chateau by the main road is the *Pihanga Cafe*.

Of course the fancy place to eat is at the *Grand Chateau Hotel*. Its Ruapehu Room is an elegant restaurant serving expensive a la carte meals; the $35 Saturday night buffet or the $19 Sunday lunch buffet are both good value.

Getting There & Away

Bus & Train Trains and InterCity buses stop at National Park Village, the main gateway to Tongariro.

Alpine Scenic Tours (☎ 386 8918) has an inexpensive shuttle departing from Turangi (7.30 am) to Whakapapa Village (arriving 8.25 am), Mangatepopo car park (for the Tongariro Crossing), National Park and Ketetahi car park (end of the Tongariro Crossing) along the way. It goes up to the ski area at the Top of the Bruce by request; its services also continue north from Turangi to Taupo and Rotorua. Since seats are limited, book in advance to guarantee a spot.

From National Park Village other shuttles run to Whakapapa, Mangatepopo and Ketetahi for the Tongariro Crossing (see the National Park section). Transport is also available from Ohakune (see that section).

Car & Motorcycle The park is encircled by roads. SH1 (at this point it's called the Desert Road) passes down the eastern side of the park; SH4 passes down the western side; SH47 crosses the northern side; and SH49 crosses the southern side. The main road up into the park is SH48, which leads to Whakapapa Village, continuing further up the mountain to the Top of the Bruce and the Whakapapa Ski Area. Ohakune Mountain Rd leads up to the Turoa Ski Area from Ohakune in the south-west.

For the Tongariro Crossing, access is from the end of Mangatepopo Rd off SH47, and SH47A from the end of Ketetahi Rd off National Park Rd, which runs between SH1 and SH47. Theft from parked vehicles is a problem at both ends: don't leave valuables in your car.

NATIONAL PARK
pop 460

At the gateway to Tongariro, this small settlement is at the junction of SH4 and SH47, 15km from Whakapapa Village. It caters to the ski season crowds, with plenty of accommodation but little else apart from great views of Ruapehu. In the quiet summer season it's a convenient base for the walks and attractions of the park. Several daily shuttles leave from here for both ends of the Tongariro Crossing and the Whakapapa Village in summer, and the ski area in winter.

CENTRAL PLATEAU

It is also a base for other ventures, such as canoe trips on the Whanganui River.

A few kilometres south on SH4 at Horopito is a monument to the Last Spike – the spike that marked the completion of the Main Trunk Railway Line between Auckland and Wellington in 1908.

Activities

Howard's Lodge, Pukenui Lodge and the Ski Haus hire out tramping boots and other gear for the Tongariro Crossing and other treks. The spa pools at Ski Haus and Pukenui Lodge can be hired by guests and nonguests.

Go For It Tours (☎ 892 2705), at the Petticoat Junction building, which is also the train station, does guided off-road motorcycle tours. Pete Outdoors (☎ 892 2773) at 8 Buddo St rents mountain bikes (from $20 for two hours) and will take guided bike trips (from $25).

There is an 8m-high indoor climbing wall (30 top ropes) at National Park Backpackers on Findlay St open from 9 am to 9 pm daily. It costs $10 to climb ($8 with your own gear).

See Whanganui National Park in the Wanganui & Manawatu chapter for details on canoe hire and operators on the Whanganui River.

Places to Stay

Prices increase dramatically in the ski season, when accommodation is tight and bookings are essential, especially on weekends. The prices below are for the summer.

Backpackers The modern *Pukenui Ski & Backpackers Lodge* (☎ 892 2882, ✉ pukenuilodge@xtra.co.nz) on Millar St has share rooms (four beds per room) for $15 per person, doubles and twins from $40 (linen available), new en suite rooms with views from $75, and new motel units for $75 for two people. Campervans and tents are catered for ($8 per person). There is a spa, a kitchen and a restaurant, as well as Internet. The lodge sells lift passes and organises Tongariro track transport, Whanganui River canoeing and trout fishing.

Howard's Lodge (☎/fax 892 2827) on Carroll St is an excellent place with a spa pool, ski hire, comfortable lounge and spotless, well-equipped kitchens. Dorms cost $15, beds in a four-bed room are $16, standard doubles and twins cost $40, and deluxe doubles or twins $65. There are also triples ($65) and suites ($90 for four). Standard rooms have made-up beds, and deluxe rooms have their own bathrooms. Breakfast is available from $6 (continental) to $12 for a full cooked one.

The *Ski Haus* (☎ 892 2854, ✉ SkiHaus@ xtra.co.nz), also on Carroll St, has a spa pool, billiards table and a sunken fireplace in the large lounge. There is also a house bar, a restaurant and a kitchen. Rooms are simple but comfortable.

Further down Carroll St, the *National Park Lodge* (☎ 0800-861 861, 892 2993), an older-style ski lodge, has a large lounge area and comfortable rooms. A bed in a shared room costs $15, twins and doubles are $40, and motel units cost from $60 for two.

The *National Park Backpackers* (☎ 892 2870, ✉ nat.park.backpackers@xtra.co.nz), next to Schnapps on Findlay St, has dorm beds for $15, beds in four-bed rooms for $17 and double rooms with en suites for $20 per person. The big attraction is the climbing wall (see Activities earlier).

Escape the ski set at *Forest Lodge* (☎/fax 895 4773) at Owhango, 24km north of Ruapehu, on the corner of Maki Rd and Ohorere St. There's a lodge that sleeps 14 for $22 a person, and a motel unit that sleeps six ($70 for a double, $15 for each extra person).

Chalets, Motels & Hotels The *National Park Hotel* (☎ 892 2805) on Carroll St has basic bunk beds at $15 per person with linen included. Hotel rooms cost $25/45 for singles/doubles. Prices remain the same all year. There's a kitchen.

Near the hotel and on Ward St, *Chalet on the Rocks* (☎ 892 2938) has two self-contained three-bedroom houses with single and double rooms for $20 per person.

The *Mountain Heights Lodge* (☎ 892 2833) on SH4, 2km south of National Park, had just changed hands at the time of writing. It's a welcoming place. The lodge costs $25 a single, $50 for twins and doubles, and $15 per person for dorm beds. There are also six self-contained motel units. A kitchen is available to guests although breakfast can be ordered ($10 for a full breakfast), as well as dinner and lunch if required. The lodge is part of a 100-hectare sheep farm; there are plenty of walks to explore. The owners will organise transport to the mountain as well.

The *Discovery Motel & Caravan Park* (☎ 892 2744) on SH47, between National Park and Whakapapa, has camp sites for $10. It has a spa pool, a restaurant and bar.

Places to Eat
All the places to stay in National Park provide either meals, kitchens or both for their guests. *Schnapps* is a congenial place for a drink and/or a meal. There is pizza, burgers, steaks, seafood and more. There are bands on Saturday night in winter.

Eivin's Cafe on SH4, on the Carroll St corner, has pizza, wedges and sandwiches as well as more substantial fare (mains from about $17).

The bar and restaurant at the *Ski Haus* are open to guests and nonguests.

Getting There & Away
Bus Daily InterCity buses arrive at and depart from outside Ski Haus on Carroll St. Tickets are sold at Ski Haus, Pukenui Lodge and Howard's Lodge. Journeys north to Auckland via Hamilton or south to Wellington via Palmerston North both take about five hours.

Alpine Scenic Tours (☎ 386 8918) operates several daily shuttles making a round trip between Turangi and National Park, with stops at Whakapapa Village, Whakapapa Ski Area by request, the Mangatepopo and Ketetahi car parks (Tongariro Crossing), and on from Turangi to Taupo and Rotorua. For the track ends, make sure you arrange transport beforehand, as there are no phones at the trail heads.

Tongariro Track Transport (☎ 892 3716), which trades as Whakapapa Shuttle in winter,

operates a daily shuttle from behind the National Park BP petrol station to either end of Tongariro Crossing, stopping at Whakapapa Village on the way ($15 return). You need to ring and book. Ski Haus, Pukenui Lodge, National Park Backpackers and Howard's Lodge also provide transport.

Train Some trains running between Auckland and Wellington stop at National Park. *Interislander* ferry tickets and train tickets are sold not from the train station, but from Ski Haus or Howard's Lodge, both on Carroll St.

Air Mountain Air Xpress (☎ 0800-922 812) flies between Auckland airport and Mt Ruapehu (from $199 same-day return per person) during the ski season.

OHAKUNE
pop 1490
Pretty Ohakune is the closest town to the Turoa Ski Area on the southern side of Ruapehu. During the ski season a lot of effort goes into catering for those who've come to enjoy the snow, but visitors are discovering that there is plenty to do at other times including hiking, canoeing, whitewater rafting and horse riding.

Ohakune's main commercial district is to the south of the town on the highway. The northern end of town by the train station (the 'junction') comes alive during the ski season but is quiet otherwise.

Check out the Big Carrot on SH49, paying homage to the town's primary product. Kids like the tank in the Clyde St park.

Information
The Ruapehu Visitor Centre (☎ 385 8427), 54 Clyde St, has an excellent 3-D model of Tongariro National Park – great for tracing where you're going to walk. The staff make bookings for activities and accommodation, for InterCity buses, the *Interislander* ferry, and for the train. It's open from 9 am to 5 pm Monday to Friday and until 3.30 pm on weekends from June to October. Its Web site (www.whakapapa.co.nz) has information on accommodation and activities.

CENTRAL PLATEAU

CENTRAL PLATEAU

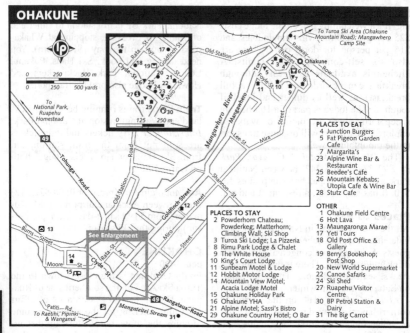

OHAKUNE

PLACES TO EAT
4 Junction Burgers
5 Fat Pigeon Garden Cafe
7 Margarita's
23 Alpine Wine Bar & Restaurant
25 Beedee's Cafe
26 Mountain Kebabs; Utopia Cafe & Wine Bar
28 Stutz Cafe

OTHER
1 Ohakune Field Centre
6 Hot Lava
13 Maungaronga Marae
17 Yeti Tours
18 Old Post Office & Gallery
19 Berry's Bookshop; Post Shop
20 New World Supermarket
22 Canoe Safaris
24 Ski Shed
27 Ruapehu Visitor Centre
30 BP Petrol Station & Dairy
31 The Big Carrot

PLACES TO STAY
2 Powderhorn Chateau; Powderkeg; Matterhorn; Climbing Wall; Ski Shop
3 Turoa Ski Lodge; La Pizzeria
8 Rimu Park Lodge & Chalet
9 The White House
10 King's Court Lodge
11 Sunbeam Motel & Lodge
12 Hobbit Motor Lodge
14 Mountain View Motel; Acacia Lodge Motel
15 Ohakune Holiday Park
16 Ohakune YHA
21 Alpine Motel; Sassi's Bistro
29 Ohakune Country Hotel; O Bar

The Ohakune Field Centre (☎ 385 8578) is on Ohakune Mountain Rd, which leads to Turoa. It's open from 8 am to 3 pm daily and from 8 am to 5 pm during school holidays and public holiday weekends. It's closed for lunch from noon to 1 pm. It offers maps, weather reports and advice about this side of the Tongariro National Park.

The Turoa Ski Area operates a phone line (☎ 385 8456) with information on ski and road conditions.

Walking

Ohakune Mountain Rd travels 17km from the northern end of Ohakune to the Turoa Ski Area on Ruapehu. Several walking tracks lead off this road into Tongariro National Park. Stop by the ranger for maps and information about the tracks. Weather on the mountains is highly changeable, so come prepared and let someone know your intentions.

Two of the most delightful walks are the short 15-minute Rimu Track and the longer one-hour Mangawhero Forest Walk, both departing from opposite the Ohakune Field Centre. They both pass through a lovely section of native forest; the Rimu Track is marked with plaques pointing out various features of the forest.

Other popular tracks leading from Ohakune Mountain Rd include a 1¼-hour return walk to the Waitonga Falls, beginning 11km past the ranger station, and the five-hour return walk to Lake Surprise, beginning 15km past the ranger station. If you continue past the falls on Waitonga Falls track, you join the Round-the-Mountain Track (see the Tongariro National Park section). Other tracks taking off from Ohakune Mountain Rd include a 10-minute return walk to the Mangawhero Falls and a four- to five-hour walk on the Old Blyth Track. You can get maps of these walks at the Ruapehu Visitor Centre.

Transport up the mountain can be arranged through Snowliner Shuttle (☎ 385 8573),

Snow Express (☎ 385 9280) or Mountain Transport (☎ 385 9045). Expect to pay about $8 one way or $15 return. Or you could go to the top with a bicycle (see Cycling, below) and do some tramping on your way down. Transport to Tongariro Crossing can be arranged through the Ohakune Holiday Park (☎ 0800-825 825; $25 return). The bus departs Ohakune at 7 am daily and the crossing at 4 pm.

Cycling

The Powderhorn Ski Shop (☎ 385 8888), at Powderhorn Chateau, hires out mountain bikes at $10 per hour, $25 for half a day or $35 per day. The Ski Shed in Clyde St also hires mountain bikes for the same prices. A cheaper and highly enjoyable way to do some cycling in Ohakune is to go with Ride the Mountain (☎ 385 8257). In summer it will take you in a van to the ski area at the top of Ohakune Mountain Rd and set you loose with a bicycle, helmet and all the other gear you need.

Bicycles are not allowed on any trails in the national park.

Other Activities

Ask at the visitor centre about activities around Ohakune – horse trekking, white-water rafting, fishing, canoeing, kayaking and jet-boat trips on the nearby Whanganui River, golf and more. You can swim in the Powderkeg restaurant-bar's hot pool.

Ohakune is a base to organise canoeing trips on the Whanganui River. Two local operators are Canoe Safaris (☎ 0800-272 335), with an office on Miro St, and Yeti Tours (☎ 0800-322 388) at 6 Tay St. See Whanganui National Park in the Wanganui & Manawatu chapter for more details.

Places to Stay

Finding a place to stay is no problem in summer, but during the ski season you should definitely book ahead. The prices listed below are for summer; they're much higher in winter. More places can be found in Raetihi, 11km west.

Camping & Cabins The *Ohakune Holiday Park (☎ 385 8561, 5 Moore St)* is a pleasant camp beside a gurgling stream, with plenty of trees and green areas and a comfortable TV lounge/dining room. Tent/powered sites are $17/20 for two, while backpackers cabins or on-site vans are $17 per person ($33 each in the ski season).

The *Raetihi Motor Camp (☎ 385 4176)* in Raetihi had at the time of writing sites for campervans and caravans (no kitchen facilities) for $15 per vehicle.

Backpackers can try the *NZ Police Ski Club (☎ 385 4003, 35 Queen St)* in Raetihi – a comfortable lodge, which has a spa in winter. There are four doubles, one single and dorms; it costs $12 per person (duvets and pillows supplied).

Another option is *Country Classic Lodge (☎ 385 4511, 14 Ameku Rd, Raetihi)*, a Victorian villa with a restaurant and bar; $50 per person including breakfast. The friendly Raetihi Information Centre (☎ 06-385 4805; open from 10 am to 4 pm on weekdays and in the afternoon on weekends), on the corner of Seddon and Ward Sts, has details on farmstays and B&Bs to suit all budgets.

The *Mangawhero Camp Site* is a simple DOC camp site ($4, children $2) on Ohakune Mountain Rd. Facilities include cold water and pit toilets.

Backpackers *Ohakune YHA (☎/fax 385 8724)* is on Clyde St, near the post shop and visitor centre. It's a good place with twin, triple and bunkrooms; guests have their own room key. During the ski season it is heavily booked; in summer it charges $16 in dorms and $36 for twin rooms.

Nearby, the *Alpine Motel* (see Lodges, Motels & Hotels) has a separate backpackers in the rear. It provides excellent accommodation in new, spotless rooms for $15 per person.

At the north end of Ohakune, the *Rimu Park Lodge & Chalets (☎ 385 9023, ✉ rimulodge@ihug.co.nz, 27 Rimu St)* is a comfortable, restored 1914 villa in a secluded spot just two minutes' walk from the train station, restaurants and nightlife. It's quiet and restful in summer and very popular with skiers in winter. The cost is $17 in dorm rooms, $19 per person in double rooms or $40 in cabins. Chalets and units next to the house cost from $80 to $140 (sleeps 10). The three quaint restored train carriages are the same as the chalets. The lodge also has rental cars ($45 per day).

The White House (☎ 385 8413, 22 Rimu St) has comfortable accommodation in a modern building; shared rooms are from $15 per person and doubles are $40 for two. Breakfast is available, and there's a nice spa.

The old, Tudor-style *King's Court Lodge* (☎ 385 8648), also on Rimu St, has rooms with shared facilities for $15 with your own linen or $25 with linen provided. There's a kitchen.

Lodges, Motels & Hotels At the southern end of town, the *Ohakune Country Hotel* (☎ 385 8268, 72 Clyde St) has singles/doubles for $55/65; doubles with private facilities are from $70.

Close by, the *Alpine Motel* (☎ 385 8758, 7 Miro St) is a popular place, with studio units, family units, chalets (and a backpackers in the rear; see Backpackers earlier), plus a spa pool and a popular restaurant-bar. Double units are $70. Chalets sleeping up to four people are $75 a double and $10 for each extra person.

Also at the southern end of town, the *Mountain View Motel* (☎ 385 8675, 2 Moore St) has units from $50. There's also a 10-bed bunkhouse for $12 per person; bring your own sleeping bag and kitchen utensils. Next door, the *Acacia Lodge Motel* (☎ 385 8729, 4 Moore St) has units without kitchens for $70 and with kitchens for $75.

Between the southern and northern ends of town, the *Hobbit Motor Lodge* (☎ 385 8248), on the corner of Goldfinch and Wye Sts, has motel units from $66 to $95, and bunk beds for $20 (linen provided).

The *Sunbeam Motel & Lodge* (☎ 385 8470, 178 Mangawhero Terrace) has backpackers beds, lodge rooms at $40 a double or $60 with private facilities, studio units from $60 and motel units from $70.

The *Turoa Ski Lodge* (☎ 385 8274, 10 Thames St) is at the 'junction', the northern end of town, in the thick of the winter nightlife. It's open only during the ski season, with doubles for $90 and bunks for $25 per person.

Top of the heap is the *Powderhorn Chateau* (☎ 385 8888), the place to be for apres-ski, with chalet rooms for $135 a double.

Four kilometres east of town on SH49 at Rangataua, the *Ruapehu Homestead* (☎ 385 8799) has a variety of fancy rooms and a licensed restaurant; it also organises horse riding through the Rangataua Forest. It has motel units ranging from $60 to $120.

Places to Eat
The 'junction' is active during the winter with the apres-ski crowd, but little is open in summer. Places on the south side of town are open year-round.

On the south side, the pleasant *Stutz Cafe* on Clyde St is open daily from breakfast until dinner, with European and Chinese food, pizza and takeaways. Nearby, the *O Bar* at the Ohakune Country Hotel is also open for long hours and has a better class of pub food.

On the opposite corner, the *Alpine Wine Bar & Restaurant* is open for wining and dining every evening. A little further along is *Beedee's Cafe* for pre-ski breakfasts. Even further west on Clyde St is *Mountain Kebabs*, and the atmospheric *Utopia Cafe & Wine Bar*, which serves focaccia, panini, bagels, cake, big breakfasts and good coffee.

On Miro St, *Sassi's Bistro* at the Alpine Motel is also open for dinner daily; it's a pleasant place with a varied, changing menu with something to suit all budgets.

There are many popular restaurants along Thames St, including *La Pizzeria*, which cooks fairly reasonable pizzas. Next door is *Junction Burgers* for a late-night hunger buster (about $6). In winter *Margarita's* has its usual brand of Tex-Mex food and lots of carousing patrons.

The *Powderkeg* and the *Matterhorn*, both restaurant-bars on the corner of Thames St and Mangawhero Terrace, are favourite apres-ski hang-outs.

The **Fat Pigeon Garden Cafe** next door is in a renovated house and has pleasant seating indoor or outside in the garden, and plenty of choice on the menu.

Entertainment

Ohakune is known as a good-fun nightlife place during the ski season; the rest of the year it's quiet. Get hold of the gig guide, available from the visitor centre and most lodges.

The **Hot Lava** nightclub on Thames St is a popular spot, open every night during the ski season, with live music on weekends and disco music on other nights (in winter it attracts some big-name bands).

Other places with live music in the ski season include the always popular **Powderkeg**, **Margarita's** and the **Turoa Ski Lodge** at the 'junction', and the **O Bar** at the Ohakune Country Hotel on Clyde St in the southern part of town.

Getting There & Away

InterCity buses serve Ohakune daily except Saturday, arriving at and departing from the Ruapehu Visitor Centre, which sells the tickets.

Auckland-Wellington trains stop at Ohakune. Buy tickets at the Ruapehu Visitor Centre, not at the station.

Getting Around

In winter several companies have transport between Ohakune and the Turoa Ski Area, charging from $15 to $18 for return door-to-door transport from wherever you're staying. The Ruapehu Mountain Tours bus also operates from the corner of Clyde and Goldfinch Sts.

Snowliner Shuttle (☎ 385 8573) and Snow Express (☎ 385 9280) offer a variety of transport around the area.

LAKE ROTOKURA

Lake Rotokura is about 11km south of Ohakune on SH49, at Karioi in the Karioi Forest, about 1km from the Karioi turn-off. It's called Lake Rotokura on the map and the sign but it's actually two lakes not one – the locals call them the Karioi Lakes. Karioi means 'places to linger' and they couldn't be more aptly named: they are two little jewels, one above the other, great for picnicking, fishing and relaxing.

WAIOURU
pop 2600

At the junction of SH1 and SH49, 27km east of Ohakune, Waiouru is primarily an army base. In a large, grey concrete building with tanks out front, the **QEII Army Memorial Museum** tells the history of the NZ army in times of war and peace, with an extensive collection of artefacts from early colonial times to the present and a 23-minute audiovisual. It's open from 9 am to 4.30 pm daily ($8, children $5).

SH1 from Waiouru to Turangi is known as the Desert Road and is often closed in winter because of snow, but can also close at other times of the year. It runs through the Rangipo Desert east of Ruapehu. It's not a true desert, but was named because of its desert-like appearance, caused by a cold, exposed and windswept location.

CENTRAL PLATEAU

Wanganui & Manawatu

The Wanganui region is dominated by the Whanganui River, historically one of the most important rivers in New Zealand. Once the sole means of access to the region, it is the only way to reach the isolated interior of Whanganui National Park. Apart from the national park, the main places of interest are Wanganui city and Palmerston North in the neighbouring Manawatu district.

The spelling difference between Whanganui and Wanganui causes much confusion. Both town and river were originally spelt Wanganui, because in the local dialect *whanga* (harbour) is pronounced 'wha-nga' not (as in the rest of the country) 'fa-nga'. However to indicate that the 'wh' sound is aspirated the 'h' was officially restored to the name of the river and national park, but not to the city or the region as a whole (the pronunciation of the two spellings is identical). The Pakeha-dominated town and region retain the old spelling, while the river area, very much Maori territory, takes the new spelling. The difference in spellings is in many ways a reflection of the split in attitudes over Maori issues, which came to a head at Moutoa Gardens in Wanganui (see Parks & Gardens under Wanganui).

Wanganui Region

☎ 06 • pop 45,300

The Wanganui region's main artery is the Whanganui River, and its main highlight is Whanganui National Park, based around the river and the parallel River Road. The estuary, over 30km long, was known to the early Maori as Whanganui, meaning 'Great Harbour' or 'Great Wait'.

WHANGANUI NATIONAL PARK

Whanganui National Park's main attraction is the Whanganui River, which winds its way 329km from its source on the flanks of Mt Tongariro in central North Island to the

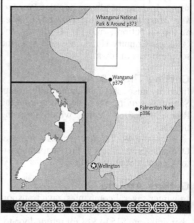

HIGHLIGHTS

- Canoeing and jet-boating on the Whanganui River
- Walking in wilderness at Matemateaonga and Mangapurua
- Driving along the Whanganui River Road to Pipiriki
- Visiting the attractive and historic river-port city of Wanganui
- Partying with students in the many pubs in Palmerston North

Whanganui National Park & Around p373

Wanganui p379

Palmerston North p386

Wellington

Tasman Sea at the city of Wanganui. The river is not the longest in the country – that honour goes to the Waikato River – but the fact that it is the longest *navigable* river in the country has been shaping its destiny for centuries. Historically a major route for travel between the sea and the interior of the North Island, first by the Maori and then by the Pakeha, the route was eventually superseded by rail and road. Recently recreational canoe, kayak and jet-boat enthusiasts have once again made the river a popular thoroughfare.

The stretch of the river from Taumarunui south to Pipiriki has been added to the NZ

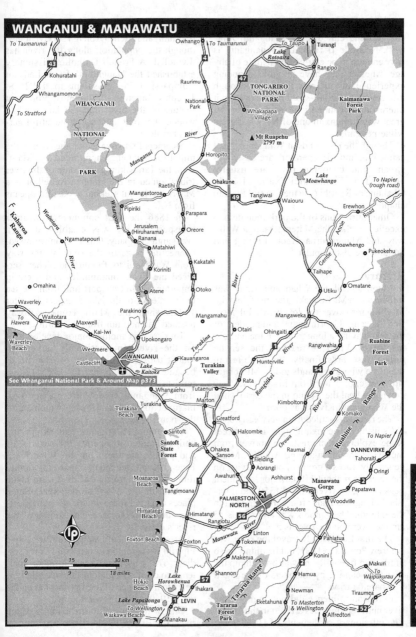

WANGANUI & MANAWATU

To Taumarunui
Tahora
43
Kohuratahi
Whangamomona
To Stratford

WHANGANUI

NATIONAL

PARK

Kaitaroa Range
Waitotara
River

Omahina

Waverley
To Hawera
Waitotara
3
Maxwell
Kai-Iwi
Waverley Beach
Westmere
Castlecliff
WANGANUI
Lake Kaitoke

See Whanganui National Park & Around Map p373

Owhango
To Taumarunui
4
Raurimu

National Park

Manganui River

Horopito

Raetihi
Mangaetoroa
Pipiriki
Jerusalem (Hiruharama)
Ranana
Matahiwi
Koriniti
Atene
Parakino

Whanganui River

Parapara
Oreore
Kakatahi
Otoko

Mangamahu
Otairi

Turakina River

Upokongaro
Kauangaroa
Turakina Valley
Rata

Whangaehu
Tutaenui
Turakina
Marton
Greatford
Turakina Beach
Santoft
Santoft State Forest
Bulls
Ohakea
Sanson
Halcombe
Moanaroa Beach
Tangimoana
Himatangi Beach
Himatangi
Rangiotu

Foxton Beach
Foxton

Awahuri
Aorangi
Fielding
Ashhurst

PALMERSTON NORTH
Aokautere

Manuwatu River
Linton
Tokomaru

0   15   30 km
0   9   18 miles

Hokio Beach
Lake Horowhenua
Ihakara
Makerua
Shannon

Lake Papaitonga
To Wellington
Ohau
Waikawa Beach
Manakau
LEVIN
Tararua Forest Park

To Taumarunui
Lake Rotoaira
Turangi
47
TONGARIRO NATIONAL PARK
Rangipo

To Taupo

Kaimanawa Forest Park

Whakapapa Village

▲ Mt Ruapehu 2797 m

Ohakune
49
Tangiwai
Waiouru

1
Lake Moawhango
To Napier (rough road)
Erewhon
Annie Road
Moawhengo
Pukeokehu
Gentle Annie
Taihape
Utiku
Omatane

Mangaweka
Ohingaiti
Ruahine
1
Rangitikei River
Rangiwahia
Ruahine Forest Park
Hunterville
54
Apiti

Oroua River
Kimbolton
Komako
Raumai
Ruahine Range
To Napier
DANNEVIRKE
Tahoraiti
Oringi
2
Manawatu Gorge
Papatawa
Woodville
56
Manawatu River

Pahiatua
Konini
Makuri
To Waipukurau
Hamua
Newman
Tiraumea
Eketahuna
To Masterton & Wellington
52
Alfredton

WANGANUI & MANAWATU

Great Walks system (see the Activities chapter) and called the 'Whanganui Journey'. A Grade II river, the Whanganui is easy enough to be enjoyed by people of any age, whether they have previous canoeing experience or not, yet there are enough movement and small-sized rapids to keep it interesting. A canoe trip down the river is a great way to relax in one of NZ's last great wilderness areas.

Though the river ends at Wanganui, most canoe hire and trip operators are based upstream and canoeing trips are usually arranged in Taumarunui, National Park, Ohakune or Raetihi (see the Central Plateau chapter).

Other attractions of the park include two excellent walks, the Matemateaonga Walkway and Mangapurua Track. Fishing and hunting are also popular.

History

In Maori legend, the Whanganui River was formed when Mt Taranaki, after his fight with Mt Tongariro over the lovely Mt Pihanga, fled the central North Island and headed for the sea, leaving a long gouge in the earth in his wake. When he reached the sea he turned westwards, finally coming to rest in the place where he stands today. Mt Tongariro sent cool water from his side, to flow down and heal the wound in the earth – and the Whanganui River was born.

The river was settled from very early on in NZ's history. The great Polynesian explorer Kupe explored some distance upriver from the river's mouth in around AD 800. Maori genealogy traces a group of people living on the river from about 1100. Major settlement began along the river around 1350 and flourished along this major route from the sea to the interior. Their motto was and still is: 'I am the river and the river is me'.

The first European to travel the river was Andrew Powers in 1831, but he didn't do so of his own free will – he was brought up the river as a captive by members of the Ngati Tuwharetoa tribe.

European influence did not begin on the river until missionaries arrived in the 1840s. The missionary settlements of Hiruharama

(Jerusalem), Ranana (London), Koriniti (Corinth) and Atene (Athens) survive today, though the population along the river has dwindled. A French Catholic missionary established the Daughters of Our Lady of Compassion in Jerusalem in 1892. St Joseph's church is still the most prominent feature of the town and the large, white wooden convent stands in a beautiful garden beside it.

Steamers first voyaged up the river in the mid-1860s, when, encouraged by Maori from the Taranaki region, some of the river tribes joined in the Hauhau Rebellion – a Maori movement seeking to oust Europeans from NZ.

In 1886 the first commercial steamer transport service was established by a Wanganui company. Others soon followed, connecting parts of the river all the way from Wanganui to Taumarunui. They serviced the river communities and grew in importance as a transport link from the sea to the interior of the island, especially after 1903, when the Main Trunk Railway reached Taumarunui from the north.

Tourism was another major development on the river. Internationally advertised tourist trips on the 'Rhine of Maoriland' became so popular that by 1905 12,000 tourists a year were making the trip upriver from Wanganui or downriver from Taumarunui to Pipiriki House (which burnt down in 1959).

The engineering feats and skippering ability required to operate the steamboats and paddle steamers on the Whanganui River became legendary, spawning something like the lore that Mark Twain made famous on the Mississippi River. Some places required some imaginative engineering, such as cables and channelling of the river's currents.

Around 1918, land along the river above Pipiriki was granted to returning WWI soldiers. This rugged area was a major challenge to clear – some families struggled for years to make a go of their farms, but by the early 1940s only a few remained.

One of the most famous features of the river, the Bridge to Nowhere, was built in

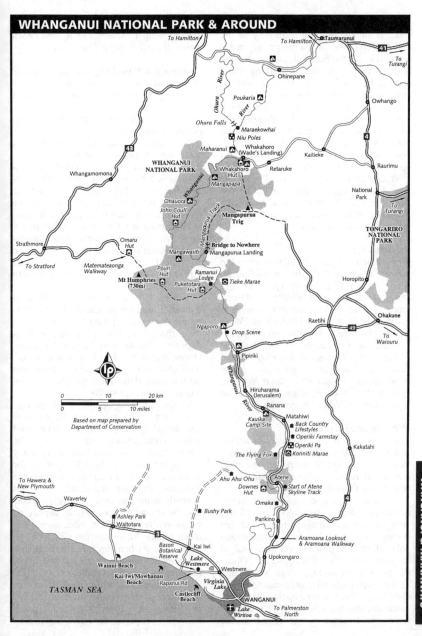

WHANGANUI NATIONAL PARK & AROUND

To Hamilton

To Hamilton — Taumarunui

41

To Turangi

Ohinepane

Ohura River

Owhango

Poukaria

Ohura River

Ohura Falls

Maraekowhai

Niu Poles

4

Maharanui

Whakahoro (Wade's Landing)

Kaitieke

Raurimu

WHANGANUI NATIONAL PARK

Whakahoro Hut

Retaruke

Whangamomona

Mangapapa

National Park

To Turangi

Ohauora

John Coull Hut

Mangapurua Trig

TONGARIRO NATIONAL PARK

Strathmore

Omaru Hut

Bridge to Nowhere

Mangawaiiti

Mangapurua Landing

To Stratford

Matemateaonga Walkway

Pouri Hut

Mt Humphries (730m)

Ramanui Lodge

Puketotara Hut

Tieke Marae

Horopito

Ohakune

Ngaporo

Drop Scene

Raetihi

49

To Waiouru

Pipiriki

Whanganui River

Hiruharama (Jerusalem)

Ranana

Matahiwi

Back Country Lifestyles

Kauika Camp Site

Operiki Farmstay

Operiki Pa

Kakatahi

The Flying Fox

Koriniti Marae

0   10   20 km

0   5   10 miles

Based on map prepared by Department of Conservation

Ahu Ahu Ohu

Atene

Downes Hut

Start of Atene Skyline Track

To Hawera & New Plymouth

Omaka

Waverley

Bushy Park

Parikino

4

Ashley Park

Waitotara

Aramoana Lookout & Aramoana Walkway

3

Bason Botanical Reserve

Kai Iwi

Upokongaro

Wainui Beach

Lake Westmere

Westmere

Kai Iwi/Mowhanau Beach

Rapanui Rd

Virginia Lake

TASMAN SEA

Castlecliff Beach

WANGANUI

To Palmerston North

Lake Wiritoa

WANGANUI & MANAWATU

1936 as part of a road from Raetihi to the river. It stands as mute testimony to the failed efforts to settle the region. The track from the Mangapurua Landing to the bridge, though now only a walking track, used to be a 4.5m-wide roadway leading down to the riverboat landing.

The Auckland–Wellington Main Trunk Railway line and improved roads gradually superseded the riverboats, the last of which made its final commercial voyage in 1959. Today only one vessel of the old fleet still operates on the river: the *Waimarie* makes river cruises on the lower reaches of the river from Wanganui. Another of the old fleet, the MV *Ongarue*, is usually on display at Pipiriki. At the time of writing it was off limits for safety reasons.

Information

Maps, brochures and information about the park are available at Department of Conservation (DOC) offices in Wanganui (☎ 345 2402), Taumarunui (☎ 07-895 8201) and Pipiriki (☎ 385 4631). Information centres in the area – at Taumarunui, Ohakune and Wanganui – also have information on the park.

Good books about the river include the *Guide to the Whanganui River* by the NZ Canoeing Association (good for canoe trips). *In and Around Whanganui National Park,* a DOC booklet, is good if you want to do some walking or tramping.

Whanganui River

The native bush is thick podocarp-broadleaf forest, with many types of trees and ferns. Occasionally you will see poplar and other introduced trees along the river, evidence of settlements that have long since vanished.

There are also traces of former Maori settlement along the river in various places, with *pa* (fortified village) sites, old *kainga* (village) sites, and the unusual Hauhau *niu* poles of war and peace at Maraekowhai, at the confluence of the Whanganui and Ohura Rivers. The Ratakura, Reinga Kokiri and Te Rerehapa Falls, all near Maraekowhai on the Ohura River, were popular places for Maori to come to catch small 'tuna riki' eels (river, or freshwater, eel found in the

Whanganui). Several of the landings marked along the Whanganui River's banks were once riverboat landings.

Canoeing & Kayaking The most popular section of the river for canoeing and kayaking is between Taumarunui and Pipiriki. Entry to the river is at Taumarunui, Ohinepane and Whakahoro (Wades Landing).

Taumarunui to Pipiriki is a five-day/four-night trip, Ohinepane to Pipiriki is a four-day/three-night trip, and Whakahoro to Pipiriki is a three-day/two-night trip. Taumarunui to Whakahoro is a popular overnight trip, especially for weekenders, or you can do a one-day trip from Taumarunui to Ohinepane or Ohinepane to Whakahoro. From Whakahoro to Pipiriki, 88km downstream, there's no road access so you're committed to the river for a few days. This is the most popular trip. Most canoeists stop in Pipiriki.

The season for canoe trips is usually from around September to Easter. Up to 5000 people make this trip each year, the majority of them doing it over the summer holidays from Christmas to the end of January. During winter the river is almost deserted, with good reason. The cold weather and shorter days deter most people, and the winter currents are swifter.

Canoe and kayak operators will provide you with everything you need for the journey, including life jackets and waterproof drums – essential if you capsize in the rapids. Prices range from about $20 per day for single-person kayaks to $35 per day for two-person Canadian canoes (transport not included). Transport in and out can be just as costly as the canoes themselves; the cost may be around $45 per person, depending where you're starting out from, sometimes much higher. Some operators include the transport cost when they hire out the canoes – ask about transport in and out and figure this amount into the overall cost.

Another option is a fully guided canoe or kayak trip – typical prices are around $250 per person for a two-day guided trip and $550-plus per person for a five-day trip.

Operators that offer independent hiring and/or guided trips include:

Blazing Paddles (☎/fax 07-895 5261) Taumarunui; canoe hire, guided trips
Canoe Safaris (☎ 0800-272 335) 5 Miro St, Ohakune; guided trips only
Pioneer Jet-Boat Tours (☎ 07-895 8074) Taumarunui; hire only
Plateau Outdoor Adventure Guides (☎ 07-892 2740) Raurimu; guided trips and hire
Rivercity Tours (☎ 344 2554) Wanganui; guided trips and hire
Wades Landing Outdoors (☎ 07-895 5995, mobile 025-797 238) Owhango; guided trips, hire and jet-boat trips
Wairua Hikoi Tours (☎ 345 3485) Jerusalem. Day tours from Jerusalem, including a picnic and a visit to the Flying Fox for coffee and muffins, are $75 per person (minimum two people). A self-guided option is $45 per person (minimum two people) and also includes coffee and muffins, and vehicle transfer if required.
Yeti Tours (☎ 0800-322 388) Ohakune; guided trips and hire

Jet-Boat Trips Jet-boat trips give you a chance to see parts of the river in just a few hours that would take you days to cover in a canoe or kayak. These depart from Pipiriki, Taumarunui and Whakahoro. All operators provide transport to the river ends of the Matemateaonga Walkway and the Mangapurua Track.

Departing from Pipiriki, you can take a number of trips including a four-hour return trip to the Bridge to Nowhere for $70 with Bridge to Nowhere Jet Boat Tours (☎ 385 4128) or River Spirit (☎ 342 1718).

From Taumarunui you can do anything from a short 15-minute jet-boat tour to a two-day run to Wanganui with Pioneer Jet-Boat Tours. Whakahoro is a bit off the beaten track – it's a long drive down an unsealed road to get there, whichever way you come – but Wades Landing Outdoors conducts trips from one day to three days that take in this area. See Canoeing & Kayaking for details of both these operators.

Tramping

Probably the most famous and best-travelled track in Whanganui National Park is the 40-minute bush walk from the Mangapurua Landing to the Bridge to Nowhere, 30km upstream from Pipiriki.

The Matemateaonga Walkway and the Mangapurua Track are excellent for longer tramps. Both are one-way tracks beginning (or ending) at remote spots on the river, so you must arrange for jet-boat transport to or from these points. Any jet-boat operator on the river will do this, but if it has to make a special trip from Pipiriki or Whakahoro to pick you up expect to pay around $200 for four people. If you arrive at Ramanui Lodge, and jet-boats are already there, it is substantially cheaper for the transfer to the Mangapurua trail head.

There are several good walks between Pipiriki and Wanganui; see the Whanganui River Road & Pipiriki section for details. The DOC offices in Wanganui, Pipiriki and Taumarunui have information and maps.

Matemateaonga Walkway Taking four days to complete, the 42km Matemateaonga Walkway has been described as one of NZ's best walks. Nevertheless it is not widely known and does not attract the crowds that can form on some of NZ's more famous tracks, probably due to its remoteness.

Penetrating deep into bush, wilderness and hill country, the track follows an old Maori track and a disused settlers' dray road between the Wanganui and Taranaki regions. It traverses the Matemateaonga Range along the route of the Whakaihuwaka Rd, started in 1911 to create a more direct link from Stratford to Raetihi and the Main Trunk Railway. The outbreak of WWI interrupted the plans and the road was never completed.

The track passes through thick and regenerating bush. Much of it follows the crest of the Matemateaonga Range. On a clear day, a 1½-hour side trip to the summit of Mt Humphries affords a panoramic view of the Wanganui region all the way to Mt Taranaki and the volcanoes of Tongariro. There's a steep section between the Whanganui River (75m above sea level) and the Puketotara Hut (427m), but much of the track is easy walking. There are five huts along the way.

WANGANUI & MANAWATU

Mangapurua Track The Mangapurua Track is a 40km track between Whakahoro and the Mangapurua Landing, both on the Whanganui River. The track runs along the Mangapurua and Kaiwhakauka Streams, both tributaries of the Whanganui River, passing through the valleys of the same names. Between these valleys a side track leads to the Mangapurua Trig, at 663m the highest point in the area, from where you can see all the way to the volcanoes of the Tongariro and Egmont National Parks on a clear day. The route passes through land that was cleared for farming by settlers earlier this century and later abandoned. The Bridge to Nowhere is 40 minutes from the Mangapurua Landing end of the track.

The track takes 20 hours and is usually walked in three to four days. Apart from the Whakahoro Hut at the Whakahoro end of the track, there are no huts, but there are many fine camping spots. Water is available from numerous small streams. There is road access to the track at the Whakahoro end and from a side track leading to the end of the Ruatiti Valley–Ohura Rd (from Raetihi).

Places to Stay

The park has several huts, a lodge and numerous camping grounds. Along the upper section of the river between Whakahoro and Pipiriki are three Category Two huts classified as Great Walks Huts: the Whakahoro Hut at Whakahoro, the John Coull Hut and the Tieke hut, which has recently been revived as a marae; you can stay here, but full marae protocol must be observed (see the 'Maori Culture & Arts' special section).

Alternatively, on the other side of the river opposite the Tieke Marae, the *Ramanui Lodge* (☎ 025-480 308) has accommodation in cabins for $18 per person; dinner, bed and breakfast in the lodge for $80 per person; or self-catering accommodation in the lodge for $30 per person (this latter option is only available to groups of 10 or more). There is also camping for $5 per person. The lodge can arrange jet-boat transfers. It's quite remote, 21km upriver from Pipiriki, near the Matemateaonga Walkway; the only way to get there is by river or by tramping.

Along the Matemateaonga Walkway are three huts, all Category Two. The others are simpler, with only two bunks. On the lower part of the river, Downes Hut is on the west bank, opposite Atene.

During the summer season from October to April, a Great Walks Pass is required for boat trips on the river involving overnight stays in the park between Taumarunui and Pipiriki; the rule applies only to this stretch of the river. The pass is valid for six nights and seven days and allows you to stay overnight in the huts, in camp sites beside the huts or in other designated camp sites along the river.

The Great Walks Pass costs $25 if purchased in advance (otherwise $35). Children aged 11 and older are half-price (under 11 free). You can book this Great 'Walk' by email (✉ greatwalksbooking@doc.govt.nz).

Jet-boaters who only spend one night in the park pay $8 (children $4). Passes are available at all DOC offices and information centres in the region, and some canoe operators also sell them. During summer, hut wardens are on duty and the river is patrolled by conservation officers, so bring your pass.

Great Walks Passes are not required in the off season from May to September. During this time, the cost is $10 in huts, $5 for camping beside the huts, and free for camping at designated river camp sites. Annual hut passes are acceptable during this time.

Getting There & Away

If you're going on a canoe or kayak trip, the canoe company will make some arrangement for transport to get you and the canoe to and from the river.

There's road access to the river at Taumarunui, Ohinepane and Whakahoro. Whakahoro is a long drive in through a remote area, along a road that is unsealed for much of its distance; roads leading to Whakahoro take off from Owhango or Raurimu, both on SH4. There isn't any further road access to the river until you reach Pipiriki. From Pipiriki, the Whanganui River Road heads south for 79km to Wanganui and east for 28km to Raetihi.

The only public transport to any part of the river is at Taumarunui, served by buses and trains, and at Pipiriki, where the mail bus makes a round trip from Wanganui on weekdays. See the Wanganui section in this chapter and the Taumarunui section in The Central West chapter for details.

WHANGANUI RIVER ROAD & PIPIRIKI

The Whanganui River Road, running along the Whanganui River most of the way from Wanganui to Pipiriki, is a scenic and historic area worth making the detour to see. The road meets SH4, the highway from Wanganui to the centre of the North Island, 14km north of Wanganui and again at Raetihi, 91km north of Wanganui.

It takes about 1½ to two hours to drive the 79km between Wanganui and Pipiriki – that's not counting stops. If you come on the mail-run bus from Wanganui to Pipiriki the trip will take most of the day, but you'll have the benefit of lots of social and historical commentary. The full circle from Wanganui to Pipiriki to Raetihi and back down SH4 through the scenic Paraparas and the Mangawhero River Gorge to Wanganui takes about four hours. The Whanganui River Road is also becoming increasingly popular with cyclists as an alternative route to SH4.

Information

The Pipiriki DOC office (☎ 385 4631) is open from 8 am to 5 pm on weekdays, but is not always staffed.

Things to See

The main attraction of the drive is the scenery and lovely views of the Whanganui River. A few notable sights include the Maori villages of **Atene**, **Koriniti**, **Ranana** and **Jerusalem** (you can visit Jerusalem's historic Catholic church and the historic flour mill at Ranana); the **Operiki Pa** and other pa sites; the **Aramoana hill** from where there's a panoramic view; and Pipiriki.

Pipiriki is beside the river at the north end of the Whanganui River Road. This is the ending point for canoe trips coming down the Whanganui River, and for jet-boat rides (see the earlier Whanganui National Park section).

The **Colonial House** in Pipiriki is a historic house now converted into a museum with many interesting exhibits on the history of Pipiriki and the river. It's open from 10 am to 4 pm between 1 November and Easter (entry $1, children $0.50). At other times ask at the DOC office.

Beside the Colonial House, some old steps and foundations are all that remain to mark the site of the old **Pipiriki House**, a glamorous hotel once popular with tourists.

Pipiriki was once a bustling place served by river steamers and paddleboats. An interesting historic relic there is the **MV Ongarue**, a 20m, 65-passenger riverboat that was once one of the A Hatrick & Co riverboat fleet (at the time of writing, off limits for safety reasons). Built by Yarrow & Co in London in 1903 and shipped in sections to Wanganui where it was assembled, the riverboat plied the river from 1903 to 1959, when Pipiriki House burned down and the riverboat fleet ceased operating. The vessel was restored in 1983 and is now on display on land, about 50m from the turn-off to the DOC office.

Walking

The Wanganui Information Centre and DOC office have brochures on a couple of good walks starting from the Whanganui River Road. Or ask for the DOC booklet *Walks In and Around Whanganui National Park*, with details on these and other walks along the river.

The Aramoana Walkway begins across the road a few metres south of the Aramoana Lookout, near the southern end of the Whanganui River Road, 3km north of its junction with SH4. A 7km, 2½-hour loop track, the walkway passes through farmland and forest to higher ground from where there's a panoramic view of the river area and all the way to Mt Ruapehu to the north, Mt Taranaki to the west and Kapiti Island to the south. At the time of writing part of the loop was closed; but you can still complete the circuit by taking the road for about 1.5km. Other features include fossilised cockleshell beds, evidence that this land – now 160m high – was once at the bottom of the sea. Take drinking water, warm clothing and be prepared for mud after wet weather. (It's closed during the lambing season in spring.)

The Atene Skyline Track begins at Atene, on the Whanganui River Road about 22km north of where it meets with SH4. The 18km track takes six to eight hours and features native forest, sandstone bluffs and the 523m Taumata Trig, commanding broad views. The track ends back on the river road, 2km downstream from where it began.

Places to Stay

At Pipiriki there's an informal camping ground with toilets and cold water. Beside the river at Ranana, the privately owned *Kauika Camp Site* (☎ 342 8061) has hot showers, a kitchen and a laundry. Tent sites are $6 per tent and powered sites are $10.

Back Country Lifestyles (☎ 342 8116), on the Wanganui side of Matahiwi, has horse riding and jet-boating. Accommodation is in restored shearers' quarters; $20 per person including linen and breakfast. There's a kitchen and a barbecue. It's signposted on the main road.

There are various other places to stay along the Whanganui River Road. The *Flying Fox* (☎ 342 8160, **@** *theflyingfox@paradise. net.nz*) is a superb little getaway on the right bank of the river across from Koriniti. You can stay in The Brewhouse or the James K, both self-contained cottages and self-cater, or dinner, bed and breakfast is $70. You can camp in a secluded bush clearing for $8.

The *Koriniti Marae* (☎ 342 8198), on the east bank, also takes prebooked visitors; you should offer *koha*, or a donation, as well as the fee – see the 'Maori Culture & Arts' special section.

About 3km north is friendly *Operiki Farmstay* (☎ 342 8159); all meals and accommodation costs $55 (children $25).

Omaka (☎ 342 5595), about 12km north of Parikino, is a delightful homestay. You can also do canoeing ($15 per person for an hour, or $30 for three hours) and horse riding ($15). Homestay accommodation with meals included is $55. A bed in the spacious woolshed (mattresses, bathroom and kitchen included) costs $12, and camping is $8; all prices per person.

The *Ahu Ahu Ohu* (☎ 345 5711) is a remote farming community about 4km up the Ahu Ahu Stream from where it meets the Whanganui River at Te Tuhi Landing, between Atene and Koriniti on the other side of the river. This alternative community welcomes campers, WWOOFers (see the Facts for the Visitor chapter) and backpackers. Contact them before you arrive to be picked up at Te Tuhi Landing.

The nuns at the *Catholic church* in Jerusalem take in travellers (you should book ahead on ☎ 342 8190). A large room has been divided by curtains into cubicles; the cost is around $10.

Getting There & Away

One of the most convenient and congenial ways of travelling the Whanganui River Road is with the mail-run bus, which goes from Wanganui to Pipiriki on weekdays and takes passengers along with the mail for an interesting tour. See under Organised Tours in the Wanganui section.

If you're travelling by car, petrol is available at Raetihi (north) and at Upokongaro and Wanganui (south), but not in between. This route is also becoming a favourite with cyclists, despite the steep hills.

WANGANUI
pop 40,700

Midway between Wellington and New Plymouth, Wanganui is an attractive city on the banks of the Whanganui River. The town has many fine old buildings and the centre has been rejuvenated by the restoration of historic buildings on the main street, Victoria Ave, down by the river. The block from Taupo Quay and Ridgway St has many restored reminders of Wanganui's days as a prominent port. This area also houses some interesting galleries, including Te Wa at 25A Drews Ave and the Wanganui Community Arts Centre at 19 Taupo Quay.

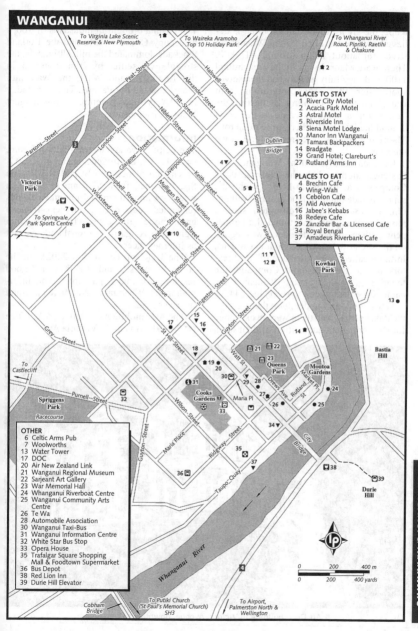

WANGANUI

PLACES TO STAY
1 River City Motel
2 Acacia Park Motel
3 Astral Motel
5 Riverside Inn
8 Siena Motel Lodge
10 Manor Inn Wanganui
12 Tamara Backpackers
14 Bradgate
19 Grand Hotel; Clareburt's
27 Rutland Arms Inn

PLACES TO EAT
4 Brechin Cafe
9 Wing-Wah
11 Cebolon Cafe
15 Mid Avenue
16 Jabee's Kebabs
18 Redeye Cafe
29 Zanzibar Bar & Licensed Cafe
34 Royal Bengal
37 Amadeus Riverbank Cafe

OTHER
6 Celtic Arms Pub
7 Woolworths
13 Water Tower
17 DOC
20 Air New Zealand Link
21 Wanganui Regional Museum
22 Sarjeant Art Gallery
23 War Memorial Hall
24 Whanganui Riverboat Centre
25 Wanganui Community Arts
    Centre
26 Te Wa
28 Automobile Association
30 Wanganui Taxi-Bus
31 Wanganui Information Centre
32 White Star Bus Stop
33 Opera House
35 Trafalgar Square Shopping
    Mall & Foodtown Supermarket
36 Bus Depot
38 Red Lion Inn
39 Durie Hill Elevator

To Virginia Lake Scenic Reserve & New Plymouth

To Waireka Aramoho Top 10 Holiday Park

To Whanganui River Road, Pipriki, Raetihi & Ohakune

Peat Street
Halswell Street
Alexander Street
Pitt Street
Nibett Street
London Street
Glasgow Street
Liverpool Street
Keith Street
Parsons Street
Campbell Street
Wicksteed Street
Mulligan Street
Harrison Street
Bell Street
Dublin Street
Victoria Avenue
Plymouth Street
Ingestre Street
Somme Parade
Anzac Parade
Grey Street
St Hill Street
Guyton Street
Watt St
Wilson Street
Maria Place
Purnell Street
Guyton Street
Ridgway Street
Taupo Quay

Dublin Bridge

Victoria Park

To Springvale Park Sports Centre

Kowhai Park

Bastia Hill

Moutoa Gardens
Queens Park
Market Pl
Rutland St
Drews Ave

Cooks Gardens
Maria Pl

Spriggens Park
Racecourse

To Castlecliff

City Bridge

Durie Hill

Whanganui River

Cobham Bridge

To Putiki Church (St Paul's Memorial Church) SH3

To Airport, Palmerston North & Wellington

0   200   400 m
0   200   400 yards

WANGANUI & MANAWATU

History

Kupe, the great Polynesian explorer, is believed to have travelled up the Whanganui River for about 20km around AD 800. There were Maori living in the area around 1100, and they fully established themselves soon after the larger migration from Hawaiki in the 14th century. By the time the first European settlers came to the coast around the late 1830s there were numerous Maori settlements scattered up and down the river.

European settlement at Wanganui was hastened along when the New Zealand Company was unable to keep up with the supply and demand for land around Wellington. In 1840 many Wellington settlers moved to Wanganui and founded a permanent settlement there; the deed was signed on the site now known as Moutoa Gardens. Initially called Petre after one of the directors of the New Zealand Company, the town's name was changed to Wanganui (the name Kupe had given the river) in 1844.

When the Maori understood that the gifts the Pakeha had given them were in exchange for the permanent acquisition of their land, seven years of bitter opposition followed. The Pakeha brought in thousands of troops to occupy Queen's Park, and the Rutland Stockade dominated the hill. Ultimately, the struggle was settled by arbitration and, in the Taranaki Land Wars, the Wanganui Maori assisted the Pakeha. The town today is still very much a centre for re-emergent Maori consciousness.

Information

The helpful Wanganui Information Centre (☎ 349 0508, @ info@wanganui.govt.nz) is on Guyton St between St Hill and Wilson Sts. It's open from 8.30 am to 5 pm on weekdays and 10 am to 2 pm on weekends (extended hours during summer). It has a great model of the area from Wanganui right up to Tongariro National Park, as well as Internet access.

The DOC office (☎ 345 2402), on the corner of Ingestre and St Hill Sts, is a good resource for maps, pamphlets and information on Whanganui National Park and the river road.

The Automobile Association (AA) office (☎ 348 9160) is at 78 Victoria Ave.

Art Deco building in Victoria Avenue, downtown Wanganui

IAN DUCKWORTH

WANGANUI & MANAWATU

Wanganui Regional Museum & Sarjeant Art Gallery

Opposite the War Memorial Hall on Watt St, near Maria Place, is one of the largest and best regional museums in NZ, containing excellent Maori exhibits. The collection includes the magnificently carved *Te Mata-o-Houroa* war canoe, other fine carvings and some mean-looking *mere* (elegant but lethal greenstone clubs). The museum also has good colonial and wildlife collections – the display of moa skeletons is particularly worth seeing. It is open from 10 am to 4.30 pm Monday to Saturday and 1 to 4.30 pm on Sunday ($2, children $0.60).

On the hill beside the museum is the Sarjeant Art Gallery, which has an extensive permanent exhibition, as well as frequent special exhibits. It's open from 10.30 am to 4.30 pm on weekdays and 1 to 4.30 pm on weekends (entry is free).

Parks & Gardens

Wanganui has several parks right in the city centre including the pleasant **Queens Park** in which the museum and gallery are situated.

Wanganui's most famous park is **Moutoa Gardens**, claimed as Maori land and subject to a four-month Maori occupation in 1995. The occupation signalled a new chapter in Maori-Pakeha relations and caused great acrimony in the town. The city council, abandoned by Wellington, fought the claim in the High Court, while some angry Pakeha counter-demonstrated under the banner of 'One New Zealand' and police raids flamed Maori anger. When the claim was eventually rejected by the High Court, the country looked on, expecting violence, but the occupation was peacefully abandoned after a moving night-long meeting addressed by Maori leaders. The gardens have acquired a sacred status in the eyes of many Maori.

The **Virginia Lake Scenic Reserve (Rotokawau)**, about 1km north from the top end of Victoria Ave, is a beautiful reserve with a lake, theme gardens, a walk-in aviary, statues and the Higginbottom Fountain. The winter gardens are open from 9 am to 5 pm daily (the aviary from 8.30 am), and the rest of the reserve is always open.

Whanganui Riverboat Centre

On the riverbank beside Taupo Quay, the Whanganui Riverboat Centre (entry is free) houses the *Waimarie* side-paddle steamer. This vessel's long history began in 1900, when it was shipped in pieces from England and reassembled at Murrays Foundry in Wanganui. After plying the Whanganui River for 50 years it sank in 1952 at its original berth. It remained submerged for 40 years until it was raised and finally relaunched, restored and proud, on the first day of the 21st century.

Durie Hill

Across the river from the town centre is the carved gateway to the Durie Hill elevator. You can follow a tunnel into the hillside and then, for $1 (children $0.50), ride up through the hill to the summit 65m above.

There are two viewpoints at the top: a lower one on the top of the lift machinery room and the higher War Memorial Tower, from where there's a fine view over the town all the way to Mt Taranaki, Mt Ruapehu or the South Island if the weather is clear. Once you have climbed the tower and returned to the elevator building there is a path around the front which takes you back to your starting point at street level.

In summer the Durie Hill elevator operates from 7.30 am to 6 pm on weekdays, 10 am to 6 pm on Saturday and 11 am to 5 pm on Sunday.

Putiki Church

If you turn right after crossing the City Bridge and continue for 1km you come to Putiki Church, also called St Paul's Memorial Church. It's a plain little place from the outside but the interior is magnificent, completely covered in **Maori carvings** and **tukutuku** (wall panels). The church is usually closed during the day; you can ask for the key at the caretaker's house on the corner of Anaua St and SH3.

Activities

The best way to get a feel for the Whanganui and its history is to take a **river cruise** on the 30.6m *Waimarie* paddle steamer (☎ 347 1863). Excursions are for one hour and leave from the Whanganui Riverboat Centre most days; check with the centre for times ($25, children $15).

A variety of other river trips are possible by canoe, kayak, jet-boat or motorised vessel, starting further up the river in Whanganui National Park. Rivercity Tours (☎ 344 2554) offers additional tours up the Whanganui River Road and on to the Drop Scene or the Bridge to Nowhere by jet-boat, returning to Wanganui via SH4. See the Whanganui National Park section earlier for more details on river activities.

If you prefer sightseeing from the air, Wanganui Aero Work (☎ 345 3994) has Tiger Moth flights, and Remote Adventures (☎ 346 5747) has scenic flights in a five-passenger Cessna.

Organised Tours

A very interesting trip up the Whanganui River Road can be made with the weekday mail run, going up the river from Wanganui to Pipiriki on weekdays. You get picked up around 7.30 am for an all-day trip along the river, stopping at many interesting and historic sites including the Kawana Flour Mill, Jerusalem church and Koriniti Marae; the river's past and present is related along the way. Coffee and tea are provided, but bring lunch (you return to town around 3 or 4 pm). The cost is $25 per person, with an optional half-hour jet-boat trip from Pipiriki to Drop Scene for another $40 or to the Bridge to Nowhere ($60, minimum of three people). Contact the mailman (☎ 344 2554) for bookings.

Places to Stay

Camping & Cabins Closest to the city centre is the *Avro Motel & Caravan Court* (☎ 345 5279, 36 Alma Rd), 1.5km west of the city centre. It has powered sites at $19 for two and single/double motel units at $65/90; there's an indoor spa pool and swimming pool but no kitchen facilities.

The *Aramoho Top 10 Holiday Park* (☎ 343 8402, 460 Somme Parade), 6km north of the Dublin St Bridge, is a peaceful, parklike camp on the town-side bank of the

Whanganui River. It has tent and caravan sites at $17 for two, cabins from $34, tourist flats at $50 and chalets at $65. Local Aramoho buses run there weekdays.

Other camps and cabins are at Castlecliff, a seaside suburb 8km north-west of Wanganui. The local Castlecliff bus runs there every day except Sunday. The *Castlecliff Motor Camp* (☎ 344 2227), by the beach on the corner of Karaka and Rangiora Sts, has tent/powered sites at $16/18 for two, backpackers cabins at $15/26 for one/two, and larger cabins at $32 for two.

Backpackers The friendly *Riverside Inn* (☎/fax 347 2529, 2 Plymouth St) opposite the river is part guesthouse and part YHA associate. It's $16 in dorms or $36 for double and twin rooms. The guesthouse half of the Riverside Inn is $50/80 for singles/doubles, including a continental breakfast. Don't confuse it with the nearby Riverside Motel.

Also overlooking the Wanganui River is *Tamara Backpackers* (☎ 347 6300, ✉ tamarabakpak@xtra.co.nz, 24 Somme Parade), a rambling old guesthouse-turned-hostel. It's a well-run, friendly place with large recreational areas. Dorm beds cost $15, singles are $23, and doubles and twins are from $32 to $34. You can organise all sorts of activities here, both on the river and elsewhere.

Motels, Hotels & Guesthouses The *River City Motel* (☎ 343 9107, 57 Halswell St) is attractively situated on a quiet, tree-lined street at the foot of St John's Hill; it charges $65 a double.

The *Astral Motel* (☎ 347 9063, 45 Somme Parade) on the corner of Dublin St has units from $65.

Across the river, the *Acacia Park Motel* (☎ 343 9093, 140 Anzac Parade) has studio units from $70.

The *Manor Inn Wanganui* (☎ 345 2180, 63 Dublin St) has studio units for $80 and luxury spa units for $99. *Siena Motor Lodge* (☎ 345 9009, 335 Victoria Ave) has good units with spa from $98.

The *Rutland Arms Inn* (☎ 347 7677) on the corner of Victoria Ave and Ridgway St

...as tastefully appointed rooms in a beautifully restored building in the heart of the city. Prices start at $140.

The **Grand Hotel** (☎ 345 0955, 99 Guyon St) is about the only hotel of the old school still surviving in Wanganui; singles/doubles are $65/77 and all rooms have private facilities.

Bradgate (☎ 345 3634, 7 Somme Parade) is a grand old home overlooking the Whanganui River, with three comfortable guestrooms; one single ($40), one queen-sized and one double ($70 each). Breakfast is included.

Places to Eat

Amadeus Riverbank Cafe (69 Taupo Quay) is an excellent place for a meal or snack and a drink. Seafood, steaks, chicken and pasta are all on the menu, along with snacks and cakes. Dining outside beside the river on a balmy evening is a particularly nice way to spend some time.

The **Redeye Cafe** (96 Guyton St) is a pleasant cafe with good light meals and snacks, as is the **Zanzibar Bar & Licensed Restaurant** in Victoria Ave.

Cebolon Cafe near Tamara Backpackers serves breakfast, lunch and dinner as well as good coffee and snacks. It's in a large house and has dining indoor and out. It also has a couple of rooms given over to collectibles, most of which are for sale.

For Mediterranean-style food, there's **Jabee's Kebabs** on Victoria Ave.

For Chinese food, the **Wing-Wah** on Victoria Ave is popular and cheap. Good Indian food at very a reasonable cost (about $12 for a main) can be found at the **Royal Bengal** on Victoria Ave.

The **Mid Avenue** on the corner of Victoria Ave and Ingestre St is a good place for fish and chips.

For pub food try **Clareburt's**, tucked away in the recesses of the Grand Hotel on the corner of Guyton and St Hill Sts, a block from Victoria Ave.

At Upokongaro, on SH3, about 12km north of Wanganui, is the **Riviera** licensed restaurant, recommended for its gelato, as well as its pasta.

Entertainment

The **Red Lion Inn** on Anzac Parade is a consistently good place, has a variety of entertainment and travellers are always made to feel welcome.

The **Rutland Arms Inn** (48 Ridgway St) is one of Wanganui's most pleasant pubs for a drink in a magnificently restored historic building.

Other cafes or bars which are popular gathering places at night are the **Celtic Arms** (432 Victoria Ave), open daily from 11 am; and the **Amadeus Riverbank Cafe** (69 Taupo Quay), also with an innovative blackboard menu.

Getting There & Away

Air Air New Zealand Link (☎ 348 3500) at 133 Victoria Ave has daily direct flights to Auckland and Wellington, with onward connections.

Bus InterCity and Newmans buses operate from the top end of Ridgway St. Both operate buses to Auckland via Hamilton, and to New Plymouth. Heading south, buses go to Palmerston North and on to Wellington or Napier. For services north to Tongariro, Taupo and Rotorua, you have to transfer at Bulls, on the way to Palmerston North.

White Star buses (☎ 347 6673) operate from in front of Avis Rent A Car, 161 Ingestre St, with buses to New Plymouth, Palmerston North and Wellington.

The mail-run bus (☎ 344 2554) heads up the Whanganui River Road to Pipiriki and back on weekdays (it picks up from hostels); see under Organised Tours earlier in this section.

Car & Motorcycle Between Wanganui and the centre of the North Island the highway (SH4) passes through the Paraparas, an area of interesting *papa* (large blue-grey mudstone) hills with some beautiful views, and also passes close by the impressive Raukawa Falls and along Mangawhero River Gorge.

Alternatively you can take the Whanganui River Road (see Whanganui River Road & Pipiriki).

Getting Around

To/From the Airport The airport is about 4km south of town, across the river towards the sea. Ash's Transport Services (☎ 343 8319, 025-958 693) operates a shuttle to the airport, bus station and other points in town. It also operates a shuttle to Palmerston North airport.

Bus Wanganui Taxi-Bus (☎ 343 5555) operates a limited local bus service on weekdays, including routes to Castlecliff and to Aramoho, all departing from the taxi-bus stop on Maria Place near Victoria Ave.

WESTMERE TO LAKE WIRITOA

Heading north-west from Wanganui on SH3 as if you were going to New Plymouth, after about 5.5km you reach Rapanui Rd. Turn towards the sea on this road and you come to some pleasant spots.

First is the **Westmere Reserve & Wildlife Refuge**, where there's lots of bird life and a 40-minute walk around Lake Westmere. Next along, **Bason Botanical Reserve** is a 25-hectare reserve with a lake, conservatory, gardens of many kinds, lookout tower and an old homestead. The reserve is open from 9.30 am until dusk daily; the conservatory is open from 10 am to 4 pm on weekdays and 2 to 4 pm on weekends.

At the end of Rapanui Rd, 9km from the SH3 turn-off, the black-sand **Mowhanau Beach**, also called Kai Iwi Beach, is beautiful. The Mowhanau Creek meets the sea here and provides a safe place for children to swim, and there's also a motor camp and scenic papa cliffs. You can walk back to Castlecliff along the coast (two to three hours).

Bushy Park

Bushy Park is 24km north-west of Wanganui. Following the signs as if you were going to New Plymouth, take SH3 to Kai Iwi, turn off where you see the signs and go 8km further on a sealed side road. Owned by the Royal Forest & Bird Protection Society, the park is a 96-hectare scenic reserve with spacious grounds, picnic and barbecue areas, bush walks and a historic 1906 homestead.

It's open from 10 am to 5 pm daily ($3, children $1).

Accommodation is available (☎ 342 9879) in the homestead; it's like staying in a well-preserved museum. Singles/doubles are $75/90 for B&B. It also has a bunkroom at $15 per person, and caravan and tent sites at $15 for two.

Ashley Park

Ashley Park (☎ 346 5917) at Waitotara, 34km north-west of Wanganui on SH3, is another attractive park, with gardens and trees surrounding a picturesque lake. Activities include fishing, eeling, bird-watching and kayaking. The park is open from 9 am to 5 pm daily (entry is free).

Accommodation is available and you can join in the farm activities, or go boating on the lake or hunting. B&B in the house is $3? per person (extra person $11), with dinner by arrangement. It also has basic cabins at $1? per person (children under 12 are $6), powered sites for $10/14.50 for one/two people and tent sites for $3 per person. Remote Adventures (☎ 346 5747) is a wilderness farm stay which organises bushwalks, jet-boating and scenic flights near Waitotara.

Lake Wiritoa

About 12.5km south-east of Wanganui, off SH3, Lake Wiritoa is popular for swimming and water-skiing. To get there, turn left at Lake Kaitoke and keep going past it to Lake Wiritoa.

Manawatu

☎ 06 • pop 147,400

The rich sheep- and dairy-farming district of Manawatu is centred around the provincial city of Palmerston North, dominated by Massey University, and includes the surrounding districts of Rangitikei to the north and Horowhenua to the south.

PALMERSTON NORTH

pop 67,400

On the banks of the Manawatu River, Palmerston North is the principal centre of he Manawatu region and a major cross-roads. With Massey University, the second-largest university in NZ, and several other colleges, Palmerston North has the relaxed feel of a rural university town. Though not really a tourist destination, it is well ordered and pleasant.

Orientation & Information

The wide open expanse of The Square with its gardens and fountains is very much the centre of town. You can get your bearings from a lookout on top of the Civic Centre building on The Square, open on weekdays.

The Destination Manawatu Visitor Centre (☎ 354 6593, ☎ manawatu.visitor-info@xtra.co.nz) at 52 The Square (in The Square Edge building) has plenty of information on the area. It's open from 9 am to 5 pm on weekdays and 10 am to 3 pm on weekends.

The DOC office (☎ 358 9004) is at 717 Tremaine Ave, on the north side of town.

The AA office (☎ 357 7039) is at 185 Broadway Ave, near Amesbury St.

Things to See & Do

The **Science Centre & Manawatu Museum** on the corner of Church and Pitt Sts has a museum specialising in the history of the Manawatu region, including its Maori history, culture and art. The Science Centre has rotating science exhibits and the hands-on displays are fun for kids and adults alike. It's open from 10 am to 5 pm daily. Entry to the museum is free, while the Science Centre costs $6 (children $4, family $15).

Next door is the modern, spacious **Manawatu Art Gallery** at 398 Main St West. It's open from 10 am to 4.30 pm on weekdays and 11.30 am to 4.30 pm on weekends (entry is free, but donations are welcome).

Rugby fans shouldn't miss the **New Zealand Rugby Museum** at 87 Cuba St, a few blocks from The Square. This interesting museum contains exhibits and memorabilia relating to the history of rugby in NZ from the first game played in the country, in Nelson in 1870, up to the present. It also has mementos from every country where rugby is played and videos of the most famous international games. The museum is open from 10 am to

noon and 1.30 to 4 pm Monday to Saturday, and 1.30 to 4 pm on Sunday ($3, children $1).

Esplanade Park is a beautiful park stretching along the shores of the Manawatu River, a few blocks south of The Square. The Manawatu Riverside Walkway & Bridle Track, extending 10km along the river, passes through the park.

Palmerston North is well supplied with sporting venues. The **Palmerston North Showgrounds** includes the Manawatu Sports Stadium, other stadiums, rugby pitches, a stockcar track, concert halls and more. Other sports venues include the Awapuni Racecourse for thoroughbred horse racing, and the Manawatu Raceway on Pioneer Highway for trotting and greyhound racing. There is an indoor rock-climbing wall, **City Rock**, at 38a Grey St ($8).

Manawatu Gorge

About 15km north of Palmerston North the SH2 to Napier runs through the spectacular Manawatu Gorge. Manawatu Jet Tours (☎ 326 8190) operates jet-boat trips on the river and will arrange transport for small groups from Palmerston North for no extra cost. The information centre has details on horse trekking, bridge swinging, abseiling and drift rafting in the area.

Places to Stay

Camping, Cabins & Hostels The *Palmerston North Holiday Park (☎ 358 0349, 133 Dittmer Drive),* off Ruha Place, is pleasantly situated beside the Esplanade Park, about 2km from The Square. It has tent sites for $8.50 per person, powered sites for $20 for two, standard cabins for $28 for two, cabins with kitchens for $39, tourist cabins for $42 and tourist flats for $55.

The *Peppertree Hostel (☎ 355 4054, ☎ peppertreehostel@clear.net.nz, 121 Grey St),* a YHA associate, has a well-appointed kitchen, off-street parking, open fireplace and a homey atmosphere. It charges $15 for a dorm, or $25 for singles and $35 for twins and doubles; it offers free pick-up from the bus/train station.

King St Backpackers (☎ 358 9595, 95 King St) is a large, lifeless backpackers. The

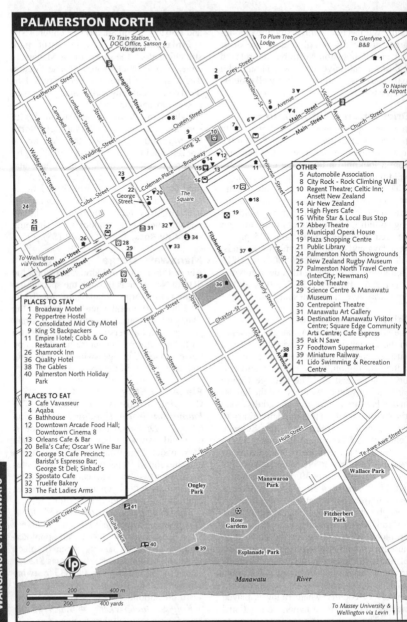

PALMERSTON NORTH

To Train Station, DOC Office, Sanson & Wanganui

To Plum Tree Lodge

To Glenfyne B&B

To Napier & Airport

To Wellington via Foxton

To Massey University & Wellington via Levin

Manawatu River

The Square

Rose Gardens

Ongley Park

Manawaroa Park

Wallace Park

Fitzherbert Park

Esplanade Park

0   200   400 m
0   200   400 yards

OTHER
5 Automobile Association
8 City Rock - Rock Climbing Wall
10 Regent Theatre; Celtic Inn; Ansett New Zealand
14 Air New Zealand
15 High Flyers Cafe
16 White Star & Local Bus Stop
17 Abbey Theatre
18 Municipal Opera House
19 Plaza Shopping Centre
21 Public Library
24 Palmerston North Showgrounds
25 New Zealand Rugby Museum
27 Palmerston North Travel Centre (InterCity; Newmans)
28 Globe Theatre
29 Science Centre & Manawatu Museum
30 Centrepoint Theatre
31 Manawatu Art Gallery
34 Destination Manawatu Visitor Centre; Square Edge Community Arts Centre; Cafe Express
35 Pak N Save
37 Foodtown Supermarket
39 Miniature Railway
41 Lido Swimming & Recreation Centre

PLACES TO STAY
1 Broadway Motel
2 Peppertree Hostel
7 Consolidated Mid City Motel
9 King St Backpackers
11 Empire Hotel; Cobb & Co Restaurant
26 Shamrock Inn
36 Quality Hotel
38 The Gables
40 Palmerston North Holiday Park

PLACES TO EAT
3 Cafe Vavasseur
4 Aqaba
6 Bathhouse
12 Downtown Arcade Food Hall; Downtown Cinema 8
13 Orleans Cafe & Bar
20 Bella's Cafe; Oscar's Wine Bar
22 George St Cafe Precinct; Barista's Espresso Bar; George St Deli; Sinbad's
23 Spostato Cafe
32 Truelife Bakery
33 The Fat Ladies Arms

cost is $15 per person in dorm and shared rooms, $25 a single and $35 a double – with reduced weekly rates.

Accommodation is also available on the *Massey University campus* (☎ 350 6180) from $20 per person.

About 25km north-west of the city, at the junction of SH3 and SH1, is Sanson. Backpacker accommodation is available at the *Golden Galleon* (☎ 329 3829) for $12.

B&Bs & Guesthouses The visitor centre has information on homestays and B&Bs. Recommended are *Glenfyne B&B* (☎ 358 1626, 413 Albert St), with singles/doubles for $45/70; *The Gables* (☎ 358 3209, 179 Fitzherbert Ave), with singles for $50 to $80 and doubles for $80 to $110; and *Plum Tree Lodge* (☎ 357 5200, 97 Russell St), with rooms for $85/105.

Motels & Hotels The *Consolidated Mid City Motel* (☎ 357 2184, 129 Broadway Ave) is a fancy, central motel with singles/doubles from $63/70.

Further along, the *Broadway Motel* (☎ 358 5051, 258 Broadway Ave) is slightly cheaper.

There's a 'motel row' on Fitzherbert Ave, south of The Square; motels along here are a bit more expensive.

The *Empire Hotel* (☎ 357 8002), on the corner of Princess and Main Sts, has nine rooms with private bath and off-street parking; doubles are $75.

The *Shamrock Inn* (☎ 355 2130, 267 Main St West) is a restored building with good budget rooms for $45 a single and $55 a double (all with en suite).

The *Quality Hotel* (☎ 356 8059, 110 Fitzherbert Ave) has 151 rooms, a gym, spa and sauna. Budget rooms are $69.

Places to Eat

Palmerston North has its fair share of cafes and bar/restaurants serving inexpensive fare to cater for the town's student population.

On Broadway Ave, *Downtown Arcade* has a food hall with counters serving Italian, Chinese, fish and chips, coffee, ice cream etc. It is open late to cater to movie-goers.

Popular student bar/restaurants with reasonably priced meals and snacks are *Orleans Cafe & Bar* on Main St and *The Fat Ladies Arms* near the visitor centre.

Behind the visitor centre is *Cafe Express*, which has a good range of cakes and snacks, as well as good coffee. The tiny *Truelife Bakery* (49 The Square) specialises in wholefoods.

Oscar's Wine Bar on the corner of Coleman Place and The Square is a fancy bar but the blackboard menu features inexpensive light meals. Next to it, *Bella's Cafe* is a popular lunch spot and the *Loaded Hog* on Coleman Place is also a busy place.

Spostato Cafe (upstairs, 213 Cuba St), the best Italian place in town, is open daily from 6 pm until late.

There's a new wave of fine cafes along Broadway Ave. *Aqaba* at No 186 is a great little bar with good bar snacks; *Cafe Vavasseur* at No 201 has a good atmosphere; and the *Bathhouse* at No 161 has periodic jazz, a couple of big open fires for winter and al fresco dining in summer.

Another trendy enclave is George St, behind the library. Here you'll find *Barista's Expresso Bar* with an international menu and a range of coffees; the *George St Deli;* and a Kurdish place, *Sinbad's*, with tasty kebabs and naan breads.

For self-caterers, the *Foodtown* supermarket is on Ferguson St at the rear of the Plaza shopping centre. *Pack N Save* is a little further along.

Entertainment

Nightlife fluctuates according to the student year and is quieter during the holidays.

The *Celtic Inn* in the Regent Arcade between Broadway Ave and King St is a small, pleasant, low-key Irish pub with live music on weekend nights.

The *Fat Ladies Arms* on the corner of Church and Linton Sts is a popular student watering hole. The cafes and bars along Broadway Ave and George St are all popular on weekends (see Places to Eat).

The *High Flyers Cafe*, on the corner of The Square and Main St, is for a more mature crowd.

Theatre and music performances are staged at the *Centrepoint Theatre, Globe Theatre* and the *Abbey Theatre*. The revamped *Regent Theatre* hosts big events. The city's people are avid movie-goers – the large *Downtown Cinema 8* complex, upstairs in the Downtown Arcade, shows the latest films and art-house selections.

Getting There & Away

Air The international airport is on the northern outskirts of town; planes often get diverted here when the weather at Wellington is bad.

Air New Zealand (☎ 351 8800) on Broadway Ave has daily direct flights to Auckland, Christchurch, Hamilton and Wellington, with onward connections. Ansett New Zealand (☎ 356 5146) is at 59 Broadway. It has daily direct flights to Auckland, Christchurch and Wellington, with connections to other centres. Freedom Air (☎ 0800-600 500) flies to Brisbane, Sydney and Melbourne in Australia. Origin Pacific (☎ 0800-302 302) has direct flights to Auckland and Nelson with connections to other centres.

Bus InterCity, Newmans and Tranzit Coachlines buses operate from the Palmerston North Travel Centre (☎ 355 4955) on the corner of Main and Pitt Sts. InterCity and Newmans buses go from Palmerston North to most places in the North Island; Tranzit Coachlines operates one route – Palmerston North via Masterton to Wellington.

White Star (☎ 358 8777) operates from a bus stop at the Courthouse, on Main St near The Square, with buses to Wellington, Wanganui and New Plymouth.

Many direct services between Auckland and Wellington bypass Palmerston North, stopping instead at the nearby township of Bulls. Wellington–Napier buses do stop at Palmerston North.

Train The train station is off Tremaine Ave, about 12 blocks north of The Square. Trains between Auckland and Wellington stop here, as do trains between Wellington and Napier. Auckland–Wellington trains run twice daily in each direction (morning and night). The Wellington–Napier train runs once daily in each direction.

Getting Around

Transit City Link minibuses operate from the bus stop in the middle of Main St, on the east side of The Square. They operate on weekdays from 7 am to 6 pm, Saturday until mid-afternoon and not at all on Sunday; all rides cost $1.50. The No 12 bus goes to Massey University but none go to the airport. One of the minibuses stops near the airport at the Milson shopping centre; from the terminal to the shopping centre is a 10- to 15-minute walk. The visitor centre has timetables. A taxi costs $9 to the centre, or $11 to Massey.

RANGITIKEI

The Rangitikei region stretches from Taihape (the self-styled 'gumboot' capital) in the north to Bulls in the south (west of Palmerston North) and also includes the towns of Hunterville and Marton. In NZ terms it is an unsung region but there is great potential for tourism, only now being realised along the banks of the untamed Rangitikei River. Visit the Rangitikei Information Centre (☎ 388 0350) on Hautapu St, Taihape, for more information and a free copy of the pamphlet *Rangitikei: The Undiscovered Secret*.

Just south of Taihape ('a gumboots throw from civilisation') is *River Valley Lodge* (☎ 388 1444), on the banks of the Rangitikei. It is quite remote, in a pristine valley, and there are many activities to engage in – white-water rafting ($79), abseiling ($20), kayaking ($40), horse trekking ($35 for two hours) and walking (free). A dorm bed in the lodge is $15, twins and doubles are $40. The lodge has a huge communal area with an open fire – grab a beer, relax and tell the person next to you about your NZ experiences.

Mangaweka

Located north on SH1, 52km south of Waiouru, Mangaweka's most noticeable attraction is the **Aeroplane Cafe**, a cafe in an old DC-3 plane right beside the highway, open daily. Beside the plane, Rangitikei River Adventures (☎ 382 5747) offers various activities including an 80m bungy jump ('High Time') over the Rangitikei; it's $120 for a jump and photos.

It also does a number of Rangitikei River trips, including jet-boating and rafting ($25 to $120), and can arrange accommodation. Bookings are essential for all activities.

Gardens

The **Cross Hills Gardens**, with one of NZ's largest and most varied collections of rhododendrons and azaleas, is 5km north of Kimbolton, on SH54 about a 45-minute drive north of Palmerston North. It's open from 10.30 am to 5 pm daily during the bloom from September to April; there is a small entry fee.

Ohakea

Ohakea is a whistle-stop town, west of Palmerston North on SH1 near Bulls. It is dominated by a large air-force base, where you'll find the **Ohakea Museum** dedicated to the exploits of the tiny Royal New Zealand Air Force. This small museum of air-force memorabilia is open from 9.30 am to 4.30 pm daily ($5, children $2).

The plus is the **Kites Kafé**, from where the kids can watch the ageing jets come and go.

HOROWHENUA

The Horowhenua region extends south from Foxton to Waikawa Beach, and is bordered by the Tasman Sea to the west and the rugged Tararuas to the east. Included in the region is the provincial centre Levin, the beautiful Papaitonga and Horowhenua Lakes, and Himatangi, Foxton, Waitarere and Hokio Beaches.

Levin
pop 19,300

Levin, 50km south of Palmerston North, is a sizable town in the centre of the fertile Horowhenua agricultural region.

The Horowhenua Visitor Information Centre (☎ 368 7148) in Regent Court on Oxford St is open from 9 am to 5.30 pm Monday to Friday and 10 am to 3 pm on weekends. It can do bookings for InterCity, Newmans, White Star, Tranzrail, and the Interislander ferry, and has DOC information. It can also provide details on B&Bs, homestays and farmstays, and activities in the area. The AA (☎ 368 2988) is at 212 Oxford St.

Lake Papaitonga, a few kilometres south of Levin and reached by Buller Rd, is a serenely beautiful place. Follow the boardwalk to the sacred lake which features heavily in the story of the Maori chief Te Rauparaha.

There are plenty of motels. They include *Bentons Motel (☎ 367 8282, 2 York St)*, which has singles/doubles from $75/85, *Bassinger Motor Lodge (☎ 367 0048, 374 Oxford St), with rooms for* $80/90, and *Mountain View Motel (☎ 368 5214, The Avenue)*, from $60 for a double.

One very pleasant homestay/B&B is *The Fantails (☎ 368 9011, 40 MacArthur St)*, which has rooms for $55/85 and self-contained cottages from $90.

Good places to eat include the *Italian Flame (104 Oxford St)*, which has a fireplace and couches, and a good wine list. Mains are around $17. It's open for dinner from 6 pm (closed Sunday).

Cafe Nua (7 Bath St) has good coffee, light meals and snacks.

Tokomaru Steam Engine Museum

The Tokomaru Steam Engine Museum, in Tokomaru on SH57 about 30km north of Levin, exhibits a large collection of working steam engines and locomotives. It's open from 9 am to noon and 1 to 3.30 pm daily ($5, children $2).

The East Coast

The East Coast is an area full of interest, with the sea on one side and towering forested hills in the hinterland. It is also a place of contrasts, from the Art Deco and Spanish Mission-style architecture of bustling Hastings and Napier to the serene, primeval forests that girt Lake Waikaremoana in Urewera National Park.

The area includes three of the North Island's larger cities and their adjoining bays: Gisborne on Poverty Bay and Napier and Hastings on Hawke Bay.

From Opotiki in the eastern Bay of Plenty, circling around to Gisborne, the East Cape is a rugged landscape with stunning coastal scenery and dense inland forest. This long-isolated region has retained its strong Maori influence, and remains largely undeveloped and well off the main tourist routes.

East Cape

☎ 07 and 06 • pop 6700
The East Cape is a scenic, isolated and little-known region of the North Island. The small communities scattered along the coast are predominantly Maori (largely of the Ngati Porou tribe) and the pace of life is peaceful and slow. Geographically, the area has few natural harbours and, until the road network was completed, goods had to be loaded off the beaches onto waiting barges. The interior is still wild bush, with the Raukumara Range extending down the centre of the cape. The western side of the range is divided into several protected forests: Raukumara Forest Park, Urutawa Forest and Waioeka Gorge Scenic Reserve.

The coast is circled by 330km of highway (SH35), which took decades to build, and is an excellent road (open year-round). The drive is worthwhile, if only for the magnificent views of this wild coast dotted with picturesque little bays, inlets and coves that change aspect with the weather. On a sunny day the water is an inviting turquoise,

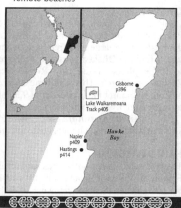

at other times a layer of clouds hangs on the craggy mountains rising straight up from the beaches and everything turns a misty green. Dozens of fresh, clear streams flow through wild gorges to meet the sea. During the summer the coastline turns crimson with the blooming of the pohutukawa trees which line the seashore.

Getting There & Around
At the time of writing shuttle services around the East Cape were in a state of flux, with new operators expected to start up and timetables expected to change. The Gisborne Visitor Information Centre has the latest information (see later in this chapter).

THE EAST COAST

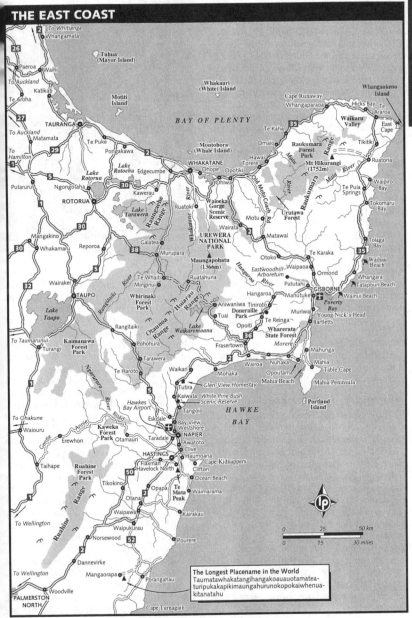

BAY OF PLENTY

HAWKE BAY

The Longest Placename in the World
Taumatawhakatangihangakoauauotamatea-
turipukakapikimaungahurunokopokaiwhenua-
kitanatahu

Cooks Couriers goes to Hicks Bay and Te Araroa from Gisborne on weekdays at 2 pm. East Light (☎ 0800-868 294) leaves Gisborne at 5 pm weekdays. Mo Reedy Transport leaves the Gisborne Visitor Information Centre for Hicks Bay at 1 pm weekdays. There is one weekend service: Downs Transport (☎ 06-868 5723), departing 9.30 am on Saturday and 7.30 am on Sunday. The one-way fare between Gisborne and Hicks Bay is about $25. Check with the drivers for return times.

All except Downs Transport leave from the towns' information centres; Downs will pick up in Gisborne given advance notice.

Coastal Pony Express (☎ 07-315 5907) runs between Opotiki and Waihau Bay (about 4km west of Cape Runaway) on weekdays.

Matakaoa Transport (☎ 06-864 4627 for details) runs between Hicks Bay and Whakatane ($30) via Opotiki ($25) on weekdays; it departs Hicks Bay at 6.30 am and arrives in Opotiki at 9.15 am before departing for Whakatane 15 minutes later. The terminal in Whakatane is at A-1 Taxis on St Georges Rd, near the Whakatane Hotel, but the bus will pick up and drop off at the visitor centre.

Hitching around the cape was once notoriously slow, but locals say the hitching situation isn't that bad these days.

OPOTIKI TO EAST CAPE

This trip is well described in *Opotiki & East Cape,* a comprehensive booklet available free from the Opotiki Information Centre. Along the first stretch of road from Opotiki there are fine views across to the steaming Whakaari (White Island) volcano. At the Waiaua River is the turn-off for the road to Gisborne via Toa Toa and the **Old Motu Coach Road**, probably more suited to mountain bikes than cars. At Ruatama Enterprise (☎ 07-315 4630) you can learn aspects of Maori culture on a *marae* stay; contact Mohi and Sonia for more details.

When you are travelling along this stretch of road keep an eye out for the magnificent carved *whakairo* gateway at Torere School.

HILARY ERICKSEN

Marae o Hawai, beside the East Coast road

The beaches at **Torere** and **Hawai** are steeply shelved and covered with driftwood; they're good spots for seascape photography. Hawai is the boundary of the Whanau-a-Apanui tribe, whose sphere of influence extends north to Cape Runaway. About 45km from Opotiki the road crosses the **Motu River**, famed for jet-boating, white-water rafting and kayaking.

Some 25km further on is **Te Kaha**, once a whaling centre but now a small town popular for boating and fishing. It has a rocky beach, a pub, a store and accommodation. At the large marae, the Tukaki meeting house is magnificently carved. A succession of picturesque bays, including the beautiful Whanarua Bay, are passed before **Whangaparaoa** and Cape Runaway are reached. You cannot miss the Raukokore Anglican Church, nestled under Norfolk pines on a lone promontory, about 100km north of Opotiki. Cape Runaway can only be reached on foot; seek permission before going onto private land.

Hicks Bay gets its name from a crew member of Captain Cook's *Endeavour*. It is a magnificent place, complemented by nearby Horseshoe Bay. Nearly 10km further on is the sizable community of **Te Araroa,**

which has an information centre. At Te Araroa there is a distinct change in geography from the volcanic rock outcrops to the sandstone cliffs standing above the town on the bay. One of NZ's largest **pohutukawa**, Te Waha o Rerekohu, reputed to be over 600 years old, stands in the school grounds.

At Te Araroa you turn off for the **East Cape Lighthouse**, at the most easterly tip of NZ.

Places to Stay & Eat

There is no shortage of accommodation along the cape's western side. Not far from Opotiki is *Tirohanga Motor Camp* (☎/fax 07-315 7942); $16 for two for a tent site, or $40 for two for tourist flats.

At Opape, which is 18km from Opotiki, is *Coral's B&B* (☎/fax 07-315 8052), which has two attractive self-contained cottages (one which sleeps six; there's a cot as well). The larger cottage ($110 for two) overlooks a delightful valley and has a deck. The smaller cottage costs $70 for two.

Te Kaha is the central point on the western side of the East Cape. *Te Kaha Holiday Park & Motels* (☎/fax 07-325 2894) has camp sites ($18 for two), cabins and tourist flats ($85 for two), and backpackers accommodation. *Te Kaha Hotel & Motel* (☎/fax 07-325 2830) has double rooms from $60 for two and luxury beachside units ($130 for two). A great place to stay is *Tui Lodge* (☎/fax 07-325 2922), which is a short distance up Copenhagen Rd (inland, off the main road). It's a spacious, modern guesthouse – originally intended as a fishing lodge – set in lovely gardens with two twin rooms and two double rooms (singles/doubles from $75/95). Two rooms have en suites.

Further along towards Whanarua Bay, and signposted on the main road, is *Waikawa B&B* (☎ 07-325 2070), in a delightful little spot overlooking a small bay. There are two comfortable en suite rooms (one double upstairs with a deck, and one twin downstairs) in a cottage flanked by a lovely garden. The upstairs room costs $75 and the downstairs $70 (prices for two).

At pretty Whanarua Bay, *Rendezvous on the Coast* (☎/fax 07-325 2899) has camp sites from $16 for two, backpacker bunks, tourist flats and on-site caravans ranging up to $65 for two.

Robyn's Place (☎ 07-325 2904) is a small backpackers which has beach access and walks. It costs $15 per person for dorm beds, $17.50 per person for a double.

At Waihau Bay, the *Waihau Bay Holiday Park* (☎ 07-325 3844) at Oruati Beach has camp sites costing $9 per person, $10 for powered sites. Cabins cost $20 per person and on-site caravans are $15 per person.

Waihau Bay Homestay (☎/fax 07-325 3674) is opposite the beach and has a double with en suite upstairs, a twin downstairs and a new self-contained unit out the front that sleeps four. It's $80 for two, including breakfast. *Oceanside Apartments* (☎ 07-325 3699) nearby has singles/doubles for $65/90.

Equidistant between Whangaparaoa and Hicks Bay is the *Lottin Point Motel* (☎ 06-864 4455) with units from $80 for two.

If you take the dirt road around the peninsula from the Hicks Bay township, you'll come to the spic-and-span *Hicks Bay Backpackers Lodge* (☎ 06-864 4731) on Onepoto Beach Rd. It's a small, friendly place with a backpackers bunkroom off to one side of the home, and fronts a beautiful beach, only 50m away. It's $15 in dorms, $45 for a double and $25 per person for a twin (the double and twin are in the main house). Horse riding, fishing and trips to the East Cape Lighthouse can be organised, and there's Internet access.

Also at Hicks Bay, up on the hill overlooking the bay, is the *Hicks Bay Motel Lodge* (☎ 06-864 4880) with doubles starting at $88.

Hicks Bay has a *takeaway* and a *general store*.

Four kilometres north of Hicks Bay is *Te Puna Frontier* (☎/fax 06-864 4862), which has cottages, horse riding and river swimming; prices on application.

Te Araroa Holiday Park (☎ 06-864 4873), midway between Te Araroa and Hicks Bay, is another lovely spot. In a sheltered 15-hectare parklike setting near the beach, the park has lots of amenities, including a cinema.

Tent/powered sites cost $8.50/9.50 per person, bunkroom accommodation is $12, cabins are $35 for two and tourist flats are $50.

EAST CAPE TO GISBORNE

Heading south from Te Araroa the first place of interest you come to is **Tikitiki**. The Anglican Church is well worth visiting for its Maori architectural design.

A few kilometres off the road is **Ruatoria**, which has powerful Mt Hikurangi as a backdrop. Ruatoria is a very important Maori town – the centre of the Ngati Porou tribe. The politician Sir Apirana Ngata (see History in the Facts about New Zealand chapter) lived here, as did Victoria Cross-winner Lt Moananui-a-Kiwa Ngarimu and All Black George Nepia.

About 25km south is **Te Puia Springs**, a pretty little town with hot springs nearby, and the pleasant **Waipiro Bay**. Another 10km further is **Tokomaru Bay**, a crumbling, picturesque town with a good beach and sweeping cliffs at the southern end of the bay. Hiking, swimming, surfing, tennis, fishing, cycling and visits to the new beachside pub are all popular activities at Tokomaru Bay.

Tolaga Bay is next and, although popular with surfers, is not particularly exciting when contrasted with Tokomaru or bays to the north. South of Tolaga Bay is the small settlement **Whangara**, the setting for Witi Ihimaera's wonderful fictional work *The Whale Rider*. It is a great little book to read for a feel of the Maori culture and mythology of the area. After passing Tatapouri and Wainui Beaches you reach Gisborne.

Places to Stay

Heading south along the east coast from Te Araroa you come to the Waiapu River and the town of Tikitiki, which has a hotel and caravan park.

Ruatoria has the old ***Manutahi Hotel*** (*☎ 06-864 8437*) with standard pub rooms from $45. At the time of writing *Mountain View Cafe* was constructing units on the premises. At Te Puia is *Te Puia Springs Hotel* (*☎ 06-864 6755*), an Historic Trust building, with singles for $35 with shared facilities and doubles with en suite for $55.

Te Puia also has a motel and the information centre (*☎ 06-864 6894*), in the council chambers, can tell you about homestays in the area.

At Waipiro Bay on the coast, *Waikawa Lodge* (*☎ 06-864 6719*) on Waikawa Rd is a small, romantic backpackers cottage, ideal for getting away from it all. It has two doubles at $20 per person. There's a kitchen where you can prepare your own food. The big plus here is the two-hour horse trek ($30) guided by Anne and Jimmy, two quintessential Kiwis. This place is hard to find. If you are coming from the Opotiki side turn off at the Kopuaroa Rd sign. If you are coming from the Gisborne side, look for the signposted turn-off to Waipiro Bay. Both roads lead to Waikawa Rd and the lodge is up a farm road at the end of Waikawa Rd. Waikawa Rd is impassable when conditions are very wet so it's *essential* to ring before you come (there's a public telephone at Te Puia Springs). The owners will pick you up from Te Puia Springs or Waipiro Bay.

On Potae St in Tokomaru Bay, the ***House of the Rising Sun*** (*☎ 06-864 5858*) is small, comfortable and homey hostel about a block from the beach. It charges $15 for dorm and $17 per person for twins and doubles. Uphill, *Brian's Place* (*☎ 06-864 870*), in a great spot overlooking the bay, has a double room ($15 per person), two lofts ($12; can sleep four) and tent site ($8). You can organise horse treks here (from $30).

Further south, the well-equipped ***Tolaga Bay Motor Camp*** (*☎ 06-862 6716*), on Wharf Rd on the beach, has sites from $1 for two and a variety of cabins.

The historic ***Tolaga Bay Inn*** (*☎ 06-86 6856*) on Cook St has singles/doubles for $40/50; and the ***Tolaga Bay Motel*** (*☎ 06 862 6888*) on the corner of Cook and Monkhouse Sts has units from $68.

RAUKUMARA & WAIOEKA

Inland, the Raukumara Range offers tramping (the highest mountain in the range is Hikurangi at 1752m) and whitewater rafting on the Waioeka and Mot Rivers – contact Wet 'n' Wild Rafting

0800-462 723) for more information on rafting. The most popular way of accessing this rugged, untamed region is via SH2 (the Waioeka Gorge Road), the 144km road which connects Opotiki to Gisborne.

There are many great walks in this region and the Department of Conservation (DOC) has plenty of information on possibilities. See its *Raukumara Forest Park* and *Waioeka Gorge Scenic Reserve* pamphlets. The rare blue duck may be seen in Raukumara, and Hochstetter's frog *(Leiopelma hochstetteri)* is quite common in the park. Some parts of the region are penetrable by mountain bike, while others are certainly not. This region is one of NZ's last frontiers, as wild as sections of south Westland.

The *Matawai Hotel* (☎ 06-862 4874), 76km from Opotiki on SH2, has backpackers beds for $20 and doubles for $50. Only 16km from Opotiki, the *Riverview Cottage* (☎/fax 07-315 5553), also on SH2, has rooms for $110 for two.

Matawai Village Cafe is a convenient place to get a bite to eat.

Poverty Bay

☎ 06 • pop 41,400

This now little-visited region got its name in 1769 from one of its earliest European visitors, James Cook (on his first expedition). While trying to replenish his ship, there were skirmishes with the local Maori, six of whom were killed. Cook decided the area had little to offer, hence 'poverty'.

The actual bay is quite small, a halfmoon stretching from Tuahine Point to Young Nicks Head. The Poverty Bay region includes the coast from Tolaga Bay south to the Mahia Peninsula, and west to the hills of the East Cape, the gem of which is Lake Waikaremoana.

GISBORNE

pop 32,700

Gisborne is NZ's most easterly city and one of the closest in the world to the International Date Line. The fertile alluvial plains around Gisborne support intensive farming of subtropical fruits, market-garden produce and vineyards. More recently, kiwi fruit and avocados have been important crops.

The city itself is on the coast at the confluence of two rivers: the Waimata and Taruheru (the short stretch below the junction is the Turanganui). Often described as 'the city of bridges', it is also noted for its fine parks.

This part of the East Coast retains a definite Maori character with great emphasis placed on the retention of culture and traditions. You'll often hear *te reo Maori* (the Maori language) being spoken here.

History

The Gisborne region has been settled for over 1000 years. Two skippers of ancestral migratory *waka* (canoes) – Paoa of the *Horo-uta* and Kiwa of the *Takitimu* – made an intermarriage pact which led to the founding of Turanganui a Kiwa (now Gisborne) soon after their arrival from Hawaiki. The newly introduced kumara (sweet potato) flourished in the fertile soil and Maori settlement spread to the hinterland.

European settlement of the region did not occur until the late 19th century. A man of considerable drive, John Williams Harris, was first to purchase a small area on the west bank of the Turanganui River. He set up the region's first whaling venture, and in 1839 began farming up the Waipaoa River near Manutuke.

As whaling became increasingly popular, missionaries also began to move into the area. Father Baty and Rev William Colenso were the first Europeans to tramp into the heart of Te Urewera and see Lake Waikaremoana.

Gradually more Pakeha arrived but organised settlement was limited due to Maori resistance. When the Treaty of Waitangi was signed in 1840 many chiefs from the east coast did not acknowledge the treaty, let alone sign it.

In the 1860s, numerous battles with the Maori broke out. The Hauhau insurrection that began in Taranaki and spread to the Bay of Plenty and the East Coast reached its height here at the battle of Waerenga-a-hika in November 1865. By the following year the government had crushed opposition and

GISBORNE

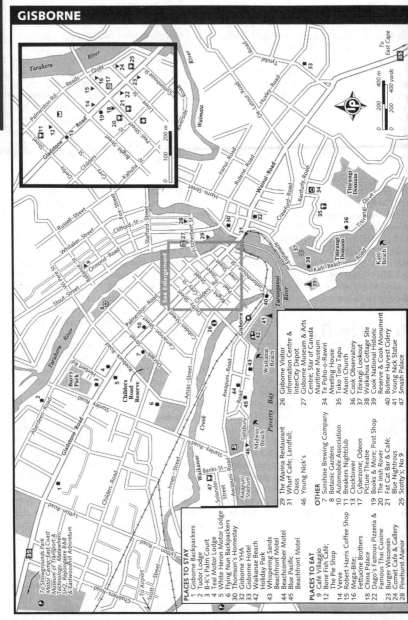

See Enlargement

To East Cape

To Showgrounds Park
Motor Camp; East Coast
Museum of Transport &
Technology; Matawhero;
SH2, Repongaere B&B
& Eastwoodhill Arboretum

To Airport

PLACES TO STAY
1   Gisborne Backpackers
2   Tudor Lodge
3   B-K's Palm Court
4   Teal Motor Lodge
5   White Heron Motor Lodge
6   Flying Nun Backpackers
30   Thomson's Homestay
32   Gisborne YHA
33   Gisborne Hotel
42   Waikanae Beach
     Holiday Park
43   Whispering Sands
     Beachfront Motel
44   Beachcomber Motel
45   Blue Pacific
     Beachfront Motel

PLACES TO EAT
9   Café Villaggio
12   Bone Fish Café;
     The Pie Shop
14   Verve
15   Robert Harris Coffee Shop
16   Mega-Bite;
     Fettucine Brothers
18   China Palace
22   Dago's Famous Pizzeria &
     Famous Thai Cuisine
23   Burger Wisconsin
24   Comet Cafe & Gallery
28   Pinehurst Manor

29   The Marina Restaurant
31   Wharf Café; Landfall;
     Oasis
46   Young Nick's

OTHER
7   Sunshine Brewing Company
8   Botanic Gardens
10   Automobile Association
11   Breakers Nightclub
13   Clocktower
17   Cyberzone; Odeon
     Picture Theatre
19   Books & More; Post Shop
20   The Irish Rover
21   Fat Cat Bar & Café;
     Blue Nightrous
25   Scotty's; No 9

26   Gisborne Visitor
     Information Centre &
     InterCity Depot
27   Gisborne Museum & Arts
     Centre; Star of Canada
     Maritime Museum
34   Te Poho-o-Rawiri
     Meeting House
35   Toko Toru Tapu
     Maori Church
36   Cook Observatory
37   Titirangi Lookout
38   Waikahua Cottage Site
39   Cook National Historic
     Reserve & Cook Monument
40   Bulmer Harvest Cidery
41   Young Nick Statue
47   Smash Palace

transported a number of the survivors, including the charismatic Te Kooti (see the boxed text), to the remote Chatham Islands. This paved the way for an influx of Europeans, who brought with them their flocks of sheep. But in 1868 Te Kooti escaped and with an army of 200 exacted revenge on the settlement at Matawhero, killing 33 Europeans and 37 Maori.

Even today, however, much of the pasture land is leased from the Maori and a large part of it is under their direct control. Unfortunately, the pioneer farmers were so anxious to profit from the land that they ripped out far too much forest cover, with disastrous results. Massive erosion occurred as the steeply sloping land was unable to hold the soil after heavy rains.

Information

The Gisborne Visitor Information Centre (☎ 868 6139, 🖂 info@eastland.tourism .co.nz) is at 209 Grey St. Look for the fine Canadian totem pole beside it. It's open from 8 am to 5 pm daily and has a Web site at www.eastland.tourism.co.nz. Children (and a fair number of adults) love the minigolf course behind the centre.

The DOC office (☎ 867 8531), 63 Carnarvon St, is open from 8 am to 4.35 pm on weekdays; you're requested to first seek information from the visitor centre. The Automobile Association (AA; ☎ 868 1424) is at 363 Gladstone Rd.

Gisborne's telephone area code is ☎ 06. There is Internet access at a couple of cafes and at Cyberzone.

Gisborne Museum & Arts Centre

This excellent regional museum is at 18 Stout St and has numerous displays relating to East Coast Maori and colonial history, as well as geology and natural history exhibits. The gallery has changing exhibitions of local, national and international art. Outside are more exhibits – a sled house, stable, the 1870 Wyllie Cottage (first house on the site), and Lysnar House with working artists' studios (not open to the public).

The **Star of Canada Maritime Museum** behind the main museum is part of the complex. One wild night in 1912 the 12,000-ton ship *Star of Canada* was blown ashore on the reef at Gisborne. The ship's bridge and captain's cabin were salvaged and eventually installed in what became the town's best-known home. This unique house was moved to its present site, restored and made into a museum. There are displays on Maori canoes, early whaling and shipping, and Cook's Gisborne visit but the most interesting items relate, of course, to the *Star of Canada*.

The museum complex is open from 10 am to 4 pm on weekdays, 1.30 to 4 pm on weekends (entry is by donation).

Statues & Views

There's a **statue** of 'Young Nick' (Nicholas Young), Cook's cabin boy, in a little park on the river mouth. A press-ganged member of Cook's crew, he was the first to sight NZ. Across the bay are the white cliffs that Cook named Young Nick's Head.

Across the river at the foot of Kaiti Hill is a **monument** to Cook, near the spot where he first set foot on NZ (9 October 1769 in 'ship time' in Cook's journal, but really the 8th). It's in the Cook National Historic Reserve. Nearby Waikahua Cottage once served as a refuge during the Hauhau unrest.

Titirangi (Kaiti Hill) has fine views of the area. There's a walking track up from the Cook monument which starts near Waikahua Cottage. Near the top is yet another monument to Cook, but it is a fine statue. At the 135m summit is the **Cook Observatory**, with a sign proclaiming it the 'World's Easternmost Observatory'. The Gisborne Astronomical Society (☎ 868 8653) meets here at 7.30 pm on Tuesday; all are welcome.

Down on **Kaiti Beach**, low tide attracts a wealth of bird life, including stilts, oystercatchers and other pelagic visitors.

Te Poho-o-Rawiri

Also at the foot of Titirangi is Te Poho-o-Rawiri Maori meeting house, one of the largest in NZ. It has a richly decorated interior and its stage is framed by carved *maihi* (ornamental carved gable boards). The

Te Kooti

The enigmatic Te Kooti was born into the Rongowhakaata tribe in Poverty Bay during the early decades of the 19th century in the shadow of a prophecy. It was foretold that if, as the second born, he outlived his brother evil would fall upon the land and its people.

Indeed, Te Kooti survived an illness that killed his sibling. Rejected by his father, he was adopted, and attended an Anglican mission school. Later, as a young man, he was accused of assisting the Hauhau in Gisborne during a siege by government troops. In 1865 Te Kooti, along with a number of others, was packed off to exile in the Chatham Islands. Here, during a bout of fever, he experienced the visions that were to eventually lead to the establishment of the Ringatu Church. In 1867 he led an escape from the Chathams; more than 200 men, women and children sailed away on a captured supply ship, the *Rifleman*.

They landed at Poverty Bay where during a ceremony of thanks for their safe return, Te Kooti urged his followers to raise their right hands to pay homage to God rather than kneel in submission. This is believed to be the first time the raised hand, from which Ringatu takes its name, was used.

The escapees intended to make their way peaceably into the interior, where Te Kooti hoped to challenge the Maori king, Tawhiao, in the Waikato for spiritual leadership. But resident magistrate Reginald Biggs demanded they give up their arms. They refused and a series of skirmishes followed, during which the government troops suffered a series of humiliating defeats. But when Te Kooti reached the Waikato he was rejected by Tawhiao.

He turned back to Poverty Bay and attacked Matawhero, killing Biggs and, later, several chiefs including the father of his first wife. He became both hated and feared; some of his prisoners decided it was prudent to become supporters.

For a while he dominated Poverty Bay, but was forced to retreat into the Urewera Ranges in the face of challenges from avenging Maori tribes. There he mustered a fighting force of some 200 warriors, and adopted the custom of sallying forth on his various raids astride a white horse.

More fighting took place during which Te Kooti moved into the King Country, back to the Ureweras and then out again to the King Country where in 1873 he finally put his fighting days behind him.

From his base in Te Kuiti he formulated the rituals of the Ringatu Church. His reputation as a prophet and a healer spread, and he made a series of predictions about a successor. He devoted the rest of his life to making peace with his former enemies and spreading the tenets of his faith. He particularly desired to return to Poverty Bay, but his old foes prevented this.

After his pardon Te Kooti lived near Ohiwa Harbour, and he spent much time visiting other Ringatu centres in the region. He never returned to Poverty Bay and he eventually died at Ohiwa in 1893.

His body was removed by his followers from its original burial place at Maromahue and to this day no-one knows for sure exactly where he was finally laid to rest.

human figure kneeling on the right knee with right hand held upwards is the *tekoteko* (carved figure) representing the ancestor who challenges those who enter the marae. It is open all the time except when a function is in progress; seek permission before entering. A little Maori church, **Toko Toru Tapu**, stands on the side of Titirangi, not far from the meeting house.

The leaflet called *Tairawhiti – Heritage Trails: Gisborne District* provides good information on historic sites in this Maori ancestral land. The Ngati Porou tribe has a Web site at www.ngatiporou.iwi.nz.

Other Attractions

The Gisborne area has a few attractive gardens to visit, including the huge **Eastwoodhill Arboretum** (☎ 863 9003), 35km west of town, which is open from 9 am to 5 pm daily ($8, children free). It contains NZ's largest collection of northern hemisphere temperate trees, shrubs and climbers. To get there follow the Ngatapa-Rere Road; there is a 45-minute marked track through the trees. The visitor information centre has details on many other private gardens.

The **Botanic Gardens** are in town beside Taruheru River off Aberdeen Rd.

Gisborne is a major wine-producing area, noted for its chardonnay. **Wineries** to visit are: Parker Methode Champenoise, 24 Bank St; Matawhero Wines on Riverpoint Rd; Millton Vineyard in Manutuke; Longbush Wines at the Esplanade; Montana Wines on Lytton Rd; and Pouparae Park Wines at 385 Bushmere Rd. The visitor information centre has details on opening hours and tours. Trev's Tours (☎ 863 9815) does a wine trail.

There is also a **natural beer brewery**, the Sunshine Brewing Company, at 109 Disraeli St, and a **cidery** (Bulmer Harvest Cidery), Customhouse St.

Near the A&P Showgrounds in Makaraka is the **East Coast Museum of Transport & Technology (ECMOT)**. It is open from 9 am to 5 pm daily ($2, children $0.50).

Matawhero is a few kilometres south along SH2. The historic Presbyterian Church here is the only building in town to have survived the conflicts of 1868.

Activities

You can swim at Waikanae Beach in the city. In fact there's good swimming, fishing and surfing all along the coast. Midway Beach has a swimming complex with a big waterslide and children's playground. Enterprise Pools on Nelson Rd is an indoor complex open to the public.

The Motu and Waioeka Rivers are in the Gisborne district, although they drain into the Bay of Plenty; ask at the visitor information centre about white-water rafting. The centre also has details on walks, horse trekking, fishing, hunting and tours.

Te Kuri Walkway is a three-hour walk through farmland and some forest to a commanding viewpoint. The walk starts 4km north of town at the end of Shelley Rd. It's closed from August to October for lambing.

You can **horse trek** with Waimoana Horse Trekking (☎ 868 8218, 025-307 216) at Wainui Beach; a trek is $30 for two hours.

The adventurous can get close up to mako sharks ('waterborne pussycats') in submersible metal cages, from $120 per person. Contact Surfit Charters (☎ 867 2970). Tamer snorkelling on the reefs around Gisborne can also be arranged.

Places to Stay

Camping & Cabins The good *Waikanae Beach Holiday Park* (☎ 867 5634) is on Grey St at Waikanae Beach. Camp sites cost from $18 for two, cabins start at $26 and tourist units from $55.

The *Poverty Bay A&P Showgrounds Park Motor Camp* (☎ 867 5299) at Makaraka is cheaper but it's not so conveniently central. Tent/powered sites are $10.50/12.50 for two, on-site caravans are $30 and basic cabins $15.

Backpackers The *Flying Nun Backpackers* (☎ 868 0461, @ eastbroke@clear.net.nz, 147 Roebuck Rd) still awaits the right winds for Sister Bertrille. Backpackers with the right equipment (the hat and healthy habits, perhaps) can alight here. It charges from $15 in dorms, $19/20 per person in twins/doubles, and $25 in singles. Dame Kiri Te Kanawa (see the boxed text later in this chapter) had her early singing lessons here.

The *Gisborne YHA* (☎ 867 3269, @ yha .gisborne@clear.net.nz, 32 Harris St), 1.5km from the town centre across the river, is in a substantial old home with spacious grounds. The nightly cost is $15 in dorms and $36 for doubles or twins.

Gisborne Backpackers (☎ 868 1000, @ gisborne@xtra.co.nz, 690 Gladstone Rd) is about 2km from the town centre. This large, neat and tidy former orphanage has dorm rooms for $18 ($16 with own linen), twins and doubles for $20 per person and singles for $25.

B&Bs & Guesthouses The visitor information centre has full details. *Thomson Homestay* (☎ 868 9675, 16 Rawiri St) is pleasantly situated in the historic riverfront district and charges $70 for two. The owners are active bridge players.

Tudor Lodge (☎ 867 7577, 573 Aberdeen Rd) is near the Taruheru River. There are two self-contained apartments and a Lockwood cottage with two bedrooms, kitchen and sitting room. Prices range from $70 to $95 and include a continental breakfast.

Repongaere (☎ 862 7717, Lavenham Rd), near Patutahi, and *Acton Estate* (☎ 867 999, 577 Back Ormond Rd) are two beautiful, upmarket guesthouses 10 to 15 minutes' drive west of Gisborne. Repongaere is on a 60-hectare farm and was built in 1909. Acton Estate, an Edwardian mansion built in 1907, was part of a large station; the tree-lined driveway is 1km long. Rooms are $100-plus.

Motels & Hotels Most Gisborne motels start from around $85 for two. Salisbury Rd, close to the city centre and right near the beach, is a good motel hunting ground. Note that prices are likely to depend on the season.

The *Blue Pacific Beachfront Motel* (☎ 868 6099, 90 Salisbury Rd) has 13 self-contained units of varying sizes. The motel is handy to the Olympic Pool, an adventure playground and a golf course. Prices range from $85 to $135 for two. Each extra person is $15.

Whispering Sands Beachfront Motel (☎ 867 1319, 18–22 Salisbury Rd) has 14 units right on Waikanae Beach and impressive views of Poverty Bay. The rates range from $85 to $150 for two. *Beachcomber Motel* (☎ 868 9349, 73 Salisbury Rd) is also located here.

Good choices on Gladstone Rd include *B-K's Palm Court* (☎ 868 5601, 671 Gladstone Rd), one of Gisborne's newest upmarket motels, with 15 units, some with their own spa. There are 11 studio units and four one-bedroom units. Prices range from $90 to $130 for two. *Teal Motor Lodge* (☎ 0800-838 325, 479 Gladstone Rd) has a saltwater swimming pool and 20 ground-floor units. Prices (depending on the season) range from $89 to $144 for two. The *White Heron Motor Lodge* (☎ 0800-997 766, 470 Gladstone Rd) has good one- and two-bedroom suites, most with a spa. Prices range from $90 to $120 for two.

The *Gisborne Hotel* (☎ 868 4109) on the corner of Tyndall and Huxley Rds, Kaiti, is a tidy enough place, if a little isolated (from $100 for a double with en suite).

Places to Eat

Gisborne has the usual selection of sandwich places, particularly along Gladstone Rd, or you could try Peel St, where there is *Mega-Bite* with good hot lunches (quiche, samosas and the like), sandwiches, rolls and drinks. Next door is *Fettucine Brothers* – you guessed it, it's an Italian pasta place.

Opposite in the pedestrian mall is the *Robert Harris Coffee Shop* with a good selection of sandwiches.

For Chinese food, the most popular place is *China Palace* on Peel St, which has a takeaway counter at the front and a no-frills dining section.

Verve (121 Gladstone Rd) has continental meals, an Internet connection and a nice ambience – it is open daily.

Comet Cafe & Gallery on the corner of Lowe St and Reads Quay is very popular, with good coffee, cakes and light meals (including a satisfying selection of vegetarian options). There's also Internet access.

For pizzas try *Dago's Famous Pizzeria*, which is also the home of *Dago's Famous Thai Cuisine;* it's a takeaway place.

For burgers it's hard to beat *Burger Wisconsin* for sheer variety (pumpkin and tofu, satay, and blue cheese, among others).

On Grey St the *Bone Fish Cafe* has indoor and courtyard dining (seafood, nachos, pasta and so on); nearby is *The Pie Shop* with a large selection of pies and sandwiches.

Down at Gisborne wharf, the *Wharf Cafe*, *Landfall* and *Oasis* all offer satisfying dining in a pleasant spot. *Young Nick's* on the beach has a big deck – pleasant for outdoor dining.

The top of the town's dining pile is *Pinehurst Manor* (4 Clifford St), a winner of several awards and justifiably so.

Out of town, in Ballance St village, is the popular *Café Villaggio*, recognisable by its

Art Deco look and with a good blackboard menu.

Entertainment
Breakers Nightclub in Derby St has occasional big-name bands as well as local artists.

The Irish Rover on Peel St also has live music occasionally. Across the road, *Blue Nightrous* and the *Fat Cat Bar & Cafe* are also options. *Scotty's* on Gladstone Rd is popular with the young, trendy set; *No 9* next door has live music on weekends.

The most interesting place in town is *Smash Palace*, set appropriately in the junkyard area of town at Bank St. A couple of beaten-up old Morris Minor cars and the hulk of a long-grounded aircraft greet you outside, while inside is a veritable Aladdin's cave of junk from all parts of the globe and Kiwi memorabilia. But the place has atmosphere, a good selection of beers and wines, and light bar meals.

During summer, bands, musicians and poets perform in the parks.

Getting There & Away
Air The Air New Zealand office (☎ 868 2700) is at 37 Bright St. It has daily direct flights to Wellington and Auckland, with onward connections to places like Napier and Hamilton.

Bus The InterCity depot (☎ 868 7600) is at the visitor information centre. InterCity has one bus daily (leaves at 9 am) to Napier via Wairoa. From Napier there are connections to Palmerston North and Wellington. InterCity also runs buses between Gisborne and Auckland via Opotiki, Whakatane and Rotorua.

The much longer, but very scenic, East Cape route to Opotiki can be done by car. Another route from Rotorua to Gisborne is the partly unsealed SH38 running through the Urewera National Park, passing Lake Waikaremoana and joining the Napier route at Wairoa, 97km south of Gisborne; there is currently no bus service along this route.

Hitching Hitching is OK from the south of the city, and not too bad through Waioeka Gorge to Opotiki – it's still best to leave early. To hitch a ride out, head along Gladstone Rd to Makaraka, 6km west, for Wairoa and Napier, or the turn-off to Opotiki and Rotorua. Hitching from Wairoa to Waikaremoana is hard going.

Beyond the Morries – the eclectic interior decorations of Smash Palace, Gisborne

JEFF WILLIAMS

Dame Kiri Te Kanawa

One of the most internationally famous Kiwis of all time is Dame Kiri Te Kanawa, the serenely beautiful opera diva. (The only equally-well-known Kiwi is perhaps mountaineer Sir Edmund Hillary.)

It's hard to imagine that this lyrical soprano who graces La Scala and Covent Garden with aplomb had her beginnings in this motley neighbourhood; she was born in Gisborne in 1944. Her first major leading role was as the Countess in *Le Nozze di Figaro* at Covent Garden (1971), and she has since embraced the roles of Donna Elvira *(Don Giovanni)*, Marguerite *(Faust)*, Mimi *(La Bohéme)*, Amelia *(Simon Boccanegra)* and Desdemona *(Otello)*. There have been many famous commercial recordings – *West Side Story* with José Carreras, and the haunting calls across the valley of Canteloube's *Songs of the Auvergne*. She also sang at Charles and Diana's wedding in 1981.

An appreciative crowd gathered to see in the new millennium at Gisborne were treated to the sound of Kiri's beautiful voice accompanied by the New Zealand Symphony Orchestra.

Getting Around

Gisborne Taxi Buses (☎ 867 2222) runs the town's bus service; buses only go on weekdays and the last run is at 5.15 pm. Taxis include Gisborne Taxis (☎ 867 2222) and Eastland Taxis (☎ 868 1133). Link Taxis (☎ 868 8385) runs to Gisborne airport ($8 to $10 from town).

For rentals try Hertz (☎ 867 9348), Budget (☎ 867 9794) or Avis (☎ 868 9084).

GISBORNE TO WAIROA

Heading south towards Napier you have two choices: SH2 is the coastal route which the bus follows, while SH36 is inland. The two routes meet in Wairoa.

The **coastal route** runs just inland most of the way south from Gisborne, before entering the Wharerata State Forest. At the southern edge of the state forest, 56km from Gisborne, Morere is a pretty little town noted for its hot springs. The **hot springs** are complemented by short walks of up to two hours through the beautiful native forest of the surrounding reserve. The hot springs are open from 10 am to 6 pm (to 7 pm Friday, Saturday and Sunday). Entry is $4, children $2.50.

You can stay in Morere at the delightful old *Peacock Lodge* (☎ 06-837 8824, @ peacocklodge@xtra.co.nz), about two minutes' walk from SH2. Follow the road next to the tearooms across the stream. This colonial farmhouse has a spacious lounge, fully equipped kitchen and a wide veranda

– it charges $15 in shared rooms, or $30 in doubles and twins.

The *Morere Springs Tavern* has a small restaurant. Opposite the springs is the *Morere Tearooms & Camping Ground* (☎ 06-837 8792), which has tent sites for $18 for two.

SH2 continues south to Nuhaka on the northern end of the sweep of Hawke Bay, where you can head west to Wairoa or east to the superb, windswept and wild **Mahia Peninsula** (said to be named after a place in Tahiti). There are long, curving beaches popular with surfers, clear water for diving and fishing, bird-watching at Mangawhio Lagoon and walks to a number of reserves. Mahia was once an island, but sand accumulation has formed NZ's largest tombolo landform (where a sand or shingle bar ties an island to another island or the mainland). The peninsula is a magical, atmospheric place, majestic in either sun or storm.

Facilities are limited and you'll need your own transport to get around. The *Mahia Beach Motels & Holiday Park* (☎ 06-837 5830) at Nuhaka has sites from $20 for two, cabins for $36 for two and motel-style units from $75.

Some 6km north from Opoutama is the *Tunanui Station Cottages* (☎ 06-837 5790, @ tunanui@xtra.co.nz), which has two fully self-contained cottages, one with three bedrooms sleeping six ($130 for two) and another with four bedrooms sleeping eight ($165 for two). It is $30 for each extra person. The views over the peninsula are stupendous.

Along SH36, the **inland route** to Wairoa, there are also several things to see and do. You can climb up **Gentle Annie Hill** for a good view over the Poverty Bay area. **Doneraille Park** (53km from Gisborne), a native bush reserve, is a popular picnic spot with good swimming when the water is clear.

There's fine trout fishing at **Tiniroto Lakes**, 61km from Gisborne, and about 10km further, **Te Reinga Falls** is worth a detour off the main road.

Hawkes Bay

☎ 06 • pop 133,900

The Hawkes Bay region (note that the body of water is 'Hawke Bay') is, sadly, missed by many visitors to NZ. Napier (like Hastings) is one of the best holiday destinations in the country, with fine Art Deco architecture.

The region also offers the 'perfect' village of Havelock North, wineries near Te Mata Peak and natural attractions such as the Cape Kidnappers gannet colony.

WAIROA
pop 5228

The two highways, SH2 and SH36, meet in Wairoa, 98km south of Gisborne. Wairoa has a reasonable beach and is a gateway to Urewera National Park. The reconstructed **lighthouse** by the river, built in 1877 of solid kauri, used to shine from Portland Island at the tip of the Mahia Peninsula. Ten kilometres east of Wairoa is Whakaki Lagoon, an important wetlands area renowned for its bird populations.

The Wairoa Information Centre (☎ 838 7440, ✉ weavic@xtra.co.nz) is on the corner of SH2 and Queen St. The DOC field centre (☎ 838 8252) is at 272 Marine Parade.

The telephone area code is ☎ 06.

Places to Stay & Eat

The *Riverside Motor Camp* (☎ 838 6301) is a pleasant place on the banks of the Wairoa River with powered sites from $16 for two and cabins for $35 a double.

Wairoa also has pub rooms ($40 for a twin room) at the *Clyde Hotel* (☎ 838 7139) on Marine Parade. The *Three Oaks Motel* (☎/fax 838 8204), on the corner of Campbell St and Clyde Rd, has doubles from $76.

For food, try *Johanna's* in Clyde Court, or *Katz* and *Oslers Bakery* on Marine Parade.

Getting There & Away

All InterCity (☎ 838 6049) buses between Gisborne and Napier pass through Wairoa.

WAIROA TO NAPIER

There are some good reserves along this stretch of road to break the twisting drive, all accessible from SH2.

There's backpacker accommodation at *Bushdale Farm* (☎/fax 06-838 6453) on Cricklewood Rd, about 9km from Wairoa heading towards Napier. Dorms are $15, doubles are $18 and a single is $23 (prices per person). Pick-up from Wairoa can be arranged.

Lake Tutira has a farmland setting; there are walkways around the lake and a bird sanctuary. The **Hawkes Bay Coastal Walkway** is 12km from SH2, down Waikari Rd. The walkway is 16km long, goes from the Waikari River to the Aropaoanui River, and involves equal portions of boulder hopping, track walking and beach walking.

Off Waipati Rd and 34km from Napier is the **Waipatiki Scenic Reserve**. The **White Pine Bush Scenic Reserve**, 29km from Napier, is notable for the dominant kahikatea (white pine). The **Tangoio Falls Scenic Reserve**, 2km south of White Pine, has Te Ana Falls, stands of ponga and whekiponga and podocarps. The White Pine and Tangoio Falls Scenic Reserves are linked by the **Tangoio Walkway**, which follows Kareaara Stream.

UREWERA NATIONAL PARK

Home of the Tuhoe people, one of NZ's most traditional tribes, Te Urewera is rich in history. The army of Te Kooti (see the boxed text earlier in this chapter) found refuge here during his battles against the government. Te Kooti's successor, Rua Kenana, led a thriving community at Maungapohatu, beneath

ALEXANDER TURNBULL LIBRARY, WELLINGTON NZ

Maori women weaving, Te Whai-a-te-Motu meeting house, Mataatua Marae, Ruatahuna (circa 1910)

the sacred mountain of the same name, from 1905 until his politically inspired arrest in 1916. Maungapohatu never recovered and only a small settlement remains; slightly larger is nearby Ruatahuna, where the extraordinary Mataatua Marae celebrates Te Kooti's exploits.

Urewera National Park is one of the country's most attractive parks. It is a marvellous area of lush forests, lakes and rivers, with lots of bushwalks ranging from half an hour to several days, and plenty of birds, trout, deer and other wildlife. The main focus of the park is the superbly scenic Lake Waikaremoana (Sea of Rippling Waters). Most visitors to the park come to go boating on the lake or walk the Lake Waikaremoana Track, one of NZ's Great Walks, but other walks are possible.

The park protects part of the largest untouched native forest area in the North Island. The rivers and lakes of the park offer good fishing for trout.

Information

The Aniwaniwa Visitor Centre (☎ 06-837 3803) is within the park on the shores of the lake. It has interesting displays on the park's natural history and supplies information on the walking tracks and accommodation around the park.

The Murupara Field Centre (☎ 07-366 5641) is the park's other main information centre, near Murupara on the park's western edge.

Hut and camping ground passes for the Lake Waikaremoana Track can also be bought at DOC offices and visitor centres in Gisborne, Wairoa, Whakatane and Napier.

Lake Waikaremoana Track

This three- to four-day tramp is one of the most popular walks in the North Island. The 46km track has spectacular views from the Panekiri Bluff, but all along the walk through fern groves, beech and podocarp forest there are vast panoramas and beautiful views of the lake. The walk is rated as easy and the only difficult section is the climb to Panekiri Bluff. Because of its popularity it is very busy from mid-December to the end of January and at Easter.

The walk can be done year-round, but the cold and rain in winter deter most people and make conditions much more challenging. Because of the altitude, temperatures can drop quickly even in summer. Walkers should take portable stoves and fuel as there are no cooking facilities in the huts. It's not recommended that you park your car at either end of the track – there have been break-ins.

Five huts and five camp sites are spaced along the track. Huts and camp sites are $12 and $8 respectively (school-age children half-price). It's essential to book through DOC (**@** greatwalksbooking@doc.govt.nz) and if you are intending doing the walk over the Christmas/New Year period, it would be wise to book as far ahead as possible.

Walking the Track The track can be done either clockwise from Onepoto in the south or anticlockwise from Hopuruahine Landing in the north. Starting from Onepoto, all the climbing is done in the first few hours. Water on this section of the track is limited so make sure you fill your water bottles before heading off. For those with a car, it is safest to leave it at Waikaremoana and then take a boat to the trail heads.

Estimated walking times are:

Onepoto to Panekiri Hut	five hours
Panekiri Hut to Waiopaoa Hut	three to four hours
Waiopaoa Hut to Marauiti Hut	4½ hours
Marauiti Hut to Waiharuru Hut	2¾ hours
Waiharuru Hut to Whanganui Hut	two hours
Whanganui Hut to Hopuruahine	three hours

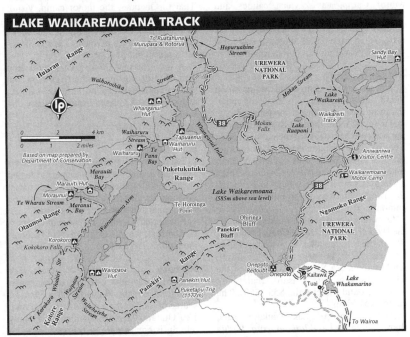

LAKE WAIKAREMOANA TRACK

Other Walks

The other major walk in the park is the **Whakatane River Round Trip**. The three- to five-day walk starts at Ruatahuna on SH38, 45km from the Aniwaniwa Visitor Centre towards Rotorua. The track follows the Whakatane River then loops back via Waikare River, Motumuka Stream and Whakatane Valley. Alternatively, you can walk on north down the Whakatane River and out of the national park at Ruatoki.

The track has six huts. At Aniwaniwa, DOC has track notes for this walk and sells topographical maps.

Another good walk is the **Lake Waikare-iti Track**, which begins near Aniwaniwa and leads to the Sandy Bay Hut. There are at least 20 other walks along the park's 600km of tracks.

Boating

Waikaremoana Guided Tours (☎ 06-837 3729), which is based at the Waikaremoana Motor Camp, has kayaks, canoes and dinghies for hire. Costs are $40 a day for a single kayak (or $10 an hour), $45 a day for a Canadian canoe, and $80/60 a day for a dinghy with/without an outboard motor.

Places to Stay

There are various camps and cabins along SH38, including a camp, cabins and motel 67km inland from the Wairoa turn-off.

There are more than 50 DOC huts along the walkways throughout the national park. The five Lake Waikaremoana Track huts are rated as Great Walks huts and cost $12 per night. There are also five DOC camping grounds, where it costs only $8 to camp. All the ranger stations have information on camping.

On the shore of Lake Waikaremoana is the *Waikaremoana Motor Camp* (☎ 06-837 3826), the most popular place to stay. Camp sites cost $7.50 per person, $9 with power, while cabins are $30 for two ($40 in the Christmas/New Year season), chalets are $55 ($65) and motel units $55 ($60). The camp has a shop.

At Tuai, 5km from Lake Waikaremoana, there is the *Lake Whakamarino Lodge* (☎ 06-837 3876) which has singles/twins/doubles for $45/50/80 and backpacker accommodation for $15. There is also a *homestay* (☎ 06-837 3701, 9 Rotten Row), which has singles/doubles for $45/70, including breakfast.

On the northern edge of the park there is a range of accommodation. There are *motels* at Ruatahuna, Taneatua and Murupara, which also has a *hotel*. At Galatea, on the Whakatane-Murupara Road, the *Galatea Estate Guest Cottage* (☎ 07-366 4703) has doubles or twins for $65.

Getting There & Around

Most of the 120km road through the park between Frasertown and Murupara is unsealed, winding and time-consuming. Traffic is light, making it slow for hitching. There is no InterCity bus service between Wairoa and Rotorua.

The Waikaremoana Shuttle service (☎ 06-837 3729) operates on demand from Tuai to Onepoto, the motor camp, visitor information centre, Mokau landing and Hopuruahine. Depending on the number of people, the cost from Tuai to Lake Waikaremoana is about $10.

A water taxi (☎ 06-837 3729) will drop you off/pick you up at the beginning and end of your walk around the lake. Contact Waikaremoana Guided Tours (see Boating earlier).

NAPIER

pop 55,000

Lying on sweeping Hawke Bay, Napier is a fascinating, architecturally rich city, blessed with a Mediterranean climate, a fine coastal position, an attractive marine parade, good restaurants and a friendly population.

It is a great city to visit but avoid domestic holidays, when it is crowded and accommodation is expensive.

History

Long before James Cook sighted the area in October 1769, the Maori found a plentiful source of food in the bay and the hinterland. The Otatara Pa, with its barricades now rebuilt, is one of the pre-European sites of habitation. It's past the Eastern Institute of Technology on Gloucester St.

The French explorer Jules Dumont d'Urville, using Cook's charts, sailed the *Astrolabe* into the bay in 1827. After whalers started using the safe Ahuriri anchorage in the 1830s, a trading base was established in 1839.

The town was planned in 1854, named after the British general and colonial administrator, Charles Napier, and soon flourished as a commercial regional centre.

In 1931 Napier was dramatically changed when a disastrous earthquake, measuring 7.9 on the Richter scale, virtually destroyed it. In Napier and nearby Hastings over 250 people died, and Napier suddenly found itself 40 sq km larger when the quake heaved that amount of seabed above sea level – in places the land level rose by over 2m. The Napier airport is built on that previously submerged area. The rebuilding program that followed has left one of the world's best examples of an Art Deco city.

Orientation

At the northern end of town Bluff Hill looms, acting as a natural boundary between the centre and the Ahuriri and port areas. The fine wooden villas on the hill that survived the quake give this district a genteel air. The coast and Marine Parade, with its many attractions, mark the eastern boundary and the main part of town is in this north-eastern corner.

The prime commercial streets are Hastings and Emerson Sts. Emerson St has been developed into a pedestrian thoroughfare with clever paving and street furniture to complement its many Art Deco features.

Information

Napier's helpful and well-informed visitor information centre (☎ 834 1911, ✆ info@ napiervic.co.nz) is at 100 Marine Parade. It's open from 8.30 am to 5 pm on weekdays and from 9 am on weekends (extended over summer).

The AA office is on Dickens St (but it is closed on weekends).

The Masonic Hotel, Napier, damaged by the 1931 Hawkes Bay earthquake (Arthur B Hurst, 1931)

The DOC office (☎ 834 3111), at 59 Marine Parade, in the Old Courthouse, has information on walkways around Napier, the Cape Kidnappers gannet colony, Urewera National Park, and the Kaweka and Ruahine Forest Parks, both 50km west of Napier.

Napier's telephone area code is ☎ 06.

Art Deco Architecture

The earthquake and fire of 1931 resulted in the destruction of most of Napier's older brick buildings. Two frantic years of reconstruction from 1931 to 1933 meant that much of the city's buildings date from the peak years of the Art Deco architectural style. Dr Neil Cossons, past president of the British Museums Association, said:

Napier represents the most complete and significant group of Art Deco buildings in the world, and is comparable with Bath as an example of a planned townscape in a cohesive style. Napier is without doubt unique.

The Napier Art Deco Trust promotes and protects the city's architectural heritage. Its excellent guided Art Deco walks cost $10 for adults and leave from the Desco Centre (☎ 835 0022), 163 Tennyson St, at 2 pm on Wednesday, Saturday and Sunday (daily in the summer months). The walk takes 1½ hours, and is preceded by a half-hour introductory talk (and illustrative slide presentation) and ends with a video.

The shop in the Desco Centre sells books, postcards and souvenirs. A one-hour walk starts at the visitor information centre at 10 am daily during summer and finishes at the Desco Centre (where a video is shown). It costs $7.

There are also quake walks every Friday in January and February at 9.30 am. They start at the visitor information centre and explore the area along Marine Parade. The cost is $15, including morning tea at the Hawke's Bay Club.

Walk leaflets ($2; in German also) are available from the visitor information centre, Desco Centre or the museum.

There's also an Art Deco Scenic Drive map to the Art Deco and Spanish Mission-style architecture around Napier and Hastings ($2.50). The *Marewa Meander* ($1.50) leads you through a suburb transformed after the quake.

As you walk around town, look on the buildings for Art Deco motifs such as zigzags, lightning flashes, geometric shapes and rising suns. Soft pastel colours are another Art Deco giveaway, employed by restorers, though many of Napier's buildings were originally monochrome plaster.

Emerson St has some excellent examples of Art Deco, though many of the shopfronts have been modernised and you'll have to look up to the second storeys to see the fine Art Deco detail. Good examples on Emerson St are the **Provincial Hotel**, **Charlie's Art Deco Restaurant**, the **Esprit buildings**, the **Criterion Hotel (Criterion Art Deco Backpackers)** and the **ASB Bank**. On Dalton St the **Hotel Central** is a superb example of the style. Round the corner on Dickens St, look for the extravagant Moorish and Spanish Mission-style building which used to be the **Gaiety de Luxe Cinema**. On the corner of Dickens and Dalton Sts is the **State Cinema** (now a shopping complex).

Tennyson St has fine, preserved buildings. The restored **Municipal Theatre** is a must with its neon light fittings and wall decorations. The **Daily Telegraph building** is one of the finest examples of Art Deco in Napier and the **Desco Centre** facing Clive Square is also impressive, despite some modifications. At the intersection of Tennyson and Hastings Sts are more fine buildings, particularly the block of **Hastings St** from Tennyson to Browning Sts. On Marine Parade the **Soundshell** is Art Deco, as is the paving of the plaza. From here you can admire the Art Deco **clock tower** (neon-lit at night) of the A&B building and also the **Masonic Hotel**, now the Masonic Establishment.

In the third week of February, Napier holds an Art Deco weekend, when there are dinners, balls and much fancy dress.

Marine Parade

Lined with Norfolk pines and some fine old wooden buildings that survived the quake, Marine Parade is one of NZ's premier seaside

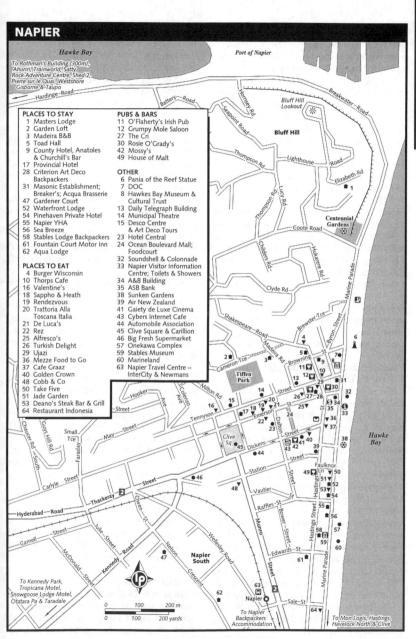

NAPIER

PLACES TO STAY
1 Masters Lodge
2 Garden Loft
3 Madeira B&B
5 Toad Hall
9 County Hotel, Anatoles & Churchill's Bar
17 Provincial Hotel
28 Criterion Art Deco Backpackers
31 Masonic Establishment; Breaker's; Acqua Brasserie
47 Gardener Court
52 Waterfront Lodge
54 Pinehaven Private Hotel
55 Napier YHA
56 Sea Breeze
58 Stables Lodge Backpackers
61 Fountain Court Motor Inn
62 Aqua Lodge

PLACES TO EAT
4 Burger Wisconsin
10 Thorps Cafe
16 Valentine's
18 Sappho & Heath
19 Rendezvous
20 Trattoria Alla Toscana Italia
21 De Luca's
22 Rez
25 Alfresco's
26 Turkish Delight
29 Ujazi
36 Mezze Food to Go
37 Cafe Graaz
40 Golden Crown
48 Cobb & Co
50 Take Five
51 Jade Garden
53 Deano's Steak Bar & Grill
64 Restaurant Indonesia

PUBS & BARS
11 O'Flaherty's Irish Pub
12 Grumpy Mole Saloon
27 The Cri
30 Rosie O'Grady's
42 Mossy's
49 House of Malt

OTHER
6 Pania of the Reef Statue
7 DOC
8 Hawkes Bay Museum & Cultural Trust
13 Daily Telegraph Building
14 Municipal Theatre
15 Desco Centre & Art Deco Tours
23 Hotel Central
24 Ocean Boulevard Mall; Foodcourt
32 Soundshell & Colonnade
33 Napier Visitor Information Centre; Toilets & Showers
34 A&B Building
35 ASB Bank
38 Sunken Gardens
39 Air New Zealand
41 Gaiety de Luxe Cinema
43 Cybers Internet Cafe
44 Automobile Association
45 Clive Square & Carillion
46 Big Fresh Supermarket
57 Onekawa Complex
59 Stables Museum
60 Marineland
63 Napier Travel Centre – InterCity & Newmans

Hawke Bay

Port of Napier

To Rothman's Building (300m), Ahuriri, Trainworld, Satty, Rock Adventure Centre, Shed 2, Pierre sur, le Quai, Westshore Gisborne & Taupo

Hardinge Road

Battery Road

Seapoint Road

Hornsey Rd

Breakwater Road

Bluff Hill Lookout

Bluff Hill

Thompson Rd

Lighthouse Road

Elizabeth Rd

Thompson Rd

Lucy Rd

Centennial Gardens

Coote Road

Childers Rd

Huiarere Rd

Marine Parade

Clyde Rd

Brewster Tce

Byron Street

Shakespeare Road

Madeira Rd

Browning

Cameron Tce

Cameron Tce

Tiffen Park

Milton Rd

Street

Colenso Ave

Hooker Ave

Emerson

Dalton Street

Tennyson

Small Tce

May Street

Faraday

Clive Sq

Dickens

Hawke Bay

Chaucer Rd

Guys Hill Rd South

Carlyle Street

Street

Thackeray Street

Owen St

Station

Faulknor Ln

Hastings Street

Vautier

Raffles St

Bower Street

Munro Street

Hyderabad Road

Julie Street

Kennedy Road

Wellesley Road

Edwards St

Garnell Street

McDonald Street

Napier South

Napier Crescent

Nelson Crescent

Sale St

Napier

To Kennedy Park, Tropicana Motel, Snowgoose Lodge Motel, Otatara Pa & Taradale

To Napier Backpackers Accommodation

To Mon Logis, Hastings, Havelock North & Clive

0   100   200 m
0   100   200 yards

boulevards. It has retained its air of an old-fashioned English seaside resort complete with pebble beach, but the strong riptide makes for hazardous swimming.

Marine Parade has parks, sunken and scented gardens, and amusements including minigolf, swimming pools and a roller-blading rink. The statue of **Pania of the Reef**, a sort of Maori equivalent of Copenhagen's Little Mermaid, is at the parade's northern end.

Marineland has performing seals and dolphins; displays take place at 10.30 am and 2 pm, with an extra 4 pm show in summer ($9, children $4).

Not far away on the parade, the **Hawkes Bay Aquarium** has sharks, crocodiles, piranha, turtles and other animals including NZ's unique tuatara. It's open from 9 am to 5 pm daily and feeding time is 3.15 pm ($7, children $3.50).

The **Stables Museum** at 321 Marine Parade covers the effects of the 1931 quake and is open from 10 am to 4.30 pm daily. Entry to the museum (including the quake simulation) costs $4.50; if you also wish to visit the waxworks it's $6 (children $2.50).

Hawkes Bay Museum & Cultural Trust

Also on Marine Parade is a well-run art gallery and museum. Quality artefacts of the East Coast's Ngati Kahungunu tribe are displayed, as well as European antiques and Art Deco items; there's also a dry but informative audiovisual of the 1931 earthquake.

There are exhibitions on Maori art and culture, colonial history and dinosaurs. The latter display records the struggle of an amateur palaeontologist, Jan Wiffen, who proved university-trained sceptics wrong and found several prehistoric species when they said there were none to be found. There's also a fascinating section on earthquakes including an audiovisual in which Napier quake survivors tell their stories. The sound effects as the quake and subsequent fires rip through the town are terrific.

The museum is open from 10 am to 4.30 pm daily ($4, children free). Its shop has good-quality souvenirs.

Bluff Hill Lookout

There's an excellent view over all of Hawkes Bay from Bluff Hill, 102m above the Port of Napier. It's a sheer cliff-face down to the port, however, and rather a circuitous route to the top. It's open daily from 7 am until one hour after sunset.

Activities

There are many water activities, including fishing, windsurfing, kayaking, canoeing, parasailing, jet-boating, water-skiing and tandem skydiving – ask at the information centre.

Although the beach along Marine Parade is too dangerous for swimming, there's great swimming and surfing on the beach up past the port. The pool on Marine Parade is closed in winter. The redeveloped Onekawa Complex has waterslides and other attractions.

At the Salty Rock Adventure Centre (☎ 834 3500) at Ahuriri there is a **climbing wall** which is open from noon to 9 pm weekdays and 10 am to 6 pm on weekends. It costs $13/9 for adults/children (price includes a harness). The centre, which is next to Shed 2 West Quay, also organises caving and kayaking trips.

Also in Ahuriri, on the corner of Bridge and Waghorne Sts, is **Trainworld**, a model railway with up to 37 trains running around 800m of track, past model villages, across bridges and through tunnels ($6, children $3).

More activities can be found at Riverland Outback Adventures (☎ 834 9756), 50km north of Napier on SH5, where there's horse trekking, white-water rafting and backpacker accommodation.

Hawkes Bay Jet Tours (☎ 874 9703) organises trips on the scenic Ngaruroro River, which range from 30 minutes to one day.

Hawkes Bay Adventure Kayaking (☎ 875 0341) does trips in the inner harbour and out to Cape Kidnappers.

Places to Stay

Camping & Cabins Napier has a number of camping grounds, but none are conveniently central. Closest to the centre is *Kennedy Park* (☎ 843 9126), on Storkey Rd, off

Kennedy Rd in Marewa, and 2.5km from the central post shop. Tent and powered sites cost $10 per person, cabins are from $40, tourist flats from $62 and motels from $60.

The *Westshore Holiday Camp* (☎ 835 9456, 1 Main Rd), near Westshore Beach, 6km north of town. Camp sites here are $8 per person, and there are powered sites, cabins and tourist flats ($70 for two).

At Taradale, 9.5km south-west, *Taradale Holiday Park* (☎ 844 2732, 470 Gloucester St) has tent sites for $8 per person, cabins, powered sites, on-site caravans, motel units and a 48-bed lodge.

Backpackers The *Napier YHA* (☎ 835 7039, **@** yhanapr@yha.org.nz, 277 Marine Parade) is a former guesthouse in an excellent location opposite the beach. It charges $16 in a dorm, and $18 per person in a twin or double. There's a courtyard (with barbecue) out the back.

Right in the centre the *Criterion Art Deco Backpackers* (☎ 835 2059, fax 835 2370, 48 Emerson St) is upstairs in what was formerly the Criterion Hotel, a classy Art Deco building. It has a large recreation area; downstairs are a bistro and bar. It charges $14 in the dorms, $16 in four-bed rooms, $34 for twin or double rooms, and $18 to $24 for a single. You can hire bikes for $10 a day. There's also a spa in winter.

The *Stables Lodge Backpackers* (☎ 835 6242, **@** stables@ihug.co.nz, 321 Marine Parade) is behind The Stables Museum complex – you enter from Hastings St after hours. It's a modern hostel with spotless rooms. A dorm is $12 and rooms with four beds $15; doubles and twins are $36.

The *Waterfront Lodge* (☎/fax 835 3429, 217 Marine Parade) offers single/double budget accommodation for $20/50 and backpacker beds for $20 ($17 in dorms). Breakfast is an extra $5.

The *Aqua Lodge* (☎ 835 4523, **@** aquaback@inhb.co.nz, 53 Nelson Crescent) has a poolside barbecue, just the ticket on a balmy evening; dorms are $15, and doubles and twins are $36.

The tiny *Napier Backpackers Accommodation* (☎ 835 8901, 19 McGrath St) donates its profits to charity. A bed in a four-bed room is $10.

Toad Hall (☎ 835 5555, **@** toad@xtra .co.nz) on the corner of Shakespeare Rd and Browning St is in the former Shakespeare Hotel. A dorm costs $15, a single or twin with shared facilities costs $30, and a double with bathroom costs $50.

The *Glen-View Farm Hostel* (☎ 836 6232, fax 836 6067) is a hill-country sheep and cattle station, where horse riding and walking are popular. You can join in farm activities. It costs $12 in a four-bed room, $15 to $18 per person in a double. The hostel is 31km north of Napier off SH2, 2km along the Arapaoanui Rd towards the sea.

B&Bs & Guesthouses Since it is a summer resort of the old-fashioned variety, Napier has some good guesthouses along Marine Parade. However, as a major thoroughfare, it can be quite noisy.

The *Pinehaven Private Hotel* (☎ 835 5575) at No 259 has singles/doubles for $55/75; it's a strictly nonsmoking place. The front rooms have fine views of the seafront.

At No 415 is the charming French-style *Mon Logis* (☎ 835 2125). Built in 1915 as a private hotel, it has delightful rooms with en suites for $160 for two ($120 a single). There is a room with an adjacent bathroom for $140 for two. Breakfast is included, and there's also the option of fine dining in the evening ($55 per person, including house wine).

Opposite Marineland on the parade, the *Sea Breeze* (☎ 835 8067) is a friendly, homely place with three attractive rooms and a comfortable upstairs sun room with sea views. It costs $55/75 a single/double, breakfast included.

Another good hunting ground for *B&Bs* is on Bluff Hill, just a short walk down to the city (but a hard walk back); see the *Napier Hill Homestays* pamphlet.

A number of fine wooden villas offer accommodation – the visitor information centre has listings. They include *Madeira B&B* (☎ 835 5185, 6 Madeira Rd), at the end of a very steep street. It's a lovely, spacious house with great views over the bay.

Singles/doubles cost $50/75. Nearby, the *Garden Loft (☎ 835 1527, 29 Cameron Rd)* is a fine old villa, with a pleasant guest bedroom and en suite upstairs in a building behind the main house. It costs $50/75 (including breakfast with the family).

The *Masters Lodge (☎ 834 1946, 10 Elizabeth Rd)* is the most upmarket place in Napier; it is the former home of Gerhard Husheer, the founder of the National Tobacco Co (now Rothmans). Swiss-style meals are served.

Motels & Hotels Napier has plenty of motels, particularly around Westshore, on the Taupo Road.

The *Marineland Motel (☎ 835 2147, 20 Meeanee Quay)* has 23 units, many with spas, including two-bedroom units suitable for families, and executive suites. There's also a heated indoor pool. Prices range from $75 to $150 for two depending on the season.

The *Fountain Court Motor Inn (☎ 835 7387, 209 Hastings St)* is in a quiet street parallel to Marine Parade. There is off-street parking, a swimming pool and spa baths. Prices for two range from $94 to $150.

The *Snowgoose Lodge Motel (☎ 843 6083, 376 Kennedy Rd)* has 18 units, including one- and two-bedroom units and executive suites with spas. It's handy to Marine Parade and the city centre. Prices range from $80 to $150.

The *Tropicana Motel (☎ 843 9153, 335 Kennedy Rd)* is a convenient motel for families and has 14 ground-floor units starting at $72 for two.

The *Gardener Court (☎ 835 5913, 16 Nelson Crescent)* is in a quiet location, five minutes' walk from the city centre. There are eight self-contained, ground-floor units, each with separate bedrooms. It charges $75 for two.

The fine old *Masonic Establishment (☎ 835 8689)* on the corner of Marine Parade and Tennyson St is very central. Single/double rooms with bathroom cost $60/85. Singles without bath are $30.

For something special, the *County Hotel (☎ 835 7800, 12 Browning St)* is a boutique hotel in a newly refurbished and converted building. Rooms offering real luxury start at $193.

Places to Eat

Restaurants & Cafes Napier has an excellent selection of restaurants, cafes and bars, and many places act as all three.

Alfresco's (65 Emerson St), upstairs, has a good range of food and great liqueur coffees.

On lower Emerson St *Sappho & Heath* is the place for good coffee and panini. *De Luca's* nearby is a good place with antipasto and dip platters on Friday evening and antipasto and tapas ($22.50 per person) on Saturday evening. *Rez* opposite is another good cafe with flans, pasta and vegetarian frittata.

Cafe Graaz at Hastings St has really great cakes (fudge espresso, chocolate whisky, Mississippi mud) as well as a good selection of other cafe fare. The *Mezze Food to Go (142 Hastings St)* has pasta sauces, Thai rice and fresh pasta if you want to make something yourself, but there are other tempting things to buy including Thai curry on rice. You can always have cake and coffee here.

Anatoles at the County Hotel on Browning St is a stylish cafe-bar.

Ujazi on Tennyson St has great coffee and a fresh, innovative blackboard menu with lots of choice for vegetarians.

Turkish Delight on Market St has charwama, kebabs and other Turkish fare as well as desserts to satisfy your sweet tooth (such as baklava, halwa, Ottoman ice cream).

Trattoria Alla Toscana Italia on Tennyson St has authentic Italian cuisine and a carefully chosen wine list. It's open from 5.30 pm till late.

If you are hankering for satay or rendang head to *Restaurant Indonesia (409 Marine Parade)*. *Jade Garden* at No 201 offers very reasonably priced Chinese fare (eat in or take out). *Take Five* at No 189 has excellent food (lamb, steaks, seafood) with the added bonus of occasional live jazz.

Deano's Steak Bar & Grill at No 255 has a good range of steaks for reasonable prices.

Acqua Brasserie and *Breakers* at the Masonic Establishment on Marine Parade enjoy a great location; at Breakers you can sit outside and watch the world go by.

The Ahuriri wharf precinct has a number of trendy eateries. *Shed 2* on West Quay and *Pierre sur le Quai (63 West Quay)* are fine dining establishments. *Sri Thai (6 Bridge St)* has various Thai dishes with mains in the $15 to $18 mark.

Fast Food Emerson St has some good sandwich bars, including *Tummy Tempters (204 Emerson St)* for healthy sandwiches and snacks.

There are plenty of Chinese places in Napier. Try the *Golden Crown* on Dickens St; the Wednesday to Friday lunchtime smorgasbord is good value.

Burgers Wisconsin (10 Shakespeare Rd) makes gourmet burgers. *Valentine's,* a family buffet chain in the style of Denny's in the USA, is on Tennyson St.

Entertainment

The Cri on Emerson St is always a good bar for a drink and an inexpensive meal.

Rosie O'Grady's on the Hastings St side of the Masonic Establishment has Guinness on tap and occasional live music.

Mossy's on Dickens St is a local venue for musicians who gather for impromptu jam sessions; it has a good range of food, coffees and beers.

O'Flaherty's Irish Pub on Hastings St is yet another Irish pub that packs them in with bands on weekends.

In the County Hotel there is a smoking bar, *Churchill's,* where you can imitate the great man by sticking a big fat cigar in your mouth.

Serious drinking bars include the *House of Malt* on Hastings St, the *Provincial Hotel* on Emerson St and the *Grumpy Mole Saloon* (with its often grumpy and fisty clientele) on the corner of Hastings and Tennyson Sts.

Getting There & Away

Air Air New Zealand (☎ 835 3288) is on the corner of Hastings and Station Sts. It has direct flights to Auckland and Wellington several times daily, and to Christchurch

daily with connections to other centres. Origin Pacific (☎ 0800-302 302) flies from Napier to Auckland and Wellington, with onward connections.

Bus InterCity and Newmans both operate from the Napier Travel Centre (☎ 834 2720) at the train station in Munro St. InterCity has services to Auckland, Hamilton, Rotorua, Taupo, Tauranga, Gisborne, Palmerston North and Wellington. The travel centre is open from 8.30 am to 5 pm weekdays, from 9 am to 5 pm on weekends.

Newmans routes head north to Taupo, Rotorua and Tauranga, through Palmerston North and Wanganui to New Plymouth, and to Wellington via Palmerston North.

There is a shuttle service from Napier to the motor camp at Lake Waikaremoana and to Mahia Peninsula (Mahia Beach). Minimum numbers apply; the bus leaves from outside the Napier Visitor Information Centre. For shuttle information including times, contact ☎ 835 0865.

Train The train station (☎ 834 2720) is on Munro St. The *Bay Express* train operates daily between Napier and Wellington, with several stops including Palmerston North.

Hitching If you're heading north catch a bus and get off at Westshore, or try thumbing closer in. If you're heading south stick to SH2. The alternative inland route (SH50) is much harder going, with less traffic.

Getting Around

The airport shuttle bus (☎ 870 9050) charges $9 from the airport to Napier city centre, and Napier Taxi Service (☎ 835 7777) charges about the same.

Nimbus (☎ 877 8133) operates the suburban bus services on weekdays, with regular buses between Napier and Hastings via Taradale, plus other local services. There's no service on weekends. All local buses depart from the corner of Dickens and Dalton Sts.

Napier Cycle & Kart Centre (☎ 835 9528) at 104 Carlyle St hires out 21-speed mountain bikes at $25/12 for a full/half-day. Marineland also hires bikes.

HASTINGS
pop 50,200

Hastings, only 20km south of Napier, shared the same fate as Napier in the 1931 earthquake and is also noted for its Art Deco and Spanish Mission-style architecture. The paved Civic Square is particularly attractive, with the Art Deco clock tower as its centrepiece (but watch out for those trains that hurtle through the square!).

Hastings is an agricultural centre. During the apple harvest season from February to April, it is popular with those seeking work (accommodation is tight at this time). There are many nearby wineries.

The Blossom Festival, a celebration of spring, is held in September/October, with parades, arts and crafts and visiting artists.

Information

The Hastings Visitor Information Centre (☎ 873 5526, @ vic@hastingstourism.co.nz) on Russell St is open from 8.30 am to 5 pm on weekdays and 10 am until 3 pm on weekends (the office plans to relocate soon). The AA office is on Heretaunga St West.

Hasting's telephone area code is ☎ 06.

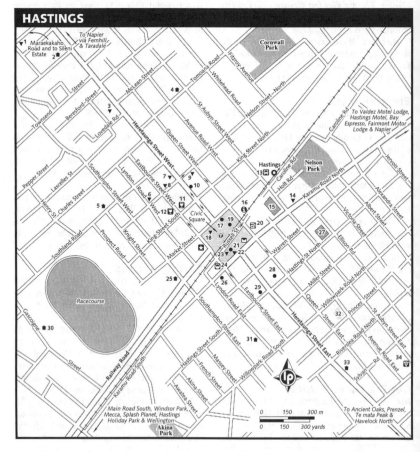

Things to See & Do

The legacy of the 1931 earthquake is an impressive collection of **Art Deco and Spanish Mission-style buildings**. The *Self Drive: Art Deco Tour* pamphlet ($2.50) is available from the visitor information centre to explore Hastings' architecture in depth.

The highlights are undoubtedly the **Westerman's building**, with its impressive bronze and leadlight shopfronts that have largely survived modernisation, and the magnificent **Municipal Theatre** on Hastings St, the most imposing example of Spanish Mission style in the region.

Travelling with children? In Windsor Park, 2km south-east of the town centre on Grove Rd, is **Splash Planet** waterpark. Its facilities include a miniature castle, go-karts, boats you can take out on the lake, a flying fox, train rides, waterslides, ice rink and hot pools. It's open from 9 am till 9 pm daily. Entry costs $15/8 for adults/children; $7.50/3.50 to the hot pools only, or $9.50/6.50 to the ice rink only.

The **Hawkes Bay Exhibition Centre** in the Civic Square on Eastbourne St hosts a wide variety of changing exhibitions. It's open from 10 am to 4.30 pm on weekdays, from 11 am to 4 pm on weekends.

Places to Stay

In Windsor Park, adjacent to Splash Planet, *Hastings Holiday Park* (☎ 878 6692) has camp sites at $10 per person. There are also cabins, tourist flats and motels. The camp is on Windsor Ave, 2.5km from the central post shop.

The *Raceview Motel & Holiday Park* (☎ 878 8837, 307 Gascoigne St), adjacent to the racecourse, has camping at $14 for two.

Backpackers are busy in the harvest season. The *Hastings Backpackers Hostel* (☎ 876 5888, 505 Lyndon Rd East) has dorm beds for $14, and doubles and twins for $28. It is in a suburban area, not far from the city centre. The staff organise cheap trips to the region's attractions, including rubber tubing on the Tuki Tuki River ($5).

AJ's Backpackers Lodge (☎ 878 2302, 405 Southland Rd) is a tidy, well-run place charging $15 for a dorm and $36 for twins.

Travellers Lodge Ltd (☎ 878 7108, fax 878 7228, 606 St Aubyn St West) is yet another suburban house; it's crammed with fruit-pickers during the season but is quiet otherwise. Dorm beds are $15, four-bed shared rooms are $16 per person, twins and doubles are $36 and singles are $24.

Sleeping Giant Backpackers (☎ 878 5393, 109 Davis St) is popular with fruit-pickers. Dorm beds in this roomy villa are $15; doubles are $18 per person.

The *Hastings Motel* (☎ 0800-806 2443, 1108 Karamu Rd) has six studio units, eight one-bedroom units, two one-bedroom luxury suites (one with a double spa), four two-bedroom units and one two-bedroom luxury suite. They are all self-contained

There's Work if you Want it

Many overseas travellers come to this region to work so they can extend their trip to other parts of the country.

If you are a competent fruit-picker you will make about $350 to $400 a week either apple-picking or thinning (both back-breaking work). Top-flight pickers can earn up to $700 but you have to be bloody good. Night packing can earn up to $8.50 an hour.

There is usually work from November (in the summer apple season), followed by peach-picking.

The hostels usually find orchard contracting work if you are staying with them.

Avoid short-term grape-picking, as it doesn't pay that well.

and serviced daily. Prices range from $55 for a single occupancy and $60 for two people to $95 for a family unit. Each extra person is $10.

Mecca (☎ *0800-664 424, 806 Heretaunga St)* is within walking distance of the city centre and Splash Planet. It has nine studio units, two one-bedroom units and plenty of parking. Rates start at $75 for two ($12 for each extra person).

Portmans Motor Lodge (☎ *0800-767 862, 401 Railway Rd)* has units from $100 for two, and *Valdez* (☎ *0800-825 339, 1107 Karamu Rd North)* has units from $98 for two.

The visitor information centre lists over 40 B&Bs, homestays and farmstays.

Places to Eat

The ice cream at *Rush Munro's Ice Cream Garden* on Heretaunga St West is a real treat; it's home-made, loaded with fresh fruit and very rich.

The ubiquitous family favourite *Cobb & Co* is on Heretaunga St. *Friends Bar* next door has a free barbecue at 7 pm on Sunday.

The *Robert Harris Coffee Shop* on Russell St has the usual cafeteria-style pastries and cakes and *Muffs* in the Kmart Plaza is good for a muffin or quick takeaway.

St Vineés Wine Bar & Cafe (108 Market St South) provides both burger-type snacks and more substantial meals.

The popular *Cat & Fiddle Ale House* (502 Karamu Rd) has good pub food but be careful that the dish doesn't run away with the spoon.

Baksters on Nelson St North has economical bar meals, such as hearty serves of nachos.

North-east of town, on Karamu Rd, is *Bay Espresso*, good for breakfasts and lunches.

Ancient Oaks, on the way to Havelock North, makes good salads.

The pleasant *Vidal Winery Brasserie* (913 St Aubyn St), open daily for lunch and dinner, is attached to the Vidal Winery.

Popular *Piccolo's*, a brasserie on the corner of Lyndon Rd and Nelson St, is also a good bet. For a quiet drink and good food, try *La Pizza Forno* on Heretaunga St West.

The *Corn Exchange* (118 Maraekakaho Rd) is open daily for all meals, and has a sunny deck and intimate bar.

For a really special experience take a trip out to the stunning *Sileni Estate* on Maraekakaho Rd, about 10 minutes' drive from the centre of Hastings. There are two restaurants (RD1 – open from 6 pm Wednesday to Saturday – and Mesa – open from 11.30 am Wednesday to Sunday and daily in summer). In addition to the fine food you can sample the fine wines (tastings at $2 per glass) daily between 10 am and 5 pm.

Another option is *Prenzel* (108 Havelock Rd), a fruit distillery a little under 1km from Hastings. You can sample and buy luscious liqueurs, schnapps, brandies and sparkling fruit wines.

Entertainment

Bentan Twisted's on Eastbourne St and *Shooter's* (with regular happy hours) on the corner of Eastbourne and King Sts are popular bars.

Getting There & Away

Nimbus (☎ 877 8133) operates a frequent local bus service from Hastings to Napier ($4.40/2.20 for adults/children one way)

Carving of Ngatoro-i-Rangi, Lake Taupo

Waiotapu Thermal Reserve, Rotorua

Mt Tongariro, Mt Ngauruhoe and Mt Ruapehu, Tongariro World Heritage Region

DAVID WALL

Volcanic White Island off the Bay of Plenty coast

DAVID WALL

Grand Chateau at the foot of Mt Ruapehu

FERGUS BLAKISTON

Mt Ruapahu threatens the main trunk line

DENNIS JOHNSON

Lawn bowls at Rotorua's Government Gardens

DAVID WALL

Early morning at Mt Maunganui

and from Hastings to Havelock North ($2.20/1.10); both run on weekdays.

All InterCity and Newmans buses going to Napier continue to Hastings, stopping at the Hastings Travel Centre (☎ 878 0213) at the train station on Caroline Rd.

HAVELOCK NORTH
pop 8510

Havelock North, 5km east of Hastings, is a great holiday destination well worth a visit for its gardens, wineries, village atmosphere and the towering backdrop of Te Mata Peak.

If you have kids in tow, there's the miniature railway in beautiful Keirunga Gardens; it operates on the first and third Sunday of the month ($1 per ride).

Te Mata Peak

Te Mata Peak is about 11km from Hastings. Dramatically sheer cliffs rise to the Te Mata trig (399m), commanding a spectacular view over the Heretaunga Plains to Hawke Bay. On a clear day you can see all of Hawke Bay up to the Mahia Peninsula, and to Mt Ruapehu in Tongariro National Park. You can also see oyster shells in the rocks at your feet!

Te Mata Peak is part of the 98-hectare Te Mata Park, with several walkways. You can drive right up to the trig at the summit.

The peak is a favourite spot for **hang-gliding**. Gliders get remarkable possibilities from the updraughts breezing in from the Pacific Ocean, about 5km away. Peak Paragliding (☎ 877 8804, 025-223 6999) offers tandem paragliding, weather permitting. Trips lasting around 15 minutes cost $120 and cross-country flights lasting up to four hours cost $200.

Places to Stay & Eat

There are some superb places to stay, all reasonable considering the high standards and backdrop of vineyards.

The **Havelock North Motor Lodge** (☎ 877 8627, 7 Havelock Rd) is within walking distance of the village cafes; doubles are from $98.

It's the quaint cottages and B&Bs that people come here for. **Telegraph Hill Villa**

(☎ 877 5140, 334 Te Mata Rd) is a peaceful hilltop retreat with great views. The villa has two bedrooms each with direct access to the en suite bathroom. There's also a sunny north-facing veranda. Breakfast provisions are supplied (there's a fully equipped kitchen) and a barbecue is also available to guests, as are a tennis court and swimming pool. It costs $150 for two (each additional person is $25).

Providencia (☎ 877 2300), a gracious old building in a picturesque rural setting on Middle Rd, starts at $195 for a double. **Endsleigh Cottages** (☎ 877 7588) on Endsleigh Rd costs $100 for the cottage without a kitchen, $150 and $200 for the others.

The **Greenhouse** (☎ 877 4904) on Te Mata Rd, and the unbeatable historic **Rush Cottage** (☎ 877 7985), are adjacent to Lombardi Estate vineyard and have magnificent views over the vineyards, Napier Hill and the bay (each costs $290).

The **Rose & Shamrock** is a great Irish pub in the centre of the village. **Cafe Diva**, across the road, is good for relaxing over a light lunch and the nearby **Turk's Bar** and **Happy Tav** are popular for a drink.

Peak House on Te Mata Rd is popular for both the spectacular view and the Sunday roast brunch.

AROUND HAWKES BAY
Wineries & Arts and Crafts

The Hawkes Bay area is one of NZ's premier wine-producing regions, with many vineyards to visit. Hawkes Bay is very much the chardonnay capital of NZ, but cabernet sauvignon grapes from the area are also highly regarded and many other varieties are produced.

Vineyards to visit include Brookfields at Meeanee, Mission at Taradale (the oldest in the country), Esk Valley Estate Winery, Vidal of Hawkes Bay, Ngatarawa Wines in Hastings and Church Road Winery in Taradale.

Havelock North has a concentration of wineries, especially out on Te Mata Rd. Included are Te Mata Estate Winery, Bradshaw Estate, Akarangi Wines, Waimarama Estate and Lombardi Wines. A number of the wineries are open for lunch and offer excellent dining.

The Hawkes Bay Vintners produces the handy *Guide to the Hawkes Bay Wineries*. Every year around February, the Harvest Hawkes Bay weekend has activities focusing on food and wine. Around the same time an international concert is held at the Mission winery (Taradale) and a special label is produced for each entertainer.

A fine way of visiting the wineries is by bicycle (you can hire one in Napier), since most of the wineries are within easy cycling distance and it's all flat land.

From Napier, Bay Tours (☎ 843 6953) does four tours (half to full day) starting at $30 for an afternoon tour through four wineries; Vince's Vineyard Tours (☎ 836 6705) takes you through the wineries for $30; and Vicky's Wine Trail Tours (☎ 877 5707) runs several trips including the Red Wine Tour, the Barrel Room Tour and the Earthquake & Art Deco Delight Tour; prices start at around $35. All tour operators will pick up in Napier and Havelock North.

Some local craftspeople open their studios to the public. Get the informative *Hawkes Bay Arts & Crafts Guide* from the visitor information centres.

Cape Kidnappers Gannet Colony

From late October until late April the Cape Kidnappers gannet colony comes to life. Elsewhere these large birds usually make their nests on remote and inaccessible islands but here (and at Muriwai near Auckland) they nest on the mainland; they are unworried by human spectators.

The gannets usually turn up in late July after the last heavy storm of the month. Supposedly, the storm casts driftwood and other handy nest-building material high up the beach so very little effort has to be expended collecting it. In October and November eggs are laid and take about six weeks to hatch. By March the gannets start to migrate and by April only the odd straggler will be left.

You don't need a permit to visit the gannet sanctuary and the best time to see the birds is between early November and late

One hazard of cycle tours through the Hawkes Bay wineries – lots of toilet stops

February (the sanctuary is closed from June to October).

Several tour operators take trips through Cape Kidnappers (so named because the local Maori tried to kidnap a Tahitian servant boy from Cook's expedition here). Gannet Beach Adventures (☎ 875 0898) at Te Awanga, on the coast near Hastings, has rides on a tractor-pulled trailer along the beach for $22 (children $15). From where they drop you, it's a 20-minute walk to the main saddle colony. The guided return trip takes about four hours. Unimog (☎ 835 4446) departs from Napier and goes along the beach in a 4WD open Mercedes Benz unimog for $25 (children half-price). The most exciting way of getting to the cape is with Quad Ventures (☎ 836 6652), which leaves from Sullivan's motor camp at Te Awanga; it is $95/140 for one/two people on a bike and the trip takes from three to four hours.

Cape Kidnappers Walks (☎ 875 0837) offers guided walks over Summerlee Station, a 2000-hectare sheep and cattle run about 2km from Te Awanga. Accommodation in renovated shearers quarters for overnight (self-guided) trips is available. Half-day walks cost $40 per person, and full-day $80; it costs about $50 to overnight (bring a sleeping bag, and food if you want to cook). You can also do 4WD trips out to the gannet colony over Summerlee, or 4WD trips around the station itself (cost for both $38; three hours each). Call ☎ 0800-427 232 for bookings. Pick-up from Napier, Hastings and elsewhere can be arranged.

Alternatively, the 8km walk along the beach from Clifton, just along from Te Awanga, takes about two hours. You must leave no earlier than three hours after high tide and start back no later than 1½ hours after low tide. It's 16km return and there are no refreshment stops, so go prepared! All trips are dependent on the tides. The tide schedule is available from the Napier Visitor Information Centre. No regular buses go to Te Awanga or Clifton from Napier, but Kiwi Shuttle (☎ 835 7802, 025-593 669) goes on demand for $15 per person. There is a rest hut selling refreshments at the colony.

The reserve is administered by DOC, which has a handy leaflet and booklets on the colony. Accommodation is available in Te Awanga at **Sullivan's Motor Camp** (☎ 875 0334), which is also good for information. At Clifton, the **Clifton No 2 Reserve** has camp sites and cabins.

Inland Ranges

The main populated area of Hawkes Bay is concentrated around Napier-Hastings. Regional Hawkes Bay does extend much further, however, both to the south and inland.

The inland region provides some of the best tramping on the North Island – in the remote, untamed Kaweka and Ruahine Ranges. There is an excellent series of DOC pamphlets on the ranges. See *North-east Kaweka, Makahu Saddle, Southern Kaweka, South-east Ruahine, Mid-east Ruahine* and *Western Ruahine*.

An ancient Maori track, now a road, runs inland from the bay, heading from Fernhill near Hastings via Omahu, Okawa, Otamauri, Blowhard Bush and the Gentle Annie Rd to Taihape. It is a three-hour return car journey from Fernhill to the top of the Kaweka Ranges.

Central Hawkes Bay

The two main towns of central Hawkes Bay are Waipukurau (almost always called simply 'Wai-puk') and Waipawa. The Waipukurau information office (☎ 858 6488, ✉ chbinfo@xtra.co.nz) is in Railway Esplanade.

The prestigious Te Aute College, 20km north of Waipukurau, was school to many influential leaders of the Young Maori Party (see History in the Facts about New Zealand chapter) such as James Carroll, Apirana Ngata, Maui Pomare and Peter Buck.

Many visit this region to see the **longest place name in the world** (yes, longer than Llanfairpwllgwyngllgogerychwyrndrobwl-lllantysiliogogogoch in Wales – see the boxed text on the following page). From Waipukurau on SH2 you head towards Porangahau on the coast. Follow this road for 40km to the Mangaorapa junction and then follow the 'Historic Sign' indicators.

The Longest Place Name in the World

Hold your breath and then spit this name out as fast as you can:
Taumatawhakatangihangakoauauotamateaturipukakapikimaungahoronukupokaiwhenuaktanatahu.

The name is a shortened form of 'The brow of a hill where Tamatea, the man with the big knees, who slid, climbed, and swallowed mountains, known as Land Eater, played his flute to his lover'.

Tamatea Pokaiwhenua (Land Eater) was a chief so famous for his long travels across the North Island that it was said he ate *(pokai)* up the land *(whenua)* as he walked. There are many other place names in the region also attributed to this ancient explorer.

The much-photographed AA road sign is a few kilometres up the hill from Mangaorapa station; the actual hill is on private property.

After contemplating the name's astronomic length you can stop off at the idyllic *Lochlea Farmstay (☎ 855 4816, 0800-186 506, ✉ lochlea.farm@xtra.co.nz, 344 Lake Rd, Wanstead)*. Twins and doubles on this laid-back and friendly farm are from $15 to $18 per person.

The *Porangahau Lodge (☎ 855 5386)* is good value at $50 to $75 per double; it does 4WD trips to the longest place name.

In Waipawa stop for tea at the *Abbotslee Tearooms* and in Waipuk try the *Stray Cat Cafe* and *Dak's Bar & Grill*.

Wellington Region

☎ 04 and 06 ● pop 415,700

Wellington, the capital of New Zealand, is on a beautiful harbour at the southern tip of the North Island. Approaching it from the north, you will pass through one of two regions – either the Kapiti Coast on the west side (SH1) or the Wairarapa on the east side (SH2) – before entering the heavily populated Hutt Valley or the city itself. Both these areas have interesting activities and places to visit.

Wellington

☎ 04 ● pop 205,500

Wellington takes part in friendly rivalry with larger Auckland. The city is hemmed in by its magnificent harbour, with wooden Victorian buildings on the steep hills. It prides itself as a centre for culture and the arts, has a plethora of restaurants, cafes, nightlife and activities, and is home to the country's government and national treasures. Apart from its importance as the capital, it's a major travel crossroads between the North and South Islands.

The city's fine harbour was formed by the flooding of a huge valley. An earthquake pushed up Miramar Peninsula in 1460.

The city runs up the hills on one side of the harbour, and so cramped is it for space that many of its workers live in two narrow valleys leading north between the steep, rugged hills – one is the Hutt Valley and the other follows SH1 through Tawa and Porirua. The city's nickname is 'Windy Wellington'.

History

Maori legend has it that the explorer Kupe was the first person to discover Wellington Harbour. The original Maori name was Te Whanga-Nui-a-Tara, Tara being the son of a Maori chief named Whatonga who had settled on the Hawkes Bay coast. Whatonga sent Tara and his half-brother to explore the southern part of the North Island. When

HIGHLIGHTS

- Enjoying Wellington Harbour, whether you are taking in the view from Mt Victoria, cruising across to Eastbourne, or walking (or rollerblading) along the city foreshore
- Taking the exhilarating cable-car ride to the Botanic Gardens and then walking on trails through stands of native trees
- Seeing the Maori collection in Te Papa
- Discovering mystical Kapiti Island and the scenic Kapiti Coast
- Visiting the vineyards of the Wairarapa and the region's rugged coastline
- Exploring the Tararua Ranges

Wellington Region p442
Wellington pp424-5
Central Wellington p430

they returned over a year later, their reports were so favourable that Whatonga's followers moved to the harbour, founding the Ngati Tara tribe.

The first European settlers arrived in the New Zealand Company's ship *Aurora* on 22 January 1840, not long after Colonel William Wakefield arrived to buy land from the Maori. The idea was to build two cities: one would be a commercial centre by the harbour (Port Nicholson) and the other, further north, would be the agricultural hub.

421

The settlers were to be allotted two blocks: a town section of an acre (less than half a hectare) and a backcountry block worth £1 an acre.

However, the Maori denied they had sold the land at Port Nicholson, or Poneke, as they called it. Founded on hasty and illegal buying by the New Zealand Company, land rights struggles followed and were to plague the country for the next 30 years, and still affect it today.

Wellington began as a settlement with very little flat land. Originally the waterfront was along Lambton Quay, but reclamation of parts of the harbour began in 1852 and has continued ever since. In 1855 an earthquake razed part of Hutt Rd and the area extending from Te Aro flat to the Basin Reserve, which initiated the first major reclamation.

In 1865 the seat of government was moved from Auckland to Wellington.

Orientation

Lambton Quay, the main business street, wriggles along almost parallel to the seafront (which it once was). The heart of the city, known as the 'Miracle Mile', stretches from the train station, at the northern end of Lambton Quay, to Cambridge and Kent Terraces. Thorndon, immediately north of the centre, is the historic area and the embassy district.

The waterfront along Jervois Quay, Cable St and Oriental Parade is an increasingly revitalised area and now houses the huge, futuristic Te Papa (Museum of New Zealand). Renovated Queens Wharf has ferries, restaurants and a few diversions, there's a new stadium on Aotea Quay (some say badly located), and Oriental Parade, past the Freyberg swimming pool, is Wellington's premier seafront boulevard and a pleasant place for a stroll.

Mt Victoria at the eastern edge of the city has hostels and cheap places to stay. Willis St, Cuba Mall, Manners Mall, Courtenay Place and Queens Wharf, as well as Lambton Quay, are important streets for shopping and restaurants.

Maps The Map Shop, near the corner of Vivian and Victoria Sts, carries Land Information NZ's complete line of maps, plus aerial photographs. It's open from 8.30 am to 5 pm on weekdays.

HILARY ERICKSEN

A quirky mural on the waterfront at Oriental Bay

Information

Tourist Offices The Wellington Visitor Information Centre (☎ 802 4860, ✆ info@ wellingtonnz.com), Web site: www .wellingtonnz.com, is on Civic Square at 101 Wakefield St. It's open from 8.30 am to 5.30 pm on weekdays and from 9.30 am to 5.30 pm on weekends (in winter until 4.30 pm). Its friendly staff book almost everything, and provide the *Wellington Visitor's Guide* and several other pamphlets.

Two excellent pamphlets for a good historical overview are *Te Ara o nga Tupuna: The Path of our Ancestors* and *Old Shoreline Wellington City*.

The information centre (☎ 385 5123) at the airport is open until around 6 or 7 pm daily, and until 11.30 pm on Saturday.

The Department of Conservation (DOC) Visitor Centre (☎ 472 7356), Web site: www.doc.govt.nz, is in The Government Buildings facing Lambton Quay opposite the Cenotaph. It has information on walks, parks, outdoor activities, camping in the region and visitor permits for Kapiti Island. The office is open from 9 am to 4.30 pm on weekdays, from 10 am to 3 pm on weekends.

The Automobile Association (AA; ☎ 470 9999), on the 1st floor, 342 Lambton Quay, has the usual maps and services as well as NZ travel books. Members receive a 10% discount.

Free tourist publications with events listings include *Wellington's What's On,* the weekly *Capital Times* and *City Voice*.

The *Dominion* and the *Evening Post* are the local daily newspapers; the entertainment sections are in Saturday's editions.

Embassies & Consulates Wellington, as the national capital, houses the consulates and embassies of many countries (see the Facts for the Visitor chapter).

Money Banks around town exchange foreign currency and are open from 9 am to 4.30 pm on weekdays. Thomas Cook (☎ 472 2848) has a foreign exchange office at 358 Lambton Quay which is open from 9 am to 5.30 pm on weekdays, 10.30 am to 2 pm on Saturday.

The American Express office (473 7766) in the Sun Alliance Centre on Lambton Quay at Grey St, near the lower cable-car terminal, is open from 9 am to 5 pm on weekdays.

Post & Communications The main post shop is in Waterloo Quay near Downtown Wellington Backpackers. Poste restante mail can be collected between 8.30 am and 5 pm on weekdays. Other post shops are spread around the centre.

Most backpackers places have Internet facilities. The NetArena Cybercafe (☎ 384 1185, ✆ cybercafe@netarena.co.nz) is at 115 Cuba St and Moving Planet (☎ 801 8119) is at 10 Majoribanks St.

Travel Agencies The YHA Travel Centre (☎ 801 7238), Web site: www.yha.org.nz, is on the corner of Courtenay Place and Taranaki St.

STA, specialising in air fares, has offices at 130 Cuba St (☎ 385 0561), 37 Willis St (☎ 472 8510) and in the Student Union building at Victoria University (☎ 499 1017).

Bookshops Dymocks, at 366 Lambton Quay opposite the BNZ Centre, is one of Wellington's largest bookshops, with armchairs for browsers.

Others with a good range of titles include Whitcoulls at 312 Lambton Quay and 91 Cuba St, and London Bookshops at 310 Lambton Quay and 89 Cuba Mall. Unity Books, 119 Willis St on the corner of Manners Mall, is something of a Wellington institution with an excellent fiction selection.

Megazines, on the ground floor of the Market at James Smith Corner, which is on the corner of Cuba and Manners Sts, has the most extensive range of magazines.

Bellamy's, 106 Cuba St, is a good second-hand bookshop, and there are more bookshops further south on Cuba St.

Cultural Centres The German cultural centre, the Goethe Institut (☎ 385 6924), is at 150 Cuba St on the corner of Garrett St. It's open from 9 am to 5 pm Monday to Thursday and 9 am to 3 pm on Friday.

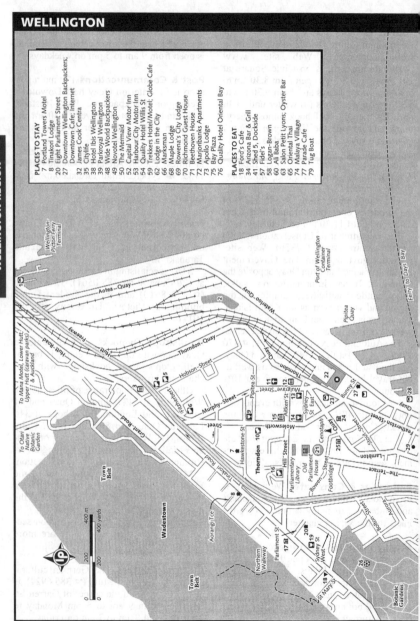

WELLINGTON

PLACES TO STAY
- 7 Portland Towers Motel
- 8 Tinakori Lodge
- 20 Eight Parliament Street
- Downtown Wellington Backpackers;
  Downtown Cafe, Internet
- 32 James Cook Centra
- 35 Citylife
- 38 Hotel Ibis Wellington
- 39 Parkroyal Wellington
- 48 Wide World Backpackers
- 49 Novotel Wellington
- 50 The Mermaid
- 52 Capital View Motor Inn
- 53 Harbour City Motor Inn
- 54 Quality Hotel Willis St
- 59 Trekkers Hotel/Motel; Globe Cafe
- 62 Lodge in the City
- 66 Marksman
- 68 Maple Lodge
- 69 Rowena's City Lodge
- 70 Richmond Guest House
- 71 Beethoven House
- 72 Marjoribanks Apartments
- 73 Apollo Lodge
- 75 Bay Plaza
- 76 Quality Hotel Oriental Bay

PLACES TO EAT
- 18 Ford's Cafe
- 34 Arizona Bar & Grill
- 41 Shed 5, Dockside
- 57 Fidel's
- 58 Logan-Brown
- 60 Ali Baba
- 63 Salon Petit Lyons; Oyster Bar
- 65 Oriental Thai
- 74 Malaya Village
- 77 Parade Cafe
- 79 Tug Boat

WELLINGTON

WELLINGTON REGION

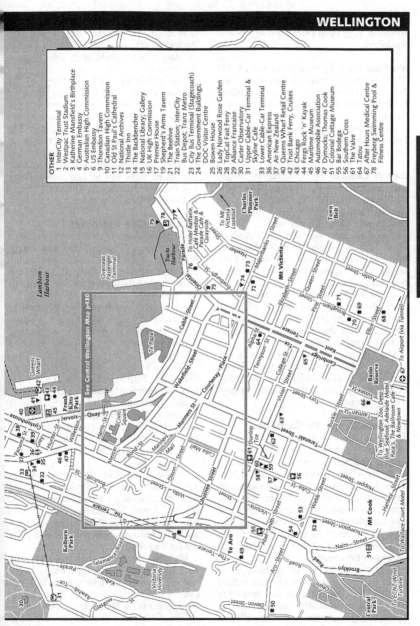

The Alliance Francaise (☎ 472 1272), 24 Johnston St, is open from 9 am to 5 pm on weekdays.

Medical The City Medical Centre (☎ 471 2161) is on the corner of Featherston and Johnston Sts, and the After Hours Medical Centre (☎ 384 4944) is at 17 Adelaide Rd, Newtown.

AIDS services include the NZ Aids Foundation Awhina Centre (☎ 801 6640), at Level 2, 45 Tory St.

Gay & Lesbian For information on gay and lesbian events, phone Boyz Nite (☎ 0800-4 BADBOYZ) or listen to 783AM Access Radio from 10 am for lesbian news and from 11.15 am for gay news.

Out! Bookshop, and the Club Wakefield, are at 15 Tory St, and Unity Bookshop on Willis St has a good gay and lesbian book section. The *Express* ($2.50) is available from these places.

Devotion is a week of gay and lesbian pride celebrations in November, which re-emerges in February with the Sprung at Devotion bash that welcomes all comers with the right attitude.

See Gay & Lesbian Travellers in the Facts for the Visitor chapter for NZ-wide organisations and useful Web sites. See Entertainment later in this chapter for gay-friendly venues.

The Beehive & Parliament

Three buildings on Bowen St form NZ's parliamentary complex. By far the most distinctive and well known is the modernist executive office building known as the Beehive – because that is just what it looks like. Designed by British architect Sir Basil Spence, its construction began in 1969 and was completed in 1980. Controversy surrounded its construction, and, while it's not great architecture, it is the architectural symbol of the country.

Next door is Old Parliament House, completed in 1922. Expensive plans to extend the Old Parliament House and move the Beehive were recently quashed after a public outcry in a country that doesn't like

spending money on its relatively small number of politicians. Beside the Old Parliament House, the neogothic Parliamentary Library building is the oldest in the complex.

Free public tours (☎ 471 9999) of the Beehive and the House of Representatives are offered most days, from 9 am to 4 pm on the hour weekdays, 10 am to 4 pm on Saturday and 1 to 4 pm on Sunday. The public can also attend sessions of the House of Representatives and are free to come and go from the public gallery. Parliament usually meets three out of four weeks every month from Tuesday to Thursday; phone ☎ 471 9999 for sitting times.

Old Wooden Buildings

Opposite the Beehive, at the northern end of Lambton Quay, stands **The Government Buildings**, one of the largest all-wooden buildings in the world – a wooden temple in Japan (the Daibutsu-den in Nara) beats it for 'the biggest' honours. With its block corners and slab wooden planking, you have to look twice to realise that it is not made of stone. The building has been restored and houses various offices, including the DOC Visitor Centre.

Wood was used widely in the construction of buildings in Wellington's early days. Fine old **wooden houses** can still be seen, especially along Tinakori Rd in the historic Thorndon area, Wellington's first suburb, just uphill from the parliament buildings. Pick up a copy of the *Thorndon Heritage Trail* brochure ($1) from the visitor information centre.

Dating from 1843, **Premier House** on Tinakori Rd is the official prime ministerial residence. An early Labour prime minister, Michael Joseph Savage, spurned such luxury, however, and the house was used for a variety of purposes between 1935 and 1990 until it was restored.

Probably the best examples of genuine 19th-century architecture are on Ascot St, just off Tinakori Rd and Sydney St West. One of the oldest pubs in NZ still on its original site is the **Thistle Inn** (1840), on the corner of Mulgrave St and Sydney St East.

National Library

Opposite the Beehive on the corner of Molesworth and Aitken Sts, the National Library (Te Puna Matauranga o Aotearoa; ☎ 474 3000) houses by far the most comprehensive book collection in NZ. Also at the National Library is the Alexander Turnbull Library, an early colonial collection with many historical photographs, often used for genealogical and other research on NZ.

The library hosts free public lectures and cultural events and the National Library Gallery has different exhibits. The library is open from 9 am to 5 pm on weekdays, 9 am to 4.30 pm on Saturday and 1 to 4.30 pm on Sunday.

National Archives

A block away, at 10 Mulgrave St at the junction of Aitken St, the National Archives (Te Whare Tohu Tuhituhinga o Aotearoa; ☎ 495 6226) displays several interesting national treasures, including the original Treaty of Waitangi and other historical documents.

The archives are open from 9 am to 5 pm on weekdays, 9 am to 1 pm on Saturday.

The Film Centre

This museum (Te Anakura Whitiahua; ☎ 384 7647), Cable St, features NZ film, television and video from the 1890s to the present. It's open from noon daily.

Old St Paul's Cathedral

Just a few doors up the hill on Mulgrave St is Old St Paul's Cathedral. It was built from 1863 to 1864 and looks quaint from the outside, but the interior is a good example of early English Gothic design in timber.

It's open from 10 am to 5 pm Monday to Saturday (admission by donation).

Museums

Te Papa (Museum of New Zealand)

The national museum (☎ 381 7000), Web site: www.tepapa.govt.nz, is in a striking building that dominates the waterfront on Cable St. The nation's pride and joy, affectionately called 'Our Place', it has an extensive Maori collection and its own *marae*. Natural history, the environment, European

Nikau palms in metal outside Wellington Central Library

settlement, among other things New Zealand, are presented in impressive gallery spaces with a touch of interactive high-tech (eg, a virtual bungy jump and TimeWarp).

It has excellent Maori and Pacific Islands collections, although the rest of the world gets a look-in with changing exhibits of international art.

Shops, restaurants and an auditorium round off this impressive complex. It's open from 10 am to 6 pm daily, until 9 pm on Thursday (free, except for special shows). It's sometimes necessary to queue for particular exhibits.

Maritime Museum On the corner of Jervois Quay and the renovated Queens Wharf, this museum has many maritime relics associated with the city, a fine three-dimensional model of the harbour and a collection of ship models.

A corner is devoted to the inter-island ferry *Wahine,* which sank in Wellington Harbour in

1968; this disaster has made a strong impression on the national psyche. Photo and video exhibits document the tragedy.

The museum is open from 9.30 am to 4 pm on weekdays and from 1 to 4.30 pm on weekends ($2, children $0.50). It was closed at the time of writing, but due to reopen.

Katherine Mansfield's Birthplace This house (Te Puakitanga), 25 Tinakori Rd, is where the famous writer was born in 1888. The excellent video *A Portrait of Katherine Mansfield* screens here and the 'Sense of Living' exhibition displays photographs of the period alongside excerpts from her writing. A doll's house has been constructed from details in the short story of the same name.

The house is open from 10 am to 4 pm daily ($5, children $2). The No 14 Wilton bus stops nearby on Park St.

Other Museums The **Colonial Cottage Museum**, 68 Nairn St, is one of the oldest colonial cottages in Wellington. It was built in 1858 by carpenter William Wallis and lived in by his family until 1977. It's open from 12 am to 4 pm on weekdays and 1 to 4.30 pm on weekends ($3, children $1).

Those familiar with the expressions 'silly mid-on', 'leg spin' and 'maiden over' will gravitate to the **National Cricket Museum** at the Basin Reserve. Aficionados will be bowled over by the 1743 Addington bat (one of the oldest) and Australian cricketer Dennis Lillee's controversial aluminium bat banned in 1979. It's open from 10.30 am to 3.30 pm daily from October to April, or on weekends from May to September ($3, children $1 – free if accompanied by an adult).

Capital E
This children's educational and entertainment centre on Civic Square has rotating exhibits, usually hands-on, a children's theatre company and a television studio.

It's great for kids and the huge **Hocus Pocus Toys shop** alone is worth a visit; it's open from 10 am to 5 pm daily (free, except for special events).

City Gallery Wellington
On Civic Square, in the Old Library Building, the City Gallery is open from 10 am to 5 pm daily and features various changing exhibits (donation).

Katherine Mansfield

Katherine Mansfield is NZ's most distinguished author, known throughout the world for her short stories and often compared to Chekhov and Maupassant.

Born Katherine Mansfield Beauchamp in 1888, she left Wellington when she was 19 for Europe, where she spent the rest of her short adult life. She mixed with Europe's most famous writers, such as DH Lawrence, TS Eliot and Virginia Woolf, and married the literary critic and author John Middleton Murry in 1918. In 1923, aged 34, she died of tuberculosis at Fontainebleau in France. It was not until 1945 that her five books of short stories (*In a German Pension*, *Bliss*, *The Garden-Party*, *The Dove's Nest* and *Something Childish*) were combined into a single volume, *Collected Stories of Katherine Mansfield*.

She spent five years of her childhood at 25 Tinakori Rd in Wellington; it is mentioned in her stories *The Aloe* (which in its final form became *Prelude*) and *A Birthday* (a fictionalised account of her own birth).

Katherine Mansfield, 1888–1923

ALEXANDER TURNBULL LIBRARY, WELLINGTON NZ

The information centre has details on other Wellington galleries.

Botanic Gardens

The tranquil Botanic Gardens are easily visited in conjunction with a cable-car ride. They contain 26 hectares of native bush and a wide variety of gardens, including the **Lady Norwood Rose Garden** with over 100 kinds of roses. Other gardens include succulents, ferns, threatened species, Australian plants, rhododendrons, fuchsias, camellias, begonias and herbs.

The large gardens have an information centre with a World Wide Fund for Nature shop and a cafe. They are open from 9 am to 4 pm on weekdays, and on weekends also from September to April.

The main entrance to the **Otari Native Botanic Garden** is at the junction of Wilton Rd and Gloucester St; get there on the No 14 bus (Wilton). Devoted to the cultivation and preservation of indigenous NZ plants, it has a number of walks through densely forested areas and flax clearings. There's also a fernery and information centre (☎ 475 3245).

Wellington Zoo

This zoo has a wide variety of native and non-native wildlife and has outdoor lion and chimpanzee parks, plus a nocturnal kiwi house which also houses tuatara and giant weta. The kiwi are on view from 10 am to 4 pm daily but the best time to see them is from 10 am to noon.

The zoo is 4km from the city centre, at the end of the Newtown Park bus route No 10. It is open from 9.30 am to 5 pm daily ($8, children $4).

Cable Car

A Wellington icon and 'must-do' attraction is the cable car that runs from an arcade off Lambton Quay up to Kelburn, overlooking the city. The cable-car service began in 1902, carried nearly half a million passengers in its first year and by 1912 was transporting a million passengers a year. In the late 1970s the track was reconstructed and the two old wooden cable cars were replaced with shiny red Swiss-made ones.

A ride to the top costs $1.50 (children $0.70) or $2.50 return ($1.40). It operates at 10-minute intervals from 7 am to 10 pm on weekdays, 9 am to 10 pm weekends and holidays.

The Skyline Cafe (☎ 475 8727), at the top, is open from 10 am to 4 pm daily, and offers great vistas. From here, you can stroll back down through the Botanic Gardens or return to town by a series of steps which interconnect with roads.

The **Carter Observatory** is in the Botanic Gardens near the top cable-car terminal. It has displays and videos about astronomy and is open from noon to 4.15 pm daily ($7/3.50 for adults/children), and from 6.30 to 10 pm on Tuesday, Thursday and Saturday, when you can view the night sky through the telescope (weather permitting; $10/5).

Views

The best view of the city, harbour and surrounding region is from the lookout at the top of **Mt Victoria** (196m), east of the city centre. It's a taxing walk but well worth the effort; otherwise take bus No 20 on weekdays from the train station or Courtenay Place and walk or ride back down. To drive, take Oriental Parade along the waterfront and then Carlton Gore St. Alternatively, head up the hill on Majoribanks St and follow the 'Lookout' signs, turning left onto Hawker St.

Other good views are from the top cable-car terminal and from the Northern, Southern and Eastern Walkways.

West of the city, the **ECNZ wind turbine** on Brooklyn Hill also has good views. Go along Victoria St to Brooklyn Rd, turn left into Ohiro Rd, then right into Todman St and follow the signposts. Bus No 7 is the closest public transport, but still leaves you with a stiff 2km walk.

Walking

Wellington has many enjoyable walks in the city and surrounds. The visitor information centre has brochures on the Eastern, Northern and Southern Walkways, Red Rocks Coastal Walk and others.

The easy **Red Rocks Coastal Walk** follows the volcanic coast from Owhiro Bay to

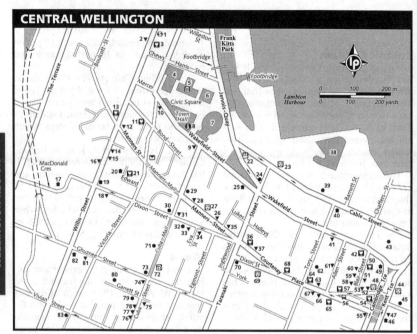

CENTRAL WELLINGTON

Red Rocks and Sinclair Head, where there is a seal colony. Take bus No 1 or 4 to Island Bay, then No 29 to Owhiro Bay Parade (or walk 2.5km along the Esplanade). From the start of Owhiro Bay Parade it is 1km to the quarry gate where the coastal walk starts.

There's a **4WD tour** to see the seals which includes a cross-country climb to the wind turbine. It departs from outside the visitor centre at 10.30 am ($30; book at the visitor centre).

The DOC Visitor Centre and the Wellington Visitor Information Centre are both good sources of information on walks, providing A4 sheets covering each walk (and there are many of them).

Mountain Biking

City biking destinations include Mt Victoria, most of the Southern Walkway, along the ridgetop at Tinakori Hill, in firebreaks around Karori Reservoir and a track to Mt Kau Kau.

Longer rides can be enjoyed in Belmont, East Harbour and Kaitoke Regional Parks; up the Rimutaka Incline to the Wairarapa and along Tunnel Gully; in Queen Elizabeth II Park (Kapiti Coast); and in the Akatarawa Forest between Upper Hutt and Paraparaumu. The visitor centre provides maps.

Water Sports

With all the wind and water, Wellington is a great place for **windsurfing** – choose from sheltered inlets, rough harbours and wave-beaten coastal areas, all within half an hour's drive of the city. Wild Winds Sail & Surf (☎ 384 1010), Chaffers Marina, Oriental Bay, has windsurfing courses for beginners. Windsurfers and boats can be hired at the Days Bay Boatshed (☎ 562 8150), opposite the pier in Eastbourne, over the harbour from Wellington.

For **kayaking** on the bay, Fergs Rock 'n' Kayak (☎ 499 8898, @ fergs.rock.n.kayak @clear.net.nz) at Shed 6, Queens Wharf,

CENTRAL WELLINGTON

PLACES TO STAY
17 Rosemere Backpackers
19 Abel Tasman
20 The Woolshed
25 Plaza International
40 Museum Hotel de Wheels
46 Halswell Lodge
49 Wellington City YHA
82 Richard Pearse

PLACES TO EAT
2 Ye-Jun
9 Felix
10 The Lido
12 Kopi
14 Armadillo's
15 Satay Time
16 Turners
18 Chevy's
26 Java
28 A Taste of France
31 Satay Noodle
33 Angkor
34 La Casa Pasta
35 Great India
37 Espressoholic 2000
41 Satay Kampong
47 Deluxe Cafe; Embassy Theatre
51 Mondo Cucina
52 ate
53 The Opera
55 Calzone
58 Beacon

59 Little India
60 Exchange
61 Cafe India
63 Axolotl Cafe
66 Sahara Cafe
67 Cinta
74 Krazy Lounge
75 Kebabholik
76 Midnight Espresso
77 Cafe Istanbul
78 Khmer Satay Noodle House
81 Flipp Brasserie

PUBS & CLUBS
3 The Malthouse
11 The Loaded Hog
13 Bouquet Garni
21 Edward Street Bars & Clubs –
    Studio 9, Lava Lounge,
    Tupelo
36 Molly Malone's; Dubliner
42 CO2 Champagne Bar
50 One Red Dog
54 CafeParadiso; Blue Room
57 Kitty O'Shea's
64 Wellington Sports Cafe
65 Coyote; The Grand
68 Big Easy

OTHER
1 BNZ Centre
4 Central Library & Continuum
    Theatre

5 City Gallery
6 Capital E
7 Michael Fowler Centre
8 Wellington Visitor
    Information Centre
22 The Film Centre
23 Circa Theatre
24 Wellington Market
27 State Opera House
29 Market at James Smith
    Corner
30 Bojangles
32 Sanctuary
38 Te Papa (Museum of New
    Zealand)
39 Crocodile Bikes
43 New World Supermarket
44 Bats Theatre
45 Moving Planet
48 Downstage Theatre
56 Bus Stop
62 Out! Bookshop;
    Club Wakefield
69 Westpac Trust St James
    Theatre
70 YHA Travel Centre
71 Bellamy's Bookshop
72 NetArena Cybercafe
73 STA
79 Goethe Institut
80 Checkmate
83 The Map Shop

---

rents out kayaks, from $7/25 per hour/day. Guided trips include night trips, usually via Somes Island, for around $40. The 'rock' part of the name refers to the 14m indoor wall for rock climbing.

Good **surfing** breaks include one near the airport and the fine breaks on Palliser Bay, south-east of Wellington.

The Freyberg Pool, 139 Oriental Parade, is the best close to the city centre. It's open from 6.30 am to 9 pm daily, except Friday when it closes at 5.30 pm.

In-line Skating

You can't beat rollerblading along the Wellington waterfront on a sunny day. Cheapskates (☎ 499 0455), Chaffers St Park opposite the New World supermarket, hires out rollerblades on weekends. Fergs Rock 'n' Kayak (see earlier) at Queens Wharf

also rents out rollerblades for $10/15 an hour/night.

Those who are a bit unsure on their feet can rent rickshaw-style bikes from Crocodile Bikes (☎ 380 9128; $50 deposit).

Organised Tours

Bus Wally Hammond (☎ 472 0869) takes a 2½-hour city highlight tour at 10 am and 2 pm for $25 (children $12.50), including hotel pick-up and drop-off. The three-hour Kapiti Coast Tour ($55, children $26) runs daily at 9 am and 1.30 pm. Full-day Wairarapa and Palliser Bay tours ($110, children $48) leave at 9 am.

Indigenous Aotearoa (☎ 560 4630) has a Maori Insight Tour to Waiwhetu (58 Guthrie St), a Maori settlement in the Hutt Valley. These tours explain Maori culture and customs, and demonstrate Maori arts and crafts ($19/9/48 for adults/children/family).

Tours further afield include 4WD safaris with All Track Adventures (☎ 0800-494 335, ✉ alltrack@xtra.co.nz).

Harbour & Fishing Cruises Trips across the harbour to Days Bay are made on the *Trust Bank Ferry* (☎ 499 1273). The ferry catamaran goes to and from Queens Wharf on a regular daily schedule. The one-way fare is $7 (children $3.50). It's a 30-minute trip to Days Bay, where there are beaches, a fine park and a couple of houses that Katherine Mansfield's family kept for summer homes; her story *At the Bay* recalls summer holidays here. At least three ferries per day also call in at Somes Island ($16 return). Somes Island was a quarantine station until 1995 and has only just been opened to the public. Now a reserve managed by DOC, the island has walking trails and beach areas.

Wellington on Water (☎ 025-732 948) has a fast boat which goes almost anywhere in the harbour, including The Heads; ring for prices.

The information centre has a list of fishing and diving charters.

Special Events

Wellington is always celebrating one event or another; various tourist publications and the information centre have current listings. Notable regular events include:

January
NZ Golf Open Paraparaumu
February
Dragon Boat Festival a festival with an international flavour held between Queens and Taranaki St Wharves
February/March
International Festival of the Arts a biennial event involving a month of culture, including theatre, music and opera performances, with many top international artists performing, and a writers festival (even-numbered years)
March
Wellington Fringe Festival innovative festival of the arts
April/May
ASB Bank Laugh Festival national and international comedians perform in venues around town
Wellington International Jazz Festival jazz concerts, workshops and street performances (odd-numbered years)
July
International Film Festival a two-week gala film event

Places to Stay

Camping & Cabins Areas of green grass (or even no grass) for pitching a tent in the city are rarities.

The *Hutt Park Holiday Village (☎ 568 5913, 95 Hutt Park Rd)* in Lower Hutt, 13km

Windy Wellington

Wellington really can get windy. When the sun's shining it can be a very attractive city, but it's not called the windy city for nothing – one of the local rock stations even calls itself Radio Windy.

At the start of winter you've got a fair chance of experiencing some gale-force days – the sort of days when strong men get pinned up against walls and little old ladies, desperately clutching their umbrellas, can be seen floating by at skyscraper height. Seriously, the flying grit and dust can be uncomfortable to the eyes and the flying rubbish can be a real mess. I was walking back from a restaurant late one windy night when a sudden gust blew several bags of garbage out of a doorway: A passing car hit one and a veritable snowstorm of soft-drink cans, pizza boxes and assorted debris rushed down the street, eventually overtaking the offending car!

One blustery day back in 1968 the wind blew so hard it pushed the almost-new Wellington–Christchurch car ferry *Wahine* onto Barrett's Reef just outside the harbour entrance. The disabled ship later broke loose from the reef, drifted into the harbour and then sank, causing the loss of 51 lives. The Wellington Maritime Museum has a dramatic model and photographic display of the disaster.

Nancy Keller

north-east of the centre of Wellington, is closest to town. It has tent/powered sites for $19/21, standard/tourist cabins for $32/42, tourist flats for $59 and motel units for $84 (all prices for two). It is a 15-minute drive from the ferry, a five-minute walk from the bus stop (take the Eastbourne bus) or a 20-minute walk from Woburn train station.

The *Harcourt Holiday Park* (☎ 526 7400, 45 Akatarawa Rd, Upper Hutt), 35km north-east of Wellington, is in a lovely native-bush setting. Sites are $18 for two, cabins $30 and tourist flats from $58.

Backpackers The *Wellington City YHA* (☎ 801 7280, @ yhawgtn@yha.org.nz), on the corner of Cambridge Terrace and Wakefield St, is conveniently situated and quite a luxurious place. Most rooms have private bathrooms and views right over the harbour. The cost is $19 in different-sized dorms, or $46 for twins and doubles.

Opposite the train station, *Downtown Wellington Backpackers* (☎ 473 8482, @ db@downtownbackpackers.co.nz), on the corner of Waterloo Quay and Bunny St, is also convenient but further from the action. It's one of the largest Art Deco buildings in the country (it was formerly the Waterloo Hotel) and the young Queen Elizabeth II stayed here in 1953. It has a big-city feel, and amenities include a restaurant, large bar with billiard table (and carved kauri fireplace), huge kitchen, lounge facilities, Internet and pubs next door. All rooms have private bathroom; the cost is $19 for a share room or $25/42/42 for singles/twins/doubles.

The Woolshed (☎ 385 9235, 19 Edward St) is an early 20th-century building with 24 dorm beds for $16.

Trekkers Hotel/Motel (☎ 385 2153, @ info@trekkers.co.nz, 213 Cuba St) is in a lively area among the delights of Cuba St. It's a large hotel, stretching through from Cuba St to Dunlop Terrace, but also popular with backpackers. Good rooms with basins cost $40/44 for backpackers; hotel rooms are from $45 to $65 (single) and $79 (twins/doubles) with linen provided. Facilities include the Parlour Bar & Cafe and the Globe Cafe.

The *Lodge in the City* (☎ 385 8560, @ litcnz@voyager.co.nz, 152 Taranaki St) is in a central location close to the controversial 'sex in the city' sign. It is friendly, has good managers, there's secure overnight parking close by, and it has a bar and rooftop garden. Comfortable dorms are $18, twins and doubles $36/45, and singles $22.50.

Wide World Backpackers (☎ 802 5590, @ wide.world@paradise.net.nz, 291 The Terrace), close to town on the corner of Ghuznee St, offers an all-you-can-eat breakfast. It's $19 for dorms, $45 for singles, and from $45 to $65 for twins and doubles.

Rosemere Backpackers (☎ 384 3041, @ rosemerebp@yahoo.com, 6 MacDonald Crescent) is a short walk uphill from the centre. It remains an old, dilapidated house, badly in need of an overhaul. The cost is $15 for dorms, $38 for twins and doubles.

There are several backpackers on and near Brougham St in the pleasant Mt Victoria area, a quiet residential suburb close to the city. From the train station catch bus No 2 or 5 to Brougham St, or No 1 or 3 to the Basin Reserve stadium. The area is only a five-minute walk from Courtenay Place.

Beethoven House (☎ 939 4678, 89 Brougham St, Mt Victoria) is one of NZ's original backpackers and many people stay just for the company of the eccentric owner, Alan. All birthdays, including Ludwig's, the house's and yours, as well as Christmas are celebrated. Alan is helpful but straight-talking, which some find hard to take. The $15 or $16 for a dorm bed and $36 double-room rate includes the now-famous breakfast heralded by a wake-up call of classical music. There's no prominent sign.

Rowena's City Lodge (☎ 385 7872, @ rowenas@iconz.co.nz, 115 Brougham St), nearby, is a larger hostel, up a driveway above the street. It's friendly, well equipped and one of the better choices. Rates are $10 for camping, $18 in dorms and from $25/44 for singles/doubles and twins.

Maple Lodge (☎ 385 3771, 52 Ellice St), around the corner, is a smaller hostel with rates of $17 in dorms and $20/38 for singles/twins and doubles. It has safe off-street parking, but a confined kitchen.

Guesthouses Wellington has a wide selection of guesthouses. *Richmond Guest House* (☎ 385 8529, 116 Brougham St, Mt Victoria) is simple but clean and comfortable with a guests' kitchen. B&B is $50/65 for singles/doubles with bathroom.

Eight Parliament Street (☎ 479 6705, @ grasenack@xtra.co.nz), in historic Thorndon, is a comfortable, central B&B with lots of character (from $95/120).

The *Tinakori Lodge* (☎ 473 3478, 182 Tinakori Rd), also in Thorndon, is good value. It offers attractive B&B rooms, each with TV, at $70/95 ($90/125 with bathroom).

The Mermaid (☎ 384 4511, 1 Epuni St) is a guesthouse for women only; it costs from $68 to $120.

South of the city, *The Lighthouse* (☎ 472 4177, @ bruce@sportwork.co.nz, 326 The Esplanade, Island Bay) is just what it says – a self-contained lighthouse for special occasions. It's $150 for two ($180 on weekends).

Motels *Halswell Lodge* (☎ 385 0196, 21 Kent Terrace) has a great location. Hotel-style rooms with en suite cost $75/89 for singles/doubles, motel units $130 and spa bathroom units $145.

The *Harbour City Motor Inn* (☎ 384 9809, 92–96 Webb St) is relatively central and has 26 suites. These are from $95 to $160, and there's a guest spa and undercover parking.

Other recommended motels close to the centre include the following: *Marksman* (☎ 385 2499, 44 Sussex St), is centrally located with one- and two-bedroom suites costing $95 to $135. *Wallace Court Motel* (☎ 385 3935, 88 Wallace St), similarly priced, is central with 10 kitchen and studio units. *Apollo Lodge* (☎ 385 1849, 49 Majoribanks St), is close to Te Papa and has 50 motel units from $95 to $140. The *Capital View Motor Inn* (☎ 385 0515, 12 Thompson St) has units from $95 and the *Adelaide Motel* (☎ 389 8138, 209 Adelaide Rd) has 10 very comfortable units from $95 to $105. The *Mana Motel* (☎ 0800-866 262, 41 Mana Esplanade), off SH1, has been recommended by readers.

Hotels Both *Downtown Wellington Backpackers* and *Trekkers Hotel/Motel* are good cheaper options, and are popular and central (see under Backpackers earlier).

Otherwise, Wellington is awash with mostly mid-range hotels. It is a business, rather than tourist, destination so there are weekend discounts from Friday to Sunday.

Portland Towers Hotel (☎ 473 2208, 24 Hawkestone St) is one of the cheaper high-rises with rooms for $150 during the week ($96 on weekends).

The *Bay Plaza* (☎ 385 7799, 40–44 Oriental Parade), with superb harbour views, charges $139/85 plus GST during the week/weekend.

The following are also good and centrally located: *Hotel Ibis Wellington* (☎ 496 1880, 153 Featherston St) is an excellent mid-range option right in the heart of the business district. The *Richard Pearse* (☎ 916 0500, 219 Willis St) has rooms with kitchen from $135 to $235. *Citylife* (☎ 472 8588, 300 Lambton Quay) has large rooms from $210 to $240.

The *Museum Hotel de Wheels* (☎ 385 2809, 80 Cable St) charges $175 to $195, dropping to a reasonable $135 to $158 on weekends.

The *Abel Tasman* (☎ 385 1304, 169 Willis St) has rooms from $99 on weekends, rising to $129 weekdays.

The *Quality Hotel Willis St* (☎ 385 9819, 355 Willis St) is central and has B&B from $105 for two, and the *Quality Hotel Oriental Bay* (☎ 385 0279, 73 Roxburgh St) is outstanding for its harbour-view rooms from $145 ($95 on weekends).

The *Novotel Wellington* (☎ 385 9829, 345 The Terrace) is one of the city's best hotels and has a pool. There are particularly good weekend deals, with rooms from $119, rising to $125-plus on weekdays.

The *Hotel Raffaele* (☎ 384 3450, 360 Oriental Parade) is also recommended; doubles are $204 during the week (weekend specials are $179).

At the top end, with rooms in the $200 to $300-plus range, are the *James Cook Centra* (☎ 499 9500, 147 The Terrace), the *Parkroyal Wellington* (☎ 472 2722) on the corner of Grey and Featherston Sts, and the *Plaza International* (☎ *473 3900, 148 Wakefield St)*; prices halve on weekends.

Apartment Hotels Wellington also has some apartment hotels, which are a cross between an apartment and a hotel. You can rent them nightly and there are often discounts for long-term stays.

Majoribanks Apartments (☎ *385 7305, 38 Majoribanks St)*, for example, has double apartments from $560 to $980 per week.

Places to Eat

Wellington has a plethora of cafes and restaurants serving a wide selection of international cuisines.

Restaurants Courtenay Place is the entertainment centre of Wellington and has a large selection of restaurants. The Manners Mall-Willis St area, Cuba St, and Riddiford St, Newtown, all have a good range. Oriental Parade is the place for seafood restaurants.

Asian Asian is the dominant international cuisine. If you like spicy Malaysian food you're in luck because the city has nearly 30 Malaysian restaurants and competition keeps prices down.

Malaya Village (17 Majoribanks St) is more a real restaurant, with pleasant decor and authentic Malaysian hawker fare for about $10 a main.

Cinta (41 Courtenay Place) and *Kopi* (☎ *499 5570, 103 Willis St)* are both stylish and more expensive; Kopi consistently gets voted as the city's best Malaysian place and it's necessary to book. (See also Cheap Eats later.)

Angkor (43 Dixon Street) is a real Cambodian restaurant, a rarity in NZ. You can sample such delights as mahope kari (a curry selection of chicken, lamb or prawn), amok trei (spicy steamed fish) and yao horn (a charcoal broiler steam boat); it's open for dinner daily.

Java (119 Manners St), upstairs, is Wellington's only Indonesian restaurant and has reasonably priced mains from $10 to $14 and a bar.

The *Oriental Thai* (☎ *801 8080, 58 Cambridge Terrace)* is the city's best authentic Thai restaurant but it's expensive.

Courtenay Place is Wellington's traditional Chinatown and, though it has now been taken over by fashionable restaurants and bars, many Chinese places remain. One place that is particularly good value, although it's not on Courtenay Place, is *Ye-Jun (40 Willis St)*, upstairs. This Cantonese restaurant has an all-you-can-eat 10-course dinner buffet for $14 and weekday lunches for $12. It's not gourmet food but it's popular with travellers.

The Indian subcontinent is also well represented. The *Great India (141 Manners St)* gets rave reviews from Wellingtonians and serves delicious tandoori specialities.

Cafe India (☎ *382 9400, 22 Allen St)* is also popular and has lunch specials for $8.50.

Little India (☎ *384 9989, 18 Blair St)*, one of several branches now in NZ, is consistently good and serves great tandoori food; it's open daily from 5.30 pm until late.

Middle Eastern *Ali Baba (203 Cuba St)* is a very pleasant place to dine, with seating on Turkish pillows or chairs if you prefer. It's casual and great for an inexpensive meal, snack, or just a baklava and coffee, and is open from 10.30 am to 9 pm daily and until 10 pm on Friday.

Cafe Istanbul (156 Cuba St) is another Turkish restaurant-cafe, with pleasant Turkish decor and mains for around $15.

Sahara Cafe (39 Courtenay Place) has Turkish, Lebanese and Syrian food.

Tex-Mex *Armadillo's (129 Willis St)* is a Wellington institution – a loud, Texas cowboy-style restaurant-bar specialising in American food like steaks, ribs, southern chicken and burgers in Texas-size portions. It's not cheap at $18-plus for mains.

Chevy's (97 Dixon St), around the corner, is a colourful pseudo-US restaurant with fancy burgers and Tex-Mex dishes. *Arizona Bar & Grill* (☎ *495 7867)*, on the corner of Grey and Featherston Sts, is a popular bar which serves Tex-Mex food.

WELLINGTON REGION

Axolotl Cafe *(34 Courtenay Place)* achieved fame for its Mexican dishes but the menu is now more eclectic. It still serves great enchiladas ($15); it's open from 3 pm to 3 am.

Seafood The **Tug Boat**, as its name suggests, is in a boat moored on the water behind the Freyberg Pool on Oriental Parade. It has a mixed menu but is noted mainly for its seafood. Mains are around $20 to $28, while the seafood platter ($70 for two) includes lobster.

The **Quayside** (☎ 801 7900), about 500m further east on Oriental Parade, has great harbour views, as it is built over the water in the old Oriental Bay Sea Baths. This is a more formal restaurant but the mains ($22 to $25) are reasonably priced for seafood.

The **Shed 5** and **Dockside** restaurants on Queens Wharf are both fine, upmarket places for seafood. They were opened as part of the city's waterfront revamp.

European & Other **La Casa Pasta** *(37 Dixon St)* is just one of several restaurants serving home-style Italian food.

Calzone on the corner of Courtenay Place and Cambridge Terrace is a yuppie sort of place serving gourmet pizzas, pastas, salads and desserts; it's open from 10 am to 1 am daily.

Café Menton *(232 Oriental Parade)*, overlooking the harbour, is a rarity – a reasonably priced French country-style restaurant with mains for around $20.

Salon Petit Lyons (☎ 384 9402, 33 Vivian St) is as 'mega-posh' as its name, but a good place to indulge if you can afford it. Also attached is the **Oyster Bar**, which has live jazz on Friday night.

On Courtenay Place, **ate** (☎ 802 5818) is a snazzy bistro which serves contemporary Kiwi food; it's open for dinner until late daily.

Logan-Brown (☎ 801 5114), on the corner of Cuba and Vivian Sts, is elegant and serves superb food. The pre-theatre and bankers' lunch set menus are $29.50. There's an excellent wine selection.

Mondo Cucina *(15 Blair St)*, mixing Californian and Italian styles, is the place to

head to if your wallet allows. It's open from 6 pm for dinner daily, and for brunch from Wednesday to Sunday.

Blair St is at the centre of the Courtenay Place restaurant scene; other fashionable restaurants here include the **Exchange** (☎ 384 1006) at No 20 for beef and lamb main courses at around $25, and the slightly cheaper **Beacon** at No 8. **The Opera** *(14 Courtenay Place)*, on the corner of Blair St, is very swish. 'Overtures' are about $12, various 'acts' (pastas and mains) are around $22, and 'finales' (desserts) are $10.

Turners, a licensed place in the Willis St Village, has an open barbecue and is the ticket for steaks. Its motto is 'If you leave us hungry, you've only got yourself to blame'. A huge steak, bottomless salad bowl and fries/baked potato is $21. It's open from 5.30 pm daily.

Cafes Wellington has many cafes – see the boxed text 'Bean There, Done That' in this section. Many restaurants are also cafes by day. **The Lido**, on the corner of Victoria and Wakefield Sts in the centre, is licensed, trendy, and always features a daily special and a soya option.

The Ballroom Cafe (☎ 389 4828, 9 Riddiford St, Newtown), upstairs in the former Five Star Ballroom, is open daily for all meals; live jazz is featured at the Sunday brunch.

Espressoholic 2000 *(128 Courtenay Place)*, near the corner of Taranaki St, is trendy and open long hours (daily from 8 am until 3 am). There's a courtyard out the back – a good place to relax in summer.

Cuba St has a string of good cafes. Check out the **Midnight Espresso** *(178 Cuba St)* near the corner of Vivian St, the 'granddaddy of cafes'; **Globe Cafe** *(213 Cuba St)*, in Trekkers Hotel, known for its potato cakes; and **Felix**, on the corner of Wakefield and Cuba Sts.

The **Krazy Lounge** *(132 Cuba St)* is one of the most popular cafes because of its good food such as Krazy chips and dips ($5.50) and 'coffee with balls'; it's open until late.

Fidel's *(234 Cuba St)* is a cool hang-out for coffee-craving, left-wing subversives. It features an all-day breakfast with great hash browns.

The **Deluxe Cafe** *(10 Kent Terrace)*, beside the Embassy Theatre, is a smaller, quieter but very hip little cafe open from 8 am to midnight most days.

Parade Cafe *(148 Oriental Parade)*, a popular cafe down by the water, has a mixed menu, reasonable prices, and outside tables and chairs.

Ford's Cafe *(☎ 472 6238, 342 Tinakori Rd, Thorndon)* is a stylish place which serves full meals and the tempting Combo with samples from all items on the dessert menu ($15.50).

The **Downtown Cafe** *(☎ 473 8482)* in Downtown Wellington Backpackers, Bunny St, is a popular resting place for travellers who sit, sip, chat and write postcards.

On the Miramar Peninsula, the **Chocolate Fish** *(☎ 388 2808, 497a Karaka Bay Rd, Scorching Bay)* attracts large crowds on sunny weekends. A second coffee is only $2.

Cheap Eats South of town, **Deep Blue Seafood** *(☎ 389 6465, 150 Adelaide Rd)* has all types of seafood for sale and its lunch specials are both cheap and delicious; it also serves sushi, tasty chicken and salads. **Raja** in Riddiford St, Newtown, is ideal for the budget-conscious; it's from $4.95 to $5.50 for a filling curry.

Satay Time *(143 Willis St)* is a no-frills takeaway with a few tables, but the food is excellent; the prices (around $5 to $7 for a meal) are hard to beat.

Satay Kampong *(262 Wakefield St)* is a basic, functional place with nothing over $8 on the menu; it's enormously popular (open for lunch daily, plus from 6 to 9.30 pm Monday to Saturday).

Khmer Satay Noodle House *(148 Cuba St)* is low on decor but great value. Noodle dishes for $6 to $8 are very tasty and a steaming dish of noodle soup with added chilli is guaranteed to clear the sinuses.

Kebabholik *(☎ 801 6693)* on Cuba St is a Turkish cafe and takeaway which has cheap vegetarian kebabs; it's open daily until late.

Wellington has a reasonable selection of food courts for cheap, varied dining but

---

Bean There, Done That

Not so long ago, you couldn't get anything other than a cup of tea or an instant coffee in a NZ cafe or tearoom (milk and sugar compulsory). Nowadays, the choice is bewildering – mochaccino, cappuccino, latte, 'mellowccino', decaf, Colombian, Kenyan and so on. An order for 'instant' is likely to send the waiter's ponytail bolt upright.

Wellington prides itself as a cultural centre and no literati could flourish without a decent cafe scene for a relaxed meal, snack, dessert or coffee. The city boasts more cafes per capita than New York City.

There are several good cafes around the city centre. Cuba St is one of the best strips, favoured by alternative society, and Courtenay Place has more than its fair share of cafe-bars. Several roasters deliver the fresh product to their doors.

Wellington's Cafe Culture ($10) is an excellent A to Z of the cafes (Arabica to Zing, no less), and it covers 52 aromatic spots.

---

most are only open during shopping hours. The **food court** *(55 Cuba St)* on the ground floor of the Market at James Smith Corner has Chinese, Mexican, pizza, burgers and other fare and is open the longest – from 9 am to 8 pm on weekdays and until late on Friday and Saturday.

For sea views, the **food court** in the Queens Wharf Retail Centre is open from 10 am to 6 pm daily. It has Thai, Chinese and Turkish food, as well as a McDonald's.

The **food court** in the Wellington Market on Wakefield St has excellent Asian food, including Indian food, but is only open from 10 am to 6 pm from Friday to Sunday. A speciality here is Maori cuisine; you can take away food prepared in a *hangi*.

A Taste of France *(101 Manners St)*, a French bakery close to the Cuba St junction, has a variety of interesting sandwiches and baked goods.

The well-stocked **supermarket**, on the corner of Cambridge Tce and Wakefield St, is open from 8 am to 10 pm daily.

Entertainment

Wellington is undisputed king (or queen) of NZ's nightlife with copious clubs, bars and other insomniac refuges (also see Cafes earlier). It also has a vibrant performing arts scene.

Pubs Brewery pubs are very popular. The *Loaded Hog (14 Bond St)*, just off Willis St, has a lively atmosphere, live music Wednesday to Sunday nights (no cover charge) and a good menu. It's open from 11 am till late daily and until 10 pm on Sunday.

The *Malthouse (47 Willis St)* is a good place for a meal but an absolute shrine for the lover of naturally brewed NZ beer.

One Red Dog (9 Blair St) is a chic variety of the brewery pub, very popular for a meal and for late-night drinking on the weekend.

Molly Malone's, an Irish pub at the Glass House on the corner of Courtenay Place and Taranaki St, is another rousing, popular pub. Live music is mostly Irish, playing Tuesday to Saturday nights with no cover charge; on Monday nights there's an Irish jam session. It's open from 11 am till late from Monday to Saturday and until 9 pm on Sunday. Traditional Irish fare is served upstairs in the *Dubliner*.

The *Backbencher* is on the corner of Molesworth St and Sydney St East, opposite the Beehive, so you might bump into a polly or two or overhear a coup being planned. It does a thriving business at lunchtime, serving large portions of food, and dinners are popular too. The atmosphere is casual, friendly and fun. It's open from 11 am until late daily.

The *Thorndon Tavern (110 Molesworth St)*, a couple of blocks up the hill, is a sports bar with a big-screen sports TV, billiards, darts and a TAB (where you can bet on horse races) downstairs. It also has pub food and laid-back bands playing on weekends.

Wine buffs should check out the *Bouquet Garni (☎ 499 1095, 100 Willis St)*, housed in an historic building with a huge wine list and expensive bistro meals.

A slightly suburban but stylish pub is the renovated *Shepherd's Arms Tavern*

(285 Tinakori Rd), not far from the main entrance to the Botanic Gardens.

Music & Dancing For gig guides pick up a copy of *City Voice* or *Capital Times*, which are free papers available around town.

Courtenay Place is the nightlife centre of Wellington with numerous bars, and crowds on weekends.

Along it you'll find the *Big Easy* (often referred to locally as the 'big sleazy'), a 'singles' venue with oversized bouncers on the door. *Kitty O'Shea's* at No 28 is a more convivial pub-bar with rock bands.

The *Wellington Sports Cafe* on the corner of Courtenay Place and Tory St is large and pleasant with interesting decor, a long twisted bar and DJs from Thursday to Saturday.

The Grand, Courtenay Place, is very popular and has a bottom-level dining area and second-level bar with pool tables.

Coyote (☎ 385 6665) next to The Grand at No 63, a 'street bar', is an alternative dance venue featuring techno and rave music. The *Blue Room*, at No 20 behind the equally popular *Cafe Paradiso*, has DJ dance music from Thursday to Saturday and occasional bands.

Blair and Allen Sts, running off Courtenay Place, are also fertile hunting grounds for booze and music. The *CO2 Champagne Bar (☎ 384 1064, 28 Blair St)* positively bubbles and is popular with the bubblier of the suited set. The *Judder Bar* on Allen St also has DJs.

Edwards St is also becoming a party venue with *Studio 9*, a dance party place; the *Lava Lounge* for rhythm and blues; and *Tupelo*, a trendy bar with whatever yuppies are listening to at the time.

Queens Wharf is away from the main nightlife areas and less frenetic. *Chicago* has bands downstairs on weekends, doing mostly 1980s covers. The dance floor is lively and there is a quieter bar upstairs.

Tatou (22 Cambridge Terrace) allows patrons to flick through musical tastes. Upstairs is the Velvet Lounge for jazz, downstairs is a disco, and The Boiler Room specialises in house music, drum and bass and techno.

Diva (37 Dixon St) attracts a loyal crowd of 30-somethings. It is open daily for meals and drinks.

For original bands, the pick of the venues is *Bar Bodega (286 Willis St)*, a cool hangout popular with alternative types (open from morning until late). Good local bands play every night of the week and on Tuesday and Sunday it is usually the last bar in town to shut. For a change of pace, Monday is jazz night and there are drinks specials on Monday and Tuesday.

Gay & Lesbian Venues *Evergreen Coffee House (144 Vivian St)* is a popular gay and lesbian cafe which stays open until late. *Flipp Brasserie (103 Ghuznee St),* in the RSA building and a great place for good Mediterranean food and company, is also gay-friendly.

The *Valve (154 Vivian St)* is a popular gay and lesbian club; *Bojangles (☎ 384 8445, 60 Dixon St),* upstairs, is probably the most popular gay bar in town; the *Sanctuary (39 Dixon St)* is a cruise club; and *Checkmate (20 Garrett St)* is a well-patronised sauna.

Out! Bookshop and the *Club Wakefield,* a men's cruise bar, are at 15 Tory St. Also see Information earlier in this chapter.

Cinemas There are plenty of cinemas: *Midcity* on Manners St, the *Hoyts 5* on Manners Mall and the *Embassy* on Kent St, which screens commercial films; the *Paramount (25 Courtenay Place),* which has 'hard-edged' and art-house movies; the *Penthouse (205 Ohiro Rd, Brooklyn),* which screens 'middle of the road' art-house films; and the *Rialto Cinemas* on Cable St, which boasts 'quality independent productions'.

Performing Arts Wellington is the most active place in NZ for live theatre, supporting a number of professional theatre companies and quality amateur companies.

Downstage Theatre (☎ 801 6946) presents plays in the Hannah Playhouse on the corner of Cambridge Terrace and Courtenay Place; the pleasant Encore cafe is here. *Circa Theatre (☎ 801 7992, 1 Taranaki St),* adjacent to Te Papa, presents a variety of drama. The *Bats Theatre (☎ 802 4176, 1 Kent Terrace)* is a more avant-garde, alternative theatre.

Reduced-price theatre tickets for the Bats, Circa and Downstage Theatres are available at the information centre, subject to availability. These tickets are one sale from 12 noon.

The *Royal New Zealand Ballet (☎ 238 5383)* performs in town, usually at the Westpac Trust St James Theatre at 77 Courtenay Place; ring for schedules. *The National Opera of Wellington (☎ 384 4434)* performs at the State Opera House (☎ 801 8209) at 111 Manners St; this has recently undergone extensive renovations.

The *Michael Fowler Centre (☎ 801 4263)* on Wakefield St, the *Wellington Town Hall (☎ 471 1573)* on Wakefield St and the *Victoria University Theatre (☎ 473 3120)* are all popular performance venues. The ritzy *Michael Fowler Centre,* part of the Civic Square complex, has its main entrance on Wakefield St. It hosts all sorts of performances, from bands to the New Zealand Symphony Orchestra. Check the newspapers or the information centre for current shows.

The amphitheatre at Frank Kitts Park on the waterfront, and the *Dell* in the Botanic Gardens are popular venues for outdoor concerts and shows.

Shopping

James Smith Corner is in the old St James building on the corner of the Cuba Mall and Manners St. Dozens of tiny shops upstairs sell African beads, Balinese jewellery, bongs, candles and other New Age stuff.

Wellington Market on Wakefield St is similar but mostly specialises in second-hand goods and furniture and is open from 10 am to 5 pm Friday to Sunday.

New Zealand's answer to Bloomingdale's or Harrods is Kirkcaldie & Stains on Lambton Quay.

Getting There & Away

Air Wellington airport has a domestic and international terminal, each one has restaurants, gift shops and its own information centre (☎ 388 5123), open until around 6 or 7 pm daily and until 11.30 pm on Saturday. Left-luggage lockers are in the domestic terminal.

Air New Zealand and Ansett offer direct domestic flights to many places in NZ, with connections to other centres. Air New Zealand has direct flights to Auckland, Blenheim, Chatham Islands, Christchurch, Dunedin, Gisborne, Hamilton, Napier, Nelson, New Plymouth, Palmerston North, Rotorua, Taupo, Tauranga, Timaru, Wanganui and Westport. Ansett has direct flights to Auckland, Blenheim, Christchurch, Dunedin, Hamilton, Invercargill, Nelson, Palmerston North and Rotorua.

The flight between Wellington and Picton in the South Island takes 25 minutes in a small plane. Soundsair (☎ 0800-505 005) has daily flights to Picton and Blenheim; and Origin Pacific (☎ 0800-302 302) has daily flights to Nelson (see the Air, Bus & Train Routes map in the Getting Around chapter for prices). All of these airlines offer discounts.

For international airlines with offices in Wellington see the Getting There & Away chapter.

Bus Wellington is an important junction for bus travel, with buses to Auckland and all major towns in between.

Buses from the two main companies, InterCity (☎ 472 5111) and Newmans (☎ 499 3261), depart from Platform 9 at the train station. Tickets for these buses are sold at the travel reservations and tickets centre in the train station.

City to City: White Star (☎ 478 4734) buses depart from Bunny St, near Downtown Wellington Backpackers opposite the train station, and run along the west coast of the North Island to Palmerston North, Wanganui and New Plymouth.

Train Wellington train station has a travel centre (☎ 0800-802 802, 498 3000) offering reservations and tickets for trains, buses, the *Interislander* ferry, airlines, tours and more. Luggage lockers are open from 6 am to 10 pm daily.

A free shuttle bus runs between the train station and the ferry terminal, departing from the station 45 minutes before each ferry leaves and meeting each arriving ferry.

Trains operate between Wellington and Auckland, running through the central North Island. The daily, daytime *Overlander* departs from each end in the morning. The overnight *Northerner* runs daily except Saturday, departing from each city in the evening and arriving early the next morning.

The *Bay Express*, between Wellington and Napier departs from Wellington in the morning, arriving in Napier in the early afternoon; it leaves from Napier an hour later to arrive back in Wellington in the evening.

Hitching It's not easy to hitch out of Wellington because the highways heading out of the city, SH1 up the Kapiti Coast and SH2 up the Hutt Valley, are motorways for a long distance and hitching is illegal on motorways. The best option is to catch a bus or train out to one of the outer suburbs on the Kapiti Coast or to Masterton and hitch from there.

Boat Departing from the ferry terminal north of town, the *Interislander* (☎ 0800-802 802) ferries shuttle back and forth between Wellington and Picton in the South Island. The trip is comfortable, takes around three hours and sailing times (subject to change) are:

leaves Wellington	leaves Picton
1.10 am*	5.30 am*
5.00 am †	8.00 am †
9.30 am	12.30 pm
1.00 pm	4.00 pm
5.30 pm	8.30 pm

* Tuesday to Saturday only
* Tuesday to Sunday only

See their Web site (www.tranzrailtravel.co .nz/interislander) for an up-to-date schedule and fares.

It's best to do the trip in daylight, if the weather's good, to see Wellington Harbour and the Marlborough Sounds. Sailing can be rough in adverse weather but ferries are large and well equipped, with lounges, cafes, bars, a movie theatre and an information centre for bookings. One-way fares (also subject to change) are:

	Standard	Economy	Sailaway Saver	Super Saver
Adult	$49	$39	$32	$23
Child (4 to 14)	$29	$23	$19	$14
Motorbikes	$49	$39	$32	$23
Cars & Campervans	$175	$140	$116	$83

Children under four years travel for free and bicycles cost $10.

All discount fares *must* be booked in advance. Only standard fares are available on the day of departure. Discounts are subject to availability and may not be available during peak travel times.

You can book up to six months in advance, either directly (☎ 0800-802 802) or at most travel agents and information centres.

A free ferry shuttle-bus service is provided on both sides of the strait. In Wellington it operates between the ferry and train station (where long-distance buses also depart), departing from the train station 35 minutes before each sailing. The shuttle meets all arriving ferries. On the Picton side, a free shuttle runs between the ferry and the Picton–Christchurch *Coastal Pacific Express* train.

The *Lynx* (☎ 0800-834 596) is a faster way of doing the crossing as it takes only 2½ hours. It departs Wellington at 8 am and 3 pm, and Picton at 11.30 am and 6.30 pm. One-way fares are:

	Standard	Economy	Sailaway Saver	Super Saver
Adult	$63	$53	$45	$32
Child (4 to 14)	$37	$32	$27	$19
Motorbikes	$63	$53	$45	$32
Cars & Campervans	$199	$169	$141	$100

Vehicle Storage If you need to store your vehicle while you go across on the ferry, Wellington has some reputable vehicle-storage services.

The ferry terminal has an overnight lock-up service. Securaport (☎ 387 3700), at 57–61 Kingsford Smith St, Lyall Bay, and Car Storage (☎ 472 3215), at 138 Old Hutt Rd, Kaiwharawhara, charge around $10 per day and pick up and drop off at the ferry and airport terminals.

Getting Around

To/From the Airport The airport is 7km south-east of the city centre. Johnstons Shuttle (☎ 569 9017) and Super Shuttle (☎ 387 8787) provide door-to-door shuttle buses between the city and the airport at $8 for one person, $10/12 for two/three.

Both companies operate scheduled services ($5 per person) from the train station to the airport, stopping at Lambton Quay, Cuba St and elsewhere. Johnstons Shuttle runs half-hourly from 8 am to 5.30 pm daily; Super Shuttle runs every half to one hour between 7.15 am and 5.45 pm on weekdays.

A taxi between the city centre and airport costs around $15.

Bus Wellington has a good local bus system, Stagecoach, with frequent buses daily from around 7 am to 11.30 pm on most routes. Most depart from beside the train station and from the major bus stop on Courtenay Place at the intersection with Cambridge Terrace. Useful colour-coded bus route maps and timetables are available at the information centre.

Phone Ridewell (☎ 0800-801 7000) for timetable and fare information from 7.30 am to 8.30 pm Monday to Saturday and 9 am to 3 pm on Sunday.

Bus fares are determined by zones. The 'Golden Mile', between the train station and the Courtenay Place/Cambridge Terrace bus stops, costs $1; otherwise it's $1.10 to ride in one section and $1.70 for two sections.

An all-day Daytripper Pass for $5 allows unlimited rides on Stagecoach Wellington buses (most local buses) after 9 am. They are available from bus drivers only and two children can ride free with each adult.

The After Midnight Bus (☎ 0800-801 7000) has three buses scheduled from 1, 2 and 3 am, leaving the entertainment district (Courtenay Place and Dixon St); it's $3 to Island Bay and Strathmore, Karori and Northland, and Khandallah and Newlands.

Train Four suburban electric train routes, with frequent trains daily from around 6 am to midnight, leave the Wellington train station. These routes are: Johnsonville, via Khandallah and Ngaio; Paraparaumu, via Porirua and Paekakariki; Melling, via Petone and Lower Hutt; and Upper Hutt, going on to Masterton. Phone Ridewell (☎ 0800-801 7000) or pick up timetables from the train station or visitor information centre.

In addition to the regular fares there is also a day pass ($15) which allows two adults and two children (or one adult and three children) to ride these suburban trains anywhere, all day long.

Car Wellington has a number of hire car operators (check the *Yellow Pages*), but the prices are nowhere near as competitive as in

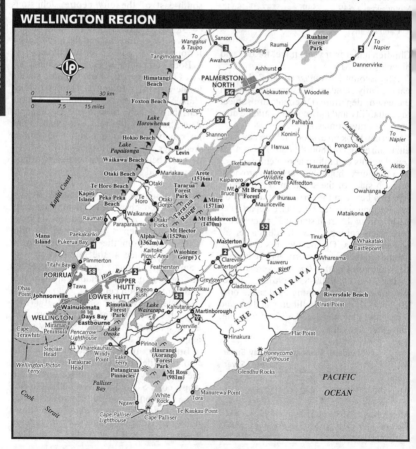

WELLINGTON REGION

Auckland. Prices start at around $40 a day for an older car. If you are landing in Wellington and heading to the South Island, it is cheaper and easier to hire a car in Picton. Prices are around the same as in Wellington but you don't have to pay the ferry charges.

Bicycle The Penny Farthing Cycle Shop (☎ 385 2279), at 89 Courtenay Place, and Pins Cycles (☎ 472 4591), on the corner of Willis and Boulcott Sts, hire mountain bikes at $25 per day, and do longer term rentals. Both shops offer a full range of bicycle gear, clothing, bicycle repairs, and bicycles for sale.

Hutt Valley

☎ 04 • pop 130,000

The Hutt River acts as the western boundary for land-starved Wellington's dormitory cities, Lower Hutt and Upper Hutt. Apart from some attractive forest parks for picnics and a few museums, they are fairly suburban. Both cities are easily reached by train from Wellington. Visitor information is available from the Council Buildings, 30 Laings Rd.

Lower Hutt has the **Petone Settlers Museum** on the Esplanade, Petone, which is open from noon to 4 pm Tuesday to Friday and 1 to 5 pm on weekends.

In Upper Hutt, the **Silver Stream Railway Museum** on Eastern Rd has NZ's largest collection of working steam locomotives. The museum also runs train rides on Sunday and public holidays ($5, children $3). The drive from Upper Hutt to Waikanae on the scenic Akatarawa road passes the **Staglands Wildlife Reserve** (☎ 526 7529) where the rare blue duck has been successfully bred.

Upper Hutt Visitors Centre (☎ 527 2141, @ uhvic@uhcc.govt.nz) is at 6 Main Rd.

To the south are the towns of Wainuiomata and Eastbourne. Wainuiomata has a **heritage trail** with 14 points of interest. At Eastbourne there's a pavilion popular with families for picnics, craft shops, an art gallery, restaurants and cafes. There's also a good swimming beach, kayaks and bikes for hire, and fishing off the wharf.

Eastbourne is a 7km bike ride or walk from Burdan's Gate at the end of Muritai Rd to the country's first permanent lighthouse, **Pencarrow Lighthouse**.

Rimutaka Forest Park (☎ 564 8551) is 30km east of Wellington and south of Wainuiomata. In the Catchpool Valley near DOC's Catchpool Visitor Centre, off Coast Rd, there's *camping* in delightful surroundings ($4, children $2). A shower block and barbecues make this better than the usual basic DOC camp.

Good cafes in this region include *Beanworx (196 Jackson St, Petone)* noted for its banana and bacon panini; and *Circus Cafe (7 Oroua St, Eastbourne)*, 1km after Days Bay pier, with economical lunches (under $10).

Kapiti Coast

☎ 04 • pop 36,700

The picturesque Kapiti Coast stretches 30km along the west coast from Paekakariki (45km north of Wellington) to Otaki (75km north of Wellington). The region takes its name from large Kapiti Island, an interesting bird and marine sanctuary 5km offshore.

The coast has fine white-sand beaches, good swimming and other water activities, and is a summer playground of the windy city, as well as a suburban extension of Wellington.

The other attraction is the Tararua Forest Park in the Tararua Range, which forms a backdrop to the coastline all along its length.

The Kapiti Coast is easily visited as a day trip from Wellington, but also has good accommodation for a few restful days.

Getting There & Away

Paraparaumu airport has direct flights down to Nelson in the South Island (including pick-up), and direct flights up to Auckland (☎ 0800-650 400).

Getting to the west coast from Wellington is a breeze – it's on the major route (SH1) north from Wellington.

WELLINGTON REGION

InterCity, White Star, Kiwi Experience and Magic Bus all stop at Paraparaumu and Otaki on their north-south routes to/from Wellington. From Wellington it's about an hour to Otaki and 45 minutes to Paraparaumu, much of it by motorway.

Trains between Wellington and the coast are easier and more frequent than buses. Electric trains between Wellington and Paraparaumu ($7.50; one hour) run hourly in both directions from around 6 am to midnight (until 8 pm on weekends), stopping at Paekakariki. Weekday off-peak fares (9 am to 3 pm) are slightly cheaper.

Three long-distance trains serving Wellington also stop at Paraparaumu and Otaki daily, as does the early morning Tranz Metro *Capital Connection* to Palmerston North.

PAEKAKARIKI
pop 1690

Paekakariki is a quiet seaside village spread out along a lovely stretch of often-deserted beach, just two blocks from the train station and the highway. This little town is home to a number of artists and is a pleasant spot to relax within striking distance of Wellington.

Fly by Wire (☎ 025-300 366) provides an adrenaline-buzz activity in the hills just behind Paekakariki. You fly yourself in a bullet-shaped contraption with a turbo fan at back, hanging from a cable that dangles 55m from an overhead suspension point. You can reach speeds of up to 120km/h. A seven-minute flight costs $99, including a video. Book at the Southern Lights Cafe or telephone direct.

Steam Inc (☎ 292 8662), by the train station and almost on SH1, contains restored steam locomotives, a must for those who love the screech of steam and the smell of smoke. It's open on Saturday from 8.30 am to 6 pm.

About 5km north of Paekakariki at MacKay's Crossing, just off SH1, the **Wellington Tramway Museum** (☎ 292 8361) has restored wooden trams that ran in Wellington until its tram system was shut down in 1964, plus interesting photographs of old-time Wellington. A 2km track runs

from the museum down to the beach with good swimming, a playground and walking tracks through the dunes. A return ride is $4 (children $2). The museum is open from 11 am to 5 pm on weekends and holidays (daily over the Christmas holidays).

An alternative way to travel between Wellington and Paekakariki is over the scenic Paekakariki Hill Rd. If you're cycling south, it's a steep climb for about 3km and then smooth sailing all the way after that.

Places to Stay & Eat
Paekakariki Holiday Park (☎ 292 8292) is about 1.5km north of the town, right on the beach in Queen Elizabeth Park. Tent or powered sites are $20, cabins are $39 and tourist flats are $56; prices are for two.

Paekakariki Backpackers (☎ 292 8749, 11 Wellington Rd), up on a hill but close to the beach, is a small, friendly and relaxed place with a magnificent view of the sea and sunset. Free use of surfboards and bicycles is included in the cost of $15 in share rooms, or from $36/38 in twins/doubles.

The main street, Beach Rd, has a take-away fish-and-chip shop and a pub for counter meals. The *Fisherman's Table* in South Paekakariki has $12.95 meal specials.

The *Paekakariki Cafe*, on Wellington St near the backpackers, has substantial and innovative meals and is open for dinner Wednesday to Saturday.

PARAPARAUMU
pop 18,900

Paraparaumu is the principal town of the Kapiti Coast, forming almost a suburban satellite of Wellington, which is within commuting distance. This modern town is made up of Paraparaumu on the main highway, Paraparaumu Beach on the coast 3km west, and Raumati Beach further south. The beach is the coast's most developed, with a beachside park and plenty of water activities. Boat trips to Kapiti Island depart from Paraparaumu Beach.

The name Paraparaumu is rather a mouthful, and locally it is shortened to 'para-par-AM', although this is a politically incorrect corruption of the original. Radio announcers and the culturally aware use the correct pronunciation ('pah-ra-pah-ra-oo-moo'), but most locals won't budge. The name means 'Scraps From an Oven' and is said to have originated when a Maori war party attacked the settlement and found only scraps of food in the oven.

Most things you'll need in Paraparaumu are on the highway. The Visitor Information Centre (☎ 298 8195) in Coastlands is open from 9 am to 4 pm Monday to Saturday.

Things to See & Do

Paraparaumu Beach, with its beachside park, good swimming and other water activities (waterslide, jet-skiing, windsurfing etc) is the main attraction.

On SH1, 2km north of Paraparaumu, the Lindale Centre (☎ 297 0916) is a large tourist complex open from 9 am to 5 pm daily. Here you'll find the **Lindale Farm Park** with weekend farm shows ($6, children $4), and an outlet for the region's famous cheese and ice cream – drop in for a taste. Helicopter tours, craft shops and cafes complete the scene.

Inquire at the NZ Geographic Shop in the centre about visiting **Nikau Gardens** further along the highway. There are landscaped gardens, coastal rainforest and a butterfly park, and NZ's prehistoric insect, the weta, is on display ($9.50, children $5).

Another kilometre north, just off SH1, the **Southward Car Museum** (☎ 297 1221) has one of the largest collections of antique and unusual cars in Australasia. Its more than 130 cars include NZ's oldest, an array of motorbikes, three-wheeled cars, inventive home-made vehicles, some antique aeroplanes, and bicycles. See also Marlene Dietrich's Rolls Royce, the 1895 Benz 'horseless carriage' and a gull-winged Mercedes Benz. It's open from 9 am to 4.30 pm daily ($5, children $2).

Nyco Chocolates (☎ 293 5146), on SH1 about 1km south of town, is open from 9 am to 5 pm daily, with all kinds of chocolates and confections for sale; tours ($1) leave at 10.30 am and 2.30 pm on weekdays.

The airport on the road to the beach has flights to Auckland and Nelson, and tandem

skydiving (☎ 298 6600), while the Kapiti Aero Club has Tiger Moth aerobatic flights from $69.

Places to Stay & Eat

The **Lindale Motor Park** (☎ 298 8046) is about 2km north of the town near SH1, just south of the Lindale Centre. It's $18/20 for two for tent/powered sites, $30 for single cabins, and from $40 to $56 for double cabins.

Barnacles Seaside Inn (☎ 298 4856, ✉ lin&lois@xtra.co.nz, 3 Marine Parade), opposite the beachside park at Paraparaumu Beach, has views of the sea. It has dorms for $18 but most rooms are singles ($25); twins/doubles are $35/45.

There are plenty of motels in the town and at the beach; most charge around $65 to $75 a double. At Paraparaumu Beach there's the **Ocean Motel** (☎ 298 6458, 42–44 Ocean Rd), with units for $84 for two, **Kapiti Court** (☎ 298 7982, 341 Kapiti Rd), with units for $65 and the **Golf View** (☎ 298 6089, 16 Golf Rd), with units from $65.

Restaurants, cafes and takeaways are plentiful near Paraparaumu Beach and include the **Beach Bar & Cafe** and **Alice's Beach Bistro** (☎ 298 9404).

KAPITI ISLAND

About 10km long and 2km wide, Kapiti Island is the coastline's dominant feature. Its name is short for Te Waewae Kapiti o Tara raua ko Rangitane, meaning 'The Place where the Boundaries of Tara and Rangitane Divide'; historically it formed the boundary between the Ngati Tara and Rangitane tribal lands. In the early 1800s the island was the base for Te Rauparaha, a mighty warrior who came down from Kawhia with his forces and took over the entire region. Later that century the main island and the three small islands between it and the mainland became bases for seven whaling stations.

Since 1897 the island has been a protected wildlife reserve. Many species of birds that are now rare or extinct on the mainland still thrive on Kapiti Island.

The island is maintained by DOC and access is limited to 50 people per day. To visit

WELLINGTON REGION

you must obtain a permit ($8, children $4) from the DOC office in Wellington (see Information in the Wellington section). You can book up to three months in advance; you might be able to arrange something on the coast at the last minute if a booking is cancelled, but don't count on it.

Transport is booked separately (DOC can advise you). Kapiti Tours (☎ 237 7965, 0800-527 484) is the main operator and has a ferry from Paraparaumu Beach to the island ($30 return).

Although access to the island itself is restricted, boat and diving trips can go *around* the island. A variety of tours around the island are offered by Kapiti Tours and Kapiti Marine Charter (☎ 297 2585). Tamarillo Sea Kayaking (☎ 025-801 7549) has all-day kayaking trips for $125.

WAIKANAE
pop 9340

About 5km north of Paraparaumu, Waikanae is another town with two sections, one on SH1 and another by the beach. The Waikanae Field Centre (☎ 293 2191), 10 Parata St, is the main DOC office for the Kapiti Coast.

Waikanae's main attraction is the **Nga Manu Sanctuary**, a 15-hectare bird sanctuary with habitats including ponds, swamp, scrubland, coastal and swamp forest, and birds such as mute swans, kea, pied stilts, parakeets, ducks and wood pigeons. Other features include picnic areas, bushwalks and a nocturnal house with kiwi, owls and tuatara. To reach the sanctuary, turn seawards from SH1 onto Te Moana Rd and then follow the signs; the sanctuary is several kilometres from the turn-off. It's open from 10 am to 5 pm daily ($9.50, children $5).

Places to Stay

Waikanae has several motels including the *Kapiti Gateway Motel (☎ 293 6053)* on SH1, with units from $65; the *Toledo Park Motel (☎ 293 6199, 95 Te Moana Rd)*, with units from $70 and the *Ariki Lodge Motel (☎ 293 6592, 4 Omahi St)*, with units from $78.

Of the many B&Bs, *Waimoana (☎ 293 7158, ✉ waimoana@nzhomestay.co.nz, 63*

Kakarirki Grove) has been recommended. Singles/doubles are from $60/100 to $90/140. This place has a pool, garden and waterfall all under the one roof.

OTAKI
pop 5600

Otaki is primarily a gateway to the Tararua Ranges. It has a strong Maori history and influence: the little town has nine marae and a Maori college. The historic Rangiatea Church, built under the guidance of Ngati Toa chief Te Rauparaha nearly 150 years ago, was tragically burnt to the ground in 1995. This was the original burial site of Te Rauparaha and also the burial place of the opera singer Inia Te Wiata.

Most services, including the train station where buses stop, are on SH1. The main centre of Otaki, with the post shop and other shops, is 2km seawards. Three kilometres further on the same road brings you to Otaki's windswept beach.

Otaki means 'The Place of Sticking In' – a story tells that the place was where Hau stuck his staff in the ground when he was pursuing his wife, though the story may have lost something in the translation.

Otaki Forks

Two kilometres south of the town, Otaki Gorge Rd takes off inland from SH1 and leads 19km to Otaki Forks, the main western entrance to Tararua Forest Park. The scenic half-hour drive up through the Otaki Gorge to Otaki Forks has a number of posted walking tracks along the way.

Otaki Forks has picnic, swimming and camping areas, a hut, and a resident conservation officer (☎ 364 3111) who has maps and information on Tararua Forest Park. Bushwalks from 30 minutes to 3½ hours long are around the immediate area; longer tracks lead to huts. Ask for advice on longer tracks in the park – you can walk across the Tararua Range, but must bring adequate clothing and be well equipped and prepared for adverse weather. Sign the intentions book.

On Otaki Gorge Rd, Tararua Outdoor Recreation Centre (☎ 364 3110, ✉ torc@ xtra.co.nz) has guided kayak and rafting trips on the Otaki River (grades II to III) for $35. Night (evening) rafting trips are very popular. You can hire river equipment or mountain bikes for $30 a day, and be dropped off by 4WD for an extra $10; abseiling is also offered. The centre is open from October to April.

Places to Stay

Byron's Resort (☎ *364 8121, 20 Tasman Rd*) has tent/powered sites at $18/20 for two, tourist flats for $60 and motels from $74. Facilities include a licensed restaurant, pool, spa, sauna, tennis and playgrounds.

Coming into Otaki from Wellington, **Toad Hall** (☎/fax *364 6906, 4 Addington Rd*) is just off SH1 about 3km before the town. This friendly backpackers is in an impressive two-storey wooden house and is surrounded by farmland. Dorms are $15 and doubles are $36. Free bikes and pick-up from town are offered.

The **Otaki Oasis & Pony Practice School** (☎ *364 6860, 33 Rahui Rd*) is a small hobby farm on the inland side of the railway tracks. The well-kept backpackers lodge next to the house charges $15 for dorms or $35 for a double. Pony treks are offered for $15 per hour.

The **Otaki Motel** (☎ *364 8469*) on SH1 has units from $62 and **Waitohu Lodge B&B** (☎ *364 5389*) a few doors along charges $50/75 for singles/doubles.

Naumai (☎ *364 8440, 112 Waerenga Rd*) is a beautiful Edwardian home with a garden and orchard; contact them for prices.

The Wairarapa

☎ 06 • pop 38,700

The large region east and north-east of Wellington is known as the Wairarapa, taking its name from Lake Wairarapa (Shimmering Waters), a shallow but vast 8000-hectare lake.

This region, very much the apotheosis of rural NZ, is principally a sheep-raising district – it boasts three million sheep within a 16km radius of Masterton, the region's main town. It also has a few interesting attractions for visitors, including the Mt Bruce National Wildlife Centre, wineries at Martinborough, and very good tramping and camping in regional and forest parks.

The route through the Wairarapa along SH2 is a pleasant, much less frenetic alternative to busy SH1 on the west coast.

MASTERTON

pop 19,900

The main town of the Wairarapa, Masterton is a fair-sized town and can be used as a base for the surrounding area. Its main claim to fame is the international Golden Shears competition held annually during the first week in March, in which sheep shearing is raised to the level of sport and art, with the world's top shearers competing in finesse as well as speed.

The office of Tourism Wairarapa (☎ 378 7373, ✉ tourwai@xtra.co.nz), 5 Dixon St, is open from 9 am to 5 pm on weekdays, 10 am to 4 pm on weekends.

The DOC field office (☎ 378 2061) on South Rd, 2km south of the town centre, is open from 8.30 am to 5 pm on weekdays. The AA (☎ 378 2222) is on the corner of Chapel and Jackson Sts.

The telephone area code is ☎ 06.

Things to See & Do

The large 32-hectare **Queen Elizabeth Park** has sportsgrounds, an aviary, an aquarium, a deer park, a small lake where boats are hired out, children's playgrounds and a miniature railway where trains run on weekends and holidays.

The **Museum of Early Childhood** (☎ 377 4743), 40 Makora Rd, has a fascinating collection of antique dolls, toys, games, books and clothing and an array of teddy bears (admission by donation). Ring for an appointment.

Places to Stay

The **Mawley Park Motor Camp** (☎ 378 6454) is on Oxford St on the bank of the Waipoua River. Tent/powered sites are $15/16, and cabins are $27 and $35 for two.

The **Masterton Backpackers** (☎ 377 2228, 22 Victoria St), is a homey, colonial-style place. A bed in this friendly place is $14 per night or $32 in a twin room.

Chanel Backpackers (☎ 378 2846, ✉ chanelcourtmotel@xtra.co.nz, 14 Herbert St) near Rugby Park has dorms for $15, singles/doubles for $20/35, as well as a pool table, darts, Internet, SKY TV and a restaurant.

The **Victoria House Guesthouse** (☎ 377 0186), a friendly place opposite, offers B&B for $42/65 for singles/doubles.

Essex House (☎/fax 378 6252, 29 Essex St) is a delightful, outstanding B&B with a pool, charging $65/95.

Inexpensive motels include the **Colonial Cottage Motel** (☎ 377 0063, 122 Chapel St) with singles/doubles from $55/65, and the **Cornwall Park Motel** (☎ 378 2939, 119 Cornwall St) with units from $70 to $100.

The **Masterton Motor Lodge** (☎ 378 2585) on SH2 in South Masterton has units for $99 to $175.

The **Copthorne Resort Solway Park** (☎ 377 5129), an upmarket establishment on High St, charges from $95 to $156, plus GST, for a double. Just about every sporting whim is satisfied here – there's even a jogging track.

The information centre has referrals for farmstays and homestays in the Wairarapa; singles/doubles start at $40/65.

Places to Eat

The Regent Bistro (232 Queen St) serves snacks and meals and is open from 10 am daily. The **Slug & Lettuce** (☎ 377 3087, 94 Queen St) doesn't (fortunately!) serve the first item of its name but does have good-value meals.

Bloomfields, on the corner of Lincoln Rd and Chapel St, is the cafe to laze in.

Getting There & Away

From Wellington, the Tranz Metro train is faster, cheaper and more frequent than the buses, with four trains daily on weekdays and two daily on weekends. An adult day excursion ticket is $15.

Tranzit Coachlines (☎ 377 1227) has one bus daily to/from Wellington, but only on weekdays. It also has two weekday buses

and a Sunday bus to/from Palmerston North, passing Mt Bruce ($6) on the way.

MT BRUCE

Thirty kilometres north of Masterton on SH2, the **Mt Bruce National Wildlife Centre** is an important sanctuary for native NZ wildlife, mostly birds. Large aviaries and outdoor reserves feature some of the country's rarest and most endangered species, which you probably won't get to see elsewhere, in addition to more common species. There's an impressive nocturnal house with kiwi (sightings are not guaranteed), tuatara and other endangered reptiles. There are breeding programs of endangered species. Each species is given as natural a habitat as possible, so you have to look closely in the dense growth to find the birds.

The centre is open from 9 am to 4.30 pm daily ($6, children $1.50). Facilities include a cafe and displays; a good audiovisual is screened. The last admissions to the centre are at 4 pm; get there much earlier as there's a lot to see.

The private **Mt Bruce Pioneer Museum** on SH2, 10km south of the wildlife centre, has a huge collection, including gramophones, farming equipment and relics of NZ's pioneering days. It's open from 9 am to 4.30 pm daily ($3, children $0.50).

Tranzit Coachlines (Wellington; ☎ 04-387 2018) runs tours to the wildlife centre from Wellington ($35) and elsewhere in the Wairarapa ($20). It's easy to hitchhike.

CARTERTON, GREYTOWN & FEATHERSTON

A number of rural communities line SH2. Carterton has the **Paua Shell Factory** at 54 Kent St, open daily. You can see shellfish in a live paua aquarium and buy tacky or tasteful shell souvenirs.

Greytown was the country's first planned inland town and good examples of **Victorian architecture** line the main street. Pick up a heritage trail brochure from the tourist office for self-guided **historic walks** in the region. The quaint **Cobblestones Museum** at 169 Main St is open from 9 am to 4.30 pm daily.

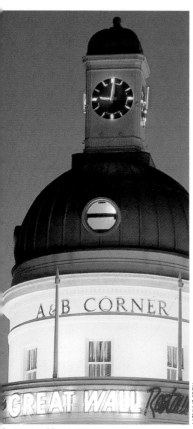

Art Deco architecture in Napier

The A&B Building in Napier

Street tile decoration

The Hawkes Bay is cabernet/merlot country – Te Mata Vineyard near Napier

Take the cable car to have a good look at the leafy hills of Wellington

Where the hot air comes from: The Beehive

Old Parliament House, Wellington

Enjoying a quiet cappuccino or soothing ale at Wellington waterfront

North-west of Greytown is the scenic **Waiohine Gorge** with a vast choice of outdoor activities conducted in an amphitheatre of native forests of rimu, kahikatea, beech and rata.

In Featherston, the **Fell Engine Museum** on the corner of Lyon and Fitzherbert Sts is worth a look. It houses the only remaining Fell locomotive in the world which once ran on three rails to climb 265m up the Rimutaka Incline. The museum is open on weekends from 10 am to 4 pm (1 to 4 pm on Sunday in winter).

Kahutara Canoe (☎/fax 06-308 8453) has sedate half-day canoe trips on the grade I Ruamahanga River ($30/15/12 for adults/students/children). There is a taxidermy museum, if you like that sort of thing.

The information centre (☎/fax 06-308 8051) is in the courthouse on Fitzherbert St.

The *Leeway Motel (☎ 06-308 9811)* has backpackers beds for $20 ($15 for two nights or more), as well as motel units for $80 a double.

Tranzit Coachlines buses from Wellington pass through all three towns and the train stops at Featherston and Carterton. Cyclists can avoid the worst of the horrors of the Rimutaka Hills on SH2 by taking the **Rimutaka Incline**, the old railway line now converted to a walking and mountain bike track. It starts 10km from Featherston along Western Lake Rd and comes out on SH2 at Kaitoke, where there is a YHA, 9km before Upper Hutt.

MARTINBOROUGH
pop 1500

Off SH2 and south of Greytown, Martinborough is the centre for tourism in the Wairarapa. Once just a sleepy town (although it still is on weekdays), it has become very popular with Wellingtonians as a weekend retreat because of the many vineyards in the area. On weekends, Gucci replaces gumboots and the town's fashionable dining establishments fill up.

Some 16 **wineries** are close to the town and are outlined in the free *Winemakers of Martinborough* pamphlet. The region produces only 2% of NZ's grapes but a wide variety of styles can be tasted. Martinborough is particularly known for its pinot noir.

Local tour operators that do winery tours include Mercury Buses (☎ 025-478 009), South Wairarapa Tours (☎ 308 9352) and Wairarapa Coach Lines (☎ 025-916 971).

Tours also run from Wellington: Wally Hammond Tours (☎ 04-472 0869) and Tranzit (☎ 04-387 2018) include Martinborough in their Wairarapa itineraries. Tranzit also has a transport-only option to Martinborough for $30 return (less for YHA members).

Other sights around Martinborough include the impressive **Patuna Chasm Walkway** through native bush and a limestone gorge. It goes through private property and can be booked ($10) through the information centre (☎ 306 9043) at 18 Kitchener St, which also has a full rundown on other activities, including glowworm cave visits.

The telephone area code is ☎ 06.

Places to Stay

Budget accommodation is nonexistent unless you count the very basic *Martinborough Camp Ground (☎ 306 9336)*, on the corner of Princes and Dublin Sts, which has tent/powered sites for $11/13.50 for two.

The information centre has a big list of B&Bs, farmstays and self-contained cottages in the area, and will book them. Cottages are popular and cost from around $60 to $120 a double. *Country Fare Cottages (☎ 306 9696, 4 Cambridge Rd)* has luxurious dwellings with extra-special touches; they are from $120 to $140.

The *Martinborough Connection (☎ 306 9708, 80 Jellicoe St)*, in a 120-year-old cottage, is a great B&B with four guestrooms. It's from $110 for a single or double.

Other notable places to stay are *The Turret House (☎ 306 8469, 21 Oxford St)*, *The Bronx (☎/fax 307 7728)*, just a short stroll from Martinborough's central square, and *McLeods (☎ 306 9032)* in Hautotara, 11km from Martinborough.

Places to Eat

The *Martinborough Hotel* in the square has been magnificently restored and includes a

WELLINGTON REGION

classy bistro. The menu is innovative, the chef is French and meals start at around $22 a main. Local wines are offered by the glass.

Ma Maison (☎ 306 8388) is open Saturday evening for dinner only, and it specialises in a nine-course French *degustation* (tasting) menu.

The *Grapevine* (☎ 306 9516, 48 Kitchener St) is a pleasant winery cafe for antipasto, cheeses and wine. The *Vineyard Cafe* (☎ 306 9889), in Puruatanga Rd, has home-cooked meals; it's open from 11 am to 5 pm Saturday, Sunday and holidays.

WAIRARAPA COAST
The Wairarapa coast from Palliser Bay to Castlepoint is one of the most remote and intriguing coasts in the North Island and well worth exploring. The road to Cape Palliser is really scenic, hemmed in as it is by the sea and the Aorangi Mountains. It also offers grand views across to the South Island, a spectacular sight in winter when the far-off hills are cloaked in snow. On the way, you pass the Wairarapa Wetlands and The Spit at Onoke – both good bird-watching sites. The coast is also the best surfing destination around Wellington.

The **Putangirua Pinnacles**, formed by rain washing silt and sand away and exposing the underlying bedrock, stand like giant organ pipes. Well worth a visit, they're accessible by a track near the car park on the Cape Palliser road. It's a one-hour return walk along a stream bed to the pinnacles, or you can take the three-hour loop track which takes in the hills and coastal views.

Not far to the south is the archetypal fishing village of **Ngawi**. The first thing that will impress you is the bulldozers pulling the fishing boats ashore. Continue on to the Cape Palliser **seal colony**, the North Island's largest breeding area. Whatever you do in your quest for that *National Geographic* shot, don't get between the seals and the sea. If you block off their escape route they are likely to have a go at you!

There are 252 steps up to the Cape Palliser **lighthouse**, from where there are even more breathtaking views of the South Island on a clear day. Occasionally you will see

surfers enjoying the southerly and south-easterly swells.

Castlepoint, with its reef and the lofty 162m-high Castle Rock, is an awesome place, with good protected swimming and plenty of walking tracks. There is a 45-minute return walk across the reef to the lighthouse, with over 70 species of fossil shells in the rock you pass over. Another 1½-hour walk goes to a huge limestone cave, or take the two-hour track from Deliverance Cove to Castle Rock. Keep well away from the lower reef when there are heavy seas; many lives have been lost here.

The telephone area code is ☎ 06.

Places to Stay
Lake Ferry, just a short detour off the road to Cape Palliser, has black sand dunes, lake fishing and surf casting, and several accommodation choices.

Lake Ferry Motor Camp (☎ 307 7873) has tent/powered sites for $9/11 and cabins from $15 per person. The *Lake Ferry Hotel* (☎ 307 7831) overlooking the water has doubles for $45 and $55.

Mangatoetoe (☎/fax 307 7728), a spacious place with a large deck, is in a beautiful location overlooking Palliser Bay ($50 for two, $10 per extra person).

At Ngawi, *Top House Tea Garden* (☎ 307 8229) has one room with en suite, TV and fridge for $55, and a self-contained unit for $65 a double. This place is also the local shop and cafe.

FOREST PARKS
Good opportunities for tramping in the Wairarapa are in the Tararua, Rimutaka and Haurangi (Aorangi) Forest Parks. There are some fine coastal walks too. Maps and information are available from DOC offices in Wellington and Masterton.

A favourite spot for tramping is at **Holdsworth**, the main eastern entrance to the Tararua Forest Park, where mountain streams run through some beautiful virgin forest. The park entrance has swimming, picnic and camping areas ($4 per night), a good hut ($8) and fine walks including: short, easy family walks; excellent one- or two-day walks; and longer, more challenging treks for experienced trampers right across to the west coast, coming out near Otaki.

The resident conservation officer (☎ 06-377 0022) has maps and information on tramping in the area, and an intentions book for you to sign. Ask about current weather and track conditions before setting off, and come prepared for all types of weather – the Tararua Forest Park has a notoriously changeable climate. The turn-off to Holdsworth is on SH2, 35km south of Masterton; from there it's 15km to the park entrance.

Closer to Wellington, the Rimutaka Incline walk is a five- to seven-hour walk (it can also be biked) each way along a historic old railway line which carried trains between Wellington and the Wairarapa between 1878 and 1955. The walk begins from SH2 (look for the signpost) 9km north of Upper Hutt. A little further north, 16km north of Upper Hutt on SH2, the **Kaitoke Regional Park** is good for swimming, rafting, camping, picnicking and walking; it has walks ranging from 20 minutes to six hours long.

The ***Black Stump YHA*** (*☎ 06-526 4626*) is at Kaitoke, 42km north of Wellington at the top of the Hutt Valley. On Marchant Rd, just off SH2, it's 1.5km from bushwalking tracks, swimming holes, horse and kayak hire, and 45 minutes' drive from Wellington (or you can take the Tranzit bus to Masterton). This rather basic hostel charges $10 a night.

SOUTH ISLAND

Marlborough & Nelson

Crossing Cook Strait from Wellington to Picton in the South Island is like entering a new country – the landscapes and people are similar yet different, and the Maori influence is less apparent. Many visitors strike out further afield immediately after crossing, but there is much of interest in this area, in particular the inlets and bays of Marlborough Sounds.

To the west is the Nelson region, with great tramping possibilities in its national parks. Nelson is a great city to relax in, as are the towns of Motueka and Takaka. If you are lucky and make it over to the far west, you can tour to remote Farewell Spit.

Marlborough Region

☎ 03 • pop 40,200

The first sight of the South Island for many visitors on the ferry is the convoluted waterways of the Marlborough Sounds. Picton is the gateway to the South Island and the many hideaways in the Marlborough Sounds, and you can set up a base there to go walking, fishing, sailing and kayaking. To the south of Picton is the sedate city of Blenheim and many nearby vineyards.

History

The first European to come across the Marlborough district was Abel Tasman, who spent five days sheltering on the eastern coast of D'Urville Island in 1642. It was to be over 100 years before the next European, the British explorer James Cook, turned up – in January 1770 – remaining there for 23 days. Between 1770 and 1777 Cook made four visits to the stretch of water he named Queen Charlotte's (now Charlotte) Sound. Near the entrance to Ship Cove a monument commemorates the explorer's visits. Because of Cook's detailed reports, the area became the best-known haven in the southern

HIGHLIGHTS

- Boating, walking and relaxing on the waterways of the Marlborough Sounds
- Walking the many tramping tracks of Kahurangi National Park
- Taking the ferry from Wellington to Picton, across Cook Strait and through the Tory Channel
- Relaxing and holidaying in Nelson
- Walking the Abel Tasman Coastal Track – undoubtedly and deservedly the most popular in the country
- Making the trip to the gannet colony and the lighthouse at the end of Farewell Spit
- Walking, boating or fishing in the Nelson Lakes National Park

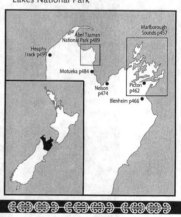

hemisphere. In 1827 the French navigator Jules Dumont d'Urville discovered the narrow strait now known as French Pass, and his officers named the island just to the north in his honour.

In the same year a whaling station was set up at Te Awaiti in Tory Channel, which brought about the first permanent European settlement in the district. In June 1840 Governor Hobson's envoy, Major Bunbury,

MARLBOROUGH & NELSON

See Marlborough Sounds Map p457

arrived on the HMS *Herald* on the hunt for Maori signatures to the Treaty of Waitangi. On 17 June Bunbury proclaimed the British Queen's sovereignty over the South Island at Horahora Kakahu Island. Towards the end of that year a Wesleyan mission was set up at Ngakuta Bay in the north-western corner of the port.

Despite this, the Marlborough area was not the site of an organised company settlement; it was more an overflow of the Nelson colony. Around 1840 the opportunistic and unscrupulous New Zealand Company tried to settle part of the Wairau Plain after

buying the alleged rights from the widow of a trader, John Blenkinsopp. He claimed he bought the land from the Maori for a 16-pound cannon, and had obtained a dubious deed signed by Maori chiefs who couldn't read English. The cannon is on display in Blenheim.

By 1843 the pressure for land from the Nelson settlers was so great that it led to conflict with the Maori, who denied all knowledge that any part of Wairau was sold. Two chiefs of the Ngati Toa tribe, Te Rauparaha and Te Rangihaeata, arrived from Kapiti to resist survey operations. The

MARLBOROUGH & NELSON

Pakeha sent out a hurriedly co-opted armed party led by Arthur Wakefield and Police Magistrate Thompson to arrest the chiefs. The party was met peacefully by the Ngati Toa at Tuamarina, but the Pakeha precipitated a brief skirmish, during which Te Rangihaeata's wife was shot. The Pakeha were then forced to surrender and Rangihaeata, mad with rage, demanded vengeance. Twenty-two of the party, including Wakefield and Thompson, were clubbed to death or shot; the rest escaped through the scrub and over the hills. The event came to be known as the Wairau Massacre.

Te Rauparaha was a formidable chief who was, indirectly, a major reason for the British government taking control of New Zealand. He cultivated the captains and crews of visiting whaling ships (they nicknamed him the 'Old Sarpint') and, with muskets and other weapons he acquired, set out on the wholesale and horrific slaughter of other South Island tribes. In his most gruesome raid he was aided by a Pakeha trader, who transported his warriors and decoyed the opposing chiefs on board, where they were set upon by Te Rauparaha's men. The ensuing slaughter virtually wiped out the local tribe. When news of this event and the captain's part in it reached Sydney, the British Government finally decided to bring some law and order to NZ and to unruly British citizens operating there.

In March 1847 Wairau was finally bought and added to the Nelson territory. It was not long before the place was deluged by settlers from Nelson and elsewhere. However, when the Wairau settlers realised that revenue from land sales in their area was being used to develop the Nelson district, they petitioned for independence. The appeal was successful and the colonial government called the new region Marlborough and approved one of the two settlements, Waitohi (now Picton) as the capital. At the same time, the other settlement, known as 'The Beaver', was renamed Blenheim. After a period of intense rivalry between the two towns, including legal action, the capital was transferred peacefully to Blenheim in 1865.

MARLBOROUGH SOUNDS

The waters of the Marlborough Sounds have many delightful bays, islands, coves and waterways, which were formed by the sea invading its deep valleys after the ice ages. Parts of the sounds are now included in the Marlborough Sounds Maritime Park, which is actually many small reserves separated by private land. To get an idea of how convoluted the sounds are, Pelorus Sound is 42km long but has 379km of shoreline.

The Queen Charlotte Track attracts many visitors, but accommodation is scattered throughout the sounds, offering delightful scenic retreats with an emphasis on water-based activities or simple relaxation.

Information

The best way to get around the sounds is still by boat, although the road system has been extended. Permits are required for hunting or camping and there's plenty of good swimming, tramping and fishing. Information is available in Picton from the visitor centre and Department of Conservation (DOC).

Queen Charlotte Track

Those put off by the hordes doing the Abel Tasman Track may wish to try this increasingly popular alternative. Though it doesn't have the beaches of the Abel Tasman, it has similarly wonderful coastal scenery. It is a 67km-long track that connects historic Ship Cove with Anakiwa, passing through privately owned land and DOC reserves. The coastal forest is lush, and from the ridges you can look down on either side to Queen Charlotte and Kenepuru Sounds.

You can do the walk in sections using local boat services or do the whole three- to four-day journey. There are many camp sites for those tenting it, as well as hostels and hotels. The route relies on the cooperation of local landowners, so respect their property and carry out what you carry in.

Endeavour Express (☎ 579 8465) has a number of day walks on the track. Ship Cove to Furneaux Lodge is the most popular ($40/30 for adults/children).

The track is well defined and suitable for people of all ages and average fitness. Ship

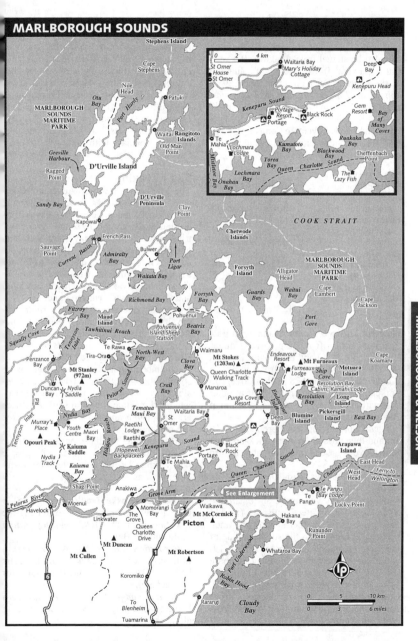

MARLBOROUGH SOUNDS

MARLBOROUGH & NELSON

Cove is the usual starting point, simply because it is easier to arrange a boat from Picton to Ship Cove than vice versa, but the walk can also be started from Anakiwa. Between Camp Bay and Torea Saddle you'll find the going toughest. For more information, get a copy of the *The Queen Charlotte Track* pamphlet from DOC in Picton. It is possible to do a leg of the trip by sea kayak; contact Marlborough Sounds Adventure Company (☎ 573 6078) for advice. Estimated distances and conservative walking times are:

Ship Cove to
Resolution Bay	4.5km	two hours
Resolution Bay to		
Endeavour Inlet	10.5km	three hours
Endeavour Inlet to		
Camp Bay/		
Punga Cove	11.5km	four hours
Camp Bay/Punga Cove to		
Torea Saddle/Portage	20.5km	nine hours
Torea Saddle/Portage to		
Mistletoe Bay	7.5km	four hours
Mistletoe Bay to		
Anakiwa	12.5km	four hours

Getting There & Away A number of boat operators drop off at Ship Cove. Cougar Line (☎ 573 7925) and Endeavour Express (☎ 579 8465), both at the Town Wharf in Picton, charge $30 to $38 to Ship Cove, and you can arrange to be dropped off at other destinations such as Resolution Bay, Camp Bay or Torea Bay (for Portage).

Boats from Picton leave around 9 to 10 am and then around 1.30 pm. Pick-up from Ship Cove is around one hour later. Return fares are $45 to $48.

At the Anakiwa end, the Mail Run (☎ 573 7389) picks up at the Anakiwa Kiosk and buses you to Picton for around $10. West Bay Water Transport (☎ 573 5597) covers the southern end of the track by boat, leaving from the southern side of the Picton ferry terminal to Anakiwa ($19) and other southern bays such as Lochmara ($15) at 9.45 am and 3.15 pm. Endeavour Express also covers Anakiwa in summer. Cougar Line also brings you back from Anakiwa, in conjunction with West Bay, as part of its return ticket.

Endeavour Express (☎ 579 8465 🅮 xprsboat@voyager.co.nz) has a good round-trip special for $45 that includes transferring your pack between accommodation daily, allowing you to walk with a day-pack only. For a day-trip walk, it will drop you off at Ship Cove and pick you up in the afternoon at Furneaux Lodge for $40. Cougar Line also has a wide range of day-walk options. West Bay has good one- and two-day specials with walks from Torea Saddle or Mistletoe Bay to Anakiwa ($29).

Sea Kayaking

The Marlborough Sounds Adventure Company (☎ 573 6078, 🅮 msac@msadventure .co.nz) in Picton organises sea-kayak trips and bushwalks around the sounds. The kayak trips range from one day ($80 including lunch) to four days ($750). It also hires out kayaks for solo trips at a daily cost of $50 for a single kayak (minimum of two days) or $75 for a double kayak. For $70 it will drive you and your kayaks to Tennyson Inlet.

Another operator running similar sea-kayaking trips out of Picton is Sea Kayaking Adventure Tours (☎ 574 2765).

Places to Stay & Eat

Accommodation is scattered throughout the sounds and, though some places are accessible only by boat, they are delightfully isolated and in some beautiful settings. Prices are reasonable and most places offer free use of dinghies.

Most popular are those on or just off the Queen Charlotte Track – even with people not walking the trail – but there are many other options.

Queen Charlotte Track Starting at Ship Cove (where camping is not permitted), the first camping is the *DOC camping ground* at Resolution Bay.

Resolution Bay Cabins (☎ 579 9411), a little further along the track, has backpackers beds for $16 and self-contained cabins for $45 and $80.

Kamahi Lodge (☎ 579 9415), nearby, is a homestay charging $65 per person including all meals.

Furneaux Lodge (☎ 579 8259) is a couple of hours' walk further on at Endeavour Inlet. This century-old place is set amid lovely gardens; chalets for two are $80, backpacker accommodation is $16 and $25 per person and camping is $6. The lodge has a shop, bar and restaurant.

The *Endeavour Resort (☎ 579 8381, ❸ endeavouresort@xtra.co.nz)*, a further 0-minute walk along, is comfortable with backpackers beds at $20, and cabins from $55 to $80 for two.

Another *DOC camping ground* is at Camp Bay on the western side of Endeavour Inlet, and other good places are a short walk off the track. These are accessible by car as well as boat.

Punga Cove Resort (☎ 579 8561), Web site: www.pungacove.co.nz, has expensive A-frame chalets for $100 to $300 but special packages may be offered. The older backpackers has twin rooms from $25 per person with linen. The resort has a pool, spa, shop and an excellent but expensive restaurant.

Homestead Backpackers (☎ 579 8373), a 10-minute walk around the bay, is open from the end of November to mid-April. This old farmhouse has a variety of beds for $16 per person, extra with linen.

Noeline's (☎ 579 8375), five minutes further up the hill, is a friendly place with great views. This well-kept homestay has beds in comfortable twin rooms for $16 per person.

The Bay of Many Coves has a *DOC camp site* on the saddle above the track.

Gem Resort (☎ 579 9771, ❸ gemresort@xtra.co.nz) is further south on the bay and charges $20 for backpackers and from $70 for units. The resort has a shop and licensed restaurant. Access to the Bay of Many Coves is only by boat or on foot.

Black Rock camp site, run by DOC, is further along the trail above Kumutoto Bay or you can continue on to the Torea Saddle and down to Portage.

The *Portage Resort (☎/fax 573 4309)*, an old stalwart on Kenepuru Sound, has doubles from $100 to $120. Improved bunkroom facilities cost $25 per person and you can cook. The hotel has sailboats, windsurfers, fishing, a spa, gym and tennis courts. The Portage Bay Shop (☎ 573 4445) also rents out yachts, dinghies, kayaks and bikes. The *DOC Cowshed Bay camp site* is just east around the bay from the resort. Portage can easily be reached by road from Picton or Havelock.

Lochmara Lodge (☎ 573 4554, ❸ lochmaralodge@xtra.co.nz) on Lochmara Bay is a superb and popular backpackers retreat, with good facilities and dorm beds from $20 to $30. More upmarket rooms are $80-plus. It's off the Queen Charlotte Track to the south and only 15 minutes by boat from Picton.

The *Mistletoe Bay Reserve (☎ 573 7582)*, towards the southern end of the track, is DOC's best local accommodation. As well as the camp site ($4), three farm cottages have beds for $10.

Te Mahia Bay Resort (☎ 573 4089, ❸ temahia@voyager.co.nz), north of the track just off the main road and in a beautiful bay facing Kenepuru Sound, has backpackers beds for $20 and self-contained units for $95. Camping is possible, and there's a store.

Anakiwa Backpackers (☎ 574 2334), at the south end of the trail, has a good self-contained backpackers unit with four beds for $16 per person. The sprawl of beds upstairs in the main house is less inviting in the busy season.

Other Sounds Accommodation There are almost 30 DOC camping grounds scattered throughout the sounds, providing water and toilet facilities but not a lot else – pick up a list in Picton. The *Marlborough Sounds Parkmap* ($13.50) shows camping locations.

Momorangi Bay Motor Camp (☎ 573 7865), 15km from Picton on the road to Havelock, is the only fully serviced camping ground near the water. Tent/powered sites are $7/8 per person, and cabins are $15/25/30 for one/two/three people.

The *Lazy Fish (☎ 579 9049, ❸ lazyfish@voyager.co.nz)* on Queen Charlotte Sound, 12km from Picton and accessible only by boat, is stylish and the most popular backpackers. This renovated homestead, now a hostel, charges $20 per person for dorms and $45 for doubles. This includes free use of the windsurfer, dinghy, canoe, fishing gear, snorkels etc. The backpackers has its own secluded beach and a spa pool underneath the palm trees. It is popular, so book ahead before you catch a boat out there.

Mary's Holiday Cottage (☎ 573 4660), on Kenepuru Sound at Waitaria Bay, 95km from Picton via Linkwater, is a YHA associate. You'll probably have the old farmhouse to yourself at $15 per person, unless a family or group rents out the whole house for $70. *Hopewell Backpackers* (☎/fax 573 4341), further along the same road, is the place to choose if you want to stay in a remote part of Kenepuru Sound. Doubles and twins are $34, and the price lets you use a full range of equipment such as rowing boats and fishing lines. Access by road is possible but it's a long, tedious and bumpy drive; better is a water taxi from Portage.

Other accommodation at Double Bay, Kenepuru Sound (accessible by road) includes the upmarket *Raetihi Lodge* (☎ 573 4300, @ hotel@raetihi.co.nz), with a variety of lodge rooms for up to $175 a double. Meals are available.

St Omer House (☎ 573 4086) has bunkroom accommodation from $25 per person, cottages from $65 a double and full board in the old-fashioned main buildings for $95 per person with excellent meals.

Te Pangu Bay Lodge (☎ 579 9755) on Te Pangu Bay, Tory Channel, rents out self-contained units for two to seven people for $25 per person (minimum unit charge $50). It can only be reached by boat.

Pohuenui Island Sheep Station (☎ 597 8161) at Pohuenui, 30km north of Havelock, comes recommended by readers and has accommodation ranging from a bunkroom at $18 to full board in the homestead for $200 including boat trips, with the bonus of staying on a working sheep station.

Soul Escape Tours (☎ 0800-737 227, @ john.jules@xtra.co.nz), Moenui Bay, has been recommended as a relaxing place to stay by readers.

The Picton Visitor Centre can advise on other places to stay in the sounds.

Getting There & Away

Scheduled boats service most of the accommodation on the Queen Charlotte Track (see that section) and are the cheapest way to get around the sounds. The Cougar Line also runs to the Lazy Fish hostel on Queen Charlotte Sound at least two days a week for a $30-return special. A water taxi costs about the same if there's a group of four or five.

Arrow Water Taxis (☎ 573 8229) is one well-known operator at Town Wharf in Picton servicing Queen Charlotte Sound. In Havelock, the Havelock Outdoors Centre (☎ 574 2114) books water taxis. These are quite expensive unless split among four or five passengers.

No scheduled buses service the sounds but much of it is accessible by car. The road to Portage is sealed, but beyond that you have to endure forever-winding, gravel roads.

PICTON
pop 3600

The ferry from the North Island comes into Picton, a pretty little port at the head of Queen Charlotte Sound. Originally called Waitohi, Picton is a small borough: a hive of activity when the ferry is in and during the peak of summer, but rather slow and sleepy any other time.

Information

The Picton Visitor Information Centre (☎5573 7477, @ pictonvin@xtra.co.nz), 200m from the ferry terminal, has good maps, information on boats and walking in the sounds area and email facilities, and makes bookings for transport and accommodation. It is open from 8.30 am to 5 pm daily in winter and until 8 pm in summer. Email is also available at the Creek Pottery, 26 High St. There is a DOC booth in the centre.

A useful website is www.marlborough .co.nz; it lists accomodation and activities.

The Railway Station (☎ 573 8857) in the Picton train station also provides information.

The ferry terminal in Picton has a rare convenience for NZ – a laundrette and public showers. The Marlin Motel (☎ 573 6784) at 33 Devon St is the Automobile Association (AA) agent.

The *Edwin Fox*

Between the information centre and the ferry wharf is the battered but still floating hull of the old East Indiaman *Edwin Fox*. Built of teak in Bengal, the 157ft (48m), 760-ton vessel was launched in 1853 and in its long and varied career carried convicts to Perth (Australia), troops to the Crimean War and immigrants to NZ.

The *Edwin Fox* is slowly being restored and the metal-sheathed hull is open to visitors from 8.45 am to 5 pm daily, closing at 4.30 pm in winter ($4, children $1). Enter through the small museum which has a few maritime exhibits and local crafts.

Other Attractions

The excellent little **Picton Museum** is on the foreshore, right below London Quay. Interesting exhibits include whaling items such as a harpoon gun, and a Dursley Pederson bicycle built around 1890. The museum is open from 10 am to 4 pm daily ($3, children $0.50).

On the eastern side of Shakespeare Bay, across the inlet from the town centre via the footbridge, is the scow (barge) **Echo**, which now houses the Maritime History Gallery. Built on the Wairau River in 1905, the *Echo* shipped around 14,000 tons of freight a year between Blenheim and Wellington, and was only retired in 1965 after the railway ferries were introduced ($3, children $1).

Tuamarina, 19km south of Picton, is historically interesting as the site of the Wairau Massacre. The tree near where the skirmish started still stands on the riverbank. In the cemetery, just above the road, is a **Pakeha monument** designed by Felix Wakefield, youngest brother of Arthur Wakefield, who was killed in the fray.

Walking

The information centre has a map showing several good walks in and near town, as well as others further afield in the sounds and the maritime park. Plenty of maps and leaflets on walks in the area are available from DOC.

An easy 1km track runs along the eastern side of Picton Harbour to Bob's Bay, where there's a barbecue area in a sheltered cove.

The **Snout Walkway** carries on along the ridge from the Bob's Bay path and has great views of the length of Queen Charlotte Sound. Allow three hours for the walk.

The **Tirohanga Walkway**, beginning on Newgate St behind the hospital, takes about 45 minutes each way and features panoramic views of Picton and the sounds.

Organised Tours

The main access around Queen Charlotte Sound is by water, serviced by innumerable cruises and fishing trips.

Round-the-bay cruises include the Beachcomber Fun Cruises' (☎ 573 6175) all-day mail-run cruise around Pelorus Sound on Tuesday, Thursday and Friday for $70, and a Queen Charlotte Sound Cruise on Wednesday and Saturday. Other options are its Round the Bays and Portage Luncheon Cruise.

Dolphin Watch Marlborough (☎ 573 8040), beside the train station, has a variety of eco-boat tours taking in the seals, sea birds and dolphins of Queen Charlotte Sound with departures at 8.45 am and 1.45 pm (from $58).

On land, Sounds Connection (☎ 573 8843) and the Corgi Bus Company (☎ 573 7125) are local tour operators; winery visits are a speciality. Deluxe Travel Lines (☎ 578 5467) operates all-day wine-trail tours from Blenheim but also picks up in Picton.

Diver's World (☎ 573 7323), on the corner of London Quay and Auckland St, and Picton Underwater Centre, at 41 Wellington St, hire out equipment and organise charters.

See the Marlborough Sounds section earlier for sea kayaking trips out of Picton.

Places to Stay

Camping & Cabins The *Blue Anchor Holiday Park* (☎ 573 7212, 78 Waikawa Rd), only 500m from the town centre, has tent/powered sites at $20/22, various cabins for $35 to $45 and tourist flats at $57 to $60; prices are for two.

Alexander's Holiday Park (☎ 573 6378) is 1km out on Canterbury St and has sites at $18 for two, plus a variety of ageing cabins at $30 to $40.

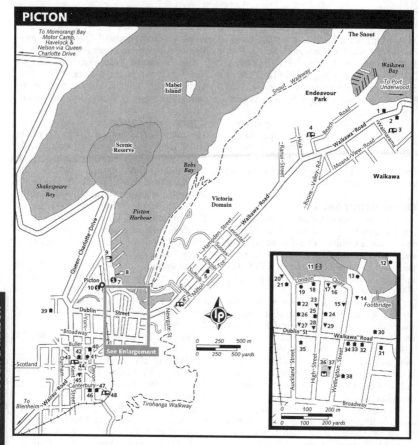

PICTON

To Momorangi Bay
Motor Camp,
Havelock &
Nelson via Queen
Charlotte Drive

The Snout

Waikawa
Bay

To Port
Underwood

Mabel
Island

Snout Walkway

Endeavour
Park

Beach Road

Waikawa Road

Scenic
Reserve

Hula

Ranui Street

Moana View Road

Waimama

Waikawa

Bobs
Bay

Shakespeare
Bay

Victoria
Domain

Boons Valley Rd

Picton
Harbour

Waikawa Road

Hampden Street

Sussex Street

Lincoln Tce

Suffolk Street

Milton Tce

London Quay

Picton
10

9

8

7

Dublin
Street

Lynch St

Newgate St

Surrey

39

Broadway

Buller

42

40

Scotland

43

Durham

Kent Street

Devon

44

45

Canterbury 47

46   48

To
Blenheim

Tirohanga Walkway

See Enlargement

0   250   500 m
0   250   500 yards

Enlargement

11

12

13

20

21

London Quay

14

Footbridge

19   18

17   16

22   23

25

15

26

24

27   28

29

Dublin St

30

35

Waikawa Road

33   34   33   32

31

Auckland Street

High Street

36   37

38

Wellington Street

Broadway

0   100   200 m
0   100   200 yards

Picton Campervan Park (☎ 573 8875) is
a small, well-equipped slice of suburbia
with powered sites for $18.

The ***Parklands Marina Holiday Park***
(☎ 573 6343) is on Beach Rd at Waikawa
Bay, 3km from town. Other possibilities include ***Waikawa Bay Holiday Park*** (☎ 573
7434) and ***Momorangi Bay Motor Camp***
(☎ 573 7865) – see the Marlborough
Sounds section for details.

Backpackers These are listed in terms of
distance from the ferry terminal, not necessarily quality.

Picton Lodge (☎ 573 7788, **ℯ** picton
.lodge@xtra.co.nz, 3 Auckland St) is 200m
from the terminal. Dorms are $15 per per-
son, and twins and doubles are $38. The fa-
cilities in this large place are good and
there's a smokers' terrace with harbour
views.

The Villa (☎ 573 6598, **ℯ** stay@
thevilla.co.nz, 34 Auckland St) is a popular
place based on a renovated villa. Dorm beds
cost $17 and $18, and doubles or twins are
$44. It books activities, provides breakfast
and has a spa. The attentive owners make
this a special place.

PICTON

PLACES TO STAY
1 Bay Vista Waterfront Motel
2 Bayview Backpackers
3 Waikawa Bay Holiday Park
4 Parklands Marina Holiday Park
5 Bell Bird Motel
6 Blue Anchor Holiday Park
18 Terminus Hotel
21 Picton Lodge
22 The Villa
24 Americano Motor Inn & Restaurant
25 Tourist Court Motel
26 Bavarian Lodge
30 Picton Beachcomber Inn; Whalers Restaurant
31 Harbour View Motel
32 Marineland Motels/ Guesthouse
33 Admiral's Lodge
34 The Gables
35 Wedgewood House

38 Jasmine Court Traveller Inn
39 Cottage International
40 Marlin Motel; Automobile Association Agent
42 Sequoia Lodge Backpackers & Car Rentals
43 Picton Campervan Park
46 Juggler's Rest
47 Sounds Paradise Backpackers
48 Alexander's Holiday Park

PLACES TO EAT
14 Kiwi Takeaways
15 Bollies Cafe
16 Seaspray Cafe
17 Sea Breezes Cafe
20 Toot 'n' Whistle
23 Le Café; Marlborough Terranean
27 Picton Bakery
28 Holty's
29 Kentucky-Eat-A-Way
37 Settler's Arms

45 Crow Tavern

OTHER
7 Picton Visitor Information Centre; DOC
8 Edwin Fox
9 Cook Strait Ferry Terminal; Laundry; Shower
10 Booking Office & Dolphin Watch
11 Picton Museum
12 Echo
13 Town Wharf - Marlborough Sounds Adventure Company; Cougar Line; Endeavour Express; Beachcomber Fun Cruises; Buzzy Bikes & Boat Rentals
19 Diver's World
36 Mariners Mall
41 Wiseway's Supermarket
44 Nelson Square

The ***Bougainvillea Lodge*** (☎ *573 6536,* **@** *bavarian@voyager.co.nz, 42 Auckland St),* formerly the Bavarian, is next to the Villa and though not as stylish it's comfortable and well run. Dorm beds cost $15 per person, doubles $34 and $36 and twins $40, including breakfast.

Wedgewood House (☎ *573 7797, 10 Dublin St),* around the corner, is a YHA associate. An old converted guesthouse with two, four or six beds to a room, it costs $16 per person or $38 for twin rooms. It's open until 11 pm for passengers from the late ferry.

The ***Sequoia Lodge Backpackers*** (☎ *0800-222 257,* **@** *stay@sequoialodge .co.nz, 3A Nelson Square),* Web site: www.sequoialodge.co.nz, named after one of the enormous trees out the front, is a breath of fresh air in Picton. It has an outdoor chess set, free email, soup in winter, fresh bread nightly, and percolated coffee morning and evening. A dorm is $16, a double $40 and a double with en suite $45 (with linen). You can rent cheap cars here ($45 insured, and everything over 30 days is $25 per day).

About five minutes' walk south of town, the ***Juggler's Rest*** (☎ *573 5570,* **@** *jugglers-rest@xtra.co.nz, 8 Canterbury St),* is a backpackers with a difference: it is run by professional jugglers and juggling lessons (even fire-eating lessons!) are offered free. The house has a nice garden and dorm beds are $14 and doubles $32.

Sounds Paradise Backpackers (☎ *573 8280),* a restored homestead, is a little further east on Canterbury St near the river; share rooms are from $14 and twins $38.

Bayview Backpackers (☎ *573 7668,* **@** *bayview.backpackers@xtra.co.nz, 318 Waikawa Rd)* on Waikawa Bay has bay views and pleasant porch areas from which to enjoy them. It's 4km from central Picton but offers free pick-up and drop-off. Doubles and twins are from $32 to $45, and dorms cost from $14.50 to $16 per person. Water sports equipment and bicycles are free for guests.

B&Bs & Guesthouses Picton has a number of B&Bs and guesthouses, including ***Cottage International*** (☎/fax *573 7935, 25 Gravesend Place)* in a comfortable private house. It's halfway between a backpackers and a B&B – singles/twins/triples are from $26/40/48, and breakfast is extra.

Marineland Motels/Guesthouse (☎ *573 6429, 28 Waikawa Rd)* has a pool. B&B

singles/doubles are $45/60, up to $45/75 in the peak season with breakfast, and motel units are $70 for two. The staff are friendly and helpful.

The *Admiral's Lodge* (☎ 573 6590, ✆ admiralb&b@xtra.co.nz, 22 Waikawa Rd) has B&B rooms for $55/85 and offers low-season discounts.

The Gables (☎ 573 6772, 20 Waikawa Rd), next door, is similarly priced, and serves some good breakfasts.

Motels & Hotels Picton has plenty of motels, many of them on Waikawa Rd just east of the city centre. Most are priced at around $65 to $85 for two; low-season discounts may apply.

The *Tourist Court Motel* (☎ 573 6331, 45 High St), very central, is a simple place with studio units from $55 for two or two-bedroom units for $70.

The *Bell Bird Motel* (☎ 573 6912, 96 Waikawa Rd) is another cheapie with units for $58.

The *Bay Vista Waterfront Motel* (☎ 573 6733), 4km out at Waikawa Bay, is also good value at $65 to $80 for two.

The *Harbour View Motel* (☎ 0800-101 133, 30 Waikawa Rd) is notable for its great views; units cost from $65 to $80.

Americano Motor Inn (☎ 573 6398, ✆ americano@xtra.co.nz, 32 High St) is a better class of motel with a spa, pool, restaurant/bar and units from $75 to $98.

Jasmine Court Travellers' Inn (☎ 573 7110, 78 Wellington St) is a very nice, up-market place with units with heated bathrooms from $95 to $115.

The *Terminus Hotel* (☎ 573 6452, 1 High St) has good pub rooms with private facilities costing $45/75 for singles/doubles.

Places to Eat

Restaurants Picton's best cluster of restaurants is on High St.

Holty's (53 High St) serves ribs, pizzas and its popular barbecued chicken.

The *Marlborough Terranean* (☎ 573 7122, 31 High St) is a sophisticated place with a very good wine selection. The European, not just Mediterranean, inspired menu features many seafood dishes at around $10 an entree and $25 a main.

The *Americano Restaurant*, nearby in the motel, has a great menu which includes the Pacific platter ($25.50) and mussels in garlic sauce ($9). *Le Café*, an artistic place next door, is very popular for its reasonable prices – mains are around $16.

Whalers Restaurant, in the Picton Beachcomber Inn, has steaks and seafood.

Along London Quay, the *Terminus Hotel* has pub food, with bistro meals from about $8 to $10. The Terminus has sticky carpets and laminated tables but the food is fine.

The *Crow Tavern* (☎ 573 6123) at Nelson Square has pub fare and fresh seafood. The *Toot 'n' Whistle* is a much classier pub with reasonable snacks and meals.

Fast Food The best *supermarket* is in Mariners Mall on High St. *Wiseway's supermarket* is on Nelson Square. *Kiwi Takeaways*, popular for fast food, is near the corner of the Quay and Wellington St. *Kentucky Eat-A-Way* (52 High St) is similar.

The *Picton Bakery*, on the corner of Dublin and Auckland Sts, bakes 'dark long-baked rye bread ... real German style', good for tramping (as it doesn't break up).

The *Seaspray Cafe*, along the waterfront, has standard Kiwi coffee-shop fare and cheap breakfasts.

Bollies Cafe on Wellington St has similarly plain but cheap and hearty meals. The *Sea Breezes Cafe* (24 London Quay) is a good spot for a snack.

The *Settler's Arms* (☎ 573 6566), Wellington St, is a cafe with an excellent local wine selection.

Getting There & Away

Air Soundsair (☎ 0800-505 005) has a regular service across the strait to and from Wellington. The short flight costs $50 and operates about six times a day. The courtesy shuttle bus from the airstrip at Koromiko, 8km south, is included in the price. There are also flights from Blenheim.

Bus Numerous buses go south to Christchurch and beyond, and west to Nelson, from where there are connections going across to the West Coast.

InterCity (☎ 573 7025), at the ferry terminal, has a service to Christchurch with connections to Dunedin and Invercargill, and another route east to Nelson via Blenheim and Havelock with connections to Greymouth and the glaciers. At least one bus daily on each of these routes connects with a ferry sailing to and from Wellington.

A profusion of small shuttle buses heads south to Christchurch and beyond. You can choose from Atomic Shuttles (☎ 573 6855), South Island Connections (☎ 578 9904), Compass Coachlines (☎ 578 7102) and Southern Link Shuttles (☎ 573 7477). They charge around $25 to $30. You can book through the information centres.

To Nelson, the main shuttles are Kiwilink (☎ 577 8332) and Knightline (☎ 528 7798), both running Blenheim-Picton-Nelson. Sounds to Coast (☎ 0800-802 225) has shuttles three days a week to Greymouth via St Arnaud. Nelson Lakes Transport (☎ 521 1877) also runs to St Arnaud and on to Westport in summer.

All buses serving Picton operate from the ferry terminal or the information centre.

Train The *Coastal Pacific* train between Picton and Christchurch, via Blenheim and Kaikoura, operates daily in each direction. The train connects with the ferry and a free shuttle service is provided between the train station and ferry terminal on both sides of the strait. This trip is highly recommended for its coastal scenery.

Hitching Hitching out on SH1 towards Blenheim is possible, but may take a few hours. Most traffic is on the road as soon as the ferry docks – there is not much between sailings. Most cars are off the ferry before you can get your thumb out and you'll have to compete with other hitchhikers.

Heading west, Queen Charlotte Drive between Picton and Havelock is the shortest way to Nelson but has little traffic. It's easier to hitch via Blenheim on the Spring Creek bypass: follow the Blenheim road (SH1) for 22km to Spring Creek, where you

turn right towards Renwick. On average it will take a day to reach Christchurch or Nelson.

Boat *Interislander* ferries (☎ 0800-802 802) shuttle back and forth between Wellington and Picton four or five times daily; the crossing takes three hours. The faster *TopCat* does the crossing in 1½ hours, twice daily in both directions. The *Lynx* operates in summer three times daily. (See the Wellington Region chapter for details.)

Getting Around

Avis, Hertz, Thrifty, Budget and Avon Cars (Shoestring Rentals) have rental offices at the ferry terminal. Pegasus (☎ 573 7733), near the train station, and other cheaper car rentals are also represented in Picton.

Nifty-fifty (50cc) motorbikes (for which you need a current car licence) can be hired from Buzzy Bikes beside the MV *Beachcomber* office or at Sounds Connection.

See the Marlborough Sounds section for details of cruises, boat connections and water taxis to the sounds. Check at the station information office or at the visitor information centre.

BLENHEIM
pop 25,900

The largest town in the Marlborough Sounds region, Blenheim is 29km south of Picton on the Wairau Plains, a contrasting landscape to the sounds. The flatness of the town, at the junction of the Taylor and Opawa Rivers, was a problem in the early days and it grew up around a swamp, now the reclaimed Seymour Square with its attractive lawns and gardens.

Blenheim doesn't have Picton's picturesque setting but it does have a large array of services and is at the centre of NZ's most famous wine-growing district.

During the second weekend in February Blenheim hosts the now famous Marlborough Food & Wine Festival at Montana's Brancott Estate. The comprehensive *Wineries of Marlborough* ($2) outlines the festival, restaurants and wineries, and has profiles on the wine makers.

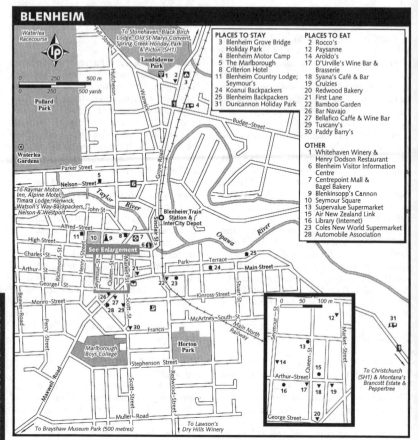

BLENHEIM

Waterlea Racecourse

To Stonehaven, Black Birch Lodge, Old St Marys Convent, Spring Creek Holiday Park & Picton (SH1)

Landsdowne Park

Pollard Park

Waterlea Gardens

Parker Street

Nelson—Street

To Raymar Motor Inn, Alpine Motel, Timara Lodge, Kenwick, Watson's Way Backpackers, Nelson & Westport

Alfred—Street

High—Street

Charles—St

Arthur—St

George—St

Monro—Street

Francis—

Marlborough Boys College

Stephenson Street

Muller—Road

To Brayshaw Museum Park (500 metres)

To Lawson's Dry Hills Winery

Budge—Street

Blenheim Train Station & InterCity Depot

Opawa   River

Park—Terrace

Kinross—Street

McArtney—South—St

Main North Railway

Horton Park

To Christchurch (SH1) & Montana's Brancott Estate & Peppertree

George-Street

PLACES TO STAY
3 Blenheim Grove Bridge Holiday Park
4 Blenheim Motor Camp
5 The Marlborough
8 Criterion Hotel
11 Blenheim Country Lodge; Seymour's
24 Koamui Backpackers
25 Blenheim Backpackers
31 Duncannon Holiday Park

PLACES TO EAT
2 Rocco's
12 Paysanne
14 Aroldo's
17 D'Urville's Wine Bar & Brasserie
18 Syana's Café & Bar
19 Cruizies
20 Redwood Bakery
21 First Lane
22 Bamboo Garden
26 Bar Navajo
27 Bellafico Caffe & Wine Bar
29 Tuscany's
30 Paddy Barry's

OTHER
1 Whitehaven Winery & Henry Dodson Restaurant
6 Blenheim Visitor Information Centre
7 Centrepoint Mall & Bagel Bakery
9 Blenkinsopp's Cannon
10 Seymour Square
13 Supervalue Supermarket
15 Air New Zealand Link
16 Library (Internet)
23 Coles New World Supermarket
28 Automobile Association

Information

The Blenheim Visitor Information Centre (☎ 578 9904, ✉ blm_info@clear.net.nz) is at 2 High St on SH1. It has a number of DOC maps and leaflets on the many walkways around the Marlborough area. The centre is open from 8.30 am to 6.30 pm daily in summer and for shorter hours in winter. Get the free *Treasured Pathway* pamphlet, a guide to the Marlborough Nelson Heritage Highway.

The AA office (☎ 578 3399) is at 23 Maxwell Rd, on the corner of Seymour St. There are email facilities at the Blenheim Library in Arthur St, and at the town's backpackers.

Things to See & Do

The 5.5-hectare **Brayshaw Museum Park**, off New Renwick Rd, has several attractions, including a reconstructed colonial village of old Blenheim, early farming equipment, a miniature railway and the Museum & Archives Building. The park is open during daylight hours (free). As regional museums go, this is a good one.

At **Pollard Park & Waterlea Gardens**, off Parker St, there is a childrens playground and a fitness trail; flowers bloom all year here.

Near Seymour Square are relics of Blenheim's violent early history, including **Blenkinsopp's cannon** in front of the council offices on Seymour St. Originally from the whaling ship *Caroline,* which Blenkinsopp captained, this is reputedly the cannon for which Te Rauparaha was persuaded to sign over the Wairau Plains and, therefore, one of the causes of the subsequent massacre at Tuamarina.

Recreation Areas There are a number of rural retreats with a variety of landforms and flora, such as native broom or prostrate kowhai. The **Robertson Range** and **Whites Bay** near Port Underwood north of Blenheim have great vistas of Cloudy Bay. **Wairau Lagoons**, to the east of Blenheim, is home to more than 70 bird species.

The **coastal road** from Blenheim to Picton is a good two-hour drive but has spectacular coastal views and remnants of early European history. Good spots for picnics are Robin Hood Bay, Ocean Bay and the head of Port Underwood (Hakahaka Bay). The narrow winding road from Waikawa to Rarangi has superb views of the North Island silhouetted on the horizon.

There are about 10 excellent **walks** in Wither Hills Farm Park, just to the south of Blenheim. Included is the Mt Vernon Loop mountain bike trail (1½ hours).

The Ramshead Farm walking track in the Waihopai Valley is a private venture with two huts (Dillon's and McNaught's). The one-/two-/three-day options are $20/35/50 (contact ☎ 572 4016 or fax 572 4046 for bookings).

Wineries The big attraction around Blenheim is the wineries – it's NZ's largest wine-producing area – and there are around 30 cellar doors for tasting. The wineries produce a variety of wines, but the Marlborough region is particularly famous for its floral sauvignon blancs, chardonnays, fruity reislings and Methode Champenoise styles.

Most wineries are open daily and some have cafes or restaurants (see Places to Eat

later). The largest winery in NZ is Montana (with a storage capacity of 20 million litres); there are tours (☎ 578 2099) from 10 am to 3 pm Monday to Saturday.

If you really want to finish yourself off, Prenzel Distillery on Sheffield St, 6km south-east of Blenheim, produces liqueurs, schnapps, fruit wines and brandies. The Cork & Keg in Renwick, 10km west of Blenheim, is ye olde English pub that brews its own malt beers. Ponder Estate, 2km south of Renwick, produces olives as well as wine.

Deluxe Travel Lines (☎ 578 5467) has a six-hour 'Scenic Wine Trail' tour of local wineries which costs $36 ($40 from Picton). Highlight Tours (☎ 578 9904) offers personalised tours for between $35 and $45 per person. Back Country Safaris (☎ 575 7525) also puts together well-regarded personalised tours for a minimum of two.

Activities

There is **skiing** at the Rainbow Valley ski area (☎ 521 1861), 130km (1½ hours) west of Blenheim. Back Country Safaris (☎ 575 7525) and JJs Ski Transport (☎ 544 7081) buses go right to the skifield (see the Activities chapter).

The more adventurous could try **white-water rafting** on some of the nearby rivers. Action in Marlborough (☎/fax 578 4531) at 59 Lakings Rd, Blenheim, can get you wet any time. The costs range from about $65 for a half-day trip to $450 for three-day expeditions. Its trips focus on the Buller and Gowan Rivers.

Horse-trekking operators include High Country Horse Treks (☎ 577 9424). The Branch Saddle and Ridge rides are $50 (both 2½ hours).

Places to Stay

Camping & Cabins The *Blenheim Grove Bridge Holiday Park (☎ 578 3667, 78 Grove Rd)* at the northern end of town has sites by the river at $20, cabins from $35 to $50 and tourist flats from $55; prices are for two.

The *Blenheim Motor Camp (☎ 578 7419, 27 Budge St),* just off SH1, is neat and fastidious. Tent/powered sites are $18/20 but there's not much grass for campers. It has mostly cabins at $30 to $40, and the backpackers lodge at $15 per person doesn't have much atmosphere.

Camping grounds further out include **Duncannon Holiday Park** (☎ 578 8193), 2km east of the town centre, where sites cost $18 and on-site caravans and cabins are $30.

The **Spring Creek Holiday Park** (☎ 570 5893), on Rapaura Rd 6km out towards Picton and about 500m off SH1, has camp sites ($18) and cabins ($28 to $40). It is peaceful and near a good fishing creek.

Backpackers Blenheim Backpackers (☎ 578 6062, ✆ rob.diana@xtra.co.nz, 29 Park Terrace) is an old maternity home. Doubles are $36 and dorms are $14 per person. The Opawa River runs behind the house and you can borrow canoes.

Koanui Backpackers (☎ 578 7487, ✆ koanui@xtra.co.nz, 33 Main St) has bunks at $16 per person, twins for $18 and $20 per person, and doubles for $40. This is a friendly place popular with itinerant fruit-pickers. It has a pool table, barbecue and electric blankets on all the beds.

Watson's Way Backpackers (☎/fax 572 8228, 56 High St), at Renwick 10km west of Blenheim (in the heart of the wine-growing district), is an excellent purpose-built place in a quiet garden setting. Shared rooms are $18 per person and the one double room is $40. Breakfast is included.

Guesthouses, Motels & Hotels The information centre lists B&Bs, homestays and self-contained accommodation. Those on vineyards are particularly popular and include **Stonehaven** (☎ 572 9730) on Rapaura Rd north-west of town, where doubles are $105 to $120.

On SH1, south of town, **Peppertree** (☎ 578 7009, ✆ thepeppertree@xtra.co.nz) has a beautiful garden setting; doubles cost $165.

Broomfield (☎ 572 8162, 35 Inkerman St), similarly priced, is in a rammed-earth house in Renwick with a lovely garden ($120 for two). It's close to 16 wineries.

The **Black Birch Lodge** (☎ 572 8876, fax 572 8806), on Jefferies Rd just north of

Rapaura Rd, is quite simply superb and in the heart of the wine country (prices on application).

Old Saint Marys Convent (☎ 570 5700, ✆ oldstmary@xtra.co.nz), Rapaura Rd, has a magnificent interior with a kauri staircase; inquire at the visitor centre.

Timara Lodge (☎ 572 8276), Web site: www.timara.co.nz, on Dog Point Rd near Renwick, is expensive but worth it ($450/550 plus GST for singles/doubles).

Reasonably priced motels include **Raymar Motor Inn** (☎ 578 5104, 164 High St) where doubles cost $55 to $65, and the similarly priced **Alpine Motel** (☎ 578 1604, 148 Middle Renwick Rd). At most other motels, doubles cost $65 to $85.

The **Criterion Hotel** (☎ 578 3299) on Market St costs $75 for two.

Upmarket hotels include **The Marlborough** (☎ 577 7333, 20 Nelson St), close to Pollard Park, with rooms from $120; and the **Blenheim Country Lodge** (☎ 578 5079) on the corner of Alfred and Henry Sts, with 52 rooms from $90 to $165.

Places to Eat

Restaurants The excellent **Seymour's** restaurant is at the Blenheim Country Lodge. The **Criterion Hotel** on the corner of Market and Alfred Sts is the place for pub food with its large carvery. **Paddy Barry's** is an Irish-style place on Scott St for seafood and steaks washed down with Guinness. **Bar Navajo** (☎ 577 7555, 70 Queen St) is another pub with cheap meals.

The **Bamboo Garden** (16 Main St) serves good Chinese food.

Aroldo's (578 0553, 57 Seymour St) serves genuine Kiwi fare and plenty of seafood; flames are a speciality.

Tuscany's (36 Scott St) specialises in Mediterranean fare. The Berrocca buzz in pineapple and orange juice is $3.50, entrees are around $7 and mains $18.

Rocco's (☎ 578 6940, 5 Dodson St), run by two brothers Piero and Gino, serves excellent Italian provincial dishes (mains are from $21 to $28 and there's a great wine selection).

The **d'Urville Wine Bar & Brasserie** (☎ 577 9945, 52 Queen St) serves regional produce (mains are about $22) and a big selection of local wines.

Bellafico Caffe & Wine Bar (☎ 577 6072, 17 Maxwell Place) has an interesting, varied European menu.

Paysanne, upstairs in the Forum building on Market St, has a blackboard menu, a selection of pizzas, and mains from $16 to $25.

Wineries Several of the wineries around Blenheim also serve meals. The *Henry Dodson Restaurant (☎ 577 6634)*, in the Whitehaven Winery north of town on Dodson St (off Grove Rd), has tasty food.

Hunters on Rapaura Rd also serves food daily. The *Twelve Trees (☎ 572 7123)* at Allan Scott's winery, Jacksons Rd, is also recommended for its innovative blackboard menu.

Lawson's Dry Hills, Alabama Rd, also serves meals, usually enjoyed after a wine tour. Other wineries serving food are *Cairnbrae Wines* on Jacksons Rd, *Cellier Le Brun* in Renwick, *Domaine Georges Michel* in Rapaura, *Forest Estate* on SH6 (for ploughman's lunches daily), *Gillan Estate* on Rapaura Rd, *Highfield Estate* in the Omaka Valley and *Wairau River Wines* on Rapaura Rd.

Out in Renwick, 10km west of Blenheim, is the *Cork & Keg*, where you can lunch and relax with a beer if you tire of wine.

Fast Food & Self-Catering *Cruizies (10 Maxwell Rd)* is an old-style cafe with filled rolls, bagels and salads. The *Redwood Bakery* on Queen St bakes continental bread for those tired of the usual Kiwi loaf.

Syana's Cafe & Bar (67 Queen St) is a small cafe and bar with ambience, good coffee and great hot chocolate served in a huge cup. *First Lane* on Main St is another salubrious cafe with good delicatessen fare.

For self-caterers, the *Supervalue supermarket*, on the corner of Charles and Queen Sts, and *Coles New World*, on Main St, are open daily until late.

Getting There & Away
Air New Zealand Link (☎ 578 4059, 0800-737 000), 29 Queen St, has direct flights to

Wellington with connections to other centres. Ansett (☎ 0800-800 146) has direct flights between Blenheim, Wellington and Palmerston North.

Soundsair (☎ 573 6184) in Picton also flies the Wellington to Blenheim route, Monday to Friday (March to August) for $50/90 one way/return.

Deluxe Travel Lines (☎ 578 5467), 45 Main St, has regular services between Blenheim and Picton. InterCity (☎ 577 2890) buses pass through Blenheim on their way to Christchurch and Nelson and stop at the train station. InterCity has connections on to the West Coast. A plethora of shuttle buses (see the Picton section) run to Nelson, Christchurch and other destinations; many leave from outside the visitor centre.

Sounds to Coast (☎ 0800-802 225) has a shuttle three days a week to Greymouth ($44) via St Arnaud ($10). Nelson Lakes Transport (☎ 521 1877) also runs to St Arnaud and on to Westport in summer.

The *Coastal Pacific* Picton-Christchurch train stops daily at Blenheim (☎ 0800-802 802).

Getting Around
The Blenheim airport is on Middle Renwick Rd, about 6km west of town. Neil's Shuttle (☎ 577 5277) has a door-to-door service for $8.

Mountain bikes can be hired for $25 per day in town from Spokesman Cycles on Queen St.

HAVELOCK
pop 500
Founded around 1860 and named after Sir Henry Havelock of Indian Mutiny fame, this small town is at the confluence of the Pelorus and Kaiuma Rivers, 43km northwest of Blenheim.

Havelock was once the hub of the timber milling and export trade, and later became the service centre for gold-mining in the area. Today it has a thriving small-boat harbour and is the place to catch a boat to more remote parts of Marlborough Sounds. Otherwise, the town's title as the 'green-shelled mussel capital of the world' pretty much sums it up. The tiny **museum** on the main street covers local history.

Information

The Havelock Outdoors Centre (☎/fax 574 2114) is on the main street. It's open from around 8 am to 5 pm daily.

Walking

There's not much to do in the town itself, but good walks include the four-hour return walk to **Takorika Summit** behind the township and the half-hour walk to **Cullen Point** for good views of Havelock and the sunset.

Extended walks include the **Mt Stokes** walk. From the 1204m summit, the highest point in the Marlborough Sounds, you can see the Kaikouras, Tararuas (in the North Island) and the sounds below.

Another walk is the three-day **Pelorus Track** to Nelson, following the Pelorus River, then over Dun Saddle via a historic railway line. Mountain bikers can test their pedal strength on the Maungatapu Track, which passes through scenic Maitai Reserve.

The **Nydia Track** starts at Kaiuma and ends at Duncan Bay. The suggested walking time is two days or 10½ hours. There are DOC *camping grounds* and the *Nydia Lodge* ($12), also run by DOC. About halfway along, *Driftwood Lodge* and *Marty Quinn* both offer accommodation for around the same price. Nydia Bay was originally the site of a Maori *pa* (fortified village) called Opouri, which means 'Place of Sadness' – the DOC pamphlet explains why. The walk passes through different habitats of various species of birds.

It is best to get dropped off at Shag Point by water taxi as it is only a five-minute trip past the mudflats, and you can arrange a water taxi for around $60 at the other end. Pelorus Sounds Water Taxi (☎ 574 2151) is one of the main operators; you can phone the water taxi or shuttle service from Driftwood Lodge. The track can be walked in either direction.

Sea Kayaking

Havelock Sea Kayaking Company (☎ 574 2114, **@** sightsounds@hotmail.com) has full-day sea-kayaking trips on the delightful Marlborough Sounds for $70, leaving from Havelock. It rents out all equipment for one day for $45, up to four days for $150. Sea Kayaking Adventure Tours (☎ 574 2765) operates from Anakiwa at the end of the Queen Charlotte Walkway and has kayaks ($45 per day), mountain bikes ($25) and one-day guided kayak tours for $70 per person.

Organised Tours

Beachcomber Cruises takes passengers on the Pelorus mail boat, stopping at isolated homesteads to deliver mail and supplies. It can drop off and pick up later anywhere along the way if you want to camp or tramp. Take supplies, although fresh water is available in some places; ask the locals.

The trips depart from Havelock at 9.30 am on Tuesday, Thursday and Friday, and return between 5 and 6 pm. The round-trip mail-run fare is $75 (children free).

The Mussel Farm Cruise (☎ 574 2144) visits the mussel farms where you can sample the product ($45, half-day). Classic Cruises also has very popular boat tours of the sounds in a 40ft kauri launch. Both can be booked at the Havelock Outdoors Centre (see Information).

Many water taxis operate out of Havelock and nature cruises can be organised to Maud Island, abode of the rare Hamilton frog, takahe and kakapo (see the 'Flora & Fauna' special section). Havelock Fishing Charters (☎ 574 2190), across the road from Havelock Outdoors Centre, organises charter boats and water taxis.

Places to Stay & Eat

Havelock Motor Camp (☎ 574 2339) on Inglis St has tent/powered sites for $16/18 per person and cabins from $25 a double.

Chartridge Park (☎ 574 2129), 6km south of Havelock at Kaiuma Bridge on SH6, has camp sites at $16 for two. It has a pool, six-hole golf course and a river running through it.

The *Rutherford YHA (☎ 574 2104, **@** stell@xtra.co.nz)*, a well-equipped place on the corner of Lawrence St and Main Rd,

Mothers of Invention

Some amazing inventors and achievers have come out of little old New Zealand. Perhaps most-famous internationally was the man who 'split the atom', Baron Ernest Rutherford. After winning the Nobel Prize for chemistry in 1908, Rutherford went on to show that atoms could be artificially broken down into sub-atomic particles, thus ushering in the nuclear age. Rutherford accomplished his greatest feats at the prestigious Cavendish Laboratory in England. Kiwis have always been 'do-it-yourself-ers', though, slipping out into their back sheds to tinker with 'number eight' fencing wire and lengths of 'four by two' timber (the building blocks of Kiwi ingenuity). While most such projects never get off the ground, some do … .

In 1902 Richard Pearse (see the boxed text 'Flights of Fancy' in the Canterbury chapter) was possibly the first person in the world to fly an aircraft, one that he literally built out of scrap in a back shed. Other inventions of his included an automatic potato driller and hydroelectric power unit.

Cantabrian Bill Hamilton was the inventor of the propellerless jet-boat which is now seen on most navigable NZ rivers (the prototype is held at the NZ National Maritime Museum in Auckland). Hamilton also dabbled with improvements to air-conditioners, air compressors and hydroelectricity, and gave the world the water sprinkler.

The thrilling sport of bungy jumping was made a commercial possibility by the ingenuity of AJ Hackett and Henry van Asch. Their improvements to the latex bungy and the safety techniques they introduced have seen jumping sites blossom all over the world. The curious zorb, an inflatable ball into which you climb before rolling down hills (see Rotorua in the Bay of Plenty chapter), is another Kiwi innovation.

Other world firsts: The NZ Liberal government (1891–1911) gave women the vote in 1893, the first country to do so, introduced the old age pension, a Conciliation and Arbitration Act, and low interest housing. The eight-hour day was first formalised in Nelson.

Thank Kiwis also for the totalisator betting system for horse racing (now used for all manner of sports), the velcro strip, crinkled hairpins so designed to stop them falling out, the lids on self-sealing paint tins, child-proof pill bottles and the delicious meringue dessert, the 'Pavlova' (named after the famous Russian ballerina; however ownership of the pavlova is disputed with Australia).

charges $15 per person in dorms, and $36 for doubles. The hostel is in an 1881 school-house once attended by Lord Ernest Rutherford (See the boxed text). The manager has information on walks and other local activities.

Havelock has a couple of small motels, both on the main road through town. The *Havelock Garden Motel* (☎ 574 2387) has units at $60 to $80 for two, with low-season discounts available.

The *Pelorus Motor Inn Hotel* (☎ 574 2412), which has a restaurant and pub, has hotel rooms for $35 for two.

Pelorus Jack Tearooms on the main road has snacks and light meals. *Darling Dill Cafe* is a little more upmarket.

Mussel Boys (☎ 574 2824, 73 Main Rd) specialises in local fresh tasty mussels, especially 'steamers' and chowders; it's open

daily from 11 am. Check out the 'mussel' team playing rugby on the roof.

Getting There & Away
Both InterCity and Newmans have Picton–Blenheim–Nelson buses at least once each day. Kiwilink has two services a day to Blenheim, Picton and Nelson. Knightline has a similar service.

HAVELOCK TO NELSON
The SH6 from Havelock to Nelson is 75km of scenic highway, passing the Wakamarina Valley, Pinedale (also known as Canvastown), the Pelorus Bridge Scenic Reserve and Rai Valley.

Pinedale
The tiny township of Pinedale, in the Wakamarina Valley 8km west of Havelock, got

the nickname Canvastown back in the 1860s, when gold was discovered in the river. By 1864 thousands of canvas tents had sprung up as miners flocked to the prosperous working goldfield, one of the richest in the country. By 1865 the boom was over. Nevertheless, gold is still found in the area and in 1986 a tourist panned a 5g nugget from the river.

Visits to the interesting indoor-outdoor **gold-mining museum, gold panning, horse trekking, bushwalking** and **trout fishing** are all popular activities. The Wakamarina Track, an old gold-miners trail which passes through the Mt Richmond Forest Park, begins from Butchers Flat, 15km into the Wakamarina Valley on the metalled road from Pinedale.

The ***Trout Hotel*** (☎ 574 2120) at the entrance to the Wakamarina Valley has doubles and motel units from $55.

The ***Pinedale Motor Camp*** (☎ 574 2349) has tent/powered sites for $14/18 for two and cabins from $25 to $35; you can hire gold pans and other equipment here and lessons can be arranged. Butchers Flat, Roadend, Wakamarina Valley is a local ***DOC camping ground***.

Pelorus Bridge
The Pelorus Bridge Scenic Reserve, 18km west of Havelock, has interesting walks of between 30 minutes and three hours on the Pelorus and Rai Rivers, with waterfalls, a suspension bridge and the Pelorus Bridge itself. Within the reserve are ***tearooms***, ***camp sites*** at $16 for two, and ***cabins*** from $24. Ask for the ranger at the Pelorus Bridge Tearoom (☎ 571 6019).

The ***Lord Lionel*** (☎ 574 2770) is on SH6 near the Pelorus Bridge Scenic Reserve; the German-speaking owners offer single/double B&B for $65/105 and budget beds.

Rai Valley
At Carluke, 1.5km from the Rai Valley township on the road leading to Tennyson Inlet, is the Rai Valley Pioneer Cottage, built in 1881 when the area was still virgin bush. The cottage was home to its owner for 28 years and had been used as a sheep shed

and chicken house before being restored in 1969 and given to the Historic Places Trust in 1980. There's no charge to see the cottage, but donations are appreciated.

Nelson Region

☎ 03 • pop 82,100

The Nelson region is one of the top destinations for travellers to NZ. In addition to its equable climate and some good beaches, it is home to some of the best and most popular national parks in the country – Kahurangi, Nelson Lakes and Abel Tasman National Parks offer a wealth of walking and other outdoor activities. The city of Nelson and the towns of Motueka, Takaka and Collingwood are great places to 'lay back' for a while.

NELSON
pop 52,300

The city of Nelson is pleasant, bright and active. The surrounding area has some of the finest beaches in NZ and more sunshine than any other part of the country, so it's a popular holiday area. Apart from beaches and bays, Nelson is noted for its fruit-growing industry and its energetic local arts and crafts community.

Nelson stages many noteworthy events throughout the year. One of the most interesting, the Wearable Art Award, is held in September and the annual Arts Festival is held around the same time. In early February the Taste Nelson Festival features locally produced food and beverages.

History
The Maori began to migrate to the South Island during the 16th century, and among the first to arrive in Nelson were the Ngati Tumatakokiri. By 1550 this tribe occupied most of the province, as Abel Tasman (see History in the Facts about New Zealand chapter) found out to his cost when he turned up in 1642 at what he later named Murderers' Bay. Other tribes followed the Tumatakokiri, settling at the mouth of the Waimea River. The Tumatakokiri remained

supreme in Tasman Bay until the 18th century, when the Ngati-apa from Wanganui and the Ngati Kahu (or Ngai Tahu) – the largest tribe in the South Island – got together in a devastating attack on the Tumatakokiri, who virtually ceased to exist as an independent tribe after 1800.

The Ngati-apa's victory was short-lived because between 1828 and 1830 they were practically annihilated by armed tribes from Taranaki and Wellington who sailed into the bay in the largest fleet of canoes ever assembled in NZ.

By the time the European settlers arrived no Maori lived at Te Wakatu – the nearest pa being at Motueka – and the decimated population that remained in the area put up no resistance. The first Pakeha settlers sailed in response to advertisements by the New Zealand Company, set up by Edward Gibbon Wakefield to systematically colonise the country. His grandiose scheme was to transplant a complete slice of English life from all social classes. In reality 'too few gentlemen with too little money' took up the challenge and the new colony almost foundered in its infancy from lack of money.

The settlement was planned to consist of small but workable farms grouped around central towns. However, the New Zealand Company's entitlement to the land was disputed and it was almost a year before this problem was sorted out. Town land was distributed early, but farmland remained unallocated for so long that landowners and labourers were forced to live in town and whittle away their capital to survive.

The Wairau Massacre (described at the beginning of the Marlborough Region section) resulted in the deaths of 22 of Nelson's most able citizens, including Captain Wakefield whose leadership was irreplaceable, and plunged the colony into deep gloom. To make matters worse, the New Zealand Company was declared bankrupt in April 1844 and, since nearly three-quarters of the population were dependent on it in some way, particularly for sustenance, the situation was so grim as to be near famine. Only the later arrival of hard-working German immigrants saved the region from economic ruin.

Information
The Nelson Visitor Information Centre (☎ 548 2304), Web site: www.nelson.co.nz, is on the corner of Trafalgar and Halifax Sts. It's open from 8.30 am to 6 pm daily in summer (8.30 am to 5 pm on weekdays and 10 am to 4 pm on weekends in winter). Pick up a copy of *Nelson; Live the Day* here.

It is also Nelson's Transit Centre – all buses arrive and depart from this office. Trafalgar St, which crosses the river just before the information centre and runs straight up to the cathedral, is the main street.

A DOC officer is at the information centre in summer for inquiries about national parks and walks. The AA (☎ 548 8339) is at 45 Halifax St.

There are Internet facilities at most of the backpackers, and coin-operated self-service Internet at Chez Eelco, Subway at 40 Bridge St and Tahuna Beach Camp.

Camping gear can be hired from most of the backpackers or from Natural High (☎ 546 6936), 52 Rutherford St, which also has bicycles and kayaks. Others with camping gear for sale or hire are Alp Sports (☎ 546 8536) at 220 Hardy St, Basecamp (☎ 548 1710) at 295 Trafalgar St and Rollo's Barbeque & Camping (☎ 548 2363) at 12 Bridge St. Hire prices are reasonable at around $6 a day for packs and boots, and $10 a day for tents.

Small Planet Recycling (☎ 545 7010, 278 Hardy St) sells all manner of second-hand items; you might find something for your fave activity.

Fruit-picking (nashi pears, apples and grapes) and other agricultural work is available from February to May; berries are picked from December to January – contact the Employment NZ office or individual growers.

Fish processors down at the port sometimes have casual daily work (the hoki season is from June to November).

Historic Buildings
The traditional symbol of Nelson is its Art Deco **cathedral** at the top of Trafalgar St. Work began in 1925 but was delayed and arguments raged in the 1950s over whether

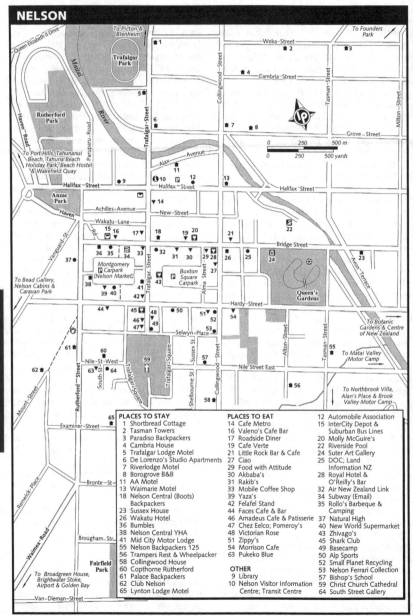

NELSON

PLACES TO STAY
1 Shortbread Cottage
2 Tasman Towers
3 Paradiso Backpackers
4 Cambria House
5 Trafalgar Lodge Motel
6 De Lorenzo's Studio Apartments
7 Riverlodge Motel
8 Borogrove B&B
11 AA Motel
13 Waimarie Motel
18 Nelson Central (Boots) Backpackers
23 Sussex House
26 Wakatu Hotel
36 Bumbles
38 Nelson Central YHA
41 Mid City Motor Lodge
55 Nelson Backpackers 125
56 Trampers Rest & Wheelpacker
58 Collingwood House
60 Copthorne Rutherford
61 Palace Backpackers
62 Club Nelson
65 Lynton Lodge Motel

PLACES TO EAT
14 Cafe Metro
16 Valeno's Cafe Bar
17 Roadside Diner
19 Cafe Verte
21 Little Rock Bar & Cafe
27 Ciao
29 Food with Attitude
30 Akbaba's
31 Rakib's
33 Mobile Coffee Shop
39 Yaza's
42 Felafel Stand
44 Faces Cafe & Bar
46 Amadeus Cafe & Patisserie
47 Chez Eelco; Pomeroy's
48 Victorian Rose
51 Zippy's
54 Morrison Cafe
63 Pukeko Blue

OTHER
9 Library
10 Nelson Visitor Information Centre; Transit Centre
12 Automobile Association
15 InterCity Depot & Suburban Bus Lines
20 Molly McGuire's
22 Riverside Pool
24 Suter Art Gallery
25 DOC; Land Information NZ
28 Royal Hotel & O'Reilly's Bar
32 Air New Zealand Link
34 Subway (Email)
35 Rollo's Barbeque & Camping
37 Natural High
40 New World Supermarket
43 Zhivago's
45 Shark Club
49 Basecamp
50 Alp Sports
52 Small Planet Recycling
53 Nelson Ferrari Collection
57 Bishop's School
59 Christ Church Cathedral
64 South Street Gallery

the building should be completed to its original design. Finally completed in 1965 to a modified design, it was consecrated in 1972, 47 years after the foundation stone was laid! The cathedral is open from 8 am to 7 pm daily.

Close to the cathedral, **South St** is home to a row of restored workers cottages dating from 1863 to 1867 (many are available as accommodation). Of prime interest is the **South St Gallery** on the corner of Nile St West, noted for its extensive collection of fine pottery. It's open daily.

Bishop's School (☎ 548 0821) served Nelson for about 90 years from 1840. On display are the notes and textbooks used in the old days. It's on Nile St East and open by appointment only.

Broadgreen House at 276 Nayland Rd in Stoke is a historic two-storey cob house built about 1855 and carefully furnished in the period. It is open daily except Monday in summer and Wednesday and weekend afternoons in winter ($3, children $0.50).

Beaches

Five kilometres west of the town centre, **Tahunanui** is an old-fashioned Kiwi holiday resort with minigolf, a playground, waterslide and a motley little zoo called Natureland. Now a suburb of Nelson, it's had a slight update, with a few fashionable cafes. A stroll along the foreshore and wide, grey-sand beach with shallow waters is pleasant. Paddle trikes can be hired in summer. It's reached on a Nelson Suburban bus.

Rabbit Island, some 20km west of Nelson, has 13km of undeveloped, much better beach backed by plantation forest. The bridge to the island is closed after 9 pm daily and camping is not allowed; opening hours depend on the fire risk.

Founders Park

This replica colonial village on Atawhai Drive reflects the town's early history. It's near the waterfront (look for the big windmill), 1km north-east of the city centre, and open from 10 am to 4 pm daily ($5, children $2). Next door are the attractive **Miyazu Japanese Gardens** (free).

Museums & Galleries

The **Suter Art Gallery** (☎ 548 4699) adjoins Queen's Gardens on Bridge St and is named after Bishop Suter, founder of the Bishopdale Sketching Club in 1889. It has a few interesting lithographs and paintings and is the city's main repository of high art, with changing exhibitions, films, musical and theatrical performances, films, a craft shop and a cafe (☎ 548 4040). It's open from 10.30 am to 4.30 pm daily ($1).

The **Nelson Ferrari Collection**, 132 Collingwood St, has six of the red devils for aficionados of Italian racing design. It's open from 10 am to 5 pm daily ($6, children $3).

The small **Nelson Provincial Museum** at Isel Park, 6km south of Nelson in Stoke, has a permanent Maori collection and tries hard with rotating exhibits that sometimes draw on the museum's large photographic collection. It's open from 10 am to 4 pm on weekdays and noon to 4 pm on weekends ($2, children $1). The beautiful **Isel Park gardens** are worth a visit in their own right, and also in the grounds is historic **Isel House**, open from 2 to 4 pm on weekends ($1, children $0.50). Get there on the Stoke bus.

Nelson is famous for its pottery and the quality of local clay, but glass-blowing, furniture, woodcarving, paintings and other arts and crafts are also represented.

Gardens

Nelson has some fine gardens, including the Botanic Gardens and Queens Gardens. The **Botanic Gardens** has a good lookout at the top of Botanical Hill, with a spire proclaiming it NZ's exact geographical centre.

Several readers have recommended **Gardens of the World** (☎ 542 3736), 95 Clover Rd East, Hope ($5, children free).

Get a free copy of *Gardens of the Nelson Region*. Some of the gardens are free, others around $2.50 for entry.

Activities

Rapid River Rafting Co (☎ 545 7076) and Ultimate Descents (☎ 546 6212), Web site: www.rivers.co.nz, both do **white-water rafting** on the Buller and Gowan Rivers for around $65/115 for a half/full day.

MARLBOROUGH & NELSON

You can go **paragliding** with Airborn (☎ 543 2669) or Nelson Paragliding (☎ 544 1182); $110 per person. Airborn also has rock climbing and abseiling in the Takaka Hills; a full day of climbing, all equipment supplied, is $110.

For a little extra try a **tandem parachute jump** with Tandem Skydive Nelson (☎ 548 7652, 0800-422 899, ✉ stuart@skydive .co.nz). It costs $195 per person including transport, 10 minutes' instruction and a certificate.

Hang-gliding with Nelson Hang Gliding Adventures (☎ 548 9151) is another aerial possibility ($130; 20 minutes).

Nelson's most popular activity is a **quad-bike tour** along farmland and high-country trails with Happy Valley Tours (☎ 545 0304), a 10-minute drive north-west along SH6. The ride takes in native bush and great views for $75 (2½ hours), including refreshments at the award-winning cafe. Try out the Skywire, a 1.6km free-fall ride on a **flying fox swing** (if it has been completed).

The Nelson visitor centre can suggest many other activities around Nelson. Two unusual activities are creating your own **bead necklace** or **bone carving**. The Bead Gallery (☎ 548 2892) is at 18 Parere St, Nelson, and the Nelson Bonecarver (☎ 546 4275) is at 87 Green St, Tahunanui ($45 for a day course).

Of the many **walks** and tramps, the riverside footpath makes a pleasant stroll through the city and the Maitai Valley Walkway is particularly restful and beautiful.

Organised Tours

Many tours around Nelson can be booked through the visitor centre. Some of the more popular are Wine Trail Tours ($50 to $65) and Craft & Scenic Tours (from $50). Two operators are JJ's Scenic Tours (☎ 544 7712, ✉ jjstours@ts.co.nz) and Bay Tours (☎ 544 4494, ✉ baytours@ts.co.nz).

Day trips from Nelson to the Abel Tasman National Park are popular and good value (see the Abel Tasman National Park section for details).

Plenty of water activities are available around Nelson. The *Cat 09* (☎ 548 0202)

does sea and game-fishing trips to all parts of the Nelson coastline; ring for details.

Places to Stay

Camping & Cabins *Tahuna Beach Holiday Park (☎ 548 5159, 70 Beach Rd),* near the airport, is a huge motor camp accommodating thousands, but there are plenty of secluded tent and powered sites for $18, cabins and lodges from $30 to $41, and units ($64); prices are for two. The site is 5km from the city centre and has its own supermarket.

Brook Valley Motor Camp (☎ 548 0399) at the end of Tasman St in the upper Brook Valley is in a superb forested setting by a stream. It's the same distance from the centre as Tahuna, but rather smaller and more personal. Tent/powered sites are $16/17, very basic two-bunk cabins are $23 and better cabins are $39.

The *Nelson Cabins & Caravan Park (☎ 548 1445, 230 Vanguard St)* has powered sites at $18, but no tent sites. Cabins with their own kitchens are $42 and you can hire linen. Tourist flats with shower and toilet are $54.

Backpackers Backpackers have been popping up like mushrooms around Nelson – plenty of good choice in this small city. *Paradiso Backpackers (☎ 546 6703, 42 Weka St),* Web site: www.backpackernelson .webnz.co.nz, is in a lovely old building with spacious grounds. It has a pool, spa, sauna and a wonderful glassed-in dining room. Seven- or eight-bed dorms with mezzanines cost $16, four-bed dorms are $17 and twins and doubles are $38. This place is extremely popular.

The *Nelson Central YHA (☎ 545 9988, ✉ yhanels@yha.org.nz, 59 Rutherford St),* very central and purpose-built, has excellent rooms and facilities. It has several quiet areas and good common rooms in a soundproofed environment, and the expansive kitchen/dining room opens onto a terrace garden. A dorm bed is $19 per person and twins and doubles are from $42 to $44.

The *Palace Backpackers (☎ 548 4691, 114 Rutherford St)* is in an early 20th-century villa set above the street with views from the balconies. The house is surrounded by garden and there are plenty of areas to sit and relax. It has a wide variety of rooms, with dorms costing $16, and twins and doubles for $38.

Club Nelson (☎ 548 3466, @ clubnelson@ xtra.co.nz, 18 Mount St), an uphill walk away from the bus station, is a big, rambling place with large dorms for $14, four-share rooms for $18 and a big selection of small/large doubles for $39/46 including linen. Singles are $25, tent sites $12 per person. Small and cosy it ain't but it's quiet, has plenty of parking and the gardens, pool and tennis court are impressive.

Tasman Towers (☎ 548 7950, 10 Weka St) is another large, purpose-built place with very good rooms and facilities. Dorms (mostly quads) are $17, and twins and doubles are $38.

Nelson Central Backpackers (also called 'Boots'; ☎ 548 9001), right in town on the corner of Trafalgar and Bridge Sts, is not the fanciest but it's clean and roomy enough. Dorms are $15 per person and doubles cost $34. There's a special sound-proofed 'Party Room' and a pool table.

Bumbles (☎ 548 2771, @ bumbles@ts .co.nz, 8 Bridge St) is a former hotel turned backpackers. It has a big common room, plenty of information and helpful staff. Dorm beds are $16 to $18 per person, and twins and doubles are $36 or $40 with en suite.

More backpackers can be found just east of the centre. The ***Trampers Rest & Wheelpacker*** (☎/fax 545 7477, 31 Alton St) is hard to beat for a small, homestay-style backpackers. The friendly owner is a keen tramper and cyclist and provides information as well as free bikes. The small, attractive house has only a few beds for $16 and $38 a double.

Nelson Backpackers 125 (☎ 548 7576, 125 Tasman St) is another friendly, smaller place in an old house with dorms for $15 and $16 and doubles for $34.

Alan's Place (☎/fax 548 4854, 42 Westbrook Terrace) is a bit further out, but not far from town. It's also an older house but has a good atmosphere and Alan, one of the

'originals' in the backpacker industry, offers pick-up, free bikes and other services. Dorm beds cost $17, and twins and doubles are $38. There's always a Japanese staff member on hand.

The roomy ***Beach Hostel*** (☎ 548 6817, @ nelsonbeachhostel@xtra.co.nz, 25 Muritai St), 4 km out at Tahunanui Beach, is a pleasant area to stay with restaurants, a pub and the airport nearby. It's friendly and laid-back with good communal areas. Free pick-up and bikes are offered. Dorms are $14, twins $36 and doubles $38.

Shortbread Cottage (☎ 546 6681, 33 Trafalgar St) is tiny with only 12 beds, but this adds to its intimacy. A dorm bed is $17, a twin $38 and a double $40. It's closed from May to September.

B&Bs & Guesthouses Nelson has plenty of B&Bs, but they may be full in the high season. ***Borogrove*** (☎ 548 9442, 27 Grove St) is an Edwardian villa with self-contained rooms for $60/85 for single/doubles.

Collingwood House (☎ 548 4481, 174 Collingwood St) has twins and doubles for $85; ***Sussex House*** (☎ 548 9972, 238 Bridge St) with a pool and spa costs from $65/90 for singles/doubles or $100 a double with en suite; and ***Northbrook Villa*** (☎ 548 3021, 174 Tasman St), another gracious old villa, has rooms with en suite for $90/120.

The Wheelhouse Inn (☎ 546 8391, @ wheelhouse@ts.co.nz, 41 Whitby Rd), a new self-contained B&B in Port Hills, has spectacular views of Tasman Bay and spacious rooms from $80 to $95.

The ***Cathedral Inn*** (☎ 548 7369, 369 Trafalgar St) is a delightful but expensive B&B option costing from $145 to $190 for doubles.

The popular ***Cambria House*** (☎ 548 4681, @ cambria@clear.net.nz, 7 Cambria St), in a 130-year-old homestead, is still as superb as ever (ring for prices).

Motels & Hotels Many of Nelson's motels, mostly of higher standard, are near the beach at Tahunanui on Beach Rd and Muritai St.

Central and reasonably priced motels include the ***Lynton Lodge Motel*** (☎ 548 7112,

25 Examiner St) with double rooms for $70 to $79. The *Riverlodge Motel (☎ 548 3094, 31 Collingwood St)* has units for $79 to $105.

The *Trafalgar Lodge Motel (☎ 548 3980, 46 Trafalgar St)* has units from $65 to $85 for doubles (less in winter), while B&B in the guesthouse section is $45 per person.

The *Waimarie Motel (☎ 548 9418, 45 Collingwood St)* is central and has units for $75 to $99. The *Mid City Motor Lodge (☎ 546 9063, 218 Trafalgar St)* has rooms from $78 to $95 for doubles.

The *AA Motel (☎ 548 8214, 8 Ajax Ave),* by the river, is conveniently located with units from $99 for two.

The *Copthorne Rutherford (☎ 548 2299),* on Nile St West, is an expensive 115-room place with everything – sauna, pool, spa and gym. The cheapest rooms cost $155, with weekend discounts.

The *Honest Lawyer (☎ 547 8850, 1 Point Rd),* in Monaco, south of the airport overlooking Tasman Bay, has luxurious units from $130 to $160 for two.

De Lorenzo's Studio Apartments (☎ 548 9774, 51 Trafalgar St) is central, luxurious and well worth the $120 to $170 for two.

Places to Eat

The wealth of local produce, particularly seafood, makes dining out in Nelson a pleasure. Deep-sea fish such as orange roughie and hoki, scallops from the bays, and mussels and oysters are available, complemented by local wines and beers.

Restaurants & Cafes *Chez Eelco (296 Trafalgar St),* near the cathedral, is a Nelson institution. This relaxed place is open from 6 am to 11 pm daily and serves everything from strong coffee, croissants and fruit juices to regular meals. It's a popular meeting place, the front window is a popular local notice board and there's Internet facilities. *Pomeroy's (☎ 548 7524),* next door, also has fresh roasted coffee.

The *Cafe Metro (☎ 546 7530),* upstairs at the State Cinema on Trafalgar St, is another trendy little place for good coffee and has an excellent wine selection.

Yaza's (☎ 548 2849) in Montgomery car park (where the weekend markets are held) is a cosy cafe which occasionally features live acoustic and jazz music.

Zippy's (☎ 546 6348, 276 Hardy St) has several vegetarian and vegan selections; it opens early in the evening, and stays open until late.

Akbaba's (☎ 548 8825, 130 Bridge St) is run by Turks and you dine at low tables surrounded by Turkish rugs and carpets; three courses will set you back $15. Try the Iskender kebab – delicious!

Rakib's (☎ 548 089, 116 Bridge St) is open in the evenings daily except Monday for takeaway or dine-in Indian and Middle Eastern food.

The *Little Rock Bar & Cafe (☎ 546 8800, 165 Bridge St),* across the road from the Wakatu Hotel, serves pizza and budget meals to good music. The cost of the original wrought-iron sculpture is added to the wide range of cocktails.

Ciao (☎ 548 9874, 94 Collingwood St) has expensive Italian and Asian-influenced food for lunch and dinner, Monday to Saturday from 6.30 pm.

Faces Cafe & Bar (☎ 548 8755, 136 Hardy St) is a bit more raunchy; it has tasty Italian food and salads and a good selection of wines.

Valeno's Cafe Bar (☎ 546 7474, 35 Bridge St) is a good place for cheap food; meals are less than $15.

The *Amadeus Cafe & Patisserie (☎ 545 7191, 284 Trafalgar St)* has breakfast from 7.30 am, and an all-day menu – it has an excellent assortment of strudels, gateaux and tortes.

Pukeko Blue (☎ 545 9931, 6 Nile St West) is a good place for hearty breakfasts; try the grilled salmon and pistachio with basil butter for lunch ($14.50).

Cafe Verte on Bridge St has comfortable old lounge chairs and a good atmosphere. It serves bagels and coffee, and has an excellent selection of mains.

Morrison Cafe (☎ 548 8110, 244 Hardy St) is in a beautiful heritage building, and there is a delightful outdoor area where breakfast is served on sunny days.

For excellent seafood by the sea and a touch of the Cote d'Azur in sunny Nelson, head to Wakefield Quay for the *Quayside Brasserie* (☎ 548 3319) at No 309, *Harbour Light Store* (☎ 546 6685) at No 341 or the *Boat Shed* (☎ 546 9783) at No 350 on the road to Tahunanui. The wonderful Boat Shed is on stilts over the sea and serves superb chilli crab for $23. Other seafood selections include crayfish and it has a cheaper lunch menu.

Pub Food The *Victorian Rose* (☎ 548 7631, 281 Trafalgar St) is a pastiche of English/Irish pub styles in airy premises. The Guinness is served with care and there is a varied selection of beers. Meals are cheap and backpackers specials are offered.

The *Honest Lawyer* (see Places to Stay earlier), an oxymoronic establishment, is out past the airport at Nayland. It's a stylish pub overlooking the estuary, with outdoor tables, great atmosphere and reasonably priced meals.

Fast Food The *Roadside Diner* is a big white pie cart that has been serving fast food in Nelson since 1933 and is reputed to have the 'biggest burgers in NZ'. It's parked on Trafalgar St near Bridge St after 6 pm daily except Sunday and is open until late most nights (until 3.30 am on Friday and Saturday).

Food with Attitude on Bridge St serves greasy burgers to alleviate the late-night hunger horrors.

There's an unnamed *mobile coffee shop* on the corner of Bridge and Trafalgar Sts, and a *felafel stand* on the corner of Hardy and Trafalgar Sts.

Entertainment
The local band scene can be summed up as: *Molly McGuire's* for Irish, folk and country; the *Victorian Rose* for blues and pop; *O'Reilly's*, in the Royal Hotel, for pop, blues and dance music; *Fresh & Funky* in the Little Rock for disco; and *Yaza's* for jazz and acoustic music.

The *Shark Club* on the corner of Hardy and Trafalgar Sts is a backpackers bar

popular with bus groups. In the middle is the lounge lizard's delight called the Ultra Lounge. In summer there's a dance bar set up at the far end called The Aquarium.

Luce (☎ 548 1818), a bar and nightclub in Buxton Mall, is fast becoming a popular venue with an outdoor adventure theme.

For information about gay and lesbian venues tune to 99.4FM Fresh on Sunday at 10 am ('Dyke FM') and 11 am ('Gaytime FM').

The *Suter Art Gallery* has theatre, music and dance, and its Stage Two theatre shows a selection of popular and international art films.

Getting There & Away
Air The Air New Zealand Link office (☎ 0800-737 000) is on the corner of Trafalgar and Bridge Sts. Direct flights go to Wellington, Auckland, Christchurch and New Plymouth, with connections to other cities. Ansett (☎ 0800-267 388) has direct flights to Wellington and Auckland.

Origin Pacific (☎ 0800-302 302) has connections to several major centres (see the Getting Around chapter).

Bus All buses serving Nelson stop and pick up from the Nelson Visitor Centre on the corner of Trafalgar and Halifax Sts, where you can also buy tickets. The main depot for InterCity (☎ 548 1539) is at 27 Bridge St.

InterCity buses run daily to Picton and Christchurch and to Greymouth via Murchison and Westport, with connections to the Franz Josef and Fox Glaciers.

White Star (☎ 546 8687) runs daily between Nelson and Picton, and Nelson and Christchurch via the Lewis Pass. To Westport, White Star takes the quicker route through Springs Junction, where you change buses.

Lazerline (☎ 0800-220 001) has a reliable shuttle service to Christchurch daily ($40); it screens videos.

Atomic Shuttles goes from Picton via Nelson and all the way down the West Coast to Queenstown. Buses stop in Greymouth for the night, so you can't get to the glaciers in one day. It's $50 to Greymouth, and $75 from Greymouth to Queenstown.

Abel Tasman Coachlines (☎ 548 0285) at 27 Bridge Rd provides transport from Nelson, Motueka and Takaka to the Abel Tasman Track (see the Abel Tasman National Park section later for details) and to the Heaphy Track. Kahurangi Bus (see Takaka later in this chapter) provides transport to the tracks and as far as Collingwood ($32).

The main shuttles to Picton and Blenheim are Kiwilink (☎ 0800-802 300), The Rose Express (☎ 548 2304) and Knightline (☎ 528 7798). They charge about $19/11 for adults/children to Picton, $2 less to Blenheim.

Wadsworths Motors (☎ 522 4248) and Nelson Lakes Transport (☎ 547 5912) have buses to St Arnaud in Nelson Lakes National Park.

A backpackers bus, the West Coast Express (☎ 546 6703), departs from Nelson for six-day trips down the 'Coast' to Queenstown, with plenty of stops along the way. Since hitching is notoriously slow and you don't see all the sights by public bus, this is a good option. It departs every Wednesday and there's only one bus per week ($99). See the Getting Around chapter for more details.

Hitching Getting out of Nelson is not easy as the city sprawls so far. It's best to take a bus to the outskirts. Hitching to the West Coast can be hard going.

Getting Around

To/From the Airport Super Shuttle Nelson (☎ 547 5782) offers door-to-door service to and from the airport (6km south-west) for $7. A taxi to the airport costs about $15. You can also take the shuttle to Tahunanui, from the visitor centre or the Hotel Rutherford.

Bus Nelson Suburban Bus Lines (☎ 548 3290) operates local services from its terminal on Lower Bridge St. Buses run out to Richmond via Tahunanui and Stoke, and also to Wakefield. They operate until about 5 or 6 pm on weekdays, with one later bus at about 7 pm on Friday.

Bicycle Bicycles can be hired from Stewart Cycle City (☎ 548 1666) at 114 Hardy St (by the half-day, day, week or month), from Fraine Cycles Ltd (☎ 548 3877) at 105 Bridge St and Natural High (☎ 546 6936), 52 Rutherford St. Thunderbike Engineering (☎ 548 7888) on Achilles Ave hires out touring motorcycles.

AROUND NELSON
Brightwater & Wakefield

The small town of Brightwater, the birthplace of Lord Rutherford, is a pleasant place to stay. It's 9km south of Richmond on SH6, and there are farmstays and homestays in the region.

Also south of Nelson, at Pigeon Valley, Wakefield, is the **Pigeon Valley Steam Museum**, with an interesting collection of vintage steam-driven machinery. It's open from 9 am to 4.30 pm daily.

Wineries

Many vineyards on the Nelson Wine Trail can be visited by doing a loop from Nelson through Richmond to Motueka, following the SH60 coast road in one direction and the inland Moutere River road in the other. Some wineries are open for visitors, including The Denton Winery (Ruby Bay), Ruby Bay Winery, Moutere Hills Winery, Neudorf Vineyards and Seifrieds. **McCashin's Brewery & Malthouse** is also nearby if you wish to sample the legendary Black Mac.

The information centres in Nelson and Motueka have wine trail maps.

NELSON LAKES NATIONAL PARK

Nelson Lakes National Park is 118km south-west of Nelson. Two beautiful glacial lakes are fringed by beech forest and flax, with a backdrop of forested mountains. There's good tramping, walking, lake scenery and also skiing (in winter) at the Rainbow Valley and Mt Robert skifields.

Information on the park is available at the Park Visitors Centre (☎ 521 1806) in St Arnaud or at the Lake Rotoroa Ranger Station (☎ 523 9369) near the northern end of Lake Rotoroa.

The park is accessible from two different areas: Lakes Rotoiti and Rotoroa. St Arnaud

Village, at Lake Rotoiti, is the main centre, while Rotoroa receives far fewer visitors (mainly trampers and fishing groups).

An excellent three-day **tramp** from St Arnaud takes you south along the eastern shore of Lake Rotoiti to Lake Head, across the Travers River and up the Cascade Track to Angelus Hut on beautiful alpine Lake Angelus. The trip back to St Arnaud goes along Roberts Ridge to the Mt Robert skifield. On a clear day this ridge walk affords magnificent alpine views all along its length. The track descends steeply to the Mt Roberts car park, from where it's a 7km road walk back to St Arnaud.

Other **walks** at Rotoiti include the Peninsula Nature Walk (1½ hours), Black Hill Track (1½ hours return), Mt Robert Lookout (20 minutes), St Arnaud Range Track (five hours), Loop Track (1½ hours return) and Lakehead Track around the lake (six hours).

There are a number of walks around Lake Rotoroa. Two short ones are the Short Loop Track (20 minutes) and the Flower Walk (10 minutes), while medium-length ones include Porika Lookout (two to three hours), Lakeside Track (six hours) and Braeburn Walk (two hours). The track along the eastern shore of the lake connects with the Sabine, Blue Lake and Lake Constance area of the walk described under Lake Rotoiti. For more information get a copy of the publications *Lake Rotoroa, Lake Rotoiti, Mt Robert* and *Peninsula Nature Walks* – these have much of the information you need to know about NZ's forests condensed into tiny, excellent volumes. For information on other walks in the Nelson Lakes region, ask at the ranger stations or refer to Lonely Planet's *Tramping in New Zealand*.

Places to Stay & Eat

Lake Rotoiti There are *DOC camping grounds* (☎ 521 1806) at the edge of the lake in West and Kerr Bays. Tent/powered sites cost $7/8 per person. There are toilets, coin-operated hot showers and a kitchen.

The *Yellow House* (☎ 521 1887), Web site: www.nelsonlakes.co.nz, in St Arnaud, is a YHA associate charging $18 per person for dorms, and $44 for doubles and twins. It

has a spa pool, hires out tramping equipment, and is only a five-minute walk to Lake Rotoiti.

The *Alpine Lodge* (☎/fax 521 1869), a 10-minute walk from the lake, has doubles for $105 to $130. Across the car park is its *Alpine Chalet* backpackers accommodation. This is a large, clean and European-style 'alpine' building costing $16 per person in dorms, and $45 for a double or twin. Guests are left to themselves.

The *St Arnaud Log Chalets* (☎ 521 1887), self-contained units which cost $90 for two people, are next door.

Nelson Lakes Homestay (☎ 521 1191) is a new place with good rooms for $50/85.

There are also several camping grounds and lodges within the park itself – contact the visitors centre. There's a *restaurant* at the Alpine Lodge, and a *snack bar* at the petrol station, which also sells limited grocery supplies.

The *Tophouse* (☎ 521 1848), 8km from St Arnaud, dates from the 1880s, when it was a hotel. It's a comfortable B&B with self-contained cottages ($85 a double) and the possibility of a round of golf.

Lake Rotoroa There is not much accommodation here. A basic *DOC camping ground* ($4 per person) by the lake has only a toilet and water point.

The *Retreat Camping Ground*, towards Gowan Bridge, is a centre for white-water rafting but you can camp for $8 per person ($9 with power) and cabins are $15 per person.

The *Gowan River Holiday Camp* (☎ 523 9921), 5km from SH6 on Gowan Valley Rd, is small, scenic and has tent/powered sites for $8/9, and cute, converted train carriages for $13.50 ($15 with en suite).

Other expensive options are the exclusive fishing retreats, the *Rotoroa Lodge* and the *Braeburn Lodge*.

Getting There & Away

See the Nelson, Blenheim and Picton sections for details of buses to St Arnaud.

Rainbow Transport (☎ 521 1861) operates in the region to Rainbow skifield; inquire at

MARLBOROUGH & NELSON

the Yellow House. JJ Ski Transport (☎ 544 7081) operates from Nelson to the Rainbow Valley skifield and the Mt Robert car park and Rainbow skifield in winter.

Getting Around

Water taxis operate on Lakes Rotoiti and Rotoroa; these can be booked on ☎ 521 1894 (Lake Rotoiti) or ☎ 523 9199 (Lake Rotoroa).

Murchison

pop 850

Murchison is on the Buller Gorge Heritage Highway, some 125km south of Nelson. It's an important service centre for the surrounding region and the starting point for adventure activities. It's also the gateway to the West Coast if you are coming from the north.

The Murchison Information Centre (☎ 523 9350) on Waller St is open from 10 am to 5 pm daily from 1 October to 30 April. The small **museum**, open from 10 am to 4 pm daily, has interesting exhibits on the 1929 earthquake.

Activities Activities in the Murchison area include fishing, rafting, kayaking, tramping, gold panning, boating, mountain biking, caving and rock climbing.

Hundreds of kayakers descend on Murchison in summer to **kayak** the Buller and its tributaries, which have easy road access. The New Zealand Kayak School (☎ 523 9611) rents out kayaks for $25, including gear, and offers four-day courses.

Whitewater Action Rafting Tours (☎ 0800-100 582) has a variety of **river adventures** (Buller Big Water $85, Ariki Falls $80 with its big-volume 3m drop, and funyaks $80).

Buller Experience (☎ 523 9696) offers 20-minute **jet-boating** trips on the Matakitaki, Mangles and Buller Rivers for $40, or $120 for two adults and three kids.

Mountain-bike trails dot the area and popular rides include the west bank of the Matakitaki (16km return) and the Upper Matakitaki (76km return). Hire bikes from Murchison Mountain Bike Hire (☎ 523 9425), 27 Grey St ($15/25 for half/full day); it has good tips for interesting trails.

The Tutaki Valley has good **horse trekking** and Tiraumea Horse Treks (☎ 523 9341) runs trips from one hour to a full day.

The **fishing** in the scenic rivers nearby is rightly said to be 'unbelievable', but a guided day out to hook a trout is not cheap – from $500 up. The information centre lists guides.

Gold panning in Lyell Creek, the Buller River and the Howard Valley is popular. The information centre rents out pans and shovels for $5, with a $20 bond.

Places to Stay *Riverview Holiday Park* (☎ 523 9591), 2km from town on the road to Nelson, is right by the river and has tent sites at $12, powered sites at $16 and well-kept cabins at $29; all prices are for two. Self-contained tourist flats are $55 and motel units $65. Showers cost $2.

The *Kiwi Park Motels* (☎ 523 9248, ✉ kiwipark@xtra.co.nz, 170 Fairfax St), a well-run place, has tent/powered sites at $15/16 for two, and basic cabins from $15 per person. Tourist flats are from $55 and excellent motel units $95 (less in the low season).

The *Lions Club Aorangi Hall Hostel* (☎ 523 9415) is at the end of Hampden St next to the sportsground. It charges $10 per person for basic accommodation, and is only open from 1 December to the end of February.

The *Commercial Hotel* (☎ 523 9490), on the main street, has regular pub rooms for only $20/38 a single/double.

Motels include the *Murchison* (☎ 523 9026, 53 Fairfax St) and the *Mataki* (☎ 523 9088, 34 Hotham St); expect to pay from $60 to $70 for two.

The *Coch-y-Bondhu Lodge* (☎ 523 9196, 15 Grey St) is a delightful, two-storey homestay.

Moonlight Lodge (☎ 523 9323), Web site: www.moonlightlodge.com, on SH65 at Shenandoah, is only for the rich. If you can afford it the DB&B is excellent, with the meals quite simply superb.

Places to Eat *Collins* (67 Fairfax St) is the ubiquitous tearoom in town, but it serves good country chicken, the 'Murch Muncher' and super dogs.

Beechwoods, on the southern edge of town, open from 6 am until about 11 pm, is licensed and there's indoor and outdoor dining.

Getting There & Away A number of bus services pass through Murchison on the way to the West Coast, Nelson, St Arnaud, Blenheim and Picton. These include Nelson Lakes Transport, White Star, Sounds to Coast and InterCity. These buses stop either at Collins tearooms on Fairfax St or outside Beechwoods on SH6.

NELSON TO MOTUEKA

From Richmond, south of Nelson, SH60 heads west to Motueka. The region fringing Tasman Bay is very popular with local holiday-makers, with plenty of accommodation, art and craft outlets, vineyards, yacht charters, fishing and swimming.

The picturesque Waimea Inlet and the twin villages of **Mapua** and **Ruby Bay** are at the mouth of the Waimea River. Facing them is Rabbit Island with great swimming beaches, boating, fishing and forest walks.

Mapua Nature Smoke, right on Mapua wharf, is a great cafe with delicious woodsmoked fish such as groper, tarakihi, moki and snapper.

On the back-road route along Wilsons Rd from Nelson to Motueka are the **tame eels** of the Moutere River that will slither out of the water to take bits of meat from your hand. The eels are about 11km from Upper Moutere Village – look for the signpost ($3, children $1).

Places to Stay

Mapua Leisure Park (☎ 540 2666, 33 Toru St, Mapua) is 'NZ's first clothes-optional leisure park'. Not for the shy perhaps, but you don't *have* to bare all and the position (next to the beach and river) and facilities are superb – nine-hole golf course, tennis and volleyball courts, pool, sauna and spa, childrens playground and waterfront cafe. Powered sites are $21, cabins are $36, on-site caravans are $46 and good chalets are

$50; prices are for two (with off-season reductions).

McKee Memorial Reserve, 2km north of the leisure park, is a very basic camping ground at the water's edge costing $8 for two. Water, toilets and barbecue pits are the only amenities.

Busch Lodge Holiday Camp (☎ 540 3542) is off SH60, north of Ruby Bay, 2km from the coast. It has tent/powered sites for $16/20 for two, and 20 twin-bed cabins at $30.

There are many homestays and farmstays in the region. *Rerenga Farm* (☎ 543 3825), out at Thorpe, accessible from Motueka, Richmond or Mapua and on the Dovedale-Woodstock Rd, is a rural retreat. In this 85-year-old homestead B&B costs $50/70 for singles/doubles and there is a self-contained cottage for $50. Dinners are $22 per person.

Doone Cottage (☎ 526 8740), nearby in Woodstock, has doubles with en suite from $110 to $130. It's close to some great fishing spots.

The Lodge at Paratiho Farms (☎ 528 2100, **@** lodge@paratiho.co.nz), Waiwhero Rd, Upper Moutere, is absolute luxury, but it should be at the hefty cost.

MOTUEKA
pop 6610

Motueka is the centre of a green tea, hops and fruit-growing area. The main picking season for apples, grapes and kiwi fruit is March to June. Motueka is also a base for trampers en route to the walks in the Abel Tasman and Kahurangi National Parks. The inhabitants are very cosmopolitan and include many craftspeople. In summer it's a bustling place, but in winter they say you could shoot a gun down the main street and not hit a thing!

Information

The helpful Motueka Visitor Information Centre (☎ 528 6543, **@** mzpvin@ xtra.co.nz) in Wallace St (just off the main road) will store packs, has Internet access and sells tickets for most things, including tours, kayaks, launches, hut bookings for Abel Tasman and transport. Its Web site is

MARLBOROUGH & NELSON

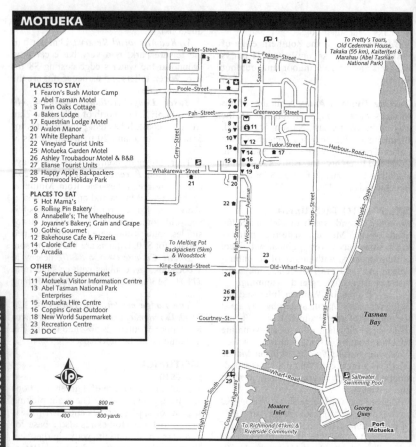

MOTUEKA

PLACES TO STAY
1 Fearon's Bush Motor Camp
2 Abel Tasman Motel
3 Twin Oaks Cottage
4 Bakers Lodge
17 Equestrian Lodge Motel
20 Avalon Manor
21 White Elephant
22 Vineyard Tourist Units
25 Motueka Garden Motel
26 Ashley Troubadour Motel & B&B
27 Elianse Tourist Units
28 Happy Apple Backpackers
29 Fernwood Holiday Park

PLACES TO EAT
5 Hot Mama's
6 Rolling Pin Bakery
8 Annabelle's; The Wheelhouse
9 Joyanne's Bakery; Grain and Grape
10 Gothic Gourmet
12 Bakehouse Cafe & Pizzeria
14 Calorie Cafe
19 Arcadia

OTHER
7 Supervalue Supermarket
11 Motueka Visitor Information Centre
13 Abel Tasman National Park
    Enterprises
15 Motueka Hire Centre
16 Coppins Great Outdoor
18 New World Supermarket
23 Recreation Centre
24 DOC

To Pretty's Tours,
Old Cederman House,
Takaka (55 km), Kaiteriteri &
Marahau (Abel Tasman
National Park)

To Melting Pot
Backpackers (5km)
& Woodstock

To Richmond (41km) &
Riverside Community

Tasman
Bay

Moutere
Inlet

George
Quay

Port
Motueka

Saltwater
Swimming Pool

0   400   800 m
0   400   800 yards

MARLBOROUGH & NELSON

www.Motueka.net.nz and the office is open from 8 am to 5 pm daily (until 7 pm in summer). Pick up a copy of the *Wine Trail* map.

Abel Tasman National Park Enterprises (☎ 528 7801), Web site: www.abeltasman .co.nz, is at 265 Main Rd. It sells a profusion of national park trips.

The DOC office (☎ 528 9117) is on the corner of High and King Edward Sts. It's an excellent source of information on the Abel Tasman and Kahurangi National Parks and sells passes for the Abel Tasman Track. Also check with DOC for tidal information.

Coppins Great Outdoor (☎ 528 7296) at 255 High St hires out tents and backpacks for use on the tracks. Backpackers rent out camping equipment.

Activities

The best beaches are outside Motueka at Kaiteriteri and Marahau. The beaches along the Abel Tasman National Park coast can be easily reached on day launch trips. You can hire **sea kayaks** from a number of places in the area. See the Abel Tasman National Park section for launch and kayak information.

Ultimate Descents (☎ 0800-748 377), based in Motueka, does **white-water rafting** trips on the Buller and Gowan Rivers for $65 (half-day) and $100 (full day). There's also an easier 1½-hour family trip on the Motueka River for $40 (children $30). The two-day Mokihinui Heli-raft trip is $450.

Places to Stay
Camping & Cabins *Fernwood Holiday Park (☎ 528 7488)* is sandwiched between SH60 and High St South at the southern end of town. Tent/powered sites in this well-equipped park are $14/16 for two and good four-person cabins are $30.

Fearon's Bush Motor Camp (☎ 528 7189, 10 Fearon St), a spacious place at the northern end of town, has tent or powered sites at $19 for two and comfortable cabins with one double and one single bed for $34 a double. Comfortable two-bedroom motel units are $75.

Vineyard Tourist Units (☎ 528 8550, 328 High St) has a variety of simple but good-value cabins for $40, on-site vans for $30 and units with kitchen and en suite for $55.

Backpackers The *Bakers Lodge (☎ 528 0102, ✉ backpackerslodge@motueka.co.nz, 4 Poole St)* is an excellent place and a YHA associate in a carefully renovated former bakery. It has all the extras imaginable and is well worth it for $17 in dorms and $40 for doubles and twins.

The *White Elephant (☎ 528 6208, fax 528 0110, 55 Whakarewa St)* is a good backpackers with room for 20 people in a big, comfortable old house. It charges $16 per person in dorms, and $40 for doubles including linen. It has tent sites, so the communal areas can come under strain in the picking season.

The *Twin Oaks Cottage (☎/fax 528 7882, 25 Parker St)* has dorms for $15 per person, twins for $36 and a caravan for $30. The backpackers is a good, if cramped, cottage in a spacious garden.

The *Happy Apple Backpackers (☎/fax 528 8652, 500 High St)*, on the southern edge of town, is a pleasant and modern hostel; it costs $15 per person ($18

with linen), mostly in twin rooms. It also has tent sites at $8 per person, but it has the facilities to handle the numbers.

Melting Pot Backpackers (☎ 528 9423) is 5km south-west of town on the SH61 to Woodstock. This large, former institutional premises has a variety of rooms costing $12.50 per person for shared rooms and $36 for doubles.

The *Riverside Community (☎ 526 7805)*, 7km out of Motueka on the Moutere Rd, has been going since 1941 (it was set up by pacifists during WWII). It has a building where visitors can stay and sample communal living, but it pays to ring in advance.

B&Bs & Motels The *Ashley Troubadour Motel & B&B (☎ 528 7318, 430 High St)* is a friendly B&B in what used to be a nunnery. All rooms have a washbasin and there's a lounge with pleasant views. It's $52/70 for singles/doubles with breakfast. Motel units cost $75 to $85 a double.

Other alternatives include the *Abel Tasman Motel (☎ 528 6688, 45 High St)* with units from $60 to $85, which also has a good-value lodge with rooms from $45. *Elianse Tourist Units (☎ 528 6629, 432 High St)* charges $75 a double.

The *Motueka Garden Motel (☎ 0800-101 911, 71 King Edward St)* near the clock tower has units from $65 to $95.

The *Equestrian Lodge Motel (☎ 528 9369)* on Tudor St is an excellent choice with a big lawn and spa pool; tidy units are from $85 to $105.

Avalon Manor (☎ 528 8320, 314 High St), close to town, is a new place with units from $85 to $95.

Places to Eat
Motueka's seemingly endless main street has the usual string of takeaways and sandwich bars, including *The Wheelhouse*, opposite the post shop, the *Rolling Pin Bakery* at No 105, *Joyanne's Bakery* at No 180 and the fancier *Calorie Cafe* at No 219.

The *Grain and Grape (☎ 528 6103, 218 High St)* is a cafe with food such as Cajun burger and ploughman's lunch.

This Kiwi country town has some surprisingly good restaurants. The **Gothic Gourmet** in the town centre was a Gothic-style Methodist church. Walk in the side door and you enter the bar. The gourmet-style meat and vegetarian dishes would be notable anywhere (about $22 for a main), and it has excellent desserts.

Annabelle's (☎ 528 8696), in the museum building, is both a cafe and an art gallery, with dining inside or out on the covered patio. It has good salads, desserts and coffee, with plenty for both meat-eaters and vegetarians.

Hot Mama's (105 High St) is a hip(py) cafe with good coffee and reasonably priced light meals. It's licensed and has live music on weekends. Note, it sometimes closes the kitchen by 9 pm.

The **Bakehouse Cafe & Pizzeria**, in a laneway off Wallace St just behind High St, is a European-style cafe with a bar with excellent pizza and Italian food. It's the town favourite and highly recommended.

Arcadia (☎ 528 7840, 265 High St) is an organic shop and cafe with grainy breads and lots of fruit and vegies.

Getting There & Away

Takaka Valley Air Services (☎ 0800-501 901) flies to Wellington in summer daily except Tuesday and Saturday (from $90 one way).

Abel Tasman Coachlines (☎ 528 8850) buses stop at the information centre. There are services from Motueka to Nelson, Takaka, Collingwood and the Abel Tasman National Park (both ends of the track all year round). It also operates a charter service into the Heaphy Track. Buses also link Motueka and Nelson with Kaiteriteri, to connect with the coastal launch that follows the Abel Tasman Track, but you *must* book ahead.

Knightline (☎ 0508-266 527) departs Motueka at 6 am and 2 pm daily and arrives in Picton at 9.10 am and 5.10 pm ($27). These services arrive back in Motueka at 1 and 9 pm.

Kahurangi Bus Services (☎ 0800-173 371) has daily buses from Takaka to Nelson via Motueka; they pick up at the visitor

centre. Buses also run to and from Totaranui by arrangement. See the Abel Tasman National Park section for more information on transport to and from the Abel Tasman Track.

Getting Around

This area is ideal to explore on bike, especially if you are going to the wineries or craft places. Think twice, however, about cycling up Takaka Hill for the views.

MOTUEKA TO TAKAKA

From Motueka, SH60 continues over Takaka Hill to Takaka and Collingwood. Before ascending Takaka Hill, on the right is the turn-off to Kaiteriteri and the southern end of Abel Tasman National Park, then a turn-off on your left to Riwaka Valley, a good area for picnicking, swimming in river pools and walks. You can walk to the spring that is the source of the Riwaka River.

Takaka Hill, 791m high, separates Tasman Bay from Golden Bay. Near the summit are the **Ngarua Caves** (☎ 528 8093) where you can see moa bones. Just before the Ngarua Caves is the Hawkes Lookout, from where there are great views of the Riwaka River headwaters. The caves are open from 10 am to 4 pm daily except Friday, and closed from mid-June to August ($10/5 for adults/children).

Also in the area is the biggest *tomo* (entrance, or cave) in the southern hemisphere, **Harwood's Hole**. It is 400m deep and 70m wide. It will take you half a day to get there from Motueka, as it is a half-hour walk one way from the car park at the end of Canaan Rd, off SH60. Exercise caution as you approach the lip of the hole – accidents have occurred.

There are many homestays and farmstays in the region. **Kairuru** (☎ 528 8091, ✉ kairuru@xtra.co.nz), on the way up Takaka Hill and 17km north-west of Motueka, is a comfortable homestay (B&B is $100 for two, dinner is $25 extra).

As you cross the crest of the hill, Harwood Lookout has fine views down the Takaka River Valley to Takaka and Golden Bay. The lookout has interesting explanations of the

MARLBOROUGH & NELSON

geography and geology of the area, from the north-west Nelson peneplain to the Anatoki Ranges. A peneplain, you ask? It is an area worn almost flat by erosion.

From the lookout you wind down through the beautiful Takaka Hill Scenic Reserve to the river valley, through Upper Takaka and on to Takaka itself.

Kaiteriteri Beach

This is one of the most popular and beautiful beaches in the area, just 13km from Motueka on a sealed road. The beach has genuine golden sand and clear, green waters. All water sports are available as well as a great childrens playground complete with minigolf. Behind the camping ground is **Withells Walk**, a 45-minute excursion into native bush from where great views look out across the bay. Otherwise walk to Kaka Pah Point at the end of the beach and find some of the secluded little coves and hideaways.

Launch and kayak trips run to the Abel Tasman National Park from Kaiteriteri, though Marahau is the usual base for the national park.

Places to Stay & Eat Summer brings many holiday-makers, mainly locals, to Kaiteriteri, but bed-space is limited.

The *Kaiteriteri Beach Camp* (☎ 527 8010), across from the beach, is large and well equipped. It has many sites at $19 for two; cabins are from $24 to $32.

The *Kimi Ora Holiday & Health Resort* (☎ 527 8027), above the beach on Martin Farm Rd, has good facilities including a vegetarian restaurant, pool, sauna, gym, tennis and more. Good units range from $55 a double to $99 with kitchen (some units sleep six). Prices are up to 20% higher from Christmas to the end of February.

Apart from the *restaurant* at Kimi Ora and the *Seafarers* (☎ 527 8114), near the beach on Inlet Rd, dining choices in Kaiteriteri are limited.

Getting There & Away Abel Tasman Coachlines buses run from Nelson and Motueka to connect with Abel Tasman National Park Enterprises cruises to the park.

With sufficient numbers the hire of a water taxi can be economical. Abel Tasman Charter Water Taxis (☎ 528 7497) at Kaiteriteri Beach can drop off at various parts of the national park or even provide transport for diving trips.

Marahau

Further north along the coast from Kaiteriteri, tiny Marahau, 18km north of Motueka, is the main gateway to the Abel Tasman National Park. It has expanded accommodation possibilities, and has water taxis, kayak hire, seal swimming and regular bus connections (see the Abel Tasman National Park section).

It's a pleasant spot and other activities include horse treks for $20 per hour with Abel Tasman Stables (☎ 527 8181), and 4WD Motorcycle Adventures (☎ 527 8400) has exciting trips through the limestone formations of the Takaka Hills.

Places to Stay The *Marahau Beach Camp* (☎ 527 8176) has tent/powered sites for $15/18, cabins for $35 for two and a self-contained backpackers lodge costing $12 (in eight- or five-bed dorms); cabins are $35. The camp has a shop, rents out kayaks and has a water-taxi service.

Marahau Lodge (☎ 527 8250, ✉ marahau .lodge@clear.net.nz), 500m past the camp, has comfortable studio units with en suite for $108 a double.

The *Ocean View Chalets* (☎ 527 8232) has excellent cottages with en suite on the hill for $88 and chalets with kitchen from $105. Prices drop in the off season.

The *Barn Backpackers* (☎ 527 8043) on Harveys Rd is a comfortable, homely place. Dorms are $14 per person, and doubles are $38; there are 15 camp sites at $17 for two. The bus service from Nelson drops you off at the Barn.

The *Park Cafe* (☎ 527 8270), near the start of the Abel Tasman Track and the park information kiosk, has good food and a great atmosphere. Gorge on cakes, muffins, blueberry crumble and milkshakes before heading out on the track. It's licensed and open for breakfast, lunch and dinner.

Old MacDonald's Farm (☎ 527 8288), further along Harveys Rd, is a simple camping ground but more facilities are being built. Tent/powered sites cost $14/18; on-site vans are $30 and $40 a double. A homestay is $35/70 per person for a bed-only/full board.

ABEL TASMAN NATIONAL PARK

The coastal Abel Tasman National Park is a very popular tramping area. The park is at the northern end of a range of marble and limestone hills extending from Kahurangi National Park, and the interior is honeycombed with caves and potholes. There are various tracks in the park, including an inland track, although the coastal track is the most popular – but beware of the sandflies.

Book accommodation for the track well in advance over summer or you will be disappointed.

Abel Tasman Coastal Track

This 51km, three- to four-day track is one of the most beautiful in the country, passing through pleasant bush overlooking beaches of golden sand lapped by bright blue water. The numerous bays, small and large, make it like a travel brochure come to life.

Once little known outside the immediate area, this track has now been 'discovered' and in summer hundreds of backpackers may be on the track at any one time – far more than can be accommodated in the huts, so bringing a tent is a good idea. At other times of the year it's not so crowded. The park has become so popular that DOC has introduced a booking system, as on the Routeburn and Milford Tracks. Check with DOC.

Information The track operates on a Great Walks Pass system – the cost is $14 per person in the huts and $7 for camp sites or, from June to October, $7 for huts or camp sites (children half-price). You can obtain the pass from DOC or information centres in Nelson, Motueka and Takaka, or by emailing DOC (@ greatwalksbooking@doc.govt.nz).

There's also a National Park Visitors Centre at Totaranui, open seasonally from late November to February; at other times the latest bus and boat schedules are posted there.

The huts (Anchorage, Bark Bay, Awaroa and Whariwharangi Homestead) have bunks for 20 or more people and are equipped with wood stoves.

Walking the Track Several sections of the main track are tidal, with long deviations during high tides, particularly at Awaroa. As the tidal stretches are all just on the northern side of huts, it is important to do the track in a southerly direction if the low tides are in the afternoons, and from south to north if they are in the mornings. Check the newspaper, subtracting 20 minutes from the Nelson tidal times. Tide tables and advice are available at the DOC office in Motueka.

Take additional food so you can stay longer should you have the inclination. Bays around all the huts are beautiful but the sandflies are a problem, except at the tiny, picturesque beach of Te Pukatea near the Anchorage Hut.

Excess luggage can be sent very cheaply by the various buses between Nelson, Motueka and Takaka. Abel Tasman National Park Enterprises has expensive, all-inclusive guided walks. Or you could parallel the track in a sea kayak.

Most walkers stop at Totaranui, the final stop for the boat services, but it is possible to keep walking around the headland from Totaranui to Whariwharangi (two hours) and then on to Wainui (1½ hours), where buses service the car park.

Estimated walking times are as follows, south to north: Marahau to Anchorage Hut (3½ hours), Anchorage Hut to Bark Bay Hut (three hours), Bark Bay Hut to Awaroa Hut (three hours), and Awaroa Hut to Totaranui (1½ hours).

Sea Kayaking

A lot of people choose to sea kayak around the relatively safe and definitely scenic waters of Abel Tasman National Park. A popular starting-point is Marahau at the southern end of the Abel Tasman Track.

The peak season is from November to Easter but you can paddle year-round. Winter

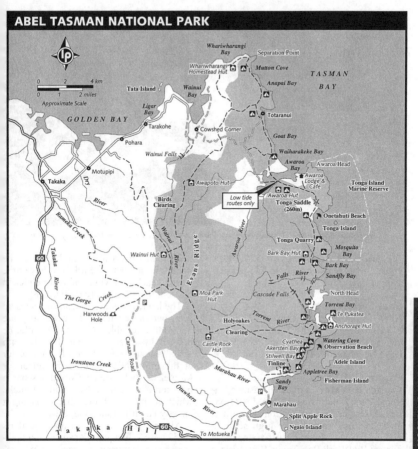

ABEL TASMAN NATIONAL PARK

Whariwharangi Bay
Separation Point
Whariwharangi Homestead Hut
Mutton Cove
Anapai Bay
T A S M A N
B A Y
0   2   4 km
0   1   2 miles
Approximate Scale
Tata Island
Wainui Bay
Ligar Bay
GOLDEN BAY
Tarakohe
Totaranui
Goat Bay
Cowshed Corner
Pohara
Wainui Falls
Waiharakeke Bay
Awaroa Bay
Awaroa Head
Motupipi
Takaka
Dry River
Awapoto Hut
Awaroa Lodge & Cafe
Tonga Island Marine Reserve
Rameka Creek
Birds Clearing
Low tide routes only
Awaroa Hut
Tonga Saddle (260m)
Onetahuti Beach
Tonga Island
Takaka River
Wainui Hut
Wainui River
Awaroa River
Tonga Quarry
Mosquito Bay
Bark Bay Hut
Bark Bay
Evans Ridge
Sandfly Bay
The Gorge Creek
Moa Park Hut
Falls River
Cascade Falls
North Head
Torrent Bay
Te Pukatea
Harwoods Hole
Torrent River
Holyoakes Clearing
Anchorage Hut
Castle Rock Hut
Cyathea
Watering Cove
Observation Beach
Ironstone Creek
Akersten Bay
Stilwell Bay
Tinline
Adele Island
Canaan Road
Marahau River
Appletree Bay
Fisherman Island
Otuwhero River
Sandy Bay
Marahau
Takaka Hill
60
To Motueka
Split Apple Rock
Ngaio Island

MARLBOROUGH & NELSON

is a really good time as you will see more bird life. Instruction is given to first-timers.

There are several sea kayaking operators in this hub of the sport, all charging about the same for specific activities. Kiwi Kayaks (☎ 0800-695 494) has guided trips for $80 per day (freedom rentals are $40 per person per day). It picks up from Nelson, Motueka and Marahau.

The Sea Kayak Company (☎ 528 7251, *e* info@seakayaknz.co.nz) has two-day rentals for $85 and a one-day tour for $80; Southern Exposure Sea Kayaking (☎ 527 8424), Web site: www.nzkayak.co.nz, has one-/two-/three-day trips for $80/195/285; and Kaiteriteri Kayaks (☎ 527 8383), Web site: www.seakayak.co.nz, based at Kaiteriteri Beach, has a sunset paddle for $40 and half-day guided trips for $40.

Ocean River Adventure Company (☎ 0800-732 529) on Main Rd, Marahau, has two-/three-day adventures for $365/565 per person all inclusive. Freedom rental for two days is $95.

Abel Tasman Kayaks (☎ 527 8022), Marahau, has a four-day kayak and walk trip for $630. Its three-day remote coast guided tour is $295.

Mosquito Bay in Abel Tasman National Park – a very pleasant place to set up your tent

Planet Earth Adventures (☎ 525 9095), Pohara, rents out kayaks from $45 per person per day.

Seal Swimming

Abel Tasman Seal Swim (☎ 0800-527 8136) takes trips to the Tonga Island seal colony ($60/45 for adults/children). Boats leave Marahau at 8.45 am and 1 pm.

Organised Tours

Cruises & Water Taxis Abel Tasman National Park Enterprises (☎ 528 7801) has launch services departing from Kaiteriteri at 9 am (also noon in the high season), picking up and dropping off trampers at Torrent Bay, Bark Bay, Tonga Bay, Awaroa and finally Totaranui (the northern end of the track), arriving back at Kaiteriteri 5½ hours later. It also picks up in Marahau but boats can't dock and you are shuttled out on a tractor trailer to meet the boat.

The launch service doubles as trampers transport and is also a pleasant day cruise. A 5½-hour cruise is $49 (children $22) and the 3½-hour cruise to Torrent Bay is $36/18. You can easily combine a walk along part of the Abel Tasman Track with the cruise, getting dropped off at one bay and picked up later at another. There are several such options, the most popular being to disembark at Torrent Bay, walk the track for two hours to Bark Bay, have time on the beach for swimming and be picked up from there for $39 (children $18).

The launch operates scheduled routes all year, but cancellations occur and they are not 100% reliable. All trips should be booked in advance, either directly with Abel Tasman National Park Enterprises or at the information centres in Nelson or Motueka. Abel Tasman Coachlines has a bus service from Nelson and Motueka which connects with the launch, making it an easy day trip from either town.

Alternatively, Abel Tasman Seafaris (☎ 527 8083, ✉ aquataxi@xtra.co.nz) operates an excellent trampers service from Marahau to Torrent Bay ($15), Bark Bay ($20), Tonga ($22), Awaroa ($25) and Totaranui ($28) and return. It also offers three-hour cruises for $40, an Awaroa return day trip for $45 and a variety of walk-cruise options. Abel Tasman Water Taxis, based in Kaiteriteri, also operates a similar drop-off service.

Sailing is a popular way to explore the coastline. Operators include Sail Tasman Yacht Charter (☎ 548 2754), with a two-day/two-night adventure for $295 per person, and Centresail (☎ 545 0548), with day sails for $85 and multiday trips from $140 each (full board).

Places to Stay & Eat
At the southern edge of the park, Marahau is the main jumping-off point. The nearest towns with accommodation at the northern end are Pohara and Takaka.

The *Awaroa Lodge & Cafe* (☎ *025-433 135)*, on the trail at Awaroa Bay, is only 300m from the water. At this place, 200m off the track, seven-bed dorms with kitchens are $22 per person, doubles are $70 with shared facilities, and private en suite units are $125. The *cafe* offers a range of health food and the proprietors will also pack lunches. Stay a while to look at the birds – white-faced herons, pied stilts, Caspian terns, tui, bellbirds and morepork are all found here. You can get to Awaroa Lodge by water taxi, walking part of the Abel Tasman Track from Totaranui, or driving to the Awaroa car park and then walking.

The *Kanuka Hill Lodge* (☎ *548 2863)* at The Anchorage is surrounded by native bush and in the heart of the park; ring for prices.

The *Totaranui Beach Camp* (☎ *525 8026)* at Totaranui, 33km from Takaka in the northern part of the national park, is administered by DOC and has no power or hot water. Camp sites are $7 per person; book during the summer holidays.

Getting There & Away
Abel Tasman Coachlines operates buses from Nelson (☎ 548 0285) to Motueka (☎ 528 8805) and on to Marahau, leaving Nelson at 7.20 am and 3.25 pm daily, picking up in Motueka one hour later. The 7.20 am bus also goes to Totaranui and the Wainui car park at the northern end of the track, returning at 1.15 pm from Totaranui. Open-dated Motueka to Marahau return tickets cost $10, while Nelson to Marahau return costs $19.

Kahurangi Bus Services (☎ 0800-173 371) also runs to and from Totaranui by arrangement.

TAKAKA
pop 1230
The small centre of Takaka is the last town of any size as you head towards the north-west corner of the South Island. It's the main centre for the beautiful Golden Bay area.

It's quite a hip little community – lots of 'Woodstock children' and artistic types have settled here.

Information
Just about everything in Takaka is along Commercial St, the main road through town. On the Motueka side of town, the helpful Golden Bay Information Centre (☎ 525 9136) is open from 9 am to 7 pm daily in summer (9 am to 5 pm in winter).

DOC (☎ 525 8026), Commercial St, has information on Abel Tasman and Kahurangi National Parks, the Heaphy and Kaituna Tracks, Farewell Spit, Cobb Valley and the Aorere goldfield. It's open from 8 am to 4 pm weekdays, but closes for lunch. Passes for the Abel Tasman Track are available here.

There's an internet cafe out the back of The Dangerous Kitchen (☎ 525 8686, @ dkitchen@voyager.co.nz).

The Quiet Revolution (☎ 525 9555) hires bikes from $15 to $25, and also does repairs and service.

Takaka has a small **museum**, open daily ($1, children $0.50). The **Begonia House** in Clifton, 8km east of town, is open in summer to show off its colourful flowers.

Watching movies ($7/9 for unwaged/waged) at the Village Theatre is good fun, and the cinema has a cafe.

Waikoropupu Springs
These springs (simply called 'Pupu') are the largest freshwater springs in NZ. Many springs are dotted around the Pupu Springs Scenic Reserve, including one with 'dancing boulders' thrown upwards by the great volume of incredibly clear water emerging from the ground.

Walking tracks through the reserve take you to the springs and a glassed viewing area, passing by **gold-mining works** from the 19th century – gold was discovered in Golden Bay in 1856. There is an excellent DOC leaflet about the reserve. To reach Pupu from Takaka, go 4km north-west on SH60, turn inland at Waitapu Bridge and continue for 3km.

Arts & Crafts Trail

Many artists and craftspeople are based in the Golden Bay area, including painters, potters, blacksmiths, screenprinters, silversmiths and knitwear designers. The large **Artisans' Shop** cooperative on Commercial St, next to the Village Theatre, displays their wares. Many other artists and craftspeople are tucked away all around the bay.

The *Golden Bay Craft Trail* leaflet gives directions to the galleries and workshops. The Whole Meal Trading Company and the Golden Bay Gallery (in the old post office) also have local art on display.

Walks

There are endless possibilities in this region. The information centre has a series of leaflets explaining the more popular options.

Kahurangi Guided Walks (☎ 525 7177), Web site: www.KahurangiWalks.webnz.co .nz, guides multiday walks along the Heaphy Track ($720 with transport and gourmet food). It also goes to the Upper Cobb ($85 per person per day), the Anatoki–Stanley ($90), Sylvester Lakes ($65 for a day walk) and The Tablelands–Mt Peel ($85).

Bush & Beyond (☎ 528 9054), Web site: www.naturetreks.co.nz, in Motueka, does similar trips.

Windsurfing

This is a popular activity on Golden Bay – all the local beaches are excellent. Windsurfers are available at Shady Rest and the Pohara Beach Camp.

Places to Stay

Takaka has accommodation, though the nearby beach resort of Pohara is more popular and has the closest camping ground (see Pohara later).

Annie's (☎ 525 8766, 25 Motupipi St), close to the town centre, is a small, peaceful haven with a homely atmosphere. It's $15 in dorms out the back, and $40 for a double. Guests can help themselves to things from the garden.

The *Shady Rest (141 Commercial St)*, in a big historic home on the main road, is friendly enough but basic, with a large dorm costing $15 per person. There's no sign and it's 'Telecom-free'.

The *River Inn (☎ 525 9425, @ riverinn@ xtra.co.nz)*, 3km west of town on the road to Collingwood, is an old pub-turned-backpackers with singles, twins and doubles for $18 per person.

About 15km west is the *Shambhala Beach Farm Hostel (☎ 525 8463)*, spectacularly set overlooking Onekaka Beach. The Kahurangi Bus and Abel Tasman Coachlines buses drop off at the Mussel Inn, Onekaka. If you're driving take the right turn 50m before the Inn (coming from Takaka), but it is then about 3km along a dirt road. Costs are only $15 per person in share rooms, and $35 in twins and doubles in the house and cottages around. There is a great German-language book exchange and much of the owner's artwork adorns the walls. A big attraction is the free use of horses.

The *Golden Bay Motel (☎ 525 9428, 113 Commercial St)* is $70 to $85 a double; *Anotaki Lodge (☎ 525 8047, 147 Commercial St)* is the town's best place to stay, with a solar-heated pool and rooms from $77 to $110.

Many B&Bs and homestays are listed at the information centre. *Amanzi (☎ 525 9615, Rangihaeata Rd)* is a self-contained unit with great bay views; a double is $75.

Kahurangi (☎ 524 8312, @ kahurangi@ xtra.co.nz) is 17km west of Takaka. It's a fascinating place to stay with massage available, and well-prepared meals employing in-season ingredients. Ring for prices.

Places to Eat

The *Wholemeal Cafe (☎ 525 9426, 60 Commercial St)* is a local institution, an enjoyable wholefood cafe, restaurant and art gallery which also sells bulk natural foods, has a bulletin board and sometimes has live music in the evenings.

Milliways (☎ 525 9636), further down Commercial St, is a fancier restaurant (mains $20 to $27.50) with a relaxed atmosphere; it's licensed and open daily in summer.

The *Takaka Tearooms (44 Commercial St)* has pastries, ice creams, pies and light meals.

The Dangerous Kitchen (☎ 525 8686, 48 Commercial St) has great coffee, pizza and cakes. The place is dedicated to Frank Zappa.

Bencarri Farm & Cafe *(☎ 525 8261)*, in a pleasant bush setting on the Anatoki River 6km from town, has a cafe serving country-style lunches and dinners.

Getting There & Away

Takaka Valley Air Services (☎ 0800-501 901) flies to Wellington summer daily except Tuesday and Saturday (from $90 one way).

Kahurangi buses (☎ 525 9434) goes from Takaka to Collingwood ($15), the beginning of the Heaphy Track ($18), and to Nelson ($20) daily. Abel Tasman Coachlines also operates from Nelson to Takaka. Both buses have daily services to Totaranui at the northern end of the Abel Tasman National Park, passing Pohara on the way.

POHARA

Small Pohara is a popular summer resort, 10km north-east of Takaka. The beautiful beach is on the way to the northern end of the Abel Tasman Track. The unsealed road to the park is scenic and passes a lookout with a pillar dedicated to Abel Tasman, the first European to enter Golden Bay (in 1642).

The **Rawhiti Caves** (☎ 525 9061) near Pohara have the largest entrance of any cave in NZ, well worth a look. A three-hour return guided tour of the caves costs $14 (children $6). To reach the caves you walk for 45 minutes past 400-year-old totara trees. It's an enjoyable and popular tour.

Planet Earth Adventures (☎ 525 9095) rents out kayaks, windsurfers, snorkelling gear and bicycles.

Pohara Fish & Dive (☎ 525 7227), on Pohara Valley Rd, has scalloping, fishing and diving trips; all gear provided.

Places to Stay & Eat

The ***Pohara Beachside Holiday Park*** *(☎ 525 9500)* is right on the beach and has sites for $20, cabins for $34 ($46 with kitchens) and motel units for $85 for two.

The Nook *(☎ 525 8501,* **ⓔ** *nook@ clear.net.nz)* is an excellent backpackers in a rendered hay-bale house. Share rooms cost $17, twins and doubles are $40 and

tent sites are available. Many people come to Pohara just to stay here. It's on the main road as you enter Pohara, five minutes' walk from the beach.

The ***Sans Souci Inn*** *(☎ 525 8663)* at Pohara Beach is an attractive rammed-earth building with a sod roof, done in Mediterranean style. This very chic place charges $65 for doubles (shared bathrooms) and there are family rooms. It has a good licensed restaurant (mains $15 to $18) and guests can use the kitchen.

Marina Motel *(☎ 525 9620)* is good value with units from $65 to $85. It has a tavern attached with good, if slightly expensive, seafood meals.

Sandcastle Seaview *(☎ 525 9087,* **ⓔ** *sandcastle@xtra.co.nz),* Haile Lane, consists of four self-contained chalets with outdoor spa pools; for what you get the price is very reasonable ($84 for two, or $104 with breakfast).

KAHURANGI NATIONAL PARK

Formerly the North-West Nelson Forest Park, this is the newest and second-largest of NZ's national parks and undoubtedly one of the greatest. Within its 500,000 hectares is an ecological wonderland – over 100 bird species, 50% of all NZ's plant species, 80% of its alpine plant species, a karst landscape and the largest known cave system in the southern hemisphere. Kahurangi means 'treasured possession'. Few keen trampers will disagree, as the many fine tracks and rugged country attracts them in droves, mostly to walk the Heaphy Track.

Information

Detailed information, park maps and Great Walks Passes for the Heaphy Track are available from these DOC offices:

Karamea Field Centre (☎ 782 6852), Main Rd, Karamea

Nelson Visitor Information Centre (☎ 548 2304), corner of Trafalgar and Halifax Sts, Nelson

Motueka Field Centre (☎ 528 9117), corner of King Edward and High Sts, Motueka

Takaka Field Centre (☎ 525 8026), 1 Commercial St, Takaka

Heaphy Track

Named after Major Charles Heaphy, the painter and soldier who was awarded the Victoria Cross during the Waikato Land Wars (1864), the Heaphy Track is one of the best-known tracks in NZ. The four- to six-day 77km track doesn't have the spectacular scenery of the Routeburn, but it still has its own beauty. Surprisingly, some people find it a disappointment if done immediately after the nearby Abel Tasman Coastal Track.

The track lies almost entirely within the Kahurangi National Park. Highlights include the view from the summit of Mt Perry (two-hour return walk from Perry Saddle Hut) and the coast, especially around the Heaphy Hut. It's worth spending a day or two resting at the Heaphy Hut, something appreciated by those travelling south from Collingwood. It is possible to cross the Heaphy River at its mouth at low tide.

Huts are set up for 20 or more people. They all have gas stoves, except Heaphy and Gouland Downs which have wood stoves. Nightly hut fees are $12 for pre-booked tickets, or $15 if they are purchased at the time of walking (children half-price). Camping is $8/6 per person (children half). You can prebook tickets by email (✪ greatwalksbooking@doc.govt.nz).

Walking the Track Most people travel south-west from Collingwood to Karamea. From Brown Hut the track passes through beech forest to Perry Saddle (but don't take the short cut uphill, unless you are fit). The country opens up to the swampy Gouland Downs, then closes in with sparse bush all the way to Mackay Hut. The bush becomes more dense towards the Heaphy Hut with the beautiful nikau palm growing at lower levels.

The final section is along the coast through heavy bush and partly along the beach. Unfortunately, the sandflies are unbearable along this, the most beautiful part of the track. The climate here is surprisingly mild, but do not swim in the sea as the undertows and currents are vicious. The lagoon at Heaphy Hut is good for swimming though, and fishing is possible in the Heaphy River.

The Heaphy has kilometre markers along its length; the zero marker is at the start of the track at the Kohaihai River near Karamea. Estimated walking times are as follows:

Brown Hut to Perry Saddle Hut	five hours
Perry Saddle Hut to Gouland Downs Hut	two hours
Gouland Downs Hut to Saxon Hut	1½ hours
Saxon Hut to Mackay Hut	three hours
Mackay Hut to Lewis Hut	three to four hours
Lewis Hut to Heaphy Hut	two to three hours
Heaphy Hut to Kohaihai River	five hours

Wangapeka & Leslie–Karamea Tracks

It is possible to return to the Nelson/Golden Bay region by the more scenic, if harder, Wangapeka Track starting just south of Karamea. Although not as well known as the Heaphy, the Wangapeka, also in Kahurangi National Park, is thought by many to be a more enjoyable walk. The track starts some 25km south of Karamea at Little Wanganui (on the West Coast side) and runs 52km east to the Rolling River near Tapawera. It takes about five days and there is a good chain of huts ($4 to $8 per night, children $2 to $4) along the track.

The 90km Leslie-Karamea Track is a medium to hard tramp of five to seven days. It connects the Cobb Valley near Takaka with Little Wanganui, south of Karamea, on the West Coast (thus including part of the Wangapeka Track on the final two days).

Cobb Valley & Mt Arthur Tablelands

The Cobb Valley and Mt Arthur Tablelands offer plenty of scope for walkers. The Cobb Valley is 28km from the Upper Takaka turn-off. You first drive up to the power station and from there it's another 13km drive to the valley. Once in the valley there are a number of walks to choose from. These

HEAPHY TRACK

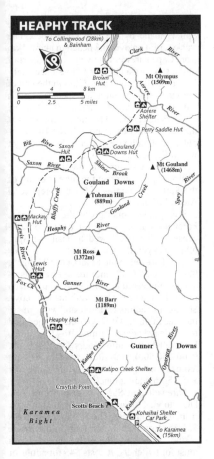

To Collingwood (28km)
& Bainham

Clark   River

Brown
Hut

Mt Olympus
(1509m)

0   4   8 km

0   2.5   5 miles

Aorere   River

Aorere
Shelter

Perry Saddle Hut

Big   River   Saxon
Hut

Gouland
Downs Hut

Shiner   Brook

Mt Gouland
(1468m)

Saxon   River

Gouland   Downs

Tubman Hill
(889m)

Gouland   Creek   River   Spey

Mackay
Hut

Bluffy Creek

Heaphy

River

Lewis   River

Lewis
Hut

Fox Ck

Mt Ross
(1372m)

Gunner   River

Mt Barr
(1189m)

Heaphy Hut

Katipo Creek

Gunner   Downs

Opawa   River

Katipo Creek Shelter

Crayfish Point

Kohaihai River

*Karamea
Bight*

Scotts Beach

Kohaihai Shelter
Car Park

To Karamea
(15km)

range from the 45-minute Mytton's Forest Walk to others of a few hours' duration, eg, Cobb Ridge to Peat Flat and Trilobite Hut to Chaffey Hut. Chaffey Hut, built in 1954, is constructed of split beech slabs.

To get to the Mt Arthur Tablelands you drive from Motueka south to Pokororo. Take the Graham Rd into the Flora car park, and from here there are a great number of walking possibilities. Walks in the area include Mt Arthur Hut (3km; one hour), Mt Arthur (8km; three hours), Mt Lodestone (5km; two hours) and Flora Hut (2km; 30 minutes).

Kaituna Track

This track is west of Collingwood and trampers have two choices: a return walk of two to three hours through the old gold workings and bush scenery, or a longer track (12km; five to seven hours) which takes you to the West Coast at Whanganui Inlet. The *Kaituna Track* pamphlet is most informative, outlining in detail the flora and fauna seen along the way, including the nikau, the world's most southerly occurring palm, and the crown fern.

The Inn-let (☎ 524 8040) guides a one-day walk through the beautiful Wakamarama Range for $70 (see the Collingwood section for details of the Inn-let backpackers).

Aorere Goldfield

The Aorere goldfield was the first major goldfield in NZ. In February 1857 five ounces (142g) of Collingwood gold were auctioned in Nelson, precipitating a gold rush which lasted three years, although various companies continued to wrest gold from the soil by sluicing and stamping batteries right up until WWI. The old goldfields are now overgrown but terraces, water races and mine shafts can still be seen.

The DOC office in Takaka has an excellent publication, *Aorere Goldfields/Caves Walk*, detailing the history of the goldfield and guiding you on a historical walk, beginning from Collingwood. The walk takes most of the day to complete. You can learn more about the local history at the small museum in town. The Inn-let backpackers in Collingwood also does tours.

Getting There & Away

Abel Tasman Coachlines (☎ 528 8805) has a service from Collingwood and Takaka to the Heaphy Track entrance in summer ($15 and $20 respectively); in winter it is on demand and expensive.

Kahurangi Bus (☎ 0800-173 371) also provides transport to the track on demand (see Takaka earlier), as will Bickley Motors (☎ 525 8352) in Takaka. There's a phone at the trail head to call buses.

Wadsworths Motors (☎ 522 4248) services the Wangapeka and Leslie–Karamea

MARLBOROUGH & NELSON

Tracks. For details on the Karamea end of the tracks see the Karamea section in The West Coast chapter.

Kahurangi Bus is very useful – it connects the walking tracks in Kahurangi National Park to Nelson ($38).

Hitchhiking to either the Karamea or Bainham end of the Heaphy Track is very difficult.

COLLINGWOOD
pop 250

Tiny Collingwood is almost at the end of the line, which is one of its main attractions. For many it's simply one jumping-off point for the Heaphy Track in the Kahurangi National Park. For others who wish to explore, there are many rewards such as the natural wonderland of Farewell Spit.

As befits a frontier town, there is a place where you can get a horse: Cape Farewell Horse Trekking (☎ 524 8031) based in Puponga. A one-hour ride is $18 and a three-hour trip to Wharariki is $55. And a kayak? A full-day trip in Whanganui Inlet with Aorere Adventure Tramps, Walks & Kayaks (☎ 524 8040) is $65 to $85, depending on numbers.

Farewell Spit

Farewell Spit is a wetland of international importance and a renowned bird sanctuary. It's the summer home to thousands of migratory waders from the Arctic tundra. On the 26km beach run there are huge crescent-shaped sand dunes from where you get panoramic views of the Spit, Golden Bay and, at low tide, the vast salt marsh.

At the Puponga car park (before the restricted section of road) there are bones from a sperm whale which beached here. You can look out over the eel grass flats and see many waders and sea birds such as pied and variable oystercatchers, turnstones, Caspian terns, eastern bar-tailed godwits, black and white-fronted terns, and big black shags. The Puponga Visitor Centre (☎ 524 8454) provides information as well as cafe refreshments, and powerful binoculars are set up to view the wetlands and the many species of wading birds.

The crossing to the northern side of the Spit is made by the tour companies. The trucks grind up over the beach to about 1km from Cape Farewell. Down towards the start of the sand are a number of fossilised shellfish. From this point it is 27km to the end of the sandy spit. Again many species of birds are seen along the way, and often a stranded pilot whale carcass. The normal trip ends at the old lighthouse compound. The 100-year-old metal lighthouse has an eight-sided light which flashes every 15 seconds.

Further east, up on the blown shell banks which comprise the far extremity of the Spit, are colonies of Caspian terns and Australasian gannets.

Two guided tours go to the remarkable Farewell Spit region. These are the only licensed vehicles allowed to visit the Spit; otherwise you'll have to walk.

The Farewell Spit Safari (☎ 524 8257, 0800-808 257, ✉ enquires@farewellspit .co.nz) pioneered travel up the sandy beach to the lighthouse. The five-hour tour costs $65/30 for adults/children and you go up the beach in a 4WD vehicle. Scheduled tours leave daily, timed to the tides. Farewell Spit Nature Tours (☎ 524 8188, 0800-250 500), Web site: www.farewell-spit .co.nz, also goes to the lighthouse for $65/35, including lunch.

Farewell Spit Safari is also licensed by DOC to visit the gannet colony, a 1km walk from the lighthouse. The 5½-hour tour costs $65/35. Its wader-watch tour on the inside of the sandy spit (the estuarine side) is a must for twitchers. It costs $45 for adults or children.

In addition to a Farewell Spit tour, Jock Lill offers a good Scenic Mail Run tour that visits isolated farming settlements and communities around Cape Farewell and the West Coast. The driver points out many points of historical and contemporary interest along the way. The 5½-hour tour departs from the Collingwood post shop at 10.30 am on weekdays ($35, $20 for children, including lunch).

Wharariki Beach

This beach is 29km to the north of Collingwood and involves a 20-minute walk from the car park. It is a wild introduction to the West Coast, with unusual dune formations, two looming, rock islets just out from shore, and a seal colony at its eastern end. A special place to get away entirely from the 'rat race' of Collingwood.

Places to Stay

The *Collingwood Motor Camp* (☎ 524 8149) on William St, near the centre of the tiny township, has tent and powered sites at $18 for two and cabins from $32 for two.

The *Pakawau Beach Park* (☎ 524 8327) is 13km north of Collingwood, which means it's even closer to the end of the road. Sites are $20 for two, large cabins with cooking facilities are $45 and motel units are $80.

The *A1 Collingwood Motel* (☎ 524 8224) on Haven Rd has units from $65 to $75 for two. The *Collingwood Beach-comber Motels* (☎ 524 8499) on Tasman St has units at $60 to $80 for two. The *Pioneer Motels* (☎ 524 8109), also on Tasman St, charges $58 to $70.

Skara Brae (☎ 524 8464) on Elizabeth St is a small B&B with two self-contained units costing $60 ($75 for B&B).

Northwest Lodge (☎ 524 8108) is an upmarket B&B 10km south of Collingwood; doubles are $120 with en suite.

In Pakawau, the *Old School House Cafe* (☎ 524 8457) has a small pool, a couple of good units for $75 a double, and cabins.

The *Inn-let* (☎ 524 8040, ✉ jhearn@ xtra.co.nz) is a friendly place on the way to Pakawau, about 10km from Collingwood. Jonathan and Katie are attuned to their environment and are full of details about the surrounding area. Comfortable beds in renovated share rooms are $16 and double rooms are $40 to $45. Another fully self-contained cottage sleeping six is $90. The owners pick up from Collingwood and also arrange 'rainforest' kayaking ($75),

caving and guided walks. Incidentally, Opua means 'Terrace', so sit on theirs above the river of that name, have a barbecue and relax in native bush surroundings.

The *World's End Backpacker Lodge* (☎ 524 8937) is a small home at Puponga, close to Farewell Spit. It's a great location; dorms are $15 and doubles $36.

The *Farewell Gardens* (☎ 524 8445, ✉ eaglenz@xtra.co.nz) is nearby. Costs per person are: backpackers accommodation $28, tent sites $10, and on-site caravans $18 (linen $5). The two-bedroom flat costs $65 for two people, $25 each extra person (up to four).

Places to Eat

The *Courthouse Cafe & Gallery* (☎ 525 8472), on the corner of Haven Rd, prepares delicious a la carte meals from locally grown organic produce, fresh seafood and herbs and spices. It's open six days a week for lunch and dinner.

The *bistro* at the tavern opposite the post office serves passable food, but meals may finish early.

The *Mussel Inn*, about halfway between Takaka (15km) and Collingwood, is a new ale house modelled on an early 1900s establishment. Good seafood, steak and salad meals are reasonably priced.

The *Old School House Cafe* in Pakawau is the best restaurant in the area. The building's decor matches its former calling, and scallops and other local seafood are featured on the menu (mains around $20).

Getting There & Away

Kahurangi Bus (☎ 0800-173 371) has a daily bus service from Collingwood to Takaka ($9) and Nelson ($20).

Abel Tasman National Coachlines (☎ 528 8850) has daily services from Nelson to Motueka, Takaka and Collingwood (and the Heaphy Track in summer).

MARLBOROUGH & NELSON

The West Coast

☎ 03 • pop 22,000

The West Coast (Westland) is a rugged land of wild, pebbled and rocky beaches and bush-clad hills sweeping up to towering icy peaks. Often the narrow coastal strip is *pakihi* (dried-up swamp) or second-class farmland, and the region is studded with jewel-like lakes mirroring the peaks above.

Pioneers hacked back the coastal bush half-successfully. Patches of native forest have escaped the axe and fire, and the rest of the scrubby farming land is always in danger of being reclaimed. The hills are still largely untamed, and scattered throughout the thick bush and by the rivers is the rusted debris of 100 years of exploitative industry – gold and coal mining and timber milling.

The two glaciers, Fox and Franz Josef, are the major drawcards, but the full stretch from Karamea to Jackson Bay is worth exploring.

The road hugs the coastline most of the way from Westport in the north to Hokitika, then runs inland until it finally joins the coast again between Knights Point and Haast, before turning east and heading over the Haast Pass. Near the coast, but a long way by road, are Mts Cook and Tasman.

Most people visit the region in summer, especially from December to January. From May to September the days can often be warm and clear, with views of snowcapped peaks, no crowds and off-peak accommodation rates. The area is worth a visit any time of year.

Westland could aptly be called 'Wetland'. Average annual rainfall is around 5m (200 inches). This said, the West Coast receives as many sunshine hours as the Christchurch region.

BULLER GORGE

The road across from Nelson to the coast via the Buller Gorge is scenic and interesting. The Buller area is still scarred from the 1929 Murchison and 1968 Inangahua earthquakes. From Inangahua Junction you can head through the lower Buller Gorge to the

- White-water and black-water rafting in the rivers and caves near Westport
- Making a foray into the many remote stands of indigenous forest which are alive with birdlife
- Walking on or aerial flightseeing over the Franz Josef and Fox glaciers
- Jet-boating, flying and walking in Mt Aspiring National Park near Makarora
- Driving the coastal road from Westport to Greymouth, and overnighting at the Pancake Rocks at Punakaiki
- Visiting the white heron *(kotuku)* colony near Whataroa
- Relaxing in one of the coast's remote fishing settlements or small towns for a few days

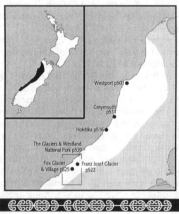

coast, or go on to Greymouth via Reefton on the inland route. The coastal route has more to offer but is longer.

Travelling from Murchison (in Nelson) to Westport takes about 1½ hours. To get onto the Buller Gorge road (SH6) you turn off at Sullivan's Bridge at the junction with SH65 to Maruia Springs and the Lewis

THE WEST COAST (WESTLAND)

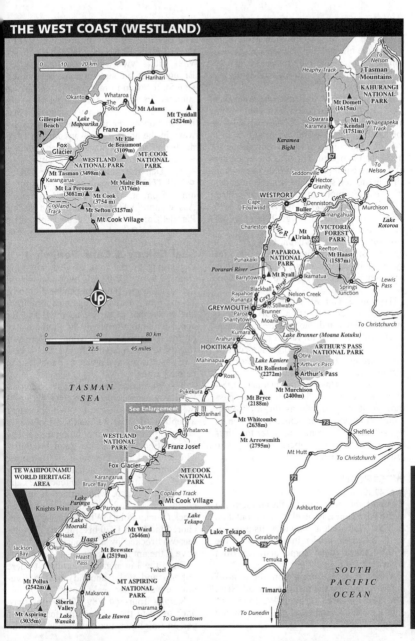

Pass. Just past the bridge, look up the valley to the left to see **Old Man Mountain**. With some imagination you see a potbellied supine fellow – the cloud above is smoke from his hidden pipe. Further on is a long swing bridge.

The homestay-style ***Brian's Backpackers*** (*☎ 523 9453*) is on SH65, just 200m from the junction with SH6. A bed costs $14 in the small farmhouse and camping is $10.

The road winds through the gorge to Inangahua Junction. This was the epicentre of a major earthquake in 1968 – over seven on the Richter scale. The scarred hillsides still bear testimony to the power of nature.

There's a ***DOC camping ground*** on SH6 at Lyell, Upper Buller Gorge, 10km north of Inangahua.

Inwood Farm Backpackers (*☎ 789 0205),* a small farmhouse and an option for cyclists, is on Inwoods Rd at Inangahua Junction; a bed costs $12 and the one twin is $26.

The Buller Gorge itself is dark and forbidding, especially on a murky day – primeval ferns and cabbage trees cling to steep cliffs, and toi toi (a tall native grass) flanks the road between gorge and river. A drive through the gorge's scenic reserve is picturesque in any weather.

The road at **Hawks Crag** has been literally hacked out of the rock. Buses pass through it very slowly as the rock overhang comes extremely close to the top of the vehicle. It is named not after the birds but a goldminer, Robert Hawks, who prospected in the area.

WESTPORT
pop 4230
Westport, the major town at the northern end of the West Coast, is developing a reputation as a base for outdoor activities. Its prosperity is based on coal mining, although the mining takes place some distance from town.

Westport is 5km north from the turn-off to Greymouth on the main coast road, SH6. The SH67 passes through Westport and ends beyond Karamea at the start of the Heaphy Track.

Information
The Westport Visitor Information Centre (*☎* 789 6658, *@* westport.info@xtra.co.nz), Web site: www.westport.org.nz, is on Brougham St, a couple of doors off Palmerston St. It's open from 9 am to 7 pm daily in summer (in winter 9 am to 5 pm on weekdays, 9 am to 3 pm on weekends). It has information on the many tracks and walkways in the area, sells tokens for the laundrette on Brougham St and handles bookings including Tranz Scenic and InterCity.

The Department of Conservation (DOC; *☎* 789 7742) on Russell St is open from 9 am to 5 pm on weekdays. The Automobile Association (AA; *☎* 789 8002) is on Marine Parade, Carters Beach. The post shop is on the corner of Brougham and Palmerston Sts.

Seal Colony & Cape Foulwind
Depending on the time of year, anything from 20 to over 100 seals may be down on the rocks at the Tauranga Bay seal colony, 12km from Westport. Pups are born from late November to early December and for about a month afterwards the mothers stay on the rocks to tend the young before setting off to sea on feeding forays. Don't venture past the marked areas, as the cliffs can be dangerous.

The 90-minute one-way **Cape Foulwind Walkway** extends along the coast 4km past the seal colony to Cape Foulwind, passing a replica of Abel Tasman's astrolabe (a navigational aid) and a lighthouse site. The information centre has a good brochure. The Maori knew the cape as Tauranga, meaning 'a sheltered anchorage or landing place'. The first European to reach the cape was Abel Tasman, who sighted it in December 1642 and named it Glyphaygen Hock (Rocky Point). When James Cook anchored in March 1770 his ship, the *Endeavour,* was rocked by a furious storm, so he gave it the apt name it retains today.

From the Tauranga Bay car park (where pukeko and weka abound) it is a five-minute walk to the seal colony.

Karaka Tours (*☎* 789 5080) runs two-hour tours to the seal colony for $15 per person (minimum two), including a scenic

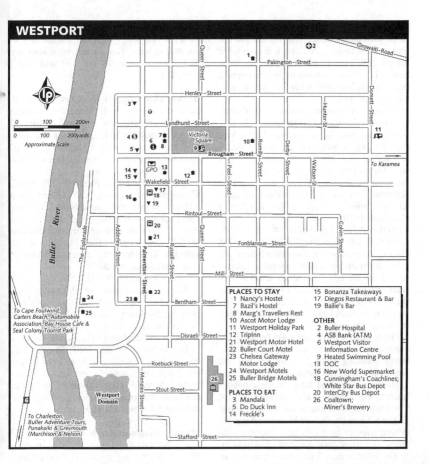

WESTPORT

Map legend:

PLACES TO STAY
1 Nancy's Hostel
7 Bazil's Hostel
8 Marg's Travellers Rest
10 Ascot Motor Lodge
11 Westport Holiday Park
12 TripInn
21 Westport Motor Hotel
22 Buller Court Motel
23 Chelsea Gateway Motor Lodge
24 Westport Motels
25 Buller Bridge Motels

PLACES TO EAT
3 Mandala
5 Do Duck Inn
14 Freckle's
15 Bonanza Takeaways
17 Diegos Restaurant & Bar
19 Bailie's Bar

OTHER
2 Buller Hospital
4 ASB Bank (ATM)
6 Westport Visitor Information Centre
9 Heated Swimming Pool
13 DOC
16 New World Supermarket
18 Cunningham's Coachlines; White Star Bus Depot
20 InterCity Bus Depot
26 Coaltown; Miner's Brewery

---

drive. It also drops off at the seal colony and picks up from the other end of the walkway ($20 per person).

Coaltown

This well laid-out museum on Queen St reconstructs aspects of coal-mining life, including a walk through a **simulated mine** complete with authentic sound effects.

There is also a one-hour film, coal- and gold-mining artefacts, and some excellent photographic exhibits. It's open from 9 am to 4.30 pm daily but closed Sunday ($6, children $4).

The locally owned **Miner's Brewery** (☎ 789 6201), open from 10 am to 5.30 pm, is on Lyndhurst St – a good place to quench your thirst after a mine tour (daily tours at 11.30 am and 1 pm).

Activities

Underworld rafting is a real New Zealand activity. From Charleston, south of Westport, Norwest Adventures (☎ 789 6686) runs trips underground into what could easily be the reaches of Xanadu on Coleridge's sacred river (the Nile actually) for $90. In the lower levels of Metro Cave you paddle rubber rafts through spectacular caverns filled with glowworms. The trip ends in the rapids of the larger Nile River and is suitable for any child over 10 who can walk for three hours. Two trips (maximum 36 passengers) depart from Westport daily in summer at 9 am and 2.30 pm.

Norwest Adventures also does thrilling, four-hour **adventure caving**, starting with a 30m abseil into Te Tahi *tomo* (hole). You then worm your way through rock squeezes and waterfalls, exploring prehistoric fossils and formations as you go (stalactites, stalagmites, straws, columns and a whale skeleton). The cost is $150 and a good standard of fitness is required. Another Metro Cave tour is $45.

Buller Adventure Tours (☎ 789 7286, 0800-697 286) on the Buller Gorge Rd (SH6), 4km east of the Greymouth turn-off, offers a variety of reasonably priced activities. They include particularly good **whitewater rafting** with grade IV trips on the Buller ($80 half-day), and grade V rapids on the Karamea ($235 one day). It arranges multiday trips also.

Other activities include **jet-boating** on the Buller River ($55 for one-plus hours), **horse trekking** ($40 for two hours) and Argo **eight-wheeler safaris** ($20).

Back and Beyond takes **mountain-bike tours** to the Denniston Incline (see later) for $79 for a full day; ask at the visitor centre. Kekeno Tours (☎ 0800-535 366) take **surf-rafting** trips to see seals and Hector's dolphins – these are good fun (from $39 to $45).

The information centre has brochures on good **bushwalks** in the region, many of which pass through old gold- and coal-mining areas. Burning Mines Tours (☎ 789 7277) goes to the opencast mines ($45, four hours).

Places to Stay
Camping & Cabins The *Westport Holiday Park (☎ 789 7043)* is on Domett St about 500m from the information centre. Tent/powered sites are $16/18, chalets (most with fridge) are $29 and chalets with en suite $39; all prices are for two. The basic bunkrooms cost $13.50 per person.

The *Seal Colony Tourist Park (☎ 789 8002)* is 6km from Westport, on the way to the seal colony. Tent or powered sites are $20, on-site caravans are $30 and motel units $88.

Backpackers *Bazil's Hostel (☎ 789 6410, 54 Russell St)* is well appointed, modern and highly regarded by its guests. Furnished shared rooms are $17, and twins and doubles are $40. There is a sheltered area of lawn for relaxing, a stylish kitchen and free herbs and spices.

Marg's Travellers Rest (☎ 789 8627, ✉ margstr@xtra.co.nz), next to Bazil's, is a YHA associate and guesthouse. The new backpackers section has excellent standards and costs $18 for dorms; twins and doubles are $47. B&B is also offered in units at $68 a double. The complex includes a restaurant with economical meals.

Nancy's Hostel (☎ 789 6565, fax 789 8015), on the corner of Pakington and Romilly Sts, is a big old house with predominant lead-lighting – down at heel but with lots of character. It's $15 in dorms and $35 for twins and doubles (it closes over winter).

The *TripInn (☎ 789 7367, ✉ tripinn@clear.net.nz, 72 Queen St)* is an even bigger old house with a new kitchen, laundry, units at the side and friendly owners. The cost in dorms (from four to 14 beds) is $15, twins and doubles are $36.

Motels *Westport Motels (☎ 789 7575, 32 The Esplanade)* has units at $75 for doubles; at this price, they are as good as anywhere else.

The *Westport Motor Hotel (☎ 789 7889, 207 Palmerston St)* has doubles from $69 to $89 and a restaurant; the *Buller Bridge Motels (☎ 789 7519, ✉ bullerbridge@clear.net.nz)* on The Esplanade – recommended by 'Coasters' – has doubles from $75; the *Buller Court Motel (☎ 789 7979, 235 Palmerston St)* charges from $70 for two; the *Ascot Motor Lodge (☎ 789 7832, ✉ bmbade@xtra.co.nz, 74 Romilly St)* charges from $70 for two; and the *Chelsea Gateway Motor Lodge (☎ 789 6835),* on the corner of Palmerston and Bentham Sts, is at the top of the heap, with units from $90 to $160 with spa bath.

Places to Eat

Palmerston St is crammed with takeaways and sandwich shops, including *Bonanza Takeaways* near the Wakefield St corner, which also has tables. Unless otherwise stated, all these places are on Palmerston St.

Freckle's is a good little cafe serving espresso, muffins and home-made food.

The *Mandala* at No 110 is a standard restaurant, but a good choice for breakfast, and the *Do Duck Inn* at No 194 does standard takeaways as well as a hearty Sunday roast.

Diego Restaurant & Bar (18 Wakefield St) is the town's culinary oasis with an innovative blackboard menu. In summer it's open daily from 6 pm until late (closed Sunday).

Bailie's Bar has live Irish music on Friday night, Guinness and very reasonable prices for barbecue meals, huge nachos and other snacks. This is where most travellers will gravitate to after bushwalks or rafting trips.

The *Bay House Cafe* at Tauranga Bay, around the bay from the seal colony, is stylish, and has great food and ocean views. The a la carte menu is interesting (mains are from $15 to $20), and the place is open for coffee and cakes during the day.

Getting There & Around

Air New Zealand Link (☎ 789 7209) has daily direct flights to Wellington (except Saturday). A taxi to the airport costs around $15.

InterCity (☎ 789 7819) runs daily between Nelson and the glaciers via Westport, and other buses make return trips between Westport and Greymouth (two hours) with a rest stop at the Punakaiki every day. InterCity buses leave from Craddock's Service Station on Palmerston St.

White Star, based at the Cunningham depot, has a Nelson–Westport–Christchurch service (via Springs Junction). This bus leaves for Springs Junction at 10.05 am every day except Saturday; the cost to Christchurch is $33, to Nelson $27.

East-West Express has a shuttle to Christchurch ($39) at 8 am from the visitor

centre. The shuttle leaves from the Christchurch station at 1.30 pm and returns to Westport at 6.30 pm.

Heading north to Karamea for the Heaphy Track, the Karamea Express makes the return trip from Monday to Friday, leaving Karamea in the morning and returning from Westport in the afternoon at 3.10 pm ($15).

For getting around Westport, you can hire bicycles from Beckers Cycles & Sports and Anderson Sports on Palmerston St, and also from Bazil's and other backpackers.

WESTPORT TO KARAMEA

This trip north along SH67 passes through a number of interesting towns. The first reached is Waimangaroa and the turn-off to **Denniston**. This town was once the largest producer of coal in NZ and can be reached by the Denniston Walkway. The track follows the original path to the town and has great views of the Denniston Incline. In its day this was a great engineering feat, as empty coal trucks were hauled back up the incline by the weight of the descending loaded trucks, sometimes at a gradient of one in one. Four kilometres north of Waimangaroa is the **Britannia Track**, a six-hour return walk to the Britannia battery and other remnants of the gold-mining era.

At Granity, head uphill for 5km to the **ghost towns** of Millerton and Stockton. The **Millerton Incline Walk** is 40 minutes return and takes in the old railway, a tunnel and an old dam. The *Drifter's Cafe* is a pleasant place to stop for a tea or coffee.

Just near Granity is another interesting walk at **Charming Creek**. This all-weather, five-hour return track follows an old coal line through the picturesque Ngakawau River Gorge. You can also walk the track all the way to **Seddonville**, a small town surrounded by bush-covered hills on the Mohikinui River. Accommodation is at the *Motor Camp* (☎ 782 1816) or *Motor Hotel* (☎ 782 1828).

Gentle Annie Beach, 3km along the gravel De Manchester Rd from the highway, has a charming little restaurant, the *Gentle Annie Seaside Cafe* (☎ 782 1826), at the mouth of the Mohikinui. Muffins, salads and steaks are specialities. It's NZ's only cowshed restaurant – 'No shit!'. It also has a rustic backpackers made of hand-hewn timbers for $15 per person, and a three-bedroom bach near the beach.

Big Raft Outdoor Activities (☎ 782 1866) rents out canoes and has guided canoe trips from $40.

Between Mohikinui and Little Wanganui you pass over the **Karamea Bluff**, a slow but magnificent scenic drive through rata and matai forest with views of the Tasman Sea below.

KARAMEA
pop 685
From Westport, SH67 continues 100km north to Karamea, an end of the road town near the Heaphy and Wangapeka Tracks. Information is available at the Karamea Information Centre (☎/fax 782 6652), the DOC office (☎ 782 6852) or the Last Resort (☎ 782 6617).

Oparara Basin & Honeycomb Caves
North of Karamea are spectacular limestone arch formations and the unique Honeycomb Caves, ancient home to the moa. Of equal interest is the area's primitive rainforest growing over the karst landscape. Moss-laden trees droop over the tannin-coloured Oparara River, illuminated by light filtering through the dense forest canopy.

Halfway along the road to the start of the Heaphy Track, turn off and go 15km past the sawmill along a rough road to the arches. From the road it is an easy 20-minute walk to the huge Oparara Arch spanning the Oparara River. The smaller but equally beautiful Moria Gate is a harder 40-minute walk along a muddy track that is not always easy to follow – take care not to get lost in the dense forest. Another arch, the Honeycomb, can only be reached by canoe.

Other interesting formations are the Mirror Tarn and the Crazy Paving and Box Canyon Caves at the end of the road. Beyond is the magnificent Honeycomb Caves, with bones of moa and other extinct species. See the bones of three of the five moa species – slender *Megalapteryx didinus*, small *Pachyornis*

elephantopus and giant *Dinornis giganteus*. This is also the cave where bones of the now-extinct giant Haast eagle, the world's largest, were discovered. This eagle, with a 3m to 4m wingspan, preyed on the moa.

Also here is the cave-dwelling spider, *gradungula*, unique to this area; it has a body length of 2.5cm and leg span of 10cm. If you're lucky you will also see the carnivorous snail *(Powelliphanta hochstetteri)*, favourite food of the weka.

Access to the cave is restricted and it can only be visited on a tour. The Last Resort organises 5½-hour tours to the cave and other features for $60 (minimum four people). Bus only to the Oparara Basin is $20.

Activities
The Karamea River offers good swimming, fishing and canoeing. The Little Wanganui, Oparara and Kohaihai Rivers also have good **swimming holes**. Tidal lagoons, 1km north and 3km south of Karamea, are sheltered and good for swimming at high tide; otherwise swimming in the sea is dangerous. The only drawback at the beautiful beaches around Karamea is the millions of sandflies. A local saying is that 'sandflies work in pairs – one pulls back the sheets, while the other eats you alive'.

Many good day **walks** are found in this area, including the five-hour Fenian Track into Adams Flat, the eight-hour return trek to 1084m Mt Stormy and the walk to Lake Hanlon. The first leg of the Wangapeka Track also makes a good day walk.

Those not keen on walking the whole **Heaphy Track** can walk all or part-way to the Heaphy Hut and return. This takes in the walk along the beach, considered by many to be the best part. Scotts Beach is 1½ hours return and passes beautiful nikau palm groves. The separate Nikau Grove Loop at the start of the track takes half an hour. For more information on the Heaphy and Wangapeka Tracks, see Kahurangi National Park in the Marlborough & Nelson chapter.

Places to Stay & Eat
The *Karamea Holiday Park (☎ 782 6758)* has tent/powered sites for $16/18, cabins

for $27 and units for $55; all prices are for two. At Kohaihai, 15km north of Karamea, is a *DOC camping ground*.

Last Resort (☎ 782 6617, @ last.resort@ xtra.co.nz) is a beautiful complex with rooms connected by walkways to the impressive central building. The buildings have sod roofs and feature massive beams of local timbers – eco-architecture at its best. Modern lodge rooms with shared facilities are $60 for a double, lodge rooms with en suite are $90 and excellent units $140.

The *Township Motels (☎ 782 6838)*, an old and fading establishment on Wharf Rd, has double units at $55, or good-value, self-contained cabins at $15 per person.

The *Karamea Village Hotel (☎ 782 6800)* has new motel units from $75, as well as a backpackers house across the road where singles are $15 and doubles with linen are $40.

The *Beachfront Farmstay (☎ 7832 6762)* has been recommended for those who like joining in farm activities.

The *Last Resort* has a licensed restaurant and a bar serving cheaper meals. The hotel has excellent food; a whitebait patty with chips is about $6. *Saracen's Cafe (☎ 782 6711)* is known for its home-made pies.

Getting There & Away

The Karamea Express (☎ 782 6617, 789 7819) leaves Karamea at 8.20 am for Westport; it returns from Westport at 11.30 am (weekdays only, $15, 1½ hours).

The ends of the Heaphy and Wangapeka Tracks have phones to arrange transport out to Karamea. Karamea Express runs on demand from the Wangapeka ($30 for up to five passengers, $5 each extra person) and Kohaihai at the end of the Heaphy ($25/5). Cheaper, scheduled summer services may be offered; ring the Karamea information centre for details.

It is also possible to fly from Karamea to Takaka and then walk back.

WESTPORT TO PUNAKAIKI

This is an interesting stretch of road. Nowadays the towns along the way are extremely small – 10 or so inhabitants. It was

a different story 130 years ago, when the gold rush was in full swing. **Charleston** was a booming town with shanties all along the pack route and gold-diggers moving out to their claims on the Nile River. Today, the raucous pubs are all closed but you can find sanctuary in the *Charleston Motel (☎ 728 7599)*, with units from $60, or the *Motor Camp (☎ 728 6773)*, with tent/powered sites for $15/16 for two and cabins for $28.

Norwest Adventures has an office next to the pub and runs its 'Underworld' rafting and tomo exploring trips from here. **Constant Bay**, once the busy port for the mining settlement, is a pleasant picnic area nearby.

The coast from Fox River to Runanga is rugged and the road will remind west coast Americans of California's Big Sur – with similarly spectacular views. Woodpecker Bay, Tiromoana, Punakaiki, Barrytown, Fourteen Mile, Motukiekie, Ten Mile, Nine Mile and Seven Mile are all beaches sculpted by the relentless fury of the Roaring Forties.

Punakaiki & Paparoa National Park

Almost midway between Westport and Greymouth, the small settlement of Punakaiki and the Paparoa National Park have the finest coastal scenery on the West Coast and a good beach. Many years of public pressure bore fruit when the area was declared a national park in December 1987, and the 30,000-hectare Paparoa National Park became NZ's 12th national park.

Punakaiki is centred around the well-known **Pancake Rocks and Blowholes**. These limestone rocks at Dolomite Point have formed into what looks like stacks of pancakes, through a weathering process known as stylobedding. When a good tide is running, the water surges into caverns below the rocks and squirts out in impressive geyser-like blowholes. A 15-minute loop walk from the road goes around the rocks and blowholes. It's best to go at high or king tide, when the blowholes perform. Heed the warning signs to keep on the track.

In addition to the rocks at Punakaiki, the park has many other natural attractions:

mountains (the Paparoa Range), **rivers, wilderness areas, limestone formations** including cliffs and caves, diverse **vegetation**, and a **Westland black petrel colony** – the world's only nesting area of this rare sea bird.

Interesting walks in the park include the 30km **Inland Pack Track**. This is a two-day track along a route established by miners around 1867 to circumvent the more rugged coastal walk. Also notable is the **Croesus Track**, a full-day or two-day tramp over the Paparoa Range from Blackball to Barrytown, passing through historic gold-mining areas. There are also many shorter river and coastal walks. If you're planning on walking, register your intentions at the park's visitor centre. Many of the tracks were closed after the Cave Creek tragedy in 1995, when several visitors were killed after a viewing platform collapsed, and the status of tracks is still under review; check at the park's visitor centre.

The Punakaiki Visitor Centre (☎ 731 1895, ✉ punakaikivc@doc.govt.nz) next to the highway is open from 9 am to 6 pm daily in summer (sometimes later) and to 4.30 pm in winter. It has interesting displays on the park and can supply information on activities, accommodation and current conditions throughout the park. Many of the inland walks are subject to river flooding and other conditions, so check before setting out.

Organised Tours Paparoa Nature Tours (☎ 731 1826) has tours to the world's only breeding colony of the Westland black petrel, the largest burrowing petrel. Tours commence 30 minutes before sunset and cost $25 per person. It also arranges other tours.

Kiwa Sea Adventures (☎ 731 1893) combines natural history and geology with an adrenaline-inducing boat ride. Hector's dolphins, seals and spotted shags may be seen. A two-hour trip to Seal Island is $95 (children $50).

Paparoa Horse Treks (☎ 731 1839) organises horse trekking at $50 for two hours. Punakaiki Canoe Hire (☎ 731 1870) is based near the bridge over the Pororari

River and hires out canoes from $15 ($5 each hour afterwards).

Places to Stay & Eat *Punakaiki Motor Camp (☎ 731 1894),* next to the beach, has tent/powered sites at $17/20, cabins from $28 to $33 and a five-bed bunkroom at $26; all prices are for two.

Punakaiki Cottages (☎ 731 1008), Dickinson Parade, has studio and family units from $82 to $110 for two.

Te Whare (☎ 731 1171) is a small, friendly backpackers close to the Punakaiki River; the twin rooms or single room are $15 per person. It's closed from May to July.

Te Nikau Retreat (☎ 731 1111) is a magnificent place, replete with 'bush' character in its thick forest setting. It's $16 in dorms and $38/40 for twin and double rooms. There is a sleepout, the *Tui,* which is $50 per couple. Te Nikau is 3km north of Punakaiki on the seaward side of the road, 200m past the entry to the Truman Track. Follow the rough no-exit drive for 450m.

The *Punakaiki Beach Hostel (☎ 731 1852, fax 731 1852),* Webb St, is in a comfortable, converted motel with spa near the village, 1km from the visitor centre and only a stone's throw from the beach. A shared room is $17 per person and singles and doubles are $39. A separate house with three doubles and two bunkrooms can be rented for $170; a double room with linen costs $42.

Hydrangea Cottage (☎ 731 1839), Web site: www.pancake-rocks.co.nz, is a self-contained cottage backed by rainforest and overlooking Pancake Rocks. It charges $80 a double.

The *Mamakau Lodge (☎ 731 1853)* near Te Nikau has B&B doubles from $70 to $90. These people run Coast & Mountain Adventures.

Paparoa Park Motel (☎ 731 1883), Web site: www.paparoa.co.nz, overlooks the Punakaiki River and has well-appointed units from $85.

The *Pancake Tearooms (☎ 731 1873),* opposite the Pancake Rocks, is open year-round from 9 am.

The *Punakaiki Tavern (☎ 731 1188),* near the Pororari River, is the local watering hole; it's open daily and has an outdoor bar (snacks are about $5, mains $15).

Getting There & Away InterCity buses between Westport and Greymouth stop at Punakaiki every day. Kea West Coast Tours (☎ 768 9292) has an 18-seater bus which goes from Greymouth to Punakaiki for $30 per person return.

THE COAST ROAD

The scenic coast road from Punakaiki to Greymouth is flanked by white-capped breakers and rugged rocks out at sea and the steep, bush-clad Paparoa Ranges, where you are forced to drive almost on the precipice. If you're looking for solitude, you'll find a number of accommodation possibilities along this coastline.

At **Barrytown**, 16km south of Punakaiki, the *All Nations (Barrytown) Tavern (☎ 731 1812)* has doubles for $55 and a bunkroom for $16 per person. There's a kitchen for guests, or takeaways and bistro meals. It's at one end of the Croesus Track.

The *Hexagon (☎ 731 1827)*, about 2km south of the tavern, is a hexagonal building where for $13 ($16 with linen) you get a mattress on the floor. It's quite basic but in a beautiful setting and very relaxing.

The township of **Runanga**, about 7km north of Greymouth, is the archetypal mining village. It is not far from Rapahoe (Seven Mile) Beach and there is a 90-minute return walk to nearby Coal Creek Falls.

The *Rapahoe Hotel (☎ 762 7701)* is 2km north of Runanga at the northern terminus of the Point Elizabeth Track. It's good for a drink, with tables outside fronting the driftwood-covered beach. The *Rapahoe Motor Camp (☎ 762 7337)* is not far away.

Kereru Lodge (☎ 762 7077, 58 Herd St, Dunollie) is near Runanga. It is a homely place with an open fire, and it has a bush hot tub. Ring for prices.

THE GREY VALLEY

From Murchison, an alternative route to the West Coast is to turn off at Inangahua Junction and travel inland via Reefton in the Inangahua Valley, then over the mountains into the Grey Valley. Despite the best efforts of a century of plunderers, abundant rainfall has fuelled regenerating bush on the green-cloaked hills and the paddocks have fast become overgrown. The small towns provide a reminder of those futile attempts to tame the land.

Reefton
pop 1050

Reefton is a pleasant little town in the heart of great walking country. Its name comes from the gold-bearing quartz reefs in the

---

Whitebait

Whitebait are small, translucent, elongated fish, the imago (immature) stage of the river smelt. They swarm up the West Coast rivers in dense schools and are caught in set seine-net traps or large, round scoop nets. Many an argument has been had along a riverbank or near a river mouth about the best rock to position yourself on to catch the biggest haul.

The season has been limited in recent years in an attempt to allow the declining stocks to breed. Usually it is September to mid-November, but may vary from year to year. Cooked in batter, these small fish are delicious and highly prized by locals.

One of the West Coast's doyennes of culinary expertise provided this perfect recipe for whitebait patties:

Take a pint of whitebait (about half a litre – yes, the fish are measured as a liquid rather than a solid, as they used to be loaded into glass pint milk bottles for sale) and pour it into a bowl. For the batter take one egg, about three tablespoons of flour, a pinch of salt and a little milk to make a smooth paste. Mix this and then pour over the whitebait; cook in smoking hot fat until golden brown and serve straight away with mint sauce and hot potato chips. Pickled onions are a fine accompaniment.

THE WEST COAST

region. As early as 1888, Reefton had its own electricity supply and street lighting, beating all other towns in NZ. Two old buildings worth exploring are the **School of Mines** and **Blacks Point Museum**.

The enthusiastic and helpful Reefton Visitor Centre (☎ 732 8391, fax 732 616, 📧 tnewman@doc.govt.nz), 67 Broadway, has lots of information on the many walks in the region and has Internet access. It is open from 8.30 am to 6 pm in summer (9 am to 4 pm in winter).

You will find DOC in the same building. The visitor centre houses an interesting re-creation of the Quartzopolis Mine.

The surrounding area has many fine **walks** and great possibilities for **mountain biking** on the Big River Track. The walks include short ones around town such as the Powerhouse Walk, Reefton Walkway and the historic Reefton Walk. The Blacks Point Walk (two to three hours) goes to abandoned coal mines. The Energetic Mine (one hour) is the closest.

There is a wealth of walking in **Victoria Forest Park**, the largest forest park in the country. The two-day Big River and the three-day Kirwans, Blue Grey River and Robinson Valley Tracks are all exciting possibilities. Reefton is close to the Lewis Pass and more excellent walking tracks (and superb trout fishing along the way).

Places to Stay & Eat The *Reefton Motor Camp* (☎ 732 8477) on Main St has tent/powered sites for $14/18 and cabins at $32 for two. The *DOC camping ground* is nearby at Slab Hut Creek, on SH7, 7km south-west of Reefton.

The *Reefton Backpackers* (☎/fax 732 8383), on the corner of Shiel and Sinnamon Sts, has beds for $16, plus free breakfasts. *Quartz Lodge* (☎ 0800-302 725) is a good B&B which specialises in hearty breakfasts (from $35/60 for singles/doubles).

The *Reef Cottage* (☎/fax 732 8440, 📧 reefton@clear.net.nz, 51 Broadway) is central and has cute B&B rooms from $50/60.

Dawsons Hotel & Motel (☎ 732 8406, 74 Broadway) has comfortable motel units for $55 and a private spa.

Broadway has a proliferation of take-aways and tearooms, and the *Electric Light Cafe* in Dawsons Hotel.

The *Al Fresco* on Broadway is, as its name suggests, an outdoor eatery with a la carte and takeaway pizzas.

Getting There & Away White Star buses operate a Westport–Springs Junction–Christchurch service and East-West Express runs a Christchurch to Westport service – both pass through Reefton.

SH7 to Greymouth

At Hukarere, 21km south of Reefton, turn east to visit **Waiuta**, now a ghost town but once the focus of a rich gold mine. Get the excellent DOC pamphlet *Waiuta: Victoria Forest Park*. The drive through beech forest to Waiuta is scenic and the views from the ghost town are well worth the time spent travelling there; watch out for cars coming in the other direction on the narrow dirt road. The *Waiuta Lodge* is a 30-bunk lodge – book at the Reefton Visitor Centre.

Further south at **Ikamatua**, the *Ikamuka Hotel* (☎ 732 3555) has a host of accommodation – bunkroom, camp sites and hotel rooms – from $13 to $40 per person. It is 50km from Greymouth, a world away from anywhere. There's no better introduction to the hidden delights of the Grey Valley.

Just before Ngahere, and 32km from Greymouth, you can turn off to beautiful **Nelson Creek** and a great swimming hole. This area is full of reminders of the gold-mining era, with a number of walks, including Callaghans which heads to a lookout. Nelson Creek has a DOC camping ground and a pub.

Blackball This town, 25km north of Grey-mouth on the road to Reefton, was estab-lished in 1866 as a service centre for the gold diggers. After that it was a coal-mining centre from the late 1880s until 1964. The national Federation of Labour (organisation of trade unions) was born here after two cataclysmic strikes in 1908 and 1931.

The *Formerly the Blackball Hilton* (☎ 732 4705, 📧 bbhilton@xtra.co.nz) offers

'Formerly the Blackball Hilton'

backpacker shared rooms from $15, serviced rooms for $25 and B&B for $60 per person. Once a hotel, the building is full of character and designated a New Zealand Historic Place. The 'formerly' has been added, as this humble backpackers was such a threat to the giant hotel chain that it mounted a challenge to force a change of name. The owners are friendly and provide lots of information on the area. Organised activities include tramping over the Croesus Track, gold panning, horse riding and a historic walk. If you ring from Greymouth they may be able to organise transport with locals.

The Salami brothers of the *Blackball Salami Co* (☎ 732 4111) lovingly produce low fat venison and beef salami.

After passing through the sawmill town of Stillwater, the former coal-mining town of Dobson and pastoral Kaiata, you arrive at the mouth of the Grey River near the Cobden Bridge and the Cobden Gap.

The *Old School Lodge* (☎ 762 5522) in Taylorville, across the Grey River from Dobson, has camp sites for $8 and classroom accommodation for $15; both are per person, and there's a free light breakfast. It's close to the **Brunner Industrial Site**, a collection of old brickworks and coke ovens.

Lake Brunner At Stillwater you can make a detour to Lake Brunner (also known as Moana Kotuku, 'Heron Sea'). The other points of access to the lake are near Jacksons on the Arthur's Pass road or near Kumara on the same road. If you have never baited a hook or gaffed an eel, then Lake Brunner offers you the big chance. They say the trout here die of old age. Fishing guides can be hired at Lake Brunner Lodge to show you the spots where the big ones shouldn't get away.

The **Moana Kiwi House & Conservation Park** (☎ 738 0009) has kiwi viewing and a large area devoted to indigenous bird species such as the white heron (*kotuku*) and other exotic animals ($8, children $3). The nearby **Velenski Walk**, which starts near the camping ground, leads through a remarkable tract of native bush consisting of totara, rimu and kahikatea.

In Moana township, the *Moana Camping Ground* (☎ 337 0572), on the shores of Lake Brunner, has tent/powered sites for $16/20 for two, and cabins from $34. The *Lake Brunner Country Motels* (☎ 738 0144), set in native forest, has self-contained chalets for $85 for two.

The *Station House Cafe* on the lakeshore is recommended.

The *Lake Brunner Lodge* (☎ 738 0163, @ fish@brunner.co.nz) is an historic, upmarket place to stay across the lake in Mitchells. It does not serve casual meals.

GREYMOUTH
pop 13,500

Greymouth was once the site of a Maori *pa* and known as Mawhera, meaning 'Widespread River Mouth'. To the Ngati Kahu people, the Cobden Gap to the north of the town is where their ancestor Tuterakiwhanoa broke the side of *Te Waka o Aoraki* (The Canoe of Aoraki), releasing trapped rainwater to the sea.

Greymouth has a long gold-mining history and still has a hint of gold-town flavour. Although it is small, it is the largest town on the West Coast. It's at the mouth of the Grey River – hence its name – and despite the high protective wall along the Mawhera Quay the river still manages to flood the town after periods of heavy rain. The Grey River meets the sea at the 'bar' (an accumulation of sand just below the waterline) between Cobden and Blaketown headlands.

The seascapes are phenomenal: to the south you can see a large sweep of beach culminating in the faint outlines of Mts Cook and Tasman, and to the north the rocky promontory of Point Elizabeth and Big Rock at the far end of Cobden Beach.

Information

The Greymouth Information Centre (☎ 768 5101, ✉ vingm@minidata.co.nz), Web site: www.westcoastbookings.co.nz, is in the Art Deco Regent Theatre on the corner of Herbert and Mackay Sts. In summer it's open from 9 am to 7 pm daily; in winter, it's open to 5 pm weekdays and from 10 am to 4 pm weekends. The AA office (☎ 768 4300) is at 84 Tainui St.

Things to See

Monteith's Brewing Co beers are now sold throughout the country – original ale, golden lager, Celtic Red, pilsener, Monteith's black and the perky Summertime Ale. Tours (costing $5) are much better than the ones you pay for in larger cities, and you get a free beer. Book at the information centre.

The **History House Museum**, open from 10 am to 4 pm Monday to Friday, has a fabulous photo collection and other bric-a-brac detailing the town's history ($3, children $1.50).

Original jade sculpture and jewellery is crafted at the **Jade Boulder Gallery** on the corner of Guinness and Tainui Sts. The gallery is open from 8.30 am to 5 pm daily and until 9 pm in summer. Also good is the **Left Bank Art Gallery** (☎ 768 0038) at 1 Tainui St, with its permanent *pounamu* (jade) collection (open 10 am to 5 pm daily, and in summer until 7.30 pm).

Interesting nearby **mining** areas include the Brunner Industrial Site and Nelson Creek. Greymouth Information Centre can give directions and historical information on both these sites, and advise on good spots for gold panning.

Activities

Good walks in the region include the three-hour return **Point Elizabeth Track**, 6km north of Greymouth, which passes through the Rapahoe Range Scenic Reserve and interesting old gold-mining areas. The quay walk from Cobden Bridge towards Blaketown is well worth doing; ask at the information centre about the route.

White-water rafting is possible in many of the coast rivers. Eco-Rafting Adventures NZ (☎ 768 4005), Web site: www.ecorafting.co.nz, is based in Greymouth on Mawhera Quay. It operates on the Arnold ($70) and Upper Grey Rivers (two days $300), and runs heli-rafts (from $210) to further afield (the Whitcombe, Whataroa, Landsborough and Perth Rivers in South Westland). **Water-skiing** and **wake-boarding** trips are operated just across from the DP One Coffee House on the Grey River – get wet!

Wild West Adventures (☎ 0800-223 456) operates a subterranean adventure into the **Taniwha Cave** which is not for the faint-hearted. The trip begins with a 30-minute walk through native beech forest. You then float on inflated tubes down through a subterranean glowworm gallery, and end the trip by sliding down a 30m natural hydroslide. The cost of this 5½-hour trip is $95.

Dolphin Watch (☎ 0800-929 991) has sea tours for spotting **dolphins** and seals (1½ hours, $67/33.50 for adults/children), and **sea kayaking** day trips for $87.

On Yer Bike (☎ 0800-669 372), at Coal Creek 5km north of Greymouth, hires out **quad bikes** and points you in the right direction. The trips are about two hours (Hour Track $45, Mighty Mud Track $80, Tramline Track $70).

There's **surfing** at Cobden Beach and at Seven Mile Beach in Rapahoe. **Fishing** safaris are especially popular activities from Greymouth and there's good fishing at Lake Brunner and in the Arnold, Orangepuke and Hohonu Rivers.

GREYMOUTH

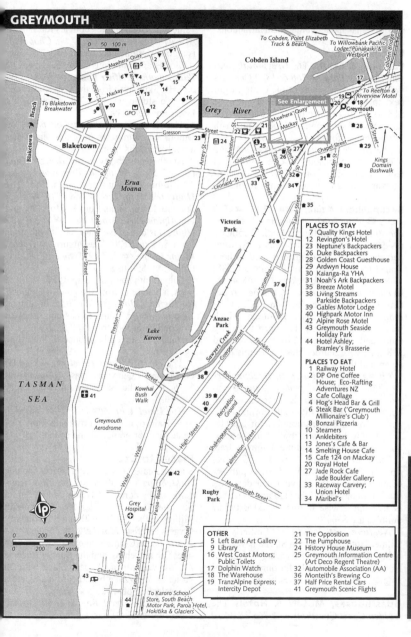

PLACES TO STAY
7 Quality Kings Hotel
12 Revington's Hotel
23 Neptune's Backpackers
26 Duke Backpackers
28 Golden Coast Guesthouse
29 Ardwyn House
30 Kaianga-Ra YHA
31 Noah's Ark Backpackers
35 Breeze Motel
38 Living Streams
    Parkside Backpackers
39 Gables Motor Lodge
40 Highpark Motor Inn
42 Alpine Rose Motel
43 Greymouth Seaside
    Holiday Park
44 Hotel Ashley;
    Bramley's Brasserie

PLACES TO EAT
1 Railway Hotel
2 DP One Coffee
   House; Eco-Rafting
   Adventures NZ
3 Cafe Collage
4 Hog's Head Bar & Grill
6 Steak Bar ('Greymouth
   Millionaire's Club')
8 Bonzai Pizzeria
10 Steamers
11 Anklebiters
13 Jones's Cafe & Bar
14 Smelting House Cafe
15 Cafe 124 on Mackay
20 Royal Hotel
27 Jade Rock Cafe
    Jade Boulder Gallery;
33 Raceway Carvery;
    Union Hotel
34 Maribel's

OTHER
5 Left Bank Art Gallery
9 Library
16 West Coast Motors;
    Public Toilets
17 Dolphin Watch
18 The Warehouse
19 TranzAlpine Express;
    Intercity Depot
21 The Opposition
22 The Pumphouse
24 History House Museum
25 Greymouth Information Centre
    (Art Deco Regent Theatre)
32 Automobile Association (AA)
36 Monteith's Brewing Co
37 Half Price Rental Cars
41 Greymouth Scenic Flights

Kea West Coast Tours (☎ 0800-532 868) runs to Punakaiki and other local attractions.

Places to Stay

Camping & Cabins The *Greymouth Seaside Holiday Park (☎ 768 6618, 2 Chesterfield St)* is 2.5km south of the centre, right next to the beach. Tent/powered sites are $18/20, cabins are from $32 to $40, tourist flats $59 and self-contained motel units $68 (all prices are for two).

The *South Beach Motor Park (☎ 762 6768)*, about 5km south of Greymouth, has tent/powered sites from $16/18 for two, on-site vans for $25 and motel units from $75.

Backpackers *Kaianga-Ra YHA (☎ 768 4951, ☻ yhagymth@yha.org.nz, 15 Alexander St)* is a spacious former Marist Brother's residence with four-bed dorms at $16 per person or a 10-bed dorm that used to be a chapel for $16. Twins and doubles are $38.

Noah's Ark Backpackers (☎ 768 4868, ☻ noahsark@xtra.co.nz, 16 Chapel St) occupies a huge edifice built in 1912 as the monastery for St Patrick's Church, which was once next door. It has been tastefully renovated and charges $16 in dorms, and $38 for twins and doubles (all rooms have an animal theme).

Living Streams Parkside Backpackers (☎ 768 7272, ☻ lsp@minidata.co.nz), close to Lake Karoro, is a large, modern hostel with good facilities and dorms at $15 per person and twins/doubles for $36/38. Duvets and linen are supplied in the doubles. Use of kayaks and the dinghy is free.

The *Duke Backpackers (☎ 768 9470, fax 768 7471)*, in Guinness St, is pub accommodation in the old vein. The deal says it all: purchase a $25 bar tab and your bed is free. Otherwise dorms are $15, twins/doubles are $36/40.

Neptune's (☎ 768 4425), formerly the Gilmer Hotel, on Gresson St, is a new place being developed by the caring owners of Noah's Ark. It costs $16 for dorms, $30 for singles and $40 for doubles/twins.

Guesthouses, Motels & Hotels The *Golden Coast Guesthouse (☎ 768 7839, 10*

Smith St), overlooking the river, is good value with B&B singles/doubles for $50/75. *Ardwyn House (☎ 768 6107, 48 Chapel St)* is a good option and charges $45/75.

Motels are numerous but expensive. The *Willowbank Pacifica Lodge (☎ 768 5339)* on SH6, 3km north from the Cobden Bridge, has two studio units at $78 a double, but larger units cost $90.

The *Riverview Motel (☎ 768 6884)* on Omoto Rd, 2km north from the centre, has a pool and units from $75.

Another possibility is the *Breeze Motel (☎ 762 5068, ☻ info@breezemotel.co.nz, 125 Tainui St)*, with units from $85. The *Highpark Motor Inn (☎ 768 4846, 90 High St)*, with luxury units from $85 to $125, and the *Alpine Rose Motel (☎ 768 7586, 139 High St)* is one of the town's best with units from $85 to $120. The luxurious *Gables Motor Lodge (☎ 768 9991, 84 High St)* has units from $90 to $120.

Greymouth has more than its fair share of pubs, a hangover from the gold-mining era. *Revington's Hotel (☎ 768 7055, ☻ revys@clear.net.nz)* on Tainui St has doubles with attached bathroom from $60 to $70. Queen Elizabeth II stayed here once (a long time ago).

The *Quality Kings Hotel (☎ 768 5085)* on Mawhera Quay has classy rooms from $115; it also has a restaurant and is very central.

The *Hotel Ashley (☎ 768 5135)*, on High St in Karoro, has very tidy units from $95, heated indoor pool, spa and sauna.

Places to Eat

Standard cafes and sandwich places include *Anklebiters* on Albert St; the *Jade Rock Cafe* on the corner of Guinness and Tainui Sts; the *Steak Bar* (aka the 'Greymouth Millionaire's Club') on Tainui St for hearty burgers and fish; *Maribel's (☎ 768 9889, 84 Tainui St)*, a Chinese takeaway which also does fish and chips; and the *Bonzai Pizzeria (29 Mackay St)*, a pleasant place with 20 varieties of pizza, a blackboard menu and a fine selection of wines and beers.

The *Hog's Head Bar & Grill (☎ 768 4093, 9 Tainui St)* has a good selection of

Kaikoura

The Leslie-Karamea Track

Sperm whale tail

Beautiful Sandfly Bay in the Abel Tasman National Park

A greenstone carver at work, Hokitika

Blowhole at Punakaiki, Paparoa National Park

Trekking on Fox Glacier, West Coast

Shantytown – a re-creation of gold-rush days near Greymouth

steaks and seafood (mains from $15) and desserts. Its speciality is whitebait in season, and it has a full range of wines and beers.

DP One Coffee House (☎ 768 4005), Mawhera Quay, has a bohemian feel and arty decor; coffee is the big plus in this 'holistic rafting' centre.

Cafe 124 on Mackay (☎ 768 7503) has delicious bacon-and-egg pie and all varieties of coffee. The food is described as 'not West Coast normal food'.

Jones's Cafe & Bar (37 Tainui St) serves fish of the day ($18), steaks ($19) and kebabs ($16).

The *Smelting House Cafe (☎ 769 0012, 132 Mackay St),* favoured by locals, serves a good range of coffees and cakes, and light meals at lunchtime only. *Steamers* is a carvery on Mackay St.

Quite a few pubs offer food, including *Ham's (☎ 762 686)* at the Paroa Hotel (see Shantytown & Paroa Beach later), the *Royal Hotel* and *Railway Hotel* on Mawhera Quay, the *Raceway Carvery* in the Union Hotel on Herbert St and the more upmarket *Bramley's Brasserie (☎ 768 5135)* in the Hotel Ashley in Karoro.

Cafe Collage (☎ 768 5497, 115 Mackay St), upstairs, is for a fancier night out. This is a BYO and quite expensive at $20 to $25 for a main. It's closed on Sunday and Monday.

The *Karoro School Store* on High St sells the best ice creams on the West Coast. Hokey Pokey Snowflake 'chocolate bombs' are less than $2!

Entertainment

In addition to the many pubs there are two nightclubs – *The Pumphouse* and across from it, appropriately, *The Opposition*. Otherwise the *Railway Hotel* karaoke nights pull in a crowd.

Getting There & Away

Air New Zealand Link flights operate only from Hokitika, 40km from Greymouth. Greymouth Taxis (☎ 768 7078) goes to Hokitika airport for $15.

InterCity (☎ 768 7080) has daily services to Westport and Nelson and to the glaciers. Buses depart from the train station.

The Coast to Coast Shuttle (☎ 0800-800 847) and Alpine Coaches (☎ 0800-274 888) operate between Greymouth and Christchurch ($35) via Arthur's Pass ($15 from Greymouth, $25 from Christchurch) and also go to Hokitika. Atomic Shuttles (☎ 322 8883) also goes to Queenstown for $75 and Sounds to Coast (☎ 0800-802 225) has shuttles to Picton.

The *TranzAlpine Express* (☎ 0800-802 802) operates daily between Christchurch and Greymouth (see the boxed text 'The *TranzAlpine*' in this chapter). If you can get it (numbers are limited), a Super Saver will cost $55 one way (otherwise it's a hefty $79).

Getting Around

Car hire sometimes works out cheaper than some of the tours. Half Price Rental Cars (☎ 768 0379) at 170 Tainui St hires out late-model cars.

Tracy Mann (☎ 768 0255), at 25 Mackay St, and Graeme Peters Cycle & Sport (☎ 768 6559), at 37 Mackay St, rent out bicycles ($25 per day), stock a full range of components and carry out repairs.

SHANTYTOWN & PAROA BEACH

Greymouth to Hokitika has great views of the wild West Coast. If you deviate from the main road to the beach you will see kilometres of salt spray and endless lines of driftwood.

Shantytown, 8km south of Greymouth and 3km inland from the main road, does a good job of re-creating an 1880s West Coast town in the gold rush. It's good family entertainment and for many the prime attraction is a ride on the 1897 steam locomotive. You can also try gold panning; everyone is assured of coming up with at least a few flakes of gold to take away.

Shantytown is open from 8.30 am to 5 pm daily (until 7 pm in summer) and entry, including train rides and gold panning, costs $11 (children $5), or $8 without the panning.

You can't go past the *Paroa Hotel & Motel (☎ 762 6860, ✉ monk@xtra.co.nz, 508 Main South Rd)* for good old-fashioned West Coast hospitality. It's on the beach

THE WEST COAST

The *TranzAlpine*

One of the great rail journeys of the world is the traverse of the Southern Alps between Christchurch and Greymouth – it begins near the Pacific Ocean and ends by the Tasman Sea.

Not so long ago, this popular rail journey, now made in the comfort of specially designed carriages, was undertaken in a ramshackle railcar. In times of bad weather and road closure, it was often the only means that West Coasters had to get to the eastern side of the Divide.

The *TranzAlpine* crossing offers a bewildering variety of scenery. It leaves Christchurch at 9 am, then speeds across the flat, alluvial Canterbury Plains to the foothills of the Alps.

In the foothills it enters a labyrinth of gorges and hills known as the Staircase, and the climb here is made possible by a system of three large viaducts and most of the tunnels which will be encountered along the line.

The train emerges into the broad Waimakariri and Bealey Valleys, and (on a good day) the surrounding vista is stupendous. The river valley is fringed with dense beech forest which eventually gives way to the snowcapped peaks of Arthur's Pass National Park.

At the small alpine village of Arthur's Pass the train enters the longest of the tunnels, the 'Otira' (8.5km), and heads under the mountains to the West Coast. (The vehicle road, which roughly parallels the line, negotiates the Otira Gorge – recently made easier by the construction of a huge viaduct.)

There are several more gems on the western side – the valleys of the Otira, Taramakau and Grey Rivers, patches of podocarp forest, and the pleasant surprise of trout-filled Lake Brunner (Moana Kotuku), fringed with cabbage trees.

The train arrives in the riverside town of Greymouth around 1.25 pm. (It departs for Christchurch an hour later, arriving at 6.35 pm.)

Few travellers who make this rail journey will have regrets, except when the weather is bad. Chances are if it's raining on one coast it's probably fine on the other.

TranzAlpine train crossing the Waimakariri River

DAVID WALL

---

opposite the turn-off to Shantytown. Motel units cost $65/75 for singles/doubles and good hearty meals are available from **Ham's** restaurant (the scallops are recommended). It's worth staying just for an evening stroll along unspoilt Paroa Beach, 100m away.

HOKITIKA
pop 3600

Hokitika, or 'Hoki' as it is affectionately known, is 40km south of Greymouth. It was settled in the 1860s after the discovery of gold and became a busy port.

Hokitika is now a major centre for the working of greenstone but the region offers more to do than just look at stone being mass-produced into bookends of *tiki* and *taniwha* images. Hoki is rich in history and nearby is a wealth of native forests, lakes and rivers.

Trivia? Hoki was the first place in NZ to have a scheduled air service. Air Travel (NZ) started flying de Havilland Fox Moths to airstrips in South Westland 60 years ago and continued doing so in biplanes until 1967.

In mid-March Hokitika hosts the increasingly popular Wildfoods Festival (@ wildfoods@westlanddc.govt.nz).

Information

The Westland Visitor Information Centre (☎ 755 6166, ✉ hkkvin@xtra.co.nz), next to the museum, is open from 8 am to 6 pm daily in summer (otherwise 9 am to 5 pm weekdays and 10 am to 3 pm weekends).

If heading south, do your banking in Hokitika, as there are no banks further south until you reach Wanaka. The next large supermarket is in Queenstown.

Things to See

Westland's Water World on Sewell St is a small aquarium with a variety of fish and other West Coast marine life, including giant whitebait. The main attraction is at 10 am, noon, 3 and 5 pm, when a diver descends into the eel tank to feed the voracious giant eels. Steel-mesh gloves have to be worn to keep fingers intact ($10, children $5). It's open from 9 am to 5.30 pm daily (until 4.30 pm in winter). You can catch salmon here (and have a local restaurant cook them for you).

Take the time to do the historical walk outlined in the museum pamphlet *Hokitika Historic Walk*. The **Custom House** and **Gibson Quay** are well worth a look – it's not hard to imagine the river and wharf choked with sailing ships many years ago. The local Heritage Hokitika group has renovated the historic wharf along Gibson Quay.

The **West Coast Historical Museum** on Tancred St, built with funds from the Carnegie Foundation, has many gold-mining relics. Medal collectors will revel in the wealth of items here. It's open from 9 am to 5 pm daily ($3, children $1), and includes an audiovisual presentation about the gold rush.

Phelp's Goldmine is 2km south of Hoki on SH6. Opencast methods are used and visitors can pan for gold. It's open from 8.30 am to 4.30 pm or later daily ($5, plus $5 to pan).

There's a **glowworm dell** right beside the road on the northern edge of the town.

Activities

Alpine Rafts (☎ 755 8156) offers various **white-water rafting** trips, including all-day 'thrill seeker' trips down some of NZ's steepest rafting rivers. Helicopters are used for access to the upper parts of the rivers, making the experience doubly exciting. Alpine Rafts does thrilling **heli-rafting** to the Frisco Canyon down one of NZ's steepest rivers for $195. A full-day trip down the Whanganui River includes a dip in the **hot pools** on the riverbank and a barbecue at the end ($285). A half-day trip on the Taipo is $155 (including a helicopter ride).

WestAir (☎ 755 7767) and Wilderness Wings (☎ 755 8118) run **scenic flights** from Hokitika over Mt Cook and the glaciers for around $150 (minimum two passengers) and local flightseeing.

The information centre and DOC have detailed brochures on the many **walks** in the area. A number of walks are near Lake Kaniere. Dorothy Falls, Kahikatea Forest and Canoe Cove are all short walks, but the Lake Kaniere Walkway is 13km and takes about four hours. Longer walks include Mt Tahua and Mt Brown, both of seven hours duration. The Mahinapua Walkway (two hours, 5.5km) goes through the scenic reserve to a swamp teeming with wildlife and to sand dunes. For the more sedentary, the *Takutai Belle,* a **paddle steamer**, operates on Mahinapua Creek to the lake and back for $20 per person.

Places to Stay

Camping, Cabins & Backpackers The *Hokitika Holiday Park* (☎ 755 8172, 242 Stafford St) has tent/powered sites for $16/18.50, cabins for $26 to $42 and tourist flats for $52 (all prices are for two).

There are *DOC camping grounds* at Goldsborough (17km) and Shanghai Bay at Lake Mahinapua (10km) – distances are from Hoki.

Beach House Backpackers (☎ 0800-755 6859, 137 Revell St) has dorm beds for $16 and doubles for $40. It's a friendly place with a restaurant attached, and there's outdoor seating and a great 'bush' bath.

Seaside Backpackers (☎ 755 7612 after hours, 197 Revell St) is a small, homestay-style backpackers with just one four-bed dorm at $15 and one double at $32.

Mountain Jade Backpackers (☎ 755 8007, ✉ mtjade@minidata.co.nz, 41 Weld St), a purpose-built place, is very central and above the souvenir shop of the same name, with a cafe downstairs. Standards are very high in dorms for $16 and doubles for $40. Internet is available.

The **Blue Spur Lodge** (☎/fax 755 8445), 5km east from town on Cement Lead Rd and reached via Hau Hau Rd, is well equipped and peaceful with dorm beds for $15 and twins/doubles for $36/38. The lodge offers free pick-up from Hokitika and free bikes, and for $35 will give you a kayak and transport to and from Lake Kaniere.

Motels & Hotels The **Jade Court Motor Lodge** (☎ 755 8855, 85 Fitzherbert St) comes recommended; a unit is from $80 to $98.

The **Heritage Highway Motel** (☎ 0800-465 484, 12 Fitzherbert St) has really nice units from $5 and a guest spa.

The **Shining Star Log Chalets** (☎ 755 8291, @ shining@xtra.co.nz, 11 Richards Drive) has great, self-contained chalets at $88 for two.

Teichelmann's Central B&B (☎ 755 8232, @ teichel@xtra.co.nz, 20 Hamilton St) is a pleasant, cosy place with doubles

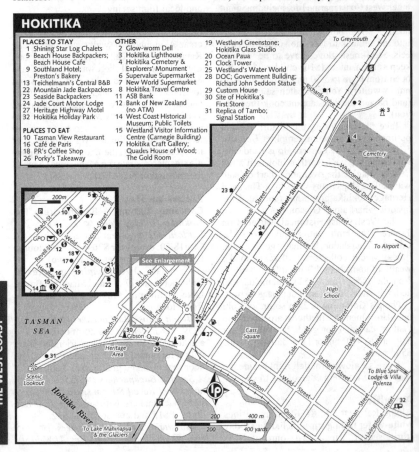

HOKITIKA

PLACES TO STAY
1 Shining Star Log Chalets
5 Beach House Backpackers; Beach House Cafe
9 Southland Hotel; Preston's Bakery
13 Teichelmann's Central B&B
22 Mountain Jade Backpackers
23 Seaside Backpackers
24 Jade Court Motor Lodge
27 Heritage Highway Motel
32 Hokitika Holiday Park

PLACES TO EAT
10 Tasman View Restaurant
16 Café de Paris
18 PR's Coffee Shop
26 Porky's Takeaway

OTHER
2 Glow-worm Dell
3 Hokitika Lighthouse
4 Hokitika Cemetery & Explorers' Monument
6 Supervalue Supermarket
7 New World Supermarket
8 Hokitika Travel Centre
11 ASB Bank
12 Bank of New Zealand (no ATM)
14 West Coast Historical Museum; Public Toilets
15 Westland Visitor Information Centre (Carnegie Building)
17 Hokitika Craft Gallery; Quades House of Wood; The Gold Room

19 Westland Greenstone; Hokitika Glass Studio
20 Ocean Paua
21 Clock Tower
25 Westland's Water World
28 DOC; Government Building; Richard John Seddon Statue
29 Custom House
30 Site of Hokitika's First Store
31 Replica of Tambo; Signal Station

To Greymouth

Richards Drive

Cemetery

Whitcombe Tce

Bonar Drive

Tudor Street

To Airport

High School

Cass Square

See Enlargement

Beach St

Revell Street

Tancred Street

Weld St

Hamilton St

Sewell Street

Fitzherbert Street

Park Street

Hampden Street

Bealey Street

Hall Street

Brittan Street

Rolleston Street

Davie Street

Jollie Street

Livingstone Street

To Blue Spur Lodge & Villa Polenza

TASMAN SEA

GPO

Gibson Quay

Heritage Area

Scenic Lookout

Hokitika River

Stafford Street

Sole Street

Weld Street

Gibson Quay

Hoffman Street

To Lake Mahinapua & the Glaciers

0   200m

0   200   400 m
0   200   400 yards

THE WEST COAST

from \$85 to \$115 (including a big continental breakfast).

The *Southland Hotel* (☎ *755 8334,* 📧 *southland@clear.net.nz, 111 Revell St)* has been considerably revamped, with 'deluxe' rooms from \$75 to \$125.

The visitor information centre has listings for homestays and farmstays in Hokitika. *Villa Polenza* (☎ *0800-241 801,* 📧 *villapolenza@xtra.co.nz),* Brickfields Rd, is a stand-out boutique lodge in a classical Italian villa 5km from the centre of town. Suites range from \$160 to \$240 for a double, and include breakfast.

Places to Eat

For snacks and sandwiches you can try *Preston's Bakery* on Revell St and *PR's Coffee Shop* (☎ *755 8379)* on Tancred St; *Porky's Takeaway* on Weld St does fish and chips.

The *Beach House Cafe* at the Beach House Backpackers has cheap breakfasts and reasonably priced meals and is a popular watering hole.

The *Tasman View Restaurant* (☎ *755 8344),* an a la carte restaurant, overlooks Hokitika's windswept and grey beach (the attraction for a lot of diners); it has a smorgasbord on Friday which is popular with locals.

The *Café de Paris* (☎ *755 6859),* on Tancred St near the corner of Hamilton St, is recommended for its French-influenced food – crepes, venison, lamb, mussels and whitebait with a hint of *'la rive gauche'*.

Entertainment

The *Mahinapua Hotel* is legendary and Les, who owns it, reflects all the trials and tribulations of Coast life in the greyness of his ample beard. They serve Hooker's Ale here and (as you'll see) they collect hats.

Shopping

Hoki's biggest attraction is the profusion of arts and crafts outlets, open from 8 am to 5 pm daily. Most of them are on Tancred St. Greenstone is the main attraction but, even with modern tools and electric power, working greenstone is not simple and good greenstone pieces will not be cheap. You can see the carvers at work.

Westland Greenstone on Tancred St has a big selection of jewellery, tiki and other greenstone ornaments.

Mountain Jade at 41 Weld St specialises in jade sculpture, as well as gold nugget jewellery (at the Heart of Gold shop within the complex).

Quades House of Wood and the Hokitika Craft Gallery on Tancred St have other crafts. Next door, the Gold Room sells handcrafted gold jewellery made from locally mined gold.

Also on Tancred St is the Hokitika Glass Studio which produces the phallic special drinking vessel.

The Sheep Station on Sewell St has a most unusual entrance – you will be engorged by a giant ram before you buy its outer coat.

Getting There & Away

Air New Zealand (☎ 0800-652 881) has daily direct flights to Christchurch, with connections to other centres.

The InterCity services travelling from Greymouth to Fox Glacier pass through Hokitika daily. Travel time is 40 minutes to Greymouth and four hours to Fox Glacier. The Coast to Coast Shuttle and Alpine Coach run to Christchurch via Arthur's Pass; all these (and the *TranzAlpine)* can be booked at the Westland Visitor Information Centre.

SOUTH FROM HOKITIKA

It's about 140km south from Hokitika to the Franz Josef Glacier, but you can make a few stops on the way. Hitching along this coast is notoriously bad, so go by bus – the InterCity buses from Greymouth to the glaciers will stop anywhere along the highway.

Ross

Ross, 30km south of Hokitika, is a small, historic gold-mining town and gold is still mined today. NZ's largest gold nugget, the 99oz 'Honourable Roddy', was found here in 1907. Grimmond House – in the gold rush era home to the Bank of New Zealand – is now the information centre (☎ 755 4077) and you can visit the small **Miner's Cottage** museum.

The cottage stands at the beginning of two historic goldfield **walkways**, the Jones Flat Walk and the Water Race Walk. Each takes about one to two hours and passes by interesting features from the gold rush era.

Near the car park in front of the cottage is a new working gold mine – you can look down on the operations. In the centre of town is a display of old gold-mining equipment and buildings.

The *Empire Hotel* (☎ 755 4005, 19 Aylmer St) has tent sites at $16, cabins at $30 and atmospheric shared/en suite rooms at $30/55; all prices for two.

The *Dahlia Cottage* (☎ 755 4160, 47 Aylmer St) gets rave reviews for both its hospitality and superb dahlia garden (which the owners are willing to guide you through). B&B is a very reasonable $40/70 for singles/doubles.

The *Roddy Nugget Cafe*, on Main Rd, is licensed and serves cappuccinos and light meals.

Ross to Okarito

From Ross it's another 109km to Franz Josef, but there are plenty of bush tracks and lakes along the way if you want to break the journey and can cope with the sandflies. Heading southwards the rainforest becomes more dense, and in many parts looks as if it would be easier to walk over the top of it than to find a way through!

Many places along here provide low-cost accommodation. About 20km south of Ross, *Kiwi Host Backpackers & Cabins* (☎ 755 4032) near Pukekura has bunkrooms ($15 each) and cabins at $30 for two ($40 in the high season), with activities including fishing and panning for gold. About 100m south of Lake Ianthe, on the eastern side of the road, is a giant **matai tree**. The short track to it is marked.

The *Bushmen's Centre* has a restaurant which serves up West Coast wild foods – this effectively excludes vegetarians – and entry to the West Coast's Castle Machismo costs $5 (children $2). Horse treks can be arranged from here.

The region has interesting **walks**. About two hours from Greens Beach is a seal colony, and the adventurous can head down to Saltwater Lagoon, a truly beautiful and remote place. The **Coastal Pack Track** goes to the end of La Fontaine Creek; get details from the 'Bush-persons' Centre.

Harihari The small town of Harihari is 22.5km south of Lake Ianthe. Harihari made headlines in 1931, when Aussie Guy Menzies completed the first solo flight across the Tasman Sea from Sydney. The landing was anything but smooth as he crash-landed *Southern Cross Junior* in the La Fontaine swamp. The aircraft turned over and when he undid his safety straps he fell head-first into the mud. He had made the trip in 11¾ hours, 2½ hours less than fellow Australian Charles Kingsford Smith and his crew in 1928.

The two- to three-hour **Harihari Coastal Walkway** (also called the Doughboy Walk) is a popular loop taking in the Poerua and Wanganui Rivers, with a lookout (atop a moraine headland) giving fine views over the coastline, forest and mountains.

You can also walk up into the **Wilberg Range** near the town (20 minutes return). Other possibilities are an old goldminers' pack track, river-mouth **fishing** for trout and salmon, or **exploring** the estuaries and wetlands of the Poerua and Wanganui Rivers.

Go **bird-watching** and try to spot native parakeets, herons, penguins, kaka and a number of migratory wading birds.

The *Harihari Motor Inn* (☎ 753 3026, ✉ hhmi@xtra.co.nz) has motel units at $70 for two, powered sites at $15 for two and a spa pool. *Tomasi Motel* (☎ 753 3116), across the road, has motel units at $60 a double. Neither has kitchen facilities, but Harihari has a *tearoom* and *fish and chips shop* and the motor inn has pub meals, a *restaurant* and takeaways.

Whataroa & the Kotuku Sanctuary

Near Whataroa, 35km south of Harihari, is a sanctuary for the white heron (kotuku), which nests from November to the end of February. It is the only NZ nesting site of this species. The herons then fly off individually to spend winter throughout the country. Access is possible only with a permit from DOC.

White Heron Sanctuary Tours (☎ 753 4120, ✉ info@whiteherontours.co.nz) at Whataroa operates jet-boat tours to the kotuku colony beside the Waitangi-taona River. Don't panic, bird lovers – the jet-boat doesn't enter the nesting area. You walk along a boardwalk to the hide, where you spend 30 to 40 minutes. The cost is $89 (children $40) including a permit for the 2½-hour return trip.

The *Sanctuary Tours Motel* also has expensive motel units (from $75 for two), cabins (from $35 for two) and tent and powered sites (but no kitchen).

The *White Heron Store & Tea Rooms* (☎ 753 4142) serves morning and afternoon teas, and you can stock up on groceries here.

Okarito

Another 15km south of Whataroa is The Forks and the turn-off to peaceful Okarito, 13km away on the coast. Much of Keri Hulme's bestseller *The Bone People* is set in this wild, isolated region. There are lots of walks along the coast from Okarito – get hold of leaflets from the visitor centres in Hokitika or Franz Josef.

Okarito Nature Tours (☎ 753 4014) on the Strand organises popular kayaking trips into the beautiful **Okarito Lagoon**, a feeding ground for the kotuku and a good place for watching all kinds of birds. The lagoon is NZ's largest unmodified wetland and consists of shallow open water and tidal flats. The lake is surrounded by rimu and kahikatea rainforest. Trips to the Okarito River delta cost from $55 per person (minimum two) to see birds up close (not in their nests). Trips are guided and include all gear and transport.

The *Okarito Hostel* (☎ 753 4124), a YHA 'original', charges $10/5 for adults/children. Hot showers are available from the nearby caravan park for multiples of $0.50. The small hostel was a schoolhouse, built in the 1870s when Okarito was a thriving gold town.

Opposite the hostel is a very basic *camping ground* with barbecues and toilets. The

ground is in a pleasant location and camp sites cost $5.

The *Royal Motel & Hostel* (☎ 753 4080) nearby has a friendly and good-value backpackers with two twins, and one double at $14 per person. Self-contained 'motel' units are $45 and $55. Okarito has no shop, so bring your own food.

Back towards The Forks turn-off, 3km in from the highway, the *Forks Lodge* (☎ 753 4122) is a simple, self-contained little lodge costing $12.50 per person or $25 for a double room (bring bedding and food). It also has tent sites.

THE GLACIERS

The two most famous glaciers in the Westland National Park – the Fox and the Franz Josef – are among the major attractions in NZ. Nowhere else in the world, at this latitude, have glaciers advanced so close to the sea. Unlike the Tasman Glacier, on the other side of the dividing range in Mt Cook National Park, these two are just what glaciers should be – mighty rivers of ice, tumbling down a valley towards the sea.

The reason for the glaciers' development is threefold. The West Coast is subject to the prevailing rain-drenched westerlies which fall as snow high up in the neves. The snow crystals fuse to form clear ice at a depth of about 20m. Secondly, the zones where the ice accumulates on the glacier are very large, so there's a lot of ice to push down the valley. Finally, the glaciers are very steep – the ice can get a long way before it finally melts.

The rate of descent is staggering: a plane that crashed on the Franz Josef in 1943, 3.5km from the terminal face, made it down to the bottom 6½ years later – a speed of 1.5m per day. At times the Franz Josef can move at up to 5m a day, over 10 times as fast as glaciers in the Swiss Alps. Generally, it moves at the rate of about 1m a day.

Heavy tourist traffic – most people stay only one night – is catered for in the twin towns of Franz Josef and Fox, 23km apart. These small, modern, tourist villages have plenty of accommodation and enough facilities at higher than average prices. Change money before you reach the glaciers (there

THE GLACIERS & WESTLAND NATIONAL PARK

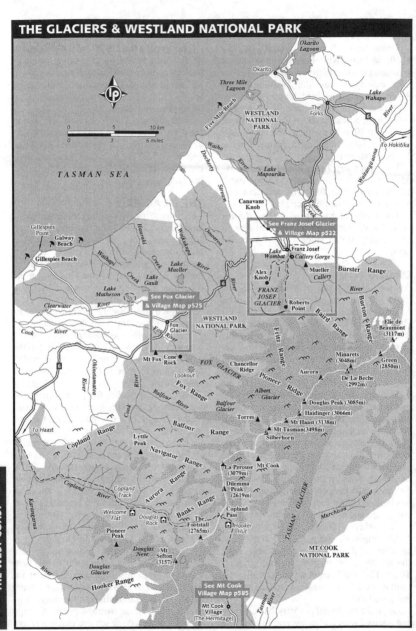

See Franz Josef Glacier & Village Map p522

See Fox Glacier & Village Map p525

See Mt Cook Village Map p585

Okarito Lagoon

Okarito

Three Mile Lagoon

Lake Wahapo

The Forks

To Hokitika

WESTLAND NATIONAL PARK

Five Mile Beach

Waitangitaona River

TASMAN SEA

Waiho

Docherty

Stream

River

Lake Mapourika

Canavans Knob

Callery Creek

Franz Josef

Lake Wombat

Callery Gorge

Alex Knob

Mueller Callery

Burster Range

Baird Range

Burton Range

River

FRANZ JOSEF GLACIER

Roberts Point

Elie de Beaumont (3117m)

Gillespies Point

Galway Beach

Gillespies Beach

Waihapi

Hauraki Creek

Creek

Waikukupa River

Omoeroa River

Lake Mueller

Lake Gault

Lake Matheson

Clearwater River

Cook River

Fox River

Fox Glacier

WESTLAND NATIONAL PARK

Mt Fox

Cone Rock

FOX GLACIER

Chancellor Ridge

Fritz Range

Pioneer Ridge

Minarets (3048m)

Aurora

De La Beche (2992m)

Green (2850m)

Ohinetamatea River

Cook River

Lookout

Fox Range

Balfour River

Balfour Glacier

Albert Glacier

Douglas Peak (3085m)

Haidinger (3066m)

To Haast

Balfour Range

Torres

Mt Haast (3138m)

Mt Tasman (3498m)

Silberhorn

Copland Range

Lyttle Peak

Navigator Range

La Perouse (3079m)

Mt Cook

Copland River

Copland Track

Aurora

Range

Banks Range

Dilemma Peak (2619m)

Copland Pass

Welcome Flat

Douglas Rock

The Footstall (2765m)

Hooker Hut

TASMAN GLACIER

Murchison River

Karangarua River

Pioneer Peak

Douglas Neve

Mt Sefton (3157m)

MT COOK NATIONAL PARK

Douglas Glacier

Hooker Range

Mt Cook Village (The Hermitage)

Tasman River

0 5 10 km
0 3 6 miles

The formidable front of the Franz Josef Glacier

are no banks between Hokitika and Wanaka) and fill up on petrol if you're driving.

Franz Josef Glacier

The Franz Josef was first explored in 1865 by Austrian Julius Haast, who named it after the Austrian emperor. Apart from short advances from 1907–09, 1921–34, 1946–59 and 1965–67, the glacier has generally been in retreat since 1865, although in 1985 it started advancing again. It has progressed well over 1.7km since 1985, moving forward by about 70cm a day, although it is still several kilometres back from the terminal point Haast first recorded.

The glacier is 5km from the town. Kamahi Tours (☎ 752 0699) has a shuttle to the car park for $5 (minimum two). From there it is a 10-minute walk to the glacier. Hope for a fine day and great views to the snowcapped peaks behind. The glaciers are roped off to stop people getting close to where there is a risk of icefall, but the ropes are a ridiculously long way back.

For $37 (children $18.50) you can walk up onto the glacier ice with an experienced guide. In the high season, guided walks (3½ hours, with 1½ hours on the glacier) depart twice daily from the Franz Josef Glacier Guides office (☎ 752 0763), Web site: www.nzguides.com, which is in the village; equipment, including boots, is included in the price.

Information The Franz Josef DOC Visitors Centre (☎ 752 0796, fax 752 0797) is open from 8.30 am to 6 pm daily in summer (until noon and 1 to 5 pm in winter). The centre has leaflets on the short walks around the glacier.

The Alpine Adventure Centre (0800-800 793) is a major booking agent for activities. Included are: Fox & Franz HeliServices; Wildtrax eight-wheeler Argo trips out to the coast ($50); fishing tours ($150 for four, two hours); glacier walks; and heli-hikes for $185. The centre screens the 20-minute *Flowing West* Helimax movie on a giant screen ($10/5 for adults/children).

There is an EFTPOS facility at the local petrol station, Glacier Motors (which has the most expensive petrol in NZ). DA's

DAVID WALL

THE WEST COAST

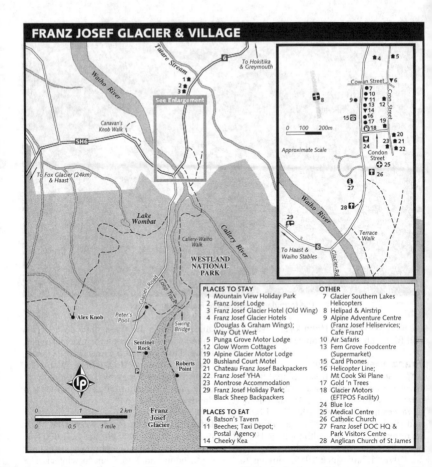

FRANZ JOSEF GLACIER & VILLAGE

PLACES TO STAY	OTHER
1 Mountain View Holiday Park	7 Glacier Southern Lakes
2 Franz Josef Lodge	Helicopters
3 Franz Josef Glacier Hotel (Old Wing)	8 Helipad & Airstrip
4 Franz Josef Glacier Hotels	9 Alpine Adventure Centre
(Douglas & Graham Wings);	(Franz Josef Heliservices;
Way Out West	Cafe Franz)
5 Punga Grove Motor Lodge	10 Air Safaris
12 Glow Worm Cottages	13 Fern Grove Foodcentre
19 Alpine Glacier Motor Lodge	(Supermarket)
20 Bushland Court Motel	15 Card Phones
21 Chateau Franz Josef Backpackers	16 Helicopter Line;
22 Franz Josef YHA	Mt Cook Ski Plane
23 Montrose Accommodation	17 Gold 'n Trees
29 Franz Josef Holiday Park;	18 Glacier Motors
Black Sheep Backpackers	(EFTPOS Facility)
	24 Blue Ice
PLACES TO EAT	25 Medical Centre
6 Batson's Tavern	26 Catholic Church
11 Beeches; Taxi Depot;	27 Franz Josef DOC HQ &
Postal Agency	Park Visitors Centre
14 Cheeky Kea	28 Anglican Church of St James

Restaurant acts as the local postal agency. The nearest doctor is a 20-minute drive north of Franz.

Walking Ask at the information centre for one of its excellent walk leaflets. There are several good glacier viewpoints close to the road leading to the glacier car park.

Other walks require a little worthwhile footslogging. The **Douglas Walk**, off the Glacier Access Rd, is an hour's stroll by the terminal moraine from the 1750 advance and Peter's Pool, a small 'kettle lake'. It's a longer walk (3½ hours) to **Roberts Point**,

which overlooks and is quite close to the terminal face.

The **Terrace Track** makes a pleasant one-hour round trip. It starts on the old Callery Track, a former gold-mining area, and leads up onto a terrace at the back of the village, with pleasant views of the Waiho River. The **Callery-Waiho Walk** is about four hours return. The **Canavan's Knob Walk**, closer to town, is about 40 minutes return.

Aerial Sightseeing The hills are alive with the sound of buzzing helicopters and planes doing runs over the glaciers (including Mt

Cook). Many flights include a snow landing, and heli-hiking is a variation on the theme (a 20-minute flight to the head of the Franz or Fox is $120; $250 for a full traverse).

Companies include Glacier Southern Lakes Helicopters (☎ 752 0755, 0800-800 732), Mt Cook Ski Plane (☎ 752 0767), The Helicopter Line (☎ 752 0767), Franz & Fox Heliservices (☎ 752 0793, 0800-800 793) and Air Safaris (☎ 752 0716). Flights up and over the glaciers are expensive but they're a superb experience.

Other Activities There are fishing trips to Lake Mapourika, a 10-minute drive north of Franz Josef.

Gold 'n' Trees (☎ 0800-752 111) organises gold prospecting and scenic walks at the Whataroa River. All aspects of prospecting (panning, sluicing and suction dredging) are explained in two hours ($20). It's as 'West Coast' as it gets.

Places to Stay The *Franz Josef Holiday Park (☎ 752 0766)* is 1km south of the township, right beside the river. Tent/powered sites are $18/19, tourist cabins and flats are $59 to $65 and motels are from $69 (all for two). See its Web site (www.fjhp.co.nz) for more details.

The *Black Sheep Backpackers (☎ 752 0766, fax 752 0066, @ fjhp@ihug.co.nz),* a friendly place adjoining the holiday park, has a variety of rooms. It's $14 in 12-bed bunkrooms, $16 in quad rooms and $40 for doubles. It has five Internet terminals, the lively Black Sheep Ba & Bar with tables overlooking a stream, and pleasant secluded areas where you can sit and write postcards.

Backpackers row is on Cron St, just off the main road. The *Franz Josef Glacier YHA (☎ 752 0754, @ yhafzjo@yha.org.nz)* at No 2–4 is a pleasant place. It charges $17 per person in dorms and $38 for doubles. There's a small shop and pool tables.

The *Chateau Franz Josef (☎ 0800-472 856, fax 752 0738)* is next door. Shared rooms are $16 per person and twins/doubles are $35/40. It's large with rooms leading off everywhere, but pleasant and well equipped with a neat spa pool.

Montrose Accommodation (☎ 752 0188), opposite, is a refurbished house with dorms for $16, doubles for $40.

Glow Worm Cottages (☎ 752 0172, 27 Cron St) is a small, comfortable place with a nice lounge/kitchen area. It's $17 for a dorm bed and $35/40 for twins/doubles.

On SH6 is *Franz Josef Lodge (☎ 752 0712),* former staff housing for the adjoining Franz Josef Glacier Hotel.

Nearby, *Mountain View Holiday Park (☎ 752 0735)* has powered sites for $20 for two, and standard/tourist/en suite cabins from $35/49/60. Very good motel units are $75 to $95.

The *Bushland Court Motel (☎ 752 0757, @ alpine.galcier@xtra.co.nz, 10 Cron St)* has units from $70 and also owns the very flash *Alpine Glacier Motor Lodge* across the street with a variety of new units, some with a spa, for $85 to $130. There are other motels costing around $75 to $85 a night.

The *Punga Grove Motor Lodge (☎ 752 0001, @ pungagrove@xtra.co.nz),* in Cron St, is in a nice rainforest setting; the 16 units cost from $65 to $130.

Franz Josef Glacier Hotels (☎ 752 0729, @ glacier.hotels@xtra.co.nz) has a large motel-style complex just north of Cowan St and the older resort-hotel wing about 1km north of the township on SH6; rooms are very expensive.

Places to Eat & Drink The shops at Franz Josef have a good selection of food supplies. *Beeches (☎ 752 0721)* has a cafe and takeaway section and a restaurant, all offering much the same menu. It specialises in a wide variety of NZ cuisine (salmon, lamb and venison). *Way Out West* in the Franz Josef Glacier Hotels serves grills and seafood mains from $15 to $20.

The *Cheeky Kea* is a good place to get country fried chicken (hopefully not the cheeky kea). The *Cafe Franz* in the Alpine Adventure Centre serves breakfast, lunch and dinner daily.

Batson's Tavern, on the corner of Cowan and Cron Sts, has a good range of bistro meals from $10 to $15 and the barbecue area is overlooked by rainforest, often cloaked in flowering rata.

Entertainment in this town is centred on the *Blue Ice* and it can get rowdy in here at times.

Getting There & Away North and south-bound InterCity buses cross between the two glaciers, with daily buses south to Fox Glacier and Queenstown and north to Greymouth. The connections are such that the trip from Nelson to Queenstown (or vice versa) by bus along the West Coast is not possible in one day. In the high season (summer) these buses can be heavily booked, so plan well ahead or be prepared to wait until there's space.

Hitching prospects can be bleak along the West Coast. If you're lucky you might do Greymouth to Queenstown in three days.

Fox Glacier

If time is short, seeing one glacier may be enough, but if you have time it's interesting to see both. Basically the same activities are offered at both glaciers – glacier walks, flights and so on. Despite consistent retreat throughout much of this century, the Fox Glacier, like the Franz Josef, has been advancing since 1985. In the last 10 years it has advanced almost 1km, and now averages about 40cm per day. Its name was given in 1872 after a visit by the NZ prime minister, Sir William Fox.

Information The Fox Glacier Visitor Centre (☎ 751 0807, fax 751 0858) is open from 8.30 am to 6 pm daily in summer, from 9 am to 5 pm in winter. The centre has displays on the glaciers and the natural environment as well as leaflets on a number of short walks around the ice.

There's a petrol station in the village – the last fuel stop until you reach Haast, 120km further on. Alpine Guides is the local postal agency and sells phonecards.

Walking The shortest and most popular walk at the Fox Glacier is the couple of minutes' stroll from the centre to the **glow-worm dell** (entry $2 at honesty box). Of course, you have to go at night to see them glowing.

Head towards the coast from the township for a lookout with a superb vista of the glacier and the Southern Alps. Before this lookout is the turn-off to **Lake Matheson** and one of the most famous panoramas in NZ. It's an hour's walk around the lake and at the far end are those unforgettable calendar and postcard views of the mountains and their reflection in the lake. The best time to see the famed reflection is very early in the morning, when the lake is at its most mirror-like calm. *Cafe Lake Matheson (☎ 752 0124),* boasting one of the most superb aspects in the world, sells pies, sandwiches, coffee and tea.

Mt Fox, off SH6 to Haast, is another excellent viewpoint – it's a four-hour walk one way.

Other interesting walks around the glacier include the short **moraine walk** over the advance of 200 years ago, the short **Minnehaha Walk** or the **River Walk**. It takes just over an hour to walk from the village to the glacier – it's 1.5km from Fox to the turn-off and the glacier is another 5km back from the main road.

At the time of writing, the Cone Rock and Ngai Tahu Tracks were closed, as was the seal colony beyond Gillespies Beach.

Aerial Sightseeing If you don't fancy walking on the ice, flightseeing may be your best option. Glacier Southern Lakes Helicopters (☎ 752 0755, 0800-800 732), Mt Cook Ski Plane (☎ 752 0747), Mountain Helicopters (☎ 751 0829), the Helicopter Line (☎ 751 0767) and Franz & Fox Heli-services (☎ 752 0793, 0800-800 793) have much the same flights and prices as at Franz Josef. These trips are expensive but provide a superb experience with amazing views.

Organised Tours As at Franz Josef you can take guided walks up onto the glacier ice. Alpine Guides (☎ 751 0825, 0800-111 600), Web site: www.foxguides.co.nz, has tours leaving at 9.30 am and 2 pm daily from the village; boots and other equipment are included in the $39 (children $26) cost.

FOX GLACIER & VILLAGE

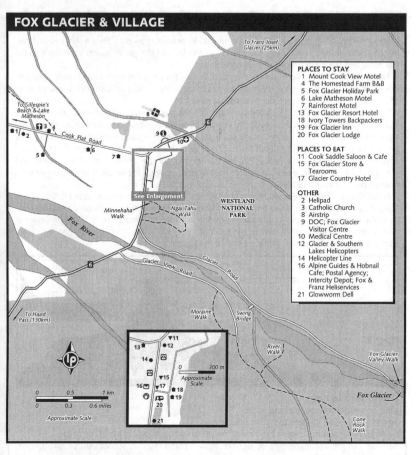

PLACES TO STAY
1 Mount Cook View Motel
4 The Homestead Farm B&B
5 Fox Glacier Holiday Park
6 Lake Matheson Motel
7 Rainforest Motel
13 Fox Glacier Resort Hotel
18 Ivory Towers Backpackers
19 Fox Glacier Inn
20 Fox Glacier Lodge

PLACES TO EAT
11 Cook Saddle Saloon & Cafe
15 Fox Glacier Store & Tearooms
17 Glacier Country Hotel

OTHER
2 Helipad
3 Catholic Church
8 Airstrip
9 DOC; Fox Glacier Visitor Centre
10 Medical Centre
12 Glacier & Southern Lakes Helicopters
14 Helicopter Line
16 Alpine Guides & Hobnail Cafe; Postal Agency; Intercity Depot; Fox & Franz Heliservices
21 Glowworm Dell

It also has full-day guided glacier walks for $65. Of course, you can just follow the marked track to the glacier from the car park, but the glacier is roped off as at Franz Josef.

Alpine Guides has three-hour ($170 each for three people) and full-day heli-hikes ($385), and an overnight trip to Chancellor Hut. The overnight trip includes hut fees, food and the flight up for $545 each for three people, $645 each for two, including a helicopter trip on each end. It also offers mountaineering instruction and full-day glacier skiing – this costs $445, which includes hut fees and a helicopter lift to the 10km ski run.

Places to Stay The *Fox Glacier Holiday Park* (☎ 751 0821) is a motor camp down Cook Flat Rd from the township. Tent/powered sites are $18/20, cabins are from $30 and $35, and tourist flats are $55; all prices are for two.

Fox Glacier Lodge (☎ 751 0888) has no tent sites, only powered sites for $20 in a pretty setting. It also has seven excellent units from $78 for two (some have double spa baths).

Advance & Retreat

Glaciers always advance, they never really retreat. Sometimes, however, the ice melts even faster than it advances, and in that case the terminal, or end face, of the glacier moves backwards up the mountain and the glacier appears to be retreating.

The great mass of ice higher up the mountain pushes the ice down the Fox and Franz Josef valleys at prodigious speeds but – like most glaciers in the world – this past century has been a story of steady retreat and only the odd short advance.

The last ice age of 15,000 to 20,000 years ago saw the glaciers reach right down to the sea. Then warmer weather came and they may have retreated even further than their current position. In the 14th century a new 'mini Ice age' started and for centuries the glaciers advanced, reaching their greatest extent around 1750. At both Fox and Franz Josef, the terminal moraines from that last major advance can be clearly seen. In the 250 years since then, the glaciers have steadily retreated and the terminal face is now several kilometres back from its position in the late 19th century or even from its position in the 1930s.

From 1965 to 1968 the Fox and Franz Josef glaciers made brief advances of about 180m, and in 1985 they once again started to advance and have been moving forward steadily and fairly dramatically ever since. Nobody is quite sure why this advance is taking place. It could be cooler or more overcast summers, or it could be the result of heavy snowfalls 10 or 15 years ago, which are now working their way down to the bottom of the glacier.

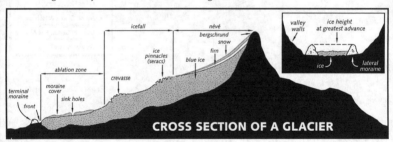

CROSS SECTION OF A GLACIER

Useful Terminology

ablation zone – where the glacier melts

accumulation zone – where the snow collects

bergschrund – large crevasse in the ice near the headwall or starting point of the glacier

blue ice – as the accumulation zone or neve snow is compressed by subsequent snowfalls, it becomes firn and then blue ice

crevasse – cracks in the glacial ice as it crosses obstacles and moves down the mountain

dead ice – as a glacier retreats, isolated chunks of ice may be left behind (sometimes these can remain for many years)

firn – partly compressed snow on the way to becoming glacial ice

glacial flour – the river of melted ice that flows off glaciers is a milky colour from the suspension of finely ground rocks

icefall – when a glacier descends so steeply that the upper ice breaks up in a jumble of iceblocks

kettle lake – lake formed by the melt of an area of isolated dead ice

moraine – walls of debris formed at the glacier's sides (lateral moraine) or end (terminal moraine)

névé – snowfield area where firn is formed

seracs – ice pinnacles formed, like crevasses, by the glacier passing over obstacles

terminal – the final ice face at the end of the glacier

The *Fox Glacier Inn* (☎ 751 0022, fax 751 0024, 39 Sullivans Rd) is a new place with an excellent bar, restaurant and cafe. It's $10 per person for campers, from $17 for a dorm and $40 for doubles and twins. Other good features are lockers in the bunkrooms, a booking office and Internet facilities.

On Sullivans Rd, the *Ivory Towers* (☎ 751 0838, ✆ ivorytowers@xtra.co.nz) is tidy and well equipped. It charges $16 a night in dorms, $40 for a twin or double and singles are from $23.

B&Bs and farmstays in the area charge around $60 to $75. *The Homestead Farm B&B* (☎ 751 0835), on Cook Flat Rd, has doubles with en suites in a 100-year-old farmhouse for $100.

The *Fox Glacier Resort Hotel* (☎ 751 0839) on Cook Flat Rd has budget rooms for $25 per person or $30 with en suite, or a better annexe with en suite doubles from $80 to $130.

Lake Matheson Motel (☎ 751 0830), close by on the Lake Matheson road, has 19 tidy units for $70 to $80. The *Mount Cook View Motel* (☎ 751 0814), nearby on Cook Flat Rd, has 12 comfortable units with spa baths; these are $80 to $110.

The *Rainforest Motel* (☎ 751 0140, ✆ rainforest@xtra.co.nz), also on Cook Flat Rd, has units for $70 to $93.

Places to Eat The *Fox Glacier Store & Tearooms* in the town centre has a reasonable selection of essentials, although not as wide a choice as at Franz Josef.

The *Cafe Neve* (☎ 751 0110) has good vegetarian food and not so good, rather greasy, pizzas (small/medium/large for $12.50/16.50/25).

The *Hobnail Cafe* in the Alpine Guides building has good sandwiches and light meals.

The *Cook Saddle Saloon & Cafe*, on the corner of SH6 and the Cook Flat Rd, is Tex-Mex in style and very popular with locals; main meals of seafood, steak and venison are from $16 to $22.

The *restaurant* in the Glacier Country Hotel serves hearty meals, and there's an open fire and a cosy atmosphere.

The *Fox Glacier Resort Hotel*, unlike the pub at the Franz Josef Glacier, is wonderfully central and you can sit with a jug of beer and discuss the day's activities.

The *Fox Glacier Inn* serves meals and takeaways, and has a lively bar.

Getting There & Away The InterCity bus services overlap – southbound services from Greymouth go to Fox Glacier, while northbound ones from Queenstown continue on to Franz Josef. Buses run every day to and from Greymouth (four hours) and Queenstown (eight hours). From Greymouth there are onward connections to Westport, Nelson and Picton.

See the Franz Josef Glacier section for the sad news on hitchhiking and a warning about the heavily booked bus services.

A local shuttle (☎ 751 0712) runs to the snout of the glacier and to Franz Josef.

SOUTH TO HAAST

Heading south from the glaciers, the rainforest is so dense on both sides of the road (SH6) that you can barely see a couple of metres into it. Further on, it opens up to reveal broad sweeps of coastline before Haast.

Just 26km south of Fox Glacier is the **Copland Valley**. This is at the end of the Copland Track, coming over from Mt Cook. It's a very pleasant six-hour walk up the valley from the highway here to the last hut at Welcome Flat, where there are hot springs. A sign on the road marks the entrance to the valley and the track. The excellent modern hut at Welcome Flat sleeps 40 and should be paid for at the DOC visitor centre in Haast or Fox. InterCity buses pass by the Copland Valley entrance.

There are a few places to stay between Fox Glacier and Haast if you wish to break up the journey.

The *Pinegrove Motel* (☎ 751 0898), 36km south of Fox Glacier, has powered sites at $16, basic/tourist cabins at $30/50 and motels at $60; all prices are for two.

Lake Paringa

Lake Paringa, about 70km south of Fox Glacier and 50km north of Haast, is a tranquil little trout-filled lake surrounded by forest, right beside the road.

The *Paringa Lodge* (☎ 751 0894) is on the lakeshore and has boats and canoes for hire. Fading, self-contained cabin units cost only $20 per person, but have no kitchens. Motel units are $75 for two. About 1km further south, still on the lakefront, is a free *DOC camping area* with basic facilities (toilets and picnic areas).

The *Lake Paringa Cafe*, beside Paringa Lodge, serves everything from sandwiches to venison pie ($10) for lunch; dinner mains for $20 to $25 are surprisingly innovative for this isolated spot. The *Salmon Farm Cafe* (☎ 751 0837), equidistant from Fox and Haast, specialises in fresh and smoked salmon dishes and home-cooked food.

The historic **Haast-Paringa Cattle Track** starts from the main road 43km north of Haast and comes out at the coast by the Waita River, just a few kilometres north of Haast. Before the Haast Pass road opened in 1965 this trail was the only link between Otago/Southland and the West Coast. The first leg of the track makes a pleasant day hike. Information on the track is available from the visitor centre in Haast.

Lake Moeraki

Lake Moeraki, 31km north of Haast, not far off the highway, is another peaceful forest lake with good fishing. It's also not far from the coast – just a 40-minute walk along a stream brings you to **Monro Beach**, where there's a breeding colony of Fiordland crested penguins; they can be found there from July to November. Also at Monro Beach are fur seals and good snorkelling. There are many other good short and long walks around the lake and the Moeraki River which runs from the lake to the sea.

The *Wilderness Lodge Lake Moeraki* (☎ 750 0881), right on the highway and just 20m from the lakeside, is a special place where visitors can fully enjoy a wilderness experience. It has rooms at $150/210 per person in the low/high season for DB&B. Daily outdoor and nature activities, such as walks to Fiordland crested penguin colonies and canoe safaris, are organised; short activities

of up to 90 minutes' duration are free for guests and half-day trips cost $50. The *Riverside Restaurant*, with its superb views of the massive trees growing outside, specialises in fish and game dishes. The canoe safaris are also open to the public.

Past Moeraki is the much-photographed **Knight's Point**, where the Haast road was eventually opened in 1965; there is an information shelter here. And who was Knight? He was a surveyor's dog.

THE HAAST REGION

The Haast region is the centre of a major wildlife refuge, where some of the biggest stands of rainforest survive alongside some of the most extensive wetlands. The kahikatea swamp forests, sand dune forests, seal and penguin colonies, kaka, Red Hills and vast sweeps of beach have ensured the listing of this hauntingly beautiful place as a World Heritage area.

In the forests you will see the flaming red rimu in flower and kahikatea thriving in swampy lagoons. Bird life abounds and the observant twitcher might see fantail, bellbird, NZ pigeon *(kereru)*, falcon, kaka, kiwi and morepork. On the beaches you are likely to see blue penguins and Fiordland crested penguins. This is the home turf of the legendary Arawata Bill, who roamed this domain as a self-styled prospector and explorer. Walk through his incredible country and take a trip back hundreds of years – raupo, ferns and cabbage trees inhibit progress if you stray off the beaten track.

Haast
pop 295

The tiny community of Haast is on the coast where the wide Haast River meets the sea, 120km south of Fox Glacier. After the magnificent scenery of the Haast Highway or the glaciers, this modern little frontier settlement comes as something of a blight on the landscape, but it makes a convenient stop and the World Heritage area has been targeted for tourist development.

A series of tracks has been developed, including the **Hapuka Estuary Walk** leading from the motor camp, and a rainforest, seacoast/wetland walk along **Ship Creek**, halfway between Haast and Lake Moeraki.

The South West New Zealand World Heritage Visitor Centre (☎ 750 0809, fax 750 0832), at the junction of SH6 and Jackson Bay Rd on the southern bank of the Haast River, has wonderful displays and information on the area. The *Edge of Wilderness* film gives an overall view of the Haast landscape ($3, children free). Check out the *kokopu* (native trout) in the large tank behind the information desk.

The supermarket is open daily from 9 am to 7 pm in summer. There are cardphones in the township and at the hotel.

Activities There are many options here including scenic flights, canoeing, fishing and diving for crayfish.

River Safaris (☎ 0800-865 382), Web site: www.riversafaris.co.nz, is based at the Red Barn. It operates exhilarating three-hour **jet-boat** trips along the true wilderness of the Waiatoto River, which rates with the Dart River as one of the best river trips in NZ. They fully describe the Maori history and legends of the region ($99 from Haast, $199/279 from Queenstown by coach/flight). Trips depart at 9 am, noon and 3 pm daily.

Heliventures (☎ 750 0866) flies over the Lost Valley and provides a unique view of the World Heritage region ($165 for 30 minutes, minimum of two).

Places to Stay & Eat The *Haast Beach Holiday Park* (☎ 750 0860) is at Okuru, 11km south of Haast township on the road to Jackson Bay. Tent/powered sites cost $16/18 for two and cabins $40 to $65 for two, with linen for hire if needed. *Acacia & Erewhon Motel* (☎ 750 0817), on the same road and 4km from Haast, has units from $68 to $110 for two.

The township, 3km east of the visitor centre and 200m from SH6, has a small supermarket and accommodation. *Wilderness Backpackers* (☎ 0800-750 029) is a neat and tidy place. It has dorm beds from $15 per person and twins and doubles for $35. *Heritage Park Lodge* (☎ 750 0868)

next door has family units with kitchen for $115. *Haast Highway Accommodation* (☎ 750 0703), a YHA associate, has beds from $16 to $19 per person.

The township also has *Smithy's Tavern* for lunches and dinners (steak and hamburgers) and the *Fantail Tearooms* for light meals.

The *Haast World Heritage Hotel* (☎ 750 0828, ✉ info@world-heritage-hotel.com) near the bridge has doubles from $90 and two-bedroom suites for about $150. There is a public bar nearby, a house bar and a restaurant with a good selection of a la carte dishes. The pub meals are really good value and $10 will see you well satisfied.

Haast to Jackson Bay & the Cascade

A road heads south from the SH6 at Haast to the Arawata River and Jackson Bay. Near Okuru is a walk to the tidal Hapuka Estuary.

The *Okuru Beach Homestay* (☎ 750 0722) is quite rustic but the owners go out of their way to make you welcome in this remote hamlet ($60 for a twin or double).

On the south side of the Arawata Bridge, turn off onto the gravel road that follows the Jackson River to the start of the scenic **Lake Ellery Track**, a one-hour return walk. Continue to Martyr Saddle, with its views of the incredible Red Hills and the Cascade River valley. The distinctive colour of the **Red Hills** is due to high concentrations of magnesium and iron in the rock forced up by the meeting of the Australo and Pacific tectonic plates at this point. Continue on from Martyr Saddle to the flats of the Cascade River, a true wilderness region.

The main road continues west from the bridge to the fishing hamlet of **Jackson Bay**, a real end-of-the-road town and perhaps the most remote in NZ. The views north to the Southern Alps are memorable and there are colonies of Fiordland crested penguins close to the road at Monro Beach. Migrants settled here in 1875 under an assisted immigrant program that was doomed. Dreams to start a farming district were shattered by rain and the lack of a wharf, which was not built until 1938. Today, fishing boats seek lobster, tuna, tarakihi, gurnard and grouper.

The ***Cray Pot***, a mobile shop selling fish and chips, venison and whitebait, was once the old Cromwell pie cart; it's open from 9 am to 6 pm.

Interesting short **walks** here include the three-hour Smoothwater Bay Track, the 15-minute Jackson Viewpoint Walk and the 20-minute Wharekai Te Kau Walk, which has great coastal rock formations. Keener trampers can walk to Stafford Bay Hut, which is a long day walk or an easier two-day walk with an overnight stop at the hut. Check tidal information with the visitor centre in Haast.

HAAST PASS

Turning inland at Haast, snaking along beside the wide Haast River and climbing up the pass, you soon enter Mt Aspiring National Park and the scenery changes again – further inland the vegetation becomes much more sparse until beyond the 563m summit, when you reach snow country covered only in tussock and scrub. Along the Haast Pass are many picturesque waterfalls, most of them just a couple of minutes' walk off the road.

The roadway over Haast Pass was opened in 1965. Prior to that the only southern link to the West Coast was by the Haast–Paringa Cattle Track, walking or on horseback. En route to Wanaka, the **Fantail** and **Thunder Creek** Waterfalls are close to the road. See the DOC booklet *Haast Pass Highway: Short Walks*.

Heading south after Haast, the next town of any size is Wanaka, 145km or 3½ hours away. If driving north, check your fuel gauge: the petrol station at Haast is the last before the Fox Glacier, 120km north.

Canterbury

☎ 03 • pop 473,300

Canterbury is the hub of the South Island and contains its largest city, Christchurch. The region extends from Kaikoura in the north to near Oamaru in the south, and from the Pacific Ocean to Arthur's Pass and Mt Cook in the Southern Alps.

This is one of the driest and flattest areas of New Zealand. The moisture-laden westerlies from the Tasman Sea hit the Southern Alps and dump their rainfall on the West Coast before reaching Canterbury, which has an annual rainfall of only 0.75m compared with 5m on the West Coast.

The region is dominated by the expansive Canterbury Plains, dead-flat farming land backed by the Southern Alps. The Alps, however, are also part of Canterbury and contain NZ's highest mountains – Mts Cook (Aoraki), Tasman and Sefton. This striking geographical contrast is the NZ of postcards – rural, sheep-strewn fields backed by rugged, snowcapped mountains.

Christchurch Region & the North

The large, ordered city of Christchurch, centrally located on the coast midway between Kaikoura and Timaru, is the focal point of Canterbury. To the west, beyond the extensive alluvial plain, are the imposing Southern Alps and Arthur's Pass National Park; to the north, beyond the rolling hills, are Hanmer Springs, more forest parks and the marine-mammal centre of Kaikoura; and to the south-east is the absorbing Banks Peninsula.

CHRISTCHURCH

pop 331,400

Christchurch is often described as the most English of NZ's cities. Punts glide down the picturesque Avon River, a grand Anglican cathedral dominates the city square and trams rattle past streets with oh-so English names.

HIGHLIGHTS

- Experiencing the beautiful city of Christchurch and seeing the fascinating Canterbury Museum – one of the best regional museums anywhere
- Visiting the charming settlement of Akaroa
- Walking in and watching the fabulous mountainscapes of Arthur's Pass National Park
- Exploring the Port Hills and Banks Peninsula region by car or on foot
- Being amazed by the grandeur of Mt Cook (Aoraki) and the glaciers in Mt Cook National Park
- Discovering the Lewis Pass region and the getaway town of Hanmer with its hot springs
- Seeing Lake Tekapo – an azure blue lake surrounded by mountains

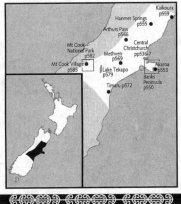

To the west, tranquil suburbs such as Fendalton, Avonhead, Bryndwr, Burnside and Ilam contain the exquisite gardens Christchurch is famous for – geraniums, chrysanthemums and carefully edged lawns with not a blade of grass out of place.

CANTERBURY

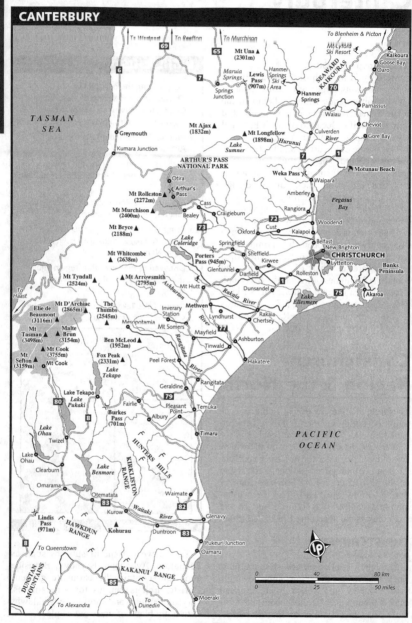

Away from the river and the gardens, much of Christchurch is a flat, typical NZ city, at the base of the Port Hills. Though it still has Gothic buildings and wooden villas, it is a modern, thriving city which has strayed somewhat from the vision of its founders: the settlement of Christchurch in 1850 was an ordered Church of England enterprise, and the fertile farming land was deliberately placed in the hands of the gentry. Christchurch was meant to be a model of class-structured England in the South Pacific, not another scruffy colonial outpost of small land-holders. Churches rather than pubs were built and wool made the elite of Christchurch wealthy. It was incorporated as a very English city in 1862, but its character slowly changed as other migrants and industry followed.

Orientation

Cathedral Square is the centre of town. To find it, just look for the spire. Once there, you can climb to the top of the tower to get your orientation.

Christchurch is compact and walking around is easy, although it is slightly complicated by the river which twists and winds through the centre and crosses your path in disconcertingly varied directions.

The network of one-way streets adds even more excitement if you're driving. Colombo St, running north-south through the square, is the main shopping street.

Information

Tourist Offices The busy Christchurch & Canterbury Visitor Centre (☎ 379 9629, ✉ info@christchurchnz.net), Web site: www.christchurchnz.net, is by the river on the corner of Worcester St and Oxford Terrace (but will soon relocate to Cathedral Square). It takes bookings for just about everything. It's open from 8.30 am to 5 pm (to 4 pm on weekends, later in the summer).

The free pamphlet *Today & Tonight Christchurch & Canterbury* is helpful. Free maps worth getting are *Avon River Drive, Port Hills Drive* and *Antarctic Heritage Trail*. Note that bus numbers refer to Canride buses unless otherwise indicated.

The Department of Conservation (DOC; ☎ 379 9758) at 133 Victoria St has leaflets and information on most national parks and walkways in the South Island. The Automobile Association (AA; ☎ 379 1280) is at 210 Hereford St.

Money Christchurch has plenty of banks for changing travellers cheques or foreign currency, but it's wise to shop around as rates vary.

Hereford St has a collection of banks, open from 9 am to 4.30 pm weekdays. Thomas Cook Forex (☎ 366 1920), on the corner of Armagh and Colombo Sts, is open from 8.30 am to 5 pm on weekdays, 10 am to 4 pm on weekends. American Express (☎ 0800-801 122) is at 773 Colombo St.

Post & Communications You will find the main post shop (☎ 0800-501 501) and pay phones in the south-west corner of the square. Credit, card and coin phones are scattered all over the city centre. All post shops have fax facilities, including the one in Ballantyne's Department Store (☎ 379 7400).

Most backpackers have Internet facilities. Other places are Ground Zero (☎ 366 0091) at 223 High St; the E-caf@the arts centre (☎ 372 9436); the Vadal Internet Fone Shop (☎ 377 2381); and Cyber Cafe Christchurch (☎ 365 5183), Web site: www.cybercafe-chch.co.nz, at 127 Gloucester St near the Theatre Royal. Vadal is probably the cheapest ($5 per hour).

Travel Agencies The YHA Travel Shop (☎ 379 9808, ✉ book@yha.org.nz) in the Cashel St Mall makes domestic and international bookings.

NZ Independent Travel (☎ 377 3155), 7 Chancery Lane, has friendly staff. It makes bookings and offers heaps of free advice to independent travellers.

Bookshops Smith's Bookshop, 133 Manchester St, is a classic second-hand bookshop with over 80,000 volumes on three floors. One room is devoted to books on NZ, including Maori culture and art, and poetry and fiction by NZ authors.

Whitcoulls in the Cashel St Mall is one of the biggest bookshops in Christchurch. Scorpio Books, 79 Hereford St, and Arnold Books at 11 New Regent St also have a wide range.

The Arts Centre Bookshop at the Arts Centre has a good range of NZ titles, including a good stock of LP guides.

Kate Sheppard Books at 145 Manchester St satisfies every New Age craving and then some.

Medical Services The Christchurch Hospital (☎ 364 0640, emergency 364 0270) is on Riccarton Ave. There's an after-hours surgery (☎ 365 7777) at 931 Colombo St, on the corner of Bealey Ave. It's open from 5 pm to 8 am on weekdays, and 24 hours on weekends.

The Travel Vaccination Clinic (☎ 364 0347), on the corner of Hagley Ave and Tuam St, is open from 8.30 am to 5 pm weekdays. The Traveller's Medical & Vaccination Centre (☎ 379 4000) is at 147 Armagh St, on the corner of Manchester St.

Disabled Facilities Christchurch is well set up with designated car parks, and most restaurants, public toilets and bars have disabled access. The city council has a Kiwi-Able Coordinator (☎ 371 1774).

Cathedral Square

Cathedral Square is the heart of Christchurch and the best place to start exploring the city. The square is dominated by **Christ Church Cathedral**, consecrated in 1881. For $4 you can see the historical display and climb 133 steps to the viewing balconies 30m up the cathedral's 63m-high spire. Study the cathedral bells and take in the views from the spire – it was damaged by earthquakes on several occasions, once sending the very top into Cathedral Square.

One of the city's most-visited attractions, the church has embraced tourism and the free market with secular zeal. The cathedral has a souvenir shop, screens videos ($2), charges for cameras (another $2) and has a good cafe open on weekdays. What would the pious founding fathers say? But the proceeds help

DENNIS JOHNSON

Statue of Captain Cook, Victoria Square

maintain this wonderful Gothic building. The cathedral is open from 8.30 am to 8 pm on weekdays, 9 am to 5 pm on Saturday and 7.30 am to 8 pm on Sunday. Free tours usually go at 11 am and 2 pm.

About the only aberration in this sea of order is **The Wizard**, a now very tired local eccentric and soap-boxer who trots out the same diatribe daily in front of the Cathedral. His patter is as dated as the 'Merlin' hat he wears.

Guided City Walks (☎ 342 7691) runs two-hour **guided walks** of the city, departing from its kiosk in the south-western section of the square. Tours leave at 10 am and 2 pm daily, cost $8 and are most informative. Independent walkers can get a copy of the free brochure *Central City Walks*.

Southern Encounter Aquarium This pseudo-landscaped warehouse in Cathedral Square has fish in acrylic tanks. There are touch tanks, divers feeding the eels and other oddities including a re-creation of a fishing lodge. The aquarium (☎ 377 3474) is well presented but quite small and, with entry at $12.50 (children $6), nothing to get too excited about. It's open from 9 am to 9 pm daily (until 6 pm in winter).

The Banks of the Avon

The invitingly calm and picturesque **Avon River** is a delight just to walk along. If you want to row down it, head to the Antigua Boatsheds by the footbridge at the southern end of Rolleston Ave. Canoes are $6, paddle boats $10 and row boats $20, all for an hour. The boatsheds are open from 7 am to 5.30 pm daily.

Or you can relax and be punted along the river. **Punts** depart from behind the visitor centre, with departures and landings also from the Antigua Boatsheds. A 30-minute trip costs $20 per person (or $12.50 for two adults, children under 12 half-price). The punts ply the river from 9 am to dusk daily (10 am to 4 pm in winter).

Beside the museum off Rolleston Ave, the **Botanic Gardens**, open from 7 am to one hour before sunset, are 30 hectares of greenery beside the Avon River. The gardens' information centre, many floral show houses and popular fern house are open from 10.15 am to 4 pm daily. Tours leave from the cafe between 11 am and 4 pm from August to April when the weather is fine.

Enchanting **Mona Vale**, an Elizabethan-style riverside homestead with 5.5 hectares of richly landscaped gardens, ponds and fountains, is open from 8 am to 7.30 pm daily from October to March, and from 8.30 am to 5.30 pm from April to September. For guided tours of the homestead book on ☎ 348 9660. It's 1.5km from the city at 63 Fendalton Rd (bus No 9). You can punt on the Avon here (45 minutes is $18 per person, children under eight half-price).

Canterbury Museum

This very good museum (☎ 366 5000), on Rolleston Ave at the entrance to the Botanic Gardens, is open from 9 am to 5.30 pm daily. Entry is by donation ($5 each family is suggested); it's $2 entry for the special Discovery Centre.

Particularly interesting are the early colonist exhibits and the Antarctic discovery section. Christchurch is the HQ for 'Operation Deep Freeze', the supply link to Antarctica (see International Antarctic Centre following). The museum has good historical exhibits on Antarctic exploration and the natural history of the Antarctic, subantarctic and Chatham islands.

The Maori gallery is very good, as is the slightly repugnant but very informative collection of stuffed birds, right across NZ's species list, including the now-extinct moa. While you're at it, check out the pull-out drawers of mounted insects for a look at NZ's unique weta, as well as huge tarantulas. The museum has a good cafe on the 4th floor with views of the gardens.

The **Robert McDougall Art Gallery** (☎ 365 0915), behind the museum, has an extensive collection of NZ and international art and is open from 10 am to 4.30 pm daily (until 5.30 pm in summer). The gallery's annexe, featuring contemporary NZ art, is in the nearby Arts Centre on Rolleston Ave.

The Centre of Contemporary Art (CoCA; ☎ 366 7261) has five galleries; the art here is for sale.

International Antarctic Centre

Near the airport, on Orchard Rd, this centre is part of a huge complex built for the administration and warehousing of the NZ, US and Italian Antarctic programs.

The centre has hands-on exhibits, video presentations and the 'sights and sounds' of the vast continent. Special effects dazzle the kids and the new Snow and Ice Experience allows you to freeze while you slide down a snow slope and explore a snow cave. Good educational family stuff, but the Canterbury Museum has better historical exhibits on Antarctic exploration and is a lot cheaper.

The latest addition to this icy theme park is a ride in a Hägglund Antarctic snowmobile vehicle through an outdoor adventure course ($20/12 for adults/children in summer, $15/8 in winter).

The centre (☎ 358 9896), Web site: www.iceberg.co.nz, is open from 9.30 am to 8.30 pm October to March, 9.30 am to 5.30 pm April to September ($12, children $6). Reach it on an airport bus.

Other Museums

Air Force World (☎ 343 9532) is exceptionally well presented. On display are aircraft

CENTRAL CHRISTCHURCH

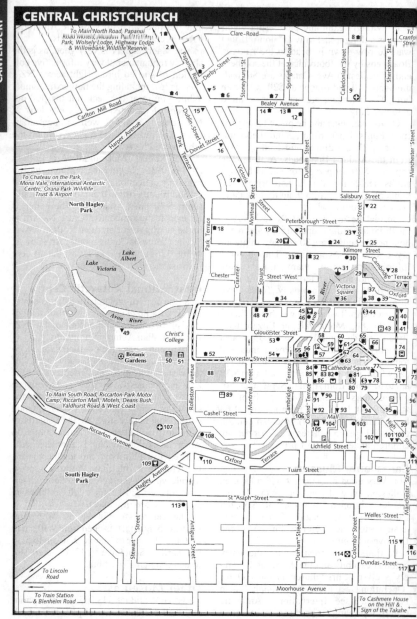

To Main North Road, Papanui
Road Motels, Meadow Park Holiday
Park, Wolsely Lodge, Highway Lodge
& Willowbank Wildlife Reserve

To Cranfo
Stree

Clare Road

Derby Street

Stoneyhurst St

Springfield Road

Caledonian Street

Sherborne Street

Manchester Street

Carlton Mill Road

Harper Avenue

Dublin Street

Dorset Street

Park Terrace

Bealey Avenue

Victoria Street

Durham Street

To Chateau on the Park,
Mona Vale, International Antarctic
Centre, Orana Park Wildlife
Trust & Airport

**North Hagley
Park**

Salisbury Street

Montreal Street

Peterborough Street

Colombo Street

Lake
Albert

Lake
Victoria

Chester Street West

Kilmore Street

Cranmer Square

Cambridge Terrace

Avon River

Victoria
Square

Oxford

Avon River

Botanic
Gardens

**Christ's
College**

Gloucester Street

Worcester Street

Rolleston Avenue

Cambridge Terrace

Cathedral Square

Montreal Street

Oxford Terrace

To Main South Road, Riccarton Park Motor
Camp, Riccarton Mall, Motels, Deans Bush,
Yaldhurst Road & West Coast

Cashel Street

Mall

High Street

Riccarton Avenue

Lichfield Street

**South Hagley
Park**

Oxford Terrace

Tuam Street

Hagley Avenue

Stewart Street

Antigua Street

St Asaph Street

Manchester Street

Durham Street

Welles Street

Colombo Street

To Lincoln
Road

Dundas Street

To Train Station
& Blenheim Road

Moorhouse Avenue

To Cashmere House
on the Hill &
Sign of the Takahe

CENTRAL CHRISTCHURCH

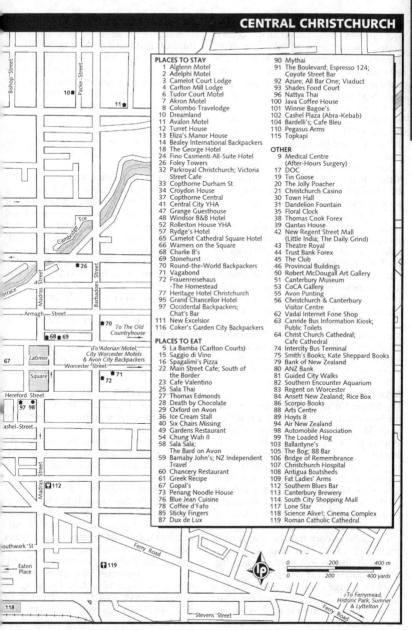

PLACES TO STAY
1 Alglenn Motel
2 Adelphi Motel
3 Camelot Court Lodge
4 Carlton Mill Lodge
6 Tudor Court Motel
7 Akron Motel
8 Colombo Travelodge
10 Dreamland
11 Avalon Motel
12 Turret House
13 Eliza's Manor House
14 Bealey International Backpackers
18 The George Hotel
24 Fino Casmenti All-Suite Hotel
26 Foley Towers
32 Parkroyal Christchurch; Victoria
   Street Cafe
33 Copthorne Durham St
34 Croydon House
37 Copthorne Central
41 Central City YHA
47 Grange Guesthouse
48 Windsor B&B Hotel
52 Rolleston House YHA
57 Rydge's Hotel
65 Camelot Cathedral Square Hotel
66 Warners on the Square
68 Charlie B's
69 Stonehurst
70 Round-the-World Backpackers
71 Vagabond
72 Frauenreisehaus
   -The Homestead
77 Heritage Hotel Christchurch
95 Grand Chancellor Hotel
97 Occidental Backpackers;
   Chat's Bar
111 New Excelsior
116 Coker's Garden City Backpackers

PLACES TO EAT
5 La Bamba (Carlton Courts)
15 Saggio di Vino
16 Spagalimi's Pizza
22 Main Street Cafe; South of
   the Border
23 Cafe Valentino
25 Sala Thai
27 Thomas Edmonds
28 Death by Chocolate
29 Oxford on Avon
36 Ice Cream Stall
40 Six Chairs Missing
49 Gardens Restaurant
54 Chung Wah II
58 Sala Sala;
   The Bard on Avon
59 Barnaby John's; NZ Independent
   Travel
60 Chancery Restaurant
61 Greek Recipe
67 Gopal's
73 Penang Noodle House
76 Blue Jean Cuisine
78 Coffee d'Fafo
85 Sticky Fingers
87 Dux de Lux

90 Mythai
91 The Boulevard; Espresso 124;
   Coyote Street Bar
92 Azure; All Bar One; Viaduct
93 Shades Food Court
96 Nattya Thai
100 Java Coffee House
101 Winnie Bagoe's
102 Cashel Plaza (Abra-Kebab)
104 Bardelli's; Cafe Bleu
110 Pegasus Arms
115 Topkapi

OTHER
9 Medical Centre
   (After-Hours Surgery)
17 DOC
19 Tin Goose
20 The Jolly Poacher
21 Christchurch Casino
30 Town Hall
31 Dandelion Fountain
35 Floral Clock
38 Thomas Cook Forex
39 Qantas House
42 New Regent Street Mall
   (Little India; The Daily Grind)
43 Theatre Royal
44 Trust Bank Forex
45 The Club
46 Provincial Buildings
50 Robert McDougall Art Gallery
51 Canterbury Museum
53 CoCA Gallery
55 Avon Punting
56 Christchurch & Canterbury
   Visitor Centre
62 Vadal Internet Fone Shop
63 Canride Bus Information Kiosk;
   Public Toilets
64 Christ Church Cathedral;
   Cafe Cathedral
74 Intercity Bus Terminal
75 Smith's Books; Kate Sheppard Books
79 Bank of New Zealand
80 ANZ Bank
81 Guided City Walks
82 Southern Encounter Aquarium
83 Regent on Worcester
84 Ansett New Zealand; Rice Box
86 Scorpio Books
88 Arts Centre
89 Hoyts 8
94 Air New Zealand
98 Automobile Association
99 The Loaded Hog
103 Ballantyne's
105 The Bog; 88 Bar
106 Bridge of Remembrance
107 Christchurch Hospital
108 Antigua Boatsheds
109 Fat Ladies' Arms
112 Southern Blues Bar
113 Canterbury Brewery
114 South City Shopping Mall
117 Lone Star
118 Science Alive!; Cinema Complex
119 Roman Catholic Cathedral

used by the NZ Air Force over the years, with figures and background scenery. Antarctic aircraft sit in the snow, aircraft are serviced, a Canberra bomber of the 1950s taxis out at night, a WWII fighter is hidden in the jungle – you can even pretend to pilot an A4 Skyhawk jet or WWII Spitfire in flight simulators. The museum is at the former Wigram air base, a 15-minute drive south of the city on Main South Rd. There is also a shuttle bus from the visitor centre. It's open from 10 am to 5 pm daily ($10, children $5).

South-east of the city centre is **Ferrymead Historic Park** (☎ 384 1970), 269 Bridle Path Rd, Heathcote. This historical village is a working museum of transport and technology with electric and steam locomotives, old household appliances, cars, machinery etc. It's open from 10 am to 4.30 pm daily ($6, children $3; steam train and tram rides are $2). Catch Canride bus No 3 from the square.

In the old train station, on Moorhouse Ave, is **Science Alive!**, an interesting hands-on science exhibit featuring numerous interactive stations. It's open from 9 am to 5 pm on weekdays and 10 am to 6 pm on weekends (all-day pass $6 for adults and kids). Its slogan is: 'If I wasn't meant to touch anything, what are these things on the end of my arms for?' A great place for kids.

Arts Centre

The former University of Canterbury town site has been transformed into the Arts Centre (☎ 366 0989), Web site: www.artscentre .org.nz. It's a great place to browse. The beautiful old Gothic buildings are now an arts, craft and entertainment complex with a good selection of cafes and restaurants thrown in. Gothic Revival Tours ($5) are conducted by the Christchurch town crier at 11 am weekdays – get tickets at the Arts Centre's information centre.

The Galleria, open from 10.30 am to 4.30 pm, has dozens of craft shops with everything from fine pottery, jewellery, weaving, woollen goods and Maori carvings to handmade toys – not cheap but one of the best craft centres in NZ and in some cases you can see the craftspeople at work. A bustling craft market is also held on weekends.

National Marae

The largest *marae* in NZ is at 250 Pages Rd, 6km north-east of the city. Nga Hau e Wha (The Four Winds) is a multicultural facility open to all people – *Nau mai haere mai* (welcome welcome). You can see the carvings, weavings and paintings in the *whare nui* (meeting house) and the *whare wananga* (house of learning).

Evening tours and concert cost $27.50 or $60 with a *hangi* (bookings essential). Take the shuttle bus from the visitor centre.

Christchurch Tramway

Trams, first introduced to Christchurch streets in 1905, only lasted as a means of transport for 60 years. Restored green and cream trams have been reintroduced as part of a 2.5km inner-city loop around many of the city's best features and shopping areas.

The trams (☎ 366 7830) operate from 9 am to 9 pm daily. Tickets cost $6 for one hour, $7 for a full day (children $3/4). It's probably quicker (certainly cheaper) to walk. One plus is that they pass through the historic **New Regent St** precinct, with many examples of Spanish mission-style architecture.

One tram has been fitted out as a restaurant allowing you to dine while sightseeing.

Christchurch Gondola

For a cost of $12 (children $6, families $29) you can be whisked up from the Heathcote Valley terminal on a 4½-minute ride to a point somewhere above the Lyttelton Rd tunnel. There are great views at the top (Mt Cavendish, around 500m) right across to the Southern Alps on a fine day.

The gondola operates from 10 am until late daily; the free Gondola bus leaves regularly from the visitor centre or take the No 28 Lyttelton bus. At the top, there's a cafe, restaurant, shop and heritage show to spend more money on. Walkways lead on to the Crater Rim Walkway (see under Walking).

You can mountain-bike down with the Mountain Bike Adventure Company or paraglide down with Nimbus Paragliding and Phoenix Paragliding. Flights are from $95; book at the visitor centre.

Christchurch Casino

NZ's first casino is in the heart of town on Victoria and Kilmore Sts. Las Vegas comes to Sleepy Hollow, but draconian dress standards (no jeans) apply and the casino thrives on pensioners from the countryside who come in on the free casino buses. It's open 24 hours. All the traditional methods of losing your money are provided.

Wildlife Reserves

Orana Park Wildlife Trust (☎ 359 7109) has an excellent walk-through aviary of native birds and a nocturnal kiwi house, as well as tuatara. Most of the extensive grounds, however, are devoted to the 'African Plains' with lions, rhino, giraffe, zebra, oryx and cheetah. Animal feeding times are scheduled daily. It's open from 10 am to 5 pm daily (last admission at 4.30 pm; $12, children $6) and includes a shuttle-bus tour. It's on McLeans Island Rd, Harewood, beyond the airport, and about 20 minutes from the city.

The **Willowbank Wildlife Reserve** (☎ 359 6226) has exotic and local animals, including a variety of domestic animals. The selection of native wildlife is extensive and there is a large nocturnal kiwi house.

The reserve, on Hussey Rd, is open from 10 am to 10 pm daily and entry is $12 (children $6). The City Circuit bus runs there from the visitor centre.

Other Attractions

The **Queen Elizabeth II Park** (☎ 383 4313) on Travis Rd, North Beach, 8km north-east of the centre, is a huge sports complex, with indoor pools, waterslides and squash courts, and was the venue for the 1974 Commonwealth Games. The adjacent fun park has a variety of amusement park attractions. Take Canride bus No 10 or 19 from the square.

Riccarton House (☎ 348 5119), an imposing Victorian mansion, is at 16 Kahu Rd, 3km west of the centre. The house is open from 1 to 4 pm on weekdays and 2 to 4 pm on Sunday, but of most interest is the six-hectare stand of native bush in the estate, a remnant of the long-since cleared Canterbury Plains.

The **Canterbury Brewery** (☎ 379 4940), at 36 St Asaph St, is the brewer of Lion beers. There are tours at 10.30 am, Monday to Thursday ($8); bookings are essential.

Out at New Brighton there's a **pier**, often crowded with local anglers. At the end of the pier is a modernistic building which includes a library and licensed cafe. Here too is the **bungy rocket**, which catapults the brave into the air before yo-yoing up and down ($35).

The *Tuhoe,* an **old steamer**, sails most Sundays down the Kaiapoi River to Kairaki on the coast and back (just over an hour). It doesn't sail every Sunday so check on ☎ 327 5786; sailings are subject to weather conditions ($8, children $4). To get to Kaiapoi take bus No 1 or 4; check times and points of departure with Bus Info (☎ 366 8855).

Swimming & Surfing

The closest beaches to the city are North Beach (10km; bus No 19), South Brighton Beach (10km; bus No 5), Sumner (11km; bus No 3), Waimairi (10km; bus No 10), New Brighton (8km; bus No 5) and Taylors Mistake – a pleasant beach further out from Sumner, popular for surfing.

Walking

The visitor centre has details and leaflets about walks around Christchurch.

Starting in the city are the **Riverside Walk** (the leaflet on this is packed with information) and various historical walks.

For great views of the city, there is a walkway from the **Sign of the Takahe**. The various 'Sign of the ...' places in this area were originally roadhouses built during the Depression as rest stops. Now they vary from the impressive tearooms at the Sign of the Takahe to a simple shelter at the Sign of the Bellbird and are referred to primarily as landmarks. This walk leads up to the **Sign of the Kiwi** through Victoria Park and then along near the Summit Rd to Scott Reserve, with several lookout points along the way. The walk is accessible by bus No 2 from Victoria Square near the Town Hall.

You can walk to Lyttelton on the **Bridle Path**. It starts from Heathcote Valley (take bus No 28) and takes one to 1½ hours at an easy pace. The **Godley Head Walkway** is a two-hour round trip from Taylors Mistake, crossing and recrossing Summit Rd with beautiful views on a clear day.

The **Rapaki Track** is an excellent walk taking just a couple of hours and offering fine views of the whole city and of Lyttelton.

The **Crater Rim Walkway** around Lyttelton Harbour goes some 14km from the Bridle Path to the Ahuriri Scenic Reserve, passing through a number of scenic reserves along the way, plus the Sign of the Bellbird and the Sign of the Kiwi. The walkway can easily be done in several short stages.

There are a number of shorter walks in and around **Nicholson Park** and **Sumner Head**, about 25 minutes by car from the square, or catch a No 3 bus. Here you'll see many inshore birds, such as the eastern bartailed godwit, gulls, shags and black swans.

Skiing

There are several ski areas within a two-hour drive of Christchurch. For more information see Skiing in the Activities chapter and individual entries for each of the resorts in this chapter.

Other Activities

There are diverse activities within Christchurch or just on its fringe. Ballooning ($200), fishing (from $150), horse trekking ($25 per hour), jet-boating ($45), tandem skydiving ($245), biplane flights (from $99) and golf tours (from $70) are all possible; inquire at the visitor centre.

Organised Tours

Great Sights (☎ 0800-744 487) has a three-hour morning highlights tour which includes Mona Vale and the Port Hills ($30, children $15), an afternoon tour to Sumner and the Port Hills ($30/15) and a 'Must See Three' including Mt Cavendish Gondola, punting and the Antarctic Centre ($55/27).

Walkaway Tours (☎ 365 6672) has interesting trips which offer activities that other trips don't. A Port Hills and crater rim tour is $30; Arthur's Pass and the Otira Gorge $125 (*TranzAlpine* option $185); and Akaroa with a sea tour is $140.

Christchurch Sightseeing Tours (☎ 366 9660) offers half-day city tours ($25) and

three-hour garden tours to the city's leading gardens on Tuesday, Thursday and Saturday from November to March ($20).

Canterbury Leisure Tours (☎ 0800-484 485) has golfing tours ($95) and tours further afield to Mt Cook ($225), Kaikoura (with dolphin swim $150) and Hanmer Springs ($145).

Readers recommend Canterbury Trails (☎ 337 1185), which offers personalised tours to various parts of the province in a 4WD vehicle.

The Christchurch Pub Crawl (☎ 021-324 537) is a tour with a difference. It leaves town at 6 pm and goes to five pubs, all diverse in character. It is designed to make you laugh at yourself, not to get drunk. You get five free beers and a T-shirt and finish at 11 pm ($30 of good value).

Places to Stay

Camping & Cabins The *Addington Accommodation Park (☎ 338 9770, 47 Whiteleigh Rd),* off Lincoln Rd, is 3km south-west of the city centre. It has tent/powered sites at $17/19 for two and a variety of cabins from as little as $25 to $49 for self-contained cabins. It's conveniently located and cheap, but not somewhere you'd want to spend a lot of time. Take bus No 7.

The *Meadow Park Holiday Park (☎ 352 9176, 39 Meadow St)* off the Main North Rd is 5km north. Camping, with power, costs $22, cabins are from $33, self-contained lodge units are $47, and 'kosy kiwi cottages' are $60; prices are for two. There's a heated pool, a spa, childrens playground and a recreation hall. Take bus No 4.

Russley Park Motor Camp (☎ 342 7021, 372 Yaldhurst Rd), opposite Riccarton Racecourse, is about 10km north-west of the square or 2km from the airport. Tent/powered sites cost $16/19, chalet cabins are from $30 to $39 and there are some fancier tourist flats from $55; all prices are for two. Take bus No 8.

South Brighton Motor Camp (☎ 388 9844, 59 Halsey St), off Estuary Rd, 10km north-east, is another attractive park. Tent/powered sites are $18/20, and standard cabins are $30. Take bus No 5.

The *All Seasons Holiday Park* (☎ 384 9490, 5 Kidbrooke St, Linwood) is about 5km east of the city. In this park powered sites are $20, budget cabins are $33 and tourist flats are $57.

Amber Park (☎ 348 3327, 308 Blenheim Rd) is only 4km west of the square. Tent and powered sites are $20 and tourist flats, which share the camp kitchen facilities but have en suites, are from $46 to $56. Take bus No 25.

North South Holiday Park (☎ 359 5993, 530 Sawyers Arms Rd), on the North-South Bypass, is 2.5km from the airport. Powered sites are $18, basic cabins are $33 and tourist cabins are $43 and $53 (with en suite).

Backpackers Christchurch has several popular backpackers, most concentrated within the Bealey, Moorhouse, Fitzgerald and Rolleston Aves grid. Some of the big, older backpackers offer very cheap rates in the off season – as low as $13 for a dorm bed.

Several stalwarts are found in the region of Latimer Square.

Stonehurst (☎ 0508-786 633, 241 Gloucester St), Web site: www.stonehurst .co.nz, is a hotel and backpackers close to the city centre. It is cleverly divided into three areas – hotel rooms, a large-group block and a delightful FIT (Free & Independent Travellers) building – The Lodge. Rates are $17 per person in the dorms, and doubles are $45; some have an en suite. Backpackers can use the pub, lounge or the pool in the main building. All attention is afforded to guests here, and there's even a TV and seating in the laundry. Tidy, fully self-contained tourist flats are $300 per week.

On the corner of Gloucester St, *Charlie B's* (☎ 379 8429, @ charlie_bees@xtra.co .nz, 268 Madras St) is very central. This large, friendly backpackers is always being upgraded, and has all the facilities, including a games room, videos, barbecue and off-street parking. A bed in the infamous big dorm costs $12 – it has been considerably improved with a skylight. Smaller shared rooms cost $15 per person, and it has a large selection of singles ($30), and twin and double rooms ($40).

Occidental Backpackers (☎ 379 9284, 208 Hereford St) is in a heritage hotel on the opposite side of Latimer Square from the previous two backpackers. Exuding old-town hospitality, this place has friendly owners and staff and sells Monteiths, the best drop in the now-known world. It has dorm beds from $15, singles ($25), twins and made-up doubles ($40).

Foley Towers (☎ 366 9720, @ foley .towers@backpack.co.nz, 208 Kilmore St), near Madras St, is a large but spacious backpackers run by the compiler of the BBH *Blue Book*. A dorm or shared room costs $15 per person, and the twin and double rooms are $30/38 without/with en suite.

Frauenreisehaus – The Homestead (☎ 366 2585, 272 Barbadoes St) is a well-equipped women-only backpackers, east of Latimer Square. It has a full kitchen and laundry, TV and video, games room, library, comfortable lounge with fire, free linen and natural spring water. Tastefully furnished rooms cost $15 for dorms, $25 for singles and $34 for twins.

Round-the-World Backpackers (☎ 365 4363, 314 Barbadoes St), also east of Latimer, is a purpose-built place with excellent fixtures and fittings. A dorm is $16 per person and twins or doubles are $38.

The *Vagabond* (☎ 379 9677, 232 Worcester St) is a small hostel just a few blocks away. It has a homey feel, has been attractively refurbished and has a sunny outdoor garden. Shared rooms are $16 per person, twins and doubles are $35 and a single is $23.

The *Old Countryhouse* (☎ 381 5504, 437 Gloucester St), well east of these, is a small, quaint old building with heated rooms and a 'help-yourself' garden. Shared rooms are from $15, and twins and doubles are $34.

The *Central City YHA* (☎ 379 9535, @ yhachch@yha.org.nz, 273 Manchester St), just west of Latimer Square, has four-bed rooms for $19 per person and twins and doubles for $44. It has a spacious common room, excellent kitchen facilities and quiet, tidy rooms with heating.

Warners on the Square (☎/fax 377 0550, 50 Cathedral Square), a little further west, has a great location, with the plus of Bailie's Bar beneath. Dorms are $15 per person and twin and double rooms are $36/40 without/with en suite.

There is another collection of places to the north. *Bealey International Backpackers* (☎ 366 6760, 70 Bealey Ave), between Montreal and Durham Sts, is a smaller place with a friendly atmosphere, an outdoor garden and barbecue area, and a cosy log fire in winter. It offers luggage storage and can book activities. It's $15 for a shared room or $34 for twins and doubles.

Dreamland (☎ 366 3519, 21 Packe St) is a relaxed, homey backpackers in a comfortable old house. Shared rooms are $15 per person, twins or doubles are $34. The owner is a keen cyclist and helps visitors repair their bikes in his workshop. It has open fireplaces, lots of information and a nice atmosphere.

In the west of the grid, *Rolleston House YHA* (☎ 366 6564, @ yhachrl@yha.org.nz, 5 Worcester St) is in an excellent position opposite the Arts Centre and only 700m from the square. A dorm bed is $17 per person and twins are $40.

The *New Excelsior Backpackers* (☎ 366 7570, @ newexcel@ihug.co.nz), on the corner of Manchester and High Sts, is a family-run, revamped pub with modern kitchen, dining room, lounge and al fresco barbecue deck. Dorm beds are from $15 to $17, singles $32 and twins/doubles are from $38 to $45.

Coker's Garden City Backpackers (☎ 379 8580, @ isabella.pavlova@xtra.co.nz, 52 Manchester St), south of the square, is large and well equipped. This former pub is an older, labyrinthine place with a huge kitchen, dining room and lounge areas, and a bar next door. Dorms are $16 per person; twins and doubles are $44 (all have en suites).

B&Bs & Guesthouses The *Thistle Guesthouse* (☎ 348 1499, 21 Main South Rd), about 6km from the city square near the junction of Riccarton and Yaldhurst Rds, is a cheap option. Singles/doubles are $30/50. Breakfast is available ($7) and there's off-street parking.

The *Windsor B&B Hotel* (☎ 366 1503, 52 Armagh St) is just five to 10 minutes'

walk from the city centre. It's meticulously clean and orderly, and rooms with shared bath cost $66/98. *Croydon House* (☎ 366 5111), on the same street at No 63, is similar and charges $70/95.

The *Wolseley Lodge* (☎ 355 6202, 107 Papanui Rd), 2km north-west of the square, is a big, old-fashioned house in a quiet setting with rooms at $40/70 including breakfast.

The *Highway Lodge* (☎ 355 5418, 121 Papanui Rd), a few doors down, has rooms for $35/50 or $49/65, and breakfast is available. This leafy area is very pleasant, with restaurants nearby and easy access to the centre (walk or take bus No 1).

The *Turret House* (☎ 365 3900, 435 Durham St North), built in 1885, has been elegantly restored. Rooms cost from $65/85, which includes breakfast and en suite.

Eliza's Manor House (☎ 366 8584, 82 Bealey Ave) is elegantly restored, and has doubles from $90 to $150. There is a licensed restaurant and a bar.

The *Grange Guesthouse* (☎ 366 2850, 56 Armagh St) is a charming old home; singles with en suite are $95, and doubles and twins with en suite are $110. It's five minutes' walk to town.

The *Locarno Gardens* (☎ 332 9987, 25 Locarno St, St Martins), 3km south of the city, has singles/doubles for $75/95, and a tennis court.

Motels Christchurch has well over 120 motels, most of them charging from $75 to $95 a double. The information centre will find one to suit your budget.

On Papanui Rd there are several motels. The *Adelphi* (☎ 355 6037) at No 49 has doubles from $80 to $100; the *Tall Trees* (☎ 352 6681) at No 454 has doubles from $69 to $89; *Camelot Court* (☎ 355 9124) at No 28 is from $90; the *Casino Court* (☎ 355 6863) at No 76 is from $85 to $130 for four; and the *Alglenn* (☎ 0800-254 536) at No 59 has doubles from $79 to $93.

Riccarton also has several good motels. The *Belle Bonne* (☎ 348 8458, 95 Yaldhurst Rd, Riccarton) has singles/doubles for $75/85; the *Earnslaw* (☎ 348 6387, 288

Blenheim Rd, Riccarton) has doubles from $70; the *Golden Mile (☎ 349 6153),* Main South Rd, Templeton, has doubles for $73; and the *Hagley Park (☎ 348 7683, 13 Darvel St, Riccarton)* has doubles for $75.

Another motel strip is Bealey Ave. The *Avalon Motel (☎ 379 9680)* at No 301 has studio units for $75 for two; the *Tudor Court Motel (☎ 379 1465)* at No 57 has good rooms from $79 to $145; the *Carlton Mill Lodge (☎ 366 1068)* at No 19 has good rooms from $85 to $140 for up to four; the *Akron Motel (☎ 0800-778 787)* at No 87 has two-bedroom units for $105; and the *Colombo Travelodge (☎ 366 3029, 965 Colombo St),* a block north of Bealey Ave, has doubles from $60 to $70.

The *Stonehurst* (see Backpackers earlier) has excellent motel rooms from $55 to $75 for up to four persons.

Hotels Top-bracket Christchurch hotels include the *Chateau on the Park (☎ 0800-808 999, 189 Deans Ave)* at the edge of Hagley Park, the *Copthorne Durham St (☎ 365 4699)* on the corner of Durham and Kilmore Sts, the *Copthorne Central (☎ 379 5880, 776 Colombo St), Rydges Hotel (☎ 379 4700)* on the corner of Worcester St and Oxford Terrace, and the *Airport Plaza (☎ 358 3139)* on Memorial Ave. In these hotels doubles are from $160 (and up).

Camelot Cathedral Square Hotel (☎ 365 2898) is a mid-range hotel with rooms from $95 to $150; the *Heritage Hotel Christchurch (☎ 379 4560, 28–30 Cathedral Square)* and the *Grand Chancellor Hotel (☎ 379 2999, 161 Cashel St)* are much flashier hotels with rooms from around $200.

The George Hotel (☎ 379 4560, 50 Park Terrace) is a small boutique hotel out of the mould and definitely in the luxury class. Rooms cost $275 to $300 and suites $350 to $550.

The *Fino Casmenti All-Suite Hotel (☎366 8444, 87 Kilmore St),* with 45 luxury two-bedroom suites, is definitely another upmarket option.

The *Parkroyal Christchurch (☎ 365 7799),* on the corner of Durham and Kilmore Sts, is right at the top of the price scale. It's imaginatively designed and wonderfully located, and a double with great views costs $350.

Places to Eat

Restaurants The largest concentration of bars, cafes and restaurants is found at 'The Terrace', the eastern side of Oxford Terrace between Hereford St and the City Mall. All of the places here have character, good vantage points and international dishes galore. *The Boulevard (☎ 374 6676),* on the corner of Hereford St, is an upmarket restaurant with continental dishes befitting its title (mains are around $20 but the light meals such as mushroom and bacon fussilli are $14).

South of there, *Espresso 124 (☎ 365 0547),* at No 124, is a brasserie and the innovative chef delights in dreaming up new Pacific Rim dishes. The *Coyote Street Bar (☎ 366 6055),* at No 126, has Tex-Mex selections (mains are about $23) and guarantees to keep you 'howlin' all night!'.

Azure (☎ 365 6088), at No 128, has many Mediterranean dishes, excellent coffee and good sounds. The menu is not all Mediterranean: how's this – oven-roasted lamb rump, stuffed with wild mushrooms and ginger served on gourmet potatoes, with manuka honey, lemon thyme and Drambuie jus ($23).

All Bar One (☎ 377 9898), at No 130, is a dance bar with meals (reef and beef, for example, $8.50).

Lastly, the *Viaduct (☎ 377 9968),* at No 136, is an old-fashioned Italian place with wood-fired pizzas, old favourite pastas, and for the adventurous, kiwi pork and kumara.

Sala Sala (184 Oxford Terrace), near the Gloucester St corner, is a good Japanese restaurant open every night for dinner.

The *Gardens Restaurant* in the wonderful Botanic Gardens is renowned for excellent smorgasbords ($13 including coffee) from noon to 2 pm daily. The restaurant is open from 10 am to 4.30 pm for snacks and other light meals.

Retour (☎ 365 2888), formerly the Thomas Edmonds, is in a band rotunda on Cambridge Terrace. You could complement the romantic atmosphere by arriving by punt! Light main courses for lunch start at around $12 (dinner $22), with both meat and vegetarian selections; it's open for lunch from Sunday to Friday, dinner from Monday to Saturday.

The *Victoria Street Cafe* (☎ 365 7799), in the inner courtyard of the ultra-expensive Parkroyal, is not as expensive as it looks – main courses, meat and vegetarian, cost around $20 and there's a salad bar.

Blue Jean Cuisine (205 Manchester St) is a bar-restaurant in a sand-blasted warehouse and is very popular for its reasonably priced fish, chicken and steak mains at around $18.

Six Chairs Missing (36 New Regent St) sounds like a best movie candidate at Cannes, but is a good little cafe with innovative mains for around $23 – the rack of lamb is excellent. It's open from 10 am to 6 pm daily except Sunday and for dinner from Wednesday to Sunday.

Mythai (84 Hereford St) serves authentic Thai cuisine and fans of Thai food will not be disappointed. *Sala Thai*, on the corner of Colombo and Kilmore Sts, is dowdy but cheap. The *Nattya Thai* (196 Hereford St) has an extensive menu with mains for around $12 to $14, and vegetarian selections for $10.

Chung Wah II (63 Worcester St) is an imposing place. This is just one of many Chinese restaurants.

La Bamba (☎ 355 3655), a South American, Cajun and Mexican restaurant on the corner of Bealey Ave and Papanui Rd in Carlton Courts, has mains from $20, up to $25 for the seafood jambalaya and tequila-infused ribeye fillet from Argentina.

South of the Border (834 Colombo St) is a reasonably priced Tex-Mex licensed restaurant.

Christchurch has a good selection of quality Italian restaurants. *Cafe Valentino* (☎ 377 1886, 813 Colombo St) is open daily from noon until late; dinner mains are around $20, less for pasta. Unfortunately, our dining experience here was ruined by the failure of management to eject noisy, aggressive people frequenting its bar, and general lack of consideration for patrons' comfort.

Spagalimi's Pizza (☎ 379 7469, 155 Victoria St) is a popular place that also does takeaways; a 12-slice is $15.95. There's another branch at 374 Riccarton Rd.

Saggio di Vino (185 Victoria St), on the corner of Bealey Ave, has a great wine selection, available by the glass, and light meals.

Sticky Fingers (☎ 366 6451) in the Clarendon Towers, Oxford Terrace, is a happy blend of NZ and Italian influences. It metamorphoses into a popular bar later in the night.

Bardelli's (☎ 353 0000, 98 Cashel St) specialises in Mediterranean food. It has blackboard and a la carte menus. The smoked salmon fettuccine is delectable ($14.50).

Death by Chocolate (☎ 365 7323, 209 Cambridge Terrace) tempts in Faustian fashion. This dessert restaurant has sinfully rich offerings for around $15.

Vegetarian *Gopal's* (143 Worcester St) is another of the Hare Krishna-run restaurants. It's open for lunch (from $3.50) on weekdays and dinner ($6) on Friday night.

The *Main Street Cafe & Bar* (☎ 365 0421, 840 Colombo St) serves exceptionally good vegan and vegetarian food. It's a relaxed and popular place with an open-air courtyard at the back. Imaginative main courses are around $10, the salads are good and the desserts mouthwatering. It's open from 10 am to late daily.

Dux de Lux is a very popular gourmet restaurant specialising in seafood but also features vegetarian taste treats. It's close to the Arts Centre, on Montreal St near Hereford St. There's an outdoor courtyard and a bar and brewery, with live music several nights a week. It's open from around 10 am until midnight.

Cafes The Arts Centre has some very pleasant cafes, including *Le Cafe* and the *Boulevard Bakehouse*, as well as more expensive dining options. Most of the chic cafes are on Oxford Terrace (see Restaurants earlier).

Coffee d'Fafo (137 Hereford St), open daily, was recommended by a reader who

DAVID WALL

Mad Cantabrian rugby fans

DAVID WALL

This is *not* white-water rafting – the Avon

DAVID WALL

Oxford Terrace in downtown Christchurch

DAVID WALL

Dunedin's historic old train station

A footbridge over the Hooker River, with Mt Sefton behind

Bienvenue á Akaroa!

Church of the Good Shepherd, Lake Tekapo

Alpenglow occurs from the reflections off snow-peaked mountains at sunset or sunrise – Mt Tasman

described themself as one of 'the fussiest and most hopelessly addicted drinkers of gourmet speciality coffees'.

Java Coffee House (☎ 366 0195) is another good cafe on the corner of High and Lichfield Sts.

Pub Food The *Oxford on Avon (☎ 379 7148, 794 Colombo St)* plays ye olde pub theme to the hilt and is in a lovely setting right by the river with an outside garden bar. It's popular for huge, hearty and cheap meals. Big English breakfasts are $10 and three-course dinner roasts are similarly oversized and cost $15. It's open daily from 6.30 am to midnight.

Other possibilities include the *Pegasus Arms (14 Oxford Terrace)* near the hospital, for a bistro lunch; *Winnie Bagoe's (83 Lichfield St)*, a lively hostelry serving pizza until 3 am; and the *Chancery Restaurant (98 Gloucester St)*, which features roasts and steaks at around $12.

Fast Food A good variety of food stalls is set up in Cathedral Square with benches and tables to eat at. *Cafe Cathedral*, in the shadow of Christchurch's centrepiece, is nothing special but it is definitely central.

The *Rice Box (78 Worcester St)* is a Japanese-style food bar which is always crammed to bursting point at lunchtime. The *Daily Grind (37 New Regent St)*, near the northern entry to the New Regent St Mall, is another popular lunchtime eatery with coffee, paninis and bagels.

There are several fast-food outlets on Manchester St between Cashel and Hereford Sts, including *McDonald's*, *Burger King* and *Dimitri's*.

Little India, on the New Regent St Mall near the corner of Gloucester St, has tandoori food and a good selection of economical vegetarian dishes such as *dhal makhani* (spicy lentils) for $12.

Topkapi (185 Manchester St) exudes the odours of an Istanbul back street and the Turkish dishes here are both filling and tasty.

The *Penang Noodle House (172 Manchester St)* is a no-frills place with good

Malaysian meals (around $6); it's open daily except Tuesday.

Barnaby John's, at the entrance to the Chancery Arcade, is an old-fashioned, not-too-tidy cheap eatery which churns out toasted sandwiches and bacon and egg breakfasts; few cellphones are heard here.

For delicious home-made ice cream check out the mobile van which is usually parked on Armagh St near Victoria Square.

In Shades Arcade, the **Shades Food Court** has a selection of food stalls; in the Cashel Plaza *(154 Cashel St)* there are cafes and an ever-reliable *Abra-Kebab;* and the *Riccarton Mall* has a wide variety of cafes and restaurants, open daily for lunch.

Entertainment

Bars, Music & Dancing Christchurch has a big selection of cafe-bars for a night on the town, and nightlife in this small city is very active on weekends.

Bailies at Warners on the Square is an old favourite. Smoke fills the room, the Guinness is carefully decanted into pint glasses, and snacks are left on the bar for patrons.

Di lusso (379 2133, 132 Oxford Tce), next door to the All Bar One dance bar, is a cigar bar and lounge in the Big Apple style.

Christchurch's liveliest area at night is around the Bridge of Remembrance where the Cashel Mall meets Oxford Terrace. Guys in check shirts and gangs of youths too young to drink cruise the mall, but inside the cafes and bars are very fashionable.

Backpackers like *Chat's Bar* in the Occidental (see Places to Stay earlier) because it's a good meeting place and the beer and food are cheap (pints are $2.50, and the barbecue/roast is $4/6). The outdoor section of the *bar* at the Stonehurst (see Places to Stay earlier) is also a popular backpacker haunt.

On the mall, *Bardelli's*, *Cafe Bleu* and *88 Bar* are popular with a more moneyed crowd. *The Bog* is a popular Irish bar which is crowded on weekends.

The Oxford Terrace conglomerate attracts the late-night crowd (see Places to Eat earlier).

Those in search of the seedy can head to the other end of the Mall and south to

Lichfield St in the red-light/bathhouse enclave. Polynesian techno and hip-hop clubs dominate.

The best place for aficionados of good blues music is the *Southern Blues Bar* on the corner of Madras and Tuam Sts. The bouncers are oversized, but it gets a mixed crowd of workers and the city's elite. At the corner of Cashel and Manchester Sts is *The Loaded Hog* (☎ 366 6674), with naturally brewed beers and piglet, piggyback and whole hog-sized meals. The popular *Lone Star* (26 Manchester St), near the corner of Dundas St, often has live music; Tex-Mex and Cajun meals are also served.

The Bard on Avon (☎ 377 1493), corner of Oxford Terrace and Gloucester St, has several English ales on tap and often features live entertainment.

The Club (☎ 377 1007, 88 Armagh St) is where you go if you haven't been there before. The food is excellent but expensive, and the staff attentive. The rack of lamb is highly recommended, as is the mussel entree.

For a good old-fashioned night out that lingers well into the 'wee' hours, *The Jolly Poacher* is opposite the casino on Victoria St. It's less pretentious than the chic *Tin Goose* nearby on the corner of Peterborough St.

Plenty of other pubs in the suburbs have bands, including the popular *Fat Ladies' Arms*, formerly Nancy's, on the corner of Riccarton and Hagley Aves.

In beachside Sumner are the *Salty Dog* (☎ 326 6609), a sports bar on the corner of Wakefield Ave and Nayland St, and the *Ruptured Duck* (4 Wakefield Ave), a popular pizzeria and bar.

Cinema & Performing Arts Dunedin may be the pub capital of the south but Christchurch is definitely the hub of the performing arts with excellent theatres and the vibrant Arts Centre.

The focus is the *town hall* (☎ 366 8899) on Kilmore St by the riverside, where you can hear a chamber or symphony orchestra.

The *James Hay Theatre* in the town hall and the *Theatre Royal* in Gloucester St are the centres of live theatre.

The *Court Theatre* (☎ 366 6992, 20 Worcester Blvd), in the Arts Centre, is the home of a very good professional theatre company. There are performances year round, from Samuel Beckett to *Cabaret*.

There's a big *cinema complex* in the old train station and the *Regent on Worcester* (☎ 377 8095) is at No 94.

Every Friday there are free *lunchtime concerts* in Cathedral Square.

Getting There & Away

Air Christchurch is the main international gateway to the South Island. For overseas airlines with offices in Christchurch see the Getting There & Away chapter.

Air New Zealand, the main domestic carrier, has an office (☎ 353 4899) at the Triangle Centre, 702 Colombo St. Daily direct flights go between Christchurch and Auckland, Blenheim, Dunedin, Hokitika, Invercargill, Mt Cook, Nelson, Queenstown, Te Anau, Timaru and Wellington, with connections to most other centres. It can also book Air Chatham flights to the Chatham Islands.

Ansett New Zealand (☎ 371 1185), on the corner of Worcester St and Oxford Terrace, has direct flights to Auckland, Dunedin, Invercargill, Palmerston North, Queenstown, Rotorua and Wellington.

Origin Pacific (☎ 0800-302 302) has daily flights to Nelson and Wellington, Napier, and to Auckland (except Saturday). There are connections to other centres.

Bus InterCity (☎ 379 9020) is the main South Island carrier and buses depart from 123 Worcestor St, between the cathedral and Manchester St. To the north, buses go to Kaikoura (three hours), Blenheim (5 hours) and Picton (5½ hours), with connections to Nelson. Daily buses go to Queenstown (10½ hours) via Mt Cook (5½ hours), with connections to Wanaka. To the south, three daily buses run along the coast via the towns of the SH1 to Dunedin (six hours), with connections to Invercargill, Te Anau and Queenstown.

The West Coast is sadly neglected by the major bus companies, but Coast to Coast Shuttle (☎ 0800-800 847) and Alpine Coach

& Courier (☎ 0800-274 888) have daily services to Greymouth or Hokitika, both $35, via Arthur's Pass. East West (☎ 0800-500 251) goes to Westport.

Myriad shuttle buses run to most destinations including Picton, Queenstown, Wanaka, Dunedin, Akaroa, Hanmer Springs and points in between. See under those towns for details. Most can be booked at the visitor centre or the bus information kiosk on Cathedral Square. See the Getting Around chapter for details on the backpacker buses.

Train The train station (☎ 0800-802 802) is on Clarence St in Addington, some way out of the city, and there is a free morning bus service; ask at the visitor centre.

Trains run daily each way between Christchurch and Picton. The *Coastal Pacific* departs Christchurch at 7.30 am and arrives at Picton at 12.50 pm, allowing plenty of time to connect with the 1.30 am *Interislander* ferry to Wellington. There is also a daily *Southerner* service each way between Christchurch and Invercargill via Dunedin.

The *TranzAlpine Express* train runs daily between Christchurch and Greymouth via Arthur's Pass (see the boxed text 'The *TranzAlpine*' in The West Coast chapter).

Hitching It's pretty good hitching on the whole but Christchurch to Dunedin can be a long day, and tends to get harder further south until you approach Dunedin. Catch a Templeton bus (No 8 or 25) to get out of the city. Christchurch to Picton can be done in a day, although there can be long waits. Hitching north, bus No 1 or 4 will get you to Redwood on SH74, a couple of kilometres before it joins SH1.

To hitch west take bus No 8 (Yaldhurst) – then keep your fingers crossed; it can be a long, hard haul, as much as two days. Pick up the train along the way if you become despondent. The first part is easily hitched, but once you leave SH1 it gets harder to find a lift.

Getting Around

To/From the Airport Christchurch airport is 11km north-west of the city centre;

it has been considerably upgraded and boasts excellent facilities. Airport banks change money.

Information centres (☎ 358 5029) are in both the domestic and international terminals. Customs staff here are zealots and are seemingly suspicious of people carrying backpacks. Departure tax on international flights is $25.

The public bus to the airport ($2.70) leaves from Cathedral Square. On weekdays buses leave every half-hour from 7.10 am to 6.40 pm, then every hour until 9.40 pm. They run every hour from 8.25 am to 9.25 pm on Saturday and until 7.25 pm on Sunday.

Door-to-door airport shuttle bus companies, such as Super Shuttle (☎ 365 5655) and Carrington (☎ 352 6369), operate 24 hours and charge from $8 per person. A taxi to or from the airport will cost about $20.

Bus Most city buses are operated by Canride and run from Cathedral Square. Unlike most NZ urban bus services, Christchurch's service is good, cheap and well organised.

The Shuttle is a free service around the central city (and as far south as Moorhouse Ave) with about 20 pick-up points; during the day (8 am to 7 pm Monday to Thursday, until 9.30 pm Friday and Saturday and 6 pm Sunday) it runs every 10 minutes. The night route is every 15 minutes (until midnight Friday and Saturday) and takes in the casino.

For bus information phone Bus Info (☎ 366 8855). Fares are $0.90, $1.80 and a maximum of $2.70. An all-day Big Red Bus Pass is $5 ($10 family). Pick up the pamphlet for the useful bus information.

The City Circuit bus (☎ 385 5386) has two circuits (Plains and Port), both leaving from the visitor centre and costing $25 for eight hours of travel or $15 on one circuit only. Plains Circuit buses leave in the morning and take in Willowbank, the International Antarctic Centre, Air Force World and Mona Vale. The afternoon Port Circuit runs to Lyttelton via the Gondola and other points of interest.

Car & Motorcycle The major rental companies all have offices in Christchurch, as do numerous smaller local companies. The *Yellow Pages* lists over 50 operators. Competition keeps the prices down and, though not as good as Auckland, Christchurch is the best place in the South Island to rent a car. Operators with national networks often want cars to be shifted from Christchurch to Auckland because most renters travel in the opposite direction. Special rates may apply. Christchurch is also a good place to rent a motor home. For reliable national rental companies see the Getting Around chapter.

Local rental companies include Pegasus Rental Cars (☎ 365 1100), 127 Peterborough St; Renny Rentals (☎ 366 6790), 156 Tuam St; and Shoestring Rentals (☎ 385 3647), 19 Bideford Place, Burwood.

Wheels ChCh – Sales (☎ 366 4855), 20 Manchester St, has cars for hire and also has a sale and buy-back scheme.

Motorcycles can be hired from Eric Wood Motorcycles (☎ 366 0129) at 35 Manchester St for around $70 a day for a new bike.

Taxi Christchurch has plenty of taxis. Catch them at ranks (there's one on the north-west side of Cathedral Square) or phone: Blue Star (☎ 379 9799), First Direct (☎ 377 5555) or Gold Band (☎ 379 5795). Flag fall is $1.90, each kilometre costs $1.70, waiting time is $0.60 per minute and a $1 airport surcharge applies.

Bicycle Trailblazers (☎ 366 6033) at 86 Worcester Boulevard and Cyclone Cycles (☎ 332 9588) at 245 Colombo St rent out bikes for $5 an hour or $20 a day; both have good mountain bikes.

LYTTELTON
pop 3100
To the south-east of Christchurch are the prominent Port Hills and, behind them, Lyttelton Harbour, Christchurch's port.

Christchurch's first settlers landed at Lyttelton in 1850 and then made the historic trek over the hills to their new promised land.

Only 12km from Christchurch, Lyttelton is an attractive small port town, with historic buildings and cafe-bars popular with

Christchurch day-trippers on weekends. It makes a good day trip, especially if you have a car and go via the scenic **Port Hills**. Drive along the narrow Summit Rd of the hills for breathtaking views of the azure waters of the harbour, the golden brown sweep of the bare hillsides and vistas of Christchurch and the Southern Alps. The route is outlined in the free *Port Hills Drive* pamphlet. Alternatively, Lyttelton can be reached more quickly from Christchurch by a road tunnel, an impressive piece of engineering with gleaming tiles reminiscent of a huge, elongated public toilet.

The Lyttelton Information Office (☎ 328 9093) is at 20 Oxford St. Pick up a copy of the self-guided historic walk pamphlet.

The **Lyttelton Museum** on Gladstone Quay has colonial displays, a maritime gallery and an Antarctic gallery. It is open from 2 to 4 pm on weekends, also from Tuesday to Thursday in summer.

On Reserve Terrace, the **Timeball Station** is one of the few remaining such places in the world. Built in 1876, it once fulfilled an important maritime duty. Daily for 58 years, the huge timeball was hoisted on a mast and then dropped at exactly 1 pm, Greenwich Mean Time, allowing ships in the harbour to set their clocks and thereby accurately calculate longitude. It's open from 10 am to 5 pm daily ($2.50, children $1).

Activities
Most popular are the **harbour cruises**. Lyttelton Harbour Cruises (☎ 328 8368) operates a cruise ($8, children $4) as well as a passenger service from B Jetty in Lyttelton to Diamond Harbour ($7.20 return), Quail Island ($9) and Ripapa Island Historic Reserve ($15) throughout the day in summer (weekends only in winter). Book at the information office. Ripapa Island was the prison for the WWI German 'sea raider' Count Felix von Luckner.

Canterbury Sea Tours (☎ 326 5607) has a jet-boat style craft departing from Lyttelton for harbour tours that also visit pods of Hector's dolphins ($35). There are also sailing tours (eg, Temptation Charters and *Fox II*); ask at the information office.

Phoenix Paragliding (☎ 326 7634) sets sail from the Gondola/Summit Rd directly above Lyttelton, and Nimbus (☎ 328 8383) is also based in Lyttelton. Tandem flights start from $95.

Places to Stay & Eat
Tunnel Vision Backpackers (☎/fax 328 7576, 44 London St) is only half an hour by bus from Christchurch if you want to stay out of the city. This attractive, refurbished old building is right in the centre, close to the harbour. The eight-bed dorm costs $14 per person, four-bed rooms are $16, and twins/doubles are $36/40.

B&Bs include *Randolf House (☎ 328 8877, 49 Sumner Rd)* with attic doubles from $80 to $110; the nearby *Dockside Accommodation (☎ 328 7344, 22 Sumner Rd),* which has rooms with decks for $75; and *Shonagh O'Hagan's (☎ 328 8577, 16 Godley Quay)* with singles/doubles for $65/95.

Lyttelton has plenty of dining choices for lunch or dinner, most of them on the main street, London St. This was once the scene of the Great Fire of Lyttelton, which on 24 October 1870 demolished the business area of town. Now the only thing burning along this street is (occasionally) the food.

Along London St are Volcano Cafe, Harvester's Cafe and Deluxe Cafe. The *Volcano (☎ 328 7077)* is a quaint place with artwork adorning the walls and the quirkiest toilet entry you are likely to see. Relax with a drink or enjoy a good range of food.

The *Lava Bar,* next door, erupts every night at 5 pm and the Black Mac flows.

Down on the waterfront (just off Norwich Quay), *Le Bistro* adds a touch of class to a street well accustomed to the nocturnal roaming of sailors. It's open from Wednesday to Saturday from 5.30 pm.

Entertainment
For a drink with a view try the *Wunderbar,* rather hidden and with a convoluted stairway entry through a doorway on London St. The *Backroom* is a music venue a couple of fire escapes away; the Wunder-barbarians will direct you there. And for those after Irish music, there's the *Harp of Erin* on London St.

Getting There & Away
Bus No 28 from Cathedral Square goes to Lyttelton every half-hour (hourly on weekends) via the road tunnel (12km). Alternatively, drive via the bayside suburb of Sumner and Evans Pass (19km) or head straight down Colombo St from the square and go up over Dyers Pass and along scenic Summit Rd (22km).

From Lyttelton by car you can continue around Lyttelton Harbour and eventually on to Akaroa. This is a very scenic, in parts treacherous, and much longer route than via SH75 between Christchurch and Akaroa.

BANKS PENINSULA
Near Christchurch, Banks Peninsula makes an interesting side trip. A change from the flat area around the city itself, this hilly peninsula was formed by two giant volcanic eruptions. Small harbours such as Le Bons, Pigeon and Little Akaloa Bays radiate out from the peninsula's centre giving it a cogwheel shape. The historic town of Akaroa is the main highlight.

The peninsula has a chequered history of settlement. James Cook first sighted it in 1770 and thought it was an island. He named it after naturalist Sir Joseph Banks. The Ngai Tahu tribe, who then occupied the peninsula, were attacked at the fortified Onawe *pa* by the Ngati Toa chief Te Rauparaha (see Kapiti Coast in the Wellington Region chapter) in 1831 and suffered a severe decline in numbers.

A few years later, in 1836, the British established a whaling station at Peraki. The most notable settlement was at Akaroa, where French immigrants arrived in 1840, spurring the British to annex all NZ under the Treaty of Waitangi, signed just before the arrival of the French settlers.

The French did settle at Akaroa, but in 1849 the French land claim was sold to the New Zealand Company and the following year the French were joined by a large group of British settlers.

Originally heavily forested, the land was cleared for timber, and dairy farming, later supplanted by sheep farming, became the main industry of the peninsula.

CANTERBURY

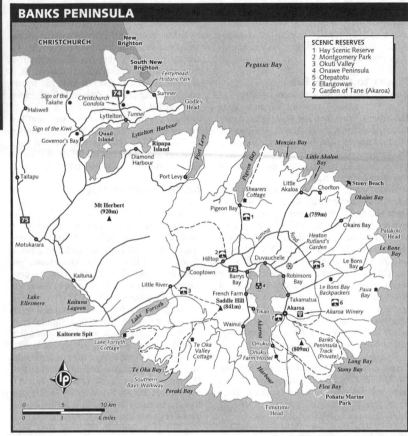

BANKS PENINSULA

SCENIC RESERVES
1 Hay Scenic Reserve
2 Montgomery Park
3 Okuti Valley
4 Onawe Peninsula
5 Otepatotu
6 Ellangowan
7 Garden of Tane (Akaroa)

Akaroa
pop 650

Akaroa, meaning 'Long Harbour' in Maori,
is the site of the first French settlement in
NZ. This charming town, 82km from
Christchurch, lies on a scenic harbour and
strives to re-create the feel of a French
provincial village.

In 1838 Jean Langlois, a whaling captain,
negotiated the sale of Banks Peninsula from
local Maori and returned to France to form
a trading company. With the backing of the
French government, 63 settlers emigrated in
1840 under escort of the warship *L'Aube,*
but only days before they arrived panicked
British officials sent their own warship to
raise the flag at Akaroa, claiming British
sovereignty under the Treaty of Waitangi.
Had the settlers arrived two years earlier,
the South Island may well have become a
French colony.

The original French colonists stayed on
and have clearly stamped their mark. Streets
(Rues Lavaud, Balguerie, Jolie) and houses
(Langlois-Eteveneaux) have French names,
and descendants of the original French settlers reside in the town. It is a delight just to
walk the streets, and to visit the delightful

gardens (such as famous Heaton Rutland Plants). Akaroa is a popular day trip from Christchurch and is also great for a longer stay.

Information The Akaroa Information Centre (☎ 304 8600, @ akaroa.info@ clear.net.nz), in the post shop building on the corner of Rues Lavaud and Balguerie, is open from 10 am to 4 pm daily (to 5 pm over summer). Check out their Web site (www.akaroa.com) for more information.

The ANZ bank has EFTPOS facilities but there's no ATM and the bank is closed weekends, so bring sufficient cash.

Things to See & Do The **Akaroa Museum** on Rue Lavaud has a 15-minute audiovisual on the history of the Banks Peninsula, and assorted colonial memorabilia. The old courthouse and **Langlois-Eteveneaux Cottage**, one of the oldest houses in NZ and partly fabricated in France, are part of the museum complex, as is the tiny **Customs House** by Daly's Wharf. The museum is open from 10.30 am to 4.30 pm daily, until 4 pm in winter ($3, children/family $1/7).

It is a short walk via either a forest trail or paved road to the **Old French Cemetery**, but the gravestones were removed in 1925 and a rather dull memorial marks the spot.

Continue further up L'Aube Hill for views across town.

For an excellent **walking tour**, pick up a copy of the *Akaroa Historic Village Walk* booklet ($3.50). The tour starts at Waeckerle Cottage at the north end of town and finishes at the lighthouse. The walk takes in all the wonderful old wooden buildings and churches that give the town so much of its character.

Advertised as 'four nights, four days, four beaches, four bays', the **Banks Peninsula Track** is a two- to four-day walk on a private walking track from Onuku Farm Hostel to the Mt Vernon Lodge across private farmland and then around the dramatic coastline of Banks Peninsula. It costs $120/140 off season/summer, including transport from Akaroa and hut accommodation. The two-day option is $75. Book in advance (☎ 304 7612); the Web site is at www.bankstrack.co.nz.

Another private track is Le Bons Bay Track (☎ 304 8533).

Daily **harbour cruises** on the *Canterbury Cat* depart from the Main Wharf at 11 am and 1.30 pm (1.30 pm only from April to November; $27, children $13). Buy tickets from the office (☎ 304 7641) on the wharf. The same company has outer bays tours at 2 pm on the *Canterbury Clipper,* an inflatable

ROSS BARNETT

A speedy backpacker walks past the Langlois-Eteveneaux house in Akaroa

CANTERBURY

naiad, from where you may see Hector's dolphins, little blue penguins and NZ fur seals. The cost is $35 (children $20). Dolphin-swimming tours are also offered at noon ($65, children $45).

Dolphin Experience (☎ 304 7207) also has popular 'swim with the dolphins' tours ($68, children $47, watching only $29).

A quiet, peaceful way to cruise the waters around Akaroa is by **boat**. Akaroa Boat Hire (☎ 304 8758) hires sea kayaks, canoes, row boats, paddle boats and motor boats.

There are trips to Pohatu Marine Reserve at Flea Bay to see **yellow-eyed penguins** and other birds ($30, $10 children); ask at the information centre.

Places to Stay Most of the places to stay on the Banks Peninsula are in or near Akaroa, but other possibilities are scattered around the various bays.

Akaroa *Akaroa Holiday Park (☎ 304 7471)* on Morgan Rd, off Old Coach Rd, has fine views. Sites cost $20 for two, and cabins are from $42.

Chez lu Mer Backpackers (☎ 304 7024, 🅰 chez_la_mer@clear.net.nz), on Rue Lavaud, is the one backpackers. It's very central, and is in a small historic house with a beautiful garden. Dorms are $16 per person, while singles/twins/doubles are $25/38/40. *Bon Accord (☎ 304 7782, 57 Rue Lavaud)* is another friendly backpackers in the heart of town ($15 per person).

Mt Vernon Lodge (☎/fax 304 7180), about 2km from town on Rue Balguerie, is a combination hostel and guest lodge. Rates are $50 for two in a five-bed unit if you supply your own bedding. Chalets are from $70 a double. There's a pool and a large comfortable common room with an open fire. In the hostel, beds are $15 per person. Horse trekking is available ($40 for two hours).

The *Madeira Hotel (☎ 304 7009),* on Rue Lavaud, has comfortable pub rooms with shared facilities for $22.50/50 for singles/doubles.

The *Oinako Lodge (☎ 304 8787, 99 Beach Rd),* Web site: www.oinako.co.nz, is a fabulous retreat in a grand old building

near the beach with B&B from $155 to $200 for two.

Two other perfect getaways are *Maison des Fleurs (☎ 304 7804, 6 Church St),* with B&B doubles for $220, and *La Belle Villa (☎ 304 7084, 113 Rue Jolie),* which has a pool ($85 to $100 a double). The information centre has details of other B&Bs and farmstays, many with lovingly tended gardens.

Cheaper motels include *La Rive Motel (☎ 304 7651, 1 Rue Lavaud),* with units for $60/80 for two in winter/summer, and the *Wai-iti Motel (☎ 304 7292, 64 Rue Jolie),* on the waterfront, with rooms from $65 to $95 off peak. The *Driftwood Motel (☎ 304 7484, 56 Rue Jolie)* and *L'Hotel (☎ 304 7559, 75 Beach Rd)* have units for two for around $100.

Loch Hill Motel (☎ 304 7195) is 1km north of Akaroa. The six country-style stone cottages are set in beautiful gardens ($120 for two).

Peninsula The *Duvauchelle Reserve Board Motor Camp (☎ 304 5777),* 8km before Akaroa off SH75 on Seafield Rd, has tent and powered sites for $8 per person.

Le Bons Bay Motor Camp (☎ 304 8533), on Le Bons Bay Valley Rd about 22km from Akaroa, has powered sites for $20 and cabins for $45 for two.

The *Okains Bay Domain (☎ 304 8635)* also has tent sites, kitchen and shower facilities. The nearby Okains Bay museum has a sacred 15th-century god stick, an Akaroa *heitiki* and a war canoe ($4, children $1).

Onuku Farm Hostel (☎ 304 7612), 6km south of Akaroa at Onuku, is on a 400-hectare sheep farm. It's $15 in the house, $10 in summer huts or $8 for camp sites.

Le Bons Bay Backpackers (☎ 304 8582) is out of the way – on the southern side of the road about 6km before Le Bons Bay. The farmhouse has commanding views down the valley. It's $15 and $16 in dorms and $36 in doubles, all including breakfast. An evening meal costs $9. Book ahead as places are limited. The owners will pick you up from Akaroa.

The *Shearers Cottage (☎ 304 6800)* sleeps 14. It's in charming little Annandale

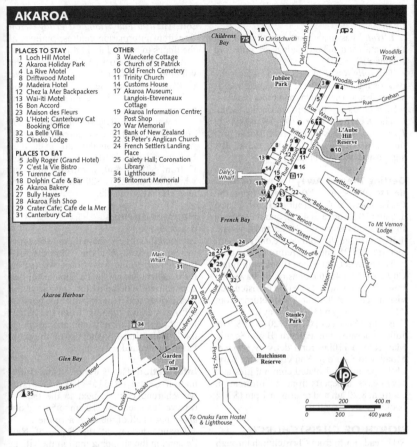

AKAROA

PLACES TO STAY
1 Loch Hill Motel
2 Akaroa Holiday Park
4 La Rive Motel
8 Driftwood Motel
9 Madeira Hotel
12 Chez la Mer Backpackers
13 Wai-iti Motel
16 Bon Accord
23 Maison des Fleurs
30 L'Hotel; Canterbury Cat
   Booking Office
32 La Belle Villa
33 Oinako Lodge

PLACES TO EAT
5 Jolly Roger (Grand Hotel)
7 C'est la Vie Bistro
15 Turenne Cafe
18 Dolphin Cafe & Bar
26 Akaroa Bakery
27 Bully Hayes
28 Akaroa Fish Shop
29 Crater Cafe; Cafe de la Mer
31 Canterbury Cat

OTHER
3 Waeckerle Cottage
6 Church of St Patrick
10 Old French Cemetery
11 Trinity Church
14 Customs House
17 Akaroa Museum;
   Langlois-Eteveneaux
   Cottage
19 Akaroa Information Centre;
   Post Shop
20 War Memorial
21 Bank of New Zealand
22 St Peter's Anglican Church
24 French Settlers Landing
   Place
25 Gaiety Hall; Coronation
   Library
34 Lighthouse
35 Britomart Memorial

on the shores of picturesque Pigeon Bay ($14 per person).

Excellent peninsula farmstays include *Kahikatea* (☎ 304 7400) at Wainui; *Kawatea* (☎ 304 8621), an Edwardian villa at Okains Bay; and *Paua Bay* (☎ 304 8511). The information centre has more listings.

Places to Eat The biggest and most fashionable selection of eateries is on Beach Road near the main wharf. Cheap eats are scarce, but the *Akaroa Bakery* is a pleasant and cheap spot for pastries, filled rolls and coffee from 7.30 am to 4 pm.

The *Turenne Cafe*, across from the Akaroa Information Centre, is good for breakfast (until 11 am) and reasonably priced lunches.

C'est la Vie Bistro (33 Rue Lavaud) caters for vegetarians, and has a wide selection of French cuisine and a BYO licence.

The *Dolphin Cafe & Bar* (6 Rue Balguerie), by the beach, has expensive fish and steak dishes.

More salubrious restaurants on Beach Rd include the chic and sunny *Bully Hayes* at No 57 with a changing blackboard menu, coffees and a good bar. *Cafe de la Mer* at

CANTERBURY

No 71 is licensed and has seafood and family meals.

L'Hotel has a pleasant bar overlooking the water and a better class of pub fare (mains $17 to $21).

The *Jolly Roger* in the Grand Hotel is the pick of the crop for good-value seafood. It serves fish, garlic prawns and other seafood; lobster occasionally crops up on the menu.

The *Akaroa Winery* (☎ 304 8990, 59 Long Bay Rd) has superb food (local produce and wines) and stunning views. It's signposted near Takamatua.

Getting There & Away The Akaroa Shuttle (☎ 0800-500 929) departs from the Christchurch & Canterbury Visitor Centre at 9 and 10.30 am and 4 pm, and the Akaroa Information Centre at 8.30 am and 2.15 and 4.30 pm in summer (only once daily in winter). It's $15/25 one way/return (1½ hours).

The French Connection (book with InterCity on ☎ 366 4556 extension 1) leaves the InterCity depot at 8.45 am (the Christchurch visitor centre at 9.10 am) and returns from Akaroa at 3.30 pm ($20 one way).

Bayline Services (☎ 304 7207), 108 Rue Jolie, operates the Eastern Bays Scenic Mail Run, a 110km rural delivery service, Monday to Saturday. You visit remote parts of the peninsula, isolated communities and seven bays. It departs from the information centre at 8.20 am and returns at 1 pm ($20); bookings are essential.

NORTH OF CHRISTCHURCH

SH1 heads north from Christchurch through Woodend to the Waipara Valley. At Waipara, 57km north of Christchurch, SH1 splits. The eastern fork goes on to Kaikoura as SH1, while the more western highway, SH7, heads via Hurunui and Culverden to the Red Post Corner where it too splits. The westerly choice leads to the Lewis Pass, Maruia Springs, and eventually either the West Coast or Nelson. If you proceed north from Red Post Corner you will reach the whale-watch capital of Kaikoura either by the inland or coastal routes. About 23km from Red Post, on the Lewis Pass route, there is a right-hand turn from SH7 to Hanmer

Springs, a well-known thermal area and resort. The *Hurunui Triangle Heritage Trail*, free from information centres, outlines all the things to see and do in this region.

The scenic Waipara Valley has a dozen **wineries**, all outlined in the free *Wineries & Wine Trail*. Sample a Mountford pinot noir or prize-winning Canterbury House sauvignon blanc.

At Waipara the *Waipara Sleepers* (☎ 314 6003, ✉ waipara.sleepers@inet.net.nz) has novel accommodation; the 'fare' in the four-bed guard's vans is $16 a person, a double is from $35 to $50, a railway hut with wheelchair access is $20 for a single, and tent sites are available.

Hanmer Springs
pop 750

Hanmer Springs, the main thermal resort on the South Island, is about 10km off SH7, the highway to the West Coast. Apart from the excellent hot pools, it's popular for outdoor activities including forest walks, horse treks, river and lake fishing, jet-boating, rafting, bungy jumping from the Waiau ferry bridge, skiing in winter and golfing at the 18-hole course. Visitors swell the population year-round.

Information The Hurunui Visitor Information Centre (☎ 315 7128), Web site: www.hurunui.com, is next to the thermal reserve. It's open from 10 am to 5 pm daily, and it books all of the local activities.

Change money at the Bank of New Zealand in the shopping mall in the village from 10.15 am to 2 pm Monday, Wednesday and Friday. There are no ATMs in town.

Thermal Reserve Hanmer Springs has been renowned for its thermal waters for over 100 years. Legend has it that the springs are a piece of the fires of Tamatea dropped from the sky after an eruption of Mt Ngauruhoe in the North Island. Centuries later it has metamorphosed into the excellent Hanmer Springs Thermal Reserve (☎ 315 7511).

Open from 10 am to 9 pm daily, hot spring water mixes with fresh water to produce

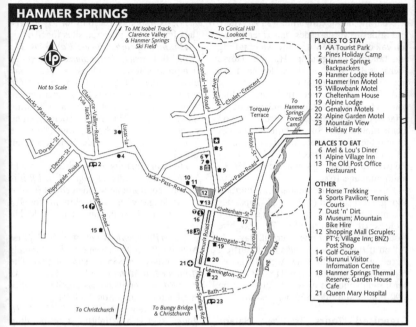

HANMER SPRINGS

To Mt Isobel Track,
Clarence Valley
& Hanmer Springs
Ski Field

To Conical Hill
Lookout

Not to Scale

To
Hanmer
Springs
Forest
Camp

Torquay
Terrace

To Christchurch

To Bungy Bridge
& Christchurch

PLACES TO STAY
1 AA Tourist Park
2 Pines Holiday Camp
5 Hanmer Springs Backpackers
9 Hanmer Lodge Hotel
10 Hanmer Inn Motel
15 Willowbank Motel
17 Cheltenham House
19 Alpine Lodge
20 Genalvon Motels
22 Alpine Garden Motel
23 Mountain View Holiday Park

PLACES TO EAT
6 Mel & Lou's Diner
11 Alpine Village Inn
13 The Old Post Office Restaurant

OTHER
3 Horse Trekking
4 Sports Pavilion; Tennis Courts
7 Dust 'n' Dirt
8 Museum; Mountain Bike Hire
12 Shopping Mall (Scruples; PT's; Village Inn; BNZ) Post Shop
14 Golf Course
16 Hurunui Visitor Information Centre
18 Hanmer Springs Thermal Reserve; Garden House Cafe
21 Queen Mary Hospital

pools of varying temperatures. There are 're-laxer' pools, landscaped rock pools, private pools, a freshwater 25m pool, sauna and steam room, a toddlers pool, massage facilities and a restaurant ($8, children $4, day pass $9). Per half-hour, private pools are $13 for two and the sauna or steam room is $13 per person.

Activities There are two main **skiing** areas near Hanmer Springs. Hanmer Springs Field is the closest, 27km from Hanmer, and Lyford is 75km away. They are not nearly as expensive as the larger resorts (see Skiing in the Activities chapter). Heliski & Heliboard (☎ 0800-888 308) takes you to exhilarating runs on the Crimea and St James ranges ($395/650 for half/full day).

The *Hanmer Forest Recreation* pamphlet outlines a number of pleasant **walks** near the town, mostly through exotic forest. The easy Woodland Walk starts from Jollies Pass Rd, 1km from the town, and goes

through Douglas fir, poplar and redwood stands. It joins the Majuba Walk, which leads to Conical Hill Lookout and then back to Conical Hill Rd – about one hour all up. The information centre has details of longer tramps and mountain-biking trails in the area, including Lake Sumner Forest Park.

Thrillseekers Canyon (☎ 315 7046) is Hanmer Springs' adrenaline centre, and is the closest to Christchurch for **bungy jumping**, here off the Waiau ferry bridge where it crosses the river of the same name. It costs $89 to hurl yourself from this bridge (37m high). **Jet-boating** ($60) and **white-water rafting** ($60) on grade II to III water are also offered at the Thrillseekers Canyon centre. It's next to the bridge where the Hanmer Springs turn-off meets SH7 and operates from 9 am to 5 pm.

Rainbow Horse Trekking (☎ 315 7444) at The Stables, Jacks Pass Rd, takes **horse treks** around Hanmer costing from $25 for one hour to $90 for a full day.

A variety of other exciting activities are offered, including **canyoning** ($39), where you slide down cascades and river pools, **fun yak canoeing** ($60), white-water rafting and **tandem paragliding**. Hurunui Horse Treks (☎ 314 4204) in Hawarden has treks from a half-day to eight days.

A fun way to see the surrounding countryside is on a **four-wheel motorbike safari**. After introductory instruction, you tackle the trails on Suzuki farm quad bikes up into the hills or along the river for magnificent views. Backtrax (☎ 315 7684) takes the two-/four-hour trips which cost $75/110 (minimum age 16).

This region is very popular for **mountain biking**. Dust 'n' Dirt (☎ 315 7233) operates two-hour guided trips for $19 and a full-day Molesworth Station ride for $75. Bike hire costs from $9/25 for one hour/full day.

And if two to four wheels don't suffice, there's always eight. The Argo 8WDs of Alpine Argo Adventures (☎ 315 7387) lumber through and beside the Waiau River on a 90-minute fun ride ($60 per person).

Organised Tours Trailways Safaris (☎ 315 7401) has trips to Molesworth Station, the largest farm in NZ (supporting the country's largest cattle herd), for $58 for a half-day and $98 for a full-day tour (lunch is provided on the latter). Harley tours and other farm tours are available – contact the information centre.

Places to Stay The *Mountain View Holiday Park* (☎ 315 7113) on the southern edge of town has tent/powered sites at $18/20, a variety of cabins at $35 to $45 and fully equipped tourist flats at $59 to $68; prices are for two.

The *AA Tourist Park* (☎ 315 7112) on Jacks Pass Rd, 3km from the town centre, is the best equipped. Tent/powered sites cost $16/18 for two, good cabins are $40 and tourist flats $58; AA members get a discount.

The *Pines Holiday Camp* (☎ 315 7152), also on Jacks Pass Rd, next to the golf course, has tent/powered sites for $16/18, cabins for $36 for two and motels for $56.

The *Hanmer River Holiday Park* (☎ 315 7111), 6km south, has cabins for $39, tourist flats for $49 and powered sites for $16.

Hanmer Springs Forest Camp (☎ 315 7202, ✉ hanmer.forest.camp@xtra.co.nz), in a pretty setting on Jollies Pass Rd 2.8km east of the village, has dozens of old forestry workers' cabins for $14 per person, and a large self-contained lodge costing $20 per person. This YHA associated camp caters mostly to school groups, but one kitchen is always set aside for independent travellers.

Hanmer Springs Backpackers (☎ 315 7196, fax 315 7520, 41 Conical Hill Rd) is a small, comfortable wooden chalet (a winter ski lodge) with two bunkrooms for $15 per person ($18 with linen) and one double for $36.

The *Willowbank Motel* (☎ 315 7211) on Argelins Rd is the cheapest of the motels with units from $55 to $65 for two. The *Hanmer Inn Motel* (☎ 315 7516, 16 Jacks Pass Rd) is central and has excellent studio/ one-bedroom units from $79/95.

Scenic View Motels (☎ 315 7281, 10 Amuri Ave) is a delightful stone building with two- and three-bedroom apartments from $89 for doubles. The *Alpine Garden Motel* (☎ 315 7332, 3 Leamington St) is another good motel with units from $79 to $115.

The *Alpine Lodge* (☎ 315 7311, 9 Harrogate St) has the zenith of luxury in its tower units (which have circular beds and spa baths); these cost a cool $180. Other units are from $75 to $95 for two.

The *Hanmer Lodge Hotel* (☎ 315 7021) is a grand old resort hotel which has just been extensively renovated (it needed it!). It wasn't quite finished when we got there; ask at the desk for prices.

Cheltenham House (☎ 315 7545) is a superb B&B with beautiful rooms for $100/130 including a substantial breakfast. All rooms have en suite and the guest lounge has a billiard table.

Glenalvon Motels (☎ 315 7475, ✉ glenalvon@xtra.co.nz), Amuri Rd, is also in a restored house and has B&B from $79 to $125 for two.

Places to Eat *Mel & Lou's Diner* is great for takeaways or a sit-down light meal, and the *Hanmer Bakery* is handy for those rushing out to one of the activities.

The shopping mall has a selection of cafes for coffee or light meals including the *Village Plus* for breakfasts and *PT's*, open daily, for breakfast and pizzas.

Scruples, also in the mall, is one of the most upmarket places with mains from $9 to $19 and desserts from $3. It is usually open late when all else shuts early with a bang.

The *Garden House Cafe* in the hot pools complex, recently revamped, has snacks and wine-bar dining in pleasant surrounds.

The Old Post Office is one of the best restaurants in town and serves tasty NZ fare, but mains will set you back around $25. Noted for its beef and lamb dishes, it is open daily for dinner.

The *Alpine Village Inn*, near the mall on Jacks Pass Rd, is the local boozer and has reasonably priced bistro meals from $11 to $15.

Getting There & Away Hanmer Connection (☎ 315 7575, 0800-377 378) runs daily between Hanmer Springs and Christchurch ($22; two hours), and also goes three days a week to Kaikoura ($25; two hours). Lazerline (☎ 315 7128) picks up in Hanmer Springs on its daily service to Nelson and Christchurch.

Ski shuttles run to Mt Lyford in winter; it is $20/15 for adults/children.

White Star and East West buses from Christchurch to the West Coast stop at the Hanmer turn-off, but the junction is 10km from town.

Hanmer Springs to the West Coast

SH7 continues west from the Hanmer Springs turn-off to Lewis Pass, Maruia Springs and Springs Junction. This is a beautiful route but, lying at the northern end of the Southern Alps, the **Lewis Pass** (907m) is not as steep or the forest as dense as the routes through the Arthur's and Haast Passes. The forest near Lewis Pass is mainly red and silver beech, though the kowhai trees which grow along the river terraces are spectacular in spring.

The Lewis Pass area has a number of interesting walks – pick up the *Lewis Pass Region* pamphlet and the *Lake Sumner Forest Park* Infomap. Most of the tracks pass through beech forest. Snowcapped mountains form the backdrop and there are lakes, alpine tarns and mountain rivers. The most popular tramps are those around Lake Sumner in the Lake Sumner Forest Park and the St James Walkway in the Lewis Pass National Reserve. Subalpine conditions apply – contact DOC in Hanmer Springs (☎ 315 7154) for advice and information before heading off.

Maruia Springs is 69km from the Hanmer turn-off. The *Maruia Springs Thermal Resort* (☎ 523 8840) has natural thermal water pumped into a sex-segregated Japanese bathhouse and outdoor rock pools that are magic in winter when the snowflakes drift down while you relax in the hot water. The complex is open from 9 am to 9 pm ($6, children $4). Private spa units (open from 11 am to 5 pm) cost $20 per hour. Accommodation at the resort ranges from the run-down backpackers costing $26.50 per person to good hotel units from $105 to $140 (includes entry to the pools and bathhouse). The resort has a licensed cafe and bar.

From Maruia the road continues to Springs Junction where it splits. SH65 heads north to SH6 and on to Nelson. SH7 continues west to Reefton, then down the Grey Valley to Greymouth and the West Coast.

In Springs Junction, *Springs Junction Alpine Inn* (☎ 523 8813) has budget rooms for $30/50 for singles/twins, and motel units for $74 a double.

There are DOC *camping grounds* in the area, including: Marble Hill, 6.5km east of Springs Junction (start of the Lake Daniells walk), and Deer Valley in Lewis Pass, 25km east of Springs Junction.

At Maruia, about 20km north of Springs Junction on SH65, *Reids Store Backpacker* (☎ 523 8869) has bunk beds for $15 and doubles and twins for $38.

CANTERBURY

Kaikoura
pop 3850

This small town, 183km north of Christchurch on SH1, is a mecca for wildlife enthusiasts. Once just a sleepy little fishing town noted mainly for its crayfish (lobster) – Kaikoura means 'To Eat Crayfish'. Then, during Christmas 1987, Nature Watch Charters began whale-watching trips, the first such commercial operation in NZ. The tours quickly became famous and put Kaikoura on the tourist map.

Kaikoura is also the home of dolphin swimming, another activity now popular in many parts of NZ. Besides whale and dolphin watching, the area has a host of other activities and Kaikoura lies in a superb setting on a beautiful bay backed by the steeply rising foothills of the Seaward Kaikouras, snowcapped in winter.

History In Maori legend, the tiny Kaikoura Peninsula (Taumanu o te Waka o Maui) was the seat upon which the demigod Maui sat when he fished the North Island up from the depths of the sea (see the 'Maori Culture & Arts' special section). The area was heavily settled before Europeans came – at least 14 Maori pa sites have been identified.

Excavations near the Fyffe House show that the area was a moa-hunter settlement about 800 to 1000 years ago. In 1857 George Fyffe came upon an early moa-hunter burial site near the present Fyffe House and among other things he found an almost complete moa eggshell, the largest moa egg ever found (240mm long, 178mm in diameter).

James Cook passed by here on 15 February 1770, but did not land. His journal states that 57 Maori in four double-hulled canoes came out from shore towards the *Endeavour,* but 'would not be prevail'd upon to put along side'. Cook called the peninsula 'Lookers on', a name which was later mistakenly ascribed to the Seaward Kaikoura Range.

In 1828 the beachfront of Kaikoura, now the site of the Garden of Memories, was the scene of a tremendous battle when a Ngati Toa war party led by the chief Te Rauparaha from Kapiti Island (see the Wellington Region chapter) bore down on Kaikoura armed with muskets, killing or capturing several hundred of the local Ngai Tahu tribe.

The first European to settle in Kaikoura was Robert Fyffe, who established a whaling station in 1842. Kaikoura was a whaling centre from 1843 until 1922, and sheep farming and agriculture flourished. After whaling ended, the sea and the farmland continued to support the community.

Information The Kaikoura Visitor Information Centre (☎ 319 5641, @ info@kaikoura .co.nz), Web site: www.kaikoura.co.nz, is on West End by the car park (on the beach side). It's open from 8 am to 6 pm daily in summer and 9 am to 5 pm in winter. The staff are very helpful and can make bookings for any tour. They screen an excellent 20-minute audiovisual ($3) on the marine environment around Kaikoura.

There is a DOC field centre (☎ 319 5714) on Ludstone Rd, but it's not always staffed.

Things to See George Fyffe, cousin of NZ's first European settler, Robert Fyffe, came to Kaikoura from Scotland in 1854 and built **Fyffe House** around 1860. The house, about 2km east of the town centre, is the only survivor from the whaling days and is protected by the Historic Places Trust. It is open from 10 am to 6 pm daily. The curator conducts tours for $5 (children free).

The **museum** on Ludstone Rd has several big sections out the back, including the old town jail (1910), historical photographs, Maori and colonial artefacts, and an exhibit on the region's whaling era. The museum is open from 12.30 to 4.30 pm weekdays in summer, and from 2 to 4 pm on weekends ($2).

Up on the hill at the eastern end of town is a water tower with a great **lookout**; you can see both sides of the peninsula and all down the coast. Take the walking track up to the tower from Torquay St or drive up Scarborough Terrace.

Tours of **Maori Leap Cave**, a limestone cave formed by the sea and discovered in 1958, take place around 10.30 and 11.30 am and 12.30, 1.45, 2.30 and 3.30 pm daily.

KAIKOURA

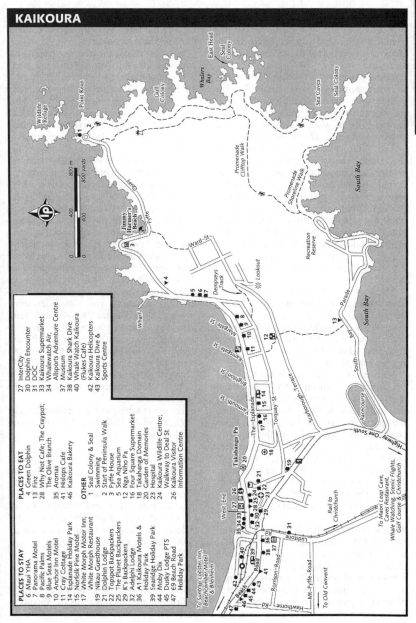

800 m
800 yards

PLACES TO STAY
6   Maui YHA
7   Panorama Motel
8   Pacific Palms
9   Blue Seas Motels
10 Anchor Inn Motel
11 Cray Cottage
14 Esplanade Holiday Park
15 Norfolk Pine Motel
17 White Morph Motor Inn;
    White Morph Restaurant
19 Nikau Guesthouse
21 Dolphin Lodge
22 Topspot Backpackers
25 The Planet Backpackers
29 K's Backpackers
32 Adelphi Lodge
36 A1 Kaikoura Motels &
    Holiday Park
39 Searidge Holiday Park
44 Moby Dix
45 Dusky Lodge PTS
47 ©9 Beach Road
    Holiday Park

PLACES TO EAT
4   Green Dolphin
13 Finz
28 Why Not Cafe; The Craypot;
    The Olive Branch
35 Aromas
41 Hislops Cafe
46 Kaikoura Bakery

OTHER
1   Seal Colony & Seal
    Swimming
2   Start of Peninsula Walk
3   Fyffe House
5   Sea Aquarium
12 Nga Niho Pa
16 Four Square Supermarket
18 Takahanga Domain
20 Garden of Memories
23 Hospital
24 Kaikoura Wildlife Centre;
    Walkway to Deal St
26 Kaikoura Visitor
    Information Centre

27 InterCity
30 Dolphin Encounter
31 DOC
33 Kaikoura Supermarket
34 Whalewatch Air;
    Allsports Adventure Centre
37 Museum
38 Kaikoura Shark Dive
40 Whale Watch Kaikoura
    (Flukes Cafe)
42 Kaikoura Helicopters
43 Kaikoura Dive &
    Sports Centre

They depart from the Caves Restaurant, 3km south of the town on SH1. The 45-minute tour costs $8.50 (children $3.50). Book at the restaurant or the visitor centre.

Marine-Mammal Watching Thousands of international visitors come for the wildlife every year and during the busy summer months, especially December to March, it pays to book whale-watching tours and dolphin swimming a few days ahead.

The 'Big Five' most likely to be seen are the sperm whale, Hector's dolphin (the smallest and rarest of dolphins), the dusky dolphin (found only in the southern hemisphere), the NZ fur seal and the bottlenose dolphin. Other animals frequently seen include the orca (killer whale), common dolphins, pilot whales and blue penguins. Sea birds include shearwaters, fulmars, petrels and royal and wandering albatross. Seals are readily seen out on the rocks at the seal colony.

There's no guarantee of seeing any specific animal on any one tour, but it's fairly certain something of interest will be sighted. Sperm whales are most likely to be seen from October to August and orcas from December to March. Most other fauna is seen year-round.

Marine animals are abundant at Kaikoura because of the currents and continental shelf formation. From land, the shelf slopes gradually to a depth of about 90m, then plunges to over 800m. Warm and cold currents converge here, and when the southerly current hits the continental shelf it creates an upwelling current, bringing nutrients up from the ocean floor and into the light zone. The waters are often red with great clouds of krill, the sperm whale's favourite food, which attract larger fish and squid.

Whale Watching Whale Watch Kaikoura (☎ 319 6767, 0800-655 121), Web site: www.whalewatch.co.nz, is at the old train station. It sets out to sea in search of the whales and other wildlife in boats equipped with hydrophones (underwater microphones) to pick up the sounds of whales below the surface. Three-hour tours run daily from 5 am to 1.30 pm most of the year for $95 (children $60, or $30 for children three to four years old).

For most people the tour is a thrilling experience – the main attraction is the sperm whale, and Kaikoura is the most accessible spot on the planet to see one (for more information see the colour 'Fauna & Flora' section). Other whales sighted include orcas, the minke, humpback and southern right. Dolphins are also usually spotted, as well as sea birds.

There is one hitch to the whale-watch experience – the weather. Nothing is more dismal than heading out for a special encounter with nature, only to have it stopped by the intervention of the uncontrollable elements.

Whale Watch depends on its spotter planes to locate the whales at sea and they can't usually find them in foggy or wet conditions. The Whale Watch office then cancels line after line of disappointed customers. The town benefits each time this happens as many people stay on to try the next day. If this trip is a *must* for you, allow a few days.

Wings over Whales (☎ 0800-226 629), based at the airport, charges $95 each (children $60, minimum two) for a half-hour flight. Kaikoura Helicopters (☎ 319 6609) at the old train station also offers 20- to 40-minute flights out over the whales for $150 to $230. Both guarantee that you see the 'whole whale'.

Try to get a copy of the excellent *Whales & Dolphins of Kaikoura, NZ* by Barbara Todd ($15).

Dolphin Swimming Dolphin Encounter (☎ 319 6777), Web site: www.dolphin.co.nz, is at 58 West End. It offers swimming with huge pods of dusky dolphins. It provides wetsuits (essential in this water), masks and snorkels for $85/65 for adults/children for a three-hour 'dolphin encounter' ($48/38 if you are just a spectator).

The Kaikoura Wildlife Centre (☎ 319 6622, ✉ nzsa@southern.co.nz), opposite the information centre, also operates dolphin-swimming trips for the same price, Monday to Friday only ($80/60 to swim, $60/40 to observe).

Dolphin Swimming

I didn't quite know what to expect when I went dolphin swimming. At the Dolphin Encounter office I was fitted out with a good-quality wetsuit, flippers, face mask and snorkel. The early hour added to the confusion and the only hint of what I was about to experience was given by the numerous photographs and postcards scattered around the office.

We went out in a powered catamaran to an area between Oaro and Goose Bay, the preferred feeding ground of the pods of dusky dolphins. There was no guarantee that the dolphins would be there but the skipper had successfully located many in the previous days. When the first pod was sighted, the atmosphere on board the boat was electric. The skipper manoeuvred in front of the pod, which was feeding on squid, and advised us to enter the water. The eight of us donned our masks and flippers and jumped into the cold water. The initial shock was quickly overcome as streaks of quicksilver flashed by. Before I knew it, a curious dusky circled below me and I gasped for air through my snorkel: I was witness to one of the most beautiful, streamlined creatures of the sea. I raised my head out of the water to see another dolphin performing, circus-like, back flip after back flip – not one or two, but 10, 11, 12 ...

I dived down to show more of me to the curious dolphins and for a brief instant I was an interloper in their underwater world. I now had a better view of their graceful forms as they darted by. It made me feel that there really is some inexplicable spiritual communication between human and dolphin.

Three pods of dusky dolphins – numbering some 450 in total – had joined together for mass feeding on that day. Later they were joined by a pod of common dolphins, and on the way back to Kaikoura, a lone bottlenose dolphin, Maui, came up to the boat. Three dolphin species in one day. The encounter was over and my satisfaction complete. I don't think I had ever experienced anything quite like it.

(Swimming with dolphins is also popular at Whakatane and Tauranga in the North Island. See the Bay of Plenty chapter for details.)

Jeff Williams

Seal Swimming Seals may appear threatening if approached on land, but under water, in their element, they are completely passive. Graeme's Seal Swim (☎ 319 6182) arranges snorkelling with NZ fur seals. These two-hour guided snorkelling tours from the shore are a great opportunity to view your mammalian cousins at close hand ($40/30 for adults/children). Topspot Backpackers (☎ 319 5440) also arranges similar trips.

You can also snorkel with the seals from a boat. From September to May, the Kaikoura Wildlife Centre organises boat-based seal swimming and supplies all equipment for $45/30 ($25/15 for observers).

Shark Diving Kaikoura Shark Dive (☎ 319 6888) takes three-hour trips out to dive with the sharks in the safety of a shark cage. All equipment is supplied and scuba experience isn't necessary as air is supplied by a tube connected to the boat ($110).

Bird-Watching Bird-watchers will relish the opportunity to see pelagic species with Ocean Wings (☎ 319 6777, @ info@oceanwings.co.nz) – species seen include shearwaters, shags mollymawks, albatross and petrels ($60, children $35).

Walking The Kaikoura Peninsula has many good walkways. There are two **peninsula walkways** starting from the seal colony, one along the seashore and one above it along the clifftop; both take 2½ hours. If you go on the seashore trail, check the tides beforehand. Both walks afford excellent views of the fur seal and red-billed seagull colonies. A trail from South Bay Rd leads over farmland and back to the town.

A walks pamphlet is available from the information centre.

Other good walks in the area are at Mt Fyffe Forest, 9km from Kaikoura; the Puhi Puhi Scenic Reserve, 18km from town; and the Omihi Lookout, 19km from town.

The **Mt Fyffe Walking Track** centres on Mt Fyffe (1602m), an outlier of the Seaward Kaikoura Range, which dominates the narrow Kaikoura plain and the town. The eastern face of Fyffe is cloaked in forest. Information about history, vegetation, birds and the walking tracks is in the *Mt Fyffe Forest: Kaikoura* pamphlet.

A popular day or overnight walk is to the summit of Fyffe and the hut of the same name for impressive views of the peninsula and plains. On a clear day you can see Banks Peninsula to the south and Cape Palliser on the North Island. The forest is accessed from the end of Mt Fyffe Rd, which leads to the short forest walk, or from the western end of Postmans Rd, the access route to the Hinau Picnic area.

The **Kaikoura Coast Track** (✆ sally@ kaikouratrack.co.nz) is a three-day walk through private farmland and along the Amuri coast, 50km south of Kaikoura. The walk has spectacular coastal views and accommodation is in comfortable farm cottages – the Staging Post at Hawkswood (☎ 319 2708), where you get information on the walk, Ngaroma near the sea, and Medina on the Conway River Flats. You can get a shuttle from Kaikoura and the cost is $110. Bring your own sleeping bag and food.

Other Activities In winter, Mt Lyford has **skiing**. Daily lift charges are quite reasonable. A day excursion from Kaikoura (☎ 319 6178) runs to the field in winter only for $75 (ski hire, field pass and transport included).

The **golf course** is on the highway south of the racecourse ($15 for green fees).

The beach in front of the Esplanade has safe **swimming** and a swimming pool. Other beaches are on the peninsula's north-east (eg, Jimmy Harmers) and at South Bay. The whole coastline, with its rocky formations and abundant marine life, is good for snorkelling and diving. Mangamanu Beach, about 15km north of Kaikoura, has good surfing.

Fishing is popular off the new and old wharves, at the Kahutara River mouth, or by surfcasting on the many beaches. Fishing charters can be arranged. *Victoria Lee* Fishing Charters (☎ 319 6478) has six- to seven-hour crayfishing trips for $750 for the boat (maximum 12 people).

Four Wheeler Safaris (☎ 319 6424) operates **quad-bike rides** on and around Mt Fyffe and the Kowhai River where you drive through rivers, hill country and bush; a three-hour/full-day trip is $85/140.

Fyffe View Horse Treks (☎ 319 5069) has half-day guided **horse treks** for $40. Ludley Horse Treks (☎ 319 5925) has two-hour trips for $20.

Sea Kayak Kaikoura (☎ 319 5641) has guided half-day **kayak** tours around the peninsula ($55).

Aitken's Picnic Tours (☎ 319 5091) has two-hour **scenic tours** ($20) and TJ's (☎ 319 6803) is both a tour operator and shuttle; book at the information centre.

Places to Stay *Camping & Cabins A1 Kaikoura Motels & Holiday Park (☎ 319 5999, 11 Beach Rd),* near the railway overpass, has tent/powered sites for $18/20, cabins from $30 and tourist flats from $55; all prices are for two.

69 Beach Road Holiday Park (☎ 319 6275) has tent/powered sites for $18/20 for two; the *Esplanade Holiday Park (☎ 319 5947, 126 The Esplanade)* has sites and cabins (from $31 for two); and *Searidge Holiday Park (☎ 319 5362, 34 Beach Rd)* has sites, cabins and motel units ($75 a double).

Goose Bay Camping Ground (☎ 319 5348), 18km south, is actually several camping areas spread over a 5km stretch of coastline. Generally the sites at each camping ground cost $7 per adult ($9.50 for power) and the cabins cost $30 for a double.

Backpackers The *Maui YHA (☎ 319 5931, ✆ yhakaikr@yha.org.nz, 270 The Esplanade)* is an attractive, modern place (recently refurbished with 40 extra beds), beside the sea about 1.5km from the town centre. The common room has superb views along the bay. Dorms cost $17 per person, twins $38 and doubles $40.

Topspot Backpackers (☎ 319 5540, 22 Deal St) has plenty of space and is a non-smokers haven. There is a sundeck and a courtesy van. The clean and tidy share rooms are $16 per person and doubles are $40. There's a sign near the post shop indicating the path to this place.

Almost directly across the road from the Topspot, *Dolphin Lodge* (☎ 319 5842, ✉ dolphinlodge@xtra.co.nz, 15 Deal St) is a well-equipped place where dorm beds are $16 per person and twins and doubles are $40.

The *Planet Backpackers* (☎ 319 6972, ✉ stay@planetbackpackers.com, 85 West End) is the most central and laid-back place. It has a large, open dorm upstairs costing $15 and doubles and twins downstairs from $36.

Adelphi Lodge (☎ 0800-472 856, 319 5141, 26 West End) is in a grand old pub of yesteryear, but they've succeeded in keeping the excellent backpackers separate. A dorm is $16, a twin with en suite from $40 to $45, and a double is $55 (with TV and video provided). Book the spa on the hill for great views and a sip of champagne.

The *Cray Cottage* (☎ 319 5152, 190 The Esplanade) is one of Kaikoura's most popular backpackers (it pays to book). The well-equipped little hostel behind the house charges $16 in the dorms, $36 in good twin rooms.

K's Backpackers (☎ 319 5538, 11 Churchill St) is small, homey and a short walk from town. The comfortable beds are a change from the old sleeping bag and there is a nice lounge and kitchen. The cost is $16 for twins or doubles with linen.

The *Dusky Lodge* (☎ 319 5959, ✉ dusky .lodge@xtra.co.nz, 67 Beach Rd) is a nice, purpose-built place with a rear deck with mountain views, a spa pool and a host of other facilities. A dorm is $16, and classy twins and doubles are $40.

Moby Dix (☎ 319 6699, ✉ isabella .pavlova@xtra.co.nz, 65 Beach Rd) has

dorms from $15.50, twins from $33, and doubles/triples for $37/47.50. It has a volleyball court, sundeck with barbecue and a creek at the back.

B&Bs & Guesthouses The *Old Convent* (☎ 319 6603), out on Mt Fyffe Rd (near the junction with Mill Rd) and about three minutes from town, is a highly regarded B&B. Its advertising says: 'Get in the habit ... nun can compare.' Singles are $50, and twins and doubles with en suite are $110.

The *Nikau Guesthouse* (☎ 319 6973, 53 Deal St), a renovated two-storey place, is another good choice right in town. B&B doubles with en suite in this pleasant establishment cost $85 (triples $95).

Pacific Palms (☎ 319 5857, 218 The Esplanade) overlooks the harbour and has B&B doubles for $75.

Fifeshire (☎ 319 5059) at The Point farm, 2.5km east of the town centre, is a great place with twins for $110; and *Donegal House* (☎ 319 5083), Mt Fyffe Rd, has singles/doubles with en suite for $45/85 and an excellent restaurant.

Motels & Inns Kaikoura has many motels, especially along The Esplanade; rooms here mostly cost around $85 a double.

Panorama Motel (☎ 319 5053, 266 The Esplanade), *Blue Seas Motels* (☎ 319 5441, 222 The Esplanade) and *Beachcomber* (☎ 319 5623, 169 Beach Rd) are similarly priced.

The *Norfolk Pine Motel* (☎ 319 6405, 124 The Esplanade) has doubles and twins from $80.

The *Anchor Inn Motel* (☎ 319 5426, 208 The Esplanade) is very good with excellent units from $100 to $130.

The *White Morph Motor Inn* (☎ 319 5014, 92 The Esplanade), next to the restaurant of the same name, is one of the better motels, with studio doubles/family units for $105/125.

The *Fyffe Country Inn* (☎ 319 6869), 5km south of Kaikoura, comes recommended and costs from $120 to $150 a double. It has a good restaurant.

Places to Eat In season, crayfish is often featured in Kaikoura restaurants and even the local takeaways.

The *Why Not Cafe (52 West End)*, a BYO, has home-made food, takeaways, pizza and sandwiches.

The *Kaikoura Bakery* out on Beach Rd (on the corner of Hawthorne Rd) is a good place to pick up a quick snack before eco-touring. *Flukes Cafe & Wine Bar (☎ 319 7733)* in the Whaleway Station has stone-grilled fish and lobster and is in a great setting overlooking the sea.

Aromas, West End, is more stylish. It's the place for coffee, quiche and cake, and has outdoor dining.

Hislops Cafe (☎ 319 5221, 33 Beach Rd) is a smart cafe, and very popular for whole-food meals and snacks.

The *Suntrap Lobster Inn (☎ 319 5743, 115 Beach Rd)*, just down from Hislops, is a licensed restaurant/bar which serves seafood meals daily.

The *Craypot*, West End, is a long-running restaurant/bar and serves good feeds of crayfish; a half crayfish is $28. It often features live music.

The *Olive Branch (☎ 319 6992, 54 West End)* is a licensed place with Mediterranean fare and changing lunch and dinner menus.

The *White Morph (☎ 319 5676, 94 The Esplanade)* is in a stately old home and has both indoor and outdoor garden tables. With local seafood so plentiful, what better place to try a paella.

The *Green Dolphin (12 Avoca St)* is opposite the Pier Hotel near the wharf. The food is continental and delicious with mains for around $16.

Finz (☎ 319 6688), out at South Bay, is a predominantly seafood place with a bar. It's open daily from 6 pm till late.

Getting There & Around The daily Inter-City bus services operating between Nelson, Picton and Christchurch all stop at Kaikoura. Buses arrive and depart from the town car park; tickets are sold at the information centre next door.

Several shuttle buses service Kaikoura, including Compass Coachlines, Southern Link, South Island Connections, East Coast Express and Atomic. They cost $15/10 for adults/children to Christchurch, Blenheim or Picton. The information centre takes bookings.

The Hanmer Connection to Hanmer Springs costs around $25/20 by shuttle.

One northbound and one southbound *Coastal Pacific* train between Picton and Christchurch stop at Kaikoura daily. The northbound arrives at 10.30 am and the southbound at 4.10 pm.

You can hire bicycles from many of the petrol stations (it costs about $20 per day). A taxi (☎ 319 6214) costs about $5 from town to accommodation.

WEST OF CHRISTCHURCH
Heading west from Christchurch on SH73 it's about a two-hour trip to Arthur's Pass National Park. The crossing from Christchurch to Greymouth, over the pass, is a very scenic route covered by both bus and the *TranzAlpine Express* train (see the boxed text 'The *TranzAlpine*' in The West Coast chapter).

Nowhere in NZ do you get a better picture of the climb from the sea to the mountains. From Christchurch, almost at sea level, the road cuts through the flat Canterbury Plains, through rural towns such as Kirwee, Darfield, Sheffield and Springfield. It then winds up into the skiing areas of Porter Heights and Craigieburn before following the Waimakariri and Bealey Rivers to Arthur's Pass, passing picturesque lakes along the way, including Pearson and Grasmere.

To the south-west of Christchurch and reached by SH73 and SH77 is the Mt Hutt ski resort and the adventure centre, Methven.

Craigieburn Forest Park
This forest park is 110km north-west of Christchurch and 42km south of Arthur's Pass, on SH73. A good system of walking tracks crosses the park, and longer tramps are possible in the valleys west of the Craigieburn Range. The nearby country is suitable for skiing (see later) and rock climbing (particularly at Castle Hill). The predominant vegetation types are beech, tussock, totara,

Moa statue at Bealey

and turpentine scrub. If you are lucky you may see patches of South Island edelweiss *(Leucogenes grandiceps)*. Get a copy of the DOC pamphlet *Craigieburn Forest Park Walks* for more information.

Smylie's YHA & Ski Lodge Accommodation (☎ 318 4740) in Springfield is a cosy place with a potbelly stove and coal range; dorms are $18 and doubles and twins $40.

The *Flock Hill Lodge* (☎ 318 8196, @ flockhilllodge@xtra.co.nz) is a high-country sheep station 44km east of Arthur's Pass on SH73, adjacent to Lake Pearson and the Craigieburn Forest Park. Bunk rooms cost $18, and twins are from $40 to $110 depending on the season; there's a fully equipped communal kitchen and a restaurant. Activities include swimming, fishing, skiing, walking and mountain biking.

Craigieburn is one of the best **skiing** areas in the country, as it has a rise of 503m. It is set in wild country and suits the advanced skier (see also Broken River, Porter Heights and Mt Cheeseman under Skiing in the Activities chapter).

The *Bealey Hotel* (☎ 318 9277, @ bealeyhotel@xtra.co.nz) is 12km east of Arthur's Pass at **Bealey**. Bealey is famous for a hoax which led people across the nation to believe that a live moa had been sighted in the area, 'confirmed' by two German tourists. Motel units cost $85 and the budget Moa Lodge costs $20 per person in double rooms.

Grasmere Lodge (☎ 318 8407), 30km east of Arthur's Pass, is a 10-room luxury place on a high-country station; several activities are provided to repay the $300 winter and $400 summer rates (DB&B per person).

The *Wilderness Lodge* (☎ 318 9245), Web site: www.wildernesslodge.co.nz, is a superb, 20-room luxury lodge on a sheep station. Guided walks are included in the price of $180/240 per person in the low/high season.

Arthur's Pass

The small settlement of Arthur's Pass is 4km from the pass of the same name. The 924m pass was on the route used by the Maori to reach Westland, but its European discovery was made by Arthur Dobson in 1864, when the Westland gold rush created enormous pressure to find a crossing over the Southern Alps from Christchurch. A coach road was completed within a year of Dobson's discovery. Later on, the coal and timber trade demanded a railway, which was completed in 1923.

The town is a fine base for walks, climbs, views and winter-time skiing (at Temple Basin) in Arthur's Pass National Park, and would make a good day trip from Greymouth or Christchurch.

Information The Arthur's Pass Visitor Centre (☎ 318 9211) in the town is open from 8 am to 5 pm daily. It has information on all the park walks, topographical maps and route guides for longer tramps with huts. Staff can also offer invaluable advice on the park's often savagely changeable weather conditions – check here before you go on any walk, and fill out an intentions card. Be sure to sign out again when you leave, otherwise they'll send a search party to find you!

The visitors centre has excellent displays. In January there's a summer program of guided walks and evening talks, discussions, films and slide shows.

Arthur's Pass National Park Day walks in the park offer 360° views of the snowcapped peaks. Many of these peaks are over 2000m, the highest being Mt Murchison (2400m). One of the most spectacular views from the road is of the Bealey Face of Mt Rolleston.

The park has huts on the tramping tracks and several areas suitable for camping. The day walks leaflet from the visitor centre lists half-day walks of one to four hours and day walks of five to eight hours. The four-hour return walk to Temple Basin provides superb views of the surrounding peaks. For skiing at Temple Basin, see Skiing in the Activities chapter.

Longer tramps with superb alpine scenery include the two-day Goat Pass Track and the difficult Harman Pass and Harpers Pass Tracks. Tracks require previous tramping experience, flooding can make rivers dangerous to cross and the weather can be extreme; always seek advice from DOC first.

Places to Stay & Eat You can camp at the basic *public shelter* for $3 per night. It has running water (must be treated) and a flush toilet. Camping is also available at the *YHA* ($10) and *Mountain House* ($10). Camping is free at Klondyke Corner, 8km east of Arthur's Pass, and Kelly Shelter, 17km west. Both have toilets and water that must be treated.

From November to March all accommodation is in demand; it is advisable to book ahead. The *Sir Arthur Dudley Dobson YHA* (☎/fax 318 9230) has bunks at $15 per night or $36 a double. You should bring your own food.

Mountain House Backpackers (☎ 318 9258, fax 318 9058), across the road, is a good backpackers with shared rooms and dorms for $16 – from May to September stay three nights for the price of two.

The *Alpine Motel* (☎ 318 9233) has doubles at $80 or $70.

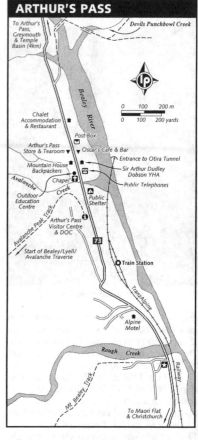

ARTHUR'S PASS

To Arthur's Pass, Greymouth & Temple Basin (4km)

Devils Punchbowl Creek

Bealey River

0   100   200 m
0   100   200 yards

Chalet Accommodation & Restaurant

Post Box

Arthur's Pass Store & Tearoom

Oscar's Cafe & Bar

Entrance to Otira Tunnel

Mountain House Backpackers

Sir Arthur Dudley Dobson YHA

Avalanche Creek

Chapel

Public Telephones

Outdoor Education Centre

Public Shelter

Avalanche Peak Track

Arthur's Pass Visitor Centre & DOC

73

Start of Bealey/Lyell/ Avalanche Traverse

Train Station

TranzAlpine

Rough Creek

Alpine Motel

Railway

Mt Bealey Track

To Maori Flat & Christchurch

The *Chalet Accommodation* (☎ 318 9236), Web site: www.arthurspass.co.nz, offers B&B for $100 for a double with shared facilities or $110 a double with en suite.

The *Otira Hotel* (☎ 738 2802) in the township of Otira, 14.5km west of Arthur's Pass, has cheap rooms. There are some great walks in the area including the Goat Pass trip which forms part of the Coast to Coast endurance race. Also nearby is the start of the Harpers Pass Track.

The *Arthur's Pass Store & Tearoom* and the *Chalet Restaurant* (☎ 0800-506 550), which has a cheaper coffee bar beyond its restaurant area, are a couple of the town's limited dining choices.

Oscar's Cafe & Bar (☎ *318 9234)* serves good-value meals, and it is the social focus of the town.

Getting There & Around Arthur's Pass is on the main run for buses between Christchurch ($25) and Greymouth ($15). Coast to Coast, Ko-Op Shuttles and Alpine Coach & Courier (☎ 0800-274 888) stop at Arthur's Pass.

The *TranzAlpine Express* train runs from Greymouth to Arthur's Pass ($35) and then on to Christchurch ($56); saver fares for backpackers and others may be available. Bus and train tickets are sold at the Arthur's Pass Store.

The road over the pass was once winding and very steep – the most tortuous of all the passes – but a new, spectacular **viaduct**, an engineering marvel in its own right, has removed many of the treacherous hairpin bends. It is slowly being extended to eliminate areas prone to rockfall.

Arthur's Pass Taxi Service (☎ 318 9266) offers transport service to the walking tracks, eg, Greyneys Shelter ($10), Klondyke Corner ($20) and Cass ($30).

Central & South Canterbury

From Christchurch, two routes go through the South Canterbury region: take SH1 south along the coast to Ashburton, Timaru, Oamaru and then Dunedin, or head inland, crossing the Mackenzie Country to the spectacular lakes and the Southern Alps.

CHRISTCHURCH TO OTAGO

The SH1 south of Christchurch is very flat and boring as you cross the Canterbury Plains, but better in an elevated bus, which allows you to see over the nearby hedges and obstructions. In clear weather there are magnificent views of the distant Southern Alps.

South of Christchurch, the road crosses many wide, glacial-fed rivers – quite a sight in flood, though the water is low at other times. The Rakaia River is popular for jet-boating, the Rangitata River attracts white-water rafters, and salmon fishing is possible in many streams in South Canterbury. The first sizable town is Ashburton.

Ashburton
pop 15,800

Ashburton is very much the service centre for the surrounding district. It is 85km south of Christchurch and lies between the Rakaia and Rangitata Rivers.

The Ashburton Visitor Centre (☎ 308 1050, @ adt@voyager.co.nz), Web site: www.adt.co.nz, is on the main road, East St, in the centre of town and handles bookings for just about everything.

The local office of the AA (☎ 308 7128) is at 119 Tancred St.

Change money at the Bank of New Zealand, 295 Stafford St.

If **museums** are your thing, six of them are in or around this town – the Ashburton Museum & Art Gallery in Baring Square East is the pick of them and it's open from 10 am to 4 pm Tuesday to Friday, 1 to 4 pm on weekends (donation). The town has some good **craft galleries** – Ashford Craft on East St is worth a look.

Places to Stay & Eat The *Coronation Holiday Park* (☎ *308 6603, 780 East St)* has tent or powered sites for $18 for two, on-site caravans for $28, cabins for $45 and motel units from $58.

The *Academy Lodge Motel* (☎ *308 5503)*, next door, has doubles from $72 to $82 for two. Several other motels, all on the highway, typically charge from $60 to $75 for a unit. The information centre lists many other options.

Some reasonable dining options exist. *Cactus Jack's* (*509 Wills St)* has Mexican food; *Kelly's* on East St has varied fare and is one of Ashburton's best restaurants; *Jesters* (☎ *308 9983, 9 Mona Square)*, formerly Chandler House, serves crayfish, lamb and venison dishes; and *Tuscany's*

(☎ 308 5039) in the Somerset Hotel on East St opposite the information centre serves Pacific Rim and Mediterranean-influenced fare, and has a fine wine selection. There's a nightclub on the side of Tuscany's called *The Somerset Boulevard*.

Getting There & Away InterCity (☎ 308 5179) buses stop outside the information centre in Ashburton on their way to Dunedin, Christchurch or Queenstown. Ashburton Shuttle (☎ 308 4889) runs three times a week between Ashburton and Christchurch for $18.

Methven
pop 1070
Inland from Ashburton on SH77 is Methven, a good centre for the Canterbury Plains or the mountains. A small town, Methven is quiet for most of the year, coming alive in winter when it fills up with skiers using it as a base for Mt Hutt and other ski areas. There's a world-class 18-hole golf course nearby.

Information The Methven Visitor Centre (☎ 302 8955) is on Main Rd. It makes bookings for accommodation, skiing packages, transport and activities. See their Web site (www.nz-holiday.co.nz/methven/info).

There is a bank near the mall and the medical centre is opposite, on the corner of Chertsey and Main Rds.

Activities The **Mt Hutt Forest**, an area of predominantly mountain beech, is 14km west of Methven. It is adjoined by the **Awa Awa Rata Reserve** and the **Pudding Hill Scenic Reserve**.

There are two access roads: Pudding Hill Rd leads to foot access for Pudding Hill Stream, and McLennan's Bush Rd leads to Pudding Hill Scenic Reserve and Awa Awa Rata Reserve. There are many **walking trails**: the Pudding Hill Stream Route, which requires many stream crossings, takes 2½ hours, and the Awa Awa Rata Reserve Loop Track takes 1½ hours. In the latter reserve, many short walks show the diverse vegetation within the surrounding forest.

It is **skiing** that has really set Methven on an upward growth curve. Nearby Mt Hutt offers six months of skiing, perhaps the longest ski season of any resort in NZ.

Beaches Restaurant on the mountain is the highest dining establishment in Australasia. (See Skiing in the Activities chapter for more details.)

White Water Jets (☎ 318 6574) and Rakaia Gorge Scenic Jet (☎ 318 6515) zip up to the Rakaia Gorge on **jet-boats** for around $40 per person. As you can only see the gorge from the river, a jet-boat is the best means of transport on this braided river system.

The Parachute Centre (☎ 025-321 135) at Pudding Hill, 5km from Methven, has **tandem skydiving** ($245, 10,000ft). More sedate is a **balloon flight** organised through Aoraki Balloon Safaris (☎ 302 8172); the $225 flights include a champagne breakfast.

Methven Heliski (☎ 302 8108) operates in winter ($660 for a day trip). Rock + Ice (☎ 302 9227), Web site: www.rockice .co.nz, has **abseiling** and night-time **rap jumping**.

The Horsepower Experience (☎ 302 4800) gives you a chance to race in a twin sulky behind a champion harness racer ($125); booking is essential. More sedate, Ranelagh Horse Trekking (☎ 302 8626) has rides for $30 for an hour.

And lastly, Planet Argo (☎ 302 8464) has two-hour **safaris** through back country in 8WD all-terrain vehicles ($60).

Places to Stay In winter Methven has over 2000 beds to cater for skiers on Mt Hutt, but many places are closed in summer. The following are open year-round unless otherwise indicated.

Methven Caravan Park (☎ 302 8005) on Barkers Rd has tent/powered sites at $13/16 for two and basic cabins at $13 per person. Bedding and cooking utensils can be hired.

The *Bedpost (☎ 302 8508),* near the corner of Main Rd and Allen St in central Methven, has hostel-style accommodation from $20 and well-appointed units from $80 in winter ($60 summer).

Redwood Lodges (☎ 302 8964, ✉ skired@voyager.co.nz, 5 Wayne Place)

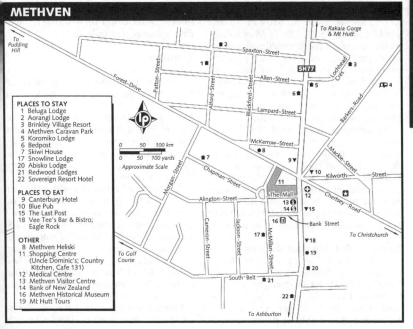

METHVEN

To Pudding Hill

To Rakaia Gorge & Mt Hutt

Spaxton Street

Forest Drive

Patton Street

Alford Street

Allen Street

Blackford Street

SH77

Lochhead Cres

Barkers Road

Lampard Street

McKerrow Street

Morgan Street

Chapman Street

Kilworth Street

Mackie Street

Alington Street

The Mall

Chertsey Road

Cameron Street

Jackson Street

Bank Street

To Christchurch

McMillan Street

South Belt

To Golf Course

To Ashburton

0   50   100 km
0   50   100 yards
Approximate Scale

PLACES TO STAY
1 Beluga Lodge
2 Aorangi Lodge
3 Brinkley Village Resort
4 Methven Caravan Park
5 Koromiko Lodge
6 Bedpost
7 Skiwi House
17 Snowline Lodge
20 Abisko Lodge
21 Redwood Lodges
22 Sovereign Resort Hotel

PLACES TO EAT
9 Canterbury Hotel
10 Blue Pub
15 The Last Post
18 Vee Tee's Bar & Bistro;
     Eagle Rock

OTHER
8 Methven Heliski
11 Shopping Centre
     (Uncle Dominic's; Country
     Kitchen, Cafe 131)
12 Medical Centre
13 Methven Visitor Centre
14 Bank of New Zealand
16 Methven Historical Museum
19 Mt Hutt Tours

are two well-appointed lodges with a communal kitchen area and good four-bed rooms with en suite for $22.50 per person in summer and $25 in winter.

On Chapman St, *Skiwi House* (☎ 302 8772, ✉ skiwihouse@xtra.co.nz, 30 Chapman St) is another main budget choice, open all year. The cost in this self-contained, older-style house is $19 per person in singles, doubles and quads.

The *Snowline Lodge* (☎ 302 8883, 17 McMillan St) has recently opened its doors to the budget market; dorms are $15 and doubles $35 to $36. We haven't seen inside, so tell us about it.

NagZski (☎ 302 1770) is a small farmhouse in Lyndhurst, 9km from Methven. It is isolated, which will suit some travellers. It's open year round and is $18 in a dorm, $20 for B&B.

Kohuia Lodge of Pudding Hill (☎ 302 8416), 5km from town on SH72, has tent/powered sites at $14/20 for two, lodge

rooms from $40, studio units from $60 and backpackers accommodation from $15 (extra in winter). There are lots of extras, including a sauna, spa, bar and restaurant.

Aorangi Lodge (☎ 302 8482, 38 Spaxton St) is a purpose-built place with B&B for $25 per person in summer, up to $48 during the ski season.

Mt Hutt Homestead (☎ 302 8130), Web site: www.the-homestead.co.nz, is part of a high-country sheep-and-deer station just outside Methven. B&B is not cheap at $90/125 for singles/doubles, but the food is excellent and it's an interesting place to stay.

Inverary Station (☎ 303 9734) on the Ashburton Gorge Rd is similar; singles/doubles are $105/170. *Pagey's Farmstay* (☎ 302 1713), a spacious home on the Methven-Chertsey Rd, has been enthusiastically recommended by several travellers.

Motel-style lodges include the comfortable *Koromiko Lodge* (☎ 302 8165) on

SH77 (Main Rd), where B&B is $75 a double in summer, closer to $100 in winter; *Abisko Lodge* (☎ *302 8875, 74 Main Road),* another in the ski lodge mould with lots of wood panelling, sauna, spa and a pleasant bar-restaurant (rooms with en suite cost from $70 to $100 for two); and *Beluga Lodge* (☎ *302 8290, 40 Allen St),* a luxurious place with gardens and hydrotherapy pool that's worth the $150 for two.

The *Sovereign Resort Hotel* (☎ *302 8724)* south of town on the Ashburton Rd (SH77) is one of the flashest places in town; a double is $110 to $160 ($20 less in summer).

Brinkley Village Resort (☎ *302 8885)* is a new, luxurious apartment complex catering to the ski crowds with rooms from $110 to $180 in winter ($80 to $140 in summer). The visitor centre lists many more places.

Places to Eat The main shopping centre has a selection of dining establishments including *Uncle Dominic's* for takeaways, *Country Kitchen* for tearoom fare and the salubrious *Cafe 131,* open until 4 pm in summer and also for dinner in winter. *Vee Tee's Bar & Bistro* on Main Rd serves good family meals.

There are two pubs: the *Canterbury Hotel,* on the corner of Main Rd and Forest Drive, and the famous *Blue Pub* opposite. The latter is very popular with ski bums during winter, but both serve good pub meals.

Many more restaurants and entertainment venues open in winter when skiers converge on the town.

Both the *Brinkley* and the *Sovereign Resorts* have classy restaurants which are open year-round.

The *Eagle Rock, Ski Time* on Racecourse Rd and *The Last Post* are really popular bars in winter, but are most likely closed in summer.

Getting There & Around InterCity has buses between Methven and Christchurch for $16. Methven Travel (☎ 0800-684 888) picks up from the Christchurch airport and will drop you off at your accommodation; other companies also offer this service during the ski season.

Many shuttles operate to Mt Hutt skifield from May to October for $18 to $22; multiday discounts are available.

Temuka
pop 3950

In 1853 William Hornbrook settled on his run Arowhenua, on the south bank of the Temuka River. His wife, who settled there a year later, was the first female European pioneer in South Canterbury. Arowhenua had long been a pa site of the Ngai Tahu people. Their earth ovens, *te umu kaha* (the fierce ovens), gave Te-umu-kaha, later Temuka, its name.

A number of relics of early settlement survive, including middens, Old Hope Cottage, Mendelssohn House and the magnificent redwood trees on the corner of King St and Wilmhurst Rd. The site of pioneer aviator Richard Pearse's first attempted flight and a replica of his plane are out on Main Waitohi Rd, 13.5km from Temuka towards Hanging Rock Bridge (see the boxed text 'Flights of Fancy' in this section).

Five kilometres south of Waitohi, **Pleasant Point**, 18km west of Timaru towards Fairlie, has an interesting railway museum (☎ 686 2269) at the old train station and a collection of steam locomotives and carriages that run along 3km of track on weekends and holidays.

The District Council Service Centre (☎ 615 9537) on Domain Ave acts as an information centre.

Places to Stay & Eat The *Temuka Holiday Park* (☎ *615 7241, 2 Fergusson Drive)* has tent/powered sites for $16/17 and cabins at $28 for two.

Temuka has five hotels and four motels. *Benny's Getaway Motel* (☎ *615 8004, 54 King St)* has reasonable units for $60 to $70.

Along King St are pubs serving meals, a number of takeaways and the omnipresent tearooms. The local cheeses are superb.

Timaru
pop 27,350

Timaru is a thriving port city, halfway between Christchurch and Dunedin. It is a

Flights of Fancy

Richard Pearse (1877–1953), a farmer and inventor, was born at Waitohi, north-west of Timaru. Once known to locals as 'Mad Pearse' and 'Bamboo Dick' (because he employed bamboo in his inventions), he may well have been the first human to fly in a heavier-than-air machine.

He was a lonely man and happy to tinker away in his shed building aircraft with home-made tools. His first plane, 8m wide, was constructed of scrap metal and bamboo braced by wire and powered by a simple two-cylinder engine which he designed himself; underneath were bicycle wheels.

It is reputed that he first flew about 1km on 31 March 1902 before ignominiously crash-landing in gorse near the Ophir River. The flight was supposedly witnessed by several people. It is also believed that he flew again 12 months later. Both flights would have been before the Wright brothers flew at Kittyhawk, North Carolina, on 17 December 1903.

After 1904 Pearse disappeared into obscurity and he died a recluse in a psychiatric hospital in Christchurch.

Richard Pearse Memorial

Interest in his inventions escalated after his death and he is remembered in Auckland's Museum of Transport & Technology and in the Timaru Museum (where there is a reconstruction of his first aircraft). There's also a memorial at the point where his first flight commenced. If only they had filmed the event – Pearse's achievement will probably never be proven.

small city, but a convenient stopping point with an attractive beach at Caroline Bay. The Caroline Bay Christmas Carnival, beginning on 26 December and running for about 10 days, is a lot of fun.

Timaru comes from the Maori name Te Maru, meaning 'The Place of Shelter', but no permanent settlement existed when the first Europeans, the Weller brothers of Sydney, set up a whaling station in 1839. The *Caroline,* a sailing ship that picked up whale oil, gave the picturesque bay its name.

The town really began to boom when a landing service was established at the foot of Strathallan St. It moved in 1868 to George St and has been renovated into a boutique brewery pub. After about 30 vessels were wrecked attempting to berth near Timaru between the mid-1860s and 1880s, an artificial harbour was built. The result is today's excellent port and Caroline Bay's beach, a result of the construction of

breakwaters. The port is an important shipping point for the surrounding agricultural region. You may see one of the huge sheep 'liners' – five-storey ships crammed with live sheep on a death cruise bound for the Middle East.

Orientation & Information Timaru's main road, SH1, is a road of many names – the Hilton Highway north of town, Evans St as it enters town and then Theodosia St and Craigie Ave as it bypasses the central business district. The central business district is around Stafford St. Continuing south, the highway becomes King St and then SH1 as it emerges from town.

The Timaru Visitor Information Centre (☎ 688 6163), Web site: www.southisland .org.nz, is at 14 George St, diagonally across from the train station. It has enthusiastic staff and is open from 8.30 am to 5 pm on weekdays and 10 am to 3 pm on weekends (summer hours may be extended).

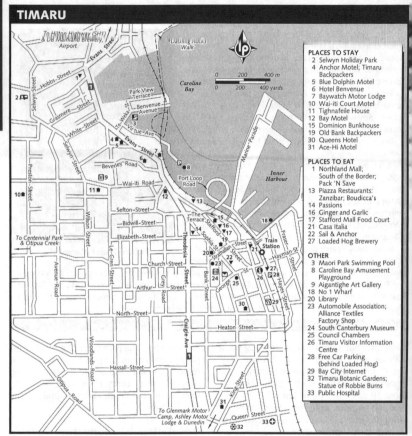

TIMARU

PLACES TO STAY
2 Selwyn Holiday Park
4 Anchor Motel; Timaru Backpackers
5 Blue Dolphin Motel
6 Hotel Benvenue
7 Baywatch Motor Lodge
10 Wai-iti Court Motel
11 Tighnafeile House
12 Bay Motel
15 Dominion Bunkhouse
19 Old Bank Backpackers
30 Queens Hotel
31 Ace-Hi Motel

PLACES TO EAT
1 Northland Mall;
   South of the Border;
   Pack 'N Save
13 Piazza Restaurants:
   Zanzibar; Boudicca's
14 Passions
16 Ginger and Garlic
17 Stafford Mall Food Court
21 Casa Italia
22 Sail & Anchor
27 Loaded Hog Brewery

OTHER
3 Maori Park Swimming Pool
8 Caroline Bay Amusement Playground
9 Aigantighe Art Gallery
18 No 1 Wharf
20 Library
23 Automobile Association; Alliance Textiles Factory Shop
24 South Canterbury Museum
25 Council Chambers
26 Timaru Visitor Information Centre
28 Free Car Parking (behind Loaded Hog)
29 Bay City Internet
32 Timaru Botanic Gardens; Statue of Robbie Burns
33 Public Hospital

Pick up a street map and the interesting pamphlet *Timaru City Historic Walk*.

The AA is on the corner of Church and Bank Sts, and for email go to Bay City Internet, 47a Stafford St.

Things to See & Do One of the few safe, sheltered beaches on the east coast is **Caroline Bay**. The park along the beach has a walk-through aviary, a maze, a pleasant walkway and other attractions, including a new landscaped piazza. A good walk heads north from town along Caroline Bay, past the Benvenue Cliffs and on to the Dashing Rocks and

rock pools at the northern end of the bay. Caroline Bay is sheltered and calm but there's good **surfing** south of town (at Patiti Point), where you might also see sea lions. An easy 45-minute walk around the bay is outlined in a map available from the information centre.

Timaru has other good parks including **Centennial Park** along the **Otipua Creek** with a pleasant 3.5km walkway along the stream bed. The information centre has leaflets outlining a scenic drive. Also of note are the **Botanic Gardens**, entered from Queen St, which include native plants and endangered species.

The **South Canterbury Museum**, in the Pioneer Hall on Perth St, is the main regional museum, with exhibits on the whalers and early settlers. Admission is free and it's open from 10 am to 4.30 pm daily except Monday, 1.30 to 4.30 pm weekends. One fascinating exhibit is a replica of the aeroplane designed and flown by Richard Pearse (see the boxed text 'Flights of Fancy').

Over 900 works of art, plus changing exhibits, feature at the **Aigantighe Art Gallery** at 49 Wai-iti Rd, open from 11 am to 4 pm Tuesday to Friday and noon to 4 pm on weekends (free, donations welcome).

The **DB Mainland Brewery** (☎ 688 2059) at Sheffield St, 6km north of town at Washdyke, has free tours at 10.30 am from Monday to Friday. Enclosed footwear must be worn.

Places to Stay The *Selwyn Holiday Park* (☎ 684 7690) on Selwyn St, 2km north of the town centre, has tent/powered sites for $18/19, cabins for $32, tourist cabins with en suite for $42 and flats for $55 to $65; prices are for two.

The *Glenmark Motor Camp* (☎ 684 3682) on Beaconsfield Rd, 3km south of Timaru town centre, has sites at $16 and cabins for $25.

There are *DOC camping grounds* at Mt Nimrod, Back Line Rd, 32km south-west, and Otaio Gorge, Back Line Rd, 29km south-west of Timaru. They cost $5 per adult; drinking water, toilets and barbecues are provided.

The *Timaru Backpackers* (☎ 684 5067, 44 Evans St), in the Anchor Motel, is a YHA associate. It's small (10 people), homey and the management goes out of its way to look after you. A bed costs $17 per person, and comfortable and well-appointed doubles are $40.

The *Old Bank Backpackers* (☎ 686 9098, 232 Stafford St), above the Old Bank bar, is a new addition to the backpackers scene with dorm beds for $14 and doubles for $34.

The *Dominion Bunkhouse* (☎/fax 684 4729, 334 Stafford St), near the piazza, has 80 beds. Dorms cost from $15, singles cost $25 and twins and doubles cost from $36 to $48.

The *Hotel Benvenue* (☎ 688 4049, ✉ benvenue@voyager.co.nz, 18 Evans St) is a better class of hotel with rooms from $95 ($85 on weekends). It has an intimate bar and a good restaurant.

The *Queens Hotel* (☎ 688 0005), on the corner of Barnard and North Sts opposite the police station, is small but has clean singles/doubles for $35/50.

Timaru has numerous motels, especially along Evans St (SH1) at the northern end of town. Most cost from around $70 a double but the *Anchor Motel* (☎ 684 5067, 42 Evans St) has double units for $60. A backpackers double is $40.

Also reasonable are the *Bay Motel* (☎ 684 3267, 9 Hewlings St); *Ace-Hi Motel* (☎ 684 3054, 51 King St), a small cosy place with spa baths; the quiet, off-street *Blue Dolphin Motel* (☎ 684 4589, 40 Evans St); and intimate *Wai-iti Court Motel* (☎ 688 8447, 5 Preston St).

The *Baywatch Motor Lodge* (☎ 688 1886, 7 Evans St) is more upmarket and charges $95 to $125. The units have bay views.

The *Ashley Motor Lodge* (☎ 688 9939, 97 King St), on the south side of town, is also a cut above the rest and charges from $90 for two; it has facilities for the disabled.

Tighnafeile House (☎ 684 3333, 62 Wai-iti Rd), pronounced 'tine-a-faylee', is an exceptional smoke-free B&B in a grand old house (singles/doubles are from $100/140). The information centre lists more homestays and farmstays.

Places to Eat The *Stafford Mall* on Stafford St has a food court for cheap Chinese, roasts or filled rolls during the day.

The *Sail & Anchor* in the Royal Arcade serves good-value, pub-style meals and the *Old Bank* (see Places to Stay) is another popular night venue, also serving meals.

The *Loaded Hog Brewery*, a boutique brewery in the former Landing Service building in George St, serves food and a veritable trough of selections for the beer lover.

Casa Italia on Strathallan St, in a beautiful historic building, has an excellent wine list and serves authentic Italian food. Pasta

CANTERBURY

Three Great Champions

The Timaru region has produced three great sporting champions – two human, the third a horse.

In the centre of Timaru, next to the ANZ Bank, is a statue of Robert Fitzsimmons, three-time world boxing champion with a record barely matched today. Fitzsimmons was born in 1862 and developed his impressive physique at his father's blacksmith's forge. He defeated Jack Dempsey (the Irish Jack Dempsey, not the illustrious 1920s American boxer of the same name) in 1891 to take the world middleweight crown and then Jim Corbett in 1897 in 14 rounds to win the heavyweight crown (held until 1899). Four years later, he took the world light-heavyweight championship. He died in 1917, three years after the last of his 350 or so professional bouts.

Dr John Edward (Jack) Lovelock, born in 1910, was the world record holder for the one mile. In 1936, in front of a crowd of 120,000 at the Berlin Olympics, he broke the record for the 1500m and took the gold medal. Hitler presented him with an oak tree, which is still growing in the grounds of Timaru Boys' High School on North St.

The racecourse at Washdyke is named after NZ's most famous galloper, Phar Lap, who was born at nearby Seadown. In the late 1920s and early 1930s Phar Lap swept all challengers before him. After winning Australia's top horse race, the Melbourne Cup, in 1930, he was later taken to the USA, where he continued his winning streak. There he died, apparently poisoned, soon after winning the richest race in the world, the Agua Caliente Handicap in Mexico. Despite racing in the Depression years, Phar Lap was for many years the greatest stakes winner in the world. Today, Phar Lap's stuffed skin is held by the Melbourne Museum in Australia, his skeleton is in the Auckland Museum and his heart is preserved at the Institute of Anatomy in Canberra (also in Australia).

---

mains cost around $16, although more expensive dishes are offered.

Passions, in an old church on Theodosia St, is a very good wine bar with a wood-fired oven for pizza.

The piazza area on Bay Hill has a couple of good places overlooking the bay. *Zanzibar* (☎ 688 4367) has seafood creole entree for $8.50 and Cajun chicken mains for $18.50. *Boudicca's* (☎ 688 8550) is a cafe and wine bar with a good kebab selection; it's open from noon to 2 pm and 6 to 10 pm Tuesday to Sunday. Local lamb is a speciality.

Ginger and Garlic (☎ 688 3981, 335 Stafford St) has great seafood ragout and venison dishes; mains are around $23 and entrees $11.

Good-value eats can be found around the Northland Mall. *South of the Border*, fronting Evans St, is a small restaurant/bar for cheap Tex-Mex food.

The mall also has a *Pack N Save supermarket*.

Shopping Fans of the 'Swannie', the check woollen shirt famed throughout NZ, should flock to the Alliance Textiles Factory Shop,

24 Church St. It's open from 10 am to 4 pm Monday to Saturday, and the items are cheaper here than anywhere else.

Other woollen clothing, duvets and oilskins are also sold. Goods are seconds, but high quality and cheaper than in the shops.

Getting There & Around Air New Zealand (☎ 688 2500) has daily flights to Christchurch and Wellington. Timaru's airport is 12km north-west of town, just off SH1. Timaru Taxis (☎ 688 8899) has an airport shuttle for $9, and a taxi (ring Call-A-Cab on ☎ 688 8811) will cost about $15.

InterCity buses stop at the train station, where AJ's Cafe (☎ 688 3597) handles bookings. InterCity passes through Timaru on the Christchurch to Dunedin or Queenstown, and Christchurch to Dunedin or Te Anau routes.

Shuttle buses between Christchurch and Dunedin, such as Catch-a-Bus (☎ 453 1480) and Atomic (☎ 322 8883), pass through Timaru. The fare is around $20 to Christchurch or Dunedin.

The *Southerner* train (Christchurch–Invercargill) passes through Timaru daily: at

0.13 am going south and 3.10 pm going orth.

For hitching north get a Canride Grantlea us to Jellicoe St.

Waimate
op 2960

This town, 45km south of Timaru, is eached by a deviation off SH1 onto SH82. t is possible to do a loop and rejoin SH1 ear the Waitaki River. The town's name ranslates as 'Stagnant Water' although here is little hint of it today.

The town has a **museum** and the historic Cuddy, a thatched cottage constructed from a ingle totara tree – contact the Waimate Information Centre (☎ 689 7771), 75 Queen St.

Waimate is the gateway to the hydro lakes f the Waitaki Valley, noted for Quinnat almon fishing.

Don't be surprised if you see wallabies in he nearby hills, as they have bred like rabits since being introduced from Australia.

The *Victoria Park Motor Camp* (☎ 689 3079, 5 Tennant St) has tent/powered sites or $10/14 for two, and basic cabins for $10 er person.

The *Lochiel Motel* (☎ 689 7570, 100 Chearman St) has units at $55 to $70 for two nd also offers rooms in a simple guesthouse.

Queen St has several tearooms and takeways.

TO THE MACKENZIE COUNTRY

Those heading to Queenstown and the lakes rom Christchurch will probably turn off SH1 onto SH79. This scenic route passes hrough the towns of Geraldine and Fairlie efore joining with SH8, which heads over Burkes Pass to Lake Tekapo.

Geraldine
op 2325

On the road inland to Mt Cook is Geraldine, a picturesque town with a country village atmosphere. Geraldine was not settled until 854, when a pioneer built the first bark hut n Talbot St; a totara tree planted at that ime still survives. A number of early setlers cottages remain.

The information centre (☎ 693 1006, @ geraldine_info@xtra.co.nz) on Talbot St is open from 8 am to 5 pm weekdays, 10 am to 2 pm on weekends.

The **Vintage Car Club & Machinery Museum** (☎ 693 8756) on Lower Talbot St has over 30 vintage and veteran cars dating from 1905. A huge shed at the back houses tractors dating back to the 1920s. The tractors are entered in the annual Geraldine tractor races and competitions. The museum is open from October to Easter daily from 10 am to 4 pm, and by arrangement at other times ($10).

Geraldine is also noted for its beautiful private gardens and active craft scene.

Buses between Christchurch and Queenstown stop in Geraldine, and the Berry Barn tourist complex in Talbot St sells souvenirs for the bus trade. Of primary interest is the Barker's Wines shop specialising in fruit wines, mulled wine, jams and preserves.

Places to Stay & Eat The *Geraldine Motor Camp* (☎ 693 8147) on Hislop St has tent and powered sites for $8 and cabins for $15 per person.

The *Farmyard Holiday Park* (☎ 693 9355), on Coach Rd 7km from Geraldine, has tent/powered sites for $15/17, cabins for $28 and units from $45 for two.

The *Olde Presbytery* (☎ 693 9644, 13 Jollie St) is a neat and tidy homestay-style backpackers with friendly owners. A bed here costs $20 per person in doubles or twins.

The *Crossing* (☎ 693 9689, @ srelax@ xtra.co.nz) on Woodbury Rd is a luxurious B&B with a licensed restaurant. Doubles cost from $125 to $160 with en suite. Geraldine has plenty of other B&Bs for around $70 a double.

The *Crown Hotel* (☎ 693 8458) on Talbot St offers B&B twins for $65 with en suite, and has backpackers singles for $25.

Geraldine Motels (☎ 693 8501, 97 Talbot St) charges $60 for two; the *Andorra* (☎ 693 8622, 16 McKenzie St) is $68 to $78 for a unit; and the *Four Peaks* (☎/fax 693 8339, 28 McKenzie St) charges $70.

Robbie's serves hearty breakfasts and great milkshakes, the *Berry Barn Bakery* has good, cheap fare, and *Plums Cafe* *(☎ 693 9770)* has Chinese food and fish and chips; all are on Talbot St.

Peel Forest & Mt Somers

The Peel Forest, 19km north of Geraldine, is one of NZ's most important areas of indigenous podocarp (conifer) forest. Mt Peel station is nearby and the road from it leads to Mesopotamia, once the run of the English writer Samuel Butler in the 1860s.

Get information, including *Peel Forest Park: Track Information,* at the Peel Forest Store *(☎ 696 3567).* The store has tearooms (open from 8 am to 7.30 pm) and also manages the excellent, fully serviced *DOC camping ground* on the banks of the Rangitata River ($6.50 each adult and an extra $2.50 for power). Ask at the store about baches to rent ($15 per person).

Other, more basic, DOC camping grounds in this region are at Orari Gorge on Yates Rd, 12km north of Geraldine; Waihi Gorge on Waihi Gorge Rd, 14km north of Geraldine; and Pioneer Park on Home Bush Rd, 14km west of Geraldine.

The magnificent native podocarp forest consists of totara, kahikatea and matai. One fine example of totara on the **Big Tree Walk** is 9m in circumference and over 1000 years old. Bird life attracted to this forest includes the rifleman, NZ pigeon *(kereru),* bellbird, fantail and grey warbler. Nesting NZ falcons are on the higher reaches of Mt Peel. There are also picturesque waterfalls in the park – Emily Falls (1½ hour), Rata Falls (two hours) and Acland Falls (20 minutes).

Mt Peel-based Rangitata Rafts (☎ 0800-251 251), Web site: www.rangitata.rafts .co.nz, operates **white-water rafting** on the nearby Rangitata River; it has budget accommodation at Mt Peel, where you can get a basic bunk bed for $13. Rangitata Gorge is one of the best white-water rafting areas because of the exhilarating grade V rapids at all water levels. The cost is $115 per person for the Rangitata Gorge, including lunch and a barbecue dinner. The trips depart from Christchurch between 9 and 9.30 am and arrive at the river base at 11.30 am. The trip on the river is about three

hours and returns to Christchurch about 7 to 8 pm. Rangitata Rafts is a 10-minute drive past Peel Forest.

The 10-hour **Mt Somers Subalpine Walkway** traverses the northern face of Mt Somers, linking the Sharplin Falls with Woolshed Creek. The highlight is walking through several altitudinal plant sequences, although there is also plenty of regenerating beech forest. Two huts, the Pinnacles and Mt Somers, on the walk cost $4 each adult. Be warned that this route is subject to sudden changes in weather and all tramping precautions should be taken. Hut tickets are available at the general store in Mt Somers township.

The *Mt Somers Holiday Park* (☎ 303 9719) in town has tent and powered sites from $16 to $18.

Stronechrubie *(☎/fax 303 9814)* has chalets from $80 to $120 (B&B plus dinner is $160 for two) and a superb, award-winning restaurant.

Lake Coleridge Lodge (☎/fax 318 5002) on the upper Rakaia River, is remote but in truly beautiful country. Single/double B&B is $60/80 (dinner $20).

Fairlie

pop 845

Fairlie is often described as 'the gateway to the Mackenzie' because just west of here the landscape changes dramatically as the road mounts Burkes Pass to the open spaces of the Mackenzie Country. It was named after the town of Fairlie in Ayrshire, Scotland, the birthplace of the town's first hotel owner in 1865.

One legacy of the early residents is the tree-lined avenues. The colonial **Mabel Binney Cottage** and **Vintage Machinery Museum** are on the main highway, just west of the town centre. A few minutes' drive west of Fairlie is the historic limestone **woolshed** of the Three Springs Sheep Station.

A good 1½-hour, 38km scenic drive from Fairlie takes in the spectacular Opihi Gorge. It goes to Allandale, then along Middle Valley Rd and Spur Rd to Opihi, and back to Fairlie. The Sunflower Centre (☎ 685 8258) 31 Main St, has information on the region.

Nearby **skiing** is at Fox Peak (☎ 685 8539), in the Two Thumb Range 37km north-west of Fairlie, a club ski area. Mt Dobson (☎ 685 8039), 26km north-west of Fairlie, is in a basin 3km wide. For information see the Skiing section in the Activities chapter.

Places to Stay & Eat The *Gateway Holiday Park (☎ 685 8375)* on Allandale Rd has tent/powered sites for $18 for two, and cabins for $32 a double or $37 with cooking facilities. It also has a spic-and-span backpackers lodge with two dorms and a kitchen/living area for $15 per person.

The *Fairlie Lodge (16 School Rd)* has six good motel units ($50 for two). Cooked breakfasts and Asian meals are also available.

The *Aorangi Motels (☎ 685 8340, 26 Denmark St)* and the *Rimuwhare Country Retreat (☎ 685 8058, 53 Mt Cook Rd)* have units from $65; the latter has a licensed restaurant.

Farmstays include *Cricklewood Farm (☎ 685 5876)* on Rockwood Rd, *Parkwood Cottage (☎ 685 8365)* on Middle Valley Rd and *Poplar Downs (☎ 685 8170)* in Kimbell.

The *Sunflower Centre* serves wholesome vegetarian food. The *Old Library Cafe (6 Allandale Rd)* is a good place for excellent coffee, snacks and main meals (around $15). It's open daily from 10 am until late.

Getting There & Away InterCity's depot is the BB Stop (☎ 685 8139), 81 Main St. Atomic Shuttles also passes through Fairlie between Christchurch and Queenstown.

THE MACKENZIE COUNTRY

The high country from which the Mt Cook park rises is known as the Mackenzie Country after the legendary James 'Jock' McKenzie (nobody's sure why the region and the chap himself have different spelling), who is said to have run his stolen flocks in this uninhabited region around 1843. See the boxed text 'The Legend of Jock McKenzie'. When he was finally caught, other settlers realised the potential of the land and followed in his footsteps. The first people to traverse the Mackenzie were the Maori, who used to trek from Banks Peninsula to Otago hundreds of years ago.

Lake Tekapo
pop 295

At the southern end of Lake Tekapo, the small settlement of Lake Tekapo has sweeping views across the turquoise lake with the hills and snowcapped mountains as a backdrop. The turquoise colour of the lake is created by 'rock flour', finely ground particles of rock held in suspension in the glacial melt water. Tekapo derives its name from *taka* (sleeping mat) and *po* (night).

Lake Tekapo is a popular first stop on a tour of the Southern Alps. The buses heading to or from Mt Cook or Queenstown stop at the cluster of tourist shops by the main road and create chaos when they arrive.

The Kiwi Express Visitor Centre (☎ 680 6224) on SH8 acts as an information and booking office.

The picturesque little **Church of the Good Shepherd** beside the lake was built of stone and oak in 1935. Further along is a statue of a collie dog, a touching tribute to the sheepdogs which helped develop the Mackenzie Country. It is not, as a lot of people believe, James Mckenzie's dog Friday. Visit after the last bus leaves.

Activities Popular activities around Lake Tekapo include fishing, boating, kayaking, water-skiing, bicycle touring and horse trekking.

In winter, Lake Tekapo is the base for downhill **skiing** at Mt Dobson or cross-country skiing on Two Thumb Range. There's ski area transport and ski hire in season. Lake Tekapo also has an open-air ice-skating rink, open from June to September.

The people at Alpine Recreation (☎ 680 6736, ✉ alprec@voyager.co.nz), Web site: www.alpinerecreation.co.nz, offer **mountaineering** and **climbing courses** and **guided treks** in the Mt Cook National Park. The challenging three-day Ball Pass Trek is $625 per person.

The Legend of Jock McKenzie

A legend this rightly is – many subsequent investigations have only helped to cloud or confuse the truth. It is thought that James (Jock) McKenzie was born in 1820 in Scotland. In his short time in this country (date of arrival unknown), possibly only two years, he achieved great notoriety. In March 1855 he was caught near present-day Mackenzie Pass in possession of 1000 sheep which had been stolen from the Levels run, north-west of Timaru.

It was believed at the time that he had stolen the sheep to stock a run he had purchased in Otago and that he was aided only by his remarkable dog, Friday. He was captured near the pass by the Levels overseer and two Maori shepherds. He escaped and made his way to Lyttelton where, while hiding in a loft, he was recaptured by a police sergeant. He was then tried for sheep stealing and sentenced to five years imprisonment. Throughout the trial McKenzie had pleaded not guilty, and nine months after the trial he was granted a pardon. He escaped from prison three times during his nine-month incarceration, always proclaiming his innocence. Even the then Superintendent of Canterbury, James Fitzgerald, remarked: 'I am inclined to believe his story.' Popular myth has it that he was then ordered to leave the country, but there is no evidence to back this belief.

Lyttelton's town clock now covers the foundations of the gaol that once held McKenzie; he was interned here after the only Supreme Court trial ever held in the town. It is believed by some that McKenzie'treasure' – well, his savings anyway – are concealed in a bush near Edendale, 39km north of Invercargill. He supposedly selected the bush as it was *tapu* (sacred) to the local Maori. As legend has it, Mackenzie was only pardoned on the condition that he leave NZ for ever – so he never returned to pick up his savings.

If you're heading to Timaru via Mackenzie Pass you will see a monument erected near the spot where McKenzie was apprehended, although no-one really knows the exact spot. The pass is said to be named after McKenzie as the discoverer, but it is now believed that it had appeared on an earlier map in the late 1840s. Similarly, there is no proof that he had ever purchased land in Otago to stock with either stolen or bought sheep. Little is known of his later life and the date of his death is a mystery.

The region has a number of good **walks**. Most popular is the one-hour walk to the top of Mt John, and you can continue on to lakes Alexandrina and McGregor, an all-day walk. Other walks are along the eastern side of the lake to the ski area road: it is a one-hour return walk to the Tekapo Lookout and 1½ hours to the power station.

Organised Tours Air Safaris (☎ 0800-806 880, ✉ sales@airsafaris.co.nz) operates aerial sightseeing flights from Lake Tekapo over Mt Cook and its glaciers for $160 (children $110). Backpackers with cards can get a 10% discount. The flights do not land on the glacier, but Air Safaris' spectacular 'Grand Traverse' takes you up the Tasman Glacier, over the upper part of the Fox and Franz Josef Glaciers, and by Mts Cook, Tasman and Elie de Beaumont ($220). Air Safaris operates the same flights from Glentanner, near Mt Cook, for the same price. These flights are much cheaper than similar flights offered by other airlines from Mt Cook itself and offer the most comprehensive aerial coverage of the national park, including the Godley River.

Places to Stay *Lake Tekapo Motels & Motor Camp* (☎ 680 6825), in a beautiful setting by the lake, has tent/powered sites at $18/19, 10 cabins at $32, tourist flats with kitchens at $58 and comfy units from $75; prices are for two.

The *Tekapo YHA* (☎ 680 6857, fax 680 6664) is on the Mt Cook side of town, beyond the shops down towards the water. It's a well-equipped, friendly little place with great views across the lake to the mountains beyond. The dorm cost is $15 per person, twins are $36 and there are limited tent sites for $9 per person. Bicycles can be hired for $15 per day.

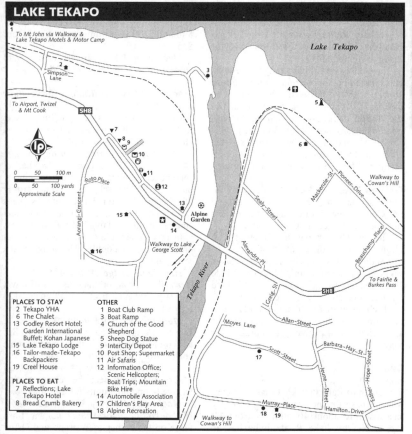

LAKE TEKAPO

To Mt John via Walkway &
Lake Tekapo Motels & Motor Camp

Lake Tekapo

To Airport, Twizel
& Mt Cook

SH8

0   50   100 m
0   50   100 yards
Approximate Scale

Roto Place

Aorangi Crescent

Walkway to
Cowan's Hill

Mackenzie St
Pioneer Drive

Sealy Street

Alpine
Garden

Walkway to Lake
George Scott

Tekapo River

Alexandra Pl

Beauchamp Place

To Fairlie &
Burkes Pass

SH8

Greig St

Moyes Lane

Allan Street

Barbara-Hay-St

Scott Street

Jeune Street

Esther-Hope-Street

Murray Place

Hamilton Drive

Walkway to
Cowan's Hill

PLACES TO STAY
2   Tekapo YHA
6   The Chalet
13 Godley Resort Hotel;
    Garden International
    Buffet; Kohan Japanese
15 Lake Tekapo Lodge
16 Tailor-made-Tekapo
    Backpackers
19 Creel House

PLACES TO EAT
7   Reflections; Lake
    Tekapo Hotel
8   Bread Crumb Bakery

OTHER
1   Boat Club Ramp
3   Boat Ramp
4   Church of the Good
    Shepherd
5   Sheep Dog Statue
9   InterCity Depot
10 Post Shop; Supermarket
11 Air Safaris
12 Information Office;
    Scenic Helicopters;
    Boat Trips; Mountain
    Bike Hire
14 Automobile Association
17 Children's Play Area
18 Alpine Recreation

Tailor-made-Tekapo Backpackers (☎ 680 6700, ☻ tailor-made-backpackers@xtra .co.nz, 9 Aorangi Crescent) has dorms for $16 per person, and doubles and twins for $36 (duvets supplied). It has full kitchen facilities, a laundry and, importantly, caring owners.

The ***Godley Resort Hotel*** (☎ 680 6848), formerly the Alpine Inn, is the largest hotel, favoured by tour groups. Singles/doubles, all with en suite, cost from $135 to $225 for the lake-view rooms (includes a cooked breakfast and dinner). It has a pool and three restaurants.

The Chalet (☎ 680 6774, ☻ speck@ clear.net.nz, 14 Pioneer Drive) has units and holiday homes from $90 to $120 for two (a cooked breakfast is $14).

Creel House (☎ 680 6516), a three-storey place, has B&B from $70/125 and ***Lake Tekapo Lodge*** (☎ 680 6566, 24 Aorangi Crescent), a purpose-built B&B (four rooms) with great views, has doubles from $160.

Near Burkes Pass and the Mt Dobson turn-off, ***Dobson Lodge*** (☎ 685 8316, ☻ dobson_lodge@xtra.co.nz) is a romantic stone cottage and a perfect hideaway (telephone for prices).

Places to Eat The business centre by the main road has takeaways and cafes, as well as a bakery. *Reflections* at the Lake Tekapo Hotel has bistro meals for around $16 for lunch or dinner daily.

The Godley Resort has a range of restaurants, including the *Garden International Buffet*, with hot buffet lunches ($16) and dinners ($29) and an a la carte menu, and the *Kohan Japanese (☎ 680 6688)* with good-value sashimi sets ($20 to $22).

Cheaper options are the *tearooms* in the Mall, and the *Bread Crumb Bakery* for all manner of fresh breads, pies and pastries.

Getting There & Away InterCity southbound services to Queenstown, Wanaka and Mt Cook come through daily, as do the northbound services to Christchurch.

The InterCity (☎ 680 6895) depot is at High Country Crafts on Main St.

Southern Link, Kiwi Discovery (takes bikes for free) and Atomic Shuttles include Lake Tekapo on their routes; it is $20 to Christchurch and $25 to Queenstown.

Hitching in or out of Lake Tekapo can sometimes be difficult, but once you've got a ride it will probably be going a fair way.

Twizel
pop 1140

Just south of Lake Pukaki, Twizel is a convenient base for the surrounding area. By car it's only about 40 minutes from Mt Cook. Nearby Lake Ruataniwha has an international rowing centre, fishing, boating and windsurfing. In the Ben Ohau Ranges there is heli-skiing in winter.

There is a black stilt captive breeding centre near Twizel. The black stilt is the rarest wader species in the world (see the colour 'Fauna & Flora' section).

Information On Wairepo Rd, the Twizel Visitor Information Centre (☎ 435 3118, ✉ wherewhatwhy@xtra.co.nz) is open from 8.30 am to 6.30 daily (in winter, weekdays only 9 am to 4.30 pm). Informative tours to DOC's black stilt breeding program hide leave from here twice daily at 10.30 am

and 2 pm (in winter, one tour only at 10.30 am and no weekend trips). It costs $12.50/5 for adults/kids, minimum charge per tour $25.

The National Bank in the Twizel Mall changes money and has an ATM.

Places to Stay The *Ruataniwha Holiday Park (☎ 435 0613)*, 4km from town right beside the lake, is a spacious place; tent/powered sites are $18/19 for two and cheap cabins from $30 to $42.

The *High Country Holiday Lodge (☎ 435 0671, 23 Mackenzie Drive)* has all sorts of accommodation in cabins originally built for the hydro scheme workers, starting with backpacker-style bunks (only two beds to a room) at $15 per person, and singles/doubles and twins at $33/48. Rooms with private facilities cost $60 and motel units are $70 a double. The lodge has a restaurant.

Heartland Lodge (☎/fax 435 0387, 19 North West Arch), on the outskirts of town, is a large but nice B&B which costs $120 for two.

Mountain Chalet Motels (☎ 435 0785, ✉ mt.chalets@xtra.co.nz), on Wairepo Rd, is a comfortable place with twin and double chalets from $80 to $95.

The *Colonial Motels (☎ 435 0100, 36 Mackenzie Drive)* near the service station has well-appointed units for $95 for two.

MacKenzie Country Inn (☎ 435 0869, ✉ bookings@mackenzie.co.nz), a flash place on the corner of Wairepo and Ostler Rds, has rooms at $150 a double. It also has an upmarket restaurant.

Glenbrook Station (☎ 438 9407) is a high-country sheep station 8km south of Twizel and 22km north of Omarama. Its DB&B is about $100/160 for singles/doubles, but there are also some bunkhouse beds for $15 per person. It offers horse riding, cross-country trail riding and bushwalks.

There's a *DOC camping ground* in Temple Forest on Lake Ohau Rd, 50km west of Twizel.

Places to Eat Market Place in the centre of town has a range of eateries. The *Black*

Stilt Coffee Shop offers croissants, takeaways, burgers and breakfast, and meals at around $10.

The *Hunter's Bar & Cafe (☎ 435 0303)* is open from 11 am until late and has a blackboard menu from 6 pm offering steak, fish, salmon and other mains for around $18.

The *Top Hut Cafe & Bar (13 Tasman Rd)* is open daily from 10 am, and has a sit-down bistro and takeaways.

Getting There & Away InterCity buses serving Mt Cook stop at Twizel, with additional buses shuttling between Twizel and Mt Cook (50 minutes).

Christchurch-Queenstown shuttles, such as Atomic and Southern Link, also stop in Twizel. GTS Country Link (☎ 435 0052) goes to Timaru on Friday and provides transport to the Lake Ohau skifield.

Lake Ohau & Ohau Forests

Six forests in the Lake Ohau area (Dobson, Hopkins, Huxley, Temple, Ohau and Ahuriri) are administered by DOC.

The walks in this vast area are too numerous to mention but are outlined in the DOC pamphlet *Ohau Forests Recreation Guide*. Huts are scattered throughout the region for the more adventurous trampers.

Lake Ohau Lodge (☎ 438 9885), Web site: www.ohau.co.nz, is on the western shore of Lake Ohau. It has good facilities and luxurious units from $154 to $180; backpackers rates in the older wing are $45 per person.

MT COOK NATIONAL PARK

Mt Cook National Park, along with Fiordland, Aspiring and Westland National Parks, has been incorporated into a World Heritage area which extends from the Cook River in Westland down to the base of Fiordland. The Mt Cook National Park is 700 sq km in area and one of the most spectacular in a country famous for its parks. Encompassed by the main divide, the Two Thumb, Liebig and Ben Ohau Ranges, more than one-third of the park is in permanent snow and glacial ice.

Of the 27 NZ mountains over 3050m, 22 are in this park, including the mighty Mt Cook – at 3755m this is the highest peak in Australasia.

Known to the Maori as Aoraki, after a deity from Maori mythology, the tent-shaped Mt Cook was named after James Cook by Captain Stokes of the survey ship HMS *Acheron*.

The Mt Cook region has always been the focus of climbing in NZ. On 2 March 1882, William Spotswood Green and two Swiss alpinists, after a 62-hour epic, failed to reach the summit of Cook. Two years later three local climbers, Tom Fyfe, George Graham and Jack Clarke, spurred into action by the news that two well-known European alpinists, Edward Fitzgerald and Matthias Zurbriggen, were coming to attempt Cook, set off to climb it before the visitors. On Christmas Day 1884 they ascended the Hooker Glacier and north ridge, a brilliant climb in those days, and stood on the summit.

In 1913 Freda du Faur, an Australian, was the first woman to reach the summit. In 1948 Edmund Hillary's party climbed the south ridge. (Hillary went on to become, with Tenzing Norgay, the first to reach the summit of Mt Everest in the Himalaya.) Since then most of the daunting face routes have been climbed. The Mt Cook region has many great peaks – Sefton, the beguiling Tasman, Silberhorn, Elie de Beaumont, Malte Brun, Aiguilles Rouges, Nazomi, La Perouse, Hicks, De la Beche, Douglas and the Minarets.

Many of the peaks can be ascended from Westland National Park, and there is a system of climbers' huts on both sides of the divide.

In the early hours of 14 December 1991, a substantial piece of the east face of Mt Cook (around 14 million cubic metres) fell away in a massive landslide. Debris spewed out over the surrounding glaciers for 7.3km, following a path down the Grand Plateau and Hochstetter Icefall and reaching as far as the Tasman Glacier.

The national park is on most itineraries of the South Island and Mt Cook is certainly an impressive sight – if you can get clear views. Most visitors to the park come on tour buses stop quickly at the Hermitage hotel for photos, and are then off again, but the park has

CANTERBURY

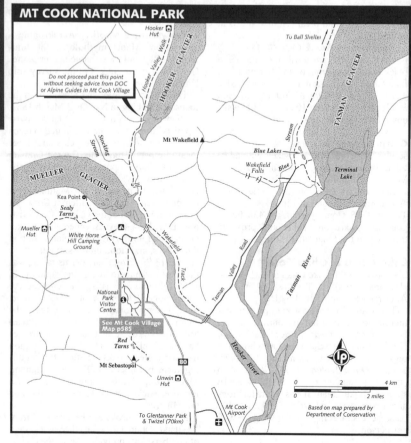

MT COOK NATIONAL PARK

Do not proceed past this point without seeking advice from DOC or Alpine Guides in Mt Cook Village

Hooker Hut

To Ball Shelter

HOOKER GLACIER

TASMAN GLACIER

Stocking Stream

Mt Wakefield

Blue Lakes

Stream

MUELLER GLACIER

Wakefield Falls

Blue

Terminal Lake

Kea Point

Sealy Tarns

Mueller Hut

White Horse Hill Camping Ground

Wakefield Track

Tasman Valley Road

Tasman River

National Park Visitor Centre

See Mt Cook Village Map p585

Red Tarns

Mt Sebastopol

Unwin Hut

Hooker River

80

To Glentanner Park & Twizel (70km)

Mt Cook Airport

| 0 | | 2 | | 4 km |
| 0 | 1 | | 2 miles | |

Based on map prepared by Department of Conservation

---

a number of accommodation options, though most are expensive and rooms are limited. The park has some excellent short walks, but is not a major tramping destination.

Information

The National Park Visitor Centre (☎ 435 1186, @ mtcookvc@doc.govt.nz), open from 8.30 am to 6 pm daily (till 5 pm in winter), will advise you on guided tours and tramping routes. It screens a 20-minute audiovisual on the history, mountaineering and human occupation of the Mt Cook region hourly from 9 am to 4 pm ($2.50).

A post shop and general store (open 9 am to 6 pm) are not far from the visitor centre. Mt Cook has no banking facilities.

The Alpine Guides Mountain Shop (☎ 435 1834) sells equipment for skiing and mountaineering, and rents out equipment, including ice axes, crampons, day-packs and sleeping bags.

The best introduction to the Mt Cook National Park is the beautifully illustrated *Alpine World of Mt Cook National Park* by Andy Dennis & Craig Potton. It has details of flora and fauna, walks and the park's history.

The Hermitage

The Hermitage is the most famous hotel in NZ, principally for its location and the fantastic views of Mt Cook. Originally constructed in 1884, when the trip up from Christchurch took several days, the first hotel was destroyed in a flash flood in 1913. You can see the foundations about 1km from the current Hermitage. Rebuilt, it survived until 1957, when it was totally burnt out; the present Hermitage was built on the same site.

Even if it is beyond your budget to stay, you can sample the bar and restaurants and look out the huge windows straight up to Mt Cook.

Tasman Glacier

Higher up, the Tasman Glacier is a spectacular sweep of ice just like a glacier should be, but further down it's ugly. Glaciers in NZ (and elsewhere in the world) have generally been retreating over the past 100 years, although they are advancing now. Normally as a glacier retreats it melts back up the mountain, but the Tasman is unusual because its last few kilometres are almost horizontal. In the process, over the last 75-or-so years it has melted from the top down, leaving stones, rocks and boulders on top as the ice around them melts. So the Tasman in its 'ablation zone' (the region it melts in) is covered in a more or less solid mass of debris, which slows down its melting rate and makes it unsightly.

Despite this considerable melt, the ice by the site of the old Ball Hut is still estimated to be over 600m thick. In its last major advance, 17,000 years ago, the glacier crept right down to Pukaki, carving out Lake Pukaki in the process. A later advance didn't reach out to the valley sides, so the Ball Hut Rd runs between the outer valley walls and the lateral moraines of this later advance.

Like the Fox and Franz Josef Glaciers on the other side of the divide, the glaciers from Mt Cook move fast. The Alpine Memorial, near the old Hermitage site on the Hooker Valley Walk, illustrates the glaciers' speed. The memorial commemorates Mt Cook's first climbing disaster, when three climbers were killed by an avalanche

in 1914. Only one of the bodies was recovered at the time but 12 years later a second body melted out of the bottom of the Hochstetter Icefall, 2000m below where the party was buried.

Alpine Guides organises sightseeing trips from September to May to the Tasman Glacier viewpoint. It's $28 for 1½-hour trips and $32 for two-hour trips (children half-price).

Walking

Various easy walks from the Hermitage area are outlined in the *Walks in Mt Cook National Park* leaflet ($1) from the visitor centre. Be prepared for sudden changes in climate.

In summer look for the large mountain buttercup, often called the Mt Cook lily, as well as mountain daisies, gentians and edelweiss. Animals include the thar, a goat-like mammal and excellent climber; the chamois, smaller and of lighter build than the thar but an agile climber; and red deer.

The trail to **Kea Point** is an easy two- to three-hour return walk with much native plant life and fine views of Cook, the Hooker Valley and the ice faces of Mt Sefton and the Footstool. You will probably see more than one cheeky kea on this walk.

The walk to **Sealy Tarns** is a three- to four-hour return walk from the village, branching off the Kea Point Track. If the weather is warm and you're feeling brave you can swim in the tarns. The Sealy Tarns Track continues up the ridge to Mueller Hut. If you intend staying up here register your intentions at the DOC visitor centre and pay the hut fee ($18 per person per night).

A good way to spend two to three hours (return) is to walk to **Red Tarns**. Climb another half-hour for spectacular views of Mt Cook and the valley.

It is a four-hour return walk up the **Hooker Valley** across a couple of swing bridges to Stocking Stream and the terminus of the Hooker Glacier. After the second swing bridge Mt Cook totally dominates the valley. For those who have never seen a glacier 'calving' ice blocks into the azure blue glacial lake, this is a must.

From here the alpine route to the Hooker Hut deteriorates rapidly and walkers without equipment (and sound advice) should go no further. Check with DOC and make sure you sign an intentions form at park headquarters.

The 3½-hour return **Wakefield Track** follows the route used by early mountaineers and sightseers, then returns by the southern section of the Hooker Valley Track. This walk has deteriorated – seek advice from DOC before heading off.

Governors Bush is a short one-hour walk through one of the last stands of silver beech in the park. A brochure on the native plants found in Governors Bush is available at the visitor centre.

Shorter walks include the 10-minute **Bowen Bush Walk** through a small patch of totara trees near the Alpine Guides shop. The 15-minute **Glencoe Walk**, beginning from the rear of the Hermitage, ascends through totara forest to a lookout point facing Mt Cook and the Hooker Valley.

The **Tasman Valley** walks are popular for a view of the Tasman Glacier. The walks start at the end of the unsealed Tasman Valley Rd, 8km from the village. It is only a 15-minute walk up from the car park to the Tasman Glacier viewpoint, passing the Blue Lakes on the way. The views of Mt Cook and the surrounding area are spectacular, but the view of the glacier is limited mostly to the icy, grey sludge of the Terminal Lake and the Tasman River. To get close to the snub of the glacier, take the Ball Shelter Track (three to four hours return) from the car park, but this track is subject to flooding (consult DOC). A few hundred metres before the car park is the side road to the **Wakefield Falls Track**, an easy 30-minute return walk to the waterfall.

Longer Walks Longer walks are only for those with mountaineering experience. Advice must be sought from DOC and intentions registered. Conditions at higher altitudes are severe, the tracks dangerous and many people have died. The majority of walkers shouldn't even consider tackling them (see Mountaineering).

Guided Walks Alpine Recreation, in Lake Tekapo, offers high-altitude guided walks in the area. The Ball Pass trip is a two- to three-day crossing over Ball Pass (2130m) from the Tasman to the Hooker Valleys; it allows you to get close to Mt Cook without requiring mountaineering experience (with a group of six to eight people it's about $500 each).

Alpine Guides (see Mountaineering later) in Mt Cook Village also offers short guided walks along the tracks.

Mountaineering

There is unlimited scope here for climbing for the experienced, but beware: there have been some 180 people killed in climbing accidents in the park.

The highly changeable weather is an important factor around here – Mt Cook is only 44km from the coast, catching the weather conditions blowing in over the Tasman Sea. The weather can change abruptly and you can suddenly find yourself in a storm. Unless you are experienced in such conditions, don't attempt to climb anywhere without a guide.

It's important to check with the park rangers before attempting any climb, and to heed their advice! Fill in a climber's intentions card before starting out on any climb, so they can check on you if you are overdue coming out.

Alpine Guides (☎ 435 1834) has ski-touring and mountaineering courses but they are costly. Alpine Recreation in Lake Tekapo also has mountaineering courses.

Heli-skiing & Heli-hiking

In the winter months, Alpine Guides (☎ 435 1834), with Mt Cook Line, offers ski-touring trips and ski-mountaineering courses, but the speciality is glacier heli-skiing. Day trips on Tasman Glacier are $595 (three skiplane flights) and the Wilderness Heli-Skiing trip takes in the Liebig or Malte Brun Ranges on four runs with a minimum of 3000 vertical metres of skiing for $650.

Another possibility is the half-day heli-hike for $325, an expensive option that takes you by helicopter up the Liebig Range for a walk and play around in the snow.

Aerial Sightseeing

The skies above Mt Cook are alive with the sound of aircraft. This is the antipodean equivalent of the Grand Canyon in the USA. The views are superb and glacier landings are a great experience – a must on any NZ adventure.

Mount Cook Ski Planes (☎ 435 1026, **@** mtcook@skiplanes.co.nz) operates trips from Mt Cook. Air Safaris does these trips from Lake Tekapo (see Lake Tekapo, earlier) and Glentanner, the Helicopter Line (☎ 435 1801) from Glentanner, and Southern Lakes Helicopters (☎ 435 0370) in Twizel.

The Mt Cook skiplane landing flights are the most expensive but still worthwhile. The 40-minute Glacier Highlights flight is $225 and a 55-minute Grand Circle flight is $305. Flights without landing are much cheaper. It also offers helicopter flights with snow landings from $140 to $295.

From Glentanner, the Helicopter Line has a 20-minute Alpine Vista flight at $125; an exhilarating 30-minute flight over the Richardson Glacier with a landing at $220; and a 45-minute Mountains High flight over the Tasman Glacier and by Mt Cook with a glacier landing for $300.

Southern Lakes Helicopters has chopper flights from Twizel for $200 (35 minutes) to $375 (70 minutes).

Organised Tours

Alpine Guides' interesting (but, at $30, rather expensive) two-hour Tasman Glacier Guided Tours go two or three times a day in season – check at the Hermitage about bookings and tour times. The rocky road follows the lateral moraines of the Tasman Glacier and the bus stops several times to see this mighty river of ice. Part of the tour involves an optional 15-minute walk to the glacier viewpoint.

If you want to go boating on a glacial lake contact Glacier Explorers (☎ 435 1809). You go out in a small motorised inflatable with about six people. Trips are over two hours and cost $60 (children $30).

From Glentanner (☎ 435 1855) you can go on horse treks over this high-country station from $30 for half an hour to $120 for

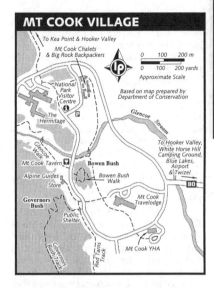

MT COOK VILLAGE

To Kea Point & Hooker Valley

Mt Cook Chalets & Big Rock Backpackers

National Park Visitor Centre

The Hermitage

Glencoe Stream

Glencoe Walk

To Hooker Valley, White Horse Hill Camping Ground, Blue Lakes, Airport & Twizel

Mt Cook Tavern

Bowen Bush

Alpine Guides Store

Bowen Bush Walk

Governors Bush

Public Shelter

Mt Cook Travelodge

Governors Bush Track

Red Tarns Track

Mt Cook YHA

0   100   200 m
0   100   200 yards
Approximate Scale

Based on map prepared by Department of Conservation

three hours. There are 4WD trips for $25 per person ($15 for children), lasting about 90 minutes, which climb up to the highest point of the station at about 1500m.

Another good 4WD trip is with Alan's 4WD Tours (☎ 435 1809), where it is guaranteed that all 'will rub knees, shoulders and bums' as the vehicle climbs up to Husky Flat above the glacier. Alan points out interesting alpine flora. The 2½-hour trip costs $60.

Places to Stay

Camping is allowed at the *White Horse Hill Camping Ground* at the old Hermitage site, the starting point for the Hooker Valley Track, 1.8km from Mt Cook Village. There's running water and toilets but no electricity, showers or cooking facilities. It's run by DOC on a first-come, first-served basis and costs $5/3 for adults/children. Contact the visitor centre.

With great views of Mt Cook, *Glentanner Park* (☎ 435 1855, **@** glentanner.park .mtcook@xtra.co.nz) is the nearest motor camp to the park; it's 23km south on the shores of Lake Pukaki. There are good facilities and it's spacious. Tent/powered sites are $18 for two, basic cabins are $40 and deluxe cabins are $65. The restaurant, open from 8 am to 5.30 pm, sells milk and bread, but the nearest store is at Mt Cook Village.

There is a booking service in the complex for Air Safaris, Helicopter Line, Glentanner Horse Trekking and heli-hikes.

About 3.5km before the village is the NZ Alpine Club's *Unwin Hut* (☎ 435 1102). Members get preference but beds are usually available ($20 per person) for intrepid travellers who wish to meet spider-person ascensionists. It's basic bunk accommodation but there is a big common room with fireplace, showers, kitchen and excellent views up the Tasman Glacier to the Minarets and Elie de Beaumont.

The *Mt Cook YHA* (☎ 435 1820, ✉ yhamtck@yha.org.nz), on the corner of Bowen and Kitchener Drives, is comfortable and well equipped with a sauna, shop and a good video collection. It's conveniently located and open all day. It can get crowded in the high season, from December to April, so try to book at least four days in advance. Dorms are $20 per person and twins/doubles are $48/54.

Big Rock Backpackers is part of the Hermitage complex and you may be able to get a bed for $20; this place caters primarily for bus groups and is often full.

Mt Cook Chalets costs $112.50 for up to four people. It has two mini-bedrooms and a fold-out double sofa/bed, so between four people it can be quite economical. Well-equipped kitchens and a dining table add to the convenience. Other places to stay here are expensive and are booked at the same place (☎ 435 1809, ✉ reservations.hermitage@ xtra.co.nz). *Mt Cook Motels* charges $140 a double and the *Mt Cook Travelodge* charges $195; the rooms have no cooking facilities but the price includes breakfast.

The *Hermitage Aoraki Mount Cook* has prices and services in line with its fame and position, not the standard of its rooms – from $275 to $320 for a double or twin.

Places to Eat

The *store* is well stocked for self-catering, but prices are higher than elsewhere. There is a *cafe* at Glentanner and a little *coffee shop* at the Mt Cook airport.

The Hermitage base line is the *coffee shop* for cheap cafeteria-style meals, pies and coffee. The *Alpine Room* has unexciting main courses for around $18 to $25 (vegetables or salad extra) and desserts are $7.50. Buffets are also offered. The *Mt Cook Travelodge* has a similarly priced restaurant for dinner.

The *Panorama Room*, at the Hermitage, is expensive. Two people can easily spend well over $100, but the view from here is up there with the world's best – you see Sefton to your left, Cook in the centre and the Ben Ohau Ranges, dark brown and forbidding, to your right.

The *Mt Cook Tavern*, open until 1 am (midnight on Sunday), has pizza ($8), pies and barbecue meals ($10) and is the place to drink, sit and talk.

Getting There & Away

Air   Air New Zealand Link operated by Mt Cook Airlines (☎ 435 1848) has daily direct flights to/from Queenstown and Christchurch, with connections to other centres. Mt Cook provides bus services to and from the airport for $4.

There's no scheduled air service to the West Coast but Air Safaris can fly between Glentanner and Franz Josef for $150 one way (minimum of two). It's a way of combining transport with a scenic flight, but the flights are weather-dependent.

Bus   InterCity buses on the daily Christchurch–Wanaka route go directly to Mt Cook, where they stop for one hour. InterCity buses stop at the YHA and at the Hermitage, both of which also handle bookings.

Hitching   Hitching is hard – expect long waits once you leave SH1 if coming from Christchurch or Dunedin, and long waits all the way if coming from Queenstown. Hardest of all is simply getting out of Mt Cook itself, since the road is a dead end. It's worth considering taking the bus down to Twizel, where there's much more traffic.

Otago

☎ 03 • pop 187,200

Exciting Queenstown and Wanaka with their adrenaline-inducing activities, the Otago Peninsula, New Zealand's first real foray into ecotourism, and Dunedin, the capital of the region with its fine architecture, make Otago a must for any visitor to NZ. Otago's history featured a major gold rush and many aspects of the region's geography hark back to an era of prosperity when rivers and creeks swarmed with prospectors.

Otago occupies a central position on the South Island. The main entry route is SH1 from Christchurch along the east coast. From Southland you can approach Otago via the southern scenic route, through the Catlins or via SH1 from Invercargill. The most scenic way, however, is via the West Coast (SH6) and across Haast Pass.

Dunedin & the Otago Peninsula

Otago Harbour's long fiord-like inlet is the hub for many ecotourism activities, especially on the Otago Peninsula and in nearby coastal areas. The fauna-rich peninsula is close to Dunedin, a quaint city with many historic buildings and a convenient base for trips further afield to Central Otago and the Catlins.

DUNEDIN
pop 110,800

Dunedin is the second city of the South Island and home of NZ's first university. During the gold-rush days it was the largest city in the country. Founded by Scottish settlers (Dunedin is Celtic for Edinburgh), Dunedin has a statue of Robert Burns guarding its city centre, produces whisky at a local distillery and still has haggis ceremonies.

Dunedin's ostentatious wealth in the latter half of the 19th century produced a grand Victorian city in the South Pacific.

HIGHLIGHTS

- Enjoying activities on water, land and air at Queenstown, Lake Wakatipu and Lake Wanaka
- Tackling the Glenorchy, Routeburn and Rees–Dart tracks amid spectacular mountain scenery
- Skiing on any of the ranges near Queenstown (The Remarkables and Coronet Peak), Wanaka (Treble Cone) and Cardrona
- Marvelling at the historic towns of the Manuherikia and Maniototo valleys and the goldfields of Central Otago
- Enjoying architecturally rich Dunedin and the best nightlife on the South Island
- Seeing albatross, rare penguins and sea lions on the Otago Peninsula

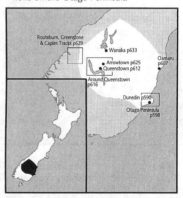

Though central Dunedin now has modern intrusions, much of the Victorian architecture survives: solid public buildings dot the city and wooden villas are scattered across the hilly suburbs. Preservation was as much a matter of fate as of planning.

After its heady start, Dunedin declined economically and much of its population

OTAGO

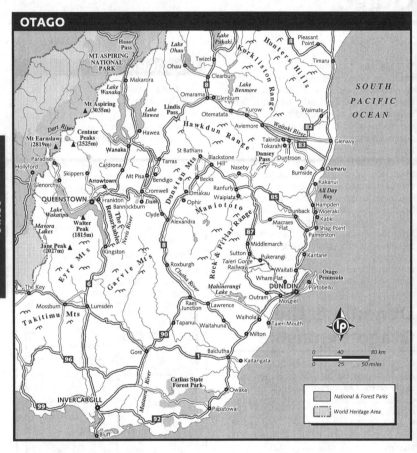

OTAGO

drifted away. Recent years have witnessed a slight revival, but local newspapers still lament the lack of economic opportunities.

Though Dunedin's boom years are gone, it is cultured, graceful and lively for its size. The 18,000 tertiary students drive the local arts, entertainment, cafe and pub scenes.

History

The early Maori history of the Dunedin area was particularly bloody, with a three-way feud between Otago Peninsula tribes and *utu* (revenge) followed attack as the Ngati Kahu and Ngatimamoe tribes' feud

escalated in the early 19th century. Then sealing and whaling along the coast brought ravaging diseases and by 1848 the once considerable population of Otakau Pa was just over 100.

The first permanent European settlers arrived at Port Chalmers in March 1848, six years after the plan for a Presbyterian settlement on the east coast of the South Island was initially mooted. Soon after, gold was discovered in Otago and the province quickly became the richest and most influential in the colony. Famous business houses were established and it was the powerhouse of the NZ economy. In 1879 it was the first city outside the USA to have its own tram system, which was not finally phased out until 1957.

Orientation & Information

Dunedin's main street changes from Princes St on the south to George St on the north as it crosses the eight-sided Octagon which marks the city centre. The Dunedin Visitor Centre (☎ 474 3300), Web site: www.cityofdunedin.com, is at 48 The Octagon, in the magnificently restored municipal chambers. It's open from 8 am to 6 pm on weekdays and 9 am to 6 pm on weekends, with shorter hours in winter.

The Department of Conservation (DOC) office (☎ 477 0677), at 77 Lower Stuart St, has pamphlets and information on walking tracks. The Automobile Association (AA; ☎ 477 5945) is at 450 Moray Place just east of Princes St.

The central post shop is on Princes St; it handles poste restante. There is an inner-city post shop on Moray Place. The Arc Cafe (☎ 474 1135), Web site: www.coffee .co.nz, is at 135 High St. It's popular with backpackers (see under Places to Eat later) and has Internet facilities, as do many of the backpackers places.

The informative, free *Focus on Dunedin* is widely available. The visitor centre also has an *Accessibility for People with Disabilities* pamphlet.

Olveston

Designed by a London architect and built between 1904 and 1906, this fine turn-of-the-century house at 42 Royal Terrace is preserved as when lived in by the Theomin family in the early 1900s. Though the building is not as extravagantly impressive as Larnach Castle (see the Otago Peninsula section), the lavish furnishings and art collections are stunning. One-hour guided tours at 9.30 and 10.45 am, noon, 1.30, 2.45 and 4 pm are a fascinating glimpse into the lifestyle of this fabulously wealthy family. Phone ☎ 477 3320 or email them at ✉ olveston@xtra.co. nz to reserve a place ($11, children $4).

Distillery & Breweries

Dunedin's most famous and popular factory tour has gone – Cadbury's no longer has chocolate tours.

Speight's Heritage Tours on Rattray St has tours of **Speight's Brewery** at 10 and 11.45 am and 2 pm from Monday to Sunday, and evening tours Monday to Thursday at 7 pm ($12, $4 for children accompanied by an adult).

Tours start from the brewery's visitor centre. The brewery is one of the smallest in the country. At the end of the one-hour tour you get to taste three beers, select one of these, and then pour it yourself. You must book (☎ 477 9480).

And 'Speights'? The locals say it stands for 'Superior Piss Enjoyed In Great Hotels Throughout Southland'.

Another good tour (free) is run by **Emerson's Brewery** (☎ 477 1812) at 4 Grange St, a boutique brewery specialising in good dark malt beers. Make sure you try the excellent London Porter or the India Pale Ale. Bookings are essential and the brewer prefers visits after 4 pm.

Museums

The **Otago Museum** (☎ 477 2372), Web site: www.otagomuseum.govt.nz, is at 419 Great King St. It has a large and varied collection, including Maori and South Pacific exhibits, a marine and maritime hall and a good Asian collection. The natural history displays of penguins, moa and extinct birds are particularly good and there is a hands-on Discovery World science centre for children (entry free). The museum is open from 10 am to 5 pm on weekdays, noon to 5 pm on weekends (free), and there's a cafe and craft shop.

The **Otago Settlers Museum** (☎ 477 5052), 31 Queens Gardens near the train station, has a photographic collection of the region's early settlers, as well as exhibits on the loss of Maori land and the role of Chinese miners.

The transport section has a variety of old vehicles. Steam locomotives in glassed-in display rooms at the train station end of the museum include *Josephine,* the first engine to run between Dunedin and Port Chalmers.

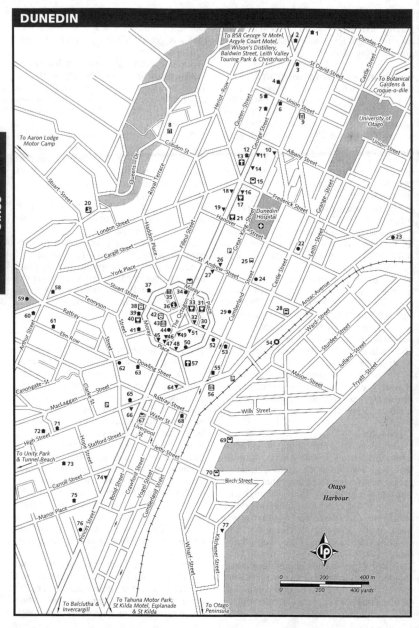

DUNEDIN

To 858 George St Motel,
Argyle Court Motel,
Wilson's Distillery,
Baldwin Street, Leith Valley
Touring Park & Christchurch

To Botanical
Gardens &
Croque-o-dile

University of
Otago

To Aaron Lodge
Motor Camp

Dunedin
Hospital

To Unity Park
& Tunnel Beach

Otago
Harbour

To Balclutha &
Invercargill

To Tahuna Motor Park,
St Kilda Motel, Esplanade
& St Kilda

To Otago
Peninsula

0   200   400 m
0   200   400 yards

OTAGO

DUNEDIN

PLACES TO STAY
1 Albatross Inn
2 Owens Motel
3 Cargill's Hotel
4 Sahara Guesthouse & Motels
5 Aunty's Backpackers
6 Farry's Motel
7 Allan Court Motel
12 Alexis Motor Lodge
37 Quality Hotel Dunedin
39 97 Motel Moray Place
41 Next Stop Dunedin
   Backpackers
53 Law Courts Hotel
55 Leviathan Hotel
58 Castlewood
60 Elm Lodge Too
61 Elm Lodge Backpackers
63 Adventurer Backpackers
   Lodge
65 Southern Cross; Casino;
   Ports O'Call; Deli Cafe
68 Penguin Palace Backpackers
71 Fletcher Lodge
72 Chalet Backpackers
73 Stafford Gables YHA
75 Manor House Backpackers

PLACES TO EAT
10 Captain Cook Hotel
11 Cafe Cena

14 Governors
16 Fast-food Restaurants (Mega
   Bite; The Reef; Khmer Satay;
   Korean Cuisine; Aspara;
   Modaks - Turkish Kebab)
18 London Lounge;
   Albert Arms Tavern
19 Steakhouse – The Huntsman
26 Little India
27 Paasha
30 Gypsy Café
32 Percolators
45 Bennu
46 Jizo Cafe
47 Etrusco at the Savoy
48 Cafe Zambezi
49 Ra Street Bar & Cafe
51 Passion Cafe/Bar
64 Palms Cafe
66 Arc Cafe
74 Bell Pepper Blues
77 High Tide

OTHER
8 Olveston
9 Otago Museum
13 Knox Church
15 Taxi Stand
17 Robbie Burns Hotel
20 Moana Pool
21 Abalone

22 Emerson's Brewery
23 Hocken Library
24 Supermarket
25 Suburban Bus Stop
28 InterCity Depot
29 Supermarket (Countdown)
31 The Woolshed
33 Ruby in the Dust
34 Library
35 Town Hall
36 Dunedin Visitor Centre;
   Rogano's Seafood
38 Fortune Theatre
40 Abbey Road
42 Stuart Street Terrace Houses
43 Dunedin Public Art Gallery;
   Café Nora
44 Air New Zealand
50 Automobile Association
52 DOC; Potpourri
54 Train & Taieri Gorge Railway
56 Otago Settlers Museum
57 First Church
59 Beverley Begg Observatory
62 Speight's Brewery
67 Central Post Shop
69 MV *Monarch* Harbour
   Cruises
70 Harbour Cruise (Blue Wave
   Cruise & Southern Spirit)
76 Newton Tours

OTAGO

The museum is open from 10 am to 5 pm on weekdays and 1 to 5 pm on weekends ($4, children free).

The **New Zealand Sports Hall of Fame** (☎ 477 7775), in the train station on Anzac Ave, is a must-see for keen sports fans.

The **Dunedin Public Art Gallery** (☎ 474 3450), at 30 The Octagon, is the oldest art gallery in NZ. Its international collection is small but has some big names – Gainsborough, Reynolds, Constable, Turner, Durer and Monet – even if some of the paintings are minor works. Excellent visiting exhibitions are staged. It's open from 10 am to 6 pm daily, except Friday (10 am to 8 pm) and Sunday (10 am to 5 pm).

The **University of Otago** (☎ 479 8247), Web site: www.otago.ac.nz, was founded in 1869, 25 years after the settlement of Otago, with 81 students. It has an interesting variety of old and new styles of architecture.

The old administration building is the most photographed building in Dunedin. Check to see if the Geology Museum and the Hocken Library (at the intersection of Anzac Ave and Parry St) are open.

Other Attractions
Dunedin parks include the extensive **Botanical Gardens** at the northern end of the city on the lower slopes of Signal Hill. There is a hothouse and an aviary with kea and other native birds.

It's possible to stargaze at the **Beverly Begg Observatory** (☎ 477 7683), in the Robin Hood Ground – it's off to your left across the lawn at the top (western end) of Rattray St. Viewing is on clear Sunday nights an hour or so after dusk in winter.

A short but definitely strenuous walk is up **Baldwin St**, listed in the *Guinness Book of Records* as the steepest street in the world

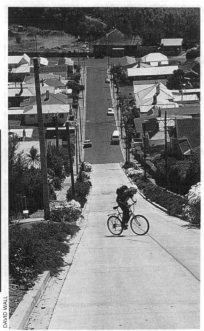

Baldwin St, Dunedin – alleged to be the
steepest street in the world

with a gradient of 1 in 1.266. From the city centre, head north up Great King St for 2km to where the road branches left to Timaru – veer right along North Rd for another kilometre. The Gut Buster race, held every year during the Dunedin Festival around February, sees the winners run up and back in around two minutes.

Swimming & Walking

The heated **outdoor saltwater pool** on the headland at the end of St Clair Beach is open in summer – catch bus No 34 from The Octagon. St Clair and St Kilda are good beaches for walking but on the shortest day (the middle of winter) you can join the famous Shortest Day Swim (in the sea, not the heated pool!).

There is a 1.5km walkway to **Tunnel Beach**, south-west of the city centre. Catch a Corstorphine bus from The Octagon to Stenhope Crescent and walk 1.4km along Blackhead Rd to Tunnel Beach Rd. It is then 400m to the start of the trail. This leads down through farmland for 20 minutes to the hand-hewn stone tunnel built by John Cargill so that his family could enjoy picnics on the small, secluded beach just over the headland. The sandstone cliffs are impressive and contain fossils if you look closely. The walkway is closed from August to October for the lambing season.

Catch a Normandy Citibus No 34 from The Octagon to the start of Norwood Rd, then walk two hours uphill (90 minutes down) to the **Mt Cargill-Bethunes Gully Walkway**, north-east of town. The highlight is the view from Mt Cargill, which is accessible by car. In Maori legend the three peaks of Cargill represent the petrified head and feet of a princess of an early Otakau tribe. Captain William Cargill was a leader of the early Otago colonists. Take warm clothes – it gets very windy at the top. From Mt Cargill a trail continues down to the 10 million-year-old Organ Pipes (half an hour), formed by cooling lava flows which left behind a crop of giant granite crystals. From here it is half an hour to the Mt Cargill Rd on the other side of the mountain.

North of Dunedin, the 5km **Pineapple Flagstaff Walk** is not accessible by public transport but offers great views of the harbour, coastline and inland ranges. If you have your own vehicle, look for the signpost at Whare Flat Rd.

Other Activities

Other Dunedin activities include golf (three 18-hole courses), tennis, ice skating and tenpin bowling. The Otago Aero Club (☎ 489 6158), Helicopters Otago (☎ 486 1784) and Mainland Air Services (☎ 486 2200) offer **flightseeing**.

The Otago Tramping & Mountaineering Club has regular meetings at 3 Young St, St Kilda; the Wilderness Shop (☎ 477 3679), 101 Stuart St, provides information.

Trojan Horseriding (☎ 465 7013) has rides along the beach north of Dunedin from $25 to $75, and Bums 'n' Saddles (☎ 488 0097) is based south of Dunedin at

Blackhead. Treks with Castle Discovery Horse Treks (☎ 0800-467 738) go to Larnach Castle ($45/35 for adults/children).

The Otago University Mountain Bike Club (☎ 479 5332) can advise on good **mountain bike** trips in the region.

For **sea kayaking** contact Heritage Boats (☎ 478 0820) at Weller Rocks on the peninsula.

Organised Tours

Taieri Gorge Railway Some visitors rate this as one of the great train journeys, similar to the Silverton to Durango line in Colorado. From October to April, four-hour excursions depart from Dunedin Station on set days at 2.30 pm and, from April to September, at 12.30 pm. The 58km trip to Pukerangi costs $53 return (students $42.40; one child free per adult). Some trains continue 19km further to Middlemarch. Tickets are available from Dunedin Station (☎ 477 4449), Web site: www.taieri.co.nz.

Most people take the train as a day trip, but you can continue on to Queenstown by bus with Pacific Tourways for a steep $99/49.50. Or take your bike on the train and cycle the Otago Central Rail Trail to Alexandra, an excellent trip along the railline extension which has been ripped up and converted into a mountain bike-walking track (see Central Otago for more details).

Cruises Otago Harbour Cruises (☎ 477 4276), Web site: www.wildlife.co.nz, is the main operator and has daily cruises from one to five hours long on the MV *Monarch* from the Rattray St wharf. The half-day Otago Harbour cruise for $59/30 for adults/children passes fur seal, shag and gull colonies and the albatross colony at Taiaroa Head.

Similar three-hour tours are available on the *Paranui* (☎ 477 8666, **@** paranui.harbour .cruises@xtra.co.nz).

Bus Tours Newton Tours (☎ 477 5577) has 1½-hour double-decker Citisights tours at 10 am and 3.30 pm from the visitor centre taking in historic buildings, the university, Baldwin St and the Botanical Gardens for $15 (children $8).

See also Organised Tours in the Otago Peninsula section.

Places to Stay

Camping & Cabins The *Tahuna Motor Park* (☎ 455 4690, 41 Victoria Rd), a large and efficiently run place, is near the showgrounds and beach at St Kilda. Tent/powered sites cost $18/18.50, cabins are $32 to $46 with en suite (prices for two). The check-out call over the loudspeakers will get you moving in the morning. St Kilda bus No 47 from The Octagon stops nearby.

The *Aaron Lodge Motor Camp* (☎ 476 4725, 162 Kaikorai Valley Rd), a well-tended place, has sites for $19, cabins at $33 to $36 and tourist flats at $54 to $61. It's 2.5km north-west of the city; take a Bradford or Brockville bus from The Octagon.

The *Leith Valley Touring Park* (☎ 467 9936, 103 Malvern St, Woodhaugh) has sites at $19, on-site caravans at $30 and tourist flats for $55.

Backpackers The *Stafford Gables YHA* (☎ 474 1919, **@** yhadndn@yha.org.nz, 71 Stafford St) is only a five-minute walk from the post shop. It's an elegant and sprawling old building, once used as a private hotel. The cost is $16 in dorm rooms and $38 for twins and doubles.

Elm Lodge Backpackers (☎ 474 1872, 74 Elm Row), with a Web site at www .elmwildlifetours.co.nz, is 10 minutes uphill (five back down) from The Octagon. It's a fine old family home with a cosy atmosphere and fantastic harbour views. It charges $14/15 per person in dorm/shared rooms and $34 for twins and doubles. This good backpackers also offers excellent wildlife tours of the Otago Peninsula. It picks up and drops off visitors (within reason) and rents out bicycles. Its overflow building nearby, *Elm Lodge Too* on Arthur St, is another fine old house with the same rates.

The central *Chalet Backpackers* (☎ 479 2075, 296 High St) is a former hospital with lots of character. Shared rooms cost $15 per person, singles $25, and twins and doubles $35, all including linen. There is plenty of information and some comfortable spots in the building's nooks and crannies to get away from it all.

The *Adventurer Backpackers Lodge* (☎ 477 7367, @ adventur@es.co.nz, 37 Dowling St) is close to the action and offers the highest standards. This large old building has been extensively renovated and the large common area with a small bar-kitchen is very chic. The rooms are immaculate and cost $14/15 in dorm/shared rooms, $32 for twin bunkrooms and $35 to $40 for doubles. Some of the rooms are small and windowless.

The *Manor House Backpackers* (☎ 477 0484, 28 Manor Place), Web site: www.manorhousebackpackers.co.nz, is in a couple of Dunedin's old stately homes. It has dorms at $15 (four to a room) and twins and doubles for $36. It operates a courtesy vehicle and has a comfortable TV common room, Internet and a nice outdoor patio.

Penguin Palace Backpackers (☎ 479 2175, fax 479 0700), on the corner of Rattray and Vogel Sts, is old but has all the facilities, including a TV room, sitting room with pool table and a pleasant dining/kitchen area upstairs. This city-style hostel has beds for $15, or $16 in less-cramped dorms. A single, when available, is $25 and doubles and twins are $34.

Aunty's Backpackers (☎ 0800-428 6897, @ auntys@xtra.co.nz, 3 Union St) is a small, pleasant place in an old colonial house. The staff are very helpful and the kitchen is a convivial meeting place. Dorm beds are from $15, and twins/doubles are from $34/36.

Next Stop Dunedin Backpackers (☎ 477 0447, @ nextstop@es.co.nz, 2 View St) is just a short walk from The Octagon up a steep street. This place is a converted church hall, with most rooms fronting the cavernous common room. There are shared rooms for $14 per person, and twins and doubles for $36.

B&Bs, Guesthouses & Motels The *Sahara Guesthouse & Motels* (☎ 477 6662, 619 George St), close to the city centre, is a grand old house with worn singles/doubles from $53/80 and better rooms with en suite for $84.

The *Albatross Inn* (☎ 477 2727, 770 George St), nearby, is superbly renovated.

Luxurious doubles with en suite and TV range from $85 to $125 for those with kitchen (less in winter).

Castlewood (☎ 477 0526, 50 Arthur St), Web site: www.castlewood.co.nz, is in a fine house and costs from $65/85 for singles/doubles.

Fletcher Lodge (☎ 477 5552, @ lodge@es.co.nz, 276 High St) is a renovated historic mansion only a few minutes from the city centre, and *The Stationmaster's Cottage* (☎ 0800-327 333, 300 York Place) is yet another historic building turned into a boutique B&B ($80/140 for singles/doubles).

Dunedin's most convenient motel row is along George St. The *Argyle Court Motel* (☎ 477 5129) on the corner of Duke and George Sts has units for $75.

The *Owens Motel* (☎ 477 7156, 745 George St) has a spa, courtesy car and units from $70 to $97.

Motels on George St charging around $90 include: *Farrys Motel* (☎ 477 9333) at No 575, *Allan Court Motel* (☎ 477 7526) at No 590, *858 George St Motel* (☎ 474 0047) and *Alexis Motor Lodge* (☎ 471 7268) at No 475.

97 Motel Moray Place (☎ 477 2050, 97 Moray Place) is central and friendly, and has been recently upgraded; good, new units cost from $89 to $140.

Moderately priced motels along Musselburgh Rise, on the Otago Peninsula side of town, include the *Arcadian Motel* (☎ 455 0992) at No 85, the *Chequers Motel* (☎/fax 455 0778) at No 119 and the *Bayfields Motel* (☎ 455 0756) at No 210. Double rooms cost $65 to $80.

The *St Kilda Motel* (☎ 455 1151, 105 Queens Drive) near St Kilda Beach charges from $55/70.

Hotels Relatively cheap hotels include the *Law Courts Hotel* (☎ 477 8036, 65 Stuart St), a very central place which has rooms with en suite for $50/75, and the *Beach Hotel* (☎ 455 4642, 134 Prince Albert Rd, St Kilda) with en suite rooms for $42/62.

The *Leviathan Hotel* (☎ 477 3160), on the corner of Cumberland and High Sts, solid, reliable, old-fashioned and central, is a Dunedin landmark. Its budget twin rooms are $70, the standard rate is $89, and studio units are $98.

Cargill's Hotel (☎ 477 7983, 678 George St) charges $112.50 to $195. It has a spa and courtyard garden.

At the top of the Dunedin listings are the *Quality Hotel Dunedin (☎ 477 6784)* on Upper Moray Place with 55 rooms, and the *Southern Cross (☎ 477 0752, 118 High St)*, with its excellent cafe (see Places to Eat later), 142 rooms and Dunedin's casino. Prices at both start at around $200.

Places to Eat

Restaurants The *Etrusco at the Savoy (☎ 477 3737, 8A Moray Place)*, stylish and very popular, serves delicious Italian food. On the upstairs floor, it's fully licensed and open from Tuesday to Sunday from 5.30 pm. Medium pastas are reasonably priced at around $13.50, pizzas are $19.50 and the desserts are excellent.

Palms Cafe, on the corner of Dowling and Lower High Sts, is a pleasant and deservedly popular place open for dinner. Mains are from $19 to $25; try the Denver leg venison or the aubergine and vegetable curry.

Rogano's Seafood, in the municipal building on The Octagon (next to the visitor centre), is an elegant restaurant with fine cuisine, priced accordingly.

Little India (☎ 477 6559, 82 St Andrew St) is a great Indian eatery specialising in tandoori dishes. Curry mains are around $16 and set meals are offered. Get there early to be sure of a table.

Steakhouse – The Huntsman (☎ 477 8009, 311 George St) is for steak-lovers, with 20 steak dishes and a fantastic selection of salads at reasonable prices.

High Tide (29 Kitchener St) is another excellent restaurant down by the waterfront with views of the harbour and peninsula. The blackboard menu features local produce, including seafood.

Bell Pepper Blues (☎ 474 0973, 474 Princes St) has a great menu with such delights as baked fresh blue cod ($26); pre-booking is recommended.

Bennu (☎ 474 5055, 12 Moray Place) has an international menu focusing mainly on Mexican and Italian dishes; try its huge chicken enchiladas.

The *Esplanade (☎ 456 2544)*, overlooking the beach at St Clair, is popular with locals on the weekend. Brunch from $5.50 to $12.50 is served from 11 am to 2 pm. There is also a good selection of pastas and pizzas.

Cafes Cafe society is well catered for in and around The Octagon. *Cafe Nova* at the Dunedin Public Art Gallery on The Octagon has good coffee, all-day breakfasts and sumptuous cakes.

The *Deli Cafe* in the Southern Cross hotel (see Places to Stay earlier) is known for its hot roast beef sandwiches.

The *Passion Cafe/Bar (☎ 477 7084, 153 Lower Stuart St)* adds a touch of European style, and the *Percolator*, across the road at No 142, specialises in good coffee. Both have reasonably priced meals and snacks, are open during the day and are popular night venues.

Paasha (31 St Andrew St) is an excellent little Turkish cafe open from 11.30 am to midnight (until 2 am on Friday and Saturday). Large mains are only $6.50 up to $9.50 for the Turkish mixed grill, and it does takeaways.

Croque-o-dile in the Botanical Gardens has good service and food in a delightful setting and is open from 10 am to 4 pm daily.

The *Gypsy Cafe* in Lower Stuart St is run by an ebullient Frenchman who tends to take your mind off his fine products. This intimate little place only seats about 20.

The *Ra Street Bar & Cafe (☎ 477 6080, 21 The Octagon)* is open daily for all meals, and it changes to a popular music and dance venue at night. As for breakfast, when did you last have lambs fry and bacon (on corn waffles)?

Cafe Cena (466 George St) also has very good, innovative NZ fare with mains costing around $22.

The *Arc Cafe* (see Information earlier) is very popular with travellers. It serves good-value meals and often has live music.

OTAGO

Pub Food The *London Lounge (☎ 477 8035, 2A Pitt St),* upstairs in the Albert Arms Tavern, is open daily for hearty pub meals – steak and seafood – for under $10. The weekday lunch roasts are only $5.50. Serves are huge and piled with chips to satisfy student appetites, and Emerson's fine brews are on tap.

The *Captain Cook Hotel,* at the intersection of Albany and Great King Sts, is another popular student pub, and has good food upstairs – if you can get in the door – and a beer garden.

Fast Food Many of Dunedin's sandwich or lunch places are along George St and around Moray Place.

Cafe Zambezi (480 Moray Place) is a BYO with an excellent selection of sandwiches and light meals.

Potpourri (97 Stuart St), near the DOC office, is a good wholefood place with salads, vegetarian burritos, quiche and other light meals. It's open from 9 am to 8 pm on weekdays and 10 am to 2 pm on Saturday.

Mega Bite (388 George St) has a similar menu, and desserts topped with frozen yoghurt. There is a collection of other places near Mega Bite on both sides of George St (between Frederick and Hanover Sts) including *Modaks* for hamburgers, *Aspara* for Cambodian dishes, the *Turkish Kebab, Korean Cuisine, The Reef* for seafood, and the *Khmer Satay*.

Governors (438 George St) is something of an institution for student meals (big breakfasts, steaks, pies etc) and low prices. Open from 8 am until midnight, it is decorated with student notices and ads. The Union Building in the university has a cheap cafeteria and a bar.

Jizo Cafe (56 Princes St) serves relatively inexpensive Japanese dishes such as udon (noodles), miso and sushi sets; it's BYO.

Entertainment
The *Otago Daily Times* back page lists what's on around the city.

Pubs, Music & Dancing Dunedin is a drinker's town and a good place for a pub crawl. Many of the pubs and bars cater to students and are packed during term but die in the university holidays.

The *Captain Cook,* or simply the 'Cook', on the corner of Albany and Great King Sts near the university, is *the* student pub, often so hopelessly crowded you can hardly get in the door. Bands often play.

The *Albert Arms* on George St is a less crowded student pub that comes into its own on Monday and Tuesday nights when bands play. Monday night's Irish band is very popular.

Other student bars are *The Woolshed* on Moray Place, a smaller place with a good atmosphere, and *The Outback* on Great King St, a cafe-bar with music.

Ruby in the Dust on The Octagon gets a mixed crowd and has acoustic and other music.

Dunedin has few bands playing original music, despite its reputation as NZ's alternative music capital.

Ports O'Call in the Southern Cross (see Places to Stay) is a popular gay bar.

Some of the liveliest drinking holes are the many bar/cafe/restaurants (see Places to Eat). *Passion Cafe/Bar* on Lower Stuart St has jazz occasionally. *Bennu* on Moray Place is an incredibly popular place with a yuppie crowd, especially on Friday and Saturday nights in the downstairs bar, which has house music.

Abalone (☎ 477 6877, 44 Hanover St), on the corner of George St, is alive with the ringing of mobile phones and the nudging of shoulder pads, especially on weekend evenings.

The *Bacchus Wine Bar (☎ 474 0824, 12 The Octagon)* would make the Roman god it's named after very happy; it has an impressive selection of NZ and imported wines. It's closed on Sunday.

The *Robbie Burns Hotel,* if you still have the energy or inclination, has live jazz on Fridays.

Theatre & Folk Music Dunedin has the professional Fortune Theatre and several amateur companies. The New Edinburgh Folk Club meets at 6 Carroll St on Friday at 8 pm.

Getting There & Away

Air Air New Zealand (☎ 477 6594) on the corner of Princes St and The Octagon has daily direct flights to/from Auckland, Christchurch and Wellington, with connections to other centres. Ansett (☎ 0800-267 388), 1 George St (on The Octagon), has direct flights to/from Auckland, Christchurch and Wellington, and from (but not to) Invercargill. Southern Air flies to Invercargill and on to Stewart Island.

Bus InterCity (☎ 474 9600), 205 St Andrews St, has services to Christchurch, Wanaka, Invercargill, Mt Cook, Queenstown and Te Anau.

Several door-to-door shuttles service Dunedin. Atomic Shuttles (☎ 474 3300) runs to Christchurch ($25) and Queenstown ($25). Southern Link (☎ 474 3398) has services from Dunedin to Christchurch, Queenstown and Te Anau and Wanaka. The drop-off and pick-up point for all shuttles is at the train station.

The Bottom Bus (☎ 471 0292, @ info@ bottombus.co.nz) and the Catlins Coastal Link (☎ 474 3398, @ info@southern-nz .co.nz) both do the scenic route through the Catlins (see The Catlins in the Southland chapter). Both of these pick up from accommodation.

Train Dunedin's magnificent train station (☎ 477 4449) is on Anzac Ave. The *Southerner* (Christchurch-Invercargill) passes through in both directions daily. Tickets are sold at the train station and the visitor centre.

Hitching To hitch northwards get a Pinehill bus to SH1 before the motorway or a Normandy bus to the Botanical Gardens from The Octagon, or walk for 30 to 40 minutes. Hitching south, take an Otago Road Services bus from Princes to Fairfield.

Getting Around

Dunedin Airport Shuttles (☎ 477 7777), Johnson's Express (☎ 476 2519) and City Airport (☎ 477 1771) offer door-to-door airport services for $11 per person (children $5.50). The 27km trip takes 40 minutes.

Citibus buses leave from The Octagon area and buses to districts around Dunedin leave from Cumberland St. Buses run regularly during the week, but routes combine on weekends to form limited services or they simply stop running. The visitor centre has timetables and the average trip costs $1.55 to $1.80.

OTAGO PENINSULA

You can spend a pleasant day, or longer, tripping around the Otago Peninsula, the most accessible wildlife area on the South Island. Stops can be made at Larnach Castle, Glenfalloch Woodland Gardens, the Portobello Westpac Trust Aquarium and Otakou Marae, where there's a Maori church and meeting house with a small museum, and there are many other historical sites, walkways and natural formations. The *Otago Peninsula* brochure and map is available at both the Dunedin and Taiaroa Visitor Centres and lists over 40 sights and activities.

Wildlife

For many people the peninsula's wealth of interesting fauna is the main reason for visiting. As well as albatross and yellow-eyed penguin tours, little blue penguins *(koroa)*, fur seals and sea lions can be seen on the peninsula.

Albatross Taiaroa Head, at the end of the peninsula, has the only northern royal albatross colony in the world close to human habitation. The birds arrive at the nesting site in September, court and mate in October, lay eggs in November, then incubate the eggs until January, when the chicks hatch. Between March and September parents leave their chicks while collecting food, returning only for feeding. By September the fledged chicks leave.

The visitor centre at Taiaroa has excellent displays on the albatross and other wildlife, with regular screenings of videos. The only access to the area is from the centre. Tours head up the hill to the glassed-in viewing area overlooking the albatross nesting sites. The tour includes a 30-minute introduction at the visitor centre and then 30 minutes

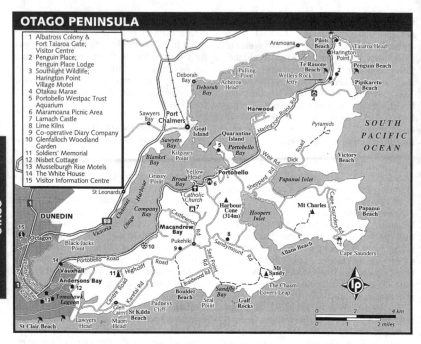

OTAGO PENINSULA

1 Albatross Colony &
  Fort Taiaroa Gate;
  Visitor Centre
2 Penguin Place;
  Penguin Place Lodge
3 Southlight Wildlife;
  Harington Point
  Village Motel
4 Otakau Marae
5 Portobello Westpac Trust
  Aquarium
6 Maramoana Picnic Area
7 Larnach Castle
8 Lime Kilns
9 Co-operative Diary Company
10 Glenfalloch Woodland
   Garden
11 Soldiers' Memorial
12 Nisbet Cottage
13 Musselburgh Rise Motels
14 The White House
15 Visitor Information Centre

viewing the birds. In calm weather it's unlikely you'll see an albatross flying, but chances are better later in the day when the wind picks up. Ask if the birds are around before you pay. Entry to just the visitor centre is free (donations please). The main viewing area is closed during the breeding season (mid-September to late November) and on Tuesday mornings.

The head is also home to the tunnels of **Fort Taiaroa**, built in 1886 and featuring a 150mm Armstrong Disappearing Gun. The gun was installed during the late 19th century to counter the improbable threat of attack from Tsarist Russia; it was so named because it could be withdrawn into its bunker after firing. Tours go to the fort for $12/6; the 1½-hour combined albatross and fort tour costs $25/12 for adults/children.

The Taiaroa Visitor Centre (☎ 478 0499, ✉ albatros@es.co.nz) is open from 9 am to 8 pm daily (shorter hours in winter). Tours go hourly until 1 pm, then roughly every half-hour. Tours run from Dunedin (see Organised Tours in this section), or you can catch a Portobello bus and hitch the remaining 11km through beautiful scenery.

Penguins The yellow-eyed penguin (in Maori: *hoiho*), one of the rarest penguin species, can be seen at close quarters on the peninsula. Tours run from Dunedin but you have more options with your own transport.

From Penguin Place (☎ 478 0286), just off the Portobello Rd, 1½-hour tours run to its unique yellow-eyed penguin conservation project. A talk on penguins and their conservation is included, and the system of trenches and hides allows viewing of the penguins from just a few metres. This is as close as you'll get anywhere, so the tours are very popular. Tours cost $25/12 and go throughout the day in peak times, though prime viewing time is a couple of hours before dark. The project is funded entirely through profits from these tours. For tour times and bookings, phone Penguin Place or the Dunedin Visitor Centre.

The operators of Penguin Place have replanted the breeding habitat, built nesting sites, cared for sick and injured birds and, importantly, trapped predators. The yellow-eyed penguin's greatest threat is loss of habitat, especially the low-lying coastal vegetation in which the birds nest. Sadly, many farmers in Southland and Otago allow cattle to trample remaining patches of vegetation favoured by yellow-eyed penguins.

If you have a car, Southlight Wildlife (☎ 478 0287), 200m past the turn-off to Penguin Place, can give you a key ($7.50, family $15) that opens the gate to a farm road starting right next to the albatross colony and leading to Penguin Beach. This beach has a colony of yellow-eyed penguins (bring binoculars).

A number of tour operators (see Organised Tours in this section) go to other yellow-eyed penguin beaches through private 'conservation reserves', ie, land owned by farmers who charge for the privilege. Yellow-eyed penguins also nest at other, public beaches but numbers are small and sightings less certain. Sandfly Bay has a small colony which can be viewed from a DOC hide at the far end of the beach. Follow all signs, don't approach the penguins and view only from the hide.

Sea Lions The New Zealand (more commonly Hooker's) sea lions can only be seen on a tour (see Organised Tours) to a 'secret' beach where the first pup was born on the NZ mainland after a breeding absence of 700 years. You will usually see six or more animals. The sea lions, visitors from Campbell Island and the Auckland Islands, are predominantly bachelor males.

Other Attractions

Larnach Castle (☎ 476 1616) is Dunedin's best-known building, a symbol of the indecent wealth that once resided in the city. This private 'castle' is a conglomeration of architectural styles and fantasies on the highest point of the peninsula. Built by JWM Larnach in 1871, its construction cost

£125,000, about $25 million by today's standards. Proving that money can't buy happiness, Larnach, a merchant and politician, committed suicide in a Parliament House committee room in 1898.

Larnach Castle is 15km from central Dunedin and can be reached by tour or by taking the Portobello bus to Company Bay and walking 4km uphill. Horse treks are operated from Broad Bay (see Other Activities under Dunedin earlier). The castle is open from 9 am to 5 pm. Entry to the castle and gardens is $12 (children $4.50) and you can explore the castle at will, or you can pay $6 (children $2) to visit only the gardens, stable and ballroom.

The **Glenfalloch Woodland Garden**, 430 Portobello Rd, 9km from Dunedin, is noted for its rhododendrons and azaleas and for the domestic birds freely wandering in the grounds. The garden is open from 9.30 am until dusk daily. There's a tearoom and a restaurant popular with wedding parties. The Portobello bus stops at the front.

The University of Otago's **Westpac Trust Aquarium** (☎ 479 5819) is on Hatchery Rd, at the end of a small peninsula near Portobello. The small room has fish and invertebrates from a variety of local marine habitats, and 'touch tanks' with animals and

Elaborate Larnach Castle

plants found in shallow waters and rock pools. The aquarium is open from noon to 4.30 pm, from 1 December to 1 March and during school holidays. The rest of the year it's open on weekends at the same hours ($5, children $2).

Walking

The peninsula has a number of scenic farmland and beach walks, though you really need your own transport to get to the trails. It is a half-hour walk from the car park at the end of Seal Point Rd down huge sand dunes to the beautiful beach at Sandfly Bay.

From the end of Sandymount Rd it is a 40-minute round-trip walk to the impressive cliff scenery of The Chasm and Lovers Leap. A one-hour side trail leads to Sandfly Bay.

Other walks include those to the Pyramids and Mt Charles (through private land). Get a copy of the *Otago Peninsula Tracks* pamphlet from the visitor centre.

Organised Tours

Elm Wildlife Tours (see Places to Stay under Dunedin) has interesting tours of five to six hours ($39). You'll usually see the royal albatross (visitor centre tours not included), little blue penguins, fur seals, yellow-eyed penguins and Hooker's sea lions. Viewing sites are at private beaches. Many other species of birds are spotted on the way, especially waders in the peninsula's eastern estuaries. This is the only tour where you will most probably see a Hooker's sea lion. (We saw the 'big five' within 90 minutes.)

Back to Nature Tours (☎ 0800-477 0484), Web site: www.backtonaturetours.co.nz, does the same type of trip for $43.

From Dunedin, Newton Tours (☎ 477 5577), 595 Princes St, has bus tours to Larnach Castle along the Highcliff Rd for $30 (children $15), and Wildlife Tours to Taiaroa has options to view the albatross on land or on water with the *Monarch* cruise, or to see the yellow-eyed penguins at Penguin Place. It's $43 (children $22) or $89 ($45), including the penguins and a *Monarch* cruise.

Otago Peninsula Express (☎ 474 3300), Web site: www.southern-nz.co.nz, provides shuttle transport to Taiaroa, Penguin Place

and Southlight Wildlife for $25 return, but not to Larnach Castle (with penguin *or* wildlife tour $50). It departs from the visitor centre and hotel pick-up can be arranged.

Wild South (☎ 474 3300) also has twilight tours to see yellow-eyed penguins at Southlight Wildlife.

For small group ecotours, Wings of Kotuku Tours nature guides (☎ 454 5169) is recommended. It has sunrise walks to see the yellow-eyed penguins ($45).

Places to Stay & Eat

The *Portobello Village Tourist Park* (☎ 478 0359, 27 Hereweka St) in Portobello township has tent/powered sites at $18/20 for two. On-site vans are $35 and tourist flats $60.

Larnach Stablestay (☎ 476 1616), in the grounds of the famous castle, has double rooms in the historic stable building at $55 and hotel-style rooms in the new lodge from $120. Meals are available.

The *Penguin Place Lodge* (☎ 478 0286), at the Penguin Place tour office on Harington Point Rd, is $15 per person in twin rooms (linen $5 extra).

Nearby, the *Harington Point Village Motel* (☎ 478 0287), on the main road near Southlight Wildlife, has self-contained units sleeping four for $85. Broad Bay has B&B accommodation and there are other homestays on the peninsula.

Nisbet Cottage (6A Elliffe Place, Shiel Hill) is a delightful new B&B. Run by Wings of Kotuku Tours, it's from $95 to $120 for two.

The Cottage (☎ 478 0073, 748 Portobello Rd, Broad Bay) is a self-contained place in a private setting; it's $80 for two (a breakfast hamper is provided). Contact 7 Frances St, Broad Bay, first.

Sleepy Hollow (☎ 478 0306, 687 Portobello Rd, Broad Bay) is another cottage option.

McFarmers Backpackers (☎ 478 0389, 78 Portobello Rd, Portobello) is a friendly place with dorms and doubles for $15 per person.

The *1908 Cafe & Bar* (☎ 478 0801) in Portobello is an excellent, if expensive, restaurant. The changing blackboard menu has a wide variety of delights, including seafood – blue cod, bay clams and mussels. Entrees cost around $9, mains around $25.

Portobello has a fish-and-chip shop, and Macandrew Bay has fish and chips and *McKenzies of Macandrew Bay* (☎ *476 1081*) with its 'international fusion' menu – how's an entree ($10) of green-lipped mussels with Creole spices and raclette cheese souffle sound?

PORT CHALMERS

On the opposite side of Otago Harbour from the peninsula, Port Chalmers was founded in 1844 and became Dunedin's port. The modern container port is no great attraction, but the town's historic streetscapes have hardly changed since its heyday as the centre of the frozen meat trade in the 19th century.

The **museum**, open from 1.30 to 4.30 pm on weekends, has nautical displays, but the main interest is the collection of old photograph albums. **Flagstaff Lookout** has expansive views of the town and harbour.

Pub accommodation is available, though Port Chalmers is primarily a day-trip destination. Stop for a drink at one of the old stone pubs, such as *Carey's Bay Hotel* overlooking the yacht harbour.

The *Port Stables Bar & Cafe* is a trendier alternative on the main street.

From Port Chalmers the narrow road hugs the coast all the way to **Aramoana**, a small settlement with a white-sand surf beach where yellow-eyed penguins nest.

Central Otago

Most Central Otago towns owe their origin to 40 years of gold mining during the 19th century. The goldfields area extends from Wanaka down to Queenstown and Glenorchy, east through Alexandra to the coast at Palmerston, and south-east from Alexandra to Milton. Interpretative pamphlets such as *Goldfields: Heritage Trail* show towns and gold-mining areas. Stone buildings, gold-mining equipment and machinery, and miles of tailings (waste left over from mining) are found throughout the area, while Queenstown, an important town

during Otago's golden days, maintains its glory in the modern gold rush – tourism.

Most of Central Otago lies on a rugged and dry plateau, sheltered by the Southern Alps. In summer, days are warm to hot and rainfall is very low. In winter, temperatures can drop to well below freezing.

CROMWELL
pop 2610

This modern little town is on the main route between Wanaka and Queenstown. Cromwell is the heart of stone fruit country – as testified by the giant Carmen Miranda's hat display in front of the town. Roadside stalls sell all manner of fruit and January to February is the main picking season.

The Cromwell & Districts Information Centre (☎ 445 0212, @ cromwellvin@ xtra.co.nz), Web site: www.cromwell .org.nz, in the Cromwell Mall, handles bookings and has displays on the hydroelectric projects in the Clutha Valley. It's open from 10 am to 4 pm daily. The information centre also houses the town **museum** with artefacts of local mining, including a section on the Chinese miners.

On Melmore Terrace, **Old Cromwell** is a row of historic buildings housing craft shops overlooking Dunstan Dam. They were painstakingly removed and restored from the original Cromwell, now flooded by the waters of the dam.

Gold-mining sites around Cromwell include Bannockburn, crumbling Bendigo and the Kawarau. Across a footbridge spanning the Kawarau Gorge, the **Goldfields Mining Centre**, 5km towards Queenstown, has tours of the tailings and old mine machinery for $14 – easily skipped at that price.

Bendigo, 18km from Cromwell on the Bendigo Loop Rd, is a classic ghost town. A hunt around in the scrub will turn up the ruins of stone cottages, but stick to obvious tracks as there are many deep mine shafts.

Tucked away above the Nevis River is the new, sensational **Nevis High Wire Bungy**, a suspended gondola and a masterpiece of engineering in its own right (see Queenstown later).

OTAGO

The Kawarau Gorge between here and Queenstown is spectacular and there's **bungy jumping** at the old Kawarau suspension bridge. Built in 1880 for access to the Wakatipu goldfields, it was used until 1963.

Places to Stay & Eat

The *Cromwell Holiday Park* (☎ 445 0164) on Alpha St, 2km from the town centre, has tent and powered sites at $19 and cabins from $30 to $48 for two.

The *Chalets* (☎ 445 1260, 102 Barry Ave), owned by the local polytechnic, was once the quarters for the dam workers. Each chalet has its own lounge and kitchen and a number of well-equipped singles/doubles with washbasin for $30/40 for two (linen $5 extra).

Hotels and motels include the *Golden Gate Lodge* (☎ 445 1777) on Barry Ave with restaurant, lounge, public bars and doubles from $80; and the *Twin Rivers Motel* (☎ 445 0035, 67 Inniscort St) with rooms for $68/75.

The *Cromwell Mall* has coffee lounges and restaurants. The *Ploughmans* is licensed and has a takeaway section.

ALEXANDRA

pop 4620

East of Cromwell is Alexandra, the hub of Central Otago. The lure of gold brought thousands of diggers to the Dunstan goldfields but the town owes its permanence to the postrush dredging boom of the 1890s. The orchardists followed and Alexandra owes its current prosperity to them. This pretty town is an oasis of trees among barren, rocky hills.

The Central Otago Visitor Information Centre (☎ 448 9515, @ info@tco.org.nz), 22 Centennial Ave, provides maps and plenty of local information like its excellent *Walk – Central Otago,* a series of seven pamphlets outlining walks in the region. See its Web site (www.tco.org.nz) for more information.

The huge clock on the hill above town, Alexandra's answer to the Hollywood Hills sign, can be reached by a walking track or by a drive to a nearby viewpoint. The DOC office (☎ 448 8874) is at 45 Centennial Ave.

The **Alexandra Historical Museum** (☎ 448 7077), on the corner of Thompson and Walton Sts, houses a comprehensive collection of mining and pioneering relics; it's open from 11 am to 5 pm on weekdays, 1 to 4 pm on weekends.

The free *Central Otago Vineyards* map has details on a dozen **vineyards**, the southernmost in the world.

Four-wheel driving enthusiasts can attempt the **Dunstan Trail**, a magnificent rugged mountain road from Alexandra to SH87 near Outram, a one-hour drive from Dunedin. The trail leaves you in awe of the tenacity of the early gold prospectors who stumbled across muddy sections and over steep hills with their bullock wagons and horse-drawn drays. Check with DOC in Alexandra first and remember to leave all gates as you found them. With time spent for stops at Paerau (Styx), Serpentine Flat and the Great Moss Swamp the trip takes five to six hours.

Mountain Biking

Alexandra is mountain bike heaven with numerous old gold trails through the Old Man, Dunstan, Raggedy and Knobby Ranges. A highlight for keen bikers is the Dunstan Trail. The *Mountain Biking* pamphlet from the information centre details five exhilarating rides but check latest track conditions (eg, the Roxburgh Gorge Track has become dangerous). The Otago Central Rail Trail (see that section later) from Clyde via Alexandra to Ranfurly is ideal for cyclists. Henderson Cycles on Limerick St and MCS Services on Shannon St rent out bikes. Guided trips are operated by MCS Services.

Places to Stay & Eat

The *Alexandra Holiday Park* (☎ 448 8297) on Manuherikia Rd has sites for $19 and basic cabins from $28 to $34 for two.

The *Pine Lodge Holiday Camp* (☎ 448 8861, 31 Ngapara St) has tent/powered sites for $17/19, basic cabins from $30 to $36 and motels for $62.

The *Two Bob Backpackers* (☎ 448 8152, 4 Dunorling St), an excellent YHA associate, overlooks the Clutha River and provides information on walks, mountain biking and kayaking. Dorm beds cost $15; there is one double for $36 and a family room.

Of the town's eight motels, the *Kiwi Motel (☎ 448 8258, 115 Centennial Ave)* is one of the cheapest, with units from $68.

Centennial Ave has the *Avenue* and the *Bakery* bakeries, and pub food is served at the *Bendigo Hotel*, Tarbert St.

Fruitlands Cafe, 10 minutes out of town towards Roxburgh, does great Devonshire teas for around $5.50.

Getting There & Away

InterCity and Atomic pass through Alexandra with connections to Wanaka, Queenstown and Dunedin. The InterCity agent is Gourleys Travel (☎ 448 8198) at 4 Centennial Ave.

CLYDE

pop 850

This attractive town, only 10km west of Alexandra, was once the centre of the Dunstan Goldfields, and historic stone buildings line the streets. Clyde has two **museums**: the Clyde Museum on Blythe St in the historic Magistrate's Courthouse features exhibits depicting domestic life on the early goldfields; the Stationary Engine Display on Upper Fraser St includes all sorts of rural machinery.

The Clyde Lookout Point, reached from a signposted road, gives great views out over the once bustling goldfields.

The massive Clyde Dam is at the edge of town and tours of the project ($5) leave at 1 pm from the Clyde Information Centre (☎ 449 2056); bookings are essential.

Places to Stay & Eat

There's not much to Clyde, but good accommodation caters for the regular tourist traffic. The *Clyde Holiday Park (☎ 449 2713)* has tent/powered sites for $16/18, on-site vans and a cabin for $36.

Dunstan House (☎ 449 2295), a beautiful old stone building on Sunderland St, is a fine place to stay and charges $45/65 for singles/doubles.

A couple of doors along, the historic *Dunstan Hotel* is one of the few left in a town that once boasted 70 pubs. It has rooms from $38/53 and meals. Clyde also has motels.

The *Post Office Cafe & Bar*, Blythe St, is a fine dining establishment as is the delightful, award-winning *Oliver's Restaurant (☎ 449 2860, 34 Sunderland St)*. Oliver's has boutique accommodation; check its Web site at www.olivers.co.nz.

OTAGO CENTRAL RAIL TRAIL

Combined with the scenic Taieri Gorge rail trip from Dunedin to Middlemarch (see Organised Tours under Dunedin for details), this track makes an excellent traffic-free route for cyclists. The former railway line from Middlemarch to Alexandra and Clyde has been taken over by DOC, the tracks ripped up and resurfaced, and the trail uses the old rail bridges, viaducts and tunnels.

The Middlemarch to Ranfurly (62km) and Lauder to Clyde (45km) sections are open. Until Ranfurly to Lauder (50km) is complete, cyclists have to use SH85 or the Ida Valley Rd on this section.

The trail can also be used by horses or walked, but the rolling farmland and rocky hill scenery is not enough to maintain interest for walkers over the entire length.

ALEXANDRA TO PALMERSTON

To the north-east of Alexandra the Manuherikia Valley bears rich evidence of Otago's golden age. At Blackstone Hill the SH85 swings south-east to the Maniototo plain and via the Pig Root to the sea and Palmerston.

Today's peacefulness belies the bustling past of the small township of **Ophir**, 27km north of Alexandra and a short side trip from Omakau on the main highway. The Manuherikia River is still spanned by the 1870s Dan O'Connell Bridge and there is a restored 1886 post and telegraph building. Ophir has the widest temperature range of any town in NZ: from -20°C in winter to 35°C in summer.

Ophir Lodge Backpackers (☎/fax 447 3339, 1 Macdonald St) is handy if you're cycling the rail trail and it will pick up from Omakau. Cabins cost $12.50 (share basis), twins are $28 and doubles are $26. It's closed June to August.

The road forks at Becks, where there is a great old pub. The left fork leads to **St Bathans**, once a thriving gold-mining town with a population of 2000 – today there are less than 20 inhabitants. This is a real get-away sort of place and has original buildings like the 'haunted' *Vulcan Hotel (☎ 447 3629)*, a quaint living museum and the only survivor of the town's 14 hotels. Rooms cost $60 a double and meals are available. In winter, curling teams compete on frozen ponds near town.

The **Blue Lake**, formed entirely by sluicing activity, is a popular nearby picnic spot.

Back on SH85, eastbound past Blackstone Hill, **Naseby** was once the largest gold-mining town on the Maniototo. There's a museum and the surrounding area is great walking country. From May to September the Maniototo Ice Rink (☎ 444 9270) is used for skating, curling and ice hockey.

The *Ancient Briton Hotel & Motel (☎ 444 9992)* on Lever St has rooms for $24 per person or motels for $68 for two; it serves bistro-style meals.

The *Larchview Camping Ground (☎ 444 9904)* has tent/powered sites for $17/18, cabins for $28 and self-contained cottages from $42 to $52 for two.

Danseys Pass, 39km north of Naseby, is another goldfields town with a great 1860s pub where it's said the stonemason was paid a pint of beer for each stone laid! The *Danseys Pass Coach Inn (☎ 444 9048)*, a quaint old place strategically located between the Maniototo and the Waitaki Valley, has been extensively refurbished. One of the 11 en suite doubles costs from $108 to $125.

Ranfurly

pop 840

This small town is the hub of the vast inland Maniototo plain, the site of a number of stud farms. Nearby Naseby with its goldfields and the more luckless Hamiltons goldfields near Waipiata were the original reasons for European settlement. When the railway line was closed in 1990, it came as another nail in the town's coffin, but the conversion of the line into the walking-cycling Otago Central Rail Trail brings a promise of tourism. The **Display Centre** at the old train station has interesting exhibits and audio-visuals on the history of the line.

The Maniototo Visitor Centre (☎ 444 9970, ✉ maniototo.vic@xtra.co.nz) is on Charlemont St.

The *Ranfurly Camping Ground (☎ 444 9144)* on Read St has tent/powered sites for $17/18 and cabins are $25 for two.

The *Ranfurly Lion Hotel (☎ 444 9140, 10 Charlemont St East)*, on the main street, has good pub rooms for $40/60 or $45/75 with en suite. It also runs the *Dew Drop Inn* backpackers opposite, a blockhouse building next to a rail line that charges $10 per person ($15 with linen). The pub's restaurant is the best in town.

Peter's Farm Hostel (☎ 444 9083) is in an old farmhouse, 3km from Waipiata and 12km from Ranfurly off the highway. Apart from the peace and quiet of the farm, the main attractions are the free horse treks and kayaking and the walking loop nearby. Dorm beds cost $14 per night, while doubles and twins are $32. Peter will pick up from Ranfurly.

Macraes Flat

Not all of the gold has disappeared, and the small town of Macraes Flat is the gateway to the huge Macraes Gold Mine. From Ranfurly it is 63km east along SH85 to Dunback and then 17km south to Macraes Flat. The open-cut mine is the largest in NZ, and tours on the first weekend of the month can be arranged through *Stanley's Hotel (☎ 465 2400)* in Macraes Flat. The hotel has DB&B for $45 per person.

ALEXANDRA TO DUNEDIN

South-east from Alexandra via SH8 to Dunedin there's more evidence of the 19th century's gold-seekers and spectacular scenery: **Fruitlands** is a restored 1866 pub where food and crafts are sold. About 1km away, via Symes Rd, the restored **Mitchells Cottage** is a fine example of the Shetland Islands stonemasons' building skills.

The next town of any size is **Roxburgh**, in an area known for fruit growing. Sales begin in early December, continuing until early winter. This small town has a camp and a couple of motels. The *Villa Rose Backpackers (☎ 485 9101, 79 Scotland St)* is a tidy converted house with all facilities;

a dorm or shared room is $14, and twins and doubles (if not taken up by itinerant fruit pickers) are $32.

Between Roxburgh and Milton, near Lawrence, is **Gabriels Gully**, the site of a frenzied stampede for gold by 10,000 miners in July 1861, after Gabriel Read discovered gold in the Tuapeka River. Interesting walks near the town include Gabriels Gully to Jacobs Ladder.

In Lawrence, the ***Oban House Backpackers*** (☎ 485 9600, 🖂 obanhouse@xtra.co.nz, 1 Oban St) has beds for $15 in shared or dorm rooms and twins and doubles for $34.

There is a takeaway and bistro in the *Coach & Horses Tavern* on Ross Place.

At Lawrence the road splits to the coast and SH1 to Dunedin via Milton or by Lake Mahinerangi and the Waipori goldfield (and Waipori Falls) with more relics of the gold rushes. Dunedin is 55km north of Milton and about half that distance from where the Waipori Falls road meets SH1.

THE CLUTHA DISTRICT
The mighty Clutha River, through the Clutha district's collection of small communities, is not NZ's longest river (the Waikato is 16km longer) but it carries the most water. Clutha is Gaelic for Clyde, alluding to that river in Scotland; to the Maori it is Mata-au (Surface Current).

The Clutha drains a huge area including Lakes Hawea, Wanaka and Wakitipu. In a number of places the river has been dammed to feed hydroelectric power stations. The Clyde Dam holds back the waters of Lake Dunstan, and generated great controversy at the drowning of such natural beauty.

The towns of Clinton, Lawrence, Milton, Waihola, Owaka, Tapanui and Balclutha are all part of the region. Owaka is covered in The Catlins section of the Southland chapter.

Balclutha
pop 4130
The largest town in South Otago, Balclutha is dominated by an impressive arched concrete bridge across the Clutha River.

The Clutha Information Centre (☎ 418 0388, 🖂 clutha.vin@cluthadc.govt.nz), at 4 Clyde St, is staffed by a friendly bunch and open from 8.30 am to 5 pm on weekdays, 9 am to 3 pm weekends.

There is a **museum** at 1 Renfrew St. The scattered collection of 10,000 old farming and household implements indicates just how much things have changed over the years.

Peggydale Leathercraft & Tea Kiosk 2km north of town is just the place if you are looking for the genuine sheep's article.

The ***Naish Park Holiday Park*** (☎ 418 0088, 56 Charlotte St) has sites for $16 and cabins for $22 to $30 for two.

Balclutha Backpackers (☎ 025-291 7466, 20 Stewart St), a former nunnery, has a long way to go to attain 'good digs' status. It's OK if you are stuck here overnight ($16 for a bed with linen).

The ***Rosebank Lodge*** (☎ 418 1490, 265 Clyde St) is the flashest place in town; a double or twin costs $85. The information centre lists other possibilities in the region.

Garvan Homestead B&B (☎ 417 8407), in Lovell's Flat north of Balclutha, has excellent rooms and food; with every little detail taken care of, it's worth the $90 to $120 for doubles.

The ***265 Restaurant*** in the Rosebank Lodge has a menu featuring locally caught salmon and trout.

The ***Hotel South Otago*** and several takeaways are along the main street.

Sinclair Wetlands
These wetlands, basically shallow peaty lagoons, are 50km south of Dunedin and near Lake Waihola. They are home to several species of waterfowl, some of NZ's rarest birds, and the secretive bittern. There are open walkways which you can follow during daylight hours. The wetlands are signposted from SH1.

North Otago

The Waitaki River, south of Waimate, marks North Otago. Continuing south from the Waitaki is Oamaru, the largest town in North Otago. Follow either SH82 from Waimate or SH83 from Pukeuri Junction

OTAGO

OTAGO

(just north of Oamaru) to reach Kurow and the Waitaki Valley. From here SH83 continues to Omarama via the hydroelectric lakes of Waitaki, Aviemore and Benmore.

OAMARU
pop 12,000

Pretty Oamaru was first settled by Europeans in 1853. It was the seventh-largest town in NZ by the 1870s and early 1880s. Refrigerated meat shipping made it prosperous, and the local sandstone was the favoured material for the many imposing buildings that still grace the town.

The novelist Janet Frame used Oamaru as the setting for some of her books (see the boxed text 'Shiver with a sense of yesterdays...' in this section).

The town comes alive during the Heritage Celebrations in late November with penny-farthing races and other events. Oamaru also has fine public gardens and colonies of little blue penguins and the rare yellow-eyed penguin.

The Oamaru Visitor Information Centre (☎ 434 1656), Web site: www.waitaki-dc .govt.nz, is on the corner of Thames and Itchen Sts. It has extremely helpful staff and is open from 9 am to 5 pm on weekdays, 10 am to 4 pm on weekends (extended hours in summer).

There's an AA agent on the corner of Thames and Usk Sts.

Harbour-Tyne Historic Precinct

Oamaru boasts the best-preserved collection of historic commercial buildings in NZ, particularly in the Harbour-Tyne Street Precinct, which has 22 classified buildings. The town's architecture is a mosaic of styles from Gothic revival to neoclassical Italianate and Greek. The local limestone was soft enough to be sawn, but it hardened when exposed to the air and so was a convenient and enduring building material. The free *Historic Oamaru* pamphlet describes this precinct. Walking tours ($7.50) leave from the visitor centre.

Several small businesses have set up in the precinct, including a bookbinder, bookshop, antique shops, cafes and the Criterion Hotel, open daily for an old-fashioned ale.

The Woolstore has souvenirs and a car museum. A good market is held on Sunday.

The **North Otago Museum** on Thames St is open from 1 to 4.30 pm on weekdays and has historic and general exhibits.

Public Gardens

Floraphiles will adore these 1876 gardens with a red Japanese bridge across Oamaru Creek, an Oriental Garden, Fragrant Garden, Rhododendron Dell, Cactus House and Azalea Lawn. The main entrance gates are on Severn St where it crosses the railway line.

Penguins

You can actually walk to the yellow-eyed penguin and little blue penguin colonies from the town centre.

Little blue penguins are numerous and nest right in the town around the Oamaru Harbour. Once considered a pest – they would nest under buildings and on council reserves – they are now the mascot for Oamaru and are the town's biggest tourist attraction. At the end of Waterfront Rd a nesting site has been fenced to keep out predators, and nesting boxes and a small grandstand have been built. This is a country town version of the Phillip Island complex in Australia, the most famous site for viewing little blue (or fairy) penguins. The small visitor centre has souvenirs and entry costs $8 (children free). The penguins waddle ashore around dusk in the nesting season from September to February, but can also be seen at other times.

The loss of coastal forest for breeding has made **yellow-eyed penguins** among the world's rarest penguins. The Bushy Beach nesting site has good natural vegetation and a hide allows undisturbed observation of these beautiful birds. The yellow-eyeds are best seen a couple of hours before sunset, when they come ashore to feed their chicks, but they are shy and easily upset, so avoid loud noises and stick to the trail and hide. It is well worth taking a tour ($5), operated under a DOC concession, that allows closer viewing. Tours leave from the car park on Bushy Beach Rd in the early evening (the information centre has times).

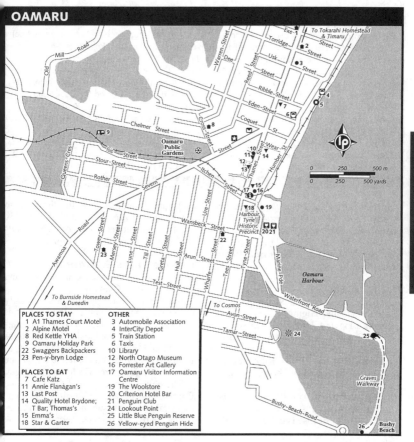

OAMARU

PLACES TO STAY	OTHER
1 A1 Thames Court Motel	3 Automobile Association
2 Alpine Motel	4 InterCity Depot
8 Red Kettle YHA	5 Train Station
9 Oamaru Holiday Park	6 Taxis
22 Swaggers Backpackers	10 Library
23 Pen-y-bryn Lodge	12 North Otago Museum
	16 Forrester Art Gallery
PLACES TO EAT	17 Oamaru Visitor Information
7 Cafe Katz	Centre
11 Annie Flanagan's	19 The Woolstore
13 Last Post	20 Criterion Hotel Bar
14 Quality Hotel Brydone;	21 Penguin Club
T Bar; Thomas's	24 Lookout Point
15 Emma's	25 Little Blue Penguin Reserve
18 Star & Garter	26 Yellow-eyed Penguin Hide

OTAGO

Places to Stay

The *Oamaru Holiday Park* (☎ 434 7666) on Chelmer St, adjacent to the large public gardens, has tent/powered sites at $18/20 and various cabins for $28 to $42 for two.

There's a *DOC camping ground* at Glencoe Reserve, adjacent to SH1, 2km west of Herbert, which is 22km south of Oamaru.

The *Red Kettle YHA* (☎/fax 434 5008) on the corner of Reed and Cross Sts is open from October to June. Dorm beds are $15 and twins are $34.

Swaggers Backpackers (☎ 434 9999, 25 Wansbeck St) is a small, homey backpackers with a good atmosphere. Dorms cost $15 and the twin room is $34.

Cosmos (☎ 434 6311, 9 Traill St) is a ladies-only place with table tennis and a pool table; it's $15/13 for the first/second day.

The *Alpine Motel* (☎ 434 5038, 285 Thames St),* conveniently located, has units from $65 to $85 for two, and the *A1 Thames Court Motel* (☎ 434 6963, 252 Thames St) has units from $68 for two.

The *Waitaki Accommodation Guide* lists many homestays and farmstays (from $80 to $100 for two).

OTAGO

Shiver with a sense of yesterdays...

The renowned novelist Janet Frame was born in Dunedin in 1924 but spent most of her early school years in Oamaru. Her Oamaru home, 56 Eden St, is mentioned in her autobiographies. She uses the name 'Waimaru' as a pseudonym for the town and it appears in some of her novels.

She first gained international repute in 1957 with *Owls Do Cry*. Many of the places alluded to in this novel can still be seen in town – the clock tower, the Opera House ('Miami' in the book), the Majestic (the 'Regent'), the local dump (now site of the Red Kettle YHA) and the Duck Pond.

All of these places can be seen on the Janet Frame Trail outlined in the free *Heritage Trails of North Otago*. Other sites relate to *Faces in the Water* (1961), *Scented Gardens for the Blind* (1963), *A State of Siege* (1967), *Intensive Care* (1970) and *The Edge of the Alphabet* (1962).

It was Jane Campion's film version of *An Angel at my Table*, based on the second volume of Janet Frame's autobiographical trilogy, that spurred current interest in her works. Frame had a somewhat tortured life as a young woman, and became rather reclusive later. She still lives in NZ.

Special B&Bs are *Tokarahi Homestead* (☎ 431 2500, e tokarahi@xtra.co.nz, 47 Dip Hill Rd, Tokarahi), *Pen-y-Bryn Lodge* (☎ 434 7939, 41 Towey St), Web site: www.penybryn.co.nz, and *Burnside Homestead* (☎ 432 4194, 17 D Rd).

Places to Eat
Most places are concentrated along Thames St and the Thames Highway.

Emma's (☎ 434 1165, 15 Thames St) is home to Oamaru's cafe society and has the best coffee in town.

Cafe Katz (☎ 434 9543), Ribble St, has fresh local food and a blackboard menu; it's a good place for lunch.

The *Last Post* (☎ 434 8080, 12 Thames St), the town's first post office, has been revived as a fully licensed restaurant (mains are about $20).

The *Star & Garter* (9 Itchen St) is an interesting licensed restaurant with a heritage theme, a pianola and changing menu.

The *T Bar* (115 Thames St) in the Quality Hotel Brydone has good-value meals (steaks $13 and pizzas around $15). *Thomas's*, also in the Brydone, is a more upmarket, a la carte restaurant.

Annie Flanagan's (84 Thames St) is an Irish bar with generous meals and a good selection of ales.

Entertainment
The *Criterion Hotel Bar* (3 Tyne St) is the town's best watering hole but is only open on Friday. From there, ask for directions to the *Penguin Club*, a hot little club run by local musos that gets some top-name bands on Friday and other special nights.

Getting There & Around
InterCity buses between Christchurch and Dunedin stop in Oamaru.

Shuttles that pass through are generally cheaper but not as reliable. Atomic Shuttles (☎ 322 8883), Southern Link Shuttles (☎ 358 8355) and South Island Connections (☎ 0800-742 669) all charge $20 to Dunedin. To Christchurch, it's $20 from the Lagonda Tearoom and $35 for door-to-door.

The only buses to Central Otago are the Canride bus to Twizel on Friday and a bus to Geraldine. The summer service (Cook Connection) runs from Oamaru to Mt Cook ($45).

The Christchurch to Invercargill rail service stops at Oamaru, with a train in each direction daily except Saturday and Sunday. Trains leave for Invercargill at 11.29 am and for Christchurch at 2.11 pm.

There is a taxi service (☎ 434 1234) but the best way to see the old part of town is on foot.

WAITAKI VALLEY
The Waitaki Valley has interesting towns between the turn-offs on SH1 and Omarama: Glenavy, Duntroon, Kurow and Otematata. **Duntroon** was established in 1859 by Robert Campbell, owner of Otekaieke Station, as a

village for his workers. Named after Duntroon Castle in Scotland, it has an authentic blacksmith shop, trout- and salmon-fishing nearby and jet-boating on the Waitaki. Accommodation is available at motor camps (including Danseys Pass) and food at the Duntroon Tavern.

There are Maori rock drawings at **Takiroa**, 50km west of Oamaru on SH83. The sandstone cliff drawings were done with red ochre and charcoal and may date back to the moa-hunting period (AD 1000 to 1500). Other rock-art sites in the region are mostly on private land and can only be visited with permission from the owners. The Oamaru visitor centre gives directions.

Kurow, at the junction of the Waitaki and Hakataramea Rivers, loosely translates as 'A Hundred Mists', as nearby Mt Bitterness is often covered with fog. From 1928, when the Waitaki power station was built, Kurow has been a service centre for Waitaki hydroelectric schemes like Benmore power station (constructed from 1956 to 1965) and Aviemore (1968), and there is fishing, boating and snow skiing nearby. Visits to the huge Benmore power station must be arranged through the Benmore Information Centre (☎ 438 9212). Check with the Kurow Community Centre (☎ 436 0812) about motels in the town and nearby farm stays. The *Glenmac Farmstay (☎ 436 0200, @ glenmac@xtra.co.nz)* has backpacker beds for $15, and B&B is $35 per person.

Fishing

The fishing season in Waitaki's rivers, hydro lakes and tributaries is usually from 1 October to 30 April but lasts all year in some rivers. Rainbow and brown trout are caught in the Waitaki, Hakataramea, Otematata and Maerewhenua Rivers, Deep Stream and Waitaki, Aviemore and Benmore Lakes; quinnat salmon are taken from the Waitaki. Anglers can toss in a Tylo, a Pheasant tail nymph, a Royal Wulff or Craig's Nighttime and wait for that elusive bite. At night, a caddis imitation will be just the ticket. The locals may reveal some of their secrets (for a few cans of beer).

Omarama

pop 355

Omarama is at the head of the Waitaki Valley, 119km north-west of Oamaru, at the junction of SH8 and SH83.

Not far from Omarama are the Paritea or **Clay Cliffs**, formed by the active Osler fault line that continually exposes clay and gravel cliffs. These clay pinnacles are quite interesting but they are 15km from Omarama down a dirt road and entry is $5. Similar formations can be seen from SH8, about 3km south of town.

Omarama has a worldwide reputation for gliding due to the area's north-west thermals – the world championships were held here in the summer of 1994–95. Alpine Soaring (☎ 438 9600) has flights costing around $135 for 20 minutes.

The Omarama Information Centre (☎ 438 9610) is open from 10 am to 4 pm daily, but closed from May to August.

Places to Stay

Omarama Holiday Park (☎ 438 9875) has tent and powered sites/cabins/tourist flats for $18/30/57 and motels for $47 for two. Glenburn, 7km away, also has a motor camp.

The *Omarama Hotel (☎ 438 9713)* has a guest TV lounge and rooms for $30/55 for singles/doubles. There are several motels in town.

Eight kilometres north of Omarama on SH8, *Buscot Station (☎ 438 9646)* has a good backpackers on a merino sheep and Hereford cattle farm. Beds in shared rooms cost $12 and twins are $30; it's closed from mid-May to mid-August.

Killermont Station (☎ 438 9864), 15km south of Omarama on SH8, has a similarly peaceful backpackers lodge and also closes in winter. Singles, twins and doubles are all $15 per person.

Dunstan Downs (☎ 438 9862, @ tim .innes@xtra.co.nz), 17km from Omarama, is yet another option. A bed is $15; it's closed from June to August.

The *Otematata Country Inn (☎ 438 7797, 11 Rata Drive),* 96km north of Oamaru, is a YHA associate, and rooms are $36 for two.

OAMARU TO MOERAKI

The coast road south from Oamaru provides a peaceful break from SH1 with fine coastal views, good beaches and resident dolphins. It joins the highway again about halfway to Moeraki.

Coastal Backpackers (☎ *439 5411),* on a farm at All Day Bay, provides very good standards of accommodation for $15 per person. It has free canoes, mountain bikes, farm activities and organic seaweed harvesting. It's 16km south of Oamaru on the coastal road, 20km north of Moeraki. Follow a signposted turn-off onto the gravel road for 6km until you reach the sealed road. Turn left and proceed 1km up the road to the old church hall. This is it – with all the facilities you need, a lagoon with prolific bird life, beach walks, yellow-eyed penguins, dolphins and fur seals. Hearty three-course meals are $9.

MOERAKI

Extraordinary spherical boulders like giant marbles can be seen at Moeraki, 30km south of Oamaru, and again further south at Katiki and Shag Point. The Ngati Kahu people tell how the canoe *Arai Te Uru,* on a voyage in search of prized *te wai pounamu* (greenstone), was wrecked near Shag Point. The round boulders are baskets and gourds (*te kai hinaki* or food baskets), and the irregularly shaped boulders to the south are kumara (sweet potatoes). The reef which extends seaward from Shag Point is the wreck of the canoe.

Scientists have a less romantic explanation that the boulders were not washed up onto the beach, but eroded from the mudstone cliffs behind. They were not moulded by the surf but formed into their spherical shape in the mudstone. Geologists refer to the boulders as septarian concretions, formed when minerals crystallised equally in all directions from an organic nuclei. Subsequent erosion often exposes an internal network of veins, which look like a turtle's shell, hence the name 'turtle back'. Further down the beach two concretions have been found to contain the bones of a 7m plesiosaur and a smaller mosasaur.

DAVID WALL

One of Moeraki's almost-spherical boulders

The township of Moeraki is 3km further south, off SH1 on a sheltered bay. From the back of the town a gravel road leads to the lighthouse for great views of the coast, and trails lead down the cliffs to a seal colony and a yellow-eyed penguin hide.

Places to Stay & Eat

The *Moeraki Motor Camp* (☎ *439 4759),* a friendly place 37km south of Oamaru and less than an hour's walk from the boulders, has tent/powered sites for $15/16, other cabins for $30 to $35, and tourist flats from $45. The German-speaking managers will find room for weary cyclists and have a cabin for $12/22 a single/double.

The *Moeraki Motels* (☎ *439 4862)* has units at $60. Meals are available from the tourist complex near the boulders.

MOERAKI TO DUNEDIN

The phallic-shaped symbol atop **Puke-tapu,** the high, pointed hill past Shag Point, is a monument to the member of parliament responsible for splitting large farms into smaller holdings. There's a track to the top signposted from the northern end of **Palmerston**.

McGregor's Bakery (126 Ronaldsay St) has food for the road, including its delectable mince pies.

From Palmerston the **Pig Root** to Central Otago leaves SH1; the name probably concerns the early road's condition. Gold miners preferred this route into the Maniototo as it was far more sheltered than the Old Dunstan Trail. The much improved road makes a great scenic trip into Central Otago.

The town of **Karitane**, 34km north of Dunedin, overlooks part of the Waikouaiti estuary. The Plunket Society, whose nurses continue to care for the country's babies, was founded in 1907 by Sir Frederic Truby King in King's Cliff, the two-storey house on the cliff. King revolutionised child care and in his lifetime saw infant mortality in NZ drop by two-thirds.

Lake Wakatipu

Queenstown is the self-styled 'adventure capital of the world' but when the party ends the Wakatipu region, with its stunning lake and surrounding mountain scenery, materialises as the real attraction. The aptly name Remarkables and the Eyre Mountains form a breathtaking backdrop. Words hardly do The Remarkables justice – they're pure magic capped with snow, at sunrise or in the afterglow of dusk.

QUEENSTOWN
pop 7500

Queenstown, on the shores of Lake Wakatipu, is nestled in what is surely one of the most scenic spots in the world. It's *the* resort town of the South Island and every tour stops here. There is plenty of hustling for the tourist dollar, but it has a fabulous range of facilities, activities, restaurants and nightlife.

There is great skiing in winter and plenty of substitute adrenaline activities in summer. Most activities are centred around the lake and many rivers nearby, especially the Dart, Shotover and Kawarau. White-water rafting and sledging, jet-boating and boogy boarding are all great ways to get wet. Bungy jumping, tandem parachuting and parapenting are similarly exciting ways to fly. But Queenstown also is a superbly equipped resort for more urbane pursuits.

Those wishing to move at a much more leisurely pace can take a trip on the *Earnslaw,* stroll through Arrowtown in autumn, play golf at Millbrook or shop in Queenstown's many (expensive) boutiques.

President Bill Clinton said it all: 'Queenstown is breathtaking. I wish I had weeks to spend here. When we flew in here, everyone on the plane was just gasping. It's just so beautiful. You are all very fortunate'.

History

When the first Pakeha arrived in the mid-1850s the region was deserted, although there is evidence of Maori settlement. Sheep farmers came first, but in 1862 two shearers, Thomas Arthur and Harry Redfern, discovered gold on the banks of the Shotover River, precipitating a rush of prospectors to the area. A year later Queenstown was a mining town with streets and permanent buildings. Then the gold petered out and by 1900 the population had dropped from several thousand to a mere 190.

The lake was the principal means of transport and at the height of the mining boom there were four paddle steamers and 30 other craft plying the waters. The Queenstown–Glenorchy Road along the lake was only completed in 1962.

Orientation & Information

Queenstown is a compact town sloping up the steep hills from the lakeside. The main streets are the pedestrian-only mall and Shotover St, with its activity booking offices.

The Queenstown Travel & Visitor Centre (☎ 442 4100, ✉ qvc@xtra.co.nz), Web site: newzealand-vacation.com, is in the Clocktower Centre on the corner of Shotover and Camp Sts. It's open from 7 am to 7 pm in summer (until 6 pm in winter). This very busy office is the biggest booking agent in

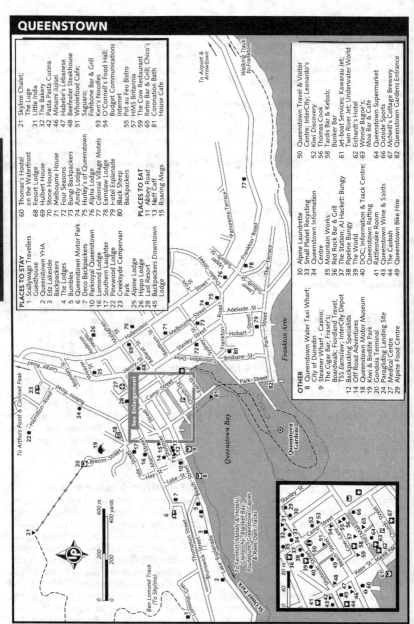

OTAGO

QUEENSTOWN

PLACES TO STAY
1 Scallywags Travellers Guesthouse
2 Queenstown YHA
3 Edz Lakeside Backpackers
4 The Lodges
5 Bumbles
6 Queenstown Motor Park
7 Deco Backpackers
10 Parkroyal Queenstown
16 Lomond Lodge
17 Southern Laughter
22 Pinewood Lodge
23 Creeksyde Campervan Park
25 Alpine Lodge
26 Hippo Lodge
28 Last Resort
45 Backpackers Downtown Lodge

60 Thomas's Hostel on the Waterfront
68 Resort Lodge
69 Hulbert House
70 Stone House
71 Melbourne House
72 Four Seasons
73 Bungi Backpackers
74 Amity Lodge
75 Hurley's of Queenstown
76 Alpha Lodge
77 Colonial Village Motels
78 Earnslaw Lodge
79 Hotel Esplanade
80 Black Sheep Backpackers

PLACES TO EAT
11 Abbey Road
13 Naff Caff
15 Roaring Megs

21 Skyline Chalet; The Luge
31 Little India
32 The Bakery
42 Pasta Pasta Cucina
46 Minami Jujisei
47 Habebe's Lebanese
48 Beefeater Steakhouse
51 Wholefood Cafe; Saguaro; Fishbone Bar & Grill
53 Ken's Noodles
54 O'Connell's Food Hall; Budget Communications Internet
55 Pot au Feu Bistro
57 HMS Britannia
59 The Cow Restaurant
65 Retro Bar & Grill; Chico's
81 Coronation Bath House Cafe

OTHER
8 Queenstown Water Taxi Wharf; City of Dunedin
9 Steamer Wharf - Casino; The Cigar Bar; Fraser's; Boardwalk; Fiordland Travel; TSS Earnslaw; InterCity Depot
12 Backpacking Specialists
14 Off Road Adventures
18 Queenstown Motor Museum
19 Kiwi & Birdlife Park
20 Gondola Terminal
24 Paragliding Landing Site
27 Medical Centre
29 Alpine Food Centre
30 Alpine Laundrette
33 Small Planet Recycling
34 Queenstown Information Centre
35 Mountain Works
36 Red Rock Bar & Grill
37 The Station; AJ Hackett: Bungy
38 Pipeline Bungy
39 The World
40 DOC; Information & Track Centre; Queenstown Rafting
41 Rattlesnake Room
43 Queenstown Wine & Spirits
44 The Casbah
49 Queenstown Bike Hire

50 Queenstown Travel & Visitor Centre; InterCity; Leonardo's
52 Kiwi Discovery
56 Thomas Cook
58 Tardis Bar & Kebab; Bunker Bar
61 Jet-boat Services: Kawarau Jet; Twin River Jet; Underwater World
62 Eichardt's Hotel
63 Winnie Bagoe's; Moa Bar & Café
64 Queenstown Supermarket
66 Outside Sports
67 McNeill's Cottage Brewery
82 Queenstown Gardens Entrance

town. Destination Queenstown (☎ 442 7440), Web site: www.queenstown-nz.co.nz, also provides copious information.

The DOC office (☎ 442 7933) on Shotover St, opposite the Trust Bank, is the place for information on the many natural attractions of the area. It's open daily, except Sunday, from 8 am to 7 pm (to 5 pm in winter).

Next door, the Information & Track Centre (☎ 442 9708), Web site: www.infotrack.co.nz, handles most of the transport to the trail heads for the Routeburn, Greenstone–Caples, Kepler, Milford and Rees–Dart Tracks. It's open in summer from 8 am to 8 pm (to 7 pm in winter).

On Camp St, Kiwi Discovery (☎ 0800-505 504, ✉ discovery@xtra.co.nz) also has track transport in summer, and ski transport and hire in winter.

On Shotover St, booking offices for activities include The Station (☎ 442 5252, ✉ the.station@xtra.co.nz), a video jungle that also houses AJ Hackett Bungy, Thomas Cook foreign exchange and 10 email terminals. Pipeline Bungy (☎ 0800-286 491) is next door. The Backpacking Specialists (☎ 442 8178) at No 35 is an agent for many activities and shuttle buses.

Fiordland Travel (☎ 0800-656 501), Web site: www.fiordlandtravel.co.nz, is in the Steamer Wharf on the waterfront. It books lake trips and tours to Fiordland.

The post shop on Camp St (with poste restante facilities) is open from 9 am to 5 pm on weekdays. Most backpackers have email facilities, and Budget Communications (☎ 441 1562, ✉ budgetc@xtra.co.nz), above McDonald's on Camp St, has 18 Internet terminals.

Queenstown has branches of all the major banks and plenty of moneychangers are open for longer hours. Thomas Cook has note-changing machines, including one on the Mall.

Things to See

Start at the top by catching the **Skyline Gondola** (☎ 441 0101) to the summit of the hill overlooking the town for incredible views over the lake. The hefty return fee is $13

(children $4). If the view isn't enough then look at *Kiwi Magic,* a hi-tech film that screens on the hour from 10 am to 8 pm. It's a chance to get rid of more change from your pocket ($8, children $4).

A new attraction is **The Luge**. You can zoom down in a three-wheel cart along two 800m tracks (Scenic and Advanced) – it's a heap of fun for all ages ($4.50 for one ride for adults and children, $22/18 for gondola and five luge rides).

The more energetic can walk up the vehicle track to Skyline from Lomond Crescent, but the ride is worth experiencing. The gondola operates from 10 am to 10 pm (until 9 pm in winter).

For views in the other direction, drive up to the back of The Remarkables. A short track leads past Lake Alta to a viewpoint at the top of The Remarkables, looking down over the lake to a diminutive Queenstown.

The private **Queenstown Motor Museum**, just below the lower gondola terminal, has a collection of old cars, motorcycles and a MiG 21 on show. It's open from 9.30 am to 5.30 pm daily, for shorter hours in winter ($8, children $4).

Right next to the gondola terminal is the **Kiwi & Birdlife Park** (☎ 442 8059). It has the NZ standard – two nocturnal kiwi houses – and a small but growing program for raising endangered species. Everyone will see a kiwi. Kea and the rare black stilt are on display in this attractive, landscaped park in the pine forest. It's open from 9 am to 5 pm daily, until 7 pm in summer ($10.50, children $4).

On the pier at the end of the Mall, near the centre of Queenstown, is **Underwater World**, a submerged observation gallery where you can see eels and trout in the clear waters of the lake. The agile little scaup or 'diving' ducks also make periodic appearances outside the windows ($5, children $2.50).

There are also **garden tours**, which include the Speight Gardens ($48), and escorted **winery tours** ($56) and Farm Scene for the kids. Queenstown even has a tourist-oriented **Maori concert** and *hangi*-style feast (☎ 442 8878), a rarity in the South Island ($45/25).

OTAGO

Bungy Jumping

The Queenstown activity that probably sparks the most interest is bungy jumping and there is no shortage of 'jumping' options. AJ Hackett (☎ 0800-286 495), Web site: www.ajhackett.com, is in The Station (see Information earlier). Hackett, world famous for his jump off the Eiffel Tower in 1986, began operating at Queenstown in November 1988.

Most jumpers are attracted to the historic **Kawarau Suspension Bridge**, 23km from Queenstown on SH6. It's 43m from the bungy jump platform down to the river. Observation platforms accommodate spectators. The Kawarau, the world's first commercial site, costs $99 (T-shirt included, video extra).

Above Queenstown on Bob's Peak (790m) is Hackett's The Ledge (30m), an urban but not urbane option – you can even jump at night ($89).

The **Skippers Canyon Bridge**, towering 71m over the narrow Shotover River gorge, is a spectacular site (but not always operating, so check). When it is, it's $110 including T-shirt.

Not high enough? Then the **Pipeline**, the second highest of the adrenaline 'highs', is 102m. Pipeline Bungy (☎ 442 5455), Web

DAVID WALL

Bungy jumping at Skippers Canyon

Nervous on the Nevis

No reassurances about safety standards can remove trepidation prior to leaping from the gondola jump pod of the 134m (440ft) Nevis Highwire bungy. The world's first gondola jump is an engineering marvel with 30 international patents on its many innovations. It spans a remote gorge on the Nevis River and the gondola is suspended by 380m-long cables.

Although all care is taken, several aspects of the construction have been deliberately designed to maximise exposure and titillate the 'fear factor'. This increases when, bedecked in a safety harness, you take the airy cable car out to the pod, and literally thunders when you peer through the glass-bottomed floor to watch the reactions of the first jumpers.

Your turn comes. You are briefed sitting in a chair, and adjustments are made to the bungy cords based on your weight. The chair is turned and you shuffle towards the abyss.

Countdown then six-plus seconds of freefall with the riverbed far beneath hurtling towards you – what an incredible groundrush! Relief as the bungy extends and you are catapulted to the top of the first bounce. At the top of the second bounce you release a rip cord and swing over into a sitting position. Now you can enjoy the bouncing and admire the view. A short bump, the clever recovery system swings into action, and you are winched back to the safety of the pod.

A relieved jumper quipped: 'This is great, you don't have to walk up from the river.'

site: www.bungy.co.nz, built the single-span suspension bridge across Skippers Canyon on the site of an 1864 gold-sluicing water pipeline. The pipeline has been reinstated and now incorporates a walkway. From the Pipeline office on Shotover St, the cost is $135 including transport to Skippers (videos and photographs extra).

And for the highest, The Nevis Highwire, see the boxed text 'Nervous on the Nevis' in this section ($149 includes jump and transport). Contact AJ Hackett Bungy (☎ 0800-286 495) in Queenstown.

The **Skippers Flying Fox** is milder than bungy but still a wild ride. It allows couples, if one is a little frightened, to select to be a 'jumper' at the bungy or 'foxer' ($39). It's possible that there will soon be jumping from hot-air balloons ($239).

Hackett and Pipeline offer combination packages that include jet-boating, helicopter flights, rafting, jumping and psychological counselling. Let's face it, after the jump the other options are chicken feed but, if you must do it all in one day, both Hackett and Pipeline charge about $340.

Jet-boating

Hurtling up and down the rivers around Queenstown in jet boats is a popular activity. The Shotover and Kawarau are the preferred rivers, with the Dart River less travelled, lengthy and more scenic (see Glenorchy later in this chapter).

Trips either depart straight from Queenstown or go by minibus to the river to board the jet boat. You can combine helicopter, jet-boat and raft rides ($229/169 on the Shotover/Kawarau). The busiest trip is the Shotover Jet, with nearly two million passengers so far. It's the boat operating in the Shotover canyons. Companies include: Dart River Jet Safaris (see Glenorchy later in this chapter); Shotover Jet (☎ 442 8570), Web site: www.shotoverjet.co.nz, which gives 30 minutes in the canyons with 360° spins for $75/35 for adults/children; Helijet, Queenstown (☎ 442 7318), which operates in conjunction with combination jet-boat and helicopter rides (the Lower Kawarau and Shotover Rivers is $119/89); and Goldfields Jet (☎ 445 1038), which operates from the Goldfields mining centre based in the historic section of the Kawarau River, 5km from Cromwell ($65/35).

Twin River Jet (☎ 442 3257, @ twinjet@ queenstown.co.nz) leaves from Frankton marina for Lower Kawarau and Shotover ($55/30); Kawarau Jet (☎ 442 6142) and Alpine Jet (☎ 442 8832) depart from the town pier for the Kawarau and Lower Shotover ($65); and Skippers Canyon Jet (☎ 442 9434), Web site: www.grandcanyon.co.nz, operates in the top of the canyon and

includes a land tour ($69/35). Kawarau Jet also offers free entry to Underwater World with its trips.

Combinations – there are too many to mention them all. The Triple Challenge, for example, includes the Shotover Jet, a helicopter ride and a raft trip with Queenstown Rafting on the Shotover ($229). An Adventure Marathon includes the Nevis and Ledge bungy jumps, Shotover Jet, rafting the Shotover, gondola ride, The Luge, *Kiwi Magic* presentation – all in 12 hours!

White-water Rafting

The rivers are equally good for rafting and again the Shotover and Kawarau Rivers are the main locations. Rivers are graded, for rafting purposes, from I (easy) to VI (unraftable). The Shotover canyon varies from III to V+, depending on the time of year and includes shooting the Oxenbridge Tunnel. The Kawarau River is a IV. On the rougher stretches there's usually a minimum age of 12 or 13 years. Rafting companies supply all equipment – it's like *Apocalypse Now* as you are lined up and given your uniform rafting gear; groups are marshalled into minibuses as others disembark from jet boats and helicopters buzz overhead.

Trips on the Shotover typically take 4½ hours or longer, but half of this time is getting there and back by minibus. Trips on the Kawarau take about an hour less ($99). On the Shotover you can do rafting only ($109), or one of several combinations.

Rafting companies include Queenstown Rafting (☎ 442 9792), which operates from Cavell's Rafting Lodge; Extreme Green Rafting (☎ 442 8517); and Challenge Rafting (☎ 442 7318, @ raftinfo@raft.co.nz) in the Queenstown Travel & Visitor Centre.

River Surfing & White-water Sledging

Perhaps the most exciting things you can do in the water near Queenstown are river surfing and white-water sledging.

Serious Fun (☎ 442 5262), 45 Camp St, takes exhilarating trips through the churning Chinese Dogleg rapid on a 7km section of the Kawarau using modified boogy

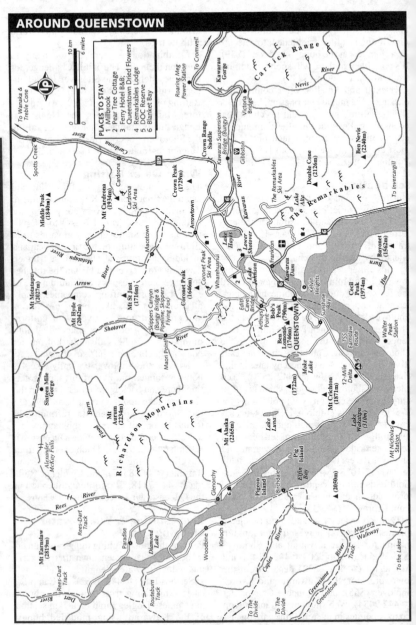

AROUND QUEENSTOWN

PLACES TO STAY
1 Millbrook
2 Pear Tree Cottage
3 Ferry Hotel B&B;
   Queenstown Dried Flowers
4 Remarkables Lodge
5 DOC Reserve
6 Blanket Bay

boards ($99). Mad Dog River Boarding (☎ 442 4117) does similar trips.

Frogz Have More Fun (☎ 0800-338 738) has trips where you get to steer highly manoeuvrable polystyrene sleds through rapids; it's a great adrenaline buzz. It operates on the Clutha ($75), Hawea ($85) and Kawarau ($95).

Paragliding & Parachuting

If you are up to it, try a tandem aerial parapente jump from Bob's Peak. Operators include Flying Cow (☎ 0800-284 376), Max Air (☎ 442 9792), Queenstown Tandems (☎ 442 7318) and Renegade Tandems (☎ 442 7640); all charge $130. Book or get hustled for business at the top of the gondola.

For those who prefer a delta wing there is Skytrek Hang Gliding (☎ 442 6311). It's not as weather dependent as skydiving and paragliding, and the launch sites at Coronet Peak and The Remarkables offer stunning views ($145). Antigravity (☎ 0800-426 445) lands its hang-gliders in town.

The Ultimate Jump (☎ 021-325 961), Web site: www.skydivetandem.co.nz, lets you tandem freefall to 'terminal' velocity before your parachute is opened and you are nursed safely to ground ($245).

Fly by Wire (☎ 025-300 474), Web site: www.flybywire.co.nz, allows you to control a high-speed tethered plane to speeds of up to 170km/hr and at forces about three times that of gravity ($129 includes a promotional video).

Paraflying on the lake is another way to see the sights from the air. Contact Paraflying (☎ 442 8507); an eight-minute flight behind its boat is $65.

Skiing

In winter The Remarkables and Coronet Peak skifields operate from Queenstown. Those who prefer motorised mobility to skis can churn up the white stuff along the Old Woman Range, in the Garvie Mountains, with Nevis Snowmobile Adventure (☎ 0800-442 4250) for $299 (3½ hours, helicopter flight included).

Heli-skiing is also popular and a full day with three runs will cost around $595.

See Skiing in the Activities chapter for more details or tune into 92 MHz FM.

Canyoning

XII-Mile Delta Canyoning (☎ 0800-222 696), Web site: www.xiimile.co.nz, has half-day trips in the 12-Mile Delta Canyons which expose you to all the fun ingredients which go with canyoning – waterslides, rock jumps, swimming through narrow channels, abseiling and a few surprises. Trips depart at 9.30 am and 1.30 pm daily, are 3½ hours and all equipment is provided ($95/69 for adults/children).

Mountain Biking

The Queenstown region has great mountain biking. If you are not that fit, avoid the strenuous uphill pedalling with an operator who takes you and your bike to a suitable high point. Gravity Action (☎ 442 8178) has a 'mega' trip into Skippers Canyon ($59, four hours).

Motorcycling

The region around Queenstown is perfect for off-road bikes, bigger touring bikes or four-wheelers on wild country tracks. Some Europeans find the freedom of these tracks a pleasant change from the restricted roads in their countries.

The rides combine thrills with a chance to see inaccessible historical areas amid the canyons and hills of Central Otago.

Dennis at Off Road Adventures (☎ 442 7858), Web site: www.offroad.co.nz, has information, prices and (especially) ideas. Three hours of the best guided biking (bikes or quads) you are ever likely to experience, in the Shotover Canyon or around Macetown, costs $225 (one/two-hour trips are $100/175).

Ask about the ATMBs (all-terrain motor boards)!

Walking

Many of Queenstown's activities are decidedly expensive but walks cost nothing. Stroll along the waterfront through town and keep going to the peaceful park on the peninsula. The lakeside walkway from Queenstown's

OTAGO

Peninsula St takes just over an hour each way through beautiful parkland.

One of the shortest climbs around Queenstown is up Queenstown Hill (900m), overlooking the town. It's a comfortable two to three hours up and back with good views. For a more spectacular view, climb Ben Lomond (1746m) – a difficult walk requiring a good level of fitness as it takes six hours return. As several people have underestimated this walk, we suggest you seek directions and advice locally.

There are many other walks in the area, especially from Arthurs Point and Arrowtown, areas rich in history – consult the DOC office for information. For longer walks you can hire camping equipment at Alpine Sports (☎ 442 7099) at 28 Shotover St; packs, sleeping bags, raincoats and boots are $5 per day, stoves and gaiters are $4. Mountain Works (☎ 442 7329) on Camp St, R&R Sports (☎ 442 7791) on the Mall and Kiwi Discovery (☎ 442 7340) at 37 Camp St all rent equipment. Small Planet Recycling (☎ 442 6393), 17 Shotover St, buys and sells all summer and winter recreational gear for tramping, skiing and biking.

Guided Nature Walks (☎ 442 7126), Web site: www.nzwalks.com, conducts excellent half-day Lakeshore & Miner's Forest ($80) and full-day Routeburn walks ($135).

Aerial Sightseeing

No possibility is ignored in Queenstown – if you can't boat up it, down it or across it, walk around it, or get a chairlift over it, then you can fly over it. Options range from short helicopter flights over The Remarkables (from $85) to plane flights to Milford Sound (from $165/100). More expensive flights to Milford include a brief landing ($176/120), or a one- or two-hour launch cruise on the sound ($195/130). Operators include: Milford Sound Fly & Cruise (☎ 442 3220), Air Fiordland (☎ 442 3404), Fiordland Travel (☎ 442 4846), Air Wakatipu (☎ 442 3148) and Milford Sound Scenic Flights (☎ 442 3065).

More exciting are aerobatic flights in a Pitts Special biplane ($195) with Actionflite Aerobatics (☎ 442 9708), or a one-hour flight in a hot-air balloon with Sunrise Balloons (☎ 0800-468 247, @ balloons@queenstown.co.nz) costing $295/175 for adults/children.

Other Activities

Still not enough activities in Queenstown? Well there's fishing, water-skiing, windsurfing, yachting, catamarans, horses, rock climbing, water-bikes, mopeds, or you can select dried flowers to send home or just collapse in a heap.

Organised Tours

Lake Cruises The stately steel-hulled TSS (Twin Screw Steamer) *Earnslaw* is the most famous of the lake's many cruise boats. Measuring 51m in length and 7.3m across the beam, it is licensed to carry 810 passengers, churns across the lake at 13 knots, burns a tonne of coal an hour and was once the major means of transport on the lake. The development of modern roads ended its career with NZ Railways. Since 1969 it has been used for lake cruises and now works harder than ever – check this schedule:

Walter Peak Sheep Station morning and afternoon tours – all year round, leaving at noon and 2 pm. They're 2½ hours long, and you see sheepdogs and sheep shearing at the station ($47/10 for adults/children).

Earnslaw Cruise only – you can't get off at Walter Peak. Daily all year at noon, 2 and 4 pm ($32/10).

Horse riding option at Walter Peak Sheep Station with Moonlight Stables – take *Earnslaw* at 10 am, noon or 2 pm (October to May) and after farm tour take scenic 40-minute horse trek before returning ($75/55).

Evening Dining Cruise – leaves at 6 pm ($75/37.50). It's four hours with a carvery buffet at Walter Peak.

Ask at the information centres about sailing trips on the lake. The *City of Dunedin* sailed around the world in 1982, taking nine months to complete the 43,500km voyage. The *City* does two-hour sailings, with every passenger (maximum 19) participating as part of the crew. The yacht sails from the water-taxi jetty opposite the Parkroyal ($45, children $20, food $10 extra).

Bus Tours There are all sorts of buses for a pleasant trip to nearby Arrowtown (see Arrowtown later).

Very popular Skippers Canyon trips take the winding 4WD road from Arthurs Point towards Coronet Peak and then above the Shotover River passing many sights from the gold-mining days. The scenery is spectacular, the road is hair-raising, and there's plenty of historical interest. Riches of Skippers Canyon (☎ 442 9434) and Outback Tours (☎ 442 7386) do 4WD trips for $55 (children $30), including a stop to try panning for gold.

Day trips via Te Anau to Milford Sound take 12 to 13 hours and cost around $155 (children $77.50), including a two-hour launch cruise on the sound. Bus-plane options are also available ($299/179.50). The main operators are Fiordland Travel, Great Sights and InterCity. Milford Sound is a long way from Queenstown and Te Anau is a better departure point. The same is true for trips to Doubtful Sound, which cost $190 (children $95) from Queenstown.

Kiwi Discovery (☎ 442 7340) has a Milford Sound day excursion for $119 ($95 without cruise, $89 from Te Anau).

The BBQ Bus (☎ 442 1045), Web site: www.milford.net.nz, charges $143/55 for adults/children, including a barbecue lunch (discount for card holders $118); from Te Anau it's $99/55. There's also a half-day Queenstown highlights tour ($69/30).

From October to March, Fiordland Travel has two-day trips ($195) to Milford Sound with a night on the *Milford Wanderer* (see Milford Sound in the Southland chapter).

Places to Stay

Despite Queenstown's 15,000 beds, finding a room at peak periods can be difficult. Prices go sky-high during the summer and ski-season peaks. Prices given are for the high season.

Camping & Cabins The *Queenstown Motor Park (☎ 442 7252)* is less than 1km from the town centre at the end of Man St. A tent site is $20, cabins cost from $35 and tourist flats from $60 (all for two). The camp is convenient and very well equipped

– good kitchen, coin-operated laundry, TV room and email facilities.

The *Creeksyde Campervan Park (☎ 442 9447)* on Robins Rd is a modern, neat place with a few tent sites and powered sites for $22, lodge rooms for $40 for two, and tourist flats and motels for $65 to $85 a double.

The *Frankton Motor Camp (☎ 442 2079)*, a tired place by the lake 6km from town, has tent/powered sites at $19/22 for two, cabins for $38 and tourist flats for $65.

The *Kawarau Falls Lakeside Holiday Park (☎ 442 3510)* is past the airport at Frankton in a beautiful setting by the lake. Tent/powered sites cost $19/20 per person, and cabins are from $35 to $48 for two.

A *DOC camping ground* at 12-Mile Creek Reserve, Glenorchy Rd, is just 15km from Queenstown.

Backpackers The *Queenstown YHA (☎ 442 8413, ✉ yhaqutn@yha.org.nz, 80 Lake Esplanade)* is right by the lake. The cost is $19 to $20 per person in four- to eight-bed dorms and from $44 to $46 for twins and doubles. It has recently been renovated with good rooms, and has email facilities.

Bumbles (☎ 442 6298), further along Lake Esplanade on the corner of Brunswick and Beach Sts, has dorm/twin bunkrooms for $17/19 per person, twins/doubles for $38/45 and good communal areas with views across the lake. It gets mixed reviews and a mixed clientele but all-in-all this is a good place.

Thomas's Hostel on the Waterfront (☎ 442 7180, 50 Beach St), Web site: www .thomashotel.co.nz, is popular for its backpackers rooms. Dorms cost $17 and $19 ($24 with linen); doubles with TV and telephone are a cut above the usual backpackers and cost $60. All rooms are heated and have their own bathrooms, TV and fridges. Regular, better-equipped hotel rooms cost from $72/85. It has a ground-floor communal kitchen and lounge with views of Lake Wakatipu. Attached is the Cafe Fat Ginger's. There's bike and sea kayak hire. Another pun is aired: 'It's the purrffect place to paws'.

OTAGO

Edz Lakeside Backpackers (☎ *442 8976,* ✉ *medward@es.co.nz, 18 Lake Esplanade)* is a dowdy lodge attached to the Lakeside Motel but it's well-kept, comfortable and reasonably priced. Dorm beds are $15, twins and doubles $40.

The *Black Sheep Backpackers* (☎ *442 7289,* ✉ *theblacksheep@queenstown.co.nz, 13 Frankton Rd),* just a short walk to town, is a former motel and has two spa pools, a deck, good outside areas and Internet facilities. Its standards are high and it has caring owners. Dorms come in a variety of sizes (up to 10-bed) and cost $18; doubles are $42 and $44. Its motto: 'Black sheep out standing in its field'. Puns aside, it's a good place.

Backpackers Downtown Lodge (☎ *442 6395, 48 Shotover St),* in the town itself, is a rambling former hotel with dorm beds for $17, and twins and doubles from $40 and $42. Many of the dorms and rooms have bathrooms, some showers only. The communal areas are cramped, but it's central.

Alpine Lodge (☎ *442 7220, fax 442 7038, 13 Gorge Rd)* is cosy with a ski-lodge feel. It charges $16 per person in dorms; twins and doubles are $40.

Deco Backpackers (☎ *442 7384, fax 442 6258, 52 Man St),* a short walk from town, is in a restored Art Deco building. It has shared rooms for $17 per person and twins and doubles for $38.

Bungi Backpackers (☎ *0800-472 856, 442 8725, 15 Sydney St)* looks dilapidated from the outside but is quite presentable inside. Dorms are only $13 and singles/doubles and twins are $30/35. Bikes can be hired for $20 per day, and there's a spa.

Southern Laughter (☎ *441 8828, 4 Isle St)* is a small place but it has all the necessary extras (email, luggage storage, booking office). Dorm beds are from $17, twins and doubles $40.

The *Hotel Esplanade* (☎ *0800-861 111, 78 Park St),* overlooking the lake, has metamorphosed into a backpackers. It has a beer garden (serving Humbug) and a good dining area for breakfast. Dorms are from $10 to $18, singles $30, and twins and doubles from $45 to $65.

Pinewood Lodge (☎ *442 8273, 48 Hamilton Rd)* is a little further from the centre. Budget accommodation costs $17 in dorms, twins/doubles are $25/40, and there's a spa. It has a variety of old lodges and the chalet backpackers with four six-bed dorms has excellent facilities.

Scallywags Travellers Guesthouse (☎ *442 7083, 27 Lomond Crescent)* is a small but good place, reached by a short cut up through the motor park. Shared rooms are $20 and doubles and twins are $55.

One delightful little place with some of the best views in town is *Hippo Lodge* (☎ *442 5785,* ✉ *hippolodge@xtra.co.nz, 4 Anderson Heights).* It is clean, has caring owners and charges $18 for dorms and $46 for doubles. To walk there head up to Shotover St, then take Turner St and stairs to Hallenstein St; Anderson Heights is just to the left.

Queenstown Lodge (☎ *442 7107),* Web site: www.qlodge.co.nz, is on Sainsbury Rd in Fernhill, 2km west of the centre, and has a magnificent view of the lake. This huge place is like a cross between a ski lodge and student college housing, with dozens of rooms on different levels down the hillside. It caters mostly to cheap tour groups. The lodge has budget meals, a licensed restaurant and bar, games and TV room. Singles/twins cost $45/50 or $55/65 with en suite. Quad shared/en suite rooms are available for $18/21 per person.

The *Last Resort* (☎ *442 4320)* at the east end of Man St is a stylish place approached across a small bridge over a stream. All rooms are shared – there are three four-bed dorms and one six-bed dorm – and the cost is $18 per person, including linen and towels. It's friendly, small and popular.

The *Resort Lodge* (☎ *0800-082 224,* ✉ *cottages@inq.co.nz, 6 Henry St)* is a former radio station with 50 beds and comfortable indoor and outdoor areas; dorms are $17, doubles and twins $42.

B&Bs & Guesthouses *Melbourne House*
(☎ *442 8431,* ✉ *melbourne@xtra.co.nz, 35 Melbourne St)* charges from $55/85 or $95/106 in the motor lodge. The guesthouse

is friendly and well organised with laundry and kitchens and a guest lounge.

Hulbert House *(☎ 442 8767, 68 Ballarat St)*, near the corner of Hallenstein St, is a wonderful old place. It offers upper-class B&B for $150/180 in a handful of gracious rooms with wonderful views.

The **Stone House** *(☎ 442 9812, ✉ storey@ xtra.co.nz, 47 Hallenstein St)* is a great B&B in a historic building (built 1874) with a cottage garden; doubles are from $195 to $220.

Haus Helga *(☎ 442 6077, ✉ haushelga@ xtra.co.nz, 107 Wynyard Crescent, Fernhill)* is a superb B&B for guestrooms, with great views over the lake and mountains. Rooms are from $139 to $219.

The **Hollyhock Inn** *(☎ 441 8037)*, Web site: www.hollyhockinn.co.nz, on Atley Rd, Arthurs Point, is surrounded by wonderful gardens and has alpine views. Doubles/ triples are $220/250.

Pear Tree Cottage *(☎ 442 9340, 51 Mountain View Rd)*, Web site: www .peartree.co.nz, is an idyllic little hideaway almost enclosed in a fine garden. Breakfast of any type at any time is included in the doubles price of $290 (or $400 for three using two bedrooms).

The **Ferry Hotel B&B** *(☎ 442 2194)*, Web site: www.ferry.co.nz, is a charming old converted hotel on Spence Rd in Lower Shotover. Doubles are $155, and the one twin room is $125.

The **Remarkables Lodge** *(☎ 442 2720)*, Web site: www.remarkables.co.nz, is in a fantastic location, 3.4km south of the ski-field entrance on SH6. A multi-award winner, the facilities are topnotch and include log fire, bar and snooker room. Lodge rooms are $540 and the cottage with jacuzzi is $620 (GST extra).

White Shadows Country Inn *(☎ 442 0871, ✉ info@whiteshadows.co.nz)* is off Hunter Rd between Arrowtown and Queenstown. It's quite simply superb and sleeps only four pampered guests. There are four separate breakfast areas, DVD and CD players in the rooms, an in-ground spa, a huge kitchen, a grand piano in the lounge, and just about every other comfort imaginable ($395 for two with breakfast).

Motels Queenstown motels are expensive but prices fluctuate with the seasons; the Queenstown Accommodation Centre *(☎ 442 5177, ✉ qac@xtra.co.nz)* maintains a full listing.

The **Colonial Village Motels** *(☎ 442 7629, ✉ colonial@queenstown.co.nz, 136 Frankton Rd)* is a good example of this genre – there are budget units at $68 and studio units from $78.

Some of the more reasonably priced motels are listed here: **Earnslaw Lodge** *(☎ 442 8728, 77 Frankton Rd)* has doubles from $80 to $108 depending on the season; **Four Seasons** *(☎ 442 8953, 12 Stanley St)* has units from $90 to $110 for two; **Hurley's of Queenstown** *(☎ 442 5999)*, corner of Frankton Rd and Melbourne St, has superb studio apartments from $145 to $300 depending on the season; **Alpha Lodge** *(☎ 442 6095, 42 Frankton Rd)* costs $85 for a double; **Amity Lodge** *(☎ 0800-556 000, 7 Melbourne St)* costs from $114 to $167 for two to five people; and **Lomond Lodge** *(☎ 442 8235, 33 Man St)* has units from $98 for two people.

Hotels The **Sherwood Manor Hotel** *(☎ 0800-220 020)*, Goldfield Heights on Frankton Rd, has a great setting next to the lake, good facilities and well-appointed doubles from $115 to $135.

Other top-range establishments are the **Novotel Queenstown** *(☎ 0800-655 557)* on Sainsbury Rd, Fernhill (from $99 plus GST); **The Lodges** *(☎ 442 7552, 8 Lake Esplanade)*; **The Heritage Queenstown** *(☎ 442 4988, 91 Fernhill Rd)*; and the **Parkroyal Queenstown** *(☎ 442 7800)* on Beach St with 139 rooms (and cheaper weekend rates).

Aspen on Queenstown *(☎ 442 7677, ✉ aspen@xtra.co.nz, 139 Fernhill Rd)* has spectacular views. The hotel section has doubles for $120 and one-/two-bed apartments for $200/260. The **Aspen Cafe** has a great selection of coffees and desserts.

Millbrook *(☎ 442 1563)*, a magnificent place on Malaghans Rd between Queenstown and Arrowtown, is top of the heap. It has beautiful scenery, luxurious accommodation and restored historic buildings.

OTAGO

There are myriad things to do nearby and the golf course is superlative, but count on $300-plus a double.

Places to Eat

Queenstown has a thriving restaurant scene, with the South Island's best dining outside Christchurch and Dunedin.

Restaurants The *Cow Restaurant* (☎ 442 8588) on Cow Lane is something of a Queenstown institution but very busy. The pasta and pizza are good if you get time seated to digest them.

Pasta Pasta Cucina (☎ 442 6762, 6 Brecon St) receives rave reviews for its pasta and pizza for around $18 and the delicious dips with house bread.

HMS Britannia (☎ 442 9600), in the Mall, is set up as an English galleon. The wide-ranging menu has a seafood emphasis. Next door is the *Moa Bar & Cafe* (☎ 442 8372) where the blackboard menu features fresh seafood, pasta dishes and good salads.

Chico's (☎ 442 8439), a bar and grill, is in a lovely old building on the Mall. It has an eclectic and reasonably priced menu.

Pot au Feu Bistro (☎ 442 8333) on Camp St serves innovative NZ cuisine and is consistently good. Mains cost $22 to $28 and reservations are essential.

Little India (☎ 442 5335, 11 Shotover St), upstairs, has good curries and reasonable prices, and with a little imagination The Remarkables will take on the appearance of the Hindu Kush or Himalaya.

Saguaro (☎ 442 8240), upstairs in the Trust Bank Arcade on Beach St, is a reasonable Mexican place with Mexican-style pizzas.

Roaring Megs (☎ 442 9676, 57 Shotover St), in an old miner's cottage, is one of the town's better restaurants noted for its lamb cuisine (mains from $19.50 to $27).

Minami Jujisei (45 Beach St) is a Japanese restaurant with salmon sashimi platters for $18 and teriyaki tuna steak for $20.

Fraser's (☎ 442 5111), in the Steamer Wharf, is stylish and known for its charcoal and wood-fired broiler (honey-glazed pork fillet is $17.50). The *Boardwalk* restaurant and bar (☎ 442 5630), upstairs in wharf village, has good but expensive seafood and barbecued lamb ($25).

The *Beefeater Steakhouse* (☎ 442 9149, 40 Shotover St) has been around for over 20 years, and attracts steak-lovers. Large rumps at around $23.50 are served with a baked potato and there is a self-serve salad bar.

The large resort hotels have numerous restaurants for fine dining. The Millbrook out towards Arrowtown has two excellent restaurants, including the less expensive *Italian Cafe* for good pizza and mains from $15.

The two best restaurants are *Gantley's* (☎ 442 8999), in an historic stone building on Malaghans Rd, Arthurs Point, the place for fine dining by candlelight, and the *Nugget Point* (☎ 442 7273), in the resort at Arthurs Point, with sumptuous seafood platters ($32.50).

Or ride the gondola to the *Skyline Chalet* where there's entertainment with dinner nightly and impressive views back down to the lights of Queenstown.

Cafes & Fast Food
Wholefood Cafe, down an arcade between Beach and Shotover Sts, has natural foods, a sandwich bar and sweets.

Ken's Noodles, on Camp St near Kiwi Discovery, is a local favourite where the hungry go for all types of udon (noodles) and sushi at reasonable prices.

Naff Caff (62 Shotover St) serves the definitive cup of coffee – it has its own roaster. Fresh croissants make the perfect accompaniment or there are reasonably priced breakfasts.

Leonardo's (☎ 442 8542, 22 Shotover St) is a good place for breakfast, lunch, afternoon tea and perfect espresso.

Abbey Road (☎ 442 8290, 66 Shotover St) also does a good full breakfast for $8 and has reasonably priced meals into the evening.

The *Coronation Bath House Cafe* (☎ 442 5625), in Marine Parade, is a little more expensive for a coffee and light meal, but is in a delightful setting next to the lake, gardens and a childrens playground.

The *Fishbone Bar & Grill* (☎ 442 6768, 7 Beach St) is good for fish lunches

($12.50) – the fish is fresh and they will cook fish that you have caught.

The Bakery *(11 Shotover St)* just beyond Camp St has baked food, sandwiches and pizzas and is open 24 hours.

Habebe's Lebanese *(☎ 442 9861)*, a tiny place on the corner of Rees and Beach Sts, serves Middle Eastern and vegetarian dishes.

O'Connell's Food Hall inside the shopping centre is open from 9 am to 9 pm daily and has an excellent collection of stalls, including Thai and Japanese.

Self-Catering For self-catering, Queenstown still doesn't have a large supermarket. **Queenstown Supermarket** is on the Mall; the **Alpine Food Centre** on Shotover St has the best range and prices.

The cheapest and largest supermarket is out at Frankton. Buy booze at **Queenstown Wine & Spirits** on Shotover St.

Entertainment

Queenstown is a small place but has a raging nightlife every night of the week.

The Mall is an excellent place to start a pub crawl. Near the waterfront is the long-running **Eichardt's Hotel**. During the 1879 floods, hard-drinking miners are said to have paddled up to the bar in rowing boats. During the Franco-Prussian war (1870–71), Herr Eichardt, being a good Prussian nationalist, ran the Prussian flag up the flagpole after every Prussian victory. Meanwhile, down the road at Monsieur Francois St Omer's bakery, the tricolour flew every time the French won. The public bar is a popular local meeting and drinking place.

On the Mall near Eichardt's is the **Moa Bar & Cafe**, more upmarket and sedate, but it still packs them in. Next along, **Winnie Bagoes** *(☎ 442 8635)* is one of Queenstown's more happening places with a good crowd, and the dance floor can get very lively. It also has good late-night pizzas to line the stomach. A few doors further along is **Chico's** (see Places to Eat). The **Retro Bar & Grill** is another venue at the top of the Mall.

McNeill's Cottage Brewery *(☎ 442 9688, 14 Church St)* is around the corner. Apart from reasonably priced pub fare, it has good beer including its own brews. Bands play on weekends but this place tends to peter out as the night wears on.

Tardis Bar & Kebab in Cow Lane has entertainment on Wednesday nights. Close by is the oh-so-swish **Bunker Bar**, solving the riddle of where all the well-heeled owners of bars and restaurants in Queenstown go to relax. Squeeze through the crowd in the bar, and head for the couches near the open fire.

On Upper Camp St, the **Red Rock Bar & Grill** is very popular in the ski season, but even in summer ski bunnies linger on, reminiscing and watching snowboarding videos.

Bus-bound backpackers congregate at **Abbey Road** (see earlier), where the emphasis is on cheap beer.

When that closes, **The Casbah** *(45 Shotover St)*, further down, is as noisy, smelly, smoky, bustling, boozy and colourful as befits a real kasbah. Here you can send video emails back home. Every night there are door prizes of adventure activities.

The **Rattlesnake Room** *(14 Brecon St)*, a great place to dine and enjoy a drink, is very popular with locals.

Last but not least, **The World** *(27 Shotover St)* is usually wall-to-wall with party goers and undoubtedly Queenstown's most popular venue. You might strike one of its foam parties, when the bar is filled thigh-deep with foam.

Teetotallers can just wander the streets and browse through souvenir shops and outrageously expensive tourist boutiques, many of which stay open until around 11 pm.

The small **Embassy Cinema** *(☎ 442 9994)* on the Mall next to Winnie Bagoes sometimes has good movies for around $10.

Queenstown's **Casino** *(☎ 441 1495)*, in the Steamer Wharf building, brings a touch of Monaco to the town that has just about everything. About 20% of your losses are returned to the local community. Nearby is **The Cigar Bar**, which has Churchill's favourites and jazz on Fridays.

Getting There & Away

Air Air New Zealand/Mt Cook Airline *(☎ 442 4600)* on Camp St has daily direct flights to Auckland, Christchurch, Te Anau, Milford Sound, Wanaka and Mt Cook, with a number of connecting flights from Christchurch.

Ansett New Zealand (☎ 0800-800 146), 76 Shotover St, has daily flights to Christchurch, Rotorua and Auckland. Tranzair flies on its behalf to Te Anau and Milford.

Bus The InterCity booking office (☎ 442 8238) is in the visitor centre on the corner of Shotover and Camp Sts. InterCity buses have several daily routes to and from Queenstown. The route to Christchurch goes via Mt Cook. The other routes are to Te Anau and Milford Sound, Invercargill and Dunedin. InterCity also has a daily West Coast service to the glaciers via Wanaka and Haast Pass. To continue up the coast from the glaciers and on to Nelson you have to overnight at Fox or Franz Josef.

'Alternative' bus tours such as the West Coast Express, Kiwi Experience, Magic Bus or the Flying Kiwi also go up the West Coast to Nelson. See the Getting Around chapter for details.

The Bottom Bus – book at the Information & Track Centre (☎ 442 9708) – offers a similar service, with a Queenstown–Te Anau–Milford leg provided by Kiwi Experience (see The Catlins section in the Southland chapter for details).

Myriad shuttle buses operate from out of Queenstown. Backpacking Specialists (☎ 442 8178) books most of them, as does the visitor centre. Atomic Shuttles goes to Christchurch ($35) and Dunedin ($25). Southern Link goes to Christchurch via Wanaka ($20). Catch-a-Bus goes to Dunedin and Topline Tours goes to Te Anau. Kiwi Discovery (☎ 442 7340) runs on weekdays between Queenstown and Christchurch for $40, dropping off at Christchurch airport and the city square, and also to Te Anau ($25) and Milford ($59). Southern Air (☎ 442 0099) has a daily shuttle to Invercargill ($38) connecting with its flights to Stewart Island.

Trampers Transport Backpacker Express (☎ 442 9939) runs to and from the

Routeburn, Greenstone, Caples and Rees–Dart Tracks, all via Glenorchy. Main Divide (☎ 442 8889) also covers these runs. Kiwi Discovery (☎ 442 7340) services the Routeburn and Greenstone Tracks from the east and the Routeburn and Milford Tracks from west of The Divide via Te Anau. Backpacker Express departs from the Track Centre on Shotover St, and Kiwi Discovery from its office on Camp St.

Approximate prices are Queenstown to Glenorchy ($10), to the Routeburn ($20) to the Rees ($20 to $30), to The Divide ($45) and to the Greenstone–Caples ($25); Glenorchy to the Greenstone–Caples ($10) and Dart River ($20); and Routeburn to the Greenstone–Caples ($15).

Services between Queenstown and Milford via Te Anau can be used for track transport or simply as a way to get to or from Milford. Buses generally run two or three times weekly but the schedule varies according to demand, with extra trips in summer and possibly none at all in winter.

Hitching Hitching into Queenstown is usually easy, but getting out may require real patience. Big wet backpacks are a real deterrent.

Getting Around
To/From the Airport The airport is at Frankton, 8km from town. Super Shuttle (☎ 442 3639, ✉ supershuttle@queenstown .co.nz) picks up and drops off in Queenstown/Fernhill for $6/7 per person. Taxis cost about $15 – phone Alpine Taxis (☎ 442 6666) or Queenstown Taxis (☎ 442 7788).

Bus The Shopper Bus (☎ 442 6647) has an airport bus that leaves from the top of the Mall. It has services to Fernhill and Frankton accommodation ($2). There is a limited service to the airport ($5). A day pass is $6.50.

Kiwi Discovery (☎ 442 7340) operates ski-season transport to Coronet Peak and The Remarkables ($23/16) and Cardrona ($30/19).

Bicycle & Moped Queenstown Bike Hire, 23 Beach St opposite Whitcoulls bookshop,

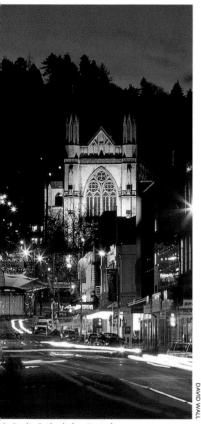
St Paul's Cathedral in Dunedin

Near Tunnel Beach on the Otago Peninsula

Beautiful old villas perched on the hillsides, Dunedin

Queenstown and the (well-named) Remarkables

Lake Harris alongside the Routeburn Track

The Taieri Gorge Railway

Skiing at Treble Cone, Lake Wanaka

NZ wool – perfect for keeping your feet warm

has a big variety of bikes, including tandems, from $14 to $28 per day. Mopeds are $35 a day and scooters are $45. Outside Sports (☎ 442 8883), on the corner of the Mall and Camp St, also has scooters for $45 a day and suspension mountain bikes for $40 to $70 a day.

ARROWTOWN
pop 1700
Between Cromwell and Queenstown (not far past the bungy bridge) is the loop road turn-off to Arrowtown. The faithfully restored early gold-mining settlement has a beautiful avenue of deciduous trees. Lined with wooden buildings (over 60 of them from the 19th century), the main street looks a lot like a movie set for a western, except for all the tourist shops.

The **Lake District Museum** has displays on gold mining and local history, and also acts as the information office (☎ 442 1824), Web site: www.arrowtown.org.nz. It's open from 9 am to 5 pm ($4, children $0.50). Get copies of *Historic Arrowtown* and *Arrowtown Walks* from the museum – the latter has information about getting to Macetown as well as historic notes about the area.

The best example of a gold-era **Chinese settlement** in NZ is near Bush Creek, at the top end of Buckingham St. A store and two huts have been restored as a reminder of the role played by Chinese 'diggers' during and after the gold rush. The Chinese were subjected to prejudice, especially during the 1880s economic depression. They often did not seek new claims but worked through the tailings looking for the fine gold undetected by earlier miners.

The **golf course** at Arrowtown is challenging, with narrow defiles and rock obstacles adding to the fun.

Macetown
Just north of Arrowtown is Macetown, a ghost town reached only via a long, unimproved and flood-prone road – the original miners' wagon track – which crosses the Arrow River 44 times! Trips are made from Queenstown on horseback or by 4WD vehicle, and allow time to do some gold panning. The main operator is Outback New Zealand (☎ 442 7386, ✉ tours@outback.org.nz). Its partner Nomad Safaris (☎ 442 6699) goes to both Skippers Canyon and Macetown ($75, four to five hours).

OTAGO

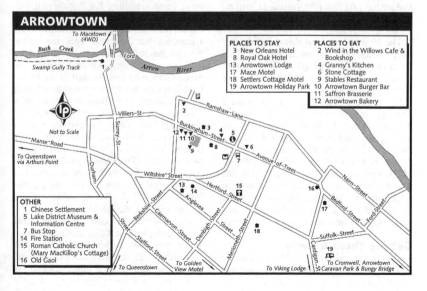

ARROWTOWN

To Macetown (4WD)
Bush Creek
Ford
Swamp Gully Track
Arrow River
Villiers St
Ramshaw Lane
Surrey St
Buckingham Street
Manse Road
Durham
Wiltshire Street
Avenue of Trees
Nairn Street
To Queenstown via Arthurs Point
Hertford Street
Bedford Street
Ford Street
Berkshire Street
Caernarvon Street
Anglesea
Denby Street
Merioneth Street
Suffolk Street
Stafford Street
Cardigan
To Queenstown
To Golden View Motel
To Viking Lodge
To Cromwell, Arrowtown Caravan Park & Bungy Bridge

Not to Scale

PLACES TO STAY
3 New Orleans Hotel
8 Royal Oak Hotel
13 Arrowtown Lodge
17 Mace Motel
18 Settlers Cottage Motel
19 Arrowtown Holiday Park

PLACES TO EAT
2 Wind in the Willows Cafe & Bookshop
4 Granny's Kitchen
6 Stone Cottage
9 Stables Restaurant
10 Arrowtown Burger Bar
11 Saffron Brasserie
12 Arrowtown Bakery

OTHER
1 Chinese Settlement
5 Lake District Museum & Information Centre
7 Bus Stop
14 Fire Station
15 Roman Catholic Church (Mary MacKillop's Cottage)
16 Old Gaol

Places to Stay & Eat

The *Arrowtown Holiday Park* (☎ 442 1876), off Suffolk St, has tent/powered sites for $18/19 and cabins at $30 for two. The *Arrowtown Caravan Park* (☎ 442 1838, 47 Devon St) has sites for $20.

Arrowtown's motels have units from $75 to $85 for doubles: the *Golden View Motel* (☎ 442 1833, 48 Adamson Drive); the *Mace Motel* (☎ 442 1825, 13 Cardigan St); *Viking Lodge* (☎ 442 1765, 21 Inverness Crescent); and top-of-the-range *Settlers Cottage Motel* (☎ 442 1734, 20–22 Hertford St).

The *New Orleans Hotel* (☎ 442 1745, 27 Buckingham St) has singles/doubles for $40/60, and a simple backpackers bunkroom for $12 per bed. The *Royal Oak Hotel* (☎ 442 1700, 42 Buckingham St) charges $25/50.

There are several good B&Bs in the vicinity of Arrowtown; contact the museum for prices.

The *Arrowtown Lodge* (☎ 442 1101, ✉ hiking@queenstown.co.nz, 7 Anglesea St) has four cottage-style suites. It also conducts alpine and historic hikes (from $80), and scenic bushwalks (from $60). Ring for prices.

Along Buckingham St, the *Arrowtown Bakery* has excellent pies, rolls and German-style bread. The *Arrowtown Burger Bar* has great fish and chips.

The *New Orleans* and *Royal Oak Hotels* have bistros with the usual pub fare. The *Wind in the Willows Cafe & Bookshop* on Ramshaw Lane is a very pleasant spot for coffee and snacks.

In gold-era dwellings are *Granny's Kitchen* for tearoom fare, the *Stables Restaurant* and the *Stone Cottage* for fine dining, and the new *Saffron Brasserie* (☎ 442 0131) for Pacific Rim fare.

The *Gibbston Valley Winery* (☎ 442 6910), 400m from the Kawarau Bridge, has a cellar restaurant and outdoor courtyard set among the vines. The blackboard menu is changed daily and the food receives rave reviews. Dine here *after* your bungy jump.

Getting There & Away

From Queenstown, the red Double Decker Bus (☎ 442 6067) makes a three-hour trip to Arrowtown at 10 am and 2 pm daily for $27 (children $10). Arrow Express (☎ 442 1535) has scheduled services that can be picked up outside the library in Buckingham St, and at the top of the Mall in Queenstown ($5, 25 minutes).

InterCity buses to Wanaka and Dunedin also can stop at Arrowtown for prebooked passengers.

It can be easy to reach Arrowtown by nifty-fifty (motorbikes) from Queenstown, or even by bicycle. The back road via Arthurs Point is steep and hard going just outside Queenstown but flat for most of the way and very scenic.

GLENORCHY
pop 215

At the head of Lake Wakatipu the picturesque, tiny hamlet of Glenorchy is 47km (a 40-minute drive) from Queenstown and offers a tranquil escape. Many people pass through briefly in their rush to knock off the Routeburn Track, and thus bypass perhaps one of the greatest tramping opportunities – the Rees and Dart River valleys.

Those with a car can explore the superb valleys north of Glenorchy. If you've always been searching for Paradise, it lies some 20km north-west of Glenorchy at the start of the Rees-Dart Track. Paradise is just a paddock but the gravel road there runs through beautiful farmland surrounded by majestic mountains. About halfway between Glenorchy and the start of the Rees–Dart Track the road passes through dripping forest where it is a five-minute walk to a small mossy waterfall. Alternatively, explore the Rees Valley or take the road to Routeburn, which goes via the Dart River Bridge, where the jet boats congregate. Near the start of the Routeburn Track in Mt Aspiring National Park there is a day hut and a couple of short walks – the Double Barrel and the Lake Sylvan walks – if you are not tackling the Routeburn.

The town has a small museum, golf course and pleasant walks around the lake. There is a DOC office (☎ 442 9937) in Glenorchy, with the latest track conditions, hut tickets and general information. It is open from 8.30 am to 5 pm daily in summer, on weekdays only in winter. Get camping gear in Queenstown or Te Anau, not here.

Jet-boating

The Dart River jet-boat trip offers a scenic trip into the heart of the Dart River wilderness, one of NZ's most beautiful places. Savour the grandeur of the slopes of Mt Earnslaw and the bush-clad mountain walls on both sides of the river. The breathtaking scenery lasts for 2½ hours plus a stop to take a walk through the beech forest at Beansburn, downriver from the turnaround point. Of course, the driver will also spin the boat and pretend to almost crash into river obstacles.

Dart River Jet Safaris (☎ 442 9992), Web site: www.dartriverjet.co.nz, departs from Queenstown at 8 am, noon and 2 pm in summer; check departure times in winter. If coming from Queenstown the five-hour trip costs $129/65 for adults/children, $119/55 from Glenorchy. The office in Glenorchy is next to the general store.

Another option is a trip by 4WD coach up to the top of the river and then return by jet boat, with an extended bushwalk along the way. This Classic Backroad Safari costs the same as the river journey.

Kayaking

You can take a 90-minute jet-boat ride up the Dart River and then descend the river in an inflatable three-seater canoe ('funyak') with Eric Billoud's Dart River Fun Yaks (☎ 0800-386 925), Web site: www.funyaks .com; the canoe section is 2½ hours. No experience is necessary and the return cost from Queenstown is $179/98.

A novel way to finish the Rees–Dart Track is to 'funyak' the last day of the four-day walk.

Other Activities

Dart Stables (☎ 442 9968) has guided **horse treks** in the spectacular high country for $40 per hour and High Country Horse Treks (☎ 442 9915) also has rides on the flats and around the lake.

Glenorchy Air (☎ 442 2207), Web site: www.glenorchy.net.nz, has a 20-minute local **flightseeing** trip around Mt Earnslaw and the Routeburn for $89. Mt Aspiring and the Olivine Ice Plateau are included in 45 minutes for $159. To Milford Sound the price is $235, including a cruise.

Glenorchy Cruising (☎ 0800-925 284, e wakatipu@xtra.co.nz) has fishing trips ($75 per person for two hours) and eco cruises and runs a water-taxi service. A cruise/horse trek combination is $160/140 from Queenstown/Glenorchy.

Places to Stay & Eat

The *Glenorchy Holiday Park* (☎ 442 9939, 2 Oban St) has tent sites for $8 per person, power sites for $9, bunkroom beds for $13 per person and cabins for $30 a double. It's well set up for trampers and runs the Backpacker Express for transport to the tracks.

The *Glenorchy Hotel* (☎ 442 9902) has doubles for $59 ($79 with en suite) plus a restaurant and bars. Out the back, its basic *Glenorchy Backpackers Retreat* consists of a 10-bed lodge and a four-bed hut for $14 per person.

The *Glen Roydon Lodge Hotel* (☎ 442 9968), nearby, has well-appointed doubles from $80 to $120. The *Mt Earnslaw Motel* (☎ 422 6993), a new place, has studio and one-bedroom units from $80 to $95.

Shirley's (☎ 442 8307) on Oban St has comfortable B&B singles/doubles in the house for $55/95 and a budget hut outside with four beds for $16 per person.

Glenorchy Cafe has $8 to $10 full breakfasts, focaccia bakes and a range of home-cooked meals; char-grills are a speciality.

The area has a few more accommodation options. On the Glenorchy-Queenstown Rd, 28km from Queenstown, *Round-the-Bend Farmstay* (☎ 442 6196) has delightful gardens, farm walks, kayaking and fishing. A variety of rooms in the eclectically styled farmhouse cost around $60.

The *Routeburn Farm Motel* (☎ 442 9901) is on the road to the Routeburn Track, 6km before the start of the walk and 21km from Glenorchy. The self-contained cottage is good value for $68 a double.

OTAGO

Blanket Bay (☎ 442 9442), Web site: www.blanketbay.com, is a new, exclusive world-class resort on the shores of Lake Wakatipu near Glenorchy. It's constructed of native timber and local schist stone, and has a Great Room with open log fire, large restaurant and a cosy bar, The Den. Splendid rooms in the Main Lodge are from $1090 to $1590 for two, and the Chalets are from $1590 to $1990.

Getting There & Away
The scenic Glenorchy-Queenstown Rd is now sealed almost all the way, but its constant hills are a killer for cyclists. In summer there are almost daily trampers' buses such as Backpacker Express, based at the Glenorchy Holiday Park, and Kiwi Discovery (see Getting There & Away in the Queenstown section).

When the weather is fine, Backpacker Express operates boats rather than buses to the Caples Track. It can also arrange boat trips to Pigeon Island and Pig Island in the middle of Lake Wakatipu.

LAKE WAKATIPU REGION TRAMPS
The mountainous region at the northern head of Lake Wakatipu combines some of the greatest scenery in NZ with some of the best tramping tracks – the famous Routeburn and lesser-known Greenstone, Caples and Rees-Dart Tracks are all here. Glenorchy is a convenient base, with excellent facilities, for all these tramps. See Getting There & Away in the Queenstown section for transport information.

Track Information
For accommodation details, transport to and from all trail heads and the location of DOC information offices and ranger stations, see the Queenstown and Glenorchy sections in this chapter and Te Anau in the Southland chapter.

Staff at the DOC office can give advice on the best maps to use, outline track conditions and sell hut and Great Walks Passes. For more detailed information on the tracks see Lonely Planet's *Tramping in New Zealand*.

The Routeburn Track
The great variety of countryside and scenery makes the three- to four-day Routeburn Track one of the best rainforest/subalpine tracks in the country. Unfortunately, it has become the surrogate for those who miss out on the Milford Track and pressures on the track have necessitated the introduction of a booking system, as on the Milford. No-one is allowed to commence the Routeburn until they have arranged accommodation.

In summer, from October to April, a Great Walks Pass ($35/17.50 per night for adults/children) allows you to stay at Routeburn Flats, Routeburn Falls, Lake Mackenzie and Lake Howden huts. In summer (December to March) it's discounted to $28/14. A camping pass (Routeburn Flats and Lake Mackenzie only) is $12/6 per person per night.

Advance bookings are required throughout the main season, either through DOC in Te Anau, Queenstown or Glenorchy, or by email at ☻ greatwalksbooking@doc.govt.nz.

Off season, from late April to late October, the Routeburn Flats and Routeburn Falls huts are $8, and Lake Mackenzie and Howden huts are $4. Note that the Routeburn Track is often closed by snow in the winter and stretches of the track are very exposed and dangerous in bad weather, so check with DOC in Glenorchy, Te Anau or Queenstown.

Routeburn Walk Ltd (☎ 442 8200, ☻ routeburn@xtra.co.nz) has a three-day walk on the Routeburn and a six-day Grand Traverse which combines the Greenstone (including return transport, accommodation and meals); ring for prices. Its one-day Routeburn Encounter is $99 per person.

There are car parks at The Divide and the Glenorchy end of Routeburn but they are not attended so don't leave valuables in your car. Glenorchy Holiday Park stores gear for free if you use its transport (otherwise it's $2.50 per day).

Walking the Track The track can be started from either end. Many people travelling from the Queenstown end attempt to reach The Divide in time to catch the bus to Milford, connecting with the launch trip across Milford Sound. Highlights of the track are the view

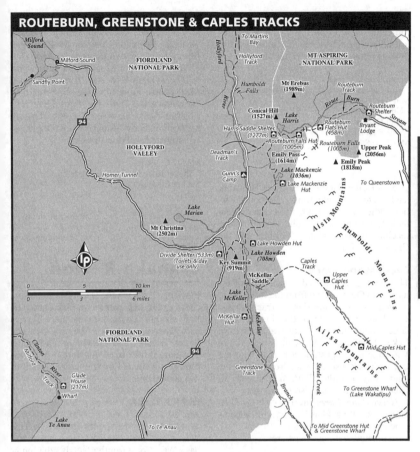

ROUTEBURN, GREENSTONE & CAPLES TRACKS

OTAGO

from the Harris Saddle and from the top of nearby Conical Hill. You can see the waves breaking on the West Coast beach at Martins Bay. The view is almost as good as the view from Key Summit, which offers a panorama not only of the Hollyford Valley but also of the Eglinton and Greenstone River valleys.

Estimated walking times are:

Routeburn Shelter to	
Flats Hut	2½ hours
Flats Hut to Falls Hut	one hour
Falls Hut to	
Mackenzie Hut	3½ hours
Mackenzie Hut to	
Howden Hut	three hours
Howden Hut to	
The Divide	one hour

Routeburn, Greenstone & Caples Tracks

The Routeburn can be combined with the Caples or Greenstone Tracks for a round trip. Access at the Caples and Greenstone end is at Greenstone Wharf. The road from Kinloch to Greenstone Wharf is unsealed and rough. The Caples and Greenstone Tracks together form a loop track. The huts on these tracks are Mid-Greenstone, McKellar, Mid-Caples and Upper Caples (all $8 per person per night) and Sly Burn ($4). Estimated walking times are:

Greenstone Wharf to	
Mid-Caples Hut	three hours
Mid-Caples Hut to	
Upper Caples Hut	2½ hours
Upper Caples Hut to	
McKellar Saddle	3½ hours
McKellar Saddle to	
Howden Hut	three hours

The McKellar Saddle to Howden Hut walk leads on to the Routeburn as mentioned earlier. Other options from McKellar Saddle include turning off for The Divide before reaching Howden Hut, or turning onto the Greenstone Track.

Greenstone Track

This track is often used as a means of returning to Queenstown from the Routeburn, or as a loop with the Caples Track. It is a 13½-hour walk down the broad, easy Greenstone Valley to Lake Wakatipu from Lake Howden. You can meet Lake Wakatipu at Greenstone Wharf (where the Caples Track also begins), from where the Glenorchy Holiday Park has a boat to Glenorchy. There are also minibuses.

   Greenstone Farmstay (☎ 442 7068) at Greenstone Wharf has backpackers accommodation for $15 per person.

   Estimated walking times are:

Greenstone Wharf to	
Sly Burn Hut	four hours
Sly Burn Hut to	
Mid-Greenstone Hut	one hour
Mid-Greenstone Hut to	
McKellar Hut	five hours
McKellar Hut to	
Howden Hut	two hours

Rees–Dart Track

This difficult four- to five-day circular route goes from the head of Lake Wakatipu by way of the Dart River, Rees Saddle and Rees River valley, with the possibility of a side trip to the Dart Glacier if you're suitably equipped. Access by vehicle is possible as far as Muddy Creek on the Rees side, from where it is two hours to 25-Mile Hut.

   You can park at Muddy Creek; transport is also available to and from the tracks. Most people go up the Rees first and then back down the Dart. The three DOC huts (Shelter Rock, Dart and Daleys Flat) are serviced and cost $8 per person a night.

   Estimated walking times are:

Muddy Creek to	
Shelter Rock Hut	six hours
Shelter Rock Hut to	
Dart Hut	seven hours
Dart Hut to	
Daleys Flat Hut	six to eight hours
Daleys Flat Hut to	
Paradise	six to eight hours

Wanaka Region

Entering Otago via the Haast Pass, you first come to the tiny hamlet of Makarora. The first sizable towns, however, are Hawea and Wanaka, reached by passing between Lakes Wanaka and Hawea at The Neck. The central feature of this region is Mt Aspiring, surrounded by the national park of the same name.

MAKARORA
pop 40

When you reach Makarora you have left the West Coast and entered Otago, but it still has a West Coast frontier feel. It's the southern gateway to the Haast Pass.

   An early traveller gave this region some terrible names. He called one of the world's most beautiful valleys Siberia and named the nearby Matterhornesque peaks Dreadful and Awful – he is not to be believed.

   Makarora can accommodate about 140 people, mostly trampers and adventure-seekers. There isn't much else in this township – which is part of its charm.

   The DOC Makaroa Visitor Centre (☎ 443 8365) on the highway has information on the Haast and should be consulted before undertaking any tramps.

'Siberia Experience'

Makarora is the base for one of NZ's great outdoor adventures – the Siberia Experience. This is one of those Kiwi extravaganzas that combine sundry thrill-seeking activities – in this case a small-plane flight (20 minutes), a three-hour bushwalk through a remote mountain valley and a jet-boat trip (45 minutes) down a river valley. Make sure you follow the markers as you descend from Siberia; people have become lost and have had to spend the night in the open.

Southern Alps Air (☎ 443 8372, 443 8292) operates the 'experience' from mid-October to mid-April ($145, minimum of three). It also has 40-minute trips over Mt Aspiring ($120 per person), 70-minute trips to Mt Cook and the glaciers ($185) and landings at Milford Sound ($205).

Jet-Boating

A 50km, one-hour jet-boating trip into Mt Aspiring National Park costs $49 (minimum five) with Wilkin River Jets (☎ 443 8351), much cheaper than Shotover jet-boat trips.

For trampers, jet boats go to Kerin Forks at the top of the Wilkin River for $40 and a ferry service goes across the Young River mouth when the Makarora floods for $17. Inquire on ☎ 443 8351 or at DOC.

Walking

The area has many walks. Shorter ones include the Old Bridal Track (1½ hours), which heads from the top of the Haast Pass to Davis Flat; a 20-minute nature walk around Makarora; and the Blue Pools River Walk, where you can see huge rainbow trout.

Longer tramps go through magnificent countryside but are not to be undertaken lightly. Alpine conditions, flooding and the possibility of avalanches mean that you must be well prepared and consult with DOC before heading off. *Tramping Guide to the Makarora Region* ($2.50) published by DOC is a good investment.

The three-day **Gillespies Pass** tramp goes via the Young, Siberia and Wilkin Rivers but this is a high pass with avalanche danger. With a jet-boat ride down the Wilkin to complete it, this surely could rate alongside the Milford Track as one of the great tramps. The **Wilkin Valley Track** heads off from Kerin Forks Hut, reached by jet boat, or you can also fly in to Top Forks, Siberia Hut and others. From Kerin Forks the track leads to Top Forks Hut, then the north branch of the Wilkin. Here you will see the picturesque Lakes Diana, Lucidus and Castalia. These are one hour, 1½ hours and three to four hours respectively from Top Forks Hut.

Places to Stay & Eat

The **Makarora Tourist Centre** (☎ 443 8372) behind the tearooms has good accommodation in a bush setting. The cost is $75 for two in the self-contained motels, $40 for two in A-frame cabins and $8.50 per person for a tent site (powered $10.50). The backpackers, off the road, is $18. The self-contained 16-bed homestead has awesome views (price based on numbers).

The **Larrivee Homestead** (☎ 443 9177) is not far from the Makarora Tourist Centre – take the road closest to the DOC office and follow it until you reach the octagonal masterpiece at the end of the drive. The cost for homestay B&B is $60 for singles and $90 to $120 for doubles. The very comfortable, self-contained cottage costs $90 for two and $20 for each extra person (maximum of six). The house and cottage are made of stone and hand-split cedar. Dinners are prepared for $30 per person.

The nearest **DOC camping grounds** are on SH6 at Cameron Flat and Davis Flat, about 14km and 17km north of Makarora respectively.

The 10-bed **hut** in Siberia Valley costs $8 per person and other huts are scattered around the park.

The **tearooms** at Makarora, open from 8.30 am to 8.30 pm in summer, has light meals and snacks and a grocery store for basic supplies.

Getting There & Away

West Coast Express, Magic Bus and Kiwi Experience buses regularly stop here. InterCity has one northbound bus (to the glaciers) and one southbound bus (to Hawea, Wanaka and Queenstown) per day.

OTAGO

HAWEA

Lake Hawea, separated from Lake Wanaka by a narrow isthmus, is 35km long and 410m deep. The lake was raised 20m in 1958 to provide those important cusecs for power stations downriver. Trout and land-locked salmon can be caught in its waters. Harry Urquhart (☎ 443 1535) has recommended fishing trips on the lake.

The small town of Hawea has yet more spectacular lake and mountain views, but is mostly just a collection of holiday and retiree homes.

At the lakeshore, *Lake Hawea Motor Camp (☎ 443 1767)* has tent/powered sites for $16/18 and cabins for $27; prices are for two people.

The *Lake Hawea Hotel (☎ 443 1224)* has a spartan hostel with beds in four-bed dorms for $20; its units are $85.

The *Glenruth Lakeview Motel (☎ 443 1440)* has doubles at $74. The pub does good food and will cook the fish you catch.

WANAKA

pop 3500

Wanaka is nirvana for adrenaline buzz seekers, with fine living and an overdose on scenery and the outdoors. Just over 100km from Queenstown, at the southern end of Lake Wanaka, it is the gateway to Mt Aspiring National Park and the Treble Cone, Cardrona, Harris Mountains and Pisa Range ski areas. This laid-back town offers a sharp contrast to the hype of Queenstown.

Long a Kiwi summer resort famous for its New Year revelries and a popular ski town in winter, Wanaka has a host of activities and natural mountain and lake splendour attracting visitors year-round.

Every second Easter on even years Wanaka hosts the popular 'Warbirds over Lake Wanaka', a huge air show.

Information

The Wanaka Visitor Information Centre (☎ 443 1233), Web site: www.wanaka .co.nz, is in the Mt Aspiring National Park Visitor Centre (☎ 443 7660) on Ballantyne Rd. It's open from 8 am to 4.45 pm daily (from 8 am to 4.30 pm and closed Sunday in winter). It has displays and audiovisua and the DOC counter is the place to inqu about walks and tramps.

The Adventure Centre (☎ 443 8174), Ardmore St, books most of the adventu activities including kayaking, parapentir rock climbing, white-water sledging a rafting, skiing and canyoning. In summ it's open from 8.30 am to 6.30 pm; in wi ter it becomes Harris Mountain Heli-Ski Treble Cone Ski Field.

Lakeland Adventures (☎ 443 7495), b side the jetty, books lake activities, re out canoes, bikes and cars, and is open fr 9 am to 6 pm daily.

The Nuovo Cinema Paradiso is worth visit just to see its quirky interior of loun chairs and converted car seats. It seats happily supine cinema-goers ($9/5 f adults/children).

Puzzling World Maze

Three-dimensional mazes have become NZ craze and an export activity. This ma was the original. The idea is to find yo way along the 1.5km of passages to t towers at each corner and then back to t exit. And it's more difficult than you thin The Tilted House, built on a 15° angle, designed to confuse the senses. The ma complex is open from 8.30 am to 5.30 p ($6, children $3.50) and includes a Puzz Centre, with a variety of puzzles to try, a the Hologram Hall. It's on the road Cromwell, 2km from Wanaka.

Museums

Wanaka airport, 8km from town, is quite aviation centre. As well as offering man aerial activities, it has the well-presente New Zealand Fighter Pilots Museu (☎ 443 7010), open from 9.40 am to 4 p ($6, children $2). It chronicles the histo and exploits of NZ's fighter pilots, but t real treasures are the war planes, loving restored and most in working order. Plan include a Mustang, Spitfire, Kittyhaw SE5A biplane, Gruman Avenger, an Japanese and Russian aircraft.

Just outside the airport, Wanaka Tran port Museum (☎ 443 8765) has interestir

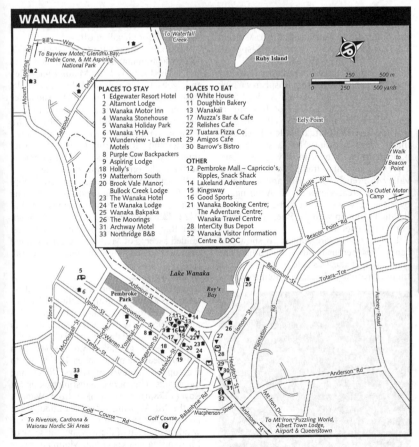

WANAKA

To Waterfall Creek

To Bayview Motel; Glendhu Bay, Treble Cone, & Mt Aspiring National Park

Ruby Island

Eely Point

Walk to Beacon Point

To Outlet Motor Camp

OTAGO

PLACES TO STAY
1 Edgewater Resort Hotel
2 Altamont Lodge
3 Wanaka Motor Inn
4 Wanaka Stonehouse
5 Wanaka Holiday Park
6 Wanaka YHA
7 Wunderview - Lake Front Motels
8 Purple Cow Backpackers
9 Aspiring Lodge
18 Holly's
19 Matterhorn South
20 Brook Vale Manor; Bullock Creek Lodge
23 The Wanaka Hotel
24 Te Wanaka Lodge
25 Wanaka Bakpaka
26 The Moorings
31 Archway Motel
33 Northridge B&B

PLACES TO EAT
10 White House
11 Doughbin Bakery
13 Wanakai
17 Muzza's Bar & Cafe
22 Relishes Cafe
27 Tuatara Pizza Co
29 Amigos Cafe
30 Barrow's Bistro

OTHER
12 Pembroke Mall – Capriccio's, Ripples, Snack Shack
14 Lakeland Adventures
15 Kingsway
16 Good Sports
21 Wanaka Booking Centre; The Adventure Centre; Wanaka Travel Centre
28 InterCity Bus Depot
32 Wanaka Visitor Information Centre & DOC

Lake Wanaka

Pembroke Park

Roy's Bay

To Riverrun, Cardrona & Waiorau Nordic Ski Areas

Golf Course

To Mt Iron; Puzzling World, Albert Town Lodge, Airport & Queenstown

aircraft ranging from a Russian Antonov to the tiny Flying Flea, motorbikes and other vehicles. It also has a collection of the type of old British cars that until recently were very much in evidence on NZ roads. The museum is open from 8 am to 6 pm daily, and 9 am to 5 pm in winter ($5, children $2). The **Wanaka Beer Works** (☎ 443 1865), also here, has guided tours and tasting.

Mt Aspiring National Park

In 1964, a mountainous area in north-western Otago and southern Westland was earmarked as a national park, named after its highest peak, 3027m Mt Aspiring, the highest peak outside the Mt Cook region. The park now extends over 3500 sq km along the Southern Alps from the Haast River in the north to its border with Fiordland National Park in the south.

The park has wide valleys, secluded flats, over 100 glaciers and towering mountains. The southern end of the park around Glenorchy is the most trafficked and includes popular tramps such as the Routeburn, but there are good short walks and more demanding tramps in the Matukituki Valley close to Wanaka.

Tracks are reached from Raspberry Creek at the end of the mostly gravel Mt Aspiring Rd, 54km from Wanaka. The Mt Aspiring Express (☎ 443 8802) runs to Raspberry Creek for $25 one way ($40 return).

The popular three-hour return **Rob Roy** walk has good views. From Raspberry Creek follow the West Matukituki Valley, from where the walk goes up the Rob Roy Stream to a point below the Rob Roy Glacier.

The **West Matukituki Valley Track** continues on to Aspiring Hut, a scenic four-hour return walk over mostly grassy flats. Overnight or longer tramps continue up the valley to French Ridge Hut and Liverpool Bivvy for great views of Mt Aspiring, or over the very scenic but difficult Cascade Saddle to link up with the Rees–Dart Track north of Glenorchy.

Longer tramps are subject to snow and can be treacherous in adverse weather. The icy slopes of the Cascade Saddle killed a tramper recently. Register intentions and

seek advice from the DOC counter at the Mt Aspiring National Park Visitor Centre in Wanaka before heading off.

Mountain Recreation (☎ 443 7330, ✆ geoff@mountainrec.co.nz) offers guided treks. The four-day West Matukituki Valley trek goes to the comfortable Shovel Flat base camp, treks up to the valley head to see glaciers and waterfalls, stops overnight in the French Ridge Hut and climbs on Mt French, with superb views of the Bonar Glacier and Mt Aspiring ($895). An easier three-day option costs $595. All equipment, accommodation and food is provided.

With all the snowy peaks, the park is popular for **mountaineering** and alpine climbing courses. Mount Aspiring Guides (☎ 443 9422, ✆ aspguide@xtra.co.nz) and Mountain Recreation offer beginners courses, guided ascents of Mt Aspiring for the more experienced and ski-mountaineering tours.

Walking

The *Wanaka Walks* brochure published by DOC has a rough map and outlines 11 walks around the town, including the easy 30-minute lakeside walk to Eely Point and on to Beacon Point, and the Waterfall Creek walk.

The fairly gentle climb up **Mt Iron** (549m), near the maze, takes 45 minutes to the top with views of rivers, lakes and mountains. The more exhausting trek up **Mt Roy** (1578m), starting 6km from Wanaka on the Mt Aspiring Rd, takes about three hours to the top if you're fit. The 8km track winds every step of the way, but the view of Mt Aspiring is a knockout. Mountain bikes can also use this track.

The **Diamond Lake Track**, a 25-minute drive from town, offers a three-hour walk to the great views from the top of Rocky Hill.

Aerial Activities

Tandem Skydive Wanaka (☎ 443 7207, ✆ skydive@skyshow.co.nz) does **tandem skydiving** from 9000ft for $225 ($195 for backpackers) and from 12,000ft for $265. As well as the adrenaline buzz, the views of the mountains are stunning.

Wanaka is ideally suited for **paragliding** and attracts paragliders from all over the

PETER HINES

Airy descent on the Cascade Saddle route, Mt Aspiring National Park

OTAGO

world. Wanaka Paragliding School (☎ 443 9193) has introductory courses for $168 (by the end of which you will be doing 100m flights from Mt Iron) and tandem flights from Treble Cone for $120. It has a complete safety record.

Kayaking

Contact Alpine River Guides (☎ 443 9023, ✉ paddle@alpinekayaks.co.nz) at 11 Mt Iron Drive to find out about kayak trips on the Hawea, Clutha, Matukituki, Makarora and Kawarau Rivers for beginners and experienced paddlers. A full day (seven hours) costs $120 and is well worth it (half-day $78), children cost $90.

Canyoning

Those with a sense of adventure and a smattering of 'derring-do' will love this unique summertime-only activity involving tobogganing, swimming and waterfall abseiling through confined, steep and wild gorges. Transport to the canyon, a picnic lunch, instruction and equipment are included for $145. These thrilling trips, operated by Deep Canyon Experience (☎ 443 7922), can be booked at the Adventure Centre.

Aerial Sightseeing

Aspiring Air (☎ 0800-100 943) at the airport has scenic flights ranging from a 50-minute flight over Mt Aspiring, the glacier and alpine country for $130 to a Mt Cook flight for $250 or Milford Sound for $225. A launch trip on the sound takes the cost to $265.

Combining adventure with sightseeing, Biplane Adventures (☎ 443 1000, ✉ biplane@skyshow.co.nz) at Wanaka airport will take you up in a stunt plane and roll, stall, fly upside down and loop with the force of four Gs for $160 (15 minutes flying). More sedate flights in a Tiger Moth cost the same, or warplane aficionados with $2000 to burn can scorch the heavens in a P51 Mustang.

Other Activities

The Wanaka and Hawea Lakes (16km away) are good for trout and salmon **fishing**. Lakeland Adventures has 2½-hour guided trips for $200, including boat hire

for three people. Alternatively, on your own, hire a motorised runabout for $55 per hour and a rod for $12 per day; a licence will cost another $12.

Alpine & Heli Mountain Biking (☎ 443 8943) does just that – high-altitude **mountain biking** in summer. Half-day trips ($70) start with a 4WD ride to 1100m and then downhill back to town. More demanding full-day trips ($95) go to 1800m in the Waiorau Nordic Ski Area for fabulous views. With your own bike it is around $15 less. Heli-biking trips from 2000m are also offered ($150 to $175).

Frogz Have More Fun (☎ 0800-338 737; in Queenstown ☎ 0800-338 738) has **whitewater sledging** on individual boogy board-styled rafts with wet suits and flippers. There are four- to five-hour trips on the Clutha ($75), Hawea ($85) and Kawarau ($95).

Pioneer Rafting (☎/fax 443 1246) has easy **white-water rafting** trips with an eco bent for $85/105 a half/full day (children half-price).

NZ Backcountry Saddle Expeditions (☎ 443 8151), 26km from Wanaka on the Cardrona Valley Rd (SH89), offers two-hour **horse treks** for $50 (children $35) and overnight wilderness trips from $135.

Mt Iron Saddle Adventures (☎ 443 7777) has two-hour treks to the top of the mountain for $55.

Criffel Peak Safaris (☎ 443 1705) has **quad-bike** trips in the Upper Clutha basin. These vary in duration, but Criffel Bluffs is $45 (two hours) and the gold diggings is $130 (4½ hours).

A 50-minute **jet-boat** trip with Lakeland Adventures across the lake and then up the Clutha River costs $50 (children $25). Jet Boat Charters (☎ 443 9126) and Edgewater Adventures (☎ 443 8422, ✉ ewa@clear .net.nz) at the Edgewater Resort Hotel also operate jet-boat trips.

The Wanaka **golf** course is quite challenging and worth playing just for the views to the mountains and lake ($10/15 for nine/18 holes).

Good **skiing** areas nearby include Treble Cone, Cardrona, the Waiorau Nordic Ski Area (for cross-country skiing) and Harris

OTAGO

Mountain for heli-skiing (see Skiing in the Activities chapter).

Other seasonal activities on the lake in summer include windsurfing, water-skiing and jet-skiing. Good Sports (☎ 443 7966) on Dunmore St hires out a vast array of sports equipment.

Just **browsing** is fun; check out the paintings of local scenery in the Artworks Gallery, upstairs at 4 Helwick St.

Organised Tours

Lakeland Adventures by the waterfront has lake cruises from $15 for 30 minutes up to $50 for its three-hour Sanctuary Island cruise (including a 30-minute walk).

Aspiring Images (☎ 443 8358) offers nature/photographic tours that teach you how to snap all that wonderful scenery (around $50 per hour).

Places to Stay

Camping & Cabins The *Wanaka Holiday Park* (☎ 443 7883, 212 Brownston St) is only 1km from town, and has lake views and treed areas. Sites cost $20 for two, cabins are $30 and tourist flats are $50 to $58.

The *Pleasant Lodge Holiday Park* (☎ 443 7360), 3km from Wanaka on Glendhu Bay Rd, has cabins and tourist flats at similar prices and a pool.

The *Glendhu Bay camp* (☎ 443 7243), right on Lake Wanaka 13km from town on Mt Aspiring Rd, has tent/powered sites for $15/17, cabins for $27 and a lodge which sleeps 16 ($13.50 per person).

The *Outlet Motor Camp* (☎ 443 7478), 6km north of Wanaka, is at the source of the Clutha River for fishing and has wonderful lake and mountain views. Tent sites cost $18 and on-site caravans $30 for two.

There are *DOC camping grounds* at Boundary Creek Reserve, adjacent to SH6, at the head of Lake Wanaka; Kidds Bush Reserve, Mead Rd, west of The Neck between Lakes Hawea and Wanaka; and Albert Town reserve, adjacent to SH6, 5km north-east of Wanaka.

Backpackers The *Matterhorn South* (☎ 443 1119, @ matterhorn@xtra.co.nz, 56 Brownston St)* is a delightful place with a cosy log fire. Dorm and shared rooms are $16 per person, doubles and twins $36. There are units (with en suite) sleeping up to four from $50 to $65 a double ($10 per extra person).

The *Wanaka YHA* (☎ 443 7405, @ yhawnka@yha.org.nz, 181 Upton St) has a relaxed, friendly atmosphere and is open all day. It charges $16 per person in dorms or twins and doubles are $36. Mountain bikes are available and there are many other activities.

The *Wanaka Bakpaka* (☎ 443 7837, @ wanakabakpaka@xtra.co.nz, 117 Lakeside Rd) is opposite the jetty on the northern side of Roy's Bay, with great views of the lake and mountains. It is well set up for travel and tramping information. Mountain bikes, kayaks and canoes can be hired. Dorms or shared rooms cost $16 per person, twins are $36 and doubles are $40.

The *Purple Cow Backpackers* (☎ 0800-772 277, @ stay@purplecow.co.nz, 94 Brownston St), formerly the Pembroke Inn, has a new kitchen and laundry, and the views are spectacular. It is spacious and friendly and the guests are afforded all the comforts. Dorms are $17, doubles from $42 to $45, and singles $25.

Holly's (☎ 443 8187, 71 Upton St) is a small converted house with friendly owners. Dorm beds are $16, and twins and doubles are $36. There are also a couple of self-contained units good for family groups.

Bullock Creek Lodge (☎/fax 443 1265, 46 Brownston St) is near a pleasant stream with trout that are almost tame. Beds in share rooms (four) are $17, and twins and doubles are $45 for two.

The *Albert Town Lodge* (☎ 443 9487), a five-minute drive east from Wanaka, is an option if Wanaka places are full.

B&Bs & Guesthouses *Altamont Lodge* (☎ 443 8864), on Mt Aspiring Rd on the edge of town towards Treble Cone, is popular with skiers in winter. It's open in summer and is good value with very comfortable singles/doubles for $30/48. Facilities include a tennis court, playground and spa pool.

Te Wanaka Lodge (☎ 443 9224, ◉ tewanakalodge@xtra.co.nz, 23 Brownston St) is a stylish place charging $90 to $120 (including breakfast), and *Aspiring Lodge (☎ 443 7816)* on Dunmore St has doubles for $120 to $160.

Riverrun (☎ 443 9049, ◉ riverrun@ xtra.co.nz), on Halliday Rd, is a magnificent luxury lodge in which all rooms have spectacular views; well-appointed singles and doubles are $240, breakfast included (DB&B is $350 for two).

A dozen or so B&B-style places (singles/doubles starting from $55/70) are in and around Wanaka; contact the visitor information centre.

Of particular note are *Northridge B&B (☎ 443 8835, ◉ s.atkinson@xtra.co.nz, 11 Botting Place),* on a ridge overlooking Wanaka, and the *Wanaka Stonehouse (☎ 443 1933, ◉ stonehouse@xtra.co.nz, 21 Sargood Drive),* an English-style manor.

The *Lady Pembroke (☎ 443 7181, ◉ gratom@xtra.co.nz)* – the perfect way to see the lake – is a self-contained houseboat with two king-size bedrooms and two bunkrooms (ring for prices).

Motels & Hotels Overlooking the reserve and close to town, *Brook Vale Manor (☎5443 8333, 35 Brownston St)* has studio/one-bedroom rooms from $80/90.

The *Archway Motel (☎ 443 7968, 64 Hedditch St)* is cheaper and has deluxe chalets from $75, and the *Wunderview – Lake Front Motels (☎ 443 7480, 122 Brownston St)* is from $75 a double. The *Bay View Motel (☎ 443 7766)* is 3km from town on Glendhu Bay Rd; all rooms have great views and cost $89 to $109 for two.

The Moorings (☎ 443 8479, 17 Lakeside Rd), Web site: www.themoorings.co.nz, has 14 new and tidy studio units with underfloor heating from $90 to $150 for two.

The *Wanaka Motor Inn (☎ 443 8216)* on Mt Aspiring Rd is a swank establishment with doubles from $142; *The Wanaka Hotel (☎ 443 7826, ◉ wanakahotel@ xtra.co.nz, 71 Ardmore St)* has doubles from $89 to $145, depending on the season; and the *Edgewater Resort Hotel (☎ 443 8311),* a flashy establishment on Sargood Drive, charges $160 to $250 and has an excellent range of activities and facilities.

Places to Eat

The *Snack Shack* in the Pembroke Mall has pizzas and the usual takeaways. The *Doughbin Bakery,* not far away, has cheap baked items.

Wanakai, on the corner of Helwick and Ardmore Sts, is a highly recommended and pleasant cafe with good coffee, cakes, quiches and panini.

Barrow's Bistro (☎ 443 8616, 20 Ardmore St), in the tavern of the same name, is a popular ski hang-out and serves good pub fare at reasonable prices.

Wanaka is surprisingly well equipped with restaurants. *Amigos Cafe (34 Ardmore St),* a pleasant place to dine inside or outside, has reasonably priced Mexican food and good margaritas.

Ripples, in the Pembroke Mall, is an upmarket licensed restaurant offering alfresco dining on the veranda. It's open for lunch and dinner (closed Sunday) and has seafood mains from $18.50.

The *Tuatara Pizza Co (☎ 443 8186, 72 Ardmore St)* is an interesting little place with friendly owners and pizzas from $15 to $25. Enjoy a game of pool while you wait.

Relishes Cafe (☎ 443 9018, 1/99 Ardmore St), a prize-winning place, is a favourite with locals. It has main courses from $16.50 and cheaper lunches, and it's great for a piece of country-style cake, muffins and a frothy cappuccino.

Capriccio's, an Italian place in the Pembroke Mall, has mains from $17 to $24 as well as fine, very popular pastas.

Muzza's Bar & Cafe, on the corner of Helwick and Brownston Sts, has an open fire and couch and table seating. It has a convivial atmosphere, probably more for drinking than eating, but the roast lamb and vegies meal ($12.95) is filling.

The *White House (☎ 443 9595),* Dungarvon St, is highly recommended. It's a chic establishment with a bar and interesting menu (vegan, vegetarian, Mediterranean and Middle Eastern cuisine are featured).

OTAGO

The ***Kingsway** (☎ 443 7663, 21 Helwick St)* is a very popular bar and diner with pool tables.

Getting There & Away

Air Aspiring Air (☎ 0800-100 943) has up to three flights daily to Queenstown, connecting with other airlines to other centres ($100, or $70 if booked seven days in advance).

Bus The InterCity bus depot at the Paper Place (☎ 443 7885), 84 Ardmore St opposite Clifford's, has daily buses from Queenstown, stopping at Wanaka on the way to Franz Josef via Haast Pass. Buses from Queenstown to Christchurch via Mt Cook stop in Wanaka and a daily bus to Cromwell connects with the Queenstown to Dunedin route.

Wanaka is well serviced by door-to-door shuttles, most of which can be booked at the Wanaka Travel Centre. Southern Link goes to Queenstown ($15) and Christchurch ($40), Wanaka Connexions (☎ 0800-879 926) goes just to Queenstown three times daily and Atomic Shuttles (☎ 442 8178 in Queenstown) goes to Dunedin ($35), Queenstown ($15) and Greymouth ($75).

Car & Motorcycle Although the Cardrona Road to Queenstown looks much shorter on the map than the route via Cromwell, it's a winding, climbing, unsealed mountain road past Cardrona. Travel is slower and rental cars, campervans and caravans are banned from this road.

Hitching The Haast Pass Road branches off the Cromwell Road 2km from Wanaka, just beyond the maze. Traffic is light and hitching is difficult to the Haast Pass and glacier country. Most traffic heads to Cromwell (for Queenstown), though you could still be in for a wait. Hitchhikers have written on stones by the roadside the sorry stories of their long waits.

Getting Around

Alpine Shuttles (☎ 443 7966) offers regular transport to Raspberry Flat at the national park for $30/45 one way/return, and to the skifields of Cardrona, Waiorau and Treble Cone ($22/15 for adults/children return). Mount Aspiring Express (☎ 443 8422) has two shuttles daily to Raspberry Creek in summer. The Bus Co (☎ 443 8775) runs to the skifields in winter.

Numerous places around town rent out mountain bikes, such as the YHA (for nonguests also) at $15 per day or $10 for half a day; Alpine Shuttles and Lakeland Adventures also rent out cars.

Southland

☎ 03 • pop 100,800

Southland is famous for the Milford Sound, but while many visit Milford on day trips from Queenstown, they get no further into this frontier province of rugged fiords, mountains, fine coastal scenery and abundant flora and fauna.

There are three main routes into Southland: via Queenstown to Fiordland; from Queenstown down SH6 to Invercargill; and from Dunedin to Invercargill on SH1. All three, however, miss spectacular scenery, so some interesting local routes are described in this chapter.

Southland has a predominantly Scottish heritage and many of its inhabitants speak with a distinctive rolling of their 'r's. There is also a considerable Maori population, whose *marae* are being re-established.

Fiordland

The spectacular Fiordland National Park, part of Te Wahipounamu World Heritage Area, includes some of New Zealand's most famous walks, including the best-known of the lot, the Milford Track. The tracks, however, barely penetrate this raw, powerful region. The immensity of it can only really be appreciated from the air or from a boat or kayak out on the sounds.

TE ANAU
pop 1785

Lake Te Anau, with its three arms that penetrate into the mountainous forested shore, was gouged out by a huge glacier. It is 417m at its deepest, 53km long and 10km across at its widest point, making it NZ's second-largest lake after Taupo in the North Island. The lake takes its name from the caves discovered on its western shore, Te Ana-au (The Cave of Rushing Water).

The township is beautifully situated on the lakeshore and is the main tourist centre of the region – a smaller, low-key version of

HIGHLIGHTS

- Cruising Lakes Te Anau and Manapouri to Te Ana-au Caves and Doubtful Sound
- Tramping the Milford and Kepler Tracks in the stunning Fiordland National Park
- Sea kayaking on magnificent Milford Sound
- Driving the Southern Scenic Route from Manapouri to Invercargill
- Exploring the flora- and fauna-rich Catlins, with its fossilised forests, native bushland, Hector's dolphins, penguins and rare birds
- Visiting Southland Museum, particularly the critters inhabiting the tuatara house

Queenstown. It offers all manner of activities and trips to keep you busy, although for many visitors the town is just a jumping-off point for Milford.

Information

The Department of Conservation's (DOC) Fiordland National Park Visitor Centre (☎ 249 7924) is on Lake Front Drive near the turn-off to Manapouri. It has a museum, park exhibits and information on tramping or

SOUTHLAND

SOUTHLAND

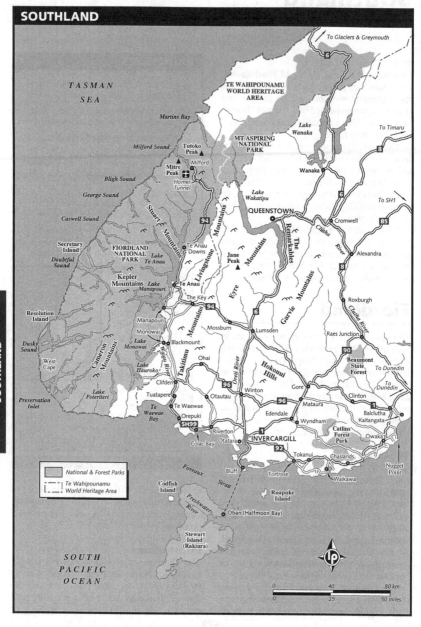

SOUTHLAND

TASMAN
SEA

To Glaciers & Greymouth

TE WAHIPOUNAMU
WORLD HERITAGE
AREA

Martins Bay

Milford Sound

Tutoko
Peak ▲

Mitre ▲
Peak

Milford

Homer
Tunnel

Bligh Sound

MT ASPIRING
NATIONAL
PARK

Lake
Wanaka

To Timaru

George Sound

Caswell Sound

Stuart Mountains

Wanaka

To SH1

Lake
Wakatipu

Secretary
Island

Doubtful
Sound

FIORDLAND
NATIONAL
PARK

Lake
Te Anau

QUEENSTOWN

Cromwell

Te Anau
Downs

Livingstone Mountains

Jane Peak ▲

Eyre Mountains

The Remarkables

Clutha River

Kepler
Mountains

Lake
Manapouri

Te Anau

The Key

Garvie Mountains

Alexandra

Resolution
Island

Dusky
Sound

Manapouri

Monowai

Lake
Monowai

Blackmount

Mossburn

Lumsden

Roxburgh

Raes Junction

Clutha River

West
Cape

Cameron Mountains

Takitimu Mountains

Waiau River

Ohai

Oreti River

Hokonui
Hills

Beaumont
State
Forest

To Dunedin

Lake
Hauroko

Clifden

Te
Waewae
Bay

Lake
Poteriteri

Preservation
Inlet

Tuatapere

Te Waewae

Orepuki

SH99

Otautau

Winton

Riverton

Colac Bay

Otatara

Edendale

INVERCARGILL

Gore

Mataura

Wyndham

To Dunedin

Clinton

Balclutha

Kaitangata

Catlins
Forest
Park

Owaka

Tokanui

Chaslands

Nugget
Point

Foveaux

Bluff

Strait

Fortrose

Waikawa

Codfish
Island

Freshwater
River

Ruapuke
Island

Oban (Halfmoon Bay)

Stewart
Island
(Rakiura)

SOUTH
PACIFIC
OCEAN

National & Forest Parks

Te Wahipounamu
World Heritage Area

0   40   80 km
0   25   50 miles

shorter walks. It's open from 8 am to 8 pm daily in summer, from 9 am to 4.30 pm in winter. Independent walkers for the Milford and Routeburn Tracks can book here (☎ 249 8514, ✉ greatwalksbooking@doc.govt.nz).

The Te Anau Visitor Information Centre (☎ 249 8900, ✉ teanau1@fiordlandtravel .co.nz) is in the Fiordland Travel office, by the waterfront on the corner of Te Anau Terrace and Milford Rd. This office is also an Inter-City bus agent. Fiordland Travel (☎ 0800-656 501) operates lake cruises and tours.

The post shop is in the centre of town on Milford Rd, and there are banks near the corner of Mokonui St and Milford Rd.

Te Anau is the jumping-off point for the Milford Track and many other walks – the Kepler, Dusky, Routeburn and Hollyford.

Bev's Tramping Gear (☎ 249 7389), 16 Homer St, rents out camping equipment (and has a Great Walks special for $75). Contact the visitor centre for guides for remote walks.

Te Anau Wildlife Centre

This DOC-run centre is just outside Te Anau on the road to Manapouri. The grounds and mostly natural enclosures house numerous birds, including the rare takahe, a flightless bird considered extinct until a colony was discovered in 1948 (see the colour 'Fauna & Flora' section). This is a good opportunity to identify birds you may see on the tramps. Entry is free, but donations are welcome.

Te Ana-au Caves

These impressive caves, on the western side of the lake, were mentioned in Maori legends but only rediscovered in 1948. On the shores of the lake and accessible only by boat, the 200m of active cave system is magical, with waterfalls, whirlpools and a glowworm grotto in the inner reaches. The heart of the caves is reached by a system of walkways and two short punt journeys. The 2½-hour trip costs $39 (children $10); departures are daily at 2 pm (also 8.15 pm September to May). Book at Fiordland Travel.

Kepler Track

This Great Walk starts just outside Te Anau and goes to the Kepler Mountains at the southern end of Lake Te Anau. Like any Fiordland track, the walk depends on the weather; when it's wet, it's very, very wet. The track is top quality, well graded and gravelled, and the three large huts are well equipped, with heating and gas stoves. Hut fees are $15 per night if prebooked, $20 otherwise, and hut wardens are on hand from the end of October to late April. Camping ($6 per person per night if prebooked, $8 if not) is available at Iris Burn and Brod Bay only (not at Mt Luxmore Hut).

The alpine sections of the track may be closed in winter due to weather conditions. These sections require a good level of fitness, though other sections are much easier. The hut fee in winter is $5 per night, and camping is free.

The walk can be done over four days and it features a variety of vegetation and terrain, including lakeside and riverside sections (good trout fishing), then a climb up out of the beech forest to the tree line and panoramic views. The alpine stretch between Iris Burn Hut and Mt Luxmore Hut goes along a high ridge line, well above the bush, offering fantastic views when it's clear. Other sections cross U-shaped, glacier-carved valleys. It's recommended that the track be done in the Mt Luxmore–Iris Burn–Moturau direction. Estimated walking times are as follows:

Fiordland National Park Visitor Centre to control gates	45 mins
Control gates to Brod Bay	1½ hours
Brod Bay to Mt Luxmore Hut	3½ to 4½ hours
Mt Luxmore to Iris Burn Hut	five to six hours
Iris Burn Hut to Moturau Hut	five to six hours
Moturau Hut to Rainbow Reach	1½ hours
Rainbow Reach to control gates	2½ to 3½ hours

Plenty of other shorter walks in the Te Anau area are outlined in DOC's *Te Anau Walks* pamphlet.

Kayaking

Kayaking trips in this enthralling natural environment are offered by Fiordland

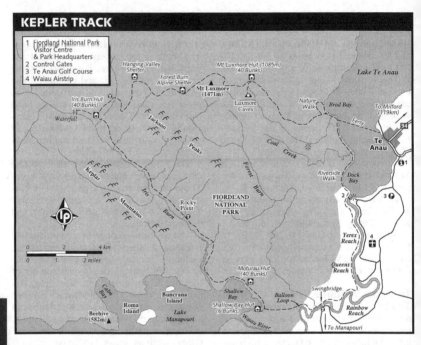

KEPLER TRACK

1 Fiordland National Park Visitor Centre & Park Headquarters
2 Control Gates
3 Te Anau Golf Course
4 Waiau Airstrip

Wilderness Experiences (☎ 249 7700), 66 Quintin Drive, which offers guided trips and independent rentals. All trips are in the World Heritage Area and could include Lakes Te Anau and Manapouri, or Doubtful and Milford Sounds. The view of the bush, lakes, waterfalls and fiords from this vantage point will overwhelm you.

Fiordland Wilderness Experiences has kayaking trips to the Milford Track trail ends and day paddles on Milford Sound ($80, including transport from Te Anau). The two-day, guided trip on serene Doubtful Sound ($230) receives rave reviews from travellers. This trip can be extended with another two days of independent paddling back across Lake Manapouri ($290). Independent rental costs around $45 per day.

Aerial Sightseeing

Waterwings Airways (☎ 249 7405) has floatplane flights from right off Te Anau Terrace in the town centre. There's a quick zip around the area for $39, a flight to Doubtful Sound for $153, and another over the Kepler Track for $80. Waterwings Airways also has a variety of Milford flights, including morning and afternoon Milford Sound Overheads ($187/112 for adults/children) and Fiordland Fantastic ($242/145).

Air Fiordland (☎ 249 7505) has short scenic flights from Milford ($50), flights to Milford Sound from Te Anau ($75 one way) and to Doubtful Sound ($120), or a 1½-hour tour over both sounds and Fiordland National Park ($250). Children's fares are 60% of adult fares. All flights are either by floatplane or normal plane.

The flight to Milford Sound goes over the Milford Track, with views of the amazing drop of the Sutherland Falls and Lake Quill.

Air Fiordland has cheaper scenic flights from Milford in summer: a 25-minute flight to Sutherland Falls is $75. Charters are also available – Milford or Hollyford to Martins Bay is $275 (four people with backpacks).

Southern Lakes Helicopters (☎ 249 7167) also has flights around the area. On one combination trip – similar to but not as good as the 'Siberia Experience' (see under Makarora in the Otago chapter) – you can 'heli-hike-sail' for $110. Southern Lakes takes you up to Mt Luxmore, then you walk to Brod Bay (about three hours) and sail back to Te Anau on the *Manuska*.

Organised Tours

Cruises on Lake Te Anau are popular. As well as Te Ana-au Caves trips, Fiordland Travel has trips to Milford and Doubtful Sounds from Te Anau. See the Milford Sound and Manapouri sections in this chapter for details.

From November to April, when the Milford Track is open, Fiordland Travel's MV *Tawera* runs from Te Anau Downs to Glade House, the starting point for the Milford Track. It connects at Te Anau Downs with the Mt Cook Line bus back to Te Anau. The one-way cruise is $32 at 10.30 am, $43 at 2 pm (children $10); the return cruise is $64/20.

Deepwater Cruises (☎ 249 7737), based at Te Anau Motor Park, also goes to Glade House at 9.30 am ($50, including the coach to Te Anau Downs). Deepwater offers Milford Track day trips for $85.

Yacht charters, scenic cruises and trampers transport are also provided on the lake by Sinbad Cruises (☎ 249 7106). Its gaff ketch, *Manuska,* sails to Glade House for $50 or Brod Bay for $15 ($25 return). Scenic lake or evening cruises are $45.

Lakeland Boat Hire (☎ 249 8364) rents out rowing boats, outboard motors, pedal boats, catamarans, canoes or jet-skis from a little caravan beside the lake. Boat transfer to Brod Bay costs $15, going on demand.

Trips 'n' Tramps (☎ 249 7081) offers a variety of things to do around Te Anau, including half-day and full-day guided walks. The Milford Track day walk, in conjunction with Fiordland Travel, is $105 (children $65).

Places to Stay

Camping & Cabins *Te Anau Holiday Park (☎ 249 7457),* opposite the lake and just 1km from Te Anau on the road to Manapouri, has tent/powered sites for two people for $20/22, tourist cabins for $51, tourist flats for $79 and five studio motel units for $95 each. Beds in the large bunkhouse cost $16 and $18. It's a large, well-equipped camping ground with attractive surroundings. Staff can organise track and boat transfers, and car, van and gear storage is available for trampers.

The *Mountain View Holiday Park (☎ 249 7462, 128 Te Anau Terrace)* is in a neat little slice of suburbia with well-tended powered sites for $22. Cabins are $41 and motel units $85.

The *Fiordland Holiday Park (☎/fax 249 7059)* is about 1.5km from town on the Milford Rd. Tent/powered sites are $14/15, basic cabins are $24, better cabins range from $35 to $45 and on-site caravans are $28.

There are over a dozen basic *DOC camping grounds* in this region, all adjacent to SH94 (see the Te Anau to Milford section).

Hostels *Te Anau Backpackers (☎ 249 7713, ❷ hostel@xtra.co.nz, 48 Lake Front Drive)* is a large, friendly place, set among the town's prime real estate with great lake views. Dorms are $14 and $17 per person and twins and doubles are $36 and $38. It has gear storage, free use of cooking utensils for trampers and coin-operated email access. The staff will help arrange transport to the tracks.

Next door, the *Lakefront Backpackers Lodge (☎ 249 7974, ❷ lakefronthostel@ xtra.co.nz, 50 Lake Front Drive)* is similar but smaller, and charges $17 for dorms and $38 and $40 in twins and doubles.

The *Te Anau YHA (☎ 249 7847, ❷ yhatanau@yha.org.nz),* once way out of town, has moved to Mokonui St in the heart of Te Anau. The hostel has dorms for $16 per person, and twins and doubles for $40. It is well set up for trampers and will store gear. There's a cafe across the road.

Tarahau Lodge (☎ 248 6182, 1 Cumberland St) in Mossburn, 52km east of Te Anau, has accommodation in a shearers' quarters. It's run by a 'gun' shearer who is only too happy to unravel shearing culture. It costs $20/30 for a single/double.

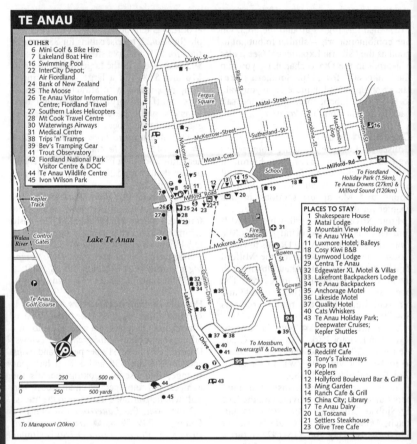

TE ANAU

OTHER
6 Mini Golf & Bike Hire
7 Lakeland Boat Hire
16 Swimming Pool
22 InterCity Depot;
     Air Fiordland
24 Bank of New Zealand
25 The Moose
26 Te Anau Visitor Information
     Centre; Fiordland Travel
27 Southern Lakes Helicopters
28 Mt Cook Travel Centre
30 Waterwings Airways
31 Medical Centre
38 Trips 'n' Tramps
39 Bev's Tramping Gear
41 Trout Observatory
42 Fiordland National Park
     Visitor Centre & DOC
44 Te Anau Wildlife Centre
45 Ivon Wilson Park

PLACES TO STAY
1 Shakespeare House
2 Matai Lodge
3 Mountain View Holiday Park
4 Te Anau YHA
11 Luxmore Hotel; Baileys
18 Cosy Kiwi B&B
29 Lynwood Lodge
29 Centra Te Anau
32 Edgewater XL Motel & Villas
33 Lakefront Backpackers Lodge
34 Te Anau Backpackers
35 Anchorage Motel
36 Lakeside Motel
37 Quality Hotel
40 Cats Whiskers
43 Te Anau Holiday Park;
     Deepwater Cruises;
     Kepler Shuttles

PLACES TO EAT
5 Redcliff Cafe
8 Tony's Takeaways
9 Pop Inn
10 Keplers
12 Hollyford Boulevard Bar & Grill
13 Ming Garden
14 Ranch Cafe & Grill
15 China City; Library
17 Te Anau Dairy
20 La Toscana
21 Settlers Steakhouse
23 Olive Tree Cafe

Lake Te Anau

Te Anau Golf Course

To Fiordland Holiday Park (1.5km),
Te Anau Downs (27km) &
Milford Sound (120km)

To Mossburn,
Invercargill & Dunedin

To Manapouri (20km)

SOUTHLAND

B&Bs & Guesthouses There are a couple of well-kept B&B places. *Shakespeare House* (☎ 249 7349, 10 Dusky St) offers B&B accommodation with a substantial breakfast. Quiet and pleasant rooms cost $80 for a single and $98 to $112 for doubles with en suite, less in the off season.

The *Matai Lodge* (☎ 249 7360, 42 Matai St) is centrally located. B&B costs $55/76 for singles/doubles with shared bathrooms. The *Cats Whiskers* (☎ 249 8112, 2 Lake Front Drive), opposite the DOC visitor centre, has B&B singles for $55, en suite doubles for $95.

The *Cosy Kiwi B&B* (☎ 249 7475, 186 Milford Rd) has lovely German-speaking hosts who love to make pancakes for breakfast; singles/doubles are from $55/80.

Motels & Hotels *Lynwood Lodge* (☎ 249 8538), on the corner of Luxmore Drive and Milford Rd, has 31 doubles for $95 ($20 for each extra person). The *Edgewater XL Motel & Villas* (☎ 249 7258, 52 Te Anau Terrace) has doubles for $83 and $92.

The *Lakeside Motel* (☎ 249 7435, ✉ Lakeside.teanau@xtra.co.nz, 36 Lake Front Drive) is in a prime position and has units for $85 to $95. The *Anchorage Motel* (☎ 249 7256, 47 Quintin Drive) has eight doubles starting at $85. There are numerous other motels at similar or higher prices.

At the top end, *Centra Te Anau* (☎ 249 7411, @ centra.teanau@xtra.co.nz), on Te Anau Terrace in the town centre, has rooms starting at $120. The *Luxmore Hotel* (☎ 249 7526), on Milford Rd near the corner of Mokonui St, has nearly 100 rooms. The *Quality Hotel* (☎ 249 7421), on Lake Front Drive and with rooms from $90 to $150, is another upmarket option.

Places to Eat

The *Pop Inn* near the lakefront has light snacks and sandwiches, and is often crammed with forlorn and starved bus travellers. Nearby, *Tony's Takeaways* is a mobile takeaway with a friendly owner.

Several places along Milford Rd and on Jailhouse Mall in the town centre serve snacks and takeaways. The *Olive Tree Cafe* has good light meals or hearty grills from $14 to $17, and *Te Anau Dairy* near the post shop is a great place to sit with a coffee and ice cream. *Baileys*, in the Luxmore Hotel, serves breakfast all day, bistro lunches and morning and afternoon teas.

Te Anau has a good restaurant scene for its size. *Keplers* on Milford Rd features venison, lamb and seafood on its menu, with main courses costing around $16 to $20. *La Toscana* (☎ 249 7756), on Milford Rd in the town centre, is an Italian pizzeria and 'spagetteria' and one of Te Anau's best dining spots. Pasta mains are around $15 and pizzas are $20. It also serves excellent desserts. *Hollyford Boulevard Bar & Grill* (☎ 249 7334) on Milford Rd looks expensive but the sizable menu is reasonably priced.

The *Settlers Steakhouse*, also on Milford Rd, is the local hunting ground for carnivores and the *Ranch Cafe & Grill* is similar, with huge steaks for $23 and good-value grill meals for $13.50.

The *Ming Garden* on Milford Crescent has reasonable Chinese food, while the licensed *China City* (☎ 249 8337), next to the library, is more upmarket.

The main entertainment venue in this sleepy town is *The Moose* (☎ 249 7100), a lakefront cafe and bar which provides a courtesy coach.

The *Redcliff Cafe* (☎ 249 7431, 12 Mokonui St) is another delightful cafe/bar with cosy indoor and outdoor dining areas. If you are lucky you might see from here the natural fireworks display of the southern lights, *aurora australis*.

Getting There & Away

Air Mt Cook Airline (☎ 249 7516) has daily direct flights to Queenstown and on to Mt Cook, Christchurch and other centres.

Waterwings Airways (☎ 249 7405), an agent for Ansett New Zealand, has flights to Queenstown and Milford. Air Fiordland (☎ 249 7505) also has flights from Milford to Te Anau and Queenstown.

Bus InterCity (☎ 249 7559) has daily services between Queenstown and Milford via Te Anau. Daily services also go to Invercargill (three hours), involving a transfer stop in Lumsden, and to Dunedin (four hours) continuing on to Christchurch. Buses arrive at and depart from the InterCity depot on Milford Rd. Mt Cook Line (☎ 249 7516) has daily buses to/from Milford, Queenstown and Christchurch.

Topline Tours (☎ 0508-832 628) operates a daily shuttle service between Te Anau and Queenstown ($35, discount $25), departing from Te Anau at 10 am and Queenstown at 2 pm.

Spitfire Shuttle (☎ 249 7505) departs from Te Anau daily for Invercargill at 8.30 am, returning at 1 pm ($40, discount $34). Catch-a-Bus (☎ 249 8900) runs to Dunedin.

Fiordland Travel (☎ 249 7419), on the lakefront, has buses to Queenstown and Milford.

Southern Explorer (☎ 249 7820) and Bottom Bus (☎ 442 9708) are good services for backpackers to get around this region. See also the Queenstown section in the Otago chapter.

Trampers' Transport Tracknet (☎ 249 7777), operating out of Te Anau Motor Park,

SOUTHLAND

Annoying Weather & Wildlife

Once you leave Te Anau, you hit two of the menaces of Fiordland: rain and sandflies. Rain in this area is very heavy – Milford gets over 6m annually! Sandflies, for those who haven't met them, are nasty little biting insects. They are smaller than mosquitoes, with a similar bite, and you will see clouds of them at Milford. Don't be put off sightseeing by rain; the masses of water hurtling down the sheer walls of Milford Sound are an incredible sight and the rain tends to keep the sandflies away. For walking and tramping it is a different story, as the rain means flooded rivers and poor visibility.

has shuttle buses from October to May for the Kepler, Routeburn and Hollyford Tracks and to Milford. The Kepler shuttle runs to the control gates and the swingbridge. The shuttle to Milford ($35) passes The Divide ($20) at the start/end of the Routeburn.

Kiwi Discovery (☎ 249 7505) from Queenstown also provides trampers' transport, passing through Te Anau at 10 am on the way to Milford. Mt Cook Line has three services a day to Milford via The Divide, and InterCity has one.

Hitching Hitching in and out of Te Anau is a bit easier than at Milford, though still fairly hard. Hitching between Manapouri and Te Anau is usually good.

Getting Around

You can hire bicycles for $25 per day from Mini Golf & Bike Hire (☎ 249 7959) on Mokonui St, and from Te Anau Motor Park.

TE ANAU TO MILFORD

It is 119km from Te Anau to Milford on one of the most scenic roads you could hope for. The first part is through relatively undulating farmland that sits atop the lateral moraine of the glacier that once gouged out Lake Te Anau. At 16km the road enters a patch of mountain beech forest, passes **Te Anau Downs Harbour** at 29km and heads towards

the entrance of Fiordland National Park and the Eglinton Valley. Again, you pass patches of beech – red, silver and mountain as well as alluvial flats and meadows.

Two interesting sights on the way are the **Avenue of the Disappearing Mountain** and the **Mirror Lakes** (58km from Te Anau). **Knobs Flat**, 5km past Mirror Lakes, is home to a new visitor centre with exhibits on the area, toilets, a dumping station and water for campers.

At the 77km mark is the area now referred to as O Tapara, but known more commonly as **Cascade Creek**. O Tapara is the original name of nearby Lake Gunn and refers to a Ngai Tahu ancestor, Tapara. The lake was a stopover for parties heading to Anita Bay in search of greenstone *(pounamu)*. A 40-minute walking track passes through tall red beech forest that shelters a variety of bird life, such as fantails, tomtits, bellbirds, parakeets, kereru and riflemen. Paradise ducks and NZ scaup are often seen on the lake. Lake Gunn is the largest of the Eglinton Valley lakes but Fergus and Lochie are higher in altitude. The forest floor is an array of mosses, ferns and lichens. In Cascade Creek you may see long-tail bats, NZ's only native land mammal.

The vegetation alters significantly as **The Divide** is approached. The size of the bush is reduced and ribbonwood and fuchsia are prominent. The Divide is the lowest east-west pass in the Southern Alps, and there is a good shelter here for walkers either finishing or starting the Routeburn and Greenstone Tracks. About a 1½-hour walk along the Routeburn brings you to **Key Summit**, where there are numerous tarns and patches of alpine bog. Three river systems – the Hollyford, Greenstone/Clutha and Eglinton/Waiau – start from the sides of this feature and radiate out to the west, east and south coasts of the island.

From The Divide, the road falls into the beech forest of the **Hollyford Valley** and there is an interesting turn-off you can take to Hollyford (Gunn's) Camp and the start of the Hollyford Track to Martins Bay. At the end of the unsealed road it is a 10-minute walk to the high **Humbolt Falls**.

FIORDLAND

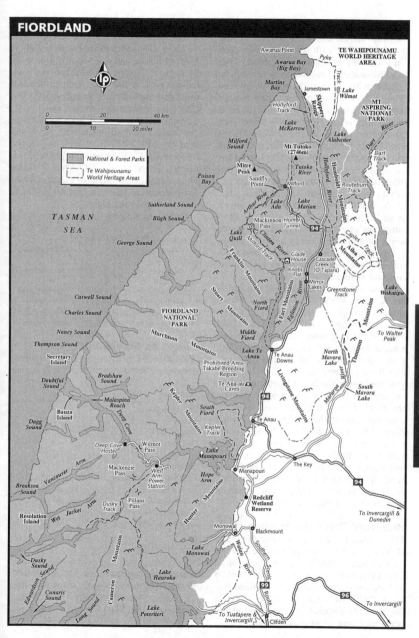

TE WAHIPOUNAMU WORLD HERITAGE AREA

Awarua Point
Awarua Bay (Big Bay)
Pyke
Track
Martins Bay
Jamestown
Lake Wilmot
MT ASPIRING NATIONAL PARK
Hollyford Track
Skippers Range
Lake McKerrow
Dart River
Lake Alabaster
Milford Sound
Mt Tutoko (2746m)
Dart Track
Poison Bay
Mitre Peak
Sandfly Point
Milford
Tutoko River
Hollyford River
Humboldt Mountains
Routeburn Track
Arthur River
Lake Ada
Lake Marian
Sutherland Sound
Mackinnon Pass
Homer Tunnel
94
TASMAN SEA
Bligh Sound
Lake Quill
Clinton River
Caples Track
Ailsa Mountains
George Sound
Milford Track
Franklin Mountains
Glade House
Cascade Creek (O Tapara)
Knobs Flat
Caswell Sound
Stuart Mountains
North Fiord
Earl Mountains
Eglinton River
Mirror Lakes
Greenstone Track
Charles Sound
FIORDLAND NATIONAL PARK
Murchison Mountains
Lake Wakatipu
Nancy Sound
Middle Fiord
Lake Te Anau
Te Anau Downs
Thompson Sound
Secretary Island
Prohibited Area-Takahe Breeding Region
North Mavora Lake
To Walter Peak
Bradshaw Sound
Te Ana-au Caves
Doubtful Sound
Livingstone Mountains
South Mavora Lake
Bauza Island
Malaspina Reach
Kepler Mountains
South Fiord
Mararoa River
Thomson Mountains
Dagg Sound
Deep Cove
Te Anau
Breaksea Sound
Deep Cove Hostel
Wilmot Pass
Kepler Track
94
Vancouver Arm
Mackenzie Pass
West Arm Power Station
Lake Manapouri
Resolution Island
Wet Jacket Arm
Pillans Pass
Hope Arm
Manapouri
The Key
Dusky Track
Hunter Mountains
Dusky Sound
Redcliff Wetland Reserve
To Invercargill & Dunedin
94
Edwardson Sound
Cameron Mountains
Lake Monowai
Monowai
Blackmount
Cunaris Sound
Waiau River
Long Sound
Lake Hauroko
Southern Scenic Route
99
96
Lake Poteriteri
To Tuatapere & Invercargill
Clifden
To Invercargill

Legend

National & Forest Parks

Te Wahipounamu World Heritage Areas

0 — 20 — 40 km
0 — 10 — 20 miles

One kilometre down the Lower Hollyford Rd from Marian Corner is a track leading to **Lake Marian**, with splendid views. You can take the three-hour return, hard tramp or a pleasant short walk to view the rapids.

Back at the corner, the road to Milford rises up to the east portal of the **Homer Tunnel**, 101km from Te Anau. The tunnel is named after Harry Homer, who discovered the Homer Saddle in 1889. Work on the tunnel didn't begin until 1935, providing relief work for unemployed people after the Depression, and it wasn't finished until 1952. Rough-hewn, the tunnel has a steep east to west gradient, but emerges after 1207m into the spectacular **Cleddau Canyon** on its Milford side. At the portals are short nature walks, with descriptions of alpine species found here. Cheeky kea greet buses.

The road is normally open year-round, but may be closed in winter by high snowfalls and avalanches.

About 10km before reaching Milford is the **Chasm Walk**. The Cleddau River plunges through eroded boulders in a narrow chasm, the Upper Fall, which is 22m deep. About 16m lower it cascades under a natural rock bridge to another waterfall. There are views of **Mt Tutoko** (2746m), Fiordland's proudest and highest peak, glimpsed above the beech forest just before you arrive in Milford. The majestic **Darrans** are in this area. A track leads off from the western side of the bridge over Tutoko River. After a two-hour walk through bush, the scenery here is overpowering. Don't venture any further unless you are a competent tramper and very well equipped. There is no development in this region – nature, swarms of gigantic sandflies and abundant rainfall seem to retort 'Just you try'.

Hollyford Track (to Martins Bay)

This is a well-known track along the broad Hollyford Valley through rainforest to the Tasman Sea at Martins Bay. Because of its length (four days one way), it should not be undertaken lightly. Check at Fiordland National Park Visitor Centre (☎ 249 7924) in Te Anau for detailed information and the latest track and weather conditions.

Hollyford Valley Walk Ltd (☎ 0800-832 226) in Queenstown has guided walks from Te Anau with transfers, including a flight to Milford Sound and a jet-boat trip on Lake McKerrow. It avoids the hardest and most tedious part of the walk, Demon Trail. A three-day trip is $1290; four days is $1570. Check out www.hollyfordtrack.co.nz.

Tracknet (☎ 249 7777) has a shuttle from Te Anau to the start of the trail. Air Fiordland (☎ 249 7505) flies from Milford to Martins Bay for $280 for a minimum of four people. There are six DOC huts (Hidden Falls, Alabaster, McKerrow Island, Demon Trail, Hokuri and the new Martins Bay Hut), each costing $4 per night.

Estimated walking times are:

Lower Hollyford Rd car park to	
Hidden Falls	2½ to three hours
Hidden Falls to	
Lake Alabaster	3½ to four hours
Lake Alabaster to	
Lake McKerrow	three hours
Lake McKerrow to Demon Trail	1½ hours
Demon Trail to Hokuri River	five hours
Hokuri River to Martins Bay	five hours

Places to Stay & Eat

Along SH94 are many *DOC camping grounds*. Their distances from Te Anau are:

location	km
Ten Mile Bush	17
Henry Creek	25
Boyd Creek	45
Walker Creek	49
McKay Creek	53
Totara Creek	53
East Branch Eglinton	56
Deer Flat	62
Kiosk Creek	65
Smithy Creek	67
Upper Eglinton	71
Cascade Creek	78
Lake Gunn	81

Barnyard Backpackers (☎ 249 8006, @ rainbowdowns@xtra.co.nz) is 9km from Te Anau on the way to Manapouri. Shared rooms are from $16 to $18, twins and doubles are $40.

Te Anau Downs Motor Inn (☎ *0800-500 805)* is at Te Anau Downs, 27km from Te Anau on the road to Milford, where boats depart for Glade House and the Milford Track. Motel units range from $90 to $119 for two. *Grumpy's Backpackers* (☎ *249 7753,* **☻** *grumpys@xtra.co.nz),* housed in the motor inn, provides good shared rooms for $18 to $20. Double and twin rooms, each with a bathroom and TV, are $43, rooms with mountain and lake views are $48.

Hollyford Camp, formerly Gunn's Camp, in the Hollyford Valley has rustic cabins (with innerspring mattresses, wood and coal-burning stoves, separate kitchen and hand basins) for $17/29 for one/two people and $15 per person share. Camping is possible but there are no kitchen facilities for campers. The camp also has a shop with basic trampers' supplies (sorted into 'pack-friendly' bags). The interesting little museum is the very personal creation of owner Murray Gunn, who has been finding things in the hills around here for over 45 years. Entry is free if you stay in his cabins.

The NZ Alpine Club's *Homer Hut* is hidden near a turn-off just before the Homer Tunnel. The club takes casual guests during the week for a minimal fee; check with the caretaker at the hut – if there is one.

Possibly the most remote homestay in NZ is *Charlie's Place* (☎ *025-893 570,* **☻** *john-p@wave.co.nz),* at Jamestown on the shores of Lake McKerrow. It's $25/40 without/with bedding. Homestay with dinner and B&B is $95.

The *Martin's Bay Lodge* (☎ *442 3760),* run by Hollyford Valley Walk, allows non-walkers to stay ($170).

MILFORD SOUND
pop 170

One of NZ's most famous tourist destinations, Milford Sound is the most visited of all the fiords, and the most instantly breathtaking. The 22km-long fiord is dominated by the beautiful, 1695m-high Mitre Peak. The calm water mirrors the sheer peaks that rise all around.

Although remote, Milford Sound has thousands of visitors each year. Some come via the Milford Track, which ends at the sound, but most come by the buses that pull into the cruise wharf. The wharf resembles an international air terminal and is as busy when all the buses arrive. A cruise on Milford Sound is a must.

Busy through much of the day, in the morning and late afternoon Milford is serene. It is definitely worth visiting, but don't expect blue skies. Milford is synonymous with rain: 5.5m of it a year is only average. Consider yourself lucky if you strike a fine day, otherwise take in the spectacular waterfalls.

In the foyer of Mitre Peak Lodge is a small display with photographs and stories relating to the history, geology and glacial formation of the fiords, as well as information

DAVID WALL

Beautiful Sutherland Falls

on Donald Sutherland (1843–1919), 'the Hermit of Milford', who ran the first accommodation at Milford Sound. The Sutherland Falls are named after him and his grave lies behind the hotel.

Milford Track

Described by some as the finest walk in the world, this four-day walk is along a very scenic track. It is the country's best-known walk and one that most Kiwis dream of doing, even if it's the *only* track they ever walk. Many overseas visitors also make a special effort to do the track though, sadly, they often leave NZ without realising that many other great tracks exist.

The number of walkers is limited each year; accommodation is only in huts, camping is not allowed and you have to follow a set itinerary. Some walkers resent the restrictions, but the benefits outweigh the inconvenience: keeping numbers down protects the environment and, though it is a hassle to book, you are guaranteed the track won't be overcrowded.

In the off season it is still possible to walk the track, but there is no trail transport, the huts are not staffed and some of the bridges are removed. In the height of winter, snow and avalanches make it unwise, but it is accessible a few weeks either side of the main season.

Expect lots of rain. And when it does rain in this country of granite, the effect is an experience not to be missed. Water cascades *everywhere* and small streams become raging torrents within minutes. Remember to bring your raincoat and pack your belongings in an extra plastic bag.

Bookings You can walk the track as an independent tramper or as part of a guided tour. The track can only be done in one direction – from Lake Te Anau to Milford. A permit is required from the DOC visitor centre in Te Anau, allowing you to enter the track on a particular day and no other. Bookings can be heavy and it pays to book as far ahead as possible. The track must be booked from late October to mid-April (bookings commence on 1 July for the following season).

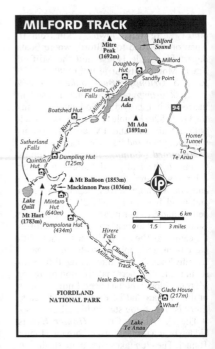

For independent bookings contact: Great Walks Booking Desk, Fiordland National Park Visitor Centre. See under Information in the Te Anau section earlier.

For independent walkers, a permit costs $105 (children $52.50), which includes three nights in the huts. The booking desk can also book transport: a bus to Te Anau Downs ($11/7), ferry to Glade House ($43/10), launch from Sandfly Point to the cruise terminal ($22/12.50) and bus back to Te Anau ($35/21). All up the cost is $196 per person (children $95).

Milford Track Guided Walk (☎ 249 7590, 🖂 mtinfo@milfordtrack.co.nz) also takes bookings. These organised parties stay at a different chain of huts from the 'independents', so there is little mingling of the two. The guided walk costs $1490/1590 in the low/high season, (children 10 to 15 years $840). It is all inclusive for five days, but walkers still only get three days on the trail.

Walking the Track The trail starts at Glade House, at the northern end of Lake Te Anau, accessed by boat from Te Anau Downs or Te Anau. The track follows the fairly flat Clinton River valley up to the Mintaro Hut, passing through rainforest. From Mintaro it passes over the scenic Mackinnon Pass, down to the Quintin Hut and through the rainforest in the Arthur River valley to Milford Sound. You can leave your pack at the Quintin Hut while you make the return walk to Sutherland Falls, NZ's highest. If the pass appears clear on arrival at Mintaro Hut make the effort to climb it – after a hot drink – as it may not be clear the next day. The highlights of Milford are the beautiful views from the **Mackinnon Pass**, the 630m **Sutherland Falls**, the rainforest and the crystal-clear streams, swarming with clever trout and eels. An amazingly intricate and very unnatural staircase has been built down beside the rapids on the descent from Mackinnon Pass. Estimated walking times are:

Glade House to Neale Burn Hut	one hour
Neale Burn Hut to Mintaro Hut	5½ hours
Mintaro Hut to Dumpling Hut	six hours
Side trip to Sutherland Falls	1½ hours return
Dumpling Hut to Sandfly Point	5½ hours

Guided walkers stop at their own huts – Glade House, Pompolona and Quintin – and for their money they have a longer walk than independent walkers on the last day (six hours from Quintin Hut out to Sandfly Point).

Transport to Glade House Mt Cook Line's 1.15 pm bus from Te Anau to Milford stops at Te Anau Downs ($11, 27km) to connect with Fiordland Travel's 2 pm boat to Glade House ($43).

Alternatively, Sinbad Cruises goes from Te Anau to Glade House for $50. You can also fly with Waterwings Airways or kayak from Te Anau. See the Te Anau section for more details.

SOUTHLAND

A stairway in the middle of nowhere – the descent from Mackinnon Pass on the Milford Track

TONY WHEELER

Transport from Sandfly Point Ferries leave Sandfly Point at 2 and 3 pm for the Milford Sound cruise wharf.

Or you could kayak to Milford. Rosco Gaudin (see the following Sea Kayaking section) has guided kayaking from Sandfly Point to Milford for $19. Fiordland Wilderness Experiences in Te Anau offers the same service.

Many operators offer complete packages covering both ends of the walk for around $100.

Sea Kayaking

The most spectacular way to see Milford Sound is at water level in a sea kayak. In a plastic shell, you fully realise your insignificance in the sound's huge natural amphitheatre. Whatever the weather, looking up to the towering bulk of the bush-clad mountains is nothing short of awesome.

Rosco Gaudin (☎ 0800-476 726) has summer trips of around six hours that include Stirling Falls, Harrison Cove beneath the bulk of the Pembroke Glacier, Bowen Falls and flora and fauna from an almost 'reach-out-and-touch-it' vantage point. Trips are great value and well within the bounds of someone with average fitness. Rosco can also arrange transport to and from Te Anau plus kayaking from the end of the Milford Track. An extended morning trip on the sound is $79, and an afternoon trip (which includes a short walk on a section of the Milford Track) is $49.

Diving

Full-day trips from Te Anau, which include two dives in Milford Sound, are operated by Tawaki Dive (☎ 249 9006). It costs $220/175 with full gear hire/weight belt and tanks only. See Tawaki's Web site at www.tawakidive.co.nz.

Milford Sound Cruises

Day Cruises Cruises on Milford Sound are popular, so it's a good idea to book a few days ahead. On all trips you can expect to see Bowen Falls, Mitre Peak, Anita Bay, the Elephant and Stirling Falls. More expensive cruises include the **underwater observatory**

moored at Harrison Cove, where you can view the reef system and have it explained.

All cruises leave from the huge wharf complex, a five-minute walk from the cafe and car park on a covered and elevated walkway through a patch of Fiordland bush.

Fiordland Travel (☎ 249 7419) has 1½-hour cruises for $44 (children $10), or $49 ($18) including the underwater observatory. *Milford Wanderer* day cruises are longer (2½ hours) and cost $49 ($10). Buffet lunch costs $23 ($15.50), a packed lunch is $11, or you can bring your own. Tea and coffee are served on all cruises.

Red Boat Cruises (☎ 0800-657 444) travels basically the same route as the Fiordland Travel boats, charges the same and also offers lunch. It has more cruises that take in the underwater observatory. The three-hour *Milford Adventurer* cruise at 12.25 pm includes the observatory and ventures out into the Tasman Sea.

Mitre Peak Cruises (☎ 249 8110) charges $48 (children $15), or $68 ($25) with the observatory.

Between them, these operators have well over a dozen cruises a day in summer between 9 am and 3 pm.

Overnight Cruises Fiordland Travel's *Milford Wanderer*, modelled on an old trading scow, carries 70 passengers overnight from 1 October to 30 April. The overnight cruise allows you to appreciate the fiord when all the other traffic has ceased. Kayaking, shore visits, fishing and swimming are offered as the boat sails the full length of the sound. You'll see wildlife such as dolphins, seals and penguins. The *Wanderer* is impressive when the sails are unfurled and it heaves its way through the Tasman swell out from Milford Sound. Staying overnight in four-bunk cabins costs $199 per person from Queenstown, $153 from Te Anau or $135/67.50 (for adults/children) from Milford; linen and meals are provided. The *Wanderer* is a YHA associate, so YHA discounts apply.

Red Boat Cruises also has a similar but slightly more upmarket cruise on the *Lady of the South Pacific* costing slightly more (in twin-share cabins).

Places to Stay & Eat

Independent walkers seeking a bit of luxury after completing the Milford Track will be disappointed. The *Mitre Peak Lodge*, formerly the Milford Hotel, caters only to those who do the guided walk.

Milford Sound Lodge (☎ 249 8071), a hostel-style place, is the only other accommodation. Tent/powered sites are $9/10 per person, but don't count on power – the generator can't handle it so it's lights off at 10.30 pm for everyone. A bed in the bunkhouse is $19, and twins and doubles with linen are $49. There is a good sitting/dining area where cheap meals are served and there's a kitchen for guest use. The lodge is a couple of kilometres from the ferry wharf, off the main road.

Mitre Peak Cafe, down on the sound near the wharf, is run by the Mitre Peak Lodge. It has good coffee and snacks, but closes around 5 pm. The *Shark in the Bar* next door is the local pub. It has pies, beer, a smattering of rowdy workers, but not much else.

Getting There & Away

You can reach Milford Sound by four methods, all interesting: hike, fly, bus or drive. The most spectacular is flying from Queenstown or Te Anau (see the Queenstown section in the Otago chapter and the Te Anau section earlier in this chapter). A good combination trip is to go to Milford by bus and return by air. (Scenic flights are also offered in Milford, starting at $50 to the head of the sound.)

The 120km road trip passing through the Homer Tunnel is also spectacular. Mt Cook Line and InterCity run daily bus services from Queenstown and Te Anau, but most passengers come on day trips which include a cruise. Trampers' buses also operate from Te Anau and Queenstown and will pick up at the Milford Sound Lodge. All these buses pass The Divide, the start/end of the Routeburn and Greenstone Tracks.

Many visitors make the return trip from Queenstown in one long 12-hour day. Te Anau is a better starting point as it is only five hours by bus. Fiordland Travel's coach–cruise–coach excursion, leaving Te Anau at 8 am and returning at 5 pm, costs $95 (children $47.50). InterCity has basically the same excursion at the same price, except the cruise is with Red Boat. It's essential to book in advance for the Milford cruises during the high season.

By car, the drive should take about 2½ hours, not allowing for stops.

Hitching on the Milford road is possible but hard going. There's little traffic and nearly all of it is tourist traffic, which is unlikely to stop.

MANAPOURI
pop 210

Just 19km south of Te Anau, on the shores of the lake of the same name, Manapouri is a popular centre for trips, cruises and walking expeditions into the Fiordland area. The lake, the second deepest in NZ after Hauroko, is in a spectacular setting, surrounded by mountains covered by native bush in their lower reaches. The town exists on a combination of hydroelectricity generation and tourism, an uneasy mix at the best of times. Now greenies work hand in hand with rednecks – the damage has been done and all are attempting to preserve their livelihoods.

Information

Fiordland Travel (☎ 0800-656 502, ✉ info@ fiordlandtravel.co.nz) is the main information and tour centre. The office at Pearl Harbour organises most of the trips, but is very busy just prior to boat departures. Buses from Te Anau connect with the West Arm Power Station and Doubtful Sound trips. See its Web site at www.fiordlandtravel.co.nz.

Doubtful Sound

Milford Sound, dominated by Mitre Peak, may be more immediately spectacular, but Doubtful Sound is larger, gets much less tourist traffic and is also a magnificent wilderness area of rugged peaks, dense forest and thundering waterfalls after rain.

Until relatively recently, only the most intrepid tramper or sailor entered the inner reaches of Doubtful Sound. Even Captain Cook, who named it, did not enter. Observing it from off the coast in 1770, he was 'doubtful' whether the winds in the sound would be sufficient to blow the ship back out to sea, and sailed on. In 1793 the Spanish entered the sound; Malsapina Reach is named after one of the leaders of this expedition, Bauza Island after another.

Doubtful Sound became accessible when the road over the Wilmot Pass was opened in 1959 to facilitate construction of the West Arm Power Station, built to provide electricity for the aluminium smelter near Bluff. A tunnel was dug through the mountain from Lake Manapouri to Doubtful Sound, and the massive flow of water into the sounds drives the power station turbines. The project sparked intense environmental battles, and in the 1970s plans to considerably raise the level of Lake Manapouri were defeated by the Save Manapouri Petition – the longest petition in NZ history. The lake is described as 'New Zealand's loveliest lake' – it's hard to imagine that anyone would want to destroy it.

Today, Doubtful Sound is exquisitely peaceful. Bottlenose and dusky dolphins and fur seals can be seen in its waters, and Fiordland crested penguins nest in October and November. Below the surface, black coral and other deep-sea life exist at unusually shallow levels because sunlight is filtered out by a permanent 3m to 4m layer of fresh water on top of the sea water. As well as the water pumped down from Lake Manapouri, Doubtful Sound receives some 6m of rain per year.

Activities

Adventure Charters (☎/fax 249 6626), next to the garage in Manapouri, rents out **kayaks** and gear at $35 per day for paddling on Lake Manapouri and can also arrange trips to Doubtful Sound. Dinghies can be hired for $7.50 per person per day.

With a dinghy you can cross the Waiau River for the best **walks** close to town – the three-hour Circle Track or further out to Hope Arm. Although Te Anau is the usual access point for the Kepler Track, the trail touches the top end of Lake Manapouri. Part of the Kepler can also be done as a day walk from Manapouri – access is via the swingbridge about 10km north of town.

Manapouri is also a staging point for the remote, five-day **Dusky Track**, a real walk into the wilderness of Dusky Sound. This challenging walk is only for experienced trampers prepared for plenty of rain. See Lonely Planet's *Tramping in New Zealand* for more details. Access to the track is by ferry to West Arm ($25), from where it is a half-hour walk to the start of the trail (you may be able to get a seat on a tour bus). Many walkers fly from Te Anau to Supper Cove, the end of the track, and then walk back. Waterwings Airways (☎ 249 7405) in Te Anau can arrange flights for around $150 per person.

For fishing tours try 4 in Fiordland (☎ 249 8070). Trolling is $75 per hour for a group of four, and fly-fishing is $55 per hour. It also organises drop-offs and pickups at several walks.

Organised Tours

Fiordland Travel has cruises from Manapouri to Doubtful Sound. After a half-hour cruise across Lake Manapouri, the next leg is by bus to Doubtful Sound with a side trip venturing 2km underground by road to the West Arm Power Station. After a tour of the power station, the bus travels over Wilmot Pass to the sea, where you then explore Doubtful Sound on a three-hour cruise. The eight-hour trip costs $160 (children $40), an additional $30 from Queenstown. You can order lunch or take your own.

Fiordland Ecology Holidays (☎ 249 6600), 1 Home St, offers a unique experience to a small number of clients. These tours are run by people who are very familiar with the flora and fauna of the area, and who sail their superbly equipped yacht into parts of the World Heritage Area only now being discovered. Experienced divers have the chance to dive in the fiords, as many visiting marine biologists do, plunging below the fresh water to see deep-water species you couldn't hope to see elsewhere. Nondivers are given many opportunities to explore the flora and fauna of this unique area. Four-day trips on Doubtful Sound cost around $600 to $700; other interesting trips go to Dusky Sound, Bluff and return. Ring for sailing dates.

The friendly seals are a highlight of boat trips through Fiordland – here at Dusky Sound

Fiordland Explorer Charters (☎/fax 249 6644) has half/full-day wilderness trips to Doubtful Sound for $60/120 (children $30/60). A full-day mountain-biking and kayaking combo is $120 (children $60).

Places to Stay & Eat

The *Manapouri Glade Motor Park* (☎ 249 6623), in a stunning location next to the river and lake, is small. Sites are $17 for two, cabins start at $30 and motel units at $70.

The *Lakeview Motor Park* (☎ 249 6624), 1km from the post office, is friendly and rather eccentric. It has tent/powered sites for $17/18 for two, standard cabins starting at $32, cute 'doll houses' for $39 and studio/one-bedroom motel units for $60/70.

Possum Lodge (☎ 249 6660, ✉ possum.lodge@xtra.co.nz, 3 Waiau St) is relaxing, and provides fine backpacker accommodation, free bikes, gear storage, and transport to the Kepler Track. Dorms cost $16, while doubles and twins are $36.

Freestone Backpackers (☎ 249 6893), 3km east of Manapouri, is a small, secluded place set back from the road. It has five four-bed huts at $15 per person. Some huts have potbelly stoves, and all have verandas.

Deep Cove Hostel (☎ 249 6602), on Doubtful Sound, charges $20 per person. It is well set up for sea and walking activities. It normally only takes groups; independent arrangements must be made in advance through the hostel.

The *Cottage* (☎ 249 6838), on Waiau St near the river, has just two very good B&B rooms for $55/75 for singles/doubles. *Murrell's Grand View House* (☎ 249 6642), built in 1889, is a fine establishment with four comfortable double en suite rooms from $165 to $185.

Cathedral Cafe, attached to the general store/post shop, has a good range of home-cooked meals and snacks. *Pearl Harbour Coffee Bar*, underneath the Fiordland Travel office, has sandwiches and other snacks.

Getting There & Away

Public transport options are limited. Spitfire Shuttle (☎ 249 7505) runs in the morning to Invercargill ($30) and in the afternoon to Te Anau ($8). Otherwise ask at Fiordland Travel if there are spare seats on its coaches to Te Anau.

The hitching between Te Anau and Manapouri is OK, but don't rely on connecting with the Doubtful Sound cruises.

SOUTHLAND

SOUTHERN SCENIC ROUTE

The Southern Scenic Route starts in Te Anau and goes via Manapouri, Blackmount and Clifden to Tuatapere. At Tuatapere, SH99 goes to Invercargill via Colac Bay and Riverton. From Invercargill to Dunedin you can take the scenic east-coast route through the Catlins (see The Catlins later in this chapter). Public transport is limited but the Bottom Bus proves a good backpacker shuttle (again, see The Catlins).

Between Manapouri and Blackmount watch out for the one sign indicating the **Redcliff Wetland Reserve** – bird-watchers will be particularly pleased to see a predatory bush falcon in action. Just before Blackmount there is a turn-off to the right (west) to **Lake Monowai** and *Borland Lodge* (☎ 225 5464), which caters primarily for school groups but individuals can stay there. Lake Monowai stands today as testament to blunder – it was flooded in 1925 for a very small power station and the lake is still unsightly.

The town of **Clifden** has a cave system nearby and the Clifden Suspension Bridge, built in 1902. The mystical Clifden (Waiau) Caves can be explored but heed all warnings. You will need at least two torches. The caves are 17km from Tuatapere; turn left towards Eastern Bush at Lime Works and continue 1km up the road. Ladders are provided in steep sections.

About 16km from Clifden there is a walk to totara trees that are 1000 years old. From Clifden you can drive out on 30km of unsealed road to **Lake Hauroko**, the deepest in NZ. Hauroko lies in a beautiful bush setting, with precipitous slopes on its sides. In 1967 an interesting example of a Maori cave burial was discovered on Mary Island, on the lake. In this *tapu* place a woman of high rank was buried, sitting upright, in about 1660.

Dusky Track starts at Hauroko Burn and leads to Supper Cove on Dusky Sound and then to the Wilmot Pass road and Lake Manapouri. This is a rugged but rewarding eight-day tramp for the well prepared. Consult DOC and Lonely Planet's *Tramping in New Zealand*. Lake Hauroko Tours (☎ 226 6681) organises four- and eight-day tramps from Hauroko to Lake Manapouri.

The **Southern Coastal Track** and the **Hump Track** are described in the DOC pamphlet *Waitutu Tracks;* both start at Te Waewae Bay. The coastal track goes via Port Craig (where there is an old schoolhouse) to Lake Hakapoua. The Hump goes to Teal Bay at the southern end of Hauroko, and then via the lake's eastern shore to the Hauroko road head.

Tuatapere
pop 740

Once a timber milling town, Tuatapere is now a farming centre on the banks of the Waiau River, famous as the 'sausage capital' of NZ. It can be used as a base for trips to Lake Hauroko or Te Waewae Bay and beyond. The woodchoppers were so effective, only the small remnant of native forest in the town's domain remains, where once most of the area looked like this.

The Tuatapere information centre (☎ 226 6349) on the main road in town has information on many activities, and it will provide a map to the Clifden Caves.

Jet boats operate on the Wairaurahiri River, and helicopter tours and trampers' transport can be arranged through the centre. The town also has a DOC field centre (☎ 226 6475).

Places to Stay & Eat *Tuatapere Motor Camp* (☎ 226 6397), in a beautiful position next to the river, charges $9 for sites. *Mickaela Motor Camp* (☎ 226 6626), on Peace St, is just a suburban block with tent/powered sites for $13/15 for two and a cabin for $25. The *Waiau Hotel* (☎ 226 6409, 47 Main St) has B&B doubles for $80. It also has good solid country fare and great Tuatap sausages.

The information centre lists B&Bs and farmstays, and along Main St there are a couple of *takeaways*.

Tuatapere to Riverton

About 10km south of Tuatapere the scenic route reaches the cliffs above **Te Waewae Bay**, where Hector's dolphins and southern

Mt Luxmore Hut on the Kepler Track, one of NZ's Great Walks

DAVID WALL

The entrance to Homer Tunnel, Fiordland

DAVID WALL

Matai Falls, near the Catlin Forest Park

DAVID WALL

Tramping the Milford Track, Clinton Valley

SALLY DILLON

Crossing Freshwater River on the magnificent North-West Circuit walking track, Stewart Island

Sea kayaking, Stewart Island

Bush-clad Paterson Inlet, Stewart Island

right whales are sometimes seen. At the eastern end of the bay is Monkey Island, or Te Poka a Takatimu (Anchor Stone of the *Taka-timu* Canoe). Nearby is **Orepuki**, where strong southerlies have had a dramatic effect on the growth of macrocarpas, trees so windblown that they grow in a direction away from the shore.

The next point of interest is **Colac Bay**, an old Maori settlement and now a popular holiday spot for Southlanders. It has a good beach and Isobel's Weaving Studio, where you can buy homespun and knitted woollen wear.

Camp Orama Lodge (☎ 234 8399), attached to the Colac Bay Tavern, has good-value budget beds for $13 per person; there's a kitchen, laundry and barbecue.

Hillcrest (☎/fax 234 5129), 7km past Orepuki on SH99, is a good little sheep farm with backpacker accommodation. Horse riding and interesting walks can be organised here. It's $16 per person, mostly in doubles and twins. Camping sites are $8 per person. Ask about 'Wayne's World'.

Riverton
pop 1850

Riverton, 38km west of Invercargill and at the mouths of the Aparima and Pourakino Rivers, is considered to be one of the oldest European settlements in NZ, dating from the sealing and whaling days. This pretty town has good beaches and proclaims itself the 'Riviera of the South'.

The **Early Settlers Museum** on Palmerston St is open daily in the afternoon. The nearby town of **Thornbury** has the Vintage Machinery Museum. The Riverton Rock area is a popular (if cold) local beach and Taramea Bay is a safe place to swim. Look for the 'big paua' on Bath Rd, where a paua factory turns out all sorts of shell souvenirs and jewellery.

The town's information centre is the Riverton Rock (☎ 234 8886). It also takes bookings for the Bottom Bus, which overnights in Riverton.

Places to Stay & Eat The *Riverton Motor Camp* (☎ 234 8526), off Roy and Hamlet Sts, has sites for $15 for two; cabins and on-site

vans are $25 to $30 for two, and the cottage is $40.

The *Globe Hotel Backpackers* (☎ 234 8527, ✉ theglobe@riverton.co.nz, 144 Palmerston St), an old pub right in the town centre, is being developed as a backpacker hostel. It is still frequented by colourful locals who roll their 'r's. Dorms are $17, singles $20 and twins and doubles $40.

The *Riverton Rock* (☎ 234 8886, 136 Palmerston St) is a beautifully renovated guesthouse, managed by the owners of the Globe. It has plenty of character and the staff provide lots of information on the area. Guesthouse doubles are $45 ($80 with en suite). Kiwi Wilderness Walks is based here, specialising in the Waitutu Track ($795, four nights) and Stewart Island ($995, five nights).

The *Riverton Beach Motel* (☎/fax 234 8181, 4 Marne St) has singles/doubles for $55/65.

The town's eateries are on Palmerston St: *Ricardo's Pizzeria* is at No 135; the *Country Nostalgia* is reliable and has home-made pies and an interesting dinner blackboard menu.

Central Southland

SH1, from Invercargill to Gore, in effect cuts the province of Southland into two. To the west of it is Fiordland and to the southeast is the Catlins. Most of Southland's population is concentrated in the centre of the province along SH1 and in the city of Invercargill.

INVERCARGILL
pop 49,300

This is the southernmost city in NZ, the main city of Southland and very much a farm-service community. It's often claimed to be the southernmost city in the world, conveniently forgetting Ushuaia in Argentina and the rest of South American Patagonia.

Invercargill has missed out on a lot of the tourism wealth you'll find in many South Island towns. Instead of a host of smart cafes and urban regeneration, Invercargill

SOUTHLAND

still has checked shirts and bad haircuts. However, an increasing number of travellers are stopping over on the way to the tramping tracks of Stewart Island, the nearby Catlins and the wild areas of southern Fiordland. It is a remarkably ordered city based on a grid pattern crisscrossing a 'flat-as-a-tack' plain.

The locals staunchly defend their city, despite snide comments from the rest of NZ about its backwardness and ennui. Spend a night in Invercargill, wander around the old-fashioned department stores and catch a glimpse of Old Zealand.

History

When the chief surveyor of Otago, JT Thomson, travelled south to settle on a site for Invercargill, the region was uninhabited and covered in a dense forest known as Taurakitewaru Wood, which stretched from the Otepuni Stream (then known as the Otarewa) in the south to the Waihopai River in the north. Realising that ships of 500 tons could sail up the estuary to the mouth of the Otepuni Stream, Thomson chose Taurakitewaru Wood as the best site for the new town. The town was laid out over 'a mile square', with four reserves just inside its boundaries and a fifth running down the banks of the Otepuni Stream. Originally, Queens Park was just over the northern boundary and 200 acres (80 hectares) of forest was set aside for this purpose. Today the only part of the forest that remains is a small area known as Thomsons Bush.

Information

In the museum building, near the entrance to Queens Park, is the office of the Invercargill Visitor Information Centre (☎ 214 6243, @ tourismandtravel.Invercargill@thenet.net.nz). It's open from 9 am to 5 pm weekdays, from 10 am on weekends. Also check out www.southland.org.nz. The chief post shop is on Don St and is open from 8.30 am to 5 pm Monday to Friday.

The Automobile Association Southland office (AA; ☎ 218 9033) is at 47 Gala St. The DOC office (☎ 214 4589) is on the 7th floor of the State Insurance building on Don St.

For sports equipment, check out H&J's Outdoor World, 27 Tay St, and the Scout Shop, which is a couple of doors along.

Internet access is available at the library on Dee St, and at Players Pool Parlour on Tay St.

Southland Museum & Tuatara House

Located at the entrance to Queens Park, the Southland Museum has natural history, technology and Maori galleries, and art galleries with temporary and touring exhibitions. Pride of place, however, goes to the exhibitions on NZ's subantarctic islands. The *Roaring Forties Experience* takes you on a 25-minute audiovisual journey to the islands between NZ and the Antarctic. Other exhibits detail life in the freezing nether-regions of NZ. Andris Apse's photography captures the remote and surreal atmosphere of the last stands of the great untouched ($2/0.50 for adults/children). The excellent Roaring Forties gallery is also worth examination.

Invercargill's most famous attraction, the tuatara house, is housed in the museum. The ancient and rare NZ reptiles on show include Henry, who is over 100 years old and going strong (a tuatara can live to 150 years in captivity).

The museum is open from 9 am to 5 pm weekdays, 10 am to 5 pm on weekends (admission is free).

Other Attractions

From the museum, wander around delightful **Queens Park**, the absolute essence of Englishness – if there were a river running through it you would most likely see punts with punters in straw boaters. Among the park's attractions are various animals, an aviary, duck ponds, rose gardens and a tea kiosk, open from 10 am to 4.30 pm daily. The 18-hole Queens Park Golf Course is good value at $25 for club hire and green fees.

Anderson Park Art Gallery (☎ 215 7432) is 7km north of town. Turn off the main road to Queenstown onto McIvor Rd and drive a further 3km; it is signposted. It's open from 1.30 to 5 pm Tuesday to Sunday

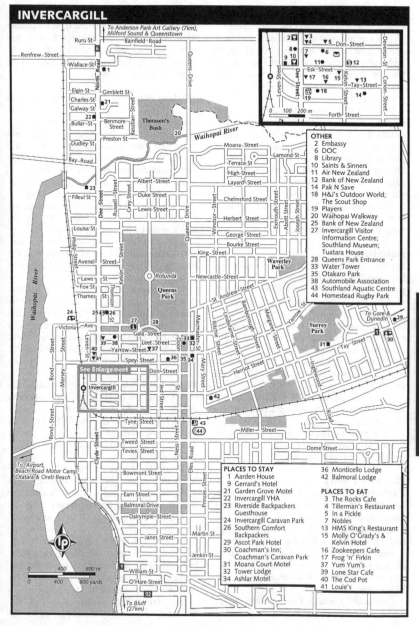

INVERCARGILL

To Anderson Park Art Gallery (7km),
Milford Sound & Queenstown

OTHER
2 Embassy
6 DOC
8 Library
10 Saints & Sinners
11 Air New Zealand
12 Bank of New Zealand
14 Pak N Save
18 H&J's Outdoor World;
   The Scout Shop
19 Players
20 Waihopai Walkway
25 Bank of New Zealand
27 Invercargill Visitor
   Information Centre;
   Southland Museum;
   Tuatara House
28 Queens Park Entrance
33 Water Tower
35 Otakaro Park
38 Automobile Association
43 Southland Aquatic Centre
44 Homestead Rugby Park

PLACES TO STAY
1 Aarden House
9 Gerrard's Hotel
21 Garden Grove Motel
22 Invercargill YHA
23 Riverside Backpackers
   Guesthouse
24 Invercargill Caravan Park
26 Southern Comfort
   Backpackers
29 Ascot Park Hotel
30 Coachman's Inn;
   Coachman's Caravan Park
31 Moana Court Motel
32 Tower Lodge
34 Ashlar Motel
36 Monticello Lodge
42 Balmoral Lodge

PLACES TO EAT
3 The Rocks Cafe
4 Tillerman's Restaurant
5 In a Pickle
7 Nobles
13 HMS King's Restaurant
15 Molly O'Grady's &
   Kelvin Hotel
16 Zookeepers Cafe
17 Frog 'n' Firkin
37 Yum Yum's
39 Lone Star Cafe
40 The Cod Pot
41 Louie's

SOUTHLAND

(shorter hours in winter). Afternoon tea is available at this elegant Georgian house.

The curious **water tower** at the eastern end of Leet St was built in 1889. It's open on Sunday afternoon if you want to climb to the top ($1) for a bird's-eye view of the town's flatness; on other days you'll need to fetch a key from next door.

Invercargill's long, sweeping beach is **Oreti**, 9.5km west of the city. The water is milder than expected because of warm currents, and you can drive on the hard sands (but take care). If you're not up to braving the sea, the **Southland Aquatic Centre** on Elles Rd is a huge swimming pool complex with slides, wave machine etc.

The Bluff Southland Seafood Festival is held in February. The visitor centre has an extensive events calendar.

Activities

For local sites of interest, pick up a walking-tour leaflet of Invercargill's historical places from the museum. Thomson's Bush, on Queens Drive, is the last remnant of Taurakitewaru Wood, the forest that once covered Invercargill. It is about 3.5km north of the chief post shop. The best of the area's short **walks** are at the Sandy Point Domain, near Oreti Beach, with a mixture of totara scrub forest, fern gullies, coastal views and bird life.

There are several other walks, scenic flights and tandem skydiving; ask at the visitor information centre.

Blue Star Taxis (☎ 218 6078) has city tours ($40, one hour) and tours to Oreti Beach, Bluff and Riverton.

Places to Stay

Camping & Cabins *Coachman's Caravan Park* (☎ 217 6046, 705 Tay St) is little more than a backyard strip behind the Coachman's Inn, with sites at $15 for two and a few cabins at $25 for two.

Beach Road Motor Camp (☎ 213 0400) is 6km west of town on Dunns Rd, on the way to Oreti Beach. Tent/powered sites are $15/16 and cabins are $26 to $40.

Lorneville Holiday Park (☎ 235 8031, 352 Lorne Dacre Rd) is a nice camping ground. From town, head north along SH6 for 8km, then turn right and travel a further 4km. This peaceful, friendly farmlet has tent/powered sites for $12/18, and a tourist flat for $55 (prices are for two). B&B in the house is $45 per person.

Hostels *Southern Comfort Backpackers* (☎ 218 3838, 30 Thomson St), consistently rated one of the best in the country, is in a late 19th-century Art Nouveau villa, with beautifully manicured gardens and tasteful decor. Pleasant, clean dorms are $16, and twins and doubles are $36. To many travellers this place is the highlight of Invercargill. There are 40 beds in two villas.

Riverside Backpackers Guesthouse (☎ 0800-302 277, 70 Filleul St), in the city's north by the Waihopai River, is a poor cousin in comparison to the Southern Comfort. Dorms cost $15, and the cabin at the back is $10 per person. This old house is down a lane off Filleul St.

The *Invercargill YHA* (☎ 215 9344, fax 215 9382, 122 North Rd, Waikiwi), on the corner of Bullar St about 3km north of the town centre, is the world's southernmost YHA. It is neat and tidy and has a variety of dorms for $15 per person, and doubles and twins from $34 to $38.

B&Bs, Hotels & Motels There are a couple of good B&Bs in Invercargill. *Aarden House* (☎ 215 8825, 193 North Rd) charges $40/65 for singles/doubles ($50/75 with en suite); *Oak Door* (☎ 213 0633, 22 Taiepa Rd, Otatara) is another good place, which charges $60/80.

Montecillo Lodge (☎ 218 2503, 240 Spey St) is an old, straightforward but well-kept guesthouse that's had a facelift. Rooms are $76/96, including a cooked breakfast served in the old dining room. It also has motel units for $65/79.

Gerrard's Hotel (☎ 218 3406) on the corner of Esk and Leven Sts is an ornate 1896 building. B&B is $50 per person, with a big breakfast, and renovated rooms with en suite are $80 per person.

The *Ascot Park Hotel* (☎ 217 6195, 🖂 ascot@ilt.co.nz) on the corner of Tay St and Racecourse Rd is very upmarket. It has an indoor pool and charges $92 for motel units or $160 for deluxe hotel rooms.

Invercargill has over 30 motels. The *Coachman's Inn* (☎ *217 6046, 705 Tay St)* has units for $65 for two.

Other reasonable motels include *Ashlar Motel* (☎ *217 9093, 81 Queens Drive)*, with singles/doubles for $70/85; *Garden Grove Motel* (☎ *215 9555, 161 North Rd)*, charging $75 for two; and *Moana Court Motel* (☎ *217 8443, 554 Tay St)*, with units starting at $75.

Tower Lodge (☎ *217 6729, 119 Queens Drive)* is also very good, as is *Balmoral Lodge* (☎ *217 6109, 265 Tay St)*, which charges $75/90.

Places to Eat
Restaurants & Cafes Invercargill does have a few fashionable cafes. *Zookeepers Cafe* (☎ *218 3373, 50 Tay St)* is chic and cool. Light meals, such as lasagne, cost around $13.50 and steaks are around $17.

The Rocks Cafe (*121 Dee St)* is similar to Zookeepers, with the temperature only slightly above cool. It is open lunch and dinner daily.

Tillerman's Restaurant (*16 Don St)* is another good local gathering spot with an Art Deco bar. It has a wide menu, including sushi and vegetarian dishes. Mains start at $16.

China City (*282 Dee St)*, next to the Pizza Hut, is an attractive licensed Chinese restaurant, with six-course meals for $14 at lunch and around $20 in the evening.

HMS King's Restaurant (*83 Tay St)* is the place to sample local seafood. It's decked out like an old sailing ship and the menu features oysters, whitebait, blue cod and salmon (mains from $20 to $25). It is open daily for lunch and dinner.

Lone Star Cafe, on the corner of Dee and Leet Sts, is open from 5.30 pm until late. It has two parts: a back bar and a dining area. It serves huge nachos, all-you-can-eat ribs and other Tex-Mex-inspired food at reasonable prices.

Frog 'n' Firkin (☎ *214 4001, 31 Dee St)* is next to a cinema complex and is open daily except Sunday. It is a restaurant and bar and you can pick up a meal for under $10. Its fiery potato wedges go well with the fine selection of ales.

Louie's, on the corner of Dee and Spey Sts, is perhaps the best place in town and very popular with locals; the food is Pacific Rim and it has a lively bar.

Pub Food & Fast Food Plenty of pubs in Invercargill serve food. *Molly O'Grady's*, in the Kelvin Hotel on Kelvin St, is classier than most and has cafe fare for lunch and a la carte dining for dinner.

Along Dee St and around the town centre there's the usual collection of fast-food and sandwich places. *Nobles* (*47 Dee St)* serves good 'mousetraps' (onion, cheese and bacon on toast) and weak cappuccinos.

In a Pickle (*16 Don St)* is the best lunch place in town and it gets crowded. It has a good range, including quiches, paninis and bagels.

The Cod Pot on Dee St turns out consistently good fish and chips, and offers delicious Bluff oysters in season.

Yum Yum's (*116 Yarrow St)* is another popular takeaway serving both fish and chips and Chinese dishes.

Entertainment
Although the town centre closes swiftly after 9 pm, there *is* entertainment if you are willing to search it out. The odd nightclub buzzes until the early hours, and a lot is happening out in the suburbs, but you'll need to ask around.

Lively places with the best atmosphere for a drink include *Zookeepers Cafe*, which has laid-back staff, some of Invercargill's brighter party animals and corrugated iron statuary, and *The Rocks Cafe* on Courtville Place. The folksy *Tillerman's, Lone Star* and the 'hits-and-memories' *Frog 'n' Firkin* are of a similar ilk. See Places to Eat earlier for details of all these venues.

Rafters Bar at the Whitehouse Hotel is possibly the best place for music, but it's right out at Lorneville, 8km north of Waikiwi (a left turn west towards Riverton); there's a cover charge.

Popular nightclubs are *Saints and Sinners (34 Dee St)* and the *Embassy (122 Dee St)*. The latter is a live music venue, which holds 500 people.

The weekend editions of the *Southland Times* will indicate what's on elsewhere. In Invercargill for the Labour Day long weekend? You can catch the Trucking & Country Music Convention.

Getting There & Away

Air Air New Zealand (☎ 214 4737), at 46 Esk St, and Ansett New Zealand (☎ 214 4644), at Invercargill airport, have daily direct flights to Dunedin, Christchurch and Wellington, with connections to other centres.

Southern Air (☎ 0800-658 876) makes flights to Stewart Island (see the Stewart Island section in the Outer Islands chapter). Southern Air and Southeast Air (SEA; ☎ 214 5522) can be chartered to remote parts such as Mason's Bay. Southern Air also flies to Dunedin twice daily on weekdays.

Bus InterCity (☎ 218 1837, 214 0598) buses are based at the train station. Buses run daily from Invercargill to Te Anau and Christchurch, with more frequent buses to Dunedin. Southern Air land service (☎ 218 9129) does the leg to Queenstown for InterCity daily ($36).

Atomic Shuttles (☎ 214 6243) has a bus to Dunedin ($20) departing Invercargill at 10 am (three hours). Buchanan Motors (☎ 218 3308) also travels daily ($20).

Spitfire Shuttle (☎ 214 1851) operates from Invercargill to Te Anau and return (see the Te Anau section earlier). Knightrider (☎ 202 5338) has coach services to Christchurch.

Catlins Coastal Link and the Bottom Bus services pass through the Catlins (see The Catlins section). The former goes north, the latter south.

Train The *Southerner* (☎ 0800-802 802 for bookings and information) operates daily between Christchurch and Invercargill, departing from each city at 8.30 am and arriving at the other around 5.20 pm.

Hitching Hitching between Dunedin and Invercargill is usually fairly simple and should only take about half a day. Queenstown or Te Anau gets steadily harder the further you go, and many people get stuck overnight in Lumsden. The Catlins coastal route between Dunedin and Invercargill is pretty hard – public transport is almost nonexistent and there's little traffic for hitching.

Getting Around

The airport is 2.5km from the centre. It is $8 by taxi or $3 with Spitfire Shuttle (☎ 214 1851), which will pick you up from accommodation. There are two taxi companies: Taxi Co (☎ 214 4478) and Blue Star (☎ 218 6079).

City buses (☎ 218 7108) run on weekdays from around 7 am to 6 pm or until around 9 or 10 pm on late shopping nights. Local bus trips cost $1.20.

Wensley's Cycles (☎ 218 6206), on the corner of Tay and With Sts, hires out bicycles.

BLUFF
pop 2100

Invercargill's port, and the departure point for the Stewart Island catamaran, Bluff is 27km to the south. A small place, its Maori name is Motupohue (*motu* because it looks like an island and *pohue* from the white convolvulus flower that grew here at the time of naming).

Popular folklore has it that Bluff is the Land's End of NZ, though it is not the South Island's southernmost point. 'From Cape Reinga to Bluff' is an oft-quoted phrase signifying the entire length of NZ. The country's main highway, SH1, runs between the two and terminates at the **Stirling Point signpost** in the south, which indicates distances to the South Pole and elsewhere in the world.

Foveaux Walk is a good 6.6km coastal walkway from the signpost to Ocean Beach (2½ hours), where there's a smelly freezing works. Alternatively, take the trail for about 1km and then return by the 1.5km Glory Track. This is as good a short walk as you'll find, uphill and then down through superb bush and ponga groves.

You can drive or walk for half an hour to the observation point at the top of 265m **Bluff Hill** for unobstructed views of the flat surrounding area and across to Stewart Island.

The **Bluff Maritime Museum** ($2) at the wharf is open from 10 am to 4.30 pm on weekdays and 1 to 5 pm on weekends. The **Paua Shell House**, 258 Marine Parade, has an amazing array of kitsch statuary (check out the fountain) and shells from all over the world. At the time of writing the house was closed to visitors.

Across the harbour from Bluff is the huge **Tiwai aluminium smelter**, a major source of employment for Invercargill's citizens. They get mighty sensitive to any hint of criticism of it. Aluminium is an important NZ export. Free tours at 10 am on weekdays can be arranged by phoning ☎ 218 5494 well in advance.

Foveaux Souvenirs & Antiques (☎ 212 8305), 74 Gore St, acts as the local information office.

Places to Stay & Eat
Bluff Motor Camp (☎ 212 8704) on Gregory St has tent/powered sites for $10/12. *Property Arcade Backpackers (☎ 212 8074, 120 Gore St)*, opposite the ferry wharf, has untidy dorms for $12 per person.

Land's End NZ (☎ 212 7575), a B&B at the end of SH1 opposite the signpost, is the best local accommodation, charging $85/95 a single/double.

The *cafe* adjoining Land's End has a wide selection of meals and wine, and *Stirling Point* restaurant, nearby, keeps variable hours. Plump Bluff oysters, the best in NZ, can be bought in season at outlets in town.

Getting There & Away
Campbelltown Passenger Services (☎ 212 7404) has a door-to-door service from Invercargill to Bluff ($10), which meets the Stewart Island ferry. See the Stewart Island section of the Outer Islands chapter for ferry details.

INVERCARGILL TO DUNEDIN
From Invercargill to Dunedin, SH1 via Gore and Balclutha is the quick, direct route. Much more scenic is the continuation of the Southern Scenic Route, SH92, via the coastal road through the Catlins.

SH1 passes through Mataura, site of a huge freezing works; Gore, home of the Big Brown Trout and country music; and Balclutha (see the Otago chapter), with a good little regional museum. The scenery is rural, which you may just have had enough of by now. If so, read about the Catlins and plan to spend some extra time there – you won't regret it.

Gore
pop 8500
This farming service town, Southland's second largest, spans the Mataura River and has the Hokonui Hills as a great backdrop. In June, Gore hosts the NZ Gold Guitars, an annual country and western festival, during which the town is booked out.

The Gore Information Centre (☎/fax 208 9908, @ goreinfo@esi.co.nz) is in the Hokonui Heritage Centre, on the corner of Hokonui Drive and Norfolk St. It's open from 9 am to 7 pm weekdays, 10 am to 7 pm on weekends (shorter hours in winter).

The **Eastern Southland Museum & Art Gallery** on Hokonui Drive is open from 10 am to 5 pm weekdays and 2 to 4 pm on Sunday. **Croydon Aircraft Company** (☎ 208 9755) at Mandeville, 16km towards Queenstown, restores vintage aircraft and offers Tiger Moth flights.

With luck, you will catch a trout the size of the 'big one' in one of the many (40 or so) excellent streams, which include the Pomahaka, Mataura, Waimea, Otamita and Waipahi. For further information get the *Anglers' Access* pamphlet from the information centre.

Places to Stay & Eat *Gore Motor Camp (☎ 208 4919, 35 Broughton St)*, at the southern end of town, has sites for $9 per person and cabins for $32 for two.

Old Fire Station Backpackers (☎/fax 208 1925, 19 Hokonui Drive) is a small, comfy place where the dorms start at $18 and double rooms are $45. The *Charlton Motel (☎ 208 9733, 9 Charlton Rd)* and

SOUTHLAND

the *Oakleigh Motel* (☎ 208 4863, 70 Hokonui Drive) both have rooms for around $65 to $80 a double. *Croydon Lodge Motor Hotel* (☎ 208 9029), Main Queenstown Highway (Waimea St), has rooms for $105. It also has a nine-hole golf course.

O Te Ika Rama Marae at McNab, a short drive north of Gore on SH1, is a special place to stay because travellers get a chance to experience Maori culture first hand.

Main St has a number of places to keep the wolf from the door, including the *Gore Pie Cart*, next to the United Video shop.

The Catlins

If you're travelling between Invercargill and Dunedin with your own transport, take the longer Catlins coastal route, allowing a couple of days for stopovers. The distance is similar to the inland route but you travel much slower as some 22km is unsealed.

The route goes through the region known as the Catlins, which stretches from Waipapa Point in Southland to Nugget Point in South Otago. It includes the Western Catlins Forest (22,250 hectares) and a number of other forests and scenic reserves. The Catlins is a totally absorbing area.

History

The area was once inhabited by moa hunters and evidence of their camp sites and middens have been found at Papatowai. Between AD 1600 and 1800 the Maori population thinned out because of the decline of the moa, the lack of kumara cultivation and fear of the *maeroero* – the wild, yeti-like creature of the Tautuku bush, reputed to snatch children and young women.

Later, whalers occupied sites along the shoreline, such as at Waikawa Harbour, Tautuku Peninsula and Port Molyneaux. Then timber millers, serving the Dunedin market, moved into the dense stands of beech forest in the 1860s. At the height of logging there were about 30 mills in the area. The railway was started in 1879 but did not reach Owaka for another 25 years. It reached Tahakopa, where it terminated,

36 years later; it was closed in 1971. As in many other parts of NZ, the pastoralists constituted the final wave of settlement.

Flora & Fauna

There are still reserves of podocarp forests in the Catlins, containing trees such as kahikatea, totara, rimu and miro. Behind the sand dunes of Tahakopa and Tautuku Bays there are excellent examples of native forest that extend several kilometres inland. The vegetation zones are best seen at Tautuku: sand-dune plants (marram, lupin, flax) are found near the beach; behind these are low trees, such as rata, kamahi and five-finger; in the peaty sands behind the dunes is young podocarp forest; and there is mature forest with emergent rimu and miro and a main canopy of kamahi beyond. A good example of young forest is found near Lake Wilkie, where growth has occurred on the sediments that have gradually filled in the lagoon.

The fauna, as much as the flora, attracts visitors. New Zealand fur seals and Hooker's sea lions are abundant. Elephant seals breed at The Nuggets, a series of remarkable wave-like pinnacles. The variety of bird life is an ornithologist's delight, with many sea, estuary and forest birds. Present here are the endangered yellow-eyed penguin *(hoiho)*, the kaka, blue ducks and the rare mohua (yellowhead).

For information contact Waikawa (☎/fax 246 8444) or Owaka (☎/fax 415 8371), or take a look at the Web site www.catlins .org.nz. The DOC pamphlet *The Catlins – Walking & Tramping Opportunities* ($2.50) is helpful.

Organised Tours

Catlins Wildlife Trackers (☎ 415 8163, ✆ catlinw@es.co.nz) has a highly recommended tour that is a specialist eco-experience. It interweaves natural history, landforms and geology with recent history, the secrets of the sea, littoral, rainforest, wetlands and sky. Nature's rare, timid creatures are also revealed. Food, land, water transport, all equipment (wet suit, snorkels etc) and a bed in Trackers' holiday home at Papatowai is included. A two-/four-night tour

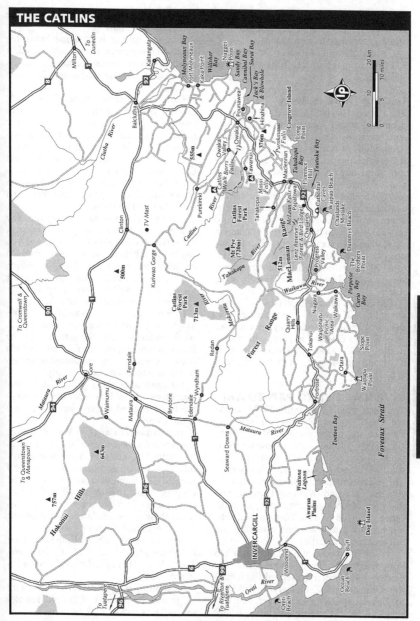

THE CATLINS

costs $250/500. Two-night tours commence at 10 am Monday, Wednesday and Saturday, and the four-night tour on Monday.

Catlins Natural Wonders (☎ 025-985 941) runs organised day trips starting in Balclutha.

Getting There & Away

The Bottom Bus (☎ 471 0292, @ bottom@ deepsouth.co.nz) specialises in the Catlins and Southern Scenic Route. It stops at all main points of interest and you can get off it and catch the next bus coming through. It runs three days a week between Dunedin and Te Anau via the Catlins, Invercargill and the Southern Scenic Route. Passes are available in conjunction with Kiwi Experience for Queenstown–Te Anau–Milford travel. Dunedin to Invercargill/Te Anau via the Catlins (or vice versa) costs $75/115 for one/two days, and various options range up to $179 for a full loop including Queenstown, Milford and back to Dunedin or Te Anau.

The Catlins Coastal Link (☎ 474 3398 in Dunedin, 214 6243 in Invercargill, @ catlins@southern-nz.co.nz) has a number of options: a day tour is $110; with a connection to Te Anau or Queenstown it is $110; and including Stewart Island flights it is $225.

INVERCARGILL TO PAPATOWAI

The road from Invercargill, SH92, meets the coast at Fortrose. Before reaching Fortrose and to the south of SH92, is the significant 14,000-hectare **Awarua Wetlands** region consisting of the Waituna, Seaward Moss and Toetoes scientific reserves. The reserves support wading bird species in Awarua Bay and Waituna Lagoon, and many vegetation types, including magnificent cushion bogs in the Waituna Wetlands, red tussock grasslands and estuarine and salt marsh communities.

At Fortrose, take a turn-off to the south to **Waipapa Point**. The lighthouse here was erected in 1884, after the second-worst maritime disaster in NZ's history. In 1881 the SS *Tararua* struck the Otara Reef, 1km offshore. Of the 151 passengers and crew only 20 survived; in the nearby graveyard the bodies of 65 victims lie.

The next detour is to **Slope Point**, the most southerly point on the South Island. A small and hard-to-see beacon lies across private land. It can also be approached from Tokanui.

Curio Bay is the next point of interest. At low tide you can see one of the most extensive fossil forests in the world – it is 160 million years old. The petrified stumps and fallen log fossils are evidence of NZ's location in the ancient supercontinent Gondwanaland, and the plant species identified here are similar to those found in South America – cycads, tree ferns and matai-like and kauri-like trees.

Just around the corner in **Porpoise Bay** you may see Hector's dolphins surfing in the waves breaking on the beach, and you can swim with them. Be careful not to touch or otherwise harry the dolphins, which come close into shore over summer to rear their young. Yellow-eyed penguins, fur seals and sea lions also inhabit the area.

In the old church at **Waikawa**, Dolphin Magic (☎ 246 8444) organises boat trips to see the dolphins ($50). Some trips go to The Brothers where there are fur seals and sea lions. A study is being conducted on the effect of human contact on the dolphins.

Waikawa also has a small district **museum** (open from 1 to 4 pm daily in summer) and a good backpacker hostel, but nothing else.

The **Cathedral Caves** on Waipati Beach, so-named for their resemblance to an English cathedral, are only accessible at low tide (tide tables are posted at the turn-off from SH92). From the road it is 2km to the car park, then a 15-minute walk to the beach and a further 25 minutes to the caves. (Currently these caves are closed, as they are the subject of a land claim.)

The turn-off to pretty **McLean Falls** is just before the parking area for Cathedral Cave. The falls are 5km up a dirt road, then a 30-minute walk.

Next along is **Lenz Reserve**, with a bird lodge and the remains of the old Tautuku sawmill just a short walk from the road.

At **Tautuku Bay** there is a 15-minute walk to the beach, a stunning sweep of sand punctuated by drifts of seaweed, and a five-minute walk to **Lake Wilkie**, where there are some unique forms of plant life. Just past Tautuku there is a good vantage point at **Florence Hill** from where you can distinguish the different vegetation types and other points of interest.

Papatowai, at the mouth of the Tahakopa River, is the next tiny town reached along this route. This is the base for Catlins Wildlife Trackers and for some amazing forays into the close forests. Also here is the **Top Track**, a two-day 26km walk through beaches and private forest. Accommodation is in a converted trolleybus (maximum six) with gas cookers and water supply. It's on top of a hill with spectacular views. The track fee is $10 ($25 if you stay overnight).

Places to Stay & Eat

At Tokanui, the turn-off to the coast leads 1.7km to *Pope's Place* (☎ 246 8420), a friendly farm backpackers with dorms for $14 and doubles and twins for $30. Right next door is the Little Shop, indeed little and the southernmost on the South Island. It's geared to the tourist trade with a sauna in the garage.

On SH92, halfway between Tokanui and the turn-off to Waikawa, is the *Egilshay Farmstay* (☎ 246 8703).

Curio Bay Camping (☎ 246 8897) is right on the beach at Curio Bay and tent/powered sites cost $7/12 for two.

The *Waikawa Holiday Lodge* (☎ 246 8552), at Waikawa opposite the dolphin centre, has a small shop and cafe. A dorm bed costs $18, and twins and doubles are $40 in this comfortable house. Located halfway along the route, this lodge is a popular place to stop.

Catlins Farmstay (☎ 246 8843) on Progress Valley Rd, which starts just past the turn-off to Waikawa, is one of the nicest places to stay. A great B&B costs $45/75 for singles/doubles in a very comfortable house; dinners cost $25.

Further along the main road and closer to Papatowai, *Chaslands Farm Motor Lodge*

(☎ 415 8501) has motel-style cabins at $55 for two. The *Tautuku Lodge* (☎ 415 8024), 6km south of Papatowai in the Lenz Reserve, is owned by the Royal Forest & Bird Protection Society. It's possible to stay for around $20 per night.

Papatowai Motor Camp (☎ 415 8500, ❷ pest@es.co.nz) has tent/powered sites for $12/14 for two, cabins for $30. Backpacker accommodation is $12 per person. *Scenic Highway Motels* (☎ 415 8147), at the entrance to the motor camp, has excellent units with kitchens for $55/65 for singles/doubles.

The *Hilltop* (☎ 415 8028, ❷ hilltop@ ihug.co.nz), a backpackers reached on the Tahakopa Rd just before the bridge near Papatowai, has fantastic views and great sunsets. It is a little over 1km from the main road and then another 500m up a steep hill. The friendly farmhouse has very high standards and accommodation is $18 in a four-bed dorm and $45 for doubles. It was rated among the top 20 accommodation places in NZ (along with Millbrook) by the *UK Observer*.

The *Papatowai Store* organises meals, sandwiches and tea or coffee, and has information on the Top Track.

PAPATOWAI TO BALCLUTHA

Between Papatowai and the regional centre of Owaka there are many interesting places to visit. First, follow SH92 north to **Matai Falls** on the Maclennan River. After looking at these, head south-east on the signposted road to the more scenic **Purakaunui Falls**. It is only a short walk through bush to these tiered falls, best viewed from a platform at their base.

In the **Catlins Forest Park** you can do the river walk, a good day trip out of Owaka. There is a track to Tawanui from the Wisp camping area – observant walkers may see the rare mohua (yellowhead) here.

Out near the mouth of the Catlins River, on the southern side, is **Jack's Blowhole**, a 55m-deep hole in the middle of paddocks. It is 200m from the sea but connected by a subterranean cavern.

On the northern side of the river, south-east of Owaka, is the **Pounawea Nature Walk**, a 45-minute loop through kahikatea,

DAVID WALL

A lighthouse looks out over jagged islands from the Catlins' Nugget Point. Next stop: South America.

ferns, kamahi, rimu, totara and southern rata. There is a salt marsh near the Catlins River estuary.

Owaka
pop 395
Owaka is the main town of the Catlins area. The Catlins Information Centre (☎ 415 8371), on Main Rd, has information on the region and accommodation listings. The DOC field office (☎/fax 415 8341) is on the corner of Ryley and Campbell Sts.

Valley View Horse Treks operates in its hill country property 24km from Owaka. Over the summer months (November to March) the two- to three-hour rides traverse tussock country, among sheep and cattle, to a lofty viewpoint. It is $85 per person and a farmer's 'smoko' (afternoon tea) is provided. Inquire at the visitor centre.

Places to Stay & Eat The *Keswick Park Camping Ground* (☎ 419 1110), Pounawea Rd, is on the waterfront. It's quite basic but is in a lovely setting. Tent/powered sites cost $10/12 for two, tourist flats start at $35 and backpacker beds are $15.

There are *DOC camping grounds* in the Catlins at Tawanui (Catlins Forest Park) and Purakaunui Bay, both in south-east Otago.

Highview Motel & Candy Cone Backpackers (☎ 415 8636, 23 Royal Terrace) has motel units for $55, and well-equipped backpacker accommodation for $12/30 in dorms/doubles. It arranges transport from Invercargill or Dunedin ($30).

Owaka Lodge Motel (☎ 415 8728) on the corner of Ryley and Campbell Sts has units for $60 to $70.

Catlins Retreat Guesthouse (☎ 415 8830, 27 Main Rd), a restored house, has rooms for $40/75 for one/two. *Blowhole Backpackers* (☎ 415 8830, 24 Main Rd) is a clean, airy backpacker place run by the B&B people across the road. It offers free vegies and a sunny veranda in summer, and a cosy fire in winter. It's $15/40 for a single/double.

The *Surat Bay Lodge* (☎ 415 8099, @ warrenc@voyager.co.nz) is in a great spot on Surat Bay Rd, Newhaven. It's 5km from Owaka and overlooks the Catlins estuary. Accommodation is $15 in dorms and $36/40 in twins/doubles.

The *Lumberjack Cafe & Bar*, the biggest thing to hit Owaka in years, is the best place for a meal.

Owaka to Balclutha
East of Owaka, **Cannibal Bay** is home to a Hooker's sea lion breeding ground, but is

SOUTHLAND

difficult to reach. Before Pounawea, cross the bridge and take the Newhaven Rd to Newhaven, from where you walk around the beach to Cannibal Bay. The bay gets its name from the surveyor Hector, who discovered human bones in a midden here and assumed it was part of a feast. Te Rauparaha is also known to have exacted revenge here.

East of Owaka at **Tunnel Hill** there is a short track that leads to NZ's most southerly railway tunnel, excavated by hand in 1893 as part of the Catlins Branch Railway.

Further around the coast, on a not-to-be-missed side track from the Kaka Point road, is **Nugget Point**, one of NZ's special places. The islands sitting out from the lighthouse promontory seem to lead off to the very edge of the world. Fur seals bask below on the rocks, as do Hooker's sea lions and elephant seals on occasions; it is the only place on the NZ mainland where these species coexist. There is a wealth of bird life: yellow-eyed and little blue penguins, gannets, shags and sooty shearwaters breed here and many other pelagic species, such as the cape pigeon, pass by. The stone lighthouse was built in 1869.

Avoid the temptation to leave the track – observe only from above with binoculars so as not to disturb the birds. Look down on the huge bladderkelp forests in the water, which fringe the Nuggets' reefs.

Only 2km from the lighthouse, *Nuggets Lodge* (☎ 412 8783) has two self-contained flats for $80 for two.

From Nugget Point the road loops back around through Kaka Point and Port Molyneaux to SH92 and Balclutha (see the Otago chapter). **Kaka Point** is a pleasant little town on a good beach. The *Kaka Point Camping Ground* (☎ 412 8814), above the town on Tarata Rd, has tent/powered sites for $8/10 per person and cabins for $15/26 for one/two.

Fernlea Backpackers (☎ 412 8834) is a cute cottage, near the beach and up the steps from Moana St. A bed is $15 per person in the two dorms or in the one double. *Nugget View Motels* (☎ 412 8602, @ nugview@ catlins.co.nz, 11 Rata St) at Kaka Point offers ocean views. Budget units are $75 and classier units $90 for two. Nugget Point Ecotours operates from here.

Outer Islands

New Zealand is often mistakenly believed to consist of just the two islands, North and South. In fact there are a number of island groups off its shores and these contain fascinating culture, unique flora and fauna, magnificent scenery and solitude for those who want to escape.

Stewart Island

☎ 03 • pop 420

Called Rakiura by the Maori, NZ's third-largest island is an increasingly popular destination for getting away from it all. Rakiura means 'Glowing Skies' in Maori, perhaps referring to the aurora australis that is often seen in this southern sky, or the spectacular blood-red sunrises and sunsets. The island is often thought of as being isolated and battered by harsh southern winds – actually Stewart Island is not so inhospitable, but it certainly is unspoilt.

The minuscule population is congregated in the only town of any size, Oban, on Halfmoon Bay. Half an hour's walk away you enter a sanctuary of forest, beaches and hills. The hardy and independent people have a healthy suspicion of the law and bureaucracy. The weather is incredibly changeable – brilliant sunshine one minute, pouring rain the next. Conditions can be very muddy underfoot and you will need boots and waterproof clothing, but the temperature is much milder than you would expect. As one islander has pointed out, the island's rainforest *is* more beautiful in the rain – and mud is 'great character-building stuff'!

History

There is evidence that parts of Rakiura were occupied by moa hunters as early as the 13th century AD. According to myth, NZ was hauled up from the ocean by Maui (see the 'Maori Culture & Arts' special section), who said 'Let us go out of sight of land, far out in the open sea, and when we have quite

HIGHLIGHTS

- Kiwi spotting on Ocean Beach, Stewart Island
- Walking on any of Stewart Island's tracks – truly a remote walking experience
- Enjoying the isolation and peace of the getaway centre of Halfmoon Bay on Stewart Island
- Seeing the rich birdlife of Stewart and Ulva islands
- Exploring Chatham Island, its isolated lagoons, ramshackle fishing settlements and wild landscapes
- Tracing Moriori culture on Chatham Island, especially the tree carvings at Te Hapupu

Chatham Islands p678
Not to scale
Oban p675
Stewart Island (Rakiura) p673

lost sight of land, then let the anchor be dropped'. The North Island was the fish that Maui caught; the South Island his canoe and Rakiura was the anchor – 'Te Punga o te Waka o Maui'.

The first European visitor was Captain Cook, who sailed around the eastern, southern and western coasts in 1770 but could not make up his mind whether it was an island or a peninsula. Deciding it was part of the South Island mainland he called it Cape

OUTER ISLANDS

South. Several decades later the sealing vessel *Pegasus,* under the command of Captain Chase, circumnavigated Stewart Island and proved it to be an island. It was named after William Stewart, first officer of the *Pegasus,* who charted the southern coast of the island in detail.

In June 1864 Stewart and the adjacent islands were bought from the Maori for £6000. Early industries consisted of sealing, timber milling, fish curing and shipbuilding. The discovery of gold and tin towards the end of the 19th century also led to an increase in settlement but the rush didn't last long and today the island's economy is based on fishing – crayfish, paua (abalone), salmon and cod – and tourism.

Flora & Fauna

Unlike the North and South Islands, there is no beech forest on Stewart Island. The predominant lowland vegetation is hardwood but there are also lots of tree ferns, a variety of ground ferns and several different kinds of orchid, including a lady's slipper orchid, two earinas and a number of spider orchids. Along the coast the vegetation consists of muttonbird scrub, grass tree, tree daisies, supplejack and leatherwood. But you are warned not to go tramping off the beaten track, as the bush is impenetrable in most places.

Stewart Island is an ornithologist's delight. Apart from the many sea birds that breed here, bush birds such as tui, parakeets, kaka, bellbirds, fernbirds, robins (the last two are seen near Freshwater Flats), dotterels and kiwi abound. The weka can sometimes be spotted, and the Fiordland crested, yellow-eyed and little blue penguins are also seen (see Ulva Island later in this section).

Two species of deer were introduced to the island early in the 20th century. They are the red deer, found mainly around Mt Anglem in the Freshwater and Rakeahua Valleys and at Toi Toi Flat in the south-east, and the Virginia (whitetail) deer which inhabits the coastal areas of the island. Also introduced were brush-tailed possums, which are very numerous in the northern

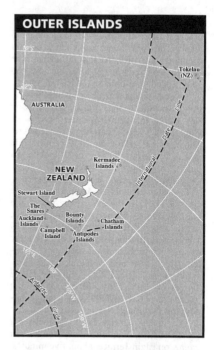

OUTER ISLANDS

half of the island and highly destructive to the native bush. Stewart Island has lots of NZ fur seals too.

Around the shores are clusters of bull kelp, common kelp, fine red weeds, delicate green thallus and bladders of all shapes and sizes.

Orientation

Stewart Island is 64km long and 40km across at its widest, has less than 20km of roads and a rocky coastline incised by numerous inlets, the largest of which is Paterson. The highest point on the island is Mt Anglem (980m). The principal settlement is Oban (named after a place in Scotland), on the shores of Halfmoon Bay, with roads extending a few kilometres further out from there.

Information

The DOC Stewart Island Visitor Information Centre (☎ 219 1218), with a Web site at www .commercial.co.nz/~rakiura, is just a few minutes' walk from the wharf. In addition to practical information on the island it has good displays on flora, fauna, walks and so on, and a summer activities program in January. The friendly staff have many ideas on how you could spend your time on the island.

Several handy and cheap pamphlets on tramps on the island, including *Halfmoon Bay Walks, Rakiura Track* and *North West Circuit* (all $1 each) can be purchased here. You can store gear at the DOC centre while you're walking ($2.50 small locker, $5 large). For online information, see *SIN: Stewart Island News* (see the Web site earlier).

The Stewart Island Adventure Centre (☎ 219 1134) at the end of the wharf is a booking agency for activities on the island.

The general store, Ship to Shore (☎ 219 1069), at Halfmoon Bay has a wide variety of supplies such as dried foods, gas canisters, fresh fruit and vegetables and hardware, as well as EFTPOS. Stewart Island Travel (☎ 219 1269, @ sam@southnet.co.nz) also has EFTPOS, fax and photocopying facilities.

The postal agency is at Southern Air (☎ 218 9129), Web site: www.southernair.co.nz, on Elgin Terrace, about five minutes' walk from the wharf. Stewart Island is a local (not long-distance) phone call from Invercargill. There are card phones outside Stewart Island Travel and at the Shearwater Inn, and coin phones in the South Sea Hotel foyer and, after hours, on the wharf at the Adventure Centre. There are public toilets at DOC, the hotel, the wharf and the public hall.

Essential companions (if you can get them) are *Stewart Island Explored* by John Hall-Jones, *The Last Refuge* by Erwin Brinkmann & Neville Peat and *Rakiura* by Basil Howard.

Ulva Island

Ever dreamed of paradise? It may well be Ulva Island in Paterson Inlet. It is only 260 hectares, but a lot is packed into it. An early naturalist, Charles Traill, was honorary postmaster here. He would hoist a flag to signal to other islands, including Stewart, that the mail had arrived and hopefuls would come from everywhere.

His postal service fell out of favour, however, and was replaced by one at Oban. A year later, in 1922, the island was declared a bird sanctuary.

Ulva is a joy for bird-watchers. As soon as you get off the launch the air is alive with the song of tui and bellbirds. You see kaka, weka, kakariki and NZ pigeon *(kereru)*. This has a lot to do with the absence of predators on the island.

The island's forest has a mossy floor and many tracks intersect the stands of rimu, miro, totara and rata – all of which, added to the delight of the birdsong, create a setting you won't forget. The birds come so close that you don't even need a telephoto lens.

Getting There & Away A number of tour operators pass here on their way to view salmon farms. If you would rather follow tracks to quiet, private beaches than visit a commercial salmon farm in Big Glory Bay, alight here while the launch excursion visits the farms. They will pick you up when they stop on the return trip to let the other passengers briefly explore the island.

You can also get to Ulva by water taxi from Golden Bay wharf; expect to pay about $15 to $20 for a return trip (see Getting Around later). You can arrange the length of your stay with booking agencies.

Things to See

The **Rakiura Museum** on Ayr St is no Victoria & Albert but it's worth a visit if you're interested in the history of the island – it features whaling, sealing, tin mining, timber milling and fishing. The collection of shipping memorabilia includes scrimshaw and photographs of the many ferries that plied across Foveaux Strait.

Particularly interesting is the section dealing with Maori heritage. It is believed that Maori have lived on Rakiura for 800 years or more. The mutton birds *(titi)* on the islands adjacent to Rakiura were an important seasonal food source for the southern Maori. Today's southern Maori population is predominantly Ngai Tahu, with earlier lineages to Kati Mamoe and Waitaho. There is a dolphin teeth necklace on display,

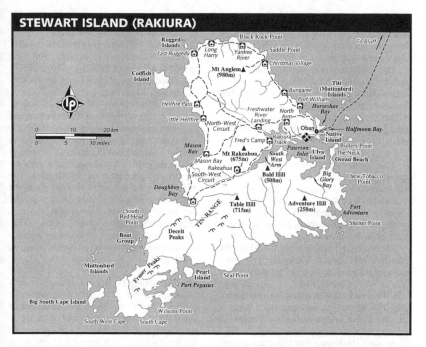

STEWART ISLAND (RAKIURA)

alongside a collection of adzes and barter goods traded between Maori and whalers, such as pipes from The Neck. The museum is open from 10 am to noon Monday to Saturday, noon to 2 pm on Sunday ($1, children $0.50).

The **library** is on Ayr St. A craft shop and gallery, **The Fernery** (☎ 219 1453), is 400m south of town in a bush setting, and housed in a new building designed to look like an original island cottage. Here, tiny fernlets from the hen-and-chicken fern, *Aplenium bulbiferum,* are placed in small egg-shaped containers and grow, ultimately, up to about 1.5m tall.

At Harrold Bay, about 3km north-east of town, is an **old stone house** built by Lewis Acker around 1835. It's one of the oldest stone buildings in NZ.

Walking

If you want to visit Stewart Island, plan on spending a few days so you can enjoy the beaches, seals and rare bird and plant life. There are many walks on the island; although some take only a couple of hours, a day trip to Stewart Island is hardly worthwhile as it is a tramper's heaven. You could spend weeks tramping here.

There is a good network of tracks and huts in the northern part of the island, but the southern part is undeveloped and can be very desolate and isolated. For the more distant walks, buy your Great Walks Pass and pay your hut fees at the DOC office. Get pamphlets before you set off – these have detailed information on the walks, the times they take, when to go and hut facilities.

You are advised not to go off on your own, particularly from the established walks, unless you have discussed your itinerary with someone beforehand. Foam rubber mattresses, wood stoves and billies are provided at each hut but you need to take food, sleeping bags, ground sheets, eating and cooking utensils, first-aid equipment and so on with you. If you have them, a tent and portable gas stove are very useful as the huts can get packed out over summer holidays and at Easter.

The **Rakiura Track**, starting from Oban, makes an interesting three-day circular tramp. Huts at Port William and North Arm have space for 30 trampers and cost $8 per night; camping is $6 if you prebook ($10 and $8 if you don't). There's a maximum stay of two nights in a hut. Huts and camping cost $4 from April to October.

This is one of the Great Walks which requires a pass; you can book by email (@ greatwalksbooking@doc.govt.nz).

The track is well defined (as it has been extensively boardwalked) and it's an easy walk, the major drawback being that it gets very crowded in summer.

The northern portion of the island has the **North-West Circuit Track** but it is long, some eight to 10 days. Fees for most of the North-West Circuit huts are $4 (children $2). The tracks further away from Halfmoon Bay can be very muddy and quite steep in places. These longer walks are detailed in Lonely Planet's *Tramping in New Zealand*.

Around Halfmoon Bay there are a number of shorter walks. Take the 15-minute walk to Observation Rock which affords good views over Paterson Inlet. You can continue past the Stone House at Harrold Bay to Ackers Point, where there are good views of Foveaux Strait. Seals and penguins can be seen near the rocks and this is the site of a shearwater colony. There are many other possible walks outlined in DOC's *Halfmoon Bay Walks*.

Organised Tours

In summer there are minibus tours around Halfmoon Bay, Horseshoe Bay and various other places. They are zippy little one-hour trips for around $15 – because there really isn't very far you can drive on Stewart Island! Check with Stewart Island Travel (☎ 219 1269) or the notice boards next to the store.

Bravo Adventure Cruises (☎ 219 1144) has daily trips to Ulva Island and salmon farms for $45. Moana Charters (☎ 219 1202)

runs half-day fishing and sightseeing trips for up to 21 people for $40 a head.

Thorfinn Charters (☎ 219 1210, @ thorfinn@southnet.co.nz) has a 30ft (9m) launch available for half-day ($50) and full-day ($70) cruises; nature tours are its speciality and it also runs fishing trips.

The *Southern Isle* (☎ 219 1133) does half-day fishing trips for $50 per person and also visits salmon farms and Ulva Island.

Kayaks can be rented for around $45 a day for independent exploring of Paterson Inlet, and guided **kayaking** is also offered; see the visitors centre for information. The inlet is 100 sq km of bush-clad sheltered waterways, with 20 islands, DOC huts and two navigable rivers. A popular trip is a paddle to Freshwater River Landing (7km upriver from the inlet) followed by a three- to four-hour walk to Mason Bay to see kiwi in the wild.

Kiwi Spotting This is one of the best eco-activities of NZ. The search for *Apteryx australis lawryi* would be a difficult one if you did not know where to look. The Stewart Island kiwi is a distinct sub-species of the brown kiwi, with larger legs and beak than its northern cousins. These kiwi are common over much of the island, particularly around beaches where they forage for sandhoppers under washed-up kelp. Unusually, *A. australis lawryi* is active during the day as well as at night – the birds are forced to forage for longer to attain breeding condition. Many trampers on the North-West Circuit spot them, especially at Mason Bay.

On any one night in summer you will probably see about three to five kiwi on Ocean Beach. Nowadays, they are quite used to human voyeurs and they even let people come close enough to take video footage.

Numbers on the tour are limited for protection of the kiwi. Only 15 people can travel to Ocean Beach on the MV *Volantis* to view this flightless marvel. Demand outstrips supply, and trips don't go every day, so make sure you book ahead with Bravo Adventure Cruises (☎ 219 1144) to avoid disappointment. The tours cost $60.

Places to Stay

The visitor centre has information on all accommodation options. The *camping ground* at Apple Bridge on Kaipipi Rd is free, but it's definitely basic, with a fireplace, wood and water supply and pit toilets only. It's about a half-hour walk from the wharf along Main Rd.

Ferndale Campsites (☎ 219 1176) at Halfmoon Bay has tent sites for $5; it has an ablution block with coin-operated showers ($2 for six minutes), a washing machine, toilets, picnic tables and rubbish collection.

Ann's Place (☎ 219 1065) offers tramping-style accommodation in a house for $12 per night. It's good value at the price, and it's a friendly place to stay.

Several homes in and around Oban offer backpacker-style accommodation at low rates. The visitor centre has the latest lists. *Joy's Place (☎ 219 1376)* on Main Rd has bunkroom beds for $15, and there is definitely no drinking or smoking here.

There are converted bachelor pads on the island. *Michael's House Hostel (☎ 219 1425)* and *Dave's (☎ 219 1078)* both charge $15.

Jo & Andy's B&B (☎ 219 1230), on the corner of Main Rd and Morris St, has one single room, one twin and two doubles. It's $17 per person with sleeping bag and $20 per person with linen provided.

The visitor centre will show you photos of all these places and direct you to them; you'll need your own sleeping bag and food.

One bachelor's place has deliberately *not* been mentioned.

The *Shearwater Inn – Katrina's Place (☎ 219 1114)* on Ayr St, in the town centre, has singles/doubles (linen included) at $36/60, or $24 per person in larger shared rooms (three or four people). More basic backpacker rooms are $14 in the dorm, or $32 for twins. The inn has a restaurant serving breakfast and dinner, and there are limited kitchen facilities for guests.

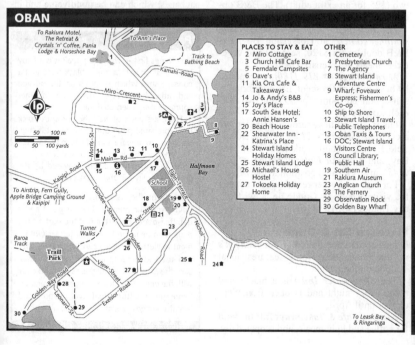

OBAN

PLACES TO STAY & EAT	OTHER
2 Miro Cottage	1 Cemetery
3 Church Hill Cafe Bar	4 Presbyterian Church
5 Ferndale Campsites	7 The Agency
6 Dave's	8 Stewart Island
11 Kia Ora Cafe &	Adventure Centre
Takeaways	9 Wharf; Foveaux
14 Jo & Andy's B&B	Express; Fishermen's
15 Joy's Place	Co-op
17 South Sea Hotel;	10 Ship to Shore
Annie Hansen's	12 Stewart Island Travel;
20 Beach House	Public Telephones
22 Shearwater Inn -	13 Oban Taxis & Tours
Katrina's Place	16 DOC; Stewart Island
24 Stewart Island	Visitors Centre
Holiday Homes	18 Council Library;
25 Stewart Island Lodge	Public Hall
26 Michael's House	19 Southern Air
Hostel	21 Rakiura Museum
27 Tokeoka Holiday	23 Anglican Church
Home	28 The Fernery
	29 Observation Rock
	30 Golden Bay Wharf

OUTER ISLANDS

The *South Sea Hotel* (☎ *219 1059),* close to the wharf, costs from $42 to $60 for singles, $80 for twins, and $95 for a room with a sea view.

The *Rakiura Motel* (☎ *219 1096),* 1.5km from the township, costs $95 for two ($15 each extra adult).

The *Beach House* (☎ *219 1059)* overlooking the bay is central and has three-bedroom motel-style units for $120 a double and $15 per extra adult.

The *Stewart Island Lodge* (☎ *219 1085),* Web site: www.stewartislandlodge.co.nz, is much more expensive. Its four rooms all have private facilities and cost about $200 per person in twin rooms (or $250 for a single), including all meals.

Another accommodation option is to hire one of the many self-contained flats or holiday homes. *Stewart Island Holiday Homes* (☎ *217 6585, 219 1057),* about a five-minute walk from town, has two houses, each sleeping up to 10 people. It's $100 for two ($25 for an extra adult). The B&B option is $90/140 for singles/doubles.

The Retreat (☎ *219 1071,* **☎** *retreat@ southnet.co.nz),* on Horseshoe Bay, has B&B doubles for $120; seafood and vegetarian meals are prepared here.

Miro Cottage (☎ *219 1180),* surrounded by bush in Miro Crescent, has comfortable, self-contained rooms for $95 for two ($15 each extra adult).

Other possibilities at around $100 for two are *Pania Lodge* (☎ *215 7733)* at Butterfield Beach, a short walk from Halfmoon Bay; and *Tokoeka Holiday Home* (☎ *219 1143),* in an elevated position in the village.

For details of other rental houses contact the visitor centre or Good Ole' Kiwi Holiday Homes (☎ 219 1116).

Places to Eat & Drink

Dining options are limited. *Annie Hansen's* in the South Sea Hotel features local seafood on the menu.

The *Shearwater Inn* has a blackboard menu every night and is open from September until April.

Kia Ora Cafe & Takeaways fills the void for coffee and light meals, and is open daily.

Church Hill Cafe Bar (☎ *219 1323)* is a good place to sip coffee as you enjoy fine views over Halfmoon Bay.

Over on Horseshoe Bay, The Retreat has *Crystals 'n' Coffee* (☎ *219 1269),* a great place for trampers to take a rest and have cake and coffee.

You can get basic necessities from the general store, buy fresh fish and crayfish from the locals, catch your own fish or bring food across from Invercargill and prepare meals yourself. Often the Fishermen's Co-op on the Halfmoon Bay wharf and Southern Seafoods at Horseshoe Bay have fresh fish and crayfish for sale.

The only place for nightlife is the pub, the South Sea Hotel – observe the evening life cycle of the endangered, white-gumbooted Stewart Islander.

Getting There & Away

For a quick look at Stewart Island, inquire at the Invercargill visitors centre about packages, which can be good value and include air fares, accommodation and tours.

Paua Recipe

First things first – what is a paua? It is a fairly large shellfish with a green-black body and a concave shell which is rough on the outside and rather beautiful on the inside. In other countries it is called abalone.

There are parts of NZ where you can pick up unprepared paua quite cheaply. It is then up to you to prepare it in a fashion that would cost about $45 for two in a restaurant.

Try the following recipe (provided by the Goomes family of Oban, Rakiura):

First, stir-fry the onion rings from one brown onion with one minced clove of garlic and a dab (teaspoon) of butter. Cut the skirt off the paua then beat the flesh until tender (with a meat mallet) – the shell can be cleaned later and used as a receptacle for knick-knacks. Slice the paua into 5mm-thick slices and cook with the onion rings for exactly three minutes. Serve on a lettuce leaf with lemon and tomato wedges. Voila!

Air Southern Air (☎ 218 9129) flies from Invercargill to Stewart Island for $60/120 one way/return (children $30/60). The student/YHA stand-by fare of $45 (return $80) is the same as the ferry. Be at the airport 30 minutes before departure; telephone ahead to see if discounted seats are available.

Flights go three times a day (8 am and 1 and 5 pm from Invercargill, returning from Stewart Island 30 minutes later) and take 20 minutes to hop over the narrow strait.

The bus from the Ryans Creek airstrip to 'town' on Stewart Island is included in the air fare. Baggage allowance is only 15kg per person (excess luggage rates apply).

Boat Stewart Island Marine's (☎ 212 7660) *Foveaux Express* runs from Bluff to Stewart Island for $45/80 one way/return (children half-price). There are departures twice daily at 9.30 am and 5 pm in summer (once on Sunday at 5 pm). In winter, there are no sailings on Saturday. Definitely book a few days ahead in summer. The crossing takes one hour across Foveaux Strait, noted for its often stormy weather.

Campbelltown Passenger (☎ 212 7404) connects with the ferry and picks up from anywhere in Invercargill.

Getting Around

Stewart Island Travel (☎ 219 1269) arranges bus tours, taxis, accommodation and rental cars. Go there for travel advice, especially air and boat charters. With a lack of roads, a boat trip is a good option to get a feel for the island.

Oban Taxis & Tours (☎ 219 1456) near the wharf provides a 24-hour taxi service and runs tours. A couple of places on the island have mountain bikes for hire.

Charter boats are available for pick-ups and drop-offs on remote parts of the island. Stewart Island Water Taxis' (☎ 219 1394) *Flyer* takes six passengers; to Ulva Island it's $20 return for one ($15 for two or more) and a half-day sightseeing trip costs about $80 per person.

Seaview Tours (☎ 219 1014) also has Ulva Island trips for up to eight passengers and offers a water-taxi service.

Chatham Islands

☎ 03 • pop 750

The Chathams are an isolated, mysterious and wild group of islands, very much off the beaten track. Named Rekohu (Misty Sun) by the Moriori, they are way out in the Pacific, about 850km east of NZ. There are 10 islands in the group but apart from the 50 or so people on Pitt Island, only Chatham Island, with 700 people, is significantly populated.

The islands offer a world of contrast – rugged coastlines and towering cliffs, volcanic peaks, lagoons and peat bogs, sweeping beaches devoid of human habitation, isolated farms, wind-stunted vegetation and dense patches of forest. Apart from farming and tourism, the other main industry is crayfish processing and there are plants at Waitangi, Kaingaroa, Owenga and Port Hutt. These four towns look like neglected junk heaps choking in the flotsam and jetsam of their raison d'etre. They may not be flash, but they exude a nuggetty, dilapidated charm.

History

The Chatham Islands were formed eons ago by volcanic upthrust. The main island is known as the home of the Moriori tribe, who settled these islands from the South Island in about AD 1000. In isolation from the mainland Maori, the Moriori maintained a more ancient Polynesian culture.

However, with the arrival of Europeans things rapidly began to go wrong. A British expedition commanded by Lieutenant Broughton first arrived at the island in 1791 and even that initial visit resulted in a clash, at aptly named Skirmish Bay (now Kaingaroa), and one Moriori was killed. Two memorials remain at the spot to this day. In the 1820s and 30s European and American whalers and sealers began to arrive and then, in 1835, a North Island tribe, Te Atiawa, was resettled in the Chathams. The impact on the peaceable Moriori was dramatic as Te Ati-awa, under Chief Pomare, established themselves by right of conquest; the Moriori population crashed from around 2000 at the time of the first European arrival in 1791 to only about 100 in the 1860s.

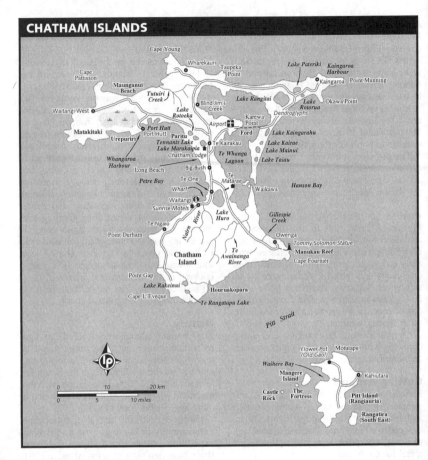

CHATHAM ISLANDS

By the beginning of the 20th century there were just 12 full-blooded Moriori left. See the boxed text 'The Last Moriori?'.

In 1865 after conflict between the Maori Hauhau movement and the government in Gisborne (North Island), many suspected Hauhau supporters were imprisoned on Chatham Island. One of them, Te Kooti, had a series of divine visions, proclaimed a new religion and led an escape of some 200 fellow prisoners. On his return to the North Island, he led East Coast tribes in a long war against the government (see the boxed text 'Te Kooti' in the East Coast chapter).

Fauna

There are 18 species of bird unique to the islands and, because of their isolation, there is a large degree of endemism, as with the local tomtit, pigeon and robin. Entry to the sanctuaries, such as those at Pitt and Rangatira (South East) Islands, is prohibited but many species can still be seen. The staff at DOC will outline the best viewing spots for birdwatchers. Rare and unusual birds include the endangered black robin, which at one stage was perilously close to extinction in its last refuge, Little Mangere Island near Pitt Island (read more about the black robin story in the

'Fauna & Flora' colour section). The rare Chatham Island taiko *(Pterodroma magentae)* was recently rediscovered nesting in the Tuku River region of the south coast of Chatham. Black swans, pukeko, weka and many species of ducks are common.

There is a fur seal colony near Kaingaroa in the north-east of Chatham Island.

Information

Waitangi is the only sizable town on the islands. There are a couple of shops, a hotel, motel, tourist lodge, small hospital, post office, ANZ bank, museum (open 8.30 am to 4.30 pm) and golf course.

Information on the islands is available from the Trust Board (☎ 305 0066, @ info@ chathams.govt.nz), PO Box 65, Waitangi; the Napier city Web site (www.chathams .napier.govt.nz); Air Chathams (☎ 305 0209); or the local information centre (☎ 305 0443). *A Land Apart,* by Michael King & Robin Morrison, provides a wealth of information about the islands.

The free fortnightly *Chatham Islander* carries the local news. The islands also have their own radio station, Radio Weka, and TV station (Chathams Television) run in conjunction with TVNZ. There is an STD and fax link with the mainland. The signposted DOC office (☎ 305 0098) is in Te One; ring before you go as it is likely to be unattended.

The Chatham Islands are very exposed but they have a temperate climate. Average daily temperatures vary from 12°C to 18°C in February and 6°C to 10°C in July. The best time to visit is in December and January; often the temperatures then reach 23°C to 24°C.

Chatham Islands time is 45 minutes ahead of mainland NZ time.

Things to See & Do

The islands have plenty of fine beaches popular for **fishing** and particularly for catching **crayfish**. Crayfish are a major industry in the Chatham Islands, and they're exported to North America and Japan. Six crayfish can be caught per person per day and 10 paua are allowed each person; check with DOC in Te One.

Scuba divers can explore the **shipwrecks** around the islands while trampers will also find interesting country to explore, particularly at the southern end of Chatham Island. Six formal reserves have been established by DOC, with **walking tracks** of anything from an hour to a full day in duration. The northern end of Chatham is flat and windswept. There's a small **museum** with Moriori artefacts in the council offices.

Three unusual attractions are the tree carvings, rock engravings and fossilised black sharks' teeth. The 200-year-old Moriori **tree carvings** (dendroglyphs) can be found in a grove adjacent to the old Te Hapupu aerodrome, in a signposted and fenced-off area. These mysterious carvings are gradually disappearing.

The **rock engravings** (petroglyphs) are found on the shores of Te Whanga Lagoon, not far from the airstrip. The **fossilised sharks' teeth** can be found at Blind Jim's Creek, also on the shores of Te Whanga Lagoon.

The sharks' teeth are about 40 million years old and a local heritage – please leave them where you see them. Their appearance here, pushed up by the waves of the lagoon, has not yet been fully explained.

One unusual sight is the **statue** of the 'last Moriori', Tommy Solomon, at Manukau Point (see the boxed text earlier in this section). Tommy's eyes seem to follow you as you scramble around the rocks below.

Places to Stay & Eat

Note that prices for accommodation and meals are invariably quoted *without* GST included (add 12.5%).

The *Hotel Chathams (☎ 305 0048),* on Waterfront Rd, Waitangi, has singles for $55 and twins and doubles for $85. The hotel also has a small souvenir shop (where you can get the highly prized Chathams T-shirt). It also hires out cars and organises trips. Meals are served and breakfast is $10, lunch $15 and an excellent dinner is $28. The same owners run *Travellers Rest Guesthouse (☎ 305 0492)* next door, offering more luxurious rooms at $100/110 for singles/doubles.

The Last Moriori?

One of the most fascinating aspects of the Chathams is the cultural legacy of the Moriori. There are still Moriori descendants on the islands and there are a few remnants of their once flourishing culture.

There has been much speculation as to where the Moriori came from (for an old-fashioned theory, see History in the Facts about New Zealand chapter). It is now scientifically accepted that the Moriori were Maori who sailed to the Chathams from NZ. The date of their arrival is in dispute, but it was some time between AD 900 and AD 1500.

Once in the Chathams, the Moriori began to develop a separate identity from the mainland Maori. They did not have rigid social divisions, they forbade tribal warfare and settled disputes on a one-to-one basis with hand-to-hand combat, and their language developed subtle differences. Most importantly, they carved their symbols into trees (dendroglyphs) and into the rocks fringing Te Whanga Lagoon (petroglyphs). When the HMS *Chatham* visited the island in 1791 there were believed to be about 2000 Moriori on these islands.

From about November 1835, groups of mainland Maori began to arrive in the Chathams and soon there were about 900 new residents made up of the Ngati Tama and Ngati Mutunga of the Taranaki Ati-awa. They began to occupy the land in a process known as *takahi*, killing about 300 Moriori who resisted, and enslaving others. By 1841 there were believed to be only 160 Moriori and over 400 other Maori and it was not until two years later that the Ngati Tama and Te Ati-awa released the last of the Moriori slaves. In 1870 the Native Land Court Hearings recognised that the two mainland tribes had sovereignty over 97% of the Chathams by right of conquest; small reserves were created for the surviving 90 Moriori. The Moriori intermarried in time and slowly the unique identity of the Moriori faded. Their language died with the last great Moriori scholar, Hirawanu Tapu, in 1900. There were only 12 full-blooded Moriori left at this stage.

The last full-blooded Moriori was Tommy Solomon, who died in 1933. His passing was seen at the time as the extinction of a particular race but it was far from that. His three sons and two daughters are identified as Moriori and there were many other families on the island who claimed Moriori ancestry.

There are now believed to be over 300 Moriori descendants and there has been a revival of Moriori consciousness, particularly strong after the building of the Solomon monument at Manukau Point near Owenga in the south-east of the island. Today Moriori, Pakeha and descendants of the mainland Maori live side by side as Chatham Islanders.

The **Sunrise Motels** (☎ 305 0157), about 500m south of Waitangi, cost $45 for singles and a self-contained unit is $65 for two. Meals are available and there are kitchens to prepare your own meals, unlike at the hotel and the lodge.

The owners also run the good **Roo's Roost Backpackers** in central Waitangi near the community hall ($25 per person).

The **Chatham Lodge** (☎ 305 0196), north of the Kaingaroa and Airport Rds junction and well signposted, has upmarket singles/doubles for $75/80 or $130/190 with all meals. There are package tour rates and a self-contained cottage (sleeps four) costs $100. The lodge hires out 4WDs and boats and activities offered include fishing,

boating, horse riding, tramping in nearby Henga Reserve and the world's most easterly windsurfing. Meals are $15 for breakfast and lunch, $25 for dinner.

The Smith family farmstay **Te Matarae** (☎ 305 0144), near the shores of Te Whanga Lagoon, is surrounded by natural bush and has a small pool. It has singles/doubles with en suite for $65/75 B&B per person; great dinners are $15.

Ask permission from the locals before camping anywhere. If you ask around, it may be possible to camp at the **Norm Kirk Centre**, just north of Waitangi on the road to the airport. The centre has showers and cooking facilities. Another option is **Owenga Campsite** (☎ 305 0271).

The *Waitangi Cafe*, between the post shop and police station, has standard take-away and tearoom fare. The *Kaingaroa Kai Kart* (☎ 305 0327) is a fast-food option for those visiting Te Hapupu, and Petre Bay has a *takeaways* (☎ 305 0132).

You can stock up at the Black Robin Breweries in Kaingaroa (☎ 305 0234 for appointment) or buy crayfish and blue cod at the packaging factory in Waitangi. Flounder and whitebait can be caught in the lagoon, and paua and kina gathered just offshore. For the true gourmet there are swan egg omelettes and weka (in season) – yes, the weka is consumed here as it is not indigenous.

Entertainment – bring your own or head to the *Hotel Chathams*, the local, to listen to a few yarns and trade friendly jibes.

Getting There & Away

Apart from a periodic freight-only cargo ship, the only transport to the islands is by air with Air Chathams (☎ 305 0209), which can also be booked through Air New Zealand. Air Chathams flies to/from Wellington on Monday, Wednesday and Friday, and Christchurch on Tuesday and Saturday. One-way fares from either destination are $354; Super Thrifty fares booked one month in advance are $212, which puts the Chathams within reach of many more travellers. The flight takes three hours and since seats are limited it's wise to book well ahead.

Getting Around

Beyond Waitangi most roads are unsealed and there is no public transport. Accommodation owners will pick you up from Karewa airport if they know of your arrival – some visitors have been left stranded at the airport.

Chatham Motors (☎ 305 0093) hires out short/long wheel base 4WDs, starting at around $56/88 per day (insurance included but not kilometres). Four wheel drive motorbikes are $52 per day, insurance included (and $0.10 per kilometre), and station wagons are $62.

Chatham Lodge, Te Matarae and Hotel Chathams hire out vehicles – expect to pay around $75 for a car, around $100 for a 4WD, inclusive of kilometres. It's also quite easy to hitch around the island.

Air Chathams operates a light aircraft (five-seat Cessna) for flightseeing and for trips to Pitt Island. It may be possible to hitch a ride with fishing vessels across to Pitt Island (19km from main Chatham), but the seas are very rough, often with mountainous waves.

Tours are available from Chatham Lodge; prices are on application. It is relatively easy to hire a car or 4WD motorbike and see most of the island's sights by yourself. Walking is a popular form of transport but check with DOC about access across private land.

Other Islands

New Zealand administers a number of outlying islands. To the south towards Antarctica are the Subantarctic Islands, and north in the Pacific Ocean are the Kermadecs.

SUBANTARCTIC ISLANDS

The Snares, Auckland, Bounty and Antipodes Islands and Campbell Island are established nature reserves. Entry is restricted to three of the five island groups and is by permit only. To get some idea of this wild environment go to the Southland Museum & Art Gallery in Invercargill and watch the *Roaring Forties Experience* audiovisual.

The islands have a colourful human history – sealing, shipwrecks and forlorn attempts at farming. Now the islands are important as a reserve for remaining areas of vegetation unmodified by humans and as breeding grounds for sea birds, penguins and mammals such as the elephant seal.

The Subantarctic Islands' remarkable wealth of birdlife saw their gazettal by UNESCO as a World Heritage Site in 1998. This recognises their outstanding value not only to NZ but to the whole world.

Few are fortunate enough to visit these remote islands but increasing ecotourism possibilities, well managed and guided, are possible by boat. They are expensive: a 15-day cruise, which takes in all the islands, will cost $2500 or more, all inclusive.

GRAHAM BELL

A group of Snares crested penguins

Fiordland Ecology Holidays (☎/fax 03-249 6600) in Manapouri takes scientific trips to the subantarctic islands every year and sells leftover berths to help fund the trips. Southern Heritage Expeditions (☎ 03-359 7711), PO Box 20219, Bishopdale, Christchurch, has a large range of tours.

Snares Islands
The uninhabited Snares Islands are most famous for the incredible number of sooty shearwaters (mutton birds) that breed there. It has been estimated that on any one evening during the season (from November to April) there will be six million in the air before they crash-land to return to their burrows.

Other birds found here are the endemic Snares crested penguin, cape pigeon and Bullers mollymawks.

Auckland Islands
These are probably the most accessible of NZ's Subantarctic Islands but some were closed to visitors in 1998 because a mystery illness was killing sea lions.

Many species of birds make Enderby Island their home (either temporary or permanent), including endemic shags, the flightless teal and the royal albatross. Skuas (gull-like birds) are ever present in the skies above the sea lion colony.

Discovered in 1806, the Auckland Islands were an infamous shipwreck risk in the 19th century. Settlement was once attempted in Erebus Cove, and it was not until 1992 that the last of the introduced cattle were destroyed.

On Disappointment Island there are some 50,000 white-capped mollymawks.

Campbell Island
This is the only inhabited island in the NZ Subantarctic Islands – there are NZ meteorological staff stationed here. Apart from these few humans it is the true domain of pelagic bird species. It is estimated that there are over 7500 pairs of southern royal albatross here, as well as colonies of greyheaded and blackbrowed mollymawks.

The Campbell Island teal is one of NZ's rarest birds (perhaps 50 to 100 remain).

Antipodes Islands
These islands get their name from the fact that they are opposite latitude 0° at Greenwich, England. The real treat on these islands is the endemic Antipodes Island parakeet, which is found with, but does not breed with, the red-crowned parakeet (similar to the NZ species of parakeet). Wandering albatross nest in the short grass at the top of the islands.

Bounty Islands
Landing is not permitted on any of the 13 Bounty Islands – there is a good chance that you would step on the wildlife anyway, as the 135 hectares of land that makes up these granite islands is covered with mammals or birds. There are literally thousands of erect crested penguins, fulmar prions and salvins mollymawks clustered in crevices, near the lower slopes and on all other available pieces of real estate.

THE KERMADECS
These islands, 1000km north-east of NZ, were annexed to NZ in 1887, and consist of Raoul, McCauley and Curtis Islands, L'Esperance Rock and several other rocky

OUTER ISLANDS

outcrops. Their Polynesian name is Rangitahua. Only Raoul has water and has been settled periodically, most notably in the early 19th century when whaling was conducted here. There are a number of protected archaeological and historical sites. Most of the islands have boulder-strewn beaches and steep, rocky cliffs.

The islands cannot be reached without difficulty and permits are not readily granted because of the frequency of earthquakes and volcanic eruptions, common in this region of the Pacific 'ring of fire'.

The Kermadec Islands constitute NZ's largest marine reserve, created in 1990, and it's interesting as it is a transitional zone between temperate and tropical waters. Diving is popular in the reserve, which has corals but not reefs, and an elusive goal is the rare spotted black groper.

TOKELAU
☎ 690 • pop 1500

These three atolls (Atafu, Nukunonu and Fakaofo), with a tiny population and covering only 12 sq km, have been administered by NZ since 1925. More recently, Samoa has aided in their administration and Tokelau is now moving more and more towards self-determination and a degree of independence.

The small atolls of Tokelau cannot support a large population and there has been a steady stream of Tokelauans leaving for overseas (Samoa or NZ) for many years. There are now many more Tokelauans living in NZ (about 5000 of them!) than on the atolls themselves. In NZ, Tokelauans maintain their culture and their language through social and church groups.

Tokelau, with other low-lying Pacific nations such as Tuvalu, Kiribati and the Marshall Islands, is at extreme risk from the effects of global warming (the greenhouse effect). With rising sea levels, increased severity of storms and the death of coral reefs all predicted, United Nations study teams do not expect Tokelau to be inhabitable for longer than another 100 years.

If you want to visit Tokelau you're probably out of luck because there's only one ship a month (from Samoa) and it's usually fully booked with islanders returning home from Samoa or NZ. If you're determined though, ask at the Tokelau Apia Liaison Office in Samoa (☎ 685-20822) or the Tokelau Office in Wellington NZ (☎ 04-494 8514) for more information.

For more information see Lonely Planet's *South Pacific* guide, which has a chapter on Tokelau.

Language

New Zealand has two official languages: English and Maori. English is the language you'll usually hear spoken, but Maori, long on the decline, is making a comeback. You can use English to speak to anyone in NZ – all Maori people speak English. There are some occasions, though, when knowing a little Maori would be useful, such as visiting a marae, where often only Maori is spoken. Maori is also useful to know since many places in NZ have Maori names.

KIWI ENGLISH

Like the people of other countries in the world who speak English, New Zealanders have a unique way of speaking the language. The flattening (Some would call it slaughtering) of vowels is the most distinctive feature of Kiwi pronunciation. The NZ treatment of 'fish and chips' – 'fush and chups' – is an endless source of delight for Australians. In the North Island sentences often have 'eh!' attached to the end. In the far south a rolled 'r' is practised widely, a holdover from that region's Scottish heritage – it's especially noticeable in Southland. See the glossary at the back of this book for an explanation of Kiwi English words and phrases.

A *Personal Kiwi-Yankee Dictionary* by Louis S Leland Jr is a fine and often hilarious book of translations and explanations of quirks between the Kiwi and American ways of speaking English. Yanks will love it.

MAORI

The Maori have a vividly chronicled history, recorded in songs and chants which dramatically recall the migration to NZ from Polynesian Hawaiki and other important events. Early missionaries first recorded the language in a written form by using only 15 letters of the English alphabet.

Maori is closely related to other Polynesian languages (including Hawaiian, Tahitian and Cook Islands Maori). In fact, NZ Maori and Hawaiian have the same lexical similarity as Spanish and French, even though over 7000km separates Honolulu and Auckland.

The Maori language was never dead – it was always used in Maori ceremonies – but over time familiarity with it was definitely on the decline. Recent years have seen a revival of interest in it, however, and this forms an integral part of the renaissance of Maoritanga (Maori culture). Many Maori people who had heard the language spoken on the marae for years but had not used it in their day-to-day lives are now studying it and speaking it fluently. Maori is now taught in schools throughout NZ, some TV programs and news reports are broadcast in it and many English place names are being renamed in Maori. Even government departments have been rechristened with Maori names: for example the Inland Revenue Department is also known as Te Tari Taake (the last word is actually *take*, meaning 'levy', but the department has chosen to stress the long 'a' by spelling it 'aa').

In many places, Maori people have come together to provide instruction in their language and culture to young children; the idea is for them to grow up speaking both Maori and English, and to develop a familiarity with Maori tradition. It's a matter of some pride to have fluency in the language. On some *marae* only Maori can be spoken, encouraging everyone to speak it and emphasising the distinct Maori character of the marae.

Pronunciation

Maori is a fluid, poetic language and surprisingly easy to pronounce once you remember to split each word (and some can be amazingly long) into separate syllables.

Most consonants in Maori – **h, k, m, n, p, t** and **w** – are pronounced much the same as in English. The Maori **r** is a flapped sound (not rolled) with the tongue near the front of the mouth. It is closer to the English 'l' in pronunciation.

Two combinations of consonants require special attention: **ng**, pronounced as in the

English words singing or running, can be used at the beginning of words as well as at the end. To practise just say 'ing' over and over, isolate the 'ng' part of it and then practise using it to begin a word rather than end one. The **wh** also has a unique pronunciation in Maori – generally as a soft English 'f'. This pronunciation is used in many place names in NZ, eg, Whakatane, Whangaroa and Whakapapa (all pronounced as if they begin with a soft 'f'). There is some regional variation, however: in the region around the Whanganui River, for example, the **wh** is pronounced as in the English words 'when' and 'why'.

When learning to speak Maori the correct pronunciation of the vowels is all-important. The examples below are only a rough guideline – to really get it right you'll have to listen carefully to someone who knows how to pronounce the language correctly. Each vowel has both a long and a short sound with long vowels often denoted in text by a macron or a double vowel. We have not indicated long/short vowel forms in this book. The approximate pronunciation of vowels is:

a	as in 'large'
e	as in 'get'
i	as in 'marine'
o	as in 'pork'
u	as the 'oo' in 'moon'

The approximate pronunciation of the diphthongs (vowel combinations) is:

ae & ai	as the 'y' in 'sky'
ao & au	as the 'ow' in 'how'
ea	as in 'bear'
ei	as in 'vein'
eo	as 'eh-oh'
eu	as 'eh-oo'
ia	as in the name 'Ian'
ie	as the 'ye' in 'yet'
io	as the 'ye o' in 'ye old'
iu	as the 'ue' in 'cue'
oa	as in 'roar'
oe	as in 'toe'
oi	as in 'toil'
ou	as the 'ow' in 'sow'
ua	as the 'ewe' in 'fewer'

Each syllable ends in a vowel and there is never more than one vowel in a syllable. There are no silent letters.

There are many Maori phrasebooks, grammar books and Maori-English dictionaries if you want to take a closer look at the language. Learning a few basic greetings is an excellent thing to do, especially if you plan to go onto a marae, where you'll be greeted in Maori.

The *Collins Maori Phrase Book* by Patricia Tauroa is an excellent book for starting to speak the language, with sections on everyday conversation and on using the language in a cultural context (such as on a marae). *Say it in Maori* compiled by Alan Armstrong is a pocket-sized book. *He Whakamarama: A New Course in Maori* by John Foster is an introductory language course and has an accompanying cassette. Lonely Planet's *South Pacific phrasebook* has a section on the Maori language as well as several Pacific languages (Tongan, Samoan, Cook Island Maori) that you may hear spoken around Wellington or South Auckland.

Other English-Maori dictionaries include the *English-Maori Maori-English Dictionary* by Bruce Biggs, and the authoritative *Reed Dictionary of Modern Maori* by PM Ryan.

Greetings & Small Talk

Maori greetings are finding increased popularity; don't be surprised if you're greeted on the phone or on the street with *Kia ora*. Try these ones:

Haere mai	Welcome
Haere ra.	Goodbye. (one staying to one going)
E noho ra.	Goodbye. (to one staying)
Kia ora.	Hello/Good luck/Good health.
Tena koe.	Hello. (to one person)
Tena korua.	Hello. (to two people)
Tena koutou.	Hello. (to three or more)
Kei te pehea koe?	
	How are you? (to one person)
Kei te pehea korua?	
	How are you? (to two people)
Kei te pehea koutou?	
	How are you? (to 3 or more)
Kei te pai.	Very well, thanks/That's fine.

Maori Geographical Terms

The following words form part of many place names in NZ:

a – of
ana – cave
ara – way, path, road
awa – river or valley
heke – descend
hiku – end, tail
hine – girl, daughter
ika – fish
iti – small
kahurangi – treasured possession; special greenstone
kai – food
kainga – village
kaka – parrot
kare – rippling
kati – shut or close
koura – crayfish
makariri – cold
manga – stream or tributary
manu – bird
maunga – mountain
moana – sea or lake
moe – sleep
moko – tattoo
motu – island

mutu – finished, ended, over
nga – the (plural)
noa – ordinary, not *tapu*
nui – big, great
nuku – distance
o – of, place of …
one – beach, sand or mud
pa – fortified village
papa – flat land, broad slab
pipi – shellfish
pohatu – stone
poto – short
pouri – sad, dark, gloomy
puke – hill
puna – spring, hole, fountain
rangi – sky, heavens
raro – north
rei – cherished possesion
roa – long
roto – lake
rua – hole in the ground, two
runga – above
tahuna – beach, sandbank
tane – man
tangata – people

tata – close to; dash against; twin islands
tautuku – bend
tawaha – entrance, opening
tawahi – the other side (of a river or lake)
te – the (singular)
titi – muttonbird
tonga – south
ure – male genitals
uru – west
wahine – woman
wai – water
waingaro – lost; waters that disappear in certain seasons
waha – broken
waka – canoe
wera – burnt or warm;floating
wero – challenge
whaka... – to act as...
whanau – extended family
whanga – harbour, bay or inlet
whare – house
whenua – land or country
whiti – east

Knowledge of just a few such words can help you make sense of many Maori place names. For example: Waikaremoana is the Sea *(moana)* of Rippling *(kare)* Waters *(wai)*; Rotorua means the Second *(rua)* Lake *(roto)*; Te Puke means The *(te)* Hill *(puke)* Urewera means Burnt *(wera)* genitals *(ure)* and Taumatawhakatangihangakoauauotamateaturipukakapikimaungahoronukupokaiwhenuakitanatahu means … well … perhaps you'd better read 'The Longest Place Name in the World' in the East Coast chapter for that translation. Some easier place names composed of words in this list are:

Aramoana – Sea *(moana)* Path*(ara)*
Awaroa – Long *(roa)* River *(awa)*
Kaitangata – Eat *(kai)* People *(tangata)*
Maunganui – Great *(nui)* Mountain *(maunga)*
Opouri – Place of *(o)* Sadness *(pouri)*

Te Araroa – The *(te)* Long *(roa)* Path *(ara)*
Te Puke – The *(te)* Hill *(puke)*
Waimakariri – Cold *(makariri)* Water *(wai)*
Wainui – Great *(nui)* Waters *(wai)*
Whangarei – Cherished *(rei)* Harbour *(whanga)*

(Note that the adjective comes after the noun in Maori constructions. Thus 'cold water' is *wai makariri* not *makariri wai*.)

Glossary

This glossary is a list of 'Kiwi English' and Maori terms you will come across often in New Zealand.

Also see the boxed text 'Maori Geographical Terms' in the Language chapter for some Maori words that pop up again and again in NZ place names.

AA – New Zealand Automobile Association; the organisation which provides road information and roadside assistance

afghan – popular homemade chocolate biscuit

All Blacks – NZ's revered national rugby union team (the name comes from 'All Backs', which the press called the NZ rugby team on an early visit to England)

Aoraki – Maori name for Mt Cook, meaning 'Cloud Piercer'. Aoraki is the South Island pronunciation; otherwise it would be Aorangi.

Aotearoa – Maori name for NZ; most often translated as 'Land of the Long White Cloud'

atua – spirits or gods

bach – a holiday home, usually a wooden cottage (pronounced 'batch'); see also *crib*

Barrier, the – local name for Great Barrier Island in the Hauraki Gulf

baths – swimming pool, often referred to as municipal baths

Beehive – Parliament House in Wellington, so-called because of its distinctive shape

Black Power – a large, well-organised and mainly Maori bikie-style gang

black-water rafting – rafting or tubing underground in a cave or *tomo*

boozer – a public bar

box of birds – an expression meaning 'on top of the world', usually in response to 'How are you?'

bro' – literally 'brother'; usually meaning mate, as in 'just off to see the bros'

bush – heavily forested areas

Buzzy Bee – a child's toy as essential to NZ child development as dinosaur models; a wooden bee dragged along by a string to produce a whirring noise

BYO – bring your own (usually applies to alcohol at a restaurant or cafe)

Captain Cooker – a large feral pig, introduced by Captain Cook and now roaming wild over most of NZ's rugged bush land (see also *kune kune*)

CHE – not the revolutionary but Crown Health Enterprise (regional, privatised health authorities)

chillie bin – cooler; esky; large insulated box for keeping food and drink cold

choice – fantastic; great

ciggies – cigarettes

crib – the name for a *bach* in Otago and Southland

cuzzie or cuz' – cousin; relative or just mate; see *bro'*

dairy – a small corner store which sells just about everything, especially milk, bread, the newspaper and ice cream

Dalmatian – a term applied to the predominantly Yugoslav gum diggers who fossicked for kauri gum (used as furniture polish) in the gum fields of Northland

DOC – Department of Conservation (or *Te Papa Atawhai*); the government department which administers national parks and thus all tracks and huts

domain – open grassed area in a town or city, often the focus of civic amenities such as gardens, picnic areas and bowling clubs

DOSLI – the former name of Land Information NZ

doss house – temporary accommodation

DPB – a government handout, increasingly used in the vernacular as more families struggle in the free market economy

dropkick – a certain method of kicking a rugby ball; a personal insult

EFTPOS – electronic funds transfer at point of sale. A facility to pay over the counter using your ATM card.

farmstay – accommodation on a typical Kiwi farm where you are encouraged to join with in the day-to-day activities

fiscal envelope – money set aside by the NZ government to make financial reparation for injustices to Maori people since the Treaty of Waitangi

football – rugby, either union or league

freezing works – slaughterhouse or abattoir for sheep and/or cattle

Gilbert – the most popular brand of rugby football

Godzone – New Zealand (from Richard Seddon who referred to NZ as 'God's own country')

good as gold, good as – very good

greenstone – jade, *pounamu*

haka – any dance but usually refers to the traditional challenge; war dance

hakari – feast

handle – a beer glass with a handle

hangi – oven made by digging a hole and steaming food in baskets over embers in the hole; a feast of traditional Maori food

hapu – sub-tribe or smaller tribal grouping

hard case – an unusual or strong-willed character

Hawaiki – the Polynesian homeland from where the Maori tribes migrated by canoe (probably Ra'iatea in the Society Islands). Also a name for the Afterworld.

hei tiki – carved, stylised human figure worn around the neck, often a carved representation of an ancestor; also called a *tiki*

hoa – friend; usually pronounced 'e hoa'

hokey pokey – a delicious variety of ice cream with butterscotch chips

hoki – a fish common in fish and chip shops

homestay – accommodation in a family house where you are treated (temporarily, thank God) as one of the family

hongi – Maori greeting; the pressing of noses and sharing of life breath

hui – gathering; meeting

huntaway – a loud-barking sheep dog, usually a sturdy black-and-brown hound

Ika a Maui, Te – (The Fish of Maui) the North Island

Instant Kiwi – state-run lottery

Interislander – any of the big old ferries which make the crossing across Cook Strait between Wellington (North Island) and Picton (South Island)

'Is it what!' – strong affirmation or agreement; 'Yes isn't it!'

iwi – a large tribal grouping with common lineage back to the original migration from Hawaiki; people; tribe

jandals – sandals; flip-flops; thongs; usually rubber footwear

jersey – a jumper, usually woollen (also the shirt worn by rugby players, eg grab him by the jersey)

judder bars – bumps in the road to make you drive slowly; speed humps

K Rd – Karangahape Rd in Auckland

kai – food; almost any word with kai in it has some food connection

kainga – village; pre-European unfortified Maori village

ka pai – good; excellent

karakia – prayer

kaumatua – highly respected members of a tribe; the people you would ask for permission to enter a *marae*.

kina – sea urchins; a Maori delicacy

kiwi – the flightless, nocturnal brown bird with a long beak which is the national symbol; the New Zealand dollar; a New Zealander; a member of the national rugby league team; an adjective to mean anything of or relating to NZ

kiwi bear – the introduced Australian brush-tailed possum

kiwi fruit – a small, succulent fruit with fuzzy brown skin and juicy green flesh; a Chinese gooseberry

koe – you (singular)

koha – a donation

kohanga reo – schools where Maori language and culture are at the forefront of the education process; also called 'language nest' schools

korua – you (two people)

koutou – you (more than two people)

kumara – Polynesian sweet potato; a Maori staple food

kunekune – another type of wild pig introduced by Chinese gold diggers in the 19th century (see *Captain Cooker*)
Kupe – an early Polynesian navigator, from *Hawaiki,* credited with the discovery of the islands that are now NZ

league – rugby league football
lounge bar – a more upmarket bar than a public bar; called a 'ladies bar' in some countries

mana – the spiritual quality of a person or object; authority of a chief or priest
manaia – a traditional carving design; literally means 'bird-headed man'
manuhiri – visitor; guest
Maori – the indigenous people of New Zealand
Maoritanga – Maori culture
marae – literally refers to the sacred ground in front of the Maori meeting house; now more commonly used to refer to the entire complex of buildings
Maui – an important figure in Maori (Polynesian) mythology
mere – flat, *greenstone* war club
metal/metalled road – gravel road (unsealed)
MMP – Mixed Member Proportional; a cumbersome electoral system used in NZ and Germany; a limited form of proportional voting
moko – tattoo; usually refers to facial tattoos
Mongrel Mob – a large, well-organised and mainly Maori bikie-style gang
Moriori – an isolated Polynesian group; inhabitants of the Chatham Islands
motor camp – well-equipped camping grounds with tent sites, caravan and campervan sites, on-site caravans, cabins and tourist flats
motorway – freeway or expressway

naiad – a rigid hull inflatable boat (used for dolphin swimming, whale-watching etc)
ngati – literally 'the people of' or 'the descendants of'; tribe; (in the South Island, it's pronounced 'kai')
nga – the (plural); see *te*
nifty-fifty – 50cc motorcycle

NZ – the universal appellation for New Zealand; pronounced 'enzed'

pa – fortified Maori village, usually on a hill top
Pacific Rim – a term used to describe modern NZ cuisine; cuisine with an innovative use of local produce, especially seafood, with imported styles
Pakeha – Maori for a white or European person; once derogatory, and still considered so by some, this term is now widely used for white New Zealanders
pakihi – unproductive and often swampy land on South Island's west coast; pronounced 'par-kee'
papa – large blue-grey mudstones; the word comes from the Maori for the Earth Mother
Papa, Te – literally 'our place', a term of endearment for the new national museum in Wellington
parapenting – paragliding
paua – abalone; tough shellfish pounded, minced, then made into patties (fritters), which are available in almost every NZ fish and chip shop
peneplain – area worn almost flat by erosion
PC – 'politically correct' (definition varies according to who you talk to)
pig islander – derogatory term used by a person from one island for someone from the other island
pillocking – 'surfing' across mud flats on a rubbish-bin lid
Plunket – an adjective to describe the Plunket Society's services to promote the health of babies eg Plunket rooms (baby clinics), Plunket nurses (baby nurses)
polly – politician
ponga – the silver tree fern; called a bungy (pronounced 'bungee', with a soft 'g', in parts of the South Island)
pounamu – the Maori name for *greenstone*
powhiri – a traditional Maori welcome onto the *marae*

quad bikes – four-wheel farm bikes

Rakiura – literally 'Land of Glowing Skies'; Maori name for Stewart Island, which is important in Maori mythology as the anchor of Maui's canoe

rap jump – face-down abseil

Ratana – a Protestant Maori church; adherents of the Ratana faith

raupo – bullrush

Rheiny – affectionate term for Rheineck beer

rigger – a refillable half-gallon plastic bottle for holding draught beer

Ringatu – an East Coast Maori church formed by Te Kooti

riptide – a dangerously strong current running away from the shore at a beach

Roaring Forties – the ocean between 40° and 50° south, known for very strong winds

scrap – a fight, not uncommon at the pub

section – a small block of land

silver fern – the symbol worn by the All Blacks and other national sportsfolk on their jerseys, representative of the underside of a *ponga* leaf. The national netball team are the Silver Ferns.

Steinie – affectionate term for Steinlager beer

Syndicate, the – the NZ defenders of the America's Cup in 2000

Tamaki Makaurau – Maori name for Auckland

tane – man

tangata – people

tangata whenua – people of the land; local people

taniwha – fear-inspiring water spirit

taonga – something of great value; a treasure

tapu – sacred; forbidden; taboo

tarseal – sealed road; bitumen

te – the (singular); see *nga*

Te Kooti – a prominent East Coast Maori prophet and rebellion leader

Te Papa Atawhai – Maori name for *DOC*

tiki – short for *hei tiki*

toi toi – a tall native grass

tohunga – priest; wizard; general expert

tomo – hole; entrance to a cave

tramp – bushwalk; trek; hike; a more serious undertaking than an ordinary walk, requiring some experience and equipment

tua tua – a type of shellfish

tuatara – a prehistoric reptile dating back to the age of the dinosaurs (perhaps 260 million years)

tukutuku – Maori wall panellings in *marae* and churches

tuna – eel

varsity – university

VIN – Visitor Information Network; the umbrella organisation of the visitor information centres and offices

wahine – woman

wai – water

waiata – song

Waikikamukau – mythical NZ town; somewhere in the *wopwops*

Wai Pounamu, Te – (The Water of Greenstone) Maori for the South Island

Waitangi – short way of referring to the Treaty of Waitangi

waka – canoe

Watties – the NZ food and canning giant; New Zealand's answer to Heinz, until Heinz took over the company

whakapapa – genealogy

whare – house

whare runanga – meeting house

whare taonga – a treasure house; a museum

whare whakairo – carved house

whenua – land

whitebait – a small elongated translucent fish which is scooped up in nets and eaten whole (head, eyes and all!) or made into patties

wopwops – remote ('out in the wopwops' is out in the middle of nowhere)

Thanks

THANKS

Many thanks to the huge number of travellers who used the last edition and wrote to us with helpful hints, useful advice and interesting anecdotes. Almost a thousand people have written to us since the last edition – a sign of how popular the book is (we hope!). The following people wrote, emailed or faxed in information:

A Bakhtair, AF Cooke, A Filshie, AJ Saddler, Abigail Watts, Achim Lieb, Adam Burk, Adrian Haas, Adrian Haysome, Adrienne Simons, Agnes Boskovitz, Aileen Murphy, Al Shearer, Alan Dibble, Alan Forbes, Alan Hakim, Alan Kendall, Alan Lloyd, Alan Morganstein, Alan Proudfoot, Alan Whittaker, Alex C Cole, Alexandria Fabbro, Alez Littlefield, Ali de Lisle, Alicia Hilario Andrade, Alison & Simon Porges, Alison Ennis, Alison Patrick, Alister Baird, Allan Jones, Amanda Beaman, Amber Hutchison, Amelia Clapton, Ami Gur, Amy Godino, Amy Wilhlemsen, Anat Oren, Anca Kruil, Andrea Brydon, Andreas Kusch, Andreas Christen, Andreas Huber, Andreas Rehm, Andrew & Rosemary Downie, Andrew Forbes, Andrew Hill, Andrew Jolly, Andrew Powell, Andrew Venton, Andy Broomfield, Andy Ganner, Angela Emslie, Anice Paterson, Anj Retter, Anja Rohlf, Ann & Bill Stoughton, Ann & Richard Edelman, Ann Campion, Ann Moorhouse, Ann Pyle, Anna Berg, Anna Day, Anna Deeley, Anna Holloway, Anna Jen Rusden, Anna Whitehead, Anne Hastings, Anne Homes, Anne Kristiansen, Anne Shepherd, Anne Vial, Anne Wilmot, Annelies Miedema, Annette Brown, Annette Pullin, Ann-Marie O'Grady, Arlene McDowell, Arthue Lister, Asaf Zahiv, Astrid Braukseipe, Astrid Schiessl, Audrey & Gerry Spencer, Avishai Weissberg, B & G Browne, B Raine, BY Yeague, Barbara Child, Barbara Couden Ochs, Barnie Jones, Barny Daley, Barry Smith, Bart Blommaert, Batya Weiser, Bea & Alan Duncan, Beat Kundig, Beate Wohlfahrt, Bede Carroll, Ben Clegg, Ben Kosse, Ben Schonthal, Bengt-Ake Ericsson, Bernd Heisterkamp, Bill Spivey, Bill Wallace, Blair Carruthers, Bo Kimstrand, Boaz Pasco, Bob Ayers, Bob Curwood, Bonnie Blacklaw, Brad Johnson, Brandon & Jo Harris, Brechin Morgan, Brenda & Kelly Rice, Brenda Davie, Brendan Nolan, Brent McFadden, Brian Graham, Brian Ware, Bridget Bannister, Bridget Fellingham, Britta Saxer-Tidswell, Bruce Driver, Bruce James, Bruce Paterson, Bryan Johnson, Buford Crites, Burkhardt Sanders, C & D Mason, C Smith-Low, Camille Favier, Carley Taylor, Carlien Melrose, Carmel Ballinger, Carol Bolt, Carol Cook, Carol Farbotko, Carol Spence, Caroline & Andre Schmidt-Lucke, Caroline Cross, Caroline Mundy, Caroll Houser, Carolyn Wincer, Carrie Charlesworth, Carrie Smetana, Catherine Robinson, Cathie Connew, Cathron Hertel, Cathy & Bob Forst, Cathy Menl, Cathy Nolan, Cecilia Fyfe, Charlene Dougherty, Charlie Marsfield, Charlie Oscroft, Charlotta Oberg, Cheryl Prinzen, Cheryl Walk, Chris Eccles, Chris Graham, Chris Walsh, Christian Jeusen, Christian Kober, Christina & Ivan Blackwell, Christina Silkstone, Christine Harris, Christine Lim, Christine Zielaika, Christoph Koenig, Christoph Lapp, Christopher Rea, Chuck Hugo, Cindy Wilkinson, Claire Harman, Clare Marston, Clare Saunders-Tack, Claudia Cleff, Claudia Gernot, Claudia Kling, Codrin Kruijne, Col Finnie, Colby Wingate, Colin Pander, Colleen Bright, Craig Wilson, DB Evans, D Elman, D Hawkins, D Maher, D McNicole, D R Howe, D Richard Owen, D Schinler, Daniel Heier, Daniel Howe, Daniela Gecchele, Danna Schwenk, Daphne Stein, Daren Bowra, Darin Miller, Darren Roberts, Daryl & Kim Hughes, Dave & Anne Evans, Dave Buckmaster, Dave Dongelmans, Dave Swannell, David & Geraldine Drabble, David & Julie Thomas, David Absdum, David Hugh Smith, David M Nelson, David Masters, David Myles, David Salmon, David Svensson, David Thompson, David Thomson, David Waters, David Whitley, Dawn & Kevin Hopkins, Dawn Rivers, Dean Davis, Debbie Gibling, Debbie Penman, Deborah Cranmer, Deborah Morris, Denis Weale, Denise Keegens, Dennis DePenning, Derek McLaughlin, Derek Newall, DF & LI Williams, Diana Fickling, Diana Korring, Diane Hill, Dianne Ferguson, Dick & April Carlton, Dirk Reiser, Dodie Stearns, Dominique Estiral, Don Ochs, Dorothy Klease, Doug Jones, Dr A Hartley, Dr Angela Kung, Dr Frank P Mechler, Dr Horst Jung, Dr Ing Frank Bendin, Dr Jane Crawley, Dr Sebastian Heintges, Druscilla Knowles, E Sesso, Eddie Salmon, Eileen Roberts, Elad Shippony, Elaine Ashton, Eleanor Puet, Eleanor Swain, Elizabeth Evenson, Elizabeth Melding, Elizabeth Smith, Ellen van Haaften, Ellen Walz, Ellie Cox, Elly de Gooyer, Emily Levan, Emma Statham, Emmanuel Vanderberghe, Emmie Thomas, Eric Fuss, Eric Malfit, Erin Zoski, Esther Menzi, FEB Fisles, F V Wilkinson, Fanney & Fertram Sigurjonsson, Faridah Tahir,

Fay Brooks, Fiona & Paul Jeffs, Fiona Hawke, Fiona Regan, Francis & Charlotte Josephs, Frank E Rose, Franklin Bloomer, Frederick Kern, Frehe Zuure, Fried Hoeben, Friederike Dewitz, GA Walker, G Patena, Gabra Drgova, Gail Braddock, Gale Buckley, Gary Malloy, Gary Spinks, Geoff & Diane Howlett, George Curry, George Dix, George Juchnowicz, George Lockyer, George Power, Georgina Lee-Elliot, Gerald Miller, Geraldine McGrane, Gerard Adamowski, Gerard Shaw, Gerhard Zwingler, Gerjan Droppers, Gerri Kenney, Gertrud Westerlund, Gil Feldman, Gim Lim, Giri Tenneti, Girry Amaya, Gisli Karl Agustsson, Glen Bacon, Glen Ditchfield, Glenn Baker, Gonda & Peter van Stralen, Gordon & Christina Bennett, Gordon Bailey, Gordon Wells, Grace Lee, Graham Lofts, Graham Monro, Graham Todd, Grant Everett, Grant Keeley, Grant Lahood, Greg Fournier, Gry Gaard, Gulielma Dowrick, Gulielma Dowrick, Guy & Janet Pinneo, Guy Channer, Gwynn Jones, HN Roberts, H Neil Zimmerman, Hanif Patni, Hanneke Luijkx, Hardi Wartenberg, Harriet Friedlander, Harry Hudson, Heather Deagle, Heather Henderson, Heidi Meyer, Heike Baumuller, Heiko Bottcher, Helen Hayes, Helen Huthchinson, Helen Stasa, Helen Woodward, Helen Wraithmell, Helena Carroll, Helena Hellidelli, Helle Hansen, Herman & Jessy Kattenberg-Batstra, Hila Bar On, Hila Keren, Hilary & Clea Gardiner, Hulda Armine Channell, Iain Mackay, Iain McAllister, Ian Carson, Ian Cliffe, Ian Garman, Ian Gunn, Ilse & Hubert Schinhleitner, Ingrid Gadermaier, Isolde Lederer, J & MJ Munro, JA Glide, JD Rimer, JD Stonham, J Fraenkel, J Grutemann, J Jensen, Jack Middleton, Jackie Carver, Jacob Nielsen, Jacqueline & Rob Klaver, Jacqui Snell, James Garnham, James Martin, James William, Jan & John Lewer, Jan John Leslie, Jan Van't Loo, Jane Battersby, Jane Churchwell, Jane Early, Jane Hole, Jane Holland, Jane Lees, Jane Matthews, Jane Pellicciotto, Jane Ross, Janet Richards, Janicke Volkmar, Jared Thomas, Jason Eady, Jason Hopper, Jason Lord, Jason Skelton, Jay Hemstapat, Jay Hoagland, Jean Burlin, Jean Starns, Jeane Carter, Jeff & Leslie Falk, Jeff Hill, Jeff Ingliss, Jen Preston, Jeni Aitken, Jennie Brightwell, Jennifer Douglas, Jennifer Heitin, Jenny Shaw, Jerome J Dambro, Jette & Rene Hoeg, Jill Anderson, Jill Brown, Jill Don, Jilles & Slavica van Werkhoven, Jim Busby, Jim Colver, Jim Ford, Jim Parker, Jo Nickson, Jo Sladen, Joan & Bob Blanchard, Joanna Jagroop, Joanna Lusty, Joanna Parker, Joanne Cable, Joanne Londbottom, Joanne Roberts, Joanne Schaefer, Joe Potter, Joel & Maria Teresa Prades, Joerg Micheel, John & Helen Wardle, John & Stephanie Kirby, John Arwe, John Have, John Howard Baker, John Irons, John Jacobsen, John Macphail, John

Mahon, John Meehan, John Morrow, John Olson, John Rennie, John Sellwood, John Steven, Jonas Wibom, Jonathan Cosgrove, Josien Dikkers, Joy Behennal, Judi Skinner, Judy & Graham Watron, Judy & Greg Klies, Judy Bell, Julia Bevin, Julia Hinde, Julia Rasche, Julie Brookes, Julie Bush, Julie Costello, Julie Hale, Julie Spiers, June Howell, Justin Nobbs, Justin Perkins, Justine Copley-Smith, Karen Anderson, Karen Bevan-Magg, Karen Collings, Karen Gallina, Karen Guest, Karen Parnell, Karin Gemeinder, Karina Severin, Karsten Mikkelsen, Kate Collinson, Kate Flanagan, Kate Newson, Kathleen Emerson, Kathryn Spall, Katie Teasdale, Katrina Alchin, Kedaar Kale, Keith & Sandy Horung, Keith Atkin, Keith Levi, Kelly Wasyluk, Ken Banwell, Ken Leong, Kenneth Chan, Kerr Family, Kerry Thompson, Kevin Barry, Kevin Crampton, Kieran Spillane, Kim & Julie Rickwood, Kimberly Schrader, Kirsten Lueders, Koty Hagai, Kristopher Clark, Kylie Granville, Kylie Watts, L & M Swart, L Seligsohn, L Smith, L Woods, Lan Lewer, Lanie Morris, Lara Bond, Larissa Wilson, Larraine Soanes, Laszlo Skultety, Laura Sobel, Laurie Agee Strauss, Laurie Morse, Lea Zore, Leanne Harrison, Lee Brownstin, Lee Elliott, Leigh Barlow, Leigh Trutwein, Leila Shahshahani, Leonie Houlahan, Leroy Jones, Les Lowe, Lesley Ngatai, Lesley Sweeney, Lester Day, Lincoln Loeln, Linda Knight, Linda Rees, Linus Fugl, Lisa Hoyland, Lisa Parrish, Lise Pekefier, Liz DeLoughrey, Liz Rodick, Liz Tibbutt, Lloyd Griscom, Lori H Johnson, Lorraine Gardner, Lou Buller, Lou Rauschenberger, Loui Strobech, Louise Bright, Louise Ford, Louise Undrill, Lousie Roberts, Lucy Tomkins, Lynda Like, Lynne Phillips, M & E Taylor, M Graive, M Grooten, M J Crozier, M Mata, Maatje Lobbezoo, Mads Kroyer, Maggi Boyer, Maggi Carstairs, Maggie Atherton, Maggie Haslinger, Magnus Koldau, Magnus Withell, Malcolm & Pat Grainper, Malcolm Rose, Marcel Vink, Marcie Louise, Marga & Theo van der Berg, Margaret Barbour, Margaret Cashman, Margaret Hampton, Margaret McOnie, Margaret Robertson, Margaret Stare, Margaret Titterington, Margrit Hugentobler, Marian Beymon, Marie-France Marais, Marijn Klijfhout, Mariolanda van der Heijden, Marion Floc'h, Marion Freijsen, Mark & Anita Voskamp, Mark Capellaro, Mark Capra, Mark Coleman, Mark Domroese, Mark Ebrey, Mark Foley, Mark Levison, Mark Meares, Mark Penny, Mark Ross, Mark Stanley, Markus Borsig, Martin & Marie Lycett, Martin Beevers, Martin Brewin, Martin McCarthy, Martin Zeh, Mary Owen, Masniza Mokhtar, Mathieu Federspiel, Matijn van der Krogt, Matt Harris, Matt Towers, Maud Mansfield, Maureen Calveley, Maureen Hodgins, Maurice Alberts, Max Roberts, Megan Looney,

Megan Middleton, Megan Wather, Meike Burgdorf-Fuhse, Melanie Harrison, Melanie Lowe, Melissa & Michael Rooney, Menieel & Alan Marshall, Menno Brouwer, Merrore Selenstoch, Michael & Patricia Clarke, Michael Adler, Michael Coggins, Michael Fawson, Michael Giacometti, Michael Grawe, Michael Krapf, Michael Mellor, Michael Ward, Michael Wilderer, Michael Winhilhotter, Micheal McEwen, Michelle & Sandra Shook, Michelle Boyde, Michelle Lee, Miho Terunuma, Mike Hughes, Mikie Edgar Nielsen, Mimi Chilcott, Miranda Sassen, Monique Wylie, Mr & Mrs AF Robilliard, Mr Baird, Murdoch King, Murray Sugden, Murray Takle, Myriam Huppert, NC Wright, Nancy & Peter Kaye, Nancy Durnford Lorimer, Nancy Ford, Natash Bristowe, Natasha Montgomery, Nathan Tidridge, Neil & Jean Webster, Neil Foord, Neil Griggs, Neil Marsh, Neil Paisnel, Neils van Dom, Nick Elliston, Nick Kolsen, Nicola Fletcher, Nicola Holmes, Nicola Smith, Nicole Burns, Nienke Groen, Nigel Rushton, Nik Janiurek, Nina O'Connell, Nina Stacmann, Nola & Paul Watson, Oliver Goldsmith, P Ledson, P McKinna, P Skinner, P Stone, Pam Coombs, Pam Tindall, Pamela Grant, Pamela Lannon, Patricia & Neil Warburton, Patricia Fuller, Patricia Knox, Patricia Richmond, Patrick Pronost, Patrick van Teooijdonk, Patti McCarthy, Paul Bloom, Paul D Varady, Paul Hulisz, Paul Kane, Paul Mitchell, Paul Morton, Paul Renee, Paul Searle, Paul Sedory, Paul Skellorn, Paul Weston, Paula Hemsley, Pedro Steneker, Penny Nelson, Pete Field, Pete Plaster, Peter & Debra Cole, Peter & Gitta Jenson, Peter & Monique Verkade, Peter Banks, Peter Bell, Peter Grimble, Peter Jaermann, Peter Monica, Peter Scholz, Petra Gaigl, Petra Meile, Petra Nolte, Petra Schleuning, Petra Wink, Phil Davies, Phil Dunnington, Philip McKernan, Philip W Smith, Phillip Meinhardt, Phillippa Reynolds, Phyllida & Bryan Isles, Piero Malaer, Prof Alan Mortimer, R Brandwood, R F Blesing, R Hamlett, R Williams, Rachel Lassman, Rachel Miles, Raewyn Owens, Rakefet & Gil Stav, Ramie Blatt, Randy & Tami Wenthold, Ray Bergfeld, Raylene Lafaele, Raymond & Wendy Mitchell, Rebecca & Mark Alsip, Rebecca Snowey, Renata Cervenkova, Rewa Kawiti, Rex Lerego, Rhianon Lloyed, Rhonda Richardson, Rich Brantingham, Richard & Lucy Hartopp, Richard A DeRosa, Richard Daly, Richard Fung, Richard Reeve, Richard Widen, Rick Molz, Rick Ruffin, Rob Bonaccorsi, Rob Gilley, Rob Kingsborough, Rob Lyle, Robert & Caro Kay, Robert Eisenstein, Robert Hjellstrom, Robert Lamb, Robert Van Oort, Robert Wright, Robin Hopf, Robyn Lindsay, Rod Daldrey, Roddy Cormack, Roger & Hilda Sturge, Roger Guy, Roger Huckle, Roland Steffen,

Ron Rosenthal, Rory & Jane Ewins, Rory Kyte, Rosalie Miller, Rosalind Power, Rose Keller, Rose Verdurmen, Ross Walker, Rou Young, Roy Carter, Roy Wiesner, Ruben Eberhardt, Russell Chan, Russell Hall, Ruth Baker, Ruth Henderson, S Isnell, S Jollivant, S Reed, Sabine & Georg Schober, Sally Tong, Sandie Caruba, Sandra Smith, Sandra Timmermans, Sandra Turner, Sandrea & Remi Cote, Sandy McClean, Sara Helm, Sarah Fisher, Sarah Fleming, Sarah Harmer, Sarah Markillie, Sarah Parker, Sarah Schnapp, Sarah Urlich, Scott Addison, Scott Albiston, Scott D Lewis, Scott Leckie, Sebastian van der Zwan, Selina Boyd, Shaan Stevens, Shacar Bazalal, Shai Goldberg, Shane Cook, Shannon Reed, Shari Robins, Sharon Adams, Sharon Meehan, Sharon Morgenstern, Sharon Robertson, Sharon Williams, Shay Gross, Shelley Rumbel, Shera Pascual, Shirley Carter, Shirley Sollis, Shmuel Babad, Shu Fen Ho, Sian Mackenzie, Silke Ruehle, Simon Blyth, Simon Brown, Simon Hicks, Simon Holliday, Simon Muckley, Simon Wallace, Sonia Beattie, Sonja Lee, SR & AE Cudworth, Stara Dietikon, Stefan VanRhyn, Stefane Mauris, Stella Bell, Stephan Waespe, Stephen Milt, Steve & Ellen Minden, Steve & Karen Williams, Steve Gibbings, Steve Layton, Steve Pitman, Steven & Diane Rose, Steven Carr, Stewart Harvey, Stuart Whitten, Sue Dayoe, Sue Masters, Sue Young, Suije Luger, Susan Bucciero, Susan Haines, Susan Robinson, Susy Kist, Suzanne & Gary Legg, Suzanne Brown, Sylvia Einsle, Sylvie Theberge, T & G Nichols, T Remmart, Tal & Eitan Segev, Tal Shchory, Tamar Shilgi, Tanja Nijhoff, Tesdorpf Family, Thad Leeper, Thomas Debris, Thomas Frick, Thomas Hoffmeister, Thomas Krahenmann, Thomas N Foster, Till Francke, Till Oberbobel, Tim Sullivan, Tina Blow, Tina Coleman, Tina Gronborg, TJ Sheeley, Tobias Runnfeldt, Toby Farrow, Tom Jones, Tony & Jan Sheppard, Tony Brunschwiler, Tony McKevitt, Tony Ooi, Treece Wright, Trevor Sze, Tristan Bailey, Trudy Germann, Trudy Hardingham, Trudy Rutgers, Ulla Peterson, Ulrik Jensen, Ulyses Cardona, Uwe & Kordula Kroll, Vanessa Smith-Holburn, Vaughan Bardell, Veerle Poels, Victoria Moss, Victoria Salmon, Vivian Cheung, Vivian Mackay, Vivienne Beddoe, Volker Probst, Wendy & Chris Webb, Wendy Davis, Wendy I Apanila, Wendy Larcombe, Wendy van Rijswijk, Wiebke van der Scheer, Wieke Myjer, Wiel Jongmans, Wil Gardner, Wilco Pruysers, Will Gardner, William K Howle, Wilma van den Bosch, Winston Bamford, Winston Jackson, Wippe Karjalainen, Yael Lahat, Yan -Christoph Pelz, Yaniv Coleman, Yashen Jones, Yong Yean Kee, Yoshiki Sato, Yowza Man, Yuri Wisniewski, Yvette & Falco Aalders, Yvette Adams and Ziv Sedbon

LONELY PLANET

ON THE ROAD

Travel Guides explore cities, regions and countries, and supply information on transport, restaurants and accommodation, regardless of your budget. They come with reliable, easy-to-use maps, practical advice, cultural and historical facts and a rundown on attractions both on and off the beaten track. There are over 200 titles in this classic series, covering nearly every country in the world.

 Lonely Planet Upgrades extend the shelf lives of existing travel guides by detailing any changes that may affect travel in a region since a book has been published. Upgrades can be downloaded for free from **www.lonelyplanet.com/upgrades**

For travellers with more time than money, **Shoestring** guides offer dependable, first-hand information with hundreds of detailed maps, plus insider tips for stretching money as far as possible. Covering entire continents in most cases, the six-volume shoestring guides have been known as 'backpackers' bibles' for over 25 years.

For the discerning short-term visitor, **Condensed** guides highlight the best a destination has to offer in a full-colour, pocket-sized format designed for quick access. From top sights and walking tours to opinionated reviews of where to eat, stay, shop and have fun.

CitySync lets travellers use their Palm™ or Visor™ handheld computers to guide them through a city with handy tips on transport, history, cultural life, major sights, and shopping and entertainment options. It can also quickly search and sort hundreds of reviews of hotels, restaurants and attractions, and pinpoint their location on scrollable street maps. CitySync can be downloaded from **www.citysync.com**

MAPS & ATLASES

Lonely Planet's **City Maps** feature downtown and metropolitan maps, as well as transit routes and walking tours. The maps come complete with an index of streets, a listing of sights and a plastic coat for extra durability.

Road Atlases are an essential navigation tool for serious travellers. Cross-referenced with the guidebooks, they also feature distance and climate charts and a complete site index.

LONELY PLANET

ESSENTIALS

Read This First books help new travellers to hit the road with confidence. These invaluable predeparture guides give step-by-step advice on preparing for a trip, budgeting, arranging a visa, planning an itinerary and staying safe while still getting off the beaten track.

Healthy Travel pocket guides offer a regional rundown on disease hot spots and practical advice on predeparture health measures, staying well on the road and what to do in emergencies. The guides come with a user-friendly design and helpful diagrams and tables.

Lonely Planet's **Phrasebooks** cover the essential words and phrases travellers may need when they're strangers in a strange land. It comes in a pocket-sized format with colour tabs for quick reference, extensive vocabulary lists, easy-to-follow pronunciation keys and two-way dictionaries.

Lonely Planet's **Travel Journal** is a lightweight but sturdy travel diary for jotting down all those on-the-road observations and significant travel moments. It comes with a handy time zone wheel, world maps and useful travel information.

Lonely Planet's eKno is an all-in-one communication service developed especially for travellers, with low-cost international calls, free email and voicemail so that you can keep in touch while on the road. Check it out on **www.ekno.lonelyplanet.com**

FOOD & RESTAURANT GUIDES

Lonely Planet's **Out to Eat** guides recommend the brightest and best places to eat and drink in top international cities. These gourmet companions are arranged by neighbourhood, packed with dependable maps, garnished with scene-setting photos and served with quirky features.

For people who live to eat, drink and travel, **World Food** guides explore the culinary culture of each country. Entertaining and adventurous, each guide is packed with detail on staples and specialities, regional cuisine and local markets, as well as sumptuous recipes, comprehensive culinary dictionaries and lavish photos good enough to eat.

OUTDOOR GUIDES

For those who believe the best way to see the world is on foot, Lonely Planet's **Walking Guides** detail everything from family strolls to difficult treks, with 'when to go and how to do it' advice supplemented by reliable maps and essential travel information.

Cycling Guides map a destination's best bike tours, long and short, in day-by-day detail. They contain all the information a cyclist needs, including advice on bike maintenance, places to eat and stay, innovative maps with detailed cues to the rides and elevation charts.

The **Watching Wildlife** series is perfect for travellers who want authoritative information but don't want to tote a field guide. Packed with advice on where, when and how to view a region's wildlife, each title features photos of over 300 species and contains engaging comments and insights into local flora and fauna.

With underwater colour photos throughout, **Pisces Books** explore the world's best diving and snorkelling areas. Each book contains listings of diving services and dive resorts, detailed information on depth, visibility and difficulty of dives, and a roundup of the marine life you're likely to see through your mask.

LONELY PLANET

OFF THE ROAD

Journeys, the travel literature series written by renowned travel authors, capture the spirit of a place or illuminate a culture with a journalist's attention to detail and a novelist's flair for words. These are tales to soak up while you're actually on the road or dip into as an at-home armchair indulgence.

The new range of lavishly illustrated **Pictorial** books is just the ticket for both travellers and dreamers. Off-beat tales and vivid photographs bring the adventure of travel to your doorstep long before the journey begins and long after it is over.

The Lonely Planet **Videos** encourage the same independent, tough-minded approach as the guidebooks. Currently airing throughout the world, this award-winning series features innovative footage and an original soundtrack.

Yes, we know, work is tough, so do a little bit of deskside-dreaming with the spiral-bound Lonely Planet **Diary**, the tearaway page-a-day **Day-to-Day Calendar** or any Lonely Planet **Wall Calendar**, filled with great photos from around the world.

TRAVELLERS NETWORK

Lonely Planet online. Lonely Planet's award-winning Web site has insider information on hundreds of destinations from Amsterdam to Zimbabwe, complete with interactive maps and relevant links. The site also offers the latest travel news, recent reports from travellers on the road, guidebook upgrades, a travel links site, an online book buying option and a lively traveller's bulletin board. It can be viewed at **www.lonelyplanet.com** or AOL keyword: lp.

Planet Talk is a quarterly print newsletter, full of gossip, advice, anecdotes and author articles. It provides an antidote to the being-at-home blues and lets you plan and dream for the next trip. Contact the nearest Lonely Planet office for your free copy.

Comet, the free Lonely Planet newsletter, comes via email once a month. It's loaded with travel news, advice, dispatches from authors, travel competitions and letters from readers. To subscribe, click on the Comet subscription link on the front page of the Web site.

LONELY PLANET

Guides by Region

onely Planet is known worldwide for publishing practical, reliable and no-nonsense travel information in our guides and on our Web site. The Lonely Planet list covers just about every accessible part of the world. Currently there are 16 series: Travel guides, Shoestring guides, Condensed guides, Phrasebooks, Read This First, Healthy Travel, Walking guides, Cycling guides, Watching Wildlife guides, Pisces Diving & Snorkeling guides, City Maps, Road Atlases, Out to Eat, World Food, Journeys travel literature and Pictorials.

AFRICA Africa on a shoestring • Cairo • Cairo City Map • Cape Town • Cape Town City Map • East Africa • Egypt • Egyptian Arabic phrasebook • Ethiopia, Eritrea & Djibouti • Ethiopian (Amharic) phrasebook • The Gambia & Senegal • Healthy Travel Africa • Kenya • Malawi • Morocco • Moroccan Arabic phrasebook • Mozambique • Read This First: Africa • South Africa, Lesotho & Swaziland • Southern Africa • Southern Africa Road Atlas • Swahili phrasebook • Tanzania, Zanzibar & Pemba • Trekking in East Africa • Tunisia • Watching Wildlife East Africa • Watching Wildlife Southern Africa • West Africa • World Food Morocco • Zimbabwe, Botswana & Namibia
Travel Literature: Mali Blues: Traveling to an African Beat • The Rainbird: A Central African Journey • Songs to an African Sunset: A Zimbabwean Story

AUSTRALIA & THE PACIFIC Auckland • Australia • Australian phrasebook • Australia Road Atlas • Bushwalking in Australia • Cycling Australia • Cycling New Zealand • Fiji • Fijian phrasebook • Healthy Travel Australia, NZ and the Pacific • Islands of Australia's Great Barrier Reef • Melbourne • Melbourne City Map • Micronesia • New Caledonia • New South Wales & the ACT • New Zealand • Northern Territory • Outback Australia • Out to Eat – Melbourne • Out to Eat – Sydney • Papua New Guinea • Pidgin phrasebook • Queensland • Rarotonga & the Cook Islands • Samoa • Solomon Islands • South Australia • South Pacific • South Pacific phrasebook • Sydney • Sydney City Map • Sydney Condensed • Tahiti & French Polynesia • Tasmania • Tonga • Tramping in New Zealand • Vanuatu • Victoria • Walking in Australia • Watching Wildlife Australia • Western Australia
Travel Literature: Islands in the Clouds: Travels in the Highlands of New Guinea • Kiwi Tracks: A New Zealand Journey • Sean & David's Long Drive

CENTRAL AMERICA & THE CARIBBEAN Bahamas, Turks & Caicos • Baja California • Bermuda • Central America on a shoestring • Costa Rica • Costa Rica Spanish phrasebook • Cuba • Dominican Republic & Haiti • Eastern Caribbean • Guatemala • Guatemala, Belize & Yucatán: La Ruta Maya • Havana • Healthy Travel Central & South America • Jamaica • Mexico • Mexico City • Panama • Puerto Rico • Read This First: Central & South America • World Food Mexico • Yucatán
Travel Literature: Green Dreams: Travels in Central America

EUROPE Amsterdam • Amsterdam City Map • Amsterdam Condensed • Andalucía • Austria • Baltic States phrasebook • Barcelona • Barcelona City Map • Belgium & Luxembourg • Berlin • Berlin City Map • Britain • British phrasebook • Brussels, Bruges & Antwerp • Brussels City Map • Budapest • Budapest City Map • Canary Islands • Central Europe • Central Europe phrasebook • Corfu & the Ionians • Corsica • Crete • Crete Condensed • Croatia • Cycling Britain • Cycling France • Cyprus • Czech & Slovak Republics • Denmark • Dublin • Dublin City Map • Eastern Europe • Eastern Europe phrasebook • Edinburgh • Estonia, Latvia & Lithuania • Europe on a shoestring • Finland • Florence • France • Frankfurt Condensed • French phrasebook • Georgia, Armenia & Azerbaijan • Germany • German phrasebook • Greece • Greek Islands • Greek phrasebook • Hungary • Iceland, Greenland & the Faroe Islands • Ireland • Istanbul • Italian phrasebook • Italy • Krakow • Lisbon • The Loire • London • London City Map • London Condensed • Madrid • Malta • Mediterranean Europe • Mediterranean Europe phrasebook • Moscow • Mozambique • Munich • the Netherlands • Norway • Out to Eat – London • Paris • Paris City Map • Paris Condensed • Poland • Portugal • Portuguese phrasebook • Prague • Prague City Map • Provence & the Côte d'Azur • Read This First: Europe • Romania & Moldova • Rome • Rome City Map • Russia, Ukraine & Belarus • Russian phrasebook • Scandinavian & Baltic Europe • Scandinavian Europe phrasebook • Scotland • Sicily • Slovenia • South-West France • Spain • Spanish phrasebook • St Petersburg • St Petersburg City Map • Sweden • Switzerland • Trekking in Spain • Tuscany • Ukrainian phrasebook • Venice • Vienna • Walking in Britain • Walking in France • Walking in Ireland • Walking in Italy • Walking in Spain • Walking in Switzerland • Western Europe • Western Europe phrasebook • World Food France • World Food Ireland • World Food Italy • World Food Spain
Travel Literature: A Small Place in Italy • After Yugoslavia • Love and War in the Apennines • On the Shores of the Mediterranean The Olive Grove: Travels in Greece • Round Ireland in Low Gear

LONELY PLANET

Mail Order

onely Planet products are distributed worldwide. They are also available by mail order from Lonely Planet, so if you have difficulty finding a title please write to us. North and South American residents should write to 150 Linden St, Oakland, CA 94607, USA; European and African residents should write to 10a Spring Place, London NW5 3BH, UK; and residents of other countries to Locked Bag 1, Footscray, Victoria 3011, Australia.

INDIAN SUBCONTINENT Bangladesh • Bengali phrasebook • Bhutan • Delhi • Goa • Healthy Travel Asia & India • Hindi & Urdu phrasebook • India • Indian Himalaya • Karakoram Highway • Kerala • Mumbai (Bombay) • Nepal • Nepali phrasebook • Pakistan • Rajasthan • Read This First: Asia & India • South India • Sri Lanka • Sri Lanka phrasebook • Tibet • Tibetan phrasebook • Trekking in the Indian Himalaya • Trekking in the Karakoram & Hindukush • Trekking in the Nepal Himalaya
Travel Literature: The Age of Kali: Indian Travels and Encounters • Hello Goodnight: A Life of Goa • In Rajasthan • A Season in Heaven: True Tales from the Road to Kathmandu • Shopping for Buddhas • A Short Walk in the Hindu Kush • Slowly Down the Ganges

ISLANDS OF THE INDIAN OCEAN Madagascar & Comoros • Maldives • Mauritius, Réunion & Seychelles
Travel Literature: Maverick in Madagascar

MIDDLE EAST & CENTRAL ASIA Bahrain, Kuwait & Qatar • Central Asia • Central Asia phrasebook • Dubai • Farsi (Persian) phrasebook • Hebrew phrasebook • Iran • Israel & the Palestinian Territories • Istanbul • Istanbul City Map • Istanbul to Cairo on a shoestring • Jerusalem • Jerusalem City Map • Jordan • Lebanon • Middle East • Oman & the United Arab Emirates • Syria • Turkey • Turkish phrasebook • World Food Turkey • Yemen
Travel Literature: Black on Black: Iran Revisited • The Gates of Damascus • Kingdom of the Film Stars: Journey into Jordan

NORTH AMERICA Alaska • Boston • Boston City Map • Boston Condensed • British Colombia • California & Nevada • California Condensed • Canada • Chicago • Chicago City Map • Deep South • Florida • Great Lakes • Hawaii • Hiking in Alaska • Hiking in the USA • Honolulu • Las Vegas • Los Angeles • Los Angeles City Map • Louisiana & The Deep South • Miami • Miami City Map • Montreal • New England • New Orleans • New York City • New York City City Map • New York City Condensed • New York, New Jersey & Pennsylvania • Oahu • Out to Eat – San Francisco • Pacific Northwest • Puerto Rico • Rocky Mountains • San Francisco • San Francisco City Map • Seattle • Southwest • Texas • Toronto • USA • USA phrasebook • Vancouver • Virginia & the Capital Region • Washington DC • Washington, DC City Map • World Food Deep South, USA • World Food New Orleans
Travel Literature: Caught Inside: A Surfer's Year on the California Coast • Drive Thru America

NORTH-EAST ASIA Beijing • Beijing City Map • Cantonese phrasebook • China • Hiking in Japan • Hong Kong • Hong Kong City Map • Hong Kong Condensed • Hong Kong, Macau & Guangzhou • Japan • Japanese phrasebook • Korea • Korean phrasebook • Kyoto • Mandarin phrasebook • Mongolia • Mongolian phrasebook • Seoul • Shanghai • South-West China • Taiwan • Tokyo • World Food – Hong Kong
Travel Literature: In Xanadu: A Quest • Lost Japan

SOUTH AMERICA Argentina, Uruguay & Paraguay • Bolivia • Brazil • Brazilian phrasebook • Buenos Aires • Chile & Easter Island • Colombia • Ecuador & the Galapagos Islands • Healthy Travel Central & South America • Latin American Spanish phrasebook • Peru • Quechua phrasebook • Read This First: Central & South America • Rio de Janeiro • Rio de Janeiro City Map • Santiago • South America on a shoestring • Santiago • Trekking in the Patagonian Andes • Venezuela
Travel Literature: Full Circle: A South American Journey

SOUTH-EAST ASIA Bali & Lombok • Bangkok • Bangkok City Map • Burmese phrasebook • Cambodia • Hanoi • Healthy Travel Asia & India • Hill Tribes phrasebook • Ho Chi Minh City • Indonesia • Indonesian phrasebook • Indonesia's Eastern Islands • Jakarta • Java • Lao phrasebook • Laos • Malay phrasebook • Malaysia, Singapore & Brunei • Myanmar (Burma) • Philippines • Pilipino (Tagalog) phrasebook • Read This First: Asia & India • Singapore • Singapore City Map • South-East Asia on a shoestring • South-East Asia phrasebook • Thailand • Thailand's Islands & Beaches • Thailand, Vietnam, Laos & Cambodia Road Atlas • Thai phrasebook • Vietnam • Vietnamese phrasebook • World Food Thailand • World Food Vietnam

ALSO AVAILABLE: Antarctica • The Arctic • The Blue Man: Tales of Travel, Love and Coffee • Brief Encounters: Stories of Love, Sex & Travel • Chasing Rickshaws • The Last Grain Race • Lonely Planet Unpacked • Not the Only Planet: Science Fiction Travel Stories • Lonely Planet On the Edge • Sacred India • Travel with Children • Travel Photography: A Guide to Taking Better Pictures

LONELY PLANET

You already know that Lonely Planet produces more than this one guidebook, but you might not be aware of the other products we have on this region. Here is a selection of titles which you may want to check out as well:

Auckland
ISBN 1 86450 092 1
US$14.95 • UK£8.99 • 110FF

Antarctica
ISBN 0 86442 772 7
US$19.99 • UK£12.99 • 149FF

Cycling New Zealand
ISBN 1 86450 031 X
US$21.99 • UK£13.99 • 169FF

South Pacific
ISBN 0 86442 717 4
US$24.95 • UK£15.99 • 190FF

South Pacific phrasebook
ISBN 0 86442 595 3
US$6.95 • UK£4.99 • 50FF

Tramping in New Zealand
ISBN 0 86442 598 8
US$17.95 • UK£11.99 • 140FF

Kiwi Tracks
ISBN 0 86442 787 5
US$12.95 • UK£6.99 • 95FF

Healthy Travel Australia, NZ & the Pacific
ISBN 1 86450 052 2
US$5.95 • UK£3.99 • 39FF

Available wherever books are sold.

INDEX

Index

Text

Bold indicates maps.

Bold indicates maps.